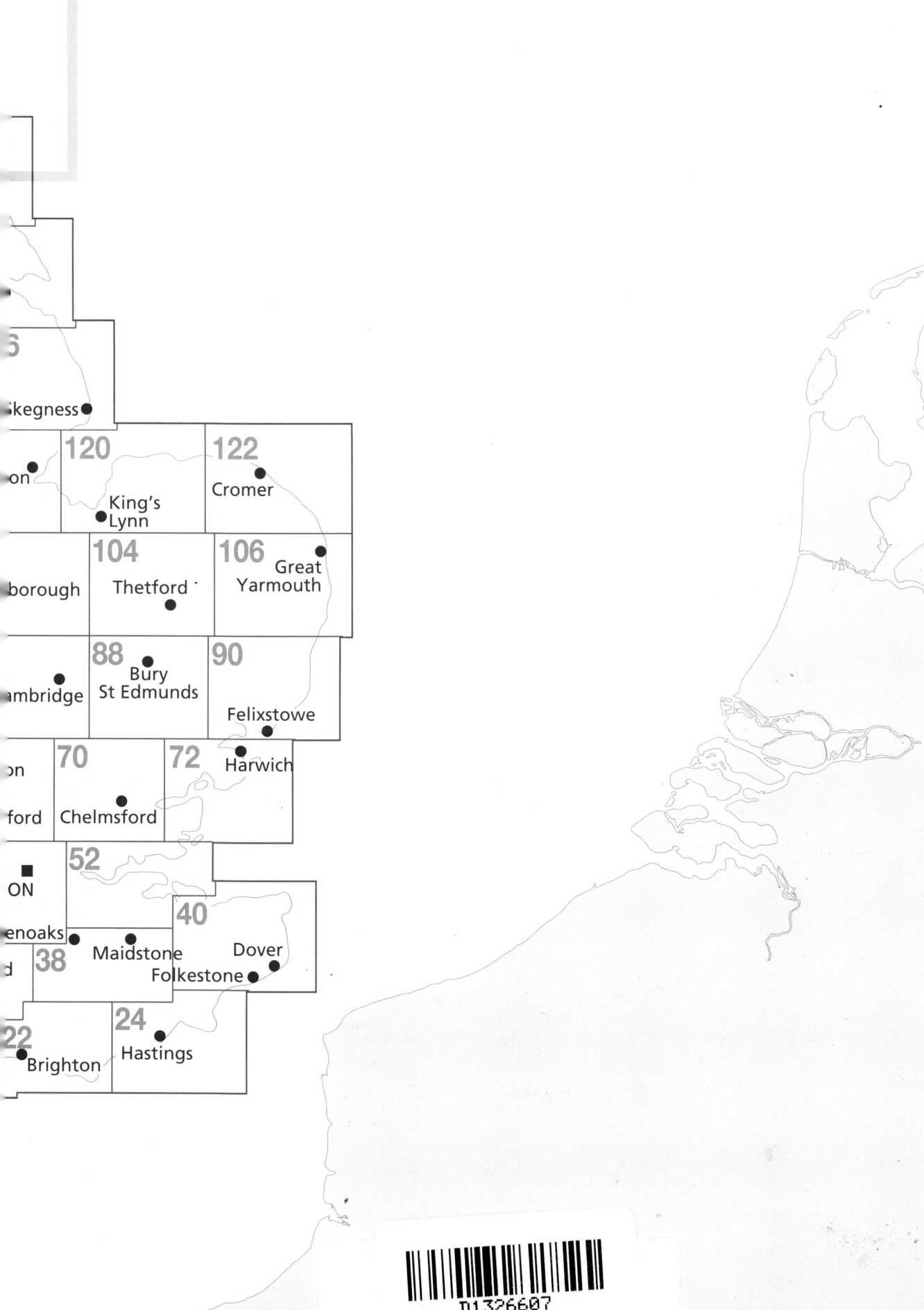

EASY READ
BRITAIN

Contents

Map pages south	inside front cover
Route planner	II–VII
Atlas symbols	VIII–1
Road maps 1:148,000 scale	2–283
Channel Islands 1:100,000 scale	9
Isle of Man 1:200,000 scale	154
Orkney Islands 1:450,000 scale	275
Shetland Islands 1:450,000 scale	281
Western Isles 1:480,000 scale	282–283
Restricted junctions	284–285
Index to place names	286–368
County, administrative area map	286–287
Map pages north	inside back cover

19th edition June 2018

© AA Media Limited 2018
Original edition printed 2000.

Cartography: All cartography in this atlas edited, designed and produced by the Mapping Services Department of AA Publishing (A05622).

This atlas contains Ordnance Survey data © Crown copyright and database right 2018.

Contains public sector information licensed under the Open Government Licence v3.0

Publisher's notes: Published by AA Publishing (a trading name of AA Media Limited, whose registered office is Fanum House, Basing View, Basingstoke, Hampshire RG21 4EA, UK. Registered number 06112600).

ISBN: 978 0 7495 7953 1

A CIP catalogue record for this book is available from The British Library.

The publishers would welcome information to correct any errors or omissions and to keep this atlas up to date. Please write to the Atlas Editor, AA Publishing, The Automobile Association, Fanum House, Basing View, Basingstoke, Hampshire RG21 4EA, UK.
E-mail: roadatlasfeedback@theaa.com

Acknowledgements: AA Publishing would like to thank the following for information used in the creation of this atlas: Cadw, English Heritage, Forestry Commission, Historic Scotland, National Trust and National Trust for Scotland, RSPB, The Wildlife Trust, Scottish Natural Heritage, Natural England, The Countryside Council for Wales. Award winning beaches from 'Blue Flag' and 'Keep Scotland Beautiful' (summer 2017 data): for latest information visit www.blueflag.org and www.keepscotlandbeautiful.org

Printer: 1010 Printing International Ltd

Scale 1:148,000
or 2.34 miles to 1 inch

ENGLAND

FRANCE

CHANNEL

Rotterdam (Europoort) Zeebrugge

Hook of Holland

Dunkirk

Calais

Calais / Coquelles Terminal

Dieppe

Cherbourg (May–Aug)

Guernsey
Jersey
St-Malo
Caen (Ouistreham)
le Havre (Jan–Oct)
Bilbao (Jan–Oct)
Santander (Jan–Oct)

Cherbourg

The Wash

THE BROADS

SOUTH DOWNS

NEW FOREST

PEAK DISTRICT

Strait of Dover

Channel Tunnel

Channel Tunnel Terminal

| 0 | 10 | 20 | 30 miles |
| 0 | 10 | 20 | 30 | 40 kilometres |

Major places: SHEFFIELD, Rotherham, Barnsley, Doncaster, Scunthorpe, Grimsby, Cleethorpes, Immingham, Chesterfield, Mansfield, Worksop, Retford, Gainsborough, Lincoln, Louth, Mablethorpe, Skegness, Horncastle, DERBY, NOTTINGHAM, Newark-on-Trent, Grantham, Sleaford, Boston, Spalding, Bourne, King's Lynn, Hunstanton, Sheringham, Cromer, North Walsham, BURTON UPON TRENT, LEICESTER, Loughborough, Melton Mowbray, Oakham, Stamford, Peterborough, Wisbech, March, Downham Market, Swaffham, Dereham, Fakenham, Aylsham, Norwich, Caister-on-Sea, Great Yarmouth, Lowestoft, COVENTRY, Rugby, Royal Leamington Spa, Warwick, Northampton, Kettering, Corby, Market Harborough, Wigston, Hinckley, Nuneaton, BIRMINGHAM, Tamworth, Lichfield, Huntingdon, Cambridge, Newmarket, Bury St Edmunds, Thetford, Attleborough, Bungay, Diss, Beccles, Southwold, Stowmarket, Aldeburgh, Woodbridge, Ipswich, Felixstowe, Harwich, Colchester, Clacton-on-Sea, Halstead, Sudbury, Haverhill, Braintree, Bishop's Stortford, Stansted, Bedford, Milton Keynes, St Neots, Royston, Baldock, Stevenage, Luton, Leighton Buzzard, Dunstable, Aylesbury, Bicester, Oxford, Thame, Banbury, Witney, Burford, Chipping Norton, High Wycombe, Beaconsfield, Maidenhead, Hertford, Hatfield, St Albans, Watford, Harlow, Chelmsford, Witham, Maldon, Brentwood, Basildon, Southend-on-Sea, Canvey Island, Burnham-on-Crouch, LONDON, Slough, Windsor, Reading, Bracknell, Newbury, Basingstoke, Woking, Guildford, Leatherhead, Dorking, Reigate, Redhill, Croydon, Staines-upon-Thames, Richmond, Heathrow, Dartford, Swanley, Gravesend, Tilbury, Sheerness, Rochester, Chatham, Maidstone, Canterbury, Margate, Ramsgate, Sandwich, Deal, Dover, Folkestone, Hythe, New Romney, Rye, Hastings, Bexhill, Sevenoaks, Tonbridge, Royal Tunbridge Wells, Crowborough, Heathfield, Uckfield, Lewes, Newhaven, Eastbourne, Brighton, Shoreham-by-Sea, Worthing, Littlehampton, Arundel, Bognor Regis, Chichester, Portsmouth, Gosport, Cowes, Ryde, Sandown, Shanklin, Newport, Freshwater, Isle of Wight, SOUTHAMPTON, Eastleigh, Romsey, Winchester, Petersfield, Midhurst, Billingshurst, Horsham, Crawley, Gatwick, East Grinstead, Ashford, Tenterden, Alton, Farnham, Andover, Amesbury, Salisbury, Ringwood, Lymington, Christchurch, Bournemouth, Swanage

EMERGENCY DIVERSION ROUTES

In an emergency it may be necessary to close a section of motorway or other main road to traffic, so a temporary sign may advise drivers to follow a diversion route.
To help drivers navigate the route, black symbols on yellowpatches may be permanently displayed on existing direction signs, including motorway signs. Symbols may also be used on separate signs with yellow backgrounds.

For further information see *theaa.com/breakdown-cover/advice/emergency-diversion-routes*

Motorway
Toll motorway
Primary route dual carriageway
Primary route single carriageway
Other A road
Vehicle ferry
Fast vehicle ferry or catamaran
National Park

0   10   20   30 miles
0   10   20   30   40 kilometres

Eyemouth
Berwick-upon-Tweed
Wooler
Alnwick
ERLAND
Amble
erburn
Morpeth
Ashington
Newcastle
Tynemouth
bridge   North Shields
South Shields
Amsterdam (IJmuiden)
Gateshead
NEWCASTLE UPON TYNE
Consett
SUNDERLAND
Chester-le-Street
Durham
Hartlepool
Bishop Auckland
Stockton-on-Tees
Middlesbrough
Barnard Castle
Darlington
Durham Tees Valley
Guisborough
Whitby
Richmond
NORTH YORK MOORS
Scarborough
Leyburn
Northallerton
DALES
Thirsk
Helmsley
Pickering
Filey
Ripon
Easingwold
Malton
Bridlington
Harrogate
Driffield
Otley
York
Wetherby
Market Weighton
eighley
Leeds Bradford
Selby
Beverley
BRADFORD
LEEDS
Halifax
Goole
KINGSTON UPON HULL
Withernsea
Pontefract
Huddersfield
Wakefield
Thorne
Scunthorpe
Immingham
Oldham
Barnsley
Humberside
Grimsby
ANCHESTER
Doncaster
Cleethorpes
Glossop
Rotherham
Doncaster Sheffield
Rotterdam (Europoort) Zeebrugge
Stockport
SHEFFIELD
Bawtry
PEAK DISTRICT
Gainsborough
Market Rasen
Louth
Mablethorpe
Buxton
Worksop
Retford
Bakewell
Chesterfield
Lincoln
Horncastle
ENGLAND
Skegness
Matlock
Alfreton
Mansfield
ngleton
Leek
Newark-on-Trent
Sleaford
Boston
Sheringham
Cromer
OKE-ON-TRENT
Ashbourne
Ilkeston
The Wash
Hunstanton
North Walsham
Uttoxeter
DERBY
Grantham
King's Lynn
Fakenham
Aylsham
Stafford
Long Eaton
NOTTINGHAM
Spalding
Dereham
Norwich
Burton upon Trent
East Midlands
Loughborough
Bourne
Swaffham
Norwich
Caister-on-Sea
Rugeley
Melton Mowbray
Wisbech
BROADS
Lichfield
Oakham
Stamford
March
Downham Market
Great Yarmouth
Walsall
LEICESTER
Wigston
Peterborough
Attleborough
Bungay
Lowestoft
Tamworth
Hinckley
Market Harborough
Chatteris
Ely
Thetford
Diss
Beccles
Nuneaton
Corby
Kettering
Huntingdon
Southwold
BIRMINGHAM
COVENTRY
Rugby
Royal Leamington
Warwick
Bury

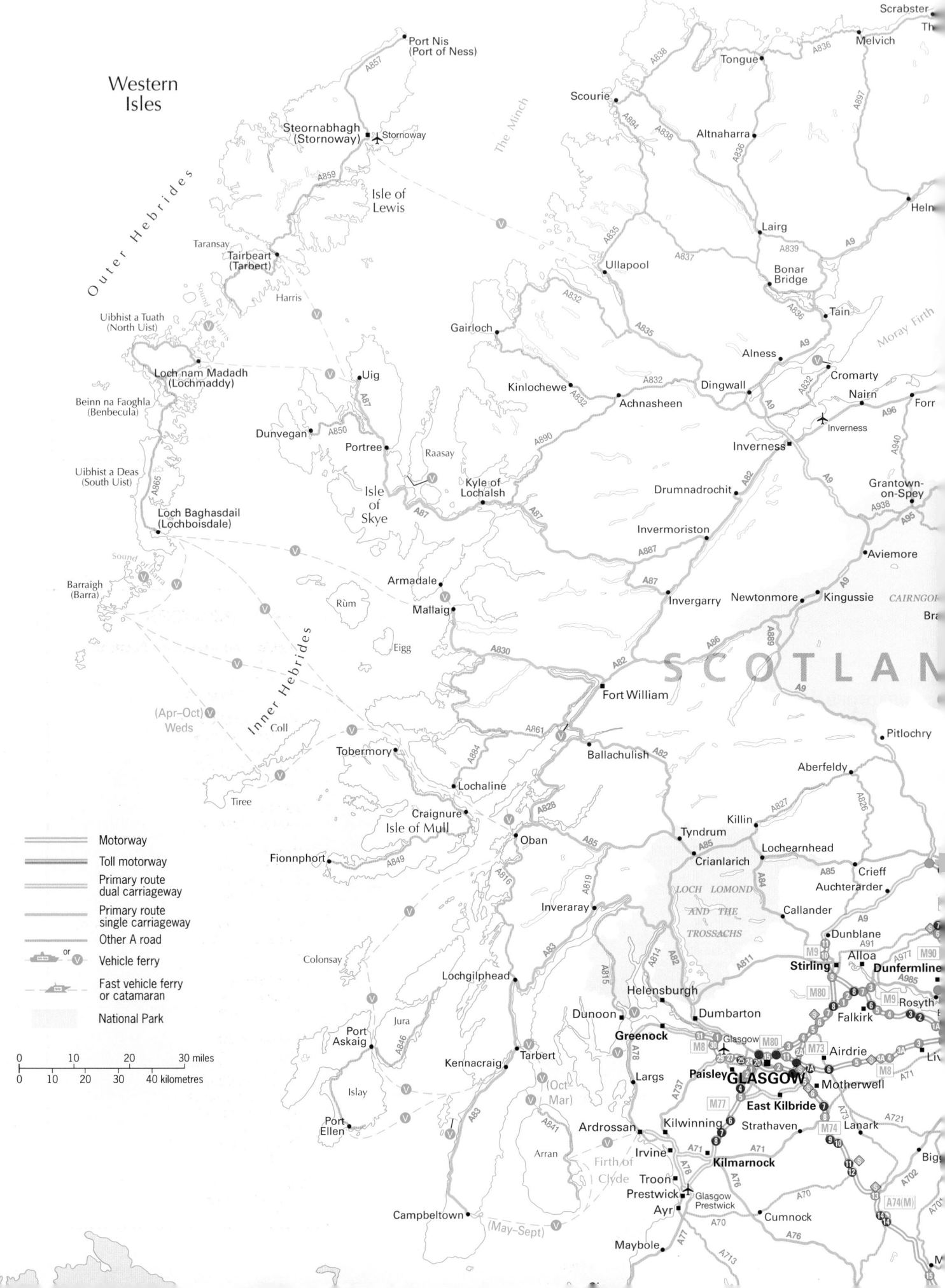

Western
Isles

Outer Hebrides

Inner Hebrides

Port Nis
(Port of Ness)

Steornabhagh
(Stornoway) — Stornoway

Isle of
Lewis

Taransay

Tairbeart
(Tarbert)

Harris

Uibhist a Tuath
(North Uist)

Beinn na Faoghla
(Benbecula)

Loch nam Madadh
(Lochmaddy)

Uig

Uibhist a Deas
(South Uist)

Dunvegan

Portree

Raasay

Isle
of
Skye

Loch Baghasdail
(Lochboisdale)

Kyle of
Lochalsh

Barraigh
(Barra)

Rùm

Armadale

Eigg

Mallaig

(Apr–Oct)
Weds

Coll

Tiree

Tobermory

Lochaline

Craignure

Isle of Mull

Oban

Fionnphort

Colonsay

Jura

Inveraray

Lochgilphead

Port
Askaig

Kennacraig

Tarbert

Islay

Port
Ellen

Arran

(May–Sept)

Campbeltown

The Minch

Scrabster

Th

Melvich

Tongue

Scourie

Altnaharra

Lairg

Bonar
Bridge

Ullapool

Heln

Gairloch

Kinlochewe

Achnasheen

Dingwall

Tain

Moray Firth

Alness

Cromarty

Nairn

Forr

Inverness

Inverness

Drumnadrochit

Grantown-
on-Spey

Invermoriston

Aviemore

Invergarry

Newtonmore

Kingussie

CAIRNGOR

Bra

Fort William

SCOTLAN

Pitlochry

Ballachulish

Aberfeldy

Killin

Tyndrum

Lochearnhead

Crianlarich

Crieff

Auchterarder

LOCH LOMOND
AND THE
TROSSACHS

Callander

Dunblane

Helensburgh

Stirling

Alloa

Dunfermline

Rosyth

Dunoon

Dumbarton

Falkirk

Greenock

Glasgow

Airdrie

Li

Paisley

GLASGOW

Motherwell

Largs

East Kilbride

Kilwinning

Strathaven

Lanark

Ardrossan

Kilmarnock

Irvine

Troon

Bigg

Prestwick

Glasgow
Prestwick

Cumnock

Ayr

Maybole

Firth of
Clyde

(Oct–
Mar)

	Motorway
	Toll motorway
	Primary route dual carriageway
	Primary route single carriageway
	Other A road
or V	Vehicle ferry
	Fast vehicle ferry or catamaran
	National Park

0   10   20   30 miles
0 10 20 30 40 kilometres

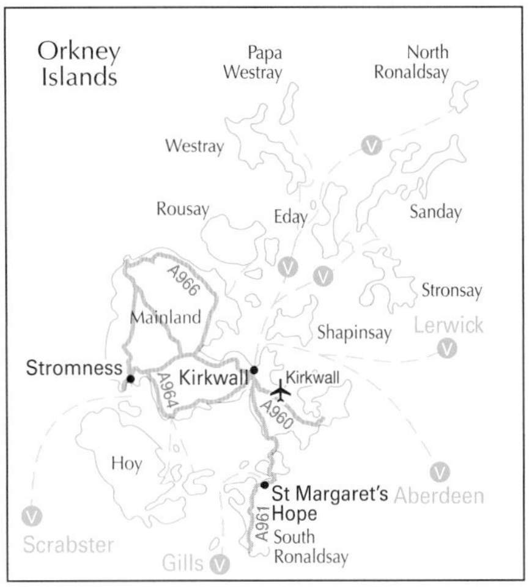

Orkney Islands

Kirkwall
Kirkwall
Orkney Islands
St Margaret's Hope
Gills
John o' Groats
Wick
A99
A90
A836
A99
A9

Orkney Islands

Papa Westray
North Ronaldsay
Westray
Rousay
Eday
Sanday
Mainland
Stronsay
Shapinsay
Lerwick
Stromness
Kirkwall
Kirkwall
A966
A965
A964
A960
Hoy
St Margaret's Hope
A961
South Ronaldsay
Aberdeen
Scrabster
Gills

Shetland Islands

Unst
A968
A970
Yell
A968
Fetlar
Out Skerries
Scatsta
Vidlin
Whalsay
Papa Stour
A971
A970
Mainland
Scalloway
Lerwick
Foula
Bressay
A970
Sumburgh
Fair Isle
Kirkwall
Aberdeen

Cullen
Banff
Fraserburgh
A98
A88
A90
Keith
Turriff
Peterhead
A941
A96
A95
A947
A952
Aberlour
Huntly
A90
Ellon
Oldmeldrum
Lerwick
ntoul
Inverurie
A90
Aberdeen
A96
Aberdeen
Ballater
Banchory
A93
A90
A92
Stonehaven
A92
Brechin
Montrose
rgowrie
Forfar
A90
A94
par Angus
A92
Arbroath
Dundee
Carnoustie
Newport-on-Tay
A90
A92
St Andrews
A91
91
Cupar
A915
A917
Glenrothes
Kirkcaldy
Firth of Forth

N O R T H

S E A

Dunbar
A1
EDINBURGH
Dalkeith
Eyemouth
A6094
A703
A68
A697
Berwick-upon-Tweed
A7
Peebles
Galashiels
A6089
Coldstream
A1
A72
Kelso
A698
Wooler
A708
Selkirk
Jedburgh
A697
Hawick
A68
Alnwick
A1
NORTHUMBERLAND
A1068
Amble

FERRY OPERATORS

Hebrides and west coast Scotland
calmac.co.uk
skyeferry.co.uk
western-ferries.co.uk

Orkney and Shetland
northlinkferries.co.uk
pentlandferries.co.uk
orkneyferries.co.uk
shetland.gov.uk/ferries

Isle of Man
steam-packet.com

Ireland
irishferries.com
poferries.com
stenaline.co.uk

North Sea (Scandinavia and Benelux)
dfdsseaways.co.uk
poferries.com

Isle of Wight
wightlink.co.uk
redfunnel.co.uk

Channel Islands
condorferries.co.uk

France and Belgium
brittany-ferries.co.uk
condorferries.co.uk
eurotunnel.com
dfdsseaways.co.uk
poferries.com

Northern Spain
brittany-ferries.co.uk

Motoring information

M4	Motorway with number
Toll / T4 / Toll	Toll motorway with toll station
6	Motorway junction with and without number
5	Restricted motorway junctions
Fleet / S / R	Motorway service area, rest area
	Motorway and junction under construction
A3	Primary route single/dual carriageway
1	Primary route junction with and without number
3	Restricted primary route junctions
S	Primary route service area
BATH	Primary route destination
A1123	Other A road single/dual carriageway
B2070	B road single/dual carriageway
	Minor road more than 4 metres wide, less than 4 metres wide
	Roundabout
	Interchange/junction
	Narrow primary/other A/B road with passing places (Scotland)
	Road under construction
	Road tunnel

Toll	Road toll
	Steep gradient (arrows point downhill)
5	Distance in miles between symbols
or V	Vehicle ferry
	Fast vehicle ferry or catamaran
	Railway line, in tunnel
	Railway/tram station and level crossing
	Tourist railway
✈ ✦ H	Airport (major/minor), heliport
F	International freight terminal
H	24-hour Accident & Emergency hospital
C	Crematorium
P+R	Park and Ride (at least 6 days per week)
	City, town, village or other built-up area
628 ▲	Height in metres
637 / Lecht Summit	Mountain pass
	Snow gates (on main routes)
	National boundary
	County, administrative boundary

Touring information

To avoid disappointment, check opening times before visiting

Symbol	Description	Symbol	Description	Symbol	Description
	Scenic route		Zoological or wildlife collection		County cricket ground
	Tourist Information Centre		Bird collection, aquarium		Rugby Union national stadium
	Tourist Information Centre (seasonal)		RSPB site		International athletics stadium
	Visitor or heritage centre		National Nature Reserve (England, Scotland, Wales)		Horse racing
	Picnic site		Local nature reserve		Show jumping/equestrian circuit
	Caravan site (AA inspected)		Wildlife Trust reserve		Motor-racing circuit
	Camping site (AA inspected)		Forest drive		Air show venue
	Caravan & camping site (AA inspected)		National trail		Ski slope (natural)
	Abbey, cathedral or priory		Waterfall		Ski slope (artificial)
	Ruined abbey, cathedral or priory		Viewpoint		National Trust site
	Castle		Hill-fort		National Trust for Scotland site
	Historic house or building		Roman antiquity		English Heritage site
	Museum or art gallery		Prehistoric monument		Historic Scotland site
	Industrial interest		Battle site with year		Cadw (Welsh heritage) site
	Aqueduct or viaduct		Steam railway centre		Other place of interest
	Garden, Arboretum		Cave or cavern		Boxed symbols indicate attractions within urban areas
	Vineyard		Windmill		World Heritage Site (UNESCO)
	Brewery or distillery		Monument		National Park and National Scenic Area (Scotland)
	Country park		Beach (award winning)		Forest Park
	Agricultural showground		Lighthouse		Sandy beach
	Theme park		Golf course (AA listed)		Heritage coast
	Farm or animal centre		Football stadium		Major shopping centre

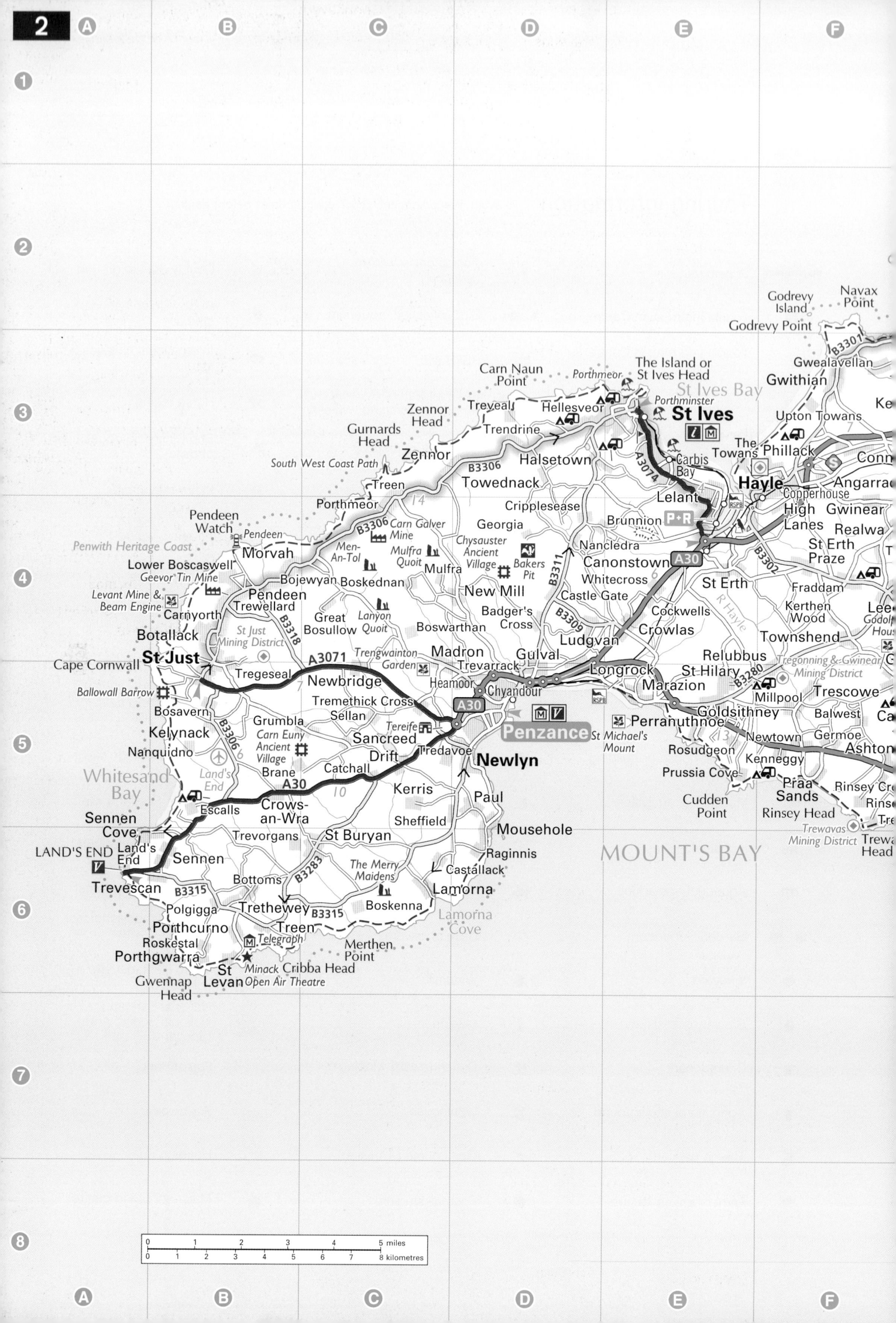

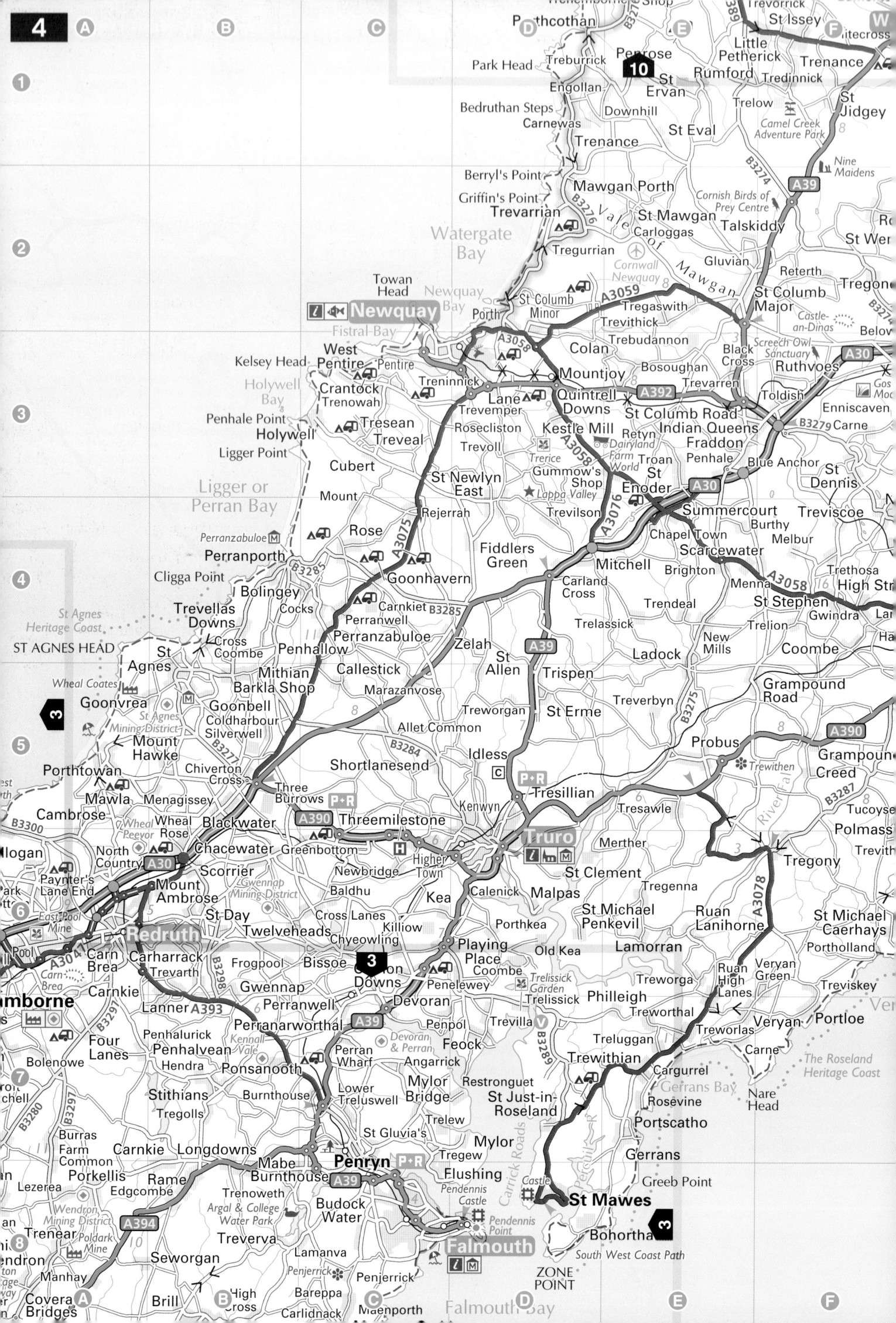

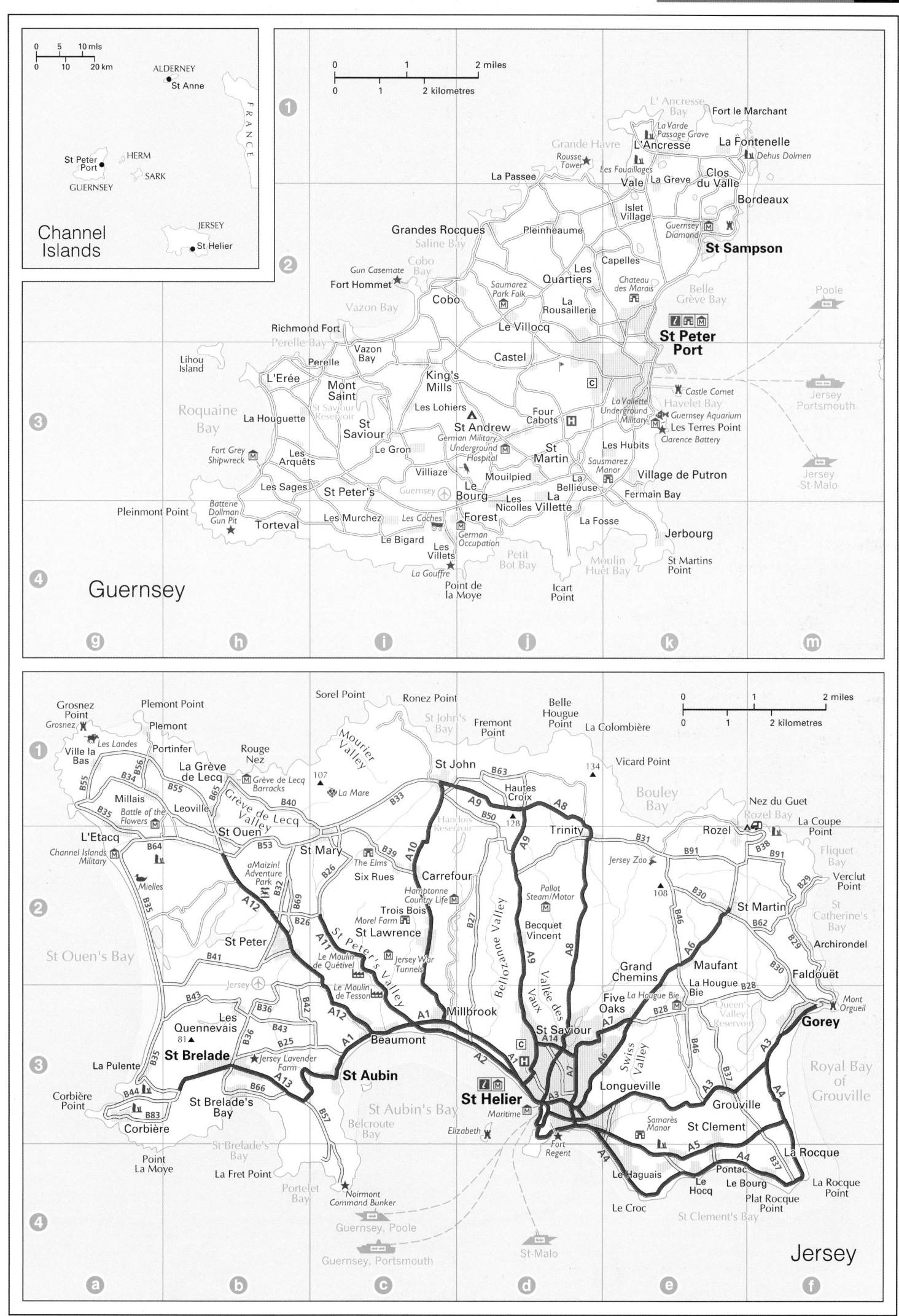

Channel Islands

ALDERNEY
● St Anne

FRANCE

St Peter ● HERM
Port ◇ SARK
GUERNSEY

JERSEY
● St Helier

Guernsey

0 5 10 mls
0 10 20 km

0   1   2 miles
0   1   2 kilometres

L' Ancresse Bay
Fort le Marchant
La Varde Passage Grave
La Fontenelle
L'Ancresse
Dehus Dolmen
Grande Havre
Rousse Tower
Les Fouaillages
La Greve
Clos du Valle
La Passee
Vale
Bordeaux
Islet Village
Guernsey Diamond
St Sampson
Grandes Rocques
Pleinheaume
Saline Bay
Les Quartiers
Capelles
Gun Casemate
Cobo Bay
Saumarez Park Folk
La Rousaillerie
Chateau des Marais
Belle Grève Bay
Fort Hommet
Cobo
Le Villocq
St Peter Port
Vazon Bay
Castel
Poole
Richmond Fort
Vazon Bay
Perelle Bay
King's Mills
Castle Cornet
Havelet Bay
Jersey Portsmouth
Lihou Island
Perelle
Les Lohiers
La Vallette Underground Military
Guernsey Aquarium
L'Erée
Mont Saint
St Saviour Reservoir
St Andrew
Four Cabots
Les Terres Point
Clarence Battery
Jersey St-Malo
Roquaine Bay
La Houguette
St Saviour
German Military Underground Hospital
St Martin
Les Hubits
Sausmarez Manor
Fort Grey Shipwreck
Les Arquêts
Le Gron
La Bellieuse
Village de Putron
Les Sages
St Peter's
Villiaze
Le Bourg
Mouilpied
La Villette
Fermain Bay
Pleinmont Point
Batterie Dollman Gun Pit
Les Murchez
Les Câches
Les Nicolles
La Fosse
Torteval
Forest
Jerbourg
Le Bigard
German Occupation
Les Villets
St Martins Point
Petit Bot Bay
Moulin Huet Bay
La Gouffre
Point de la Moye
Icart Point

Jersey

0   1   2 miles
0   1   2 kilometres

Grosnez Point
Grosnez
Plemont Point
Sorel Point
Ronez Point
St John's Bay
Belle Hougue Point
La Colombière
Nez du Guet
Ville la Bas
Les Landes
Plemont
Portinfer
Rouge Nez
Mourier Valley
Fremont Point
Vicard Point
Bouley Bay
Rozel Bay
La Coupe Point
Millais
Battle of the Flowers
La Grève de Lecq
Grève de Lecq Barracks
La Mare
St John
Hautes Croix
Trinity
Rozel
Fliquet Bay
Leoville
Grève de Lecq Valley
St Ouen
Handois Reservoir
Verclut Point
L'Etacq
Channel Islands Military
Mielles
St Mary
The Elms
Six Rues
Carrefour
Jersey Zoo
St Martin
St Catherine's Bay
aMaizin! Adventure Park
Hamptonne Country Life
Trois Bois
Morel Farm
St Lawrence
Pallot Steam/Motor
Bellozanne Valley
Becquet Vincent
Maufant
Archirondel
St Ouen's Bay
St Peter
Jersey War Tunnels
Vallée des Vaux
Grand Chemins
La Hougue Bie
Faldouët
Le Moulin de Quétivel
Le Moulin de Tesson
Millbrook
Five Oaks
Queen's Valley Reservoir
Mont Orgueil
Les Quennevais
St Brelade
Jersey Lavender Farm
Beaumont
St Saviour
Longueville
Gorey
La Pulente
St Aubin
Swiss Valley
Grouville
Royal Bay of Grouville
Corbière Point
Corbière
St Brelade's Bay
St Aubin's Bay
Maritime
St Clement
La Rocque
Belcroute Bay
Elizabeth
Fort Regent
Samarès Manor
La Rocque Point
Point La Moye
La Fret Point
Portelet Bay
Noirmont Command Bunker
Le Haguais
Pontac
Plat Rocque Point
St Brelade's Bay
Guernsey, Poole
Le Croc
Le Hocq
Le Bourg
St Clement's Bay
St Helier
Guernsey, Portsmouth
St-Malo

Isles of Scilly

White Island

ST MARTIN'S

King Charles's Castle

Old Grimsby

38

49 ▲ St Martin's Head

BRYHER
Cromwell's Castle

Old Blockhouse

Higher Town

42 ▲

New Lizard Point

Pool

Grimsby

Great Ganilly

Isles of Scilly Heritage Coast

Tresco Abbey

TRESCO

Crow Bar

Innisidgen Tomb

Eastern Isles

Great Arthur

Samson

Crow Sound

Bant's Carn Burial

North West Passage

St Mary's Sound

Harry's Walls

A3110

ST MARY'S

Higher & Lower Moors

Deep Point

Hugh Town

Porth Hellick Down Tombs

Garrison Walls ★

ℹ Ⓜ

Old Town

Isles of Scilly (St Mary's)

Middle Town

Peninnis Head

Annet

Gugh

ST AGNES

Broad Sound

Smith Sound

Horse Point

Western Rocks

```
0        1        2 miles
0    1       2 kilometres
```

a   **b**   **c**   **d**

Pentire Point - Widemouth Heritage Coast

Witchcraft & Magic Ⓜ

Boscastle

Trevalga

B3263

Castle

TINTAGEL HEAD 🏰

Tintagel

Trethevey

Bossiney

Old Post Office Ⓜ

Tregatta

Penhallic Point

Treknow

Trewarmett

Trebarwith

Penpethy

Rockhead

Treligga

Delabole

Pengelly

South West Coast Path

Trevia

Valley Truckle

Westdowns

Lanteglos

Port Isaac Bay

Trewalder

Helstone

Rumps Point

Kellan Head

Varley Head

Port-Gaverne

B3314

B3267

Port Quin Bay

Port Quin

Port Isaac

Trewetha

St Teath

Knightsmill

Pentire Point

New Polzeath

Bee Centre

Long Cross

Treburgett

Treveigha

Padstow Bay

Plain Street

Trelights

Pendoggett

Michaels

Hayle Bay

Polzeath

Stepper Point

Treharrock

Trevose Head Heritage Coast

Trebetherick

B3314

St Endellion

Trelill

Trenewth

Mother Ivey's Bay

Gunver Head

Hawker's Cove

Trevanger

Pityme

St Minver

Tregellist

Trequite

TREVOSE HEAD

Crugmeer

Prideaux Place

Rock

Tredrizzick

Trewethern

St Tudy

Dinas Head

Trevose

Harlyn Bay

Splatt

Trewethen

St Kew

St Kew Highway

Lank

Constantine Bay

Harlyn

Trevone

Treator

Stoptide

Hendra

Ro

Windmill

Padstow ℹ

Dinas

Chapel Amble

Wenfordbridge

Constantine Bay

Towan

St Merryn

8

Trevorrick

Tregonce

Tregunna

Trevanson

Bodieve

St Mabyn

B3266

Penpo

Treyarnon

A3389

Edmonton

Blisland

Trehemborne

Shop

St Issey

Whitecross

Wadebridge 🐂

Egloshayle

Croanford

Tredethy

Porthcothan

B3276

Little Petherick

Trenance

Royal Cornwall

St Breock

Pencarrow House

Hellandbridge

Park Head

Treburrick

Penrose

Rumford

Tredinnick

Treneague

Sladesbridge

Burlawn

A3389

Colquite

Helland

Bedruthan Steps

Engollan

St Ervan

Trelow

St Jidgey

Hay

St Breock Downs Monolith

Polbrock

Lane End

Washaway

Carne

Downhill

▽ **4**

Nine

▽ **5**

Brocton

Dunmere

```
0   1   2   3   4        5 miles
0  1  2  3  4  5  6  7   8 kilometres
```

A   **B**   **C**   **D**   **E**   **F**

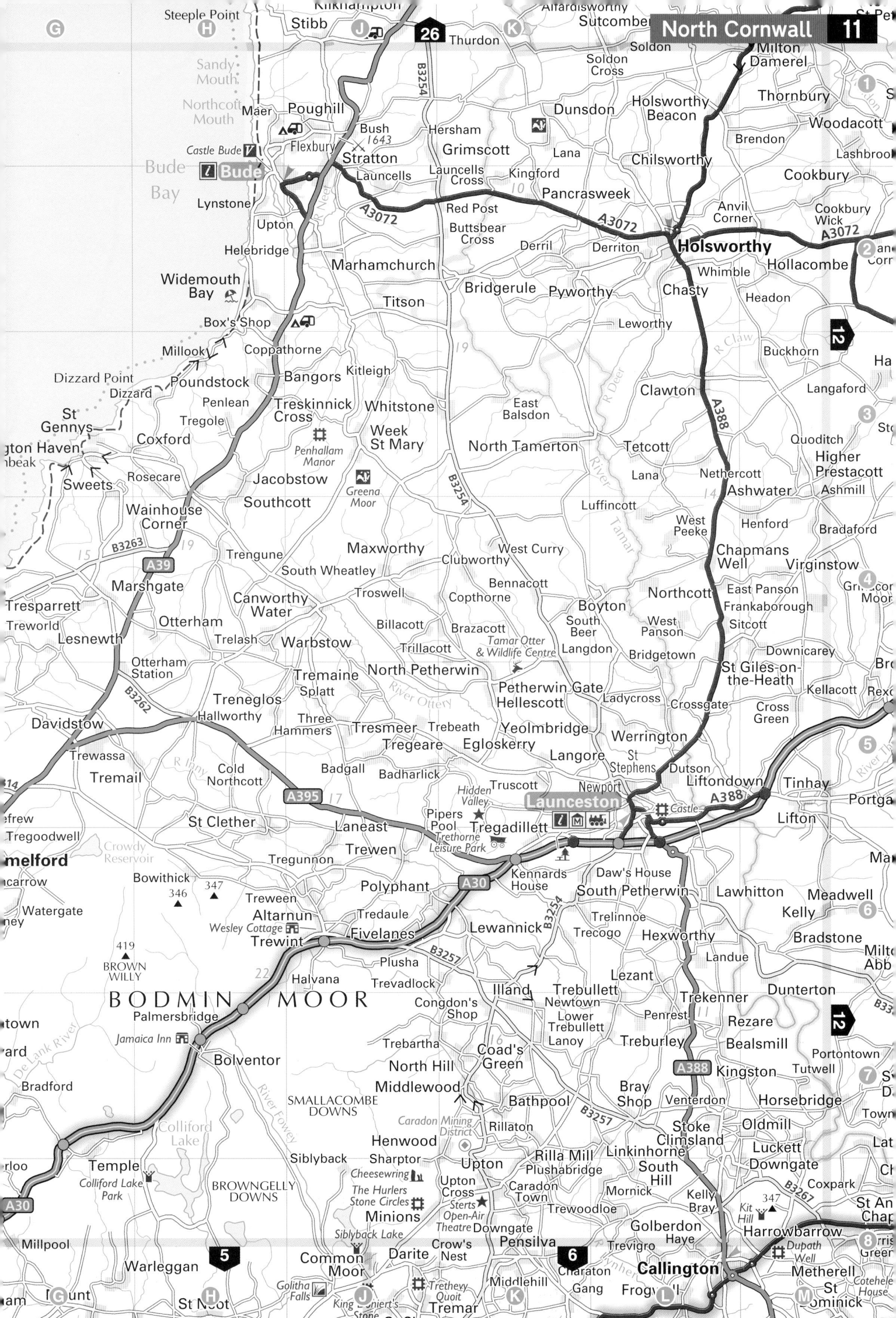

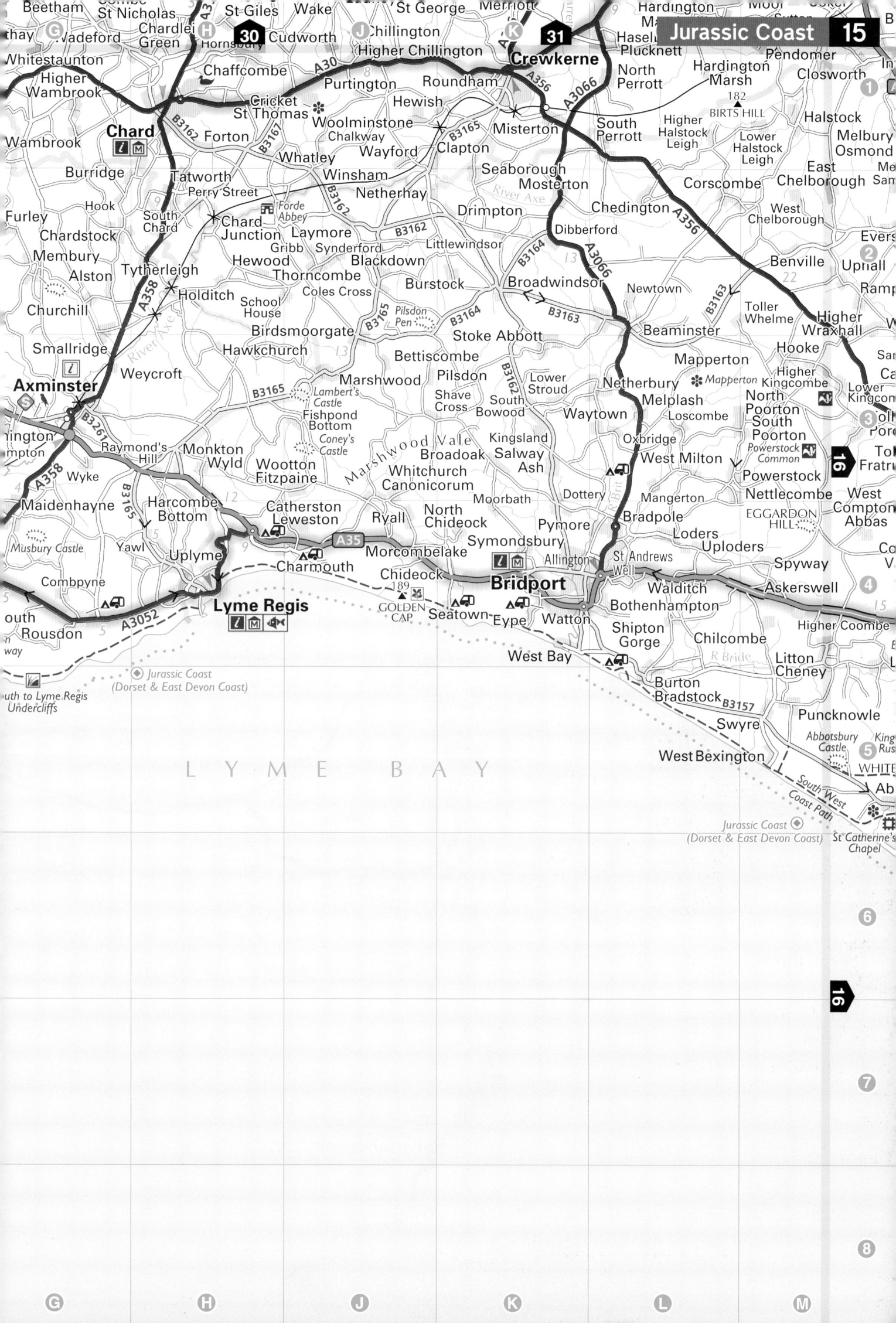

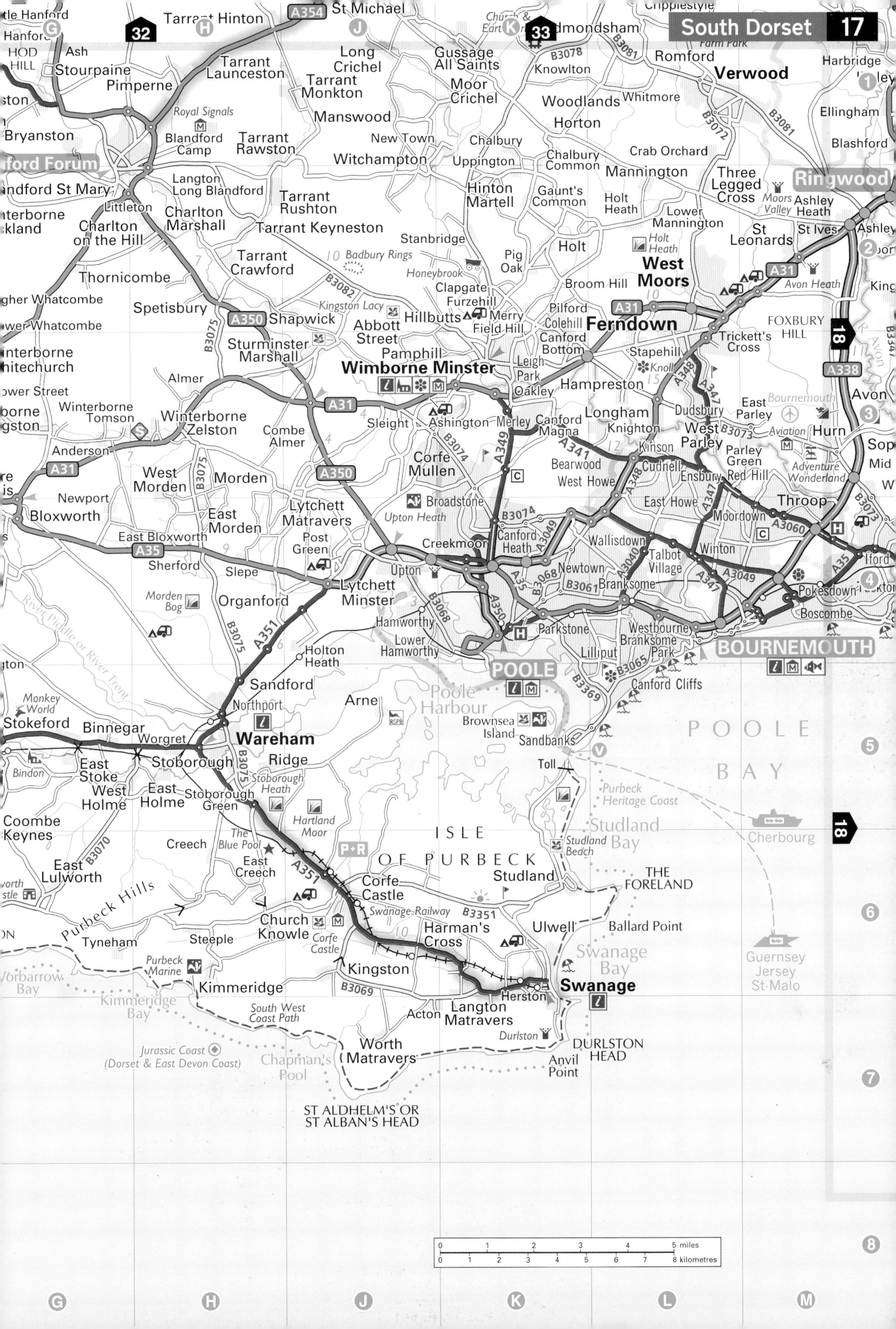

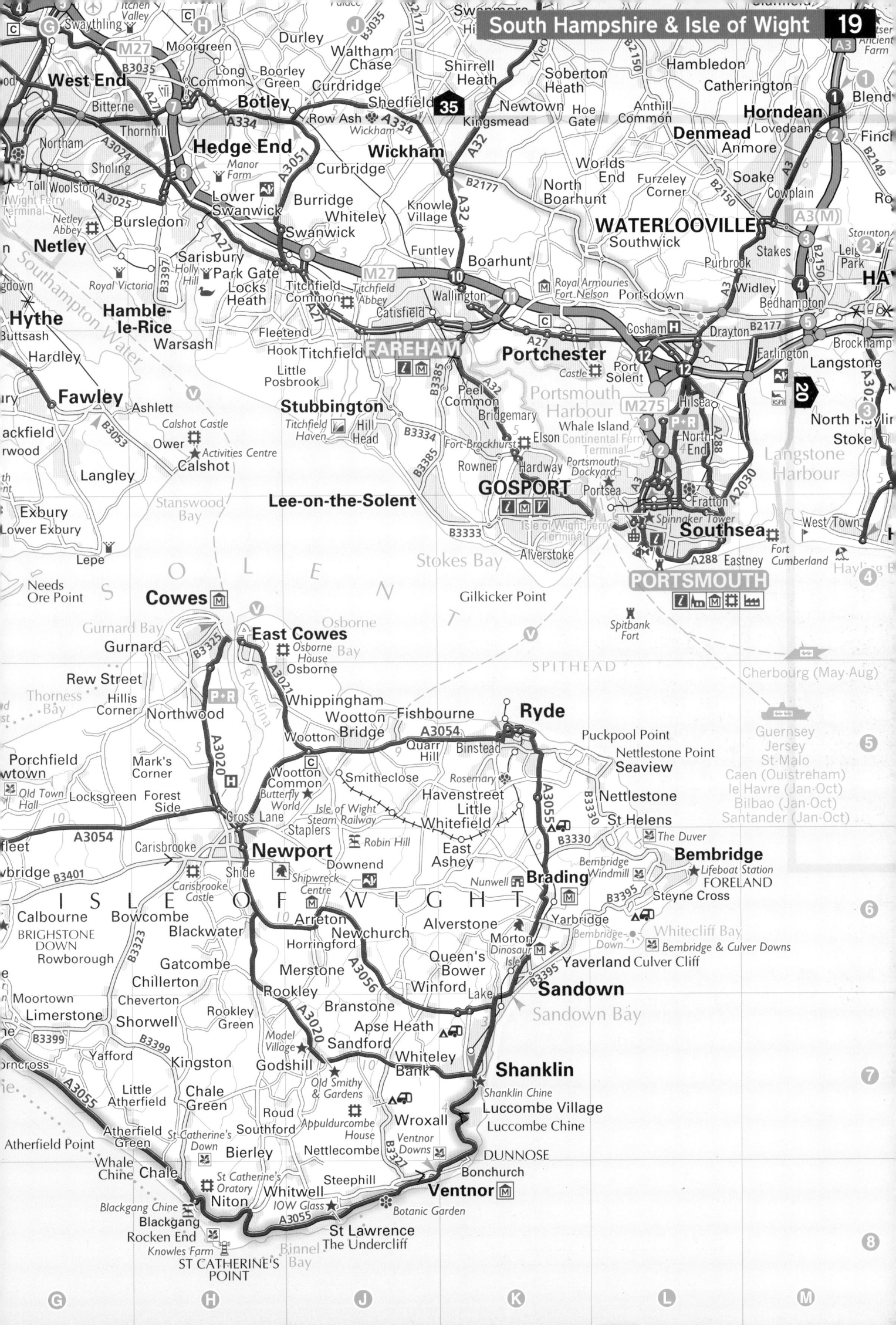

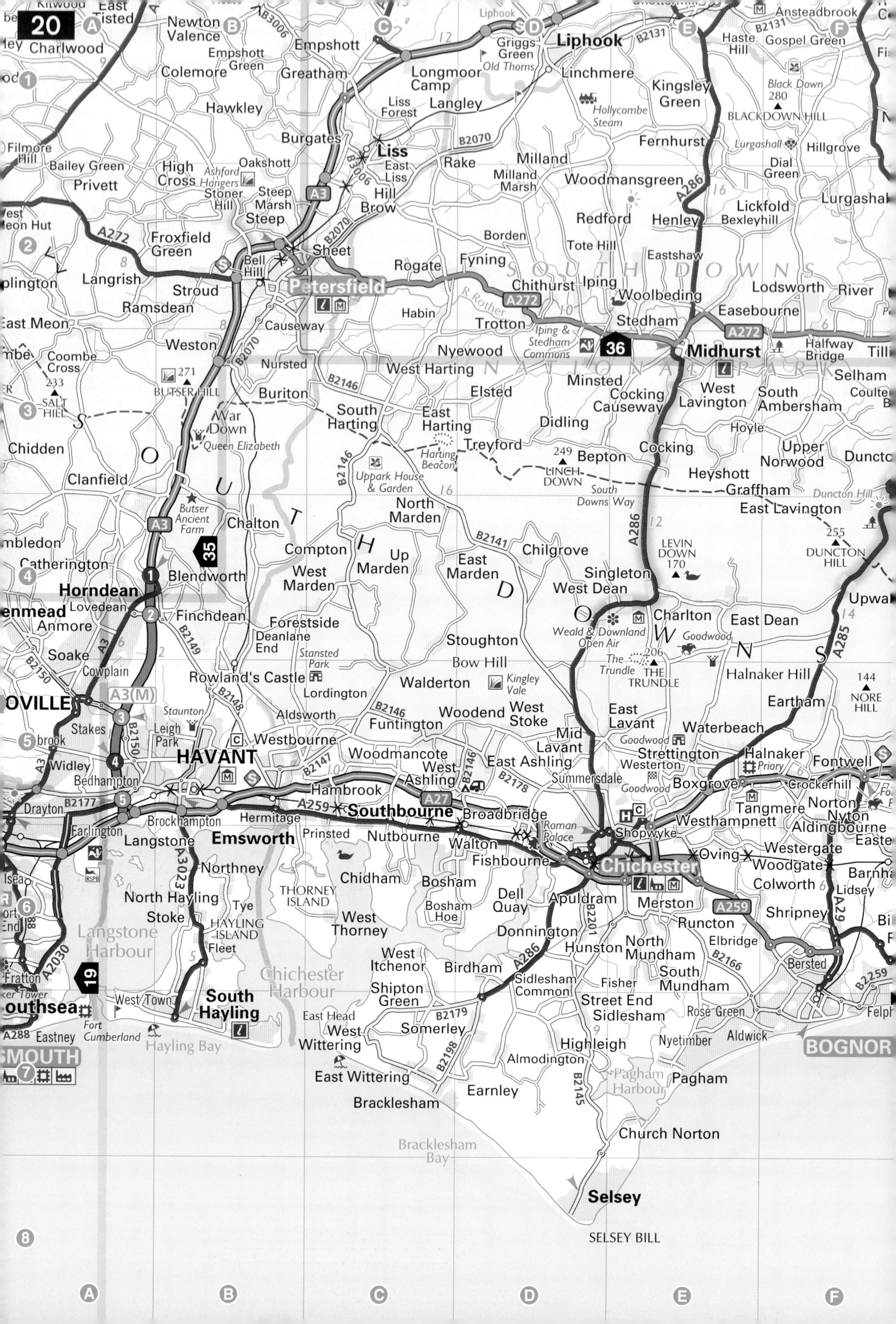

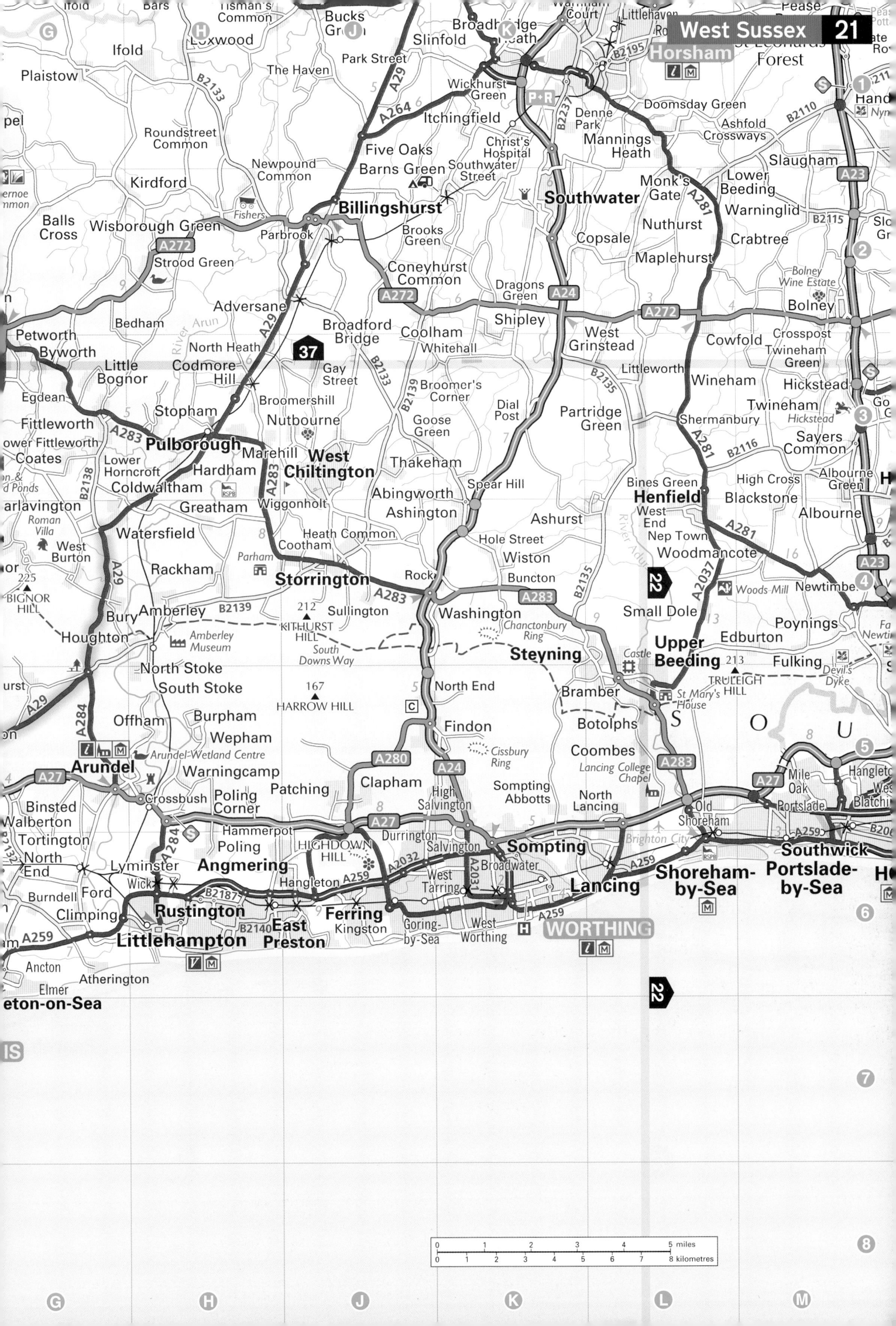

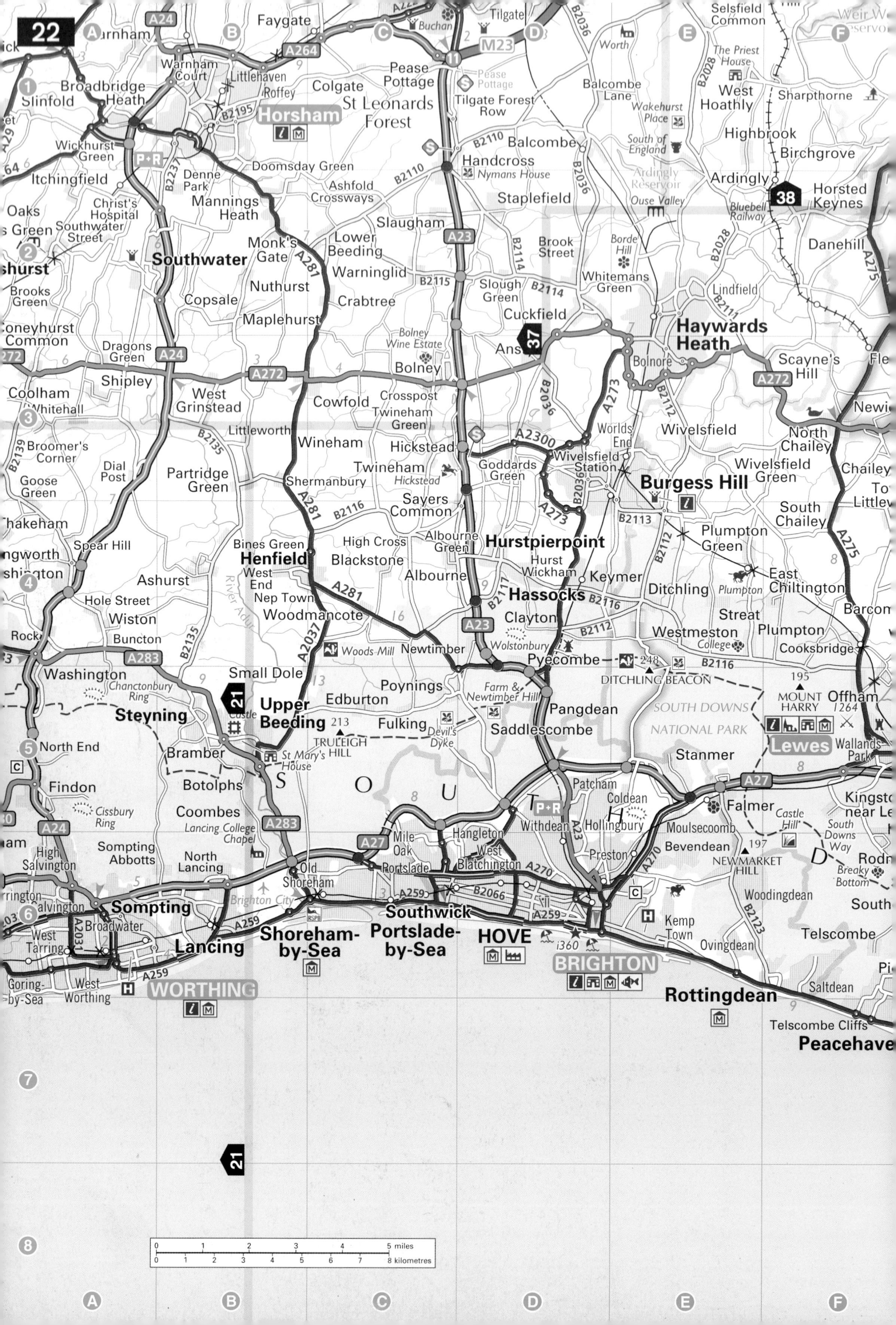

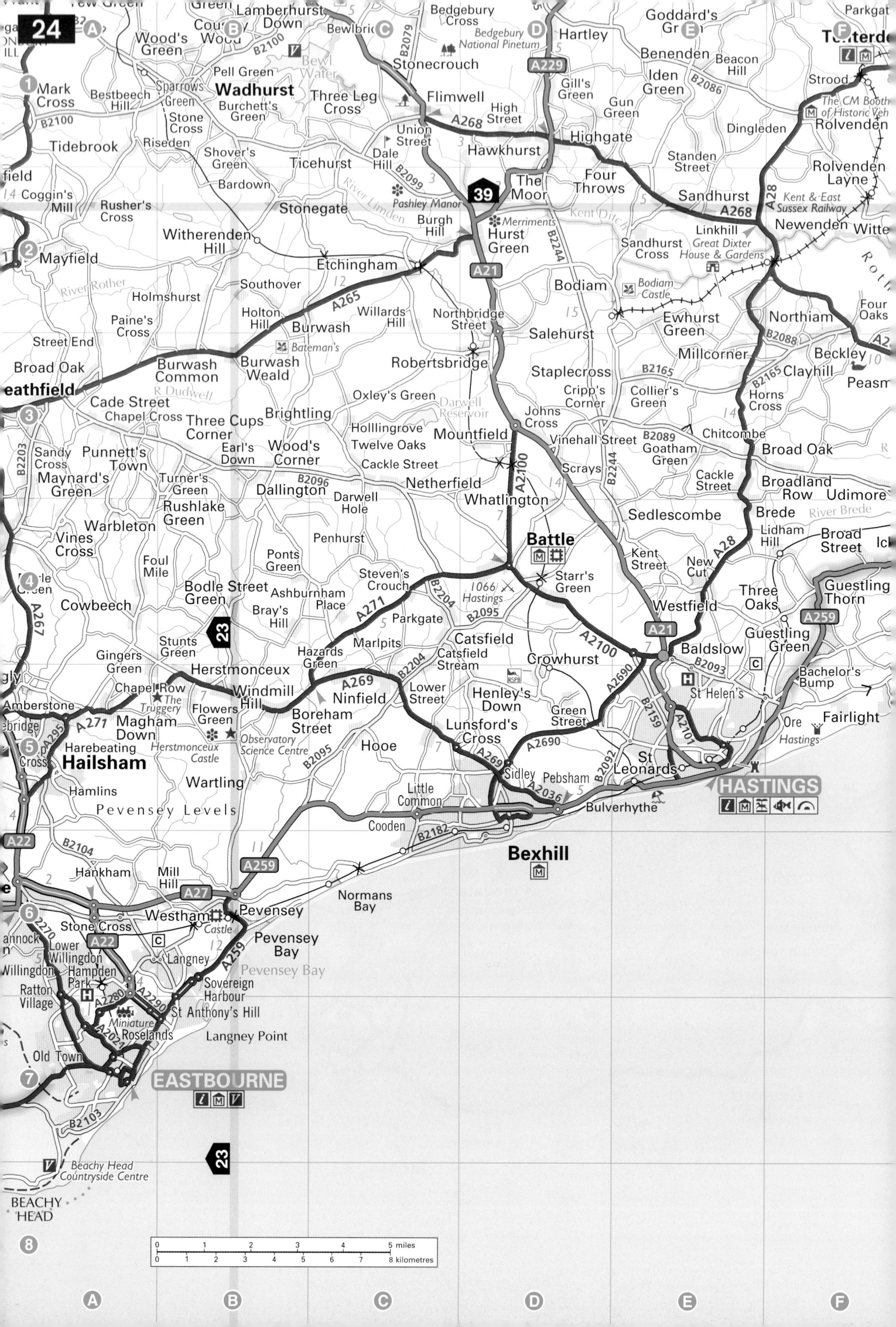

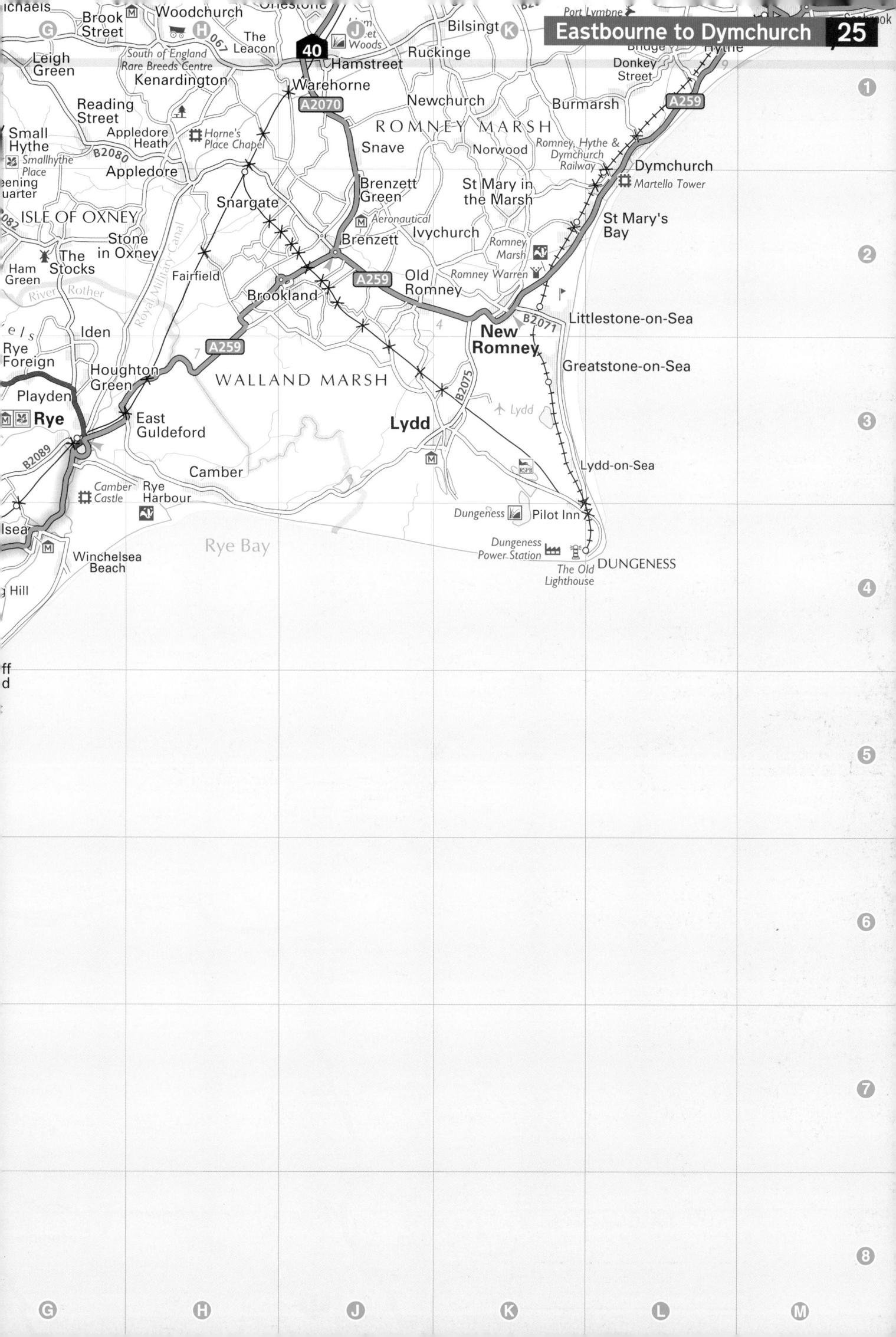

G   Brook Street   Woodchurch   Onestone

Leigh Green

H 067   The Leacon   Bilsingt K   Port Lymbne   Hythe

Small Hythe   Kenardington   40   Hamstreet   Ruckinge   et Woods   Donkey Street

Reading Street   Warehorne   A259   Newchurch   Burmarsh

Appledore Heath   A2070   ROMNEY MARSH   Romney, Hythe & Dymchurch Railway   Dymchurch

Smallhythe Place   Horne's Place Chapel   Snave   Norwood   Martello Tower

ening quarter   B2080   Appledore

ISLE OF OXNEY   Snargate   Brenzett Green   St Mary in the Marsh   St Mary's Bay

Stone in Oxney   Brenzett   Aeronautical   Ivychurch   Romney Marsh

The Stocks   Fairfield   A259   Old Romney   Romney Warren

Ham Green   Brookland   New Romney   Littlestone-on-Sea

River Rother   e l s   Iden   A259   WALLAND MARSH   B2071

Rye Foreign   Houghton Green   4   Greatstone-on-Sea

Playden   A259   Lydd   B2075   Lydd

Rye   East Guldeford   RSPB   Lydd-on-Sea

B2089   Camber

Isea   Camber Castle   Rye Harbour

Winchelsea Beach   Dungeness   Pilot Inn

g Hill   Rye Bay   Dungeness Power Station   DUNGENESS

The Old Lighthouse

1 2 3 4 5 6 7 8

North West
Point

*Lundy
Heritage Coast*

LUNDY

142

*Marine
Reserve*

Marisco

Shutter Point

Surf Point

B A R N S T A P L E

O R

B I D E F O R D   B A Y

*Shipload
Bay*

HARTLAND POINT

Titchberry

Brownsham

Damehole
Point

*Hartland Abbey
& Gardens*

Velly

Clovelly

*Hartla
Heritage*

Stoke

B3248

Buck's
Mills

Hartland Quay

Higher
Clovelly

H
C

*Speke's Mill
Mouth*

Hartland

4

Milford

*Docton
Mill*

Philham

Milky Way

Buck's
Cross

A39

Elmscott

Edistone

Woolfardisworthy

Cranford

Par

Hardisworthy

Tosberry

Parkha
Ash

South
Hole

Welcombe

Ashmanswort

Mead

Darracott

Meddon

East
Putford

Gooseham
Mill

Woolley

Gnome
Reserve

Wes
Putf

Gooseham

Eastcott

16

East
Youlstone

Dinworthy

Morwenstow

West Youlstone

Colscott

Higher Sharpnose Point

Shop

A39

Bradworthy

*South West
Coast Path*

Woodford

Lower Sharpnose Point

*Tamar
Lakes*

Kimworthy

Sutcombe

Steeple Point

Kilkhampton

Alfardisworthy

Stibb

Sutcombemill

Thurdon

Soldon

River

M
Da

Soldon
Cross

B325

G H J K

1

2

3

4

5

6

7

8

Ilfracombe
Hele
Water Mouth
Combe Martin Bay
Watermouth Castle
Haggington Hill
Woody Bay
Martinhoe
Trentishoe
Hunter's Inn
Kemacott
Killington
Heale
Woody Bay
Toll
D

Lee
Slade
Chambercombe Manor
Hele Corn Mill
Berrynarbor
Combe Martin
Dean
Parracombe
Lynton & Barnstaple Railway

Bull Point
Lincombe
Rockham Bay
Morte Point
Mortehoe
Two Pots
Mullacott Cross
A3123
Lynton Cross
A399
Kentisbury
Dean
Kentisbury Ford
Blackmoor Gate
Churntow

Woolacombe
Trimstone
B3343
West Down
Wildlife & Dinosaur Park
Berry Down Cross
Patchole
Kentisbury Ford
Blackmoor Gate
28
Stowford

Morte Bay
Bradwell
Chapel Wood
North Buckland
Bittadon
Clifton
East Down
Arlington Beccott
Arlington
Exmoor Zoo
landpound ervoir
Barto Tow

Baggy Point
Pickwell
Putsborough
Nethercott
Halsinger
Higher Muddiford
Milltown
Churchill
Arlington Court
Loxhore
Knightacott
Leworthy
Fulla

Croyde Bay
Georgeham
Darracott
Winsham
Knowle
Marwood
Muddiford
Loxhore Cott
Lower Loxhore
Bratton Fleming
River Bray
Ly

Croyde Bay
Croyde
B3231
Saunton
Lobb
Boode
Pippacott
Marwood Hill
Kingsheanton
Guineaford
Shirwell
Benton
A399
Brayford

Braunton
Heanton Punchardon
Prixford
Stoke Rivers
Gunn
Charle

North Devon Heritage Coast
Braunton Burrows
Wrafton
Chivenor
Ashford
Bradiford
Pilton
Burridge
Goodleigh
Northleigh
Stoodleigh
4

River Taw
Derby
Barnstaple
Willesleigh
Bradninch
Elwell
East Buckland

Isley Marsh
Fremington
B3233
Bickington
A3125
Roundswell
C
Lake
Landkey
Swimbridge Newland
West Buckland
Swimbridge
A361
5

Crow Point
Yelland
Horsacott
P+R
Yarnacott
Castle Hill
Alle Cross

Northam Burrows
Instow
Bickleton
Tawstock
St John's Chapel
Bishop's Tawton
Hannaford
Kerscott
8

Westward Ho!
Northam
Tapeley Park
Westleigh
Horwood
Newton Tracey
Harracott
Week
Herner
Cobbaton
East Stowford
Filleigh

Abbotsham
The Big Sheep
Eastleigh
Pillhead
East-the-Water
Lower Lovacott
Hiscott
Ensis
Chapelton
Chittlehampton
B3227
Clapworthy
Geo Nymp

Bideford
Yeo Vale
Landcross
Alverdiscott
Delley
Atherington
A377
Umberleigh
Warkleigh
Satterleigh
6

Ford oss oodtown
Littleham
Saltrens
Weare Giffard
Huntshaw
Yarnscombe
Langridgeford
Chittlehamholt
B3226
28

ldworthy
Cabbacott
Monkleigh
Huntshaw Cross
High Bullen
B3227
High Bickington
Portsmouth Arms
Kings Nympton

Buckland Brewer
Frithelstock
A386
Great Torrington
Dodscott
St Giles in the Wood
Kingscott
Burrington
River Taw

ry
Frithelstock Stone
Taddiport
RHS Rosemoor
Roborough
Colleton Mills
Cadbu Barto

ehillhead
Southcott
Little Torrington
Beaford
B3217
7

lkworthy
Langtree
Langtree Week
Great Potheridge
A3124
Ashreigney
Elstone

Stibb Cross
Berry Cross
Little Potheridge
Riddlecombe
Bridge Reeve

A388
Peters Marland
Winswell
Halsdon
Merton
Huish
Dolton
Hollocombe
Ashley

n green
Newton St Petrock
Little Marland
North Town
Petrockstow
Meeth Quarry
Dowland
Wembwort
Eggesford

G H 12 J K L M 8

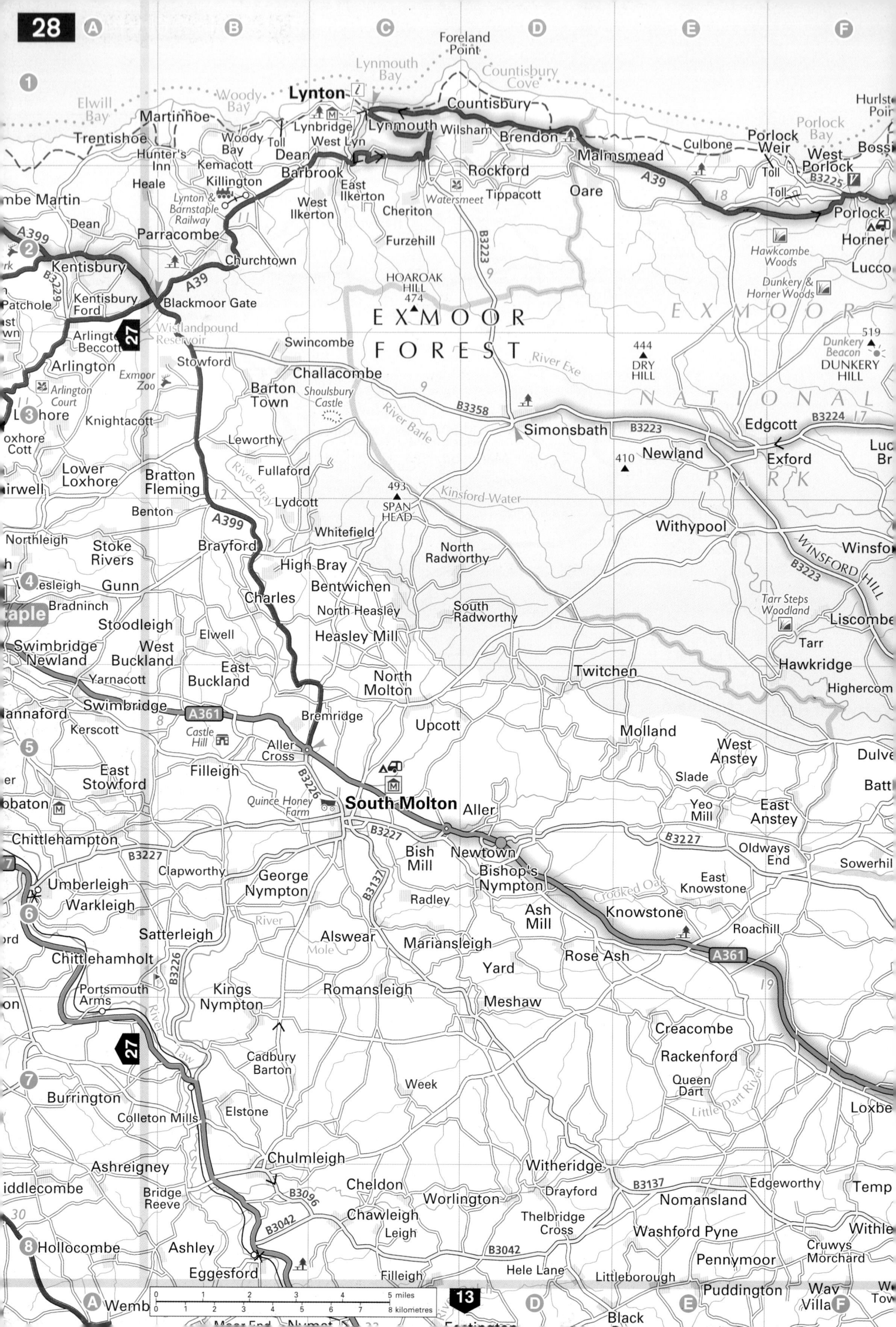

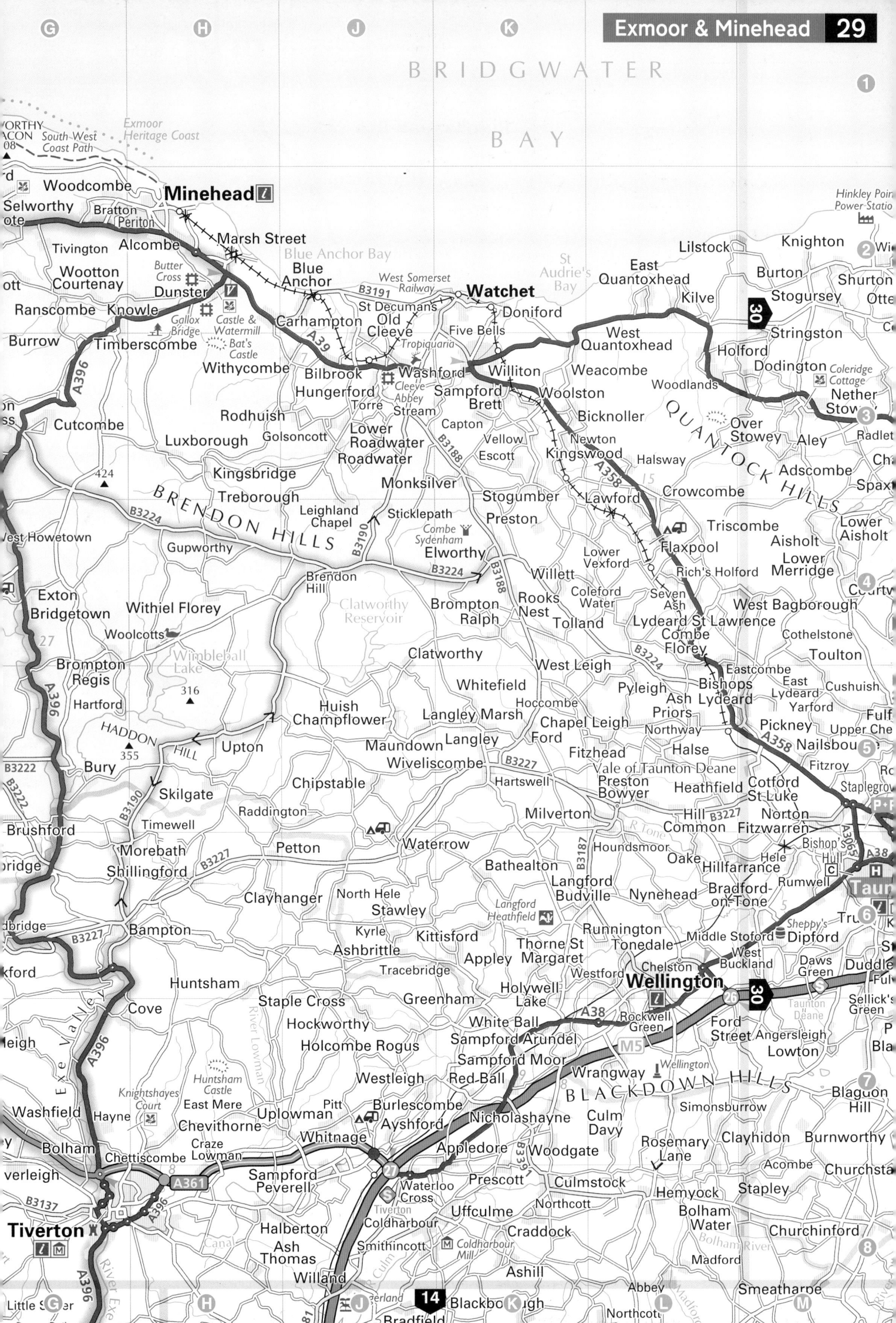

1

BRIDGWATER BAY

Berrow

East Brent Sedgemoor Badgworth
44 Tarnock Rooks Bridge Sutton
Brent Knoll Stone Allerton Chapel Allerton Ashton West Stoughton

Burnham-on-Sea Edithmead 22 Battleborough Northwick
Highbridge Mark Causeway Mark Blackford Yarrow
Bridgwater Bay Alstone Hackness Watchfield Southwick Westham Heath House

2 Lilstock Knighton Wick Stockland Bristol West Huntspill Huntspill Walrow Bason Bridge East Huntspill Burtle Hill Catcott Burtle
East Quantoxhead Burton Shurton Stogursey Stretcholt M5 Cote Secret World Wildlife Rescue Edington Burtle
Kilve 29 Otterhampton Cockwood Coultings Combwich Pawlett Puriton Woolavington Chilton Polden Edington Catcott
West Quantoxhead Stringston Holford Rodway Walpole Dunball 23 Cossington Polden Hills Catcott Sha
Dodington Coleridge Cottage Fiddington Chilton Trinity Horsey Bawdrip Stawell Moorlinch Greinton Pe
3 Nether Stowey A39 Cannington Wembdon Bradney Chedzoy Sutton Mallet
Over Stowey Aley Radlet Bradley Green Bridgwater East Bower Bussex Liney A361
Halsway Charlinch Durleigh Huntworth Westonzoyland River Cary
Crowcombe Adscombe Spaxton Lexworthy 24 Andersea Middlezoy Greylake
QUANTOCK HILLS Four Forks Enmore Rhode Compass Thorngrove Othery Hi
Triscombe Lower Aisholt Andersfield Woolmerston Moorland Langport
4 Flaxpool Aisholt Goathurst North Newton Little Moor A372
Rich's Holford Lower Merridge Courtway Huntstile North Petherton St Michael Church Burrow Bridge Pathe Beer
Seven Ash West Bagborough Broomfield Shearston West Newton Hedging Lyng Burrow Mump Stathe Lo
Lydeard St Lawrence Cothelstone Toulton Clavelshay Thurloxton Hedging A361 Aller A372
Combe Florey Fyne Court Cushuish Kingston St Mary Adsborough Durston Athelney Woodhill Wearn
5 Eastcombe East Lydeard Fulford Gotton West Monkton West Lyng Willows & Wetlands Stoke St Gregory Oath
Bishops Lydeard Yarford Hestercombe Cheddon Fitzpaine Creech Heathfield Meare Green Wick Epi
Ash Priors Pickney Upper Cheddon Sidbrook Charlton Curry Rivel
Northway Nailsbourne Rowford Monkton Heathfield Langaller Creech St Michael Knapp Heale
Halse Fitzroy Staplegrove Bathpool Huntham
Preston Bowyer Cotford St Luke Norton Fitzwarren 25 Ruishton North Curry Swell Wood
Heathfield Hill Bishop's Hull Taunton Henlade Thornfalcon Greenway Willtown Drayton
Oake Hillfarrance Hele Rumwell Haydon Ash Wrantage Curry Mallet Fivehead Thor
Nynehead Bradford-on-Tone Shoreditch Stoke St Mary Meare Green Isle Brewers Hambridge
6 Tonedale Middle Stoford Kibbear West Hatch Beercrombe Westport
Chelston West Buckland Staplehay Orchard Portman Thurlbear Hatch Beauchamp West Lambrook Blado
Wellington Daws Green Duddlestone Fulwood Heale Stewley Puckington New Cross
26 Sellick's Green Corfe Slough Green Ashill Stocklinch Barrington Court
29 West Buckland Angersleigh Pitminster Staple Fitzpaine Abbey Hill Ilton Ilford Shepton Beauchamp
Rockwell Green Lowton Blagdon Kenny Windmill Hill Rapps Atherstone Seaving
7 M5 Wellington BLACKDOWN HILLS Blagdon Hill Curland Barrington Hill Ashwell Seavington St Mich
Simonsburrow Clayhidon Burnworthy STAPLE HILL Hastings Southtown A303
Rosemary Lane Acombe Fyfett Buckland St Mary Blackwater Broadway Horton S Whitelackington Ilminster
Hemyock Churchstanton Birch Wood Horton Cross Townsend Seavington St Mary
Stapley Bishopswood Donyatt Kingstone Dowlish Ford Allowensha
Bolham Water Churchinford Newtown Crock Street Knowle St Giles Dowlish Wake Hinton St George
8 Madford Bishopswood Marsh Northay Beetham Combe St Nicholas Chardleigh Green Hornsbury Cudworth Chillington St Georg
Abbey Northcott Whitestaunton Wadeford Peasmarsh Sea Higher Chilling Purtington Roun
15 Chaff nbe A30

Wells · **Shepton Mallet** · **Glastonbury** · **Street** · **Somerton** · **Yeovil** · **Sherborne** · **Wincanton**

Draycott · Priddy · East Water · Chewton Mendip · Bathway · Emborough · Clapton · Chilcompton · Stratton-on-the-Fosse · Newbury · Kilmersdon · Mells

Clewer · Cocklake · Rodney Stoke · Old Ditch · Ebbor Gorge · Westbury-sub-Mendip · Green Ore · Gurney Slade · Downside · Holcombe · Highbury · Upper Vobster · Little

Wedmore · Latcham · Theale · Panborough · Henton · Wookey Hole · Walcombe · Lower Milton · West Horrington · East Horrington · Ashwick · Oakhill · Stoke St Michael · East End · Coleford · Vobster · Downhead · Whatley · Chantry Castle

Bagley · Bleadney · Yarley · Worth · Coxley Wick · Dulcote · Dinder · Darshill · Shepton Mallet · Dean · Leighton · Cloford · Trudoxh · Nunn Catcn

Westhay Moor · Lower Godney · Upper Godney · Polsham · Coxley · Southway · North Town · West Compton · Croscombe · Charlton · Doulting · Cranmore · East Cranmore · Wanstrow

Westhay · Godney · Meare Fish House · North Wootton · Westholme · Pilton · East Compton · Prestleigh · Chesterblade · Higher Alham · West Town · Upton Nobl

Meare · Stileway · Northload Bridge · Brindham · Glastonbury Tor · Havyatt · West Pennard · Street on the Fosse · Pylle · Royal Bath & West · Stoney Stratton · Westcombe · Batcombe · North Brewham · King Alfred's Tower

Glastonbury · Northover · Edgarley · Woodland Street · Coxbridge · West Bradley · East Pennard · Hembridge · Evercreech · Milton Clevedon · South Brewham · Hardwa

Walton · Asney · Street · Butleigh Wootton · West Town · Tilham Street · Parbrook · Huxham Green · Wraxall · Ditcheat · Lamyatt · West End · Bruton · Hardwa

Overleigh · Baltonsborough · Gosling Street · Ham Street · Catsham · Southwood · Stone · Alhampton · Hornblotton Green · Clanville · Wyke Champflower · Ansford · Cole · Redlynch · Stoney Stoke

Compton Dundon · Butleigh · Silver Street · West Lydford · East Lydford · Alford · Lovington · Pitcombe · Bratton Seymour · Shepton Montague · Charlton Ble · Musgrove · Penselw

Dundon · Littleton · Barton St David · Kingweston · Lydford on Fosse · Wheathill · Foddington · Castle Cary · Galhampton · Yarlington · Bayford · Wincanton

Somerton · Midney · Keinton Mandeville · Charlton Mackrell · Babcary · North Barrow · South Barrow · Brookhampton · Woolston · Lattiford · Wincanton

Upton · South Hill · Catsgore · Charlton Adam · Lytes Cary Manor · Kingsdon · North Cadbury · Little Weston · Blackford · Holton · Compton Pauncefoot · Maperton · North Cheriton · South Cheriton

Long Sutton · Knole · Little Load · Downhead · West Camel · Queen Camel · Sparkford · South Cadbury · Horsington · Abbas Combe

Long Load · Northover · Ilchester · Podimore · RNAS Yeovilton · Bridgehampton · Wales · Marston Magna · Sutton Montis · Corton Denham · Stowell · Charlton Horethorne · Templecombe · Yenston

Witcombe · Draycott · Yeovilton · Limington · Chilton Cantelo · Ashington · Rimpton · Milborne Wick · Henstridge Ash · Henstridge

Ash · Tintinhull Garden · Fleet Air Arm · Yeovil Marsh · West Mudford · Adber · Sandford Orcas · Milborne Port · Oborne

Treasurer's House · Chilthorne Domer · Mudford Sock · Mudford · Trent · Poyntington · Purse Caundle · Stalbridge Weston

Martock · Hurst · Priory · Stoke sub Hamdon · Tintinhull · Odcombe · Preston Plucknett · Up Mudford · Nether Compton · Goathill · Sherborne Old Castle · Haydon · Stourton Caundle

Norton sub Hamdon · Montacute · Yeovil · Over Compton · Trent · Stallen · Sherborne · North Wootton · Allweston · Bishop's Caundle

Wigborough · Little Norton · Chiselborough · West Coker · Brympton · Barwick · Bradford Abbas · Sherborne Castle & Gardens · Folke · Lydlin

East Chinnock · Burton · Thornford · Lillington · Longburton · Caundle Marsh · Holwell

Middle Chinnock · Hardington Moor · East Coker · Sutton Bingham · Stoford · Beer Hackett · Knighton · Crouch Hill · Pleck · King's

Crewkerne · North Perrott · Haselbury Plucknett · Pendomer · Closworth · Ryme Intrinseca · Yetminster · Boys Hill · Sandhills · East Pulham · Packers · Hamlet · Holnest

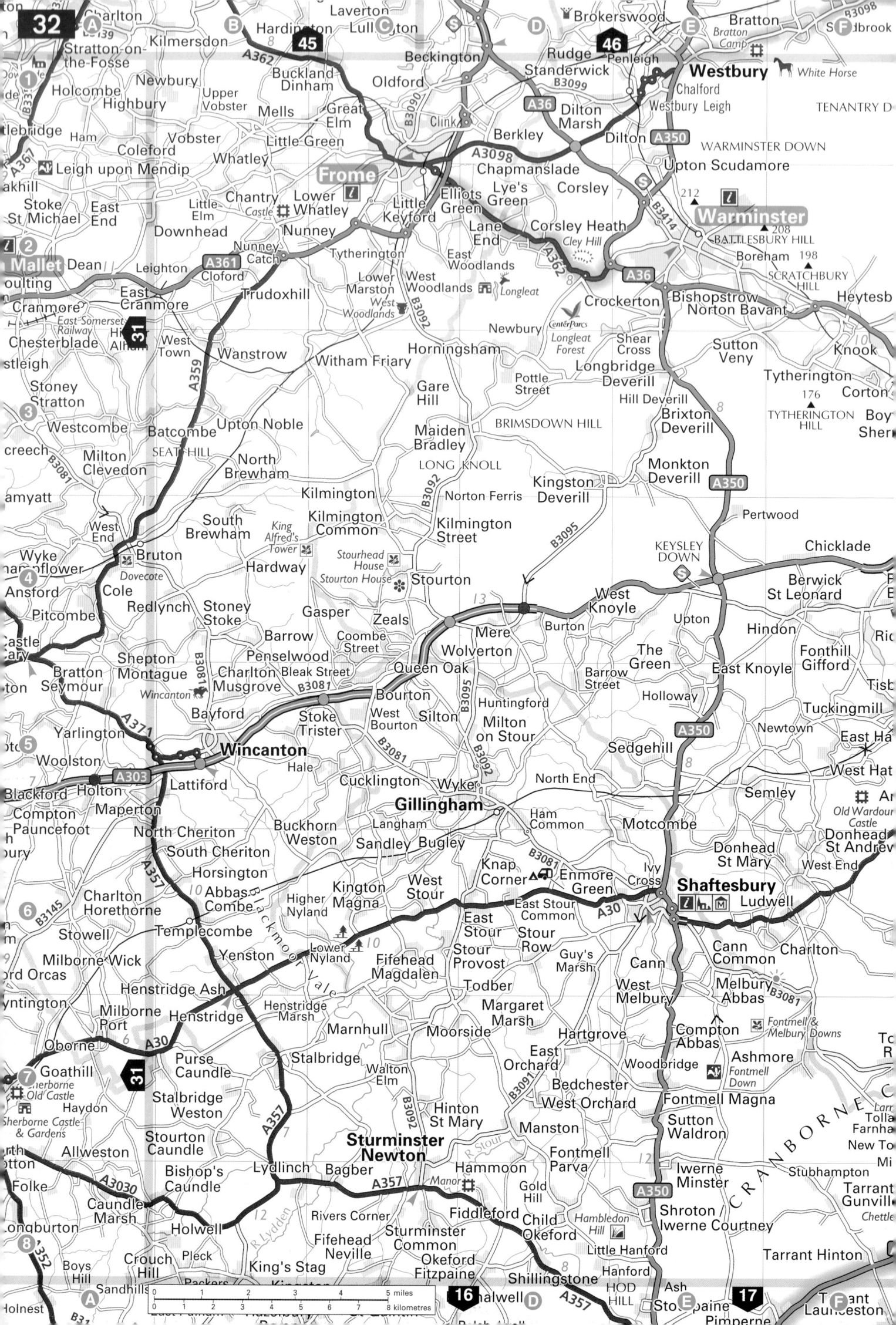

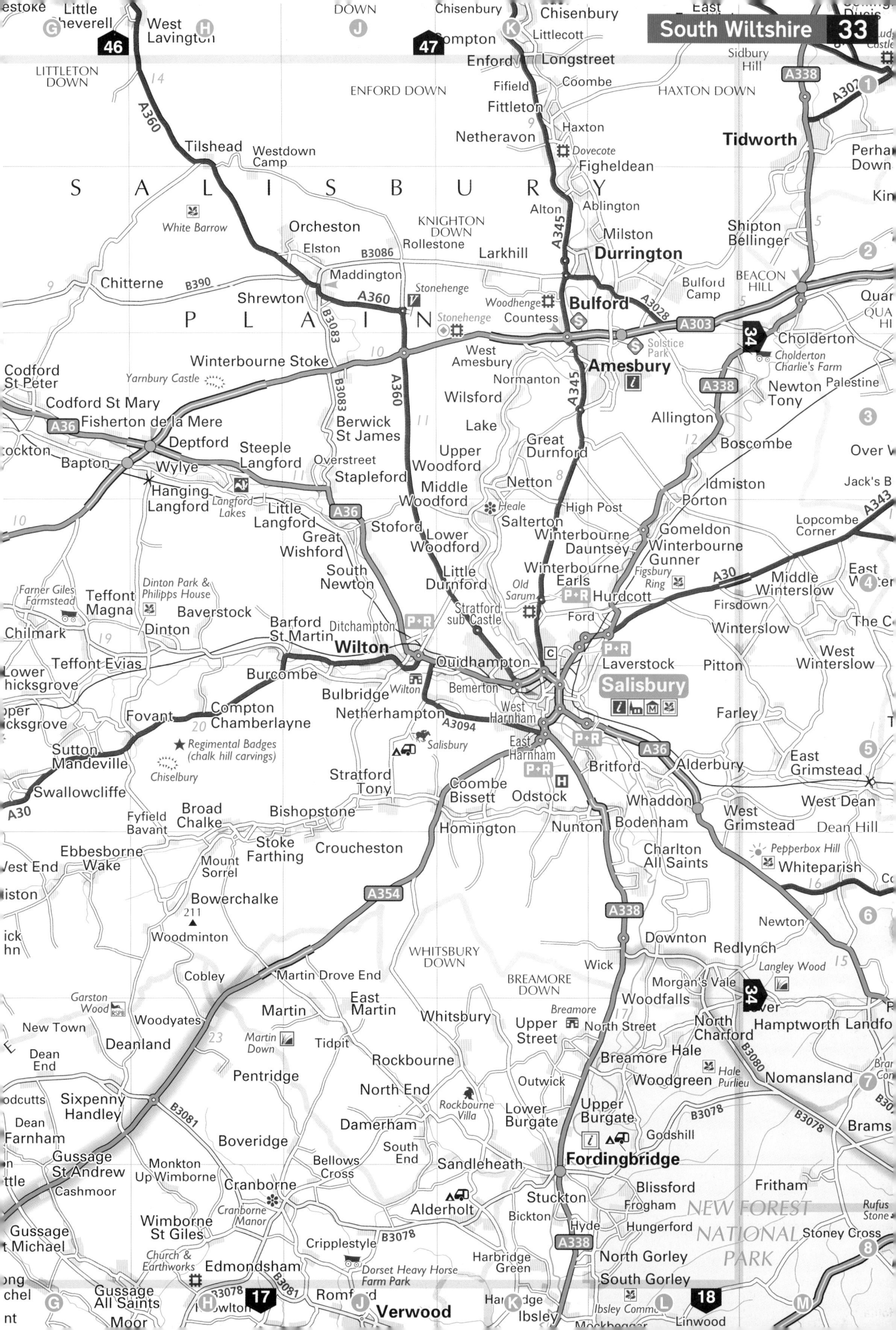

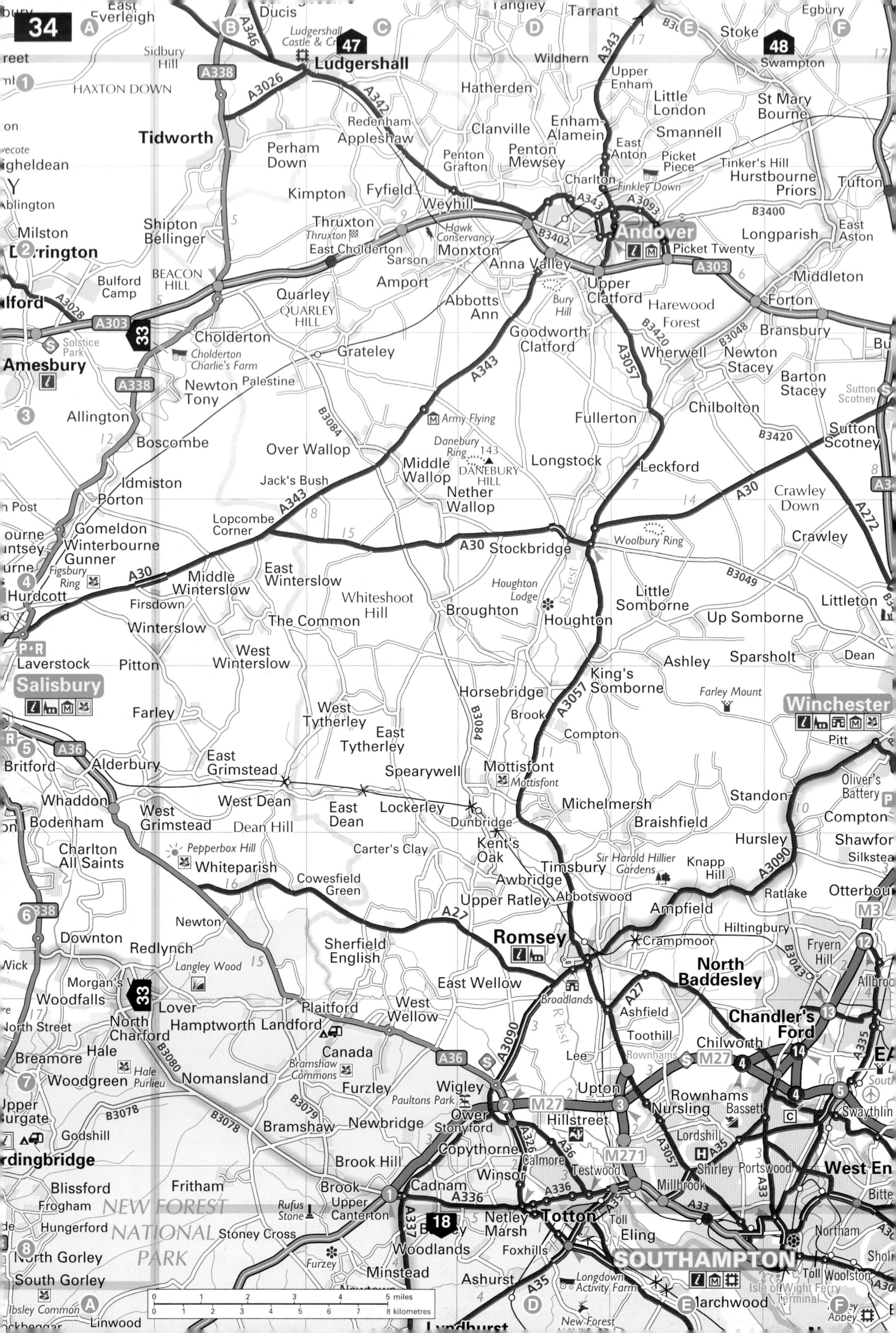

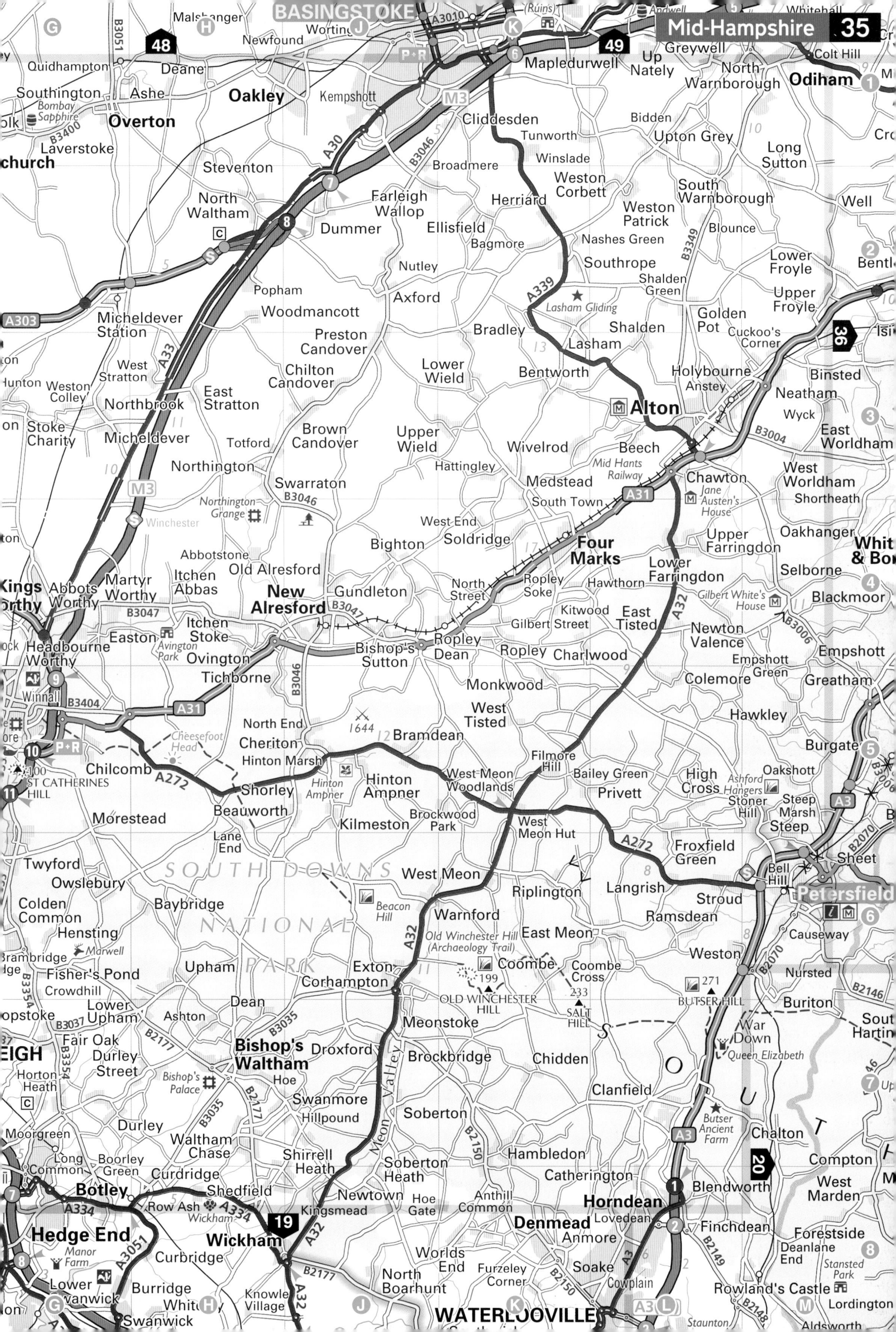

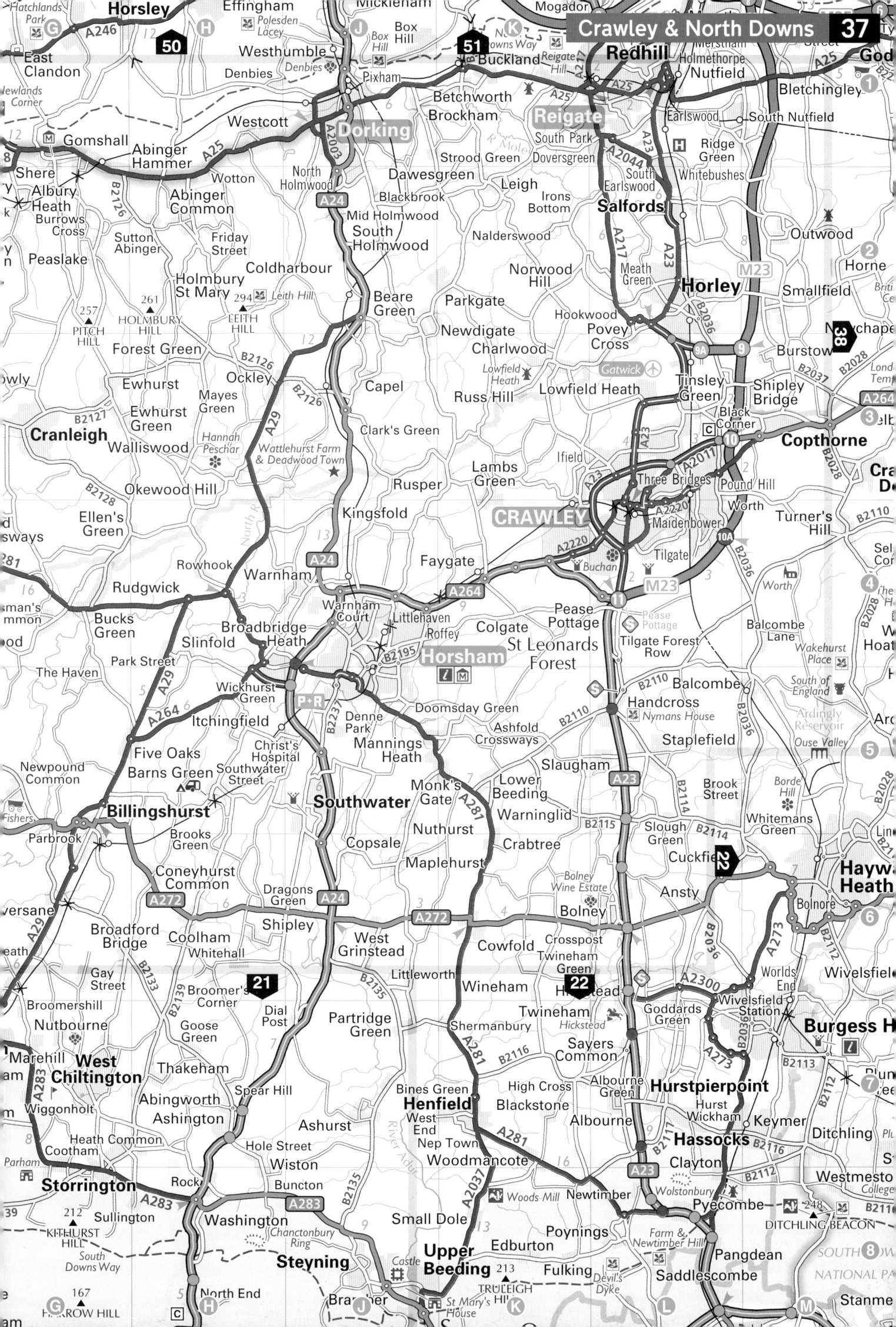

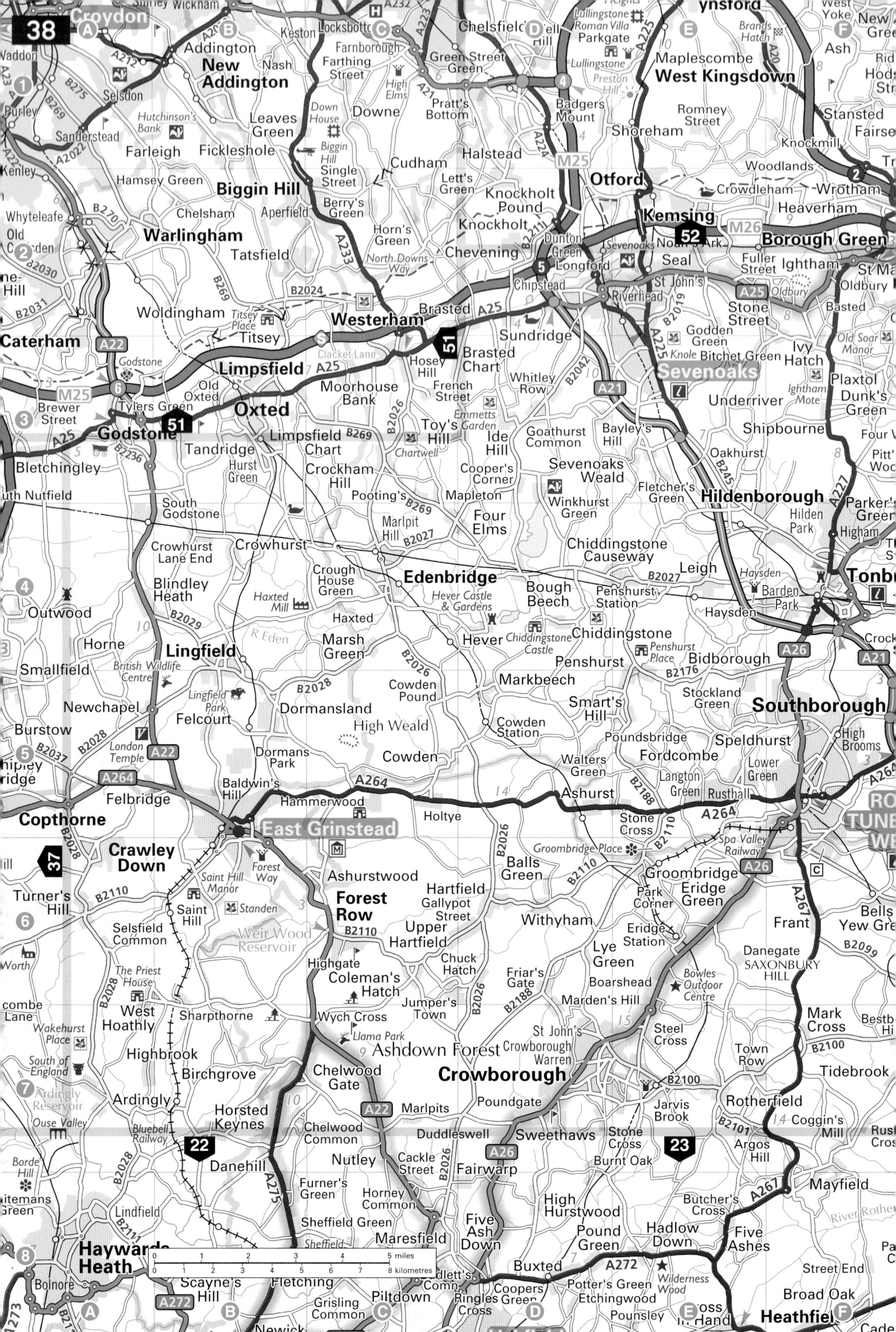

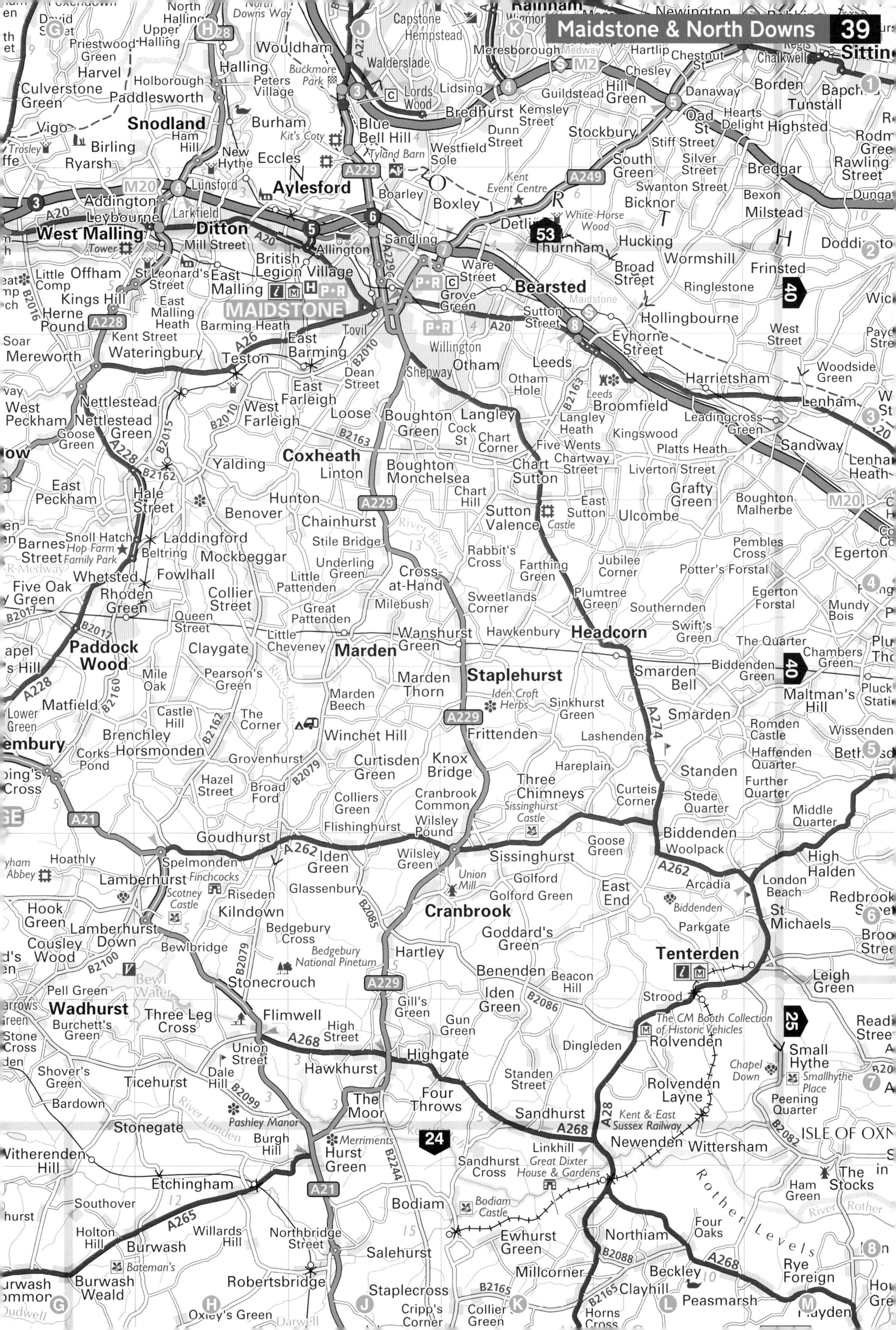

Wouldham
Capstone
Hempstead
Rainham
Newington
Sittingbourne
Halling
Upper Halling
Priestwood Green
Harvel
Culverstone Green
Holborough
Paddlesworth
Peters Village
Buckmore Park
Walderslade
Lords Wood
Lidsing
Meresborough
Hartlip
Chestnut St
Chalkwell
Bapchild
Borden
Tunstall
Chesley
Hill Green
Guildstead
Danaway
Oad St
Hearts Delight
Highsted
Snodland
Vigo
Trosley
Birling
Ryarsh
Ham Hill
New Hythe
Burham
Kit's Coty
Eccles
Blue Bell Hill
Tyland Barn
Bredhurst
Kemsley Street
Dunn Street
Westfield Sole
Stockbury
Stiff Street
Silver Street
South Green
Bredgar
Rawling Street
Rodmersham Green
Lunsford
Aylesford
Boarley
Boxley
Kent Event Centre
Swanton Street
Bexon
Milstead
Addington
Leybourne
Larkfield
West Malling
Tower
Ditton
Mill Street
Sandling
Allington
British Legion Village
Detling
White Horse Wood
Thurnham
Bicknor
Hucking
Wormshill
Frinsted
Doddington
Little Comp
Offham
St Leonard's Street
East Malling
Kings Hill
Herne Pound
East Malling Heath
MAIDSTONE
Barming Heath
Ware Street
Grove Green
Bearsted
Broad Street
Ringlestone
Maidstone
Sutton Street
Hollingbourne
West Street
Soar
Mereworth
Kent Street
Wateringbury
Teston
East Barming
Tovil
Dean Street
Willington
Otham
Shepway
Leeds
Eyhorne Street
Otham Hole
Harrietsham
Woodside Green
Lenham
West Peckham
Nettlestead
Nettlestead Green
Goose Green
West Farleigh
East Farleigh
Loose
Boughton Green
Langley
Leeds Broomfield
Langley Heath
Leadingcross Green
Kingswood
Cock St
Chart Corner
Five Wents
Platts Heath
Sandway
Lenham Heath
Coxheath
Yalding
Linton
Boughton Monchelsea
Chart Sutton
Chartway Street
Liverton Street
Grafty Green
Boughton Malherbe
East Peckham
Hale Street
Hunton
Benover
Chart Hill
Sutton Valence
Castle
East Sutton
Ulcombe
Chainhurst
River Beult
Barnes Street
Snoll Hatch
Hop Farm Family Park
Beltring
Laddingford
Stile Bridge
Mockbeggar
Rabbit's Cross
Jubilee Corner
Pembles Cross
Egerton
Whetsted
Fowlhall
Underling Green
Farthing Green
Potter's Forstal
Five Oak Green
Rhoden Green
Collier Street
Little Pattenden
Cross-at-Hand
Plumtree Green
Sweetlands Corner
Egerton Forstal
Mundy Bois
Queen Street
Great Pattenden
Milebush
Southernden
Paddock Wood
Claygate
Little Cheveney
Marden
Wanshurst Green
Hawkenbury
Headcorn
Swift's Green
The Quarter
Chambers Green
Pluckley
Mile Oak
Pearson's Green
River Teise
Marden Thorn
Staplehurst
Smarden Bell
Biddenden Green
Matfield
Marden Beech
Iden Croft Herbs
Sinkhurst Green
Maltman's Hill
Lower Green
Castle Hill
The Corner
Winchet Hill
Frittenden
Lashenden
Smarden
Romden Castle
Wissenden
Brenchley
Horsmonden
Corks Pond
Grovenhurst
Curtisden Green
Knox Bridge
Hareplain
Standen
Haffenden Quarter
Bethersden
Hazel Street
Broad Ford
Colliers Green
Cranbrook Common
Three Chimneys
Curteis Corner
Stede Quarter
Further Quarter
Middle Quarter
Flishinghurst
Wilsley Pound
Sissinghurst Castle
Biddenden
Woolpack
Goudhurst
Spelmonden
Iden Green
Wilsley Green
Sissinghurst
Goose Green
High Halden
Hoathly
Bayham Abbey
Lamberhurst
Finchcocks
Scotney Castle
Riseden
Glassenbury
Union Mill
Golford
Golford Green
East End
Arcadia
London Beach
Redbrook Street
Hook Green
Kilndown
Cranbrook
Biddenden
Parkgate
St Michaels
Lamberhurst Down
Cousley Wood
Bewlbridge
Bedgebury Cross
Goddard's Green
Broomfield Street
Bedgebury National Pinetum
Hartley
Tenterden
Bewl Water
Pell Green
Stonecrouch
Benenden
Beacon Hill
Leigh Green
Wadhurst
Burchett's Green
Three Leg Cross
Flimwell
Gill's Green
Iden Green
Strood
The CM Booth Collection of Historic Vehicles
Reading Street
Union Street
High Street
Gun Green
Rolvenden
Small Hythe
Dingleden
Smallhythe Place
Chapel Down
Dale Hill
Hawkhurst
Highgate
Standen Street
Shover's Green
Ticehurst
Bardown
Rolvenden Layne
Peening Quarter
Four Throws
Pashley Manor
The Moor
Sandhurst
Kent & East Sussex Railway
Stonegate
River Limden
Merriments
Burgh Hill
Hurst Green
Linkhill
Newenden
Wittersham
ISLE OF OXNEY
Witherenden Hill
Sandhurst Cross
Great Dixter House & Gardens
Etchingham
The Stocks
Ham Green
Southover
Bodiam
Bodiam Castle
River Rother
Rother Levels
Holton Hill
Burwash
Willards Hill
Northbridge Street
Ewhurst Green
Northiam
Four Oaks
Salehurst
Bateman's
Robertsbridge
Millcorner
Beckley
Rye Foreign
Burwash Weald
Burwash Common
Staplecross
Clayhill
Peasmarsh
Oxley's Green
Cripp's Corner
Collier Green
Horns Cross
Playden
Dudwell
Darwell
M20
M2
A20
A26
A228
A229
A249
A274
A262
A21
A268
A265
A28
B2010
B2015
B2016
B2017
B2160
B2162
B2163
B2079
B2085
B2086
B2099
B2100
B2244
B2082
B2088
B2165
53
40
24
25

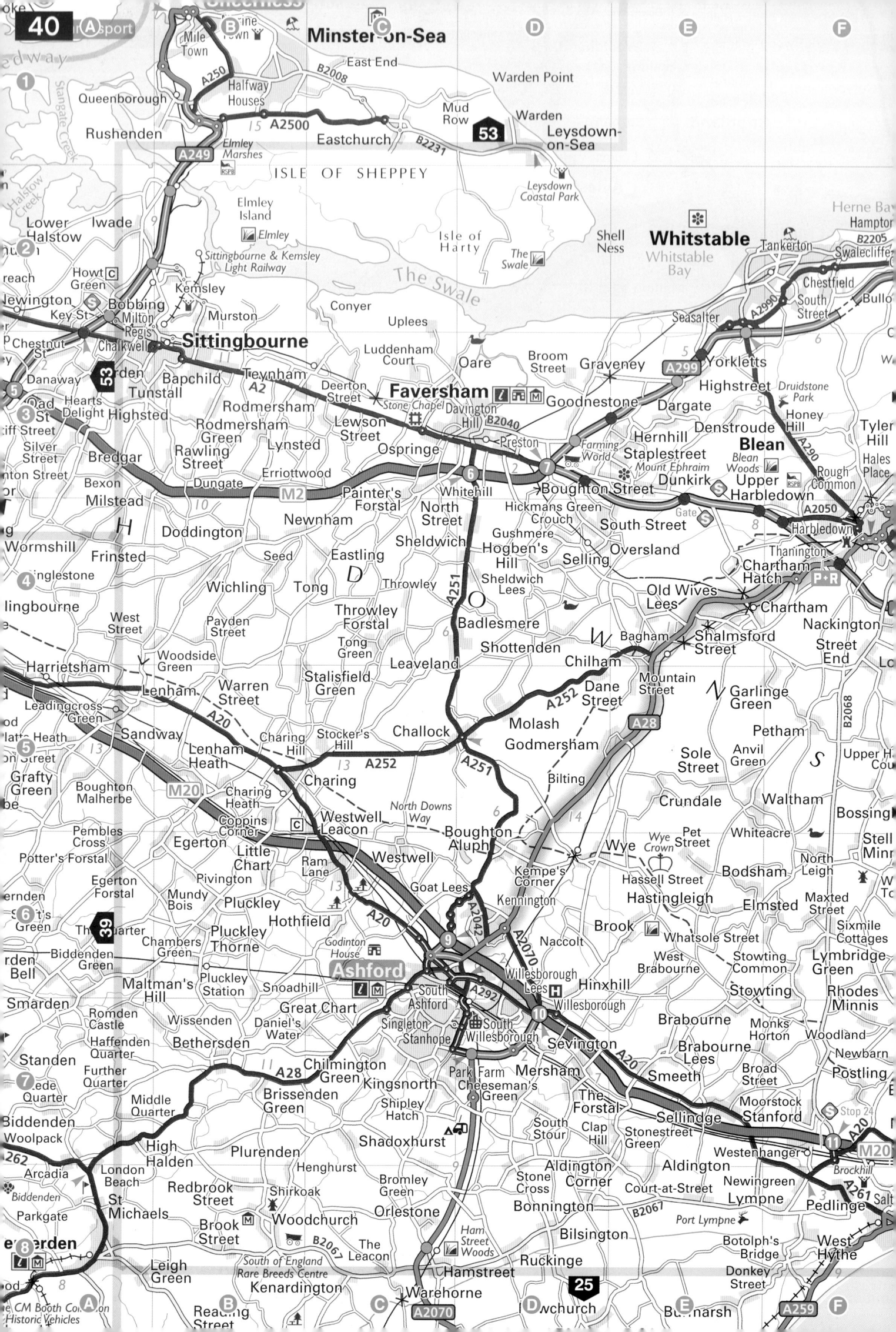

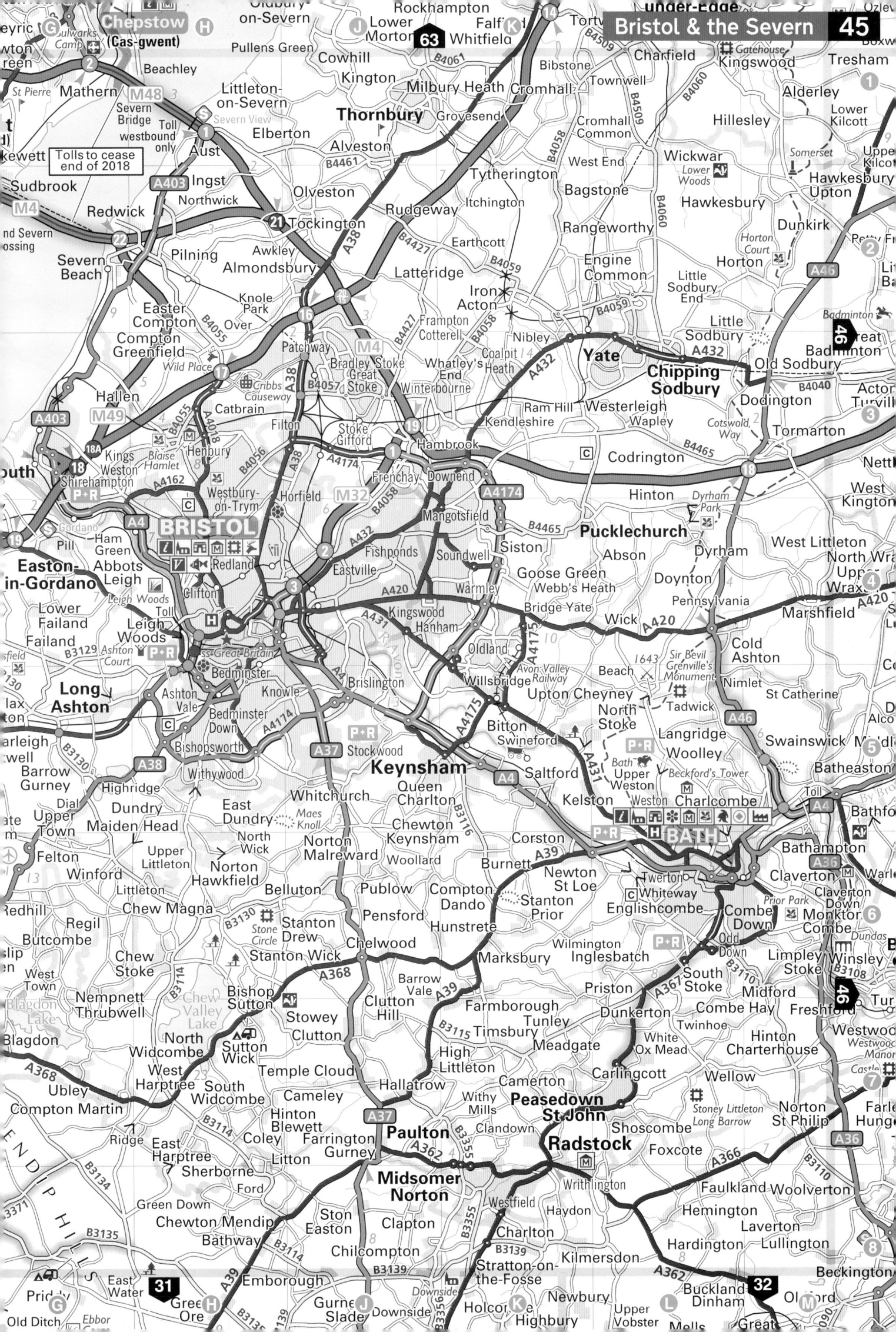

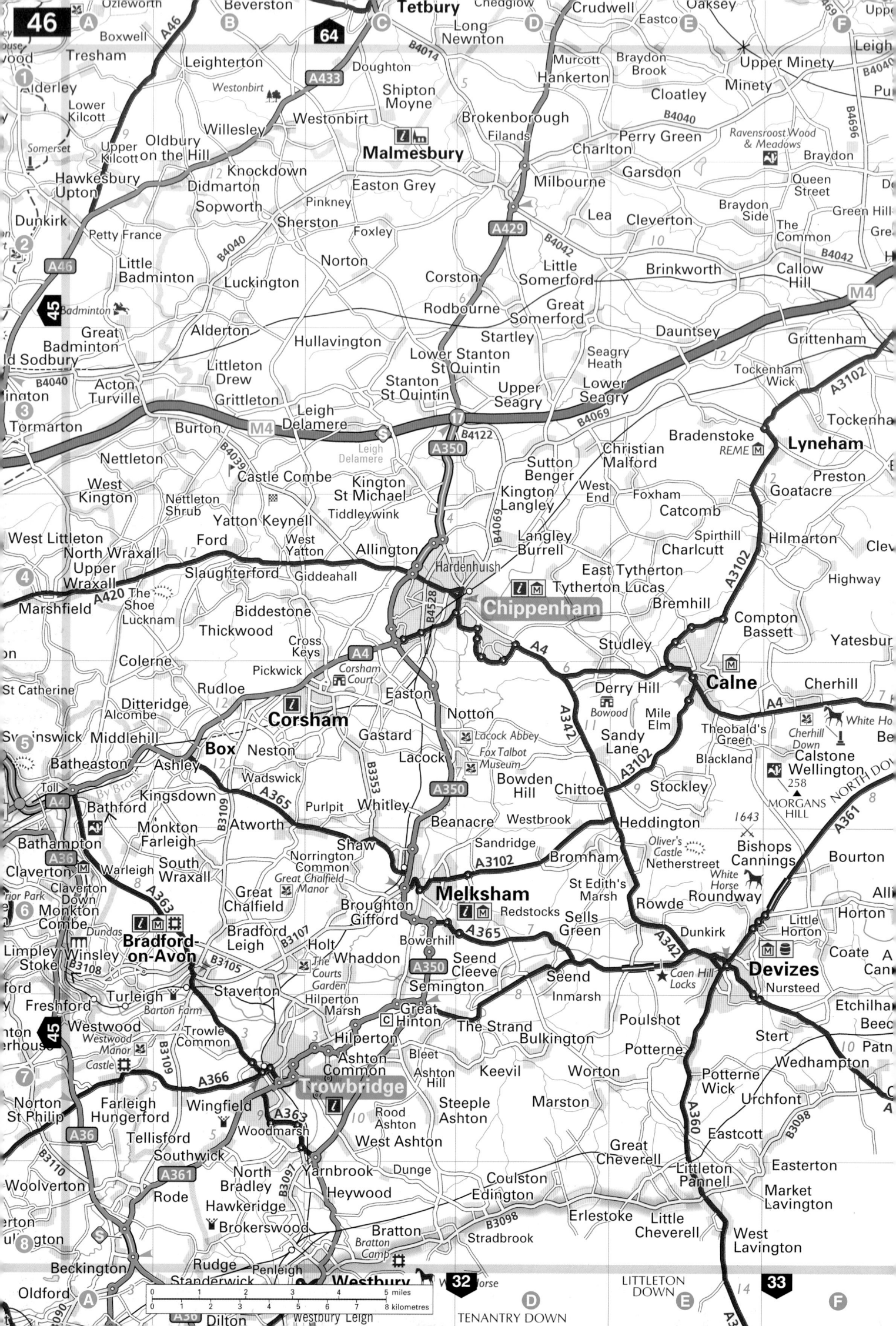

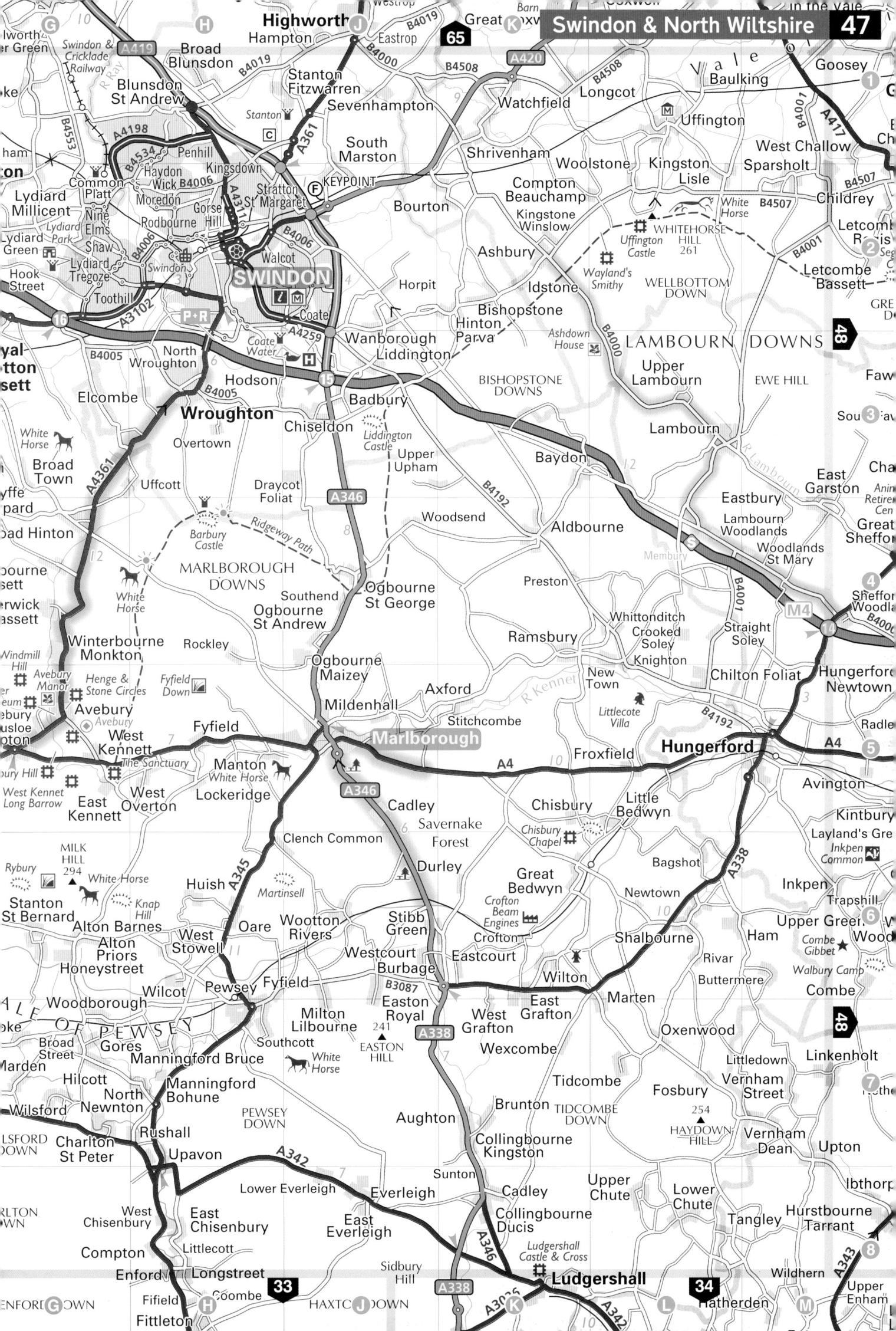

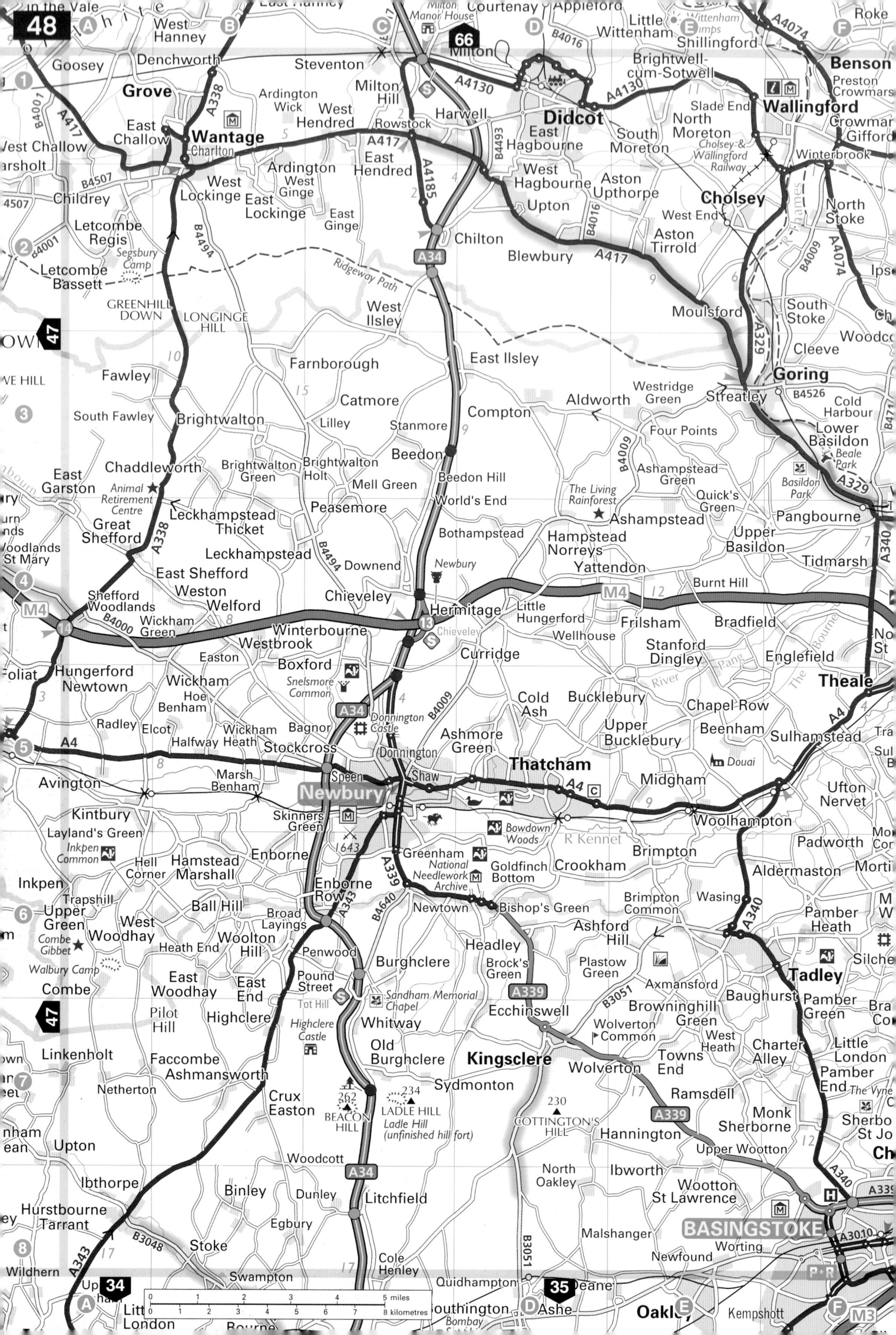

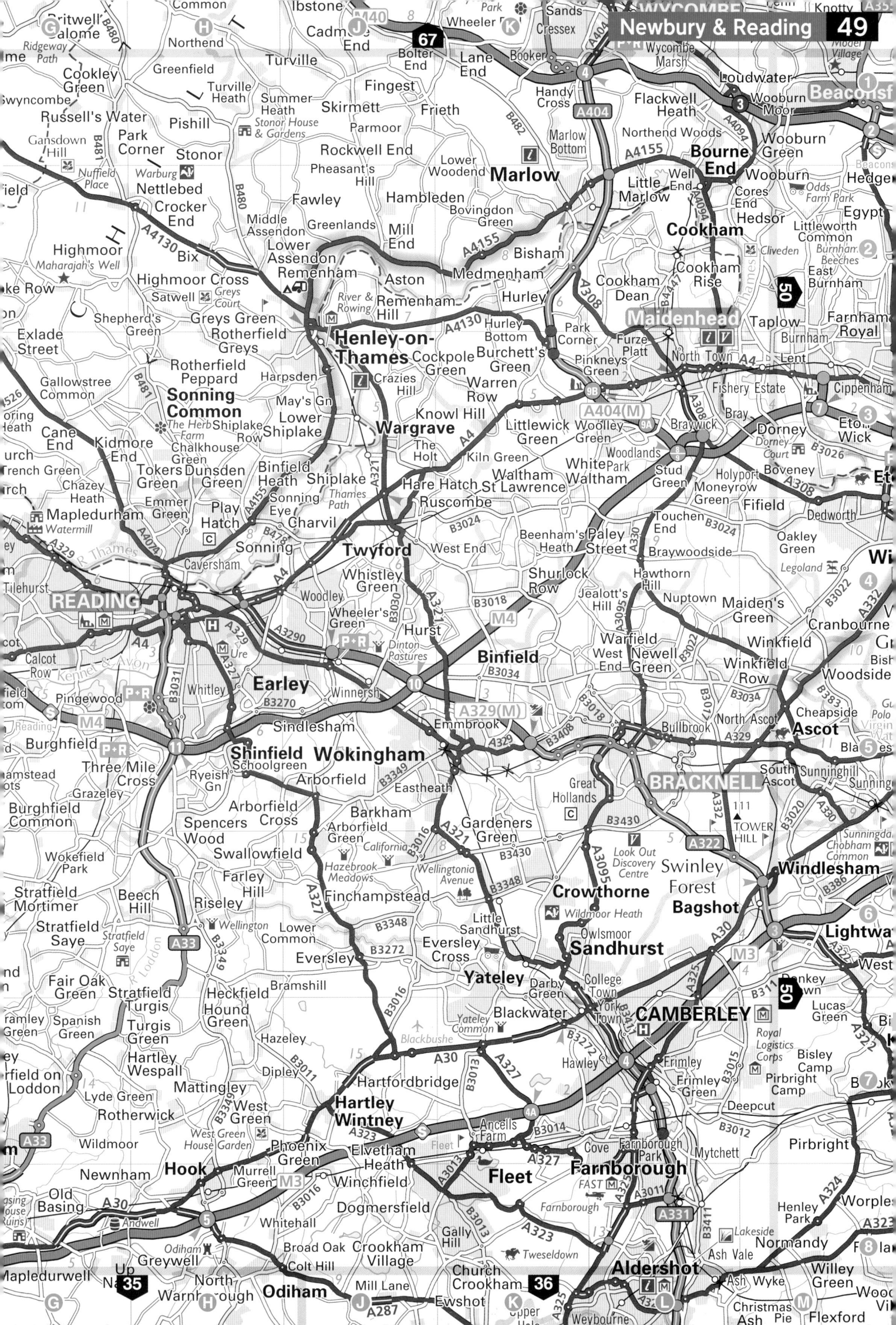

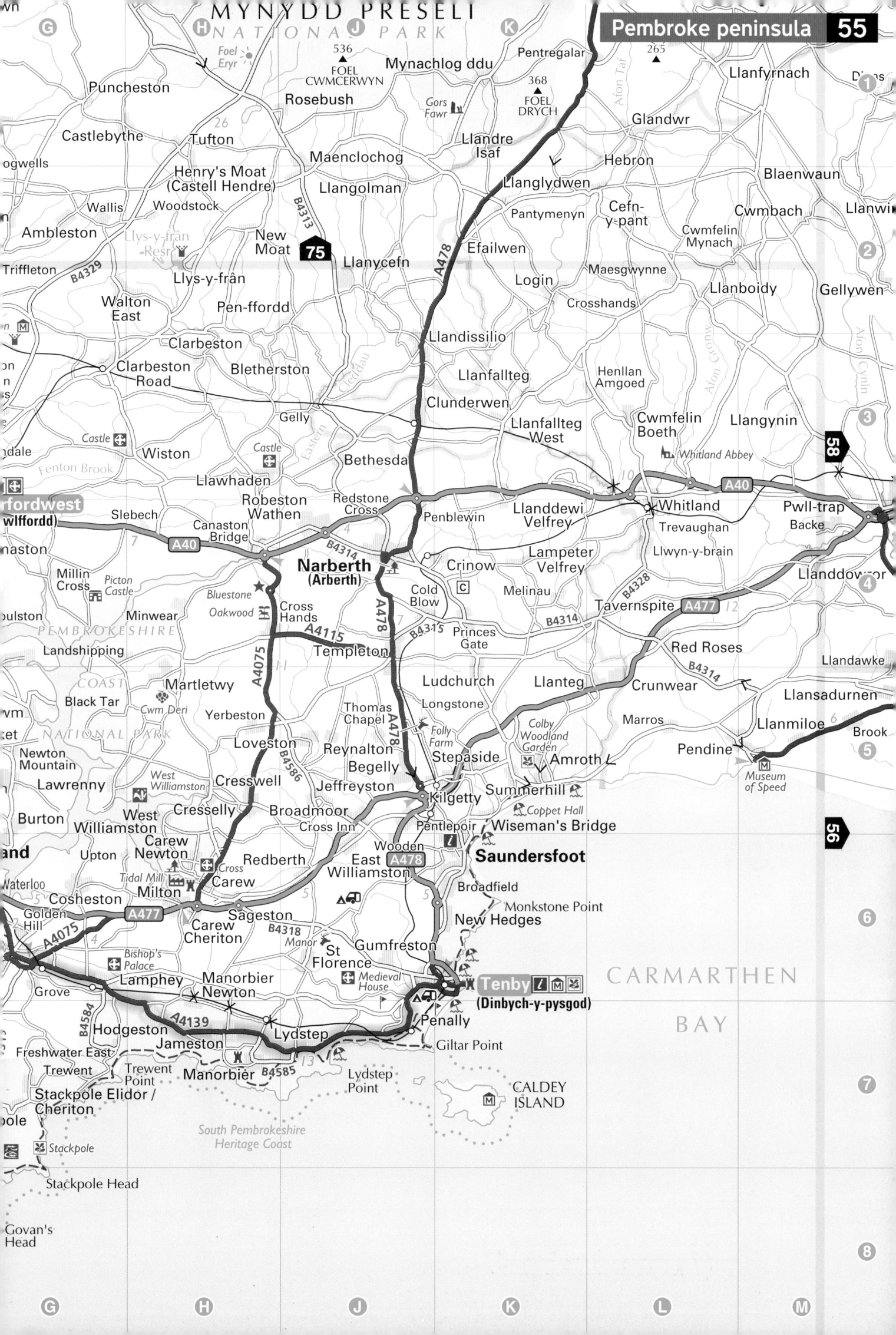

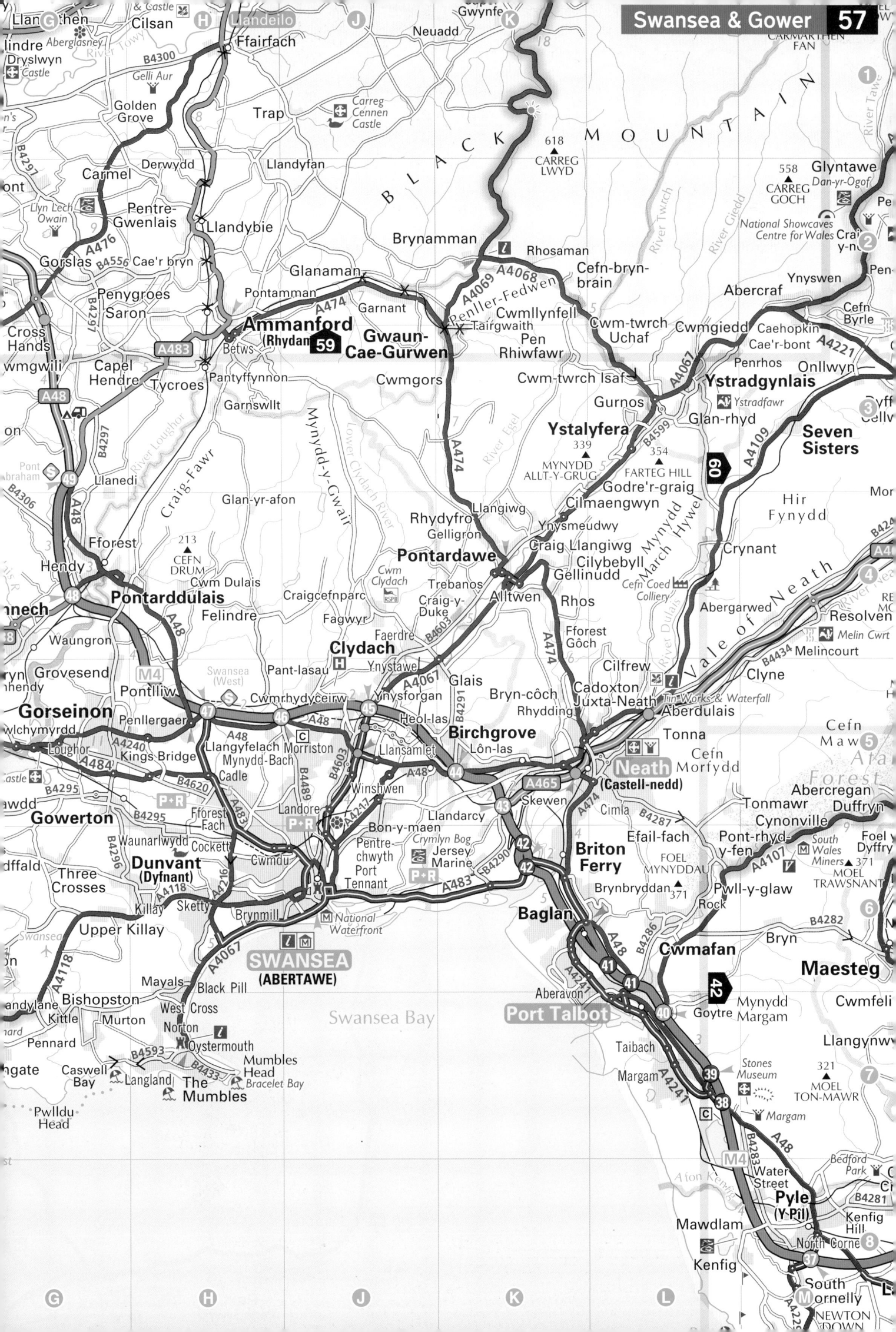

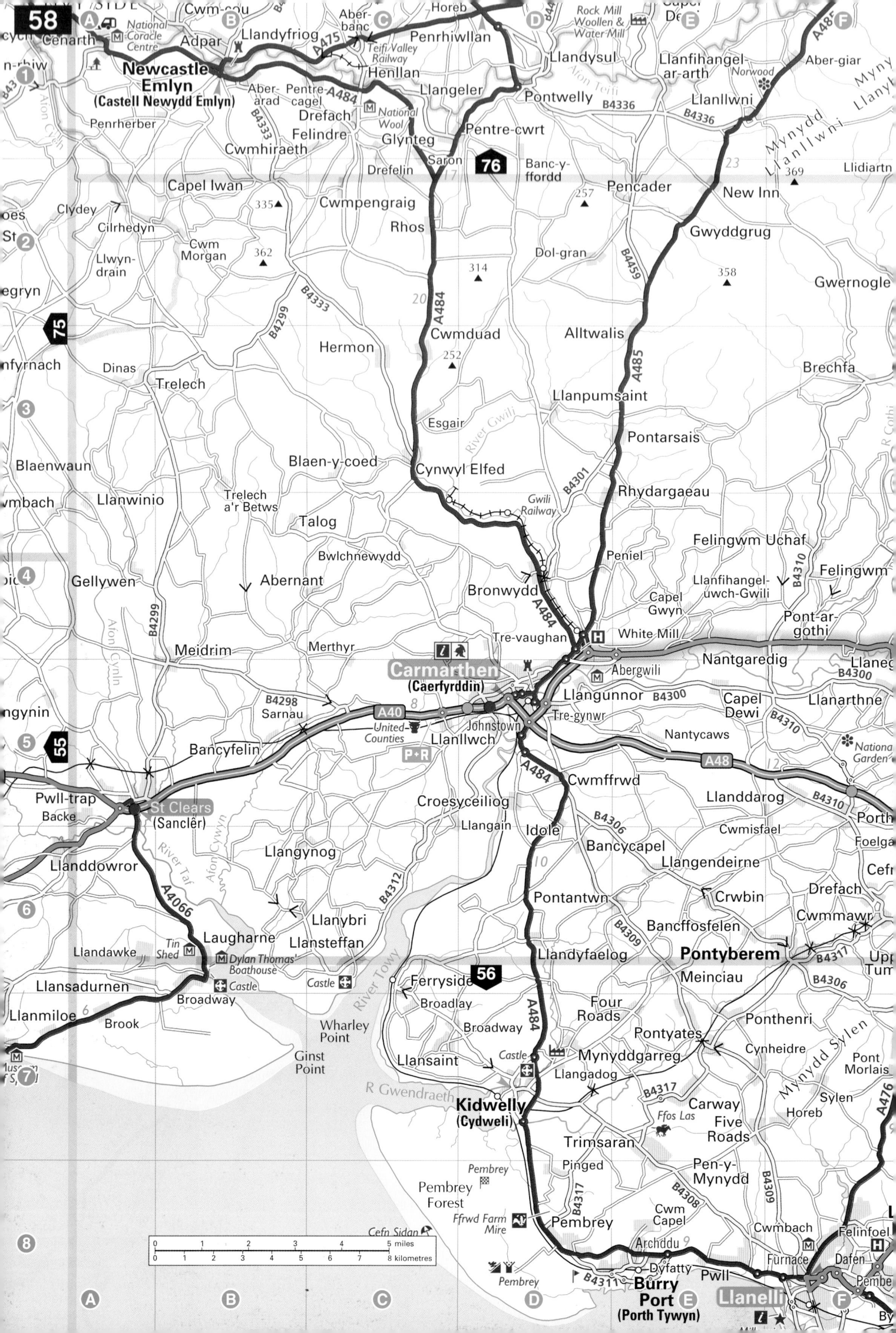

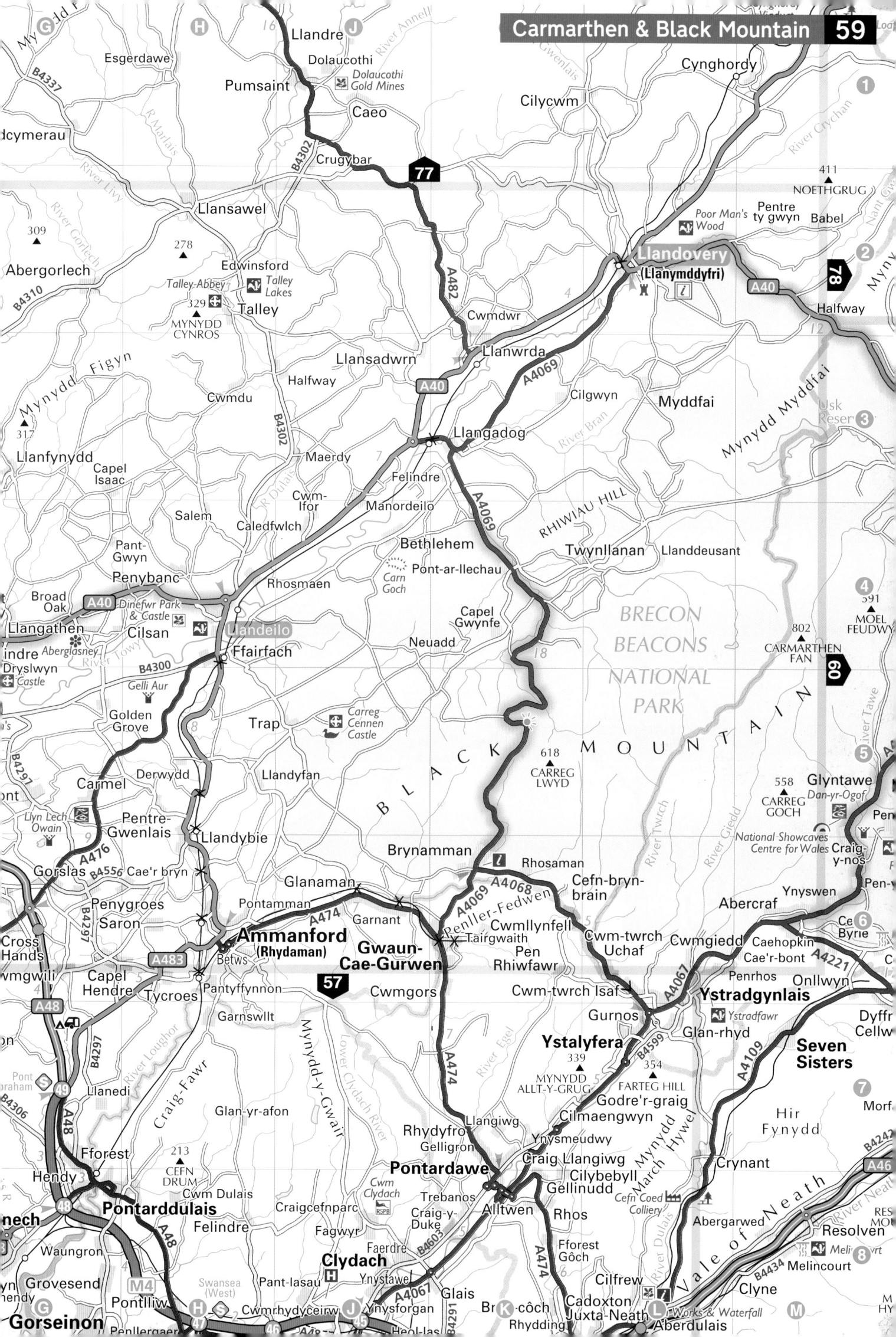

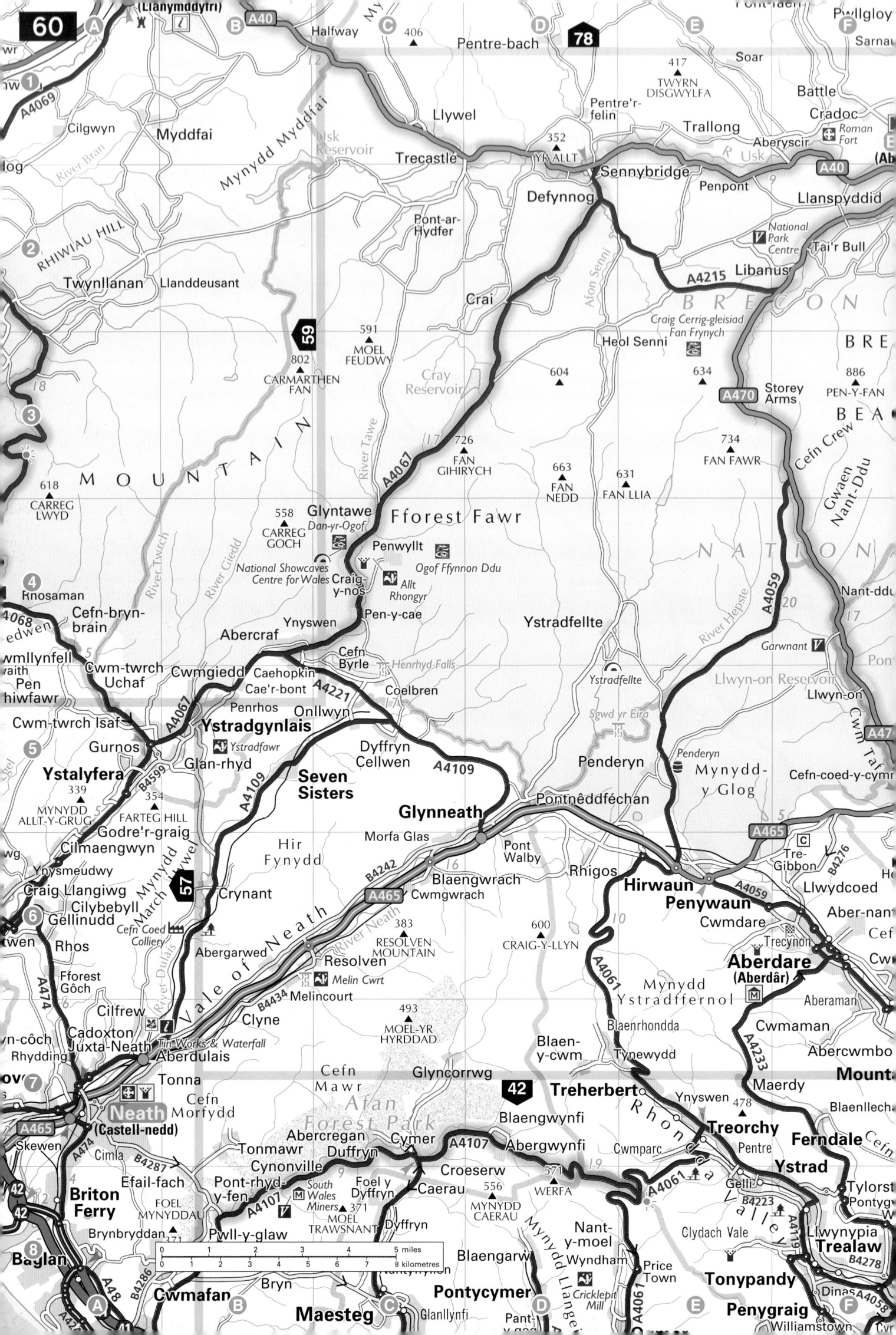

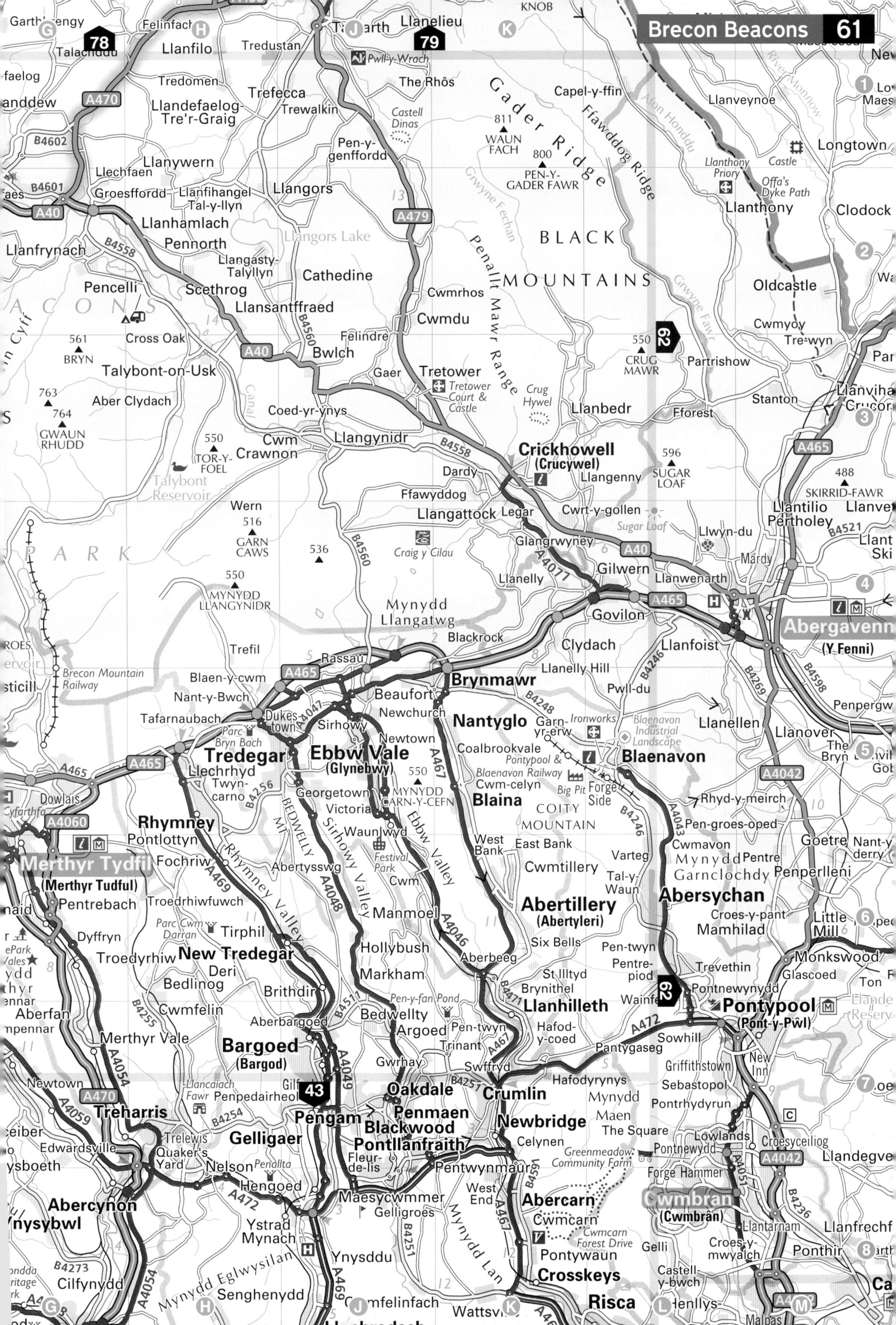

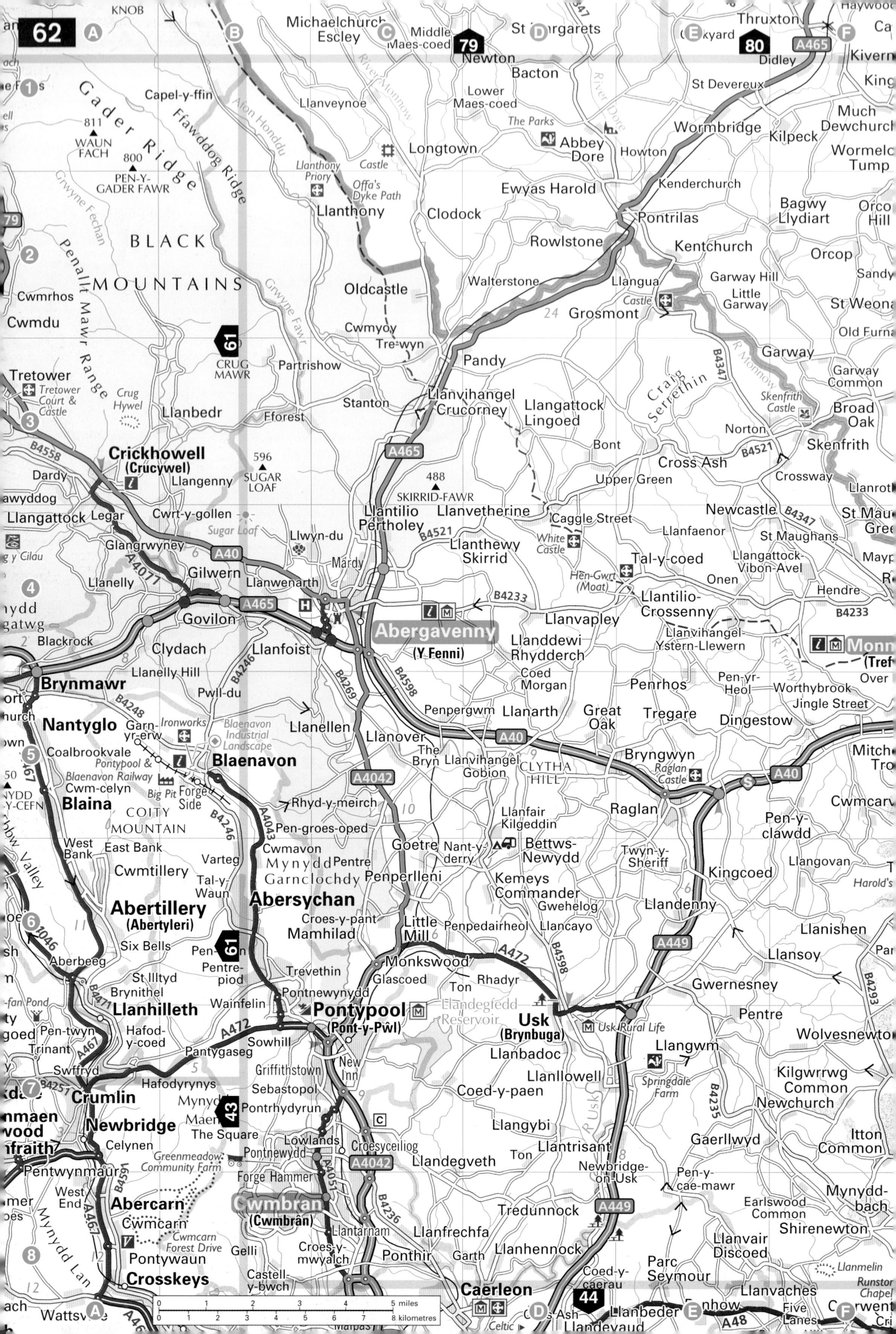

Aconbury
Common
Easy
Fownhope
B4224
Lower
Buckenhill
Donnington
Bromsberrow
Kings
Berro
White
Newtown
Little
Dewchurch
Peartree
Green
Sollers Hope
80
Hellens
Westons
Cider
Tillers Green
Much
Marcle
B4024
Dymock
Bromsberrow
Heath
Playley Green
Lowbands
Pendock
Eld
Ladyridge
Stocking
Lyne
Down
St Mary's
Church
Kempley
Green
Redmarley
D'Abitot
Staunton
1
Ballingham
Brockhampton
Carey
How Caple
Perrystone
Hill
Kempley
Kempley
Green
Three
Choirs
Poolhill
Brand
Green
Corse
Lin
Stre
Snig
End

Little Birch
Much Birch
Pen-allt
Fawley
Chapel
Crow
Hill
Upton
Bishop
Gorsley
Four
Oaks
Shaw Common
Upleadon
A49
Hoarwithy
King's
Caple
Foy
Hole-in-
the-Wall
Upton
Crews
Gorsley
Common
Kilcot
Newent
Birds of
Prey Centre
Malswick
Kent's
Green
Highleadon
Blackwellsend
Green
2
A17

Llandinabo
Harewood
End
Strangford
Brampton
Abbotts
Phocle
Green
4
Linton
Linton Hill
Little
Gorsley
Clifford's
Mesne
Taynton
Hartpury
A449
Ross-on-Wye
Aston
Crews
Aston
Ingham
Glasshouse
64
Sellack
Baysham
Upper Grove
Common
Bridstow
Rudhall
Bromsash
Weston under
Penyard
Lea
B4222
Dursley
Cross
Glasshouse
Taynton
Tibberton
Rudford
Maisemo
Highnam
Gree
3

St Owen's
Cross
Peterstow
Wilton
Ashfield
Tudorville
Hom
Green
Ryeford
Pontshill
Boxbush
May Hill
Glasshouse
Hill
Huntley
B4216
B4215
Vho
ou
Ove
A40
Three
Ashes
Glewstone
A4137
Llangarron
Ruxton
Green
Pencraig
Goodrich
Castle
Walford
Kerne
Bridge
Coughton
Howle
Hill
East Dean
Hope
Mansell
Longhope
Dick
Whittington
Little
London
Blaisdon
Northwood
Green
Churcham
GLOUC
Highnam
Huntley
Birdwood
A40
Oakle
Street
Hemp
Minsterw

Old Forge
B4234
Ruardean
Drybrook
Ruardean
Hill
A4136
Mitcheldean
Abenhall
Plump
Hill
Flaxley
Chaxhill
Stantway
Bollow
Farleys
End
Quedgele
Welsh
Newton
Symonds
Yat (East)
Symonds
Yat
Lower
Lydbrook
Ruardean
Woodside
Brierley
Harrow Hill
Nailbridge
Broadmoor
Westbury-
on-Severn
Elton
Littledean
4
Symonds
Yat (West)
English
Bicknor
Upper
Lydbrook
Cinderford
A4151
Littledean
Westbury Court
Garden
Boxbush
Rodley
Hardwicke
Epney
Longney

Crocker's Ash
Ganarew
Little
Doward
Hillersland
Christchurch
Worrall
Hill
Edge
End
Sculpture
Trail
Forest
Broadoak
Milton
End
Staunton
Berry
Hill
A4136
Mile End
Beechenhurst
Lodge
B4226
Ruspidge
Newnham
on Severn
Arlingham
Fretherne
Saul
Upper
Framilode
Moreton
Valence
Whitminster
The Kymin
Wyesham
Monmouthshire
Broadwell
Coleford
Dean
Upper Soudley
Lower Soudley
Brain's Green
Ruddle
The Dean
Northington
A48
Putlo

Penallt
Redbrook
Whitecliffe
Newland
Milkwall
New
Fancy
Northington
Westend
Nupend
Nasten
Stonehouse
Pen-twyn
re-eagle
Perrygrove Railway
Highbury
Wood
Puzzlewood
Clearwell
Meend
Clearwell
Parkend
Yorkley
Nibley
Blakeney
Purton
Awre
Frampton-
on-Severn
Claypits
Alkerton
Eastington
Cambridge
Middle
Street
6
Whitebrook
Maryland
Narth
Ellwood
Marsh
Lane
Stowe
Whitecroft
Etloe
Slimbridge
Wetland Centre
Shepherds
Patch
Frocester

Broadstone
Llandogo
St Briavels
Castle
B4231
Bream
Allaston
Dean Forest Railway
B4234
Purton
Slimbridge
Moorend
Coaley
Nympsfield
Leonar
Stanle
Catbrook
Lower Meend
St Briavels
Lydney
Sharpness
Hinton
Purton
Halmore
Lower
Cam
Far
Green
64

Tintern
Brockweir
Coldharbour
Hewelsfield
Aylburton
Newtown
Gossington
Wanswell
A38
Lower
Cam
Cam
Ashmead
Green
Uley Long
Nym
Chapel Hill
Tintern
Abbey
Woolaston
Common
Park
Hill
Alvington
Smallbrook
Breadstone
Berkeley
Heath
Stinchcombe
Wotton-
under-Edge

Offa's
Dyke
Path
High
Woolaston
Netherend
Woolaston
Hook Street
Berkeley
Road
The Quarry
Newport
Woodmancote
A4135
Boughspring
Lancaut
Stroat
Wibdon
River Severn
Berkeley
Dr Jenner's
Ham
B4066
North
Nibley
Millend
Uley
Owl
Woodcroft
National Diving Centre
Shepperdine
Bevington
Nupdown
Woodford
Stone
Michaelwood
Bournstream
Coombe
Lasb
Tidenham
Tutshill
Sedbury
Chepstow
(Cas-gwent)
Bulwarks
Camp
Hill
Oldbury
Naite
Hystfield
Lower
Stone
Lower
Wick
Pitt
Court
M5
Tortworth
B4058
Boxw

Port Wall
Beachley
Oldbury-
on-Severn
Rockhampton
Falfield
Whitfield
14
B4509
Charfield
Kingswood
Ozlev
St Pierre
M48
Littleton
Cowhill
Lower
Morton
Pullens Green
45
B4061
Milbury Heath
Cromhall
Townwell
Bibstone
Abbey
Newark
Park
Gatehouse
Tresham
Mathern

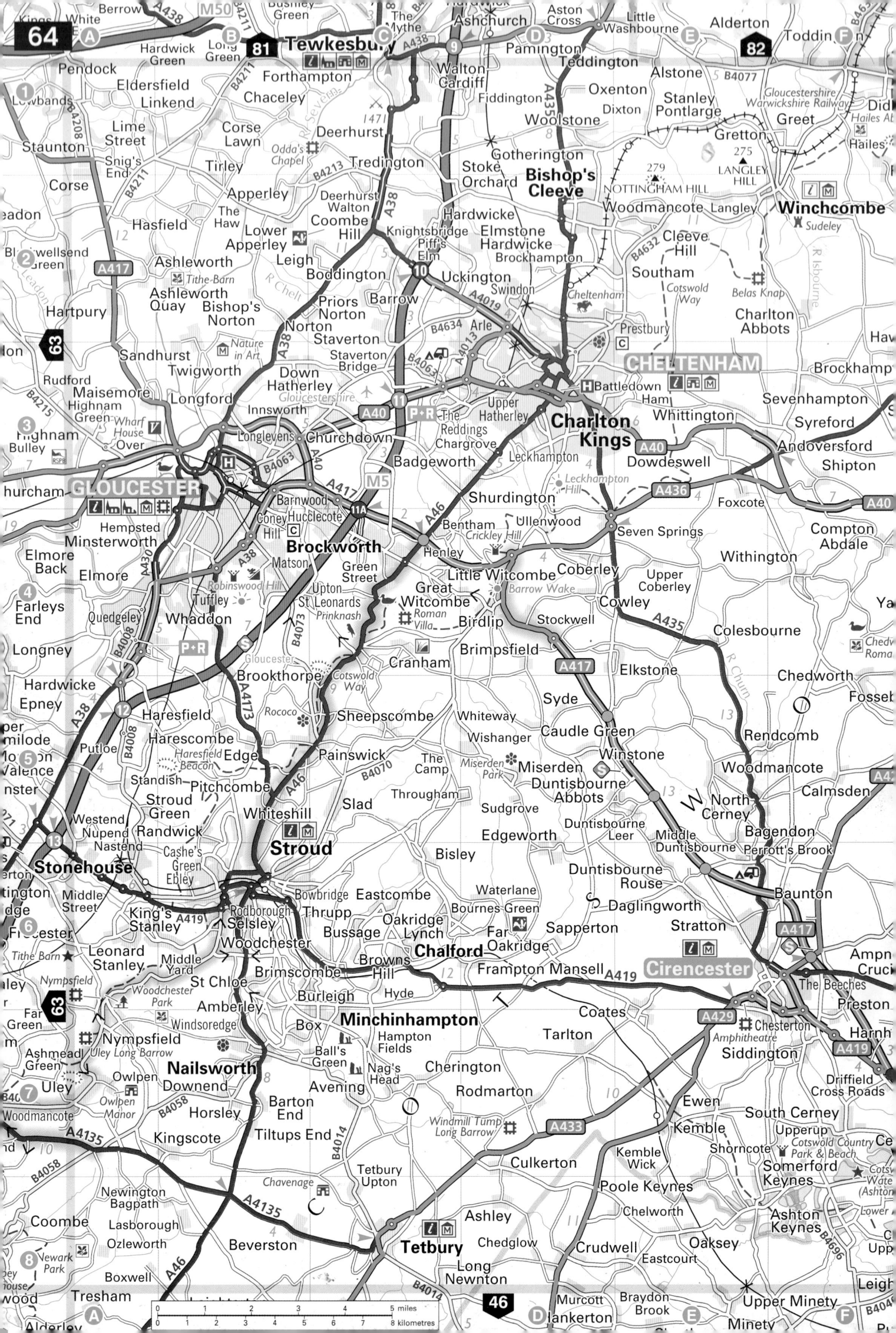

Snowshill
Cotswold Lavender
G
Taddington
Cutsdean
Ford
Temple Guiting
Adam Henson's Cotswold
Barton
Naunton
Aylworth
Notgrove
Hazleton
Cold Aston
Turkdean
Northleach
World of Mechanical Music
Coln St Dennis
Calcot
Coln Rogers
Winson
Ablington
Arlington
Bibury
Coln St Aldwyns
Hatherop
Quenington
Ampney St Mary
Poulton
Milton End
Horcott
Meysey Hampton
Whelford
Fairford
Marston Meysey
Dunfield
Down Ampney
Latton
Castle Eaton
Kempsford
Cricklade
Calcutt
Swindon & Cricklade Railway
Blunsdon
Broad Blunsdon
Blunsdon St Andrew

Batsford
Lemington
Wolford
Cotswold Falconry Centre
82
Bourton-on-the-Hill
Bourton House
Sezincote
Bourton Downs
Longborough
Condicote
Donnington
Evenlode
Broadwell
Moreton-in-Marsh
Four Shire Stone
Kitebrook
Chastleton
Chastleton House
Adlestrop
Stow 1646
Stow-on-the-Wold
Upper Swell
Lower Swell
Maugersbury
Oddington
Kingham
Icomb
Bledington
Wyck Rissington
Westcote
Nether Westcote
Idbury
Fifield
Upper Rissington
Great Rissington
Little Rissington
Clapton-on-the-Hill
Model Village
Motor & Toy
Miniatures
Bourton-on-the-Water
HABBER GALLOWS HILL
Milton-under-Wychwood
Farmington
Sherborne
Windrush
Great Barrington
Little Barrington
Upton
Taynton
Eastington
Lodge Park
Aldsworth
Holwell
Westwell
Signet
Burford
Shilton
B4425
Eastleach Turville
Eastleach Martin
Filkins
Kencot
Broughton Poggs
Southrop
Langford
Little Faringdon
Fairford Park
Fairford
Cotswold Water Park (Fairford/Lechlade)
Inglesham
Upper Inglesham
Hannington Wick
Hannington
Lechlade on Thames
Buscot
Kelmscott
Buscot Park
Coleshill
Westrop
Eastrop
Great Coxwell
Great Coxwell Barn
Little Coxwell
Highworth
Hampton
Stanton Fitzwarren

Compton
Wiggin
Barton-on-the-Heath
Little Rollright
Great Rollright
Rollright Stones
Little Compton
Salford
Over Norton
Swerford
Dunthrop
Heythrop
Chipping Norton
Enstone
Cornwell
Daylesford
The Common
Churchill
Sarsden
Chadlington
Dean
Taston
Foscot
Foxholes
Lyneham
Spelsbury
Greenend
Bruern Abbey
Chilson
Ascott-under-Wychwood
Ascott Earl
Shipton-under-Wychwood
Wychwood
Langley
Leafield
Whiteoak Green
Delly End
North Leigh
Hailey
Asthall Leigh
Crawley
Fordwells
Swinbrook
Fulbrook
Asthall
Minster Lovell
Minster Lovell Hall
Witney
Charterville Allotments
Cogges
Curbridge
Brize Norton
Ducklington
Carterton
Brize Norton
Lew
Alvescot
Black Bourton
Broadwell
Bampton
Aston
Brighthampton
Cote
Yelford
Clanfield
Little Clanfield
Weald
Grafton
Radcot
Thrup
Carswell Marsh
Chimney
Hinton Waldrist
Buckland
Eaton Hastings
Littleworth
Faringdon
Badbury Hill
Hatford
Pusey
Charney Bassett
Stanford in the Vale
Fernham
Shellingford
Longcot
Baulking
Goosey

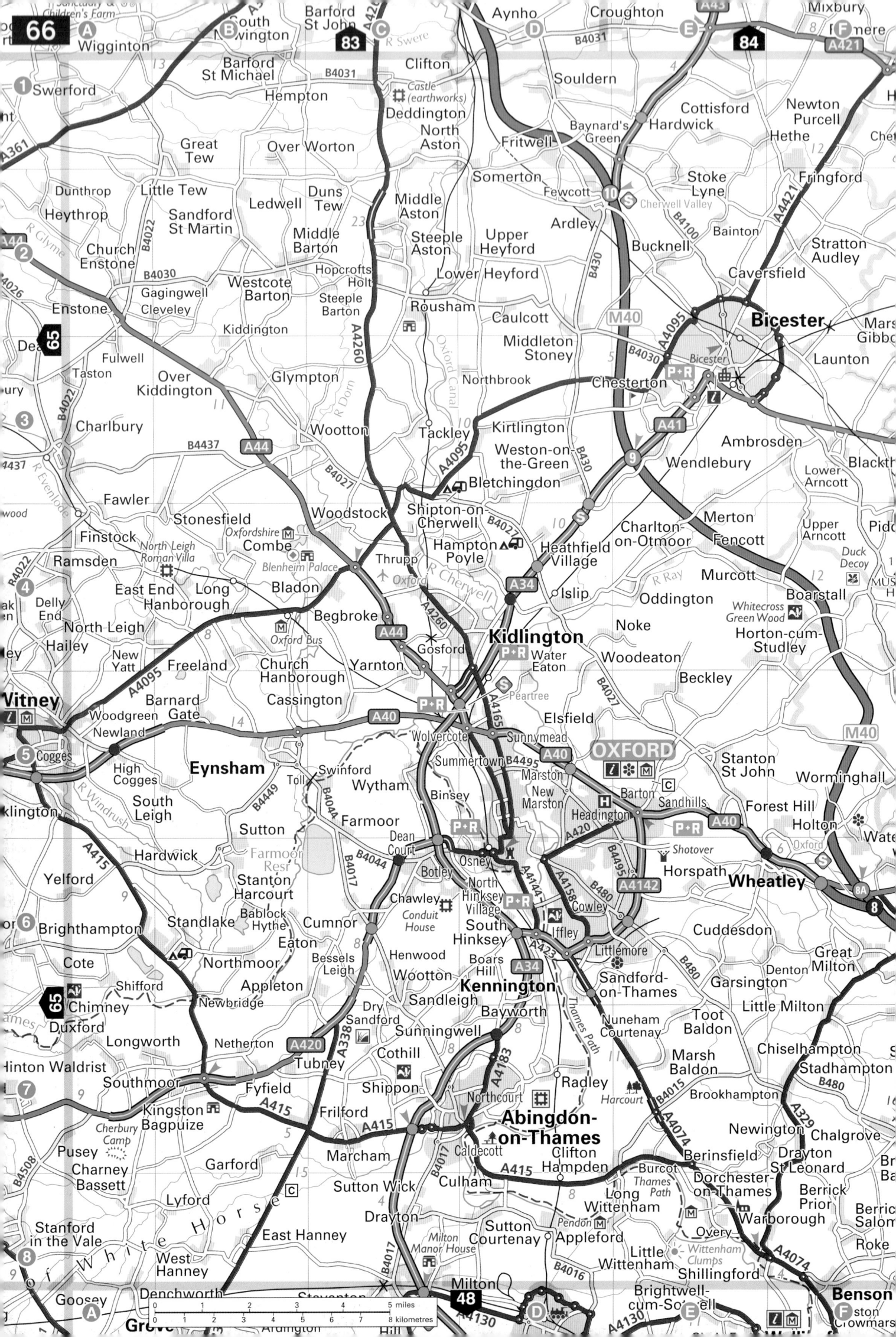

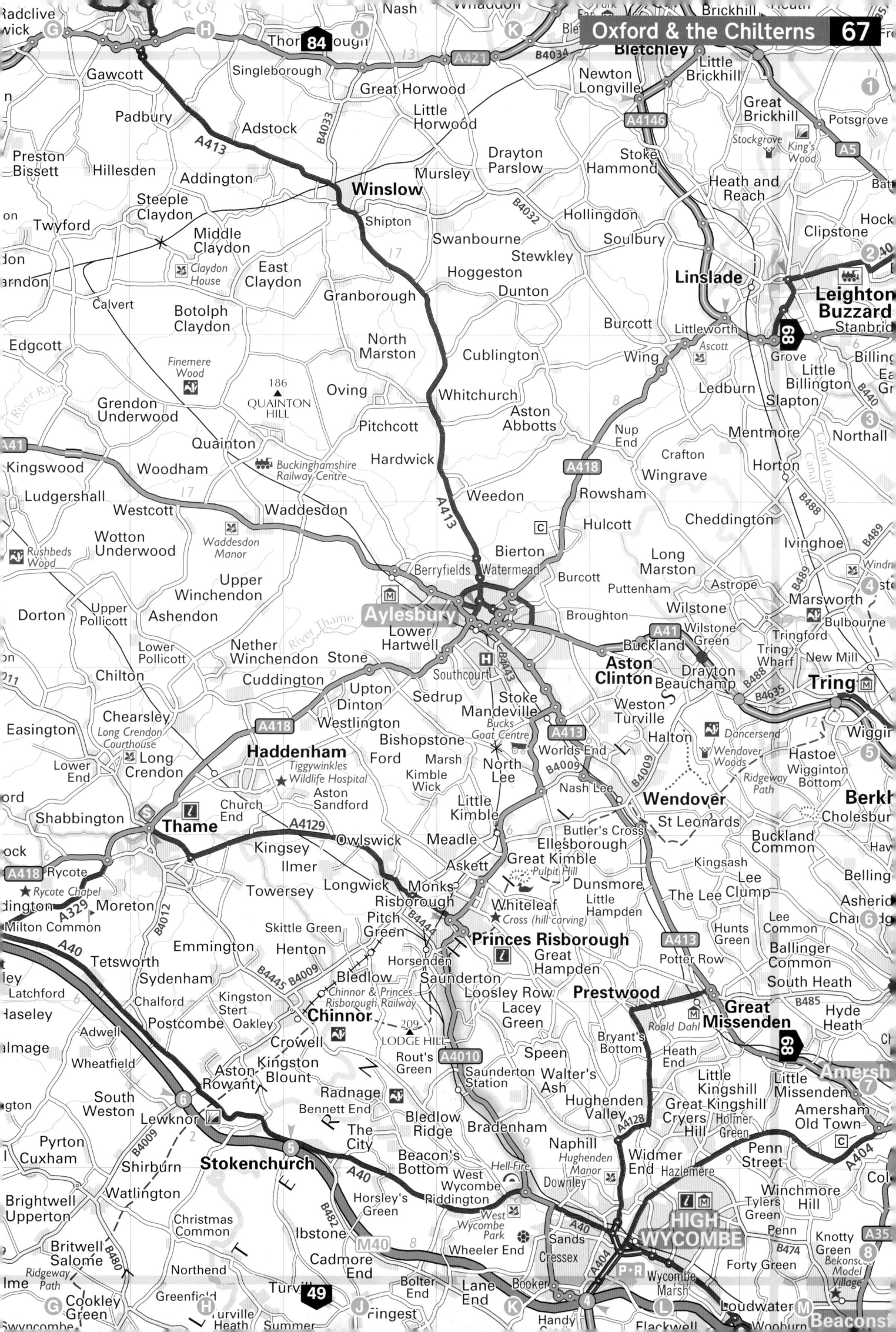

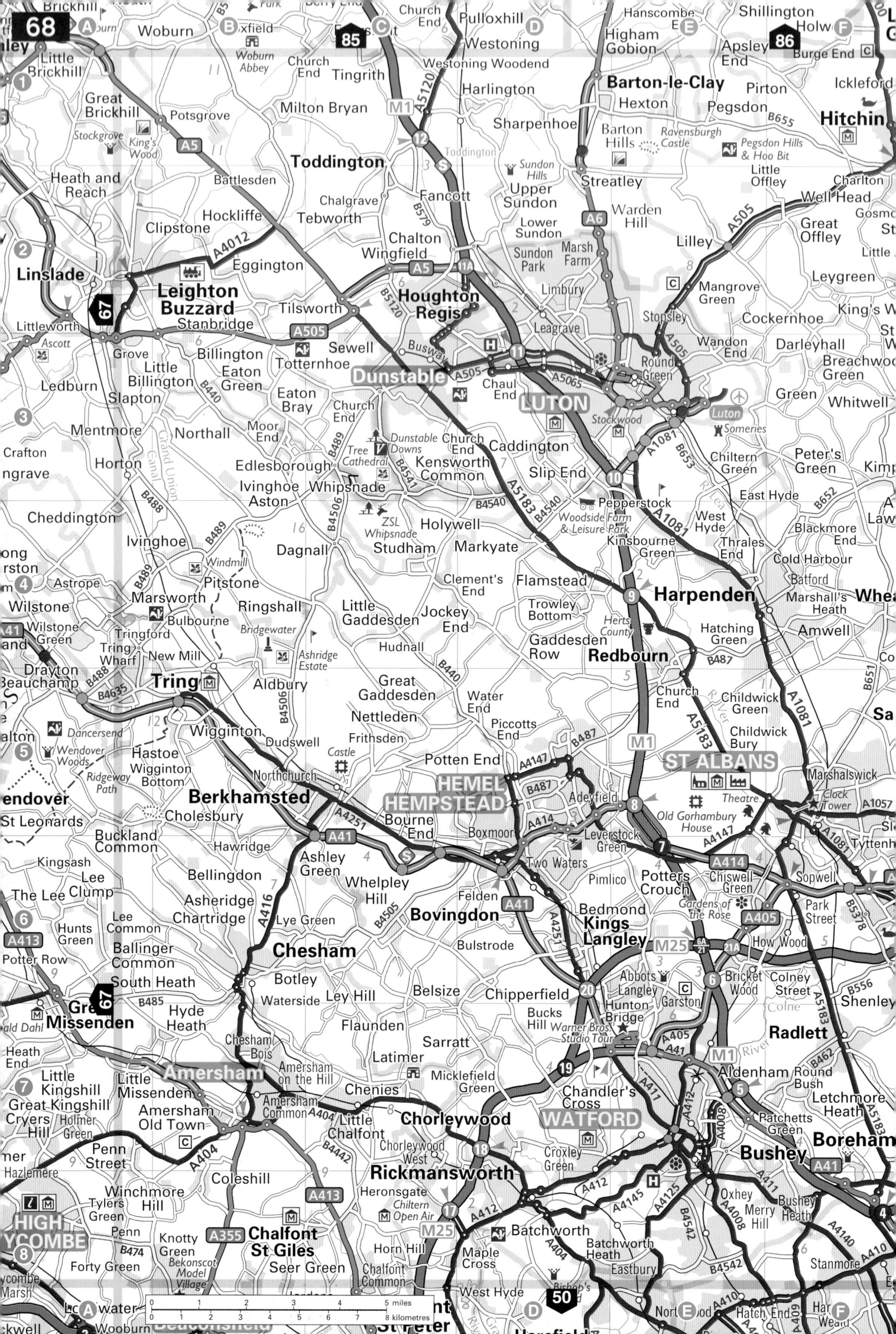

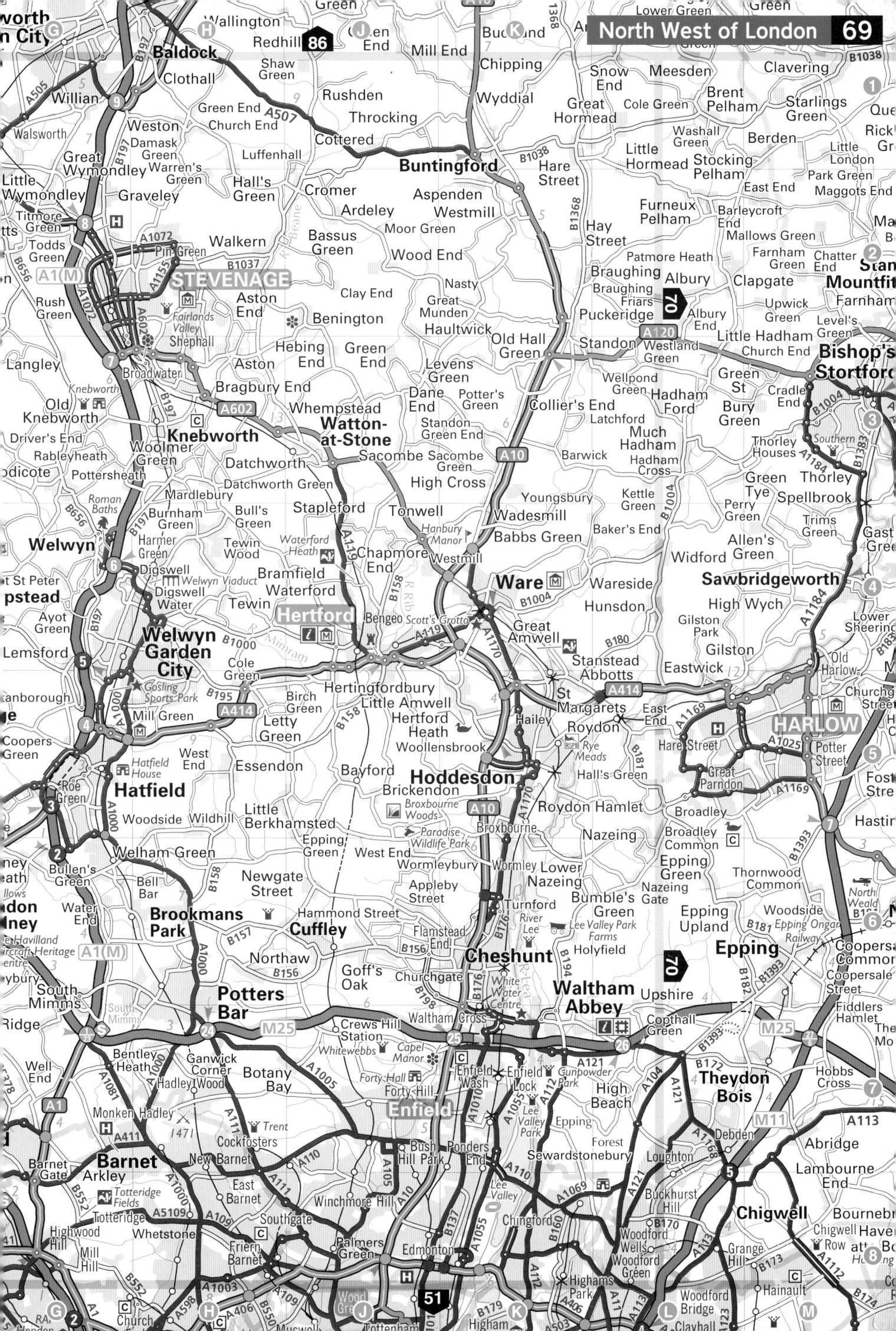

Duck End • Howe Street • **Sible Hedingham** • Maplestead • Little Maplestead • Bures • Wormingford • Little Horkesley

Finchingfield • **J** • **88** • Mount Bures • Countess Cross

Brickkiln Green • Whiteash Green • Boose's Green • Colne Engaine • White Colne • Wakes Colne • Fordham

Waltham's Cross • Wethersfield • Blackmore End • **Halstead** • **A1124** • Chappel • Swan Street • Rose Green • Fordstreet • Fordham Heath • Eight Ash • Beacon End

Bridge End • Great Bardfield • Parkgate • Shalford • Gosfield • **Earls Colne** • Great Tey • Aldham • Seven Star Green

Oxen End • Shalford Green • Church End • Jasper's Green • High Garrett • **C** • Greenstead Green • Burton's Green • **72** • Little Tey • Marks Tey • Stanway

Bardfield Saling • Duck End • Great Saling • **C** • Tumbler's Green • Marks Hall • **B1024** • Broad Green • **25** • **B1408** • Pott's Green • Copford Green • Heckford

Bran End • Crow's Green • Panfield • **Braintree** • Bocking Churchstreet • Stisted • Pattiswick • **Coggeshall** • Surrex • Langley Green • Easthorpe

Stebbing • Blake End • Duckend Green • **M** • Bocking • **A131** • **B1256** • Bradwell • Paycocke's • Coggeshall Grange Barn • Skye Green • Hardy's Green • Smythe's Green • Birch

Stebbing Green • **B1256** • Rayne • Perry Green • Cressing • R Blackwater • Feering • Gore Pit • **24** • Messing • Birch Green

Gransmore Green • **A120** • Bartholomew Green • Great Notley • Tye Green • Hawbush Green • **Silver End** • **Kelvedon** • **B1024** • Inworth • Tiptree • Layer Marney • Lay

Felsted • Bannister Green • Molehill Green • Black Notley • Cressing Temple • **23** • **A12** • Rivenhall End • Tiptree Heath • Tower • Paternoster Heath

Causeway End • Coblers Green • Cock Green • Willows Green • Row Green • Young's End • Rank's Green • The Green • White Notley • Faulkbourne • Chipping Hill • **22** • Little Braxted • Great Braxted • Oxley Green • Tollesbunt Knights • Salcott Virle

North End • **B1417** • Hartford End • Little Leighs • Great Leighs • Fuller Street • Fairstead • **Witham** • Great Totham • Little Totham • Tollesbunt D'Arcy

Littley Green • Leighs • Church End • Gambles Green • Terling • **B1389** • **21** • Wickham Bishops • Tollesbunt Major • Tollesbunt

Howe Street • Chatham Green • Flack's Green • **20B** • **S** • Great Totham • Tollesbury

Great Waltham • Russell Green • **20A** • **Hatfield Peverel** • Langford • Broad Street Green • Goldhanger

Broad's Green • **A130** • **B1137** • Boreham • Nounsley • **B1019** • Museum of Power • Heybridge • Heybridge Basin

Little Waltham • **P+R** • **H** • Broomfield • Little Baddow • Ulting Wick • Woodham Walter • **B1026** • Northey • Osea Is • **River Bla**

Chignall Smealy • **B1008** • **A1016** • **19** • R Chelmer • Maldon • Ramsey Island

Chignall St James • Springfield • **Maldon** • St Lawrence

H • **M** • **CHELMSFORD** • Woodham Mortimer • **A414** • **i**

Oxney Green • **A1016** • **A138** • **P+R** • Elm Green • Runsell Green • **A414** • St Lawren

Writtle • **C** • **A111** • **1** • Danbury • Sandon • Howe Green • **Danbury** • Hazeleigh • Rudley Green • Mundon Hill

Widford • Highlands House & Park • Great Baddow • **17** • Gay Bowers • **B1010** • New Hall • Mundon • Maylandsea

dley Green • **A414** • **B1007** • Galleywood • Butt's Green • Bicknacre • Cock Clarks • Purleigh • Roundbush • Steeple

14 • **15** • Margaretting • **A12** • East Hanningfield • Chapel Row • Howegreen • Mayland

B1002 • Margaretting Tye • **11** • Farther Howegreen • Latchingdon

Stock • West Hanningfield • **A130** • RHS Hyde Hall • Woodham Ferrers • Stow Maries • Cold Norton • **72** • Althorne

atestone • Coalhill • Chapel Row • Rettendon • **B1012** • **B1010** • Ostend

Queen's Park • **B1007** • South Hanningfield • Downham • Tropical Wings • **South Woodham Ferrers** • North Fambridge • Bridgemarsh Island • Creeksea • Bu

Ramsden Heath • Norsey Wood • Ramsden Bellhouse • Marsh Farm • **Hullbridge** • South Fambridge • Canewdon

Billericay • South Green • Runwell • Battlesbridge • **A132** • Paglesham

52 • **Wickford** • Rawreth • **Hockley** • **Ashingdon** • Halesville • Ballards Gore

A127 • Crays Hill • Nevendon • **A129** • **B1013** • **Hawkwell** • Great Stambridge

Great Burstead • Noak Bridge • **H** • **J** • **53** • **Rayleigh** • **K** • **Rochford** • **L** • **M**

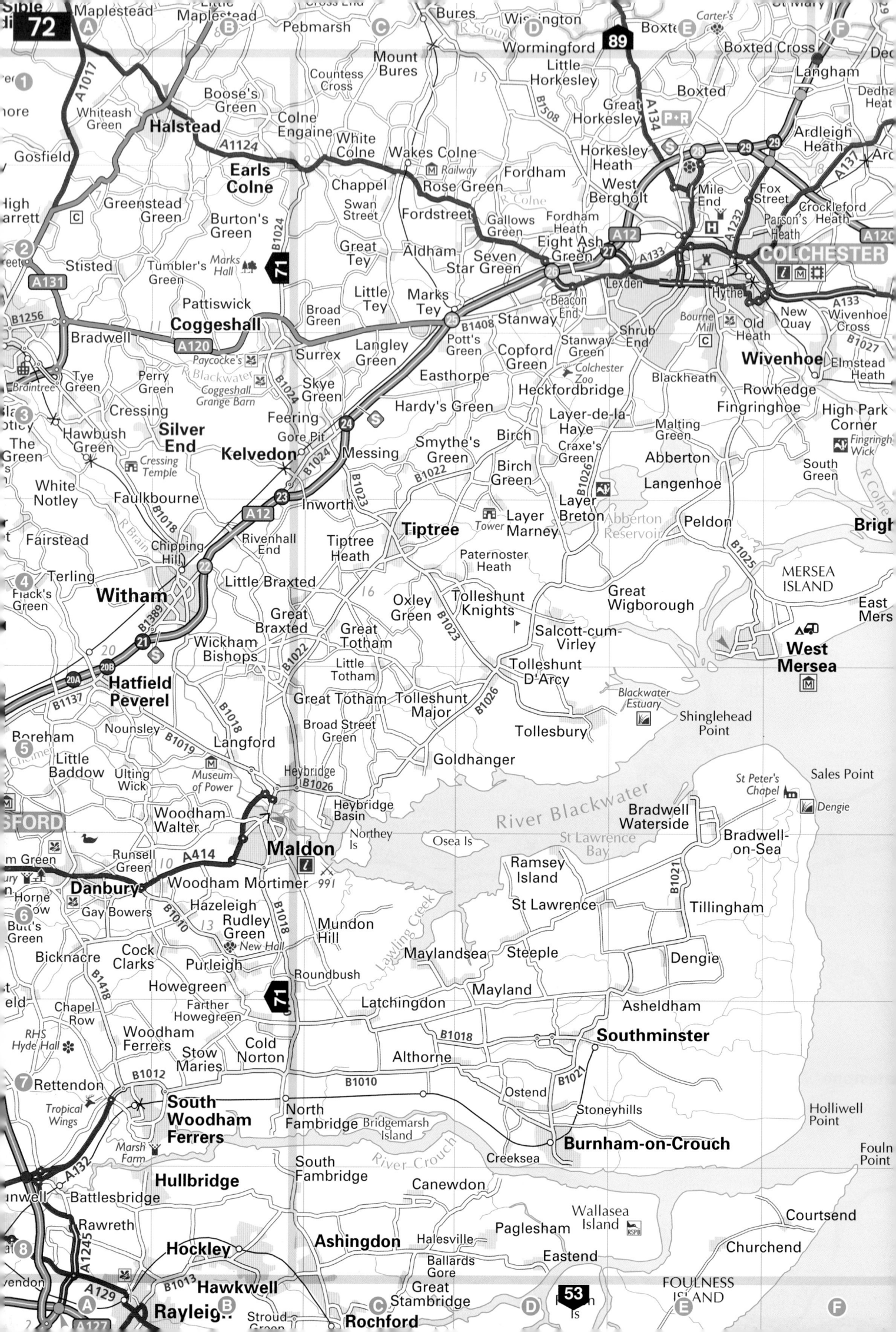

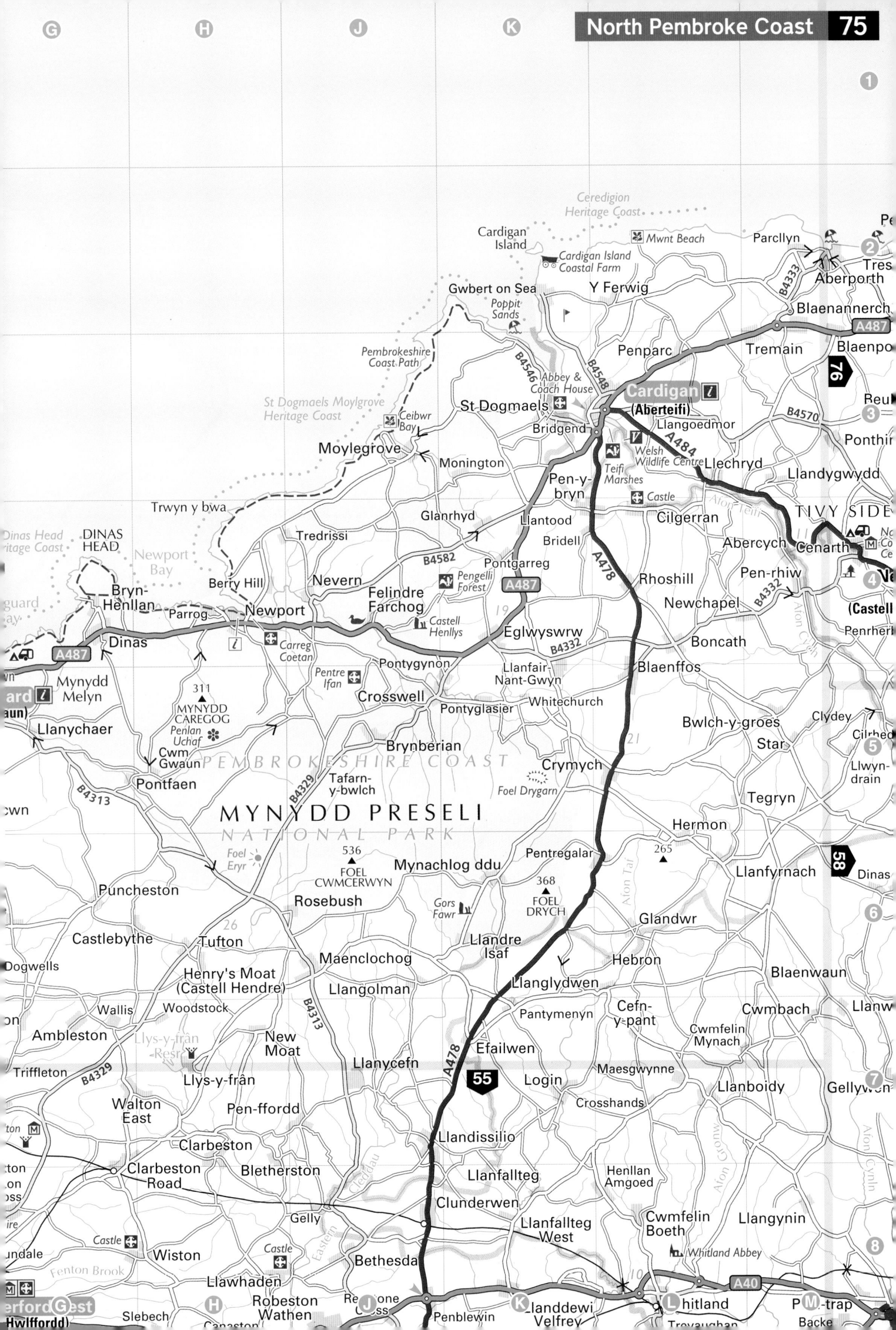

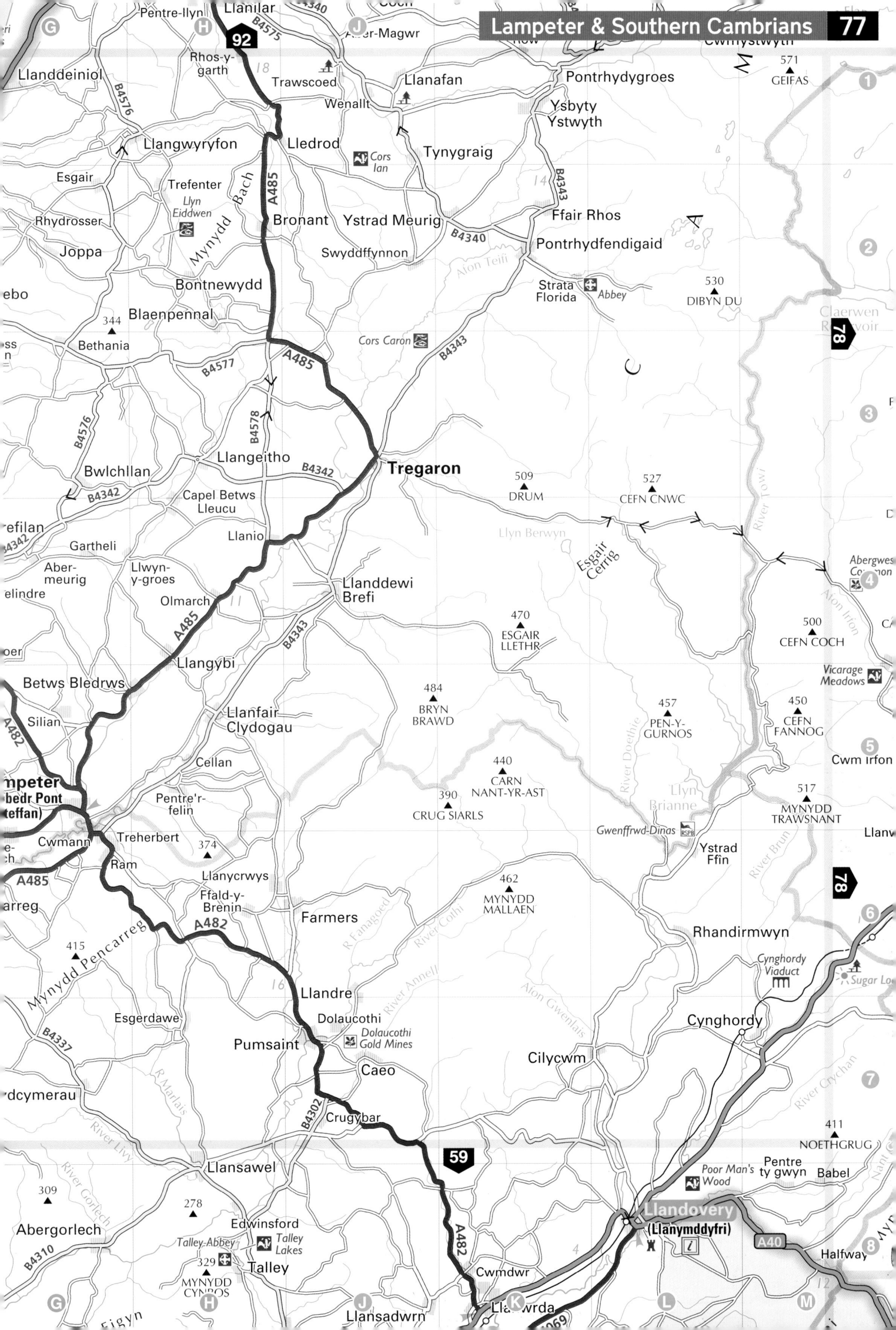

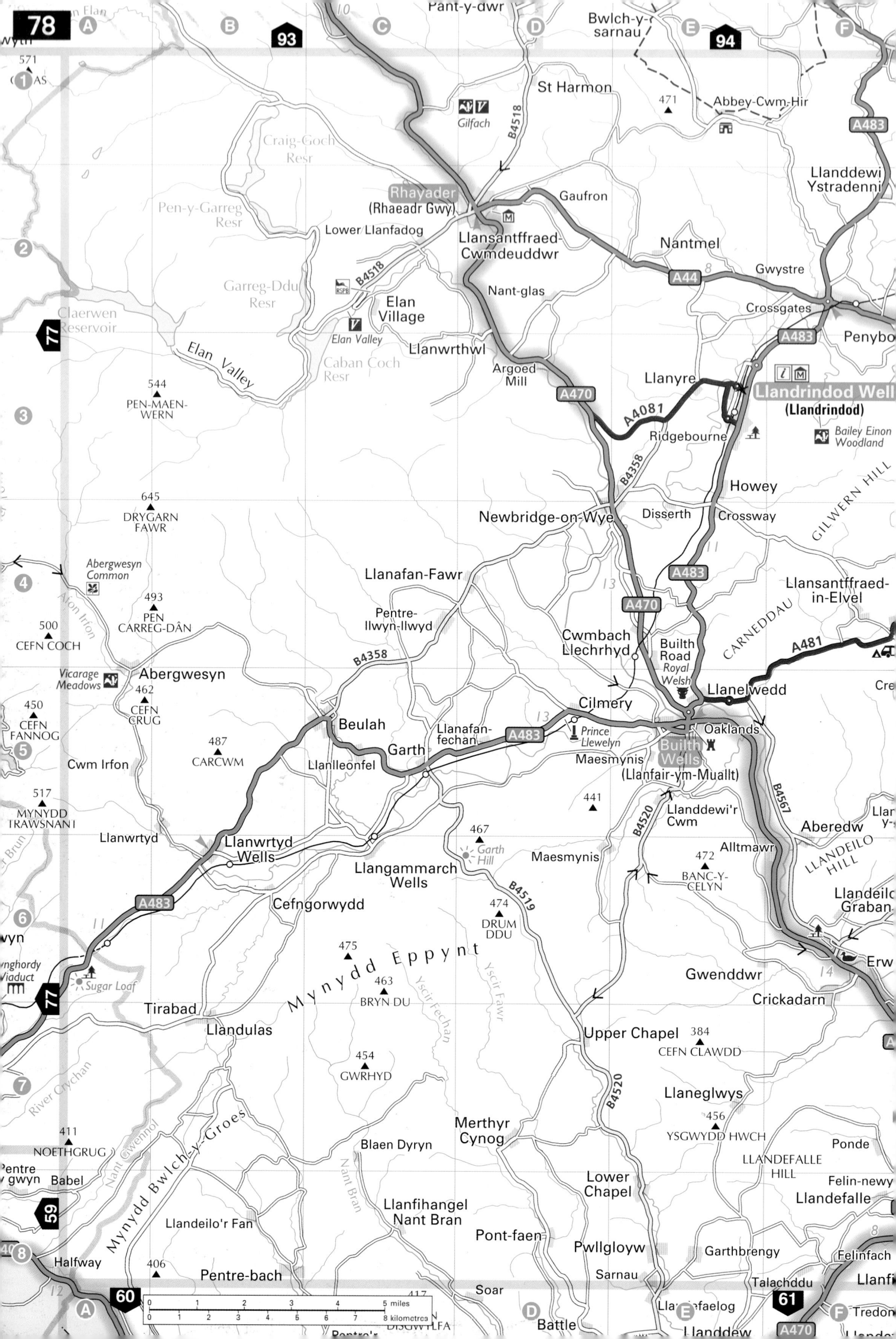

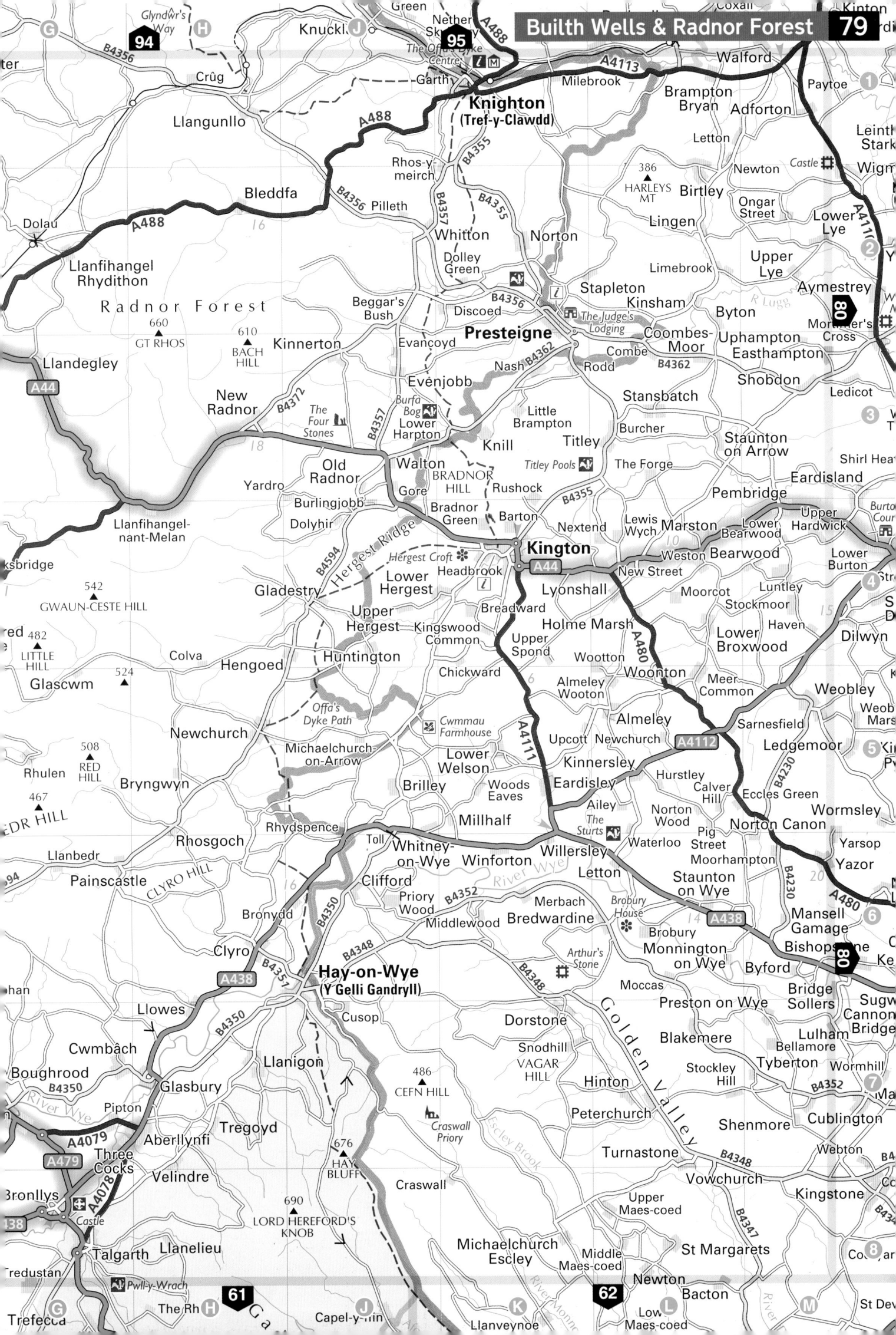

95
79

A · B · Forest
Geology Trail
C
P+R
D
96
E · F

Kinton
Wardine
Ludlow
Ludford
Knowbury
Hints
Dudnill
Bransley
Coreley
Milson
Bayt

Paytoe
Burrington
Overton
Ashford
Carbonell
Greete
Nash
Bickley
Broombank
Knighton on Teme
A456
Comm

Leinthall
Starkes
Pipe Aston
Ashford Bowdler
Middleton
Bleathwood
Little Hereford
Boraston
Newnham Bridge
Rochford
Upper Rochford

Castle
Wigmore
Richards Castle
Woofferton
Brimfield Cross
Burford
Tenbury Wells
Kyrewood
Stoc

Lower Lye
Yatton
Oreleton Common
Comberton
Wyson
Brimfield
Berrington
Callows Grave
Hanley Child
Hanley Or William

Aymestrey
Croft Ambrey
Croft Castle
Ashley Moor
B4362
Orleton
Stony Cross
Berrington Green
St Michaels
Miles Hope
Kyre Park
Bank Street
Broadheath
Upper Stoke Sapey

Mortimer's Cross
Water Mill
Bircher
A49
Middleton on the Hill
Leysters
Sweet Green

Lucton
Yarpole
Moreton Eye
Ashton
A4112
Woonton
Kyre Green
Wolferlow

Ledicot
Bicton
Luston
Berrington Hall
The Hundred
Grafton
Bockleton
Collington

Kingsland
Lugg Green
Aston
Kimbolton
Stockton
Whyle
Old Church
Tedstone Wafer

West Town
Cobnash
The Broad
Grantsfield
Hatfield
Thornbury
Edvin Loach
Sandy Cross

Shirl Heath
Lawton
Cholstrey
Ebnall
Leominster
Steen's Bridge
A44
Grendon Green
Edwyn Ralph
Bredenbury
Bromyard Downs

Eardisland
Monkland
A44
Baron's Cross
Stretford
Docklow
Bromyard

Upper Hardwick
Wall End
Newtown
Ivington
Humber
Risbury
Marston Stannett
Hegdon Hill

Lower Burton
Ivington Green
Brierley
Stoke Prior
Risbury
A465
B4214

Sollers Dilwyn
Aulden
Wharton
Marlbrook
Newton
Bowley Town
Pencombe
Munderfield Row
Stanford Bishop

Dilwyn
Birley
Hope under Dinmore
Bowley
England's Gate
Little Cowarne
Stoke Cross
Munderfield Stocks

Weobley
Knapton Green
Bush Bank
Upper Hill
Queenswood Country Park
Bodenham
Maund Bryan
Ullingswick
Stoke Lacy
Bishop's Frome

Weobley Marsh
King's Pyon
Westhope
Highway
Bodenham Moor
Pool Head
A417
Upper Town
Panks Bridge
Much Cowarne
Five Bridges

Wormsley
Canon Pyon
Wellington
Urdimarsh
The Vauld
Felton
Moreton Jeffries
Halmond Frome

Canon
Yarsop
Yazor
Auberrow
Walker's Green
Preston Wynne
Hillhampton
Burley Gate
Lower Egleton
Castle Frome

Mansell Lacy
Tillington Common
Portway
Wellington Marsh
Marden
Sutton St Nicholas
Ocle Pychard
Newtown
Upper Egleton
Stretton Grandison

Mansell Gamage
Brinsop
Tillington
Moreton on Lugg
Franklands Gate
A465
Westhide
Monkhide
Canon Frome

Bishopstone
Credenhill
Kenchester
Burghill
Upper Lyde
Pipe and Lyde
Sutton Marsh
Withington Marsh
Withington
Yarkhill
Ashperton

Bridge Sollers
Sugwas Pool
Stretton Sugwas
A49
Holmer
Nunnington
A4103
Shucknall
Lower Town
Swinmore Common

Cannon Bridge
Swainshill
Huntington
Westfields
Shelwick
White Stone
Hagley
Weston Beggard
A417
Munsley

Lulham
Bellamore
Upper Breinton
King's Acre
Lugwardine
A465
Tarrington
Trumpet

Wormhill
Breinton
Waterworks
A438
Bartestree
Tupsley
Dormington
Stoke Edith
A438

Madley
Eaton Bishop
Ruckhall
Hereford
Hampton Bishop
Perton
Clouds
Durlow Common
Aylton

Clehonger
Warham
Belmont
Blackmarstone
Lower Bullingham
Rotherwas Chapel
Checkley
Putley Green
Little Marcl

Webton
B4349
Goose Pool
Grafton
Dinedor
Mordiford
Putley
Kynaston

Kingstone
Coldwell
Bullinghope
Portway
DINEDOR HILL
Holme Lacy
Woolhope
Rushall

Hungerstone
Cobhall Common
Allensmore
Twyford Common
B4224
Lower Buckenhill
Sollers Hope
Hellens Manor

Thruxton
Cockyard
Haywood
Callow
Aconbury
Newtown
Peartree Green
Westons Cider
Tillers Gre

St Dever
A465
Didley
Kivernoll
Little
Balling
Ladyridge
63
Brockhampton
Lyne
Dym

0   1   2   3   4   5 miles
0 1 2 3 4 5 6 7 8 kilometres

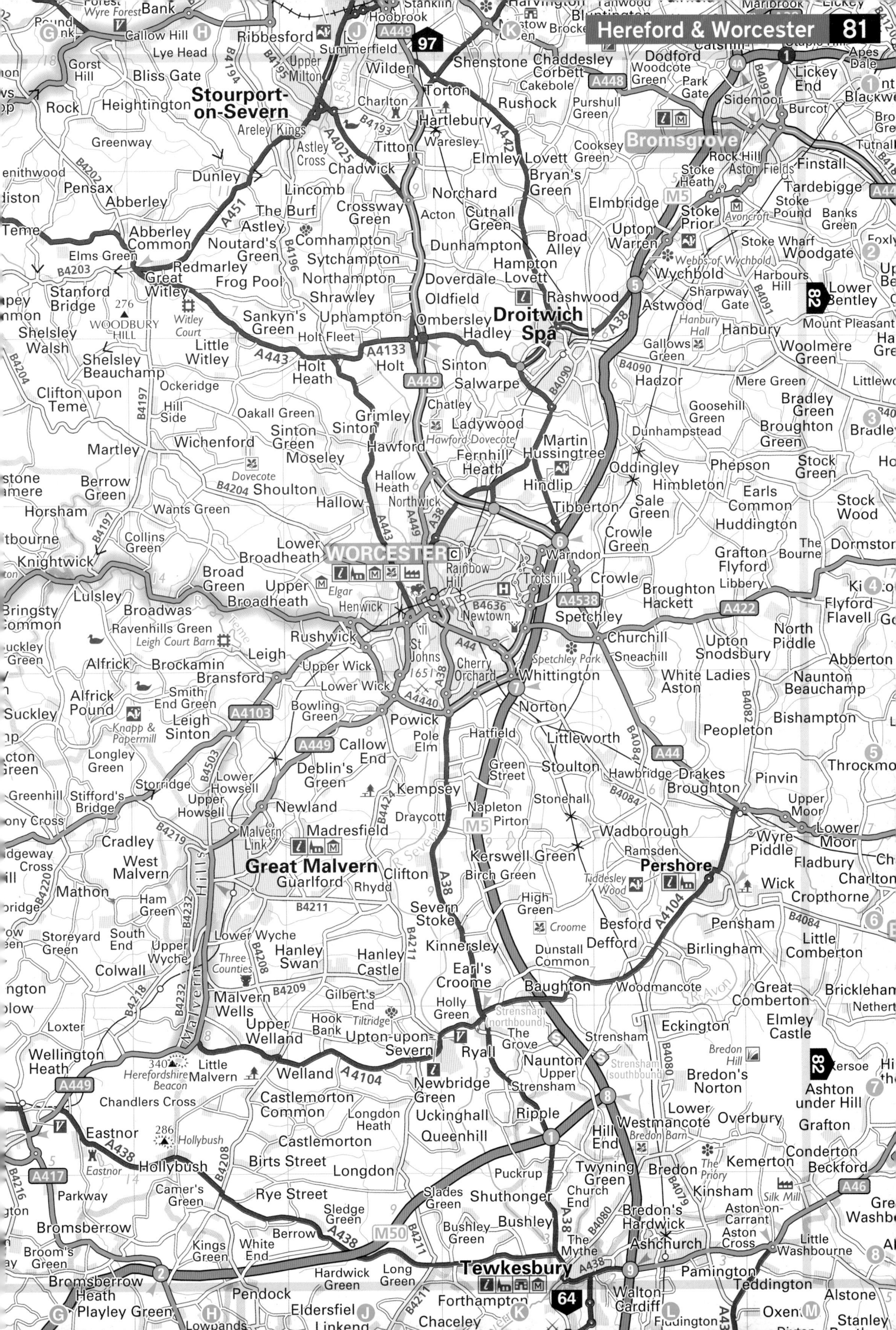

Maribrook • Lickey • Arrowfield Top • Hopwood Park • Tanner's Green • Darley Green • Fen End
A • Staple Hill • Lickey Rock • Barnt Green • Weatheroak Hill • Forshaw Heath • Edgwood • Four Ashes • Cheswick Green • Chadwick End • A417
Apes Dale • Withybed Green • M42 • Portway • Wood End • 98 • Terry's Green • Hockley Heath • Packwood House • Cheletts Wood • Baddesley Clinton
Sidemoor • Burcot • Linthurst • Blackwell • Rowney Green • Heath Green • Branson's Cross • Aspley Heath • Tanworth in Arden • Kemps Green • Kingswood • Baddesley Clinton • Wroxall
Rock Hill • Finstall • Broad Green • Beoley • B4101 • Holt End • Trap's Green • Danzey Green • Kingswood Brook • Lapworth • M40 • Turner's Green • Rowington
Aston Fields • Tardebigge • Stoke Pound • Banks Green • REDDITCH • A435 • Blunts Green • Lowsonford • High Cross • Shrewley • Little Shrewley
Stoke Wharf • Foxlydiate • Webheath • A4023 • A4189 • Ullenhall • Henley-in-Arden • Beaudesert • Preston Bagot • Holywell • Lye Green • Pinley Green
Woodgate • Headless Cross • Crabbs Cross • Green Lane • Mappleborough Green • Oldberrow • Preston Green • Claverdon • Lower Norton
Harbours Hill • Upper Bentley • Callow Hill • Walkwood • Studley Common • Studley • Thomas Town • Spernall • Wootton Wawen • Langley • Wolverton • Norton Lindsey
Hanbury • 81 • Mount Pleasant • Ham Green • Hunt End • A448 • Shelfield • Edstone • Langley Green
Coolmere Green • Astwood Bank • B4092 • New End • Coughton Court • Shelfield Green • Little Alne • Bearle Cross • Snitterfield Bushes • Pigeon Green
Mere Green • Bradley Green • Feckenham • Edgiock • Sambourne Ridgeway • Coughton • Great Alne • Aston Cantlow • Bearley • Snitterfield • Heath End
Broughton Green • Bradley • Shurnock • Holberrow Green • B4090 • King's Coughton • Mary Arden's Farm • Wilmcote • Alveston
Stock Green • Stock Wood • Bouts • Cladswell • Cookhill • Alcester • Kinwarton Dovecote • Walcot • Haselor • Upton • Shottery • Stratford-upon-Avon
Earls Common • Huddington • Dormston • Kington • Abbots Morton • Weethley • Arrow • A422 • Oversley Green • Exhall • Red Hill • Temple Grafton • Anne Hathaway's Cottage • Billesley • Bishopton • Tiddington
Grafton Flyford • The Bourne • Flyford Flavell • Goom's Hill • Wood Bevington • Ragley Hall • Wixford • Ardens Grafton • A46 • Butterfly Farm
North Piddle • Naunton Beauchamp • Abberton • Rous Lench • Cock Bevington • Dunnington • Broom • Bidford-on-Avon • Cranhill • Binton • Luddington
Upton Snodsbury • Bishampton • Church Lench • Ab Lench • Iron Cross • Salford Priors • Welford-on-Avon • Weston-on-Avon • Clifford Chambers
Peopleton • Throckmorton • Atch Lench • Abbot's Salford • Marlcliff • Barton • Atherstone on Stour • Preston on Stour
Pinvin • Harvington • B4088 • B439 • Dorsington • Long Marston • Willicote • Wimpstone • Crimscote
Upper Moor • Lower Moor • Norton • Lenchwick • B4085 • Cleeve Prior • North Littleton • Pebworth • Lower Quinton • Admington • Newbold on Stour
Wyre Piddle • A44 • Offenham • Middle Littleton • Broad Marston • Upper Quinton • Armscote
Fladbury • Charlton • Chadbury • Tithe Barn • South Littleton • Honeybourne • Hidcote Bartrim • Blackwell
Wick • Cropthorne • B4084 • Evesham • Aldington • Bretforton • Mickleton • Kiftsgate Court • Ilmington
Little Comberton • A46 • Bengeworth • Badsey • The Fleece Inn • Aston-sub-Edge • Hidcote Boyce • Darlingscott
Great Comberton • 81 • Bricklehampton • Netherton • Hampton • B4035 • Weston-sub-Edge • Ebrington • Charingworth
Elmley Castle • Hinton Green • Wickhamford • Vale of Evesham • Saintbury • Chipping Campden • A429
Bredon Hill • Kersoe • Hinton on the Green • Murcot • Willersey • Broad Campden • Stretton on Fosse
Overbury • Ashton under Hill • Grafton • Childswickham • Cotswold Way • Paxford
Kemerton • Conderton • Beckford • Sedgeberrow • Aston Somerville • Weston-sub-Edge • Ebrington • Tidmington
Ashton-on-Carrant • Silk Mill • Dumbleton • A46 • Broadway • Broadway Tower • Blockley • Aston Magna • Lower Lemington
Aston Cross • Great Washbourne • Buckland • Rectory • B4081 • Draycott • Dorn
Teddington • Little Washbourne • Alderton • B4078 • Laverton • Stanton • Snowshill • Cotswold Lavender • Batsford • Four Shires
A46 • Toddington • B4632 • Snowshill Manor • A44 • Cotswold Falconry Centre
Oxenton • Stanway • Warwickshire Railway • Bourton-on-the-Hill • 65 • Bourton House • Bourton-on-the-Water • Moreton-in-Marsh

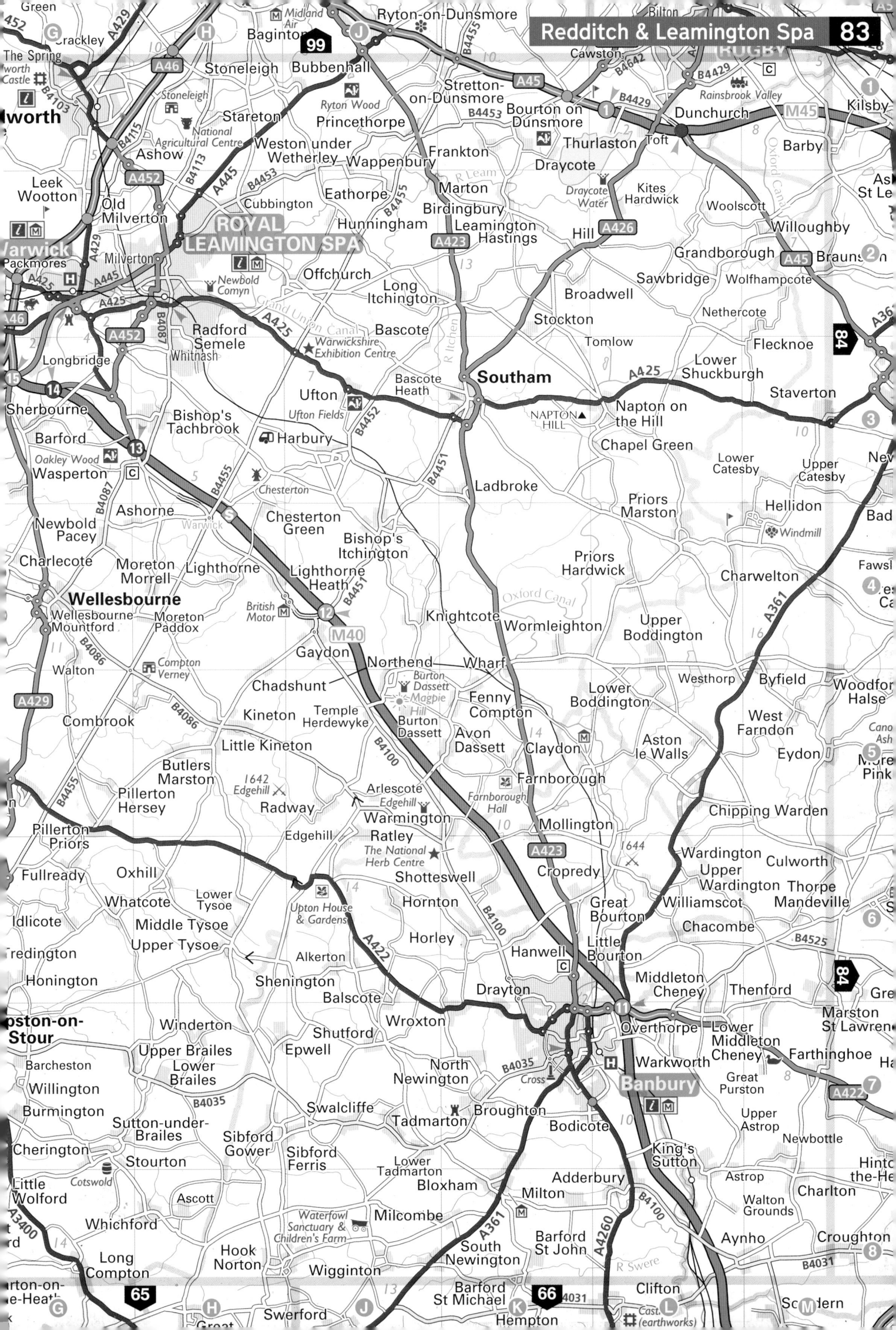

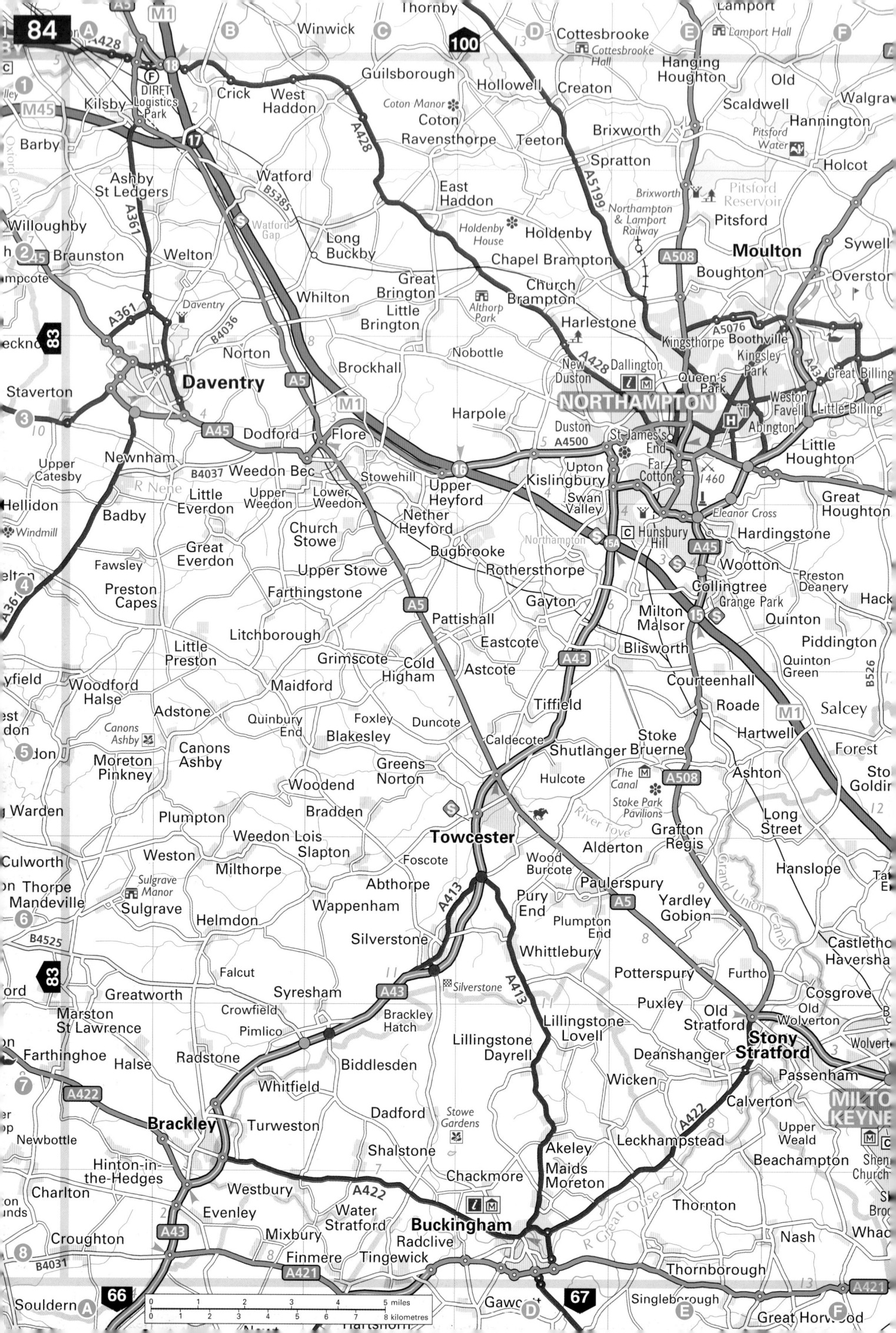

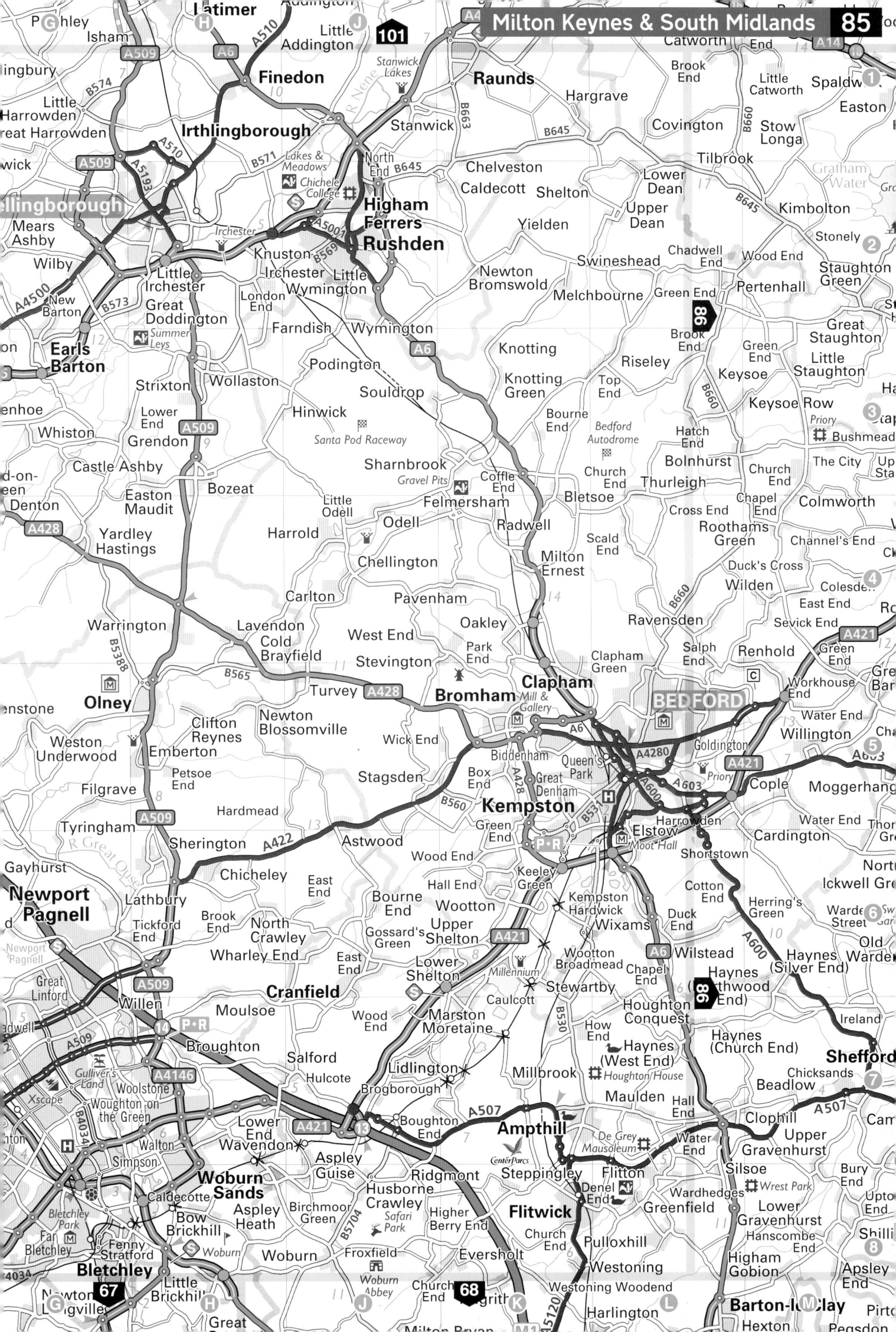

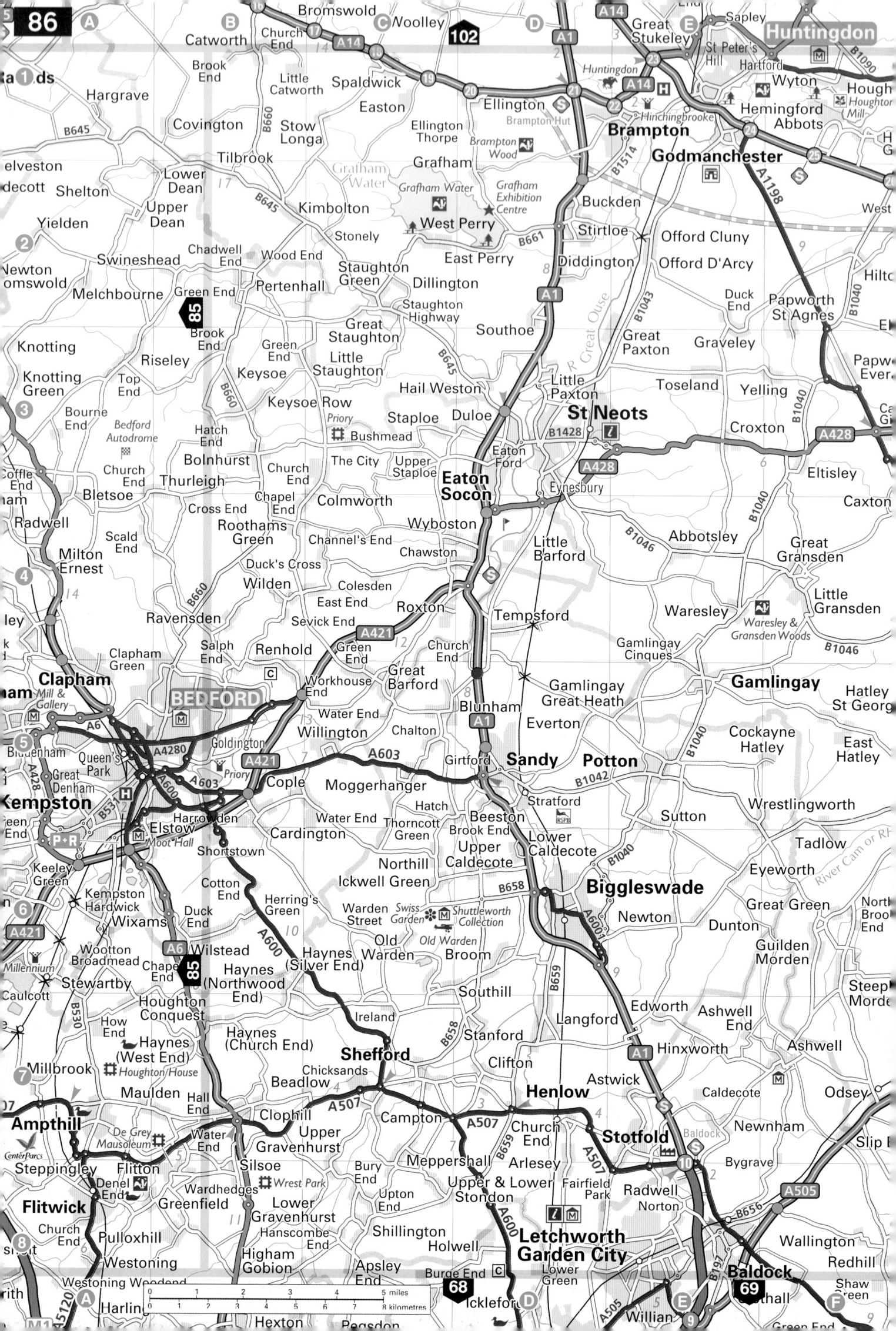

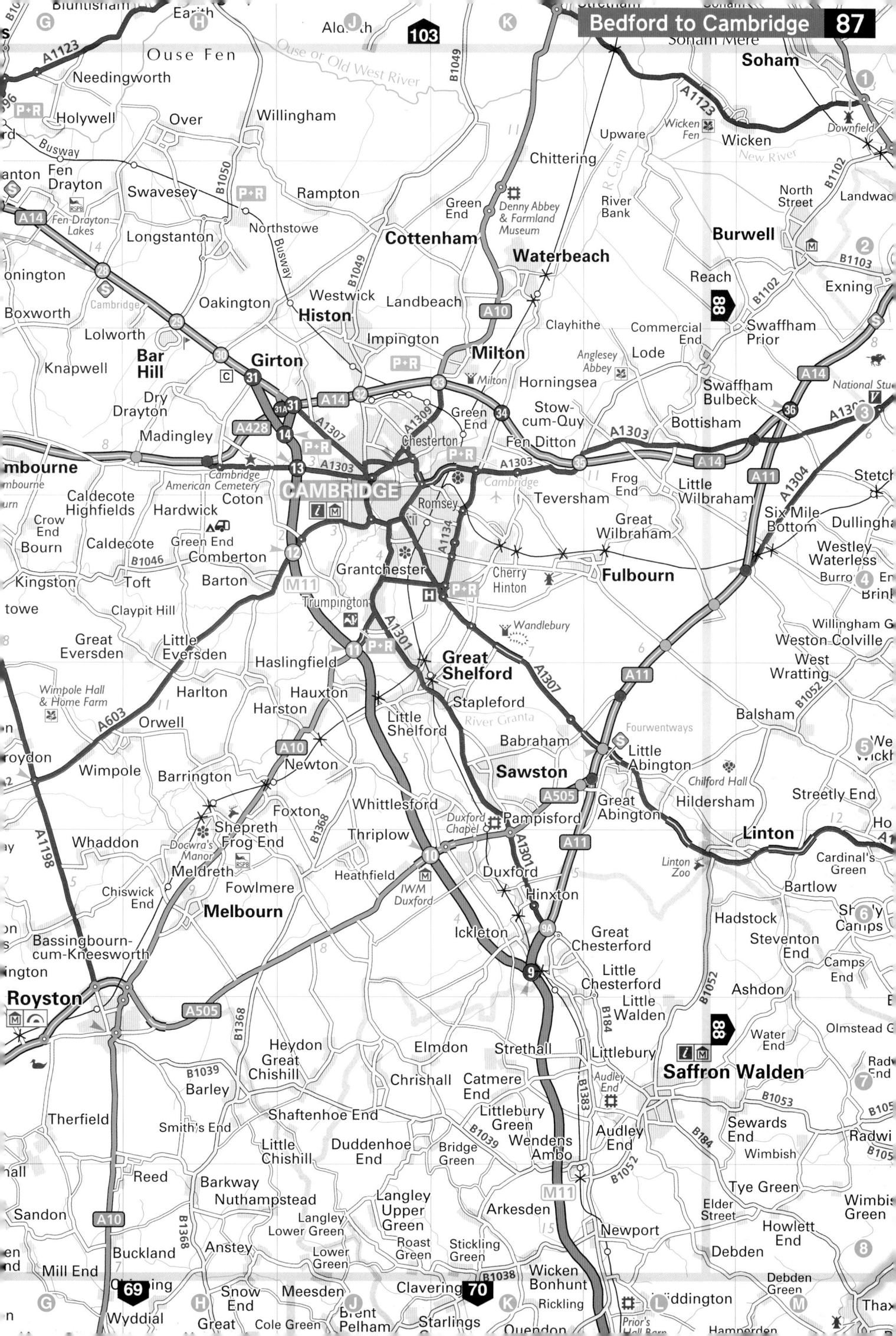

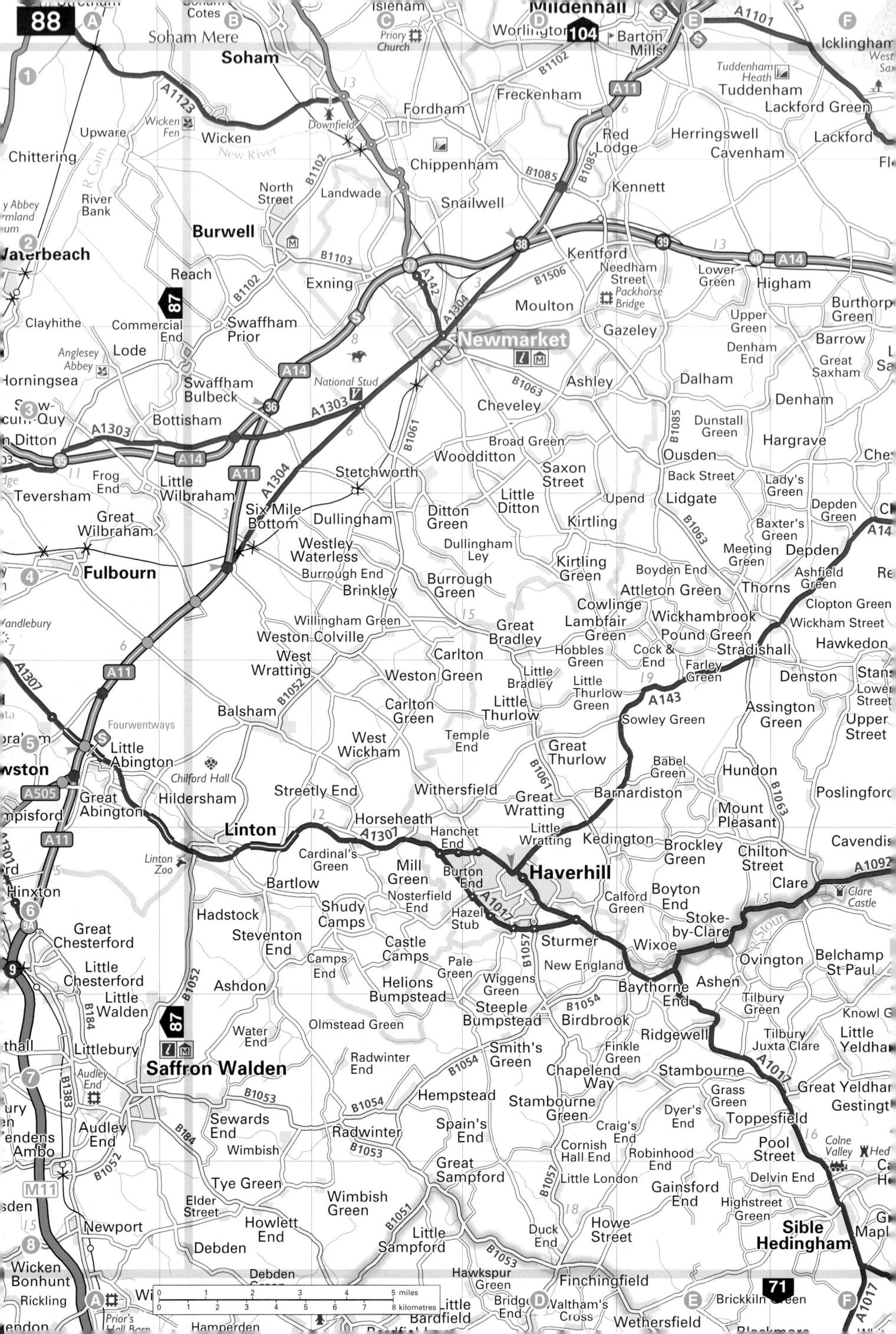

G 12 Honington Bardwe J Stanton Wattisfield K Allwood Green A1113 Mill Street Thornham Parva 1

B1106 H Ixworth Thorpe Bangrove 105 Upthorpe Walsham le Willows Cranmer Green Gislingham Thornham Magna Wickham Street A

Brockley Troston Ampton Great Livermere Wyken A143 West Street Badwell Ash Crowland Finningham Westhorpe Wickham Skeith Wickham Green 12

Culford Ingham Timworth Ixworth Langham Hunston Four Ashes Badwell Green Long Thurlow Wyverstone Street Wyverstone Cotton Brockford Stre 2

Timworth Green Conyer's Green Upper Town Grimstone End A1088 Stowlangtoft Great Ashfield Hunston Green Earl's Green Bacton Ford's Green Mendlesham A1

River Lark Fornham St Martin Watermill Pakenham Stanton Street Norton Little Green Bacton Green Cow Green Canhams Green Mendlesham Green

B1106 6 Great Barton Thurston Great Green 12 Norton Haughley Green B1113 Brown Street Gipping

A1101 C A143 Cattishall Battlies Green Thurston Planch Tostock Elmswell Base Green 06 Old Newton Middlewoo Green

42 43 44 45 Beyton Gn 46 Beyton 16 Woolpit 47 Broadgrass Gn Wetherden Haughley A14 Saxham Street Lit Stonham 3

Bury St Edmunds Blackthorpe Kingshall Street Hessett Woolpit Green Borley Green Harleston A1308 Stowupland Forward Green Earl Stonham

Horringer Nowton Park Rushbrooke Rougham Drinkstone Clopton Green Onehouse Buxhall Fen Street Stowmarket Dagworth 51

High Green Nowton Sicklesmere Bradfield St George Drinkstone Green Gedding Poystree Green Buxhall Mill Green Great Finborough Combs Ford Creeting St Mary

Pinford End Hawstead Little Welnetham Maypole Green Felsham Hightown Green B1115 Combs Needham Market 4

Hawstead Green Great Welnetham Bradfield St Clare Bush Green Bradfield Woods Brettenham Moats Tye Needham Lake A1078

Mickley Green Bradfield Combust Oldhall Green Great Green Cross Green Bird Street Battisford Tye Battisford Barking

Melon Green Hoggards Green Cockfield Thorpe Green Cooks Green Charles Tye Ringshall Lower Street Baylham

Harrow Green Stanningfield Cross Green Thorpe Morieux Hitcham Causeway Wattisham Barking Tye Ringshall Stocks Upper Street Great Blakenh 5

Lawshall Windsor Green Lawshall Green Preston St Mary Hitcham Street Hitcham Nedging Tye Great Bricett Offton Somersham

B1066 Cross Green Audley End Shimpling Street A1141 A1071 Kettlebaston Greenstreet Green Naughton Little Blakenh

A134 Shimpling Alpheton Guildhall Bildeston Nedging Flowton

Boxted Bridge Street Lavenham Little Hall Brent Eleigh Monks Eleigh B1115 Ash Street Elmsett Bramfor

Stanstead Kentwell Hall & Gardens Chelsworth Whatfield

Glemsford B1065 B1066 Melford Hall Swingleton Green Semer B1115 B1078

entlow Long Melford Little Waldingfield Milden Lindsey Tye Aldham Sproughton 6

Acton Rose Green Lindsey Stone Street Wolves Wood RSPB Burstall

A134 Great Waldingfield St James's Chapel A1071 10 Duke Street Hintlesham

Borley Newman's Green Kersey Tye Kersey Washbro Coles Green

Borley Green A134 Chilton Mill Green Wicker Street Green Kersey Upland Coram Street Hadleigh Chattisham

Sudbury B1115 Edwardstone Groton Horners Green 06 B1070 Copdock

Ballingdon Cornard Tye Newton Boxford Calais Street Hadleigh Heath Layham Great Wenham Little Wenham

Bulmer Great Cornard A1071 12 Stone Street Bower House Tye Raydon S 7

Bulmer Tye Middleton Great Cornard Little Cornard Hagmore Green Whitestreet Green Polstead Heath Shelley Lower Raydon Capel St Mary A12

Great Henny Workhouse Green Rose Green Assington Leavenheath Polstead Holton St Mary Bentley

Wickham St Paul Henny Street Twinstead Dorking Tye B1068 Stoke-by-Nayland Higham Stratford St Mary East End

A131 Alphamstone Lamarsh Honey Tye 15 Thorington Street B1068 East Bergholt

Little Maplestead Cross End B1508 Nayland B1087 Carter's Flatford Mill & Bridge Cottage 8

Pebmarsh Bures Wissington Boxted Dedham Mistley To

Boose's G H Mount Bures J 72 K Boxted L Manningtree M

Stanton Wattisfield Mellis Yaxley Denham Stradbroke Gree
Upthorpe Andle Street Mill Street Thornham Parva Denham Green
Wyken Walsham le Willows Cranmer Green Allwood Green Braiseworth Horham Wootten Green
West Street Langham Badwell Ash Four Ashes Long Thurlow Crowland Gislingham Finningham Thornham Magna Eye 106 Redlingfield Green Athelington Street
Hunston Stowlangtoft Great Ashfield Badwell Green Wyverstone Street Wickham Street Stoke Ash Standwell Green Occold Redlingfield Stanway Green
Stanton Street Hunston Green Norton Little Green Wyverstone Bacton Wickham Skeith Wickham Green Thorndon Thwaite Rishangles Bedingfield Coal Street
Norton Elmswell Bacton Green Earl's Green Cow Green Cotton Mendlesham Hestley Green Bedingfield Green Monk Soham Bedfield
Woolpit Norton Little Green Haughley Green Ward Green Canhams Green Ford's Green Brockford Street Aspall Kenton Bedfield Little Green Post Mill
Broadgrass Gn Wetherden Base Green Brown Street Gipping Mendlesham Green Park Green Wetherup Street Debenham Earl Soham
Woolpit Green Haughley Dagworth Old Newton Middlewood Green Mickfield Winston Ashfield cum Thorpe
Clopton Green Onehouse Saxham Street Stowupland Little Stonham Mill Green Cretingham
Rattlesden Harleston Stowmarket Forward Green Stonham Aspal Pettaugh Framsden Monewden
Buxhall Fen Street Combs Ford Earl Stonham Mid Suffolk Suffolk Owl Sanctuary
Poystreet Green Great Finborough Crowfield Green Helmingham Hall Otley Green Charsfield
Mill Green Buxhall Combs Creeting St Mary Crowfield Helmingham Gosbeck Otley Clopton Corner Dalli
Hightown Green Battisford Tye Battisford Needham Lake Coddenham Hemingstone Swilland Ashbocking Clopton
Brettenham Cross Green Bird Street Charles Tye Ringshall Barking Needham Market Lower Street Barham Bells Cross Grundisburgh Burgh
Cooks Green Wattisham Barking Tye Baylham Henley Witnesham Boot Street Great Bealing
Hitcham Street Hitcham Nedging Tye Great Bricett Ringshall Stocks Upper Street Great Blakenham Claydon Akenham Tuddenham Culpho Hasketon
Bildeston Nedging Greenstreet Green Offton Somersham Little Blakenham Whitton Playford Little Bealings
Monks Eleigh Ash Street Naughton Flowton Bramford Castle Hill Westerfield Rushmere St Andrew Kesgrave
Chelsworth Semer Whatfield Elmsett Sproughton Chantry IPSWICH
Lindsey Tye Lindsey Aldham Burstall Hintlesham Belstead
Rose Green St James's Chapel Stone Street Wolves Wood Duke Street Washbrook Coles Green Copdock
Kersey Tye Kersey Coram Street Hadleigh Chattisham Jimmy's Farm Wherstead Orwell Bridge Nacton
Wicker Street Green Kersey Upland Hadleigh Heath Layham Great Wenham Little Wenham Belstead Freston Levington Woolverstone
Horners Green Bower House Tye Polstead Heath Raydon Capel St Mary Bentley Tattingstone White Horse Tattingstone Holbrook Chelmondiston
Stone Street Whitestreet Green Shelley Lower Raydon Holton St Mary East End Holbrook Lower Holbrook Erwarton
Thorington Street Polstead Stoke-by-Nayland Higham Stratford St Mary East Bergholt Brantham Upper Street Stutton Harkstead Shotley Street
Boxted Carter's Langham Dedham Cattawade Mistley Towers Wrabness Parkeston Quay
Boxted Cross Boxted Manningtree New Mistley Mistley Parkeston 73

River Gipping River Brett River Box River Stour Holbrook Bay River Orwell Pin Mill Stour Estuary
Alton Water Suffolk

G H B1117 Walpole J K B1387
Huntingfield Walpole
Bramfield 107 ington
A144 A12 A6

Laxfield Heveningham
Ubbeston Green
ndish Street Pouy High Street Dunwich
Owl's Street Darsham Forest Suffolk Coast
Green Sibton Westleton
ndish Peasenhall Yoxford Heath Dunwich
Goddard's Corner A1120 B1122 Middleton Grey Friars
Capon's Badingham Middleton Moor Westleton
Green A12 North Green Minsmere
Dennington B1120 Bruisyard Theberton Dunwich
xtead Bruisyard Carlton Meres East Eastbridge Heath
Brabling Cransford Street Rendham Green Kelsale Poplar Street
Green Castle Shawsgate B1119 Carlton Leiston Power
ham Swefling Saxmundham Abbey Station
North Green Great Benhall Knodishall Sizewell
Mill Glemham Street Benhall B1119 Sternfield Coldfair Leiston
Green Green Green
Parham Stratford Benhall Friston Knodishall Thorpe
ettleburgh St Andrew Green Aldringham Ness
Easton Silverlace Farnham Friday B1121 Friston Knodishall Thorpeness
Green Street Common A1094 B1122
Hacheston Snape North
Marlesford Little Gromford A1094 Warren
Glemham Snape
Lower Street Aldeburgh
Wickham Hacheston Blaxhall B1069 Snape Aldeburgh
Market Campsea Maltings Iken
Pettistree Ash Snape High Aldeburgh
Upper Tunstall Street Bay
Ufford Rendlesham A1152 B1078
10 Ufford Chillesford Sudbourne
Lower Ufford Friday B1084
A12 Street B1084
B1438 Eyke Butley Orford
Melton Bromeswell B1084 12 Castle
Butley High Orford Ness
Woodbridge Corner Orford Ness
Capel Butley Orford Ness
Green Capel
Sutton Hoo St Andrew Orfordness-
sham Havergate
Sutton Boyton
ham River Ore
Waldringfield Shottisham Suffolk Heritage Coast
Newbourne Hollesley
Hemley Hollesley
B1083 Bay
Ramsholt North Weir Point
Kirton Alderton Shingle
Falkenham Bawdsey Street
59 Trimley
St Mary Felixstowe
60 Ferry
Walton Old
61 Felixstowe
62 Felixstowe
A154 i
bt Landguard Fort
G Landguard H J K L M
Point

0 1 2 3 4 5 miles
0 1 2 3 4 5 6 7 8 kilometres

1
2
3
4
5
6
7
8

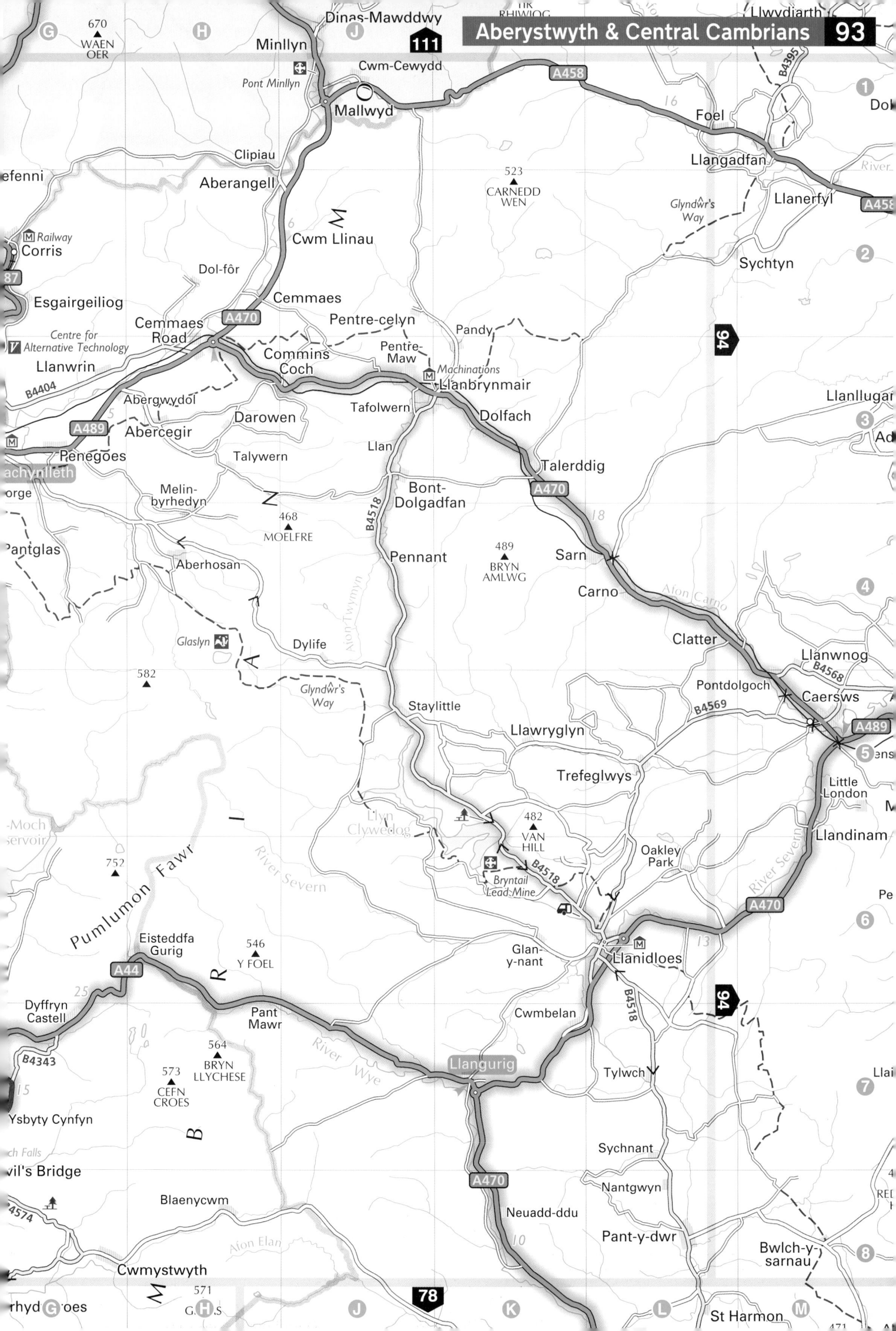

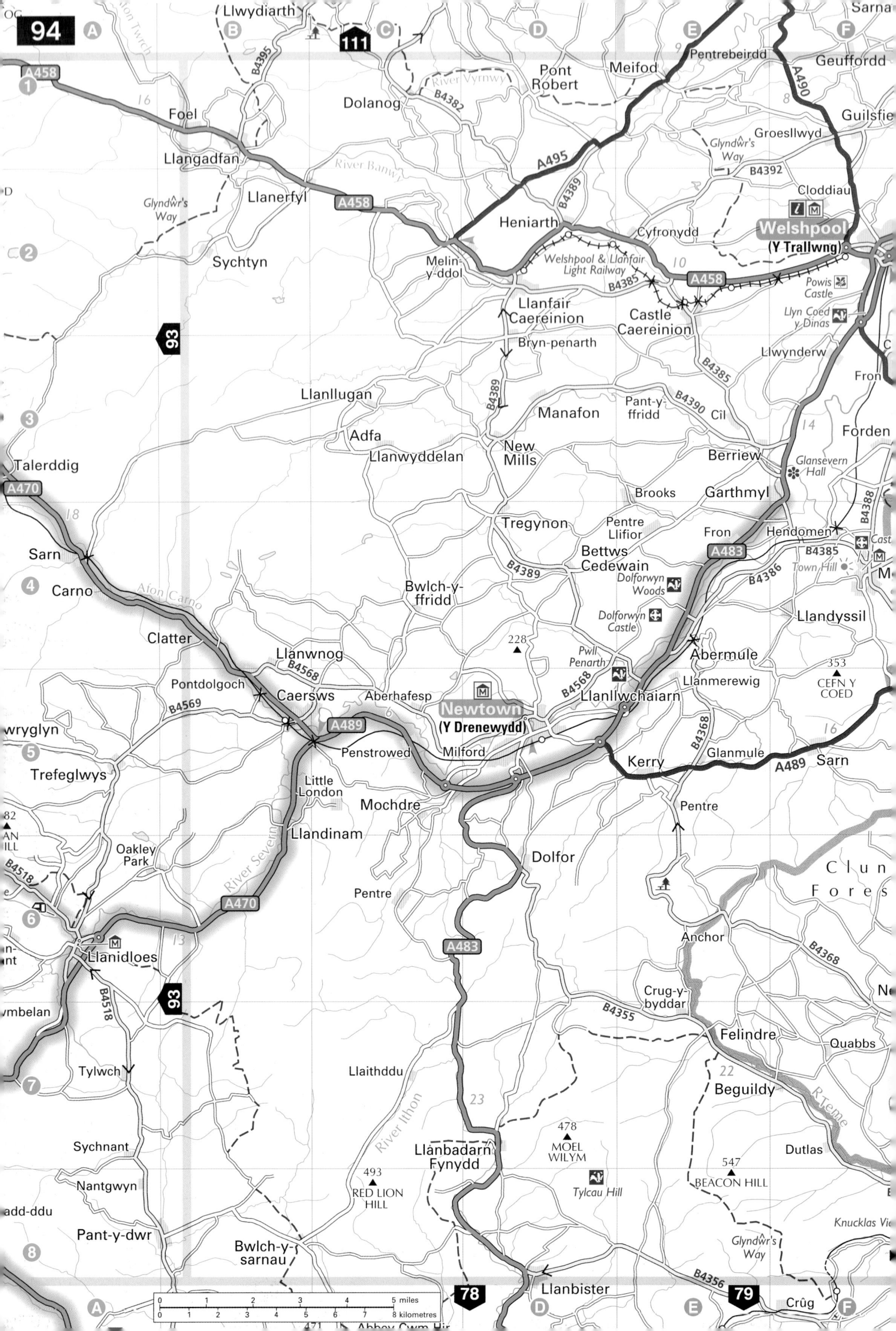

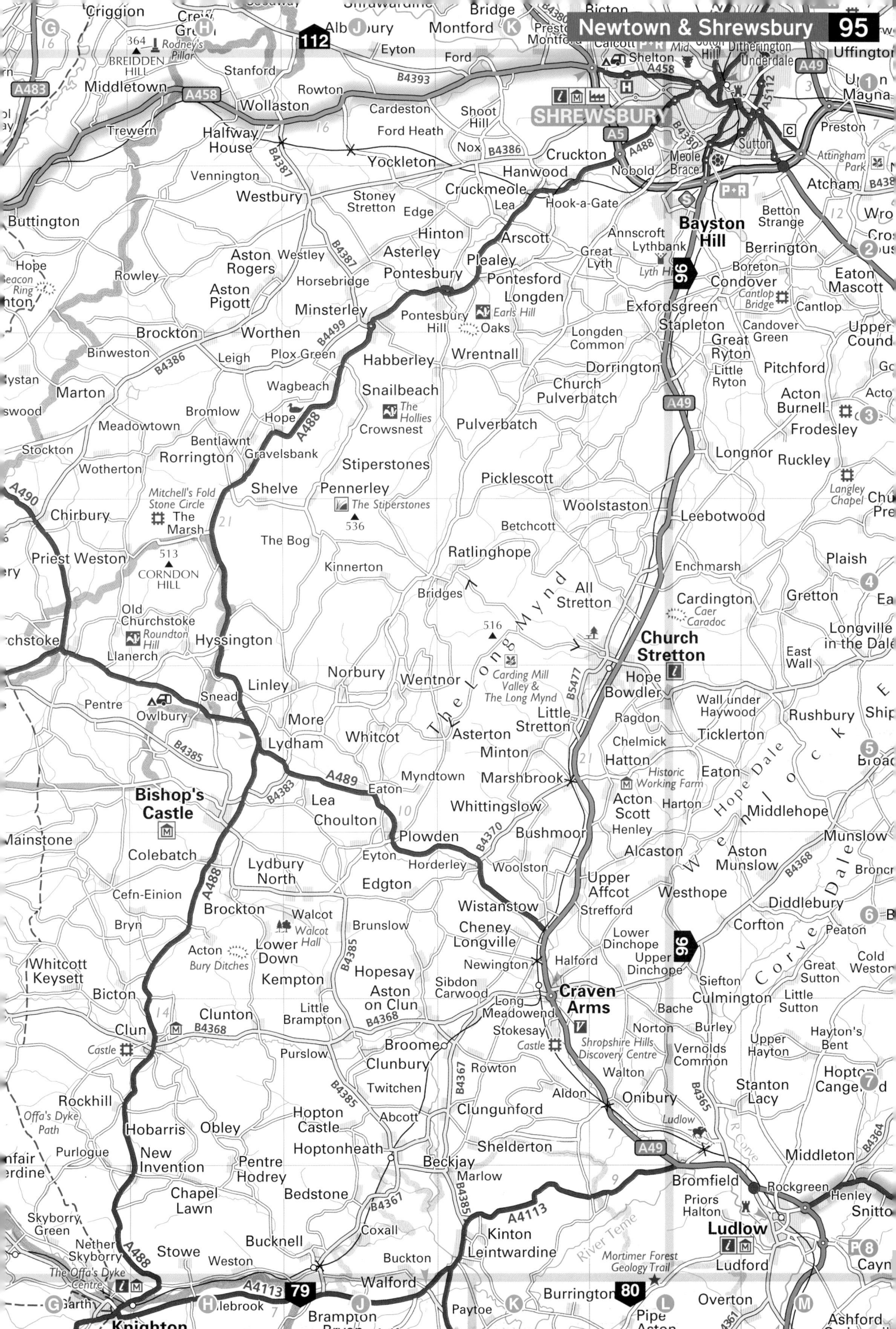

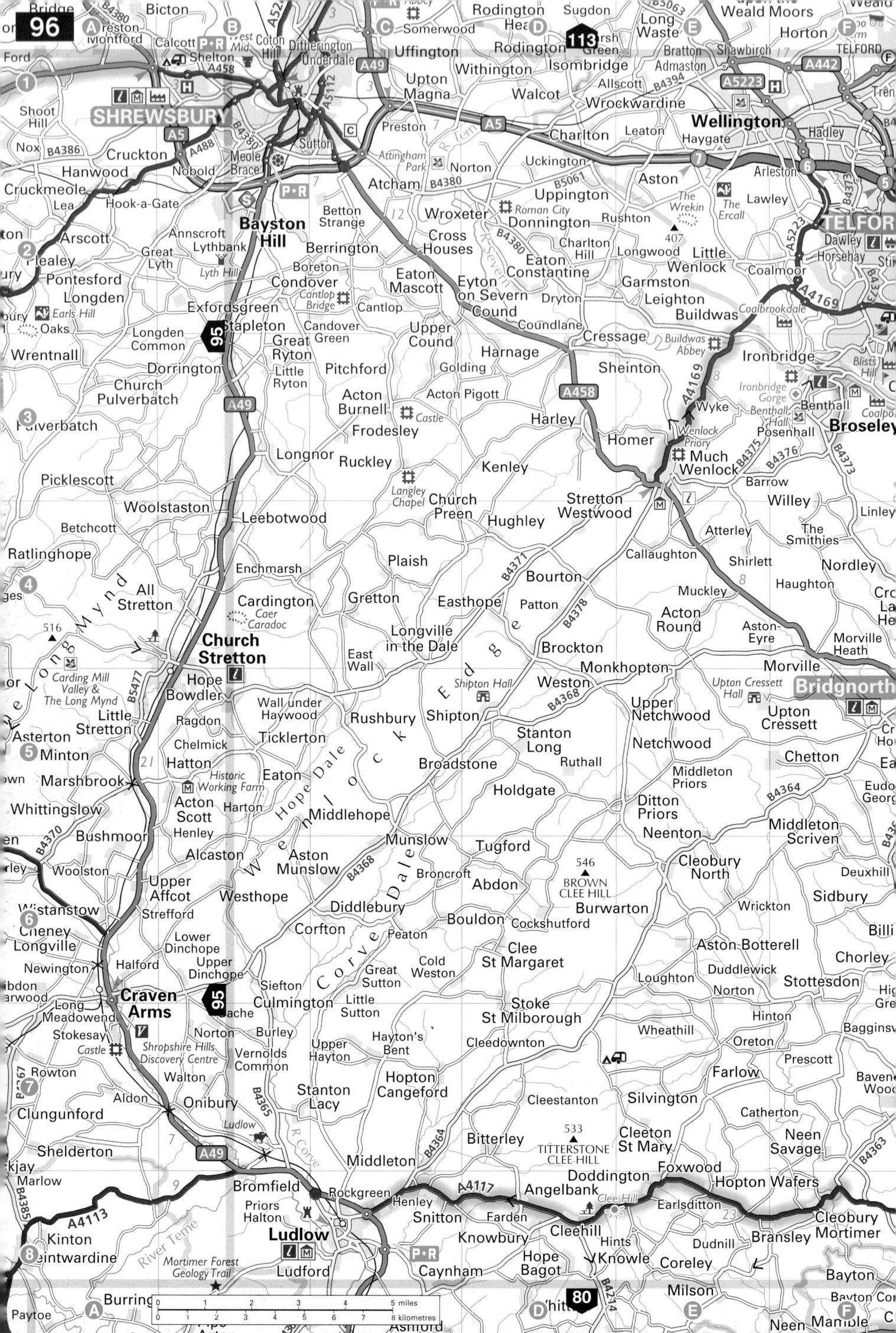

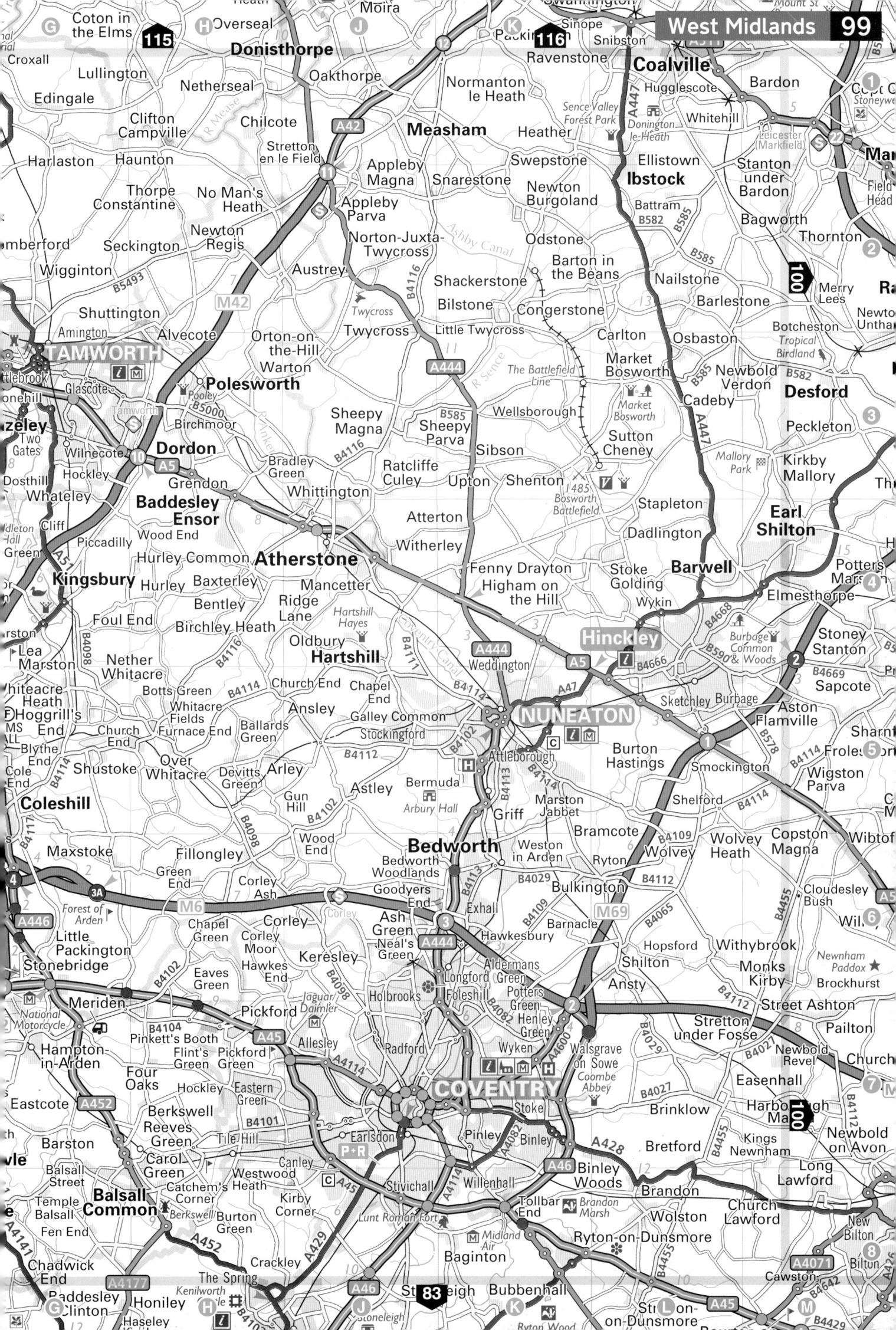

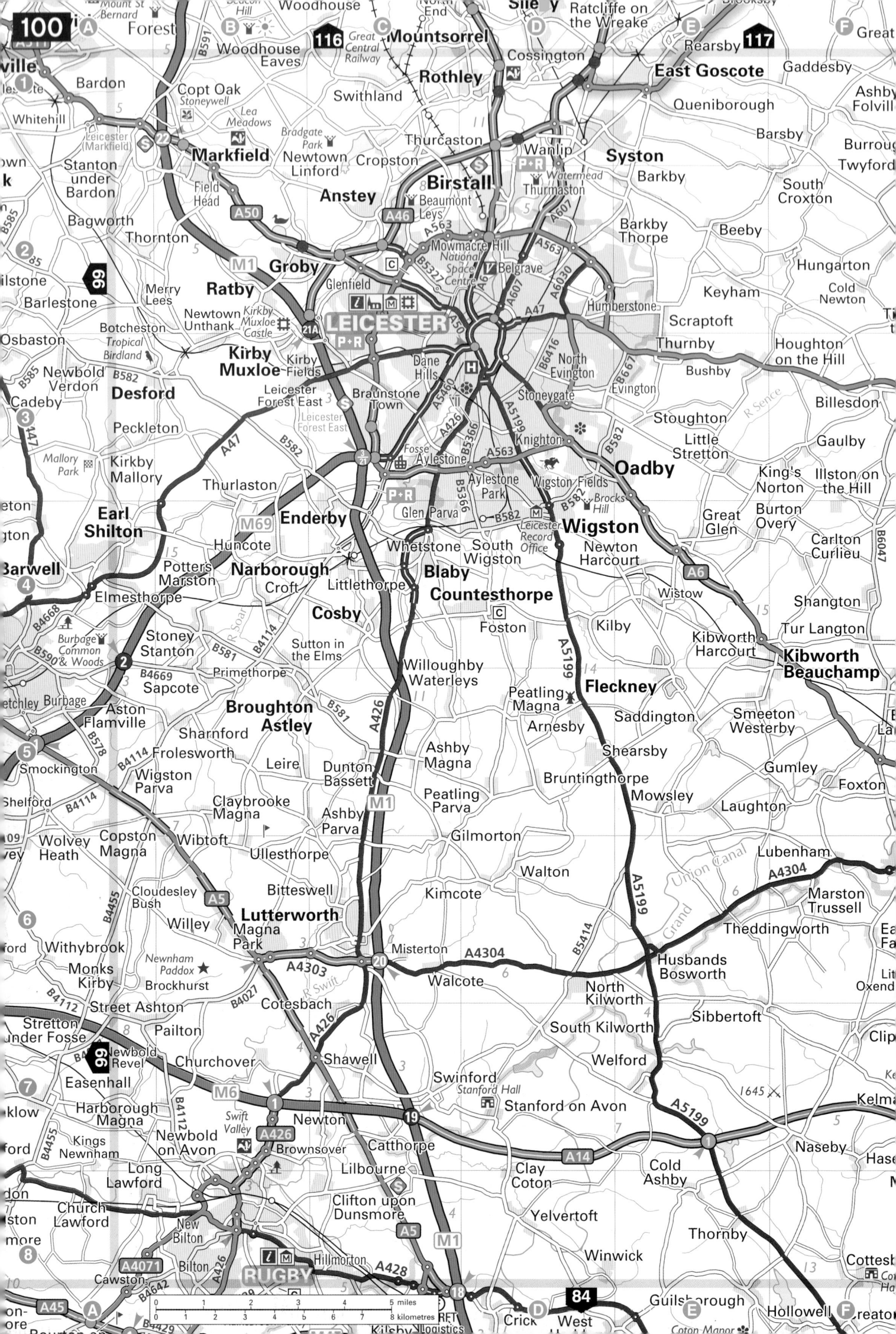

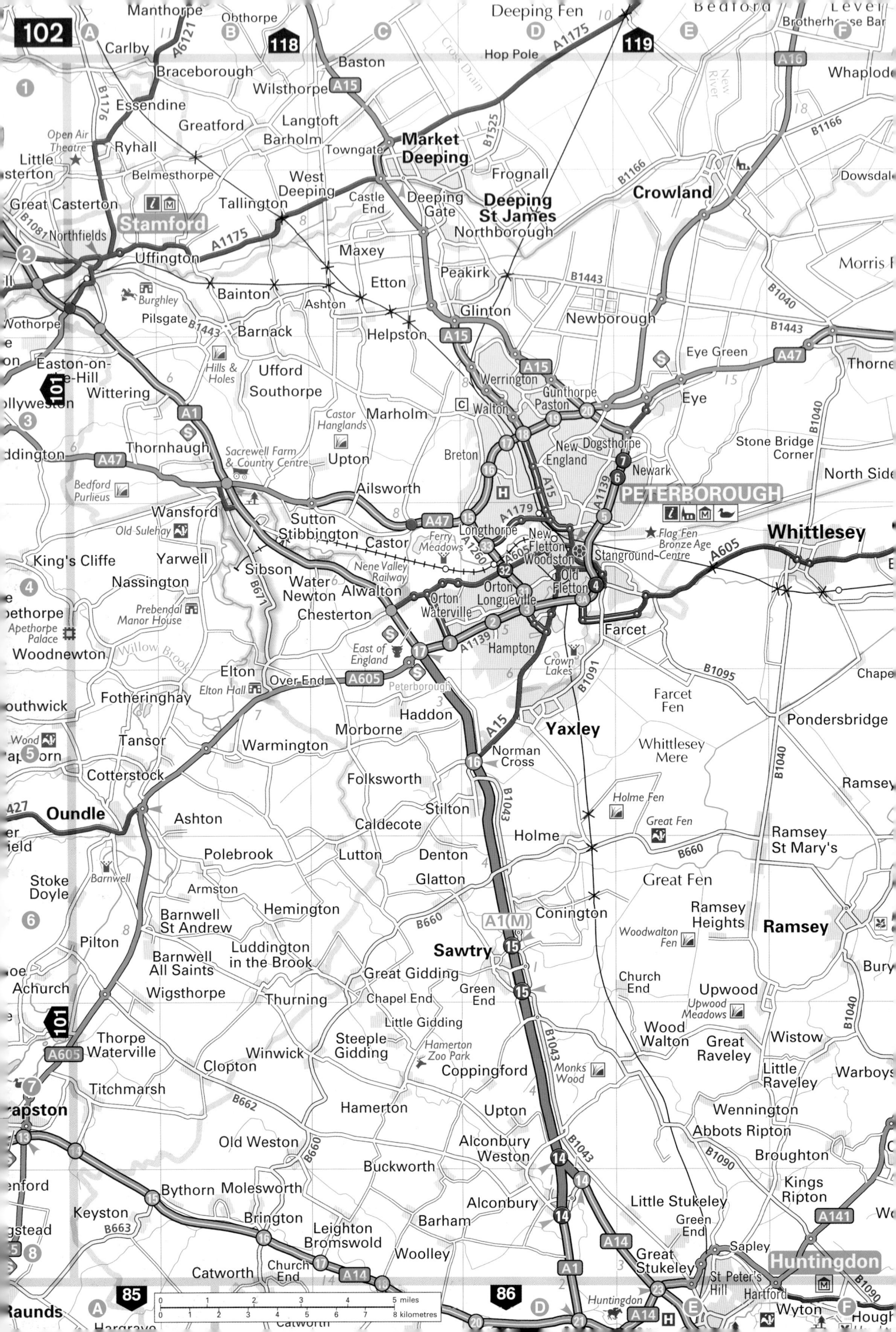

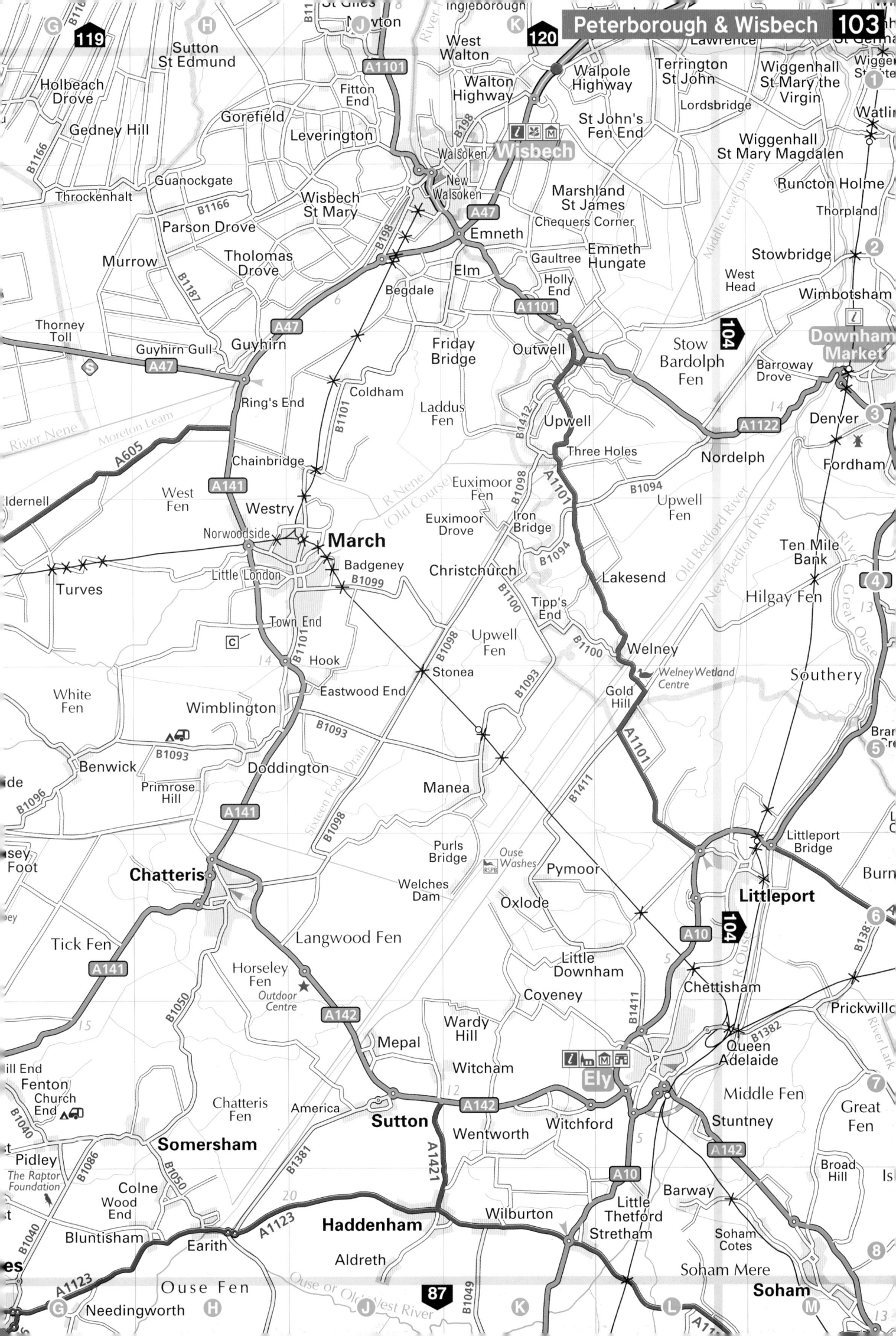

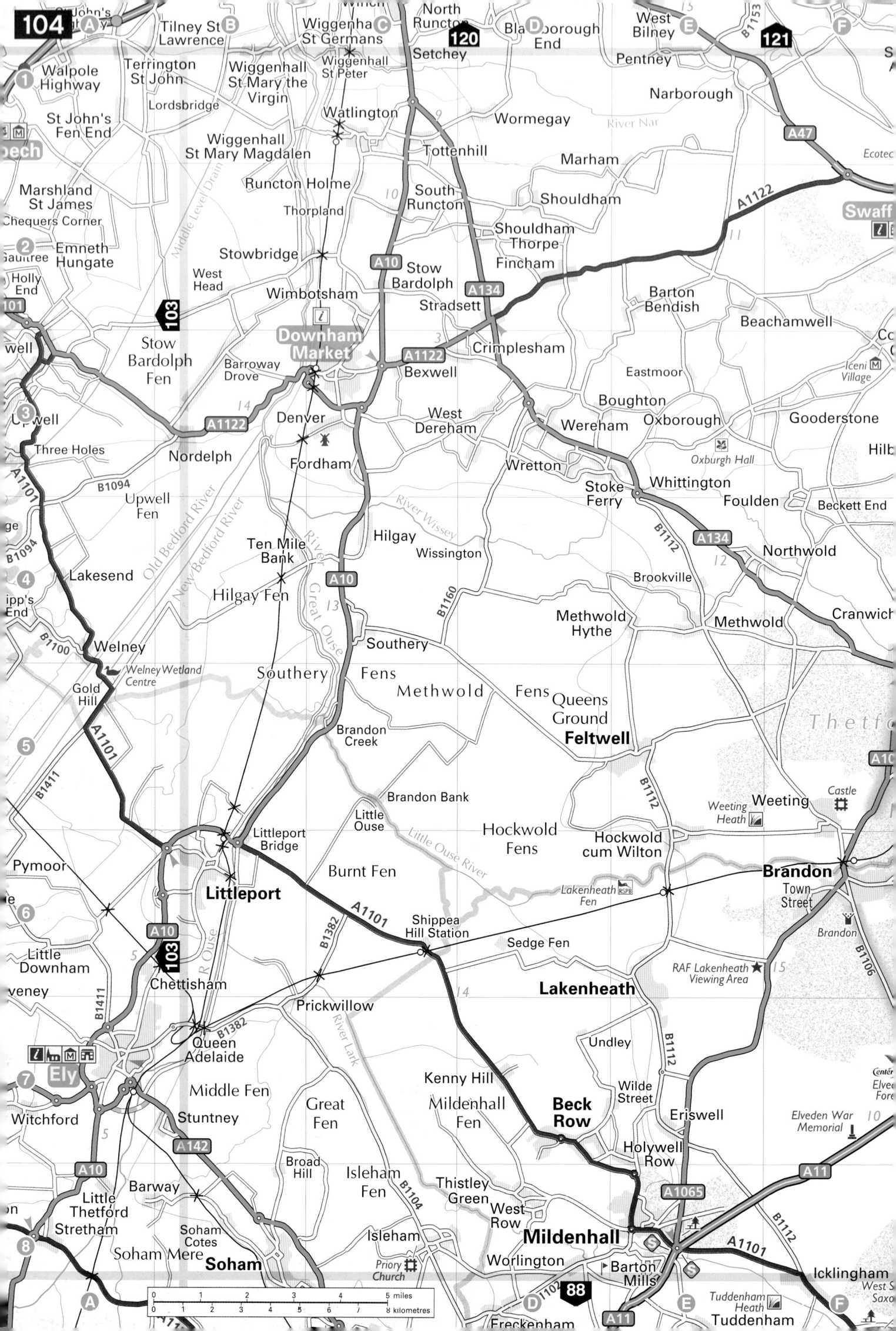

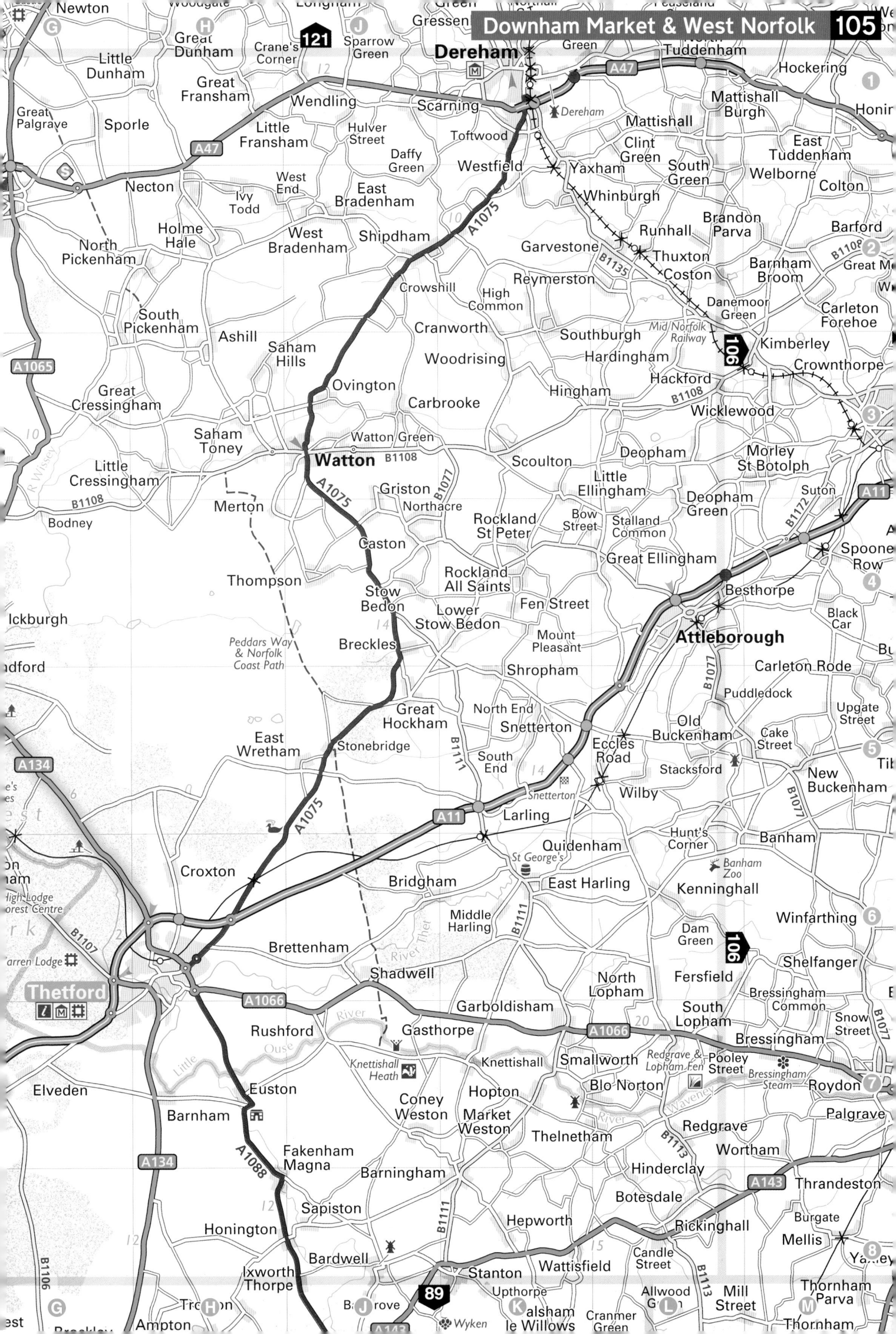

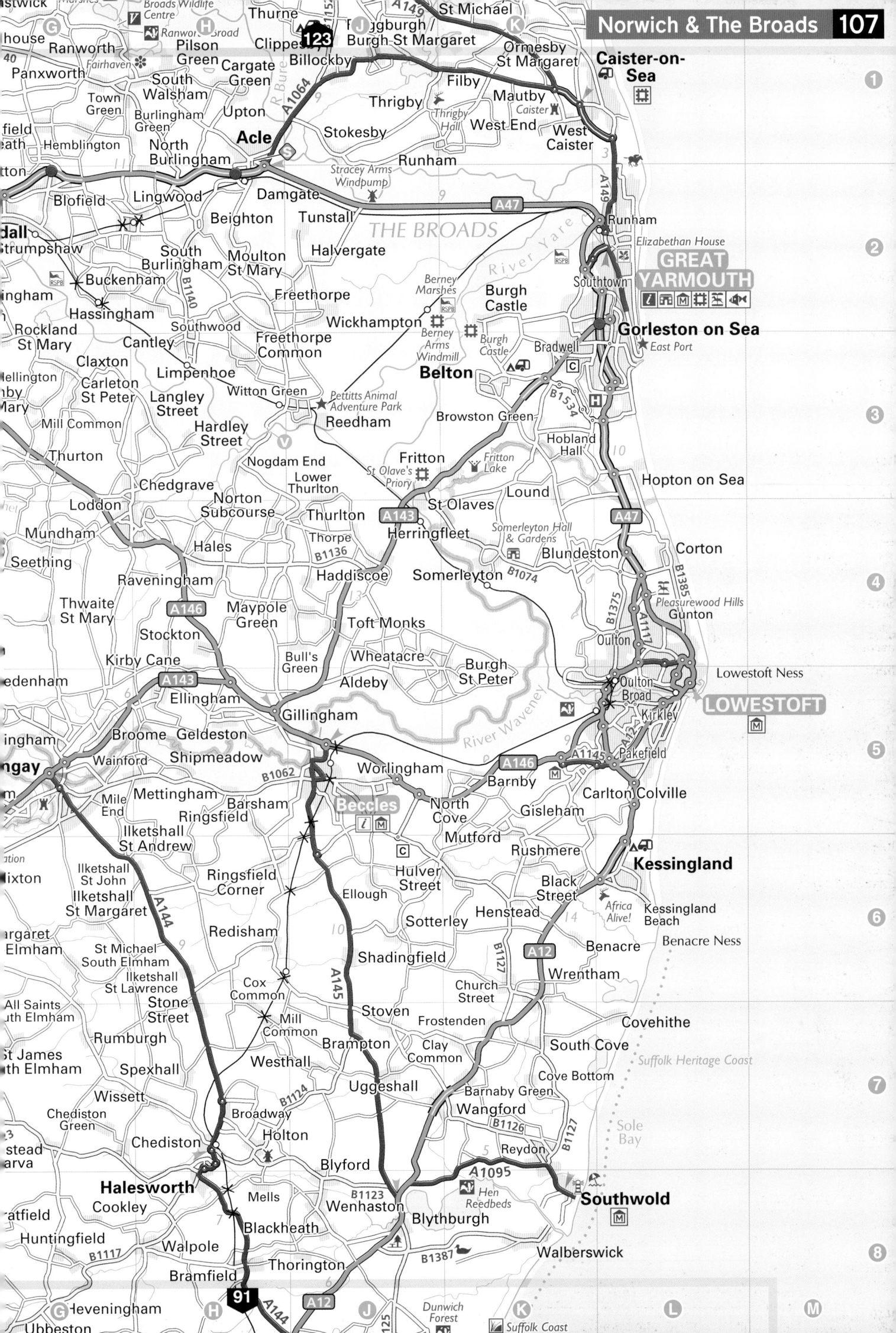

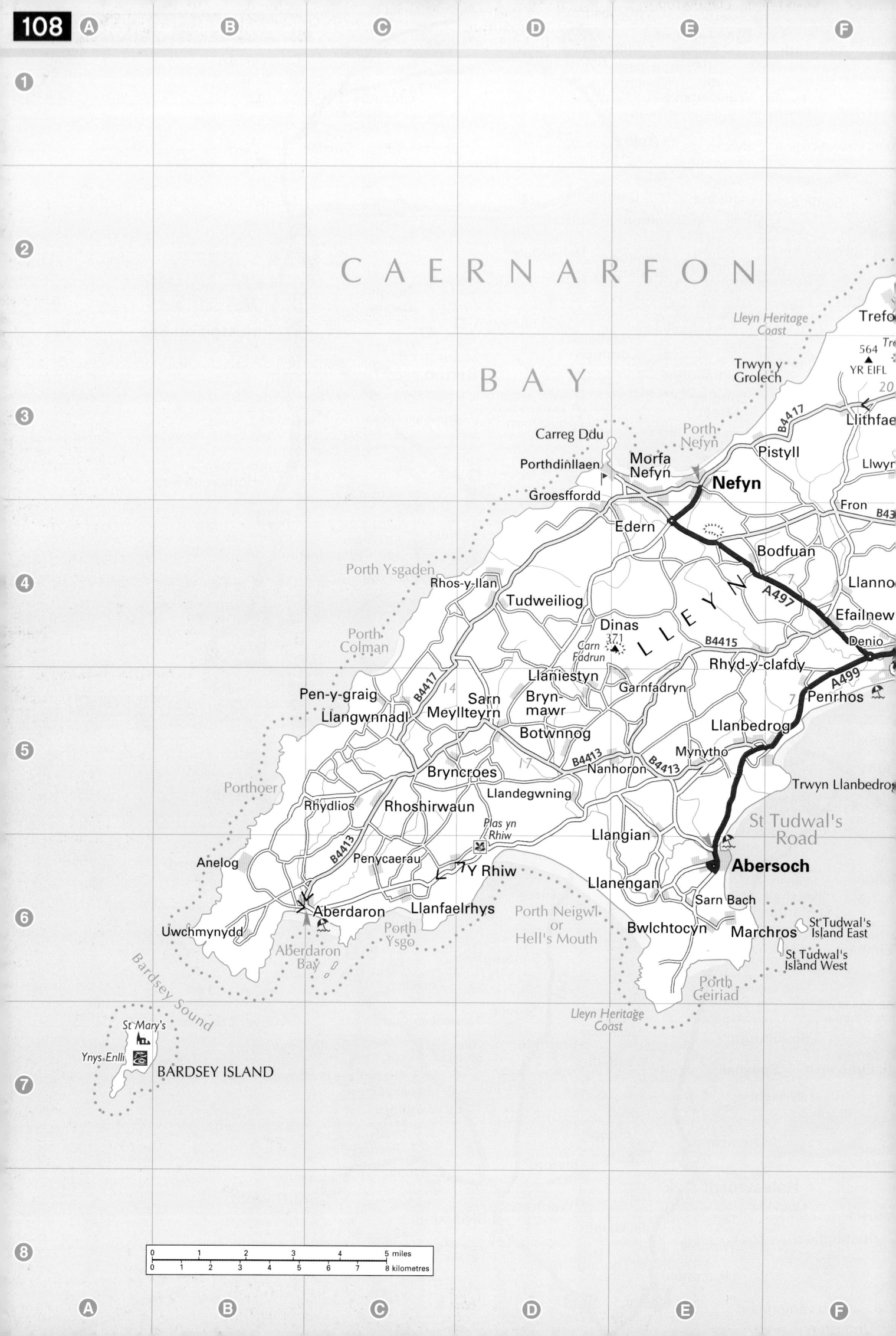

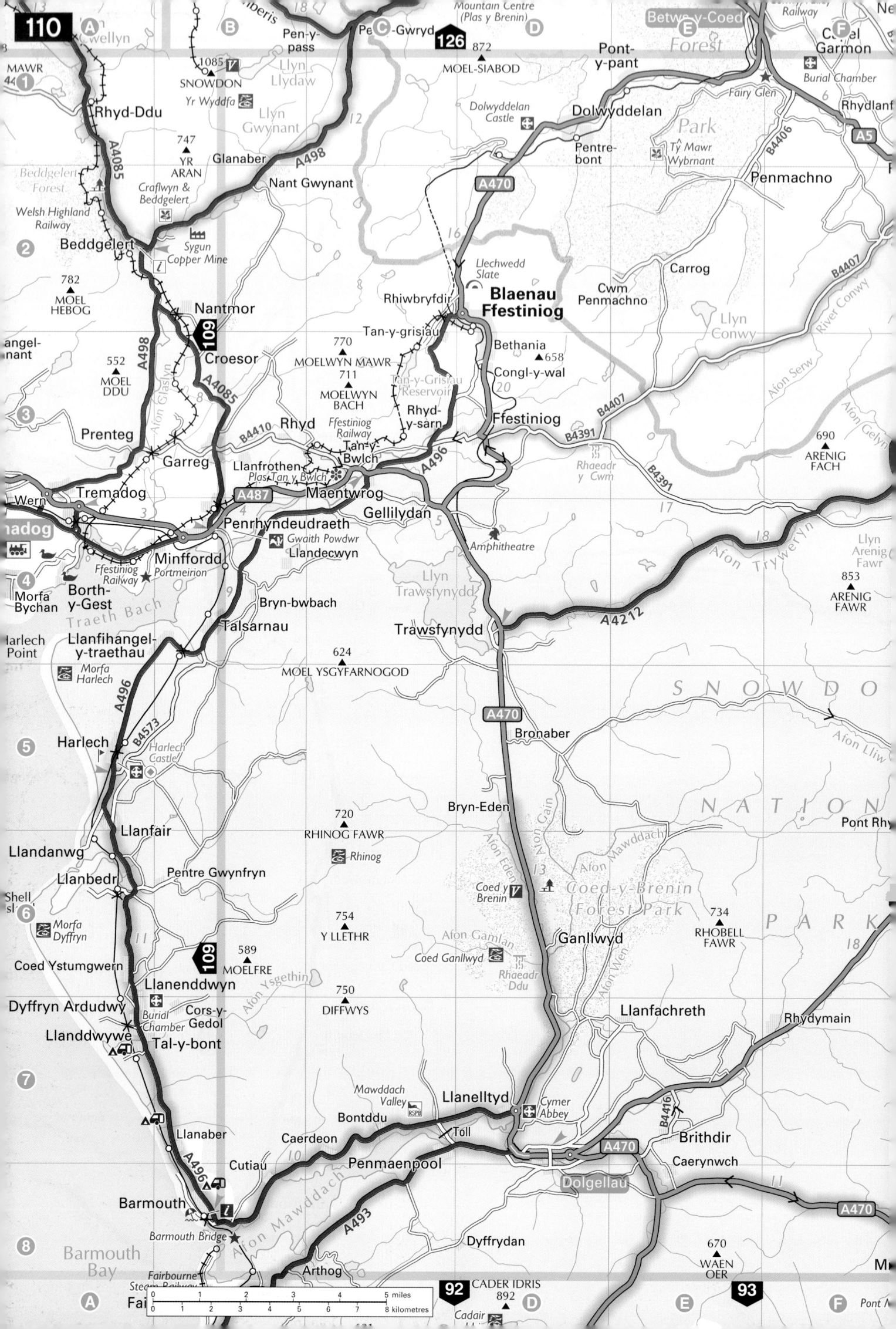

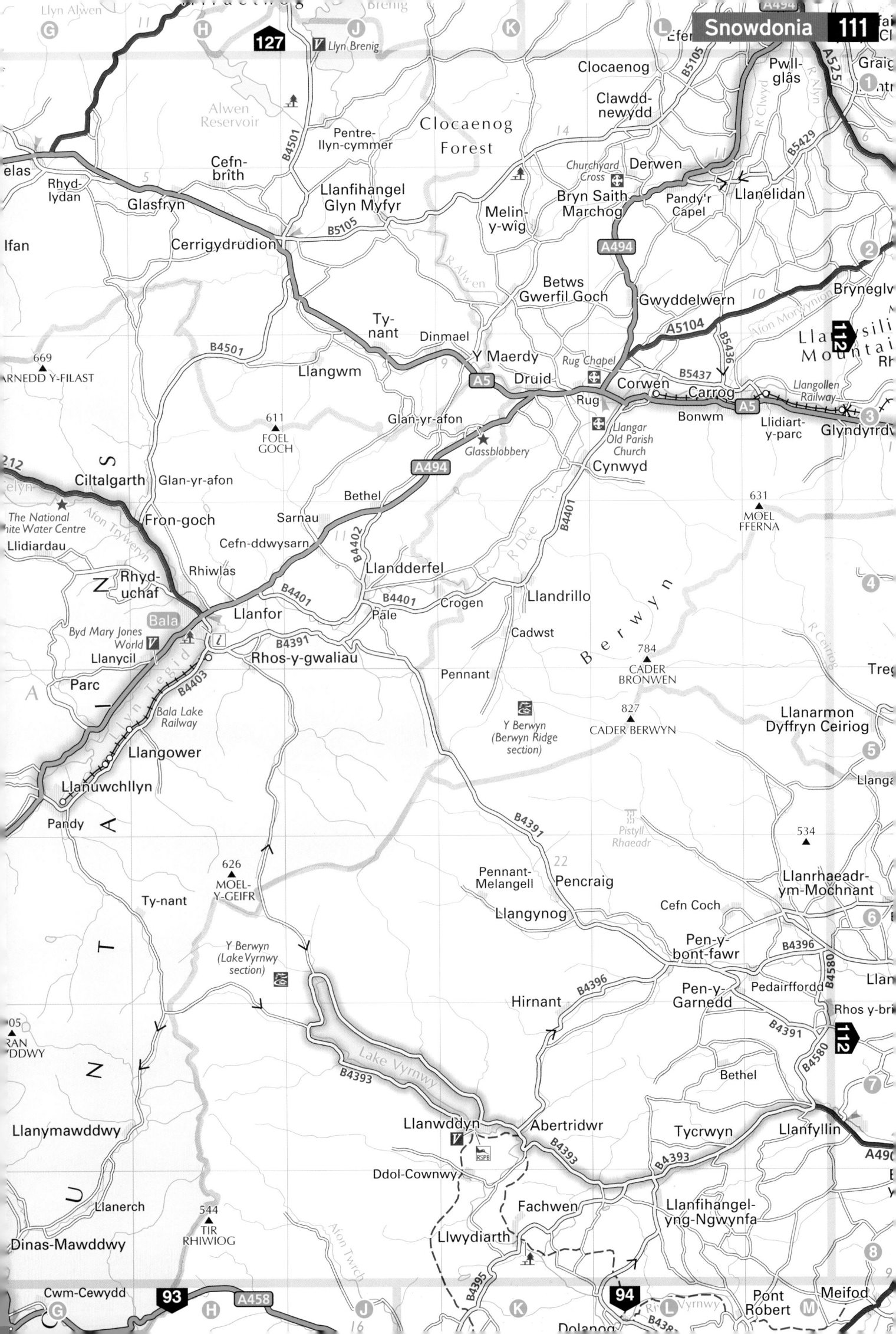

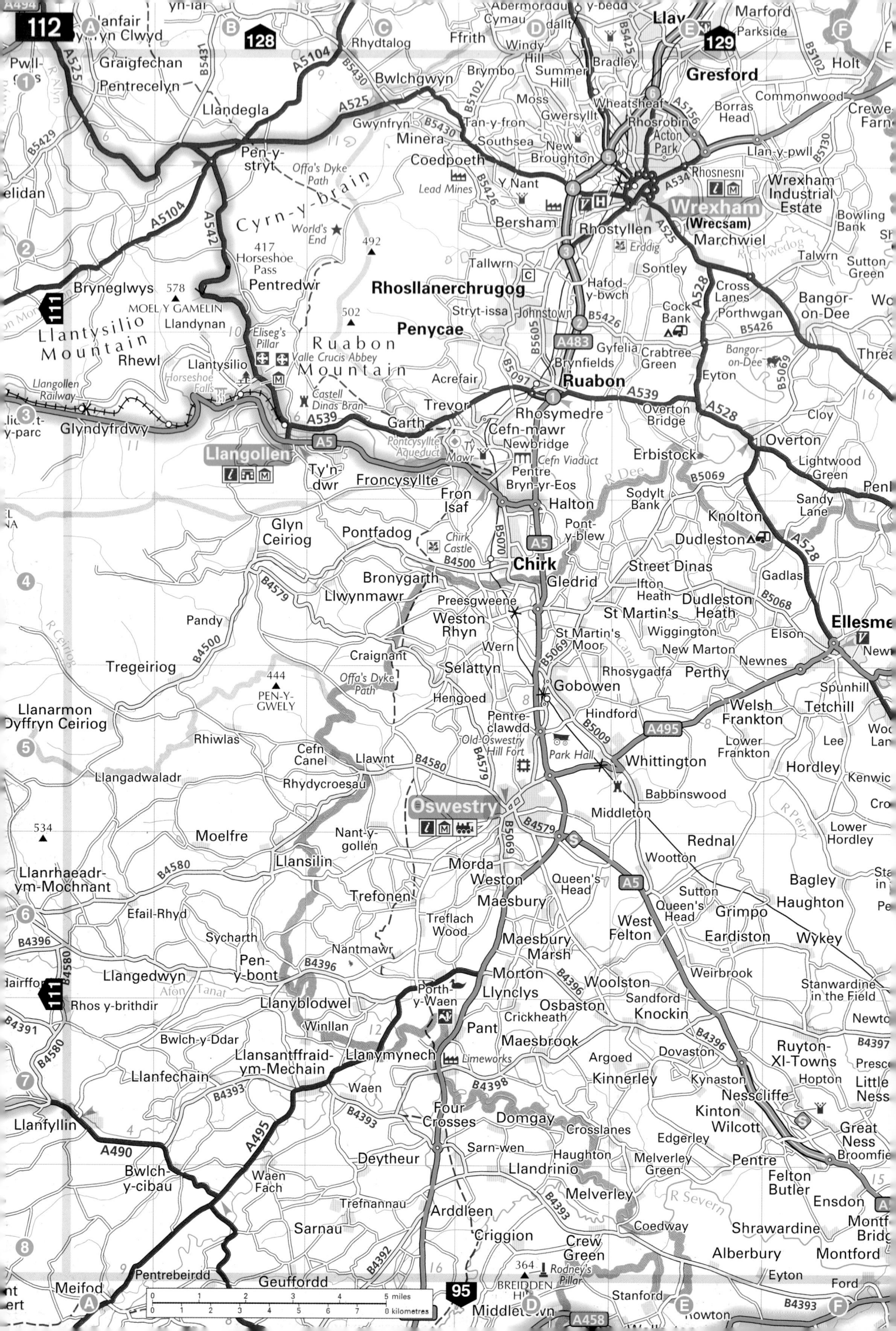

Chowley
Barbridge
G Chowley Harthill H Higher Peckfort J Radmore K
ngton Clutton 129 Broxton Hurwardsley Bulkeley Ridley Green 130 Green
Barton Barnhill Green Reaseheath
4 Barton Fuller's Gallantry Brindley Burland A51 Wistaston Wells Crewe
Watermill Moor Bank Bickerton Croxton Faddiley B5341 Green Green
Stretton A41 Duckington Cholmondeley Green Acton Nantwich Willaston Shavington
stletown Edge Castle A49 Chorley Stoneley Butt Haymoor Weston
Tilston Green Hampton Hetherson Green Gradeley Green Ravensmoor Green Hough
Horton Green Green Green Bickley Norbury Green Stapeley Chorlton Wybunbury
Shocklach Ebnal Hampton Moss Common Hack Green Wybunbury Buddi
Chorlton Malpas Heath No Man's Bickley Gaunton's Wrenbury Secret Bunker Sound Hatherton Walgherton
Lane Bradley Heath Norbury Bank Pinsley Broomhill Blake
ngton Heath Common Marbury Green Green Aston Hankelow Hunsterson
Upper Oldcastle Bickley Marley Green Newhall Bridgemere Checkle
Threapwood Heath Higher Hall Farm Bell o' Green Dodd's Audlem Buerton Check
Tallarn Wych th' Hill Wirswall Hollyhurst Green Royal's Green Woore
Green Grindley Green Lightwood Kinsey Heath A525
man's Eglwys Brook Whitchurch Burleydam Green Coxbank Dorrington
en Cross The Chequer A525 Broughall Wilkesley Knighton
mer Bronington Redbrook Catteralslane Ash Magna Adderley Bearstone
Arowry A495 Alkington Ash Ightfield Calverhall Norton
Tilstock Parva Longslow in Hales Muckl
aden Fenn's, Whixall & Platt Prees Heath Moreton Betton Sandylane
ath Bettisfield Bettisfield Mosses Lane Steel Prees Say Longford Almington Hook
Balmer Heath Heath Higher Heath Blore
hampton Welsh End Hollinwood Sandford Bletchley Market Hales
Heath Whixall Coton Prees Darliston Drayton The Fouralls Chipnall
Northwood Quina Prees Lower Heath Fauls Ternhill Sutton Woodseaves Liple
Lyneal Newtown Brook Prees Green Marchamley Lostford Old Colehurst Cheswardine
Wolverley Paddolgreen Edstaston Wood Manor Wistanswick
English Ryebank Hawkstone Wollerton Lockleywood Grea
rankton Lowe Creamore Weston-under- Marchamley Hodnet Stoke Millgreen Goldstone Soud
Brownheath Horton Bank Redcastle Heath Heathcote Little
Loppington Wem Aston Wixhill Hodnet Hall Stoke Hungryhatton Soudley
kshutt Noneley Commonwood Barkers Bury upon Tern Hinstock
A528 Sleap Green Lee Walls Booley High Ollerton Stanford Sambrook
Burlton Myddle Brockhurst Moston Hatton Peplow Bridge
eston Alderton Preston Besford Stanton upon Child's Eaton Picks
ngfields Clive Brockhurst Hine Heath Ercall upon Tern
Eyton Grinshill High Hatton Howle Chetwynd
Newton on Yorton Moreton Castle Moretonmill Ellerdine Great Bolas Edamon
church the Hill Heath Corbet Edgebolton Heath A442 Meeson Ma
ford Old Harmer Shawbury Cold Hatton Tibberton
Woods Hill Rowton Cold Hatton Church
Fitz Merrington Little Great Heath Cherrington Aston
Rosehill Preston Hadnall Wytheford Wytheford Walton Moortown Waters Edgmond
Bicton Gubbals Bomere Heath Bings B5063 Upton Adeney Longford
Walford Leaton Astley Poynton Crudgington
Heath Albrighton Green High Kynnersley Preston upon
ton Battlefield Poynton Ercall Cotwall Tern the Weald Moors
Rosehill West Haughton Longdon Sleapford Eyton on Church
ford Calcott Mid Coton Somerwood B5062 Roden upon Tern Sugdon the Weald Moors Aston
Shelton Hill Rodington Long Horton
G H Ditherington Uffington Heath Marsh Waste Telford F Donnington
Underdale A49 Upton 96 Rodington Green Bratton Shawbirch A442 M
Magna Sombridge Admaston A5223 Trench Granville
Walcot Wrockwardine Donnington

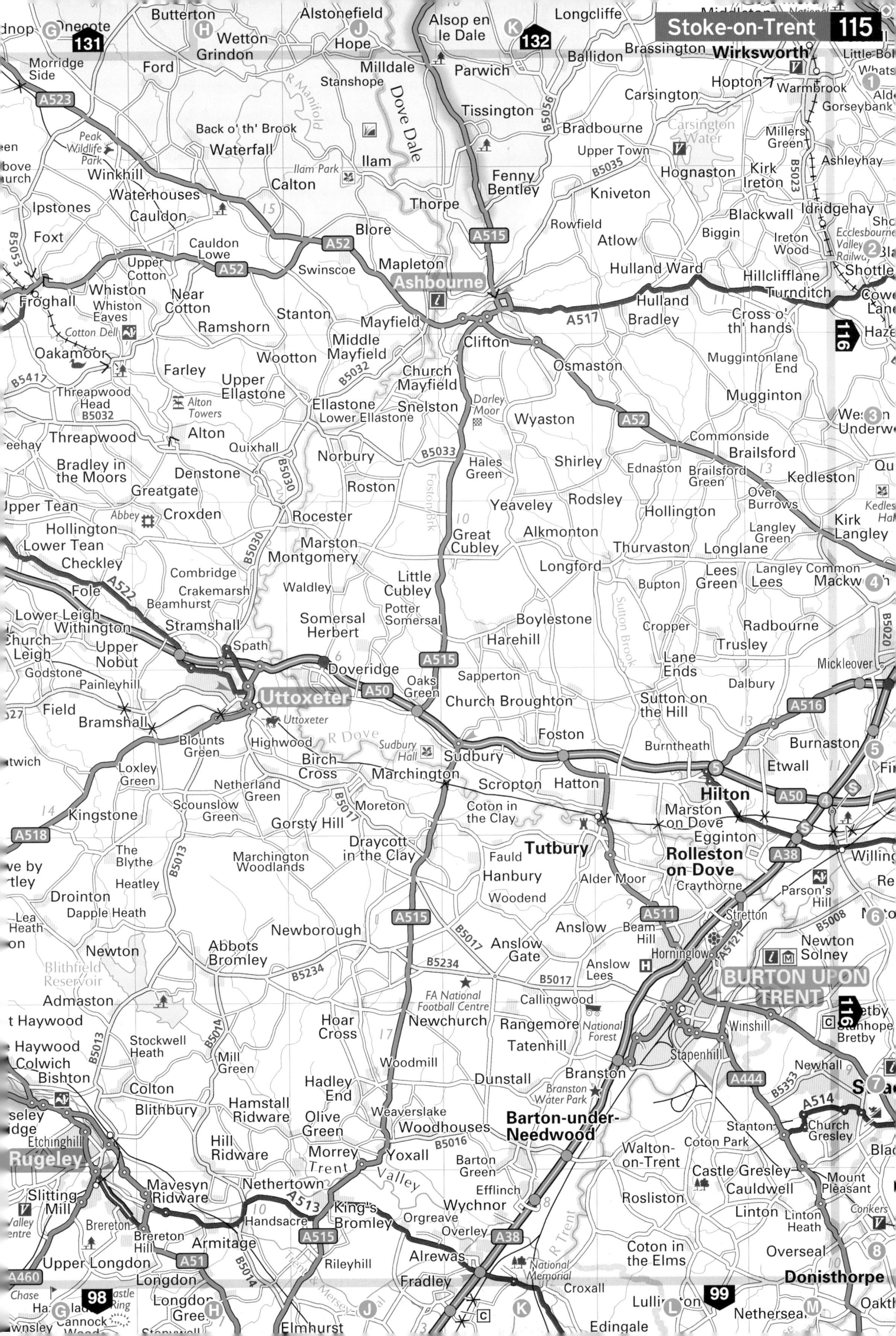

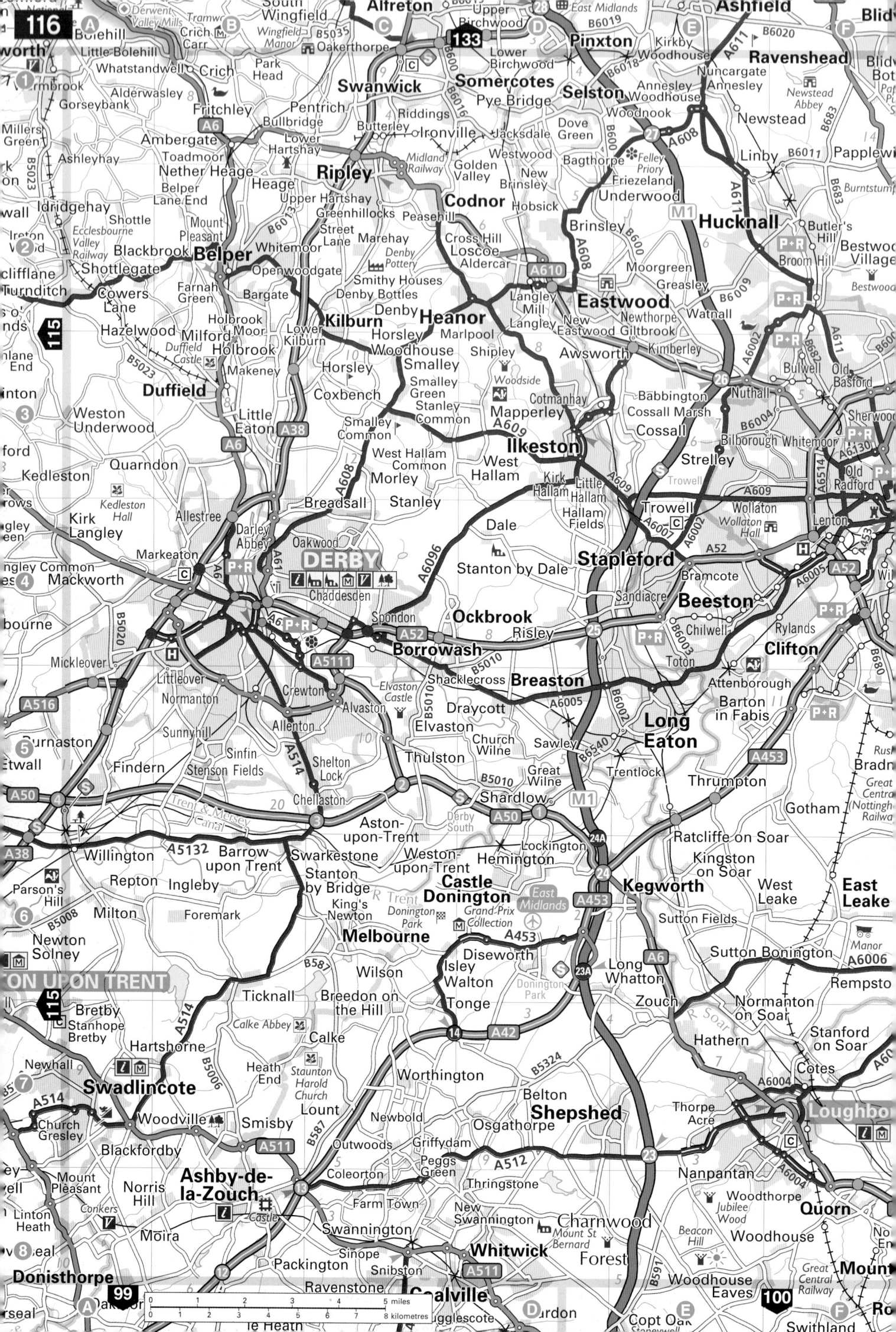

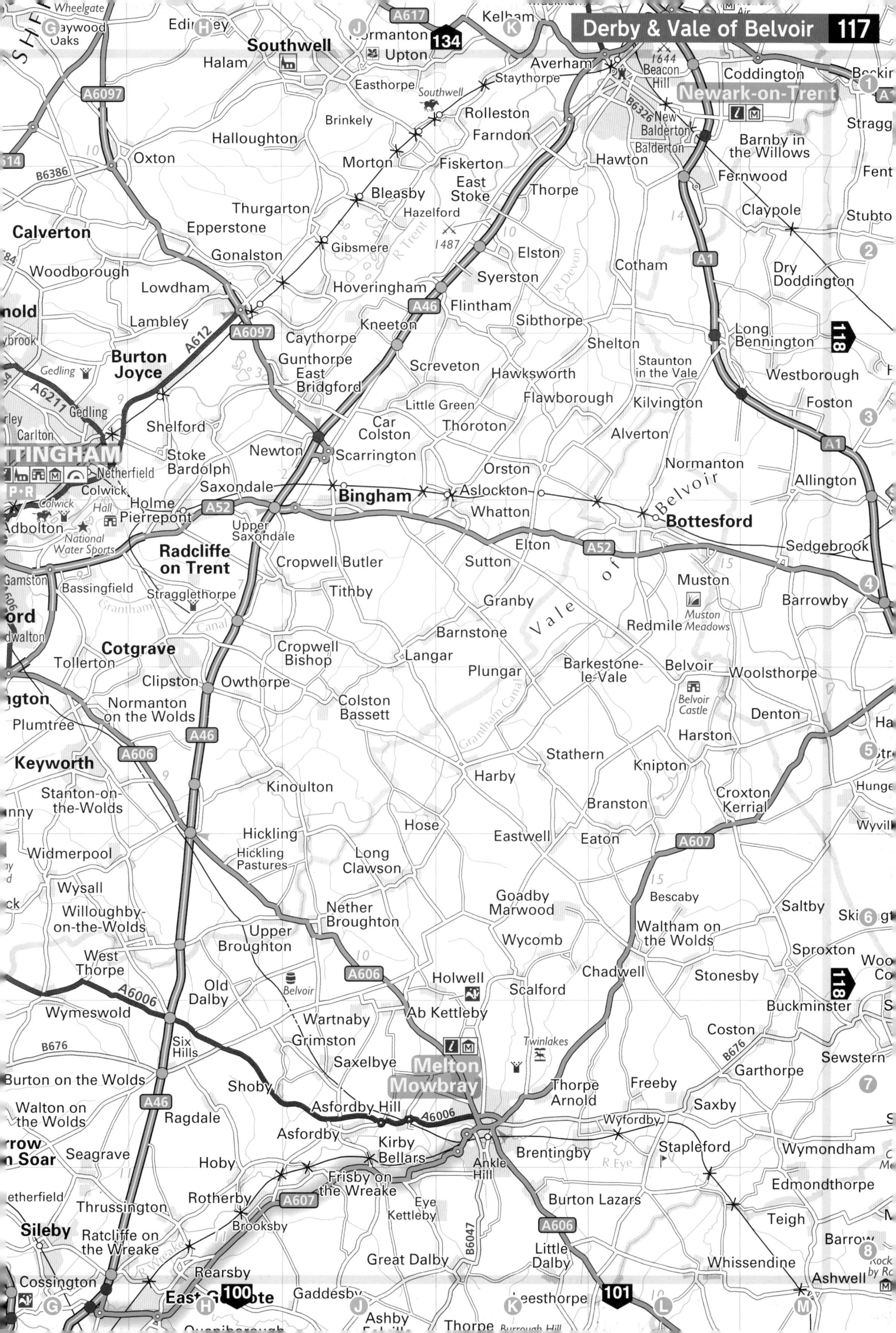

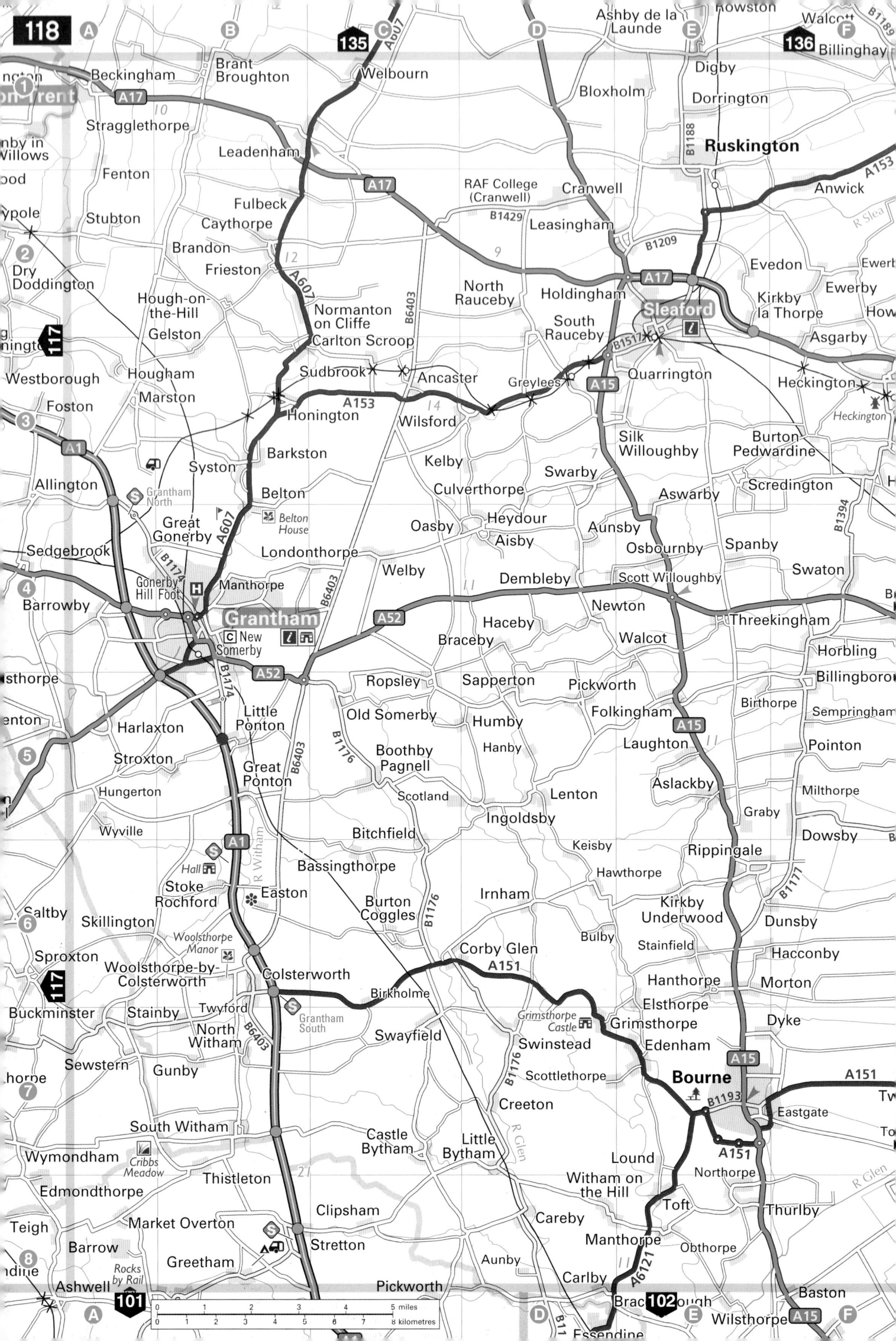

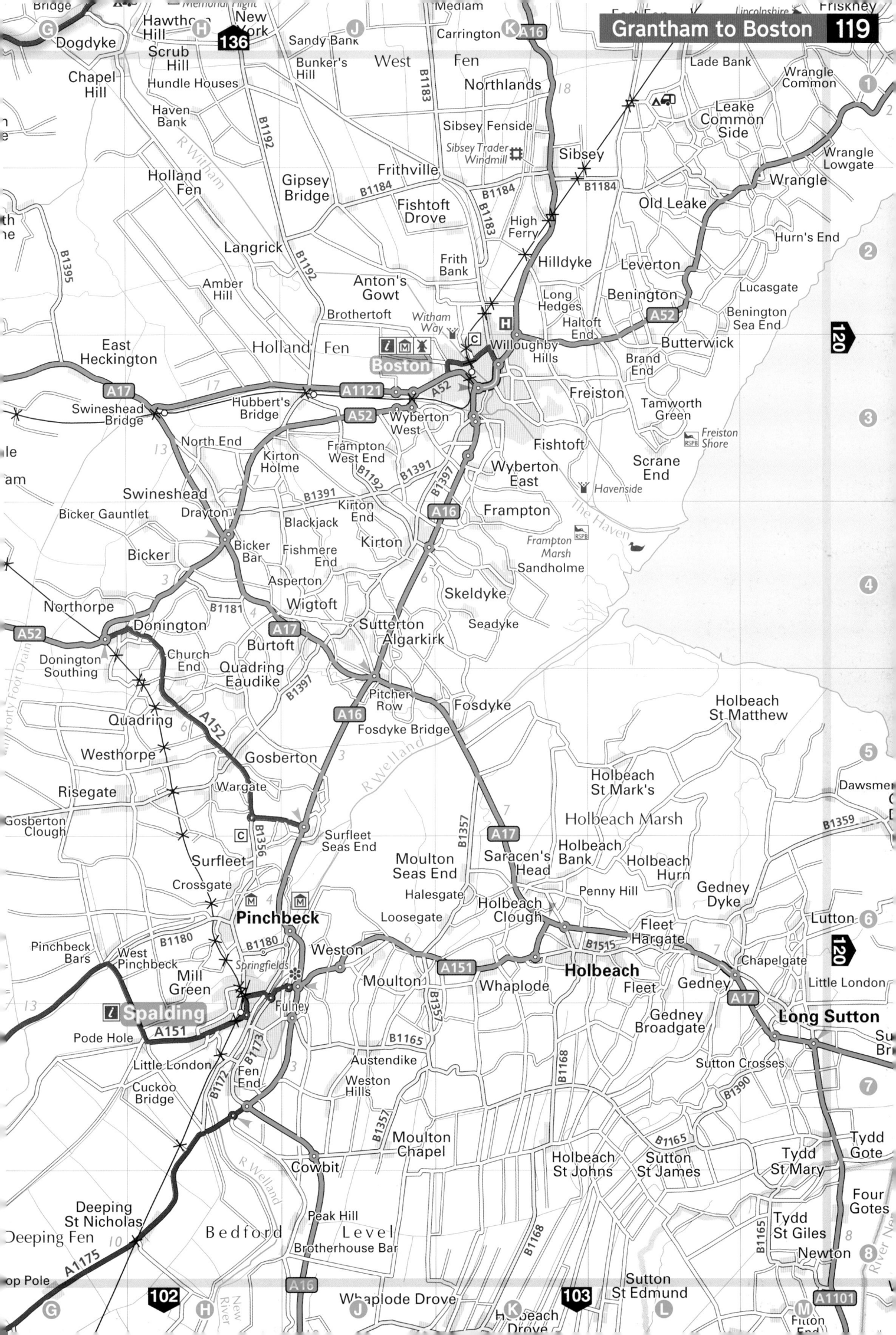

A B C D E F

120

137

119

1

2

asgate

gton
End

119

3

THE WASH

4

5

Dawsmere

Gedney
Drove End

B1359

6 Lutton

119

pelgat

Little London

Long Sutton

Sutton
Bridge

Wingland

Walpole
Cross Keys

Little
London

Terrington
St Clement

West
Lynn

Clenchwarton

7

sses

Tydd
St Mary

Tydd
Gote

Walpole
St Andrew

Hay Green

Tilney
All Saints

South
Lynn

A17

11

A47

Four
Gotes

Walpole
St Peter

Tilney High End

Saddlebow

West
Winch

8 Newton

A1101

103

West
Walton

Ingleborough

St John's
Highway

Tilney St
Lawrence

Wiggenhall
St Germans

Wiggenhall
St Mary the
Virgin

104

Fitton
End

Highway

Friskney Friskney Eaudike

Wrangle
Common

Wrangle
Lowgate

Wrangle

Hurn's End

Holme
Dunes

Holme n
the Se

Old
Hunstanton

Hunstanton

Ringstead

A149

Norfolk
Lavender

Heacham

Sedgeford

Snettisham

Park

Southgate

Shernb

RSPB Snettisham

Ingoldisthorpe

12

B1440

Dersingham

Doddshill

Dersingham Bog

Wolferton

Sandringh
West New

A149

B1439

B1440

Babingley River

Castle Rising

North
Wootton

Castle

A148

Congham

Roydon

South Wootton

A1078

A148

Roydon
Common

Pott
Row

Gaywood

H

4

C

Bawsey

B1145

Gayton

B1153

King's Lynn

Fairstead

Bawsey

Brow-of-
the-Hill

Ashwicke

A148

A47

Fair Green

East
Winch

A10

North
Runcton

Middleton

Blackborough
End

West
Bilne

Setchey

Pentne

Na

River Nene

12

8

0 1 2 3 4 5 miles
0 1 2 3 4 5 6 7 8 kilometres

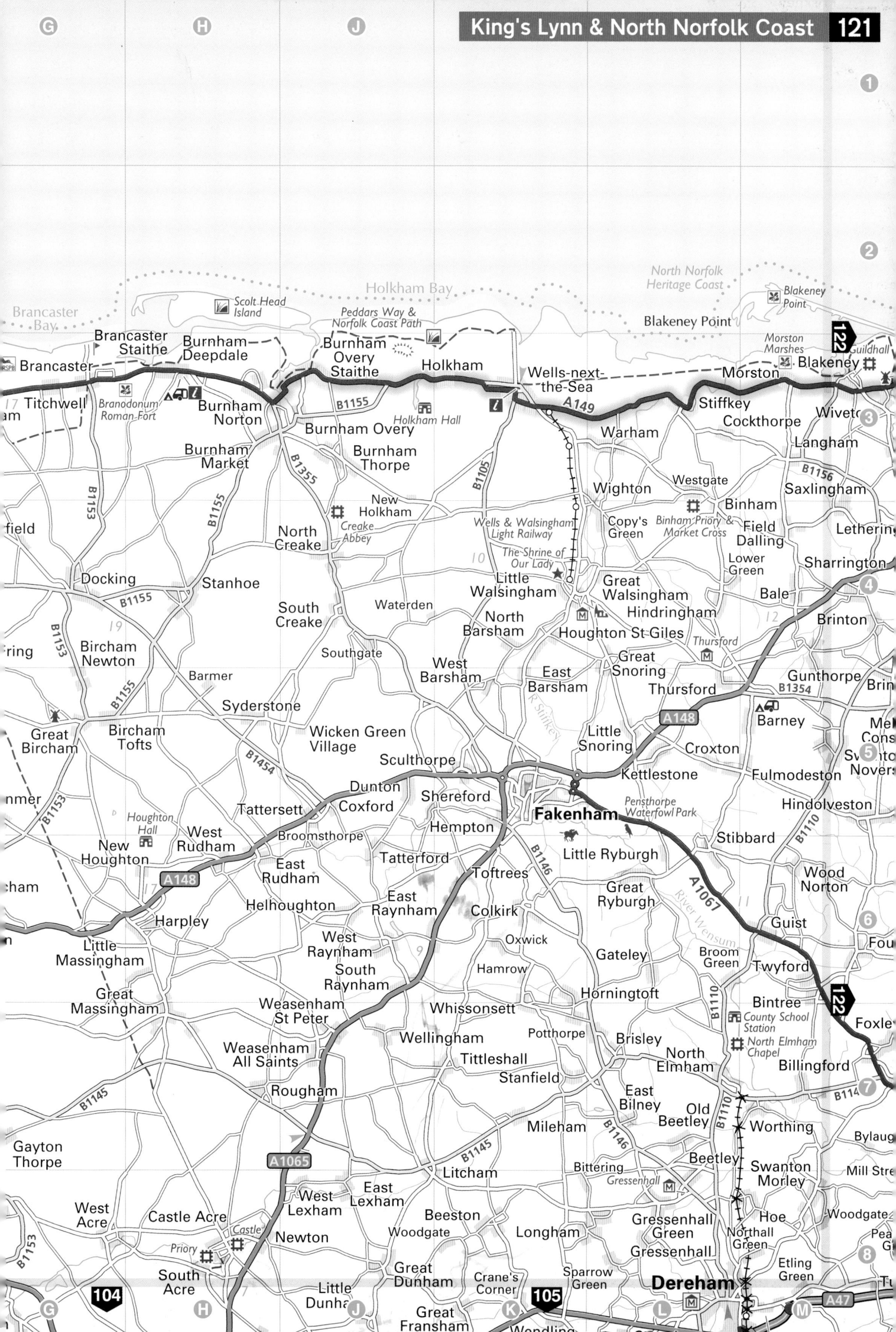

Brancaster Bay

North Norfolk Heritage Coast

Blakeney Point

Holkham Bay

Scolt Head Island

Peddars Way & Norfolk Coast Path

Morston Marshes

Blakeney Point

RSPB Brancaster

Brancaster Staithe

Burnham Deepdale

Burnham Overy Staithe

Holkham

Wells-next-the-Sea

Morston

Blakeney

Guildhall

122

Titchwell

Branodunum Roman Fort

Burnham Norton

B1155

Burnham Overy

Holkham Hall

A149

Warham

Stiffkey

Cockthorpe

Wiveton

Langham

Burnham Market

Burnham Thorpe

New Holkham

Creake Abbey

Wells & Walsingham Light Railway

Wighton

Copy's Green

Westgate

Binham

Binham Priory & Market Cross

Field Dalling

Saxlingham

Letherin

B1153

B1355

B1155

North Creake

B1105

The Shrine of Our Lady

Little Walsingham

Great Walsingham

Hindringham

Lower Green

Sharrington

Docking

Stanhoe

South Creake

Waterden

North Barsham

Houghton St Giles

Thursford

Bale

Brinton

B1155

B1156

Bircham Newton

Southgate

West Barsham

East Barsham

Great Snoring

Thursford

Gunthorpe

Brin

B1354

Barney

Great Bircham

Bircham Tofts

Barmer

Syderstone

Wicken Green Village

Sculthorpe

Little Snoring

Kettlestone

Croxton

Fulmodeston

Hindolveston

Me Cons Swanto Nover

B1153

B1454

Houghton Hall

Tattersett

Dunton Coxford

Shereford

Hempton

R Stiffkey

A148

Penthorpe Waterfowl Park

Fakenham

Stibbard

Wood Norton

New Houghton

West Rudham

Broomsthorpe

Tatterford

Toftrees

Little Ryburgh

Great Ryburgh

Broom Green

Twyford

122

A1067

River Wensum

Guist

Fou

Harpley

A148

East Rudham

Helhoughton

East Raynham

Colkirk

B1146

Oxwick

Gateley

Bintree

County School Station

North Elmham Chapel

Foxle

Little Massingham

West Raynham

South Raynham

Hamrow

Horningtoft

Great Massingham

Weasenham St Peter

Whissonsett

Potthorpe

Brisley

North Elmham

Billingford

B1110

B1145

Weasenham All Saints

Wellingham

Tittleshall

Stanfield

East Bilney

Old Beetley

Worthing

B114

B1145

Rougham

Mileham

Beetley

Swanton Morley

Bylaug

Mill Stre

B1146

A1065

Gayton Thorpe

West Acre

Castle Acre

Castle

Newton

West Lexham

East Lexham

Litcham

Beeston

Woodgate

Bittering

Gressenhall

Hoe

Northall Green

Woodgate

Pea G

Priory

South Acre

Little Dunha

Great Dunham

Crane's Corner

Longham

Sparrow Green

Gressenhall Green

Gressenhall

Etling Green

Dereham

A47

B1153

104

105

A47

Great Fransham

Wendling

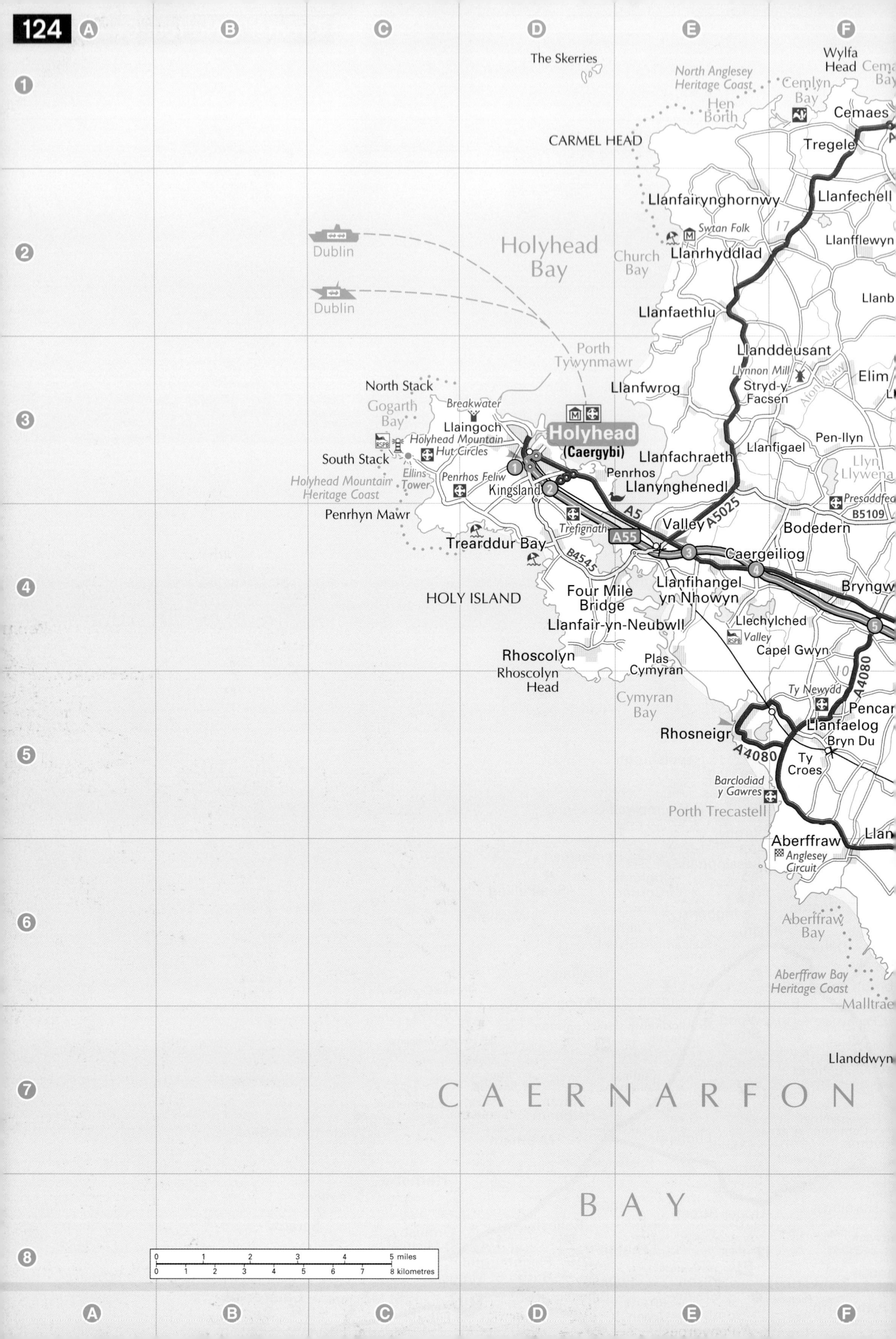

The Skerries

North Anglesey
Heritage Coast

Wylfa
Head

Cemlyn
Bay

Cemaes

CARMEL HEAD

Tregele

Llanfairynghornwy

Llanfechell

Hen
Borth

Llanfflewyn

Holyhead
Bay

Church
Bay

Swtan Folk

Llanrhyddlad

Llanb

Llanfaethlu

Holyhead
Bay

Porth
Tywynmawr

Llanddeusant

Llynnon Mill

Elim

North Stack

Breakwater

Llanfwrog

Stryd-y-
Facsen

L

Gogarth
Bay

Llaingoch

Holyhead

(Caergybi)

Holyhead Mountain

Llanfachraeth

Llanfigael

Pen-Ilyn

Llyn
Llywena

South Stack

RSPB

Penrhos Feliw

Hut Circles

Penrhos

Llanynghenedl

Presaddfe

B5109

Holyhead Mountain
Heritage Coast

Ellins
Tower

Kingsland

A5

Valley

A5025

Bodedern

Penrhyn Mawr

Trefignath

Caergeiliog

Trearddur Bay

B4545

A55

Bryngw

Four Mile
Bridge

Llanfihangel
yn Nhowyn

HOLY ISLAND

Llechylched

Llanfair-yn-Neubwll

RSPB Valley

Capel Gwyn

A4080

Rhoscolyn

Plas
Cymyran

Rhoscolyn
Head

Ty Newydd

Pencar

Llanfaelog

Cymyran Bay

Bryn Du

Rhosneigr

A4080

Ty
Croes

Barclodiad
y Gawres

Porth Trecastell

Aberffraw

Llan

Anglesey
Circuit

Aberffraw
Bay

Aberffraw Bay
Heritage Coast

Malltrae

Llanddwyn

C A E R N A R F O N

B A Y

Dublin

Dublin

0   1   2   3   4   5 miles
0 1 2 3 4 5 6 7 8 kilometres

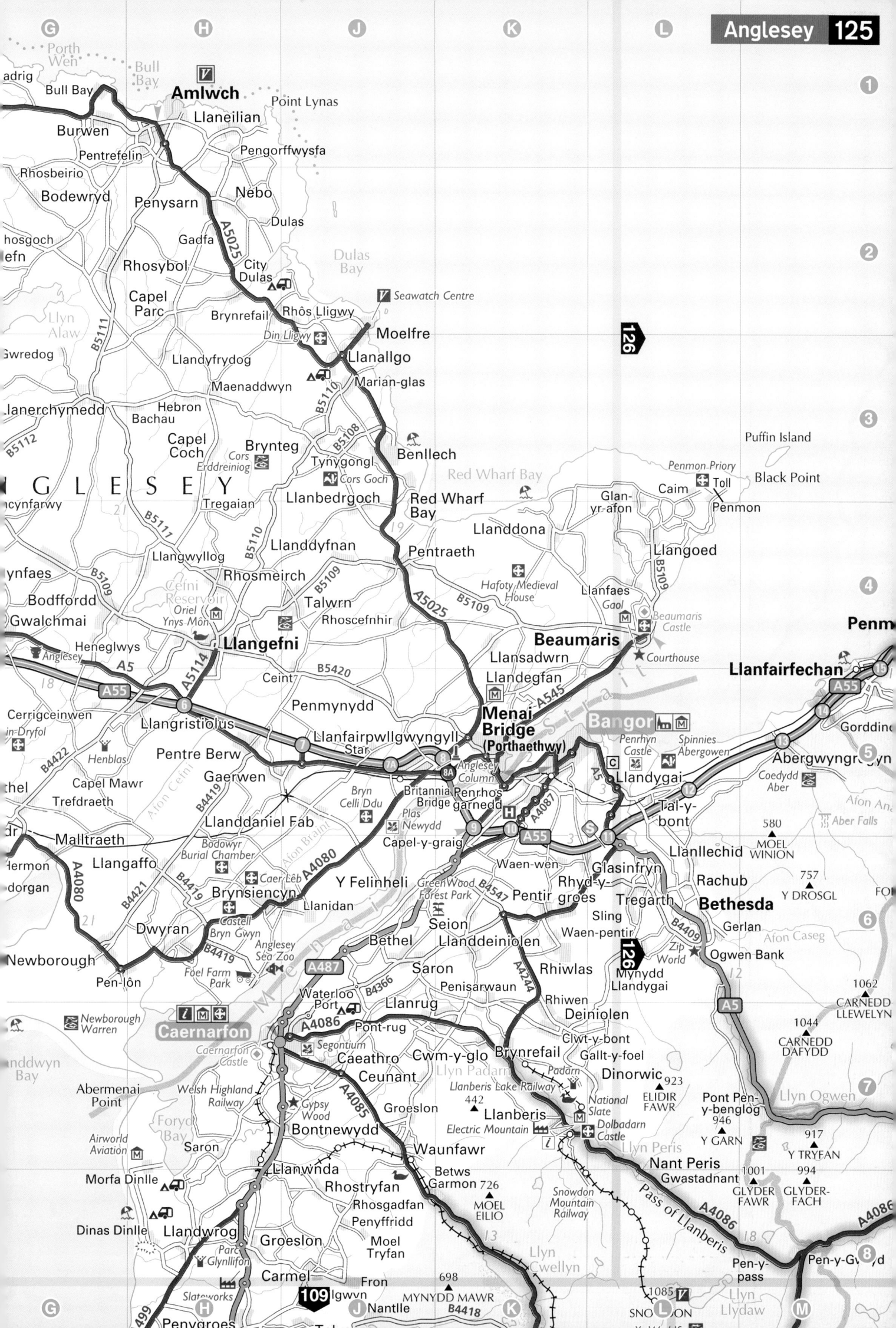

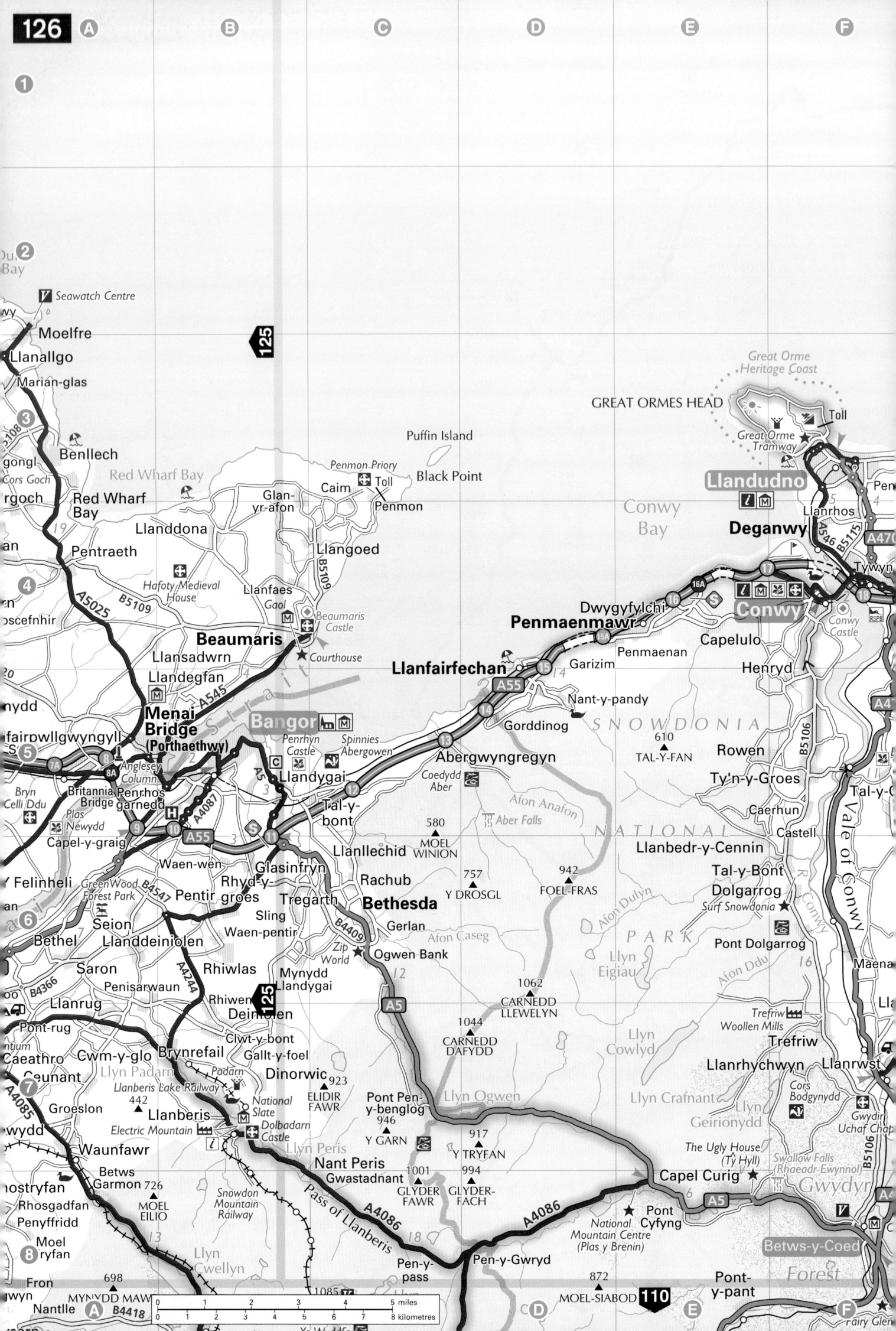

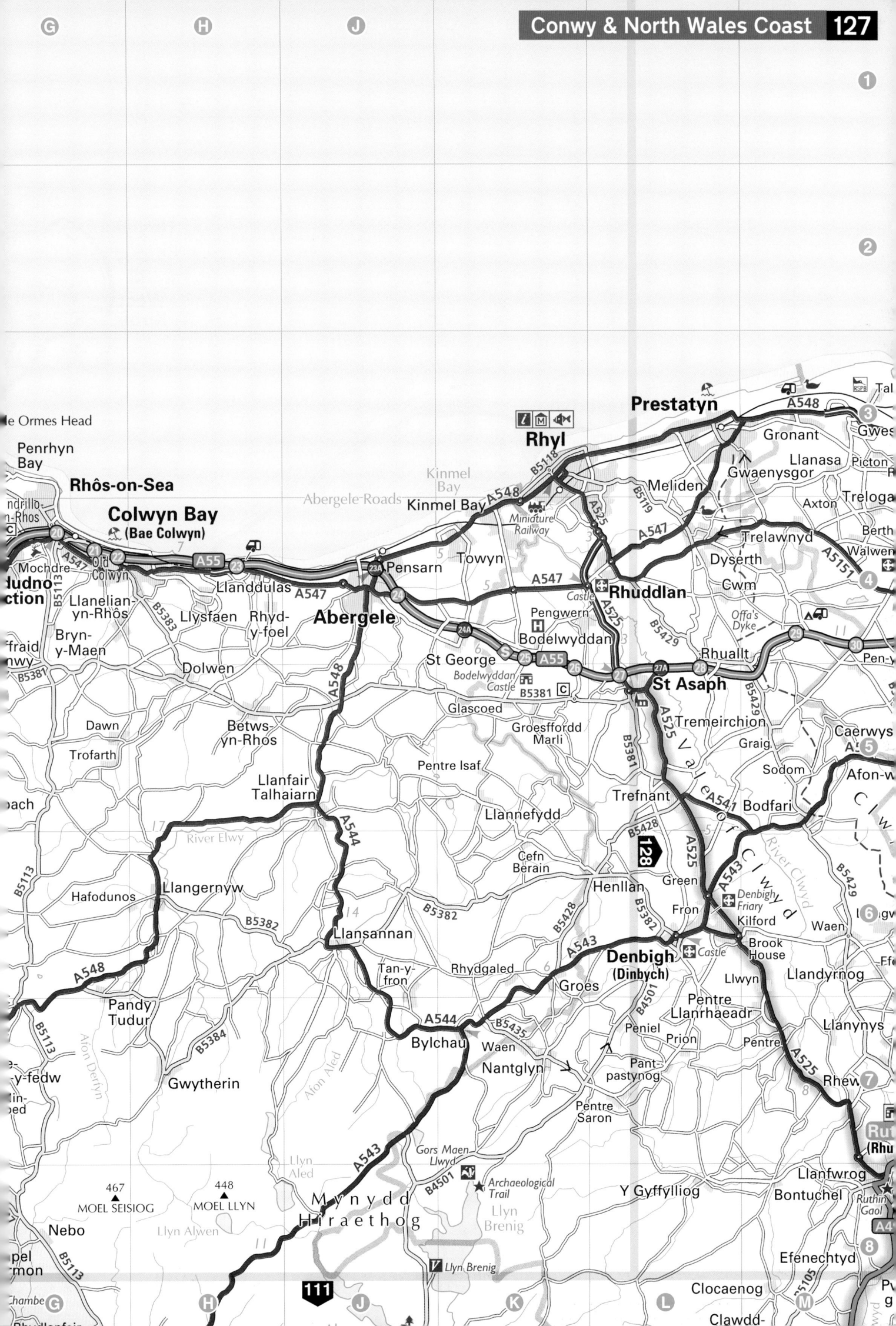

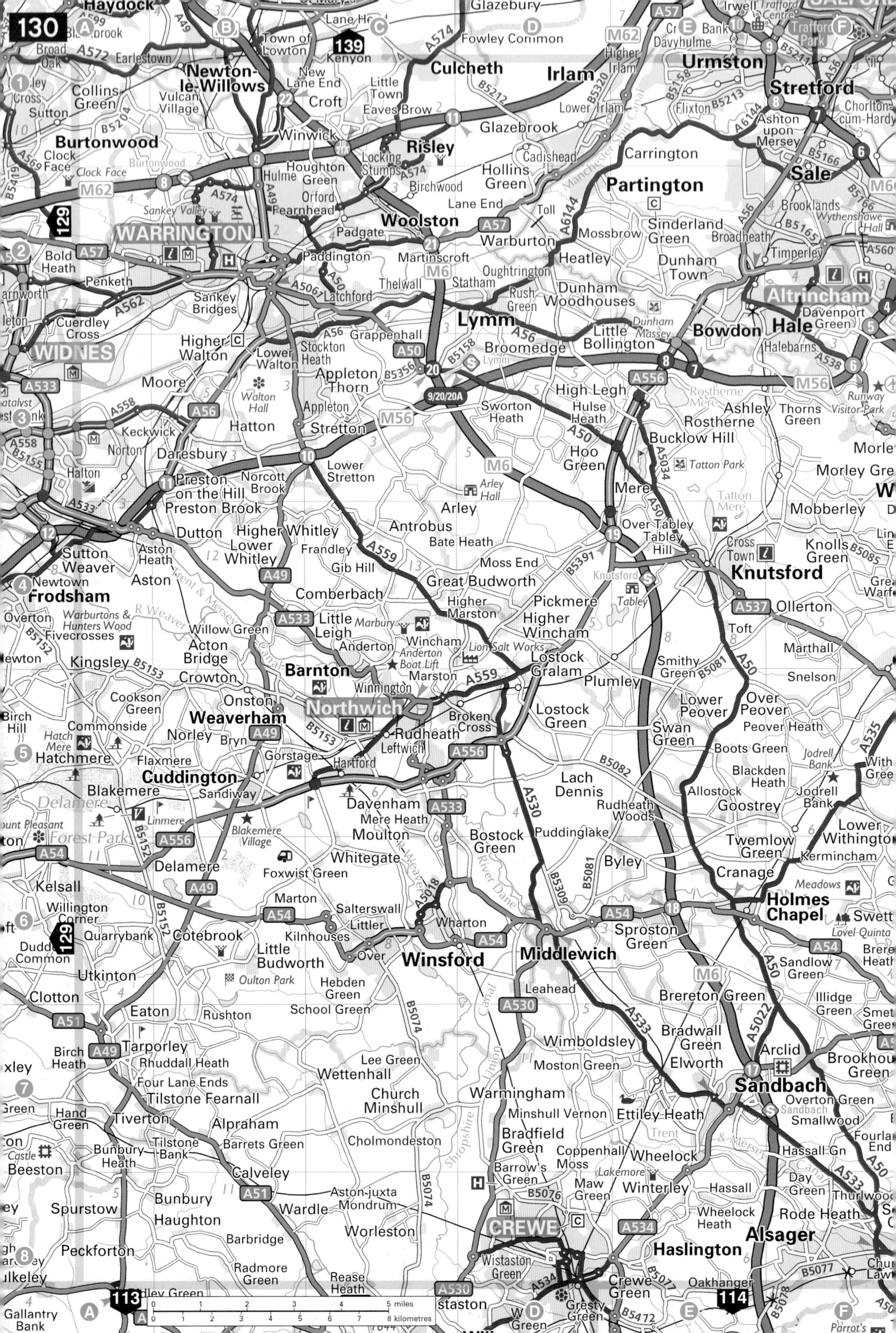

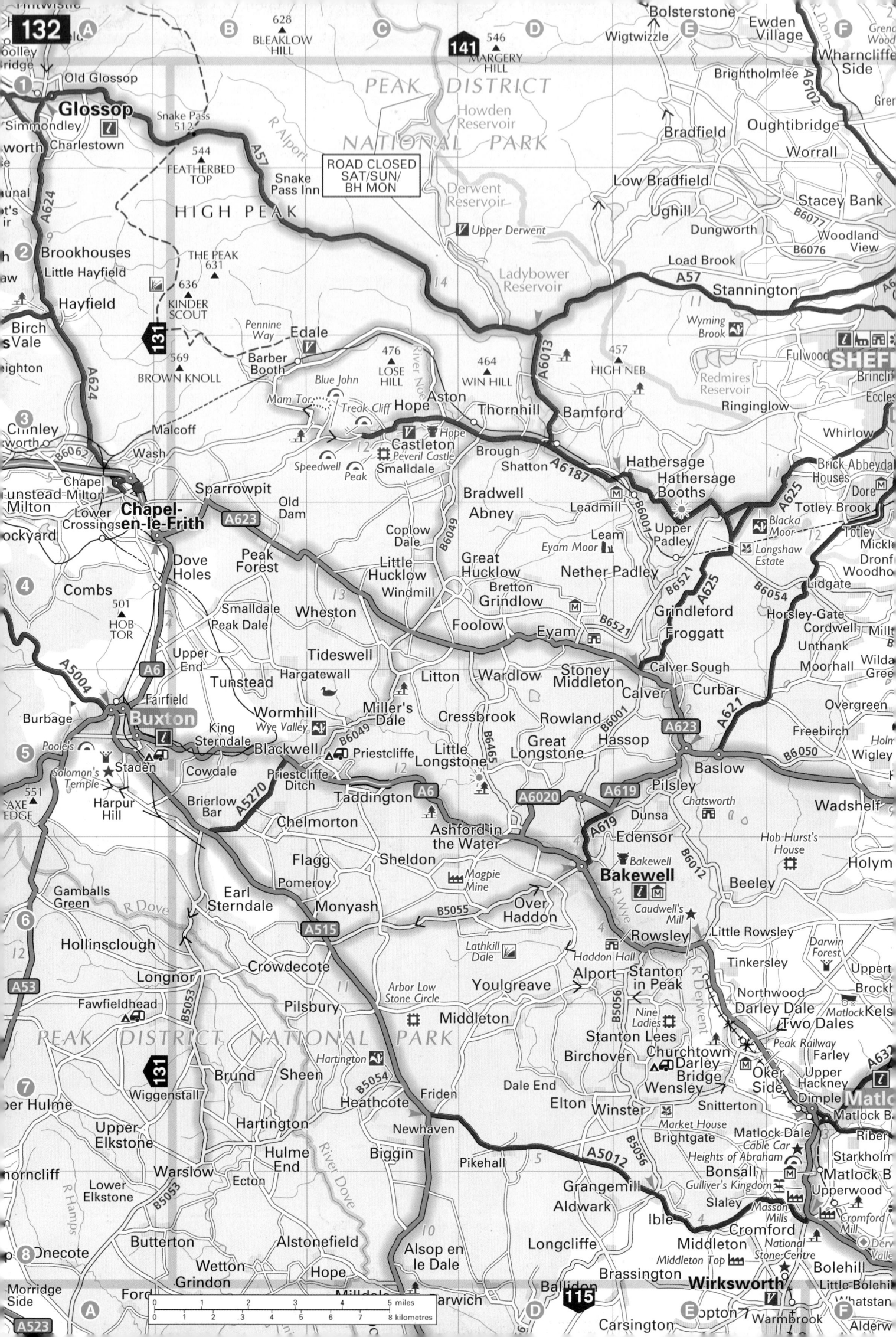

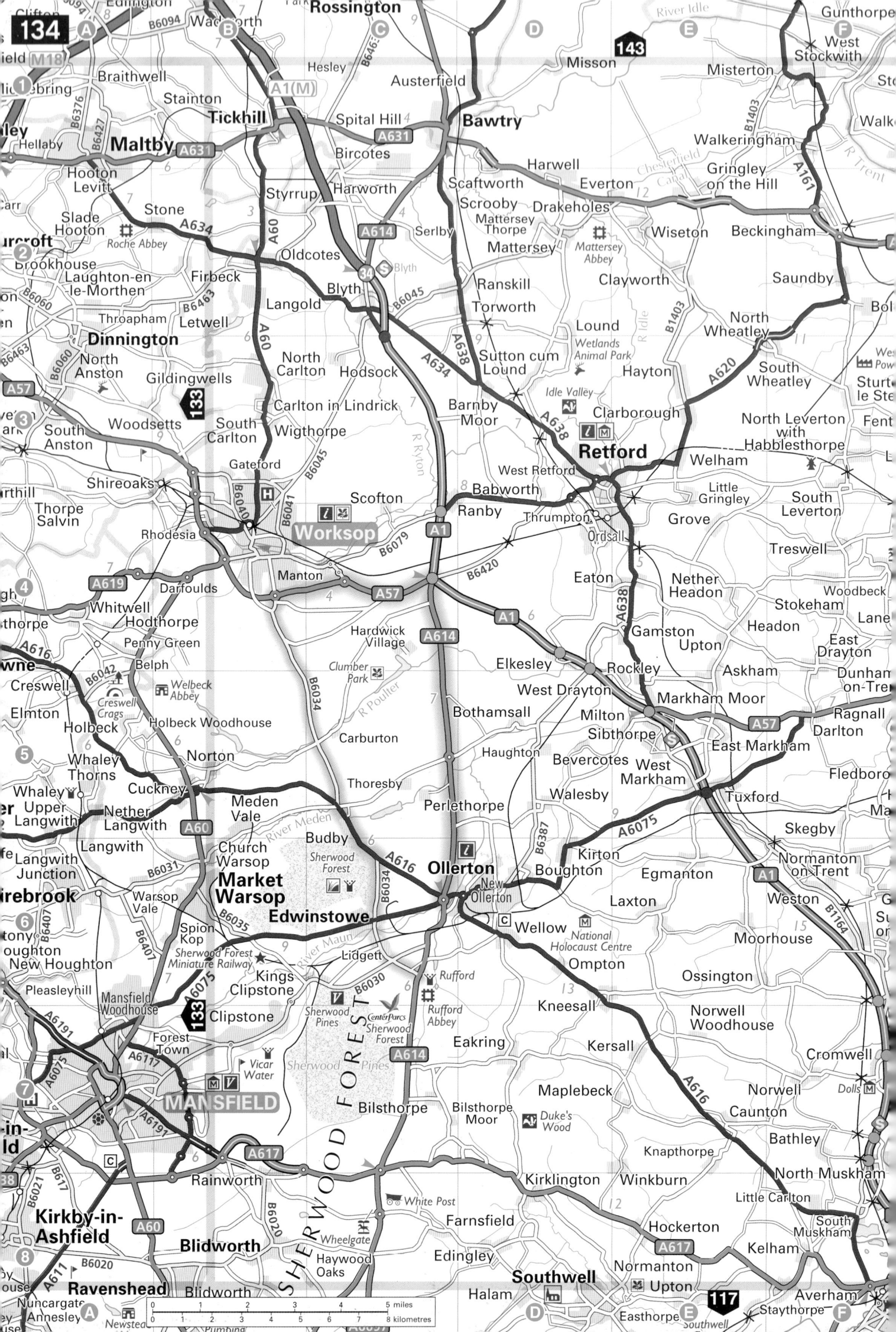

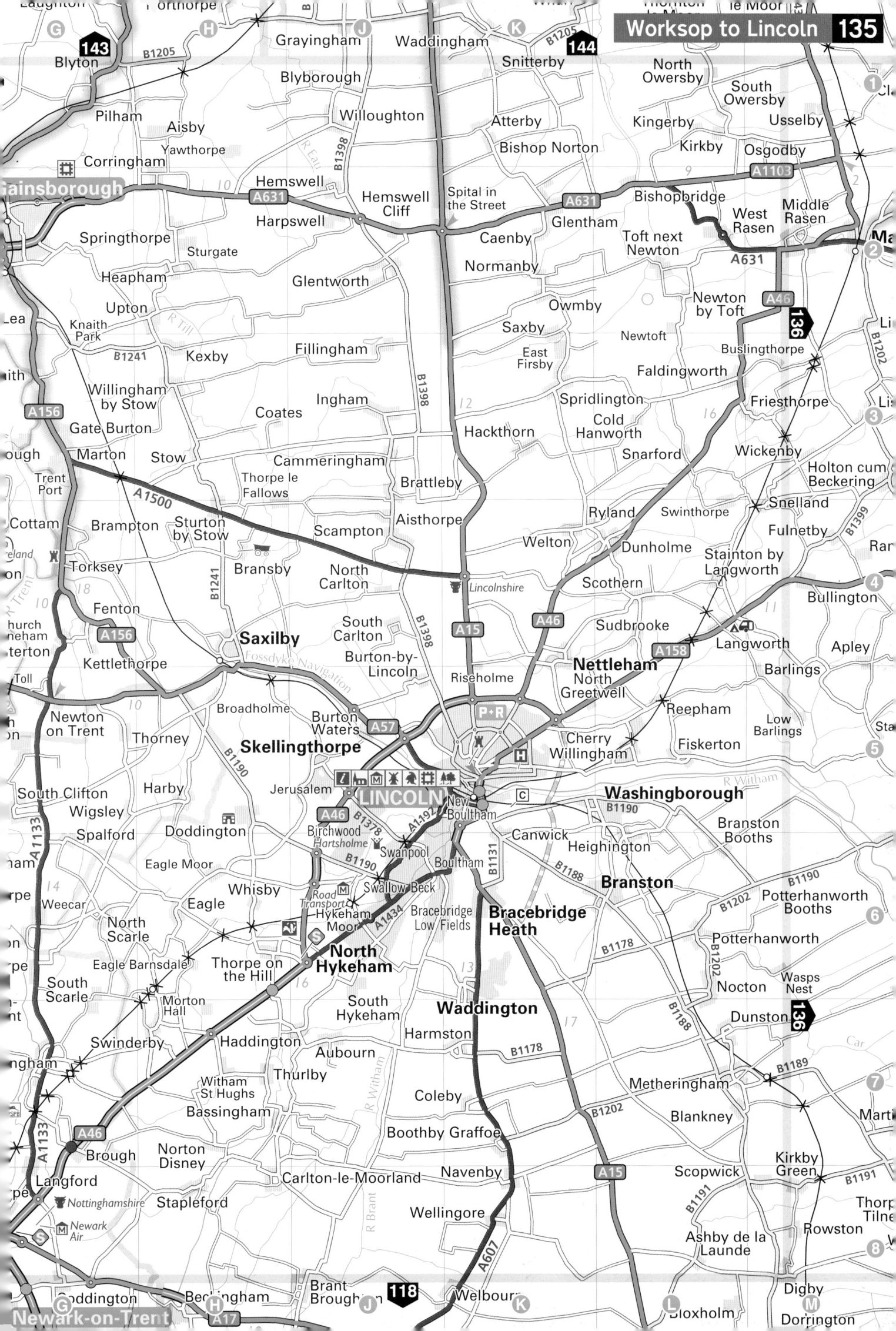

A **B** 144 **C** **D** 145 **E** A16 **F**

1

le Moor | A34 | 25 | Moresway | Swinhope | Wold Newton | 15 | Fulsto...

South Owersby | Normanby le Wold | Brookenby | Lincolns. Wolds Railway | Co... St...

...by | Usselby | Claxby | Stainton le Vale | B1203 | North Ormsby | Covenham St Mary

Kirkby | Osgodby | Walesby | Binbrook | Utterby | Little Grimsby

A1103 | Kirmond le Mire | Great Tows | Kelstern | North Elkington | Kedding Cor

2

...bridge | Middle Rasen | B1203 | Tealby | Ludford | A631 | South Elkington | Welton le Wold | Little Welton | Lo...

West Rasen | A631 | **Market Rasen** | North Willingham | Burgh on Bain | A157 | 15 | B1520 | B1...

Newton by Toft | A46 | 135 | A631 | Sixhills | Hallington | Raithby | i

3

...gworth | Friesthorpe | Linwood | Legsby | B1225 | South Willingham | Biscathorpe | Maltby | A16

Wickenby | B1202 | Bleasby | Hainton | Donington on Bain | Withcall | A153 | Tathwell

Holton cum Beckering | East Torrington | Benniworth | Stenigot | Haugham

West Torrington | East Barkwith | Market Stainton | Cawkwell | Cadwell Park | Maidenwell | Burw...

...inthorpe | Snelland | West Barkwith | Goulceby | Asterby | Farforth | Ruck... W...

Fulnetby | B1399 | Rand | A157 | Panton | Sotby | Ranby | Scamblesby | Oxcombe | Worlaby

4

Stainton by Langworth | Wragby | Hatton | B1225 | Scamblesby | 14 | A153 | Belchford | Little London

8 | Langworth | Bullington | 11 | Langton by Wragby | Low Langton | Great Sturton | Hemingby | Tetford | Salmo...

Barlings | Apley | Kingthorpe | 10 | A158 | Baumber | Fulletby | Somersby

Low Barlings | Stainfield | Bardney Limewoods | Minting | Wispington | West Ashby | Tetford

5

...eepham | ...erton | B1202 | Gautby | Edlington | Furzehills | **Horncastle** i | Ashby Puerorum

...borough | Branston Booths | Bardney | Bucknall | Thimbleby | Langton | Low Toynton | Greetham | A158 | 10

6

R Witham | B1190 | B1190 | Horsington | Old Woodhall | Thornton | High Toynton | Scrafield | 1643 | Hag...

Potterhanworth Booths | B1202 | Southrey | Stixwould | Martin | Mareham on the Hill | Winceby | L...

Potterhanworth | Sots Hole | Reeds Beck | Scrivelsby | Asgarby | Hareby

...88 | 135 | Wasps Nest | The National Golf Centre | Dalderby | B1183 | Moorby | Old Bolingbrok...

Nocto... | Kirkstead | Roughton | Wood Enderby | Miningsby | Bolir...

Dunston | Kirkby on Bain | B1191 | **Woodhall Spa** i m | Toft Hill | Wilksby | East Kirkby | V

7

...am | B1189 | Martin Dales | B1192 | A153 | A155 | Mareham le Fen | Revesby | Lincoln Avia...

...lankney | Martin | Timberland Delph | Wood Side | Tumby | Stick...

Kirkby Green | B1191 | Timberland | Tattershall Thorpe | Tumby Woodside | New Bolingbroke | ARK

Thorpe Tilney | Rowston | B1189 | Tattershall | Tattershall Castle | **Coningsby** | Moor Side | Medlam | B1183

8

Ashby de la ...aunde | Walcott | Tattershall Bridge | Tattershall College | Battle of Britain Memorial Flight | Hawthorn Hill | New York | Sandy Bank | Carrington

...oxholm | Digby | Dorrington | Billinghay | Chapel Hill | Scrub Hill | Bunker's Hill | West Fen | ...nthland

119

0 1 2 3 4 5 miles
0 1 2 3 4 5 6 7 8 kilometres

A **B** **C** D Le Houses **E** **F**

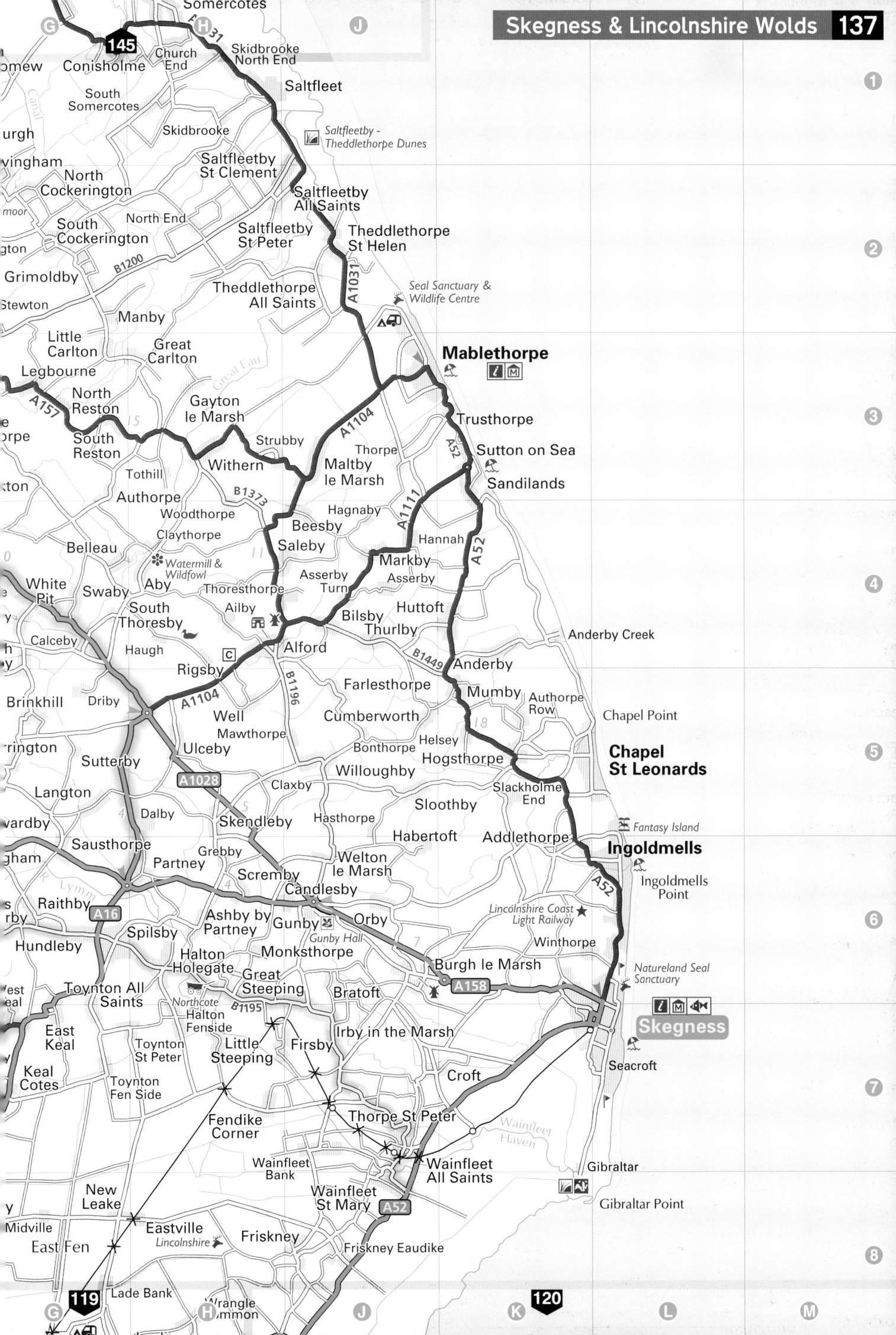

G · H · J

145
Conisholme
Somercotes
Church End
Skidbrooke North End
Saltfleet
South Somercotes
Skidbrooke
Saltfleetby – Theddlethorpe Dunes
North Cockerington
North End
Saltfleetby St Clement
Saltfleetby All Saints
Theddlethorpe St Helen
South Cockerington
Saltfleetby St Peter
Theddlethorpe All Saints
Grimoldby
Manby
Seal Sanctuary & Wildlife Centre
Stewton
Little Carlton
Great Carlton
Mablethorpe
Legbourne
North Reston
Gayton le Marsh
Trusthorpe
South Reston
Strubby
Thorpe
Sutton on Sea
Withern
Maltby le Marsh
Sandilands
Tothill
Authorpe
Hagnaby
Hannah
Woodthorpe
Beesby
Claythorpe
Saleby
Markby
Belleau
Watermill & Wildfowl
Asserby Turn
Asserby
White Pit
Swaby
Aby
Thoresthorpe
Huttoft
Calceby
South Thoresby
Ailby
Bilsby
Thurlby
Anderby Creek
Haugh
Alford
Anderby
Driby
Rigsby
Farlesthorpe
Mumby
Authorpe Row
Brinkhill
Well
Cumberworth
Chapel Point
Mawthorpe
Ulceby
Bonthorpe
Helsey
Chapel St Leonards
Sutterby
Willoughby
Hogsthorpe
Langton
Dalby
Claxby
Slackholme End
Fantasy Island
Sausthorpe
Skendleby
Hasthorpe
Sloothby
Raithby
Grebby
Habertoft
Addlethorpe
Ingoldmells
Spilsby
Partney
Welton le Marsh
Ingoldmells Point
Hundleby
Ashby by Partney
Scremby
Candlesby
Lincolnshire Coast Light Railway
Halton Holegate
Gunby
Orby
Winthorpe
Toynton All Saints
Monksthorpe
Gunby Hall
Burgh le Marsh
Natureland Seal Sanctuary
Northcote
Great Steeping
Bratoft
Skegness
East Keal
Halton Fenside
Irby in the Marsh
Keal Cotes
Toynton St Peter
Little Steeping
Firsby
Croft
Seacroft
Toynton Fen Side
Fendike Corner
Thorpe St Peter
New Leake
Wainfleet Bank
Wainfleet All Saints
Gibraltar
Eastville Lincolnshire
Wainfleet St Mary
East Fen
Friskney
Friskney Eaudike
Gibraltar Point
119
Lade Bank
Wrangle Common
120

G · H · J · K · L · M

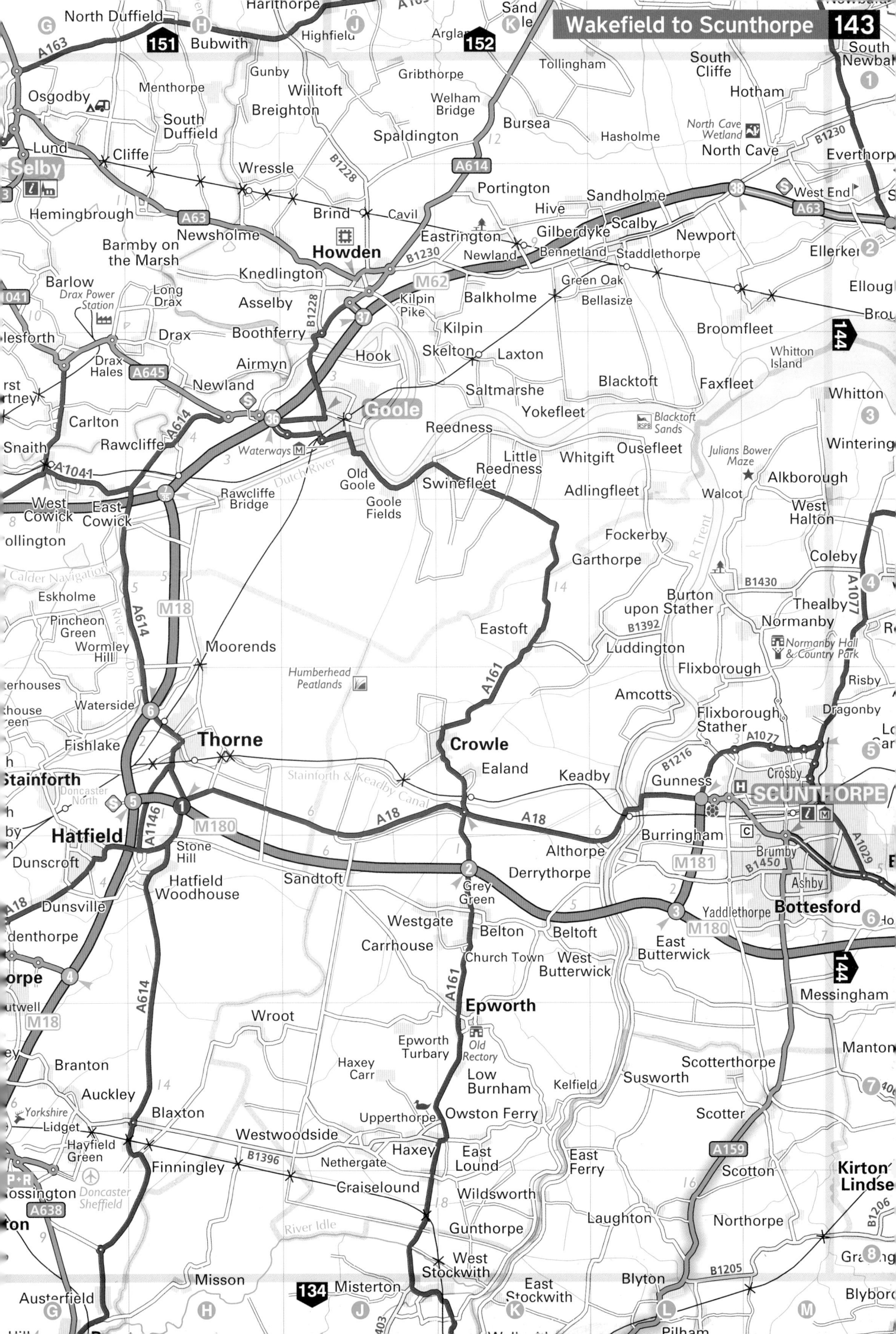

North Duffield
Harithorpe
Sand Ile
South Newba
South Newbal
1
Osgodby
151 Bubwith
Highfield
J
Arglan
152 K
Tollingham
South Cliffe
Hotham
A163
G
H
A165
Menthorpe
Gunby
Willitoft
Gribthorpe
Welham Bridge
Bursea
Hasholme
North Cave Wetland
North Cave
Everthorp
B1230
Lund
Cliffe
South Duffield
Breighton
Spaldington
Portington
Sandholme
38
West End
S
A63
S
Selby
Hemingbrough
Newsholme
Wressle
B1228
Brind
Cavil
Hive
Eastrington
Gilberdyke
Scalby
Newport
Staddlethorpe
Ellerker
2
Barmby on the Marsh
Howden
B1230
Newland
Bennetland
A63
Elloug
Brou
Barlow
Knedlington
Asselby
M62
Kilpin Pike
Balkholme
Green Oak
Bellasize
Broomfleet
Whitton Island
Whitton
Drax Power Station
Long Drax
37
Kilpin
Skelton
Laxton
Blacktoft
Faxfleet
Wintering
3
lesforth
Drax
Boothferry
Hook
Saltmarshe
Yokefleet
Blacktoft Sands RSPB
Julians Bower Maze
Alkborough
rst
Drax Hales
A645
Airmyn
Reedness
Little Reedness
Whitgift
Ousefleet
Walcot
West Halton
Coleby
rtney
Newland
S
36
Goole
Swinefleet
Adlingfleet
Fockerby
A1077
4
Carlton
A614
Waterways M
Old Goole
Garthorpe
Burton upon Stather
Thealby Normanby
B1430
Snaith
Rawcliffe
Dutch River
Goole Fields
B1392
Normanby Hall & Country Park
Risby
A1041
7
Rawcliffe Bridge
Luddington
Flixborough
Dragonby
West Cowick
East Cowick
Eastoft
Amcotts
Flixborough Stather
Lo
Car
ollington
Calder Navigation
Eskholme
A614
M18
Moorends
Humberhead Peatlands
A161
A1077
Crosby
5
Pincheon Green
Wormley Hill
Waterside
6
Thorne
Crowle
Ealand
Keadby
Gunness
B1216
H
SCUNTHORPE
i M
erhouses
Fishlake
Stainforth & Keadby Canal
Burringham
C
Stainforth
Doncaster North
S
5
1
A18
A18
Althorpe
M181
Brumby
Hatfield
A1146
M180
Stone Hill
Sandtoft
Derrythorpe
Ashby
A1029
Dunscroft
Hatfield Woodhouse
2
Grey Green
3
Yaddlethorpe
East Butterwick
Bottesford
Dunsville
Westgate
Belton
Beltoft
M180
6
denthorpe
Carrhouse
Church Town
West Butterwick
A161
East Butterwick
144
orpe
4
A614
Wroot
Westwoodside
Epworth
Old Rectory
Messingham
M18
Branton
Haxey Carr
Epworth Turbary
Low Burnham
Kelfield
Scotterthorpe
Manton
Auckley
Susworth
Scotter
7
40
Yorkshire
Lidget
Blaxton
Upperthorpe
Owston Ferry
Scotton
Kirton Lindse
Hayfield Green
Finningley
B1396
Nethergate
Haxey
East Lound
East Ferry
A159
P+R
ossington
Doncaster Sheffield
Graiselound
Wildsworth
Laughton
Northorpe
8
ton
A638
River Idle
Gunthorpe
B1205
Blyborg
Austerfield
West Stockwith
Misson
134 Misterton
East Stockwith
Blyton
L
M
G
H
J
K
403
Pilham
Grain

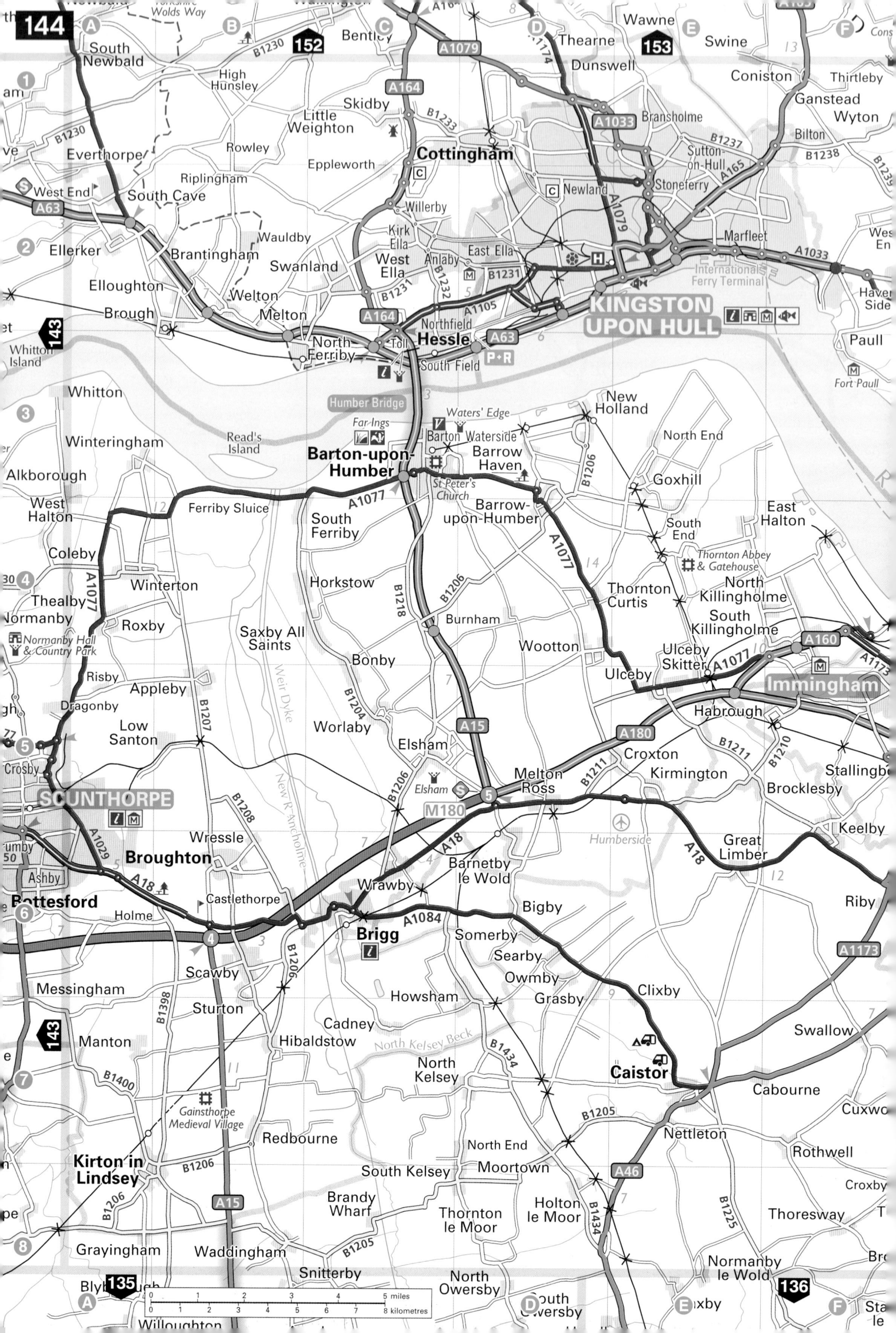

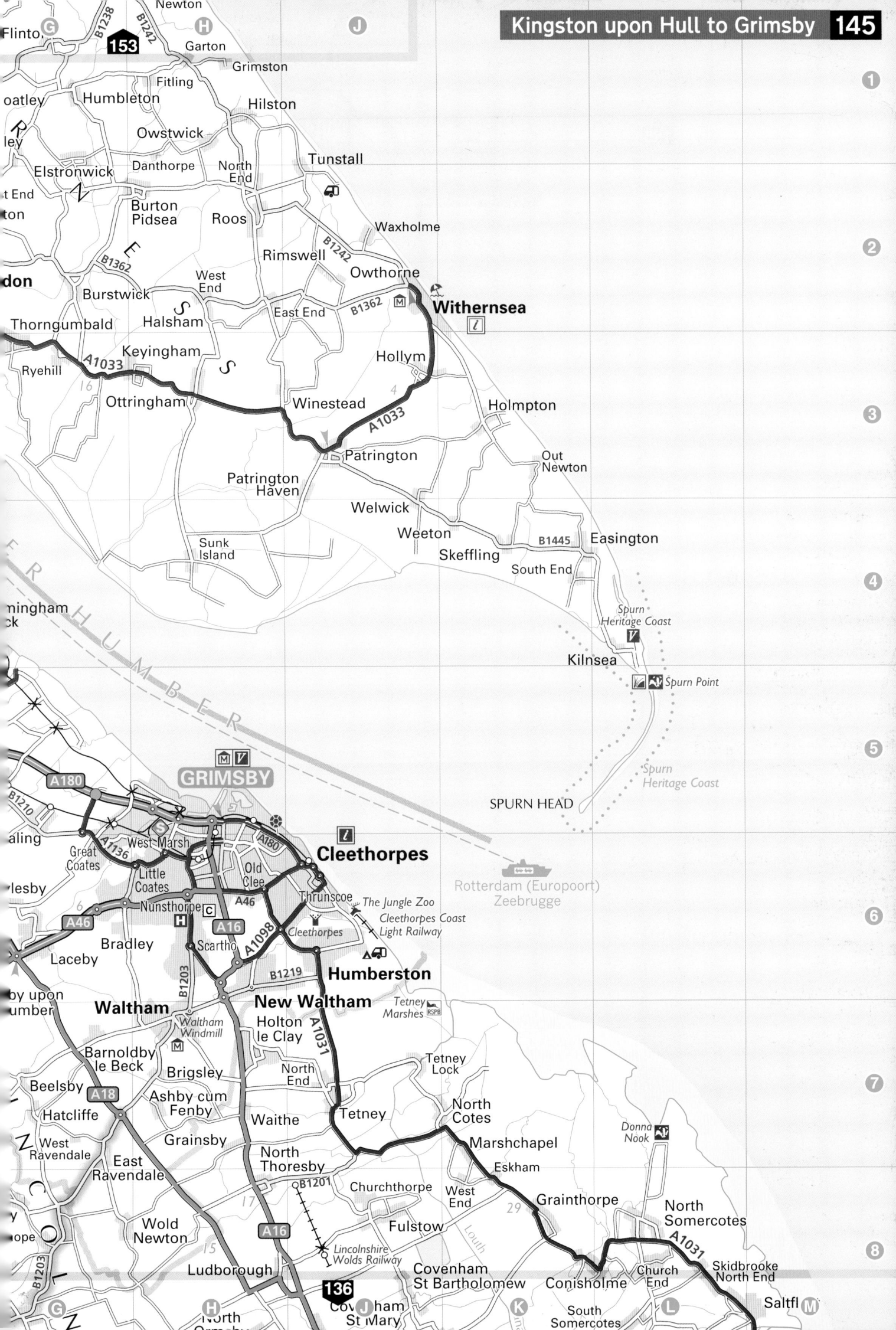

G H J

Flinto

Newton

B1238 B1242

153

Garton

Grimston

Fitling

Humbleton

Hilston

oatley

Owstwick

Elstronwick

Danthorpe

North End

Tunstall

t End
ton

Burton
Pidsea

Roos

Waxholme

Ryehill

Thorngumbald

A1033

Keyingham

Rimswell

West End

Owthorne

B1242

M

Withernsea

i

B1362

Halsham

East End

B1362

Burstwick

Hollym

Ottringham

Winestead

A1033

Holmpton

Patrington

Out
Newton

Patrington
Haven

Welwick

Weeton

B1445

Easington

Sunk
Island

Skeffling

South End

Spurn
Heritage Coast

V

Kilnsea

Spurn Point

Spurn
Heritage Coast

R HUMBER

SPURN HEAD

A180

GRIMSBY

M V

B1210

Cleethorpes

i

aling

Great
Coates

West Marsh

A1136

Old
Clee

A180

Rotterdam (Europoort)
Zeebrugge

Little
Coates

Thrunscoe

The Jungle Zoo

lesby

Nunsthorpe

A46

C

A46

H

Scartho

A16

Cleethorpes

A1098

Cleethorpes Coast
Light Railway

Bradley

Laceby

B1219

Humberston

by upon
umber

Waltham

B1203

New Waltham

A1031

Tetney
Marshes

RSPB

Barnoldby
le Beck

Waltham
Windmill

M

Brigsley

Holton
le Clay

North
End

Tetney
Lock

Beelsby

A18

Ashby cum
Fenby

Tetney

North
Cotes

Hatcliffe

Waithe

Donna
Nook

West
Ravendale

Grainsby

West
End

Marshchapel

East
Ravendale

North
Thoresby

Eskham

Churchthorpe

Grainthorpe

Wold
Newton

B1201

A16

Fulstow

North
Somercotes

A1031

Lincolnshire
Wolds Railway

Covenham
St Bartholomew

Conisholme

Church
End

Skidbrooke
North End

B1203

Ludborough

136

ham
St Mary

South
Somercotes

Saltfl

M

G H J K L M

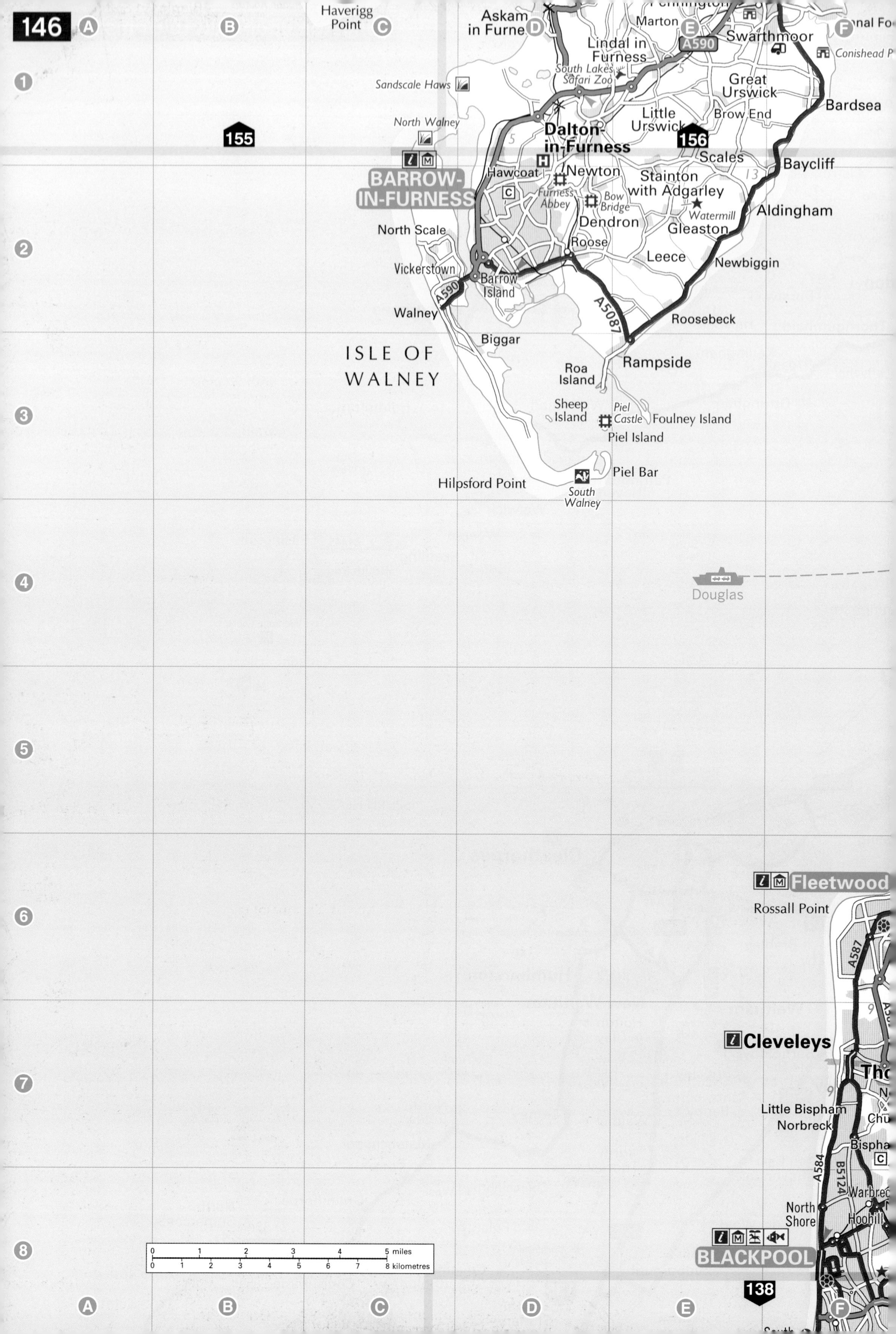

1

Haverigg
Point

Sandscale Haws

North Walney

155

156

BARROW-
IN-FURNESS

Hawcoat

C

North Scale

2

Vickerstown

Walney

A590

Barrow
Island

ISLE OF
WALNEY

Biggar

3

Hilpsford Point

Sheep
Island

Piel
Castle

Piel Island

South
Walney

Piel Bar

Askam
in Furne

Lindal in
Furness

South Lakes
Safari Zoo

Dalton-
in-Furness

H

Newton

Furness
Abbey

Bow
Bridge

Dendron

Roose

Marton

A590

Great
Urswick

Little
Urswick

Brow End

Stainton
with Adgarley

★ Watermill

Gleaston

Leece

Roose

A5087

Rampside

Roa
Island

Foulney Island

Swarthmoor

Conishead P

Bardsea

Scales

13

Baycliff

Aldingham

Newbiggin

Roosebeck

4

Douglas

5

6

Fleetwood

Rossall Point

A587

7

Cleveleys

Th

Little Bispham

Norbreck

Bispha

C

A584

B5124

Warbre

North
Shore

Hoohill

8

5 miles

8 kilometres

BLACKPOOL

138

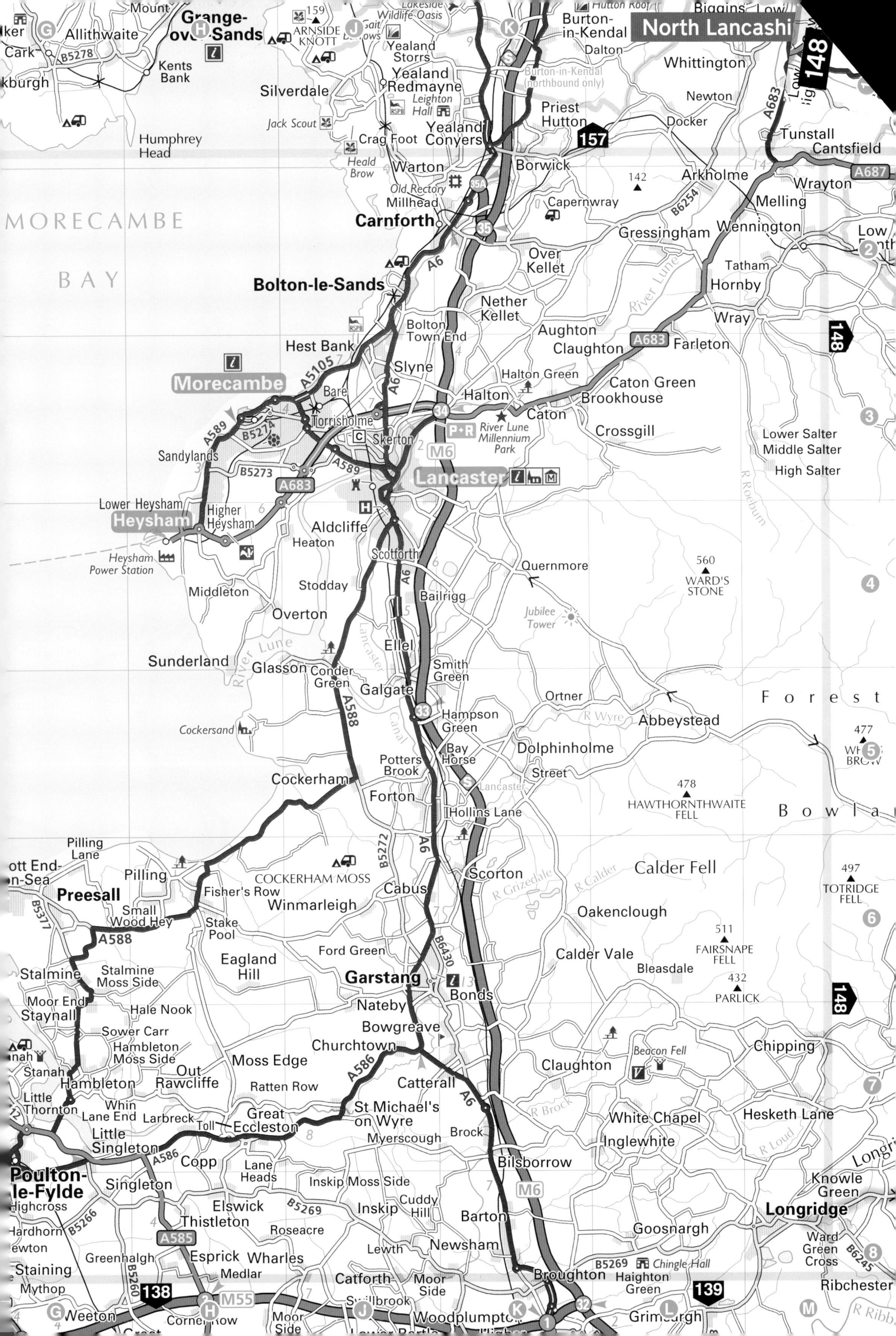

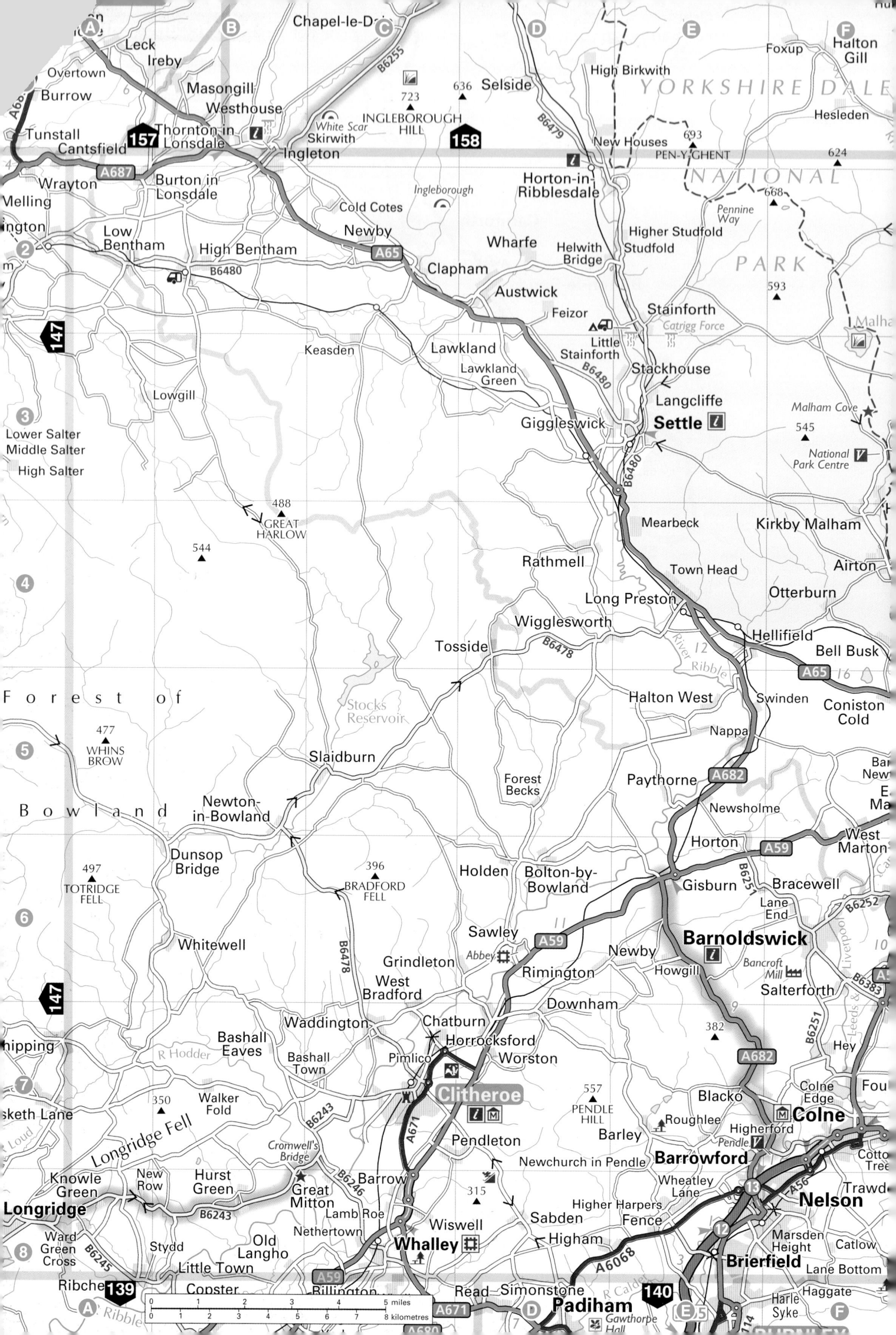

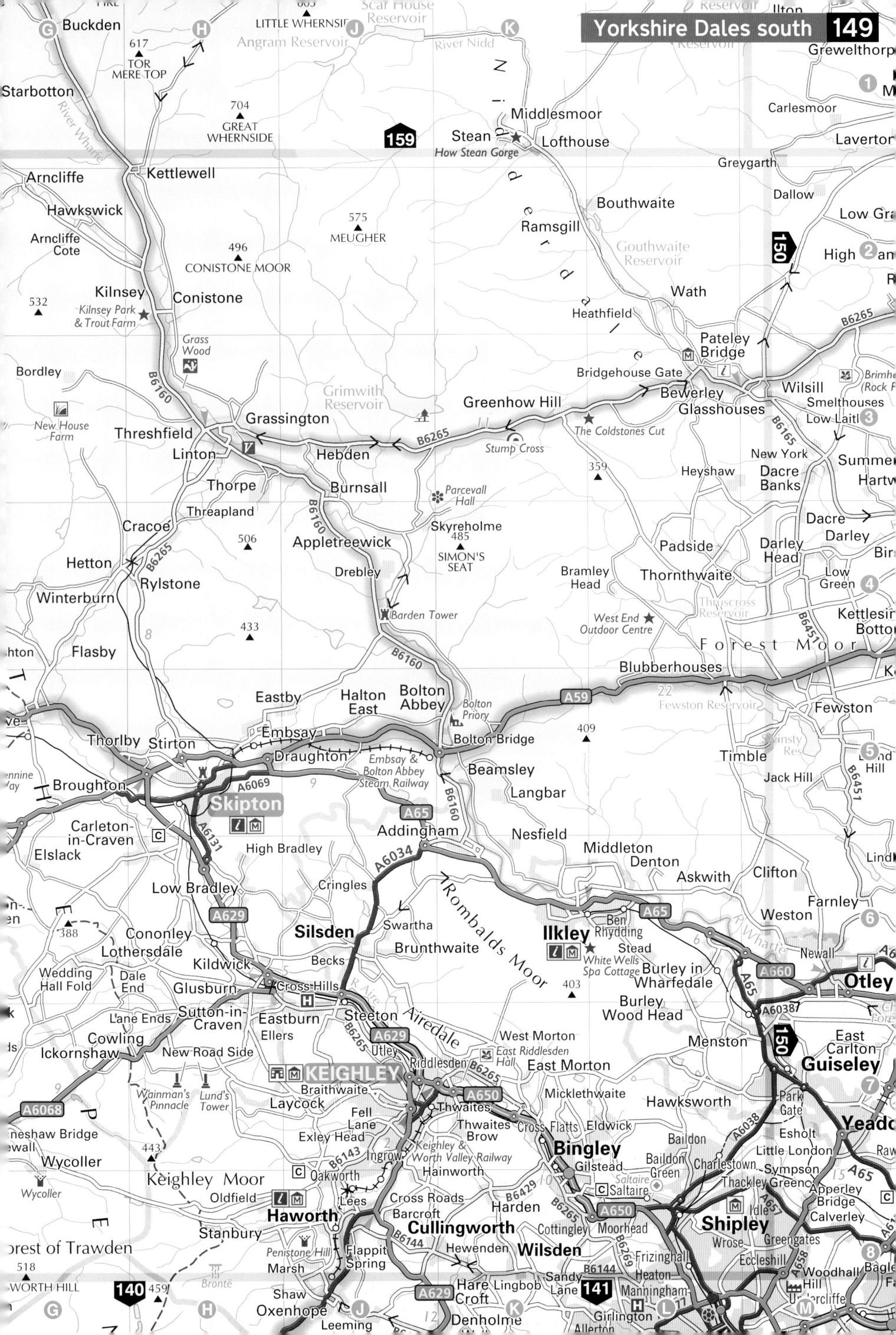

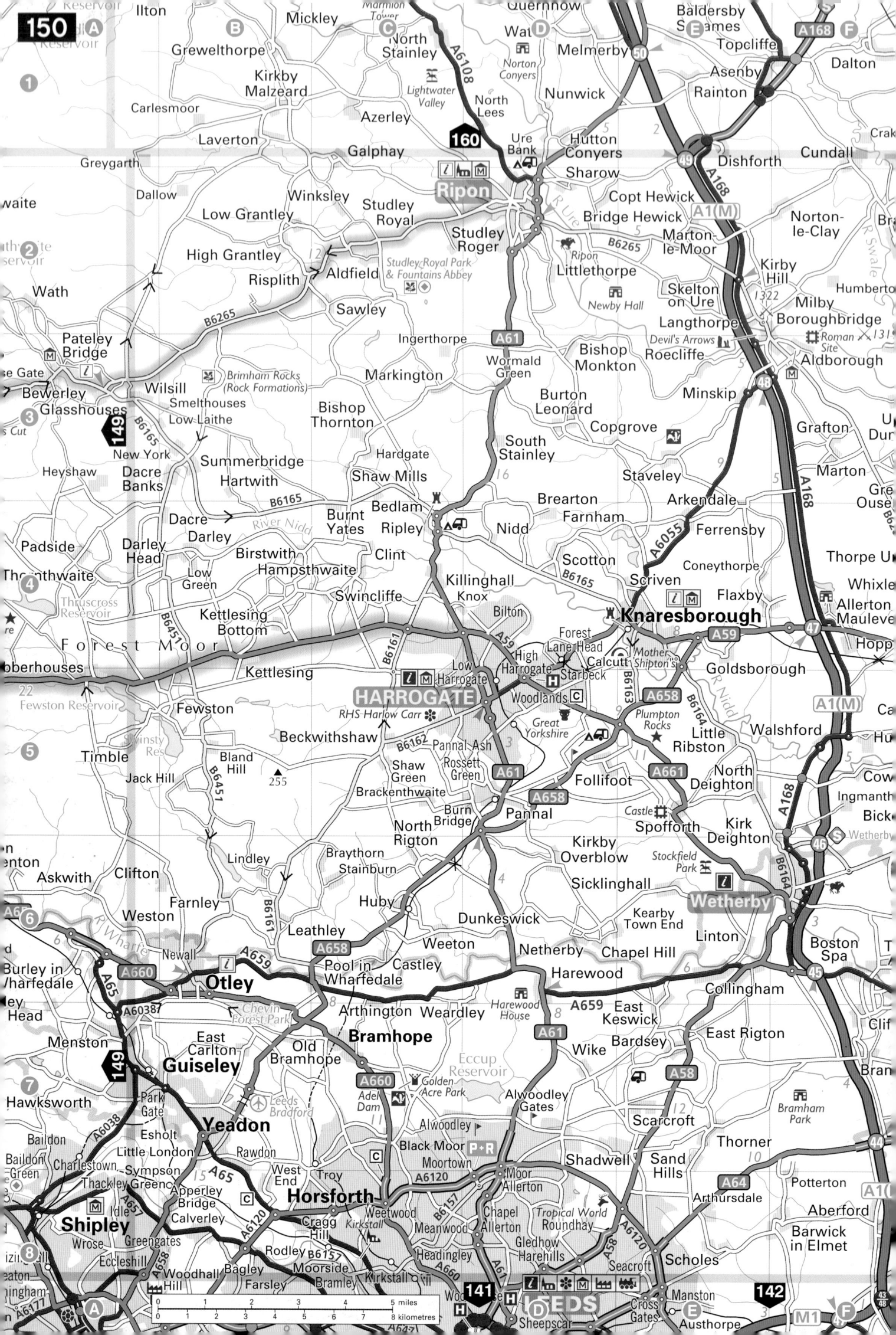

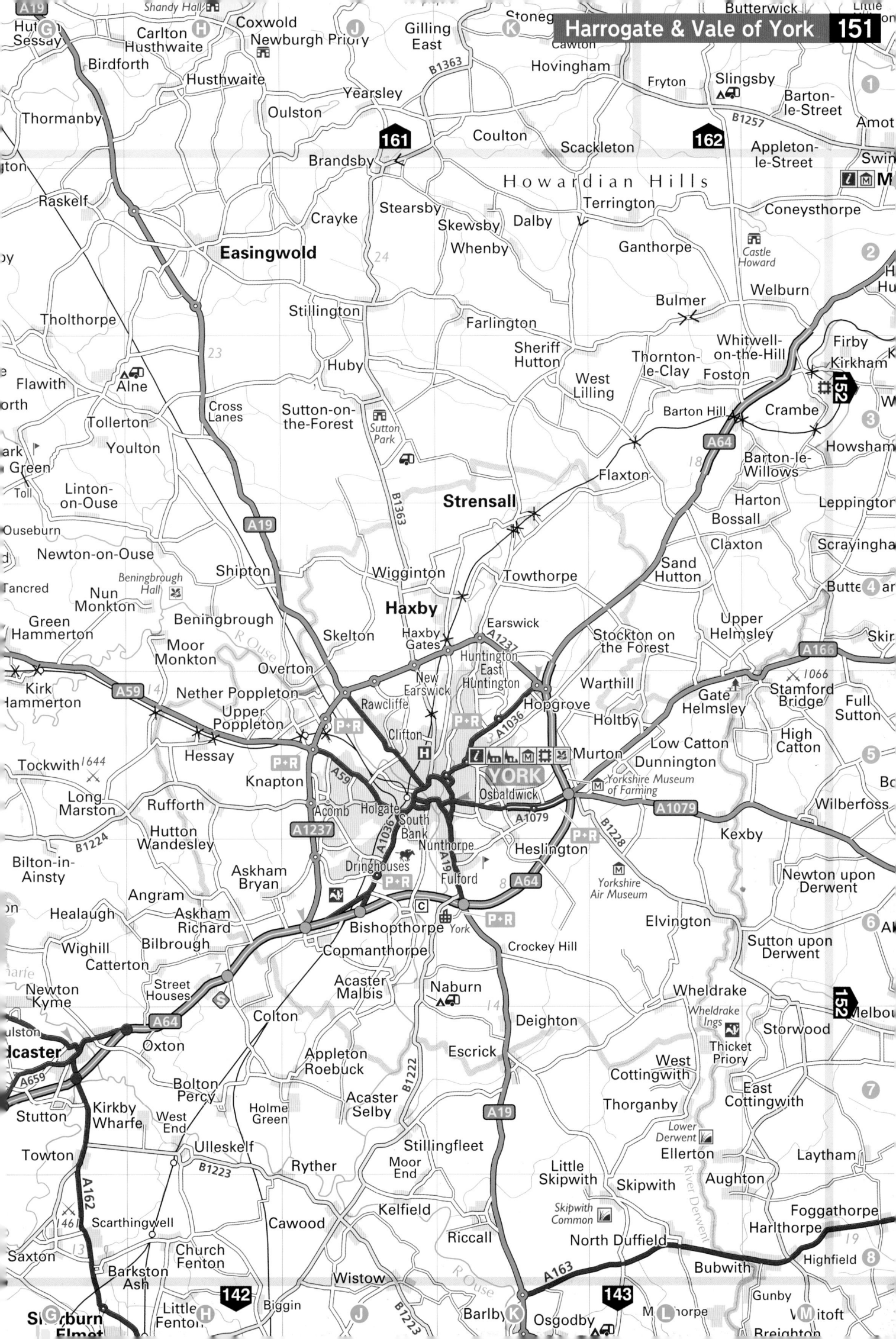

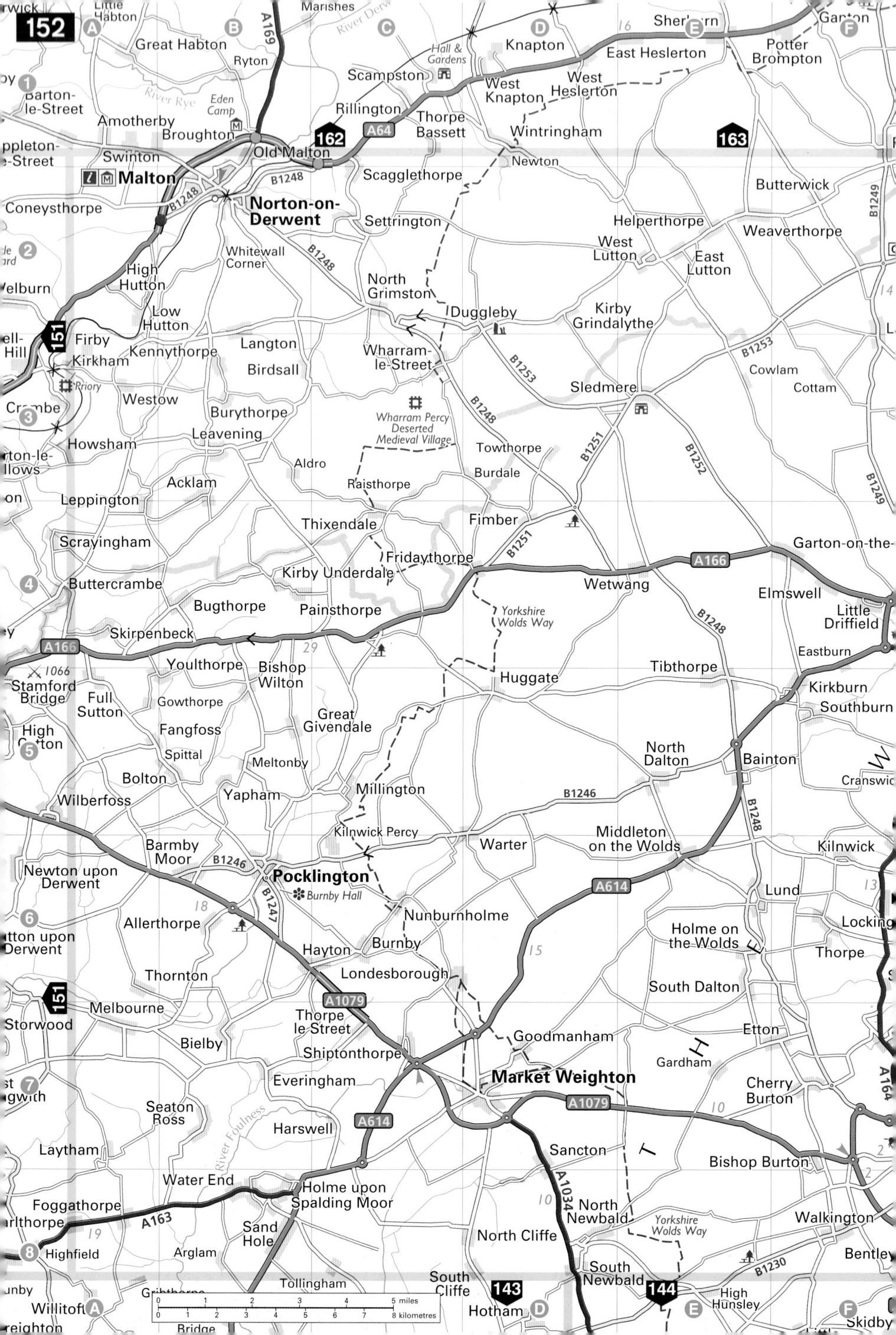

Hunmanby

Fordon

Wold Newton

Burton Fleming

Reighton

Speeton

Flamborough Head Heritage Coast

Bempton Cliffs RSPB

Thornwick Bay

Buckton

Bempton

North Landing

Flamborough Cliffs

Selwicks Bay

FLAMBOROUGH HEAD

Grindale

A165

163

B1229

Marton

Flamborough

B1255

B1259

Sewerby

Bondville Miniature Village

Rudston

Monolith

Boynton

B1253

Bessingby

Bridlington

Hilderthorpe

BRIDLINGTON BAY

Haisthorpe

Thornholme

Carnaby

Bridlington

Kilham

Burton Agnes

Norman Manor House

Harpham

A165

Huston Parva

Lowthorpe

Fraisthorpe

A614

Nafferton

Little Kelk

Gransmoor

Great Kelk

Lissett

Barmston

field

Wansford

Gembling

B1242

Ulrome

Skerne

Foston on the Wolds

Skipsea Castle

Skipsea

B1249

Brigham

Beeford

Upton

Skipsea Brough

North Frodingham

A165

Dunnington

Rotsea

Atwick

Hempholme

Bewholme

B1242

Nunkeeling

Burshill

Honeysuckle Farm

Hornsea

Brandesburton

Seaton

Hornsea Mere

Aike

Foss Hill

A1035

Sigglesthorne

Rolston

Leven

Catwick

Goxhill

Mappleton

Mappleton Sands

Eske

High Farm

Little Catwick

Long Riston

B1243

Little Hatfield

Great Hatfield

Great Cowden

rley

A1035

Routh

Rise

North End

Hull Bridge

Tickton

Arnold

Withernwick

Arram

Meaux

New Ellerby

Marton

Mount Pleasant

Weel

Skirlaugh

West Newton

Aldbrough

Woodmansey

Old Ellerby

East Newton

B1238

B1242

Wawne

A165

Burton Constable Hall

Flinton

Garton

A1174

Thearne

Swine

Coniston

Thirtleby

145

Grimston

A1079

Dunswell

144

Constable

Sproatley

Humbleton

Hilston

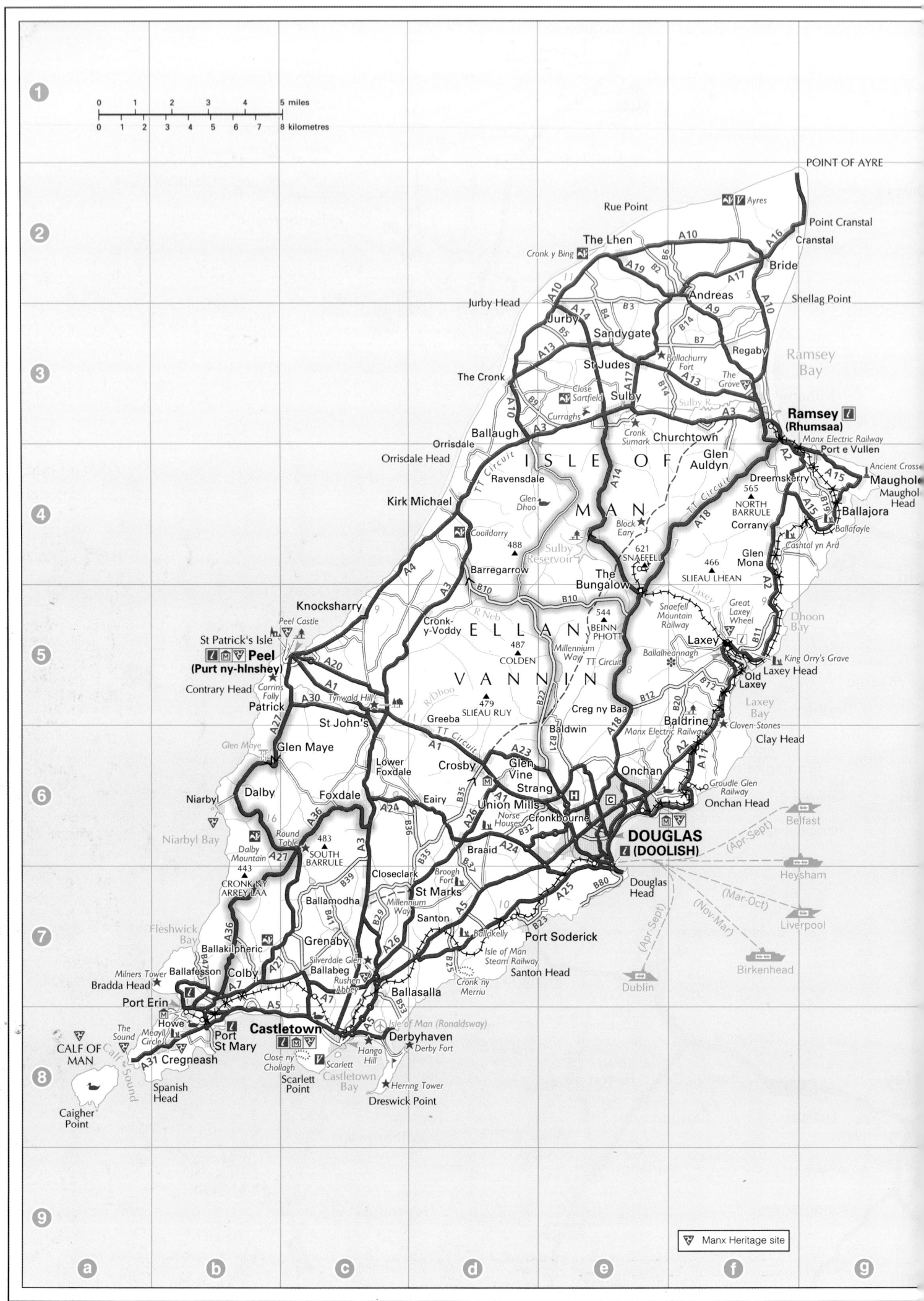

POINT OF AYRE

Rue Point

The Lhen
Cronk y Bing

Ayres

A10

Point Cranstal
Cranstal

Bride

A16

A19

B6

B2

A17

Jurby Head

Jurby

A14

A10

Sandygate

B4

B3

B5

Andreas

A9

A13

Shellag Point

Regaby

B14

B7

A10

Ramsey Bay

St Judes

Ballachurry Fort

A13

The Grove

Ramsey
(Rhumsaa)

Manx Electric Railway

Port e Vullen

Ancient Cross

The Cronk

Close Sartfield

Sulby

B14

Sulby R.

A3

A2

A15

Maughole
Maughol Head

Orrisdale

Ballaugh

A3

A10

Cronk Sumark

Churchtown

Glen Auldyn

Dreemskerry

A15

B19

Ballajora

Ballafayle

Orrisdale Head

ISLE OF

A14

TT Circuit

565
NORTH BARRULE

Corrany

A15

Cashtal yn Ard

Kirk Michael

Ravensdale

MAN

Glen Dhoo

488

Sulby Reservoir

Block Eary

621
SNAEFELL

466
SLIEAU LHEAN

A18

Glen Mona

A2

Dhoon Bay

Cooildarry

Barregarrow

B10

The Bungalow

B10

544
BEINN PHOTT

Snaefell Mountain Railway

Great Laxey Wheel

Knocksharry

R.Neb

Cronk-y-Voddy

ELLAN

487
COLDEN

Millennium Way

Ballalheannagh

Laxey

King Orry's Grave

St Patrick's Isle

Peel Castle

Peel
(Purt ny-hInshey)

A20

VANNIN

TT Circuit

B22

Old Laxey

Laxey Head

Laxey Bay

Contrary Head

Corrins Folly

A1

Tynwald Hill

Greeba

479
SLIEAU RUY

Creg ny Baa

Baldrine

Cloven Stones

Patrick

A30

St John's

Clay Head

Glen Maye

Glen Maye

A1

Lower Foxdale

Crosby

Glen Vine
Strang

Baldwin

B21

A18

Manx Electric Railway

A11

Niarbyl

Dalby

Foxdale

A24

Eairy

Union Mills

A1

Cronkbourne

Onchan

Groudle Glen Railway

Onchan Head

Niarbyl Bay

A36

Round Table

483
SOUTH BARRULE

A3

B36

B35

Norse Houses

B32

DOUGLAS
(DOOLISH)

Belfast

443
CRONK NY ARREY LAA

Dalby Mountain

A27

Braaid

A24

Heysham

Fleshwick Bay

Closeclark

Brough Fort

St Marks

A25

Douglas Head

(Mar-Oct)

Liverpool

Ballamodha

B39

B41

A5

Millennium Way

Santon

B23

A25

B80

(Nov-Mar)

Ballakilpheric

Grenaby

A26

Ballakelly

Port Soderick

Dublin

Birkenhead

Ballafesson

Colby

A21

A7

Ballabeg

Silverdale Glen

Rushen Abbey

Ballasalla

B25

Isle of Man Steam Railway

Santon Head

Cronk ny Merriu

Milners Tower

Bradda Head

Port Erin

A5

A7

A5

Howe

The Sound

Meayll Circle

Port St Mary

Castletown

Isle of Man (Ronaldsway)

Derbyhaven

Derby Fort

CALF OF MAN

Calf Sound

A31

Cregneash

Close ny Chollagh

Scarlett

Castletown Bay

Hango Hill

Spanish Head

Scarlett Point

Herring Tower

Caigher Point

Dreswick Point

Manx Heritage site

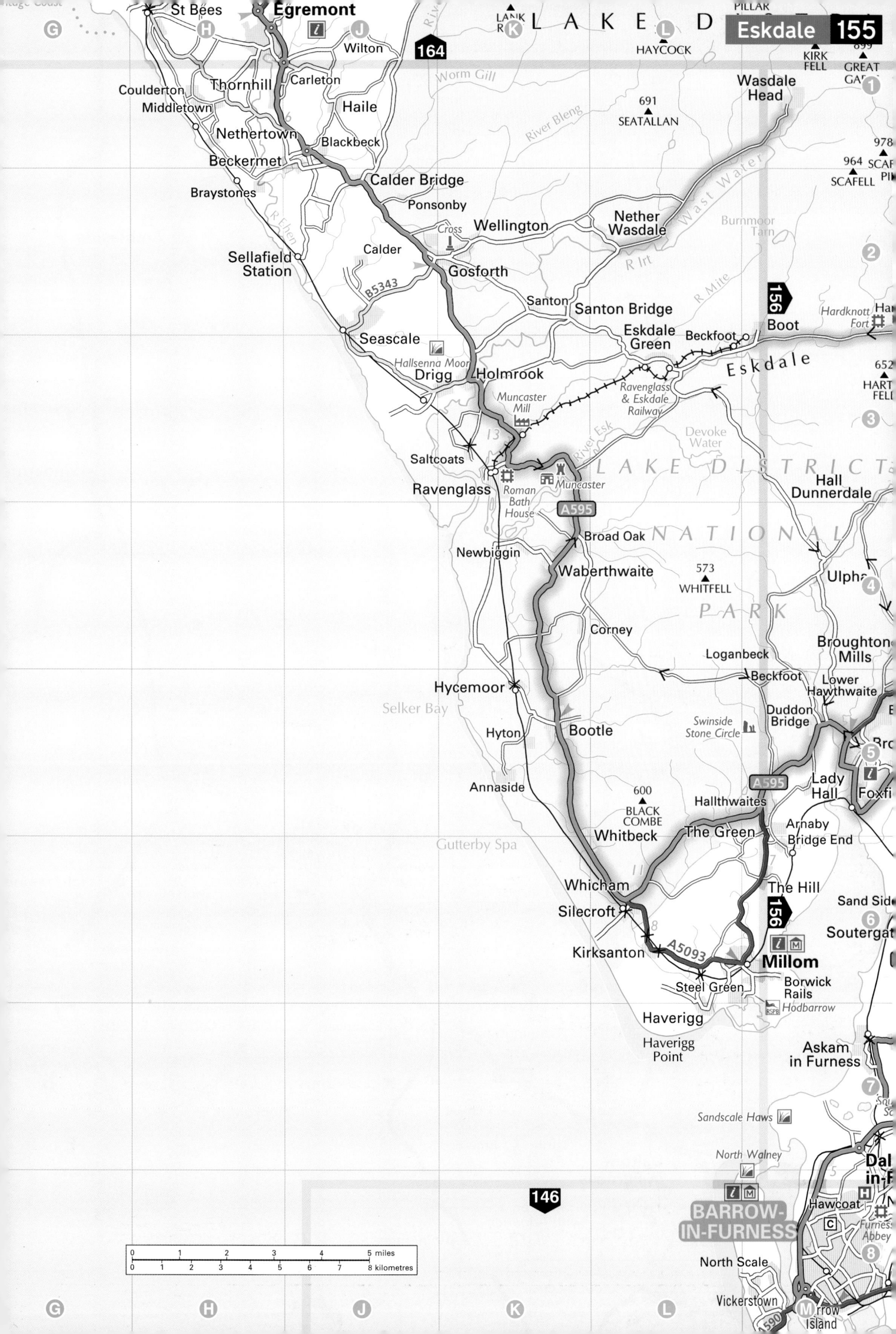

St Bees
Egremont
Wilton

G   H   J

Thornhill
Carleton
Haile
Coulderton
Middletown
Nethertown
Blackbeck
Beckermet
Braystones
Calder Bridge
Ponsonby
Calder
Cross
Wellington
Nether Wasdale
Sellafield Station
B5343
Gosforth
Santon
Santon Bridge
Eskdale Green
Beckfoot
Seascale
Hallsenna Moor
Drigg
Holmrook
Muncaster Mill
Ravenglass & Eskdale Railway
Devoke Water
Saltcoats
13
Ravenglass
Roman Bath House
Muncaster
A595
Broad Oak
Newbiggin
Waberthwaite
Corney
Hycemoor
Hyton
Bootle
Annaside
Whitbeck
Whicham
Silecroft
Kirksanton
A5093
Steel Green
Haverigg
Haverigg Point

LANK K
LAKE D
PILLAR
HAYCOCK L
Eskdale 155
KIRK FELL
GREAT GA
Wasdale Head
691
SEATALLAN
978
964 SCAF
SCAFELL   PI
R Irt
Worm Gill
River Bleng
R Mite
Burnmoor Tarn
West Water
156
Boot
Hardknott Fort
Ha
ESKDALE
652
HART FELL
River Esk
LAKE DISTRICT
Hall Dunnerdale
NATIONAL
573
WHITFELL
Ulph
PARK
Loganbeck
Beckfoot
Broughton Mills
Lower Hawthwaite
Swinside Stone Circle
Duddon Bridge
Bro
5
600
BLACK COMBE
Hallthwaites
The Green
Lady Hall
Foxfi
Arnaby
Bridge End
The Hill
Sand Side
156
Sougat
Soutergat
6
Millom
Borwick Rails
Hodbarrow
RSPB
Askam in Furness
7
Sandscale Haws
North Walney
146
BARROW-IN-FURNESS
Hawcoat
Furness Abbey
North Scale
Vickerstown
rrow Island
Dal in-F
8

R Ehen
River Irt
Selker Bay
Gutterby Spa
164

0   1   2   3   4   5 miles
0   1   2   3   4   5   6   7   8 kilometres

G   H   J   K   L   M

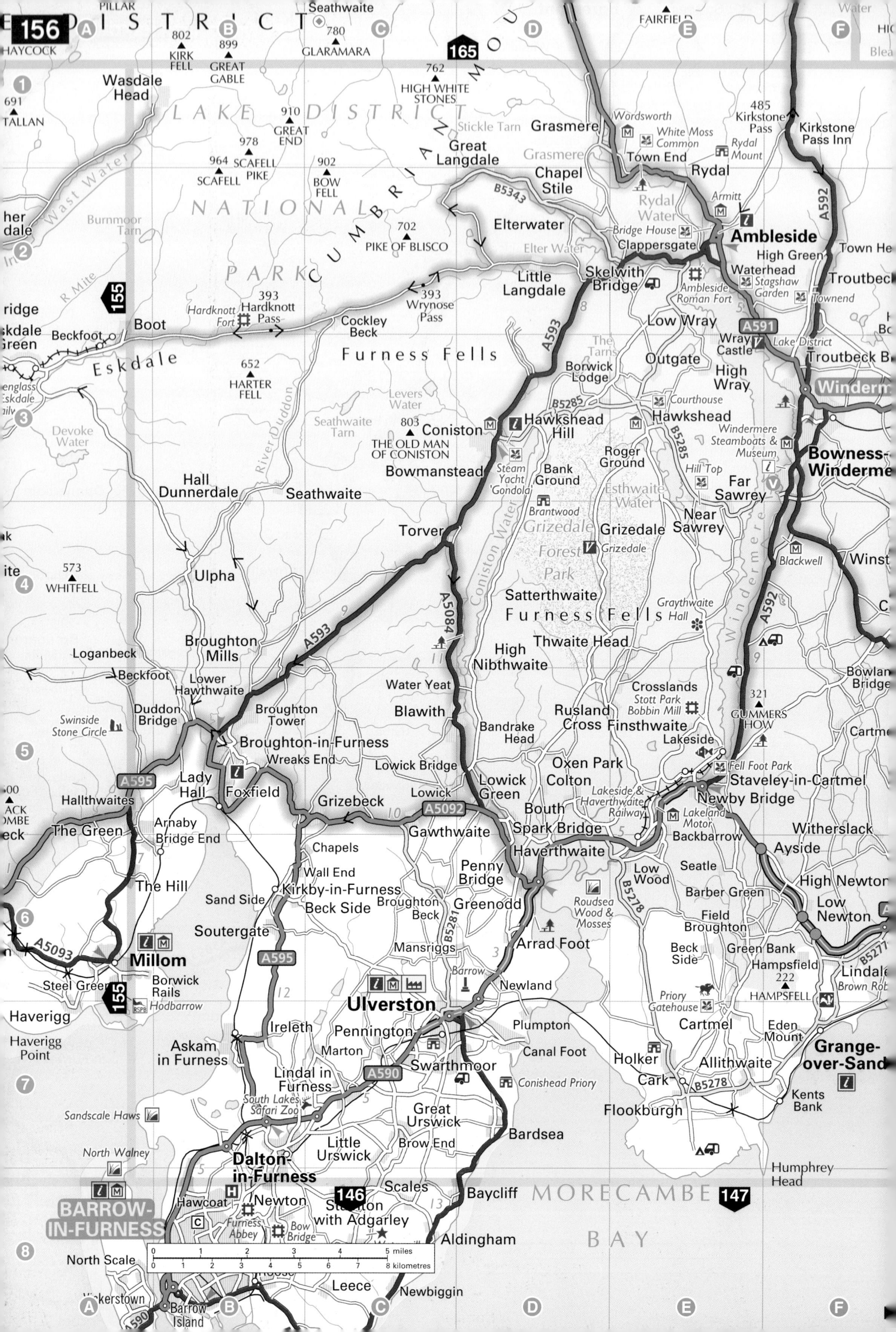

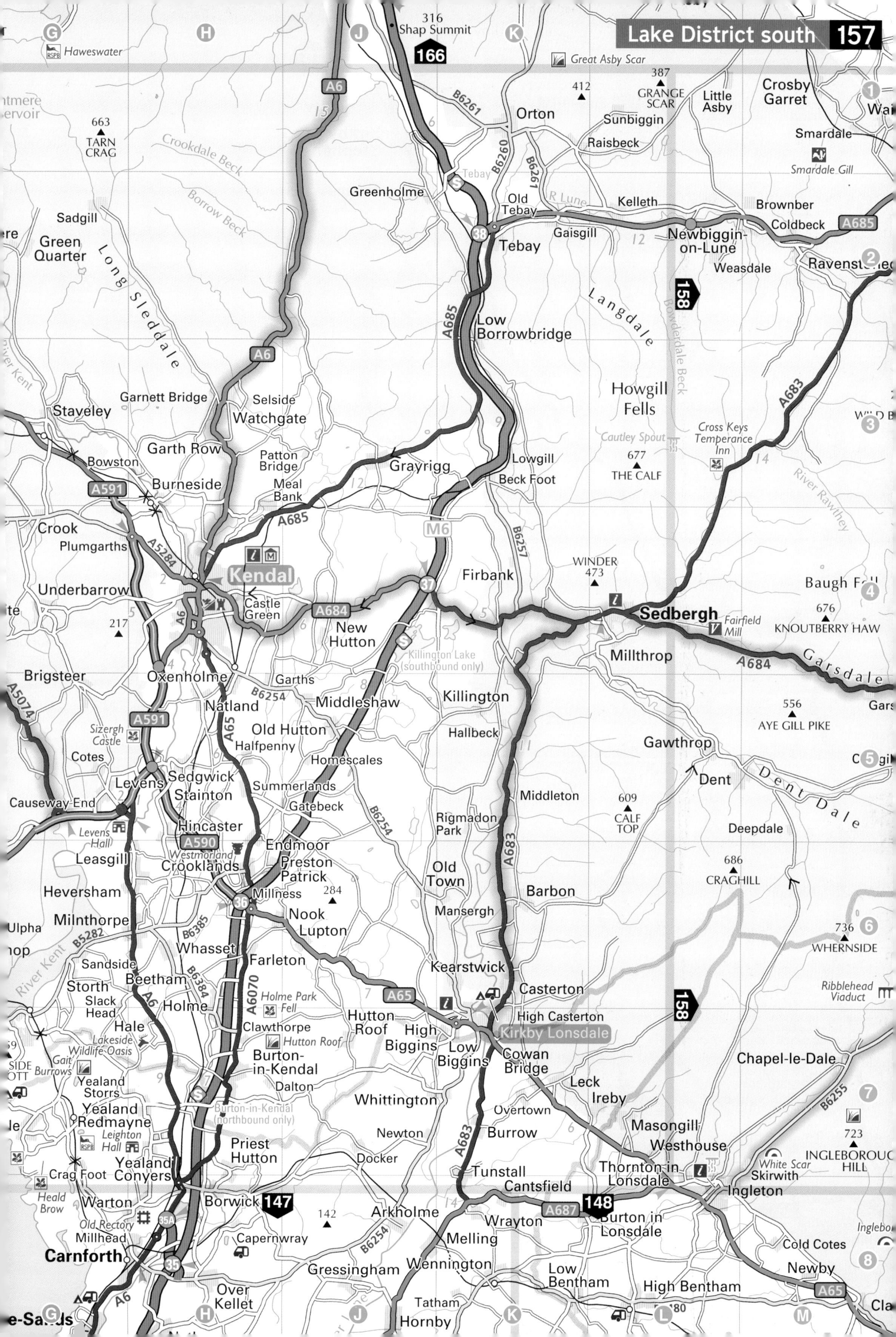

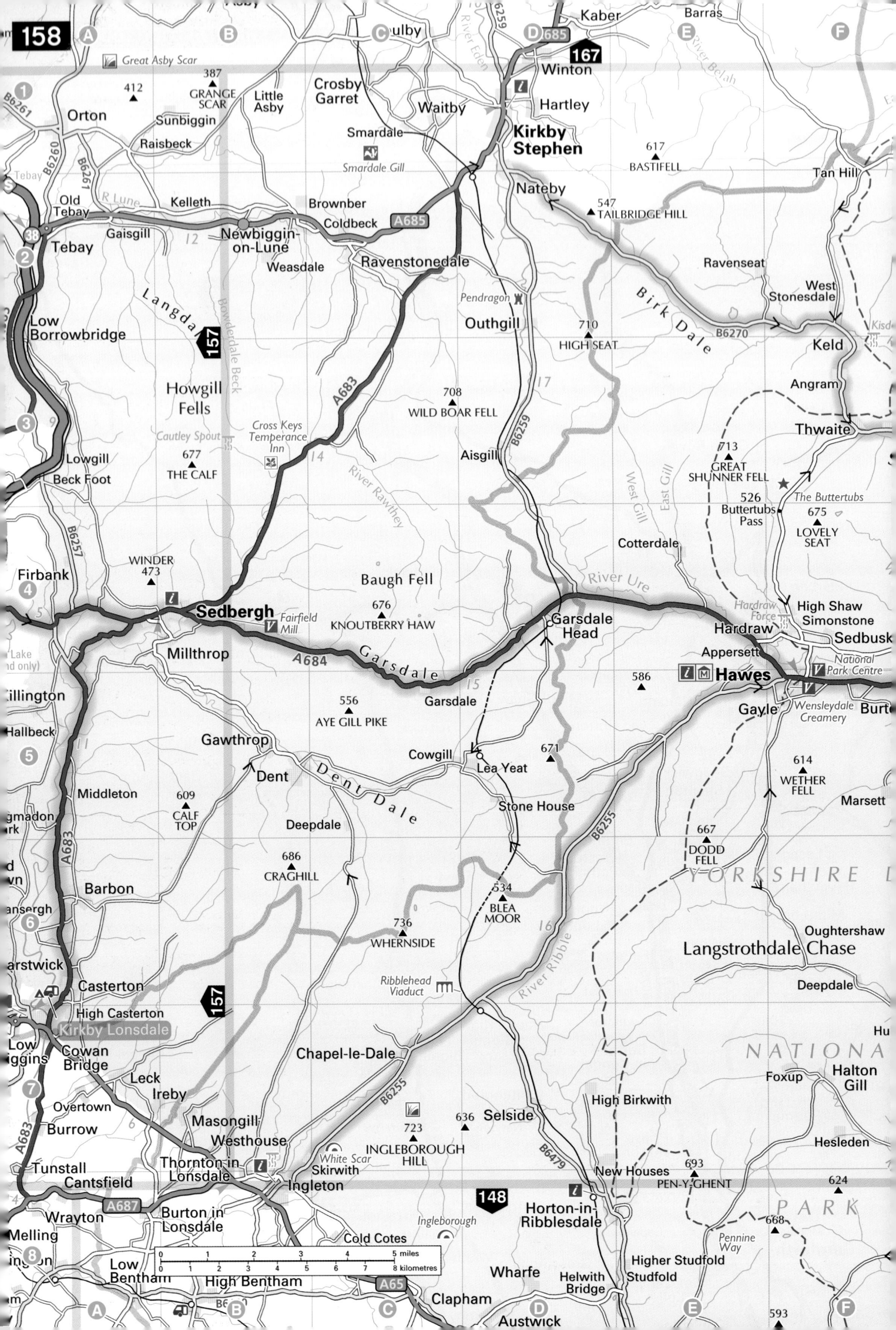

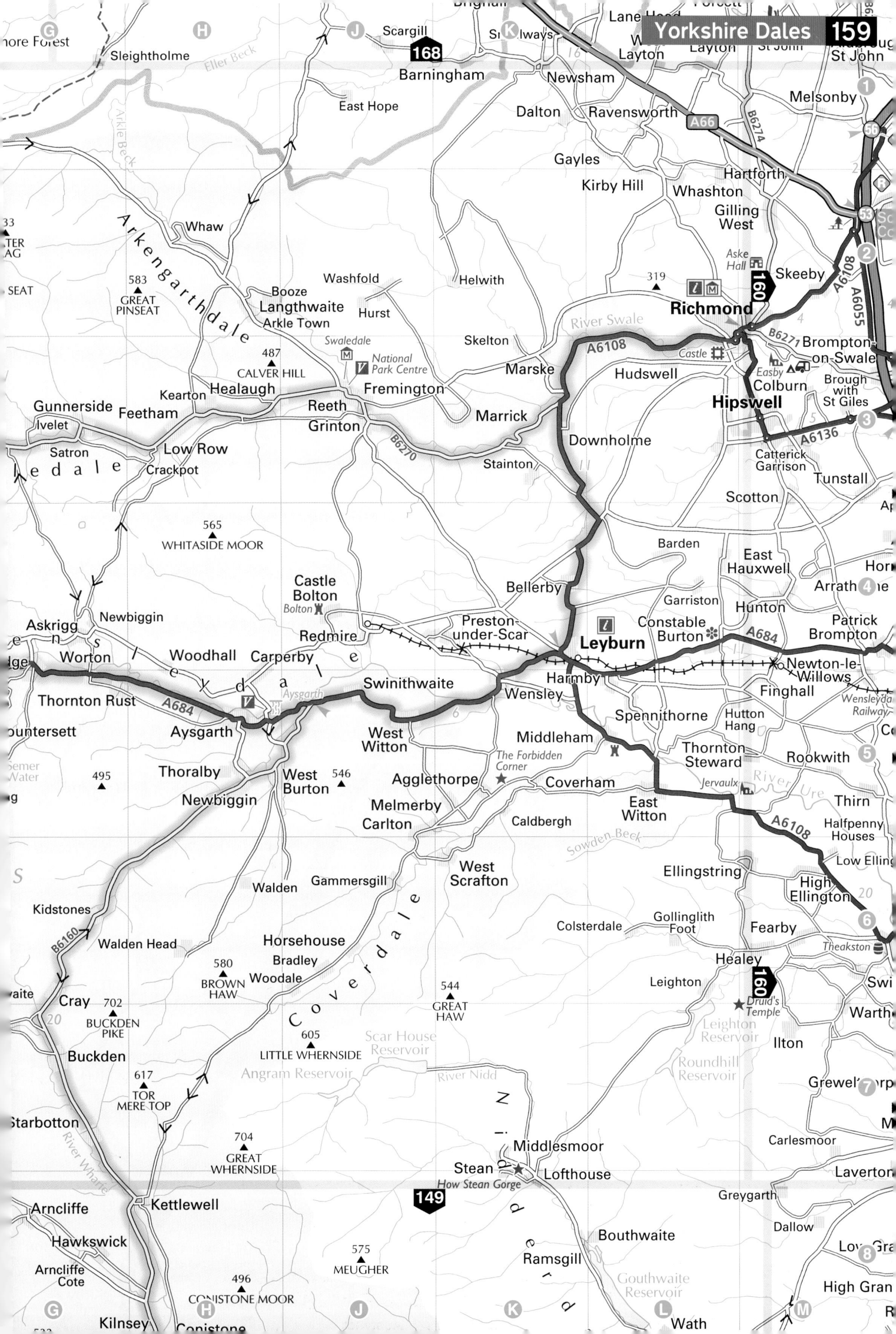

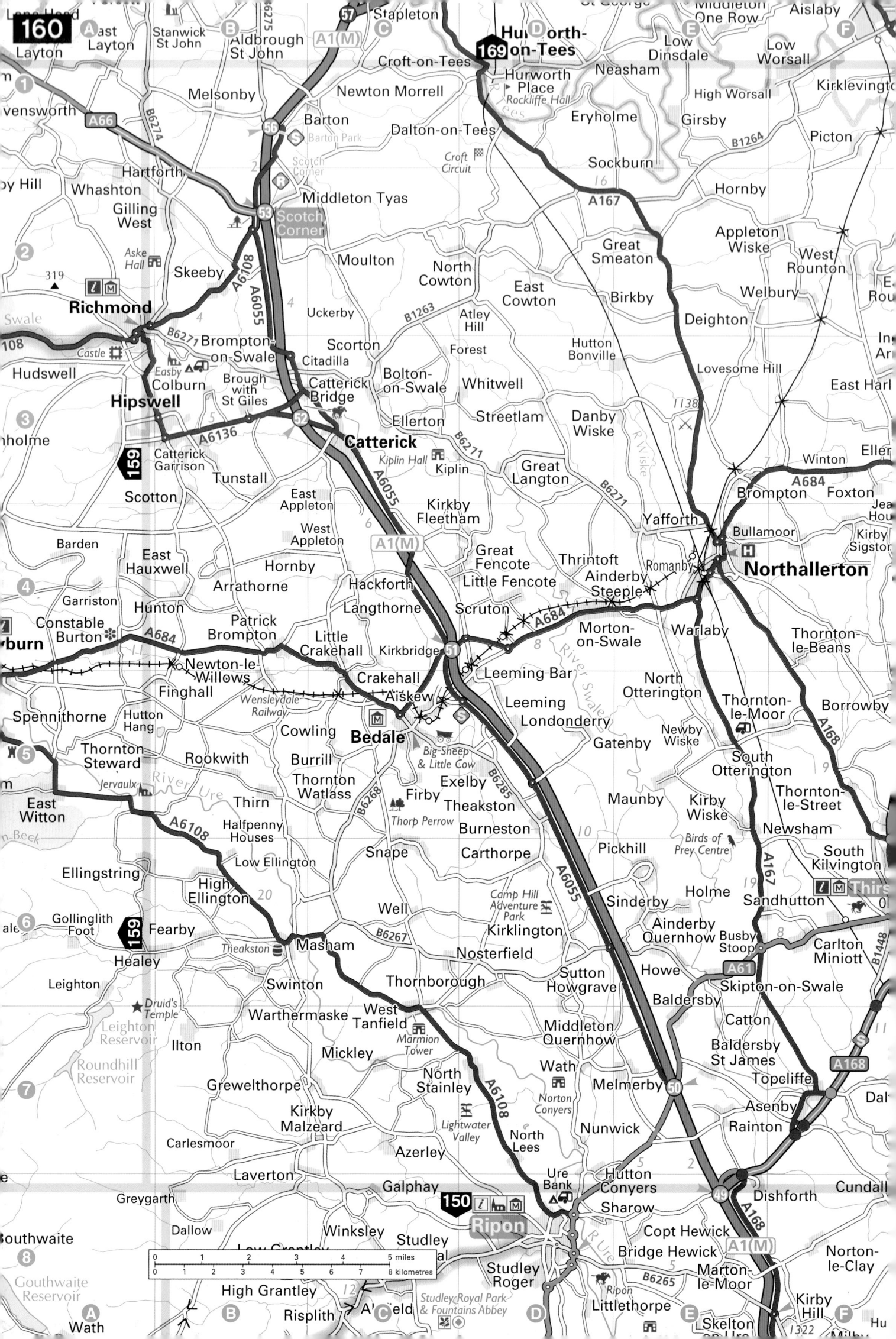

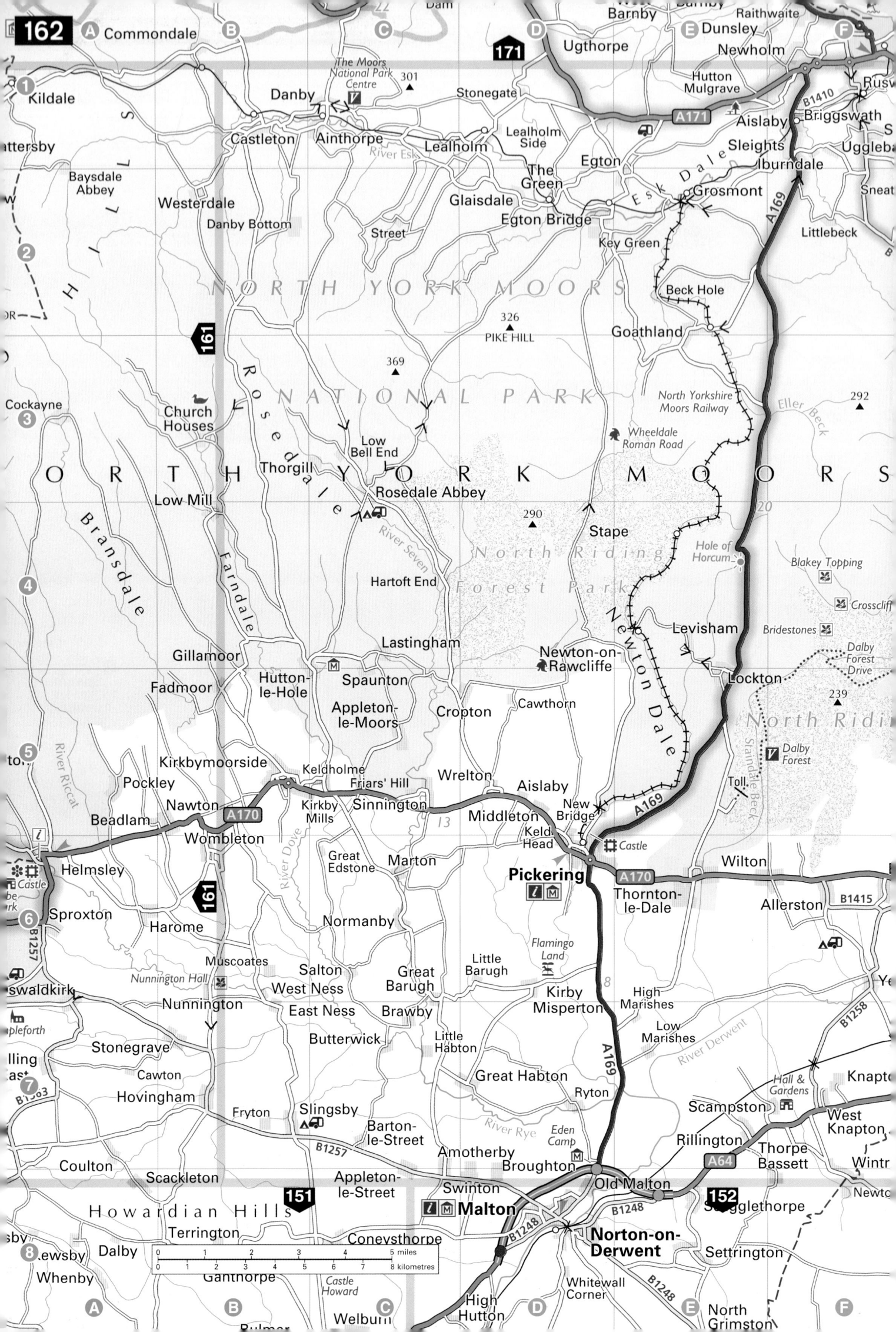

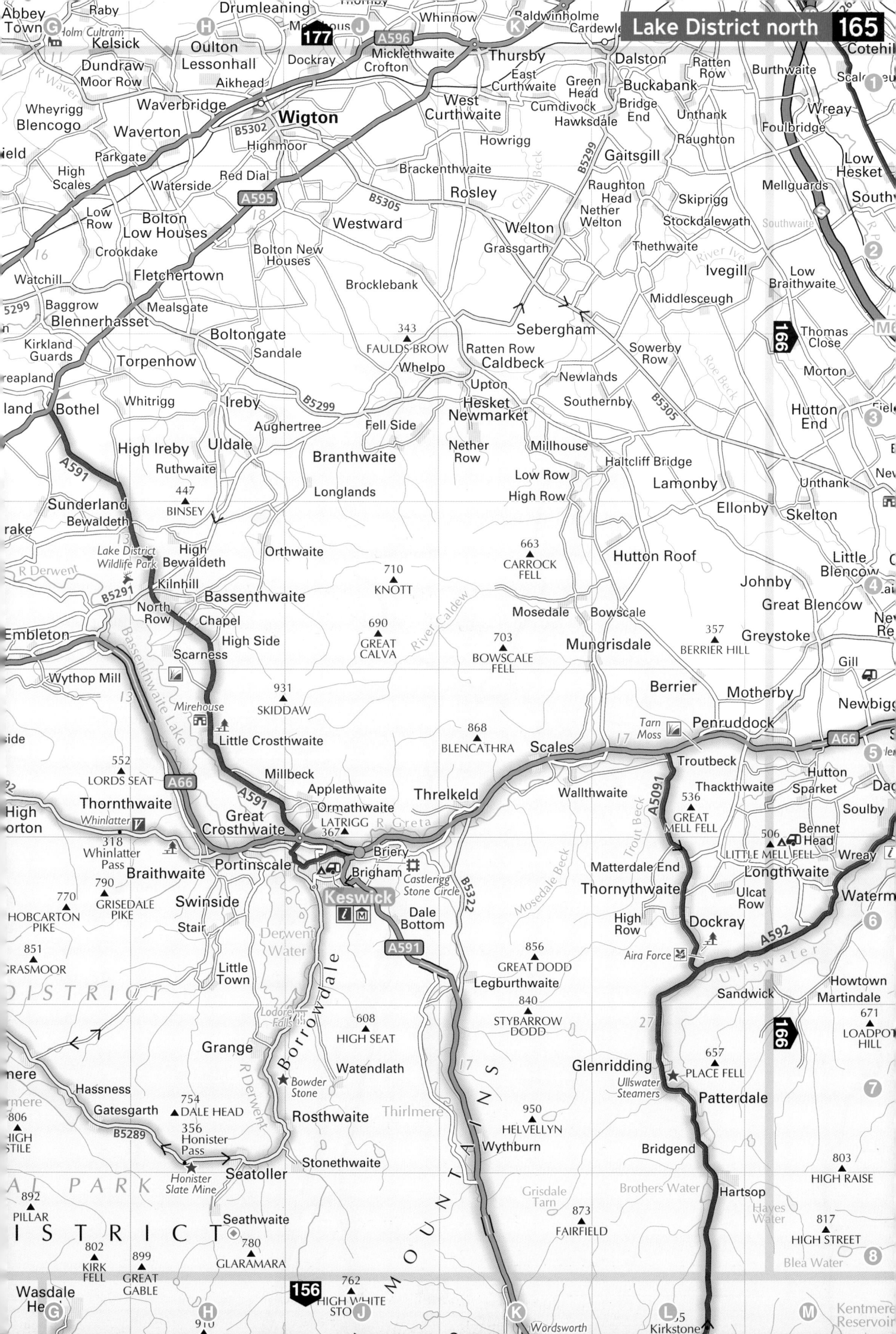

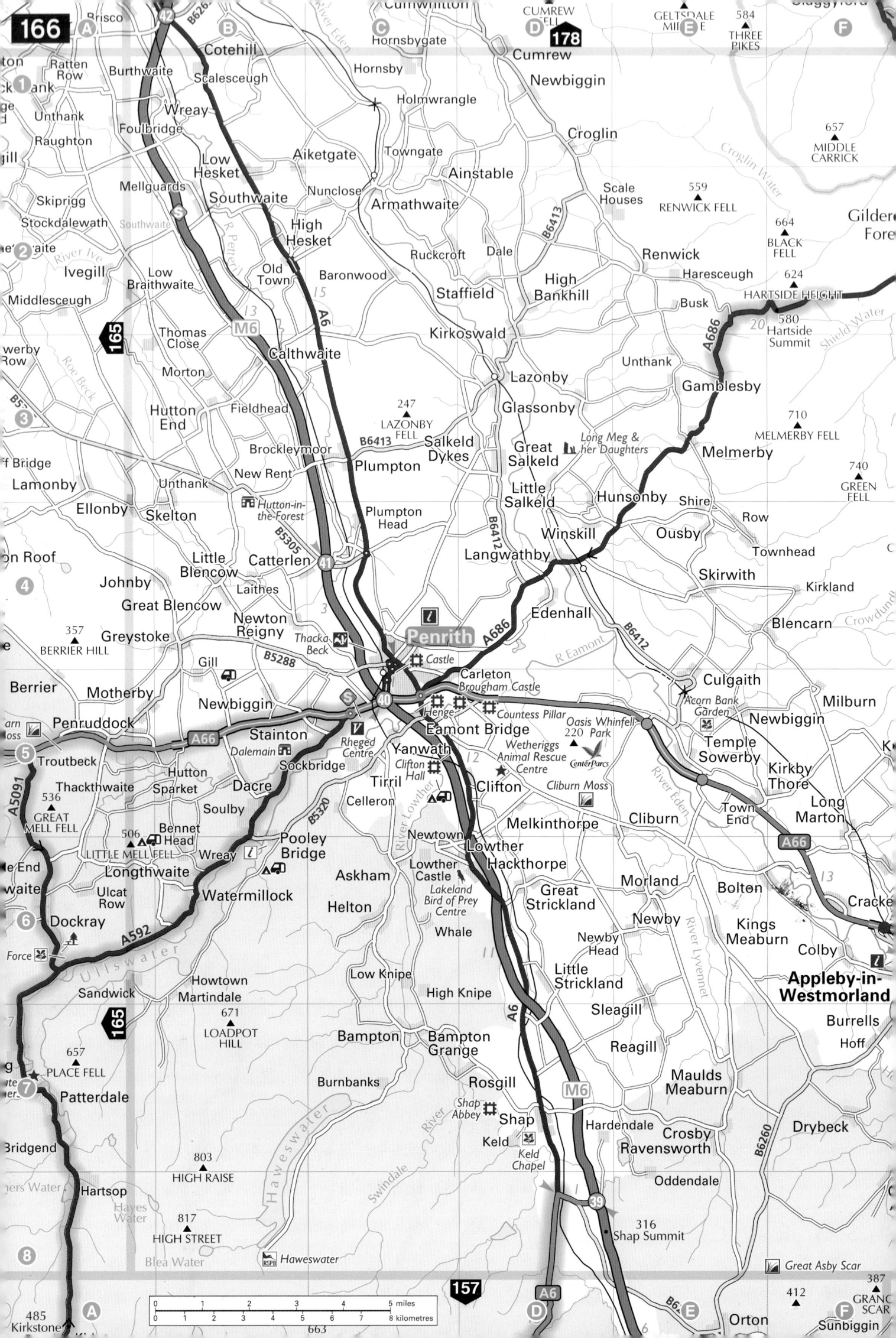

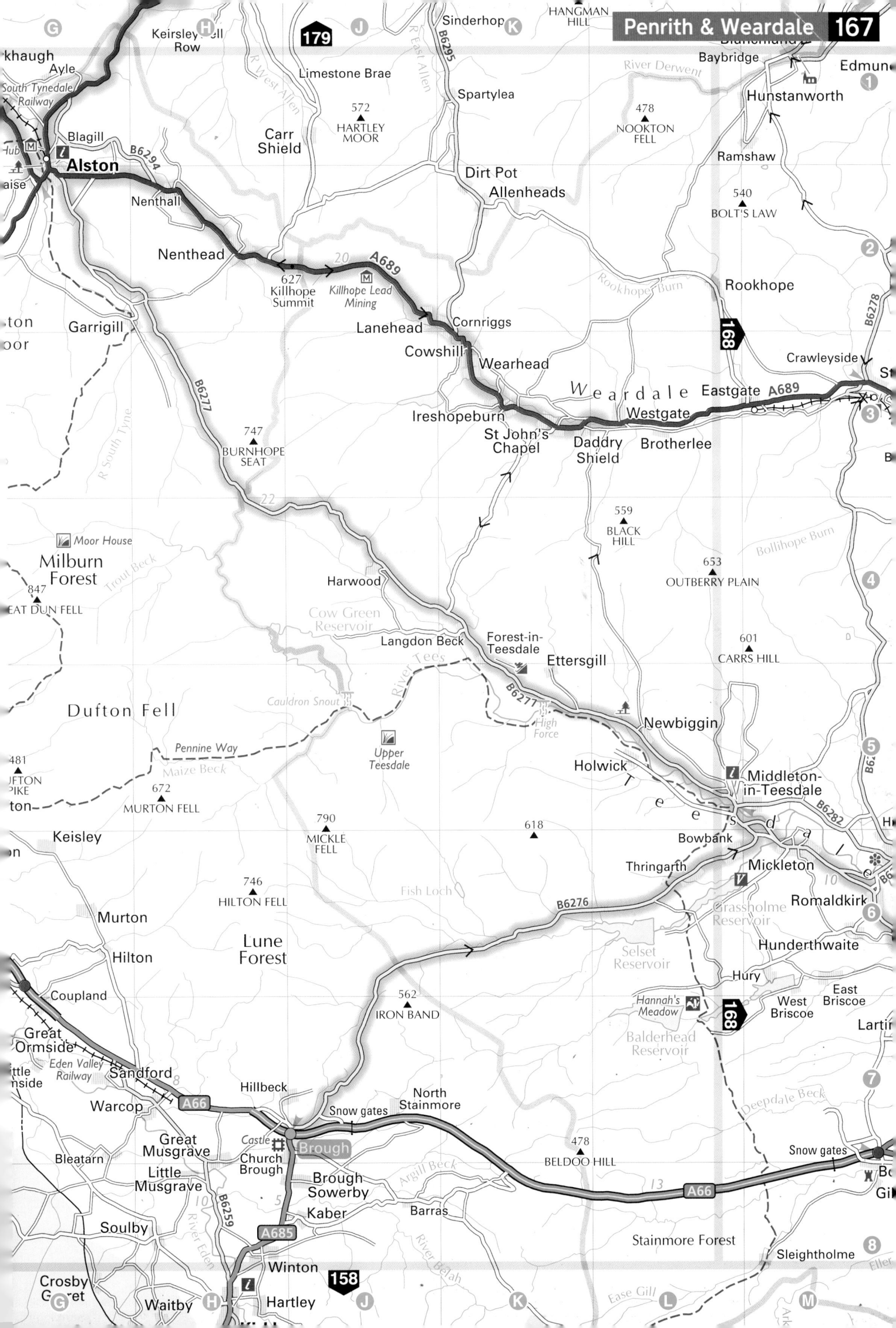

G
khaugh
Ayle
South Tynedale Railway
aise
M
Hub
Blagill
Alston
B6294
Nenthall
Nenthead

Keirsley Bell Row
H
Limestone Brae
179
J
Carr Shield
572
HARTLEY MOOR

B6295
R East Allen
Sinderhop
K
HANGMAN HILL
Blanchland
Baybridge
River Derwent
Edmun
1
Hunstanworth
478
NOOKTON FELL
Ramshaw
540
BOLT'S LAW
2

Spartylea
Dirt Pot
Allenheads

20
A689
627
Killhope Summit
Killhope Lead Mining
M
Lanehead
Cowshill
Cornriggs
Wearhead
Weardale
Eastgate A689
Rookhope Burn
B6278
168
Crawleyside
S
3

Garrigill
B6277

BURNHOPE SEAT
747
Ireshopeburn
St John's Chapel
Westgate
Daddry Shield
Brotherlee
B

22

Moor House
Milburn Forest
847
EAT DUN FELL
R South Tyne
Trout Beck
Harwood
Cow Green Reservoir
Langdon Beck
Forest-in-Teesdale
Ettersgill
B6277
559
BLACK HILL
653
OUTBERRY PLAIN
Bollihope Burn
4
601
CARRS HILL

Dufton Fell
Cauldron Snout
River Tees
High Force
Newbiggin
5
B6

Pennine Way
481
UFTON PIKE
ton
Maize Beck
672
MURTON FELL
Upper Teesdale
Holwick
T
e
e
s
d
a
l
e
Middleton-in-Teesdale
B6282
H

Keisley
on
Murton
Hilton
790
MICKLE FELL
746
HILTON FELL
Fish Loch
618
Bowbank
Thringarth
Mickleton
Romaldkirk
6
V
10

Lune Forest
B6276
Grassholme Reservoir
Hunderthwaite
Hury
West Briscoe
East Briscoe
Lartin
7

Coupland
562
IRON BAND
Selset Reservoir
Hannah's Meadow
168
Balderhead Reservoir
Deepdale Beck

Great Ormside
Eden Valley Railway
Sandford
8
Warcop
A66
Hillbeck
North Stainmore
Snow gates
Argill Beck
478
BELDOO HILL
Snow gates
A66
13
Bo
Gi

Bleatarn
Great Musgrave
Little Musgrave
Castle
Church Brough
Brough
Brough Sowerby
Kaber
Barras
Stainmore Forest
Sleightholme

Soulby
B6259
River Eden
A685
5
River Belah
Ease Gill

Crosby Garret
G
Waitby
H
Winton
Hartley
158
J
K
L
River
M
8

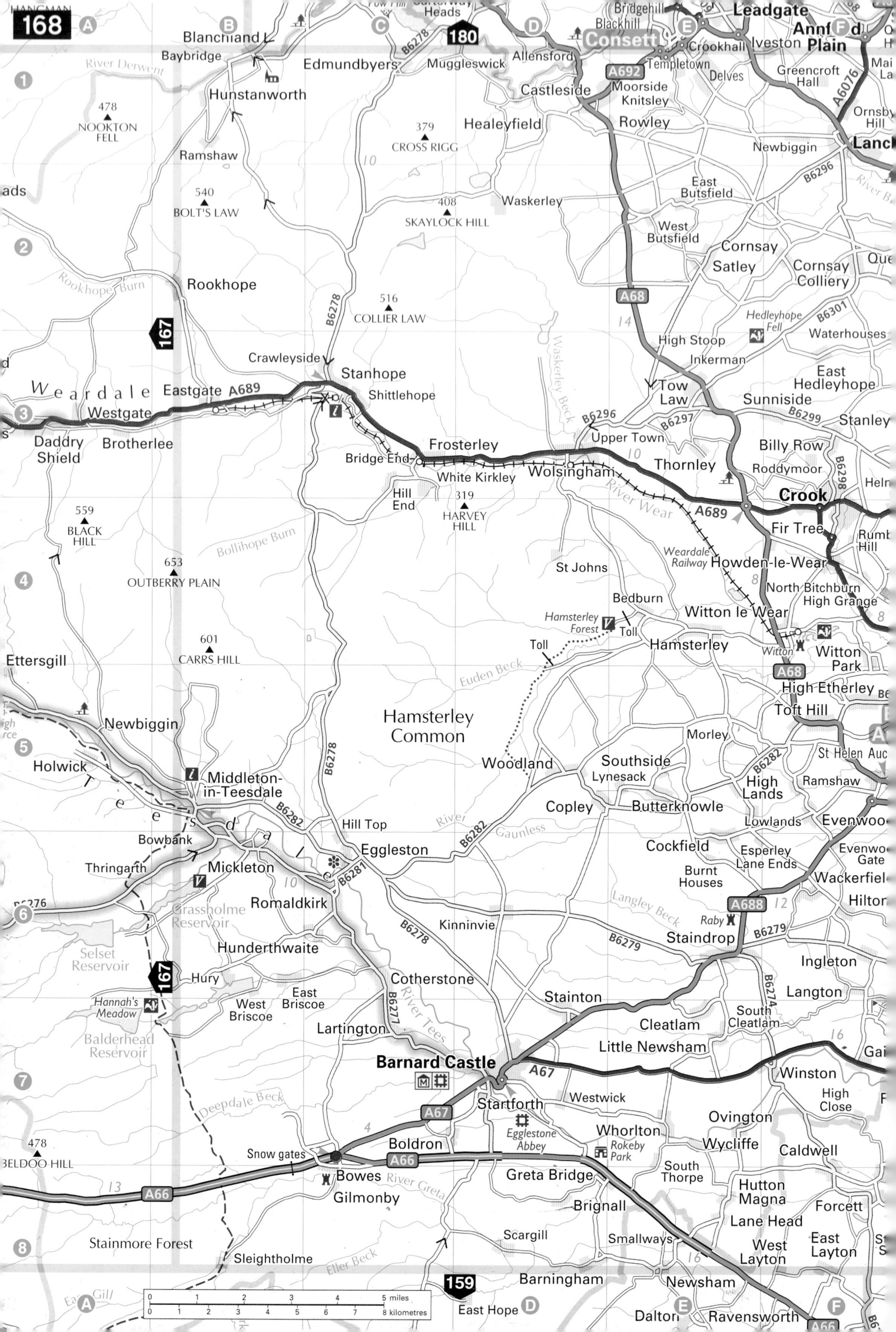

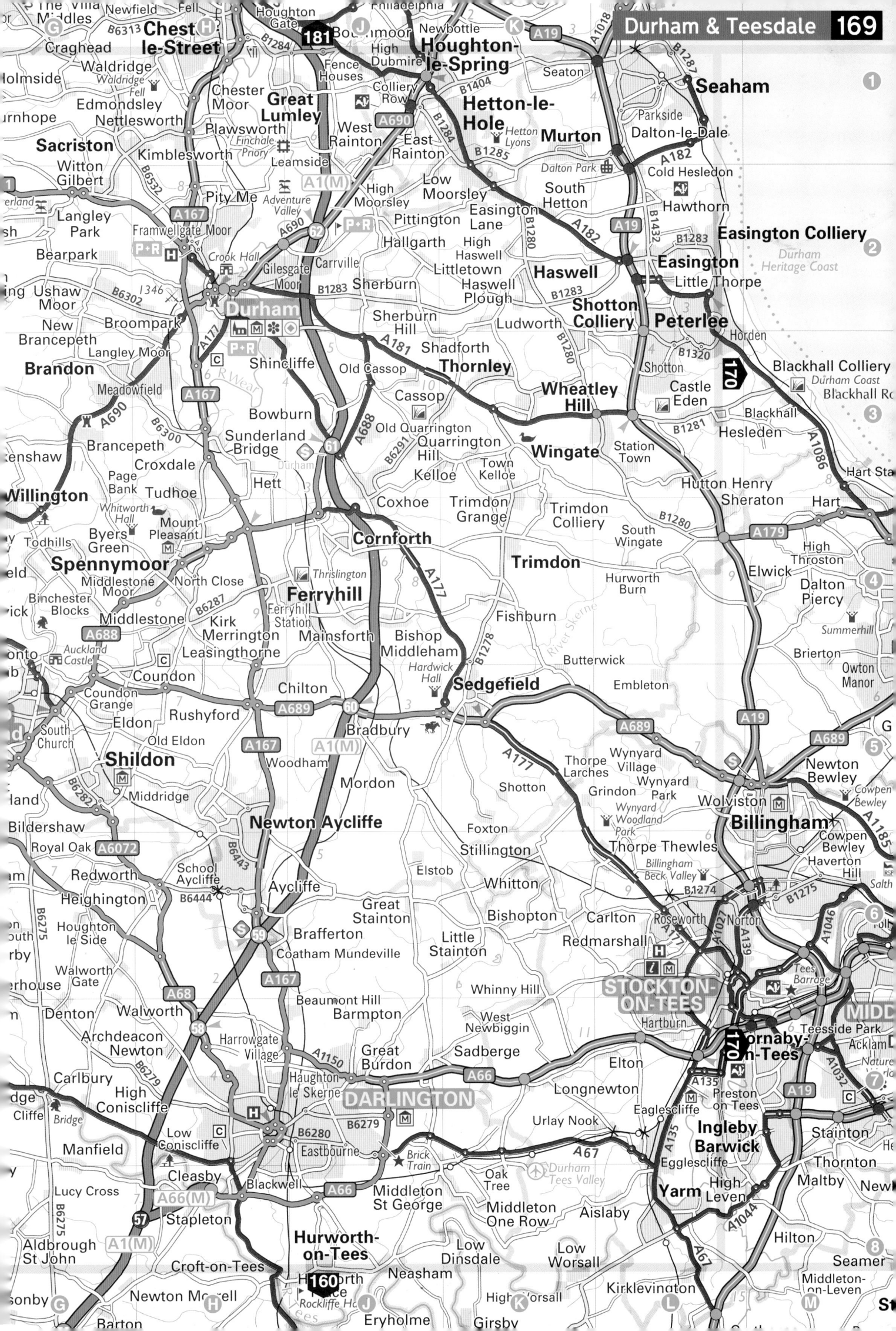

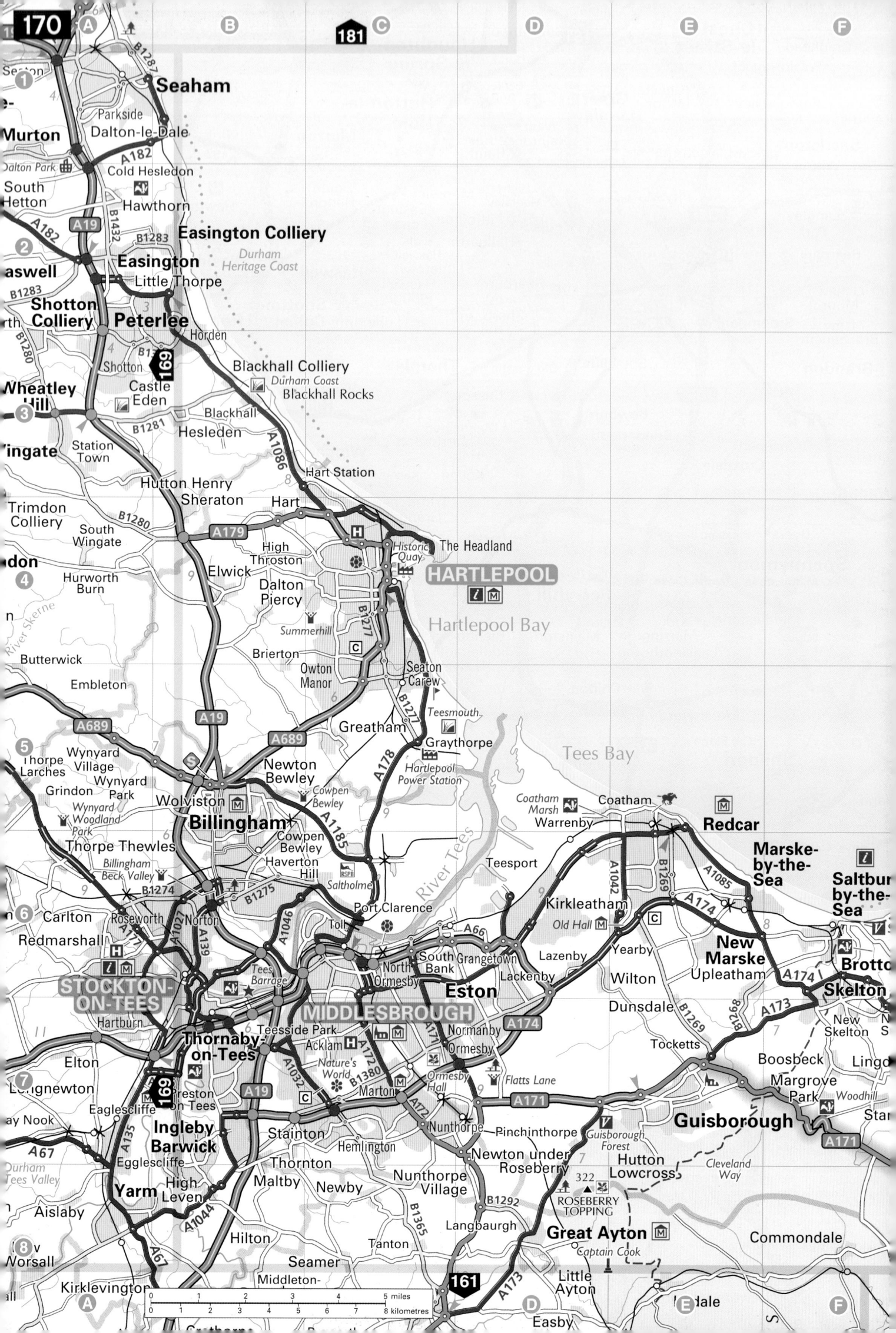

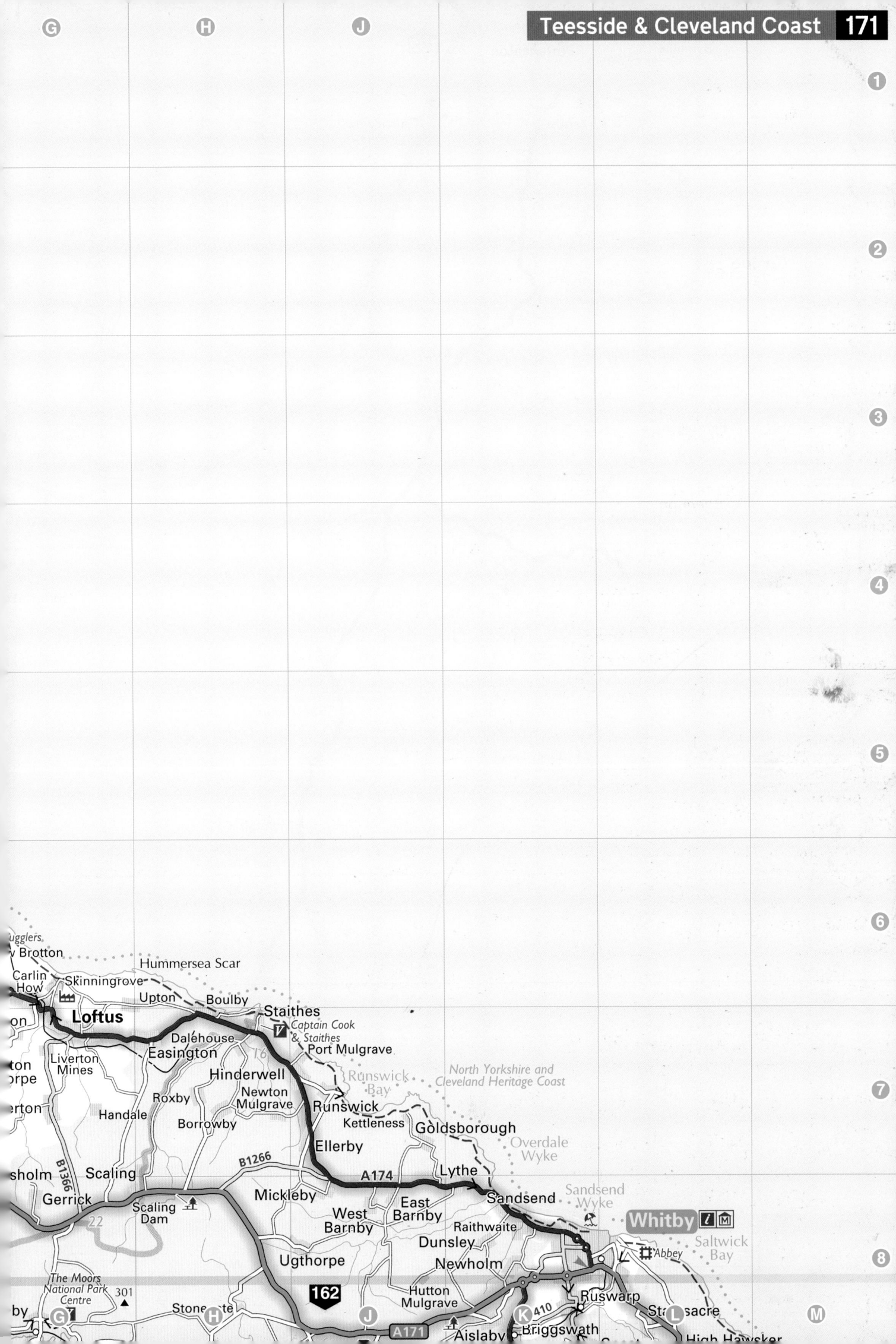

G   H   J

1

2

3

4

5

6

ugglers
y Brotton
Carlin   Hummersea Scar
How   Skinningrove
                Upton   Boulby
Loftus   Staithes
on   *Captain Cook*
                Dalehouse   *& Staithes*
                Easington   Port Mulgrave
Liverton   North Yorkshire and
Mines   Cleveland Heritage Coast
ton   Hinderwell   Runswick
rpe   Newton   Bay
        Roxby   Mulgrave
rton   Runswick
        Handale   Kettleness   Goldsborough
Borrowby   Overdale
                                Ellerby   Wyke
sholm   B1266   A174   Lythe
        Scaling   Sandsend
B1366   Wyke
Gerrick   Mickleby   Sandsend
        Scaling   East   **Whitby** ℹ 🏛
22   Dam   West   Barnby
                Barnby   Raithwaite   Saltwick
                        Dunsley   *Abbey*   Bay
                Ugthorpe   Newholm
The Moors
National Park   301   Ruswarp
Centre   **162**   Hutton   St sacre
by   Mulgrave
G   7   H   te   J   A171   K 410   L   High Hawsker
                        Aislaby Briggswath   M

7

8

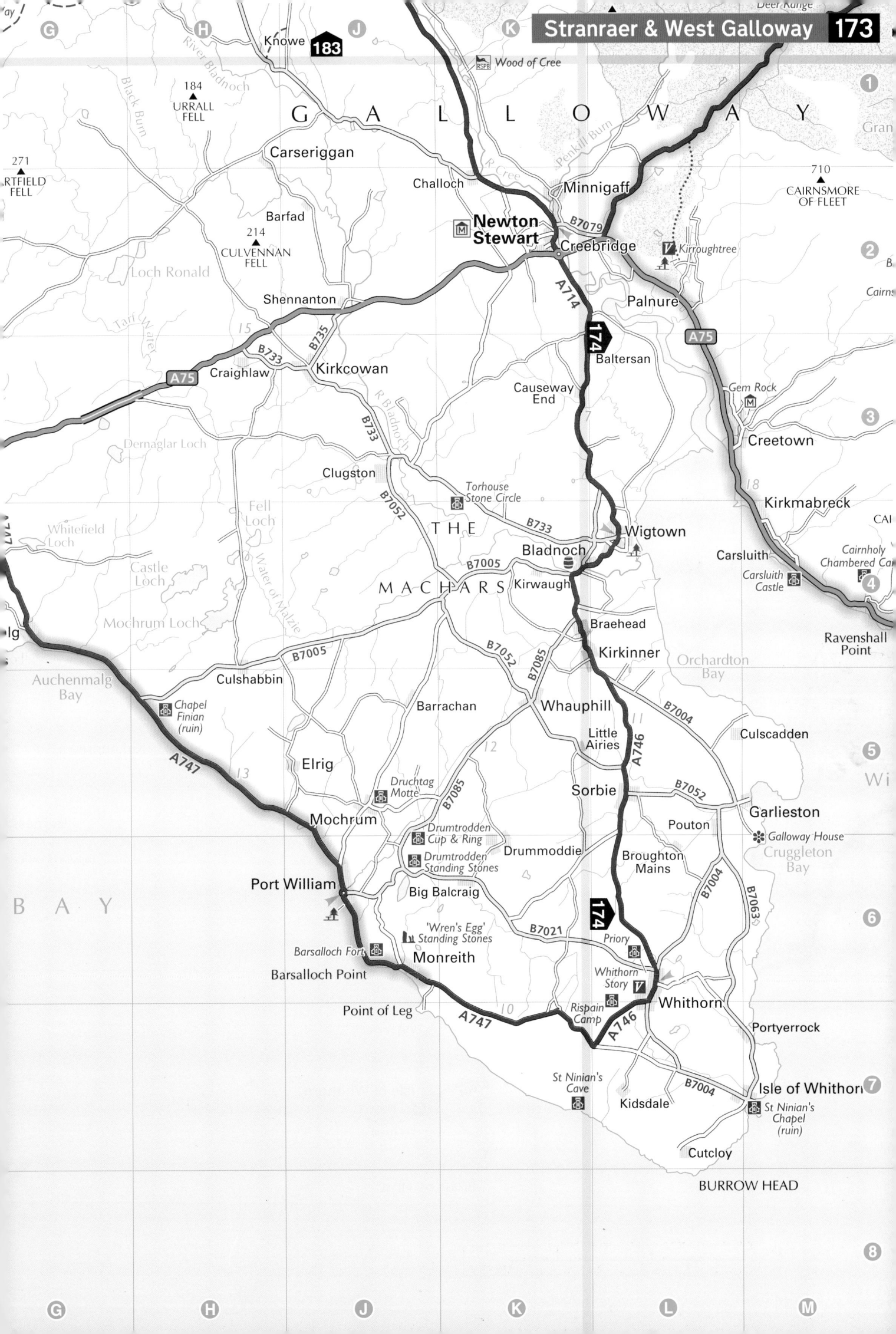

G   H   J   183

Knowe

River Bladnoch

184
URRALL
FELL

271
RTFIELD
FELL

Black Burn

G A L L O W A Y

Carseriggan

Challoch

Wood of Cree
RSPB

Minnigaff

CAIRNSMORE
OF FLEET
710

Gran

Cairns

Barfad

214
CULVENNAN
FELL

Loch Ronald

Shennanton

Tarf Water

15

B735

A75

B733

Craighlaw

Kirkcowan

R Cree

B7079

**Newton
Stewart**

Creebridge

Kirroughtree

Palnure

A714

A75

174

Baltersan

Causeway
End

Gem Rock

Creetown

Kirkmabreck

18

CAI

Dernaglar Loch

Whitefield
Loch

Castle
Loch

Fell
Loch

Water or Malzie

Mochrum Loch

Clugston

R Bladnoch

B7052

Torhouse
Stone Circle

B733

T H E

B7005

Bladnoch

Kirwaugh

M A C H A R S

Wigtown

Carsluith

Cairnholy
Chambered Ca

Carsluith
Castle

Ravenshall
Point

Braehead

Kirkinner

Orchardton
Bay

Ig

A747

Auchenmalg
Bay

Culshabbin

B7005

Barrachan

B7052

B7085

Whauphill

Little
Airies

B7004

A746

Culscadden

5

Wi

Chapel
Finian
(ruin)

13

Elrig

Druchtag
Motte

B7085

Sorbie

B7052

Garlieston

Galloway House

Cruggleton
Bay

Mochrum

Drumtrodden
Cup & Ring

Drummoddie

Pouton

Drumtrodden
Standing Stones

Broughton
Mains

B7004

B7063

B A Y

Port William

Big Balcraig

B7021

174

Priory

'Wren's Egg'
Standing Stones

Barsalloch Fort

Monreith

Barsalloch Point

Point of Leg

A747

10

Rispain
Camp

St Ninian's
Cave

Whithorn
Story

A746

Whithorn

Portyerrock

Isle of Whithorn

Kidsdale

B7004

St Ninian's
Chapel
(ruin)

Cutcloy

BURROW HEAD

G   H   J   K   L   M

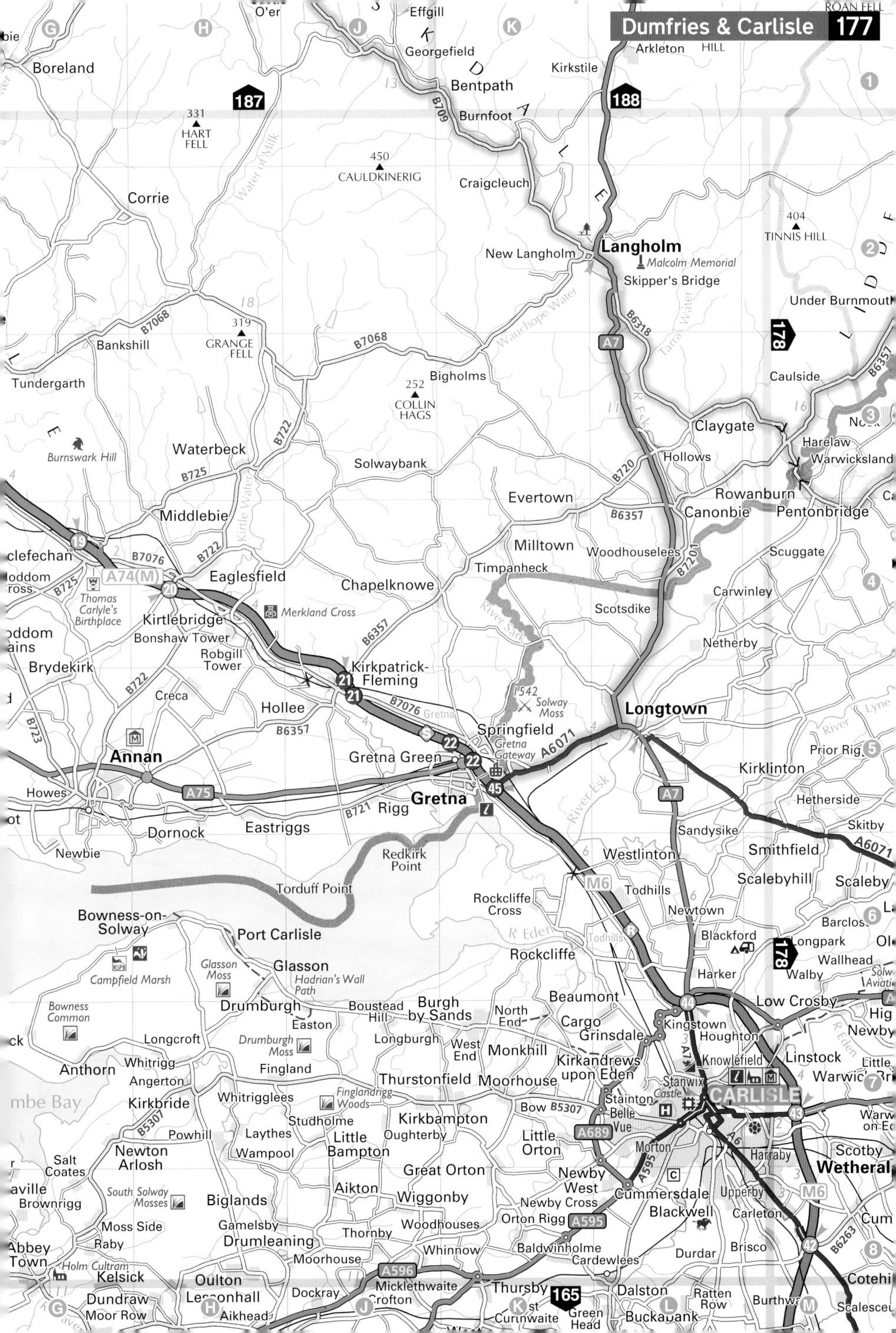

G   H   J   K

1

O'er
Effgill
Georgefield
Kirkstile
Arkleton   ROAN FELL
HILL
187
Bentpath
Burnfoot   B709
188
331
HART
FELL
450
CAULDKINERIG
Craigcleuch
TINNIS HILL   404
New Langholm
Langholm
Malcolm Memorial
Skipper's Bridge   Under Burnmouth
2
Corrie
Bankshill   B7068
319
GRANGE
FELL
B7068
Bigholms   A7   B6318   Caulside
B6357
Tundergarth
252
COLLIN
HAGS
Claygate   3
Burnswark Hill
Waterbeck   B722   Solwaybank   Harelaw
Warwicksland
Evertown   B720   Rowanburn
Hollows   Canonbie   Pentonbridge   4
Middlebie   B725   B6357
19   B7076   Eaglesfield   Chapelknowe   Milltown   Woodhouselees   Scuggate
clefechan   2   B722   Merkland Cross   Timpanheck   Carwinley
addom   20   Thomas Carlyle's   Scotsdike   Netherby
ross   B725   Birthplace   Kirtlebridge   B6357
addom   Bonshaw Tower   1542   Prior Rig   5
ains   Robgill   Kirkpatrick-   Solway   Longtown   Kirklinton
Brydekirk   B722   Tower   21   Fleming   Moss   Hetherside
Creca   21   B7076   Gretna   A6071   A7   Skitby
B723   Hollee   B6357   Springfield   Sandysike   A6071
Annan   22   Gretna   Smithfield
Howes   A75   Gretna Green   22   Gateway   Scalebyhill   Scaleby
45   Westlinton
Dornock   Eastriggs   B721   Rigg   **Gretna**   Todhills   Newtown   6
Newbie   Redkirk   M6   Blackford   Longpark
Point   Rockcliffe   178   Wallhead
Torduff Point   Cross   Todhills   Harker   Walby
Bowness-on-   R Eden   Rockcliffe   44   Low Crosby
Solway   Port Carlisle   Beaumont   Kingstown   Hig
RSPB   Glasson   Hadrian's Wall   Cargo   Houghton   Newby
Campfield Marsh   Moss   Path   Grinsdale   Knowlefield   Linstock
Bowness   Drumburgh   Boustead   Burgh   North   Kirkandrews   7
Common   Hill   by Sands   End   upon Eden   Warwic
Longcroft   Drumburgh   Longburgh   West   Monkhill   Stanwix   on Ed
Anthorn   Moss   End   Moorhouse   Castle   CARLISLE   43   Warw
Whitrigg   Fingland   Thurstonfield   H   Stainton   on Ed
Kirkbride   Angerton   Whitrigglees   Finglandrigg   Bow   B5307   Belle   A6   Harraby   Wetheral
Woods   Kirkbampton   Vue   Morton   Upperby   M6
Newton   Studholme   Little   Oughterby   A689   Carleton
Arlosh   B5307   Bampton   Great Orton   Newby   C   Cummersdale   Scotby
Salt   Powhill   Laythes   Wiggonby   West   Blackwell   Cum
aville   Coates   Wampool   Woodhouses   Newby Cross   A595   Carleton   42   B6263
Brownrigg   South Solway   Biglands   Aikton   Orton Rigg   Baldwinholme   Durdar   Brisco   Cotehi
Mosses   Moss Side   Gamelsby   Thornby   Whinnow   Cardewlees   Dalston   8
Raby   Drumleaning   Moorhouse   A596   Micklethwaite   Ratten   Scalescei
Abbey   A596   Dockray   Crofton   Thursby   165   Green   Buckabank   Burthwa
Town   Kelsick   Oulton   st   Head   Cum
Holm Cultram   Dundraw   Lessonhall   Aikhead   Curthwaite
Moor Row   G   H   J   K   L   M

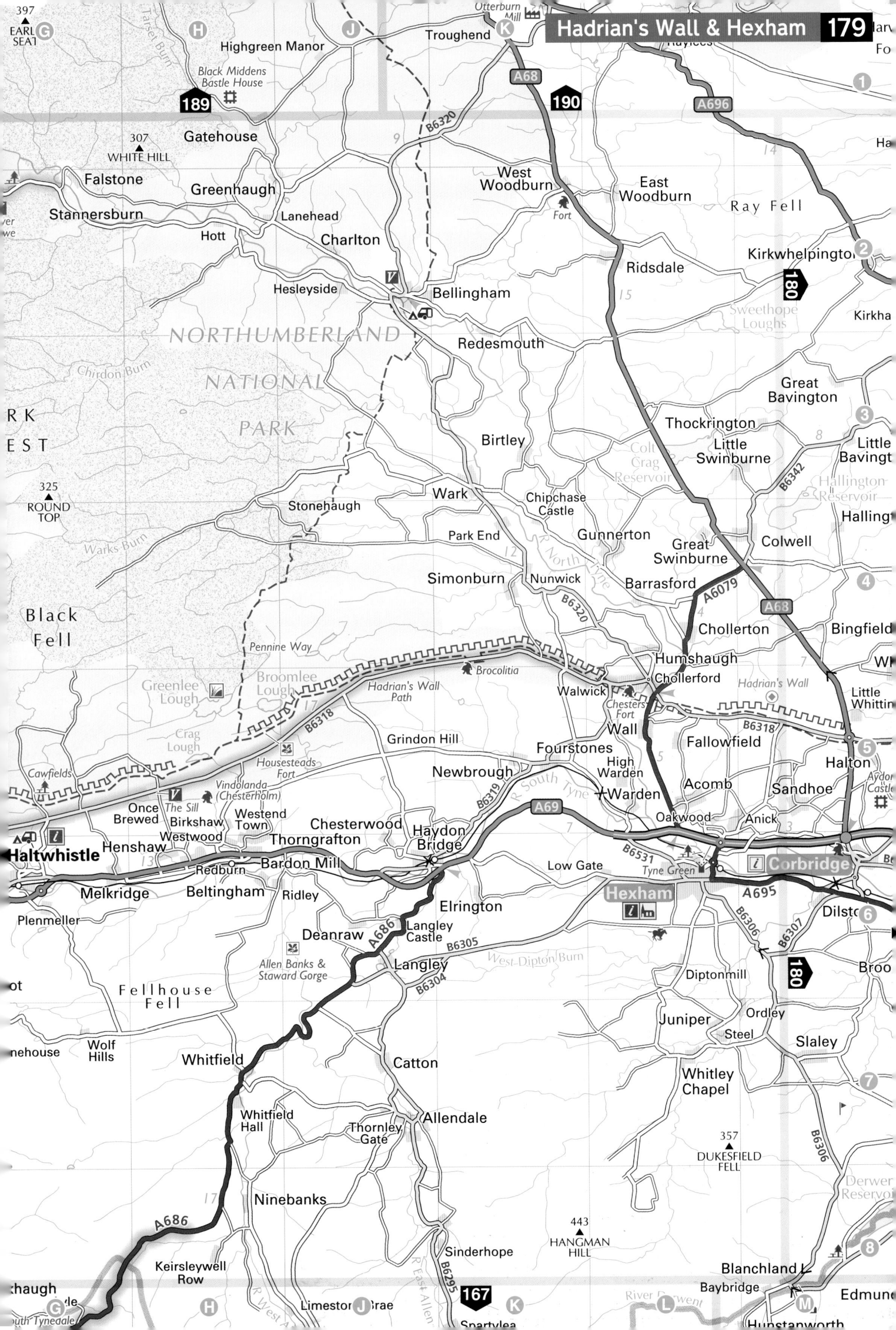

A B C D E F

1

2

Maide
B
Mai

Turnberry
Turnberry
Turnberry
Bay

A77

Ailsa
Craig

3

340 ▲

RSPB

Girvan

Dounepa

Woodland

Pinmi

4

297 ▲
GREY
HILL

Pinmore

8

13

Lendalfoot

5

A77

Bennane Head

Colmonell *9* B734

River Stincha

B734

B734

6

Ballantrae

Heronsford

Water of Tig

Belfast

Currarie
Port

437 ▲
BENERAIRD

7

321 ▲
CARLOCK HILL

Larne

387 ▲
ALTIMEG HILL

Milleur
Point

Glen App

Corsewall Point

*Lady
Bay*

8

Barnhills   **Portencalzie**

Glenwhilly

*Lagga
Standing*

A B C D E F

| 0 | 1 | 2 | 3 | 4 | 5 miles |
| 0 | 1 | 2 | 3 | 4 | 5 | 6 | 7 | 8 kilometres |

172

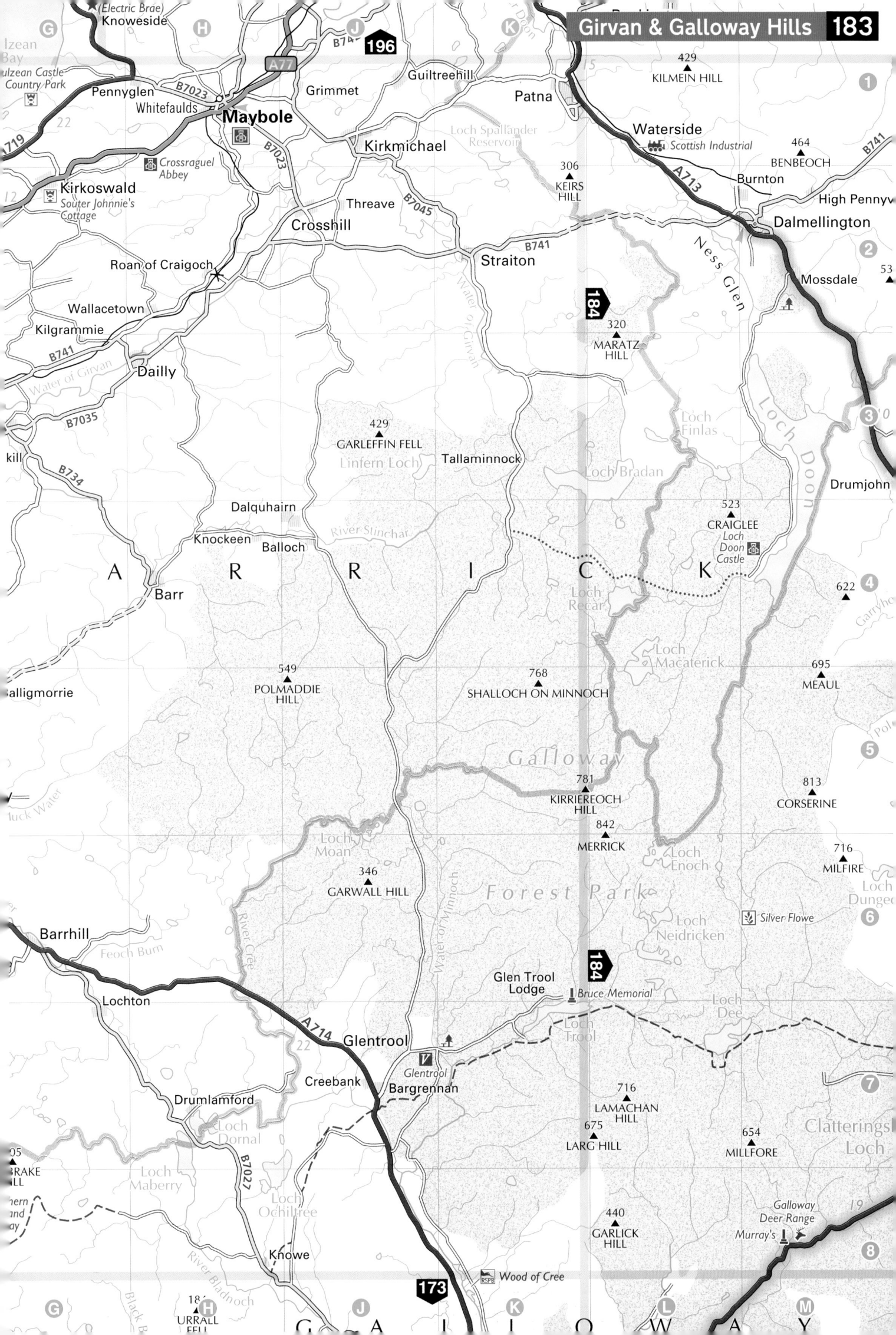

(Electric Brae)
Knoweside
Knoweside
G
H
J
196
K
Izean
Bay
B7023
A77
Guiltreehill
Patna
429
KILMEIN HILL
1
ulzean Castle
Country Park
Pennyglen
B7023
Grimmet
Waterside
Scottish Industrial
464
BENBEOCH
B741
Whitefaulds
Maybole
B7023
Kirkmichael
306
KEIRS
HILL
Burnton
High Pennyv
A719
22
Crossraguel
Abbey
Loch Spallander
Reservoir
A713
Dalmellington
Kirkoswald
Souter Johnnie's
Cottage
B7045
Threave
B741
184
Ness Glen
Mossdale
53
12
Crosshill
Straiton
320
MARATZ
HILL
2
Roan of Craigoch
Wallacetown
Water of Girvan
Loch Finlas
Loch Doon
Drumjohn
Kilgrammie
B741
Loch Bradan
523
CRAIGLEE
Loch
Doon
Castle
3
Dailly
Water of Girvan
429
GARLEFFIN FELL
Linfern Loch
Tallaminnock
Loch Recar
B7035
Dalquhairn
River Stinchar
A
R
R
I
C
K
622
4
kill
B734
Knockeen
Balloch
Loch
Macaterick
Barr
695
MEAUL
alligmorrie
549
POLMADDIE
HILL
768
SHALLOCH ON MINNOCH
5
Galloway
813
CORSERINE
781
KIRRIEREOCH
HILL
Luck Water
Loch
Moan
842
MERRICK
Loch
Enoch
716
MILFIRE
Loch
Dunge
Barrhill
346
GARWALL HILL
Forest Park
Loch
Neidricken
Silver Flowe
6
Feoch Burn
River Cree
Water of Minnoch
184
Loch
Dee
7
Lochton
A714
Glen Trool
Lodge
Bruce Memorial
Loch
Trool
Glentrool
716
LAMACHAN
HILL
Clatterings
Loch
Creebank
Bargrennan
Drumlamford
Glentrool
675
LARG HILL
654
MILLFORE
Loch
Dornal
Loch
Maberry
B7027
440
GARLICK
HILL
Galloway
Deer Range
Murray's
RAKE
LL
Loch
Ochiltree
Knowe
River Bladnoch
173
Wood of Cree
8
hern
and
y
18
URRALL
FELL
G
H
J
K
L
M
CRAI
LO
W
Y

Barr
A

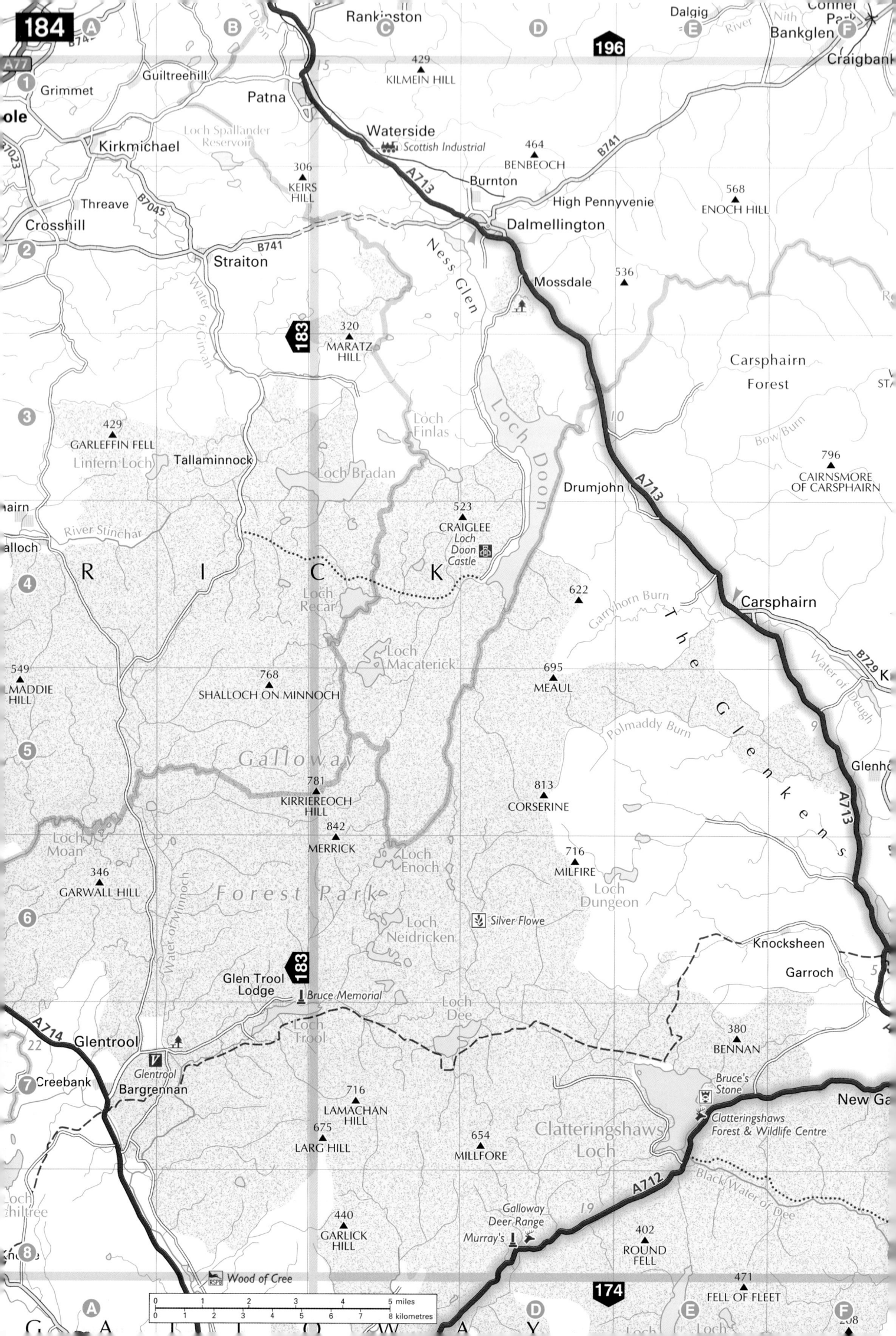

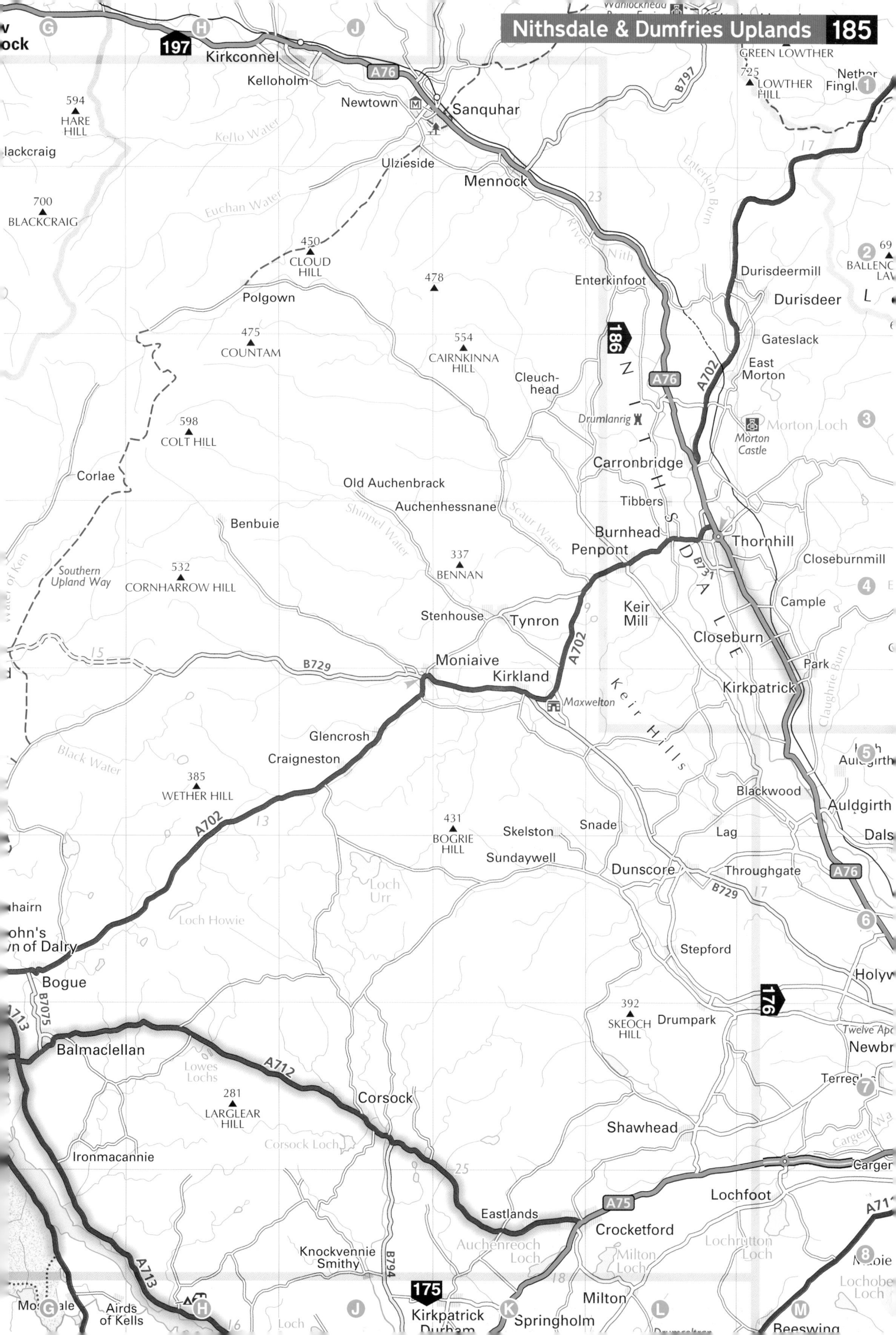

G   H   197   J   Kirkconnel
Kelloholm
Newtown
Sanquhar
Ulzieside
Mennock
A76

GREEN LOWTHER
725
LOWTHER HILL
Nether Fingl...   1

594
HARE HILL

lackcraig

700
BLACKCRAIG

BALLENC...
LAW   69   2

Durisdeermill
Durisdeer   L

450
CLOUD HILL
Polgown

478

Enterkinfoot

Gateslack
East Morton   3

475
COUNTAM

554
CAIRNKINNA HILL

Cleuch-head

186
A76

Drumlanrig

A702

Morton Loch
Morton Castle

598
COLT HILL

Old Auchenbrack
Auchenhessnane

Carronbridge

Corlae

Benbuie

Tibbers

Burnhead
Penpont

Thornhill   4
B731
Closeburnmill

Southern Upland Way

532
CORNHARROW HILL

337
BENNAN

Stenhouse   Tynron

Keir Mill

Cample

Closeburn

Water of Ken

B729

Moniaive
Kirkland

A702

Maxwelton

Kirkpatrick
Park

5
Auldgirth

Black Water

Glencrosh
Craigneston

385
WETHER HILL

A702   13

Keir Hills

Blackwood

Auldgirth
Dals

hairn

431
BOGRIE HILL

Skelston

Snade

Lag

A76

ohn's
n of Dalry

Loch Urr

Sundaywell

Dunscore
Throughgate

B729   17

6

Bogue
B7075

Stepford

Holyw

A713

392
SKEOCH HILL

Drumpark

176

Twelve Ap...
Newbr...   7

Balmaclellan

Lowes Lochs

A712

Corsock

Shawhead

Terre...

281
LARGLEAR HILL

Ironmacannie

Corsock Loch

25

A75

Lochfoot

Garger

A71...

Mo...   G   H

Airds of Kells

A713

Knockvennie Smithy

B794

175   J

Eastlands

Crocketford

A75   K   Springholm

Milton

18

L

Auchenreoch Loch

Lochrutton Loch

Milton Loch

M   Beeswing

Kirkpatrick Durham

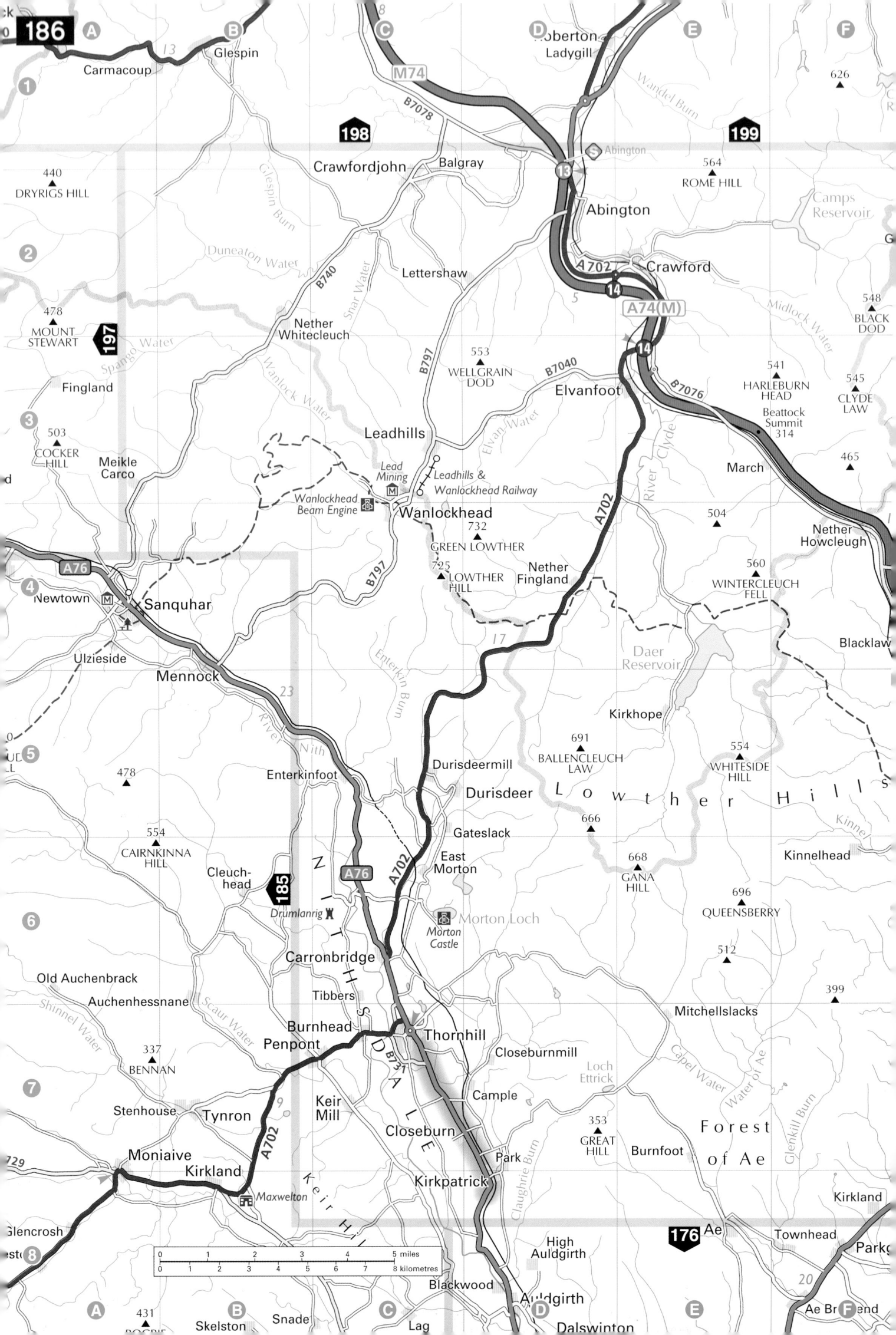

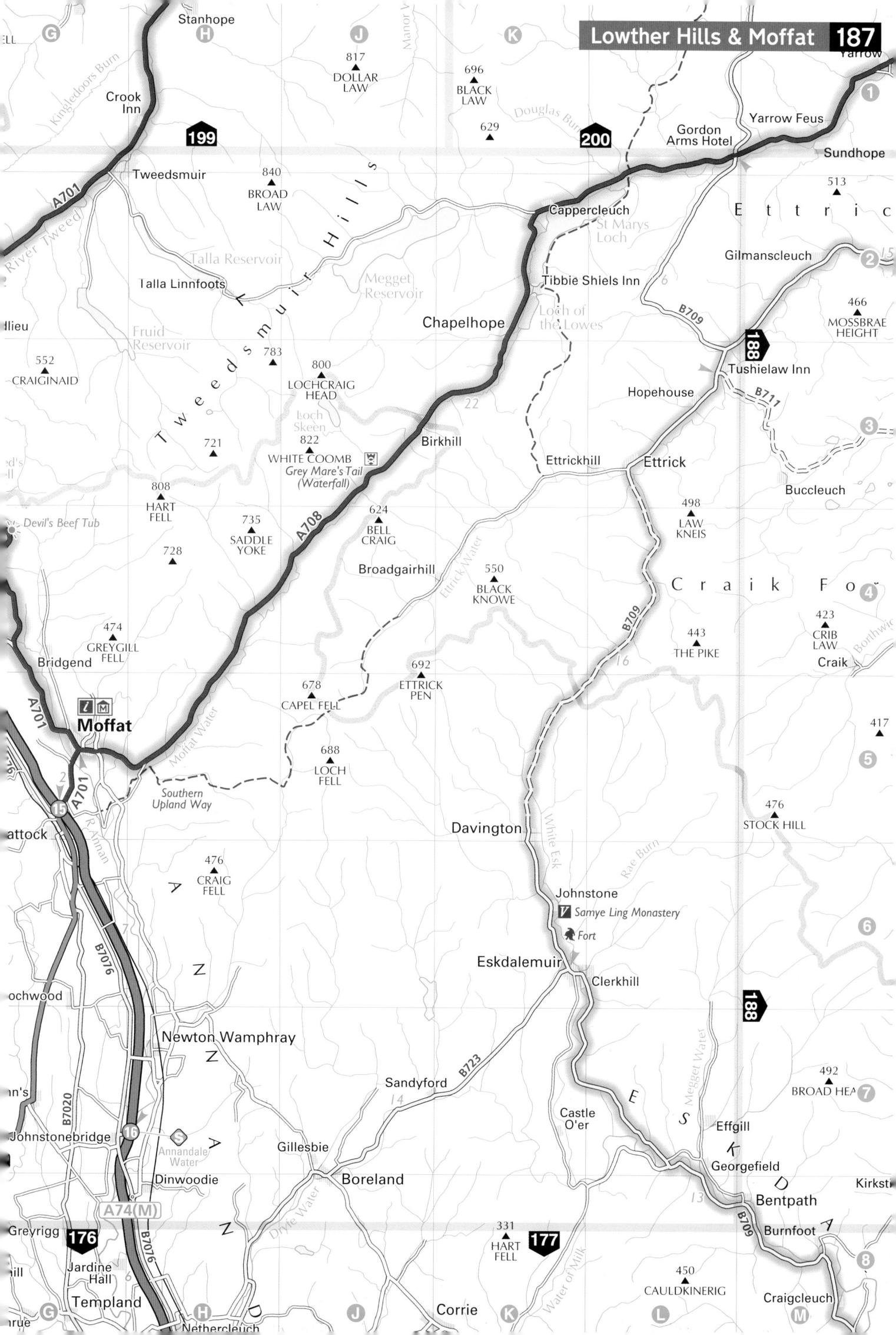

Stanhope

G

H

J

K

817
DOLLAR
LAW

696
BLACK
LAW

Yarrow

1

Crook
Inn

199

629

200

Gordon
Arms Hotel

Yarrow Feus

Sundhope

A701

Tweedsmuir

840
BROAD
LAW

Cappercleuch

Ettric

St Marys
Loch

513

River Tweed

Talla Reservoir

Talla Linnfoots

Tibbie Shiels Inn

Gilmanscleuch

2

Megget
Reservoir

Chapelhope

Loch of
the Lowes

B709

466
MOSSBRAE
HEIGHT

llieu

Fruid
Reservoir

552
CRAIGINAID

783

800
LOCHCRAIG
HEAD

188

Tushielaw Inn

Hopehouse

B711

3

d's

Loch
Skeen

721

822
WHITE COOMB
Grey Mare's Tail
(Waterfall)

Birkhill

Ettrickhill

Ettrick

Buccleuch

808
HART
FELL

735
SADDLE
YOKE

A708

624
BELL
CRAIG

Ettrick Water

498
LAW
KNEIS

Devil's Beef Tub

728

Broadgairhill

550
BLACK
KNOWE

Craik Fo

4

474
GREYGILL
FELL

B709

443
THE PIKE

423
CRIB
LAW

Craik

Bridgend

A701

692
ETTRICK
PEN

16

417

5

678
CAPEL FELL

Moffat

688
LOCH
FELL

476
STOCK HILL

attock

A701

15

Moffat Water

Southern
Upland Way

Davington

White Esk

Rae Burn

R Annan

476
CRAIG
FELL

Johnstone

Samye Ling Monastery

6

A

Fort

B7076

Eskdalemuir

Clerkhill

188

ochwood

Z

Newton Wamphray

Z

B723

492
BROAD HEA

7

B7020

Sandyford

14

E

S

Effgill

n's

Johnstonebridge

16

S

Gillesbie

Castle
O'er

Georgefield

Annandale
Water

Dinwoodie

Boreland

13

Bentpath

Kirkst

A74(M)

331

177

B7076

Burnfoot

B7076

Greyrigg

176

HART
FELL

Water of Milk

B709

8

Jardine
Hall

Templand

450
CAULDKINERIG

Craigcleuch

rue

Nethercleuch

G

H

J

Corrie

K

L

M

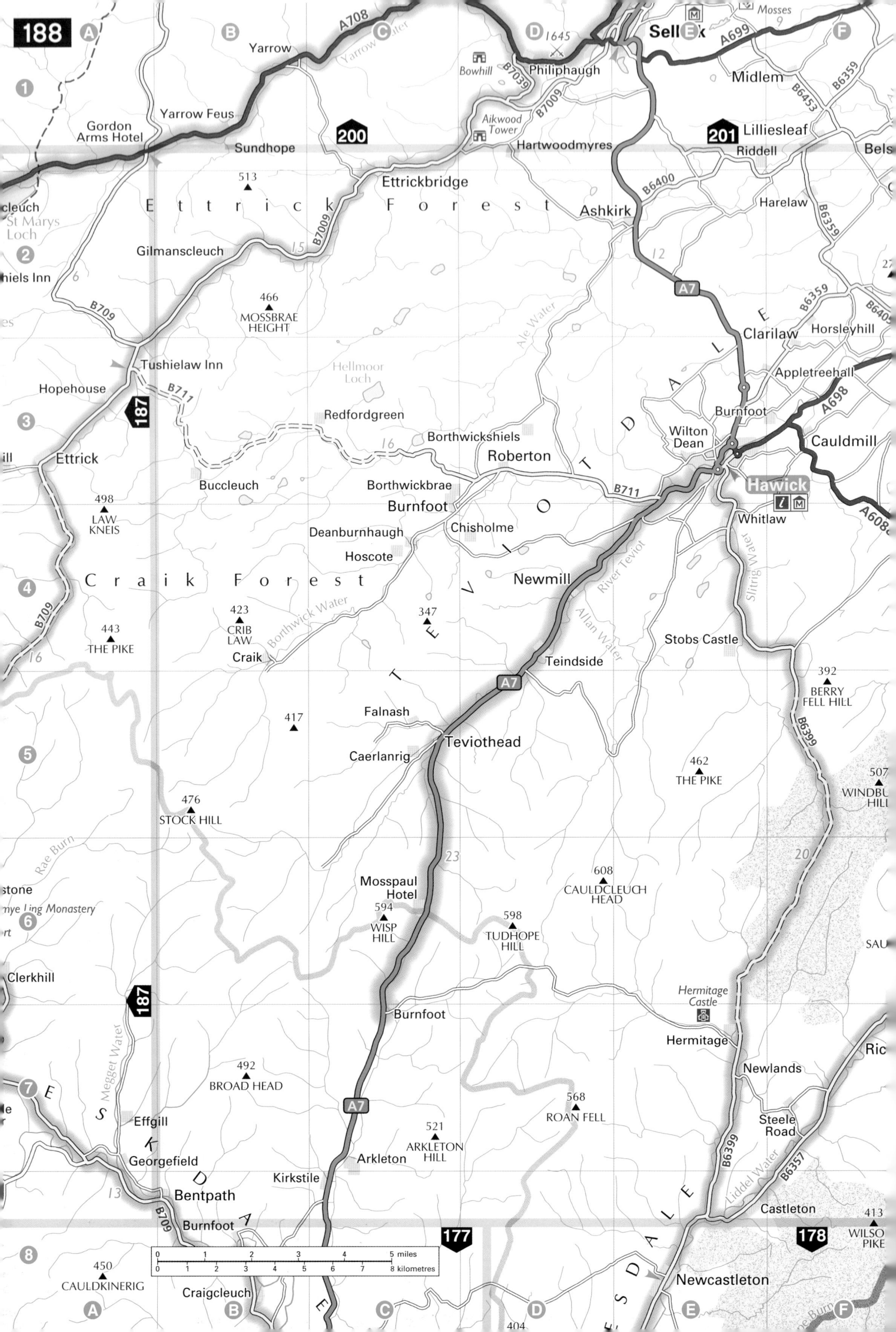

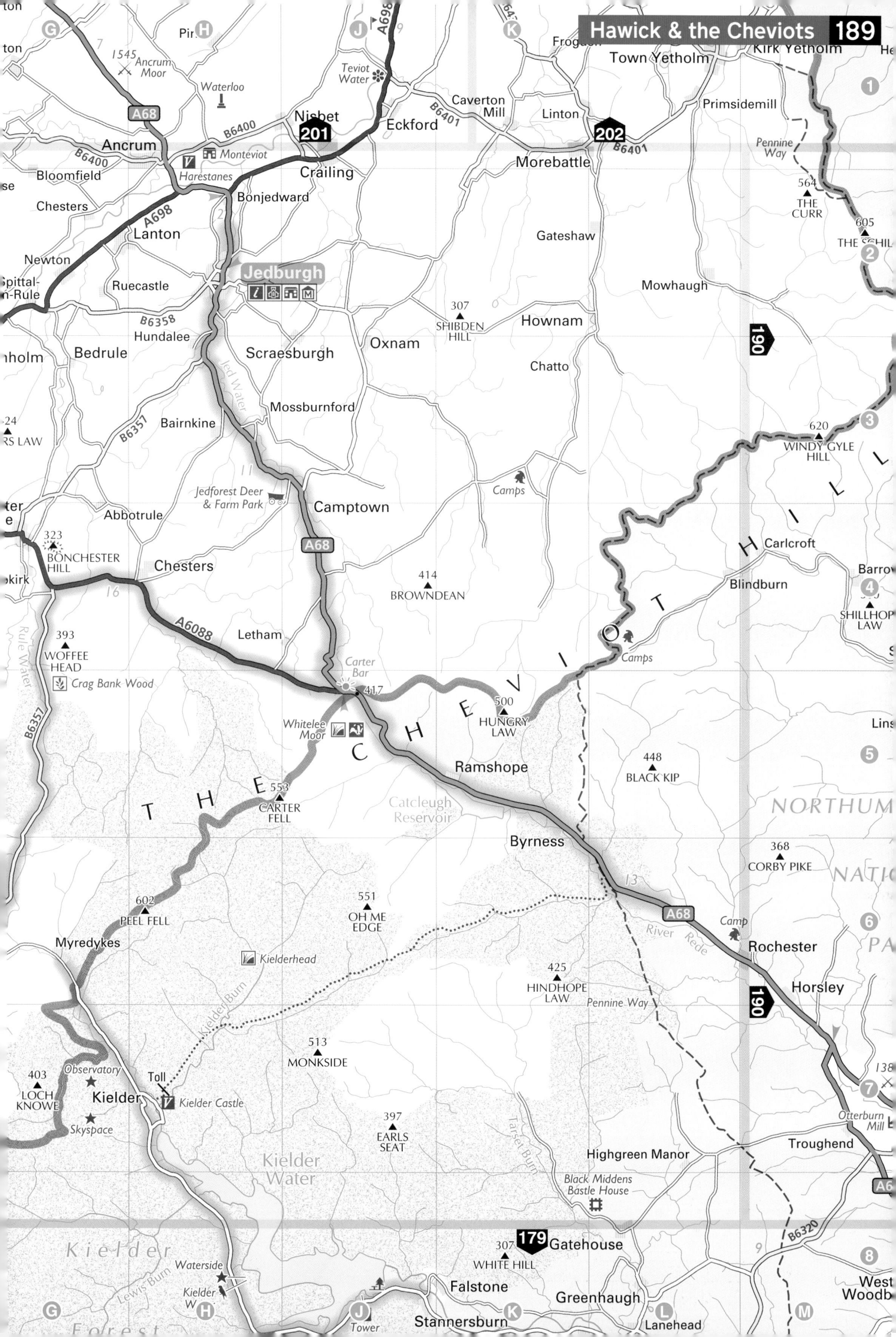

G
H
Pir
J
A698
K
Frogden
Kirk Yetholm
Town Yetholm
1545
Ancrum
Moor
Waterloo
Teviot
Water
Caverton
Mill
Linton
Primsidemill
1
A68
B6400
Nisbet
Eckford
B6401
201
202
Pennine
Way
Ancrum
Monteviot
Crailing
Morebattle
564
THE
CURR
Bloomfield
Harestanes
Bonjedward
Gateshaw
605
THE SCHIL
Chesters
A698
Lanton
Mowhaugh
2
Newton
B6358
Jedburgh
Hownam
Spittal-
on-Rule
Ruecastle
307
SHIBDEN
HILL
Bedrule
Hundalee
Scraesburgh
Oxnam
Chatto
holm
B6357
Bairnkine
Mossburnford
620
WINDY GYLE
HILL
3
ter
Jedforest Deer
& Farm Park
Camptown
Camps
Carlcroft
Abbotrule
Blindburn
Barro
323
BONCHESTER
HILL
Chesters
A68
414
BROWNDEAN
4
SHILLHOP
LAW
kirk
393
WOFFEE
HEAD
A6088
Letham
Camps
Rule Water
Crag Bank Wood
Carter
Bar
Whitelee
Moor
417
C
500
HUNGRY
LAW
Lins
B6357
THE
448
BLACK KIP
5
E
553
CARTER
FELL
Catcleugh
Reservoir
Ramshope
NORTHUM
602
PEEL FELL
551
OH ME
EDGE
Kielderhead
Byrness
368
CORBY PIKE
NATI
Myredykes
13
A68
River Rede
Camp
6
PA
425
HINDHOPE
LAW
Rochester
403
LOCH
KNOWE
Observatory
Toll
Kielder Burn
513
MONKSIDE
Pennine Way
190
Horsley
Skyspace
Kielder
Kielder Castle
397
EARLS
SEAT
Highgreen Manor
138
7
Otterburn
Mill
Troughend
Kielder
Water
Black Middens
Bastle House
A6
179
Gatehouse
B6320
9
Waterside
307
WHITE HILL
Falstone
West
Woodb
Kielder
W
Greenhaugh
G
H
J
Tower
K
Stannersburn
Lanehead
L
M
Forest

A B C **205** D E F

Muasdale

1

Glenacardoch Point

Belloch

Barr Water

Glenbarr

Clan MacAlister

454
BEINN AN TUIRC

Tor

Br

Cleongart

319

408
BORD MOR

Sadd

2

Bellochantuy Bay

Bellochantuy

194 N

Lussa Loch

396
SGREADAN HILL

Ugadale

Sadd

Tangy Loch

Glen Lussa

3

Kilkenzie

Peninver

Ardnac Bay

B842

A83

Kilmichael

Machrihanish Bay

Campbeltown

i

Campbeltown

4

Machrihanish

Drumlemble

B843

B842

6

V

Stewarton

Campbeltown Loch

Island Da

Kilkerran

Kildalloig

Earadale Point

385
THE STATE

352
BEINN GHUILEAN

Achinhoan

446
CNOC MOY

K

5

10

Conie Glen

Glen Kerran

Ru

Dalsmeran

Glen Breakevie

B842

6

Strone Glen

Cattadale

Polliwilline Bay

BEINN NA LICE

Macharioch

428

Carskey

Southend

MULL OF KINTYRE

Dunaverty

Sanda Sound

Sheep Island

Carskey Bay

7

Borgadalemore Point

Sanda Island

A B C D E F

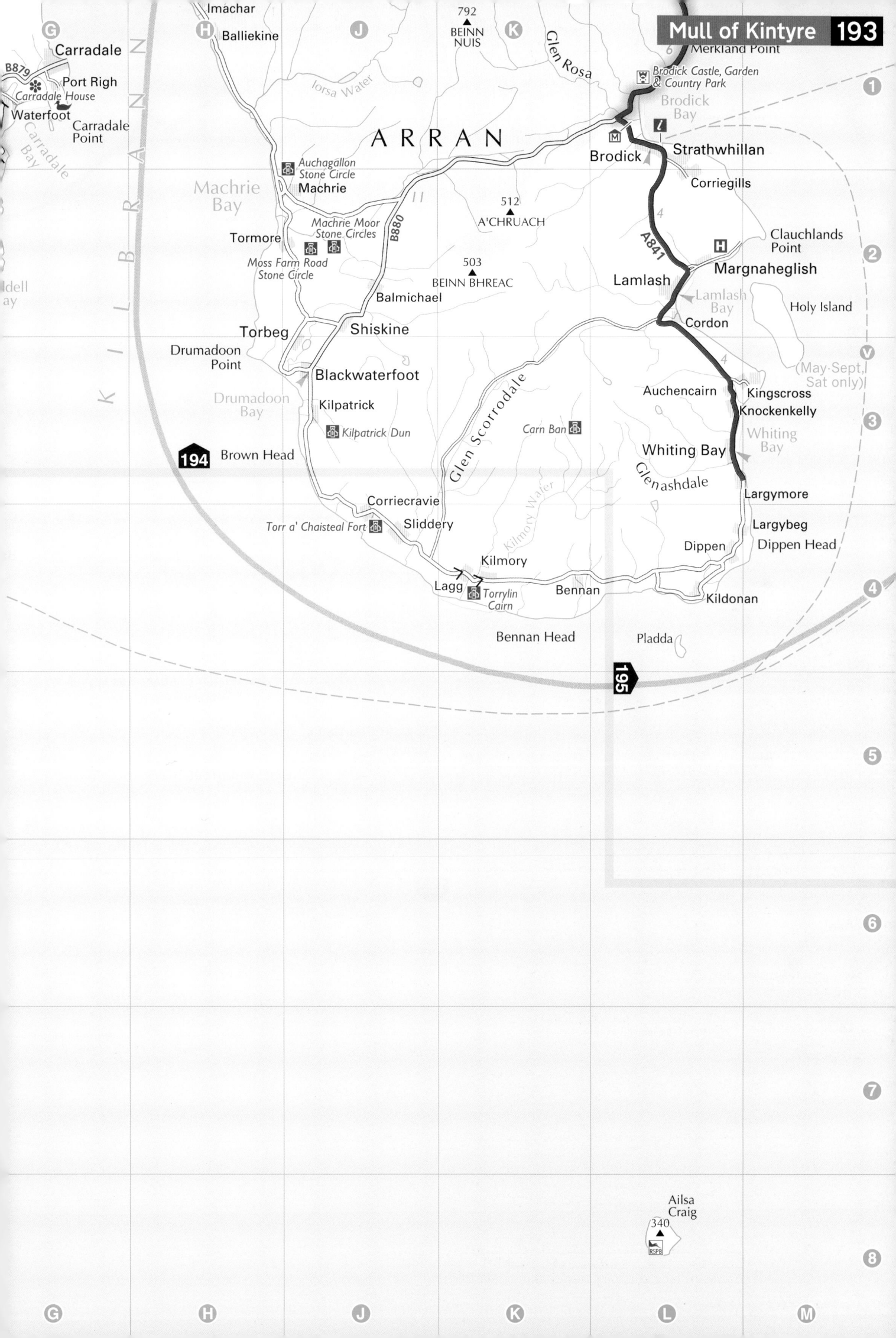

A B C D E F

1

Loch Ciaran

Loch Garasdale

Cock of Arran

Crossaig

Lochranza
Castle

Catacol

Isle of Arran

247
CRUACH MHIC
GOUGAIN

Rhunahaorine

264
CNOC-AN T-
SAMHLAIDH

Cour Bay

Cour

Glen Chalmadale 8

A841

2

Grogport

Barmollack

Pirnmill

Penrioch

North Arran

834
CAISTEAL ABHAIL

354
CRUACH
NAN GABHAR

Whitefarland

715
BEINN
BHARRAIN

Loch
Tanna

Glen Catacol

Glen Iorsa

792
BEINN
NUIS

874
GOATFELL

3

Carradale Water

B842

39

Carradale

B879

Bridgend

Dippen

Port Righ

Carradale House

Waterfoot

Imachar

Balliekine

Iorsa Water

Glen Rosa

4

319

454
BEINN-AN TUIRC

Torrisdale

Carradale
Point

Carradale
Bay

ARRAN

Auchagallon
Stone Circle

Machrie
Bay

Machrie

512
A'CHRUACH

408
BORD
MOR

Saddell

Saddell Water

Tormore

Machrie Moor
Stone Circles

B880

192

Lussa
Loch

396
SGREADAN
HILL

Ugadale

Saddell
Bay

Moss Farm Road
Stone Circle

903
BEINN BHREAC

Balmichael

Torbeg

Shiskine

5

Glen Lussa

Peninver

B842

Ardnacross
Bay

Drumadoon
Point

Drumadoon
Bay

Blackwaterfoot

Kilpatrick

Kilpatrick Dun

Glen Scorrodale

Carn Ban

Brown Head

6

Ki...chael

Campbeltown

Corriecravie

Sliddery

Torr a' Chaisteal Fort

Kilmory Water

Kilmory

B842

tewarton

Campbeltown
Loch

Island Davaar

Lagg

Bennan

Torrylin
Cairn

Bennan Head

Kilkerran

Kildalloig

7

352

BEINN GHUILEAN

Achinhoan

Glen Kerran

8

0   1   2   3   4   5 miles
0 1 2 3 4 5 6 7 8 kilometres

Ru Stafnish

A B C D E F

Gar**H**nty

Garroch Head

Little
Cumbrae
Island

207

Fairlie Road

K

Hunterston
Power Station

12

Drakemyre

Dalry

Munnoch

B784

B780

1

B7048

Portencross
Farland Head

B7047

**West
Kilbride**

B781

A737

C

U

N

Dalgarven

B780

Dalgarven
Mill

2

B714

Seamill

A78

B780

Kilwinning

A78

A738

B778

Corrie

Cannox

A78

Ardrossan

Horse Isle

A738

A738

Stevenston

Ardeer

B779

Saltcoats

196

B780

Merkland Point

6

V

3

Irvine

Maritime

rodick Castle, Garden
Country Park

Fulla

Brodick
Bay

F I R T H

Irvine

Strathwhillan

O F

Bay

Corriegills

4

Baras

C L Y D E

Clauchlands Point

H

Margnaheglish

Lamlash
Bay

Holy Island

Troon

Cordon

Lady Isle

5

4

(May-Sept, Sat only)

(May-Sept)

chencairn

Kingscross

V

Knockenkelly

P

hiting Bay

Whiting
Bay

V

ashdale

Largymore

M

Ayr

Largybeg

6

Dippen

Dippen Head

Bay

Kildonan

196

A

da

Heads
of Ayr

Doonfo

Burns Cotta

Heads of Ayr

7

A719

Fisherton

Allo

Culroy

Dunure

Drumshang

Croy Brae
(Electric Brae)

Knoweside

Culzean
Bay

182

Culzean Castle
& Country Park

L

Pennyglen

M

Whitefaulds

A

8

G

H

J

K

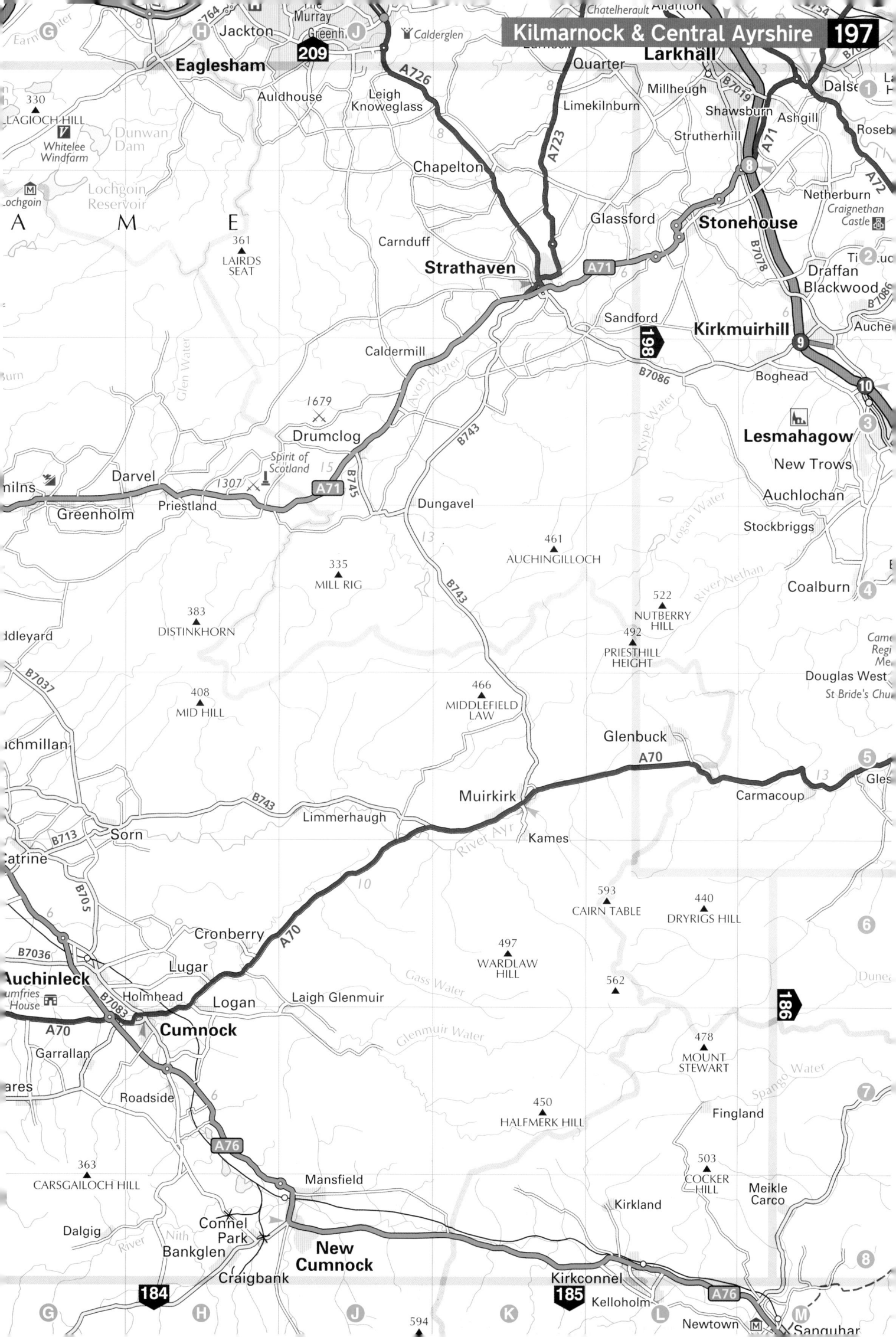

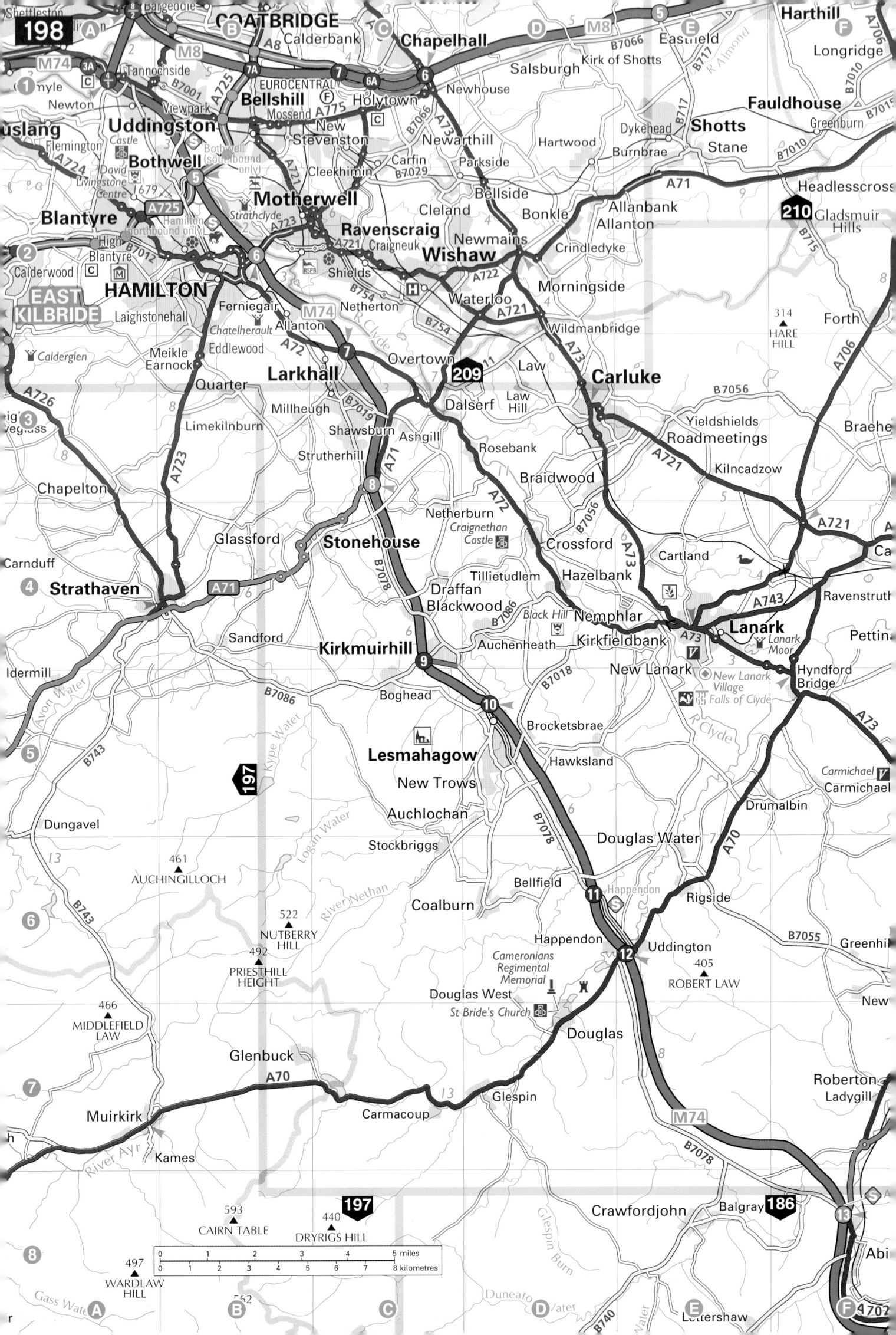

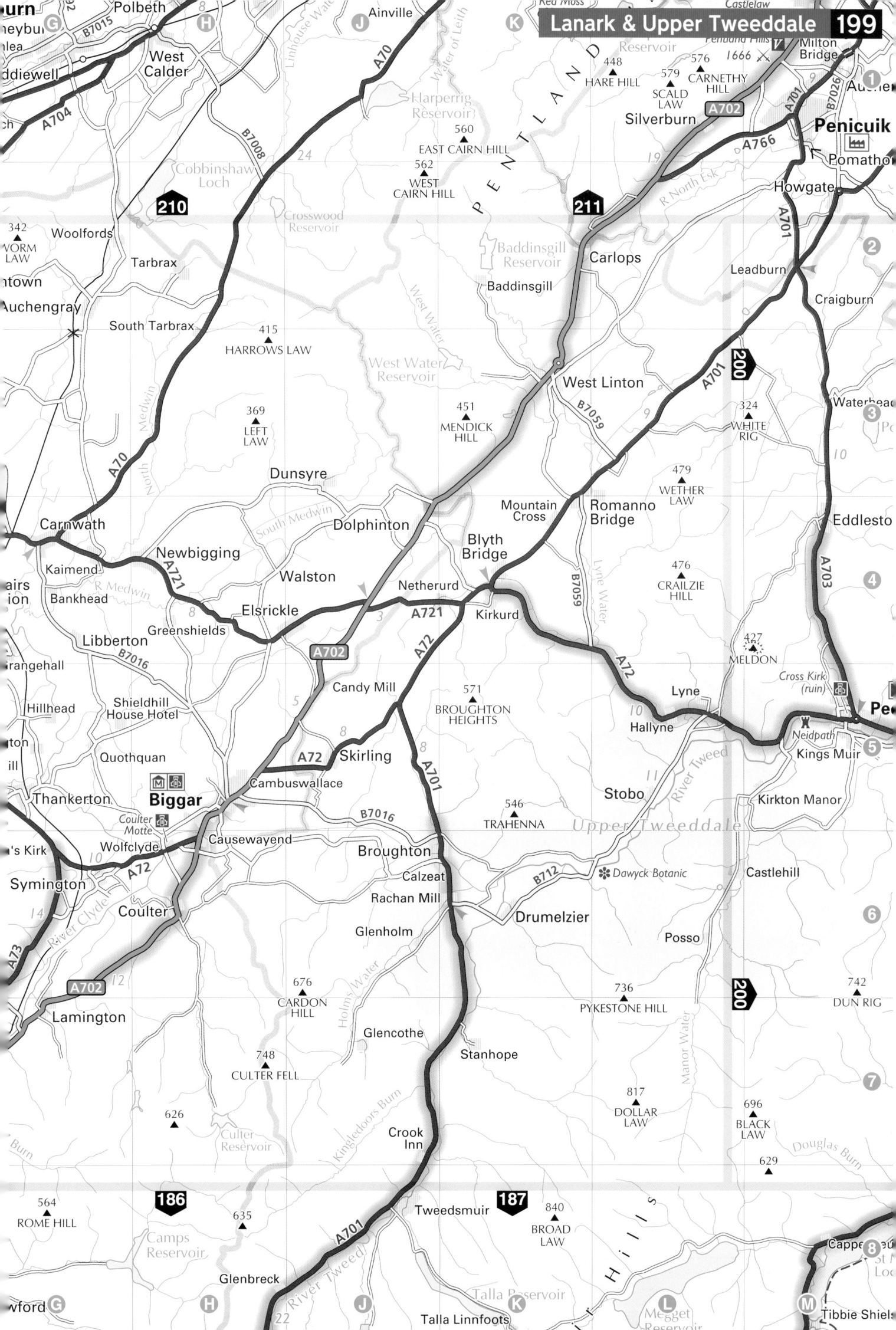

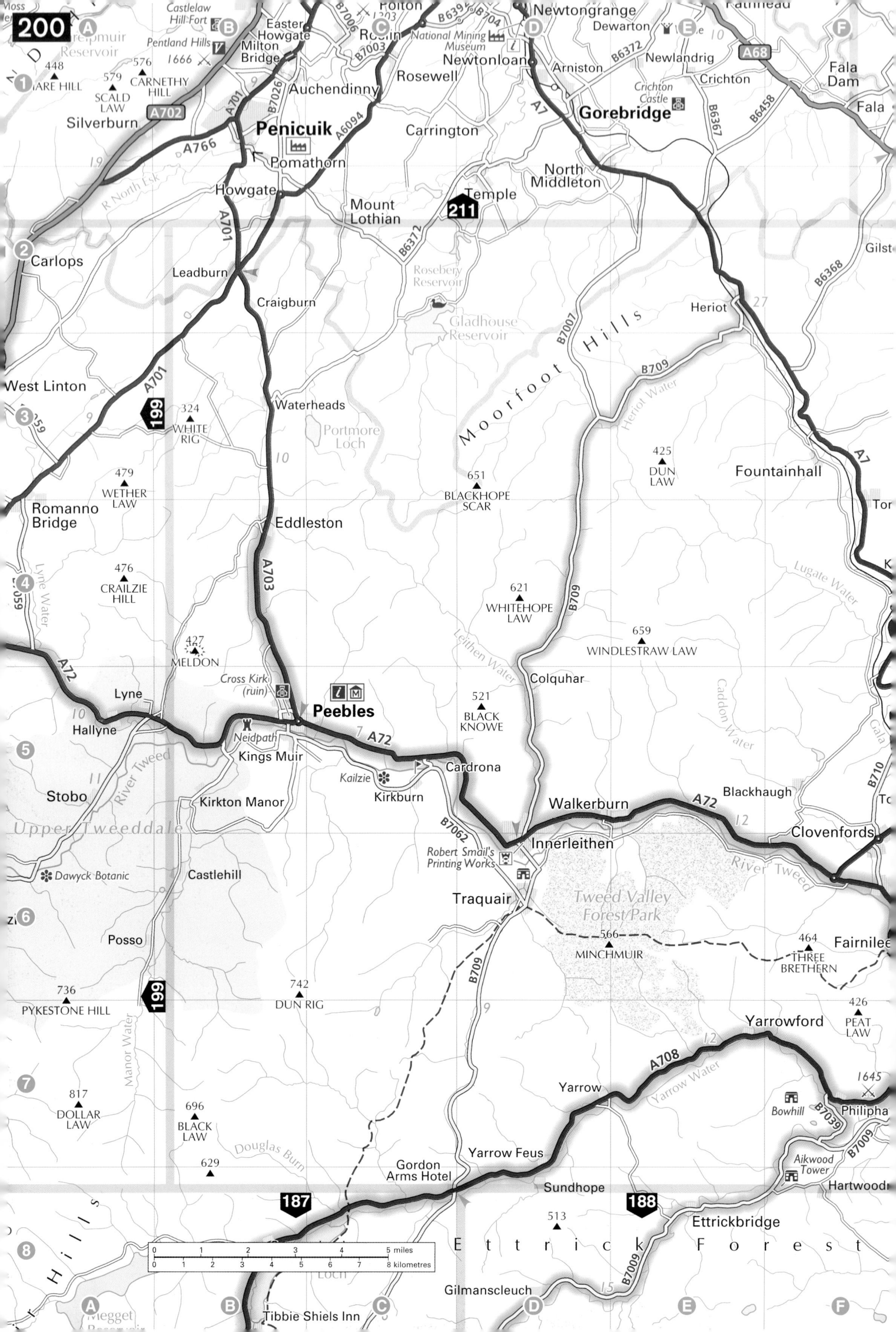

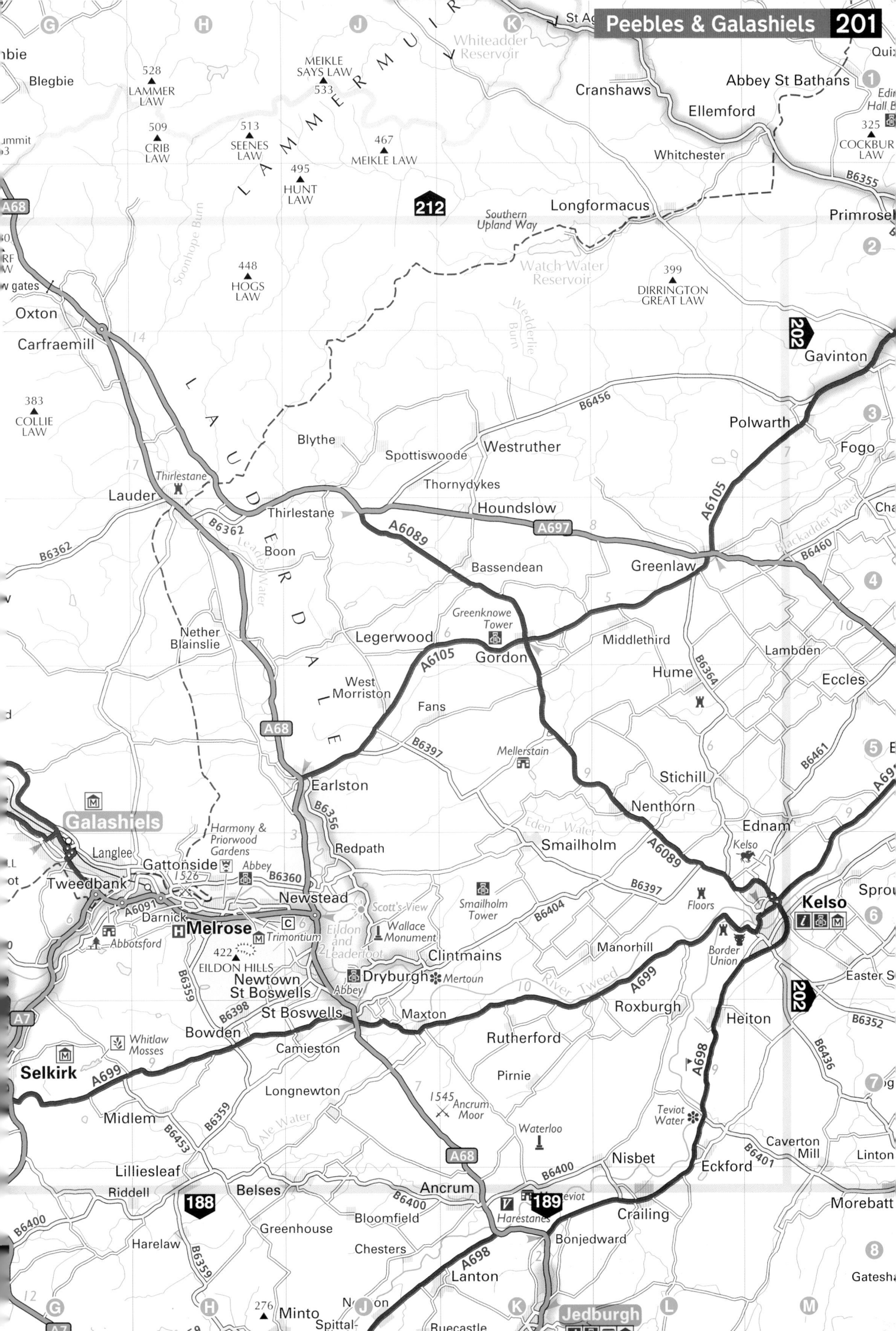

LAMMERMUIR

Whiteadder Reservoir

Abbey St Bathans

Cranshaws

Ellemford

Whitchester

Blegbie

528 ▲ LAMMER LAW

533 ▲ MEIKLE SAYS LAW

Longformacus

Primrosel

325 COCKBUR LAW

509 ▲ CRIB LAW

513 ▲ SEENES LAW

467 ▲ MEIKLE LAW

B6355

A68

212

Southern Upland Way

495 ▲ HUNT LAW

399 ▲ DIRRINGTON GREAT LAW

gates

Oxton

Carfraemill

14

Watch Water Reservoir

Wedderlie Burn

202

Gavinton

383 ▲ COLLIE LAW

L A U D E R D A L E

Thirlestane

Lauder

B6362

B6362

B6362

Thirlestane

Boon

Blythe

Spottiswoode

Westruther

Thornydykes

Houndslow

A6089

A697

Polwarth

Fogo

A6105

Bassendean

Greenlaw

7

B6456

B6460

Nether Blainslie

Legerwood

Greenknowe Tower

Gordon

Middlethird

Lambden

Eccles

A68

A6105

West Morriston

Fans

Hume

B6364

B6461

Galashiels

Harmony & Priorwood Gardens

Earlston

B6356

Redpath

Mellerstain

Smailholm

Stichill

Nenthorn

Ednam

A6089

Langlee

1526

Gattonside

Abbey

B6360

Newstead

Scott's View

Smailholm Tower

B6397

Kelso

Tweedbank

A6091

Darnick

Melrose

Trimontium

Eildon and Leaderfoot

Wallace Monument

B6404

Floors

Kelso

Border Union

Abbotsford

422 EILDON HILLS

Newtown St Boswells

Dryburgh Abbey

Mertoun

Clintmains

River Tweed

Manorhill

10

A699

Roxburgh

202

B6359

St Boswells

Maxton

Rutherford

Heiton

Bowden

Camieston

Pirnie

A698

9

B6352

Whitlaw Mosses

Longnewton

7

1545 Ancrum Moor

Waterloo

B6436

Selkirk

A699

Midlem

B6359

B6453

A68

Nisbet

Eckford

Caverton Mill

Linton

Lilliesleaf

188

Belses

B6400

Ancrum

189

Teviot Water

Crailing

B6401

Morebatt

Riddell

Bloomfield

Greenhouse

Harestanes

Nisbet

A698

Harelaw

B6359

Chesters

Teviot

Bonjedward

2

Gatesh

12

A7

276 ▲ Minto

Spittal-

Lanton

Jedburgh

L

M

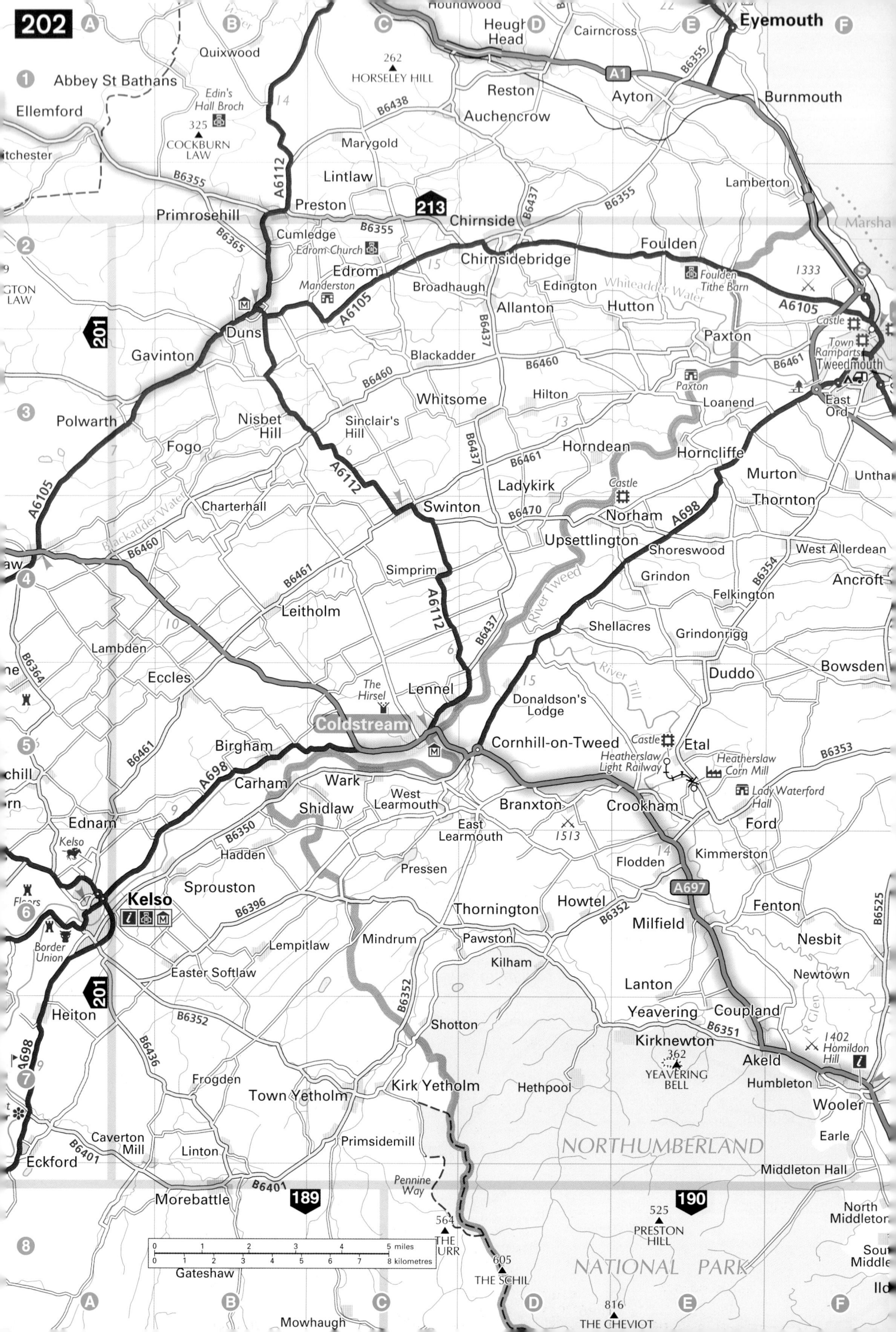

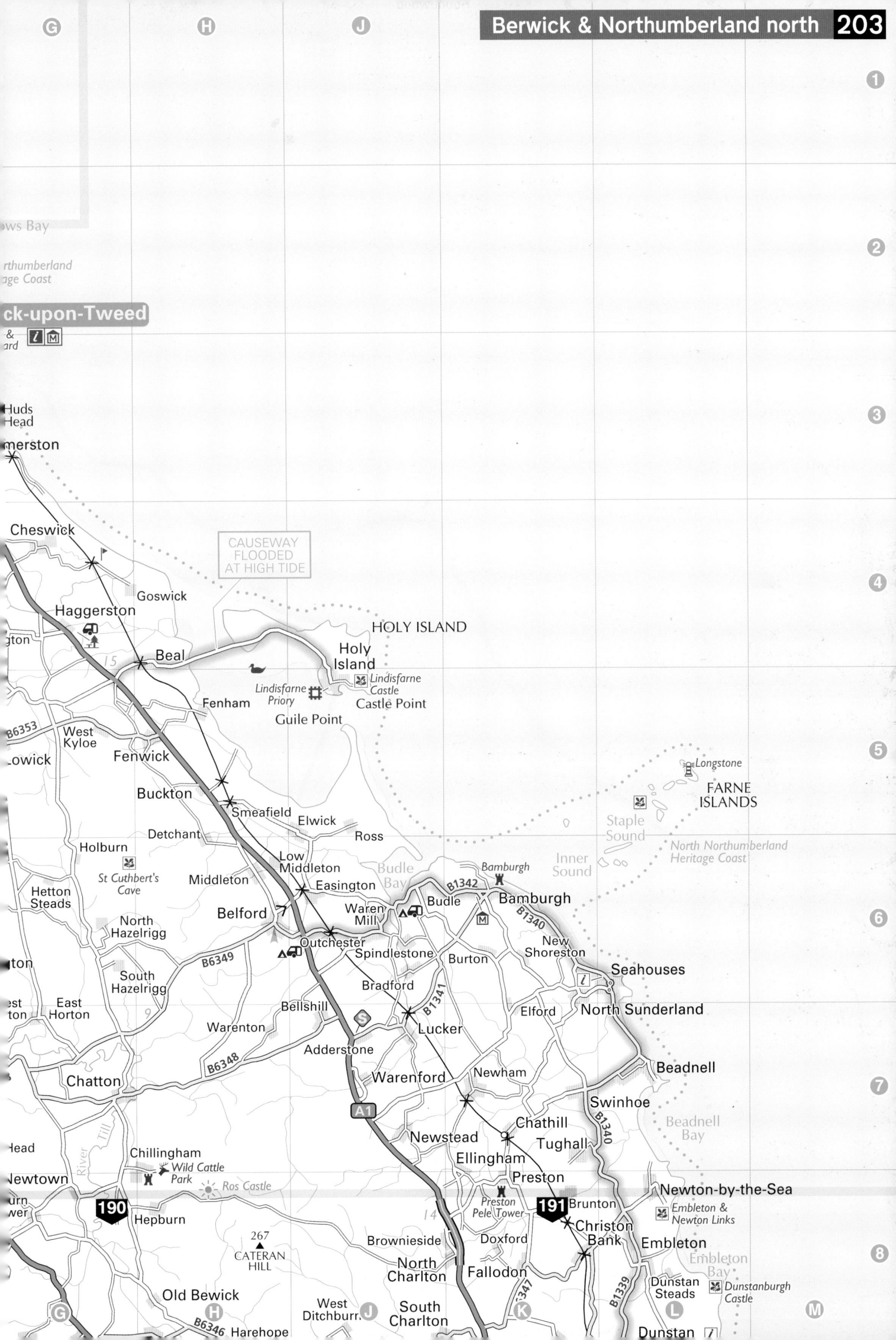

G   H   J

1

ows Bay

2

rthumberland
age Coast

ck-upon-Tweed
&
ard

3
Huds
Head

merston

Cheswick

CAUSEWAY
FLOODED
AT HIGH TIDE

Goswick

HOLY ISLAND

4

Haggerston

ton

Beal

Holy
Island

Lindisfarne
Castle

Fenham

Lindisfarne
Priory

Castle Point

B6353

West
Kyloe

Guile Point

Longstone

5

owick

Fenwick

FARNE
ISLANDS

Buckton

Smeafield

Elwick

Staple
Sound

North Northumberland
Heritage Coast

Detchant

Ross

Holburn

Low
Middleton

Budle
Bay

Bamburgh

Inner
Sound

St Cuthbert's
Cave

Middleton

Easington

B1342

Bamburgh

6

Hetton
Steads

Belford

Waren
Mill

Budle

North
Hazelrigg

Outchester

Spindlestone

Burton

New
Shoreston

B6349

B1341

Seahouses

South
Hazelrigg

Bradford

ton

East
ton

Horton

Bellshill

Lucker

Elford

North Sunderland

Warenton

Adderstone

7

Chatton

B6348

Warenford

Newham

Beadnell

Head

Newtown

Chillingham
Wild Cattle
Park

Ros Castle

Chathill

Swinhoe

Beadnell
Bay

Newstead

Tughall

urn
ower

190

Hepburn

Ellingham

Preston

Newton-by-the-Sea

267
CATERAN
HILL

Preston
Pele Tower

191

Brunton

Embleton &
Newton Links

8

Brownieside

Doxford

Christon
Bank

Embleton

Old Bewick

North
Charlton

Fallodon

B1339

Embleton
Bay

B6346   Harehope

West
Ditchburn

South
Charlton

B6347

Dunstan
Steads

Dunstanburgh
Castle

G   H   J   K   L   M

Dunstan

214

A B C D E F

Rubha
Bholsa

363
SGARB
BREA

1

Nave Island
Ardnave
Point
Gortantaoid
Point

Bunnahabhair

316
GUIR-
BHEINN

2

Ton Mhòr
Kilnave
Eilean Mòr
Sanaigmore

Finlaggan
F
A
Keills

Rubha Lamanais
Loch
Gorr
Lecht Gruinart
B8018
B8017
Loch Gruinart
Loch
Finlaggan

Ballygrant
8

3

Saligo Bay
Loch
Gorm
Gruinart
Gleann Mòr
RSPB
A846
Lo
Bally
Lo
Lo

Coul Point
Sunderland
Kilchoman
B8018
A847
Bridgend
Gartachossan

4

Machir
Bay
Bruichladdich
**Loch
Indaal**
3

Kilchiaran Bay
Bowmore
Kilennan Burn

**Port
Charlotte**
15
M
ISLAY

5

Lossit Bay
231
BEINN TART A'MHILL
Nereabolls
Laggan
Point
River Laggan
B8016
Duich R
A846
454
BEINN URARAI
Loch U

Rubha na
Faing
A847
Portnahaven
11

6

Port Wemyss
Orsay
RHINNS
POINT
L a g g a n
B a y
Glenegedale
Islay
346
BEINN SHOLUM

Rubha Mòr
Kintra
**Port
Ellen**
A846
3
Lagav

7

165
MAOL BUIDHE
T H E   O A
Risabus
Kilnaughton Bay
Laphroaig
Texa

Lower
Killeyan
RSPB
Loch
Kinnabus

Kinnabus
American
MULL
OF OA
Rubha nan Leacan

8

0   1   2   3   4   5 miles
0   1   2   3   4   5   6   7   8 kilometres

A B C D E F

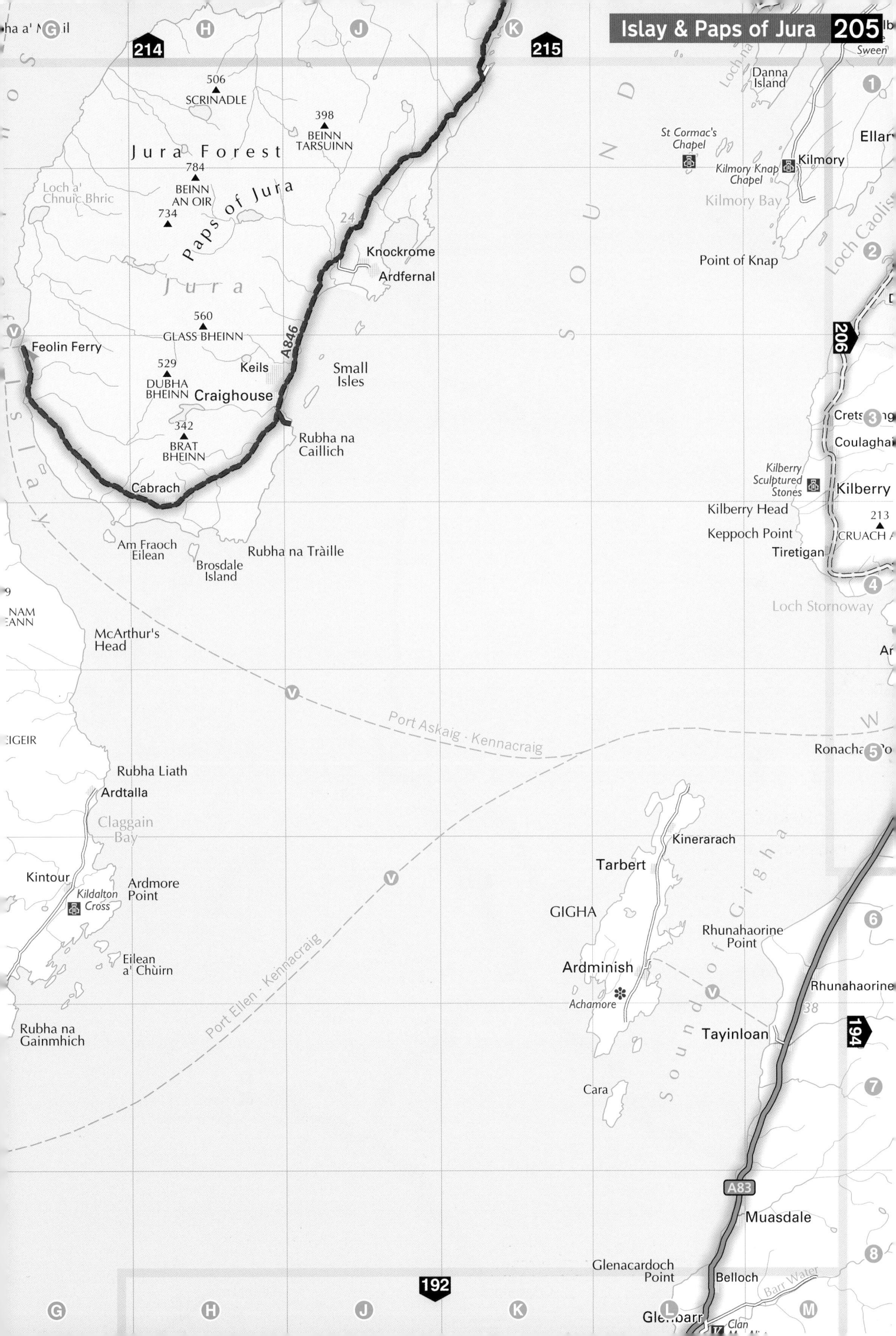

ha a' M G il
H
J
K

214
215

Sween

1

506
SCRINADLE

Danna
Island

398
BEINN
TARSUINN

St Cormac's
Chapel

Ellar

Jura Forest

784
BEINN
AN OIR

Paps of Jura

Loch a'
Chnuic Bhric

Kilmory Knap
Chapel

Kilmory

734

Kilmory Bay

2

Jura

Point of Knap

Knockrome

Ardfernal

24

SOUND

V

Feolin Ferry

560
GLASS BHEINN

A846

206

529
DUBHA
BHEINN

Keils

Small
Isles

Crets ng

3

Craighouse

Coulagha

342
BRAT
BHEINN

Rubha na
Caillich

Kilberry
Sculptured
Stones

Kilberry

Cabrach

Kilberry Head

Keppoch Point

213
CRUACH A

Am Fraoch
Eilean

Rubha na Tràille

Tiretigan

Brosdale
Island

4

Loch Stornoway

9

NAM
EANN

McArthur's
Head

V

Port Askaig - Kennacraig

W

EIGEIR

Ronacha Po

5

Rubha Liath

Ardtalla

Claggain
Bay

Kinerarach

Tarbert

SOUND

Kintour

Kildalton
Cross

Ardmore
Point

V

GIGHA

Rhunahaorine
Point

of

6

Gigha

Eilean
a' Chùirn

Ardminish

Rhunahaorine

V

Rubha na
Gainmhich

Port Ellen - Kennacraig

Achamore

Tayinloan

194

Cara

7

A83

Muasdale

8

Glenacardoch
Point

Belloch

Bart Water

192

Glen barr

G
H
J
K
L
M

Clan

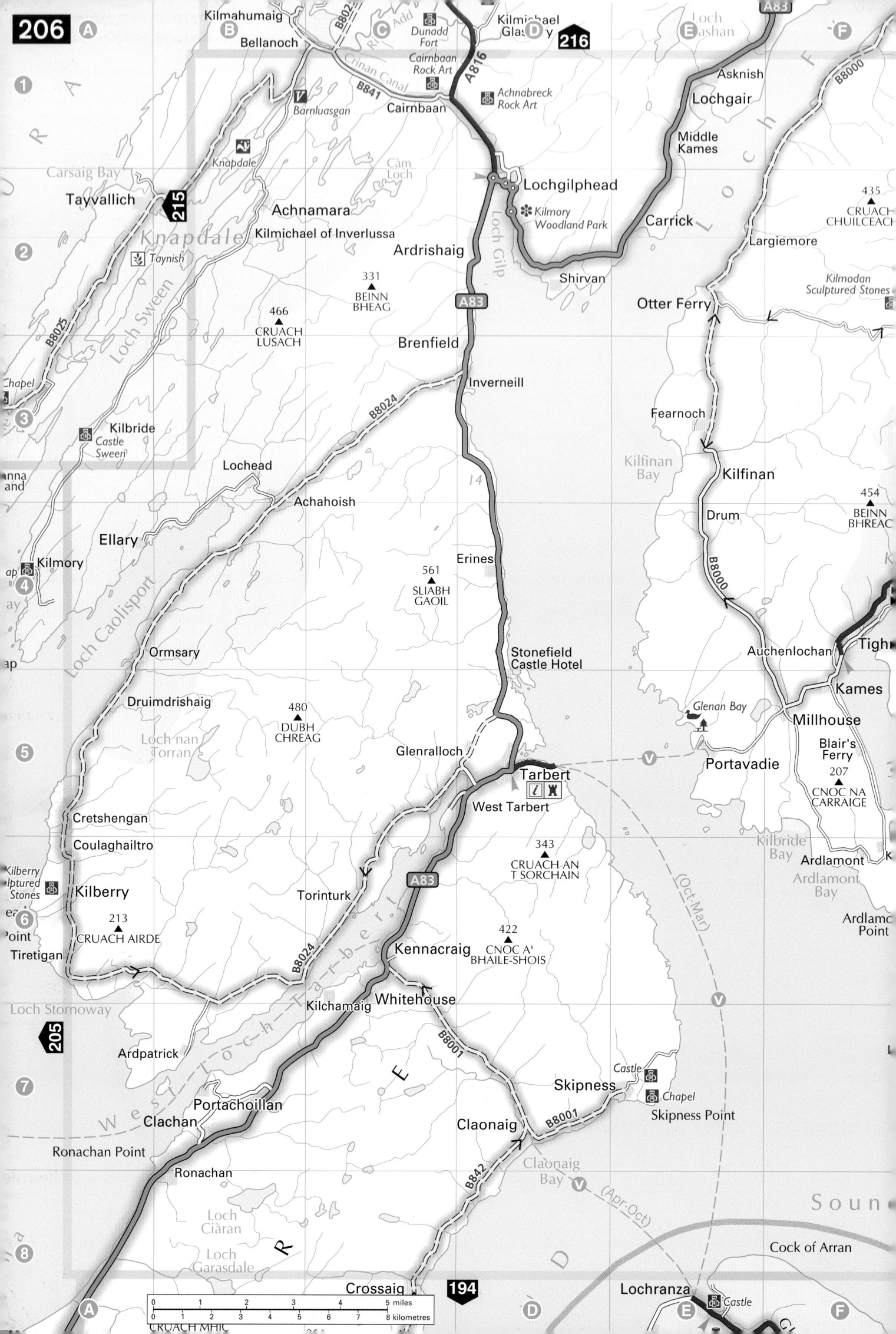

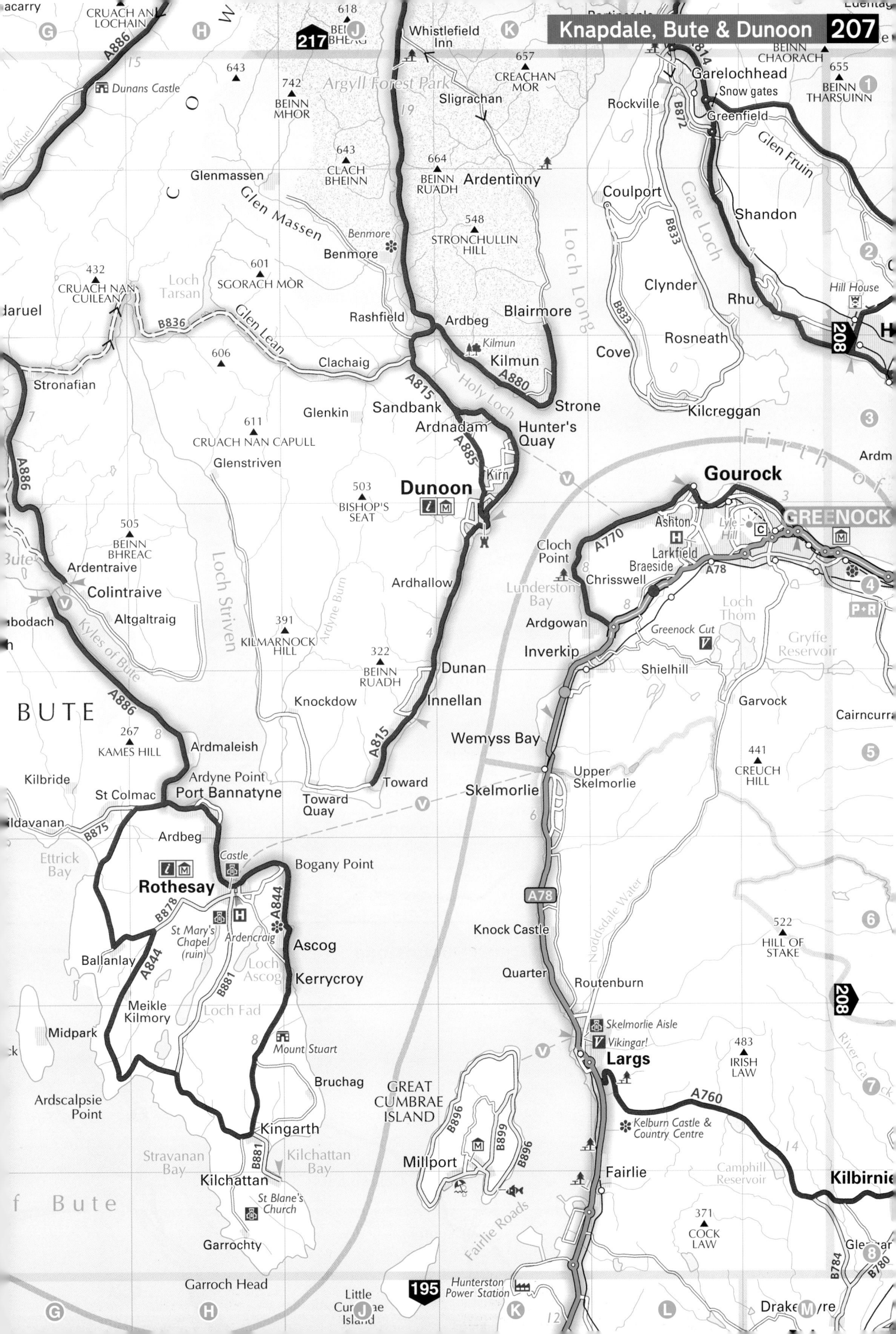

G **H** W **J** **K**

acarry
CRUACH AN
LOCHAIN
A886
618
217 BEINN
BHEAG
Whistlefield
Inn
Argyll Forest Park
657
CREACHAN
MOR
Portincaple
A814
BEINN
CHAORACH
655
BEINN
THARSUINN
1

643
742
BEINN
MHOR
Sligrachan
Rockville
Garelochhead
Snow gates
Greenfield
B872
Glen Fruin

Dunans Castle
Glenmassen
643
CLACH
BHEINN
664
BEINN
RUADH
Ardentinny
Coulport
B833
Shandon
2

Glen Massen
Benmore
548
STRONCHULLIN
HILL
Clynder
Hill House
208
H

601
SGORACH MÒR
Benmore
Rashfield
Ardbeg
Blairmore
Rosneath
Rhu

432
CRUACH NAN
CUILEAN
Loch
Tarsan
B836
Glen Lean
Clachaig
Kilmun
Kilmun
A880
Cove
Kilcreggan
3

606
Strone
Firth of

Stronafian
Glenkin
Sandbank
Ardnadam
Holy Loch
Hunter's
Quay
Gourock
GREENOCK
Ardm

611
CRUACH NAN CAPULL
Glenstriven
A885
Kirn
Ashton
Lyle
Hill
C

A886
503
BISHOP'S
SEAT
Dunoon
Cloch
Point
A770
Larkfield
Braeside
A78

505
BEINN
BHREAC
Ardentraive
Ardhallow
Lunderston
Bay
Chrisswell
8
4
P+R

Bute
Colintraive
Altgaltraig
391
KILMARNOCK
HILL
Ardyne Burn
Ardgowan
Inverkip
Greenock Cut
Loch
Thom
Gryffe
Reservoir

bodach
Kyles of Bute
322
BEINN
RUADH
Dunan
Innellan
Shielhill
Garvock
Cairncurra

BUTE
A886
267
KAMES HILL
8
Ardmaleish
Knockdow
Wemyss Bay
441
CREUCH
HILL
5

Kilbride
St Colmac
Ardyne Point
Port Bannatyne
Toward
Skelmorlie
Upper
Skelmorlie

ildavanan
B875
Ardbeg
Toward
Quay
6

Ettrick
Bay
Castle
Bogany Point
A78
522
HILL OF
STAKE
6

Rothesay
B878
St Mary's
Chapel
(ruin)
Ardencraig
A844
Knock Castle

Ballanlay
A844
B881
Ascog
Kerrycroy
Quarter
Routenburn

Midpark
Meikle
Kilmory
Loch
Ascog
Loch Fad
Skelmorlie Aisle
Vikingar!
483
IRISH
LAW

Ardscalpsie
Point
Mount Stuart
Bruchag
GREAT
CUMBRAE
ISLAND
Largs
A760
Kelburn Castle &
Country Centre

Kingarth
B881
B896
B899
B896
Fairlie
Camphill
Reservoir
Kilbirnie

Stravanan
Bay
Kilchattan
Bay
Millport
371
COCK
LAW

f Bute
Kilchattan
St Blane's
Church
Hunterston
Power Station
B784
B780

Garrochty
Garroch Head
195
Little
Cumbrae
Island
Drakemyre
Glen ar
8

G **H** **J** **K** **L** **M**

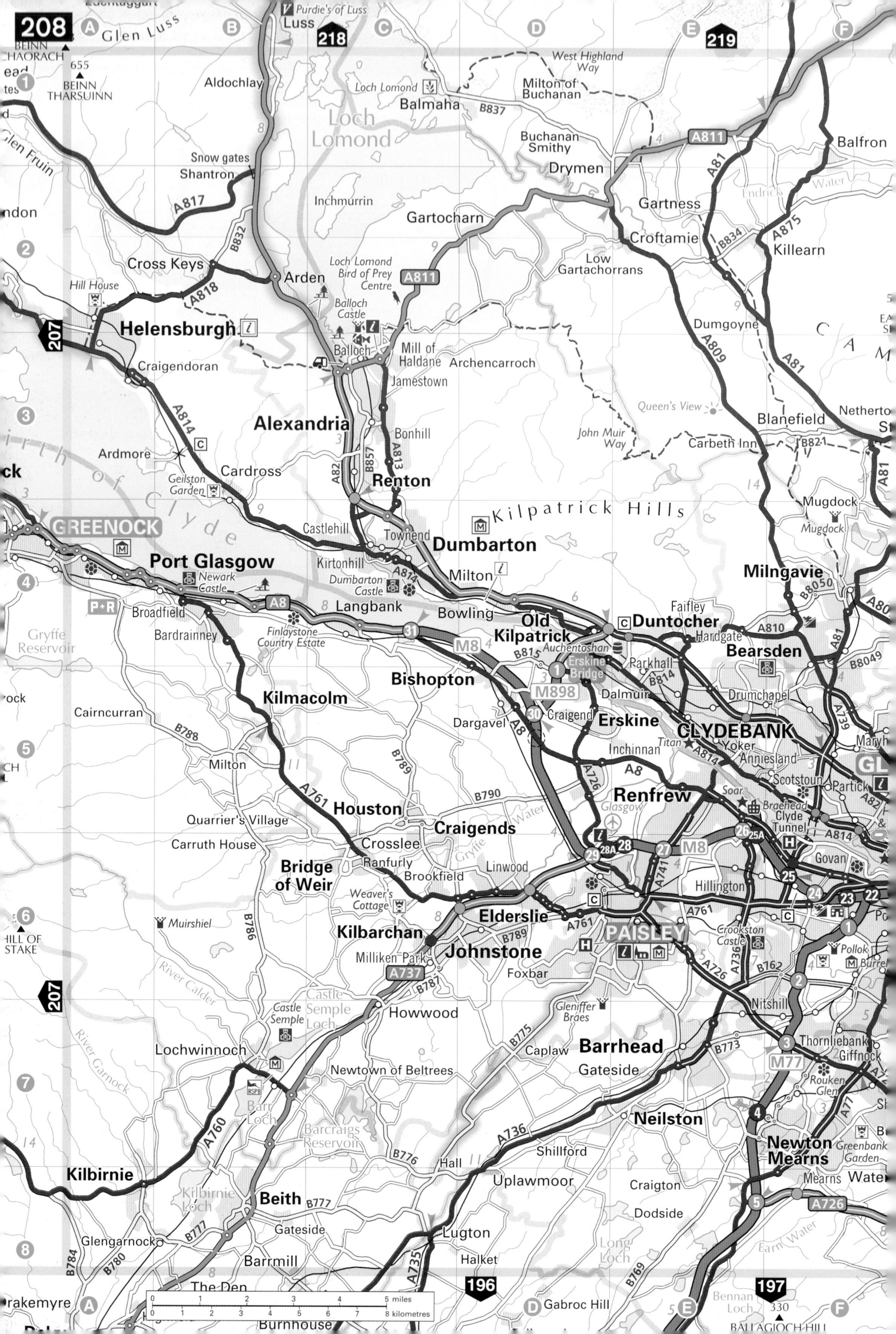

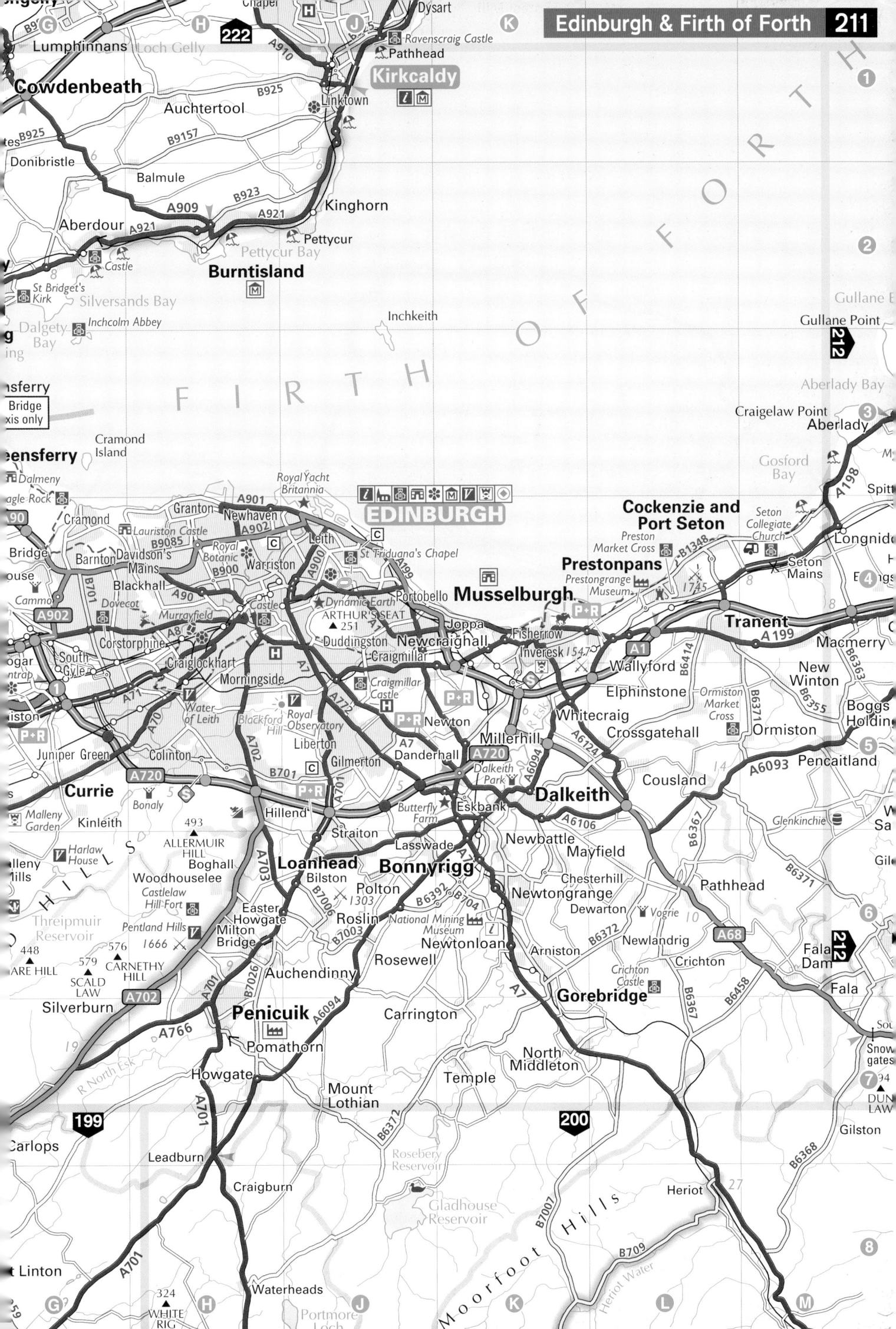

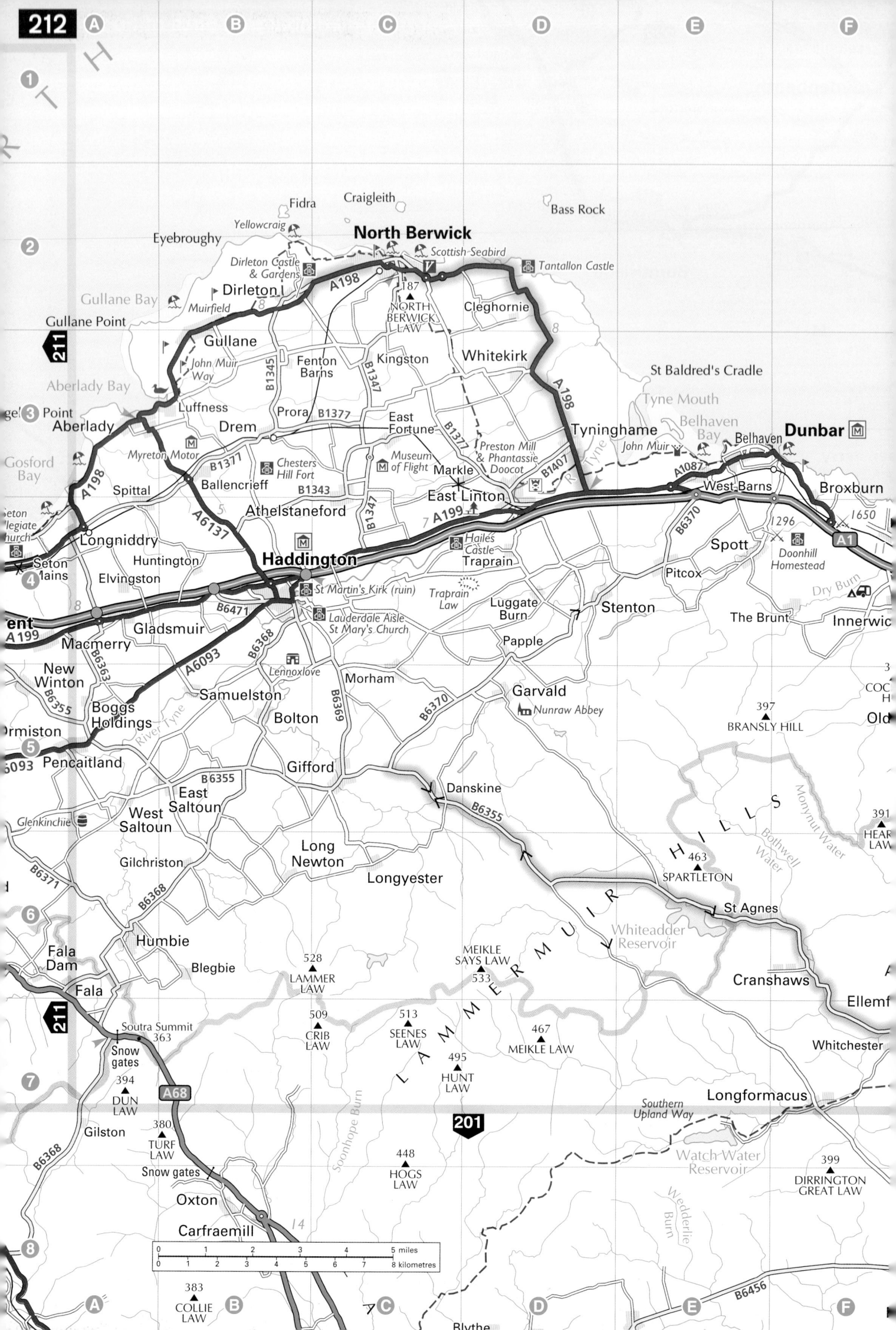

G H J

1

2

3

4

Chapel Point

Torness
Power Station
Thorntonloch

owhill

Reed
Point
Cove   Pease
Bay

Dunglass
Collegiate
Church

Siccar
Point

Fast Castle Head

Cockburnspath

A1107

Pease Dean

196 ▲
BROWN
RIG

Coldingham
Loch

ST ABB'S HEAD

Ecclaw

5

St Abbs

Grantshouse

Southern
Upland Way

Butterdean

Coldingham

Coldingham
Bay

A1107

22

Eye Water

Houndwood

Heugh
Head

B6438

Eyemouth

6

Quixwood

Heugh
Head

Cairncross

Bathans

Edin's
Hall Broch

262 ▲
HORSELEY HILL

B6438

Reston

A1

Ayton

B6355

Burnmouth

325 ▲
COCKBURN
LAW

Marygold

Auchencrow

14

Lintlaw

A6112

Lamberton

7

Primrosehill

B6365

Preston

B6355

Chirnside

B6437

B6355

Marshall Meadows Bay

North Northumberland
Heritage Coast

Cumledge

Edrom Church

B6355

Chirnsidebridge

202

Foulden

1333

S

Edrom

15

Broadhaugh

Edington

Whiteadder Water

Foulden
Tithe Barn

Manderston

A6105

Allanton

Hutton

A6105

Berwick-upo

Castle

Barracks &
Main Guard

Duns

A6105

Blackadder

Paxton

Town
Ramparts

Tweedmouth

Gavinton

B6460

Whitsome

Hilton

Paxton

Loanend

East
Ord

Spittal

Huds
Head

Nisbet
Hill

Sinclair's
Hill

13

Scremerston

G H J K L M

8

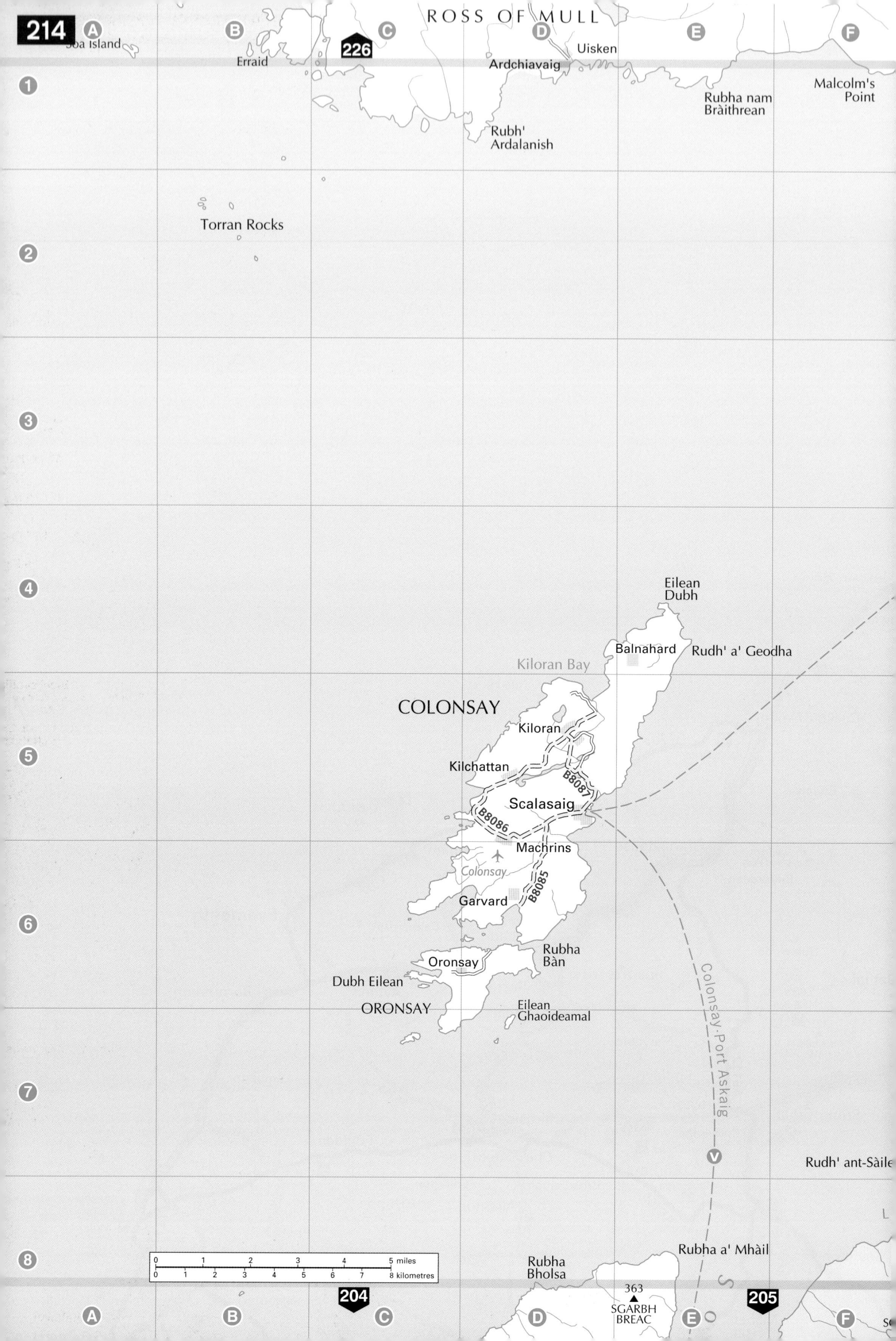

ROSS OF MULL

Soa Island

Erraid

226

Uisken

Ardchiavaig

Rubh'
Ardalanish

Rubha nam
Bràithrean

Malcolm's
Point

Torran Rocks

Eilean
Dubh

Balnahard

Rudh' a' Geodha

Kiloran Bay

COLONSAY

Kiloran

Kilchattan

B8087

Scalasaig

B8086

Machrins

Colonsay

B8085

Garvard

Rubha
Bàn

Oronsay

Dubh Eilean

ORONSAY

Eilean
Ghaoideamal

Colonsay-Port Askaig

Rudh' ant-Sàile

Rubha a' Mhàil

Rubha
Bholsa

363
▲
SGARBH
BREAC

0	1	2	3	4	5 miles
0	1 2 3 4 5 6 7				8 kilometres

G H J K

227

1

Dubh

Insh Island

Clachan

Clachan-Seil
SEIL
Ellenabeich *Seafari* ★ Easdale
Balvicar
Easdale
B844
Ardmaddy
B8003

V Cuan

Cullipool Torsa

Seil Sound

2

Loch Melfort

Degnish

Garbh Eileach

Eilean Dubh Mòr

LUING

Arduaine Garden
Arduaine

A81

GARVELLACHS
Monastery & Beehive Cells

Eileach an Naoimh

Toberonochy

216

Craob' Haven
3

SHUNA

Craigdhu

LUNGA

Scarba, Lunga and the Garvellachs

Sound of Luing

Shuna Sound

Ardfern
Kint

SCARBA

448 ▲
CRUACH SCARBA

Shuna Point

En Mhic

En Rig
4
Ca

Aird

Loch Craignish

Gulf of Corryvreckan

Craignish Point

Island Macaskin
Slockavulli
Temple Wood Stone Circles

Glengarrisdale Bay

295 ▲
CRUACH NA SEILCHEIG

Ri Cruin C
Poltalloc
5

Loch Crinan

Glendebadel Bay

364 ▲
BEN GARRISDALE

Crinan
Kilmahumaig

B8025

Corpach Bay

466 ▲
BEINN BHREAC

Glen Grundale

Lussa River

Lealt Burn

Bellanoch

B841

Crinan C

Barnluasgai
6

Knapdale

V

nian Bay

453 ▲
RAINBERG MÒR

Carsaig Bay

Tayvallich

Achnamara

Ardlussa

Lussa Point
Lussagiven

A846

FIRTH OF JURA

Kilmichael of Inverlus

Knapdale
Taynish
206

Loch Sween

7 31
▲
BEINN BHEA

h Mòr

466 ▲
CRUACH LUSACH

Keills Chapel

B8025

Loch na Cille

Kilbride
Castle Sween

Lochead
8

arbert

205

B8

398

G H J K L M chahoish

JURA

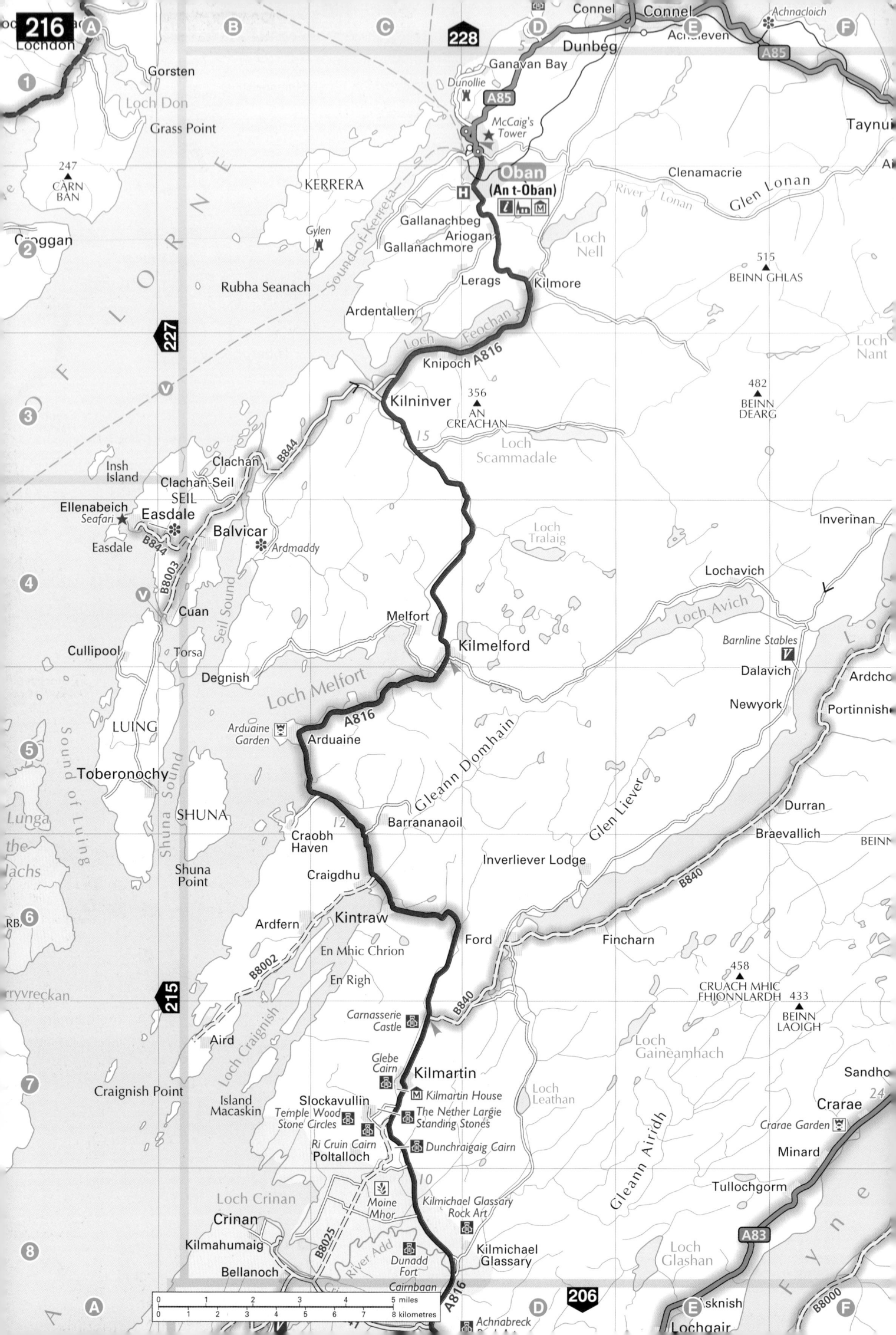

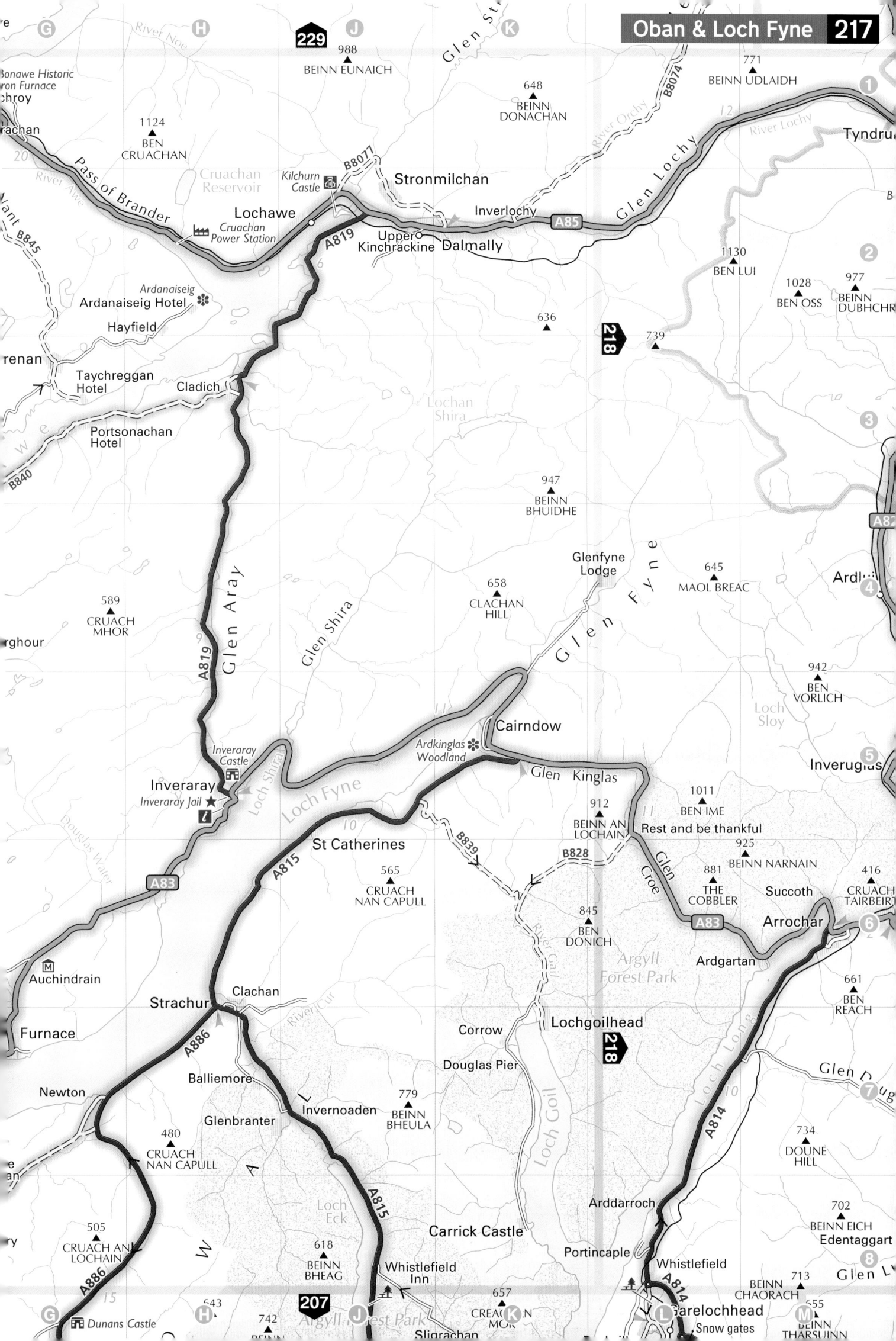

G
H
229
J
K

River Noe
Glen St
988
BEIN EUNAICH
B8074
771
BEINN UDLAIDH
1
Bonawe Historic
on Furnace
chroy
648
BEINN
DONACHAN
River Orchy
B8074
12
River Lochy
Tyndru
1124
BEN
CRUACHAN
Glen Lochy
A85
River Awe
Pass of Brander
B845
Cruachan
Reservoir
Kilchurn
Castle
B8077
Stronmilchan
Inverlochy
A85
B
1130
BEN LUI
2
Lochawe
Cruachan
Power Station
A819
Upper
Kinchrackine
Dalmally
1028
BEN OSS
977
BEINN
DUBHCHR
636
218
739
Ardanaiseig
Ardanaiseig Hotel
Hayfield
3
renan
Taychreggan
Hotel
Cladich
Lochan
Shira
Portsonachan
Hotel
B840
947
BEINN
BHUIDHE
Glenfyne
Lodge
645
MAOL BREAC
Ardl
4
589
CRUACH
MHOR
Glen Aray
A819
658
CLACHAN
HILL
Glen Fyne
942
BEN
VORLICH
rghour
Glen Shira
Loch
Sloy
Cairndow
Inverugias
5
Inveraray
Castle
Ardkinglas
Woodland
Glen Kinglas
1011
BEN IME
Inveraray
Inveraray Jail
Loch Shira
Loch Fyne
912
BEINN AN
LOCHAIN
Rest and be thankful
925
BEINN NARNAIN
Douglas Water
A83
St Catherines
A815
565
CRUACH
NAN CAPULL
B839
B828
Glen
Croe
881
THE
COBBLER
Succoth
416
CRUACH
TAIRBEIR
6
Auchindrain
845
BEN
DONICH
A83
Arrochar
Argyll
Forest Park
Ardgartan
661
BEN
REACH
Furnace
Strachur
Clachan
River Cur
Corrow
Lochgoilhead
218
Glen Du
7
A886
Balliemore
Douglas Pier
Loch Long
Newton
Invernoaden
779
BEINN
BHEULA
Glen Du
734
DOUNE
HILL
Glenbranter
A815
W
A
Loch
Goil
Arddarroch
A814
702
BEINN EICH
Edentaggart
505
CRUACH AN
LOCHAIN
A886
Loch
Eck
A815
618
BEINN
BHEAG
Carrick Castle
Portincaple
Whistlefield
713
BEINN
CHAORACH
8
G
Dunans Castle
H
742
207
J
Argyll Forest Park
Whistlefield
Inn
657
CREAC
MOR
K
N
A814
arelochhead
Snow gates
M
655
BEINN
THARSUINN

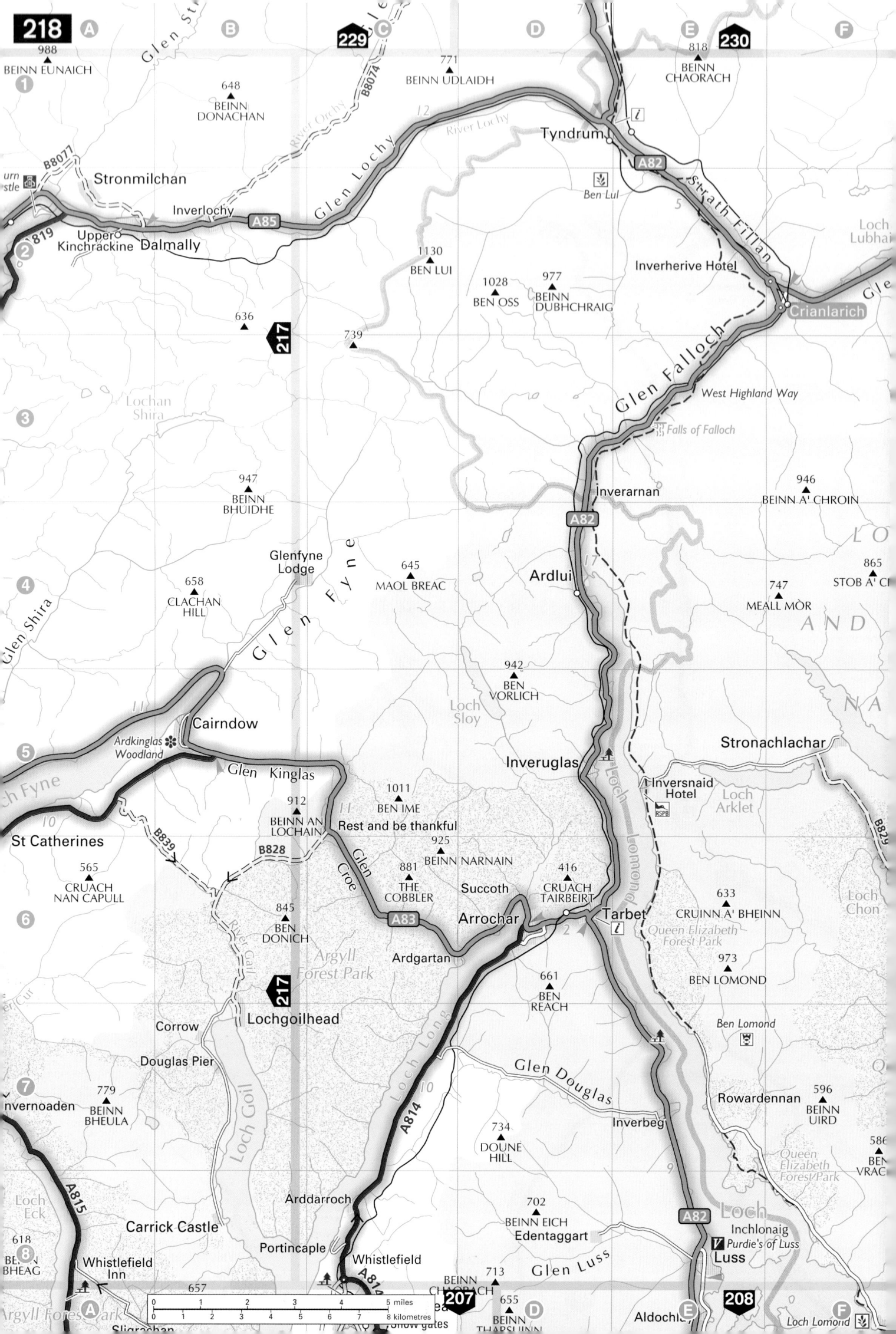

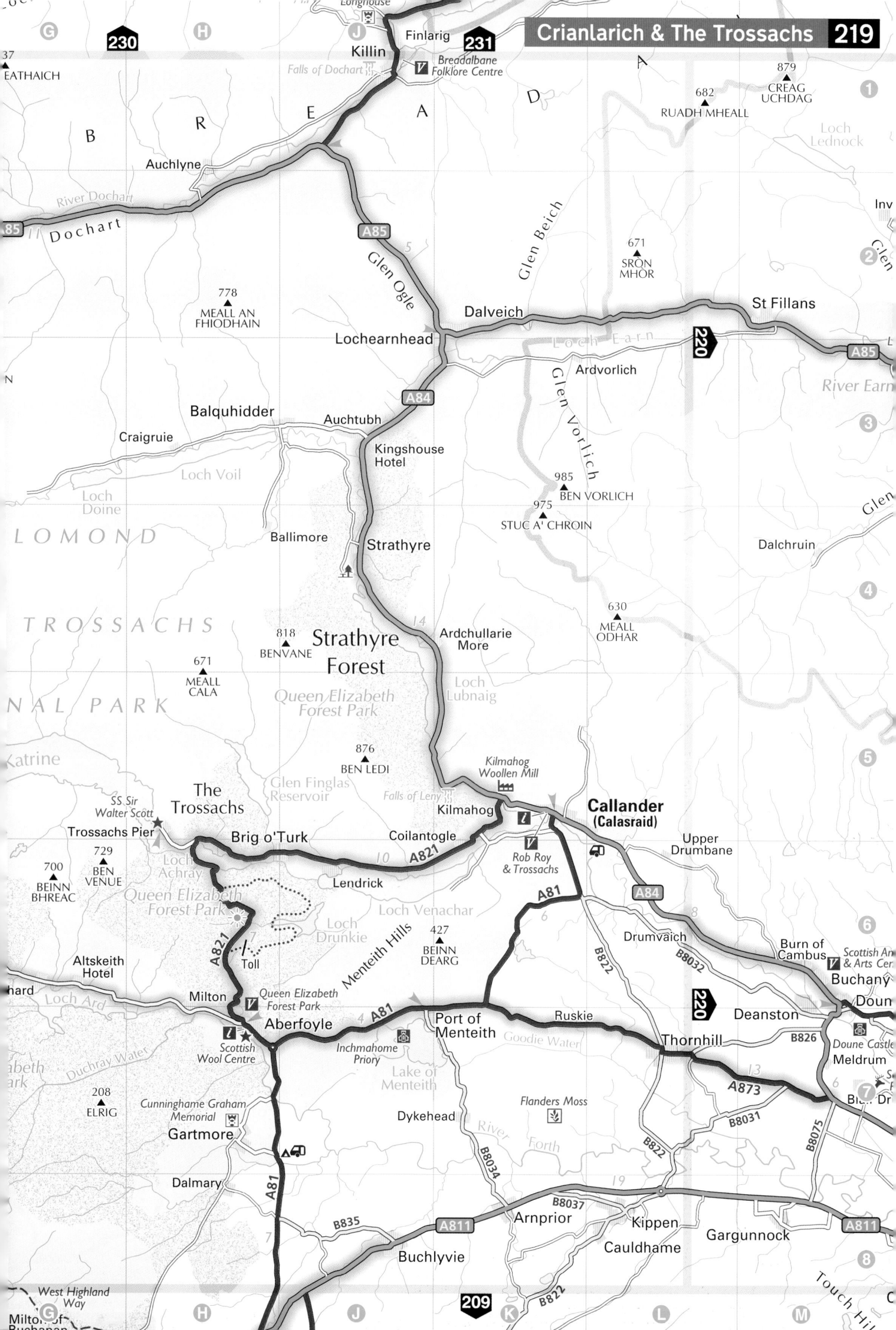

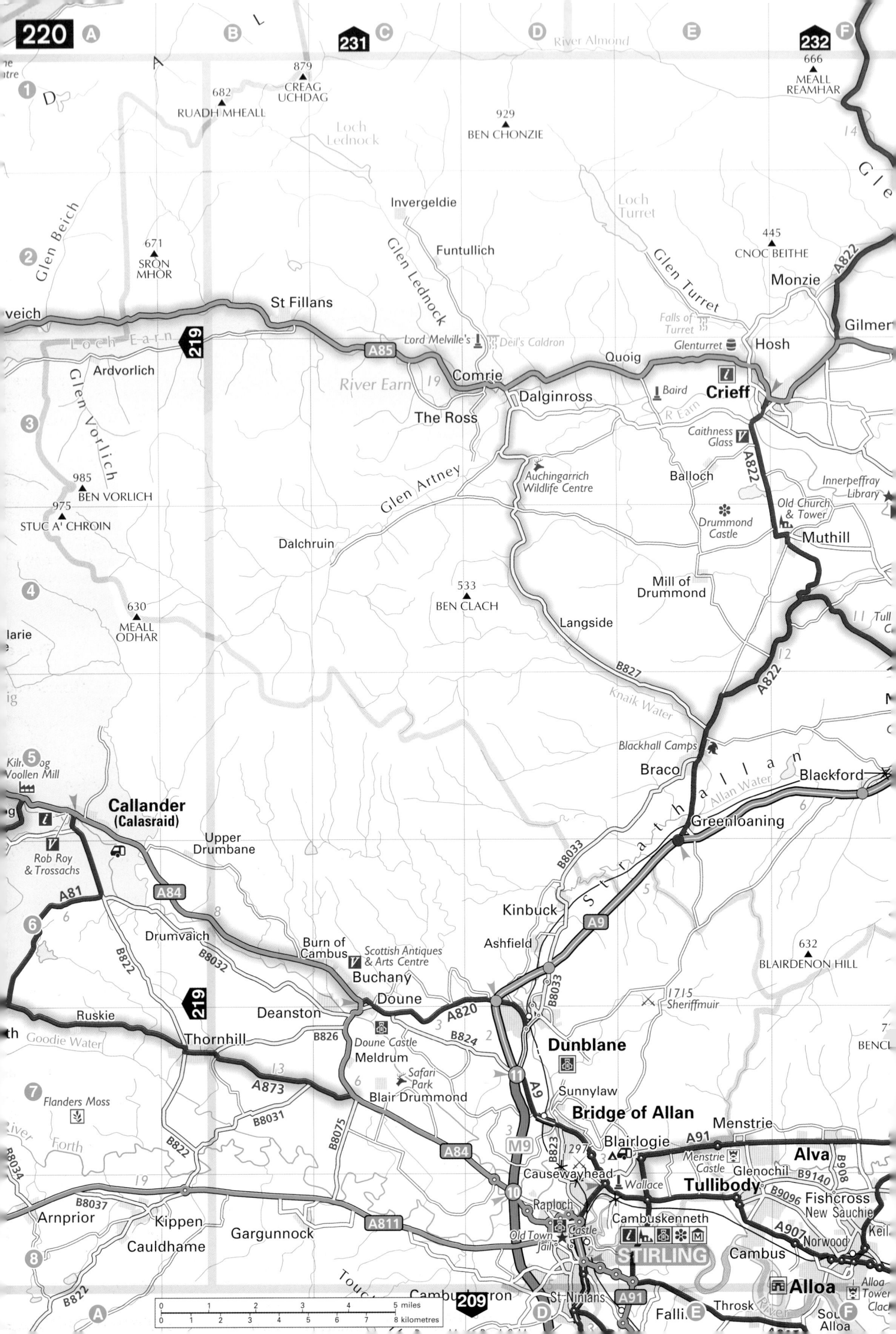

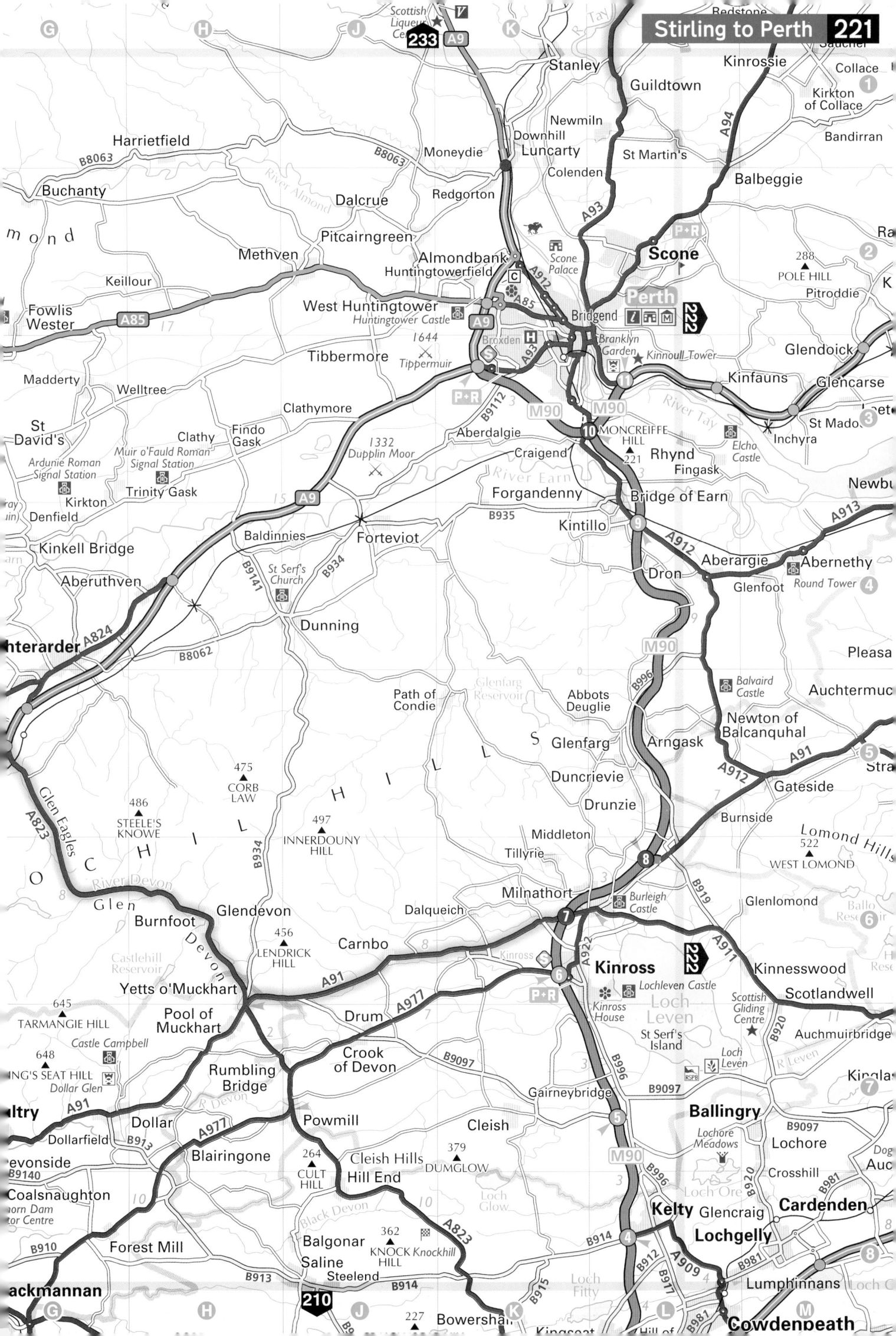

G
H
J
K

1

Mains of
Fintry
Whitfield
Douglas
and Angus
Baldovie
Murroes
Ardestie
Earth-House
234
B962
Barry
J
West Haven
K
Carnoustie
Carnoustie
B961
A92
A930

Claypotts
Castle
Barnhill
Monifieth

DUNDEE
Broughty
Ferry
Broughty
Castle
HMS
Unicorn

BUDDON
NESS

North Carr
Lightship
Tay Bridge
A92

Tayport

Tentsmuir Point

Newport-
on-Tay
B945
Morton Locks

2

Wormit
A914
Tentsmuir
Forest & Beach
Tentsmuir Point

B946

St Michaels
A919

cklawhill
13
Leuchars

ST ANDREWS
BAY

3

A914
Balmullo
13
10
Guardbridge
Kincaple
A91
St Andrews
Castle
St Andrews

River Eden

rae
irsie
Strathkinness
B939
Botanic
Brownhills
A917
Boarhills

4

Blebocraigs
Craigtoun
Denhead
A915
B9131
10

back
Pitscottie
Kingsbarns
Cambo
Kingsbarns

Ceres
ridgend
B939
Baldinnie
B940
Cameron
Reservoir
Dunino
Balcomie
Links
FIFE NESS

5

Peat
Inn
Radernie
12
Kingsmuir
10
Scotland's
Secret Bunker
B940

New
Gilston
B941
Lathones
B940
Lochty
Carnbee
B9171
Easter Pitkierie
Crail

Woodside
Largoward
Kellie
Castle
A917

Upper
Largo
A915
Arncroach
B9171
Wester
Pitkierie
B9131
Kilrenny
Cellardyke

6

Lundin
Mill
Colinsburgh
B942
Newton of
Balcormo
Fisheries
Anstruther

Lower
Largo
Drumeldrie
A917
B941
Kilconquhar
B942
Pittenweem
St Monans

undin
Links
Largo Bay
Earlsferry
Elie
Isle of May

7

8

G
H
J
K
L
M

A B C D E F

1

2

3

Gris
Clabhach

Hogh Bay   Bally

Totrona

Bagh a Chaisteil
(Castlebay)   Coll   Ac

V   Arileod   Ach
                                    Feall
                                    Bay   Uig

                                              RSPB
                                                        Crossapol   Rubh
Calgary Point   Bay   Fàsac

                                                                Loch Breachacha
Gunna

Caoles   Rubha Dubh
Rubha Port
Bhiosd   Clachan   B8069
            Mor   Balephetrish   Ruaig
Loch   Bay   B8068
Bhasapoll
Haugh   Gott
Bay   Ballevullin   Cornoigmore   Kenovay   Bay

Kilkenneth   Tiree
                                            Scarinish
            Moss   B8068   B8065
Middleton   Heylipoll
                        B8065   Crossapol   TIREE
Barrapoll
Loch a'   B8065
Phuill   B8067   Balemartine
                    Mannal   Hynish Bay
Rinn
Thorbhais   Balephuil   V
            Bay   Hynish

0   1   2   3   4   5 miles
0 1 2 3 4 5 6 7 8 kilometres

A B C D E F

G H J K L

1

Sanna Point

Sanna Bay

Sanna

Portuairk   Achnaha

Ardnamurchan Point      Achosnich

MEAL

B8007

2

342
▲
BEINN
NA SEILG

236
Eilean Mòr

Bagh a Chaisteil
(Castlebay)
Loch Baghasdail
(Lochboisdale)

236

Ormsaigmore

Kil

Rubha
Mòr

Rubha
Sgor-innis

Bousd   Sorisdale

3

B8072

Ardmore
Point

*Cliad
Bay*

Sorne
Point

Quinish Point   Glengorm Castle

Ru
na

ost

B8071

COLL

Tobe o

4

rinagour

292
▲
'S AIRDE
BEINN

Eilean
Ornsay

B8070

Caliach Point

Dervaig

Achnadrish House

Coll : Oban

5   4

5

B8073

6

Calgary

Calgary Bay

Loch Frisa

SPEINN

Treshnish Point

Ensay

342
▲
CÀRN MÒR

Rudh' a' Chaoil

Burg

390   6
▲
CNOC AN DÀ CHINN

Fanmore

Fladda

226

Ballygown

Loch Tuath

Eas Fors

19

Lunga

TRESHNISH
ISLES

Gometra

ULVA

Oskamull

7

Eorsa

Bac Mòr or Dutchman's Cap

Loch

Bac Beag

Little Colonsay

Inch Kenneth
Inchkenneth Chapel
(ruin)

B8035   17

Staffa

*Loch na Keal
Isle of Mull*

Balnahard

Fingal's

8

226

G H J K L M

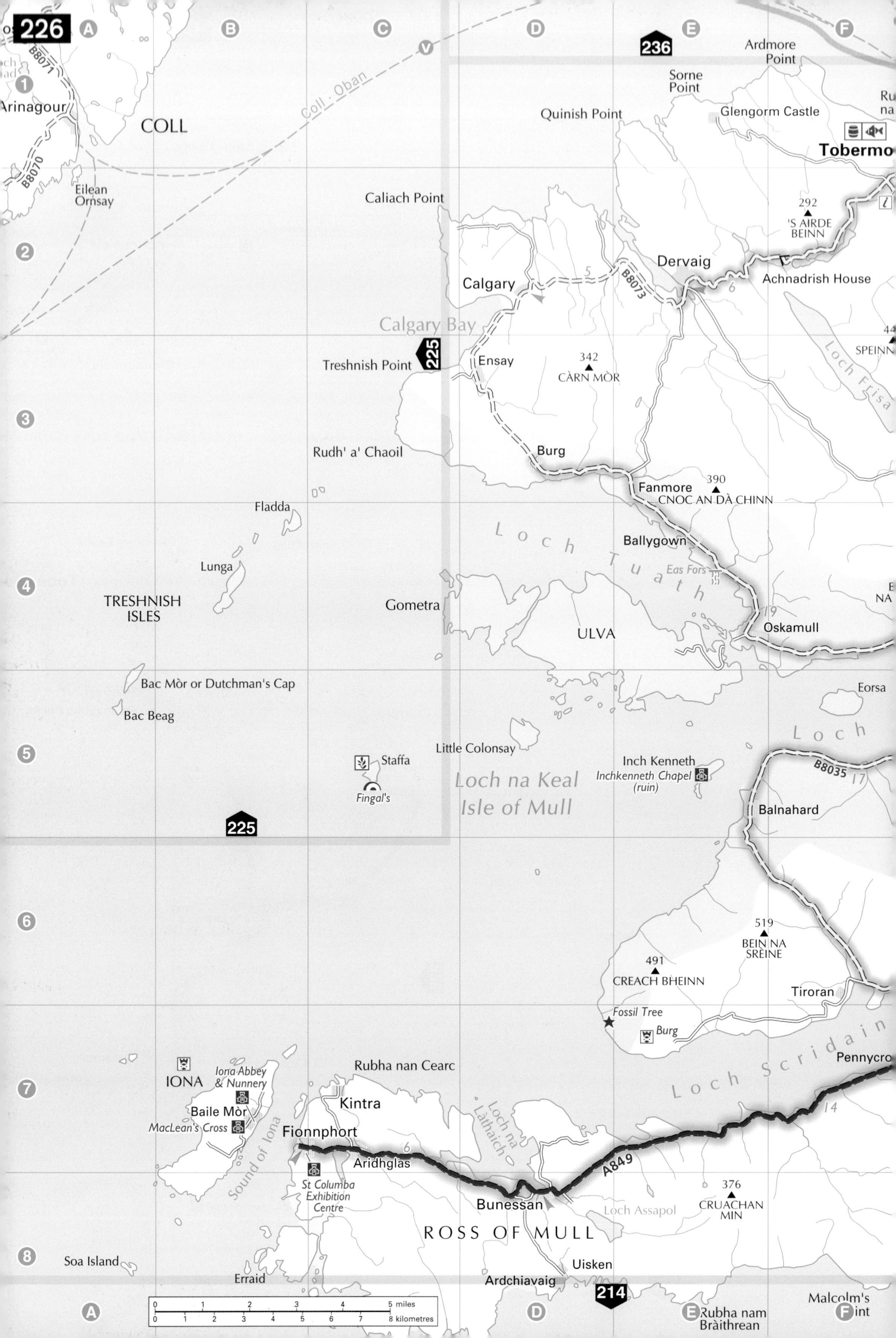

A B C D E F

226

1

Arinagour

B8071

B8070

COLL

Eilean
Ornsay

2

Caliach Point

236

Ardmore
Point

Sorne
Point

Quinish Point

Glengorm Castle

Tobermo

292 ▲
'S AIRDE
BEINN

Dervaig

Calgary

B8073

Achnadrish House

SPEINN

Calgary Bay

Loch Frisa

3

Treshnish Point **225**

Ensay

342 ▲
CÀRN MÒR

Rudh' a' Chaoil

Burg

Fanmore

390 ▲
CNOC AN DÀ CHINN

Fladda

Ballygown

Loch Tuath

Eas Fors

4

Lunga

**TRESHNISH
ISLES**

Gometra

ULVA

Oskamull

NA

Bac Mòr or Dutchman's Cap

Eorsa

Bac Beag

Loch

5

Little Colonsay

Inch Kenneth

Staffa

Inchkenneth Chapel
(ruin)

B8035 17

Loch na Keal

Isle of Mull

Balnahard

Fingal's

6

519 ▲
BEIN NA
SREINE

491 ▲
CREACH BHEINN

Tiroran

Fossil Tree ★

Burg

Pennycro

7

Rubha nan Cearc

IONA

Iona Abbey
& Nunnery

Kintra

Loch Scridain

A849

14

Baile Mòr

MacLean's Cross

Fionnphort

Sound of Iona

Loch na Làthaich

Aridhglas

6

St Columba
Exhibition
Centre

Bunessan

376 ▲
CRUACHAN
MIN

Loch Assapol

8

Soa Island

ROSS OF MULL

Erraid

Ardchiavaig

Uisken

214

Rubha nam
Bràithean

Malcolm's
Point

A B

0   1   2   3   4   5 miles
0 1 2 3 4 5 6 7 8 kilometres

D E F

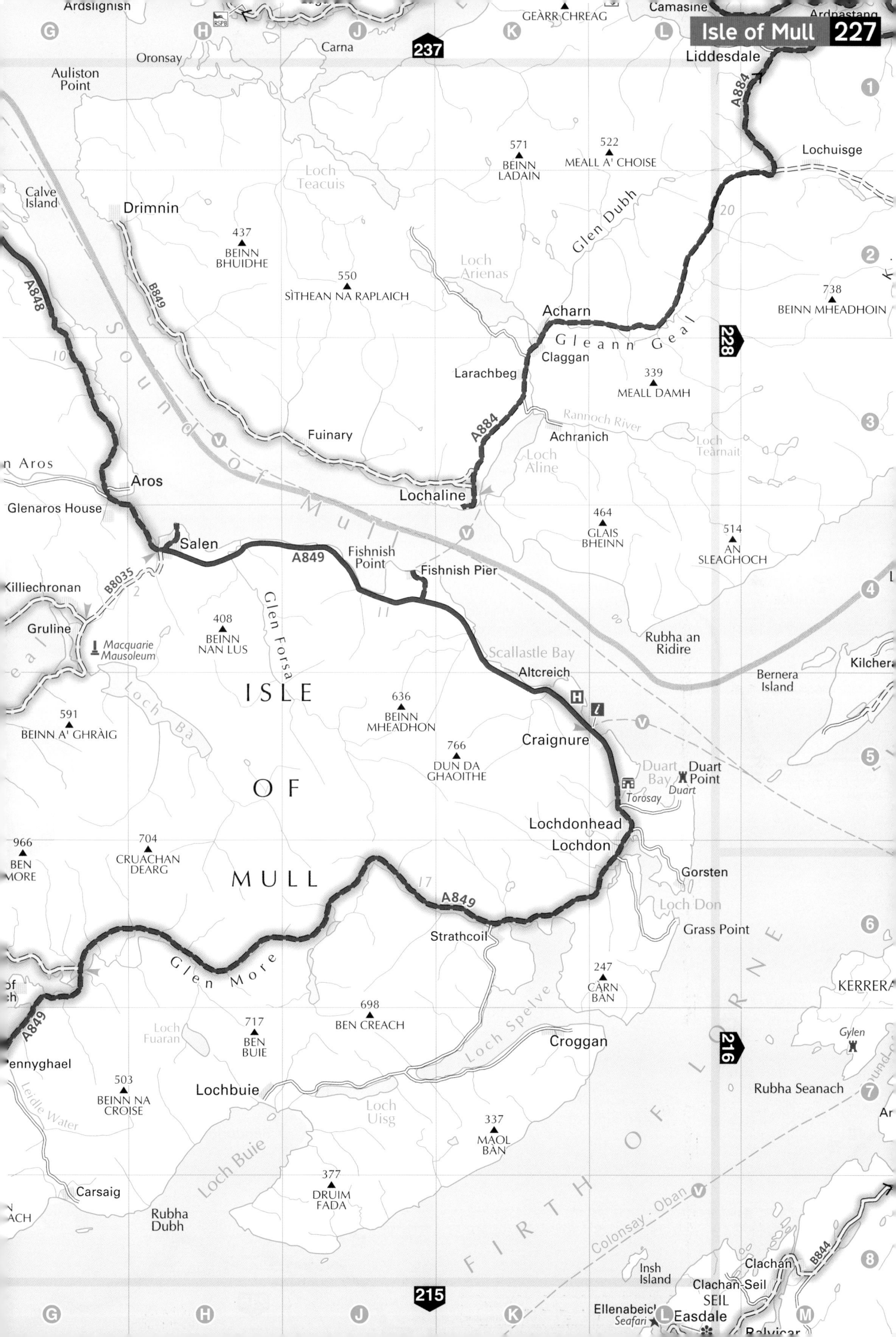

G · H · J · K · L

Ardslignish
GEÀRR CHREAG
Camasine
Ardnastang

Carna
237
Liddesdale

Oronsay
A884

Auliston
Point

571
BEINN
LADAIN
522
MEALL A' CHOISE
Lochuisge

Calve
Island
Drimnin
Loch
Teacuis
Glen Dubh
20

437
BEINN
BHUIDHE
550
SÌTHEAN NA RAPLAICH
Loch
Arienas

738
BEINN MHEADHOIN

A848
B849
Acharn
228

Gleann Geal

Claggan

Larachbeg
339
MEALL DAMH

Fuinary
A884
Achranich
Rannoch River

Loch
Teàrnait

n Aros

Aros

Glenaros House
Loch
Àline
Lochaline

464
GLAIS
BHEINN
514
AN
SLEAGHOCH

Salen
A849
Fishnish
Point
Fishnish Pier

Killiechronan
B8035
2
Gruline

Macquarie
Mausoleum

408
BEINN
NAN LUS
Glen Forsa
11
Scallastic Bay
Altcreich
Rubha an
Ridire
Bernera
Island
Kilchera

ISLE

636
BEINN
MHEADHON
H
i
V
Craignure

591
BEINN A' GHRÀIG
Loch Bà

766
DUN DA
GHAOITHE
Duart
Bay
Duart
Point
Duart
Torosay

OF

Lochdonhead
Lochdon

966
BEN
MORE
704
CRUACHAN
DEARG
Gorsten
Loch Don

MULL
17
A849
Grass Point

Strathcoil
247
CARN
BAN
KERRERA

Glen More
698
BEN CREACH
Loch Spelve
Croggan
216

717
BEN
BUIE
503
BEINN NA
CROISE
Loch
Fuaran
Gylen

ennyghael
Lochbuie
Loch
Uisg
Rubha Seanach

Leidle Water
Carsaig
Rubha
Dubh
Loch Buie
337
MAOL
BÀN

377
DRUIM
FADA
Colonsay · Oban
V
Insh
Island
Clachan
B844

FIRTH OF LORNE
Clachan-Seil
SEIL
Ellenabeich
Seafari
Easdale

215

G · H · J · K · L · M

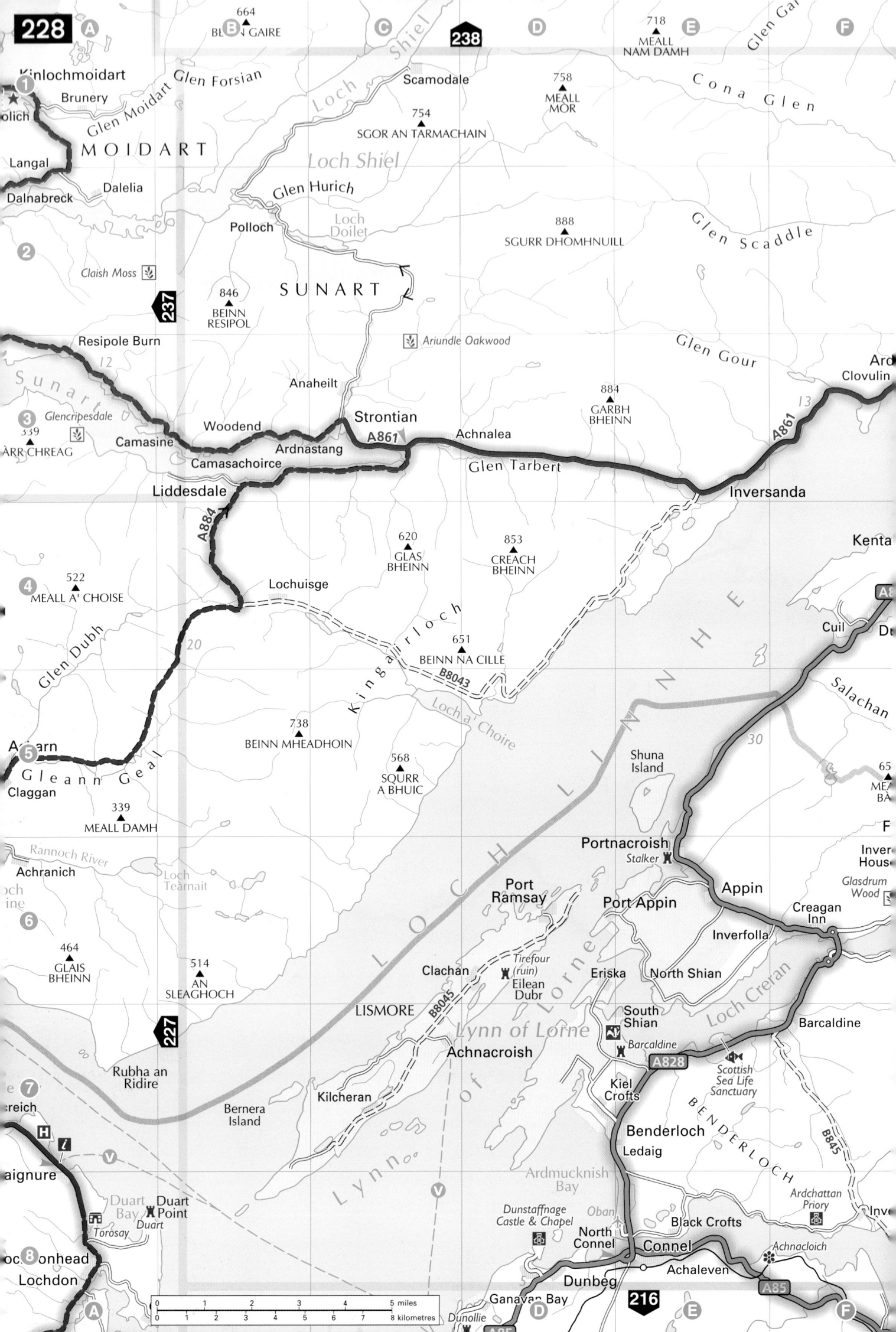

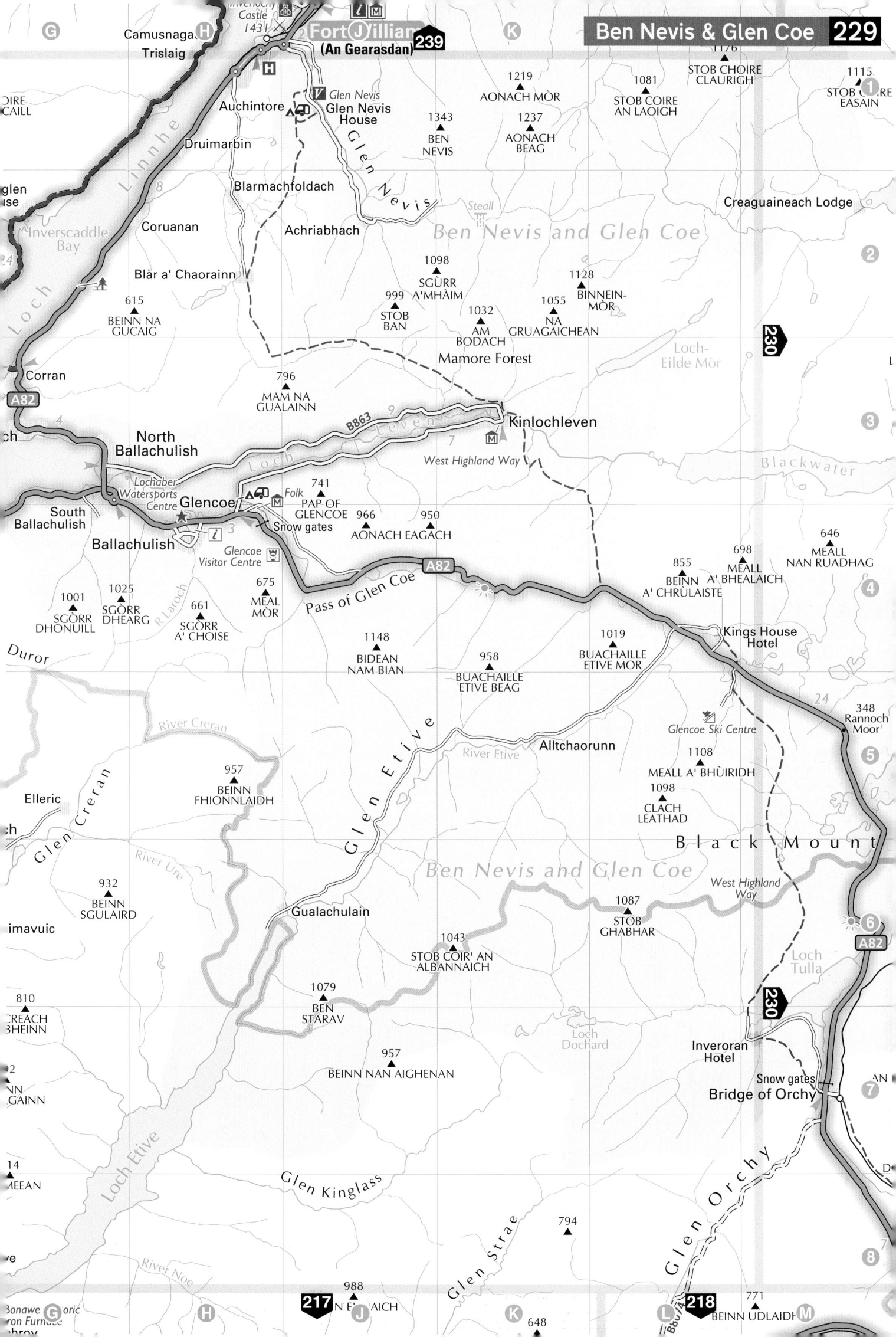

G   H   J   K

Camusnagaul
Trislaig

OIRE
CAILL

Inverscaddle
Bay

Corran

A82

North
Ballachulish

Lochaber
Watersports
Centre

South
Ballachulish

Ballachulish

Duror

Elleric

imavuic

Inverlochy
Castle
1431

Fort William
(An Gearasdan)   239

Glen Nevis

Glen Nevis
House

Auchintore

Druimarbin

Blarmachfoldach

Achriabhach

Blàr a' Chaorainn

615
BEINN NA
GUCAIG

796
MAM NA
GUALAINN

Glencoe

Folk

741
PAP OF
GLENCOE

Snow gates

Glencoe
Visitor Centre

966
AONACH EAGACH

950

675
MEAL
MOR

1148
BIDEAN
NAM BIAN

958
BUACHAILLE
ETIVE BEAG

1001
SGORR
DHONUILL

1025
SGÒRR
DHEARG

661
SGORR
A' CHOISE

R Laroch

957
BEINN
FHIONNLAIDH

Glen Creran

River Creran

River Ure

932
BEINN
SGULAIRD

Gualachulain

Glen Etive

River Etive

Alltchaorunn

810
REACH
BHEINN

988
N E....AICH

Glen Kinglass

1079
BEN
STARAV

957
BEINN NAN AIGHENAN

Loch Etive

River Noe

Bonawe
oric
ron Furnace
ebro

STOB CHOIRE
CLAURIGH   1176

STOB COIRE
EASAIN   1115

1219
AONACH MÒR

1081
STOB COIRE
AN LAOIGH

1343
BEN
NEVIS

1237
AONACH
BEAG

Steall

Ben Nevis and Glen Coe

Creaguaineach Lodge

1098
SGÙRR
A'MHÀIM

999
STOB
BAN

1032
AM
BODACH

1128
BINNEIN-
MÒR

1055
NA
GRUAGAICHEAN

Mamore Forest

Loch-
Eilde Mòr

230

B863   Leven   Kinlochleven

West Highland Way

Blackwater

646
MEALL
NAN RUADHAG

698
MEALL
A' BHEALAICH

855
BEINN
A' CHRÙLAISTE

A82

Pass of Glen Coe

1019
BUACHAILLE
ETIVE MOR

Kings House
Hotel

348
Rannoch
Moor

24

Glencoe Ski Centre

1108
MEALL A' BHÙIRIDH

1098
CLACH
LEATHAD

Black Mount

Ben Nevis and Glen Coe

West Highland
Way

1087
STOB
GHABHAR

1043
STOB COIR' AN
ALBANNAICH

Loch
Dochard

Loch
Tulla

230

Inveroran
Hotel

Snow gates

Bridge of Orchy

Glen Orchy

794

Glen Strae

217   218

648

771
BEINN UDLAIDH

1   2   3   4   5   6   7   8

A' MHARCONAICH

241

G 1008 **▲**
BEINN
UDLAMAIN 991 **▲**
SGAIRNEACH
MHOR

Dalnaspidal

H

J

K

Loch Eric...

Loch Garry

20

Snow gates
Dalnacardoch

Glen Garry

A9

491 **▲**
CRAIG
BHAGAILTEACH

Gle...

Loch Con

Clan
Donnachaidh
M Bruar

Calvine
Struan

Old
Struan

Bla

232

Loch
Errochty

841 **▲**
BEINN
MHOLACH

Glen Errochty

B847

Trinafour

Tay Forest Park

14

511 **▲**
TORR
DUBH

892 **▲**
BEINN
A' CHUALLAICH

Tressait B8019

B846

7

Loch Tummel

R Tummel

ichonan

16

Loch Rannoch

Kinloch
Rannoch

Drumchastle

Dunalastair

Tummel
Bridge

Foss
Daloist

Frenich

Loch Tum

13

Inverhadden

Tempar

Dunalastair
Water

Carie

Camghouran

Tay Forest Park

1081 **▲**
SCHIEHALLION

Tay Forest
Park

780 **▲**
FARRAGON
HILL

780 **▲**
MEALL
TAIRNEACHAN

Loch
Glassie

Loch Rannoch and Glen Lyon

745 **▲**
MEALL A' MHUIC

824 **▲**
BEINN
DEARG

1027 **▲**
CARN
GORM

1042 **▲**
CARN
MAIRG

Glengoulandie
Deer Park

B846

14

Camserney
Dull

Menzies

W

G

Coshieville

Keltneyburn

en Lyon

Bridge of Balgie

River Lyon

780 **▲**
MEALL
LUAIDHE

924 **▲**
MEALL A' CHOIRE
LEITH

1116 **▲**
MEALL
GARBH

1000 **▲**
MEALL
GREIGH

Fortingall

Tay Forest
Park

Kenmore

Fearnan

Croftmoraig
Stone Circle

A827

River Tay

232

E

Glen Qua

ME

IGHREAG

1214 **▲**
BEN LAWERS

Lochan na
Làirige

Leckbuie

713 **▲**
BEINN
BHREAC

Acharn

The Crannog
Centre **M**

A

N

7

Lawers

Ben Lawers

A827

25

Loch Tay

864 **▲**
SRON A' CHAOINEIDH

802 **▲**
MEALL NAM
FUARAN

River Quaich

Milton
Morenish

Morenish

Ardeonaig

B

Moirlanich
Longhouse

Killin

Finlarig

Breadalbane
Folklore Centre **V**

Dochart

G

H

219

D

A

J

682 **▲**

879 **▲**
CREAG
UCHDAG

K

220

L

River Almond

M

1

2

3

4

5

6

7

8

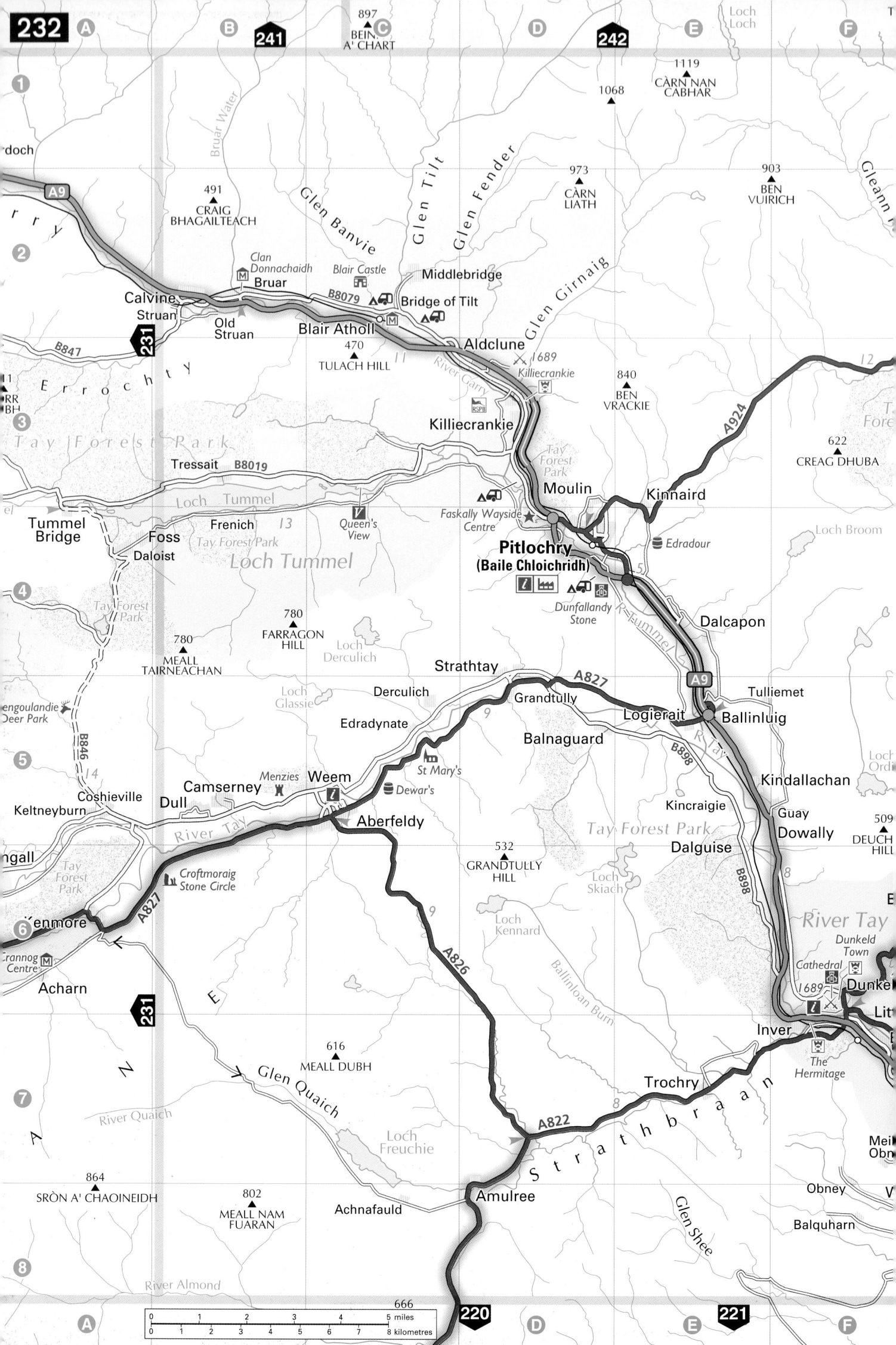

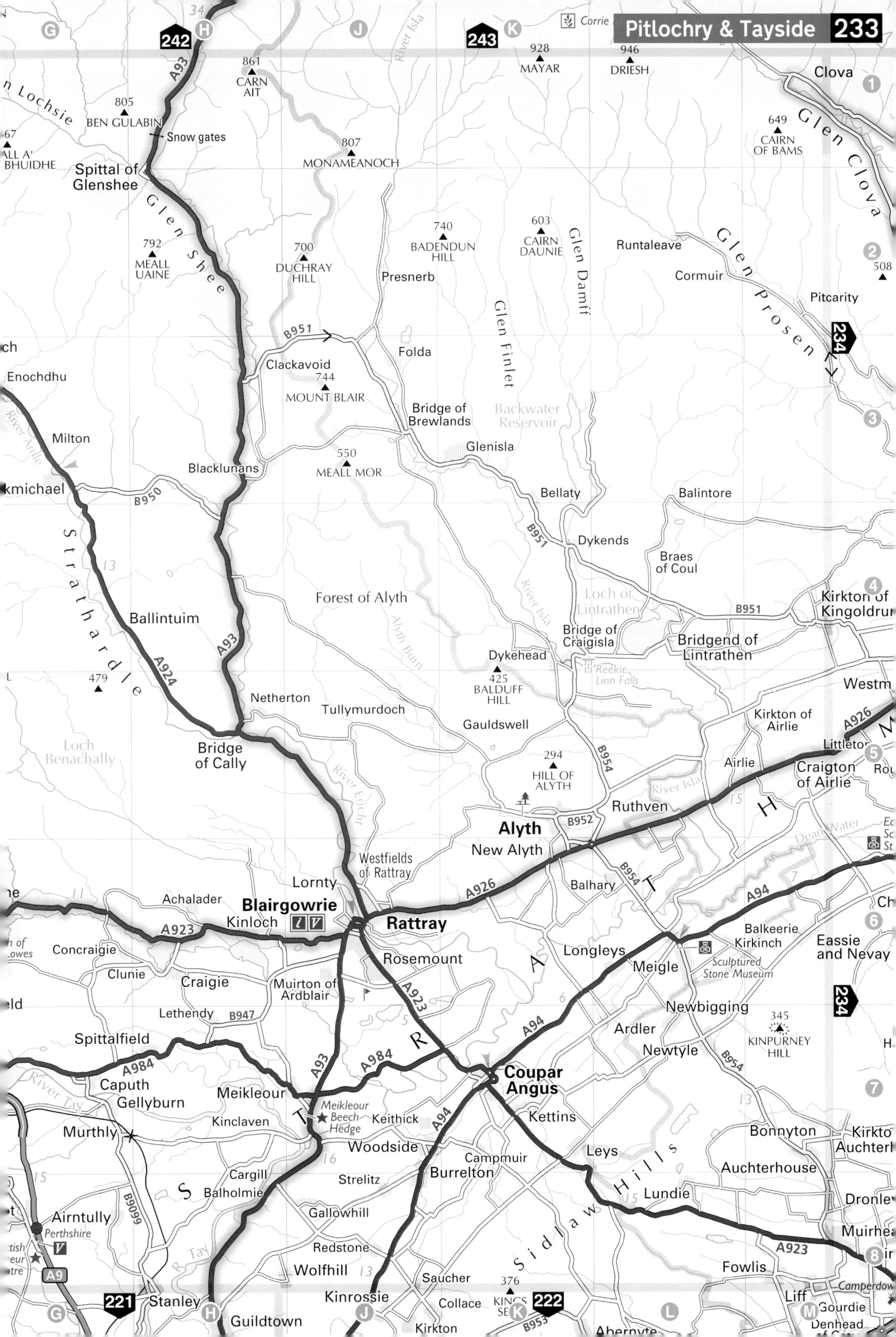

Corrie

G   242 H   J   243 K

Clova

34

River Isla

928
▲ MAYAR

946
▲ DRIESH

861
▲ CARN
AIT

67
▲
ALL A'
BHUIDHE

805
▲ BEN GULABIN

Snow gates

649
▲ CAIRN
OF BAMS

Glen Clova

807
▲ MONAMEANOCH

603
▲ CAIRN
DAUNIE

Runtaleave

Spittal of
Glenshee

792
▲ MEALL
UAINE

700
▲ DUCHRAY
HILL

740
▲ BADENDUN
HILL

Presnerb

Glen Damff

Cormuir

Pitcarity

508
▲

234

Enochdhu

River Ardle

B951

Clackavoid

Folda

Glen Finlet

Backwater
Reservoir

Glenisla

744
▲ MOUNT BLAIR

Bridge of
Brewlands

Milton

550
▲ MEALL MOR

Bellaty

Balintore

Blacklunans

B950

kmichael

Strathardle

13

Ballintuim

Forest of Alyth

Alyth Burn

River Isla

Dykends

Braes
of Coul

Loch of
Lintrathen

B951

Kirkton of
Kingoldrur

479
▲

A924

A93

Netherton

Tullymurdoch

Bridge of
Craigisla

Bridgend of
Lintrathen

Westm

Loch
Benachally

Bridge
of Cally

Dykehead

425
▲ BALDUFF
HILL

Gauldswell

Reekie
Linn Falls

Kirkton of
Airlie

A926

Airlie

Littleto

Craigton
of Airlie

Rou

294
▲ HILL OF
ALYTH

B954

River Isla

Ruthven

H

15

M

Westfields
of Rattray

Alyth

New Alyth

B952

A94

Balkeerie
Kirkinch

Eassie
and Nevay

Ch

Lornty

Achalader

A923

Blairgowrie

Kinloch i V

Rattray

A926

Balhary

B954

Longleys

Meigle

Sculptured
Stone Museum

345
▲ KINPURNEY
HILL

6

234

Concraigie

of
owes

Clunie

Craigie

Muirton of
Ardblair

Rosemount

A923

A

Newbigging

Ardler

Newtyle

B954

H

Spittalfield

Lethendy

B947

A984

5

R

Caputh

River Tay

Meikleour

Gellyburn

Kinclaven

Meikleour
Beech
Hedge

Keithick

A984

Woodside

Kettins

Campmuir

Burrelton

**Coupar
Angus**

Leys

Bonnyton

Kirkto
Auchter

Auchterhouse

Dronle

Murthly

15

Cargill

Balholmie

Strelitz

Sidlaw Hills

Lundie

13

15

Muirhe

Airntully

Perthshire

B9099

tish
eur
tre

V

A9

Gallowhill

Redstone

Wolfhill   13

Saucher

376
▲ KINGS
SE

A923

Fowlis

Liff

Gourdie

Camperdow

G   221 H   J   222 K   L   M

Stanley

Guildtown

Kinrossie

Kirkton

Collace

B953

Abernyte

Denhead

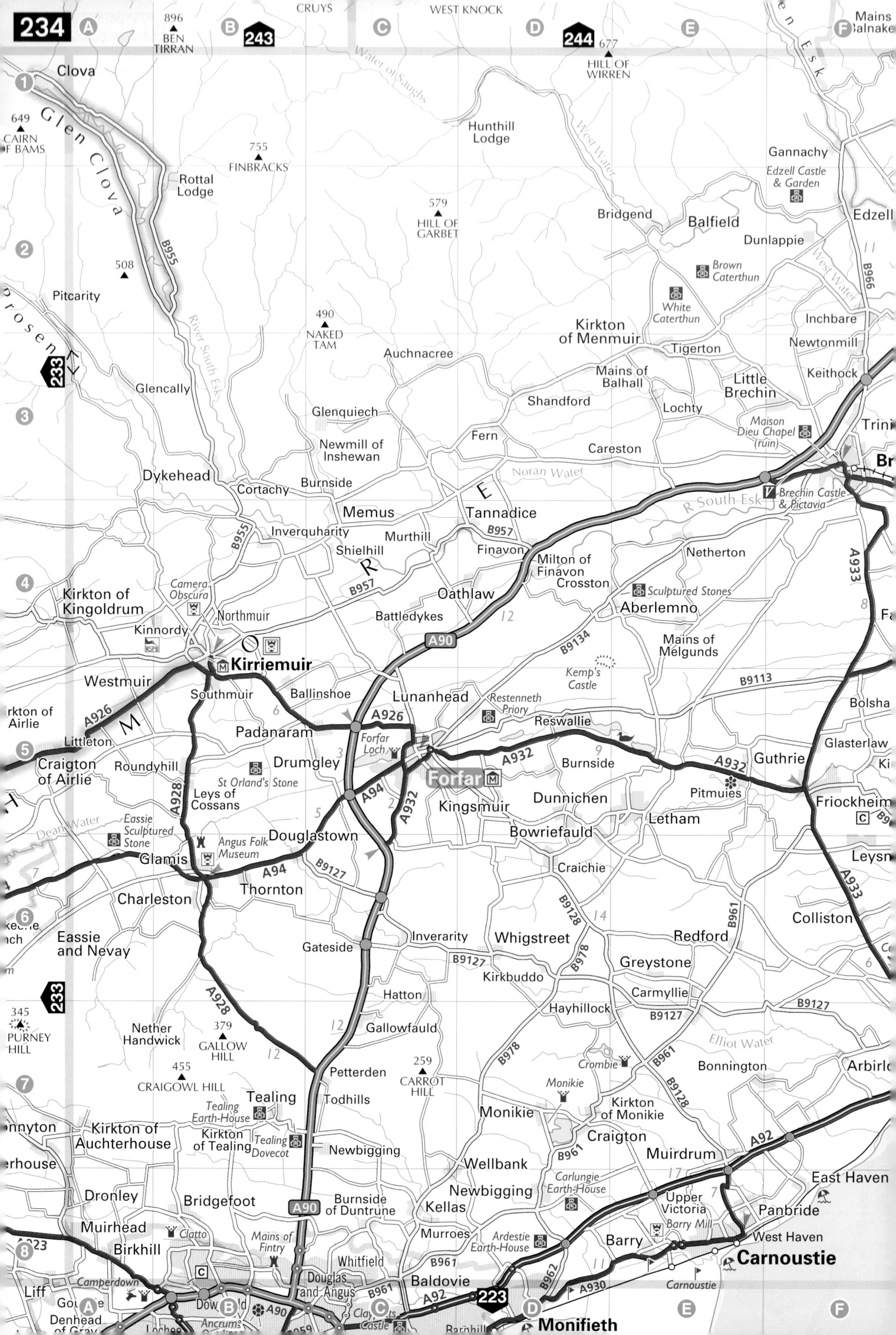

Pittarrow

Redmyre Arbuthnott Centre

G 244 H J 245 K

1

Inverbervie

Bervie Bay

Mains of Haulkerton

Gourdon

B9120

Laurencekirk

25

B974

B9120

Redford

Sauchieburn

A90 B974

North Esk

Benholm

2

Dykelands

A937

Johnshaven

Logie Pert

Marykirk

Craigo

Bush

Lochside

Milton Ness

Logie

Morphie

St Cyrus

3

Hillside

A92

House of Dun

Dun

A935 9

Montrose Air Station M

Montrose

Montrose Basin

M

4

Barnhead

Scurdie Ness

Maryton

A934

Ferryden

Craig

Usan

Westerton of Rossie

Boddin Point

Braehead

Lunan

5

Lunan Bay

Inverkeilor

Water 13

Red Head

6

A92

Marywell

eans

Auchmithie

Carlingheugh Bay

The Deil's Head

Arbroath

i M

7

| 0 | 1 | 2 | 3 | 4 | 5 miles |
| 0 | 1 2 | 3 | 4 | 5 6 | 7 8 kilometres |

8

G H J K L M

A' Bhrìdeanach

RÙM

570
ORVAL

246

MULLACH
MÒR

Rubha
na Roinne

Kinloch

Loch
Scresort

810
ASKIVAL

Harris
Bay

763
SGÙRR NAN
GILLEAN

Rubha nam
Meirleach

The Small Isles

Sound of Rùm

Bay of
Laig

Cleadale

299
AN
CRUACHAN

Rubha an
Fhasaidh

Laig

EIGG

Kildon

393
AN SGÙRR

Galmisda

Eilean
Chatha

Sound of Eigg

Eilean
nan Each

MUCK

Port Mòr

Sanna Point

Sanna
Bay

Sanna

Portuairk

Achnaha

Ardnamurchan
Point

Achosnich

MEALL

B8007

Eilean Mòr

Bagh a Chaisteil
(Castlebay)
Loch Baghasdail
(Lochboisdale)

Rubha
Mòr

Rubha
Sgor-innis

342
BEINN
NA SEILG

Kil

225

Bousd

Sorisdale

Ormsaigmore

Cliad
Bay

B8072

COLL

0   1   2   3   4   5 miles
0 1 2 3 4 5 6 7 8 kilometres

B8071

Ardmore
Point

Sorne
Po

226

rinagour

Coll–Oban

Quinish Point

Glengorm Castle

KNOYD

Sleat

G   H   J   V   K   Sandai

247

Ard
Thurinish

Point
of Sleat

Inverie
Bay

Rubha
Raonuill

Courteachan

Mallaig
(Malaig)

Mallaigvaig

547
CÀRN A'GHOBHAIR

Glasnacardoch Bay

Loch an
Nostaire

437
SGÙRR BHUIDHE

Beoraidbeg

Morar

Bracorina

Bracora

Tarbet

B8008

238 ► Swordland

Loch Nevis

Kyle

Glenancross

Loch Morar

Lettermorar

Meoble

A830

Bunacaimb

503
CÀRN A'
MHÀDAIDH-RUAIDH

MEITH

River Meoble

Eilean Ighe

Back of
Keppoch

Loch nan Ceall

Arisaig

600
SIDHEAN
MÒR

Luinga Mhòr

10

Prince Charlie's
Cairn

Kinlochnanuagh

Loch

Rubh' Arisaig

Druimindarroch

Arisaig
House

Loch nan Uamh

Polnish

Lochailort

Loch
Eilt

103
CRUACH
DOIRE

Ardnish

Inverailort

Sound of Arisaig

Rubha
Choalais

Loch Ailort

A861

877
ROIS-BHEINN

712

664
BEINN GAIRE

Smearisary

Glenuig

21

Eilean
Shona

Kinlochmoidart

Glen Forsian

Rubha Àird
Druimnich

Loch Moidart

Tioram

Seven Men
of Moidart

Brunery

Glen Moidart

Loch

Ockle
Point

Morar, Moidart and
Ardnamurchan

239
BEINN
BHREAC

Ardmolich

M O I D A R T

Imory

Ockle

Ardtoe

Shielfoot

Langal

Dalelia

Glen Hurich

Branault

356
BEINN
BHREAC

B8044

Kentra

Mingarrypark

Blain

Dalnabreck

228 ► Polloch

A R D N A M U R C H A N

Arevegaig

Acharacle

Claish Moss

S U N A

437

A861

846
BEINN
RESIPOL

7

Loch
Mudle

Salen

Resipole Burn

12

527
BEN
HIANT

Natural
History

Glenbeg

512
BEN
LAGA

B8007

Loch Sunart

Anaheilt

19

Glenborrodale

Laga

339
GEÀRR CHREAG

Glencripesdale

Woodend

Ardnastang

Ardslignish

RSPB

Carna

Camasine

Camasachoire

Auliston
Point

Oronsay

Liddesdale

A884

227

G   H   J   K   L   M

8

A   B   C   248   D   E   F   S TERS

1

BEINN NA SEAMRAIG

Sleneig Glen Beag
Brochs

1011
▲
THE SADDLE

Ornsay

974
▲
BEINN
SGRITHEAL

773
▲
BEINN NAN CAORACH

945
▲
SGURR
NA SGINE

Sandaig
Island

Rubha
Buidhe

Arnisdale

Glen Arnisdale

Rubh' Ard
Slisneach

Corran

2

247

Inverguseran

784
▲
BEINN NA
CAILLICH

614
▲

709
▲
DRUM
FADA

Kinloch
Hourn

Airor

Glen Guseran

Barrisdale
Bay

102
SGURR
MHAO

3

518
▲
DRUIM NA
CLUAIN-AIRIDHE

1019
▲
LADHAR
BHEINN

Sandaig

Knoydart

Sandaig Bay

K N O Y D A R T

940
▲
LUINNE BHEINN

Inverie

Loch an
Dubh-Lochain

Inverie
Bay

946
▲
MEALL BUIDHE

1003
▲
SGURR MÒR

Rubha
Raonuill

4

allaigvaig

547
▲
CÀRN A'GHOBHAIR

854
▲
BEINN BHUIDHE

1039
▲
SGURR NA CICHE

Loch an
Nostaire

437
▲
SGURR BHUIDHE

raidbeg

Bracora

Bracorina

Kylesmorar

859
▲
SGURR NAH-AIDE

Glen Dessarry

5

oss

Tarbet

723
▲
SGURR BREAC

Swordland

503
▲
CÀRN A'
MHÀDAIDH-RUAIDH

Lettermorar

Loch   Morar

Glen Pean

716
▲
AN STAC

6

Meoble

710
▲
MEITH BHEINN

949
▲
SGURR NAN
COIREACHAN

964
▲
SGÙRR
THUILM

600
▲
SIDHEAN
MÒR

237

River Meoble

Prince Charlie's
Cairn

Loch Beoriad

633
▲

796
▲
SGURR
AN UTHA

Glen Finnan

Arisaig
House

Kinlochnanuagh

Polnish

7

Ardnish

Lochailort

Inverailort

Loch
Eilt

A830

14

Glenfinnan
Viaduct

Glenfinnan

Kinlocheil

Drimsallie

Loch Ailort

A861

877
▲
ROIS-BHEINN

882
▲
BEINN
ODHAR BHEAG

Glenfinnan
Monument

Garvan

8

712
▲

664
▲
BEINN GAIRE

718
▲
MEALL
NAM DAMH

758

Glen Garvan

Ki ochmoi

0   1   2   3   4   5 miles
0 1 2 3 4 5 6 7 8 kilometres

A   Scamodale   228   D   E   F   Co

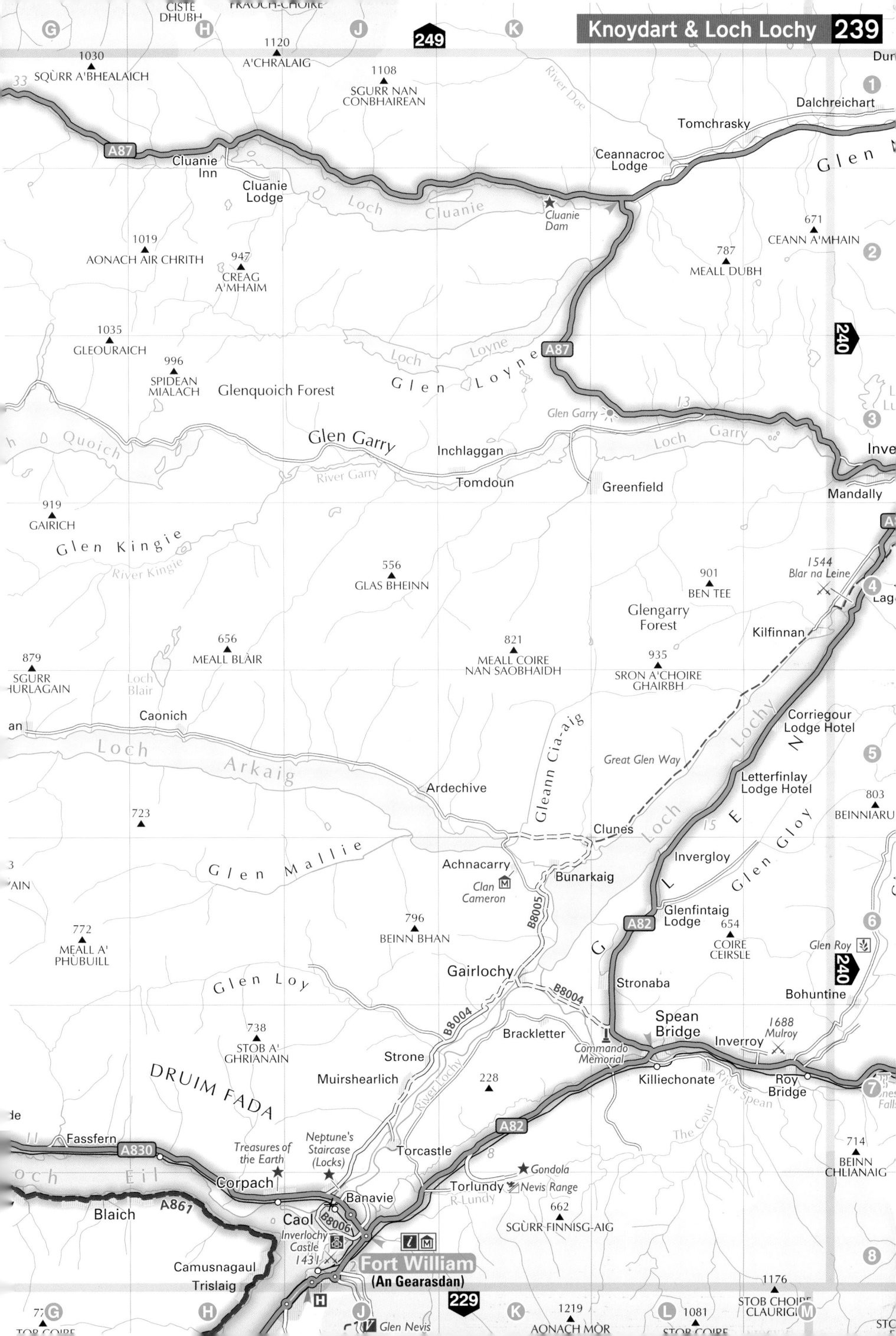

249

G H J K

1030
SQÙRR A'BHEALAICH
33

1120
A'CHRALAIG

1108
SGURR NAN
CONBHAIREAN

A87 Cluanie
Inn
Cluanie
Lodge

Loch Cluanie

Cluanie
Dam

River Doe

Dalchreichart

Tomchrasky

Ceannacroc
Lodge

Glen

671
CEANN A'MHAIN

Dur

1

2

1019
AONACH AIR CHRITH

947
CREAG
A'MHAIM

787
MEALL DUBH

1035
GLEOURAICH

996
SPIDEAN
MIALACH

Glenquoich Forest

Loch Loyne

Glen Loyne

A87

240

3

Glen Garry
h Quoich

Glen Garry

Inchlaggan

River Garry

Tomdoun

Greenfield

Glen Garry

Loch Garry

Inve

Mandally

A

919
GAIRICH

Glen Kingie

River Kingie

556
GLAS BHEINN

901
BEN TEE

Glengarry
Forest

1544
Blar na Leine

Lag

4

879
SGURR
HURLAGAIN

656
MEALL BLÀIR

Loch
Blair

821
MEALL COIRE
NAN SAOBHAIDH

935
SRON A'CHOIRE
GHAIRBH

Kilfinnan

Corriegour
Lodge Hotel

5

Caonich

Loch Arkaig

Ardechive

Great Glen Way

Letterfinlay
Lodge Hotel

803
BEINNIARU

723

Gleann Cia-aig

Clunes

Loch Lochy N

15

Glen Gloy

E

Glen Mallie

Achnacarry

Clan
Cameron

Bunarkaig

Invergloy

B8005

Glenfintaig
Lodge

A82

654
COIRE
CEIRSLE

Glen Roy

240

6

AIN

772
MEALL A'
PHÙBUILL

796
BEINN BHAN

G

Stronaba

Bohuntine

3

Glen Loy

738
STOB A'
GHRIANAIN

B8004

Gairlochy

B8004

Brackletter

Commando
Memorial

Spean
Bridge

1688
Mulroy

Inverroy

Roy
Bridge

7

Strone

Muirshearlich

River Lochy

228

A82

8

Killiechonate

River Spean

The Cour

Fassfern

A830

Treasures of
the Earth

Neptune's
Staircase
(Locks)

Torcastle

Gondola

Nevis Range

714
BEINN
CHLIANAIG

Loch Eil

Corpach

Banavie

R-Lundy

Torlundy

662
SGÙRR FINNISG-AIG

STO

8

A861

Blaich

B8006

Caol

Inverlochy
Castle
1431

Fort William
(An Gearasdan)

229

1176
STOB CHOIRE
CLAURIGI

Camusnagaul

Trislaig

G H J K L M

77

Glen Nevis

1219

1081

STOB COIRE

TOB COIRE

AONACH MÒR

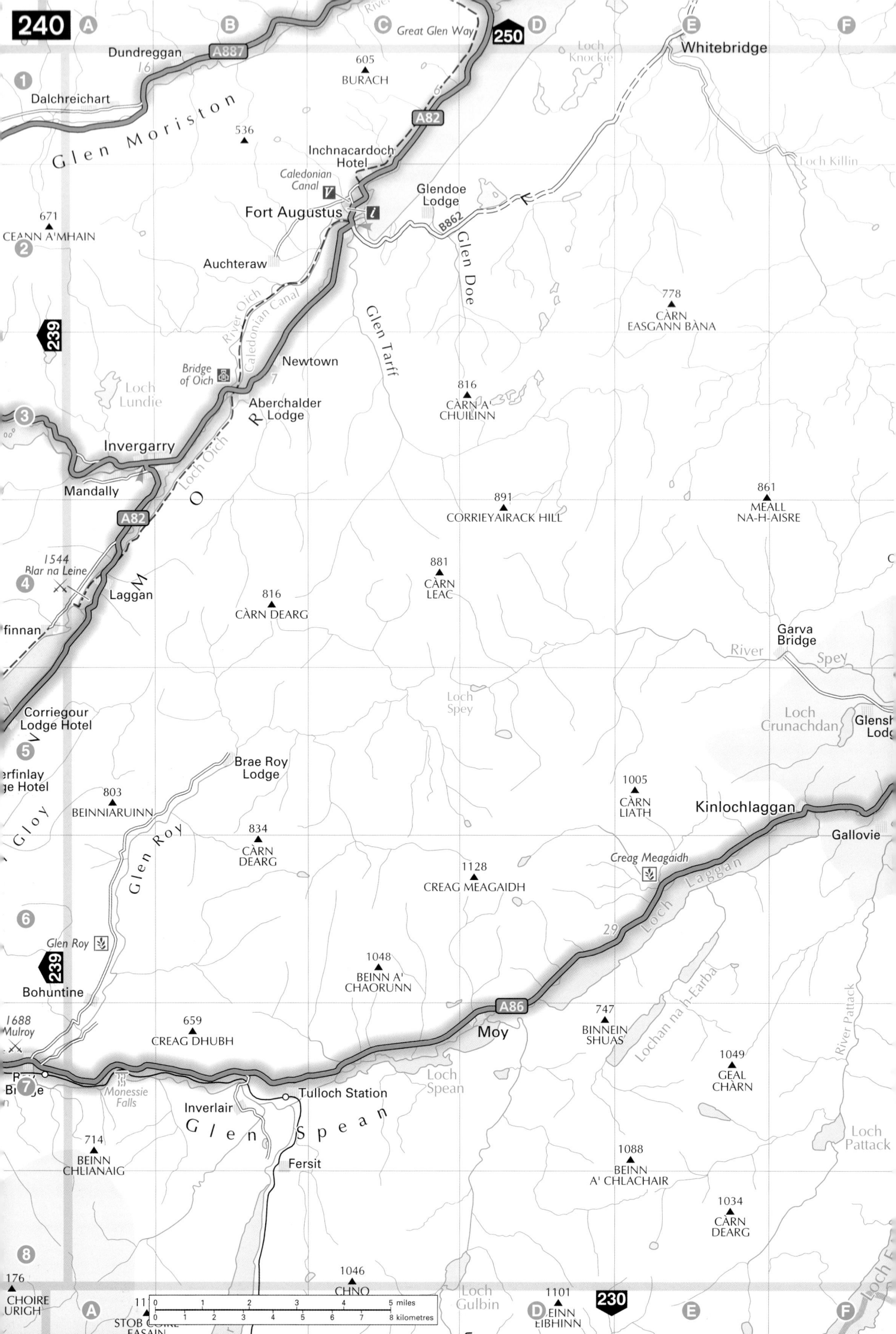

A   B   C   250   D   E   F

1

Dalchreichart
Dundreggan
A887
Great Glen Way
Whitebridge
Loch
Knockie
605
BURACH
A82
Inchnacardoch
Hotel
Loch Killin
Glen Moriston

536

Caledonian
Canal

Glendoe
Lodge
Fort Augustus   *i*
Ceann a'mhain
671
CEANN A'MHAIN

2

Auchteraw
B862
Glen Doe

Glen Tarff

778
CÀRN
EASGANN BÀNA

239

Newtown

Bridge
of Oich
Caledonian Canal

7
Aberchalder
Lodge

816
CÀRN A'
CHUILINN

Loch
Lundie

3

Invergarry

Loch Oich

861
MEALL
NA-H-AISRE

Mandally

891
CORRIEYAIRACK HILL

A82

1544
Blar na Leine

881
CÀRN
LEAC

4

Laggan

816
CÀRN DEARG

finnan

Garva
Bridge

River   Spey

Corriegour
Lodge Hotel

Loch
Spey

Loch
Crunachdan
Glensh
Lodg

5

erfinlay
ge Hotel

Brae Roy
Lodge

1005
CÀRN
LIATH

Kinlochlaggan

803
BEINNIARUINN

Gloy

Glen Roy

834
CÀRN
DEARG

Gallovie

Creag Meagaidh

1128
CREAG MEAGAIDH

Loch Laggan

6

Glen Roy

29

239

1048
BEINN A'
CHAORUNN

Bohuntine

1688
Mulroy

659
CREAG DHUBH

A86

Moy

747
BINNEIN
SHUAS

Lochan na h-Earba

1049
GEAL
CHÀRN

River Pattack

7

Bri   ge
*Monessie
Falls*

Inverlair

Tulloch Station
Loch
Spean

Glen   Spean

Fersit

1088
BEINN
A' CHLACHAIR

Loch
Pattack

714
BEINN
CHLIANAIG

1034
CÀRN
DEARG

8

176
CHOIRE
URIGH

1046
CHNO

Loch
Gulbin

1101
230
EINN
EIBHINN

STOB COIRE
EASAIN

Loch E

11

0   1   2   3   4   5 miles
0   1   2   3   4   5   6   7   8 kilometres

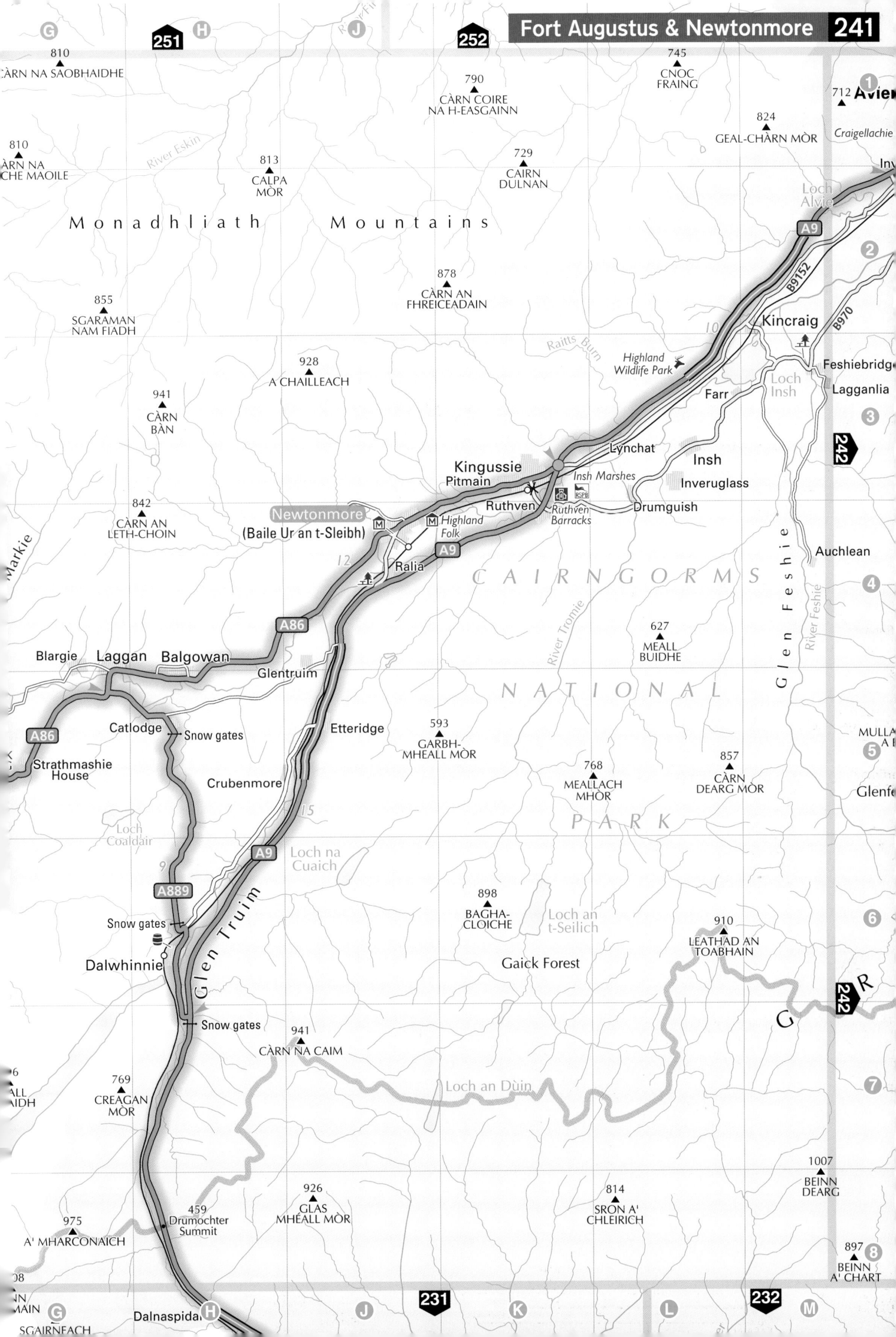

251

252

1
810
CÀRN NA SAOBHAIDHE

790
CÀRN COIRE
NA H-EASGAINN

745
CNOC
FRAING

712 Avie

824
GEAL-CHÀRN MÒR

810
ÀRN NA
CHE MAOILE

813
CALPA
MÒR

729
CAIRN
DULNAN

Inv

Craigellachie

Loch
Alvie

A9

Monadhliath Mountains

878
CÀRN AN
FHREICEADAIN

B9152

B9970

2

855
SGARAMAN
NAM FIADH

Raitts Burn

Highland
Wildlife Park

Kincraig

Feshiebridg

928
A CHAILLEACH

Loch
Insh

Farr

Lagganlia

3

941
CÀRN
BÀN

Lynchat

Insh

Inveruglass

242

842
CÀRN AN
LETH-CHOIN

Kingussie
Pitmain

Insh Marshes

RSPB

Drumguish

Auchlean

4

Newtonmore
(Baile Ur an t-Sleibh)

Ruthven
Ruthven
Barracks

Highland
Folk

A9

CAIRNGORMS

Glen Feshie

River Feshie

Ralia

627
MEALL
BUIDHE

River Tromie

Blargie Laggan Balgowan

A86

Glentruim

NATIONAL

MULLA
A

5

A86

Catlodge → Snow gates

Etteridge

593
GARBH-
MHEALL MÒR

768
MEALLACH
MHÒR

857
CÀRN
DEARG MÒR

Glenfe

Strathmashie
House

Crubenmore

PARK

Loch
Coaldair

15

A9

Loch na
Cuaich

898
BAGHA-
CLOICHE

Loch an
t-Seilich

910
LEATHAD AN
TOABHAIN

6

A889

Glen Truim

Snow gates →

Gaick Forest

G
R

242

Dalwhinnie

Snow gates

941
CÀRN NA CAIM

Loch an Dùin

7

6
LL
IDH

769
CREAGAN
MÒR

1007
BEINN
DEARG

975
A' MHARCONAICH

459
Drumochter
Summit

926
GLAS
MHEALL MÒR

814
SRON A'
CHLEIRICH

897
BEINN
A' CHART

8

N
MAIN

231

232

SGAIRNFEACH

Dalnaspida

231

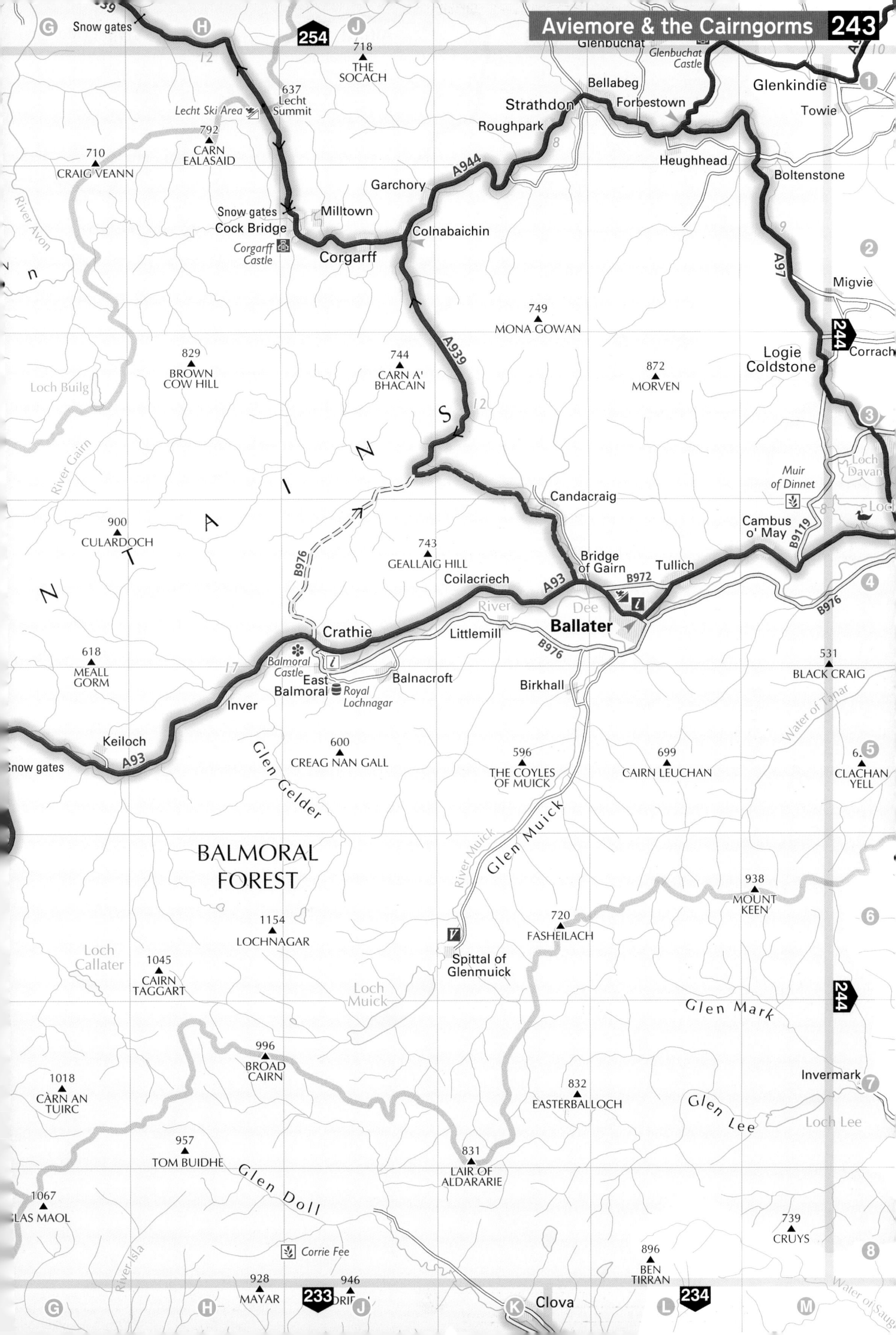

G | H | J

Snow gates

254

718
THE SOCACH

Glenbuchat

Glenbuchat Castle

Bellabeg
Strathdon
Forbestown
Glenkindie

Roughpark
Towie

Heughhead
Boltenstone

637
Lecht Summit

Lecht Ski Area

792
CARN EALASAID

710
CRAIG VEANN

A944

Garchory
Colnabaichin

Milltown

Snow gates
Cock Bridge

Corgarff Castle

Corgarff

9

A97

Migvie

244

Corrach

1

2

3

749
MONA GOWAN

829
BROWN COW HILL

744
CARN A' BHACAIN

A939

872
MORVEN

Logie Coldstone

Loch Davan

Loch

12

N

S

Candacraig

900
CULARDOCH

743
GEALLAIG HILL

Coilacriech

Bridge of Gairn

Tullich

Cambus o' May

B9119

B972

A93

B976

Crathie

River Dee

Ballater

4

B976

618
MEALL GORM

17

Balmoral Castle

East Balmoral

Inver

Littlemill

Keiloch

A93

Balnacroft

Royal Lochnagar

Birkhall

596
THE COYLES OF MUICK

699
CAIRN LEUCHAN

531
BLACK CRAIG

Snow gates

600
CREAG NAN GALL

Glen Gelder

BALMORAL FOREST

Glen Muick

River Muick

938
MOUNT KEEN

5

CLACHAN YELL

1154
LOCHNAGAR

720
FASHEILACH

6

Loch Callater

1045
CAIRN TAGGART

V

Spittal of Glenmuick

Loch Muick

832
EASTERBALLOCH

Glen Mark

244

7

996
BROAD CAIRN

1018
CARN AN TUIRC

Invermark

Glen Lee

Loch Lee

957
TOM BUIDHE

Glen Doll

831
LAIR OF ALDARARIE

1067
GLAS MAOL

739
CRUYS

8

Corrie Fee

928
MAYAR

946
DRIF

233

896
BEN TIRRAN

234

Clova

G | H | J | K | L | M

River Isla

Water of Saug

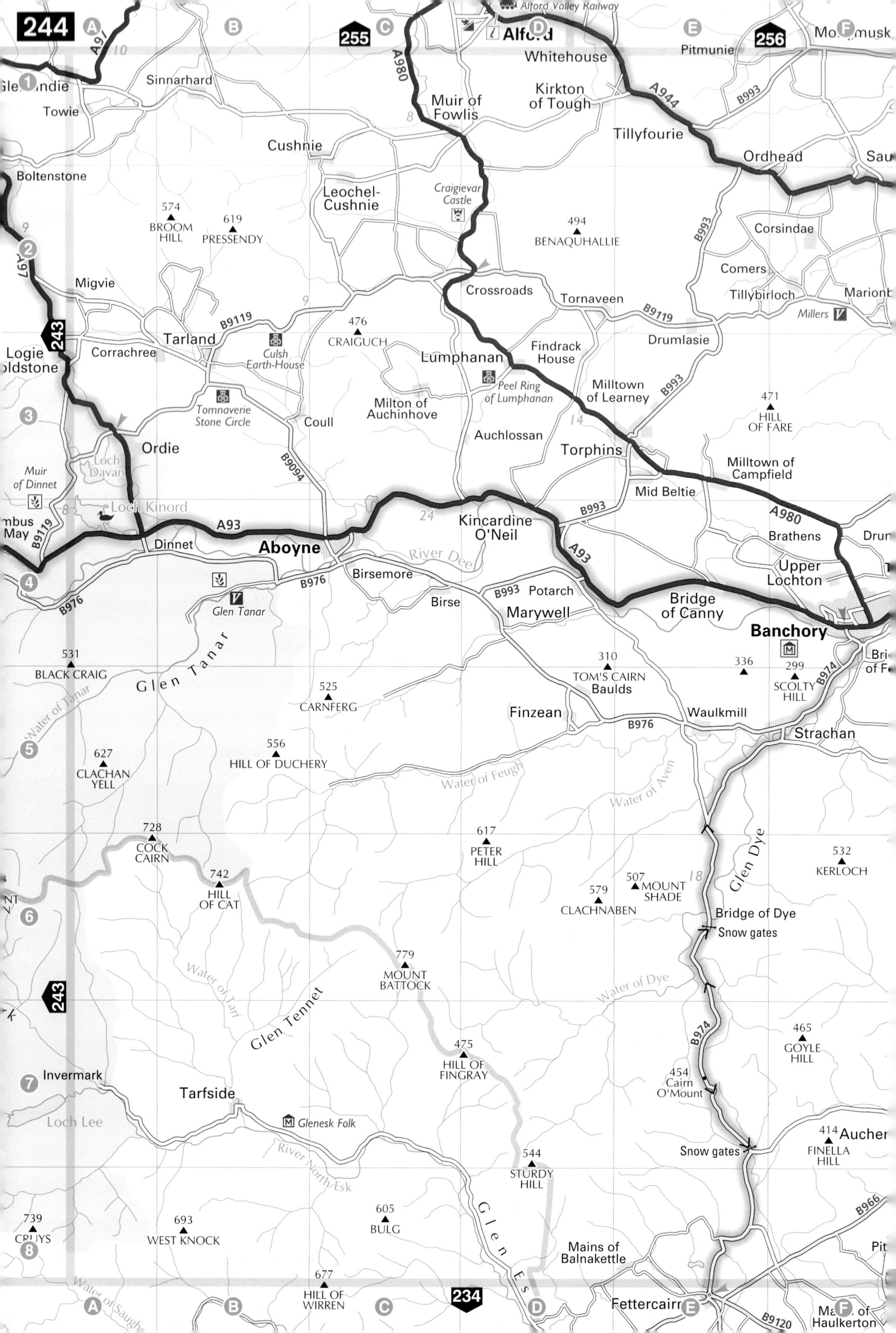

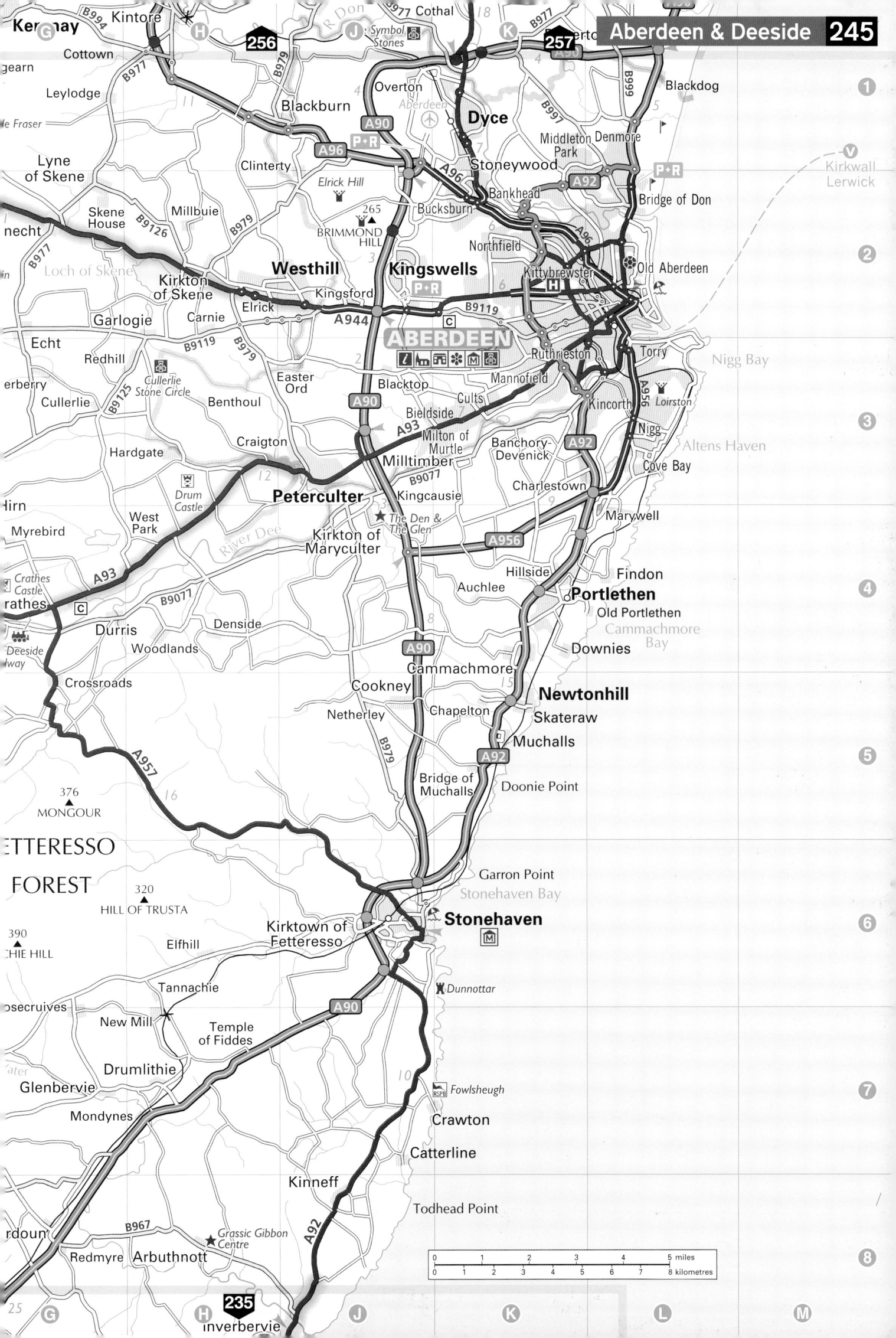

Kemnay
Kintore
B994
Cottown
gearn
Leylodge
le Fraser
Lyne
of Skene
necht
Skene
House
Millbuie
B9126
Kirkton
of Skene
Garlogie
Echt
Redhill
erberry
Cullerlie
Cullerlie
Stone Circle
Hardgate
Hirn
Myrebird
West
Park
Crathes
Castle
rathes
Durris
Denside
Woodlands
Deeside
way
Crossroads

B977
Cothal
18
B977
Overton
Aberdeen
Dyce
Stoneywood
Bankhead
Buckfrom
Northfield
Kittybrewster
Westhill
Kingswells
Kingsford
B9119
Elrick
A944
Carnie
Benthoul
B9119
B979
Easter
Ord
Blacktop
Blacktop
Craigton
Bieldside
Milton of
Murtle
Milltimber
Peterculter
Kingcausie
B9077
Kirkton of
Maryculter
The Den &
The Glen
Drum
Castle

Kintore
256
Blackburn
Clinterty
A90
A96
P+R
Elrick Hill
265
BRIMMOND
HILL
257
Blackdog
Middleton Denmore
Park
A92
P+R
Bridge of Don
Kirkwall
Lerwick
Old Aberdeen
Ruthrieston
Mannofield
ABERDEEN
Cults
Banchory-
Devenick
Charlestown
Marywell
Kincorth
Loirston
Nigg
Nigg Bay
Altens Haven
Cove Bay
Hillside
Auchlee
Portlethen
Old Portlethen
Cammachmore
Bay
Downies

MONGOUR
376
FETTERESSO
FOREST
HILL OF TRUSTA
320
390
CHIE HILL
Elfhill
osecruives
Tannachie
New Mill
Temple
of Fiddes
Drumlithie
Glenbervie
Mondynes
rdoun
B967
Redmyre
Arbuthnott
Grassic Gibbon
Centre

Cammachmore
Cookney
Netherley
Chapelton
Bridge of
Muchalls
Newtonhill
Skateraw
Muchalls
Doonie Point
Garron Point
Stonehaven Bay
Kirktown of
Fetteresso
Stonehaven
Dunnottar
Fowlsheugh
Crawton
Catterline
Kinneff
Todhead Point

235
inverbervie
A90
A92
A957
A93
B9071
B9125
B979
B979
B9126
A96
A90
A92
A956
A956
B9077
B9119
A944
A90
A93
B979
25

| 0 | 1 | 2 | 3 | 4 | 5 miles |
| 0 | 1 | 2 | 3 | 4 | 5 | 6 | 7 | 8 kilometres |

B HEALAVAL
BHFAG

C Harlosh

258

Colbost
Point

Harlosh
Island

368
▲
BEINN NA
BOINEID

Tarner
Island

Loch Bracadale

Wiay

Ullinish
Lodge Hotel

Struan

Dun
Beag

Bracadale

Coillore

D

E

F

Loch
Duagrich

Mug

23

439
▲
ROINEVAL

Idrigill
Point

Oronsay

Portnalong

Fiskavaig

Rubha nan Clach

Loch Harport

B8009

Fernilea

Talisker

369
▲
ARNAVAL

Carbost

Drynoch

A863

Merkadale

Glen Dryn

Talisker
Bay

Talisker

Minginish

Glen Eynort

Glen
Brittle

369
▲
BEINN BHR

447
▲
BEINN
BHREAC

Grula

Forest

Fair

Loch Eynort

434
▲
AN CRUACHIN

Glenbrittle

Bualintur

Cu

9

SGU
A' GHE

S
AL

Loch Brittle

225
▲
CEANN NA BEINNE

Rubha an Dùnain

Soay Soun

V

Loch Baghasdail
(Lochboisdale)

Ru
Aon

C U I L L I N

CANNA

210
▲
CÀRN A' GHAILL

A'Chill

Garrisdale Point

Canna
Harbour

Kilmory
Bay

Rubha
Shamhnan Insir

Sanday

Sound of Canna

RÙM

302
▲
MULLACH
MÒR

Rubha
na Roinne

| 0 | 1 | 2 | 3 | 4 | 5 miles |
| 0 | 1 | 2 | 3 | 4 | 5 | 6 | 7 | 8 kilometres |

A' Bhrideanach

236

570
▲
ORVAL

Kinloch

Loch
Scresort

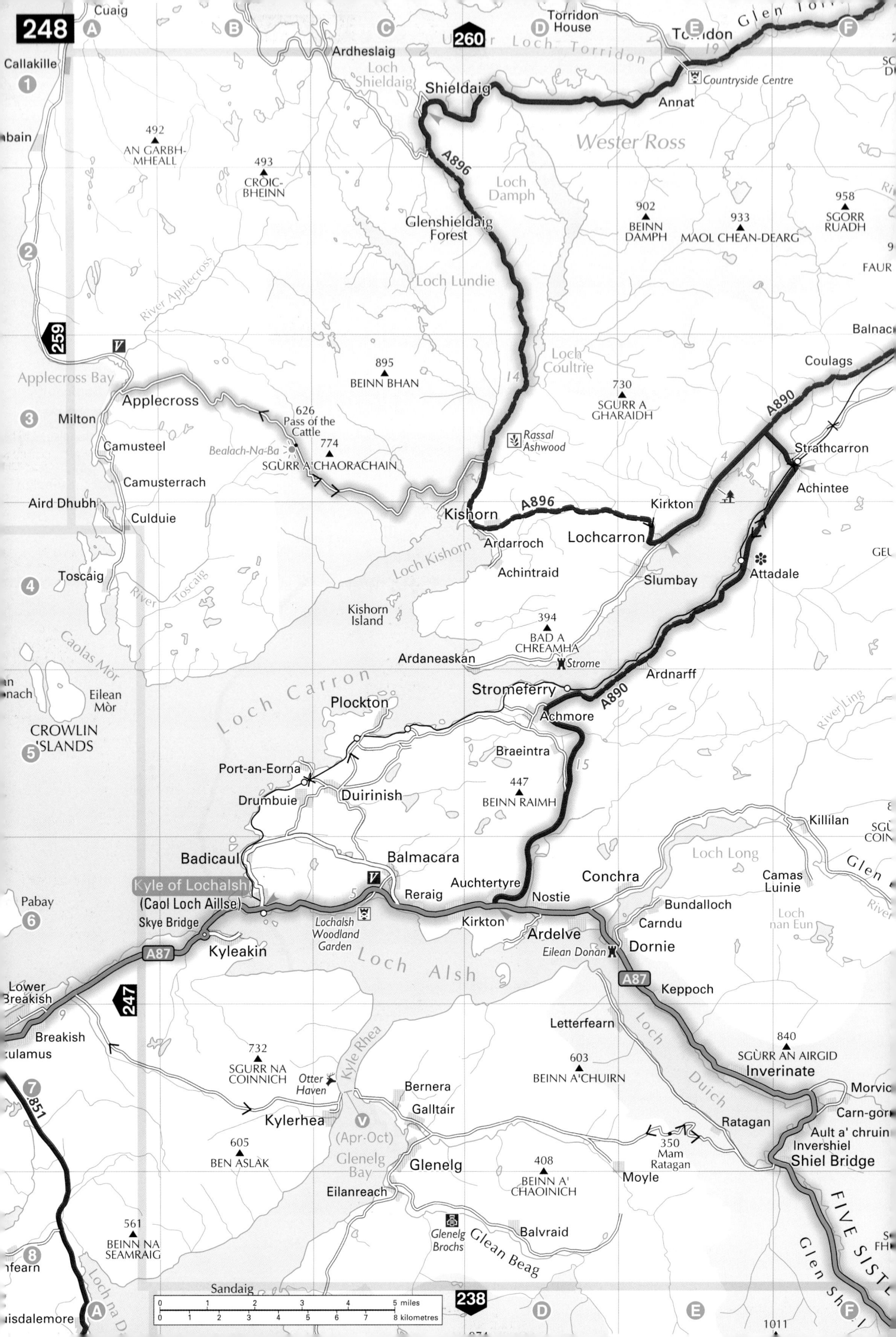

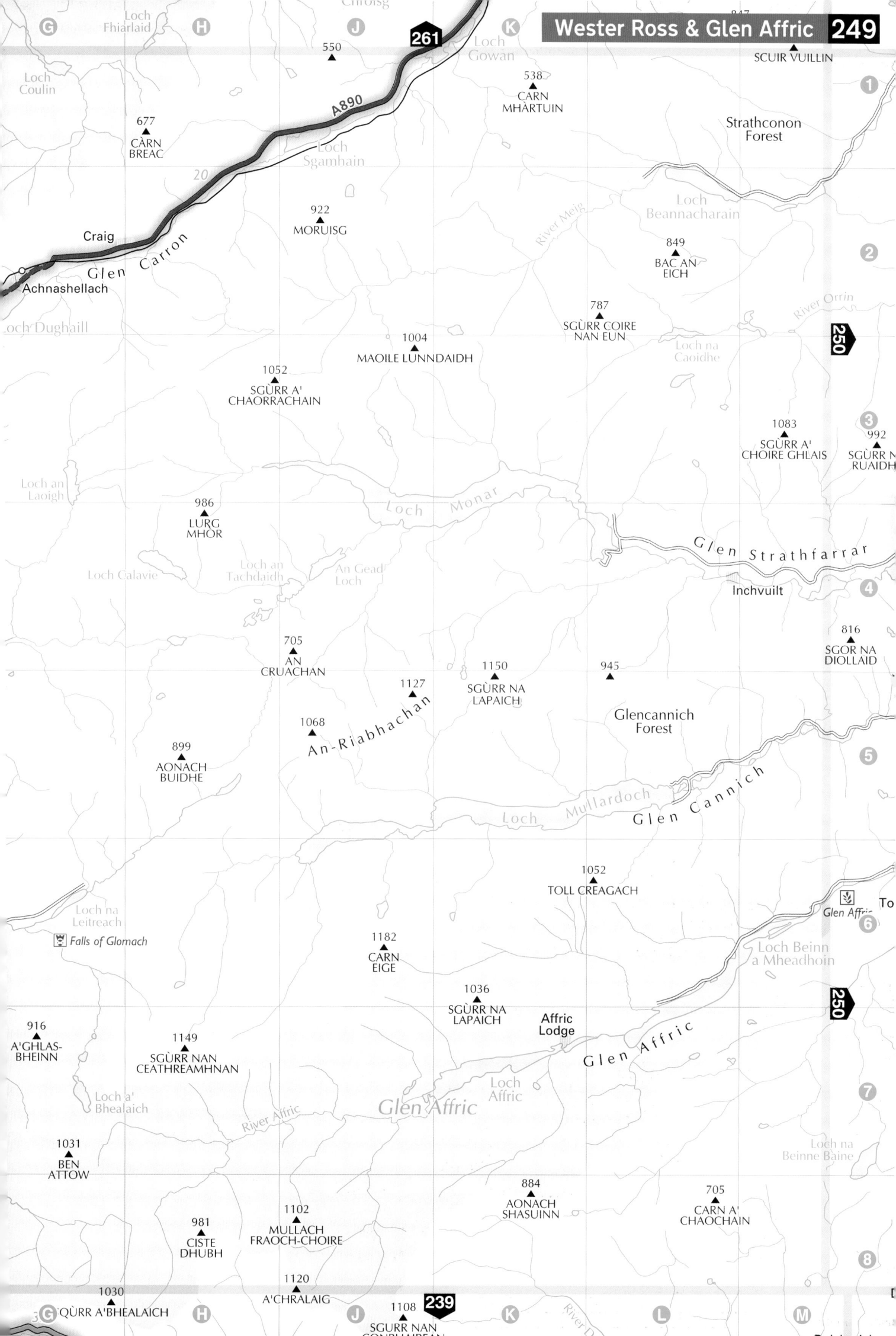

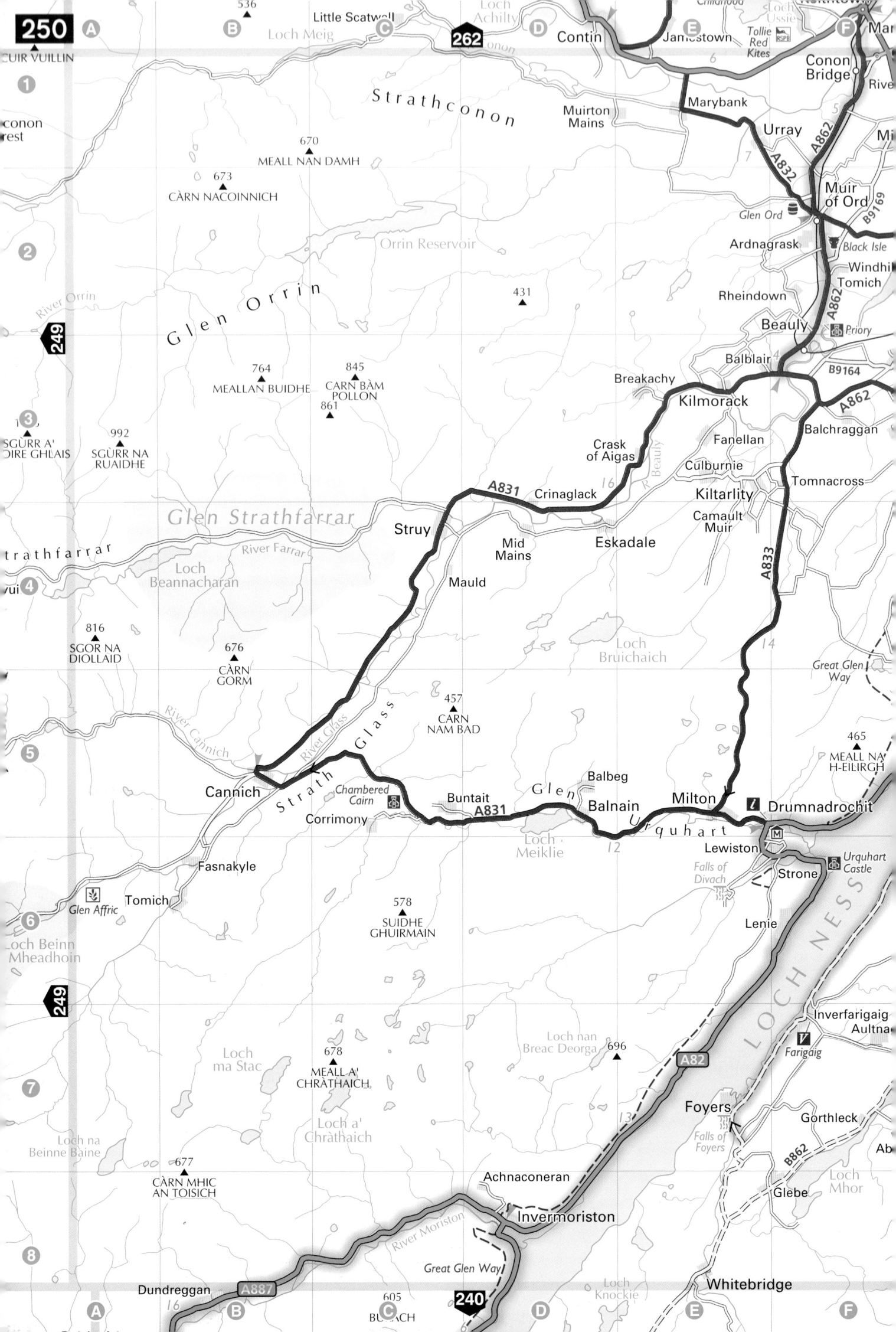

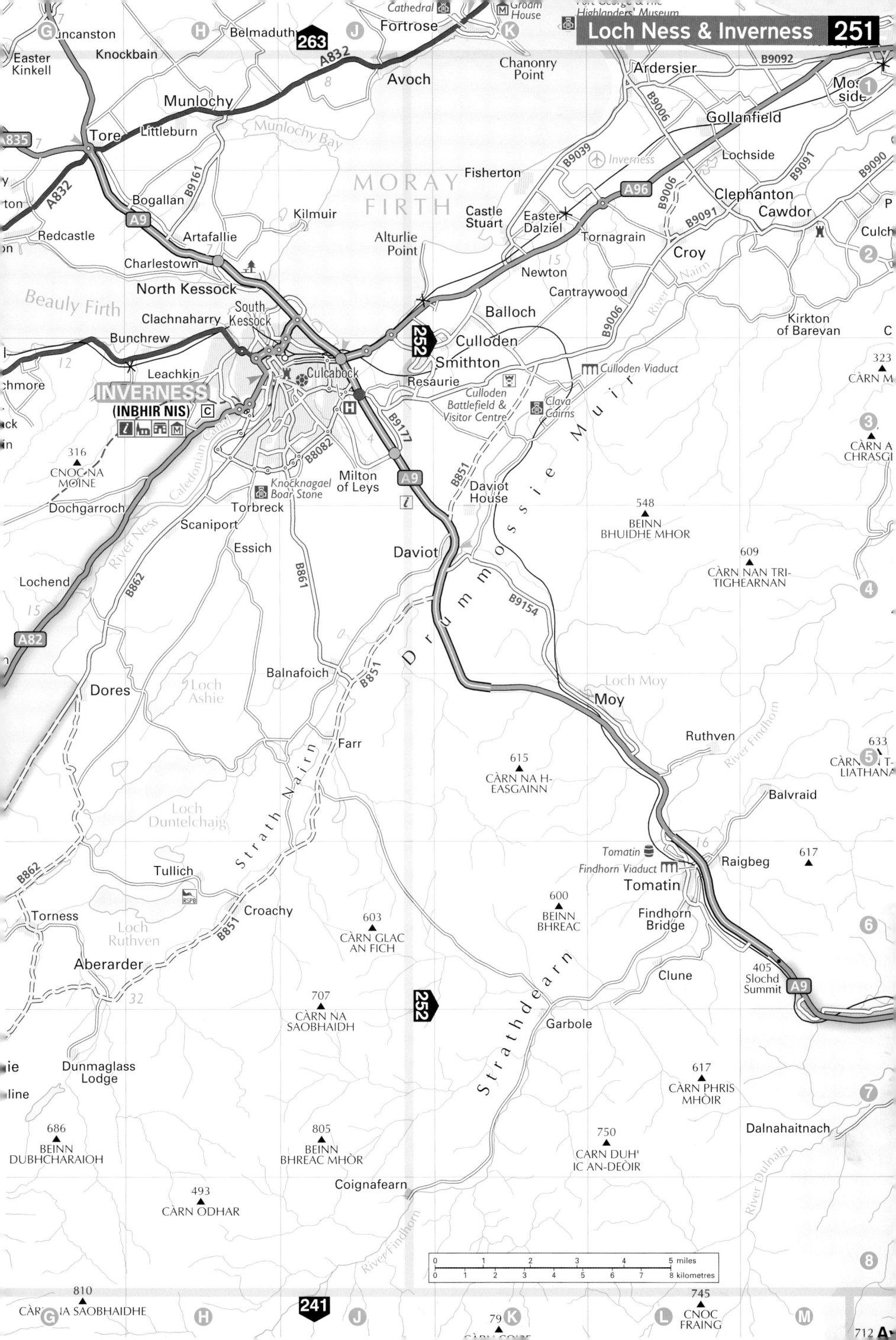

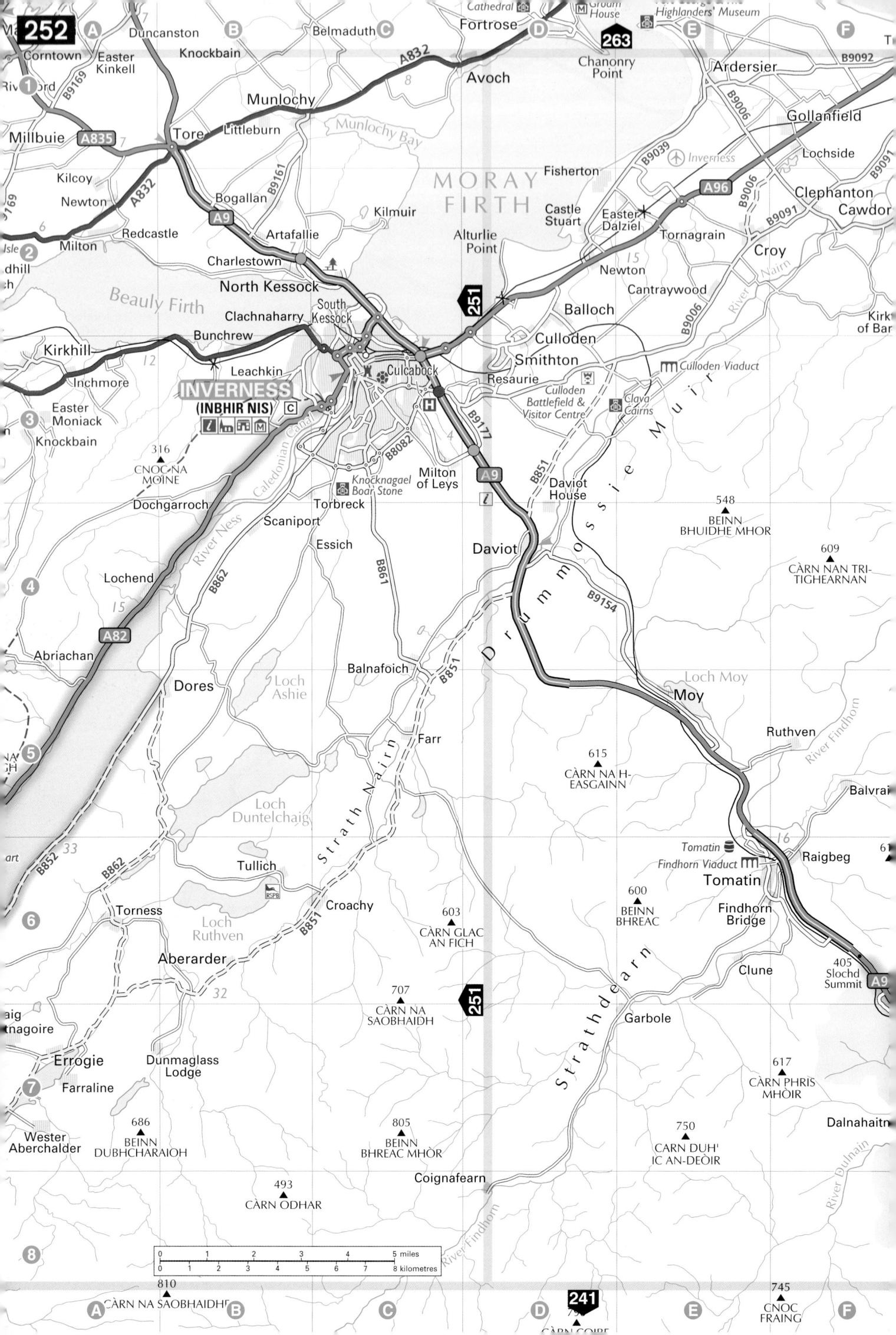

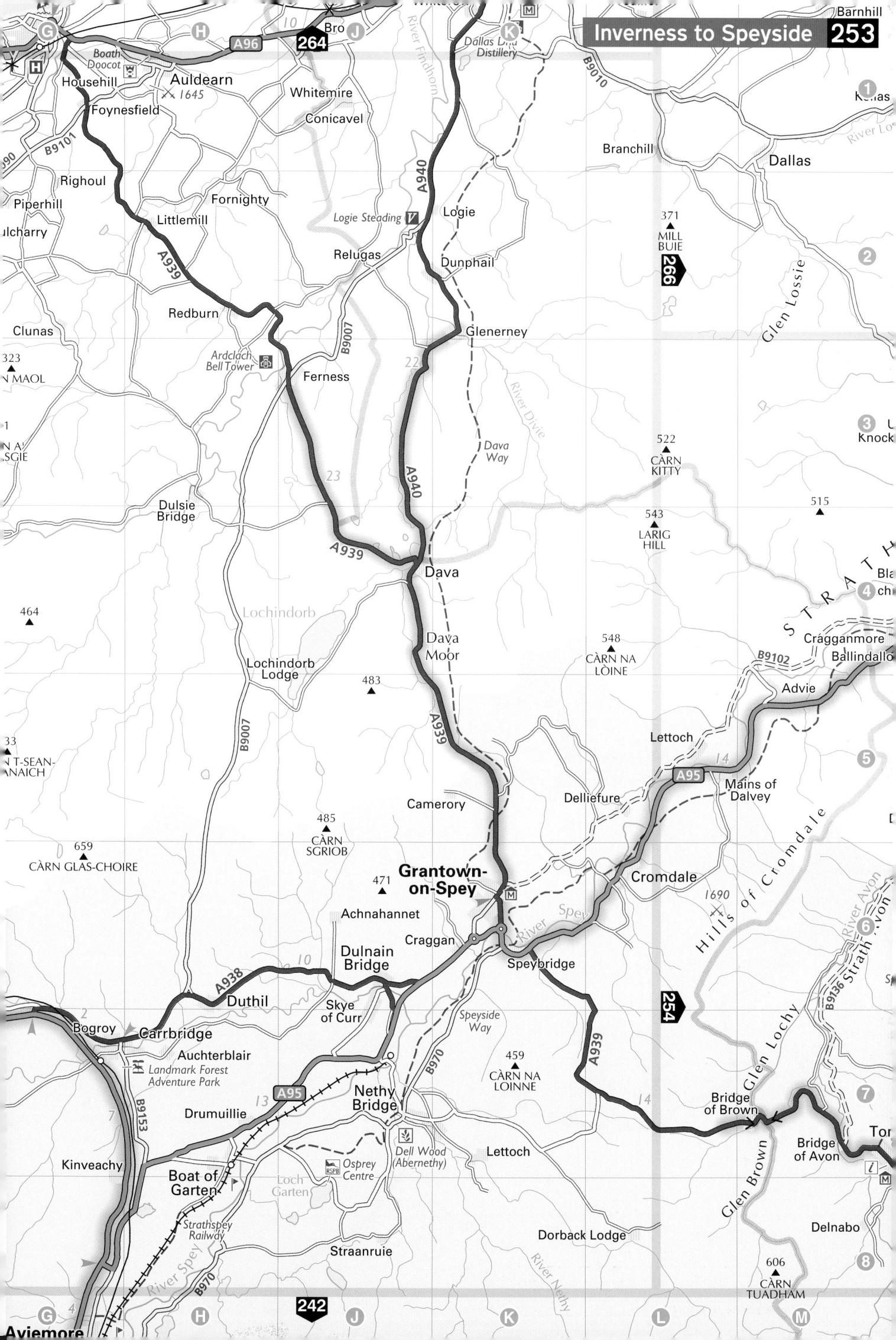

Barnhill

G H A96 10 Bro J 264

Boath Doocot
Househill
Auldearn
1645
Whitemire
Conicavel

Whit...
Dallas Dhu Distillery K
B9010

Branchill
Dallas

River Lo...
Kellas 1

Foynesfield
Piperhill
Righoul
Fornighty
B9101
Littlemill
B9090
A939
Logie Steading V
Logie
371 MILL BUIE 266
Glen Lossie
2

Clunas
Redburn
Relugas
B9007
Dunphail
3
Knock

N MAOL 323
Ardclach Bell Tower
Ferness
22..
Glenerney
River Divie
522 CÀRN KITTY
515

N A SGIE 1
Dava Way
543 LARIG HILL

Dulsie Bridge
23
A939
A940

464
Lochindorb
Dava
548 CÀRN NA LÒINE
STRATH
Bla ch 4
Crágganmore
B9102
Ballindallo

33
N T-SEAN-ANAICH
Lochindorb Lodge
483
Dava Moor
A939
Advie
Lettoch
A95 14
5

B9007
Camerory
Delliefure
Mains of Dalvey

485 CÀRN SGRIOB
Grantown-on-Spey
M
Cromdale
Hills of Cromdale

659 CÀRN GLAS-CHOIRE
471
Achnahannet
River Spey
1690
River Avon
B9136 Strath Avon
6

Dulnain Bridge
Craggan
Speybridge
A939
254
Glen Lochy

A938
Duthil
Skye of Curr
Speyside Way
Bogroy
Carrbridge
Auchterblair
Landmark Forest Adventure Park
B9153
A95 13
Drumuillie
Nethy Bridge
B970
459 CÀRN NA LOINNE
A939
14
Bridge of Brown
7

Kinveachy
7
2
Boat of Garten
Loch Garten
Osprey Centre RSPB
Dell Wood (Abernethy)
Lettoch
Glen Brown
Bridge of Avon
Tor
i M

Strathspey Railway
River Spey
B970
Dorback Lodge
Delnabo

Straanruie
River Nethy
606 CÀRN TUADHAM
8

AVIEMORE
G 4 H 242 J K L M

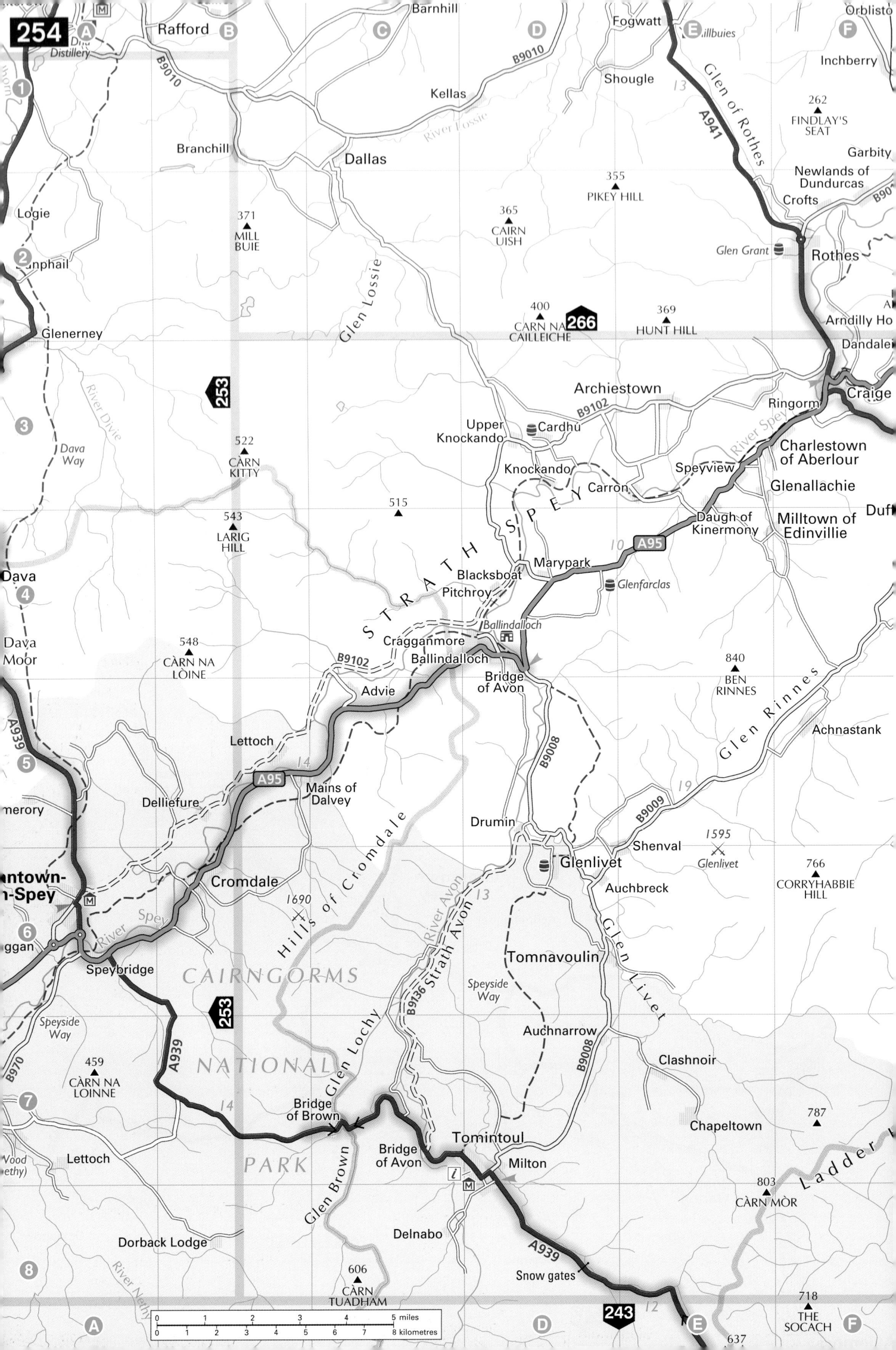

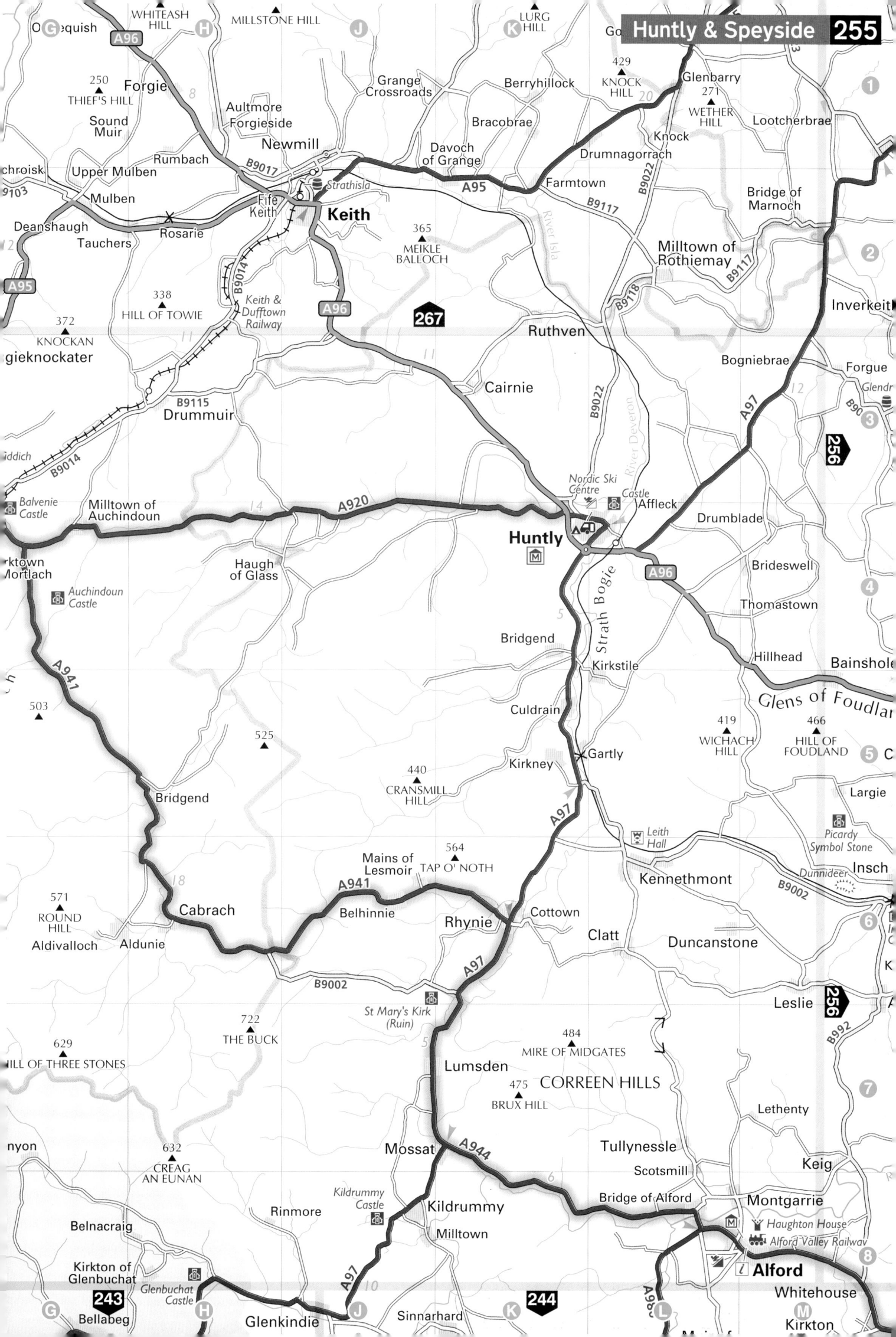

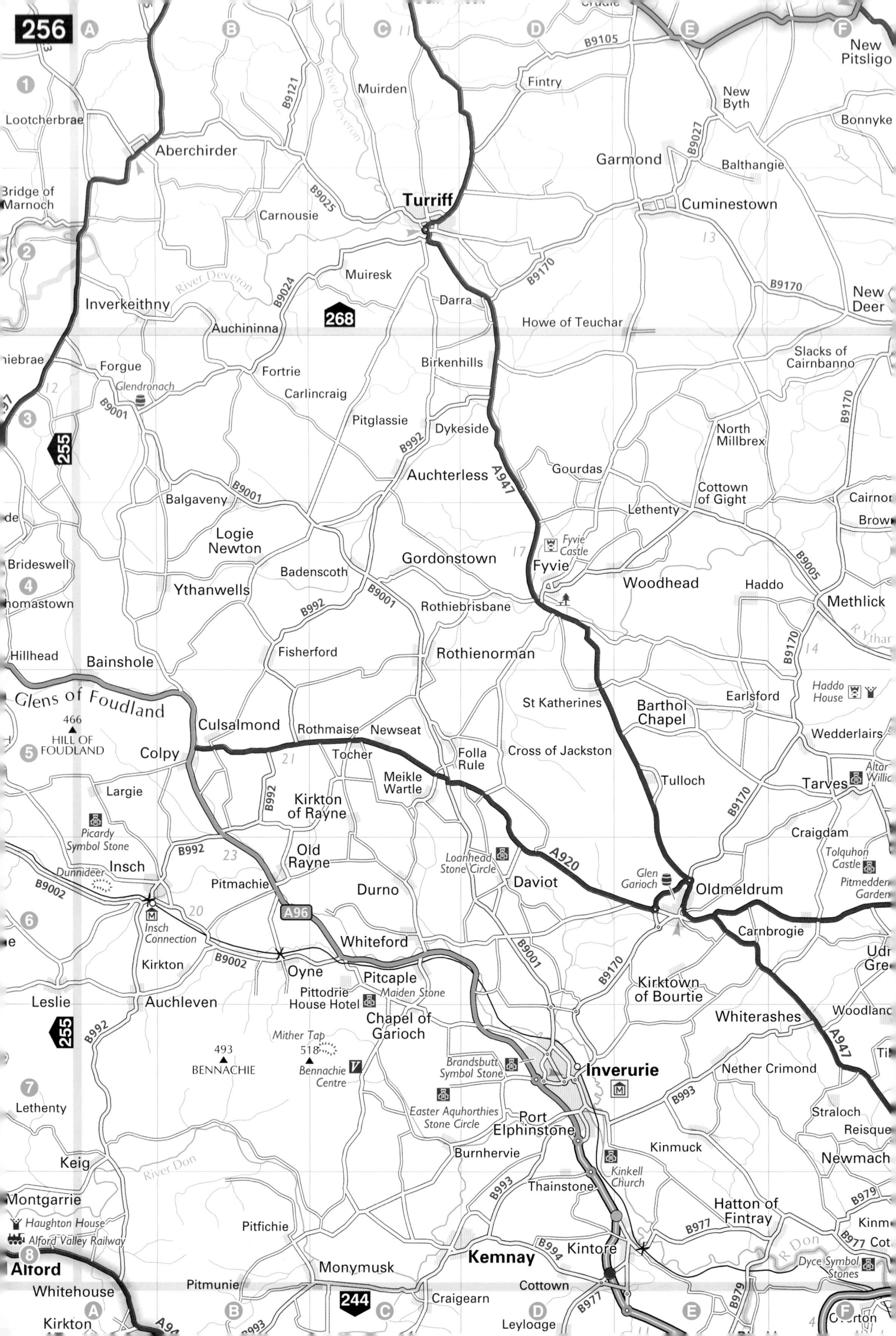

A   B   C   D   E   F

1

2

3

4

5

6

7

8

Fladda-chùain

Rubha Hur

Du

Tairbeart
(Tarbert)

Lùb Score

Borneskitaig

Kilmuir

Kilva

Balgown

Lin

Loch nam Madadh
(Lochmaddy)

Totscore

Rubha Bhatairnis

Idrigill

Ascrib
Islands

Uig Bay

283
BEN
GEARY

Geary

Loch Snizort

Earlish

A87

Trumpan

16

Ardmore
Point

Gillen

Hallin

Waternish

Isay   Mingay

DUNVEGAN
HEAD

Stein   Lusta

214
BEN
DIUBAIG

Ki

Loch
Bay

Greshornish

Loch Snizor

Claigan

Bay

Treaslane

Loch Greshornish

22

Loch
Pooltiel

Boreraig

327
BEINN
BHREAC

B886

Flashader

A850

Uig

Upperglen

Edinbane   Bernisdale

Feriniquarrie

Totaig

Oisgill
Bay

Glendale

Colbost

ISLE   OF

Milovaig

B884

Lephin

Colbost Croft

Dunvegan

Dunvegan

A850

Waterstein

Skinidin

Giant Angus MacAskill

Kilmuir

S

Neist
Point

Lonmore

Roskhill

265
BEN
AKETIL

271
CRUACHAN BEINN
A' CHEARCAILL

SKYE

Moonen Bay

Caroy River

Duirnish

469
HEALAVAL
MORE

Roag

Orbost

Ramasaig

Vatten

Hoe
Rape

Glen Ose

Loch Caroy

A863

488
HEALAVAL
BHEAG

Harlosh

Ose

Hoe Point

368

BEINN NA

246

Harlosh
Island

Colbost
Point

Dun
Beag

Bracadale

A   B   C   D   Tarner Island   E   F

0   1   2   3   4   5 miles
0   1   2   3   4   5   6   7   8 kilometres

G H J K L

260

n Trodday

Kilmaluag

Flodigarry

Eilean Flodigarry

useum
d Life

a

Poldorais

542
▲
MEAL NA   Digg
SUIREAMACH

*Staffin
Bay*   Staffin Island

Brogaig

464
▲
BIODA   Stenscholl   Staffin
BUIDHE   *Trotternish*

Kilt Rock
Ellishader

Maligar

Marishader   Valtos

Garros   Rubha nam Brathairean

Culnaknock

611
▲
BEINN
EDRA   Lealt

Tote

River Conon

608
▲
CREAG A' LAIN

A855

inlich

sdal

451
▲
BEINN
A' SGA

Òb
Chuaig

*Old Man
of Storr*
719
▲ ★
THE
STORR

RONA

Rubha
na Fearn

C g

Callakille

esdal   *River Romesdal*

Kensaleyre

River Haulton

*Loch
Leathan*

Eilean
Tigh

Lonbain

16

*Loch
Fada*

Eilean
Fladday

3
11
11   Carbost   Borve

Manish
Point   *Loch
Arnish*   Torran

S O U N D   O F   R A A S A Y

I N N E R   S O U N D

248

Drumuie

A855

Glengrasco

Arnish

der

Brochel

312
▲

Portree   Torvaig

Milton

7

Applecross Bay

RAASAY

Aros **V**

i

417
▲
BEINN NA
GREINE   Penifiler   412
▲
BEN
TIANAVAIG

Ap

Glenmore

Glenvarragill   **A87**

444
▲
247 DÙN CAAN

Aird Dhubh

G Mugeary   H

Camastianava
Tianavaig   J   Oskaig   K   Rubha na' Leac   L   M   Toscaig   Ca

Camu

1

2

3

4

5

6

7

8

A B C D E **270** F

1

2

3

4

5

6

7

8

Rubha Rèidh

Foura

Cove

Mellon
Udrigle

Rubha Beag

Stattic Point

**GRUINARD
ISLAND**

Bad

*Gruinard
Bay*

A832

296
▲
AN CUAIDH

Mellon
Charles

Ormiscaig

Laide

Gruinard

Melvaig

Aultgrishin

Aultbea

B8057

**ISLE
OF EWE**

Loch Ewe

Loch
Fada

Little Gruinard River

34
▲
CREA
MHEAL

293
▲
CNOC
BREAC

Inverasdale

Naast

681
▲
BEINN A'
CHAISGEIN B

B8021

*Inverewe
Garden*

250
▲
MEALL NA MEINE

Weste

North Erradale

Poolewe

Londubh

13

Fionn

Big Sand

Strath

A832

791
▲
BEINN
AIRIDH CHARR

Smithstown

Lonemore

Auchtercairn
M *Heritage*

421
▲
MEALL AN
DOIREIN

Longa
Island

*Loch
Gairloch*

Gairloch

Charlestown

Loch

Eilean
Horrisdale

Port
Henderson

B8056

Loch Bad
an Sgalaig

*Loch
Maree
Islands*

Lette
Fo

Badachro

Letterewe

Opinan

South Erradale

Talladale

A832

Maree

Redpoint

19

Red
Point

Loch Ghaineamhach

B

Loch na
A-Oidhche

Loch a'
Ghodhainn

875
▲
BAOSBHEINN

855
▲
BEINN
AN EÒIN

724
▲

619
▲
BEINN BHREAC

Loch a'
Bhealaich

Rubha
na Fearn

*Loch
Torridon*

Lower
Diabaig

985
▲
BEINN
ALLIGIN

914
▲
BEINN DEARG

1009
▲
RUADH-
STAC MÒR

Fearnmore

*Loch
Diabaig*

Inveralligin

1024
▲

1053
▲
LIATHACH

BEINN

Fearnbeg

Arrina

Kenmore

Alligin Shuas

Torridon
House

Torridon

Glen Torridon

Ob
Chuaig

Cuaig

19

Callakille

Ardheslaig

Upper Loch Torridon

248

Shieldaig

Countryside Centre

St
D

0 1 2 3 4 5 miles
0 1 2 3 4 5 6 7 8 kilometres

A B C D E F

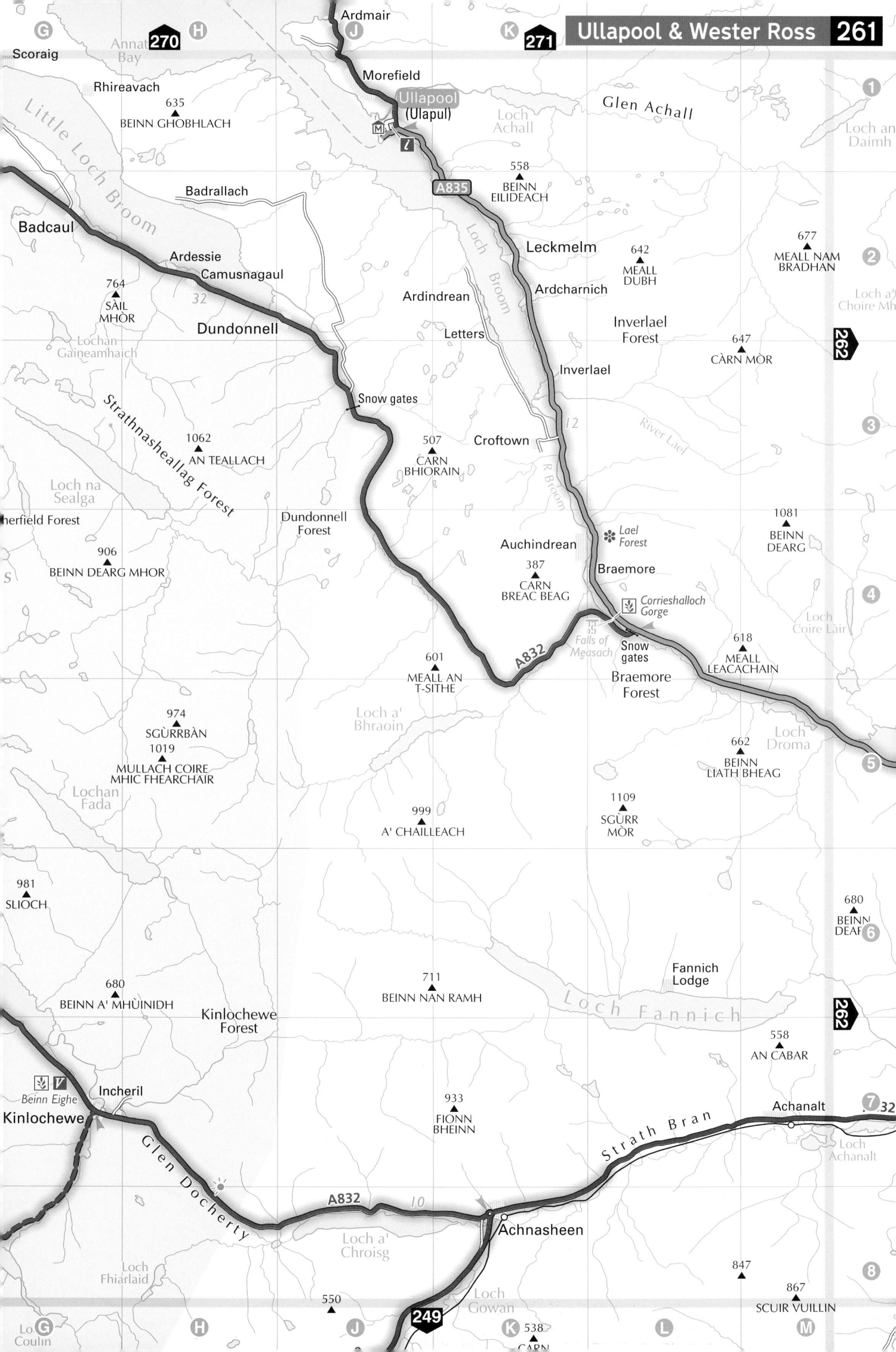

G 270 H

J

K 271

Scoraig

Annat Bay

Rhireavach

Ardmair

Morefield

Ullapool (Ulapul)

Glen Achall

Loch an Daimh

1

635
BEINN GHOBHLACH

Loch Achall

A835

558
BEINN EILIDEACH

Badrallach

Leckmelm

642
MEALL DUBH

677
MEALL NAM BRADHAN

2

Badcaul

Ardessie

Camusnagaul

Ardcharnich

Loch a' Choire Mh

764
SÀIL MHÒR

Dundonnell

Ardindrean

Letters

Inverlael Forest

647
CÀRN MÒR

262

Lochan Gaineamhaich

32

Loch Broom

Inverlael

12

R Broom

River Lael

3

Strathnasheallag Forest

Snow gates

507
CARN BHIORAIN

Croftown

Loch na Sealga

1062
AN TEALLACH

Dundonnell Forest

1081
BEINN DEARG

herfield Forest

S

906
BEINN DEARG MHOR

Auchindrean

Lael Forest

387
CARN BREAC BEAG

Braemore

4

Loch Coire Lair

Corrieshalloch Gorge

601
MEALL AN T-SITHE

Falls of Measach

A832

Snow gates

618
MEALL LEACACHAIN

Braemore Forest

974
SGÙRRBÀN

Loch a' Bhraoin

Loch Droma

Lochan Fada

1019
MULLACH COIRE MHIC FHEARCHAIR

662
BEINN LIATH BHEAG

5

999
A' CHAILLEACH

1109
SGÙRR MÒR

981
SLIOCH

680
BEINN DEAR

6

680
BEINN A' MHÙINIDH

711
BEINN NAN RAMH

Fannich Lodge

262

Kinlochewe Forest

Loch Fannich

558
AN CABAR

Beinn Eighe

Incheril

933
FIONN BHEINN

Achanalt

7

Kinlochewe

Glen Docherty

Strath Bran

Loch Achanalt

32

A832

10

Loch a' Chroisg

Achnasheen

847

8

Lo Coulin

Loch Fhiarlaid

550

249

Loch Gowan

867
SCUIR VUILLIN

G H J K 538 L M
CARN

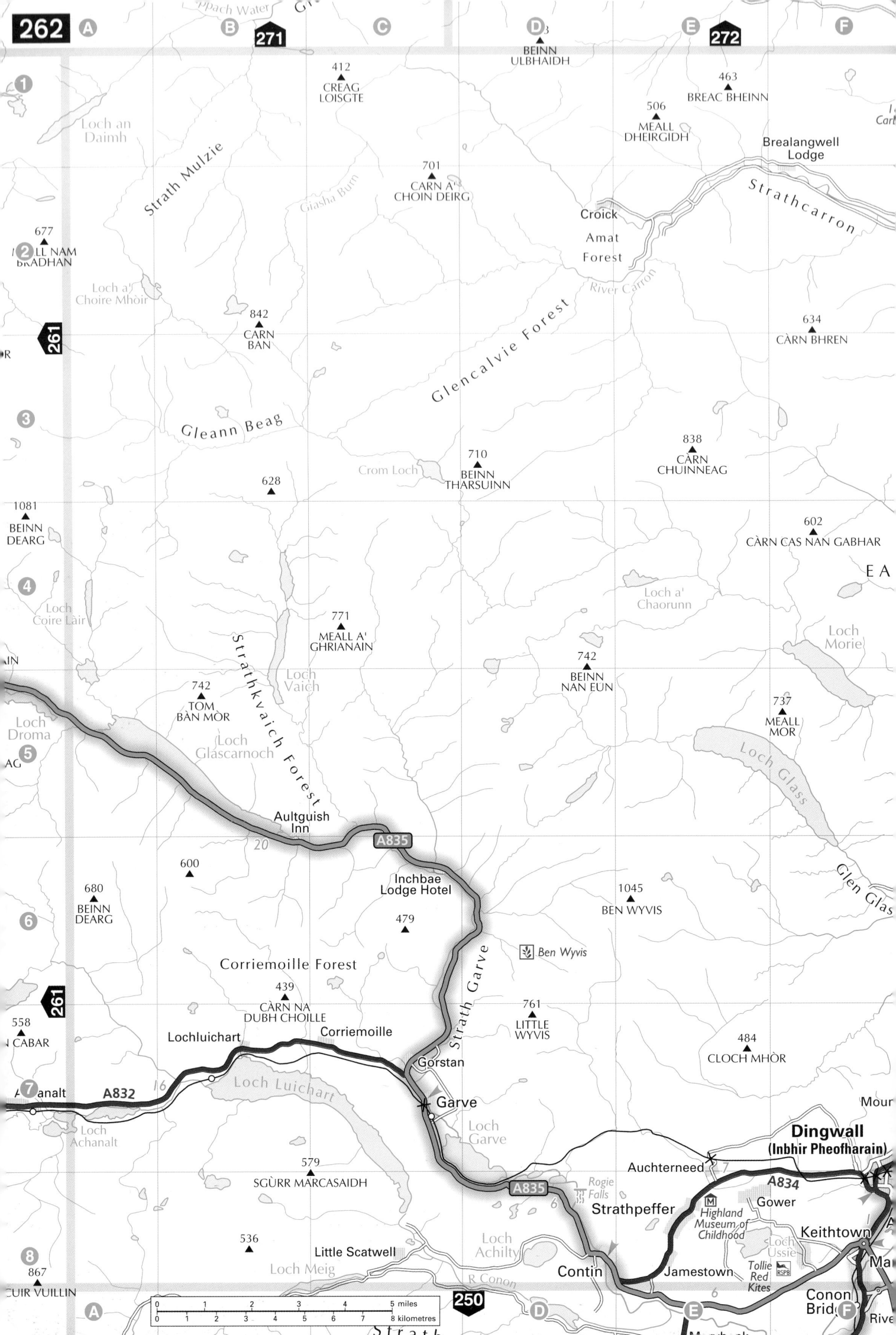

Ppach Water

412 ▲
CREAG
LOISGTE

D 3
BEINN
ULBHAIDH

463 ▲
BREAC BHEINN

506 ▲
MEALL
DHEIRGIDH

Brealangwell
Lodge

Strathcarron

677 ▲
LL NAM
bRADHAN

Strath Mulzie

Giasha Burn

701 ▲
CARN A'
CHOIN DEIRG

Croick

Amat
Forest

River Carron

261

Loch an
Daimh

Loch a'
Choire Mhòir

842 ▲
CARN
BAN

Glencalvie Forest

634 ▲
CÀRN BHREN

Gleann Beag

628 ▲

710 ▲
BEINN
THARSUINN

Crom Loch

838 ▲
CÀRN
CHUINNEAG

602 ▲
CÀRN CAS NAN GABHAR

1081 ▲
BEINN
DEARG

E A

771 ▲
MEALL A'
GHRIANAIN

Loch a'
Chaorunn

Loch
Morie

Loch
Coire Làir

Loch
Vaich

742 ▲
BEINN
NAN EUN

737 ▲
MEALL
MOR

IN

742 ▲
TOM
BÀN MÒR

Strathkvaich Forest

Loch
Glascarnoch

Loch Glass

Loch
Droma

AG

Glen Glas

Aultguish
Inn

20

A835

Inchbae
Lodge Hotel

600 ▲

680 ▲
BEINN
DEARG

479 ▲

1045 ▲
BEN WYVIS

Corriemoille Forest

Strath Garve

🌿 Ben Wyvis

261

439 ▲
CÀRN NA
DUBH CHOILLE

Corriemoille

761 ▲
LITTLE
WYVIS

484 ▲
CLOCH MHÒR

558 ▲
CABAR

Lochluichart

Gorstan

A832

16

Loch Luichart

Garve

Loch
Garve

Dingwall
(Inbhir Pheofharain)

analt

Auchterneed

A834

Loch
Achanalt

579 ▲
SGÙRR MARCASAIDH

A835

Rogie
Falls

Strathpeffer

Gower

Highland Museum of Childhood

Keithtown

536 ▲

Little Scatwell

Loch Meig

Loch
Achilty

M Highland
Museum of
Childhood

Loch
Ussie

Jamestown

Tollie
Red
Kites

RSPB

Ma

867 ▲
CUIR VUILLIN

Contin

Conon
Brid

Rive

R Conon

0 1 2 3 4 5 miles
0 1 2 3 4 5 6 7 8 kilometres

Strath

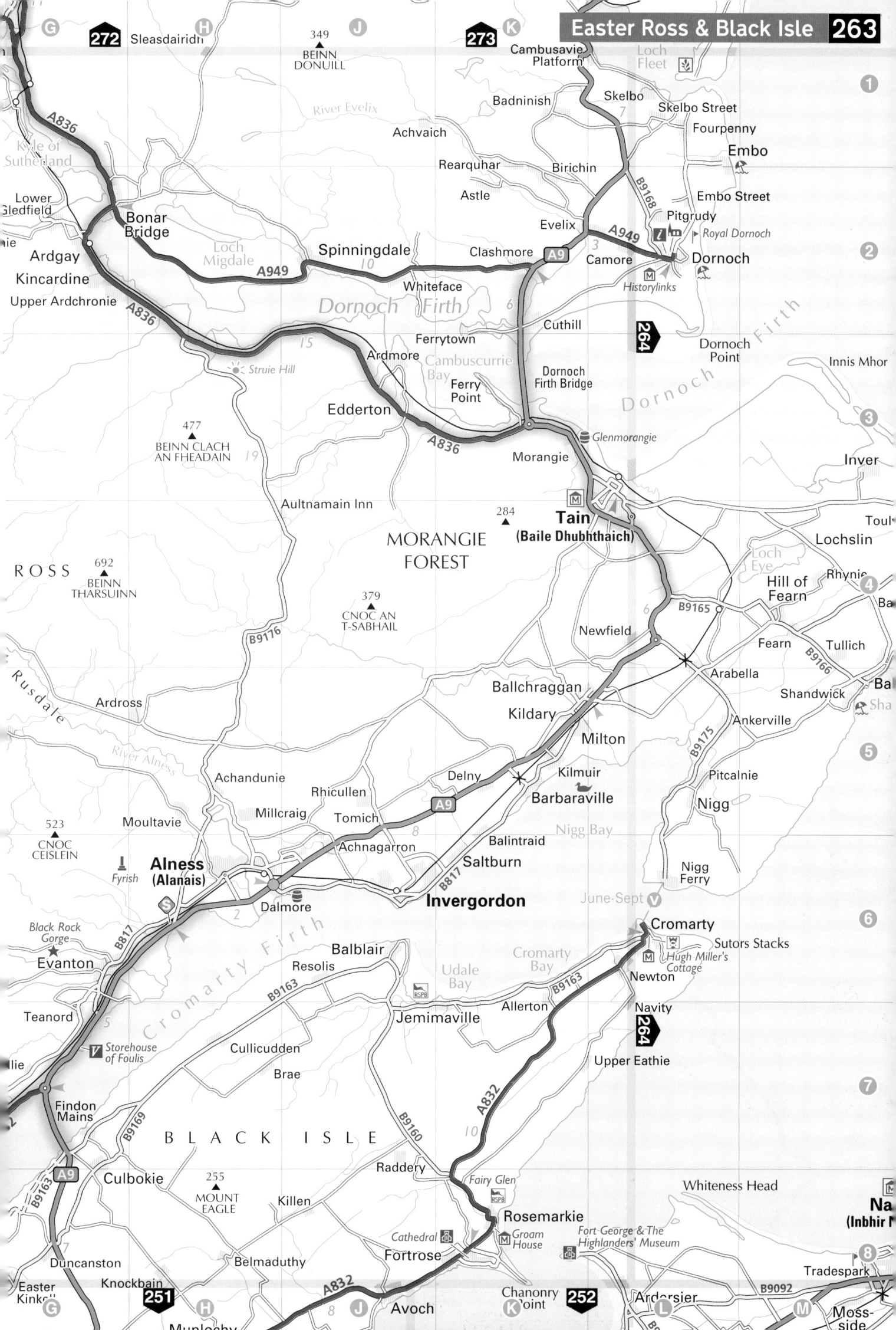

G H J K L

1
2
3
4
5
6
7
8

Fisheries & Community
Branderburgh
Stotfield
Lossiemouth

B9040

Burghead Well
Hopeman
Burnside
Burghead
St Peter's Kirk & Parish Cross
Duffus
B9012
Cummingston
Roseisle
B9013
B9012
Duffus Castle
Loch Spynie
B9135

College of Roseisle
Spynie Palace
Stonewells
Lochill
A941
B9103
Viewfield
Calcots
Innesmill

Burghead Bay

Findhorn
Hempriggs
B9089
Quarrywood
Newton
Bishopmill
Elgin
Urquhart
Lhanbryde
The Lochs

V
B9011
Kinloss
Coltfield
A96
Alves
Glen Moray
New Elgin
Linkwood
A96
Mosstodl
Cro of Dipp

Kincorth House
266
Grange Hall
Kilbuiack
Muir of Miltonduff
Clackmarras

Sueno's Stone
Forres
Califer
Pluscarden
Barnhill
Longmorn
B9103

Dallas Dhu Distillery
253
Rafford
B9010
Fogwatt
Millbuies
Orbliston

Kellas
Shougle
Inchberry
Glen

G H J K L M

262

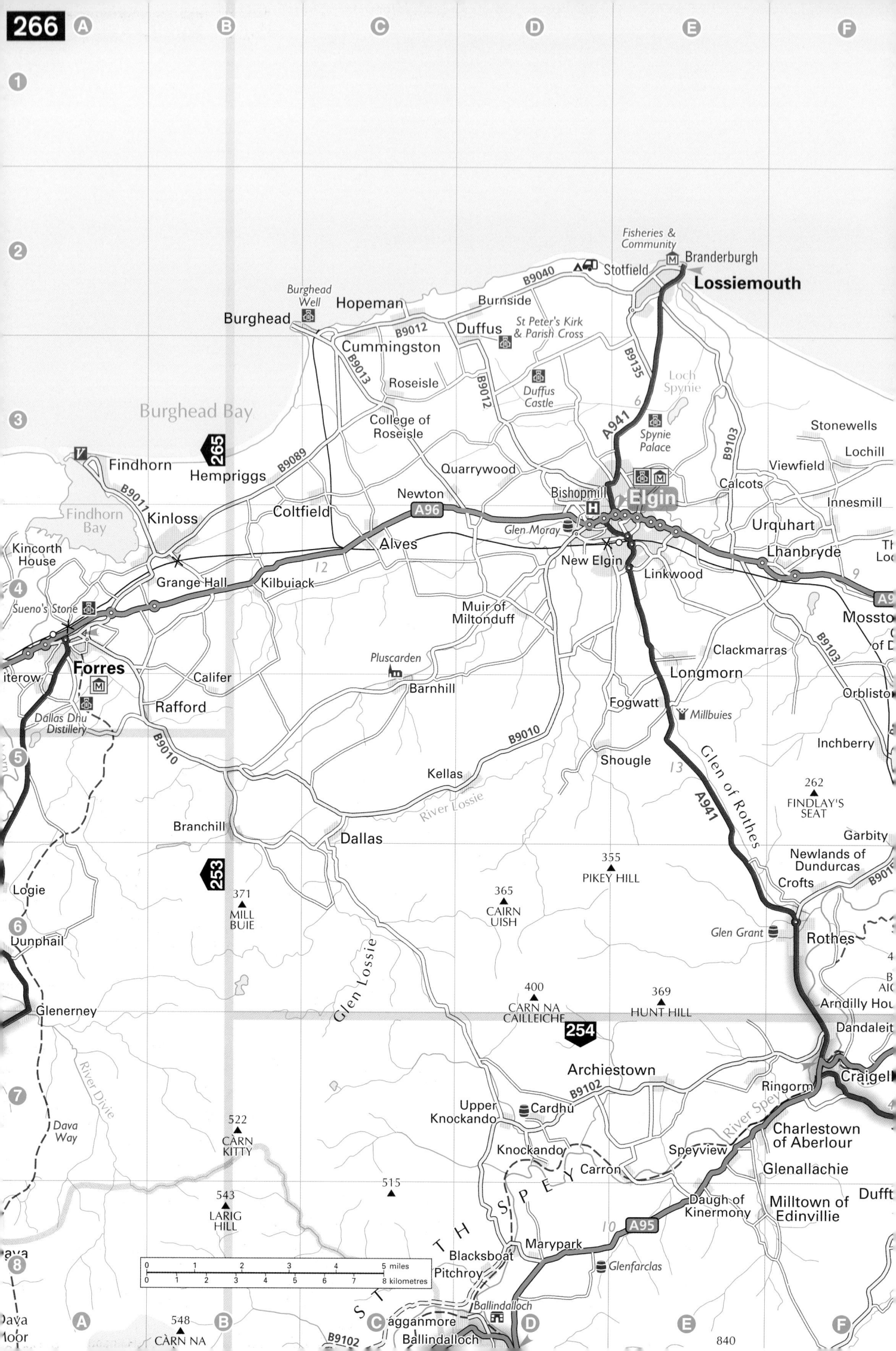

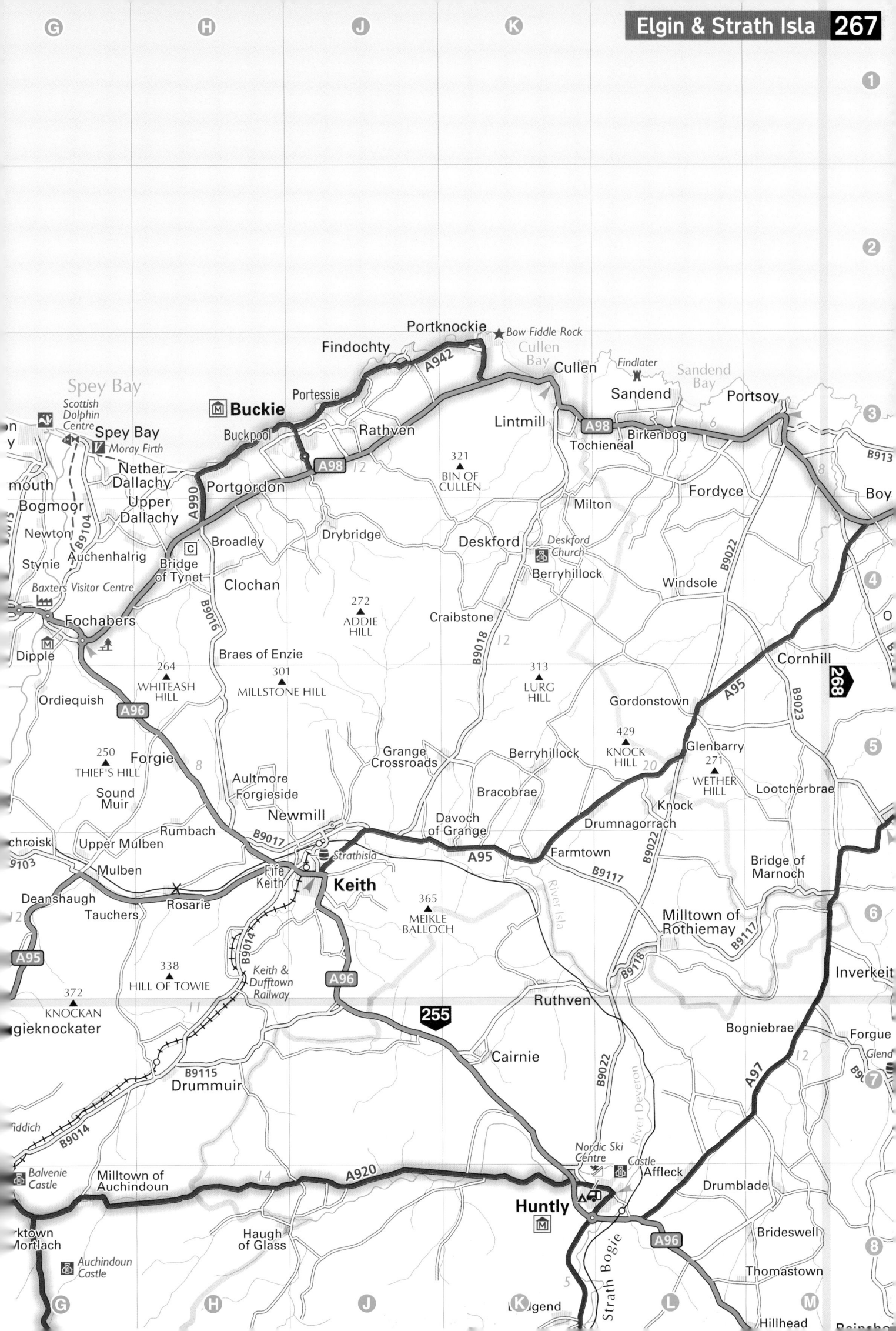

Portknockie
Findochty
Bow Fiddle Rock
Cullen
Bay
Findlater
Sandend
Bay
Portessie
A942
Cullen
Sandend
Portsoy
Buckie
Lintmill
B913
Buckpool
Rathven
A98
Birkenbog
Boy
Spey Bay
Tochieneal
Scottish
Dolphin
Centre
321
Milton
Fordyce
Spey Bay
Moray Firth
BIN OF
CULLEN
Nether
Dallachy
Portgordon
Deskford
Deskford
Church
B9022
Upper
Dallachy
Drybridge
Berryhillock
Windsole
mouth
Bogmoor
Broadley
A990
Newton
Auchenhalrig
Clochan
272
Craibstone
Cornhill
Stynie
Bridge
of Tynet
ADDIE
HILL
B9018
268
Baxters Visitor Centre
B9016
12
Dipple
Fochabers
313
A95
Braes of Enzie
LURG
HILL
B9023
264
301
Gordonstown
Glenbarry
Ordiequish
WHITEASH
HILL
MILLSTONE HILL
429
271
A96
KNOCK
HILL
WETHER
HILL
Lootcherbrae
250
Forgie
Grange
Crossroads
Berryhillock
20
THIEF'S HILL
Sound
Muir
Aultmore
Forgieside
Bracobrae
Knock
Drumnagorrach
Bridge of
Marnoch
chroisk
Upper Mulben
Rumbach
Newmill
B9017
Davoch
of Grange
9103
Mulben
Fife
Keith
Strathisla
A95
Farmtown
B9117
Deanshaugh
Tauchers
Rosarie
Keith
365
B9022
B9118
Milltown of
Rothiemay
A95
MEIKLE
BALLOCH
Inverkeit
12
338
B9014
Keith &
Dufftown
Railway
Ruthven
372
HILL OF TOWIE
B9117
255
Bogniebrae
KNOCKAN
Cairnie
Forgue
gieknockater
B9115
B9022
Glend
Drummuir
River Deveron
A97
12
B9L
7
fiddich
B9014
Nordic Ski
Centre
Castle
Affleck
Drumblade
Balvenie
Castle
Milltown of
Auchindoun
14
A920
Huntly
Brideswell
cktown
Mortlach
Haugh
of Glass
A96
Thomastown
Auchindoun
Castle
Strath Bogie
Legend
Hillhead
5

G   H   J   K   L   M

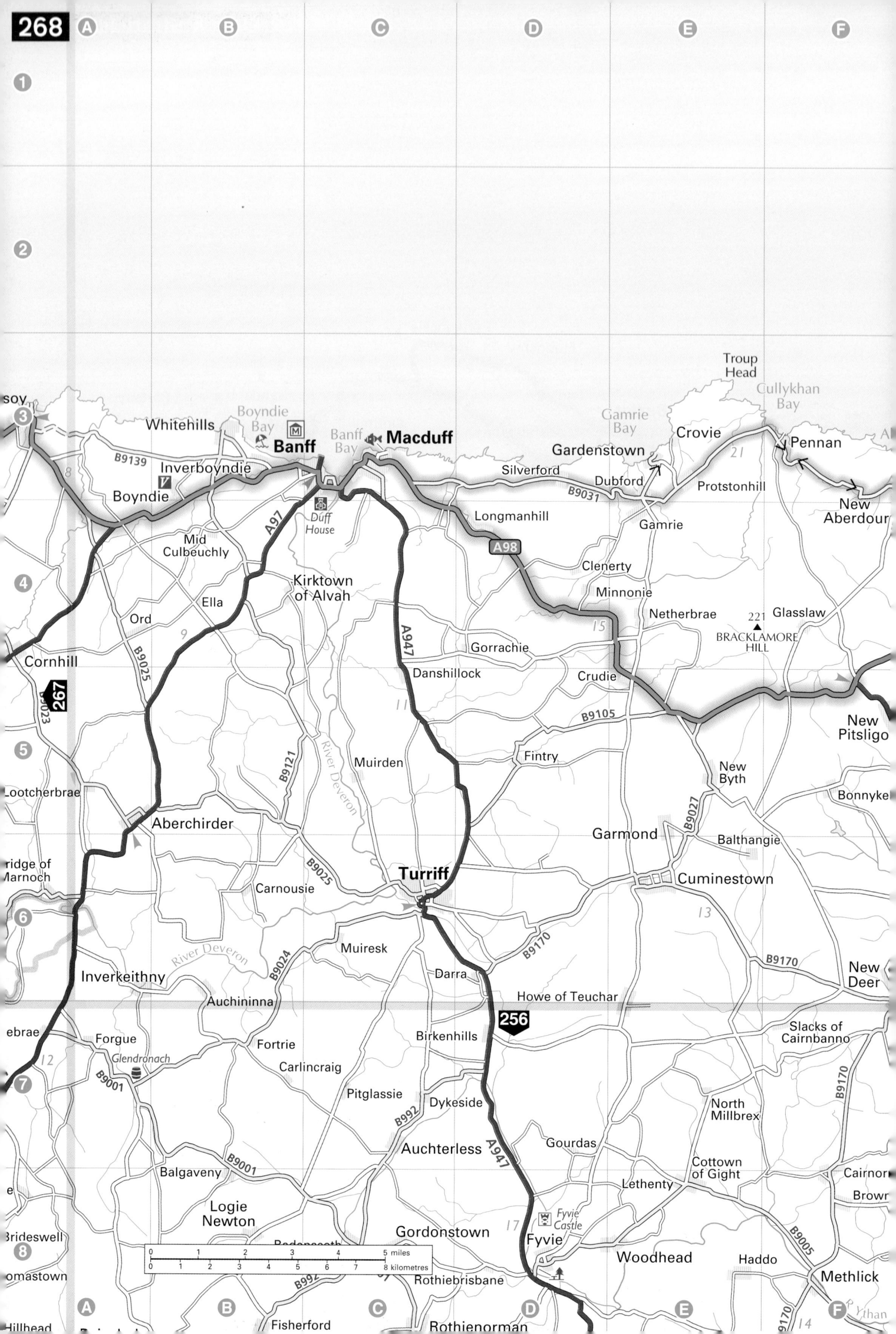

A B C D E F

1 2 3 4 5 6 7 8

Point of Stoer

Old Man
of Stoer

Culkein

Achnacarnin

Clashmore

Clashnessie

OLDANY
ISLAND

Eddrach
Bay

Culkein
Drumbeg

Oldany

Drumbeg

Nedd

Clashnessie
Bay

Loch
Poll

Stoer

Clachtoll

Bay of Clachtoll

B869

Rhicarn

Loch
Beannac

Achmelvich
Bay

Achmelvich

A837

Baddidarrach

Soyea Island

Loch Inver

Lochinver

Assyn

Strathan

Inverkirkaig

River Kirkaig

Fionn
Loch

Rubha
Còigeach

Eilean Mòr

Enard Bay

Rubha Mòr

Reiff

Achnahaird

Loch
Sionasc

Altandhu

Eilean Mullagrach

Loch
Osgaig

Isle Ristol

Polbain

612

STAC POLLAIDH

Glas-leac Mòr

SUMMER ISLES

Badentarbet

Achiltibuie

769

CUL BE

Tanera
Beg

Badentarbat
Bay

Polglass

Loch
Lurgainn

V

Steornabhagh
(Stornoway)

Tanera
Mòr

Ben Mor
Coigach

COIGACH

Glas-leac Beag

Horse
Island

Horse
Sound

Achduart

652

BEN MORE
COIGACH

Eilean Dubh

Culnacraig

Strathcanai

Priest
Island

Strath

Greenstone
Point

Leac Dhonn

Isle
Martin

A835

Cailleach Head

Rubha Beag

Ardmair

A
ellon
Udrigle

0 1 2 3 4 5 miles
0 1 2 3 4 5 6 7 8 kilometres

261

D Rhireavach

Scoraig

Annat
Bay

E

F Mor
field

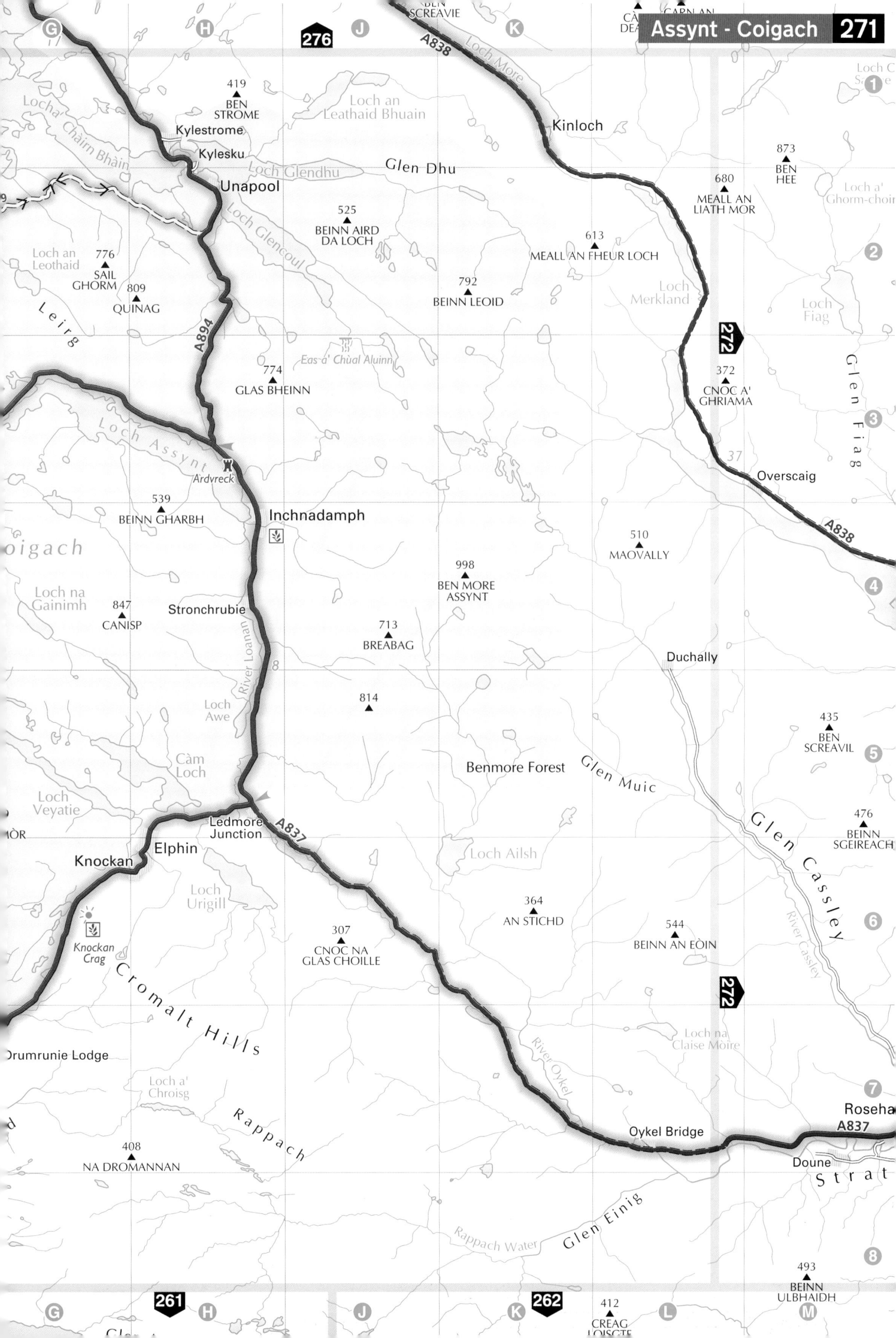

G H 276 J A838 K DEA CARN AN

BEN SCREAVIE

Loch More

1

419 ▲
BEN STROME

Loch an Leathaid Bhuain

Kinloch

873 ▲
BEN HEE

Loch a' Ghorm-choir

Kylestrome

Kylestrome

Kylesku

Glen Dhu

680 ▲
MEALL AN LIATH MOR

2

Unapool

Loch Glendhu

525 ▲
BEINN AIRD DA LOCH

613 ▲
MEALL AN FHEUR LOCH

Loch Merkland

Loch a' Chàirn Bhàin

Loch Glencoul

A894

Loch Fiag

776 ▲
SAIL GHORM

Loch an Leothaid

792 ▲
BEINN LEOID

272

Leirg

809 ▲
QUINAG

Glen Fiag

774 ▲
GLAS BHEINN

Eas-a' Chùal Aluinn

372 ▲
CNOC A' GHRIAMA

3

Loch Assynt

Ardvreck

Overscaig

A838

539 ▲
BEINN GHARBH

Inchnadamph

510 ▲
MAOVALLY

4

Coigach

847 ▲
CANISP

Stronchrubie

998 ▲
BEN MORE ASSYNT

Loch na Gainimh

River Loanan

713 ▲
BREABAG

Duchally

435 ▲
BEN SCREAVIL

5

8

Loch Awe

814 ▲

Benmore Forest

Glen Muic

Glen Cassley

476 ▲
BEINN SGEIREACH

Càm Loch

Loch Veyatie

Ledmore Junction

A837

Loch Ailsh

River Cassley

6

MÒR

Elphin

Knockan

364 ▲
AN STICHD

544 ▲
BEINN AN EÒIN

Loch Urigill

307 ▲
CNOC NA GLAS CHOILLE

Knockan Crag

272

Loch na Claise Mòire

7

Drumrunie Lodge

Cromalt Hills

Rappach

River Oykel

Rosehall

A837

408 ▲
NA DROMANNAN

Oykel Bridge

Doune

Strat

Glen Einig

8

Rappach Water

493 ▲
BEINN ULBHAIDH

G 261 H J K 262 L 412 ▲ M
CREAG LOISGTE

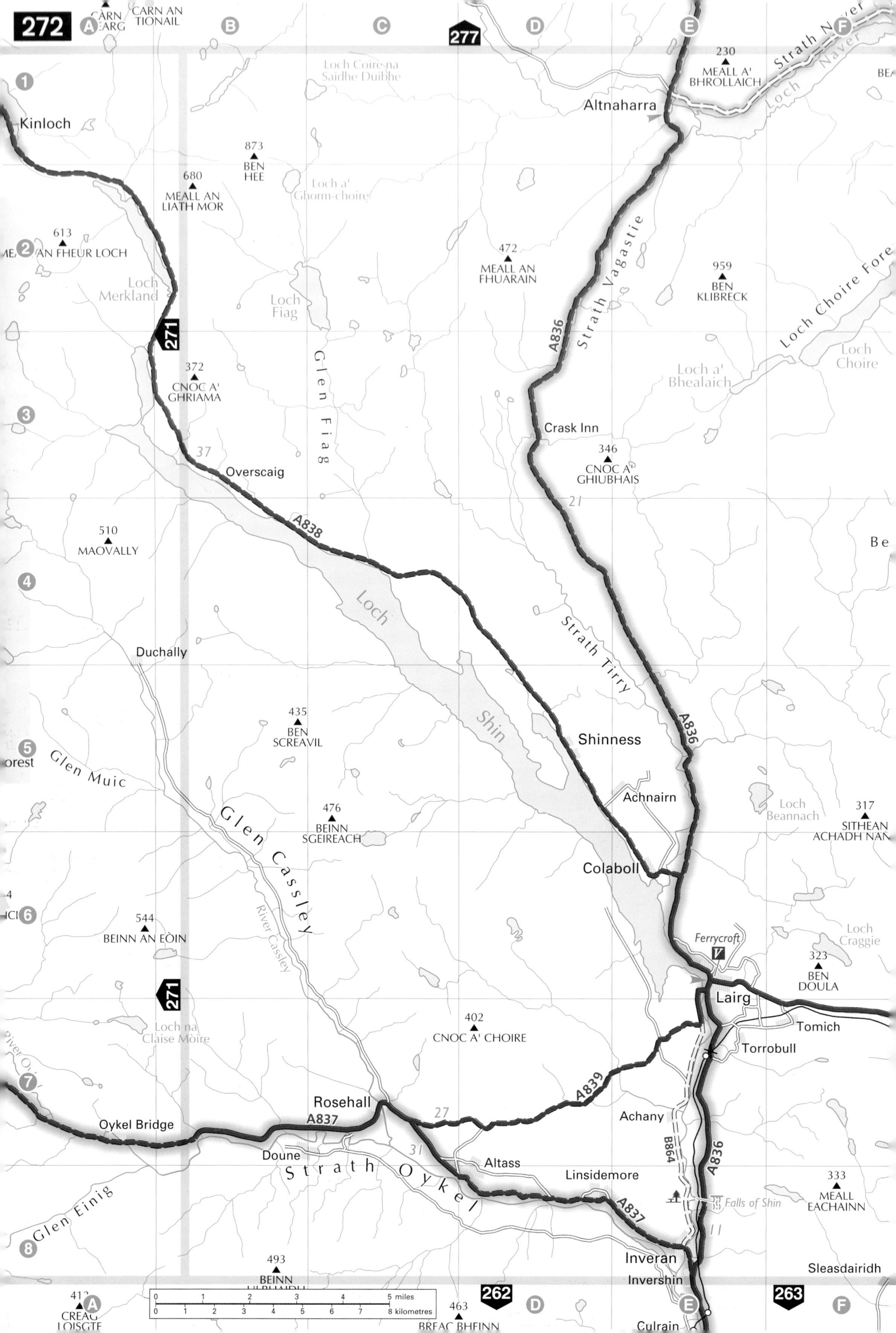

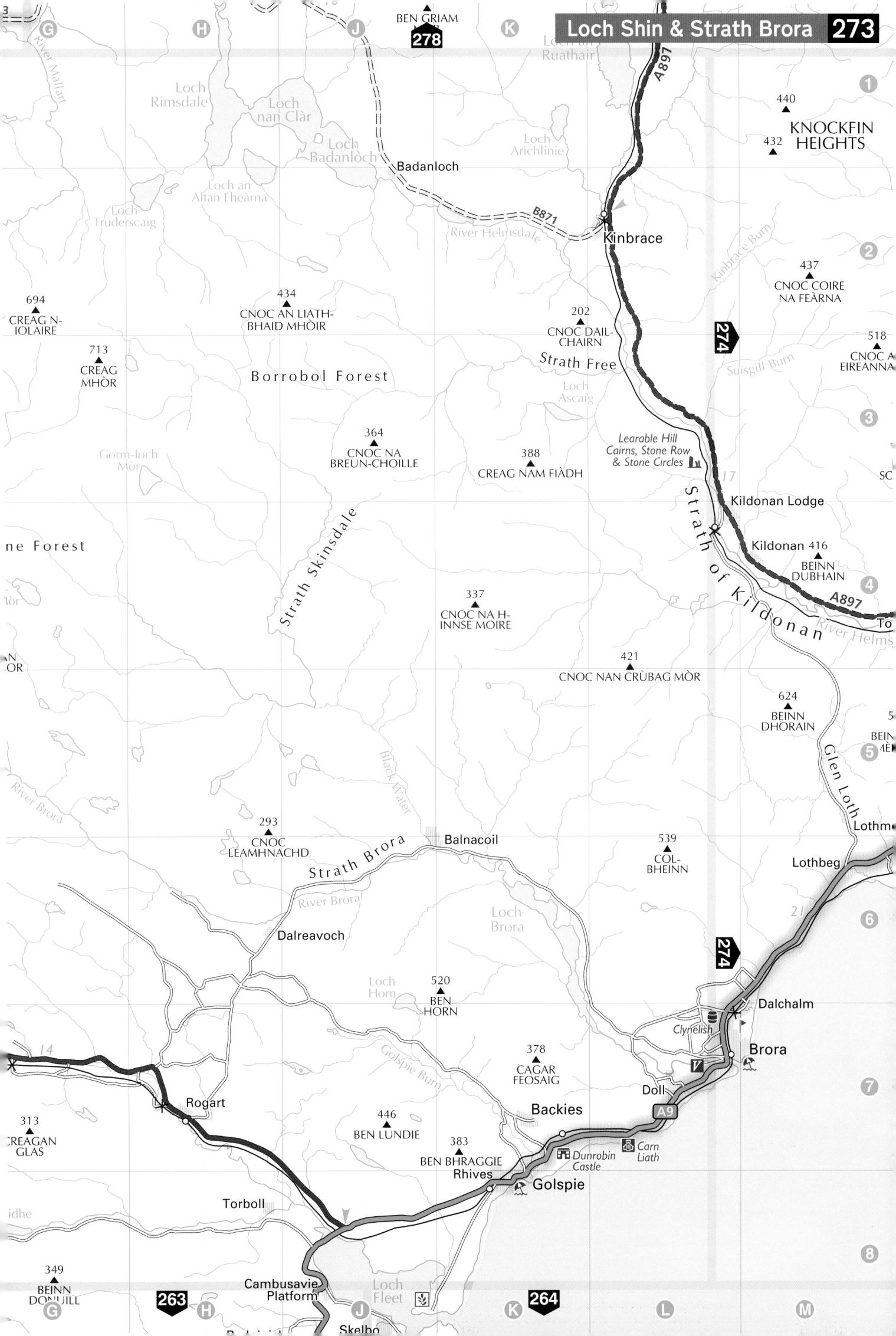

278

G H J K

BEN GRIAM

Loch an
Ruathair

A897

KNOCKFIN
HEIGHTS

440 ▲

432 ▲

1

Loch Rimsdale

Loch nan Clàr

Loch
Badanlòch

Badanloch

Loch
Arichlinie

437 ▲
CNOC COIRE
NA FEÀRNA

2

Loch an
Altan Fheàrna

Loch
Truderscaig

B871

River Helmsdale

✦ Kinbrace

Kinbrace Burn

274

518 ▲
CNOC A
EIREANNA

694 ▲
CREAG N-
IOLAIRE

434 ▲
CNOC AN LIATH-
BHAID MHÒIR

202 ▲
CNOC DAIL-
CHAIRN

Strath Free

713 ▲
CREAG
MHÒR

Borrobol Forest

Loch
Ascaig

Suisgill Burn

3

Gorm-loch
Mòr

ne Forest

364 ▲
CNOC NA
BREUN-CHOILLE

388 ▲
CREAG NAM FIÀDH

*Learable Hill
Cairns, Stone Row
& Stone Circles* ⚲

17

SC

Kildonan Lodge

Kildonan 416
✦ BEINN
DUBHAIN ▲

A897

River Helms

To

4

Strath Skinsdale

337 ▲
CNOC NA H-
INNSE MOIRE

Strath of Kildonan

OR

624 ▲
BEINN
DHORAIN

BEIN
ME

5

5

River Brora

Black Water

421 ▲
CNOC NAN CRÙBAG MÒR

Glen Loth

293 ▲
CNOC
LEAMHNACHD

Strath Brora

Balnacoil

539 ▲
COL-
BHEINN

Lothm

Lothbeg

River Brora

Loch
Brora

21

6

Dalreavoch

Loch
Horn

520 ▲
BEN
HORN

274

Clynelish 🛢

Dalchalm
✦

Brora

7

313 ▲
CREAGAN
GLAS

14
✦

Rogart
✦

Golspie Burn

378 ▲
CAGAR
FEOSAIG

Backies

🅅

Doll

A9

446 ▲
BEN LUNDIE

383 ▲
BEN BHRAGGIE

Rhives

🏰 *Dunrobin
Castle*

*Carn
Liath*

Torboll

Golspie 🏖

349 ▲
BEINN
DÒNUILL

263

Cambusavie
Platform

Loch
Fleet

264

8

G H J K L M

Skelbo

A B C D 279 E F

1

348
BEN
ALISKY

Glutt Lodge

440
▲

KNOCKFIN
HEIGHTS

264
▲
CNOCAN
CONACHREAG

432
▲

2

B871

Kinbrace

CNOC LOCH
MHADADH
317
▲

Berriedale Water

Braemore

CNOC COIRE
NA FEÀRNA
437
▲

484
▲
MAIDEN
PAP

Knock

202
▲
CNOC DAIL-
CHAIRN

705
▲
MORVEN

273

Ramscr

Strath Free

Loch
Ascaig

518
▲
CNOC AN
EIREANNAICH

626
▲
SCARABEN

3

Langwell Forest

Newport

20

M FIÀDH

Learable Hill
Cairns, Stone Row
& Stone Circles

554
CREAG
SCALABSDALE

Langwell
House

Berriec

17

Kildonan Lodge

4

Strath of Kildonan

Kildonan
416
▲
BEINN
DUBHAIN

401
▲
CNOC NA
MAOILE

A9
Badbea
Historic Village

A897

CNOC NAN CRÙBAG MÒR
421
▲

Torrish

River Helmsdale

404
▲
CREAG
THORARAIDH

Ord of Caithness

Navidale
Timespan M
Snow gates

5

624
▲
BEINN
DHORAIN

591
▲
BEINN NA
MÈILICH

West
Helmsdale

East Helmsdale

Helmsdale

Gartymore

Portgower

Glen Loth

6

539
▲
COL-
BHEINN

Lothmore

21

Lothbeg

273

Dalchalm

Clynelish

Brora

78
GAR
SA

Doll

7

Backies

A9

Dunrobin
Castle

Carn
Liath

8

Golspie

| 0 | 1 | 2 | 3 | 4 | 5 miles |
| 0 | 1 | 2 | 3 | 4 | 5 | 6 | 7 | 8 kilometres |

A B C D E F

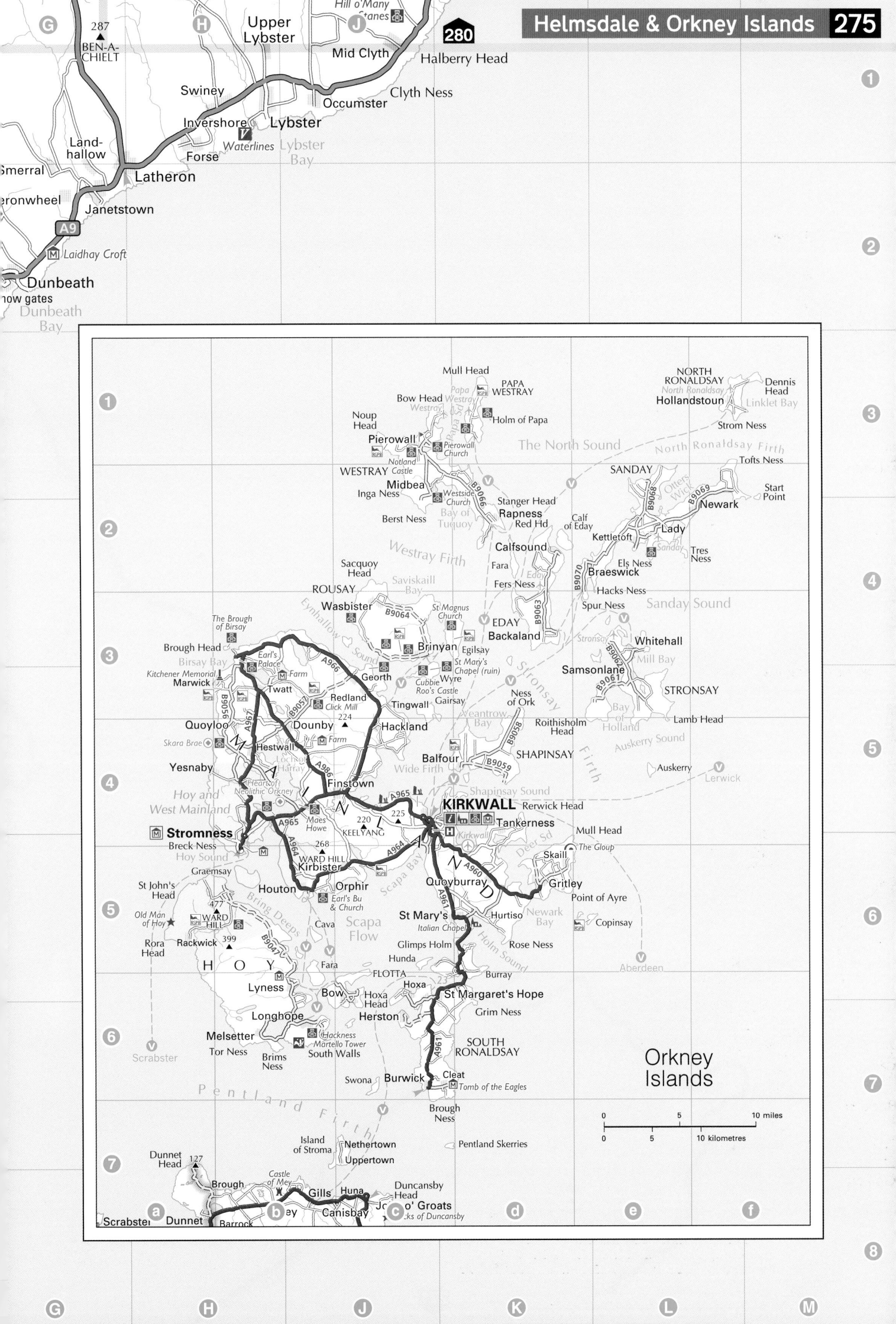

Map labels

280

287
BEN-A-
CHIELT
G

Upper
Lybster

H

Hill o'Many
Stanes

Mid Clyth
Swiney
Occumster
Clyth Ness
Halberry Head
Invershore   Lybster
Waterlines   Lybster
Forse   Bay
Land-
hallow
Latheron
Smerral
eronwheel   Janetstown
A9
Dunbeath
now gates
Laidhay Croft
Dunbeath
Bay

Orkney Islands

Mull Head
NORTH
RONALDSAY
North Ronaldsay
Dennis
Head
Bow Head PAPA
Papa   WESTRAY
Westray
Westray   Hollandstoun
Linklet Bay
Noup
Head   Holm of Papa   The North Sound   North Ronaldsay Firth
Strom Ness
Pierowall
Pierowall
Church   SANDAY   Tofts Ness
Notland
Castle   B9066
WESTRAY   Otters
Wick   B9068   Start
Point
Midbea   Stanger Head   B9069   Newark
Inga Ness   Westside
Church   Rapness   Calf   Kettletoft   Lady
Berst Ness   Bay of   Red Hd   of Eday   Els Ness   Tres
Tuquoy   Sanday   Ness
Sacquoy   Calfsound   Braeswick
Head   Westray Firth   Fara   B9070   Hacks Ness
Saviskaill   Fers Ness   Spur Ness   Sanday Sound
Bay   ROUSAY   St Magnus   EDAY   B9063
Wasbister   Church   B9061   Whitehall
The Brough   B9064   Backaland   Mill Bay
of Birsay   Egilsay   Samsonlane
Brough Head   RSPB   Brinyan   St Mary's   STRONSAY
Birsay Bay   Earl's   Chapel (ruin)   Bay
Kitchener Memorial   Palace   Georth   Wyre   Cubbie   of
Marwick   Farm   Roo's Castle   Ness   Holland
RSPB   Twatt   Redland   Tingwall   Gairsay   of Ork   Roithisholm   Lamb Head
Quoyloo   B9056   B9057   Click Mill   Veantrow   Head
Dounby   224   Bay   B9058   Auskerry Sound
Skara Brae   Hestwall   Farm   Hackland   Auskerry
Yesnaby   Heart of   Balfour   SHAPINSAY   Lerwick
Neolithic Orkney   Finstown   Wide Firth   B9059
Hoy and   Maes   A965   Shapinsay Sound
West Mainland   Howe   220   225   KIRKWALL   Rerwick Head
Stromness   KEELYANG   Tankerness   Mull Head
Breck Ness   A965   Kirkwall   The Gloup
Hoy Sound   A964   268   A964   Skaill
Graemsay   WARD HILL   Deer Sd
St John's   Kirbister   Quoyburray   Gritley
Head   477   Houton   Orphir   A960   Point of Ayre
Old Man   WARD   Earl's Bu   Scapa Bay   Newark
of Hoy   HILL   & Church   St Mary's   Hurtiso   Bay   Copinsay
Rora   Rackwick   399   B9047   Cava   Scapa   Italian Chapel   RSPB
Head   Flow   Glimps Holm   Rose Ness   Aberdeen
HOY   Fara   Hunda   Burray
Lyness   FLOTTA   Hoxa   Burray
Bow   Hoxa   St Margaret's Hope
Head   A961
Longhope   Herston   Grim Ness
Melsetter   Hackness   SOUTH
Tor Ness   Martello Tower   RONALDSAY
Brims   South Walls   A961
Ness   Swona   Burwick   Cleat
Scrabster   Tomb of the Eagles

Orkney
Islands

0   5   10 miles
0   5   10 kilometres

Pentland Firth
Island
Dunnet   of Stroma   Nethertown   Brough
Head   127   Uppertown   Ness   Pentland Skerries
Brough   Castle   Duncansby
of Mey   Gills   Huna   Head
Scrabster   Dunnet   bey   Canisby   Jo' Groats
Barrock   Cks of Duncansby

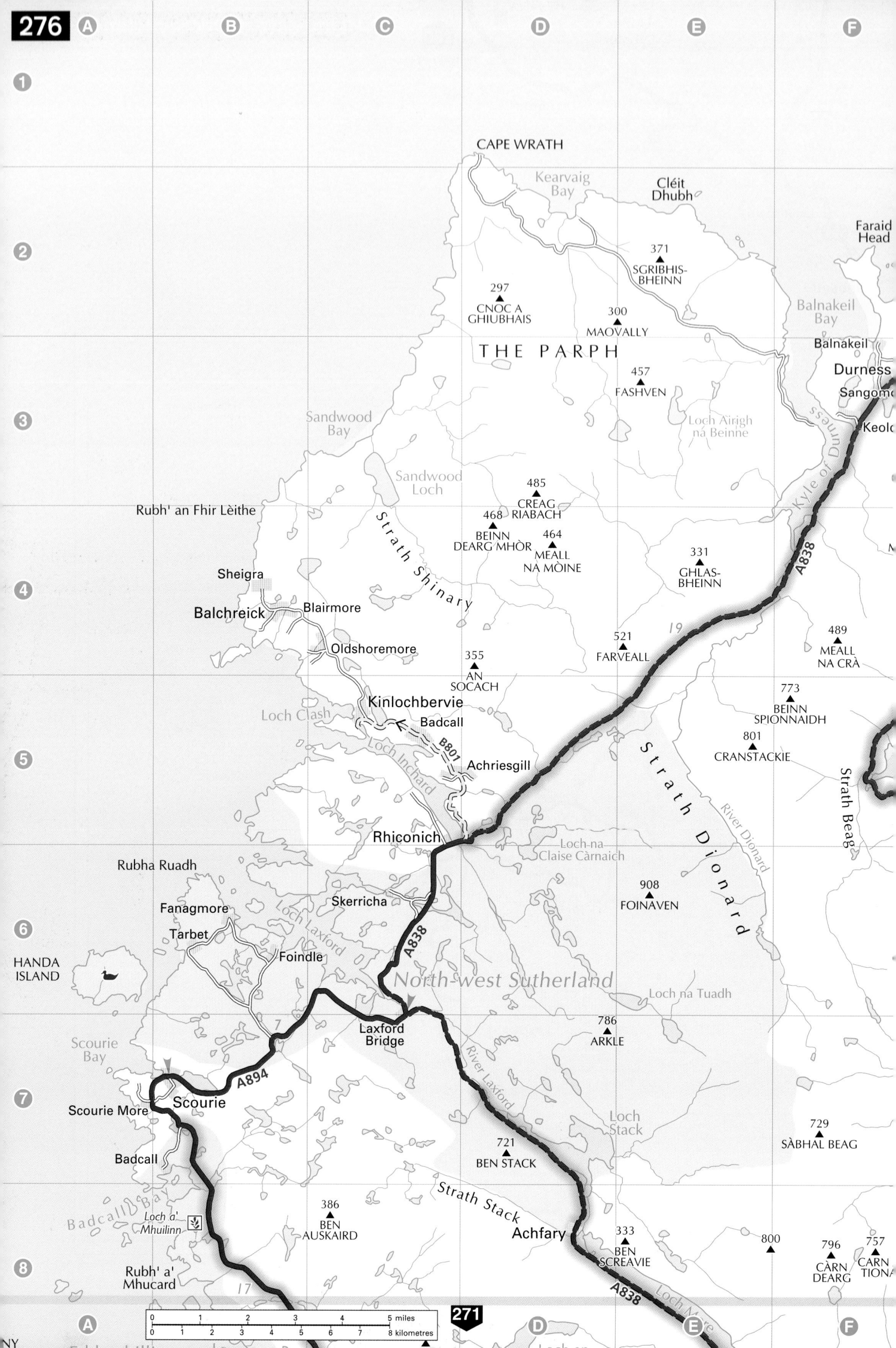

CAPE WRATH

Kearvaig
Bay

Cléit
Dhubh

Faraid
Head

371 ▲
SGRIBHIS-
BHEINN

297 ▲
CNOC A
GHIUBHAIS

300 ▲
MAOVALLY

Balnakeil
Bay

THE PARPH

Balnakeil

457 ▲
FASHVEN

Durness

Sangomo

Loch Airigh
ná Beinne

Keolo

Sandwood
Bay

Sandwood
Loch

485 ▲
CREAG
RIABACH

Rubh' an Fhir Lèithe

468 ▲
BEINN
DEARG MHÒR

464 ▲
MEALL
NA MÒINE

331 ▲
GHLAS-
BHEINN

A838

Sheigra

Strath Shinary

19

489 ▲
MEALL
NA CRÀ

Balchreick

Blairmore

521 ▲
FARVEALL

Oldshoremore

355 ▲
AN
SOCACH

773 ▲
BEINN
SPIONNAIDH

Loch Clash

Kinlochbervie

Badcall

801 ▲
CRANSTACKIE

Loch Inchard

B801

Achriesgill

Strath Dionard

River Dionard

Strath Beag

Rhiconich

Loch-na
Claise Càrnaich

Rubha Ruadh

Skerricha

908 ▲
FOINAVEN

Fanagmore

Loch Laxford

A838

Tarbet

North-west Sutherland

Loch na Tuadh

Foindle

HANDA
ISLAND

7

786 ▲
ARKLE

Laxford
Bridge

River Laxford

Scourie
Bay

A894

Loch
Stack

729 ▲
SÀBHAL BEAG

Scourie

Scourie More

721 ▲
BEN STACK

Badcall

Strath Stack

Badcall Ba

386 ▲
BEN
AUSKAIRD

Achfary

333 ▲
BEN
SCREAVIE

800 ▲

796 ▲
CÀRN
DEARG

757 ▲
CARN
TIONA

Loch a'
Mhuilinn

Rubh' a'
Mhucard

17

A838

Loch Mòre

NY

| 0 | 1 | 2 | 3 | 4 | 5 miles |
| 0 | 1 | 2 | 3 | 4 | 5 | 6 | 7 | 8 kilometres |

A B C D E F

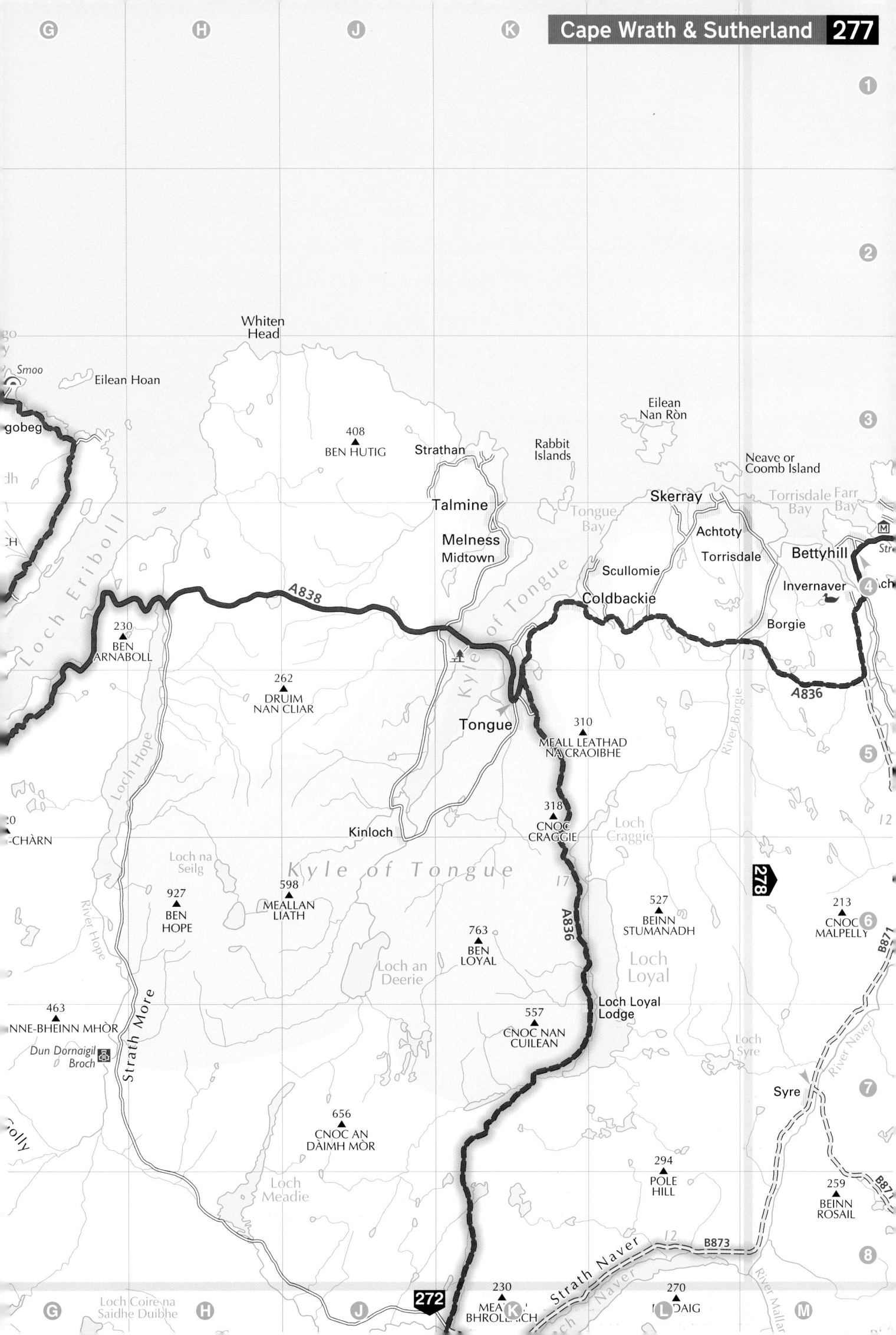

G · H · J · K

1
2
3
4
5
6
7
8

Smo
Eilean Hoan

gobeg

Whiten Head

408 ▲
BEN HUTIG

Strathan

Rabbit Islands

Eilean Nan Ròn

Neave or Coomb Island

Torrisdale Farr Bay

Skerray

Achtoty

Talmine

Torrisdale

Bettyhill

Melness
Midtown

Scullomie

Invernaver

A838

Coldbackie

Borgie

Loch Eriboll

230 ▲
BEN ARNABOLL

Tongue Bay

Kyle of Tongue

13

A836

262 ▲
DRUIM NAN CLIAR

River Borgie

Tongue

310 ▲
MEALL LEATHAD NA CRAOIBHE

Loch Hope

Kinloch

318 ▲
CNOC CRAGGIE

Loch Craggie

12

-CHÀRN

Loch na Seilg

Kyle of Tongue

17

278

927 ▲
BEN HOPE

598 ▲
MEALLAN LIATH

527 ▲
BEINN STUMANADH

213 ▲
CNOC MALPELLY

River Hope

Loch an Deerie

763 ▲
BEN LOYAL

Loch Loyal

B871

463 ▲
NNE-BHEINN MHÒR

557 ▲
CNOC NAN CUILEAN

Loch Loyal Lodge

Loch Syre

A836

River Naver

Strath More

Dun Dornaigil Broch

656 ▲
CNOC AN DÀIMH MÒR

Syre

Golly

Loch Meadie

294 ▲
POLE HILL

259 ▲
BEINN ROSAIL

B87

Strath Naver

B873

12

272

230 ▲
MEA...
BHROLL..CH

270 ▲
..DAIG

Loch Coire na Saidhe Duibhe

Loch Naver

G · H · J · K · L · M

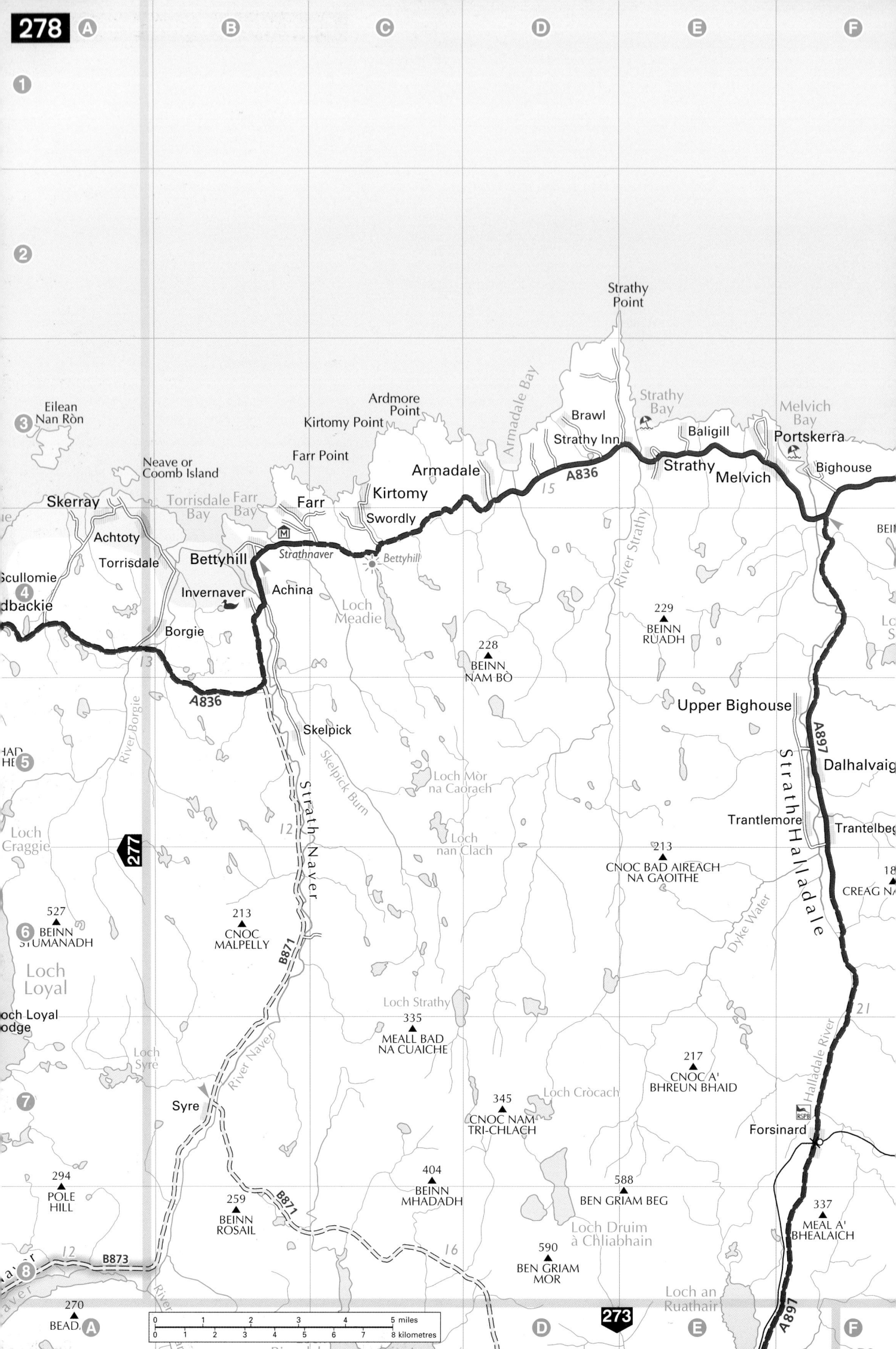

A B C D E F

1

2

Strathy
Point

3 Eilean
Nan Ròn

Ardmore
Point
Kirtomy Point
Brawl
Strathy
Bay
Melvich
Bay
Baligill
Portskerra
Farr Point
Strathy Inn
Bighouse
Neave or
Coomb Island
Armadale
Strathy
Melvich
Skerray
Torrisdale Farr
Bay Bay
Farr
Kirtomy
A836
15
Achtoty
Swordly
River Strathy
Torrisdale

Scullomie
Bettyhill
Strathnaver
Bettyhill
4 dbackie
Invernaver
Achina
Loch
Meadie
229
BEINN
RUADH
Borgie
A836
13
228
BEINN
NAM BÒ
Upper Bighouse

River Borgie
Skelpick
Strath Halladale
A897
Dalhalvaig
5 HAD
HE
Skelpick Burn
Loch Mòr
na Caorach
Trantlemore
Trantelbeg
Loch
Craggie
277
12
Strath Naver
Loch
nan Clach
213
CNOC BAD AIREACH
NA GAOITHE
18
CREAG NA

527
6 BEINN
STUMANADH
213
CNOC
MALPELLY
B871
Dyke Water
217
CNOC A'
BHREUN BHAID
21
Loch
Loyal
Loch Strathy
Halladale River

och Loyal
odge
Loch
Syre
River Naver
335
MEALL BAD
NA CUAICHE
Loch Cròcach
RSPB
7 Syre
345
CNOC NAM
TRI-CHLACH
Forsinard

294
POLE
HILL
404
BEINN
MHADADH
588
BEN GRIAM BEG
337
MEAL A'
BHEALAICH
259
BEINN
ROSAIL
B871
Loch Druim
à Chliabhain
8 aver 12 B873
270
BEAD.
590
BEN GRIAM
MOR
Loch an
Ruathair
A897

0 1 2 3 4 5 miles
0 1 2 3 4 5 6 7 8 kilometres
273
A D E F

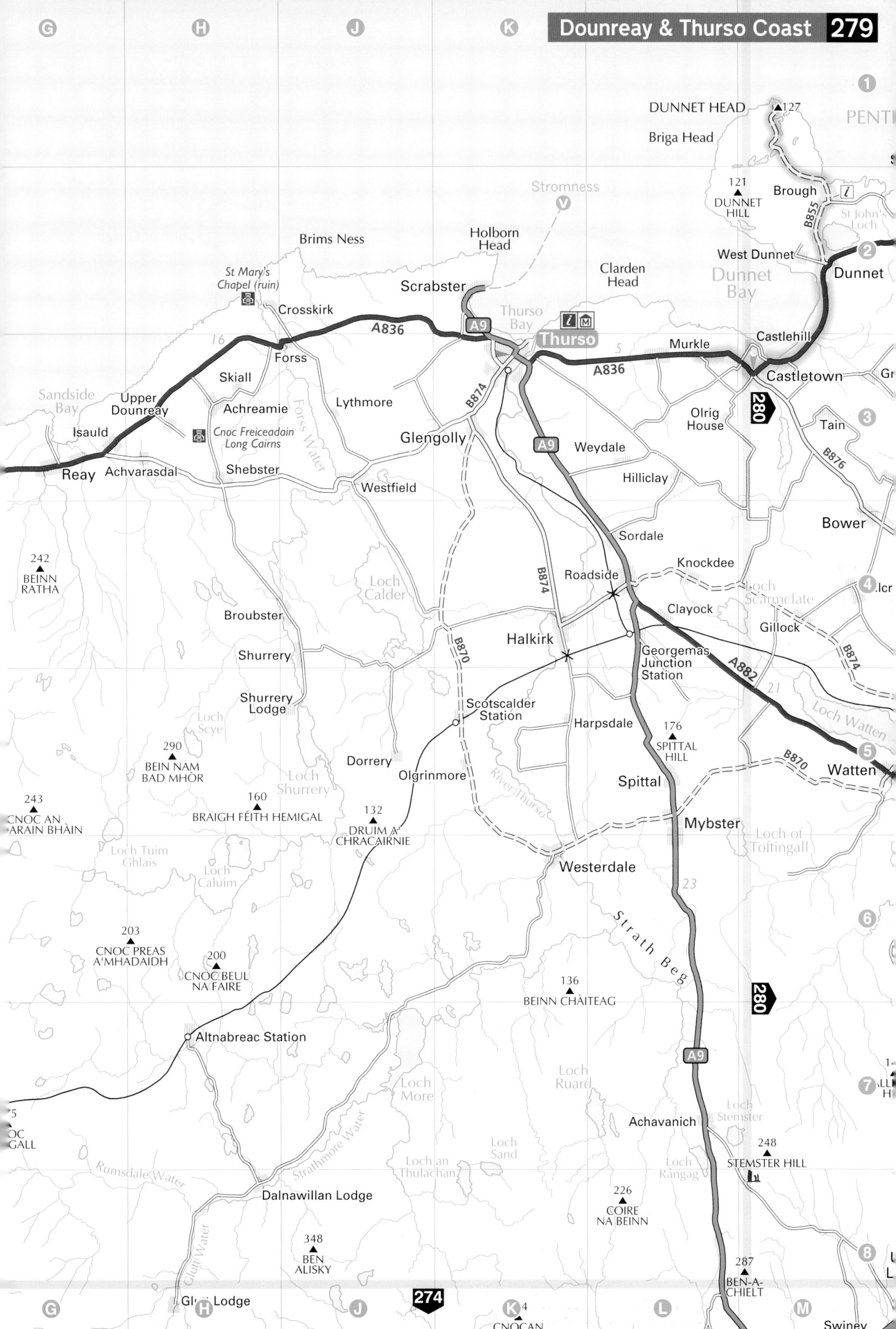

G   H   J   K

1

DUNNET HEAD ▲127

Briga Head

PENT

Brough

121
▲ DUNNET
HILL

i

St John's
Loch

2

West Dunnet

Dunnet

Stromness
V

Dunnet
Bay

Holborn
Head

Clarden
Head

Brims Ness

St Mary's
Chapel (ruin)

Scrabster

Thurso
Bay

i M

Castlehill

Murkle

Crosskirk

A836

A9

Thurso

A836

Castletown

Gr

Forss

16

Skiall

Lythmore

B874

Olrig
House

280

Tain

3

Sandside
Bay

Upper
Dounreay

Achreamie

Cnoc Freiceadain
Long Cairns

Glengolly

A9

Weydale

B876

Isauld

Forss Water

Hilliclay

Bower

Reay

Achvarasdal

Shebster

Westfield

Sordale

Knockdee

Loch
Scarmclate

lcr

4

242
▲
BEINN
RATHA

Broubster

Loch
Calder

Roadside

Clayock

Gillock

B874

B870

Shurrery

B874

Halkirk

Georgemas
Junction
Station

A882

21

Loch Watten

Shurrery
Lodge

Loch
Scye

Dorrery

Scotscalder
Station

Harpsdale

176
▲
SPITTAL
HILL

B870

5

290
▲
BEIN NAM
BAD MHÒR

Olgrinmore

River Thurso

Spittal

Watten

243
▲
CNOC AN
ARAIN BHÀIN

160
▲
BRAIGH FÉITH HEMIGAL

132
▲
DRUIM A'
CHRACAIRNIE

Mybster

Loch of
Toftingall

Loch Tuim
Ghlais

Loch
Caluim

Loch
Shurrery

Westerdale

Strath Beg

23

280

6

203
▲
CNOC PREAS
A'MHADAIDH

200
▲
CNOC BEUL
NA FAIRE

136
▲
BEINN CHÀITEAG

A9

75
OC
GALL

Altnabreac Station

Loch
More

Loch
Ruard

Loch
Stemster

7
LL
H

Strathmore Water

Loch
Sand

Achavanich

Loch an
Thulachan

248
▲
STEMSTER HILL

Rumsdale Water

Dalnawillan Lodge

226
▲
COIRE
NA BEINN

Loch
Rangag

348
▲
BEN
ALISKY

287
▲
BEN-A-
CHIELT

8

Gl   Lodge

CNOCAN

Swiney

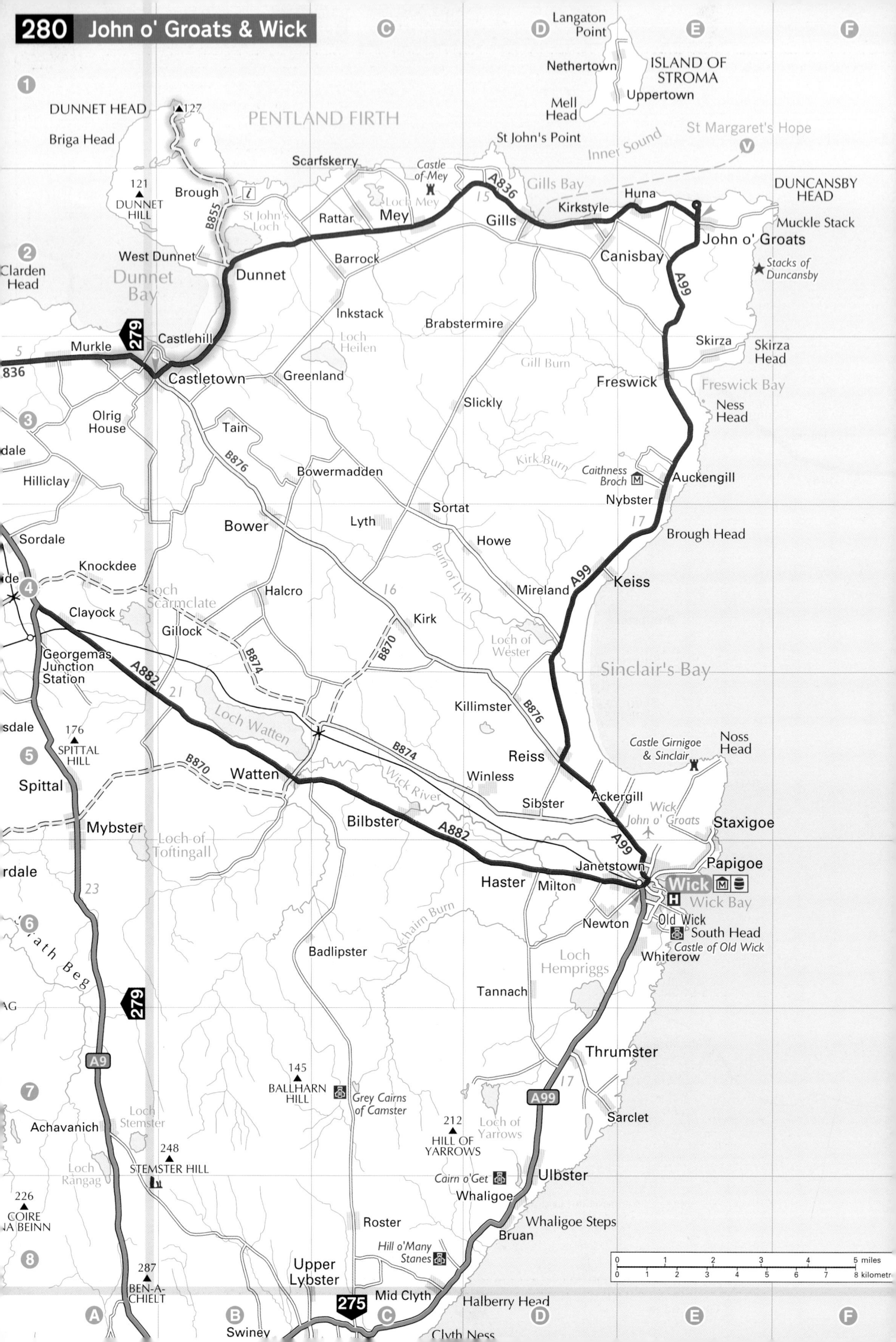

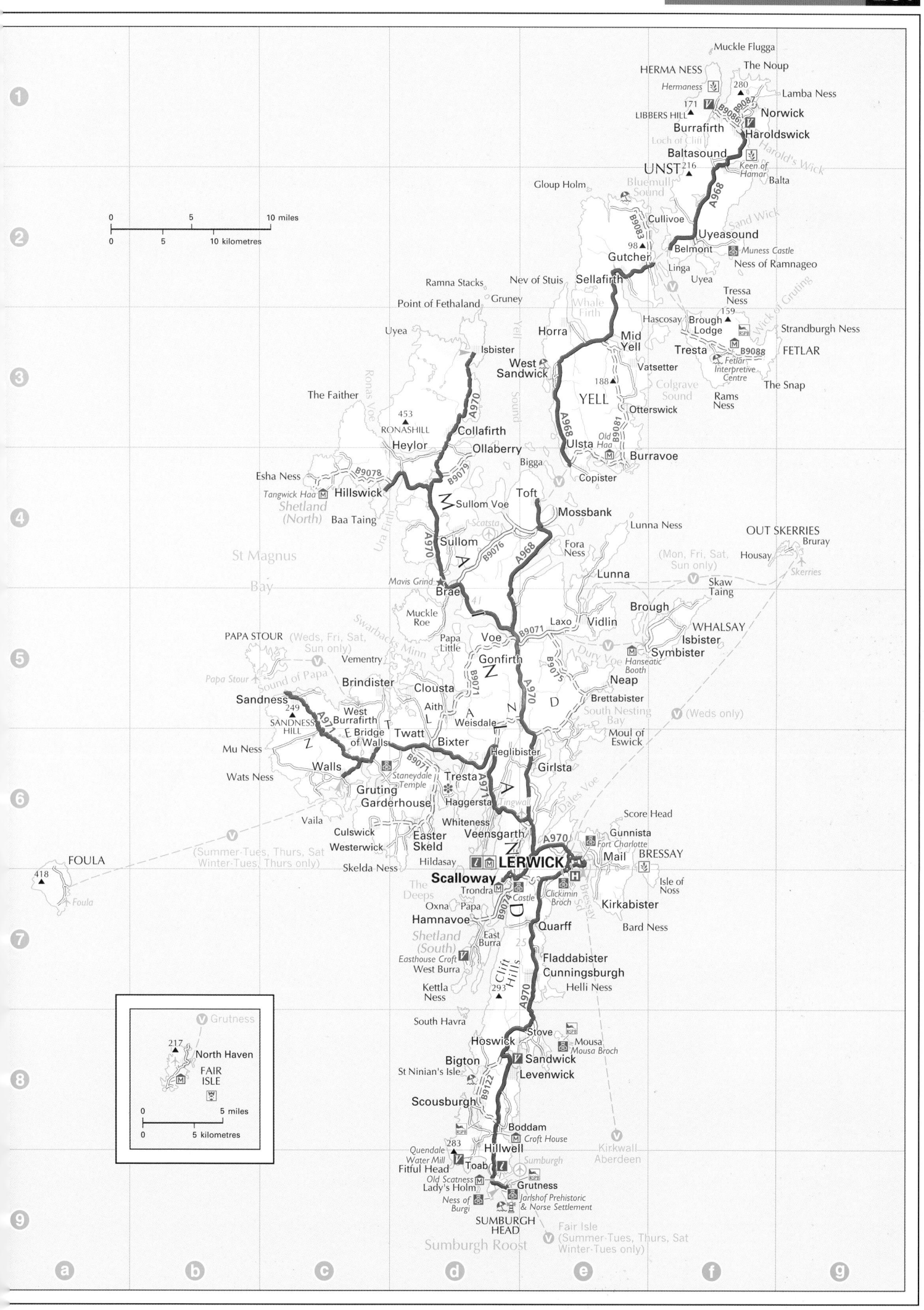

Muckle Flugga
The Noup
HERMA NESS
Hermaness 280
171 Lamba Ness
LIBBERS HILL Norwick
Burrafirth Haroldswick
Loch of Cliff Balta
Baltasound
UNST 216
Gloup Holm *Keen of Hamar*
Bluemull Sand Wick
Sound
Cullivoe
B9083 Uyeasound
98 Belmont Muness Castle
Gutcher Linga Ness of Ramnageo
Ramna Stacks Nev of Stuis Sellafirth Uyea Tressa
Point of Fethaland Gruney Ness
Uyea Horra 159
Whale Hascosay Brough Strandburgh Ness
Firth Lodge
Horra Mid Tresta B9088 FETLAR
Isbister Yell Fetlar
West Interpretive
A970 Sandwick Vatsetter Centre The Snap
The Faither 188 Colgrave
453 YELL Sound
RONASHILL Rams
Collafirth Otterswick Ness
Heylor Ollaberry Old
Esha Ness B9078 B9079 Bigga Haa
Tangwick Haa Hillswick Ulsta Burravoe
Shetland Baa Taing Sullom Voe Toft Copister
(North) A970 Mossbank
Sullom Lunna Ness
St Magnus B9076 A968 Fora OUT SKERRIES
Bay A Ness Bruray
Mavis Grind (Mon, Fri, Sat, Housay
Brae Lunna Sun only) Skaw Skerries
Taing
Muckle Brough
Roe B9071 Laxo Vidlin WHALSAY
PAPA STOUR (Weds, Fri, Sat, Papa Voe Isbister
Sun only) Little Symbister
Vementry B9075 Hanseatic
Brindister Clousta Gonfirth Booth
Sandness Aith Neap
249 West Weisdale Brettabister
SANDNESS Burrafirth Twatt South Nesting (Weds only)
HILL Bridge Bixter Bay
Mu Ness of Walls Moul of
Walls B9071 Heglibister Eswick
Wats Ness Tresta Girlsta
Gruting Staneydale Score Head
Garderhouse Temple A971
Vaila Haggersta Tingwall Gunnista
Culswick Whiteness Fort Charlotte
Westerwick Veensgarth A970 Mail BRESSAY
Easter Clickimin Isle of
FOULA Skeld Hildasay LERWICK Broch Noss
418 Scalloway Kirkabister
Foula The Trondra Castle
Deeps Oxna Papa Bard Ness
Hamnavoe Quarff
Shetland East Fladdabister
(South) Burra Cliff Cunningsburgh
Easthouse Croft Hills Helli Ness
West Burra A970
Kettla Stove Mousa
Ness 293 Sandwick Mousa Broch
South Havra Hoswick
Bigton Sandwick
St Ninian's Isle B9122 Levenwick
Scousburgh Kirkwall
Aberdeen
Boddam
283 Hillwell Croft House
Quendale Toab
Water Mill Grutness
Fitful Head Old Scatness
Lady's Holm Jarlshof Prehistoric
Ness of & Norse Settlement
Burgi
SUMBURGH Fair Isle
HEAD (Summer-Tues, Thurs, Sat
Sumburgh Roost Winter-Tues only)

Grutness
217 North Haven
FAIR
ISLE

0 5 miles
0 5 kilometres

0 5 10 miles
0 5 10 kilometres

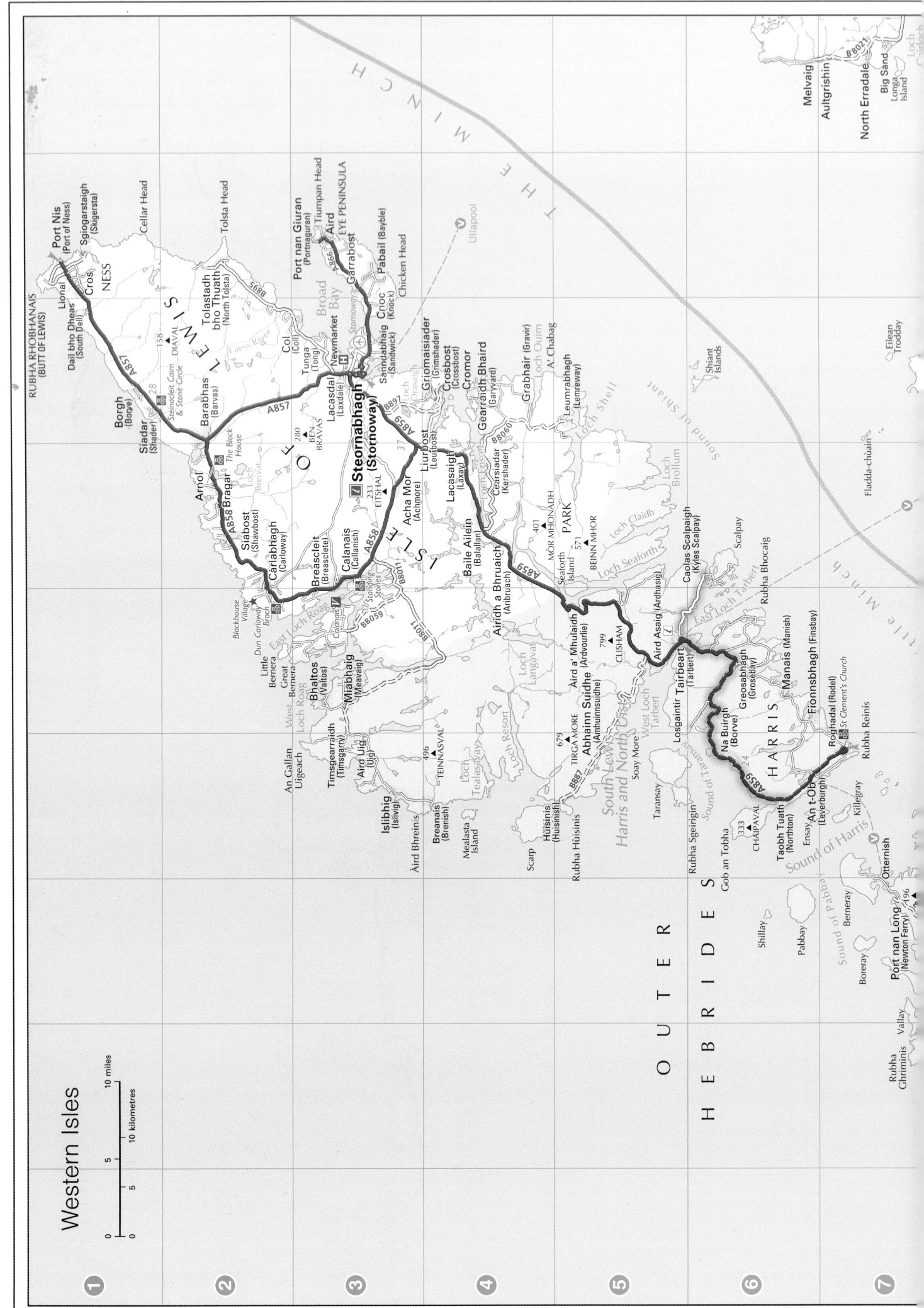

Western Isles

THE MINCH

The Minch

Sound of Shiant

Little Minch

RUBHA RHOBHANAIS
(BUTT OF LEWIS)

Port Nis
(Port of Ness)
Sgiogarstaigh
(Skigersta)
Lional
Dail bho Dheas
(South Dell)
Cros
NESS

Cellar Head

Tolsta Head

Tolastadh
bho Thuath
(North Tolsta)

Port nan Giuran
(Portnaguran)
Tiumpan Head
Aird
EYE PENINSULA
Garrabost
Pabail
(Bayble)
Chicken Head
Cnoc
(Knock)

Ullapool

Siadar
(Shader)
Borgh
(Borve)
Arnol
Barabhas
(Barvas)
A857

Steinacleit Cairn
& Stone Circle
158
DIAVAL
BEN
BRAVAS
280

Bragar
A858
Siabost
(Shawbost)
Carlabhagh
(Carloway)
Breascleit
(Breasclete)
The Block
House
Loch
Breivat

Col
(Coll)
Tunga
(Tong)
Lacasdal
(Laxdale)

LEWIS

LOCH

ISLE

Steornabhagh
(Stornoway)
Newmarket
Broad Bay

Sanndabhaig
(Sandwick)
Griomaisiader
(Grimshader)
Crosbost
(Crossbost)
Cromor
Gearraidh Bhaird
(Garyvard)

Grabhair
(Gravir)
Loch Odhairn
A'Chabag
Leumrabhagh
(Lemreway)

Liurbost
(Leurbost)
Lacasaigh
(Laxay)
Cearsiadar
(Kershader)

A859

233
EITSHAL
Acha Mor
(Achmore)
Calanais
(Callanish)
Standing
Stones

OF

Baile Ailein
(Balallan)
Airidh a Bhruaich
(Aribruaich)

PARK

MOR MHONADH
401
Seaforth
Island
BEINN MHOR
571

Loch Seaforth

Loch Shell

Shiant
Islands

Eilean
Trodday

Fladda-chùain

Dun Carloway
Broch
East Loch Roag
Calanais
B8011
B8059
B8011

Little
Bernera
Great
Bernera
West Loch Roag

Loch Roag

Loch
Langavat

Loch
Claidh

Loch
Brollum

Scalpay

Caolas Scalpaigh
(Kyles Scalpay)
Rubha Bhocaig

An Gallan
Uigeach

Aird Uig
(Uig)
Timsgearraidh
(Timsgarry)

TEINNASVAL
496

Loch
Resort

Aird a' Mhulaidh
(Ardvourlie)
799
CLISHAM

Aird Asaig
(Ardhasig)

Scalpay

Islibhig
(Islivig)
Breanais
(Brenish)
Mealasta
Island
Àird Bhreinis

Scarp

Hùisinis
(Huisinish)
Rubha Hùisinis

TIRGA MORE
679
B887
Abhainn Suidhe
(Amhuinnsuidhe)

Soay More
West Loch
Tarbert

Losgaintir
(Luskentyre)
Tairbeart
(Tarbert)

East Loch Tarbert

Manais
(Manish)
Greosabhagh
(Grosebay)
Fionnsbhagh
(Finsbay)

Na Buirgh
(Borve)

HARRIS

Roghadal (Rodel)
St Clement's Church
Rubha Reinis

SOUTH LEWIS

Taransay

South Lewis,
Harris and North Uist

Rubha Sgeirigin

Gob an Tobha

CHAIPAVAL
333

Taobh Tuath
(Northton)
Ensay
Killegray
Otternish
196
Port nan Long
(Newton Ferry)

An t-Ob
(Leverburgh)

Sound of Harris

A859
24

OUTER

HEBRIDES

Shillay

Pabbay

Boreray

Sound of Pabbay
Berneray

Rubha Ghrìminis
Vallay

Rubha
Ghrìminis

Melvaig
Aultgrishin
North Erradale
Big Sand
Longa
Island
B8021

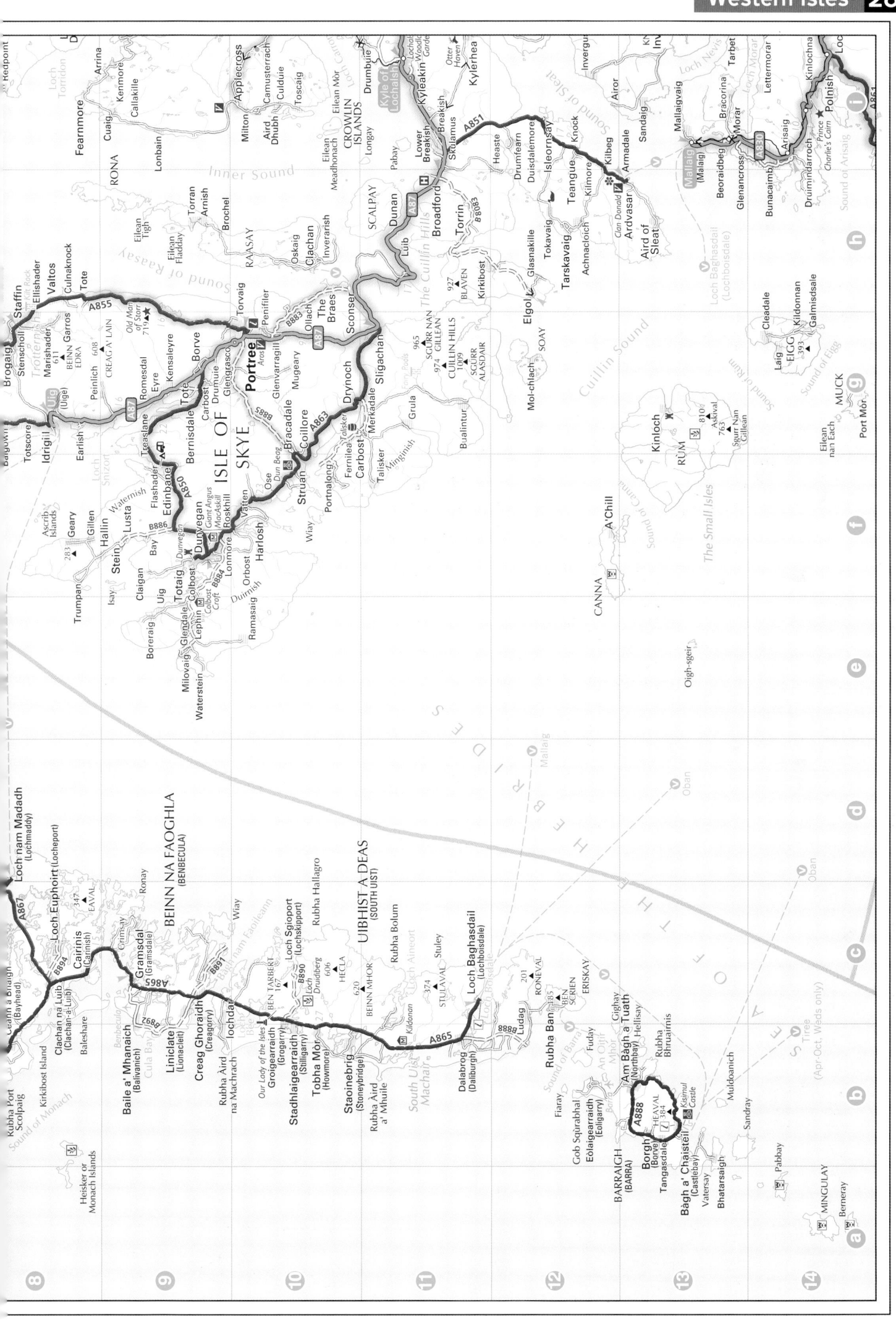

Motorway and primary route junctions which have access or exit restrictions are shown on the map pages thus:

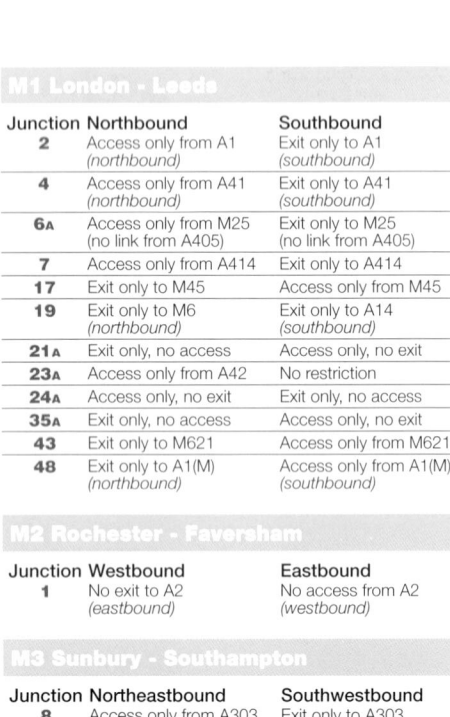

M1 London - Leeds

Junction	Northbound	Southbound
2	Access only from A1 (northbound)	Exit only to A1 (southbound)
4	Access only from A41 (northbound)	Exit only to A41 (southbound)
6A	Access only from M25 (no link from A405)	Exit only to M25 (no link from A405)
7	Access only from A414	Exit only to A414
17	Exit only to M45	Access only from M45
19	Exit only to M6 (northbound)	Exit only to A14 (southbound)
21A	Exit only, no access	Access only, no exit
23A	Access only from A42	No restriction
24A	Access only, no exit	Exit only, no access
35A	Exit only, no access	Access only, no exit
43	Exit only to M621	Access only from M621
48	Exit only to A1(M) (northbound)	Access only from A1(M) (southbound)

M2 Rochester - Faversham

Junction	Westbound	Eastbound
1	No exit to A2 (eastbound)	No access from A2 (westbound)

M3 Sunbury - Southampton

Junction	Northeastbound	Southwestbound
8	Access only from A303, no exit	Exit only to A303, no access
10	Exit only, no access	Access only, no exit
14	Access from M27 only, no exit	No access to M27 (westbound)

M4 London - South Wales

Junction	Westbound	Eastbound
1	Access only from A4 (westbound)	Exit only to A4 (eastbound)
2	Access only from A4 (westbound)	Access only from A4 (eastbound)
21	Exit only to M48	Access only from M48
23	Access only from M48	Exit only to M48
25	Exit only, no access	Access only, no exit
25A	Exit only, no access	Access only, no exit
29	Exit only to A48(M)	Access only from A48(M)
38	Exit only, no access	No restriction
39	Access only, no exit	No access or exit
42	Exit only to A483	Access only from A483

M5 Birmingham - Exeter

Junction	Northeastbound	Southwestbound
10	Access only, no exit	Exit only, no access
11A	Access only from A417 (westbound)	Exit only to A417 (eastbound)
18A	Exit only to M49	Access only from M49
18	Exit only, no access	Access only, no exit

M6 Toll Motorway

Junction	Northwestbound	Southeastbound
T1	Access only, no exit	No access or exit
T2	No access or exit	Exit only, no access
T5	Access only, no exit	Exit only to A5148 (northbound), no access
T7	Exit only, no access	Access only, no exit
T8	Exit only, no access	Access only, no exit

M6 Rugby - Carlisle

Junction	Northbound	Southbound
3A	Exit only to M6 Toll	Access only from M6 Toll
4	Exit only to M42 (southbound) & A446	Exit only to A446
4A	Access only from M42 (southbound)	Exit only to M42
5	Exit only, no access	Access only, no exit
10A	Exit only to M54	Access only from M54
11A	Access only from M6 Toll	Exit only to M6 Toll
with M56 (jct 20A)	No restriction	Access only from M56 (eastbound)
20	Exit only to M56 (westbound)	Access only from M56 (eastbound)
24	Access only, no exit	Exit only, no access
25	Exit only, no access	Access only, no exit

30	Access only from M61	Exit only to M61
31A	Exit only, no access	Access only, no exit
45	Exit only, no access	Access only, no exit

M8 Edinburgh - Bishopton

Junction	Westbound	Eastbound
6	Exit only, no access	Access only, no access
6A	Access only, no exit	Exit only, no access
7	Access only, no exit	Exit only, no access
7A	Exit only, no access	Access only from A725 (northbound), no exit
8	No access from M73 (southbound) or from A8 (eastbound) & A89	No exit to M73 (northbound) or to A8 (westbound) & A89
9	Access only, no exit	Exit only, no access
13	Access only from M80 (southbound)	Exit only to M80 (northbound)
14	Access only, no exit	Exit only, no access
16	Exit only to A804	Access only from A879
17	Exit only to A82	No restriction
18	Access only from A82 (eastbound)	Exit only to A814
19	No access from A814 (westbound)	Exit only to A814 (westbound)
20	Exit only, no access	Access only, no exit
21	Access only, no exit	Exit only to A8
22	Exit only to M77 (southbound)	Access only from M77 (northbound)
23	Exit only to B768	Access only from B768
25	No access or exit from or to A8	No access or exit from or to A8
25A	Exit only, no access	Access only, no exit
28	Exit only, no access	Access only, no exit
28A	Exit only to A737	Access only from A737

M9 Edinburgh - Dunblane

Junction	Northwestbound	Southeastbound
2	Access only, no exit	Exit only, no access
3	Exit only, no access	Access only, no exit
6	Access only, no exit	Exit only to A905
8	Exit only to M876 (southwestbound)	Access only from M876 (northeastbound)

M11 London - Cambridge

Junction	Northbound	Southbound
4	Access only from A406 (eastbound)	Exit only to A406
5	Exit only, no access	Access only, no exit
8A	Exit only, no access	No direct access, use jct 8
9	Exit only to A11	Access only from A11
13	Exit only, no access	Access only, no exit
14	Exit only, no access	Access only, no exit

M20 Swanley - Folkestone

Junction	Northwestbound	Southeastbound
2	Staggered junction; follow signs - access only	Staggered junction; follow signs - exit only
3	Exit only to M26 (westbound)	Access only from M26 (eastbound)
5	Access only from A20	For access follow signs - exit only to A20
6	No restriction	For exit follow signs
11A	Access only, no exit	Exit only, no access

M23 Hooley - Crawley

Junction	Northbound	Southbound
7	Exit only to A23 (northbound)	Access only from A23 (southbound)
10A	Access only, no exit	Exit only, no access

M25 London Orbital Motorway

Junction	Clockwise	Anticlockwise
1B	No direct access, use slip road to jct 2 Exit only	Access only, no exit
5	No exit to M26 (eastbound)	No access from M26
19	Exit only, no access	Access only, no exit
21	Access only from M1 (southbound) Exit only to M1 (northbound)	Access only from M1 (southbound) Exit only to M1 (northbound)
31	No exit (use slip road via jct 30), access only	No access (use slip road via jct 30), exit only

M26 Sevenoaks - Wrotham

Junction	Westbound	Eastbound
with M25 (jct 5)	Exit only to clockwise M25 (westbound)	Access only from anticlockwise M25 (eastbound)
with M20 (jct 3)	Access only from M20 (northwestbound)	Exit only to M20 (southeastbound)

M27 Cadnam - Portsmouth

Junction	Westbound	Eastbound
4	Staggered junction; follow signs - access only from M3 (southbound). Exit only to M3 (northbound)	Staggered junction; follow signs - access only from M3 (southbound). Exit only to M3 (northbound)
10	Exit only, no access	Access only, no exit
12	Staggered junction; follow signs - exit only to M275 (southbound)	Staggered junction; follow signs - access only from M275 (northbound)

M40 London - Birmingham

Junction	Northwestbound	Southeastbound
3	Exit only, no access	Access only, no exit
7	Exit only, no access	Access only, no exit
8	Exit only to M40/A40	Access only from M40/A40
13	Exit only, no access	Access only, no exit
14	Access only, no exit	Exit only, no access
16	Access only, no exit	Exit only, no access

M42 Bromsgrove - Measham

Junction	Northeastbound	Southwestbound
1	Access only, no exit	Exit only, no access
7	Exit only to M6 (northwestbound)	Access only from M6 (northwestbound)
7A	Exit only to M6 (southeastbound)	No access or exit
8	Access only from M6 (southeastbound)	Exit only to M6 (northwestbound)

M45 Coventry - M1

Junction	Westbound	Eastbound
Dunchurch (unnumbered)	Access only from A45	Exit only, no access
with M1 (jct 17)	Access only from M1 (northbound)	Exit only to M1 (southbound)

M48 Chepstow

Junction	Westbound	Eastbound
21	Access only from M4 (westbound)	Exit only to M4 (eastbound)
23	No exit to M4 (eastbound)	No access from M4 (westbound)

M53 Mersey Tunnel - Chester

Junction	Northbound	Southbound
11	Access only from M56 (westbound) Exit only to M56 (eastbound)	Access only from M5 (westbound) Exit only to M56 (eastbound)

M54 Telford - Birmingham

Junction	Westbound	Eastbound
with M6 (jct 10A)	Access only from M6 (northbound)	Exit only to M6 (southbound)

M56 Chester - Manchester

Junction	Westbound	Eastbound
1	Access only from M60 (westbound)	Exit only to M60 (eastbound) & A34 (northbound)
2	Exit only, no access	Access only, no exit
3	Access only, no exit	Exit only, no access
4	Exit only, no access	Access only, no exit
7	Exit only, no access	No restriction
8	Access only, no exit	No access or exit
9	No exit to M6 (southbound)	No access from M6 (northbound)
15	Exit only to M53	Access only from M5
16	No access or exit	No restriction

M57 Liverpool Outer Ring Road

Junction	Northwestbound	Southeastbound
3	Access only, no exit	Exit only, no access
5	Access only from A580 (westbound)	Exit only, no access

M58 Liverpool - Wigan

Junction	Westbound	Eastbound
1	Exit only, no access	Access only, no exit

M60 Manchester Orbital

Junction	Clockwise	Anticlockwise
2	Access only, no exit	Exit only, no access
3	No access from M56	Access only from A34 (northbound)
4	Access only from A34 (northbound). Exit only to M56	Access only from M56 (eastbound). Exit only to A34 (southbound)
5	Access and exit only from and to A5103 (northbound)	Access and exit only from and to A5103 (southbound)
7	No direct access, use slip road to jct 8. Exit only to A56	Access only from A56. No exit, use jct 8
14	Access from A580 (eastbound)	Exit only to A580 (westbound)
16	Access only, no exit	Exit only, no access
20	Exit only, no access	Access only, no exit
22	No restriction	Exit only, no access
25	Exit only, no access	No restriction
26	No restriction	Exit only, no access
27	Access only, no exit	Exit only, no access

M61 Manchester - Preston

Junction	Northwestbound	Southeastbound
3	No access or exit	Exit only, no access
with M6 (jct 30)	Exit only to M6 (northbound)	Access only from M6 (southbound)

M62 Liverpool - Kingston upon Hull

Junction	Westbound	Eastbound
23	Access only, no exit	Exit only, no access
32A	No access to A1(M) (southbound)	No restriction

M65 Preston - Colne

Junction	Northeastbound	Southwestbound
9	Exit only, no access	Access only, no exit
11	Access only, no exit	Exit only, no access

M66 Bury

Junction	Northbound	Southbound
with A56	Exit only to A56 (northbound)	Access only from A56 (southbound)
1	Exit only, no access	Access only, no exit

M67 Hyde Bypass

Junction	Westbound	Eastbound
1	Access only, no exit	Exit only, no access
2	Exit only, no access	Access only, no exit
3	Exit only, no access	No restriction

M69 Coventry - Leicester

Junction	Northbound	Southbound
2	Access only, no exit	Exit only, no access

M73 East of Glasgow

Junction	Northbound	Southbound
1	No exit to A74 & A721	No exit to A74 & A721
2	No access from or exit to A89. No access from M8 (eastbound)	No access from or exit to A89. No exit to M8 (westbound)

M74 and A74(M) Glasgow - Gretna

Junction	Northbound	Southbound
3	Exit only, no access	Access only, no exit
3A	Access only, no exit	Exit only, no access
4	No access from A74 & A721	Access only, no exit to A74 & A721
7	Access only, no exit	Exit only, no access
9	No access or exit	Exit only, no access
10	No restriction	Access only, no exit

M77 Glasgow - Kilmarnock

Junction	Northbound	Southbound
with M8 (jct 22)	No exit to M8 (westbound)	No access from M8 (eastbound)
4	Access only, no exit	Exit only, no access
6	Access only, no exit	Exit only, no access
7	Access only, no exit	No restriction
8	Exit only, no access	Exit only, no access

M80 Glasgow - Stirling

Junction	Northbound	Southbound
4A	Exit only, no access	Access only, no exit
6A	Access only, no exit	Exit only, no access
8	Exit only to M876 (northeastbound)	Access only from M876 (southwestbound)

M90 Edinburgh - Perth

Junction	Northbound	Southbound
1	No exit, access only	Exit only to A90 (eastbound)
2A	Exit only to A92 (eastbound)	Access only from A92 (westbound)
7	Access only, no exit	Exit only, no access
8	Exit only, no access	Access only, no exit
10	No access from A912. No exit to A912 (southbound)	No access from A912 (northbound). No exit to A912

M180 Doncaster - Grimsby

Junction	Westbound	Eastbound
1	Access only, no exit	Exit only, no access

M606 Bradford Spur

Junction	Northbound	Southbound
2	Exit only, no access	No restriction

M621 Leeds - M1

Junction	Clockwise	Anticlockwise
2A	Access only, no exit	Exit only, no access
4	No exit or access	No restriction
5	Access only, no exit	Exit only, no access
6	Exit only, no access	Access only, no exit
with M1 (jct 43)	Exit only to M1 (southbound)	Access only from M1 (northbound)

M876 Bonnybridge - Kincardine Bridge

Junction	Northeastbound	Southwestbound
with M80 (jct 5)	Access only from M80 (northeastbound)	Exit only to M80 (southwestbound)
with M9 (jct 8)	Exit only to M9 (eastbound)	Access only from M9 (westbound)

A1(M) South Mimms - Baldock

Junction	Northbound	Southbound
2	Exit only, no access	Access only, no exit
3	No restriction	Exit only, no access
5	Access only, no exit	No access or exit

A1(M) Pontefract - Bedale

Junction	Northbound	Southbound
41	No access to M62 (eastbound)	No restriction
43	Access only from M1 (northbound)	Exit only to M1 (southbound)

A1(M) Scotch Corner - Newcastle upon Tyne

Junction	Northbound	Southbound
57	Exit only to A66(M) (eastbound)	Access only from A66(M) (westbound)
65	No access. Exit only to A194(M) & A1 (northbound)	No exit. Access only from A194(M) & A1 (southbound)

A3(M) Horndean - Havant

Junction	Northbound	Southbound
1	Access only from A3	Exit only to A3
4	Exit only, no access	Access only, no exit

A38(M) Birmingham, Victoria Road (Park Circus)

Junction	Northbound	Southbound
with B4132	No exit	No access

A48(M) Cardiff Spur

Junction	Westbound	Eastbound
29	Access only from M4 (westbound)	Exit only to M4 (eastbound)
29A	Exit only to A48 (westbound)	Access only from A48 (eastbound)

A57(M) Manchester, Brook Street (A34)

Junction	Westbound	Eastbound
with A34	No exit	No access

A58(M) Leeds, Park Lane and Westgate

Junction	Northbound	Southbound
with A58	No restriction	No access

A64(M) Leeds, Clay Pit Lane (A58)

Junction	Westbound	Eastbound
with A58	No exit (to Clay Pit Lane)	No access (from Clay Pit Lane)

A66(M) Darlington Spur

Junction	Westbound	Eastbound
with A1(M) (jct 57)	Exit only to A1(M) (southbound)	Access only from A1(M) (northbound)

A74(M) Gretna - Abington

Junction	Northbound	Southbound
18	Exit only, no access	No exit

A194(M) Newcastle upon Tyne

Junction	Northbound	Southbound
with A1(M) (jct 65)	Access only from A1(M) (northbound)	Exit only to A1(M) (southbound)

A12 M25 - Ipswich

Junction	Northeastbound	Southwestbound
13	Access only, no exit	No restriction
14	Exit only, no access	Access only, no exit
20A	Exit only, no access	Access only, no exit
20B	Access only, no exit	Exit only, no access
21	No restriction	Access only, no exit
23	Exit only, no access	Access only, no exit
24	Access only, no exit	Exit only, no access
27	Exit only, no access	Access only, no exit
Dedham & Stratford St Mary (unnumbered)	Exit only	Access only

A14 M1 - Felixstowe

Junction	Westbound	Eastbound
with M1/M6 (jct19)	Exit only to M6 and M1 (northbound)	Access only from M6 and M1 (southbound)
4	Exit only, no access	Access only, no exit
31	Exit only to M11 (for London)	Access only, no exit
31A	Exit only to A14 (northbound)	Access only, no exit
34	Access only, no exit	Exit only, no access
36	Exit only to A11, access only from A1303	Access only from A11
38	Access only from A11	Exit only to A11
39	Exit only, no access	Access only, no exit
61	Access only, no exit	Exit only, no access

A55 Holyhead - Chester

Junction	Westbound	Eastbound
8A	Exit only, no access	Access only, no exit
23A	Access only, no exit	Exit only, no access
24A	Access only, no exit	No access or exit
27A	No restriction	No access or exit
33A	Exit only, no access	No access or exit
33B	Exit only, no access	Access only, no exit
36A	Exit only to A5104	Access only from A5104

This index lists places appearing in the main map section of the atlas in alphabetical order. The reference following each name gives the atlas page number and grid reference of the square in which the place appears. The map shows counties, unitary authorities and administrative areas, together with a list of the abbreviated name forms used in the index.

Scotland

Abers	**Aberdeenshire**
Ag & B	**Argyll and Bute**
Angus	**Angus**
Border	**Scottish Borders**
C Aber	**City of Aberdeen**
C Dund	**City of Dundee**
C Edin	**City of Edinburgh**
C Glas	**City of Glasgow**
Clacks	**Clackmannanshire (1)**
D & G	**Dumfries & Galloway**
E Ayrs	**East Ayrshire**
E Duns	**East Dunbartonshire (2)**
E Loth	**East Lothian**
E Rens	**East Renfrewshire (3)**
Falk	**Falkirk**
Fife	**Fife**
Highld	**Highland**
Inver	**Inverclyde (4)**
Mdloth	**Midlothian (5)**
Moray	**Moray**
N Ayrs	**North Ayrshire**
N Lans	**North Lanarkshire (6)**
Ork	**Orkney Islands**
P & K	**Perth & Kinross**
Rens	**Renfrewshire (7)**
S Ayrs	**South Ayrshire**
S Lans	**South Lanarkshire**
Shet	**Shetland Islands**
Stirlg	**Stirling**
W Duns	**West Dunbartonshire (8)**
W Isls	**Western Isles**
	(Na h-Eileanan an Iar)
W Loth	**West Lothian**

Wales

Blae G	**Blaenau Gwent (9)**
Brdgnd	**Bridgend (10)**
Caerph	**Caerphilly (11)**
Cardif	**Cardiff**
Carmth	**Carmarthenshire**
Cerdgn	**Ceredigion**
Conwy	**Conwy**
Denbgs	**Denbighshire**
Flints	**Flintshire**
Gwynd	**Gwynedd**
IoA	**Isle of Anglesey**
Mons	**Monmouthshire**
Myr Td	**Merthyr Tydfil (12)**
Neath	**Neath Port Talbot (13)**
Newpt	**Newport (14)**
Pembks	**Pembrokeshire**
Powys	**Powys**
Rhondd	**Rhondda Cynon Taff (15)**
Swans	**Swansea**
Torfn	**Torfaen (16)**
V Glam	**Vale of Glamorgan (17)**
Wrexhm	**Wrexham**

Channel Islands & Isle of Man

Guern	**Guernsey**
Jersey	**Jersey**
IoM	**Isle of Man**

England

BaNES	**Bath & N E Somerset (18)**
Barns	**Barnsley (19)**
Bed	**Bedford**
Birm	**Birmingham**
Bl w D	**Blackburn with Darwen (20)**
Bmouth	**Bournemouth**
Bolton	**Bolton (21)**
Bpool	**Blackpool**
Br & H	**Brighton & Hove (22)**
Br For	**Bracknell Forest (23)**
Bristl	**City of Bristol**
Bucks	**Buckinghamshire**
Bury	**Bury (24)**
C Beds	**Central Bedfordshire**
C Brad	**City of Bradford**
C Derb	**City of Derby**
C KuH	**City of Kingston upon Hull**
C Leic	**City of Leicester**
C Nott	**City of Nottingham**
C Pete	**City of Peterborough**
C Plym	**City of Plymouth**
C Port	**City of Portsmouth**
C Sotn	**City of Southampton**
C Stke	**City of Stoke-on-Trent**
C York	**City of York**
Calder	**Calderdale (25)**
Cambs	**Cambridgeshire**
Ches E	**Cheshire East**
Ches W	**Cheshire West and Chester**
Cnwll	**Cornwall**
Covtry	**Coventry**
Cumb	**Cumbria**
Darltn	**Darlington (26)**
Derbys	**Derbyshire**
Devon	**Devon**
Donc	**Doncaster (27)**
Dorset	**Dorset**
Dudley	**Dudley (28)**
Dur	**Durham**
E R Yk	**East Riding of Yorkshire**
E Susx	**East Sussex**
Essex	**Essex**
Gatesd	**Gateshead (29)**
Gloucs	**Gloucestershire**
Gt Lon	**Greater London**
Halton	**Halton (30)**
Hants	**Hampshire**
Hartpl	**Hartlepool (31)**
Herefs	**Herefordshire**
Herts	**Hertfordshire**
IoS	**Isles of Scilly**
IoW	**Isle of Wight**
Kent	**Kent**
Kirk	**Kirklees (32)**
Knows	**Knowsley (33)**
Lancs	**Lancashire**
Leeds	**Leeds**
Leics	**Leicestershire**
Lincs	**Lincolnshire**
Lpool	**Liverpool**
Luton	**Luton**
M Keyn	**Milton Keynes**

Manch	**Manchester**
Medway	**Medway**
Middsb	**Middlesbrough**
N Linc	**North Lincolnshire**
N Som	**North Somerset (34)**
N Tyne	**North Tyneside (35)**
N u Ty	**Newcastle upon Tyne**
N York	**North Yorkshire**
NE Lin	**North East Lincolnshire**
Nhants	**Northamptonshire**
Norfk	**Norfolk**
Notts	**Nottinghamshire**
Nthumb	**Northumberland**
Oldham	**Oldham (36)**
Oxon	**Oxfordshire**
Poole	**Poole**
R & Cl	**Redcar & Cleveland**
Readg	**Reading**
Rochdl	**Rochdale (37)**
Rothm	**Rotherham (38)**
Rutlnd	**Rutland**
S Glos	**South Gloucestershire (39)**
S on T	**Stockton-on-Tees (40)**
S Tyne	**South Tyneside (41)**
Salfd	**Salford (42)**
Sandw	**Sandwell (43)**
Sefton	**Sefton (44)**
Sheff	**Sheffield**
Shrops	**Shropshire**
Slough	**Slough (45)**
Solhll	**Solihull (46)**
Somset	**Somerset**
St Hel	**St Helens (47)**
Staffs	**Staffordshire**
Sthend	**Southend-on-Sea**
Stockp	**Stockport (48)**
Suffk	**Suffolk**
Sundld	**Sunderland**
Surrey	**Surrey**
Swindn	**Swindon**
Tamesd	**Tameside (49)**
Thurr	**Thurrock (50)**
Torbay	**Torbay**
Traffd	**Trafford (51)**
W & M	**Windsor & Maidenhead (52)**
W Berk	**West Berkshire**
W Susx	**West Sussex**
Wakefd	**Wakefield (53)**
Warrtn	**Warrington (54)**
Warwks	**Warwickshire**
Wigan	**Wigan (55)**
Wilts	**Wiltshire**
Wirral	**Wirral (56)**
Wokham	**Wokingham (57)**
Wolves	**Wolverhampton (58)**
Worcs	**Worcestershire**
Wrekin	**Telford & Wrekin (59)**
Wsall	**Walsall (60)**

ORKNEY ISLANDS

SHETLAND ISLANDS

WESTERN ISLES (Na h-Eileanan an Iar)

HIGHLAND

MORAY

S C O T L A N D

• Aberdeen

ABERDEENSHIRE

ANGUS

PERTH & KINROSS

• Dundee

ARGYLL AND BUTE

STIRLING

FIFE

1

8 2 FALK

4 Glasgow W LOTH Edinburgh • E LOTH

7 6 5

3

NORTH AYRSHIRE

S LANS

E AYRS

SCOTTISH BORDERS

S AYRS

DUMFRIES & GALLOWAY

NORTHUMBERLAND

Newcastle upon Tyne • 35
29 41
• Sunderland

CUMBRIA

DURHAM

31
26 40 R & CL
• Middlesbrough

IoM

NORTH YORKSHIRE

Blackpool • LANCASHIRE

Bradford • York • EAST RIDING OF YORKSHIRE
• Kingston upon Hull

20 25 Leeds •
53
21 24 37 32 N LINC NE LIN
55 36 19
44 47 42 49 27
Liverpool • 33 54 51 Manchester • 38
56 30 48 Sheffield •

IoA

CONWY

FLINTS

DENBGS

CHES W

CHES E

DERBYS

NOTTS

LINCOLNSHIRE

WREXHAM

GWYNEDD

Stoke-on-Trent •

STAFFS

Derby • Nottingham •

NORFOLK

59

SHROPSHIRE

LEICS

RUTLAND

Leicester • Peterborough •

CERDGN

POWYS

58 60
28 43 Birmingham •
46 Coventry •

WORCS

WARWKS

NHANTS

CAMBS

SUFFOLK

BED

Milton Keynes •

PEMBKS

CARMTH

HEREFS

W A L E S E N G L A N D

BEDS • Luton

HERTS

ESSEX

Swansea •

13 12 9 MONS

15 16

10 11

14

17 Cardiff •

Bristol •

39

GLOUCS

OXON

BUCKS

GREATER LONDON

Southend-on-Sea •

50

34 18

Swindon •

Reading •
52 45
W BERK 57 23

MEDWAY

WILTSHIRE

SURREY

KENT

SOMERSET

HAMPSHIRE

W SUSX

E SUSX

22

DEVON

DORSET

Southampton •
Bournemouth • • Portsmouth
Poole • IoW

Guernsey

CORNWALL

• Torbay

CHANNEL ISLANDS

Jersey

Plymouth •

IoS

A

Abbas Combe Somset ... 32 B6
Abberley Worcs ... 81 H2
Abberley Common Worcs ... 81 G2
Abberton Essex ... 72 E3
Abberton Worcs ... 82 A4
Abberwick Nthumb ... 191 G3
Abbess Roding Essex ... 70 E5
Abbey Devon ... 14 D1
Abbey-Cwm-Hir Powys ... 78 E1
Abbeydale Sheff ... 132 F3
Abbey Dore Herefs ... 62 D1
Abbey Green Staffs ... 131 J8
Abbey Hill Somset ... 30 D7
Abbey St Bathans Border ... 213 G6
Abbeystead Lancs ... 147 L5
Abbey Town Cumb ... 177 G8
Abbey Valley Crematorium
 Derbys ... 116 C1
Abbey Village Lancs ... 139 J3
Abbey Wood Gt Lon ... 52 A3
Abbotrule Border ... 189 G4
Abbots Bickington Devon ... 27 G8
Abbots Bromley Staffs ... 115 H6
Abbotsbury Dorset ... 16 A5
Abbot's Chair Derbys ... 131 K2
Abbots Deuglie P & K ... 221 K5
Abbotsham Devon ... 27 G5
Abbotskerswell Devon ... 8 C1
Abbots Langley Herts ... 68 E6
Abbotsleigh Devon ... 8 B5
Abbots Leigh N Som ... 45 G4
Abbotsley Cambs ... 86 E4
Abbots Morton Worcs ... 82 B4
Abbots Ripton Cambs ... 102 E7
Abbot's Salford Warwks ... 82 C5
Abbotstone Hants ... 35 H4
Abbotswood Hants ... 34 D6
Abbots Worthy Hants ... 35 G4
Abbotts Ann Hants ... 34 D2
Abbott Street Dorset ... 17 J3
Abcott Shrops ... 95 J7
Abdon Shrops ... 96 D6
Abenhall Gloucs ... 63 K4
Aberaeron Cerdgn ... 76 E3
Aberaman Rhondd ... 60 F7
Aberangell Gwynd ... 93 J2
Aber-arad Carmth ... 76 B7
Aberarder Highld ... 251 H6
Aberargie P & K ... 222 B4
Aberarth Cerdgn ... 76 E3
Aberavon Neath ... 57 K7
Aber-banc Cerdgn ... 76 C7
Aberbargoed Caerph ... 61 J7
Aberbeeg Blae G ... 61 K6
Abercanaid Myr Td ... 61 G6
Abercarn Caerph ... 43 K3
Abercastle Pembks ... 74 D5
Abercegir Powys ... 93 H3
Aberchalder Lodge Highld ... 240 B3
Aberchirder Abers ... 268 A5
Aber Clydach Powys ... 61 H3
Abercorn W Loth ... 210 E3
Abercraf Powys ... 59 M6
Abercregan Neath ... 42 C2
Abercwmboi Rhondd ... 60 F7
Abercych Pembks ... 75 M4
Abercynon Rhondd ... 43 G3
Aberdalgie P & K ... 221 K3
Aberdare Rhondd ... 60 F6
Aberdaron Gwynd ... 108 C6
Aberdeen C Aber ... 245 L2
Aberdeen Crematorium
 C Aber ... 245 K2
Aberdesach Gwynd ... 109 G1
Aberdour Fife ... 211 G2
Aberdulais Neath ... 57 L5
Aberdyfi Gwynd ... 92 D4
Aberedw Powys ... 78 F6
Abereiddy Pembks ... 74 C6
Abererch Gwynd ... 109 G4
Aberfan Myr Td ... 61 G7
Aberfeldy P & K ... 232 C5
Aberffraw IoA ... 124 F6
Aberffrwd Cerdgn ... 92 E7
Aberford Leeds ... 150 F8
Aberfoyle Stirlg ... 219 H7
Abergarw Brdgnd ... 42 D5
Abergarwed Neath ... 60 B6
Abergavenny Mons ... 62 C4
Abergele Conwy ... 127 J4
Aber-giar Carmth ... 76 F7
Abergorlech Carmth ... 59 G2
Abergwesyn Powys ... 78 A4
Abergwili Carmth ... 58 D5
Abergwydol Powys ... 93 G3
Abergwynfi Neath ... 42 D3

Abergwyngregyn Gwynd ... 126 C5
Abergynolwyn Gwynd ... 92 E2
Aberhafesp Powys ... 94 C5
Aberhosan Powys ... 93 H4
Aberkenfig Brdgnd ... 42 D5
Aberlady E Loth ... 212 A3
Aberlemno Angus ... 234 E4
Aberllefenni Gwynd ... 93 G2
Aberllynfi Powys ... 79 H7
Aberlour, Charlestown of
 Moray ... 254 E3
Aber-Magwr Cerdgn ... 92 E8
Aber-meurig Cerdgn ... 77 G4
Abermorddu Flints ... 129 G8
Abermule Powys ... 94 E4
Abernant Carmth ... 58 C4
Aber-nant Rhondd ... 60 F6
Abernethy P & K ... 222 C4
Abernyte P & K ... 222 D1
Aberporth Cerdgn ... 76 A5
Abersoch Gwynd ... 108 E6
Abersychan Torfn ... 62 B6
Aberthin V Glam ... 42 F7
Abertillery Blae G ... 61 K6
Abertridwr Caerph ... 43 H4
Abertridwr Powys ... 111 K7
Abertysswg Caerph ... 61 H6
Aberuthven P & K ... 221 H4
Aberyscir Powys ... 60 F1
Aberystwyth Cerdgn ... 92 C7
Aberystwyth Crematorium
 Cerdgn ... 92 D6
Abingdon-on-Thames Oxon ... 66 C7
Abinger Common Surrey ... 37 H2
Abinger Hammer Surrey ... 37 G2
Abington Nhants ... 84 F3
Abington S Lans ... 186 D2
Abington Pigotts Cambs ... 86 F6
Abingworth W Susx ... 21 J3
Ab Kettleby Leics ... 117 J7
Ab Lench Worcs ... 82 B5
Ablington Gloucs ... 65 G5
Ablington Wilts ... 33 K2
Abney Derbys ... 132 D4
Above Church Staffs ... 115 G2
Aboyne Abers ... 244 C4
Abhainn Suidhe W Isls ... 282 d5
Abram Wigan ... 139 J7
Abriachan Highld ... 250 F4
Abridge Essex ... 70 C7
Abronhill N Lans ... 209 L4
Abson S Glos ... 45 L4
Abthorpe Nhants ... 84 C6
Aby Lincs ... 137 H4
Acaster Malbis C York ... 151 J6
Acaster Selby N York ... 151 J7
Accrington Lancs ... 139 M2
Accrington Crematorium
 Lancs ... 140 A2
Acha Ag & B ... 224 F4
Achahoish Ag & B ... 206 B3
Achalader P & K ... 233 H6
Achaleven Ag & B ... 228 E8
Acha Mor W Isls ... 282 f3
Achanalt Highld ... 261 M7
Achandunie Highld ... 263 H5
Achany Highld ... 272 E7
Acharacle Highld ... 237 K7
Acharn Highld ... 227 K2
Acharn P & K ... 231 L7
Achavanich Highld ... 279 L7
Achduart Highld ... 270 D7
Achfary Highld ... 276 D8
A'Chill Highld ... 246 C7
Achiltibuie Highld ... 270 D6
Achina Highld ... 278 B4
Achinhoan Ag & B ... 192 F5
Achintee Highld ... 248 F3
Achintraid Highld ... 248 D4
Achmelvich Highld ... 270 E3
Achmore Highld ... 248 D5
Achmore W Isls ... 282 f3
Achnacarnin Highld ... 270 D2
Achnacarry Highld ... 239 K6
Achnacloich Highld ... 247 J6
Achnaconeran Highld ... 250 D8
Achnacroish Ag & B ... 228 C7
Achnadrish House Ag & B ... 226 F2
Achnafauld P & K ... 232 C8
Achnagarron Highld ... 263 J6
Achnaha Highld ... 236 F6
Achnahaird Highld ... 270 D5
Achnahannet Highld ... 253 J6
Achnairn Highld ... 272 E5
Achnalea Highld ... 228 C3
Achnamara Ag & B ... 206 B2
Achnasheen Highld ... 261 K8
Achnashellach Highld ... 249 G2
Achnastank Moray ... 254 F5

Achosnich Highld ... 236 E7
Achranich Highld ... 227 K3
Achreamie Highld ... 279 H3
Achriabhach Highld ... 229 J2
Achriesgill Highld ... 276 D5
Achtoty Highld ... 277 M4
Achurch Nhants ... 102 A6
Achvaich Highld ... 263 J1
Achvarasdal Highld ... 279 H3
Ackergill Highld ... 280 E5
Acklam Middsb ... 170 C7
Acklam N York ... 152 B3
Ackleton Shrops ... 97 H4
Acklington Nthumb ... 191 J6
Ackton Wakefd ... 142 C3
Ackworth Moor Top Wakefd ... 142 C4
Acle Norfk ... 107 H1
Acock's Green Birm ... 98 E6
Acol Kent ... 41 J2
Acomb C York ... 151 J5
Acomb Nthumb ... 179 L5
Acombe Somset ... 30 B8
Aconbury Herefs ... 80 C8
Acre Lancs ... 140 B3
Acrefair Wrexhm ... 112 D3
Acton Ches E ... 113 K1
Acton Dorset ... 17 J7
Acton Gt Lon ... 51 G3
Acton Shrops ... 95 H6
Acton Staffs ... 114 C4
Acton Suffk ... 89 H6
Acton Worcs ... 81 J2
Acton Beauchamp Herefs ... 80 F5
Acton Bridge Ches W ... 130 B4
Acton Burnell Shrops ... 96 C3
Acton Green Herefs ... 81 G5
Acton Park Wrexhm ... 112 E1
Acton Pigott Shrops ... 96 C3
Acton Round Shrops ... 96 E4
Acton Scott Shrops ... 95 L5
Acton Trussell Staffs ... 114 E7
Acton Turville S Glos ... 46 A3
Adbaston Staffs ... 114 B6
Adber Dorset ... 31 K6
Adbolton Notts ... 117 G4
Adderbury Oxon ... 83 L8
Adderley Shrops ... 113 L3
Adderstone Nthumb ... 203 J7
Addiewell W Loth ... 210 C6
Addingham C Brad ... 149 K6
Addington Bucks ... 67 H2
Addington Gt Lon ... 51 K6
Addington Kent ... 52 E7
Addiscombe Gt Lon ... 51 J5
Addlestone Surrey ... 50 D6
Addlestonemoor Surrey ... 50 D6
Addlethorpe Lincs ... 137 K6
Adeney Wrekin ... 113 M7
Adeyfield Herts ... 68 D5
Adfa Powys ... 94 C3
Adforton Herefs ... 79 M1
Adisham Kent ... 41 H4
Adlestrop Gloucs ... 65 K2
Adlingfleet E R Yk ... 143 L3
Adlington Ches E ... 131 H4
Adlington Lancs ... 139 J5
Admaston Staffs ... 115 G7
Admaston Wrekin ... 96 E1
Admington Warwks ... 82 E6
Adpar Cerdgn ... 76 B7
Adsborough Somset ... 30 D5
Adscombe Somset ... 30 B3
Adstock Bucks ... 67 H1
Adstone Nhants ... 84 B5
Adswood Stockp ... 131 H2
Adversane W Susx ... 37 G6
Advie Highld ... 254 C5
Adwalton Leeds ... 141 K2
Adwell Oxon ... 67 G7
Adwick le Street Donc ... 142 E6
Adwick upon Dearne Donc ... 142 D7
Ae D & G ... 176 C1
Ae Bridgend D & G ... 176 D2
Affetside Bury ... 139 M5
Affleck Abers ... 255 L4
Affpuddle Dorset ... 16 F4
Affric Lodge Highld ... 249 K7
Afon-wen Flints ... 128 D5
Afton Devon ... 8 C2
Afton IoW ... 18 E6
Agecroft Crematorium Salfd ... 140 B7
Agglethorpe N York ... 159 K5
Aigburth Lpool ... 129 J2
Aike E R Yk ... 153 G6
Aiketgate Cumb ... 166 B1
Aikhead Cumb ... 165 H1
Aikton Cumb ... 177 J8
Ailby Lincs ... 137 H4
Ailey Herefs ... 79 L5

Ailsworth C Pete ... 102 C4
Ainderby Quernhow N York ... 160 E6
Ainderby Steeple N York ... 160 E4
Aingers Green Essex ... 73 G3
Ainsdale Sefton ... 138 C5
Ainsdale-on-Sea Sefton ... 138 C5
Ainstable Cumb ... 166 C2
Ainsworth Bury ... 139 M5
Ainthorpe N York ... 162 C1
Aintree Sefton ... 138 D8
Ainville W Loth ... 210 F6
Aird Ag & B ... 216 B7
Aird D & G ... 172 D3
Aird W Isls ... 282 h3
Aird a' Mhulaidh W Isls ... 282 e5
Aird Asaig W Isls ... 282 e5
Aird Dhubh Highld ... 248 A4
Airdeny Ag & B ... 216 F1
Aird of Kinloch Ag & B ... 227 G6
Aird of Sleat Highld ... 247 J8
Airdrie N Lans ... 209 K6
Airdriehill N Lans ... 209 K5
Airds of Kells D & G ... 175 G1
Aird Uig W Isls ... 282 d3
Airidh a bhruaich W Isls ... 282 f4
Airieland D & G ... 175 J3
Airlie Angus ... 233 M5
Airmyn E R Yk ... 143 J3
Airntully P & K ... 233 G8
Airor Highld ... 247 M2
Airth Falk ... 210 B2
Airton N York ... 148 F4
Aisby Lincs ... 118 D4
Aisby Lincs ... 135 H1
Aisgill Cumb ... 158 F2
Aish Devon ... 7 K3
Aish Devon ... 8 C3
Aisholt Somset ... 30 B4
Aiskew N York ... 160 E5
Aislaby N York ... 162 D5
Aislaby N York ... 162 F1
Aislaby S on T ... 169 L8
Aisthorpe Lincs ... 135 J4
Aith Shet ... 281 d5
Akeld Nthumb ... 202 E7
Akeley Bucks ... 84 D7
Akenham Suffk ... 90 D5
Albaston Cnwll ... 12 A8
Alberbury Shrops ... 112 E8
Albourne W Susx ... 22 C4
Albourne Green W Susx ... 22 C4
Albrighton Shrops ... 97 H3
Albrighton Shrops ... 113 H7
Alburgh Norfk ... 106 F6
Albury Herts ... 70 B2
Albury Oxon ... 67 G6
Albury Surrey ... 37 G2
Albury End Herts ... 70 B2
Albury Heath Surrey ... 37 G2
Alby Hill Norfk ... 122 D5
Alcaig Highld ... 263 G8
Alcaston Shrops ... 95 L6
Alcester Warwks ... 82 C4
Alcester Lane End Birm ... 98 D7
Alciston E Susx ... 23 H6
Alcombe Somset ... 29 H2
Alcombe Wilts ... 46 A5
Alconbury Cambs ... 102 D8
Alconbury Weston Cambs ... 102 D7
Aldborough N York ... 150 F3
Aldborough Norfk ... 122 D5
Aldbourne Wilts ... 47 K4
Aldbrough E R Yk ... 153 L8
Aldbrough St John N York ... 169 G8
Aldbury Herts ... 68 B4
Aldcliffe Lancs ... 147 J4
Aldclune P & K ... 232 D3
Aldeburgh Suffk ... 91 K4
Aldeby Norfk ... 107 J5
Aldenham Herts ... 68 F7
Alderbury Wilts ... 33 L5
Aldercar Derbys ... 116 D2
Alderford Norfk ... 122 C4
Alderholt Dorset ... 33 K8
Alderley Gloucs ... 45 M1
Alderley Edge Ches E ... 131 G4
Aldermans Green Covtry ... 99 K6
Aldermaston W Berk ... 48 E6
Alderminster Warwks ... 82 F5
Alder Moor Staffs ... 115 L6
Aldersey Green Ches W ... 129 K8
Aldershot Hants ... 36 C1
Alderton Gloucs ... 82 B8
Alderton Nhants ... 84 E6
Alderton Shrops ... 113 H6
Alderton Suffk ... 91 H7
Alderton Wilts ... 46 B2
Alderwasley Derbys ... 116 A1
Aldfield N York ... 150 C2

Aldford Ches W 129 K7
Aldgate Rutlnd 101 L3
Aldham Essex 72 D2
Aldham Suffk 90 B6
Aldingbourne W Susx 20 F5
Aldingham Cumb 146 E2
Aldington Kent 40 E8
Aldington Worcs 82 C6
Aldington Corner Kent 40 E8
Aldivalloch Moray 255 G6
Aldochlay Ag & B 208 B1
Aldon Shrops 95 K7
Aldoth Cumb 164 F1
Aldreth Cambs 103 J8
Aldridge Wsall 98 D3
Aldringham Suffk 91 K3
Aldro N York 152 B3
Aldsworth Gloucs 65 H5
Aldsworth W Susx 20 C5
Aldunie Moray 255 G6
Aldwark Derbys 132 E8
Aldwark N York 151 G3
Aldwick W Susx 20 E7
Aldwincle Nhants 101 M7
Aldworth W Berk 48 E3
Alexandria W Duns 208 C3
Aley Somset 30 B3
Alfardisworthy Devon 26 E8
Alfington Devon 14 D3
Alfold Surrey 36 F4
Alfold Bars W Susx 36 F4
Alfold Crossways Surrey 36 F4
Alford Abers 255 M8
Alford Lincs 137 H4
Alford Somset 31 K4
Alford Crematorium Lincs 137 H4
Alfreton Derbys 133 H8
Alfrick Worcs 81 H4
Alfrick Pound Worcs 81 G5
Alfriston E Susx 23 H6
Algarkirk Lincs 119 J4
Alhampton Somset 31 K4
Alkborough N Linc 143 M3
Alkerton Gloucs 63 M6
Alkerton Oxon 83 J6
Alkham Kent 41 H6
Alkington Shrops 113 H4
Alkmonton Derbys 115 K4
Allaleigh Devon 8 B4
Allanaquoich Abers 242 F5
Allanbank N Lans 209 M7
Allanton Border 202 D2
Allanton N Lans 209 M7
Allanton S Lans 209 K8
Allaston Gloucs 63 J6
Allbrook Hants 34 F6
All Cannings Wilts 46 F6
Allendale Nthumb 179 J7
Allen End Warwks 98 F4
Allenheads Nthumb 167 K2
Allensford Dur 168 D1
Allen's Green Herts 70 C4
Allensmore Herefs 80 B8
Allenton C Derb 116 B5
Aller Devon 28 D5
Aller Somset 30 F5
Allerby Cumb 164 E3
Allercombe Devon 14 B4
Aller Cross Devon 28 B5
Allerford Somset 28 F2
Allerston N York 162 F6
Allerthorpe E R Yk 152 B6
Allerton C Brad 141 H1
Allerton Highld 263 K6
Allerton Lpool 129 J2
Allerton Bywater Leeds 142 C2
Allerton Mauleverer N York 150 F4
Allesley Covtry 99 J7
Allestree C Derb 116 B4
Allet Common Cnwll 4 C5
Allexton Leics 101 H3
Allgreave Ches E 131 J6
Allhallows Medway 53 H3
Allhallows-on-Sea Medway 53 H3
Alligin Shuas Highld 260 D8
Allimore Green Staffs 114 D7
Allington Dorset 15 K4
Allington Kent 53 G7
Allington Lincs 117 M3
Allington Wilts 33 L3
Allington Wilts 46 C4
Allington Wilts 46 F6
Allithwaite Cumb 156 E7
Alloa Clacks 220 E8
Allonby Cumb 164 E2
Allostock Ches W 130 E5
Alloway S Ayrs 196 C7
Allowenshay Somset 30 F8
All Saints South Elmham Suffk 107 G7

Allscott Shrops 97 G4
Allscott Wrekin 96 E1
All Stretton Shrops 95 L4
Alltami Flints 129 G6
Alltchaorunn Highld 229 K5
Alltmawr Powys 78 F6
Alltwalis Carmth 58 E3
Alltwen Neath 57 K4
Alltyblaca Cerdgn 76 F6
Allweston Dorset 31 L8
Allwood Green Suffk 90 B1
Almeley Herefs 79 L5
Almeley Wooton Herefs 79 L5
Almer Dorset 17 H3
Almholme Donc 142 F6
Almington Staffs 113 M4
Almodington W Susx 20 D7
Almondbank P & K 221 J2
Almondbury Kirk 141 J5
Almondsbury S Glos 45 J2
Alne N York 151 G3
Alness Highld 263 H6
Alnham Nthumb 190 E4
Alnmouth Nthumb 191 J4
Alnwick Nthumb 191 H3
Alperton Gt Lon 50 F2
Alphamstone Essex 89 H8
Alpheton Suffk 89 H5
Alphington Devon 13 L4
Alpington Norfk 106 F3
Alport Derbys 132 D6
Alpraham Ches E 130 B7
Alresford Essex 72 F3
Alrewas Staffs 115 K8
Alsager Ches E 130 F8
Alsagers Bank Staffs 114 C2
Alsop en le Dale Derbys 132 C8
Alston Cumb 167 G2
Alston Devon 15 G2
Alstone Gloucs 64 E1
Alstone Somset 30 D2
Alstonefield Staffs 132 C8
Alston Sutton Somset 44 E8
Alswear Devon 28 C6
Alt Oldham 140 E7
Altandhu Highld 270 C5
Altarnun Cnwll 11 J6
Altass Highld 272 D8
Altcreich Ag & B 227 K5
Altgaltraig Ag & B 207 G4
Altham Lancs 140 A1
Althorne Essex 72 D7
Althorpe N Linc 143 L6
Altnabreac Station Highld 279 H7
Altnaharra Highld 272 E1
Altofts Wakefd 142 B3
Alton Derbys 133 G6
Alton Hants 35 L3
Alton Staffs 115 H3
Alton Wilts 33 K2
Alton Barnes Wilts 47 G6
Alton Pancras Dorset 16 D2
Alton Priors Wilts 47 G6
Altrincham Traffd 130 E2
Altrincham Crematorium Traffd 130 E2
Altskeith Hotel Stirlg 219 G6
Alva Clacks 220 F7
Alvanley Ches W 129 L5
Alvaston C Derb 116 C5
Alvechurch Worcs 82 B1
Alvecote Warwks 99 H3
Alvediston Wilts 33 G6
Alveley Shrops 97 G6
Alverdiscott Devon 27 J6
Alverstoke Hants 19 K4
Alverstone IoW 19 K6
Alverthorpe Wakefd 141 M3
Alverton Notts 117 L3
Alves Moray 266 C4
Alvescot Oxon 65 K6
Alveston S Glos 45 J1
Alveston Warwks 82 F4
Alvingham Lincs 137 G2
Alvington Gloucs 63 J7
Alwalton C Pete 102 C4
Alwinton Nthumb 190 C5
Alwoodley Leeds 150 C7
Alwoodley Gates Leeds 150 D7
Alyth P & K 233 K5
Am Bàgh a Tuath W Isls 283 b13
Ambergate Derbys 116 B1
Amber Hill Lincs 119 H2
Amberley Gloucs 64 B6
Amberley W Susx 21 H4
Amber Row Derbys 133 G8
Amberstone E Susx 23 K5
Amble Nthumb 191 K5
Amblecote Dudley 97 K6

Ambler Thorn C Brad 141 H2
Ambleside Cumb 156 E2
Ambleston Pembks 75 G7
Ambrosden Oxon 66 F3
Amcotts N Linc 143 L5
America Cambs 103 J7
Amersham Bucks 68 B7
Amersham Common Bucks 68 B7
Amersham Old Town Bucks 68 B7
Amersham on the Hill Bucks 68 B7
Amerton Staffs 114 F6
Amesbury Wilts 33 K3
Amhuinnsuidhe W Isls 282 d5
Amington Staffs 99 G3
Amisfield D & G 176 D2
Amlwch IoA 125 H1
Ammanford Carmth 59 H6
Amotherby N York 162 C7
Ampfield Hants 34 E6
Ampleforth N York 161 J7
Ampney Crucis Gloucs 64 F6
Ampney St Mary Gloucs 65 G6
Ampney St Peter Gloucs 65 G6
Amport Hants 34 C2
Ampthill C Beds 85 K7
Ampton Suffk 89 H1
Amroth Pembks 55 K5
Amulree P & K 232 D8
Amwell Herts 68 F4
Anaheilt Highld 228 C3
Ancaster Lincs 118 C3
Ancells Farm Hants 49 K7
Anchor Shrops 94 E6
Ancroft Nthumb 202 F4
Ancrum Border 189 H1
Ancton W Susx 21 G6
Anderby Lincs 137 K4
Anderby Creek Lincs 137 K4
Andersea Somset 30 E4
Andersfield Somset 30 C4
Anderson Dorset 17 G3
Anderton Ches W 130 C4
Anderton Cnwll 6 E4
Andover Hants 34 D2
Andoversford Gloucs 64 F3
Andreas IoM 154 f2
Anelog Gwynd 108 B6
Anerley Gt Lon 51 J5
Anfield Lpool 129 J1
Anfield Crematorium Lpool 129 J1
Angarrack Cnwll 2 F3
Angarrick Cnwll 3 K4
Angelbank Shrops 96 D8
Angersleigh Somset 30 B7
Angerton Cumb 177 H7
Angle Pembks 54 D6
Anglesey IoA 125 G3
Angmering W Susx 21 H6
Angram N York 151 H6
Angram N York 158 F3
Angrouse Cnwll 3 H7
Anick Nthumb 179 L5
Ankerville Highld 264 C5
Ankle Hill Leics 117 K7
Anlaby E R Yk 144 C2
Anmer Norfk 121 G5
Anmore Hants 19 L1
Annan D & G 177 G5
Annaside Cumb 155 K5
Annat Highld 248 E1
Annathill N Lans 209 J5
Anna Valley Hants 34 D2
Annbank S Ayrs 196 E6
Annesley Notts 116 E1
Annesley Woodhouse Notts 116 E1
Annfield Plain Dur 180 E8
Anniesland C Glas 208 F5
Annitsford N Tyne 181 G4
Annscroft Shrops 95 L2
Ansdell Lancs 138 D2
Ansford Somset 31 L4
Ansley Warwks 99 J5
Anslow Staffs 115 L6
Anslow Gate Staffs 115 K6
Anslow Lees Staffs 115 K6
Ansteadbrook Surrey 36 D4
Anstey Hants 35 L3
Anstey Herts 87 H8
Anstey Leics 100 C2
Anstruther Fife 223 K6
Ansty W Susx 37 L6
Ansty Warwks 99 L6
Ansty Wilts 33 G5
Ansty Cross Dorset 16 E2
Anthill Common Hants 19 L1
Anthonys Surrey 50 C6
Anthorn Cumb 177 G7
Antingham Norfk 122 E5
An t-Ob W Isls 282 d6

Anton's Gowt Lincs 119 J2
Antony Cnwll 6 D4
Antrobus Ches W 130 C4
Anvil Corner Devon 11 M2
Anvil Green Kent 40 E5
Anwick Lincs 118 F2
Anwoth D & G 174 F4
Aperfield Gt Lon 51 L7
Apes Dale Worcs 82 A1
Apethorpe Nhants 102 A4
Apeton Staffs 114 D7
Apley Lincs 136 B5
Apperknowle Derbys 133 H4
Apperley Gloucs 64 B2
Apperley Bridge C Brad 150 B8
Apperley Dene Nthumb 180 C7
Appersett N York 158 E4
Appin Ag & B 228 E6
Appleby N Linc 144 B5
Appleby-in-Westmorland Cumb 166 F6
Appleby Magna Leics 99 J2
Appleby Parva Leics 99 J2
Appleby Street Herts 69 J6
Applecross Highld 248 A3
Appledore Devon 27 H5
Appledore Devon 29 K7
Appledore Kent 25 H2
Appledore Heath Kent 25 H1
Appleford Oxon 66 D8
Applegarth Town D & G 176 F2
Applehaigh Wakefd 142 A5
Appleshaw Hants 34 C1
Applethwaite Cumb 165 J5
Appleton Halton 129 M2
Appleton Oxon 66 C6
Appleton Warrtn 130 B3
Appleton-le-Moors N York 162 C5
Appleton-le-Street N York 162 C7
Appleton Roebuck N York 151 J7
Appleton Thorn Warrtn 130 C3
Appleton Wiske N York 160 F2
Appletreehall Border 188 F3
Appletreewick N York 149 J4
Appley Somset 29 K6
Appley Bridge Lancs 139 G6
Apse Heath IoW 19 J7
Apsley End C Beds 86 C8
Apuldram W Susx 20 D6
Arabella Highld 264 C5
Arbirlot Angus 234 F7
Arboll Highld 264 D3
Arborfield Wokham 49 H5
Arborfield Cross Wokham 49 J5
Arborfield Green Wokham 49 J6
Arbourthorne Sheff 133 G3
Arbroath Angus 235 G7
Arbuthnott Abers 245 H8
Arcadia Kent 39 L6
Archddu Carmth 56 E4
Archdeacon Newton Darltn 169 H7
Archencarroch W Duns 208 C3
Archiestown Moray 254 E3
Archirondel Jersey 9 f2
Arclid Ches E 130 F7
Ardallie Abers 257 J4
Ardanaiseig Hotel Ag & B 217 H2
Ardaneaskan Highld 248 D4
Ardarroch Highld 248 D4
Ardbeg Ag & B 204 F7
Ardbeg Ag & B 207 H5
Ardbeg Ag & B 207 K2
Ardcharnich Highld 261 K2
Ardchiavaig Ag & B 214 D1
Ardchonnel Ag & B 216 F5
Ardchullarie More Stirlg 219 K4
Arddarroch Ag & B 218 C8
Arddleen Powys 112 C8
Ard Dorch Highld 247 J3
Ardechive Highld 239 J5
Ardeer N Ayrs 196 B3
Ardeley Herts 69 J2
Ardelve Highld 248 D6
Arden Ag & B 208 B2
Ardens Grafton Warwks 82 D4
Ardentallen Ag & B 216 C2
Ardentinny Ag & B 207 K2
Ardentraive Ag & B 207 G4
Ardeonaig Stirlg 231 J8
Ardersier Highld 252 E1
Ardessie Highld 261 H2
Ardfern Ag & B 216 C6
Ardfernal Ag & B 205 J2
Ardgartan Ag & B 218 D6
Ardgay Highld 263 G2
Ardgour Highld 229 G3
Ardgowan Inver 207 L4
Ardhallow Ag & B 207 K4
Ardhasig W Isls 282 e5

Ardheslaig Highld....260 C8
Ardindrean Highld....261 K2
Ardingly W Susx....38 A7
Ardington Oxon....48 B1
Ardington Wick Oxon....48 B1
Ardlamont Ag & B....206 F6
Ardleigh Essex....72 F1
Ardleigh Heath Essex....72 F1
Ardler P & K....233 L7
Ardley Oxon....66 D2
Ardley End Essex....70 D4
Ardlui Ag & B....218 D4
Ardlussa Ag & B....215 J6
Ardmair Highld....270 F8
Ardmaleish Ag & B....207 H5
Ardminish Ag & B....205 L6
Ardmolich Highld....237 K6
Ardmore Ag & B....208 A3
Ardmore Highld....263 J3
Ardnadam Ag & B....207 K3
Ardnagrask Highld....250 F2
Ardnarff Highld....248 E4
Ardnastang Highld....228 B3
Ardpatrick Ag & B....206 B7
Ardrishaig Ag & B....206 D2
Ardross Highld....263 H5
Ardrossan N Ayrs....195 L3
Ardsley Barns....142 B6
Ardsley East Leeds....141 M3
Ardslignish Highld....237 H8
Ardtalla Ag & B....205 G5
Ardtoe Highld....237 J6
Arduaine Ag & B....216 B5
Ardullie Highld....263 G7
Ardvasar Highld....247 K7
Ardvorlich P & K....219 K3
Ardvourlie W Isls....282 e5
Ardwell D & G....172 D5
Ardwick Manch....140 C8
Areley Kings Worcs....81 H1
Arevegaig Highld....237 J7
Arford Hants....36 B3
Arglam E R Yk....152 B8
Argoed Caerph....61 J7
Argoed Shrops....112 E7
Argoed Mill Powys....78 D3
Argos Hill E Susx....23 J2
Aribruach W Isls....282 f4
Aridhglas Ag & B....226 C7
Arileod Ag & B....224 F4
Arinagour Ag & B....225 G4
Ariogan Ag & B....216 D2
Arisaig Highld....237 J3
Arisaig House Highld....237 K4
Arkendale N York....150 E4
Arkesden Essex....87 K8
Arkholme Lancs....147 L2
Arkleby Cumb....164 F3
Arkleton D & G....188 C7
Arkle Town N York....159 H2
Arkley Gt Lon....69 G7
Arksey Donc....142 F6
Arkwright Town Derbys....133 H5
Arle Gloucs....64 D2
Arlecdon Cumb....164 D7
Arlescote Warwks....83 J5
Arlesey C Beds....86 D7
Arleston Wrekin....96 F1
Arley Ches E....130 C3
Arley Warwks....99 H5
Arlingham Gloucs....63 L5
Arlington Devon....27 L3
Arlington E Susx....23 J5
Arlington Gloucs....65 G5
Arlington Beccott Devon....27 L3
Armadale Highld....247 K7
Armadale Highld....278 D3
Armadale W Loth....210 B5
Armaside Cumb....164 F5
Armathwaite Cumb....166 C2
Arminghall Norfk....106 E3
Armitage Staffs....115 H8
Armitage Bridge Kirk....141 H5
Armley Leeds....141 L1
Armscote Warwks....82 F6
Armshead Staffs....114 E2
Armston Nhants....102 B6
Armthorpe Donc....143 G6
Arnabost Ag & B....225 G3
Arnaby Cumb....156 A5
Arncliffe N York....149 G1
Arncliffe Cote N York....149 G2
Arncroach Fife....223 J6
Arndilly House Moray....266 F6
Arne Dorset....17 J5
Arnesby Leics....100 D5
Arngask P & K....221 L5
Arnisdale Highld....238 D2
Arnish Highld....259 K7

Arniston Mdloth....211 K6
Arnol W Isls....282 f2
Arnold E R Yk....153 H7
Arnold Notts....117 G2
Arnprior Stirlg....219 K8
Arnside Cumb....157 G3
Aros Ag & B....227 G3
Arowry Wrexhm....113 G4
Arrad Foot Cumb....156 D6
Arram E R Yk....153 G7
Arran N Ayrs....194 E4
Arrathorne N York....160 B4
Arreton IoW....19 J6
Arrina Highld....260 B8
Arrington Cambs....87 G5
Arrochar Ag & B....218 D6
Arrow Warwks....82 C4
Arrowfield Top Worcs....98 C8
Arscott Shrops....95 K2
Artafallie Highld....251 H2
Arthington Leeds....150 C6
Arthingworth Nhants....101 G7
Arthog Gwynd....110 C8
Arthrath Abers....257 H4
Arthursdale Leeds....150 E8
Artrochie Abers....257 J5
Arundel W Susx....21 G5
Asby Cumb....164 E6
Ascog Ag & B....207 J6
Ascot W & M....50 A5
Ascott Warwks....83 H8
Ascott Earl Oxon....65 L3
Ascott-under-Wychwood
   Oxon....65 L3
Asenby N York....160 F7
Asfordby Leics....117 J7
Asfordby Hill Leics....117 J7
Asgarby Lincs....118 F3
Asgarby Lincs....136 F6
Ash Devon....8 C5
Ash Devon....12 C1
Ash Dorset....32 E8
Ash Kent....41 J4
Ash Kent....52 D6
Ash Somset....30 D6
Ash Somset....31 G6
Ash Surrey....36 D1
Ashampstead W Berk....48 E4
Ashampstead Green W Berk....48 E3
Ashbocking Suffk....90 E4
Ashbourne Derbys....115 K2
Ashbrittle Somset....29 J6
Ashburnham Place E Susx....24 C4
Ashburton Devon....13 H8
Ashbury Devon....12 C3
Ashbury Oxon....47 K2
Ashby N Linc....143 M6
Ashby by Partney Lincs....137 H6
Ashby cum Fenby NE Lin....145 H2
Ashby de la Launde Lincs....135 L8
Ashby-de-la-Zouch Leics....116 B8
Ashby Folville Leics....100 F1
Ashby Magna Leics....100 C5
Ashby Parva Leics....100 C5
Ashby Puerorum Lincs....136 F5
Ashby St Ledgers Nhants....84 B2
Ashby St Mary Norfk....107 G3
Ashchurch Gloucs....81 L8
Ashcombe Devon....13 L6
Ashcombe N Som....44 C6
Ashcott Somset....31 G4
Ashdon Essex....88 B6
Ashe Hants....35 H1
Asheldham Essex....72 E6
Ashen Essex....88 B4
Ashendon Bucks....67 H4
Asheridge Bucks....68 B6
Ashfield Hants....34 E7
Ashfield Herefs....63 H2
Ashfield Stirlg....220 D6
Ashfield cum Thorpe Suffk....90 F3
Ashfield Green Suffk....88 F4
Ashfield Green Suffk....106 F8
Ashfold Crossways W Susx....37 K5
Ashford Devon....7 K5
Ashford Devon....27 J4
Ashford Kent....40 D6
Ashford Surrey....50 D4
Ashford Bowdler Shrops....80 C1
Ashford Carbonell Shrops....80 C1
Ashford Hill Hants....48 E6
Ashford in the Water Derbys....132 D5
Ashgill S Lans....198 C3
Ash Green Surrey....36 D1
Ash Green Warwks....99 H6
Ashill Devon....29 K8
Ashill Norfk....105 H3
Ashill Somset....30 D7
Ashingdon Essex....72 C8

Ashington Nthumb....181 G1
Ashington Poole....17 K3
Ashington Somset....31 J6
Ashington W Susx....21 K4
Ashkirk Border....188 E2
Ashlett Hants....19 G3
Ashleworth Gloucs....64 A2
Ashleworth Quay Gloucs....64 B2
Ashley Cambs....88 D3
Ashley Ches E....130 F3
Ashley Devon....28 B8
Ashley Dorset....18 A3
Ashley Gloucs....64 D8
Ashley Hants....18 C4
Ashley Hants....34 E4
Ashley Kent....41 J5
Ashley Nhants....101 H5
Ashley Staffs....114 B4
Ashley Wilts....46 B5
Ashley Green Bucks....68 B6
Ashleyhay Derbys....115 M1
Ashley Heath Dorset....17 M2
Ashley Moor Herefs....80 B2
Ash Magna Shrops....113 J4
Ashmansworth Hants....48 B7
Ashmansworthy Devon....26 F7
Ashmead Green Gloucs....63 M7
Ashmill Devon....11 M3
Ash Mill Devon....28 D6
Ashmore Dorset....32 F7
Ashmore Green W Berk....48 D5
Ashorne Warwks....83 G4
Ashover Derbys....133 G7
Ashover Hay Derbys....133 G7
Ashow Warwks....83 H1
Ash Parva Shrops....113 J4
Ashperton Herefs....80 E7
Ashprington Devon....8 B3
Ash Priors Somset....29 L5
Ashreigney Devon....27 L8
Ash Street Suffk....89 K6
Ashtead Surrey....50 F7
Ash Thomas Devon....29 H8
Ashton C Pete....102 B2
Ashton Ches W....129 L6
Ashton Cnwll....2 F5
Ashton Devon....13 K5
Ashton Hants....35 H7
Ashton Herefs....80 C2
Ashton Inver....207 L4
Ashton Nhants....84 E5
Ashton Nhants....102 B5
Ashton Somset....30 F1
Ashton Common Wilts....46 C7
Ashton Hill Wilts....46 C7
Ashton-in-Makerfield Wigan....139 H7
Ashton Keynes Wilts....64 F8
Ashton under Hill Worcs....82 A7
Ashton-under-Lyne Tamesd....140 E7
Ashton upon Mersey Traffd....130 F1
Ashton Vale Bristl....45 H5
Ashurst Hants....18 E2
Ashurst Kent....38 D5
Ashurst Lancs....138 F6
Ashurst W Susx....21 L4
Ashurstwood W Susx....38 B6
Ash Vale Surrey....49 L8
Ashwater Devon....11 M4
Ashwell Herts....86 F7
Ashwell Rutlnd....101 J1
Ashwell Somset....30 E7
Ashwell End Herts....86 E7
Ashwellthorpe Norfk....106 C4
Ashwick Somset....31 K1
Ashwicken Norfk....120 F7
Ashwood Staffs....97 K5
Askam in Furness Cumb....156 B7
Askern Donc....142 F5
Askerswell Dorset....15 M4
Askett Bucks....67 K6
Askham Cumb....166 C6
Askham Notts....134 E5
Askham Bryan C York....151 H6
Askham Richard C York....151 H6
Asknish Ag & B....206 E1
Askrigg N York....159 G4
Askwith N York....149 L6
Aslackby Lincs....118 E5
Aslacton Norfk....106 D5
Aslockton Notts....117 K3
Asney Somset....31 G3
Aspall Suffk....90 E2
Aspatria Cumb....164 F2
Aspenden Herts....69 K2
Aspenshaw Derbys....131 K2
Asperton Lincs....119 J4
Aspley Staffs....114 C5
Aspley Guise C Beds....85 J8
Aspley Heath C Beds....85 H8

Aspley Heath Warwks....82 C1
Aspull Wigan....139 J6
Aspull Common Wigan....139 J8
Asselby E R Yk....143 H2
Asserby Lincs....137 J4
Asserby Turn Lincs....137 J4
Assington Suffk....89 J7
Assington Green Suffk....88 F5
Astbury Ches E....131 G7
Astcote Nhants....84 D4
Asterby Lincs....136 E4
Asterley Shrops....95 J2
Asterton Shrops....95 H5
Asthall Oxon....65 L3
Asthall Leigh Oxon....65 L4
Astle Highld....263 K2
Astley Shrops....113 H7
Astley Warwks....99 J5
Astley Wigan....139 L7
Astley Worcs....81 H2
Astley Abbots Shrops....96 F4
Astley Bridge Bolton....139 L5
Astley Cross Worcs....81 J1
Astley Green Wigan....139 L7
Aston Birm....98 D5
Aston Ches E....113 K4
Aston Ches W....130 A4
Aston Derbys....132 D3
Aston Flints....129 G6
Aston Herefs....80 B3
Aston Herts....69 H3
Aston Oxon....65 M6
Aston Rothm....133 J3
Aston Shrops....97 H5
Aston Shrops....113 H6
Aston Staffs....114 B3
Aston Staffs....114 D6
Aston Wokham....49 J2
Aston Wrekin....96 E2
Aston Abbotts Bucks....67 K3
Aston Botterell Shrops....96 E6
Aston-by-Stone Staffs....114 E6
Aston Cantlow Warwks....82 D3
Aston Clinton Bucks....67 L4
Aston Crews Herefs....63 K3
Aston Cross Gloucs....81 L8
Aston End Herts....69 H2
Aston-Eyre Shrops....96 E4
Aston Fields Worcs....81 M2
Aston Flamville Leics....100 A5
Aston Heath Ches W....130 A4
Aston Ingham Herefs....63 K3
Aston juxta Mondrum Ches E....130 C8
Aston le Walls Nhants....83 L5
Aston Magna Gloucs....82 E8
Aston Munslow Shrops....96 C6
Aston-on-Carrant Gloucs....81 L8
Aston on Clun Shrops....95 J7
Aston Pigott Shrops....95 H2
Aston Rogers Shrops....95 H2
Aston Rowant Oxon....67 H7
Aston Sandford Bucks....67 J5
Aston Somerville Worcs....82 B7
Aston-sub-Edge Gloucs....82 D7
Aston Tirrold Oxon....48 E2
Aston-upon-Trent Derbys....116 C5
Aston Upthorpe Oxon....48 E2
Astrop Nhants....83 L7
Astrope Herts....67 L4
Astwick C Beds....86 E7
Astwith Derbys....133 J6
Astwood M Keyn....85 J5
Astwood Worcs....81 L2
Astwood Bank Worcs....82 B3
Aswarby Lincs....118 E4
Aswardby Lincs....137 G5
Atcham Shrops....96 C2
Atch Lench Worcs....82 B5
Athelhampton Dorset....16 E4
Athelington Suffk....90 F1
Athelney Somset....30 E5
Athelstaneford E Loth....212 C3
Atherfield Green IoW....19 G7
Atherington Devon....27 L6
Atherington W Susx....21 G6
Atherstone Somset....30 F7
Atherstone Warwks....99 J4
Atherstone on Stour Warwks....82 F5
Atherton Wigan....139 K7
Atley Hill N York....160 D2
Atlow Derbys....115 L2
Attadale Highld....248 E4
Attenborough Notts....116 E5
Atterby Lincs....135 K1
Attercliffe Sheff....133 G2
Atterley Shrops....96 E4
Atterton Leics....99 K4
Attleborough Norfk....105 L4
Attleborough Warwks....99 K5

Attlebridge Norfk 122 C8
Attleton Green Suffk 88 E4
Atwick E R Yk 153 K5
Atworth Wilts 46 B6
Auberrow Herefs 80 C6
Aubourn Lincs 135 J7
Auchbreck Moray 254 D6
Auchedly Abers 257 G7
Auchenblae Abers 244 F7
Auchenbowie Stirlg 209 L2
Auchencairn D & G 175 K4
Auchencairn D & G 176 C2
Auchencairn N Ayrs 195 G5
Auchencrow Border 213 J7
Auchendinny Mdloth 211 H6
Auchengray S Lans 199 G2
Auchenhalrig Moray 267 H4
Auchenheath S Lans 198 D4
Auchenhessnane D & G 185 K4
Auchenlochan Ag & B 206 F3
Auchenmade N Ayrs 196 C2
Auchenmalg D & G 173 G4
Auchentiber N Ayrs 196 D2
Auchindrain Ag & B 217 G6
Auchindrean Highld 261 K4
Auchininna Abers 268 B6
Auchinleck E Ayrs 197 G6
Auchinloch N Lans 209 H4
Auchinstarry N Lans 209 J4
Auchintore Highld 229 H1
Auchiries Abers 257 K4
Auchlean Highld 241 M4
Auchlee Abers 245 K4
Auchleven Abers 256 A6
Auchlochan S Lans 198 D5
Auchlossan Abers 244 D3
Auchlyne Stirlg 219 H1
Auchmillan E Ayrs 197 G5
Auchmithie Angus 235 G6
Auchmuirbridge Fife 222 C7
Auchnacree Angus 234 C3
Auchnagatt Abers 257 G3
Auchnarrow Moray 254 D7
Auchnotteroch D & G 172 B3
Auchroisk Moray 267 G6
Auchterarder P & K 221 G4
Auchteraw Highld 240 B2
Auchterblair Highld 253 H7
Auchtercairn Highld 260 C4
Auchterderran Fife 222 C8
Auchterhouse Angus 233 M7
Auchterless Abers 256 C3
Auchtermuchty Fife 222 D5
Auchterneed Highld 262 E7
Auchtertool Fife 211 H1
Auchtertyre Highld 248 D6
Auchtubh Stirlg 219 J3
Auckengill Highld 280 E3
Auckley Donc 143 G7
Audenshaw Tamesd 140 D8
Audlem Ches E 113 L3
Audley Staffs 114 C2
Audley End Essex 87 L7
Audley End Essex 89 G7
Audley End Suffk 89 G4
Audmore Staffs 114 C7
Audnam Dudley 97 K6
Aughertree Cumb 165 H3
Aughton E R Yk 151 L8
Aughton Lancs 138 E6
Aughton Lancs 147 L2
Aughton Rothm 133 J2
Aughton Wilts 47 K7
Aughton Park Lancs 138 E6
Auldearn Highld 253 H1
Aulden Herefs 80 B4
Auldgirth D & G 176 B2
Auldhouse S Lans 197 J1
Ault a' chruinn Highld 248 F7
Aultbea Highld 260 D2
Aultgrishin Highld 260 B3
Aultguish Inn Highld 262 B6
Ault Hucknall Derbys 133 J6
Aultmore Moray 267 H5
Aultnagoire Highld 250 F7
Aultnamain Inn Highld 263 J4
Aunby Lincs 118 D8
Aunk Devon 14 B3
Aunsby Lincs 118 D4
Aust S Glos 45 H1
Austendike Lincs 119 J7
Austerfield Donc 134 D1
Austerlands Oldham 140 E6
Austhorpe Leeds 142 B1
Austonley Kirk 141 H6
Austrey Warwks 99 J2
Austwick N York 148 D2
Authorpe Lincs 137 G3
Authorpe Row Lincs 137 K5

Avebury Wilts 47 G5
Avebury Trusloe Wilts 47 G5
Aveley Thurr 52 C3
Avening Gloucs 64 C7
Averham Notts 117 K1
Aveton Gifford Devon 7 K5
Aviemore Highld 242 B1
Avington W Berk 48 A5
Avoch Highld 251 J1
Avon Hants 18 A4
Avonbridge Falk 210 B4
Avon Dassett Warwks 83 K5
Avonmouth Bristl 45 G3
Avonwick Devon 7 K3
Awbridge Hants 34 D6
Awkley S Glos 45 H2
Awliscombe Devon 14 D2
Awre Gloucs 63 L5
Awsworth Notts 116 E3
Axborough Worcs 97 J7
Axbridge Somset 44 E8
Axford Hants 35 J2
Axford Wilts 47 K5
Axmansford Hants 48 E6
Axminster Devon 15 G3
Axmouth Devon 14 F4
Axton Flints 128 D4
Aycliffe Dur 169 H6
Aydon Nthumb 180 B5
Aylburton Gloucs 63 J6
Ayle Nthumb 167 G1
Aylesbeare Devon 14 B4
Aylesbury Bucks 67 K4
Aylesbury Crematorium Bucks 67 K4
Aylesby NE Lin 145 G6
Aylesford Kent 52 F7
Aylesham Kent 41 H5
Aylestone C Leic 100 C3
Aylestone Park C Leic 100 D3
Aylmerton Norfk 122 D4
Aylsham Norfk 122 D6
Aylton Herefs 80 F7
Aylworth Gloucs 65 G3
Aymestrey Herefs 80 A2
Aynho Nhants 83 L8
Ayot Green Herts 69 G4
Ayot St Lawrence Herts 69 G4
Ayot St Peter Herts 69 G4
Ayr S Ayrs 196 C6
Aysgarth N York 159 H5
Ayshford Devon 29 J7
Ayside Cumb 156 F6
Ayston Rutlnd 101 J3
Aythorpe Roding Essex 70 E4
Ayton Border 213 K6
Azerley N York 160 C7

B

Babbacombe Torbay 8 D2
Babbington Notts 116 E3
Babbinswood Shrops 112 E5
Babbs Green Herts 69 K4
Babcary Somset 31 J5
Babel Carmth 59 M2
Babel Green Suffk 88 E5
Babell Flints 128 E5
Babeny Devon 12 F7
Bablock Hythe Oxon 66 B6
Babraham Cambs 87 K5
Babworth Notts 134 D3
Bachau IoA 125 H3
Bache Shrops 95 L7
Bacheldre Powys 94 F5
Bachelor's Bump E Susx 24 D5
Backaland Ork 275 d3
Backbarrow Cumb 156 E5
Backe Carmth 58 A5
Backfolds Abers 269 J5
Backford Ches W 129 J5
Backford Cross Ches W 129 J5
Backies Highld 273 K7
Back of Keppoch Highld 237 J3
Back o' th' Brook Staffs 115 H1
Back Street Suffk 88 E3
Backwell N Som 44 F5
Backworth N Tyne 181 H4
Bacon's End Solhll 98 F6
Baconsthorpe Norfk 122 C4
Bacton Herefs 62 D1
Bacton Norfk 123 H5
Bacton Suffk 90 C2
Bacton Green Suffk 90 B2
Bacup Lancs 140 C2
Badachro Highld 260 C5
Badanloch Highld 273 J2
Badbury Swindn 47 J3

Badby Nhants 84 A3
Badcall Highld 276 B7
Badcall Highld 276 C5
Badcaul Highld 261 G2
Baddeley Edge C Stke 114 E1
Baddeley Green C Stke 114 E1
Baddesley Clinton Warwks 82 F1
Baddesley Ensor Warwks 99 H4
Baddidarrach Highld 270 E3
Baddinsgill Border 199 K2
Badenscoth Abers 256 C4
Badentarbet Highld 270 D6
Badenyon Abers 255 G7
Badersfield Norfk 122 E6
Badgall Cnwll 11 J5
Badgeney Cambs 103 J4
Badger Shrops 97 H3
Badger's Cross Cnwll 2 D4
Badgers Mount Kent 52 B6
Badgeworth Gloucs 64 C3
Badgworth Somset 44 E8
Badharlick Cnwll 11 J5
Badicaul Highld 248 B6
Badingham Suffk 91 G2
Badlesmere Kent 40 D4
Badlieu Border 187 G2
Badlipster Highld 280 B6
Badluarach Highld 261 G1
Badninish Highld 263 K1
Badrallach Highld 261 H2
Badsey Worcs 82 C6
Badshot Lea Surrey 36 C1
Badsworth Wakefd 142 D5
Badwell Ash Suffk 89 K2
Badwell Green Suffk 89 K2
Bagber Dorset 32 C8
Bagby N York 161 G6
Bag Enderby Lincs 136 F5
Bagendon Gloucs 64 E5
Bagginswood Shrops 96 F7
Baggrow Cumb 165 G2
Bàgh a' Chaisteil W Isls 283 b13
Bagham Kent 40 E4
Bagillt Flints 128 F4
Baginton Warwks 99 K8
Baglan Neath 57 K6
Bagley Leeds 141 K1
Bagley Shrops 112 F6
Bagley Somset 31 G2
Bagmore Hants 35 K2
Bagnall Staffs 114 E1
Bagnor W Berk 48 C5
Bagshot Surrey 49 M6
Bagshot Wilts 47 L6
Bagstone S Glos 45 K2
Bagthorpe Notts 116 D1
Bagworth Leics 99 M2
Bagwy Llydiart Herefs 62 F2
Baildon C Brad 149 L7
Baildon Green C Brad 149 L7
Baile Ailein W Isls 282 f4
Baile a' Mhanaich W Isls 283 c9
Baile Mòr Ag & B 226 B7
Bailey Green Hants 35 K5
Baileyhead Cumb 178 C3
Bailiff Bridge Calder 141 J3
Baillieston C Glas 209 H6
Bailrigg Lancs 147 J4
Bainbridge N York 159 G4
Bainshole Abers 256 A5
Bainton C Pete 102 B2
Bainton E R Yk 152 E5
Bainton Oxon 66 E2
Baintown Fife 222 F6
Bairnkine Border 189 H3
Baker's End Herts 69 L4
Baker Street Thurr 52 D3
Bakewell Derbys 132 D6
Bala Gwynd 111 H4
Balallan W Isls 282 f4
Balbeg Highld 250 D5
Balbeggie P & K 222 B1
Balblair Highld 250 E3
Balblair Highld 263 J5
Balby Donc 142 E7
Balcary D & G 175 K5
Balchraggan Highld 250 F3
Balchreick Highld 276 B4
Balcombe W Susx 37 M5
Balcombe Lane W Susx 37 M4
Balcomie Links Fife 223 L5
Baldersby N York 160 E7
Baldersby St James N York 160 E7
Balderstone Lancs 139 J1
Balderstone Rochdl 140 D5
Balderton Notts 117 L1
Baldhu Cnwll 4 C6
Baldinnie Fife 223 G5
Baldinnies P & K 221 J4

Baldock Herts 86 E8
Baldovie C Dund 234 C8
Baldrine IoM 154 f5
Baldslow E Susx 24 E4
Baldwin IoM 154 e6
Baldwinholme Cumb 177 K8
Baldwin's Gate Staffs 114 B3
Baldwin's Hill W Susx 38 B5
Bale Norfk 121 M4
Baledgarno P & K 222 D1
Balemartine Ag & B 224 C7
Balerno C Edin 211 G5
Balfarg Fife 222 D6
Balfield Angus 234 E2
Balfour Ork 275 d4
Balfron Stirlg 208 F1
Balgaveny Abers 256 B4
Balgonar Fife 221 J8
Balgowan D & G 172 E6
Balgowan Highld 241 H4
Balgown Highld 258 F3
Balgracie D & G 172 B3
Balgray S Lans 186 C2
Balham Gt Lon 51 H4
Balhary P & K 233 L6
Balholmie P & K 233 H8
Baligill Highld 278 E3
Balintore Angus 233 L4
Balintore Highld 264 D5
Balintraid Highld 263 K5
Balivanich W Isls 283 c9
Balk N York 161 G6
Balkeerie Angus 233 M6
Balkholme E R Yk 143 K2
Ballabeg IoM 154 c7
Ballachulish Highld 229 H4
Ballafesson IoM 154 b7
Ballajora IoM 154 g4
Ballakilpheric IoM 154 b7
Ballamodha IoM 154 c7
Ballanlay Ag & B 207 G6
Ballantrae S Ayrs 182 D6
Ballards Gore Essex 72 C8
Ballards Green Warwks 99 H5
Ballasalla IoM 154 c7
Ballater Abers 243 L4
Ballaugh IoM 154 d3
Ballchraggan Highld 263 K5
Ballencrieff E Loth 212 B3
Ballevullin Ag & B 224 B6
Ball Green C Stke 114 D1
Ball Haye Green Staffs 131 K8
Ball Hill Hants 48 B6
Ballidon Derbys 115 K1
Balliekine N Ayrs 194 D3
Balliemore Ag & B 217 H7
Balligmorrie S Ayrs 183 G5
Ballimore Stirlg 219 H4
Ballindalloch Moray 254 D4
Ballindean P & K 222 D2
Ballingdon Suffk 89 H7
Ballinger Common Bucks 67 M6
Ballingham Herefs 63 H1
Ballingry Fife 222 B7
Ballinluig P & K 232 E5
Ballinshoe Angus 234 B5
Ballintuim P & K 233 G4
Balloch Highld 252 D2
Balloch N Lans 209 K4
Balloch P & K 220 E3
Balloch S Ayrs 183 J4
Balloch W Duns 208 C3
Balls Cross W Susx 36 E5
Balls Green E Susx 38 D6
Ball's Green Gloucs 64 B7
Ballygown Ag & B 226 E4
Ballygrant Ag & B 204 E3
Ballyhaugh Ag & B 224 F4
Balmacara Highld 248 C6
Balmaclellan D & G 185 G2
Balmae D & G 175 H6
Balmaha Stirlg 208 C1
Balmalcolm Fife 222 E5
Balmangan D & G 175 G5
Balmedie Abers 257 H8
Balmer Heath Shrops 113 G4
Balmerino Fife 222 F2
Balmerlawn Hants 18 D3
Balmichael N Ayrs 194 E5
Balmore E Duns 209 G4
Balmuchy Highld 264 D4
Balmule Fife 211 H2
Balmullo Fife 223 G2
Balnacoil Highld 273 K6
Balnacra Highld 248 F3
Balnacroft Abers 243 J5
Balnafoich Highld 251 J4
Balnaguard P & K 232 D5
Balnahard Ag & B 214 E4

Balnahard Ag & B 226 E5
Balnain Highld 250 D5
Balnakeil Highld 276 F3
Balne N York 142 F4
Balquharn P & K 232 F8
Balquhidder Stirlg 219 H3
Balsall Common Solhll 99 G8
Balsall Heath Birm 98 D6
Balsall Street Solhll 99 G8
Balscote Oxon 83 J6
Balsham Cambs 88 B5
Baltasound Shet 281 f1
Balterley Staffs 114 B2
Balterley Green Staffs 114 B2
Balterley Heath Staffs 114 B2
Baltersan D & G 174 C3
Balthangie Abers 268 E6
Baltonsborough Somset 31 J4
Balvicar Ag & B 216 B4
Balvraid Highld 248 D8
Balvraid Highld 252 F5
Balwest Cnwll 2 F5
Bamber Bridge Lancs 139 H3
Bamber's Green Essex 70 E3
Bamburgh Nthumb 203 K6
Bamford Derbys 132 D3
Bamford Rochdl 140 C5
Bampton Cumb 166 C7
Bampton Devon 29 G6
Bampton Oxon 65 L6
Bampton Grange Cumb 166 C7
Banavie Highld 239 J8
Banbury Oxon 83 K7
Banbury Crematorium Oxon 83 K6
Bancffosfelen Carmth 58 E6
Banchory Abers 244 F4
Banchory-Devenick Abers 245 K3
Bancycapel Carmth 58 D6
Bancyfelin Carmth 58 B5
Banc-y-ffordd Carmth 76 D7
Bandirran P & K 222 C1
Bandrake Head Cumb 156 D5
Banff Abers 268 C3
Bangor Gwynd 125 K5
Bangor Crematorium Gwynd 125 L5
Bangor-on-Dee Wrexhm 112 F2
Bangors Cnwll 11 H3
Bangor's Green Lancs 138 D6
Bangrove Suffk 89 J1
Banham Norfk 106 B6
Bank Hants 18 D2
Bankend D & G 176 D5
Bankfoot P & K 233 G8
Bankglen E Ayrs 197 H8
Bank Ground Cumb 156 D3
Bankhead C Aber 245 K2
Bankhead S Lans 199 G4
Bank Newton N York 148 F5
Banknock Falk 209 K3
Banks Cumb 178 D6
Banks Lancs 138 E4
Banks Green Worcs 82 A2
Bankshill D & G 177 G3
Bank Street Worcs 80 E3
Bank Top Calder 141 H3
Bank Top Lancs 139 G6
Banningham Norfk 122 E5
Bannister Green Essex 71 G3
Bannockburn Stirlg 209 L1
Banstead Surrey 51 H7
Bantham Devon 7 K6
Banton N Lans 209 K3
Banwell N Som 44 E7
Bapchild Kent 40 B3
Bapton Wilts 33 G3
Barabhas W Isls 282 g2
Barassie S Ayrs 196 C4
Barbaraville Highld 263 K5
Barber Booth Derbys 132 B3
Barber Green Cumb 156 F6
Barbieston S Ayrs 196 E7
Barbon Cumb 157 K6
Barbridge Ches E 130 B8
Barbrook Devon 28 C2
Barby Nhants 84 A1
Barcaldine Ag & B 228 F7
Barcheston Warwks 83 G7
Barclose Cumb 178 B6
Barcombe E Susx 22 F4
Barcombe Cross E Susx 23 G4
Barcroft C Brad 149 J8
Barden N York 159 L4
Barden Park Kent 38 F4
Bardfield End Green Essex 70 F1
Bardfield Saling Essex 71 G2
Bardney Lincs 136 B6
Bardon Leics 99 M1
Bardon Mill Nthumb 179 H6
Bardowie E Duns 209 G4

Bardown E Susx 39 G7
Bardrainney Inver 208 B4
Bardsea Cumb 156 D7
Bardsey Leeds 150 E7
Bardsey Island Gwynd 108 A7
Bardsley Oldham 140 D7
Bardwell Suffk 105 J8
Bare Lancs 147 J3
Bareppa Cnwll 3 K5
Barfad D & G 173 J2
Barford Norfk 106 C2
Barford Warwks 83 G3
Barford St John Oxon 83 K8
Barford St Martin Wilts 33 J4
Barford St Michael Oxon 83 K8
Barfrestone Kent 41 H5
Bargate Derbys 116 B2
Bargeddie N Lans 209 J6
Bargoed Caerph 61 J7
Bargrennan D & G 183 J7
Barham Cambs 102 C8
Barham Kent 41 G5
Barham Suffk 90 D5
Barham Crematorium Kent 41 H5
Bar Hill Cambs 87 H3
Barholm Lincs 102 B1
Barkby Leics 100 E2
Barkby Thorpe Leics 100 E2
Barkers Green Shrops 113 H6
Barkestone-le-Vale Leics 117 K4
Barkham Wokham 49 J5
Barking Gt Lon 51 L2
Barking Suffk 90 C4
Barkingside Gt Lon 51 L1
Barking Tye Suffk 90 C5
Barkisland Calder 141 G4
Barkla Shop Cnwll 4 B5
Barkston Lincs 118 B3
Barkston Ash N York 151 G8
Barkway Herts 87 H8
Barlanark C Glas 209 H6
Barlaston Staffs 114 D4
Barlavington W Susx 21 G4
Barlborough Derbys 133 J4
Barlby N York 143 G1
Barlestone Leics 99 L2
Barley Herts 87 H7
Barley Lancs 148 E7
Barleycroft End Herts 70 B2
Barley Hole Rothm 142 B8
Barleythorpe Rutlnd 101 J2
Barling Essex 53 K1
Barlings Lincs 135 M5
Barlochan D & G 175 K3
Barlow Derbys 133 G5
Barlow Gatesd 180 E6
Barlow N York 143 G2
Barmby Moor E R Yk 152 B6
Barmby on the Marsh E R Yk 143 H2
Barmer Norfk 121 H5
Barming Heath Kent 39 J2
Barmollack Ag & B 194 C2
Barmouth Gwynd 109 L8
Barmpton Darltn 169 J7
Barmston E R Yk 153 J4
Barnaby Green Suffk 107 K7
Barnacarry Ag & B 216 F8
Barnack C Pete 102 B2
Barnacle Warwks 99 K6
Barnard Castle Dur 168 D7
Barnard Gate Oxon 66 B5
Barnardiston Suffk 88 E5
Barnbarroch D & G 175 L3
Barnburgh Donc 142 D7
Barnby Suffk 107 K5
Barnby Dun Donc 142 F6
Barnby in the Willows Notts 117 M1
Barnby Moor Notts 134 D3
Barncorkrie D & G 172 D7
Barnehurst Gt Lon 52 B4
Barnes Gt Lon 51 G4
Barnes Street Kent 39 G4
Barnet Gt Lon 69 H7
Barnetby le Wold N Linc 144 D6
Barnet Gate Gt Lon 69 G8
Barney Norfk 121 M5
Barnham Suffk 105 H7
Barnham W Susx 20 F6
Barnham Broom Norfk 106 B2
Barnhead Angus 235 G4
Barnhill C Dund 223 H1
Barnhill Ches W 113 H1
Barnhill Moray 266 C5
Barnhills D & G 182 B8
Barningham Dur 168 D8
Barningham Suffk 105 K8
Barnoldby le Beck NE Lin 145 G7
Barnoldswick Lancs 148 F6
Barnsdale Bar Donc 142 D5

Barns Green W Susx 37 H5
Barnsley Barns 142 A6
Barnsley Gloucs 65 G6
Barnsley Crematorium Barns 142 B6
Barnsole Kent 41 J4
Barnstaple Devon 27 K4
Barnston Essex 70 F3
Barnston Wirral 129 G3
Barnstone Notts 117 J4
Barnt Green Worcs 98 C8
Barnton C Edin 211 G4
Barnton Ches W 130 C5
Barnwell All Saints Nhants 102 A6
Barnwell St Andrew Nhants 102 A6
Barnwood Gloucs 64 D3
Baron's Cross Herefs 80 B4
Baronwood Cumb 166 C2
Barr S Ayrs 183 H4
Barra W Isls 283 b13
Barrachan D & G 173 J5
Barraigh W Isls 283 b13
Barrananaoil Ag & B 216 C5
Barrapoll Ag & B 224 B6
Barras Cumb 167 J8
Barrasford Nthumb 179 L4
Barregarrow IoM 154 d4
Barrets Green Ches E 130 B7
Barrhead E Rens 208 E7
Barrhill S Ayrs 183 G6
Barrington Cambs 87 H5
Barrington Somset 30 F7
Barripper Cnwll 3 G3
Barrmill N Ayrs 196 D1
Barrock Highld 280 C2
Barrow Gloucs 64 C2
Barrow Lancs 148 C8
Barrow Rutlnd 118 A8
Barrow Shrops 96 E3
Barrow Somset 32 B4
Barrow Suffk 88 F3
Barroway Drove Norfk 104 B3
Barrow Bridge Bolton 139 K5
Barrow Burn Nthumb 190 B4
Barrowby Lincs 118 A4
Barrowden Rutlnd 101 L3
Barrowford Lancs 148 E7
Barrow Gurney N Som 45 G5
Barrow Haven N Linc 144 D3
Barrow Hill Derbys 133 H4
Barrow-in-Furness Cumb 146 D2
Barrow Island Cumb 146 D2
Barrow Nook Lancs 138 F7
Barrow's Green Ches E 130 D8
Barrow Street Wilts 32 D5
Barrow-upon-Humber N Linc 144 D4
Barrow upon Soar Leics 116 F8
Barrow upon Trent Derbys 116 B6
Barrow Vale BaNES 45 J7
Barry Angus 234 E2
Barry V Glam 43 H7
Barry Island V Glam 43 H8
Barsby Leics 100 F1
Barsham Suffk 107 H5
Barston Solhll 99 G7
Bartestree Herefs 80 D7
Barthol Chapel Abers 256 E5
Bartholomew Green Essex 71 H3
Barthomley Ches E 114 B1
Bartley Hants 18 D1
Bartley Green Birm 98 C7
Bartlow Cambs 88 B6
Barton Cambs 87 H4
Barton Ches W 113 G1
Barton Gloucs 65 G2
Barton Herefs 79 K4
Barton Lancs 138 D6
Barton Lancs 147 K8
Barton N York 160 C1
Barton Oxon 66 E5
Barton Torbay 8 D2
Barton Warwks 82 D5
Barton Bendish Norfk 104 E2
Barton End Gloucs 64 B7
Barton Green Staffs 115 K7
Barton Hartshorn Bucks 66 F1
Barton Hill N York 151 L3
Barton in Fabis Notts 116 B5
Barton in the Beans Leics 99 L2
Barton-le-Clay C Beds 68 D1
Barton-le-Street N York 162 C7
Barton-le-Willows N York 151 M3
Barton Mills Suffk 104 E8
Barton-on-Sea Hants 18 C5
Barton-on-the-Heath Warwks 65 K1
Barton St David Somset 31 J4
Barton Seagrave Nhants 101 J7
Barton Stacey Hants 34 F3
Barton Town Devon 28 B3
Barton Turf Norfk 123 G7

Barton-under-Needwood Staffs 115 K7
Barton-upon-Humber N Linc 144 C3
Barton upon Irwell Salfd 140 A8
Barton Waterside N Linc 144 C3
Barugh Barns 141 M6
Barugh Green Barns 141 M6
Barvas W Isls 282 g2
Barway Cambs 103 L8
Barwell Leics 99 L4
Barwick Devon 12 E1
Barwick Herts 69 K3
Barwick Somset 31 J8
Barwick in Elmet Leeds 150 F8
Baschurch Shrops 112 F7
Bascote Warwks 83 J3
Bascote Heath Warwks 83 J3
Base Green Suffk 89 L3
Basford Green Staffs 114 F1
Bashall Eaves Lancs 148 B7
Bashall Town Lancs 148 C7
Bashley Hants 18 C4
Basildon Essex 52 F1
Basildon & District Crematorium Essex 53 G2
Basingstoke Hants 48 F8
Basingstoke Crematorium Hants 35 H2
Baslow Derbys 132 E5
Bason Bridge Somset 30 E2
Bassaleg Newpt 44 B2
Bassendean Border 201 K4
Bassenthwaite Cumb 165 H4
Bassett C Sotn 34 F7
Bassingbourn-cum-Kneesworth Cambs 87 G6
Bassingfield Notts 117 G4
Bassingham Lincs 135 H7
Bassingthorpe Lincs 118 C2
Bassus Green Herts 69 J2
Basted Kent 38 F2
Baston Lincs 102 C1
Bastwick Norfk 123 J8
Batch Somset 44 C7
Batchworth Herts 68 D8
Batchworth Heath Herts 68 D8
Batcombe Dorset 16 B2
Batcombe Somset 31 M3
Bate Heath Ches E 130 D4
Batford Herts 68 F4
Bath BaNES 45 L6
Bathampton BaNES 45 M5
Bathealton Somset 29 K6
Batheaston BaNES 45 M5
Bathford BaNES 46 A5
Bathgate W Loth 210 C5
Bathley Notts 134 F7
Bathpool Cnwll 11 K7
Bathpool Somset 30 C5
Bath Side Essex 73 K1
Bathville W Loth 210 B5
Bathway Somset 45 H8
Batley Kirk 141 K3
Batsford Gloucs 82 E8
Batson Devon 7 L7
Battersby N York 161 K1
Battersea Gt Lon 51 H4
Battisborough Cross Devon 7 H5
Battisford Suffk 90 C4
Battisford Tye Suffk 89 L4
Battle E Susx 24 D4
Battle Powys 60 F1
Battleborough Somset 30 E1
Battledown Gloucs 64 D3
Battledykes Angus 234 C4
Battlefield Shrops 113 H8
Battlesbridge Essex 71 J8
Battlesden C Beds 68 B2
Battleton Somset 29 G5
Battlies Green Suffk 89 H2
Battram Leics 99 L2
Battramsley Cross Hants 18 E4
Batt's Corner Hants 36 B3
Baughton Worcs 81 K6
Baughurst Hants 48 E7
Baulds Abers 244 D5
Baulking Oxon 47 L1
Baumber Lincs 136 D5
Baunton Gloucs 64 E6
Baveney Wood Shrops 96 F7
Baverstock Wilts 33 H4
Bawburgh Norfk 106 D2
Bawdeswell Norfk 122 A7
Bawdrip Somset 30 E3
Bawdsey Suffk 91 H7
Bawsey Norfk 120 E7
Bawtry Donc 134 C1
Baxenden Lancs 140 A4
Baxterley Warwks 99 H4

Name	Page	Grid
Baxter's Green Suffk	88	E4
Bay Highld	258	D6
Bayble W Isls	282	h3
Baybridge Hants	35	H6
Baybridge Nthumb	168	B1
Baycliff Cumb	146	F2
Baydon Wilts	47	L3
Bayford Herts	69	J5
Bayford Somset	32	B5
Bayhead W Isls	283	b8
Bay Horse Lancs	147	K5
Bayley's Hill Kent	38	D3
Baylham Suffk	90	C5
Baynard's Green Oxon	66	E1
Baysdale Abbey N York	161	K1
Baysham Herefs	63	H2
Bayston Hill Shrops	96	B2
Baythorne End Essex	88	E6
Bayton Worcs	96	F8
Bayton Common Worcs	81	G1
Bayworth Oxon	66	D6
Beach S Glos	45	L5
Beachampton Bucks	84	E7
Beachamwell Norfk	104	E2
Beachley Gloucs	45	H1
Beacon Devon	14	E2
Beacon End Essex	72	D2
Beacon Hill Kent	39	K6
Beacon Hill Notts	117	L1
Beacon Hill Surrey	36	C3
Beacon's Bottom Bucks	67	J8
Beaconsfield Bucks	50	B1
Beadlam N York	161	L5
Beadlow C Beds	86	C7
Beadnell Nthumb	203	L7
Beaford Devon	27	K7
Beal N York	142	E3
Beal Nthumb	203	H4
Bealbury Cnwll	6	D2
Bealsmill Cnwll	11	L7
Beam Hill Staffs	115	L6
Beamhurst Staffs	115	H4
Beaminster Dorset	15	L2
Beamish Dur	180	F8
Beamsley N York	149	K5
Bean Kent	52	C4
Beanacre Wilts	46	C5
Beanley Nthumb	190	F3
Beardon Devon	12	C5
Beardwood Bl w D	139	K2
Beare Devon	14	A2
Beare Green Surrey	37	J2
Bearley Warwks	82	E3
Bearley Cross Warwks	82	E3
Bearpark Dur	169	G2
Bearsden E Duns	208	F4
Bearsted Kent	39	K2
Bearstone Shrops	114	A4
Bearwood Birm	98	C6
Bearwood Herefs	79	M4
Bearwood Poole	17	L3
Beattock D & G	187	G6
Beauchamp Roding Essex	70	E5
Beauchief Sheff	132	F3
Beaudesert Warwks	82	E2
Beaufort Blae G	61	J5
Beaulieu Hants	18	F3
Beaulieu Road Station Hants	18	E2
Beauly Highld	250	F2
Beaumaris IoA	126	B4
Beaumont Cumb	177	K7
Beaumont Essex	73	H2
Beaumont Jersey	9	c3
Beaumont Hill Darltn	169	J7
Beaumont Leys C Leic	100	C2
Beausale Warwks	82	F1
Beauworth Hants	35	J5
Beaworthy Devon	12	B3
Beazley End Essex	71	H1
Bebington Wirral	129	H3
Bebside Nthumb	181	G3
Beccles Suffk	107	J5
Becconsall Lancs	138	F3
Beckbury Shrops	97	H3
Beckenham Gt Lon	51	K5
Beckenham Crematorium Gt Lon	51	K5
Beckermet Cumb	155	J1
Beckett End Norfk	104	F4
Beckfoot Cumb	155	L3
Beckfoot Cumb	156	B5
Beck Foot Cumb	157	K3
Beckfoot Cumb	164	E1
Beckford Worcs	82	A8
Beckhampton Wilts	47	G5
Beck Hole N York	162	E2
Beckingham Lincs	118	A1
Beckingham Notts	134	F2
Beckington Somset	46	A8
Beckjay Shrops	95	J7
Beckley E Susx	24	F3
Beckley Hants	18	C4
Beckley Oxon	66	E5
Beck Row Suffk	104	D7
Becks C Brad	149	J6
Beck Side Cumb	156	B6
Beck Side Cumb	156	E6
Beckton Gt Lon	51	L3
Beckwithshaw N York	150	C5
Becontree Gt Lon	52	A2
Becquet Vincent Jersey	9	d2
Bedale N York	160	C5
Bedburn Dur	168	E4
Bedchester Dorset	32	E7
Beddau Rhondd	43	G4
Beddgelert Gwynd	109	L2
Beddingham E Susx	23	G5
Beddington Gt Lon	51	J6
Beddington Corner Gt Lon	51	H5
Bedfield Suffk	90	F2
Bedfield Little Green Suffk	90	F2
Bedford Bed	85	L5
Bedford Crematorium Bed	86	B5
Bedgebury Cross Kent	39	H6
Bedham W Susx	36	F6
Bedhampton Hants	20	A5
Bedingfield Suffk	90	E2
Bedingfield Green Suffk	90	E2
Bedlam N York	150	C3
Bedlington Nthumb	181	G3
Bedlinog Myr Td	61	H6
Bedminster Bristl	45	H5
Bedminster Down Bristl	45	H5
Bedmond Herts	68	E6
Bednall Staffs	114	F7
Bedrule Border	189	G3
Bedstone Shrops	95	J8
Bedwas Caerph	43	J4
Bedwellty Caerph	61	J7
Bedworth Warwks	99	K6
Bedworth Woodlands Warwks	99	K6
Beeby Leics	100	E2
Beech Hants	35	L3
Beech Staffs	114	D4
Beech Hill W Berk	49	G6
Beechingstoke Wilts	47	G7
Beedon W Berk	48	C3
Beedon Hill W Berk	48	C3
Beeford E R Yk	153	H5
Beeley Derbys	132	E6
Beelsby NE Lin	145	G7
Beenham W Berk	48	E5
Beenham's Heath W & M	49	K4
Beeny Cnwll	11	G4
Beer Devon	14	F5
Beer Somset	30	F4
Beercrocombe Somset	30	D6
Beer Hackett Dorset	31	K8
Beesands Devon	8	B6
Beesby Lincs	137	J4
Beeson Devon	8	B6
Beeston C Beds	86	D5
Beeston Ches W	129	M7
Beeston Leeds	141	L2
Beeston Norfk	121	K8
Beeston Notts	116	E4
Beeston Regis Norfk	122	D3
Beeswing D & G	176	A5
Beetham Cumb	157	H6
Beetham Somset	30	D8
Beetley Norfk	121	L8
Began Cardif	43	K5
Begbroke Oxon	66	C4
Begdale Cambs	103	J2
Begelly Pembks	55	J5
Beggarington Hill Leeds	141	L3
Beggar's Bush Powys	79	J2
Beguildy Powys	94	F7
Beighton Norfk	107	H2
Beighton Sheff	133	J3
Beinn Na Faoghla W Isls	283	c9
Beith N Ayrs	208	B8
Bekesbourne Kent	41	G4
Bekesbourne Hill Kent	41	G4
Belaugh Norfk	122	F7
Belbroughton Worcs	97	L7
Belchalwell Dorset	16	F1
Belchalwell Street Dorset	16	F1
Belchamp Otten Essex	88	F6
Belchamp St Paul Essex	88	F6
Belchamp Walter Essex	89	G7
Belchford Lincs	136	E4
Belford Nthumb	203	H6
Belgrave C Leic	100	D2
Belhaven E Loth	212	E3
Belhelvie Abers	257	H8
Belhinnie Abers	255	J6
Bellabeg Abers	243	K1
Bellamore Herefs	79	M7
Bellanoch Ag & B	216	B8
Bellasize E R Yk	143	K2
Bellaty Angus	233	K3
Bell Bar Herts	69	H6
Bell Busk N York	148	F4
Belleau Lincs	137	G4
Bell End Worcs	97	L7
Bellerby N York	159	K4
Bellever Devon	12	F7
Belle Vue Cumb	177	L7
Belle Vue Wakefd	142	A4
Bellfield S Lans	198	D6
Bell Heath Worcs	97	L7
Bell Hill Hants	35	M6
Bellingdon Bucks	68	B6
Bellingham Nthumb	179	J2
Belloch Ag & B	192	D1
Bellochantuy Ag & B	192	D2
Bell o' th' Hill Ches W	113	H2
Bellows Cross Dorset	33	J8
Bells Cross Suffk	90	D5
Bellshill N Lans	209	J7
Bellshill Nthumb	203	J7
Bellside N Lans	209	L7
Bellsquarry W Loth	210	D6
Bells Yew Green E Susx	38	F6
Belluton BaNES	45	J6
Belmaduthy Highld	263	H8
Belmesthorpe Rutlnd	102	A2
Belmont Bl w D	139	K4
Belmont Gt Lon	51	H6
Belmont S Ayrs	196	C7
Belmont Shet	281	f2
Belnacraig Abers	255	H8
Belowda Cnwll	4	F3
Belper Derbys	116	B2
Belper Lane End Derbys	116	B2
Belph Derbys	133	L4
Belsay Nthumb	180	D3
Belses Border	201	J8
Belsford Devon	7	L3
Belsize Herts	68	D7
Belstead Suffk	90	D7
Belstone Devon	12	E4
Belthorn Lancs	139	L3
Beltinge Kent	41	G2
Beltingham Nthumb	179	H6
Beltoft N Linc	143	K6
Belton Leics	116	D7
Belton Lincs	118	B3
Belton N Linc	143	K6
Belton Norfk	107	K3
Belton Rutlnd	101	H3
Beltring Kent	39	H4
Belvedere Gt Lon	52	B3
Belvoir Leics	117	L5
Bembridge IoW	19	L6
Bemerton Wilts	33	K5
Bempton E R Yk	153	K2
Benacre Suffk	107	K6
Benbecula W Isls	283	c9
Benbuie D & G	185	H4
Benderloch Ag & B	228	D7
Benenden Kent	39	K6
Benfieldside Dur	180	D8
Bengates Norfk	122	F6
Bengeo Herts	69	J4
Bengeworth Worcs	82	B6
Benhall Green Suffk	91	J3
Benhall Street Suffk	91	H3
Benholm Abers	235	K2
Beningbrough N York	151	H4
Benington Herts	69	J2
Benington Lincs	119	L2
Benington Sea End Lincs	119	L2
Benllech IoA	125	J3
Benmore Ag & B	207	J2
Bennacott Cnwll	11	K4
Bennan N Ayrs	193	K4
Bennet Head Cumb	166	B6
Bennetland E R Yk	143	L2
Bennett End Bucks	67	J7
Benniworth Lincs	136	D3
Benover Kent	39	H4
Ben Rhydding C Brad	149	L6
Benslie N Ayrs	196	C2
Benson Oxon	66	F8
Bentfield Green Essex	70	D2
Benthall Shrops	96	F3
Bentham Gloucs	64	C4
Benthoul C Aber	245	H3
Bentlawnt Shrops	95	H3
Bentley Donc	142	E6
Bentley E R Yk	152	F8
Bentley Hants	36	A2
Bentley Suffk	90	D7
Bentley Warwks	99	H4
Bentley Crematorium Essex	70	E7
Bentley Heath Herts	69	H7
Bentley Heath Solhll	98	F8
Benton Devon	28	B4
Bentpath D & G	188	B8
Bentwichen Devon	28	C4
Bentworth Hants	35	K3
Benvie Angus	222	E1
Benville Dorset	15	M2
Benwick Cambs	103	G5
Beoley Worcs	82	C1
Beoraidbeg Highld	237	K2
Bepton W Susx	20	D3
Berden Essex	70	C1
Berea Pembks	74	C6
Bere Alston Devon	6	E2
Bere Ferrers Devon	6	E2
Berepper Cnwll	3	G6
Bere Regis Dorset	17	G4
Bergh Apton Norfk	106	F3
Berhill Somset	31	G4
Berinsfield Oxon	66	E7
Berkeley Gloucs	63	K7
Berkeley Heath Gloucs	63	K7
Berkeley Road Gloucs	63	L7
Berkhamsted Herts	68	C5
Berkley Somset	32	D1
Berkswell Solhll	99	H7
Bermondsey Gt Lon	51	J3
Bermuda Warwks	99	K5
Bernera Highld	248	C7
Bernisdale Highld	258	F6
Berrick Prior Oxon	66	F8
Berrick Salome Oxon	66	F8
Berriedale Highld	274	F3
Berrier Cumb	165	L5
Berriew Powys	94	E3
Berrington Nthumb	202	F4
Berrington Shrops	96	C2
Berrington Worcs	80	D2
Berrington Green Worcs	80	D2
Berrow Somset	44	C8
Berrow Worcs	81	H8
Berrow Green Worcs	81	H3
Berry Brow Kirk	141	H5
Berry Cross Devon	27	H7
Berry Down Cross Devon	27	K2
Berryfields Bucks	67	J4
Berry Hill Gloucs	63	H4
Berry Hill Pembks	75	H4
Berryhillock Moray	267	K4
Berryhillock Moray	267	K5
Berrynarbor Devon	27	K2
Berry Pomeroy Devon	8	B3
Berry's Green Gt Lon	51	L7
Bersham Wrexhm	112	D2
Bersted W Susx	20	F6
Berthengam Flints	128	D4
Berwick E Susx	23	H6
Berwick Bassett Wilts	47	G4
Berwick Hill Nthumb	180	E4
Berwick St James Wilts	33	J3
Berwick St John Wilts	32	F6
Berwick St Leonard Wilts	32	F4
Berwick Station E Susx	23	J6
Berwick-upon-Tweed Nthumb	202	F3
Bescaby Leics	117	L6
Bescar Lancs	138	E5
Besford Shrops	113	J6
Besford Worcs	81	L6
Bessacarr Donc	142	F7
Bessels Leigh Oxon	66	C6
Besses o' th' Barn Bury	140	B6
Bessingby E R Yk	153	J3
Bessingham Norfk	122	D4
Bestbeech Hill E Susx	38	F7
Besthorpe Norfk	106	B4
Besthorpe Notts	135	G6
Bestwood Village Notts	116	F2
Beswick E R Yk	152	F6
Betchcott Shrops	95	K4
Betchworth Surrey	37	K1
Bethania Cerdgn	77	G3
Bethania Gwynd	110	D3
Bethel Gwynd	111	J4
Bethel Gwynd	125	J6
Bethel IoA	125	G5
Bethel Powys	111	L7
Bethersden Kent	40	B7
Bethesda Gwynd	126	C6
Bethesda Pembks	55	J3
Bethlehem Carmth	59	J4
Bethnal Green Gt Lon	51	K2
Betley Staffs	114	B2
Betsham Kent	52	D4
Betteshanger Kent	41	J5
Bettiscombe Dorset	15	J3
Bettisfield Wrexhm	113	G4
Betton Shrops	113	M4
Betton Strange Shrops	96	C2

Bettws Newpt 44 C1
Bettws Cedewain Powys 94 D4
Bettws Ifan Cerdgn 76 B5
Bettws-Newydd Mons 62 D6
Bettyhill Highld 278 B4
Betws Brdgnd 42 D4
Betws Carmth 59 H6
Betws Bledrws Cerdgn 77 H5
Betws Garmon Gwynd 125 K8
Betws Gwerfil Goch Denbgs 111 K2
Betws-y-Coed Conwy 126 F8
Betws-yn-Rhos Conwy 127 H5
Beulah Cerdgn 76 B5
Beulah Powys 78 C5
Bevendean Br & H 22 E6
Bevercotes Notts 134 D5
Beverley E R Yk 153 G7
Beverston Gloucs 64 B8
Bevington Gloucs 63 K7
Bewaldeth Cumb 165 H4
Bewcastle Cumb 178 D4
Bewdley Worcs 97 H8
Bewerley N York 149 L3
Bewholme E R Yk 153 J6
Bewlbridge Kent 39 H6
Bexhill E Susx 24 D5
Bexley Gt Lon 52 B4
Bexleyheath Gt Lon 52 A4
Bexleyhill W Susx 36 D6
Bexon Kent 53 J7
Bexwell Norfk 104 C3
Beyton Suffk 89 J3
Beyton Green Suffk 89 J3
Bhaltos W Isls 282 e3
Bhatarsaigh W Isls 283 b13
Bibstone S Glos 45 K1
Bibury Gloucs 65 G5
Bicester Oxon 66 E3
Bickenhill Solhll 99 G7
Bicker Lincs 119 H4
Bicker Bar Lincs 119 H4
Bicker Gauntlet Lincs 119 H4
Bickershaw Wigan 139 J7
Bickerstaffe Lancs 138 F7
Bickerton Ches E 113 H1
Bickerton Devon 8 B7
Bickerton N York 151 G5
Bickerton Nthumb 190 E6
Bickford Staffs 114 D8
Bickington Devon 13 J8
Bickington Devon 27 J4
Bickleigh Devon 7 G2
Bickleigh Devon 13 M1
Bickleton Devon 27 J5
Bickley Ches W 113 J2
Bickley Gt Lon 51 L5
Bickley N York 163 G4
Bickley Worcs 80 E1
Bickley Moss Ches W 113 J2
Bicknacre Essex 71 J6
Bicknoller Somset 29 K3
Bicknor Kent 53 J7
Bickton Hants 33 K8
Bicton Herefs 80 B2
Bicton Shrops 95 G6
Bicton Shrops 113 G8
Bidborough Kent 38 E5
Bidden Hants 35 L1
Biddenden Kent 39 L5
Biddenden Green Kent 39 M5
Biddenham Bed 85 K5
Biddestone Wilts 46 B4
Biddisham Somset 44 D8
Biddlesden Bucks 84 C7
Biddlestone Nthumb 190 H4
Biddulph Staffs 131 H7
Biddulph Moor Staffs 131 H8
Bideford Devon 27 H5
Bidford-on-Avon Warwks 82 D5
Bidston Wirral 129 G2
Bielby E R Yk 152 B7
Bieldside C Aber 245 K3
Bierley IoW 19 H8
Bierton Bucks 67 K4
Big Balcraig D & G 173 K6
Bigbury Devon 7 K5
Bigbury-on-Sea Devon 7 J6
Bigby Lincs 144 D6
Biggar Cumb 146 D3
Biggar S Lans 199 H5
Biggin Derbys 115 L2
Biggin Derbys 132 C7
Biggin N York 142 E1
Biggin Hill Gt Lon 51 L7
Biggleswade C Beds 86 D6
Bigholms D & G 177 K3
Bighouse Highld 278 F3
Bighton Hants 35 J4
Biglands Cumb 177 H8

Bignor W Susx 21 G4
Bigrigg Cumb 164 D8
Big Sand Highld 260 B4
Bigton Shet 281 d8
Bilborough C Nott 116 E3
Bilbrook Somset 29 J3
Bilbrook Staffs 97 K3
Bilbrough N York 151 H6
Bilbster Highld 280 C5
Bildershaw Dur 169 G6
Bildeston Suffk 89 K5
Billacott Cnwll 11 J4
Billericay Essex 71 G8
Billesdon Leics 100 F3
Billesley Warwks 82 D4
Billingborough Lincs 118 F5
Billinge St Hel 139 G7
Billingford Norfk 106 D7
Billingford Norfk 121 M7
Billingham S on T 170 B6
Billinghay Lincs 136 C6
Billingley Barns 142 C6
Billingshurst W Susx 37 G5
Billingsley Shrops 97 G6
Billington C Beds 68 B3
Billington Lancs 148 C8
Billington Staffs 114 D7
Billockby Norfk 107 J1
Billy Row Dur 168 F3
Bilsborrow Lancs 147 K7
Bilsby Lincs 137 J4
Bilsham W Susx 21 G6
Bilsington Kent 40 D8
Bilsthorpe Notts 134 C7
Bilsthorpe Moor Notts 134 C7
Bilston Mdloth 211 J6
Bilston Wolves 98 B4
Bilstone Leics 99 K2
Bilting Kent 40 D5
Bilton E R Yk 144 F1
Bilton N York 150 D4
Bilton Nthumb 191 J4
Bilton Warwks 100 B8
Bilton Banks Nthumb 191 J4
Bilton-in-Ainsty N York 151 G5
Binbrook Lincs 136 D1
Binchester Blocks Dur 169 G4
Bincombe Dorset 16 D5
Binegar Somset 31 K1
Bines Green W Susx 21 L3
Binfield Br For 49 K4
Binfield Heath Oxon 49 H3
Bingfield Nthumb 180 A4
Bingham Notts 117 J3
Bingham's Melcombe Dorset 16 E2
Bingley C Brad 149 K7
Bings Shrops 113 J7
Binham Norfk 121 L4
Binley Covtry 99 K7
Binley Hants 48 B8
Binley Woods Warwks 99 L7
Binnegar Dorset 17 G5
Binniehill Falk 209 M4
Binscombe Surrey 36 E2
Binsey Oxon 66 C5
Binstead IoW 19 K5
Binsted Hants 36 A3
Binsted W Susx 21 G5
Binton Warwks 82 D4
Bintree Norfk 121 M7
Binweston Shrops 95 H3
Birch Essex 72 D3
Birch Rochdl 140 C6
Bircham Newton Norfk 121 G5
Bircham Tofts Norfk 121 G5
Birchanger Essex 70 D3
Birch Cross Staffs 115 J5
Birchencliffe Kirk 141 H4
Bircher Herefs 80 B2
Birchfield Birm 98 D5
Birch Green Essex 72 D3
Birch Green Herts 69 J5
Birch Green Worcs 81 K6
Birchgrove Cardif 43 J5
Birchgrove Swans 57 K5
Birchgrove W Susx 38 B7
Birch Heath Ches W 130 A7
Birch Hill Ches W 129 M5
Birchington Kent 41 J2
Birchington-on-Sea Kent 41 J2
Birchley Heath Warwks 99 H4
Birchmoor Warwks 99 H3
Birchmoor Green C Beds 85 J8
Birchover Derbys 132 E7
Birch Vale Derbys 131 K2
Birchwood Lincs 135 J6
Birch Wood Somset 30 C8
Birchwood Warrtn 130 C2
Bircotes Notts 134 C2

Birdbrook Essex 88 E7
Birdforth N York 161 G7
Birdham W Susx 20 D6
Birdingbury Warwks 83 K2
Birdlip Gloucs 64 D4
Birdoswald Cumb 178 E5
Birdsall N York 152 B3
Birds Edge Kirk 141 K6
Birds Green Essex 70 E5
Birdsgreen Shrops 97 H6
Birdsmoorgate Dorset 15 J3
Bird Street Suffk 89 K5
Birdwell Barns 142 A7
Birdwood Gloucs 63 L3
Birgham Border 202 B5
Birichin Highld 263 K2
Birkacre Lancs 139 H5
Birkby N York 160 D2
Birkdale Sefton 138 C5
Birkenbog Abers 267 L3
Birkenhead Wirral 129 H2
Birkenhead (Queensway)
  Tunnel Lpool 129 H2
Birkenhills Abers 256 D3
Birkenshaw Kirk 141 K2
Birkhall Abers 243 K5
Birkhill Angus 234 A8
Birkhill D & G 187 J3
Birkholme Lincs 118 C6
Birkin N York 142 E2
Birks Leeds 141 L2
Birkshaw Nthumb 179 H5
Birley Herefs 80 B4
Birley Carr Sheff 133 C1
Birling Kent 52 E6
Birling Nthumb 191 K5
Birling Gap E Susx 23 J8
Birlingham Worcs 81 L6
Birmingham Birm 98 D6
Birnam P & K 232 F7
Birness Abers 257 H5
Birse Abers 244 C4
Birsemore Abers 244 C4
Birstall Kirk 141 K3
Birstall Leics 100 D2
Birstwith N York 150 B4
Birthorpe Lincs 118 E5
Birtley Gatesd 181 G7
Birtley Herefs 79 L2
Birtley Nthumb 179 K3
Birtley Crematorium Gatesd 181 G7
Birts Street Worcs 81 H7
Bisbrooke Rutlnd 101 J3
Biscathorpe Lincs 136 D3
Biscovey Cnwll 5 H4
Bisham W & M 49 K2
Bishampton Worcs 82 A5
Bish Mill Devon 28 C6
Bishop Auckland Dur 169 G5
Bishopbridge Lincs 135 L2
Bishopbriggs E Duns 209 G5
Bishop Burton E R Yk 152 F7
Bishop Middleham Dur 169 J4
Bishopmill Moray 266 E3
Bishop Monkton N York 150 D3
Bishop Norton Lincs 135 K1
Bishopsbourne Kent 41 G5
Bishops Cannings Wilts 46 F6
Bishop's Castle Shrops 95 H5
Bishop's Caundle Dorset 32 B8
Bishop's Cleeve Gloucs 64 D2
Bishop's Frome Herefs 80 F5
Bishops Gate Surrey 50 B5
Bishop's Green Essex 70 F3
Bishop's Green Hants 48 D6
Bishop's Hull Somset 30 B6
Bishop's Itchington Warwks 83 J4
Bishops Lydeard Somset 29 M5
Bishop's Norton Gloucs 64 B2
Bishop's Nympton Devon 28 D6
Bishop's Offley Staffs 114 B5
Bishop's Stortford Herts 70 C3
Bishop's Sutton Hants 35 J4
Bishop's Tachbrook Warwks 83 H3
Bishop's Tawton Devon 27 K5
Bishopsteignton Devon 13 L7
Bishopstoke Hants 34 F7
Bishopston Swans 57 G7
Bishopstone Bucks 67 J5
Bishopstone E Susx 23 G7
Bishopstone Herefs 80 A6
Bishopstone Kent 41 G2
Bishopstone Swindn 47 K2
Bishopstone Wilts 33 J5
Bishopstrow Wilts 32 E2
Bishop Sutton BaNES 45 H7
Bishop's Waltham Hants 35 H7
Bishopswood Somset 30 C8
Bishop's Wood Staffs 97 J2

Bishopsworth Bristl 45 H5
Bishop Thornton N York 150 C3
Bishopthorpe C York 151 J6
Bishopton Darltn 169 K6
Bishopton Rens 208 D5
Bishopton Warwks 82 E4
Bishop Wilton E R Yk 152 B5
Bishton Newpt 44 D2
Bishton Staffs 115 G7
Bisley Gloucs 64 C6
Bisley Surrey 50 B7
Bisley Camp Surrey 50 B7
Bispham Bpool 146 F7
Bispham Green Lancs 138 F5
Bissoe Cnwll 3 K3
Bisterne Hants 18 A3
Bitchet Green Kent 38 E3
Bitchfield Lincs 118 C6
Bittadon Devon 27 K3
Bittaford Devon 7 K3
Bittering Norfk 121 K8
Bitterley Shrops 96 D7
Bitterne C Sotn 34 F8
Bitteswell Leics 100 C6
Bitton S Glos 45 K5
Bix Oxon 49 H2
Bixter Shet 281 d6
Blaby Leics 100 C4
Blackadder Border 202 C3
Blackawton Devon 8 B5
Blackbeck Cumb 155 J1
Blackborough Devon 14 C1
Blackborough End Norfk 120 E8
Black Bourton Oxon 65 L6
Blackboys E Susx 23 J3
Blackbrook Derbys 116 B2
Blackbrook St Hel 139 G8
Blackbrook Staffs 114 B4
Blackbrook Surrey 37 J2
Blackburn Abers 245 J1
Blackburn Bl w D 139 K2
Blackburn Rothm 133 H1
Blackburn W Loth 210 C6
Black Callerton N u Ty 180 E5
Black Car Norfk 106 B4
Black Corner W Susx 37 L3
Blackcraig E Ayrs 185 G1
Black Crofts Ag & B 228 E8
Black Cross Cnwll 4 E3
Blackden Heath Ches E 130 F5
Blackdog Abers 245 L1
Black Dog Devon 13 J1
Blackdown Devon 12 C6
Blackdown Dorset 15 J2
Blackdyke Cumb 176 F8
Blacker Barns 142 A5
Blacker Hill Barns 142 B7
Blackfen Gt Lon 51 M4
Blackfield Hants 19 G3
Blackford Cumb 177 L6
Blackford P & K 220 F5
Blackford Somset 30 F2
Blackford Somset 31 L5
Blackfordby Leics 116 B7
Blackgang IoW 19 H8
Blackhall C Edin 211 H4
Blackhall Dur 170 B3
Blackhall Colliery Dur 170 B3
Blackhall Mill Gatesd 180 D7
Blackhaugh Border 200 F5
Blackheath Essex 72 E3
Blackheath Gt Lon 51 K4
Blackheath Sandw 98 B6
Blackheath Suffk 107 J8
Blackheath Surrey 36 F2
Black Heddon Nthumb 180 C4
Blackhill Abers 257 K3
Blackhill Abers 269 K5
Blackhill Dur 180 D8
Blackhill of Clackriach Abers 269 G7
Blackhorse Devon 14 A4
Blackjack Lincs 119 H4
Blackland Wilts 46 E5
Black Lane Ends Lancs 149 G7
Blacklaw D & G 186 F4
Blackley Manch 140 C7
Blackley Crematorium Manch 140 C7
Blacklunans P & K 233 H3
Blackmarstone Herefs 80 C7
Blackmill Brdgnd 42 E4
Blackmoor Hants 36 A4
Black Moor Leeds 150 D7
Blackmoor N Som 44 F6
Blackmoorfoot Kirk 141 H5
Blackmoor Gate Devon 28 A2
Blackmore Essex 70 F6
Blackmore End Essex 71 H1
Blackmore End Herts 68 F4
Blackness Falk 210 E3

Blacknest Hants 36 B3
Blacknest W & M 50 B5
Black Notley Essex 71 J3
Blacko Lancs 148 E7
Black Pill Swans 57 H6
Blackpool Bpool 146 F8
Blackpool Devon 8 C5
Blackpool Devon 13 J7
Blackpool Gate Cumb 178 C3
Blackridge W Loth 210 A5
Blackrock Cnwll 3 G4
Blackrock Mons 61 K4
Blackrod Bolton 139 J5
Blacksboat Moray 254 D4
Blackshaw D & G 176 D5
Blackshaw Head Calder 140 E2
Blacksmith's Green Suffk 90 D2
Blacksnape Bl w D 139 L3
Blackstone W Susx 22 C4
Black Street Suffk 107 K6
Black Tar Pembks 55 G5
Blackthorn Oxon 66 F3
Blackthorpe Suffk 89 H3
Blacktoft E R Yk 143 L3
Blacktop C Aber 245 J3
Black Torrington Devon 12 B2
Blackwall Derbys 115 L2
Blackwall Tunnel Gt Lon 51 K3
Blackwater Cnwll 4 B5
Blackwater Hants 49 K7
Blackwater IoW 19 H6
Blackwater Somset 30 C7
Blackwaterfoot N Ayrs 194 D5
Blackwell Cumb 177 L8
Blackwell Darltn 169 H8
Blackwell Derbys 132 C5
Blackwell Derbys 133 J7
Blackwell Warwks 82 F6
Blackwell Worcs 82 A1
Blackwellsend Green Gloucs 63 M2
Blackwood Caerph 43 J2
Blackwood D & G 176 B2
Blackwood S Lans 198 C4
Blackwood Hill Staffs 131 H8
Blacon Ches W 129 J6
Bladbean Kent 41 G6
Bladnoch D & G 174 C4
Bladon Oxon 66 C4
Bladon Somset 30 F6
Blaenannerch Cerdgn 75 M2
Blaenau Ffestiniog Gwynd 110 D2
Blaenavon Torfn 61 L5
Blaen Dyryn Powys 78 C7
Blaenffos Pembks 75 L5
Blaengarw Brdgnd 42 D3
Blaengeuffordd Cerdgn 92 E7
Blaengwrach Neath 60 C6
Blaengwynfi Neath 42 D2
Blaenllechau Rhondd 42 F2
Blaenpennal Cerdgn 77 H2
Blaenplwyf Cerdgn 92 C8
Blaenporth Cerdgn 76 A5
Blaenrhondda Rhondd 60 D7
Blaenwaun Carmth 75 M6
Blaen-y-coed Carmth 58 C3
Blaen-y-cwm Blae G 61 H5
Blaenycwm Cerdgn 93 H8
Blaen-y-cwm Rhondd 60 D7
Blagdon N Som 45 G7
Blagdon Somset 30 B7
Blagdon Torbay 8 C3
Blagdon Hill Somset 30 B7
Blagill Cumb 167 G1
Blaguegate Lancs 138 F6
Blaich Highld 239 G8
Blain Highld 237 K6
Blaina Blae G 61 K5
Blair Atholl P & K 232 C2
Blair Drummond Stirlg 220 C7
Blairgowrie P & K 233 J6
Blairhall Fife 210 C2
Blairingone P & K 221 H7
Blairlogie Stirlg 220 E7
Blairmore Ag & B 207 K2
Blairmore Highld 276 B4
Blair's Ferry Ag & B 206 F5
Blaisdon Gloucs 63 K4
Blakebrook Worcs 97 J8
Blakedown Worcs 97 K7
Blake End Essex 71 H3
Blakeley Lane Staffs 114 F2
Blakemere Ches W 130 A5
Blakemere Herefs 79 L7
Blakemore Devon 7 M3
Blakenall Heath Wsall 98 C3
Blakeney Gloucs 63 K5
Blakeney Norfk 122 A3
Blakenhall Ches E 114 A2
Blakenhall Wolves 97 K4

Blakeshall Worcs 97 J7
Blakesley Nhants 84 C5
Blanchland Nthumb 180 A8
Blandford Camp Dorset 17 H1
Blandford Forum Dorset 17 G1
Blandford St Mary Dorset 17 G2
Bland Hill N York 150 B5
Blanefield Stirlg 208 F3
Blankney Lincs 135 L7
Blantyre S Lans 209 J7
Blàr a' Chaorainn Highld 229 H2
Blargie Highld 241 G4
Blarmachfoldach Highld 229 H2
Blashford Hants 18 A2
Blaston Leics 101 H4
Blatherwycke Nhants 101 L4
Blawith Cumb 156 C5
Blawquhairn D & G 184 F6
Blaxhall Suffk 91 J4
Blaxton Donc 143 H7
Blaydon Gatesd 180 F6
Bleadney Somset 31 H2
Bleadon N Som 44 C7
Bleak Street Somset 32 C4
Blean Kent 40 F3
Bleasby Lincs 136 B3
Bleasby Notts 117 J2
Bleasdale Lancs 147 L6
Bleatarn Cumb 167 G7
Bleathwood Herefs 80 D1
Blebocraigs Fife 223 G4
Bleddfa Powys 79 H2
Bledington Gloucs 65 K3
Bledlow Bucks 67 J6
Bledlow Ridge Bucks 67 J7
Bleet Wilts 46 C7
Blegbie E Loth 212 B6
Blencarn Cumb 166 E4
Blencogo Cumb 165 G1
Blendworth Hants 35 L8
Blenheim Cumb 165 G2
Blennerhasset Cumb 165 G2
Bletchingdon Oxon 66 D3
Bletchingley Surrey 38 A3
Bletchley M Keyn 85 G8
Bletchley Shrops 113 K5
Bletherston Pembks 55 H3
Bletsoe Bed 85 K4
Blewbury Oxon 48 D2
Blickling Norfk 122 D6
Blidworth Notts 134 B8
Blidworth Bottoms Notts 117 G1
Blindburn Nthumb 189 L4
Blindcrake Cumb 164 F4
Blindley Heath Surrey 38 A4
Blisland Cnwll 10 F8
Blissford Hants 33 L8
Bliss Gate Worcs 81 G1
Blisworth Nhants 84 D4
Blithbury Staffs 115 H7
Blitterlees Cumb 176 F8
Blockley Gloucs 82 E8
Blofield Norfk 107 G2
Blofield Heath Norfk 107 G1
Blo Norton Norfk 105 K7
Bloomfield Border 189 G2
Blore Staffs 114 A4
Blore Staffs 115 J2
Blounce Hants 35 L2
Blounts Green Staffs 115 H5
Blowick Sefton 138 D4
Bloxham Oxon 83 K8
Bloxholm Lincs 118 E1
Bloxwich Wsall 98 C3
Bloxworth Dorset 17 G4
Blubberhouses N York 149 L5
Blue Anchor Cnwll 4 E3
Blue Anchor Somset 29 J2
Blue Bell Hill Kent 52 F6
Blundellsands Sefton 138 C7
Blundeston Suffk 107 L4
Blunham C Beds 86 C5
Blunsdon St Andrew Swindn 47 H1
Bluntington Worcs 97 K8
Bluntisham Cambs 103 H8
Blunts Cnwll 6 C2
Blunts Green Warwks 82 D2
Blurton C Stke 114 D3
Blyborough Lincs 135 J1
Blyford Suffk 107 J8
Blymhill Staffs 97 H1
Blymhill Lawn Staffs 97 J1
Blyth Notts 134 C2
Blyth Nthumb 181 H3
Blyth Bridge Border 199 K4
Blythburgh Suffk 107 J8
Blyth Crematorium Nthumb 181 H3
Blythe Border 201 J3
Blythe Bridge Staffs 114 F3
Blythe End Warwks 99 G5

Blythe Marsh Staffs 114 F3
Blyton Lincs 135 G1
Boarhills Fife 223 K4
Boarhunt Hants 19 K2
Boarley Kent 53 G7
Boarsgreave Lancs 140 C4
Boarshead E Susx 38 E6
Boar's Head Wigan 139 H6
Boars Hill Oxon 66 D6
Boarstall Bucks 66 F4
Boasley Cross Devon 12 C4
Boath Highld 263 G5
Boat of Garten Highld 253 H7
Bobbing Kent 53 J6
Bobbington Staffs 97 H5
Bobbingworth Essex 70 D6
Bocaddon Cnwll 5 L3
Bocking Essex 71 J2
Bocking Churchstreet Essex 71 J2
Bockleton Worcs 80 D3
Boconnoc Cnwll 5 K3
Boddam Abers 257 L3
Boddam Shet 281 d8
Boddington Gloucs 64 C2
Bodedern IoA 124 F4
Bodelwyddan Denbgs 127 K4
Bodenham Herefs 80 C5
Bodenham Wilts 33 L5
Bodenham Moor Herefs 80 D5
Bodewryd IoA 125 G2
Bodfari Denbgs 128 C5
Bodffordd IoA 125 G4
Bodfuan Gwynd 108 E4
Bodham Norfk 122 C3
Bodiam E Susx 24 E2
Bodicote Oxon 83 K7
Bodieve Cnwll 10 D7
Bodinnick Cnwll 5 K4
Bodle Street Green E Susx 23 L4
Bodmin Cnwll 5 H2
Bodney Norfk 105 G4
Bodorgan IoA 125 G6
Bodsham Kent 40 E6
Bodwen Cnwll 5 H3
Bodymoor Heath Warwks 99 G4
Bogallan Highld 251 H2
Bogbrae Abers 257 J4
Bogend S Ayrs 196 D4
Boggs Holdings E Loth 212 A5
Boghall Mdloth 211 H6
Boghall W Loth 210 C5
Boghead S Lans 198 C4
Bogmoor Moray 267 G4
Bogmuir Abers 235 G1
Bogniebrae Abers 255 M3
Bognor Regis W Susx 20 F7
Bogroy Highld 253 G7
Bogue D & G 185 G6
Bohetherick Cnwll 6 E1
Bohortha Cnwll 3 L4
Bohuntine Highld 240 A6
Bojewyan Cnwll 2 B4
Bokiddick Cnwll 5 H2
Bolam Dur 169 G6
Bolam Nthumb 180 D2
Bolberry Devon 7 K7
Bold Heath St Hel 129 M2
Boldmere Birm 98 E4
Boldon Colliery S Tyne 181 J6
Boldre Hants 18 E4
Boldron Dur 168 C7
Bole Notts 134 F2
Bolehill Derbys 132 F8
Bole Hill Derbys 133 G5
Bolenowe Cnwll 3 H3
Bolham Devon 29 G7
Bolham Water Devon 29 L8
Bolingey Cnwll 4 C4
Bollington Ches E 131 J4
Bollington Cross Ches E 131 H4
Bollow Gloucs 63 L4
Bolney W Susx 37 L6
Bolnhurst Bed 86 B3
Bolnore W Susx 22 E3
Bolshan Angus 234 F7
Bolsover Derbys 133 J5
Bolster Moor Kirk 141 G5
Bolsterstone Sheff 141 L8
Boltby N York 161 H5
Boltenstone Abers 243 M2
Bolter End Bucks 67 J8
Bolton Bolton 139 L6
Bolton Cumb 166 E6
Bolton E Loth 212 B5
Bolton E R Yk 152 B5
Bolton Nthumb 191 G3
Bolton Abbey N York 149 K5
Bolton Bridge N York 149 K5
Bolton-by-Bowland Lancs 148 D6

Boltonfellend Cumb 178 B5
Boltongate Cumb 165 H3
Bolton-le-Sands Lancs 147 J2
Bolton Low Houses Cumb 165 H2
Bolton New Houses Cumb 165 H2
Bolton-on-Swale N York 160 C3
Bolton Percy N York 151 H7
Bolton Town End Lancs 147 J2
Bolton upon Dearne Barns 142 C7
Bolventor Cnwll 11 H7
Bomarsund Nthumb 181 G2
Bomere Heath Shrops 113 H8
Bonar Bridge Highld 263 G2
Bonawe Ag & B 228 F8
Bonby N Linc 144 C5
Boncath Pembks 75 L4
Bonchester Bridge Border 189 G4
Bonchurch IoW 19 K8
Bondleigh Devon 12 F2
Bonds Lancs 147 J6
Bonehill Devon 13 G7
Bonehill Staffs 99 G3
Bo'ness Falk 210 D3
Boney Hay Staffs 98 D2
Bonhill W Duns 208 C3
Boningale Shrops 97 J3
Bonjedward Border 189 H2
Bonkle N Lans 209 M7
Bonnington Angus 234 F7
Bonnington Kent 40 D8
Bonnybank Fife 222 F6
Bonnybridge Falk 209 L3
Bonnykelly Abers 268 F5
Bonnyrigg Mdloth 211 J6
Bonnyton Angus 233 M7
Bonsall Derbys 132 E8
Bonshaw Tower D & G 177 H4
Bont Mons 62 D3
Bontddu Gwynd 110 C7
Bont-Dolgadfan Powys 93 J3
Bont-goch Cerdgn 92 E6
Bonthorpe Lincs 137 J5
Bontnewydd Cerdgn 77 H2
Bontnewydd Gwynd 125 J7
Bontuchel Denbgs 128 C8
Bonvilston V Glam 43 G7
Bonwm Denbgs 111 L3
Bon-y-maen Swans 57 J6
Boode Devon 27 J3
Booker Bucks 49 K1
Booley Shrops 113 J6
Boon Border 201 J4
Boon Hill Staffs 114 C2
Boorley Green Hants 35 G8
Boosbeck R & Cl 170 F7
Boose's Green Essex 71 K1
Boot Cumb 155 M3
Booth Calder 141 G2
Boothby Graffoe Lincs 135 K7
Boothby Pagnell Lincs 118 C5
Boothferry E R Yk 143 J3
Booth Green Ches E 131 H3
Boothstown Salfd 139 L7
Booth Town Calder 141 G2
Boothville Nhants 84 F2
Bootle Cumb 155 K5
Bootle Sefton 138 D8
Boots Green Ches W 130 E5
Boot Street Suffk 90 F5
Booze N York 159 H2
Boraston Shrops 80 E1
Bordeaux Guern 9 k2
Borden Kent 53 J6
Borden W Susx 36 B6
Border Cumb 177 G8
Borders Crematorium Border 201 H6
Bordley N York 149 G3
Boreham Essex 71 J5
Boreham Wilts 32 E2
Boreham Street E Susx 24 B5
Borehamwood Herts 69 G7
Boreland D & G 187 J8
Boreraig Highld 258 B6
Boreton Shrops 96 C2
Borgh W Isls 282 g1
Borgh W Isls 283 b13
Borgie Highld 278 B4
Borgue D & G 175 G5
Borgue Highld 274 F5
Borley Essex 89 G6
Borley Green Essex 89 G6
Borley Green Suffk 89 K3
Borneskitaig Highld 258 F2
Borness D & G 174 F5
Boroughbridge N York 150 E3
Borough Green Kent 38 F2
Borras Head Wrexhm 112 E1
Borrowash Derbys 116 C4
Borrowby N York 160 F5

Borrowby N York 171 H7
Borrowstoun Falk 210 D3
Borstal Medway 52 F5
Borth Cerdgn 92 D5
Borthwickbrae Border 188 C3
Borthwickshiels Border 188 D3
Borth-y-Gest Gwynd 109 K4
Borve Highld 259 G7
Borve W Isls 282 d6
Borve W Isls 282 g1
Borve W Isls 283 b13
Borwick Lancs 147 K1
Borwick Lodge Cumb 156 E3
Borwick Rails Cumb 156 A6
Bosavern Cnwll 2 B5
Bosbury Herefs 80 F6
Boscarne Cnwll 5 H1
Boscastle Cnwll 10 F4
Boscombe Bmouth 17 M4
Boscombe Wilts 33 L3
Boscoppa Cnwll 5 H4
Bosham W Susx 20 C6
Bosham Hoe W Susx 20 D6
Bosherston Pembks 54 F7
Boskednan Cnwll 2 C4
Boskenna Cnwll 2 C6
Bosley Ches E 131 H6
Bosoughan Cnwll 4 E3
Bossall N York 151 M4
Bossiney Cnwll 10 F5
Bossingham Kent 40 F5
Bossington Somset 28 F1
Bostock Green Ches W 130 C6
Boston Lincs 119 K3
Boston Crematorium Lincs 119 K3
Boston Spa Leeds 150 F6
Boswarthan Cnwll 2 C4
Boswinger Cnwll 5 G6
Botallack Cnwll 2 B4
Botany Bay Gt Lon 69 J7
Botcheston Leics 100 B2
Botesdale Suffk 105 L8
Bothal Nthumb 180 F2
Bothampstead W Berk 48 D4
Bothamsall Notts 134 D5
Bothel Cumb 165 G3
Bothenhampton Dorset 15 L4
Bothwell S Lans 209 J7
Botley Bucks 68 B6
Botley Hants 35 G8
Botley Oxon 66 C6
Botolph Claydon Bucks 67 H2
Botolphs W Susx 21 L5
Botolph's Bridge Kent 40 F8
Bottesford Leics 117 L4
Bottesford N Linc 143 M6
Bottisham Cambs 87 L3
Bottomcraig Fife 222 F2
Bottom of Hutton Lancs 138 F2
Bottom o' th' Moor Bolton 139 K5
Bottoms Calder 140 D3
Bottoms Cnwll 2 B6
Botts Green Warwks 99 H5
Botusfleming Cnwll 6 E3
Botwnnog Gwynd 108 D5
Bough Beech Kent 38 D4
Boughrood Powys 79 G7
Boughspring Gloucs 63 H7
Boughton Nhants 84 E2
Boughton Norfk 104 D3
Boughton Notts 134 D6
Boughton Aluph Kent 40 D6
Boughton End C Beds 85 J7
Boughton Green Kent 39 J3
Boughton Malherbe Kent 39 M3
Boughton Monchelsea Kent 39 J3
Boughton Street Kent 40 D3
Boulby R & Cl 171 H7
Boulder Clough Calder 140 F3
Bouldnor IoW 18 F5
Bouldon Shrops 96 C6
Boulmer Nthumb 191 K3
Boulston Pembks 55 G4
Boultham Lincs 135 J6
Bourn Cambs 87 G4
Bourne Lincs 118 E7
Bournebridge Essex 70 D8
Bournebrook Birm 98 D6
Bourne End Bed 85 K3
Bourne End Bucks 49 L2
Bourne End C Beds 85 J6
Bourne End Herts 68 C6
Bournemouth Bmouth 17 L4
Bournemouth Crematorium
  Bmouth 17 M4
Bournes Green Gloucs 64 C6
Bournes Green Sthend 53 K2
Bournheath Worcs 98 B8
Bournmoor Dur 181 H8

Bournstream Gloucs 63 L8
Bournville Birm 98 D7
Bourton Dorset 32 C5
Bourton N Som 44 D6
Bourton Oxon 47 K2
Bourton Shrops 96 D4
Bourton Wilts 46 F6
Bourton on Dunsmore
  Warwks 83 K1
Bourton-on-the-Hill Gloucs 65 J1
Bourton-on-the-Water Gloucs 65 H3
Bousd Ag & B 225 H3
Boustead Hill Cumb 177 J7
Bouth Cumb 156 D5
Bouthwaite N York 149 L2
Bouts Worcs 82 B3
Boveney Bucks 50 B3
Boveridge Dorset 33 J7
Bovey Tracey Devon 13 J7
Bovingdon Herts 68 C6
Bovingdon Green Bucks 49 K2
Bovinger Essex 70 D6
Bovington Dorset 16 F5
Bovington Camp Dorset 16 F5
Bow Cumb 177 K7
Bow Devon 8 B3
Bow Devon 13 G2
Bow Gt Lon 51 K2
Bow Ork 275 c6
Bowbank Dur 168 B6
Bow Brickhill M Keyn 85 H8
Bowbridge Gloucs 64 B6
Bowburn Dur 169 J3
Bowcombe IoW 19 H6
Bowd Devon 14 D4
Bowden Border 201 H7
Bowden Devon 8 C5
Bowden Hill Wilts 46 D5
Bowdon Traffd 130 E2
Bower Highld 280 B4
Bowerchalke Wilts 33 H6
Bowerhill Wilts 46 C6
Bower Hinton Somset 31 G7
Bower House Tye Suffk 89 K7
Bowermadden Highld 280 B3
Bowers Staffs 114 C4
Bowers Gifford Essex 53 G1
Bowershall Fife 210 E1
Bower's Row Leeds 142 B2
Bowes Dur 168 C7
Bowgreave Lancs 147 K7
Bowhouse D & G 176 D5
Bowithick Cnwll 11 H6
Bowker's Green Lancs 138 E6
Bowland Border 200 F5
Bowland Bridge Cumb 156 F5
Bowley Herefs 80 C5
Bowley Town Herefs 80 C5
Bowlhead Green Surrey 36 D3
Bowling C Brad 141 J2
Bowling W Duns 208 D4
Bowling Bank Wrexhm 112 F2
Bowling Green Worcs 81 J5
Bowmanstead Cumb 156 D3
Bowmore Ag & B 204 D4
Bowness-on-Solway Cumb 177 H6
Bowness-on-Windermere
  Cumb 156 F3
Bow of Fife Fife 222 E4
Bowriefauld Angus 234 D6
Bowscale Cumb 165 K4
Bowsden Nthumb 202 F5
Bowston Cumb 157 H3
Bow Street Cerdgn 92 D6
Bow Street Norfk 105 L4
Bowthorpe Norfk 106 D2
Box Gloucs 64 B7
Box Wilts 46 B5
Boxbush Gloucs 63 K3
Boxbush Gloucs 63 L4
Box End Bed 85 K5
Boxford Suffk 89 K7
Boxford W Berk 48 B4
Boxgrove W Susx 20 E5
Box Hill Surrey 51 G8
Boxley Kent 53 G7
Boxmoor Herts 68 D6
Box's Shop Cnwll 11 H2
Boxted Essex 72 E1
Boxted Essex 89 K8
Boxted Suffk 89 G5
Boxted Cross Essex 72 E1
Boxwell Gloucs 64 A8
Boxworth Cambs 87 G2
Boyden End Suffk 88 E4
Boyden Gate Kent 41 H2
Boylestone Derbys 115 K4
Boyndie Abers 268 B3
Boyndlie Abers 269 G4

Boynton E R Yk 153 J2
Boysack Angus 234 F5
Boys Hill Dorset 16 C1
Boythorpe Derbys 133 G5
Boyton Cnwll 11 L4
Boyton Suffk 91 J6
Boyton Wilts 32 F3
Boyton Cross Essex 70 F5
Boyton End Suffk 88 E6
Bozeat Nhants 85 H3
Braaid IoM 154 d6
Brabling Green Suffk 91 G2
Brabourne Kent 40 E7
Brabourne Lees Kent 40 E7
Brabstermire Highld 280 D2
Bracadale Highld 246 E1
Braceborough Lincs 102 B1
Bracebridge Heath Lincs 135 K6
Bracebridge Low Fields Lincs 135 J6
Braceby Lincs 118 D4
Bracewell Lancs 148 F6
Brackenfield Derbys 133 G7
Brackenhirst N Lans 209 K5
Brackenthwaite Cumb 165 J1
Brackenthwaite N York 150 C5
Brackla Brdgnd 42 D5
Bracklesham W Susx 20 C7
Brackletter Highld 239 K7
Brackley Nhants 84 B7
Brackley Hatch Nhants 84 C7
Bracknell Br For 49 L5
Braco P & K 220 E5
Bracobrae Moray 267 K5
Bracon Ash Norfk 106 D3
Bracora Highld 237 L2
Bracorina Highld 237 L2
Bradaford Devon 11 M4
Bradbourne Derbys 115 K1
Bradbury Dur 169 J5
Bradden Nhants 84 C5
Braddock Cnwll 5 K2
Bradeley C Stke 114 D1
Bradenham Bucks 67 K7
Bradenstoke Wilts 46 E3
Bradfield Devon 14 B1
Bradfield Essex 73 H1
Bradfield Norfk 122 F5
Bradfield Sheff 132 E1
Bradfield W Berk 48 F4
Bradfield Combust Suffk 89 H4
Bradfield Green Ches E 130 D7
Bradfield Heath Essex 73 H1
Bradfield St Clare Suffk 89 H4
Bradfield St George Suffk 89 H3
Bradford C Brad 141 J1
Bradford Cnwll 11 G7
Bradford Devon 12 A1
Bradford Nthumb 180 C3
Bradford Nthumb 203 J6
Bradford Abbas Dorset 31 K8
Bradford Leigh Wilts 46 B6
Bradford-on-Avon Wilts 46 B6
Bradford-on-Tone Somset 30 B6
Bradford Peverell Dorset 16 C4
Bradiford Devon 27 K4
Brading IoW 19 K6
Bradley Derbys 115 L2
Bradley Hants 35 K3
Bradley Kirk 141 J4
Bradley N York 159 J6
Bradley NE Lin 145 G6
Bradley Staffs 114 D7
Bradley Wolves 98 B4
Bradley Worcs 82 A3
Bradley Wrexhm 112 E1
Bradley Common Ches W 113 H2
Bradley Green Somset 30 C3
Bradley Green Warwks 99 H3
Bradley Green Worcs 82 A3
Bradley in the Moors Staffs 115 H3
Bradley Stoke S Glos 45 J3
Bradmore Notts 117 G5
Bradney Somset 30 E3
Bradninch Devon 14 A2
Bradninch Devon 27 L4
Bradnop Staffs 131 K8
Bradnor Green Herefs 79 K4
Bradpole Dorset 15 L4
Bradshaw Bolton 139 L5
Bradshaw Calder 141 G2
Bradshaw Kirk 141 G5
Bradstone Devon 11 M6
Bradwall Green Ches E 130 E7
Bradwell Derbys 132 C3
Bradwell Devon 27 J2
Bradwell Essex 71 K3
Bradwell M Keyn 85 G7
Bradwell Norfk 107 K3
Bradwell Crematorium Staffs 114 D2

Bradwell-on-Sea Essex 72 E5
Bradwell Waterside Essex 72 E5
Bradworthy Devon 26 E8
Brae Highld 263 H7
Brae Shet 281 d4
Braeface Falk 209 K3
Braehead Angus 235 H5
Braehead D & G 173 K4
Braehead S Lans 198 F3
Braeintra Highld 248 D5
Braemar Abers 243 G5
Braemore Highld 261 L4
Braemore Highld 274 D4
Brae Roy Lodge Highld 240 B5
Braeside Inver 207 L4
Braes of Coul Angus 233 L4
Braes of Enzie Moray 267 H4
Braeswick Ork 275 e2
Braevallich Ag & B 216 E5
Brafferton Darltn 169 H6
Brafferton N York 150 F2
Brafield-on-the-Green Nhants 84 F3
Bragar W Isls 282 f2
Bragbury End Herts 69 J3
Braidwood S Lans 198 D3
Brailsford Derbys 115 L3
Brailsford Green Derbys 115 L3
Brain's Green Gloucs 63 K5
Braintree Essex 71 J2
Braiseworth Suffk 90 D1
Braishfield Hants 34 E6
Braithwaite C Brad 149 J3
Braithwaite Cumb 165 H6
Braithwell Donc 133 K1
Braken Hill Wakefd 142 C4
Bramber W Susx 21 L5
Brambridge Hants 35 G6
Bramcote Notts 116 E4
Bramcote Warwks 99 L5
Bramcote Crematorium Notts 116 E4
Bramdean Hants 35 J5
Bramerton Norfk 106 F2
Bramfield Herts 69 H4
Bramfield Suffk 107 H8
Bramford Suffk 90 D6
Bramhall Stockp 131 H3
Bramham Leeds 150 F7
Bramhope Leeds 150 C7
Bramley Hants 49 G7
Bramley Leeds 141 K1
Bramley Rothm 133 K1
Bramley Surrey 36 F2
Bramley Corner Hants 48 F7
Bramley Green Hants 49 G7
Bramley Head N York 149 L4
Bramling Kent 41 H4
Brampford Speke Devon 13 L3
Brampton Cambs 86 E1
Brampton Cumb 166 F6
Brampton Cumb 178 C6
Brampton Lincs 135 G4
Brampton Norfk 122 E5
Brampton Rothm 142 C7
Brampton Suffk 107 J1
Brampton Abbotts Herefs 63 J3
Brampton Ash Nhants 101 H6
Brampton Bryan Herefs 79 L1
Brampton-en-le-Morthen
  Rothm 133 J2
Bramshall Staffs 115 H5
Bramshaw Hants 34 C7
Bramshill Hants 49 H6
Bramshott Hants 36 C4
Bramwell Somset 31 G5
Branault Highld 237 G1
Brancaster Norfk 121 G3
Brancaster Staithe Norfk 121 H3
Brancepeth Dur 169 G3
Branchill Moray 266 B5
Brand End Lincs 119 L4
Branderburgh Moray 266 E2
Brandesburton E R Yk 153 H6
Brandeston Suffk 90 F4
Brand Green Gloucs 63 K2
Brandis Corner Devon 12 A1
Brandiston Norfk 122 C7
Brandon Dur 169 G2
Brandon Lincs 118 B3
Brandon Nthumb 190 F2
Brandon Suffk 104 F6
Brandon Warwks 99 L8
Brandon Bank Norfk 104 C5
Brandon Creek Norfk 104 C5
Brandon Parva Norfk 106 B2
Brandsby N York 151 J2
Brandy Wharf Lincs 144 C2
Brane Cnwll 2 C5
Bran End Essex 71 G2
Branksome Poole 17 L4

Branksome Park Poole 17 L4
Bransbury Hants 34 F2
Bransby Lincs 135 H4
Branscombe Devon 14 E5
Bransford Worcs 81 H5
Bransgore Hants 18 B4
Bransholme C KuH 144 E1
Bransley Shrops 96 E8
Branson's Cross Worcs 82 C1
Branston Leics 117 L6
Branston Lincs 135 L6
Branston Staffs 115 L6
Branston Booths Lincs 135 L6
Branstone IoW 19 J7
Brant Broughton Lincs 118 B1
Brantham Suffk 90 D8
Branthwaite Cumb 164 E5
Branthwaite Cumb 165 J3
Brantingham E R Yk 144 B2
Branton Donc 143 G7
Branton Nthumb 190 F3
Branton Green N York 150 F3
Branxton Nthumb 202 D5
Brassey Green Ches W 129 M7
Brassington Derbys 115 L1
Brasted Kent 38 D2
Brasted Chart Kent 51 M8
Brathens Abers 244 F4
Bratoft Lincs 137 J6
Brattleby Lincs 135 J3
Bratton Somset 29 G2
Bratton Wilts 46 C8
Bratton Wrekin 96 E1
Bratton Clovelly Devon 12 B4
Bratton Fleming Devon 27 M3
Bratton Seymour Somset 31 L5
Braughing Herts 69 K2
Braughing Friars Herts 70 B2
Braunston Nhants 84 A4
Braunston Rutlnd 101 H2
Braunstone Town Leics 100 C3
Braunton Devon 27 J4
Brawby N York 162 C7
Brawl Highld 278 D3
Braworth N York 161 H1
Bray W & M 49 L3
Braybrooke Nhants 101 G6
Braydon Wilts 46 F1
Braydon Brook Wilts 64 E8
Braydon Side Wilts 46 E2
Brayford Devon 28 B4
Bray's Hill E Susx 24 B4
Bray Shop Cnwll 11 L7
Braystones Cumb 155 H2
Braythorn N York 150 C6
Brayton N York 142 F2
Braywick W & M 49 L3
Braywoodside W & M 49 L4
Brazacott Cnwll 11 K4
Breach Kent 41 G6
Breach Kent 53 H6
Breachwood Green Herts 68 F3
Breaden Heath Shrops 113 J4
Breadsall Derbys 116 B4
Breadstone Gloucs 63 L7
Breadward Herefs 79 K4
Breage Cnwll 3 H5
Breakachy Highld 250 E3
Breakish Highld 247 L4
Breakspear Crematorium
Gt Lon 50 D1
Brealangwell Lodge Highld 262 F1
Bream Gloucs 63 J6
Breamore Hants 33 L7
Brean Somset 44 C7
Breanais W Isls 282 d4
Brearley Calder 140 F3
Brearton N York 150 D4
Breascleit W Isls 282 f3
Breasclete W Isls 282 f3
Breaston Derbys 116 D5
Brechfa Carmth 58 F3
Brechin Angus 234 F3
Breckles Norfk 105 J4
Brecon Powys 61 G2
Bredbury Stockp 131 H2
Brede E Susx 24 E4
Bredenbury Herefs 80 E4
Bredfield Suffk 91 G4
Bredgar Kent 53 J7
Bredhurst Kent 53 L6
Bredon Worcs 81 L7
Bredon's Hardwick Worcs 81 L8
Bredon's Norton Worcs 81 L7
Bredwardine Herefs 79 L6
Breedon on the Hill Leics 116 C7
Breich W Loth 210 C7
Breightmet Bolton 139 L6
Breighton E R Yk 143 H1

Breinton Herefs 80 B7
Bremhill Wilts 46 E4
Bremridge Devon 28 B5
Brenchley Kent 39 H5
Brendon Devon 11 L1
Brendon Devon 28 D1
Brendon Hill Somset 29 J4
Brenfield Ag & B 206 D3
Brenish W Isls 282 d4
Brenkley N u Ty 180 F4
Brent Cross Gt Lon 51 G2
Brent Eleigh Suffk 89 J5
Brentford Gt Lon 50 F3
Brentingby Leics 117 K7
Brent Knoll Somset 30 E1
Brent Mill Devon 7 K3
Brent Pelham Herts 70 B1
Brentwood Essex 70 E8
Brenzett Kent 25 J2
Brenzett Green Kent 25 J2
Brereton Staffs 115 G8
Brereton Green Ches E 130 F6
Brereton Heath Ches E 130 F6
Brereton Hill Staffs 115 G8
Bressay Shet 281 e6
Bressingham Norfk 106 B7
Bressingham Common Norfk 106 B7
Bretby Derbys 116 A7
Bretby Crematorium Derbys 115 M7
Bretford Warwks 99 J2
Bretforton Worcs 82 C6
Bretherton Lancs 138 F4
Breton C Pete 102 D3
Brettabister Shet 281 e5
Brettenham Norfk 105 J6
Brettenham Suffk 89 K4
Bretton Derbys 132 D4
Bretton Flints 129 H7
Brewers End Essex 70 E3
Brewer Street Surrey 51 J8
Brewood Staffs 97 K2
Briantspuddle Dorset 16 F4
Brick End Essex 70 E2
Brickendon Herts 69 J5
Bricket Wood Herts 68 E6
Brick Houses Sheff 132 F3
Brickkiln Green Essex 71 H1
Bricklehampton Worcs 82 A6
Bride IoM 154 f2
Bridekirk Cumb 164 F4
Bridell Pembks 75 L4
Bridestowe Devon 12 C5
Brideswell Abers 255 M4
Bridford Devon 13 J3
Bridge Kent 41 G4
Bridge End Cumb 156 A6
Bridge End Cumb 165 L1
Bridge End Devon 7 K5
Bridge End Dur 168 C3
Bridge End Essex 71 G1
Bridge End Lincs 118 F4
Bridgefoot Angus 234 B8
Bridgefoot Cumb 164 E5
Bridge Green Essex 87 K7
Bridgehampton Somset 31 J6
Bridge Hewick N York 150 D2
Bridgehill Dur 180 D8
Bridgehouse Gate N York 149 L3
Bridgemary Hants 19 K3
Bridgemere Ches E 113 M2
Bridgend Abers 255 K4
Bridgend Ag & B 194 B3
Bridgend Ag & B 204 E4
Bridgend Angus 234 E2
Bridgend Brdgnd 42 D5
Bridgend Cerdgn 75 L3
Bridgend Cumb 165 L7
Bridgend D & G 187 G4
Bridgend Devon 7 G5
Bridgend Fife 223 G5
Bridgend Moray 255 H5
Bridgend P & K 221 L2
Bridgend W Loth 210 D4
Bridgend of Lintrathen Angus 233 L4
Bridge of Alford Abers 255 L8
Bridge of Allan Stirlg 220 D7
Bridge of Avon Moray 254 C7
Bridge of Avon Moray 254 D4
Bridge of Balgie P & K 231 G6
Bridge of Brewlands Angus 233 J3
Bridge of Brown Highld 254 C7
Bridge of Cally P & K 233 H5
Bridge of Canny Abers 244 E4
Bridge of Craigisla Angus 233 K4
Bridge of Dee D & G 175 J3
Bridge of Don C Aber 245 L2
Bridge of Dye Abers 244 E6
Bridge of Earn P & K 221 L3
Bridge of Ericht P & K 230 F4

Bridge of Feugh Abers 244 F4
Bridge of Gairn Abers 243 K4
Bridge of Gaur P & K 230 F4
Bridge of Marnoch Abers 267 M6
Bridge of Muchalls Abers 245 K5
Bridge of Orchy Ag & B 230 B7
Bridge of Tilt P & K 232 C2
Bridge of Tynet Moray 267 H4
Bridge of Walls Shet 281 c6
Bridge of Weir Rens 208 C5
Bridge Reeve Devon 28 B8
Bridgerule Devon 11 K2
Bridges Shrops 95 J4
Bridge Sollers Herefs 80 A7
Bridge Street Suffk 89 H5
Bridgetown Cnwll 11 L5
Bridgetown Somset 29 G4
Bridge Trafford Ches W 129 K5
Bridge Yate S Glos 45 K4
Bridgham Norfk 105 J6
Bridgnorth Shrops 97 G5
Bridgwater Somset 30 D3
Bridlington E R Yk 153 K3
Bridport Dorset 15 K4
Bridstow Herefs 63 H2
Brierfield Lancs 148 E8
Brierley Barns 142 B5
Brierley Gloucs 63 J4
Brierley Herefs 80 C4
Brierley Hill Dudley 97 L6
Brierlow Bar Derbys 132 B5
Brierton Hartpl 170 B5
Briery Cumb 165 J6
Brigg N Linc 144 C6
Briggate Norfk 123 G6
Briggswath N York 162 F1
Brigham Cumb 164 E4
Brigham Cumb 165 J6
Brigham E R Yk 153 H5
Brighouse Calder 141 J3
Brighstone IoW 19 G7
Brightgate Derbys 132 E7
Brighthampton Oxon 66 A6
Brightholmlee Sheff 132 F1
Brightley Devon 12 E3
Brightling E Susx 24 C3
Brightlingsea Essex 73 G4
Brighton Br & H 22 D6
Brighton Cnwll 4 E4
Brighton le Sands Sefton 138 C7
Brightons Falk 210 B3
Brightwalton W Berk 48 B3
Brightwalton Green W Berk 48 B3
Brightwalton Holt W Berk 48 B3
Brightwell Suffk 90 F6
Brightwell Baldwin Oxon 67 G8
Brightwell-cum-Sotwell Oxon 48 E1
Brightwell Upperton Oxon 67 G8
Brignall Dur 168 D8
Brig o'Turk Stirlg 219 J6
Brigsley NE Lin 145 H7
Brigsteer Cumb 157 G5
Brigstock Nhants 101 L6
Brill Bucks 67 G4
Brill Cnwll 3 J5
Brilley Herefs 79 J5
Brimfield Herefs 80 C2
Brimfield Cross Herefs 80 C2
Brimington Derbys 133 H5
Brimley Devon 13 J7
Brimpsfield Gloucs 64 D4
Brimpton W Berk 48 E6
Brimpton Common W Berk 48 E6
Brimscombe Gloucs 64 C6
Brimstage Wirral 129 G3
Brincliffe Sheff 132 F3
Brind E R Yk 143 J2
Brindham Somset 31 H3
Brindister Shet 281 c5
Brindle Lancs 139 J3
Brindley Ches E 113 K1
Brineton Staffs 97 H1
Bringhurst Leics 101 J5
Bringsty Common Herefs 81 G4
Brington Cambs 102 B8
Briningham Norfk 122 A5
Brinkely Notts 117 J1
Brinkhill Lincs 137 G5
Brinkley Cambs 88 C4
Brinklow Warwks 99 J1
Brinkworth Wilts 46 E2
Brinscall Lancs 139 J3
Brinscombe Somset 44 E8
Brinsea N Som 44 F7
Brinsley Notts 116 D2
Brinsop Herefs 80 B6
Brinsworth Rothm 133 H2
Brinton Norfk 122 A4
Brinyan Ork 275 c3

Brisco Cumb 178 A8
Brisley Norfk 121 L7
Brislington Bristl 45 J5
Brissenden Green Kent 40 B7
Bristol Bristl 45 H4
Briston Norfk 122 B5
Brisworthy Devon 7 G2
Britannia Lancs 140 C3
Britford Wilts 33 L5
Brithdir Caerph 61 J6
Brithdir Gwynd 110 E7
British Legion Village Kent 52 F7
Briton Ferry Neath 57 K6
Britwell Salome Oxon 67 G8
Brixham Torbay 8 D4
Brixton Devon 7 G4
Brixton Gt Lon 51 J4
Brixton Deverill Wilts 32 E3
Brixworth Nhants 84 E1
Brize Norton Oxon 65 L5
Broad Alley Worcs 81 K2
Broad Blunsdon Swindn 47 H1
Broadbottom Tamesd 131 K1
Broadbridge W Susx 20 D6
Broadbridge Heath W Susx 37 H4
Broad Campden Gloucs 82 E7
Broad Carr Calder 141 H4
Broad Chalke Wilts 33 H5
Broad Clough Lancs 140 C3
Broadclyst Devon 14 A3
Broadfield Inver 208 B4
Broadfield Pembks 55 K6
Broadford Highld 247 K4
Broad Ford Kent 39 H5
Broadford Bridge W Susx 37 G6
Broadgairhill Border 187 K4
Broadgrass Green Suffk 89 K3
Broad Green Cambs 88 D3
Broad Green Essex 72 C2
Broad Green Worcs 81 H4
Broad Green Worcs 82 A1
Broadhaugh Border 202 D2
Broad Haven Pembks 54 D4
Broadheath Traffd 130 E2
Broadheath Worcs 80 F2
Broadhembury Devon 14 C2
Broadhempston Devon 8 B2
Broad Hill Cambs 104 B8
Broad Hinton Wilts 47 G4
Broadholme Lincs 135 H5
Broadland Row E Susx 24 F3
Broadlay Carmth 56 C3
Broad Layings Hants 48 B6
Broadley Essex 70 B5
Broadley Lancs 140 C4
Broadley Moray 267 H4
Broadley Common Essex 70 B5
Broad Marston Worcs 82 D6
Broadmayne Dorset 16 D5
Broad Meadow Staffs 114 C2
Broadmere Hants 35 J2
Broadmoor Gloucs 63 J4
Broadmoor Pembks 55 J5
Broadnymett Devon 13 G2
Broad Oak Carmth 59 G4
Broad Oak Cumb 155 K4
Broadoak Dorset 15 K3
Broad Oak E Susx 23 K3
Broad Oak E Susx 24 E3
Broadoak Gloucs 63 K4
Broad Oak Hants 49 H8
Broad Oak Herefs 62 F3
Broad Oak Kent 41 G3
Broad Oak St Hel 139 G8
Broadoak Wrexhm 129 J7
Broad Road Suffk 106 F8
Broadsands Torbay 8 D3
Broad's Green Essex 71 G4
Broadstairs Kent 41 L2
Broadstone Mons 63 G6
Broadstone Poole 17 K3
Broadstone Shrops 96 C5
Broad Street E Susx 24 E4
Broad Street Essex 70 E4
Broad Street Kent 39 L2
Broad Street Kent 40 F7
Broad Street Medway 53 G4
Broad Street Wilts 47 G7
Broad Street Green Essex 71 L5
Broad Town Wilts 47 G3
Broadwas Worcs 81 H4
Broadwater Herts 69 H3
Broadwater W Susx 21 K6
Broadwaters Worcs 97 J7
Broadway Carmth 56 B3
Broadway Carmth 56 C3
Broadway Pembks 54 E4
Broadway Somset 30 D7
Broadway Suffk 107 H7

Broadway Worcs 82 C7
Broadwell Gloucs 63 H5
Broadwell Gloucs 65 J2
Broadwell Oxon 65 K6
Broadwell Warwks 83 K2
Broadwey Dorset 16 C6
Broadwindsor Dorset 15 K2
Broadwood Kelly Devon 12 E2
Broadwoodwidger Devon 12 E3
Brobury Herefs 79 L6
Brochel Highld 259 K7
Brochroy Ag & B 216 F1
Brock Lancs 147 K2
Brockamin Worcs 81 H4
Brockbridge Hants 35 J7
Brockdish Norfk 106 E7
Brockencote Worcs 97 K8
Brockenhurst Hants 18 D3
Brocketsbrae S Lans 198 D5
Brockford Green Suffk 90 D2
Brockford Street Suffk 90 D2
Brockhall Nhants 84 C3
Brockham Surrey 37 J1
Brockhampton Gloucs 64 D2
Brockhampton Gloucs 64 F3
Brockhampton Hants 20 B5
Brockhampton Herefs 63 H1
Brockhampton Green Dorset 16 D2
Brockholes Kirk 141 J5
Brockhurst Derbys 133 G6
Brockhurst Warwks 100 A6
Brocklebank Cumb 165 J2
Brocklesby Lincs 144 K5
Brockley N Som 44 F5
Brockley Suffk 89 G1
Brockley Green Suffk 88 E6
Brockley Green Suffk 89 G4
Brockleymoor Cumb 166 C3
Brockmoor Dudley 97 K5
Brockscombe Devon 12 B4
Brock's Green Hants 48 D6
Brockton Shrops 95 H3
Brockton Shrops 95 H6
Brockton Shrops 96 D4
Brockton Shrops 97 G3
Brockton Staffs 114 C5
Brockweir Gloucs 63 G6
Brockwood Park Hants 35 K5
Brockworth Gloucs 64 C4
Brocton Cnwll 5 G1
Brocton Staffs 114 F7
Brodick N Ayrs 195 G4
Brodie Moray 264 F8
Brodsworth Donc 142 D6
Brogaig Highld 259 H3
Brogborough C Beds 85 J7
Brokenborough Wilts 46 D1
Broken Cross Ches E 131 H5
Broken Cross Ches W 130 D5
Brokerswood Wilts 46 B8
Bromborough Wirral 129 H3
Brome Suffk 106 C8
Brome Street Suffk 106 C8
Bromeswell Suffk 91 G5
Bromfield Cumb 165 G1
Bromfield Shrops 96 B8
Bromham Bed 85 K5
Bromham Wilts 46 D6
Bromley Barns 141 M7
Bromley Dudley 97 K5
Bromley Gt Lon 51 L5
Bromley Shrops 97 G4
Bromley Common Gt Lon 51 L5
Bromley Cross Bolton 139 L5
Bromley Cross Essex 72 F2
Bromley Green Kent 40 C8
Bromlow Shrops 95 H3
Brompton Medway 53 G5
Brompton N York 160 E3
Brompton-by-Sawdon N York 163 G6
Brompton-on-Swale N York 160 B3
Brompton Ralph Somset 29 K4
Brompton Regis Somset 29 G4
Bromsash Herefs 63 J2
Bromsberrow Gloucs 81 G8
Bromsberrow Heath Gloucs 81 G8
Bromsgrove Worcs 81 M1
Bromstead Heath Staffs 114 B8
Bromyard Herefs 80 F4
Bromyard Downs Herefs 80 F4
Bronaber Gwynd 110 D5
Bronant Cerdgn 77 H2
Broncroft Shrops 96 C6
Brongest Cerdgn 76 B6
Bronington Wrexhm 113 H3
Bronllys Powys 79 G8
Bronwydd Carmth 58 D4
Bronydd Powys 79 J6
Bronygarth Shrops 112 C4

Brook Carmth 56 A3
Brook Hants 34 C8
Brook Hants 34 D5
Brook IoW 18 F6
Brook Kent 40 E6
Brook Surrey 36 D3
Brook Surrey 37 G2
Brooke Norfk 106 F3
Brooke Rutlnd 101 J2
Brookenby Lincs 145 G8
Brook End Bed 86 B3
Brook End C Beds 86 D5
Brook End Cambs 86 B3
Brook End M Keyn 85 H6
Brookfield Rens 208 C6
Brookhampton Oxon 66 F7
Brookhampton Somset 31 K5
Brook Hill Hants 34 C7
Brook House Denbgs 128 C6
Brookhouse Lancs 147 K3
Brookhouse Rothm 133 K2
Brookhouse Green Ches E 130 F7
Brookhouses Derbys 131 K2
Brookland Kent 25 J2
Brooklands Traffd 130 F2
Brookmans Park Herts 69 H6
Brooks Powys 94 E3
Brooksby Leics 117 H8
Brooks End Kent 41 J2
Brooks Green W Susx 37 H6
Brook Street Essex 70 E8
Brook Street Kent 40 B8
Brook Street Suffk 89 G5
Brook Street W Susx 22 D2
Brookthorpe Gloucs 64 B4
Brookville Norfk 104 E4
Brookwood Surrey 50 B7
Broom C Beds 86 D6
Broom Rothm 133 J1
Broom Warwks 82 C4
Broombank Worcs 80 F1
Broome Norfk 107 G5
Broome Shrops 95 K7
Broome Worcs 97 K7
Broomedge Warrtn 130 D3
Broome Park Nthumb 191 G4
Broomer's Corner W Susx 21 K3
Broomershill W Susx 21 H3
Broomfield Essex 71 H5
Broomfield Kent 39 L3
Broomfield Kent 41 G2
Broomfield Somset 30 B4
Broomfields Shrops 112 F7
Broomfleet E R Yk 143 M2
Broom Green Norfk 121 L6
Broomhall W & M 50 B5
Broomhaugh Nthumb 180 B6
Broom Hill Barns 142 C7
Broom Hill Dorset 17 K2
Broom Hill Notts 116 F2
Broomhill Nthumb 191 K6
Broom Hill Worcs 97 L8
Broomhill Green Ches E 113 K2
Broomley Nthumb 180 C6
Broompark Dur 169 H2
Broom's Green Gloucs 81 G8
Broomsthorpe Norfk 121 J6
Broom Street Kent 40 D3
Brora Highld 274 B7
Broseley Shrops 96 F3
Brotherhouse Bar Lincs 119 J8
Brotherlee Dur 167 L3
Brothertoft Lincs 119 J2
Brotherton N York 142 D3
Brotton R & Cl 170 F6
Broubster Highld 279 J4
Brough Cumb 167 J7
Brough Derbys 132 D3
Brough E R Yk 144 B2
Brough Highld 280 B2
Brough Notts 135 G7
Brough Shet 281 f5
Brough Lodge Shet 281 f3
Brough Sowerby Cumb 167 J8
Broughton Border 199 K6
Broughton Bucks 67 K4
Broughton Cambs 102 F7
Broughton Flints 129 H7
Broughton Hants 34 C4
Broughton Lancs 139 G1
Broughton M Keyn 85 H7
Broughton N Linc 144 B6
Broughton N York 149 G5
Broughton N York 162 D8
Broughton Nhants 101 H8
Broughton Oxon 83 K7
Broughton Salfd 140 B7
Broughton Staffs 114 B5

Broughton V Glam 42 D7
Broughton Astley Leics 100 B5
Broughton Beck Cumb 156 C6
Broughton Gifford Wilts 46 C6
Broughton Green Worcs 81 M3
Broughton Hackett Worcs 81 L4
Broughton-in-Furness Cumb 156 B5
Broughton Mains D & G 174 C6
Broughton Mills Cumb 156 B4
Broughton Moor Cumb 164 E4
Broughton Poggs Oxon 65 K6
Broughton Tower Cumb 156 B5
Broughty Ferry C Dund 223 H1
Brough with St Giles N York 160 B3
Brow End Cumb 156 C7
Brownber Cumb 158 B2
Brown Candover Hants 35 J3
Brown Edge Lancs 138 D5
Brown Edge Staffs 114 E1
Brown Heath Ches W 129 K6
Brownheath Shrops 113 G5
Brownhill Abers 256 F4
Brownhills Fife 223 J4
Brownhills Wsall 98 D2
Brownieside Nthumb 191 H2
Browninghill Green Hants 48 E7
Brown Lees Staffs 131 G8
Brownlow Heath Ches E 131 G7
Brownrigg Cumb 164 D6
Brownrigg Cumb 177 G8
Brownsea Island Dorset 17 K5
Brown's Green Birm 98 D5
Brownsham Devon 26 E5
Browns Hill Gloucs 64 C6
Brownsover Warwks 100 B7
Brownston Devon 7 K4
Brown Street Suffk 90 C3
Brow-of-the-Hill Norfk 120 E7
Browston Green Norfk 107 K3
Broxa N York 163 G4
Broxbourne Herts 69 K5
Broxburn E Loth 212 F3
Broxburn W Loth 210 E4
Broxfield Nthumb 191 J3
Broxted Essex 70 E2
Broxton Ches W 113 H1
Broyle Side E Susx 23 G4
Bruan Highld 280 D8
Bruar P & K 232 B2
Bruchag Ag & B 207 J7
Bruera Ches W 129 K7
Bruern Abbey Oxon 65 K3
Bruichladdich Ag & B 204 C4
Bruisyard Suffk 91 H2
Bruisyard Street Suffk 91 H2
Brumby N Linc 143 M6
Brund Staffs 132 B7
Brundall Norfk 107 G2
Brundish Suffk 91 G1
Brundish Street Suffk 91 G1
Brunery Highld 237 L6
Brunnion Cnwll 2 D4
Brunslow Shrops 95 J6
Brunswick Village N u Ty 180 F4
Bruntcliffe Leeds 141 L2
Brunthwaite C Brad 149 J6
Bruntingthorpe Leics 100 D5
Brunton Fife 222 E3
Brunton Nthumb 191 J1
Brunton Wilts 47 K7
Brushford Devon 12 F1
Brushford Somset 29 G5
Bruton Somset 31 L4
Bryan's Green Worcs 81 K2
Bryanston Dorset 17 G1
Bryant's Bottom Bucks 67 L7
Brydekirk D & G 177 G5
Bryher IoS 10 b2
Brymbo Wrexhm 112 D1
Brympton Somset 31 H7
Bryn Carmth 57 G5
Bryn Ches W 130 B5
Bryn Neath 42 B3
Bryn Shrops 95 H6
Bryn Wigan 139 H7
Brynamman Carmth 59 K6
Brynberian Pembks 75 J5
Brynbryddan Neath 57 L6
Bryn-bwbach Gwynd 110 B4
Bryncae Rhondd 42 F5
Bryncethin Brdgnd 42 D5
Bryncir Gwynd 109 H3
Bryn-côch Neath 57 K5
Bryncroes Gwynd 108 C5
Bryncrug Gwynd 92 D3
Bryn Du IoA 124 F5
Bryn-Eden Gwynd 110 D5
Bryneglwys Denbgs 112 A2
Brynfields Wrexhm 112 D3

Brynford Flints 128 E5
Bryn Gates Wigan 139 J7
Bryn Golau Rhondd 42 F4
Bryngwran IoA 124 F4
Bryngwyn Mons 62 D5
Bryngwyn Powys 79 H5
Bryn-Henllan Pembks 75 G4
Brynhoffnant Cerdgn 76 B5
Bryning Lancs 138 E2
Brynithel Blae G 61 K6
Brynmawr Blae G 61 J5
Bryn-mawr Gwynd 108 D3
Brynmenyn Brdgnd 42 D5
Brynmill Swans 57 H6
Brynna Rhondd 42 F5
Bryn-penarth Powys 94 D3
Brynrefail Gwynd 125 K7
Brynrefail IoA 125 H1
Brynsadler Rhondd 42 F5
Bryn Saith Marchog Denbgs 111 L2
Brynsiencyn IoA 125 H6
Brynteg IoA 125 J3
Bryn-y-bal Flints 128 F6
Bryn-y-Maen Conwy 127 G4
Bryn-yr-Eos Wrexhm 112 D3
Bualintur Highld 246 F2
Buarth-draw Flints 128 E4
Bubbenhall Warwks 83 J1
Bubwith E R Yk 151 M8
Buccleuch Border 188 B3
Buchanan Smithy Stirlg 208 D1
Buchanhaven Abers 269 L6
Buchanty P & K 221 G2
Buchany Stirlg 220 C6
Buchlyvie Stirlg 219 J8
Buckabank Cumb 165 L1
Buckden Cambs 86 D2
Buckden N York 159 G2
Buckenham Norfk 107 G2
Buckerell Devon 14 D3
Buckfast Devon 7 L2
Buckfastleigh Devon 7 L2
Buckhaven Fife 222 F7
Buckholt Mons 63 G4
Buckhorn Devon 11 M3
Buckhorn Weston Dorset 32 C6
Buckhurst Hill Essex 69 L8
Buckie Moray 267 J3
Buckingham Bucks 84 D8
Buckland Bucks 67 L4
Buckland Devon 7 K6
Buckland Gloucs 82 C8
Buckland Hants 18 E4
Buckland Herts 87 G3
Buckland Kent 41 J6
Buckland Oxon 65 M7
Buckland Surrey 37 K1
Buckland Brewer Devon 27 G6
Buckland Common Bucks 68 A5
Buckland Dinham Somset 32 C1
Buckland Filleigh Devon 12 B1
Buckland in the Moor Devon 13 G7
Buckland Monachorum Devon 6 F1
Buckland Newton Dorset 16 D2
Buckland Ripers Dorset 16 C6
Buckland St Mary Somset 30 C8
Buckland-Tout-Saints Devon 7 L5
Bucklebury W Berk 48 E5
Bucklers Hard Hants 18 F4
Bucklesham Suffk 90 F6
Buckley Flints 129 G7
Buckley Green Warwks 82 E2
Bucklow Hill Ches E 130 E3
Buckminster Leics 118 A7
Bucknall C Stke 114 E2
Bucknall Lincs 136 C6
Bucknell Oxon 66 E2
Bucknell Shrops 95 J8
Buckpool Moray 267 J3
Bucksburn C Aber 245 K2
Buck's Cross Devon 26 F6
Bucks Green W Susx 37 G4
Buckshaw Village Lancs 139 H4
Bucks Hill Herts 68 D7
Bucks Horn Oak Hants 36 B3
Buck's Mills Devon 26 F6
Buckton E R Yk 153 K1
Buckton Herefs 95 J8
Buckton Nthumb 203 H5
Buckworth Cambs 102 C8
Budby Notts 134 C5
Buddileigh Staffs 114 B2
Bude Cnwll 11 H2
Budge's Shop Cnwll 6 A3
Budlake Devon 14 A3
Budle Nthumb 203 J6
Budleigh Salterton Devon 14 C6
Budlett's Common E Susx 23 H3
Budock Water Cnwll 3 K5

Buerton Ches E 113 L3
Bugbrooke Nhants 84 D4
Bugford Devon 8 B5
Buglawton Ches E 131 G7
Bugle Cnwll 5 G3
Bugley Dorset 32 C6
Bugthorpe E R Yk 152 B4
Buildwas Shrops 96 E2
Builth Road Powys 78 E4
Builth Wells Powys 78 E5
Bulbourne Herts 68 B4
Bulbridge Wilts 33 J5
Bulby Lincs 118 D6
Bulford Wilts 33 L2
Bulford Camp Wilts 33 L2
Bulkeley Ches E 113 J1
Bulkington Warwks 99 K6
Bulkington Wilts 46 D7
Bulkworthy Devon 27 G8
Bullamoor N York 160 F4
Bull Bay IoA 125 G1
Bullbridge Derbys 116 B1
Bullbrook Br For 49 L5
Bullen's Green Herts 69 G6
Bulley Gloucs 63 M3
Bullgill Cumb 164 E3
Bullinghope Herefs 80 C7
Bullington Hants 34 F3
Bullington Lincs 136 A4
Bullockstone Kent 41 G2
Bull's Green Herts 69 H4
Bull's Green Norfk 107 J4
Bulmer Essex 89 G7
Bulmer N York 151 L2
Bulmer Tye Essex 89 G7
Bulphan Thurr 52 D2
Bulstone Devon 14 E4
Bulstrode Herts 68 C6
Bulverhythe E Susx 24 D5
Bulwark Abers 257 G3
Bulwell C Nott 116 F3
Bulwick Nhants 101 L4
Bumble's Green Essex 69 L6
Bunacaimb Highld 237 J3
Bunarkaig Highld 239 K6
Bunbury Ches E 130 A8
Bunbury Heath Ches E 130 A8
Bunchrew Highld 251 H3
Buncton W Susx 21 K4
Bundalloch Highld 248 E6
Bunessan Ag & B 226 D8
Bungay Suffk 107 G5
Bunker's Hill Lincs 119 J1
Bunnahabhain Ag & B 204 F2
Bunny Notts 117 G5
Buntait Highld 250 C5
Buntingford Herts 69 K1
Bunwell Norfk 106 C4
Bunwell Hill Norfk 106 C5
Bupton Derbys 115 L4
Burbage Derbys 131 L5
Burbage Leics 99 L5
Burbage Wilts 47 K6
Burcher Herefs 79 L3
Burchett's Green E Susx 39 G7
Burchett's Green W & M 49 K3
Burcombe Wilts 33 J5
Burcot Oxon 66 E7
Burcot Worcs 82 A1
Burcote Shrops 97 G4
Burcott Bucks 67 K4
Burcott Bucks 67 L2
Burdale N York 152 D3
Bures Essex 89 H8
Burford Oxon 65 K5
Burford Shrops 80 D2
Burg Ag & B 226 D3
Burgate Suffk 106 B8
Burgates Hants 36 A5
Burge End Herts 68 F1
Burgess Hill W Susx 22 E3
Burgh Suffk 90 F5
Burgh by Sands Cumb 177 K7
Burgh Castle Norfk 107 K2
Burghclere Hants 48 C6
Burghead Moray 266 C2
Burghfield W Berk 49 G5
Burghfield Common W Berk 49 G5
Burgh Heath Surrey 51 H7
Burgh Hill E Susx 24 C2
Burghill Herefs 80 B6
Burgh Island Devon 7 J6
Burgh le Marsh Lincs 137 J6
Burgh next Aylsham Norfk 122 E6
Burgh on Bain Lincs 136 D2
Burgh St Margaret Norfk 123 J8
Burgh St Peter Norfk 107 K5
Burghwallis Donc 142 E5
Burham Kent 52 F6

Buriton Hants 20 B3
Burland Ches E 113 K1
Burlawn Cnwll 10 D8
Burleigh Gloucs 64 C6
Burlescombe Devon 29 K7
Burleston Dorset 16 E4
Burlestone Devon 8 B5
Burley Hants 18 C3
Burley Rutlnd 101 J1
Burley Shrops 96 B7
Burleydam Ches E 113 K3
Burley Gate Herefs 80 E6
Burley in Wharfedale C Brad 149 L6
Burley Lawn Hants 18 C3
Burley Street Hants 18 B3
Burley Wood Head C Brad 149 L7
Burlingham Green Norfk 107 H1
Burlingjobb Powys 79 J4
Burlington Shrops 97 H1
Burlton Shrops 113 G6
Burmarsh Kent 25 L1
Burmington Warwks 83 G7
Burn N York 142 F2
Burnage Manch 131 G1
Burnaston Derbys 115 M5
Burnbanks Cumb 166 C7
Burnbrae N Lans 210 A7
Burn Bridge N York 150 D5
Burnby E R Yk 152 C6
Burn Cross Sheff 142 A8
Burndell W Susx 21 G6
Burnden Bolton 139 L6
Burnedge Rochdl 140 D5
Burneside Cumb 157 H3
Burneston N York 160 D5
Burnett BaNES 45 K6
Burnfoot Border 188 C4
Burnfoot Border 188 F3
Burnfoot D & G 177 K1
Burnfoot D & G 186 E7
Burnfoot D & G 188 C6
Burnfoot P & K 221 H6
Burnham Bucks 50 A3
Burnham N Linc 144 D4
Burnham Deepdale Norfk 121 H3
Burnham Green Herts 69 H4
Burnham Market Norfk 121 H3
Burnham Norton Norfk 121 H3
Burnham-on-Crouch Essex 72 D7
Burnham-on-Sea Somset 30 D1
Burnham Overy Norfk 121 J3
Burnham Overy Staithe Norfk 121 J3
Burnham Thorpe Norfk 121 J3
Burnhead D & G 186 C7
Burnhervie Abers 256 C7
Burnhill Green Staffs 97 H3
Burnhope Dur 169 G1
Burnhouse N Ayrs 196 D1
Burniston N York 163 H4
Burnley Lancs 140 C1
Burnley Crematorium Lancs 140 B2
Burnmouth Border 213 L6
Burn Naze Lancs 147 G7
Burn of Cambus Stirlg 220 C6
Burnopfield Dur 180 E7
Burnrigg Cumb 178 C7
Burnsall N York 149 J3
Burnside Angus 234 C3
Burnside Angus 234 D5
Burnside Fife 222 B5
Burnside Moray 266 D2
Burnside W Loth 210 E4
Burnside of Duntrune Angus 234 C8
Burntcommon Surrey 50 D8
Burntheath Derbys 115 L5
Burnt Heath Essex 72 F2
Burnt Hill W Berk 48 E4
Burnthouse Cnwll 3 K4
Burnt Houses Dur 168 E6
Burntisland Fife 211 H2
Burnt Oak E Susx 23 H2
Burnton E Ayrs 184 D2
Burntwood Staffs 98 D2
Burntwood Green Staffs 98 D2
Burnt Yates N York 150 C4
Burnworthy Somset 30 B7
Burpham Surrey 50 C8
Burpham W Susx 21 H5
Burradon N Tyne 181 G4
Burradon Nthumb 190 D5
Burrafirth Shet 281 f1
Burras Cnwll 3 H4
Burraton Cnwll 6 E2
Burravoe Shet 281 e4
Burrells Cumb 166 F7
Burrelton P & K 233 J7
Burridge Devon 15 H2
Burridge Devon 27 K4
Burridge Hants 19 J2

Burrill N York 160 C5
Burringham N Linc 143 L6
Burrington Devon 27 L7
Burrington Herefs 80 B1
Burrington N Som 44 F7
Burrough End Cambs 88 C4
Burrough Green Cambs 88 C4
Burrough on the Hill Leics 101 G1
Burrow Lancs 157 K7
Burrow Somset 29 G2
Burrow Bridge Somset 30 E5
Burrowhill Surrey 50 B6
Burrows Cross Surrey 37 G2
Burry Swans 56 E6
Burry Green Swans 56 E6
Burry Port Carmth 56 E5
Burscough Lancs 138 E5
Burscough Bridge Lancs 138 F5
Bursea E R Yk 143 K1
Burshill E R Yk 153 H6
Bursledon Hants 19 H2
Burslem C Stke 114 D2
Burstall Suffk 90 C6
Burstock Dorset 15 K2
Burston Norfk 106 C6
Burston Staffs 114 E5
Burstow Surrey 37 M3
Burstwick E R Yk 145 G2
Burtersett N York 158 F5
Burtholme Cumb 178 D6
Burthorpe Green Suffk 88 F2
Burthwaite Cumb 165 M1
Burthy Cnwll 4 E4
Burtle Hill Somset 30 F2
Burtoft Lincs 119 J4
Burton Ches W 129 H5
Burton Ches W 129 L7
Burton Dorset 16 D4
Burton Dorset 18 B5
Burton Nthumb 203 K6
Burton Pembks 55 G5
Burton Somset 30 B2
Burton Somset 31 H8
Burton Wilts 32 D4
Burton Wilts 46 B3
Burton Agnes E R Yk 153 H3
Burton Bradstock Dorset 15 L5
Burton-by-Lincoln Lincs 135 J5
Burton Coggles Lincs 118 C6
Burton Dassett Warwks 83 J5
Burton End Essex 70 D2
Burton End Suffk 88 D6
Burton Fleming E R Yk 153 H2
Burton Green Warwks 99 H8
Burton Green Wrexhm 129 H7
Burton Hastings Warwks 99 L5
Burton-in-Kendal Cumb 157 H7
Burton in Lonsdale N York 148 A2
Burton Joyce Notts 117 H3
Burton Latimer Nhants 101 K8
Burton Lazars Leics 117 K8
Burton Leonard N York 150 D3
Burton on the Wolds Leics 117 G7
Burton Overy Leics 100 E4
Burton Pedwardine Lincs 118 F3
Burton Pidsea E R Yk 145 H2
Burton Salmon N York 142 D2
Burton's Green Essex 71 K2
Burton upon Stather N Linc 143 L4
Burton upon Trent Staffs 115 L6
Burton Waters Lincs 135 J5
Burtonwood Warrtn 130 A1
Burwardsley Ches W 129 L8
Burwarton Shrops 96 E6
Burwash E Susx 24 B2
Burwash Common E Susx 23 L3
Burwash Weald E Susx 23 L3
Burwell Cambs 88 B2
Burwell Lincs 137 G4
Burwen IoA 125 G1
Burwick Ork 275 c6
Bury Bury 140 B3
Bury Cambs 102 F6
Bury Somset 29 G5
Bury W Susx 21 G4
Bury End C Beds 86 C8
Bury Green Herts 70 C3
Bury St Edmunds Suffk 89 G2
Burythorpe N York 152 B3
Busby E Rens 208 F7
Busby Stoop N York 160 E6
Buscot Oxon 65 J7
Bush Abers 235 J2
Bush Cnwll 11 J1
Bush Bank Herefs 80 B5
Bushbury Wolves 97 L3
Bushbury Crematorium
  Wolves 97 L3
Bushby Leics 100 E3

Bushey Herts 68 E8
Bushey Heath Herts 68 F8
Bush Green Norfk 106 E6
Bush Green Suffk 89 H4
Bush Hill Park Gt Lon 69 J7
Bushley Worcs 81 K8
Bushley Green Worcs 81 K8
Bushmead Bed 86 C3
Bushmoor Shrops 95 K6
Bushton Wilts 46 F3
Busk Cumb 166 E2
Buslingthorpe Lincs 135 M3
Bussage Gloucs 64 C6
Bussex Somset 30 E4
Butcher's Cross E Susx 23 J2
Butcombe N Som 45 G6
Bute Ag & B 207 G5
Butleigh Somset 31 H4
Butleigh Wootton Somset 31 H4
Butler's Cross Bucks 67 K5
Butler's Hill Notts 116 F2
Butlers Marston Warwks 83 H5
Butley Suffk 91 J5
Butley High Corner Suffk 91 J5
Buttercrambe N York 152 A4
Butterdean Border 213 H6
Butterknowle Dur 168 E5
Butterleigh Devon 14 A1
Butterley Derbys 116 C1
Buttermere Cumb 165 G7
Buttermere Wilts 47 M6
Butters Green Staffs 114 C2
Buttershaw C Brad 141 H2
Butterstone P & K 233 G6
Butterton Staffs 114 C3
Butterton Staffs 131 L8
Butterwick Dur 169 K5
Butterwick Lincs 119 L3
Butterwick N York 152 F2
Butterwick N York 162 C7
Butt Green Ches E 113 L1
Buttington Powys 95 G2
Buttonbridge Shrops 97 G7
Buttonoak Shrops 97 G7
Buttsash Hants 19 G2
Buttsbear Cross Cnwll 11 K2
Butt's Green Essex 71 J6
Buxhall Suffk 89 K4
Buxhall Fen Street Suffk 89 K3
Buxted E Susx 23 H3
Buxton Derbys 131 L5
Buxton Norfk 122 E7
Buxton Heath Norfk 122 D7
Buxworth Derbys 131 K3
Bwlch Powys 61 J3
Bwlchgwyn Wrexhm 112 C1
Bwlchllan Cerdgn 77 G3
Bwlchnewydd Carmth 58 C4
Bwlchtocyn Gwynd 108 E6
Bwlch-y-cibau Powys 112 B8
Bwlch-y-Ddar Powys 112 B7
Bwlchyfadfa Cerdgn 76 D5
Bwlch-y-ffridd Powys 94 C4
Bwlch-y-groes Pembks 75 M5
Bwlchymyrdd Swans 57 G5
Bwlch-y-sarnau Powys 94 B8
Byermoor Gatesd 180 F7
Byers Green Dur 169 G4
Byfield Nhants 83 M4
Byfleet Surrey 50 D6
Byford Herefs 79 M6
Bygrave Herts 86 F7
Byker N u Ty 181 G6
Byland Abbey N York 161 J6
Bylaugh Norfk 122 A7
Bylchau Conwy 127 K7
Byley Ches W 130 E6
Bynea Carmth 57 G5
Byrness Nthumb 189 K5
Bystock Devon 14 B6
Bythorn Cambs 102 B8
Byton Herefs 79 L2
Bywell Nthumb 180 C6
Byworth W Susx 36 E6

C

Cabbacott Devon 27 G6
Cabourne Lincs 144 E7
Cabrach Ag & B 205 H3
Cabrach Moray 255 H6
Cabus Lancs 147 J6
Cackle Street E Susx 23 G2
Cackle Street E Susx 24 C3
Cackle Street E Susx 24 E3
Cadbury Devon 13 L2
Cadbury Barton Devon 28 B7

Cadder E Duns 209 G4
Caddington C Beds 68 D3
Caddonfoot Border 200 F6
Cadeby Donc 142 E7
Cadeby Leics 99 L3
Cadeleigh Devon 13 L1
Cade Street E Susx 23 K3
Cadgwith Cnwll 3 J8
Cadham Fife 222 D6
Cadishead Salfd 130 D1
Cadle Swans 57 H5
Cadley Lancs 139 G2
Cadley Wilts 47 J5
Cadley Wilts 47 K8
Cadmore End Bucks 67 J8
Cadnam Hants 34 C8
Cadney N Linc 144 C7
Cadole Flints 128 E7
Cadoxton V Glam 43 H7
Cadoxton Juxta-Neath Neath 57 L5
Cadwst Denbgs 111 K4
Caeathro Gwynd 125 J7
Caehopkin Powys 59 M6
Caenby Lincs 135 K2
Caeo Carmth 77 J7
Caerau Brdgnd 42 C3
Caerau Cardif 43 H6
Cae'r-bont Powys 59 M6
Cae'r bryn Carmth 59 H6
Caerdeon Gwynd 110 C7
Caer Farchell Pembks 74 C6
Caergeiliog IoA 124 E4
Caergwrle Flints 129 G8
Caerhun Conwy 126 F5
Caerlanrig Border 188 C5
Caerleon Newpt 44 D1
Caernarfon Gwynd 125 H7
Caerphilly Caerph 43 J4
Caersws Powys 94 B5
Caerwedros Cerdgn 76 C4
Caerwent Mons 44 F1
Caerwys Flints 128 D5
Caerynwch Gwynd 110 E8
Caggle Street Mons 62 D4
Caim IoA 126 C3
Cairinis W Isls 283 c8
Cairnbaan Ag & B 206 C1
Cairnbulg Abers 269 J3
Cairncross Border 213 K6
Cairncurran Inver 208 A5
Cairndow Ag & B 217 K5
Cairneyhill Fife 210 D2
Cairngarroch D & G 172 C5
Cairnie Abers 255 K3
Cairnorrie Abers 256 F3
Cairnryan D & G 172 D1
Cairnty Moray 267 G5
Caister-on-Sea Norfk 107 L1
Caistor Lincs 144 E7
Caistor St Edmund Norfk 106 E3
Cakebole Worcs 81 K1
Cake Street Norfk 106 B5
Calais Street Suffk 89 K7
Calanais W Isls 282 f3
Calbourne IoW 19 G6
Calceby Lincs 137 G4
Calcot Flints 128 E5
Calcot Gloucs 65 G5
Calcot W Berk 49 G4
Calcot Row W Berk 49 G4
Calcots Moray 266 E3
Calcott Kent 41 G3
Calcott Shrops 113 G8
Calcutt N York 150 E4
Calcutt Wilts 65 G8
Caldbeck Cumb 165 K3
Caldbergh N York 159 K5
Caldecote Cambs 87 G4
Caldecote Cambs 102 C5
Caldecote Herts 86 E7
Caldecote Nhants 84 D5
Caldecote Highfields Cambs 87 G3
Caldecott Nhants 85 K2
Caldecott Oxon 66 D7
Caldecott Rutlnd 101 J4
Caldecotte M Keyn 85 H8
Calder Cumb 155 J2
Calderbank N Lans 209 K6
Calder Bridge Cumb 155 J2
Calderbrook Rochdl 140 E4
Caldercruix N Lans 209 L5
Calder Grove Wakefd 141 M4
Caldermill S Lans 197 J3
Caldermore Rochdl 140 D4
Calder Vale Lancs 147 K6
Calderwood S Lans 209 H7
Caldey Island Pembks 55 K7
Caldicot Mons 44 F1
Caldmore Wsall 98 C4

Caldwell N York 168 F8
Caldy Wirral 128 F3
Caledfwlch Carmth 59 J4
Calenick Cnwll 4 D6
Calf of Man IoM 154 a8
Calford Green Suffk 88 D6
Calfsound Ork 275 d2
Calgary Ag & B 226 D2
Califer Moray 265 H8
California Falk 210 B4
California Norfk 123 K8
California Cross Devon 7 K4
Calke Derbys 116 B7
Callakille Highld 259 M5
Callander Stirlg 219 K5
Callanish W Isls 282 f3
Callaughton Shrops 96 E4
Callerton N u Ty 180 E5
Callestick Cnwll 4 C5
Calligarry Highld 247 K7
Callington Cnwll 6 D1
Callingwood Staffs 115 K6
Callow Herefs 80 C8
Callow End Worcs 81 J5
Callow Hill Wilts 46 F2
Callow Hill Worcs 82 B2
Callow Hill Worcs 97 G8
Callows Grave Worcs 80 D2
Calmore Hants 34 D7
Calmsden Gloucs 64 F5
Calne Wilts 46 E5
Calow Derbys 133 H5
Calshot Hants 19 H3
Calstock Cnwll 6 E1
Calstone Wellington Wilts 46 F5
Calthorpe Norfk 122 D5
Calthorpe Street Norfk 123 H6
Calthwaite Cumb 166 B3
Calton N York 148 F4
Calton Staffs 115 H2
Calveley Ches E 130 B7
Calver Derbys 132 E5
Calverhall Shrops 113 K4
Calver Hill Herefs 79 L5
Calverleigh Devon 29 G8
Calverley Leeds 150 B8
Calverley Shrops 96 C2
Calver Sough Derbys 132 E5
Calvert Bucks 67 G2
Calverton M Keyn 84 F7
Calverton Notts 117 G2
Calvine P & K 232 B2
Calvo Cumb 176 F8
Calzeat Border 199 K6
Cam Gloucs 63 M7
Camasachoirce Highld 228 B3
Camasine Highld 237 L8
Camas Luinie Highld 248 F6
Camastianavaig Highld 247 G1
Camault Muir Highld 250 E4
Camber E Susx 25 H3
Camberley Surrey 49 L6
Camberwell Gt Lon 51 J4
Camblesforth N York 143 G3
Cambo Nthumb 180 B2
Cambois Nthumb 181 H2
Camborne Cnwll 3 G3
Cambourne Cambs 87 G3
Cambridge Cambs 87 J3
Cambridge Gloucs 63 L6
Cambridge City Crematorium
Cambs 87 H3
Cambrose Cnwll 4 A5
Cambus Clacks 220 E8
Cambusavie Platform Highld .. 263 J3
Cambusbarron Stirlg 209 K1
Cambuskenneth Stirlg 220 D8
Cambuslang S Lans 209 H7
Cambus o' May Abers 243 M4
Cambuswallace S Lans 199 H5
Camden Town Gt Lon 51 H2
Cameley BaNES 45 J7
Camelford Cnwll 10 F6
Camelon Falk 209 M3
Camerory Highld 253 K5
Camer's Green Worcs 81 H8
Camerton BaNES 45 K7
Camerton Cumb 164 D4
Camghouran P & K 231 G4
Camieston Border 201 J7
Cammachmore Abers 245 K4
Cammeringham Lincs 135 J3
Camore Highld 263 L2
Campbeltown Ag & B 192 E4
Camperdown N Tyne 181 G4
Cample D & G 186 D2
Campmuir P & K 233 K7
Camps W Loth 210 E5
Campsall Donc 142 E5
Campsea Ash Suffk 91 H4

Camps End Cambs 88 C6
Campton C Beds 86 C7
Camptown Border 189 J4
Camrose Pembks 54 F3
Camserney P & K 232 B5
Camusnagaul Highld 239 H8
Camusnagaul Highld 261 H2
Camusteel Highld 248 A3
Camusterrach Highld 248 A3
Canada Hants 34 C7
Canal Foot Cumb 156 D7
Canaston Bridge Pembks 55 H4
Candacraig Abers 243 K4
Candlesby Lincs 137 H6
Candle Street Suffk 105 L8
Candover Green Shrops 96 C2
Candy Mill Border 199 J5
Cane End Oxon 49 G3
Canewdon Essex 72 C8
Canford Bottom Dorset 17 K3
Canford Cliffs Poole 17 L5
Canford Crematorium Bristl .. 45 H3
Canford Heath Poole 17 K4
Canford Magna Poole 17 K3
Canhams Green Suffk 90 C2
Canisbay Highld 280 D2
Canklow Rothm 133 H2
Canley Covtry 99 J7
Canley Crematorium Covtry .. 99 J8
Cann Dorset 32 E6
Canna Highld 246 B7
Cann Common Dorset 32 E6
Cannich Highld 250 B5
Cannington Somset 30 C3
Canning Town Gt Lon 51 L3
Cannock Staffs 98 B2
Cannock Wood Staffs 98 D1
Cannon Bridge Herefs 80 A7
Canonbie D & G 177 L4
Canon Frome Herefs 80 F6
Canon Pyon Herefs 80 B5
Canons Ashby Nhants 84 B5
Canonstown Cnwll 2 E4
Canterbury Kent 40 F4
Cantley Norfk 107 H3
Cantlop Shrops 96 C2
Canton Cardif 43 J6
Cantraywood Highld 252 E2
Cantsfield Lancs 147 M1
Canvey Island Essex 53 G2
Canwick Lincs 135 K6
Canworthy Water Cnwll 11 J4
Caol Highld 239 J8
Caolas Scalpaigh W Isls 282 f6
Caoles Ag & B 224 D5
Caonich Highld 239 H5
Capel Kent 39 G4
Capel Surrey 37 J3
Capel Bangor Cerdgn 92 E7
Capel Betws Lleucu Cerdgn .. 77 H4
Capel Coch IoA 125 H3
Capel Curig Conwy 126 E8
Capel Cynon Cerdgn 76 C5
Capel Dewi Carmth 58 E5
Capel Dewi Cerdgn 76 E6
Capel-Dewi Cerdgn 92 D7
Capel Garmon Conwy 127 G8
Capel Green Suffk 91 J5
Capel Gwyn Carmth 58 E4
Capel Gwyn IoA 124 F4
Capel Gwynfe Carmth 59 K4
Capel Hendre Carmth 59 G6
Capel Isaac Carmth 59 G3
Capel Iwan Carmth 58 B2
Capel-le-Ferne Kent 41 H7
Capelles Guern 9 j2
Capel Llanilltern Cardif 43 H5
Capel Mawr IoA 125 G5
Capel Parc IoA 125 H2
Capel St Andrew Suffk 91 J5
Capel St Mary Suffk 90 C7
Capel Seion Cerdgn 92 D7
Capel Trisant Cerdgn 92 F8
Capeluchaf Gwynd 109 H2
Capelulo Conwy 126 E4
Capel-y-ffin Powys 61 L1
Capel-y-graig Gwynd 125 K6
Capenhurst Ches W 129 J5
Capernwray Lancs 147 K2
Capheaton Nthumb 180 C3
Caplaw E Rens 208 D7
Capon's Green Suffk 91 G2
Cappercleuch Border 187 K2
Capstone Medway 53 G6
Capton Devon 8 C4
Capton Somset 29 K3
Caputh P & K 233 G7
Caradon Town Cnwll 11 K8
Carbeth Inn Stirlg 208 E3

Carbis Cnwll 5 G3
Carbis Bay Cnwll 2 E3
Carbost Highld 246 E2
Carbost Highld 259 G7
Carbrook Sheff 133 G2
Carbrooke Norfk 105 J3
Carburton Notts 134 C5
Carclaze Cnwll 5 H4
Car Colston Notts 117 J3
Carcroft Donc 142 E6
Cardenden Fife 222 D6
Cardeston Shrops 95 J1
Cardewlees Cumb 177 K8
Cardhu Moray 254 D3
Cardiff Cardif 43 J6
Cardiff & Glamorgan
Crematorium Cardif 43 J5
Cardigan Cerdgn 75 L3
Cardinal's Green Cambs 88 C5
Cardington Bed 86 B5
Cardington Shrops 96 C4
Cardinham Cnwll 5 J1
Cardrain D & G 172 B5
Cardrona Border 200 C5
Cardross Ag & B 208 B3
Cardross Crematorium Ag & B .. 208 B3
Cardryne D & G 172 B5
Cardurnock Cumb 177 G7
Careby Lincs 118 D8
Careston Angus 234 E3
Carew Pembks 55 H6
Carew Cheriton Pembks 55 H6
Carew Newton Pembks 55 H6
Carey Herefs 63 H1
Carfin N Lans 209 K7
Carfraemill Border 201 G2
Cargate Green Norfk 107 H1
Cargenbridge D & G 176 C4
Cargill P & K 233 G7
Cargo Cumb 177 L7
Cargreen Cnwll 6 E2
Cargurrel Cnwll 3 M4
Carham Nthumb 202 B4
Carhampton Somset 29 H2
Carharrack Cnwll 3 J3
Carie P & K 231 H4
Carinish W Isls 283 c8
Carisbrooke IoW 19 H6
Cark Cumb 156 E7
Carkeel Cnwll 6 E3
Càrlabhagh W Isls 282 e2
Carland Cross Cnwll 4 D4
Carlbury Darltn 169 G7
Carlby Lincs 102 A1
Carlcroft Nthumb 190 B4
Carlecotes Barns 141 J7
Carleen Cnwll 3 G5
Carlesmoor N York 160 B7
Carleton Cumb 155 J1
Carleton Cumb 166 C5
Carleton Cumb 178 A8
Carleton Lancs 146 F7
Carleton Wakefd 142 D4
Carleton Crematorium Bpool .. 146 F7
Carleton Forehoe Norfk 106 B2
Carleton-in-Craven N York .. 149 H6
Carleton Rode Norfk 106 C4
Carleton St Peter Norfk 107 G3
Carlidnack Cnwll 3 K5
Carlincraig Abers 256 B3
Carlingcott BaNES 45 K7
Carlin How R & Cl 171 G6
Carlisle Cumb 177 L7
Carlisle Crematorium Cumb .. 177 L8
Carloggas Cnwll 4 E3
Carlops Border 199 K2
Carloway W Isls 282 e2
Carlton Barns 142 B5
Carlton Bed 85 J4
Carlton Cambs 88 C4
Carlton Leeds 142 A2
Carlton Leics 99 L2
Carlton N York 143 G3
Carlton N York 159 J5
Carlton N York 161 K5
Carlton Notts 117 G3
Carlton S on T 169 K5
Carlton Suffk 91 J2
Carlton Colville Suffk 107 K5
Carlton Curlieu Leics 100 F4
Carlton Green Cambs 88 C5
Carlton Husthwaite N York .. 161 H7
Carlton-in-Cleveland N York .. 161 H2
Carlton in Lindrick Notts 134 B3
Carlton-le-Moorland Lincs .. 135 H8
Carlton Miniott N York 160 F6
Carlton-on-Trent Notts 134 D7
Carlton Scroop Lincs 118 B3
Carluke S Lans 198 D3

Carlyon Bay Cnwll 5 H4
Carmacoup S Lans 198 C7
Carmarthen Carmth 58 D5
Carmel Carmth 59 G5
Carmel Flints 128 E4
Carmel Gwynd 125 J8
Carmichael S Lans 198 F5
Carmountside Crematorium C Stke 114 E2
Carmunnock C Glas 209 G7
Carmyle C Glas 209 H6
Carmyllie Angus 234 E6
Carnaby E R Yk 153 J3
Carnbee Fife 223 J6
Carnbo P & K 221 J6
Carn Brea Cnwll 3 H3
Carnbrogie Abers 256 F6
Carndu Highld 248 E6
Carnduff S Lans 197 J2
Carne Cnwll 3 K6
Carne Cnwll 4 E7
Carne Cnwll 4 F3
Carnell E Ayrs 196 F4
Carnewas Cnwll 4 D1
Carnforth Lancs 147 K2
Carn-gorm Highld 248 F7
Carnhedryn Pembks 74 C6
Carnhell Green Cnwll 3 G4
Carnie Abers 245 H2
Carnkie Cnwll 3 H3
Carnkie Cnwll 3 H4
Carnkiet Cnwll 4 C4
Carno Powys 93 L4
Carnock Fife 210 D1
Carnon Downs Cnwll 3 K3
Carnousie Abers 268 B6
Carnoustie Angus 234 E8
Carnsmerry Cnwll 5 G3
Carnwath S Lans 199 G4
Carnyorth Cnwll 2 B4
Carol Green Solhll 99 H7
Carpalla Cnwll 4 F4
Carperby N York 159 H5
Carr Rothm 133 K2
Carradale Ag & B 194 C3
Carrbridge Highld 253 G7
Carrbrook Tamesd 140 E7
Carrefour Jersey 9 c2
Carreglefn IoA 125 G2
Carr Gate Wakefd 141 M3
Carrhouse N Linc 143 K6
Carrick Ag & B 206 E2
Carrick Castle Ag & B 217 K8
Carriden Falk 210 D3
Carrington Lincs 136 F8
Carrington Mdloth 211 K7
Carrington Traffd 130 E1
Carrog Conwy 110 E2
Carrog Denbgs 111 L3
Carron Falk 210 A3
Carron Moray 254 E3
Carronbridge D & G 186 C6
Carron Bridge Stirlg 209 K2
Carronshore Falk 210 A2
Carrow Hill Mons 44 E1
Carr Shield Nthumb 167 J1
Carrutherstown D & G 176 E4
Carruth House Inver 208 B6
Carr Vale Derbys 133 J5
Carrville Dur 169 J2
Carsaig Ag & B 227 G8
Carseriggan D & G 173 H1
Carsethorn D & G 176 C7
Carshalton Gt Lon 51 H6
Carsington Derbys 115 L1
Carskey Ag & B 192 D6
Carsluith D & G 174 D4
Carsphairn D & G 184 E4
Carstairs S Lans 198 F4
Carstairs Junction S Lans 198 F4
Carswell Marsh Oxon 65 L7
Carter's Clay Hants 34 C6
Carters Green Essex 70 D5
Carterton Oxon 65 L5
Carterway Heads Nthumb 180 C8
Carthew Cnwll 5 G4
Carthorpe N York 160 D6
Cartington Nthumb 190 E5
Cartland S Lans 198 E4
Cartledge Derbys 132 F4
Cartmel Cumb 156 E7
Cartmel Fell Cumb 156 F5
Carway Carmth 56 E3
Carwinley Cumb 177 L4
Cashe's Green Gloucs 64 D6
Cashmoor Dorset 33 G8
Cassington Oxon 66 C5
Cassop Dur 169 K3
Castallack Cnwll 2 C6

Castel Guern 9 j3
Castell Conwy 126 F6
Castell-y-bwch Torfn 62 B8
Casterton Cumb 157 K6
Castle Cnwll 5 J3
Castle Acre Norfk 121 H8
Castle Ashby Nhants 85 G3
Castlebay W Isls 283 b13
Castle Bolton N York 159 J4
Castle Bromwich Solhll 98 F5
Castle Bytham Lincs 118 C7
Castlebythe Pembks 75 H6
Castle Caereinion Powys 94 E2
Castle Camps Cambs 88 C6
Castle Carrock Cumb 178 D7
Castlecary Falk 209 L3
Castle Cary Somset 31 L4
Castle Combe Wilts 46 B3
Castle Donington Leics 116 D6
Castle Douglas D & G 175 J2
Castle Eaton Swindn 65 H7
Castle Eden Dur 169 L3
Castle End C Pete 102 C2
Castleford Wakefd 142 C3
Castle Frome Herefs 80 F6
Castle Gate Cnwll 2 D4
Castle Green Cumb 157 H4
Castle Green Surrey 50 B6
Castle Gresley Derbys 115 M7
Castle Hedingham Essex 88 F8
Castlehill Border 200 B6
Castlehill Highld 280 B3
Castle Hill Kent 39 H5
Castle Hill Suffk 90 D6
Castlehill W Duns 208 C4
Castle Kennedy D & G 172 D3
Castle Lachlan Ag & B 217 G8
Castlemartin Pembks 54 E7
Castlemilk C Glas 209 G7
Castle Morris Pembks 74 E6
Castlemorton Worcs 81 H7
Castlemorton Common Worcs 81 H7
Castle O'er D & G 187 K7
Castle Rising Norfk 120 E6
Castleside Dur 168 D1
Castle Stuart Highld 252 D2
Castlethorpe M Keyn 84 F6
Castlethorpe N Linc 144 B6
Castleton Border 188 E8
Castleton Derbys 132 C3
Castleton N York 162 B1
Castleton Newpt 43 L5
Castleton Rochdl 140 C5
Castletown Ches W 113 G1
Castletown Dorset 16 D7
Castletown Highld 280 A3
Castletown IoM 154 c8
Castletown Sundld 181 J7
Castley N York 150 C6
Caston Norfk 105 J4
Castor C Pete 102 C4
Caswell Bay Swans 57 G7
Catacol N Ayrs 194 E1
Cat and Fiddle Derbys 131 K5
Catbrain S Glos 45 H3
Catbrook Mons 63 G6
Catch Flints 128 F5
Catchall Cnwll 2 C5
Catchem's Corner Solhll 99 H8
Catchgate Dur 180 E8
Catcliffe Rothm 133 H2
Catcomb Wilts 46 E4
Catcott Somset 30 F3
Catcott Burtle Somset 30 F2
Caterham Surrey 51 J7
Catfield Norfk 123 H7
Catfield Common Norfk 123 H7
Catford Gt Lon 51 K4
Catforth Lancs 138 F1
Cathcart C Glas 209 G7
Cathedine Powys 61 J2
Catherine-de-Barnes Solhll 98 F7
Catherine Slack C Brad 141 G2
Catherington Hants 35 L8
Catherston Leweston Dorset 15 J4
Catherton Shrops 96 F7
Catisfield Hants 19 J2
Catley Herefs 80 F6
Catley Lane Head Rochdl 140 C4
Catlodge Highld 241 H5
Catlow Lancs 148 F8
Catlowdy Cumb 178 B3
Catmere End Essex 87 K7
Catmore W Berk 48 C5
Caton Devon 13 H8
Caton Lancs 147 K3
Caton Green Lancs 147 L3
Cator Court Devon 13 G7
Catrine E Ayrs 197 G6

Cat's Ash Newpt 44 D1
Catsfield E Susx 24 C4
Catsfield Stream E Susx 24 C4
Catsgore Somset 31 H5
Catsham Somset 31 J4
Catshill Worcs 98 B8
Catstree Shrops 97 G4
Cattadale Ag & B 192 D6
Cattal N York 150 F5
Cattawade Suffk 90 C8
Catterall Lancs 147 K7
Catterick N York 160 C3
Catterick Bridge N York 160 B3
Catterick Garrison N York 160 B3
Catterlen Cumb 166 B4
Catterline Abers 245 J7
Catterton N York 151 H6
Catteshall Surrey 36 E2
Catthorpe Leics 100 C7
Cattishall Suffk 89 H2
Cattistock Dorset 16 B3
Catton N York 160 E7
Catton Nthumb 179 J7
Catwick E R Yk 153 J6
Catworth Cambs 86 B1
Caudle Green Gloucs 64 D5
Caulcott C Beds 85 K6
Caulcott Oxon 66 D2
Cauldcots Angus 235 G6
Cauldhame Stirlg 219 L8
Cauldmill Border 188 F3
Cauldon Staffs 115 H2
Cauldon Lowe Staffs 115 H2
Cauldwell Derbys 115 L8
Caulkerbush D & G 176 B7
Caulside D & G 178 B3
Caundle Marsh Dorset 31 L8
Caunsall Worcs 97 J7
Caunton Notts 134 E7
Causeway Hants 35 M6
Causeway End Cumb 157 G5
Causeway End D & G 173 K3
Causeway End Essex 71 G3
Causewayend S Lans 199 H6
Causewayhead Cumb 176 F8
Causewayhead Stirlg 220 D8
Causeyend Abers 257 H7
Causey Park Nthumb 191 H7
Causey Park Bridge Nthumb 191 H7
Cavendish Suffk 88 F6
Cavenham Suffk 88 F1
Caversfield Oxon 66 E2
Caversham Readg 49 H4
Caverswall Staffs 114 F3
Caverton Mill Border 202 A7
Cavil E R Yk 143 J2
Cawdor Highld 252 F2
Cawkwell Lincs 136 E4
Cawood N York 151 J8
Cawsand Cnwll 6 E5
Cawston Norfk 122 C6
Cawston Warwks 100 A8
Cawthorn N York 162 D5
Cawthorne Barns 141 L6
Cawton N York 161 K7
Caxton Cambs 86 F3
Caxton End Cambs 87 G4
Caxton Gibbet Cambs 86 F3
Caynham Shrops 80 D1
Caythorpe Lincs 118 B2
Caythorpe Notts 117 J2
Cayton N York 163 J6
Ceann a Bhaigh W Isls 283 b8
Ceannacroc Lodge Highld 239 L1
Cearsiadar W Isls 282 f4
Ceciliford Mons 63 G6
Cefn Newpt 44 B1
Cefn Berain Conwy 127 K6
Cefn-brith Conwy 111 H2
Cefn-bryn-brain Carmth 59 K6
Cefn Byrle Powys 60 C5
Cefn Canel Powys 112 C5
Cefn Coch Powys 111 L6
Cefn-coed-y-cymmer Myr Td 60 F5
Cefn Cribwr Brdgnd 42 C5
Cefn Cross Brdgnd 42 C5
Cefn-ddwysarn Gwynd 111 J4
Cefn-Einion Shrops 95 G6
Cefneithin Carmth 59 G6
Cefngorwydd Powys 78 B6
Cefn-mawr Wrexhm 112 D3
Cefnpennar Rhondd 61 G7
Cefn-y-bedd Flints 129 H8
Cefn-y-pant Carmth 75 L7
Ceint IoA 125 J4
Cellan Cerdgn 77 H5
Cellardyke Fife 223 K6
Cellarhead Staffs 114 F2

Celleron Cumb 166 C5
Celynen Caerph 43 K3
Cemaes IoA 124 F1
Cemmaes Powys 93 H2
Cemmaes Road Powys 93 H3
Cenarth Cerdgn 76 A7
Cerbyd Pembks 74 D6
Ceres Fife 223 G5
Cerne Abbas Dorset 16 C2
Cerney Wick Gloucs 65 G7
Cerrigceinwen IoA 125 G5
Cerrigydrudion Conwy 111 J2
Cess Norfk 123 J7
Ceunant Gwynd 125 J7
Chaceley Gloucs 64 B1
Chacewater Cnwll 4 B6
Chackmore Bucks 84 D8
Chacombe Nhants 83 L6
Chadbury Worcs 82 B6
Chadderton Oldham 140 D6
Chadderton Fold Oldham 140 D6
Chaddesden C Derb 116 C4
Chaddesley Corbett Worcs 81 K1
Chaddlehanger Devon 12 B7
Chaddleworth W Berk 48 B3
Chadlington Oxon 65 M3
Chadshunt Warwks 83 H5
Chadwell Leics 117 K6
Chadwell Shrops 114 B8
Chadwell End Bed 86 B2
Chadwell Heath Gt Lon 52 A1
Chadwell St Mary Thurr 52 E3
Chadwick Worcs 81 J2
Chadwick End Solhll 99 G8
Chadwick Green St Hel 139 G7
Chaffcombe Somset 15 H1
Chafford Hundred Thurr 52 D3
Chagford Devon 13 G5
Chailey E Susx 22 F3
Chainbridge Cambs 103 J3
Chainhurst Kent 39 J4
Chalbury Dorset 17 K1
Chalbury Common Dorset 17 K2
Chaldon Surrey 51 J7
Chaldon Herring Dorset 16 F6
Chale IoW 19 H8
Chale Green IoW 19 H7
Chalfont Common Bucks 68 C8
Chalfont St Giles Bucks 68 C8
Chalfont St Peter Bucks 50 C1
Chalford Gloucs 64 C6
Chalford Oxon 67 H7
Chalford Wilts 32 E1
Chalgrave C Beds 68 C2
Chalgrove Oxon 66 F7
Chalk Kent 52 E4
Chalk End Essex 70 F5
Chalkhouse Green Oxon 49 H3
Chalkway Somset 15 J1
Chalkwell Kent 53 J6
Challaborough Devon 7 J6
Challacombe Devon 28 B3
Challoch D & G 173 K2
Challock Kent 40 C5
Chalmington Dorset 16 B2
Chalton C Beds 68 C2
Chalton C Beds 86 C5
Chalton Hants 20 B4
Chalvey Slough 50 B3
Chalvington E Susx 23 H5
Chambers Green Kent 40 B6
Chandler's Cross Herts 68 D7
Chandlers Cross Worcs 81 H7
Chandler's Ford Hants 34 F7
Channel's End Bed 86 C4
Channel Tunnel Terminal Kent 41 G7
Chanterlands Crematorium C KuH 144 D2
Chantry Somset 32 B2
Chantry Suffk 90 D6
Chapel Cumb 165 H4
Chapel Fife 222 D8
Chapel Allerton Leeds 150 D8
Chapel Allerton Somset 30 F1
Chapel Amble Cnwll 10 D7
Chapel Brampton Nhants 84 D2
Chapelbridge Cambs 102 F4
Chapel Chorlton Staffs 114 C4
Chapel Cross E Susx 23 K3
Chapel End Bed 86 B4
Chapel End C Beds 85 L6
Chapel End Cambs 102 C6
Chapel End Warwks 99 J5
Chapelend Way Essex 88 E7
Chapel-en-le-Frith Derbys 131 L3
Chapel Field Bury 140 B6
Chapelgate Lincs 119 L6
Chapel Green Warwks 83 L3
Chapel Green Warwks 99 H6

Chapel Haddlesey N York ... 142 F3
Chapelhall N Lans ... 209 K6
Chapel Hill Abers ... 257 K4
Chapel Hill Lincs ... 119 G1
Chapel Hill Mons ... 63 G7
Chapel Hill N York ... 150 D6
Chapelhope Border ... 187 K2
Chapelknowe D & G ... 177 K4
Chapel Lawn Shrops ... 95 H8
Chapel-le-Dale N York ... 158 C7
Chapel Leigh Somset ... 29 L5
Chapel Milton Derbys ... 131 L3
Chapel of Garioch Abers ... 256 C7
Chapel Rossan D & G ... 172 D6
Chapel Row E Susx ... 23 L5
Chapel Row Essex ... 71 J7
Chapel Row W Berk ... 48 E5
Chapels Cumb ... 156 B6
Chapel St Leonards Lincs ... 137 K5
Chapel Stile Cumb ... 156 D2
Chapelton Abers ... 245 K5
Chapelton Angus ... 234 F6
Chapelton Devon ... 27 K5
Chapelton S Lans ... 197 K1
Chapeltown Bl w D ... 139 L4
Chapeltown Moray ... 254 E3
Chapeltown Sheff ... 142 A8
Chapmanslade Wilts ... 32 D1
Chapmans Well Devon ... 11 L4
Chapmore End Herts ... 69 J4
Chappel Essex ... 72 C2
Charaton Cnwll ... 6 B1
Chard Somset ... 15 H1
Chard Junction Somset ... 15 H1
Chardleigh Green Somset ... 30 D8
Chardstock Devon ... 15 G2
Charfield S Glos ... 63 L8
Chargrove Gloucs ... 64 D3
Charing Kent ... 40 B5
Charing Crematorium Kent ... 40 B5
Charing Heath Kent ... 40 B5
Charing Hill Kent ... 40 B5
Charingworth Gloucs ... 82 E7
Charlbury Oxon ... 66 A3
Charlcombe BaNES ... 45 L5
Charlcutt Wilts ... 46 E4
Charlecote Warwks ... 83 G4
Charlemont Sandw ... 98 C4
Charles Devon ... 28 B4
Charleshill Surrey ... 36 D2
Charleston Angus ... 234 B6
Charlestown C Aber ... 245 L3
Charlestown C Brad ... 149 L8
Charlestown Calder ... 140 E2
Charlestown Cnwll ... 5 H4
Charlestown Derbys ... 131 L1
Charlestown Dorset ... 16 C6
Charlestown Fife ... 210 E2
Charlestown Highld ... 251 H2
Charlestown Highld ... 260 C5
Charlestown Salfd ... 140 B7
Charlestown of Aberlour
　　Moray ... 254 E3
Charles Tye Suffk ... 89 L5
Charlesworth Derbys ... 131 K1
Charlinch Somset ... 30 C3
Charlottetown Fife ... 222 E5
Charlton Gt Lon ... 51 L3
Charlton Hants ... 34 D2
Charlton Herts ... 68 F2
Charlton Nhants ... 83 M8
Charlton Nthumb ... 179 J2
Charlton Oxon ... 48 B1
Charlton Somset ... 30 D5
Charlton Somset ... 31 K2
Charlton Somset ... 45 K8
Charlton Surrey ... 50 D5
Charlton W Susx ... 20 E4
Charlton Wilts ... 32 F6
Charlton Wilts ... 46 D1
Charlton Worcs ... 81 J1
Charlton Worcs ... 82 B6
Charlton Wrekin ... 96 D1
Charlton Abbots Gloucs ... 64 F2
Charlton Adam Somset ... 31 J5
Charlton All Saints Wilts ... 33 L6
Charlton Down Dorset ... 16 C4
Charlton Hill Shrops ... 96 D2
Charlton Horethorne Somset ... 31 L6
Charlton Kings Gloucs ... 64 D3
Charlton Mackrell Somset ... 31 H5
Charlton Marshall Dorset ... 17 H2
Charlton Musgrove Somset ... 32 B5
Charlton-on-Otmoor Oxon ... 66 E4
Charlton on the Hill Dorset ... 17 H2
Charlton St Peter Wilts ... 47 G7
Charlwood Hants ... 35 K4
Charlwood Surrey ... 37 K3

Charminster Dorset ... 16 C4
Charmouth Dorset ... 15 H4
Charndon Bucks ... 67 G2
Charney Bassett Oxon ... 66 A8
Charnock Green Lancs ... 139 H4
Charnock Richard Lancs ... 139 H4
Charnock Richard
　　Crematorium Lancs ... 139 H4
Charsfield Suffk ... 90 F4
Chart Corner Kent ... 39 K3
Charter Alley Hants ... 48 E7
Charterhall Border ... 202 B4
Charterhouse Somset ... 45 G7
Charters Allotments Oxon ... 65 L5
Chartham Kent ... 40 E4
Chartham Hatch Kent ... 40 E4
Chart Hill Kent ... 39 K3
Chartridge Bucks ... 68 B6
Chart Sutton Kent ... 39 K3
Chartway Street Kent ... 39 L3
Charvil Wokham ... 49 J4
Charwelton Nhants ... 83 M4
Chase Terrace Staffs ... 98 D2
Chasetown Staffs ... 98 D2
Chastleton Oxon ... 65 K1
Chasty Devon ... 11 L2
Chatburn Lancs ... 148 D7
Chatcull Staffs ... 114 B4
Chatham Caerph ... 43 K4
Chatham Medway ... 53 G5
Chatham Green Essex ... 71 H4
Chathill Nthumb ... 203 K7
Chatley Worcs ... 81 J3
Chattenden Medway ... 53 G4
Chatter End Essex ... 70 C2
Chatteris Cambs ... 103 H6
Chatterton Lancs ... 140 B4
Chattisham Suffk ... 90 C6
Chatto Border ... 189 K3
Chatton Nthumb ... 203 G7
Chaul End C Beds ... 68 D3
Chawleigh Devon ... 28 C8
Chawley Oxon ... 66 C5
Chawston Bed ... 86 C4
Chawton Hants ... 35 L3
Chaxhill Gloucs ... 63 L4
Chazey Heath Oxon ... 49 G3
Cheadle Staffs ... 115 G3
Cheadle Stockp ... 131 G2
Cheadle Heath Stockp ... 131 G2
Cheadle Hulme Stockp ... 131 G2
Cheam Gt Lon ... 51 H6
Cheapside W & M ... 50 B5
Chearsley Bucks ... 67 H5
Chebsey Staffs ... 114 D6
Checkendon Oxon ... 49 G2
Checkley Ches E ... 114 A2
Checkley Herefs ... 80 E7
Checkley Staffs ... 115 G4
Checkley Green Ches E ... 114 A2
Chedburgh Suffk ... 88 F4
Cheddar Somset ... 44 F8
Cheddington Bucks ... 68 A4
Cheddleton Staffs ... 114 F1
Cheddleton Heath Staffs ... 114 F1
Cheddon Fitzpaine Somset ... 30 C5
Chedglow Wilts ... 64 D8
Chedgrave Norfk ... 107 H3
Chedington Dorset ... 15 L2
Chediston Suffk ... 107 G7
Chediston Green Suffk ... 107 G7
Chedworth Gloucs ... 64 F5
Chedzoy Somset ... 30 E3
Cheeseman's Green Kent ... 40 D7
Cheetham Hill Manch ... 140 C4
Cheldon Devon ... 28 C8
Chelford Ches E ... 130 F5
Chellaston C Derb ... 116 C5
Chellington Bed ... 85 J4
Chelmarsh Shrops ... 97 G5
Chelmick Shrops ... 95 L5
Chelmondiston Suffk ... 90 E7
Chelmorton Derbys ... 132 B5
Chelmsford Essex ... 71 H5
Chelmsford Crematorium
　　Essex ... 71 G6
Chelmsley Wood Solhll ... 98 F6
Chelsea Gt Lon ... 51 H3
Chelsfield Gt Lon ... 52 A6
Chelsham Surrey ... 51 K7
Chelston Somset ... 29 L6
Chelsworth Suffk ... 89 K5
Cheltenham Gloucs ... 64 D3
Cheltenham Crematorium
　　Gloucs ... 64 E3
Chelveston Nhants ... 85 K1
Chelvey N Som ... 44 F5
Chelwood BaNES ... 45 J6

Chelwood Common E Susx ... 38 B7
Chelwood Gate E Susx ... 38 B7
Chelworth Wilts ... 64 E8
Chelworth Lower Green Wilts ... 65 G8
Chelworth Upper Green Wilts ... 65 G8
Cheney Longville Shrops ... 95 K6
Chenies Bucks ... 68 C7
Chepstow Mons ... 63 G8
Chequerbent Bolton ... 139 K6
Chequers Corner Norfk ... 103 K2
Cherhill Wilts ... 46 F5
Cherington Gloucs ... 64 C7
Cherington Warwks ... 83 G7
Cheriton Devon ... 28 C2
Cheriton Hants ... 35 J5
Cheriton Kent ... 41 G7
Cheriton Pembks ... 55 G7
Cheriton Swans ... 56 E6
Cheriton Bishop Devon ... 13 H4
Cheriton Fitzpaine Devon ... 13 K2
Cherrington Wrekin ... 113 L7
Cherry Burton E R Yk ... 152 F7
Cherry Hinton Cambs ... 87 K4
Cherry Orchard Worcs ... 81 K4
Cherry Willingham Lincs ... 135 L5
Chertsey Surrey ... 50 D5
Cheselbourne Dorset ... 16 E3
Chesham Bucks ... 68 B6
Chesham Bury ... 140 B5
Chesham Bois Bucks ... 68 B7
Cheshunt Herts ... 69 K6
Chesley Kent ... 53 J6
Cheslyn Hay Staffs ... 98 B2
Chessetts Wood Warwks ... 99 G8
Chessington Gt Lon ... 50 F6
Chester Ches W ... 129 J6
Chesterblade Somset ... 31 L3
Chester Crematorium Ches W ... 129 J6
Chesterfield Derbys ... 133 G5
Chesterfield Staffs ... 98 E2
Chesterfield Crematorium
　　Derbys ... 133 H5
Chesterhill Mdloth ... 211 L6
Chester-le-Street Dur ... 181 G8
Chester Moor Dur ... 169 H1
Chesters Border ... 189 G2
Chesters Border ... 189 H4
Chesterton Cambs ... 87 K3
Chesterton Cambs ... 102 C4
Chesterton Gloucs ... 64 E7
Chesterton Oxon ... 66 E3
Chesterton Shrops ... 97 H4
Chesterton Staffs ... 114 C2
Chesterton Green Warwks ... 83 H4
Chesterwood Nthumb ... 179 J6
Chestfield Kent ... 40 F2
Chestnut Street Kent ... 53 J6
Cheston Devon ... 7 K3
Cheswardine Shrops ... 114 A5
Cheswick Nthumb ... 203 G4
Cheswick Green Solhll ... 98 E8
Chetnole Dorset ... 16 B1
Chettiscombe Devon ... 29 H7
Chettisham Cambs ... 103 L6
Chettle Dorset ... 32 F8
Chetton Shrops ... 96 F5
Chetwode Bucks ... 66 F1
Chetwynd Wrekin ... 114 A7
Chetwynd Aston Wrekin ... 114 B8
Cheveley Cambs ... 88 D3
Chevening Kent ... 52 A7
Cheverton IoW ... 19 G6
Chevington Suffk ... 88 F3
Chevithorne Devon ... 29 H7
Chew Magna BaNES ... 45 H6
Chew Moor Bolton ... 139 K6
Chew Stoke BaNES ... 45 H6
Chewton Keynsham BaNES ... 45 K5
Chewton Mendip Somset ... 45 H8
Chichacott Devon ... 12 E3
Chicheley M Keyn ... 85 H6
Chichester W Susx ... 20 E6
Chichester Crematorium
　　W Susx ... 20 E5
Chickerell Dorset ... 16 C6
Chickering Suffk ... 106 E8
Chicklade Wilts ... 32 F4
Chicksands C Beds ... 86 C7
Chickward Herefs ... 79 K4
Chidden Hants ... 35 K7
Chiddingfold Surrey ... 36 E4
Chiddingly E Susx ... 23 L4
Chiddingstone Kent ... 38 D4
Chiddingstone Causeway
　　Kent ... 38 E4
Chideock Dorset ... 15 K4
Chidham W Susx ... 20 C6
Chidswell Kirk ... 141 L3
Chieveley W Berk ... 48 C4

Chignall St James Essex ... 71 G5
Chignall Smealy Essex ... 71 G5
Chigwell Essex ... 70 B8
Chigwell Row Essex ... 70 C8
Chilbolton Hants ... 34 E3
Chilcomb Hants ... 35 G5
Chilcombe Dorset ... 15 M4
Chilcompton Somset ... 45 J8
Chilcote Leics ... 99 H1
Childer Thornton Ches W ... 129 J4
Child Okeford Dorset ... 32 D8
Childrey Oxon ... 48 A2
Child's Ercall Shrops ... 113 L6
Childswickham Worcs ... 82 C7
Childwall Lpool ... 129 K2
Childwick Bury Herts ... 68 F5
Childwick Green Herts ... 68 F5
Chilfrome Dorset ... 16 B3
Chilgrove W Susx ... 20 D4
Chilham Kent ... 40 E4
Chilla Devon ... 12 B2
Chillaton Devon ... 12 B6
Chillenden Kent ... 41 J4
Chillerton IoW ... 19 G6
Chillesford Suffk ... 91 J5
Chillingham Nthumb ... 203 H7
Chillington Devon ... 8 C8
Chillington Somset ... 30 F8
Chilmark Wilts ... 33 G4
Chilmington Green Kent ... 40 C7
Chilson Oxon ... 65 L3
Chilsworthy Cnwll ... 12 A8
Chilsworthy Devon ... 11 L1
Chiltern Green C Beds ... 68 E3
Chilterns Crematorium Bucks ... 68 B7
Chilthorne Domer Somset ... 31 H7
Chilton Bucks ... 67 G5
Chilton Devon ... 13 K2
Chilton Dur ... 169 H5
Chilton Kent ... 41 J4
Chilton Oxon ... 48 C2
Chilton Suffk ... 89 H6
Chilton Candover Hants ... 35 J3
Chilton Cantelo Somset ... 31 J6
Chilton Foliat Wilts ... 47 L5
Chilton Polden Somset ... 30 E3
Chilton Street Suffk ... 88 E6
Chilton Trinity Somset ... 30 D3
Chilwell Notts ... 116 E4
Chilworth Hants ... 34 E7
Chilworth Surrey ... 36 F2
Chimney Oxon ... 65 M7
Chineham Hants ... 49 G7
Chingford Gt Lon ... 69 K8
Chinley Derbys ... 131 L3
Chinnor Oxon ... 67 J6
Chipchase Castle Nthumb ... 179 K4
Chipnall Shrops ... 114 A5
Chippenham Cambs ... 88 D1
Chippenham Wilts ... 46 D4
Chipperfield Herts ... 68 D6
Chipping Herts ... 69 K1
Chipping Lancs ... 147 M7
Chipping Campden Gloucs ... 82 E7
Chipping Hill Essex ... 71 K4
Chipping Norton Oxon ... 65 L2
Chipping Ongar Essex ... 70 E6
Chipping Sodbury S Glos ... 45 L3
Chipping Warden Nhants ... 83 L5
Chipshop Devon ... 12 B7
Chipstable Somset ... 29 J5
Chipstead Kent ... 38 D2
Chipstead Surrey ... 51 H7
Chirbury Shrops ... 95 G4
Chirk Wrexhm ... 112 D4
Chirnside Border ... 202 D2
Chirnsidebridge Border ... 202 C2
Chirton Wilts ... 47 G7
Chisbury Wilts ... 47 K5
Chiselborough Somset ... 31 G7
Chiseldon Swindn ... 47 J3
Chiselhampton Oxon ... 66 E7
Chisholme Border ... 188 D4
Chislehurst Gt Lon ... 51 L5
Chislet Kent ... 41 H2
Chisley Calder ... 140 F2
Chiswell Green Herts ... 68 E6
Chiswick Gt Lon ... 51 G3
Chiswick End Cambs ... 87 H6
Chisworth Derbys ... 131 K2
Chitcombe E Susx ... 24 E3
Chithurst W Susx ... 36 C5
Chittering Cambs ... 87 K1
Chitterne Wilts ... 33 G2
Chittlehamholt Devon ... 28 B6
Chittlehampton Devon ... 27 L5
Chittoe Wilts ... 46 D5
Chivelstone Devon ... 8 A7
Chivenor Devon ... 27 J4

Chiverton Cross Cnwll 4 B5
Chlenry D & G 172 E3
Chobham Surrey 50 B6
Cholderton Wilts 34 B2
Cholesbury Bucks 68 B5
Chollerford Nthumb 179 L5
Chollerton Nthumb 179 L4
Cholmondeston Ches E 130 C7
Cholsey Oxon 48 E2
Cholstrey Herefs 80 B3
Chop Gate N York 161 J3
Choppington Nthumb 181 G2
Chopwell Gatesd 180 D7
Chorley Ches E 113 J1
Chorley Lancs 139 H4
Chorley Shrops 96 F6
Chorley Staffs 98 D1
Chorleywood Herts 68 D7
Chorleywood West Herts 68 C7
Chorlton Ches E 114 A2
Chorlton-cum-Hardy Manch 130 F1
Chorlton Lane Ches W 113 G2
Choulton Shrops 95 J5
Chowley Ches W 129 L8
Chrishall Essex 87 J7
Chrisswell Inver 207 L4
Christchurch Cambs 103 K4
Christchurch Dorset 18 B5
Christchurch Gloucs 63 H4
Christchurch Newpt 44 D1
Christian Malford Wilts 46 D3
Christleton Ches W 129 K6
Christmas Common Oxon 67 H8
Christmas Pie Surrey 36 D1
Christon N Som 44 D7
Christon Bank Nthumb 191 J2
Christow Devon 13 J5
Christ's Hospital W Susx 37 H5
Chuck Hatch E Susx 38 D6
Chudleigh Devon 13 K6
Chudleigh Knighton Devon 13 K7
Chulmleigh Devon 28 B8
Chunal Derbys 131 L2
Church Lancs 139 L2
Churcham Gloucs 63 M3
Church Aston Wrekin 114 A8
Church Brampton Nhants 84 D2
Church Brough Cumb 167 J7
Church Broughton Derbys 115 K5
Church Cove Cnwll 3 H8
Church Crookham Hants 49 K8
Churchdown Gloucs 64 C3
Church Eaton Staffs 114 C8
Church End Bed 85 L3
Church End Bed 86 C3
Church End Bucks 67 H5
Church End C Beds 68 C3
Church End C Beds 68 C3
Church End C Beds 85 J8
Church End C Beds 85 K8
Church End C Beds 86 D4
Church End C Beds 86 D7
Church End Cambs 102 B8
Church End Cambs 102 E6
Church End Cambs 103 G7
Church End Essex 70 F3
Church End Essex 71 H2
Church End Essex 71 H4
Churchend Essex 72 E8
Church End Gloucs 81 K8
Church End Gt Lon 51 H1
Church End Herts 68 E5
Church End Herts 69 H1
Church End Herts 70 C3
Church End Lincs 119 H5
Church End Lincs 145 L8
Church End Warwks 99 H5
Church End Warwks 99 H5
Church Enstone Oxon 66 A2
Church Fenton N York 151 H8
Churchfield Sandw 98 C5
Churchgate Herts 69 K6
Churchgate Street Essex 70 C5
Church Green Devon 14 E3
Church Gresley Derbys 115 M7
Church Hanborough Oxon 66 B4
Church Hill Staffs 98 C1
Church Houses N York 161 L3
Churchill Devon 15 G2
Churchill Devon 27 L3
Churchill N Som 44 E7
Churchill Oxon 65 L2
Churchill Worcs 81 L4
Churchill Worcs 97 K7
Churchinford Somset 30 B8
Church Knowle Dorset 17 H6
Church Laneham Notts 135 G4
Church Langton Leics 100 F5
Church Lawford Warwks 99 M8

Church Lawton Ches E 130 F8
Church Leigh Staffs 115 G4
Church Lench Worcs 82 B5
Church Mayfield Staffs 115 J3
Church Minshull Ches E 130 C7
Church Norton W Susx 20 E7
Churchover Warwks 100 B7
Church Preen Shrops 96 C4
Church Pulverbatch Shrops 95 K3
Churchstanton Somset 30 B7
Churchstoke Powys 95 G4
Churchstow Devon 7 K5
Church Stowe Nhants 84 C4
Church Street Essex 88 F6
Church Street Kent 52 F4
Church Street Suffk 107 K6
Church Stretton Shrops 95 L4
Churchthorpe Lincs 145 J8
Churchtown Bpool 146 F7
Churchtown Cnwll 10 F7
Churchtown Derbys 132 E7
Churchtown Devon 28 B2
Churchtown IoM 154 f3
Churchtown Lancs 147 J7
Church Town N Linc 143 K6
Churchtown Sefton 138 D4
Church Village Rhondd 43 G4
Church Warsop Notts 133 L6
Church Wilne Derbys 116 D5
Churnsike Lodge Nthumb 178 F3
Churston Ferrers Torbay 8 D4
Churt Surrey 36 C3
Churton Ches W 129 K8
Churwell Leeds 141 L2
Chwilog Gwynd 109 H4
Chyandour Cnwll 2 D5
Chyanvounder Cnwll 3 G6
Chyeowling Cnwll 3 K3
Chyvarloe Cnwll 3 G6
Cil Powys 94 E3
Cilcain Flints 128 E6
Cilcennin Cerdgn 76 F3
Cilcewydd Powys 94 F3
Cilfrew Neath 57 L5
Cilfynydd Rhondd 43 H3
Cilgerran Pembks 75 L4
Cilgwyn Carmth 59 K3
Cilgwyn Gwynd 109 J1
Ciliau-Aeron Cerdgn 76 F4
Cilmaengwyn Neath 57 K4
Cilmery Powys 78 D5
Cilrhedyn Pembks 58 A2
Cilsan Carmth 59 H4
Ciltalgarth Gwynd 111 G3
Cilycwm Carmth 77 L7
Cimla Neath 57 L5
Cinderford Gloucs 63 K4
Cinder Hill Wolves 97 L4
Cippenham Slough 50 B3
Cirencester Gloucs 64 F6
Citadilla N York 160 B3
City Gt Lon 51 J3
City V Glam 42 F6
City Dulas IoA 125 H2
City of London Crematorium
    Gt Lon 51 L2
Clabhach Ag & B 224 F3
Clachaig Ag & B 207 J3
Clachan Ag & B 206 B7
Clachan Ag & B 216 B3
Clachan Ag & B 217 H6
Clachan Ag & B 228 D6
Clachan Highld 247 H1
Clachan-a-Luib W Isls 283 C8
Clachan Mor Ag & B 224 C5
Clachan na Luib W Isls 283 C8
Clachan of Campsie E Duns 209 G3
Clachan-Seil Ag & B 216 B3
Clachnaharry Highld 251 H2
Clachtoll Highld 270 D3
Clackavoid P & K 233 H3
Clackmannan Clacks 210 B1
Clackmannanshire Bridge Fife 210 B2
Clackmarras Moray 266 E4
Clacton-on-Sea Essex 73 J4
Cladich Ag & B 217 H3
Cladswell Worcs 82 C3
Claggan Highld 227 K3
Claigan Highld 258 C6
Clandown BaNES 45 K7
Clanfield Hants 35 L7
Clanfield Oxon 65 L6
Clannaborough Devon 13 H2
Clanville Hants 34 D1
Clanville Somset 31 K4
Claonaig Ag & B 206 D7
Clapgate Dorset 17 K2
Clapgate Herts 70 C2
Clapham Bed 85 K5

Clapham Devon 13 L5
Clapham Gt Lon 51 H4
Clapham N York 148 C2
Clapham W Susx 21 J5
Clapham Green Bed 85 K4
Clap Hill Kent 40 D7
Clappersgate Cumb 156 E2
Clapton Somset 15 J1
Clapton Somset 45 J8
Clapton-in-Gordano N Som 44 F4
Clapton-on-the-Hill Gloucs 65 H3
Clapworthy Devon 28 B6
Clarach Cerdgn 92 D6
Claravale Gatesd 180 E6
Clarbeston Pembks 55 H3
Clarbeston Road Pembks 55 G3
Clarborough Notts 134 E3
Clare Suffk 88 F6
Clarebrand D & G 175 J2
Clarencefield D & G 176 E5
Clarewood Nthumb 180 B5
Clarilaw Border 188 F3
Clark's Green Surrey 37 J3
Clarkston E Rens 208 F7
Clashmore Highld 263 K2
Clashmore Highld 270 D2
Clashnessie Highld 270 E2
Clashnoir Moray 254 E7
Clathy P & K 221 H3
Clathymore P & K 221 H3
Clatt Abers 255 L6
Clatter Powys 94 B4
Clatterford End Essex 70 F4
Clatworthy Somset 29 J4
Claughton Lancs 147 K7
Claughton Lancs 147 L3
Claughton Wirral 129 G2
Clavelshay Somset 30 C4
Claverdon Warwks 82 E2
Claverham N Som 44 F5
Clavering Essex 70 C1
Claverley Shrops 97 H5
Claverton BaNES 46 A6
Claverton Down BaNES 45 M6
Clawdd-coch V Glam 43 G6
Clawdd-newydd Denbgs 111 L1
Clawthorpe Cumb 157 H7
Clawton Devon 11 L3
Claxby Lincs 136 B1
Claxby Lincs 137 H5
Claxton N York 151 L4
Claxton Norfk 107 G3
Claybrooke Magna Leics 100 B5
Clay Common Suffk 107 K7
Clay Coton Nhants 100 D8
Clay Cross Derbys 133 H7
Claydon Oxon 83 K5
Claydon Suffk 90 D5
Clay End Herts 69 J2
Claygate D & G 177 L3
Claygate Kent 39 H4
Claygate Surrey 50 F6
Claygate Cross Kent 38 F2
Clayhall Gt Lon 51 L1
Clayhanger Devon 29 J6
Clayhanger Wsall 98 D3
Clayhidon Devon 29 L7
Clayhill E Susx 24 F3
Clayhill Hants 18 D2
Clayhithe Cambs 87 K2
Clayock Highld 279 L4
Claypit Hill Cambs 87 G4
Claypits Gloucs 63 M6
Claypole Lincs 117 M2
Claythorpe Lincs 137 H4
Clayton C Brad 141 H2
Clayton Donc 142 C6
Clayton W Susx 22 D4
Clayton Green Lancs 139 H3
Clayton-le-Moors Lancs 139 M2
Clayton-le-Woods Lancs 139 H3
Clayton West Kirk 141 L5
Clayworth Notts 134 E2
Cleadale Highld 236 F3
Cleadon S Tyne 181 J6
Clearbrook Devon 7 G2
Clearwell Gloucs 63 H5
Clearwell Meend Gloucs 63 H5
Cleasby N York 169 H8
Cleat Ork 275 c6
Cleatlam Dur 168 E7
Cleator Cumb 164 D7
Cleator Moor Cumb 164 D7
Cleckheaton Kirk 141 J3
Cleedownton Shrops 96 D7
Cleehill Shrops 96 D8
Cleekhimin N Lans 209 K7
Clee St Margaret Shrops 96 D6
Cleestanton Shrops 96 D7

Cleethorpes NE Lin 145 J6
Cleeton St Mary Shrops 96 E7
Cleeve N Som 44 F5
Cleeve Oxon 48 F3
Cleeve Hill Gloucs 64 E2
Cleeve Prior Worcs 82 C5
Cleghornie E Loth 212 D2
Clehonger Herefs 80 B7
Cleish P & K 221 K7
Cleland N Lans 209 L7
Clement's End C Beds 68 C4
Clement Street Kent 52 B5
Clenamacrie Ag & B 216 E2
Clench Common Wilts 47 H6
Clenchwarton Norfk 120 D7
Clenerty Abers 268 D4
Clent Worcs 97 L7
Cleobury Mortimer Shrops 96 F8
Cleobury North Shrops 96 E6
Cleongart Ag & B 192 D2
Clephanton Highld 252 F2
Clerkhill D & G 187 L6
Cleuch-head D & G 185 K3
Clevancy Wilts 46 F4
Clevedon N Som 44 E5
Cleveley Oxon 66 B2
Cleveleys Lancs 146 F7
Cleverton Wilts 46 E2
Clewer Somset 31 G1
Cley next the Sea Norfk 122 A3
Cliburn Cumb 166 E5
Cliddesden Hants 35 K1
Cliff Warwks 99 G4
Cliffe Lancs 139 L1
Cliffe Medway 52 F4
Cliffe N York 143 G2
Cliffe N York 169 G7
Cliff End E Susx 25 G4
Cliffe Woods Medway 52 F4
Clifford Herefs 79 J6
Clifford Leeds 150 F7
Clifford Chambers Warwks 82 E5
Clifford's Mesne Gloucs 63 K2
Cliffsend Kent 41 K2
Clifton Bristl 45 H4
Clifton C Beds 86 D7
Clifton C Nott 116 F4
Clifton C York 151 J5
Clifton Calder 141 J3
Clifton Cumb 166 C5
Clifton Derbys 115 K3
Clifton Devon 27 L3
Clifton Donc 142 E8
Clifton Lancs 138 F2
Clifton N York 150 B6
Clifton Nthumb 180 F2
Clifton Oxon 66 C1
Clifton Salfd 140 A7
Clifton Worcs 81 J6
Clifton Campville Staffs 99 H1
Clifton Hampden Oxon 66 D7
Clifton Reynes M Keyn 85 H5
Clifton upon Dunsmore
    Warwks 100 C8
Clifton upon Teme Worcs 81 G3
Cliftonville Kent 41 L1
Climping W Susx 21 G6
Clink Somset 32 C1
Clint N York 150 C4
Clinterty C Aber 245 J1
Clint Green Norfk 105 L1
Clintmains Border 201 J6
Clipiau Gwynd 93 H1
Clippesby Norfk 123 J8
Clipsham Rutlnd 118 C8
Clipston Nhants 100 F7
Clipston Notts 117 H5
Clipstone C Beds 68 B2
Clipstone Notts 134 B7
Clitheroe Lancs 148 C7
Clive Shrops 113 H6
Clixby Lincs 144 E7
Cloatley Wilts 46 E1
Clocaenog Denbgs 111 L1
Clochan Moray 267 H4
Clock Face St Hel 129 M2
Cloddiau Powys 94 F2
Clodock Herefs 62 C2
Cloford Somset 32 B2
Clola Abers 257 J3
Clophill C Beds 86 B7
Clopton Nhants 102 B7
Clopton Suffk 90 F4
Clopton Corner Suffk 90 F4
Clopton Green Suffk 88 F4
Clopton Green Suffk 89 K3
Clos du Valle Guern 9 k1
Closeburn D & G 186 D7
Closeburnmill D & G 186 D7

Closeclark IoM ... 154 C7
Closworth Somset ... 16 A1
Clothall Herts ... 69 H1
Clotton Ches W ... 129 M6
Cloudesley Bush Warwks ... 100 A6
Clouds Herefs ... 80 D7
Clough Oldham ... 140 E6
Clough Foot Calder ... 140 D3
Clough Head Calder ... 141 H4
Cloughton N York ... 163 H4
Cloughton Newlands N York ... 163 H3
Clousta Shet ... 281 d5
Clova Angus ... 233 M1
Clovelly Devon ... 26 E6
Clovenfords Border ... 200 F6
Clovulin Highld ... 228 F3
Clow Bridge Lancs ... 140 B2
Clowne Derbys ... 133 K4
Clows Top Worcs ... 81 G1
Cloy Wrexhm ... 112 F3
Cluanie Inn Highld ... 239 H1
Cluanie Lodge Highld ... 239 H2
Clubworthy Cnwll ... 11 K4
Clugston D & G ... 173 J3
Clun Shrops ... 95 H7
Clunas Highld ... 253 G2
Clunbury Shrops ... 95 J7
Clunderwen Carmth ... 55 J3
Clune Highld ... 252 E6
Clunes Highld ... 239 K6
Clungunford Shrops ... 95 K7
Clunie P & K ... 233 H6
Clunton Shrops ... 95 H7
Cluny Fife ... 222 D8
Clutton BaNES ... 45 J7
Clutton Ches W ... 113 G1
Clutton Hill BaNES ... 45 J7
Clwt-y-bont Gwynd ... 125 K7
Clydach Mons ... 61 K4
Clydach Swans ... 57 J4
Clydach Vale Rhondd ... 42 E3
Clydebank W Duns ... 208 E5
Clydebank Crematorium
   W Duns ... 208 E4
Clydey Pembks ... 75 M5
Clyffe Pypard Wilts ... 47 G3
Clynder Ag & B ... 207 L2
Clyne Neath ... 60 B7
Clynnog-fawr Gwynd ... 109 G2
Clyro Powys ... 79 H6
Clyst Honiton Devon ... 14 A4
Clyst Hydon Devon ... 14 B2
Clyst St George Devon ... 14 A5
Clyst St Lawrence Devon ... 14 B3
Clyst St Mary Devon ... 14 A4
Cnoc W Isls ... 282 g3
Cnwch Coch Cerdgn ... 92 E8
Coad's Green Cnwll ... 11 K7
Coal Aston Derbys ... 133 G4
Coalbrookvale Blae G ... 61 K5
Coalburn S Lans ... 198 D6
Coalburns Gatesd ... 180 D6
Coaley Gloucs ... 63 M6
Coalhill Essex ... 71 J7
Coalmoor Wrekin ... 96 F2
Coalpit Heath S Glos ... 45 K3
Coal Pool Wsall ... 98 C3
Coalport Wrekin ... 96 F3
Coalsnaughton Clacks ... 221 G8
Coal Street Suffk ... 90 F1
Coaltown of Balgonie Fife ... 222 E7
Coaltown of Wemyss Fife ... 222 E8
Coalville Leics ... 99 L1
Coanwood Nthumb ... 178 F7
Coat Somset ... 31 G6
Coatbridge N Lans ... 209 J6
Coatdyke N Lans ... 209 K6
Coate Swindn ... 47 J2
Coate Wilts ... 46 F6
Coates Cambs ... 102 F4
Coates Gloucs ... 64 E7
Coates Lincs ... 135 H3
Coates Notts ... 135 G3
Coates W Susx ... 21 G3
Coatham R & Cl ... 170 E5
Coatham Mundeville Darltn ... 169 H6
Cobbaton Devon ... 27 L5
Coberley Gloucs ... 64 D4
Cobhall Common Herefs ... 80 B8
Cobham Kent ... 52 E5
Cobham Surrey ... 50 E7
Coblers Green Essex ... 71 G3
Cobley Dorset ... 33 H6
Cobnash Herefs ... 80 B3
Cobo Guern ... 9 j2
Cobridge C Stke ... 114 D2
Coburby Abers ... 269 G3
Cock Alley Derbys ... 133 H5
Cockayne N York ... 161 K3

Cockayne Hatley C Beds ... 86 F5
Cock Bank Wrexhm ... 112 E2
Cock Bevington Warwks ... 82 C5
Cock Bridge Abers ... 243 J2
Cockburnspath Border ... 213 G5
Cock Clarks Essex ... 71 K6
Cock & End Suffk ... 88 E4
Cockenzie and Port Seton
   E Loth ... 211 L4
Cocker Bar Lancs ... 139 G3
Cocker Brook Lancs ... 139 L3
Cockerham Lancs ... 147 J5
Cockermouth Cumb ... 164 F4
Cockernhoe Herts ... 68 E2
Cockersdale Leeds ... 141 K2
Cockett Swans ... 57 H6
Cockfield Dur ... 168 E6
Cockfield Suffk ... 89 H4
Cockfosters Gt Lon ... 69 H7
Cock Green Essex ... 71 G3
Cocking W Susx ... 20 E3
Cocking Causeway W Susx ... 20 E3
Cockington Torbay ... 8 D2
Cocklake Somset ... 31 G1
Cockley Beck Cumb ... 156 C2
Cockley Cley Norfk ... 104 F3
Cock Marling E Susx ... 24 F3
Cockpole Green Wokham ... 49 J3
Cocks Cnwll ... 4 C4
Cockshutford Shrops ... 96 D6
Cockshutt Shrops ... 113 G5
Cock Street Kent ... 39 K3
Cockthorpe Norfk ... 121 L3
Cockwells Cnwll ... 2 E4
Cockwood Devon ... 14 A6
Cockwood Somset ... 30 B2
Cockyard Derbys ... 131 L4
Cockyard Herefs ... 80 A8
Coddenham Suffk ... 90 D4
Coddington Ches W ... 129 K8
Coddington Herefs ... 81 G6
Coddington Notts ... 117 L1
Codford St Mary Wilts ... 33 G3
Codford St Peter Wilts ... 33 G3
Codicote Herts ... 69 G3
Codmore Hill W Susx ... 21 H3
Codnor Derbys ... 116 C2
Codrington S Glos ... 45 L3
Codsall Staffs ... 97 K3
Codsall Wood Staffs ... 97 J2
Coedely Rhondd ... 42 F4
Coedkernew Newpt ... 44 B2
Coed Morgan Mons ... 62 D5
Coedpoeth Wrexhm ... 112 D1
Coed Talon Flints ... 129 G7
Coedway Powys ... 112 E8
Coed-y-Bryn Cerdgn ... 76 C6
Coed-y-caerau Newpt ... 44 D1
Coed-y-paen Mons ... 62 C7
Coed-yr-ynys Powys ... 61 J3
Coed Ystumgwern Gwynd ... 109 K6
Coelbren Powys ... 60 C5
Coffinswell Devon ... 8 D1
Coffle End Bed ... 85 K3
Cofton Devon ... 13 M6
Cofton Hackett Worcs ... 98 C8
Cogan V Glam ... 43 J7
Cogenhoe Nhants ... 84 F3
Cogges Oxon ... 65 M5
Coggeshall Essex ... 71 K3
Coggin's Mill E Susx ... 23 K2
Coignafearn Highld ... 251 J8
Coilacriech Abers ... 243 K4
Coilantogle Stirlg ... 219 K5
Coillore Highld ... 246 E1
Coity Brdgnd ... 42 D5
Col W Isls ... 282 g3
Colaboll Highld ... 272 E6
Colan Cnwll ... 4 D4
Colaton Raleigh Devon ... 14 C5
Colbost Highld ... 258 C7
Colburn N York ... 160 B3
Colby Cumb ... 166 F6
Colby IoM ... 154 b7
Colby Norfk ... 122 E5
Colchester Essex ... 72 E2
Colchester Crematorium
   Essex ... 72 E3
Cold Ash W Berk ... 48 D5
Cold Ashby Nhants ... 100 A8
Cold Ashton S Glos ... 45 L4
Cold Aston Gloucs ... 65 H3
Coldbackie Highld ... 277 K4
Coldbeck Cumb ... 158 C2
Cold Blow Pembks ... 55 J4
Cold Brayfield M Keyn ... 85 H5
Cold Cotes N York ... 148 C2
Coldean Br & H ... 22 E5
Coldeast Devon ... 13 J7

Colden Calder ... 140 E2
Colden Common Hants ... 35 G6
Coldfair Green Suffk ... 91 K3
Coldham Cambs ... 103 J3
Cold Hanworth Lincs ... 135 L3
Coldharbour Cnwll ... 4 B5
Coldharbour Devon ... 29 J8
Coldharbour Gloucs ... 63 H6
Cold Harbour Herts ... 68 F4
Cold Harbour Oxon ... 48 F3
Coldharbour Surrey ... 37 H2
Cold Hatton Wrekin ... 113 K7
Cold Hatton Heath Wrekin ... 113 K7
Cold Hesledon Dur ... 169 L2
Cold Hiendley Wakefd ... 142 B5
Cold Higham Nhants ... 84 C4
Coldingham Border ... 213 K6
Cold Kirby N York ... 161 N6
Coldmeece Staffs ... 114 D5
Cold Newton Leics ... 100 F2
Cold Northcott Cnwll ... 11 H5
Cold Norton Essex ... 71 K7
Cold Overton Leics ... 101 H2
Coldred Kent ... 41 J6
Coldridge Devon ... 13 G1
Coldstream Border ... 202 C5
Coldwaltham W Susx ... 21 H3
Coldwell Herefs ... 80 A8
Coldwells Abers ... 257 H4
Cold Weston Shrops ... 96 C6
Cole Somset ... 31 L4
Colebatch Shrops ... 95 H6
Colebrook C Plym ... 7 G3
Colebrook Devon ... 14 B2
Colebrooke Devon ... 13 H3
Coleby Lincs ... 135 K7
Coleby N Linc ... 143 M4
Cole End Warwks ... 99 G5
Coleford Devon ... 13 H2
Coleford Gloucs ... 63 H5
Coleford Somset ... 31 L1
Coleford Water Somset ... 29 L4
Colegate End Norfk ... 106 D6
Cole Green Herts ... 69 H5
Cole Green Herts ... 70 B1
Cole Henley Hants ... 34 F1
Colehill Dorset ... 17 K2
Coleman Green Herts ... 69 G4
Coleman's Hatch E Susx ... 38 C6
Colemere Shrops ... 113 G5
Colemore Hants ... 35 L5
Colemore Green Shrops ... 97 G4
Colenden P & K ... 221 K1
Coleorton Leics ... 116 C8
Colerne Wilts ... 46 B5
Colesbourne Gloucs ... 64 E4
Cole's Cross Devon ... 8 A5
Coles Cross Dorset ... 15 J2
Colesden Bed ... 86 C4
Coles Green Suffk ... 90 C7
Coleshill Bucks ... 68 B8
Coleshill Oxon ... 65 K8
Coleshill Warwks ... 99 G5
Colestocks Devon ... 14 C3
Coley BaNES ... 45 H7
Colgate W Susx ... 37 K4
Colinsburgh Fife ... 223 H6
Colinton C Edin ... 211 H5
Colintraive Ag & B ... 207 G4
Colkirk Norfk ... 121 K6
Coll Ag & B ... 225 G2
Coll W Isls ... 282 g3
Collace P & K ... 222 C1
Collafirth Shet ... 281 d3
Collaton Devon ... 7 L7
Collaton St Mary Torbay ... 8 C3
College of Roseisle Moray ... 266 C3
College Town Br For ... 49 K6
Collessie Fife ... 222 D4
Colleton Mills Devon ... 28 B7
Collier Row Gt Lon ... 52 B1
Collier's End Herts ... 69 K3
Collier's Green E Susx ... 24 E3
Colliers Green Kent ... 39 J5
Collier Street Kent ... 39 H4
Colliery Row Sundld ... 169 J1
Collieston Abers ... 257 J6
Collin D & G ... 176 D4
Collingbourne Ducis Wilts ... 47 K8
Collingbourne Kingston Wilts ... 47 K7
Collingham Leeds ... 150 E6
Collingham Notts ... 135 G7
Collington Herefs ... 80 F3
Collingtree Nhants ... 84 E4
Collins Green Warrtn ... 130 A1
Collins Green Worcs ... 81 G4
Colliston Angus ... 234 F6
Colliton Devon ... 14 C2
Collyweston Nhants ... 101 M3

Colmonell S Ayrs ... 182 E5
Colmworth Bed ... 86 C4
Colnabaichin Abers ... 243 J2
Colnbrook Slough ... 50 C3
Colne Cambs ... 103 H8
Colne Lancs ... 148 F7
Colne Bridge Kirk ... 141 J4
Colne Edge Lancs ... 148 F7
Colne Engaine Essex ... 71 K1
Colney Norfk ... 106 D2
Colney Heath Herts ... 69 G6
Colney Street Herts ... 68 F6
Coln Rogers Gloucs ... 65 G5
Coln St Aldwyns Gloucs ... 65 H6
Coln St Dennis Gloucs ... 65 G5
Colonsay Ag & B ... 214 D5
Colpy Abers ... 256 B5
Colquhar Border ... 200 D5
Colquite Cnwll ... 10 E8
Colscott Devon ... 26 F7
Colsterdale N York ... 159 L6
Colsterworth Lincs ... 118 B6
Colston Bassett Notts ... 117 J5
Coltfield Moray ... 266 C3
Colt Hill Hants ... 49 H8
Coltishall Norfk ... 122 F7
Colton Cumb ... 156 D5
Colton Leeds ... 142 B1
Colton N York ... 151 H6
Colton Norfk ... 106 C2
Colton Staffs ... 115 G7
Colt's Hill Kent ... 39 G4
Columbjohn Devon ... 13 M3
Colva Powys ... 79 H4
Colvend D & G ... 175 J4
Colwall Herefs ... 81 H6
Colwell Nthumb ... 179 M4
Colwich Staffs ... 115 G6
Colwick Notts ... 117 G3
Colwinston V Glam ... 42 E6
Colworth W Susx ... 20 F6
Colwyn Bay Conwy ... 127 G4
Colwyn Bay Crematorium
   Conwy ... 127 G4
Colyford Devon ... 14 F4
Colyton Devon ... 14 F4
Combe Devon ... 7 L7
Combe Herefs ... 79 L3
Combe Oxon ... 66 B4
Combe W Berk ... 48 A6
Combe Almer Dorset ... 17 J3
Combe Common Surrey ... 36 E4
Combe Down BaNES ... 45 M6
Combe Fishacre Devon ... 8 C2
Combe Florey Somset ... 29 L4
Combe Hay BaNES ... 45 L7
Combeinteignhead Devon ... 13 L8
Combe Martin Devon ... 27 K2
Combe Raleigh Devon ... 14 E2
Comberbach Ches W ... 130 C4
Comberford Staffs ... 99 G2
Comberton Cambs ... 87 H4
Comberton Herefs ... 80 C2
Combe St Nicholas Somset ... 30 D8
Combpyne Devon ... 15 G4
Combridge Staffs ... 115 H4
Combrook Warwks ... 83 H5
Combs Derbys ... 131 L4
Combs Suffk ... 90 B4
Combs Ford Suffk ... 90 B4
Combwich Somset ... 30 C2
Comers Abers ... 244 F2
Comhampton Worcs ... 81 J2
Commercial End Cambs ... 87 L3
Commins Coch Powys ... 93 H3
Commondale N York ... 170 F8
Common Edge Bpool ... 138 C1
Common End Cumb ... 164 D6
Common Moor Cnwll ... 6 A1
Common Platt Wilts ... 47 G2
Commonside Ches W ... 130 A5
Commonside Derbys ... 115 L3
Common Side Derbys ... 133 G4
Commonwood Shrops ... 113 H6
Commonwood Wrexhm ... 112 F1
Compass Somset ... 30 D4
Compstall Stockp ... 131 J2
Compstonend D & G ... 175 G4
Compton Devon ... 8 C2
Compton Hants ... 34 D5
Compton Hants ... 34 E8
Compton Staffs ... 97 J6
Compton Surrey ... 36 E2
Compton W Berk ... 48 D3
Compton W Susx ... 20 C4
Compton Wilts ... 47 H8
Compton Abbas Dorset ... 32 E7
Compton Abdale Gloucs ... 64 F4
Compton Bassett Wilts ... 46 F4

Compton Beauchamp – Cox Common 305

mpton Beauchamp Oxon 47 K2
mpton Bishop Somset 44 E7
mpton Chamberlayne Wilts 33 H5
mpton Dando BaNES 45 J6
mpton Dundon Somset 31 H4
mpton Durville Somset 30 F7
mpton Greenfield S Glos 45 H3
mpton Martin BaNES 45 G7
mpton Pauncefoot Somset 31 L5
mpton Valence Dorset 16 B4
mrie Fife 210 D1
mrie P & K 220 D3
naglen House Highld 229 G2
nchra Highld 248 E6
ncraigie P & K 233 G6
nder Green Lancs 147 J4
nderton Worcs 81 M7
ndicote Gloucs 65 H2
ndorrat N Lans 209 K4
ndover Shrops 96 B2
ney Hill Gloucs 64 B3
neyhurst Common W Susx 37 H6
neysthorpe N York 151 M2
neythorpe N York 150 E4
ney Weston Suffk 105 J7
nford Hants 36 B4
ngdon's Shop Cnwll 11 K7
ngerstone Leics 99 K2
ngham Norfk 120 F6
ngleton Ches E 131 G7
ngl-y-wal Gwynd 110 D3
ngresbury N Som 44 E6
ngreve Staffs 97 K1
nheath D & G 176 C5
nicavel Moray 253 J1
ningsby Lincs 136 D8
nington Cambs 87 G2
nington Cambs 102 D6
nisbrough Donc 142 D8
nisholme Lincs 145 K8
niston Cumb 156 D3
niston E R Yk 144 F1
niston Cold N York 148 F5
nistone N York 149 H2
nnah's Quay Flints 129 G6
nnel Ag & B 228 E8
nnel Park E Ayrs 197 H8
nnor Downs Cnwll 2 F3
non Bridge Highld 250 F1
nonley N York 149 H6
nsall Staffs 114 F2
nsett Dur 180 D8
nstable Burton N York 159 L4
nstable Lee Lancs 140 B3
nstantine Cnwll 3 J5
nstantine Bay Cnwll 10 B7
ntin Highld 262 D8
nwy Conwy 126 F4
nyer Kent 40 C2
nyer's Green Suffk 89 H2
oden E Susx 24 C6
okbury Devon 12 A2
okbury Wick Devon 11 M2
okham W & M 49 L2
okham Dean W & M 49 L2
okham Rise W & M 49 L2
okhill Worcs 82 C3
okley Suffk 107 G8
okley Worcs 97 J7
okley Green Oxon 49 G1
okney Abers 245 J5
oksbridge E Susx 22 F4
ooksey Green Worcs 81 L1
ok's Green Essex 73 J3
oks Green Suffk 89 K4
okshill Staffs 114 E3
oksland Cnwll 5 J1
oksmill Green Essex 70 F6
okson Green Ches W 130 B5
olham W Susx 37 H6
oling Medway 53 G4
oling Street Medway 52 F4
ombe Cnwll 3 G3
ombe Cnwll 3 L3
ombe Cnwll 4 F4
ombe Devon 13 J6
ombe Devon 13 L7
ombe Devon 14 C4
ombe Gloucs 63 M8
ombe Hants 35 K6
ombe Wilts 33 K1
ombe Bissett Wilts 33 K5
ombe Cellars Devon 13 L8
ombe Cross Hants 35 K6
ombe Hill Gloucs 64 C2
ombe Keynes Dorset 17 G6
ombe Pafford Torbay 8 D2
ombes W Susx 21 L5
ombes-Moor Herefs 79 L3
Coombe Street Somset 32 C4
Coombeswood Dudley 98 B6
Coopersale Common Essex 70 C6
Coopersale Street Essex 70 C6
Cooper's Corner Kent 38 D3
Coopers Green E Susx 23 H3
Coopers Green Herts 69 G5
Cooper Street Kent 41 J3
Cooper Turning Bolton 139 J6
Cootham W Susx 21 J4
Copdock Suffk 90 D7
Copford Green Essex 72 D3
Copgrove N York 150 D3
Copister Shet 281 e4
Cople Bed 86 C5
Copley Calder 141 G3
Copley Dur 168 D5
Copley Tamesd 140 E8
Coplow Dale Derbys 132 C4
Copmanthorpe C York 151 J6
Copmere End Staffs 114 C5
Copp Lancs 147 H7
Coppathorne Cnwll 11 H3
Coppenhall Staffs 114 E7
Coppenhall Moss Ches E 130 D8
Copperhouse Cnwll 2 F3
Coppicegate Shrops 97 G7
Coppingford Cambs 102 D7
Coppins Corner Kent 40 B5
Copplestone Devon 13 H2
Coppull Lancs 139 H5
Coppull Moor Lancs 139 H5
Copsale W Susx 37 J6
Copster Green Lancs 139 K1
Copston Magna Warwks 99 M5
Cop Street Kent 41 J3
Copthall Green Essex 70 B7
Copt Heath Solhll 98 F7
Copt Hewick N York 150 D2
Copthorne Cnwll 11 K4
Copthorne W Susx 37 M3
Copt Oak Leics 100 B1
Copy's Green Norfk 121 L4
Copythorne Hants 34 C8
Coram Street Suffk 89 K6
Corbets Tey Gt Lon 52 C2
Corbière Jersey 9 a3
Corbridge Nthumb 180 B6
Corby Nhants 101 K5
Corby Glen Lincs 118 C6
Corby Hill Cumb 178 B7
Cordon N Ayrs 195 G5
Cordwell Derbys 132 F4
Coreley Shrops 96 E8
Cores End Bucks 49 L2
Corfe Somset 30 C7
Corfe Castle Dorset 17 J6
Corfe Mullen Dorset 17 J3
Corfton Shrops 96 B6
Corgarff Abers 243 J2
Corhampton Hants 35 J6
Corks Pond Kent 39 G5
Corlae D & G 185 G3
Corley Warwks 99 J6
Corley Ash Warwks 99 J6
Corley Moor Warwks 99 H6
Cormuir Angus 233 L2
Cornard Tye Suffk 89 H7
Corndon Devon 13 G5
Corner Row Lancs 138 E1
Corney Cumb 155 K4
Cornforth Dur 169 J4
Cornhill Abers 267 M4
Cornhill-on-Tweed Nthumb 202 D5
Cornholme Calder 140 D3
Cornish Hall End Essex 88 D7
Cornoigmore Ag & B 224 C6
Cornriggs Dur 167 K2
Cornsay Dur 168 F2
Cornsay Colliery Dur 168 F2
Corntown Highld 262 F8
Corntown V Glam 42 D6
Cornwell Oxon 65 K2
Cornwood Devon 7 H3
Cornworthy Devon 8 B4
Corpach Highld 239 H8
Corpusty Norfk 122 C5
Corrachree Abers 244 B3
Corran Highld 229 G3
Corran Highld 238 D2
Corrany IoM 154 f4
Corrie D & G 177 G2
Corrie N Ayrs 195 G2
Corriecravie N Ayrs 193 J4
Corriegills N Ayrs 195 G4
Corriegour Lodge Hotel Highld 239 M5
Corriemoille Highld 262 C7
Corrimony Highld 250 C5
Corringham Lincs 135 H2
Corringham Thurr 52 F2
Corris Gwynd 93 G2
Corris Uchaf Gwynd 92 F2
Corrow Ag & B 217 K7
Corry Highld 247 K4
Corscombe Devon 12 E3
Corscombe Dorset 15 L2
Corse Gloucs 64 A2
Corse Lawn Gloucs 64 B1
Corsham Wilts 46 C5
Corsindae Abers 244 F2
Corsley Wilts 32 D2
Corsley Heath Wilts 32 D2
Corsock D & G 185 J7
Corston BaNES 45 K6
Corston Wilts 46 D2
Corstorphine C Edin 211 G4
Cors-y-Gedol Gwynd 109 L7
Cortachy Angus 234 B3
Corton Suffk 107 L4
Corton Wilts 32 F3
Corton Denham Somset 31 K6
Coruanan Highld 229 H2
Corwen Denbgs 111 L3
Coryates Dorset 16 B5
Coryton Devon 12 B6
Coryton Thurr 52 F2
Cosby Leics 100 C4
Coseley Dudley 97 L4
Cosford Shrops 97 H2
Cosgrove Nhants 84 F6
Cosham C Port 19 L3
Cosheston Pembks 55 G6
Coshieville P & K 231 L5
Cossall Notts 116 E3
Cossall Marsh Notts 116 E3
Cossington Leics 100 D1
Cossington Somset 30 E3
Costessey Norfk 106 D1
Costock Notts 116 F6
Coston Leics 117 M7
Coston Norfk 106 B2
Cote Oxon 65 M6
Cote Somset 30 E2
Cotebrook Ches W 130 B6
Cotehill Cumb 166 B1
Cotes Cumb 157 G5
Cotes Leics 116 F7
Cotes Staffs 114 C4
Cotesbach Leics 100 C7
Cotes Heath Staffs 114 C4
Cotford St Luke Somset 30 A5
Cotgrave Notts 117 H4
Cothal Abers 256 F8
Cotham Notts 117 L2
Cothelstone Somset 30 B4
Cotherstone Dur 168 C6
Cothill Oxon 66 C7
Cotleigh Devon 14 E2
Cotmanhay Derbys 116 D3
Coton Cambs 87 H3
Coton Nhants 84 D1
Coton Shrops 113 J4
Coton Staffs 98 F2
Coton Staffs 114 C7
Coton Staffs 114 F5
Coton Clanford Staffs 114 D7
Coton Hayes Staffs 114 F5
Coton Hill Shrops 96 B1
Coton in the Clay Staffs 115 K5
Coton in the Elms Derbys 115 L8
Coton Park Derbys 115 M7
Cott Devon 8 B3
Cottam E R Yk 152 F3
Cottam Lancs 139 G1
Cottam Notts 135 G4
Cottenham Cambs 87 J2
Cotterdale N York 158 E4
Cottered Herts 69 J1
Cotteridge Birm 98 D7
Cotterstock Nhants 102 A5
Cottesbrooke Nhants 100 F8
Cottesmore Rutlnd 101 K1
Cottingham E R Yk 144 D1
Cottingham Nhants 101 J5
Cottingley C Brad 149 K8
Cottingley Hall Crematorium Leeds 141 L2
Cottisford Oxon 66 E1
Cotton Suffk 90 C2
Cotton End Bed 86 B6
Cotton Tree Lancs 148 F7
Cottown Abers 255 K6
Cottown Abers 256 D8
Cottown of Gight Abers 256 E4
Cotts Devon 6 E2
Cotwall Wrekin 113 K8
Cotwalton Staffs 114 E4
Couch's Mill Cnwll 5 K3
Coughton Herefs 63 H3
Coughton Warwks 82 C3
Coulaghailtro Ag & B 206 A6
Coulags Highld 248 F3
Coulderton Cumb 155 H1
Coull Abers 244 B3
Coulport Ag & B 207 L2
Coulsdon Gt Lon 51 J7
Coulston Wilts 46 D8
Coulter S Lans 199 H6
Coultershaw Bridge W Susx 21 G3
Coultings Somset 30 C3
Coulton N York 161 K7
Coultra Fife 222 F3
Cound Shrops 96 D2
Coundlane Shrops 96 D2
Coundon Dur 169 G5
Coundon Grange Dur 169 G5
Countersett N York 159 G5
Countess Wilts 33 K2
Countess Cross Essex 72 C1
Countess Wear Devon 13 M5
Countesthorpe Leics 100 D4
Counties Crematorium Nhants 84 E4
Countisbury Devon 28 C1
Coupar Angus P & K 233 K7
Coup Green Lancs 139 H2
Coupland Cumb 167 G7
Coupland Nthumb 202 E7
Cour Ag & B 194 C2
Court-at-Street Kent 40 E8
Courteachan Highld 237 K1
Courteenhall Nhants 84 E4
Court Henry Carmth 59 G4
Courtsend Essex 72 F8
Courtway Somset 30 B4
Cousland Mdloth 211 L5
Cousley Wood E Susx 39 G6
Cove Ag & B 207 L3
Cove Border 213 G4
Cove Devon 29 G7
Cove Hants 49 L7
Cove Highld 260 C2
Cove Bay C Aber 245 L3
Cove Bottom Suffk 107 K7
Covehithe Suffk 107 L7
Coven Staffs 97 K2
Coveney Cambs 103 K7
Covenham St Bartholomew Lincs 136 F1
Covenham St Mary Lincs 136 F1
Coven Heath Staffs 97 K2
Coventry Covtry 99 J7
Coverack Cnwll 3 K7
Coverack Bridges Cnwll 3 H5
Coverham N York 159 K5
Covington Cambs 85 L1
Covington S Lans 199 G5
Cowan Bridge Lancs 157 K7
Cowbeech E Susx 23 K4
Cowbit Lincs 119 H7
Cowbridge V Glam 42 F6
Cowdale Derbys 132 B5
Cowden Kent 38 C5
Cowdenbeath Fife 211 G1
Cowden Pound Kent 38 C5
Cowden Station Kent 38 D5
Cowers Lane Derbys 116 A2
Cowes IoW 19 H4
Cowesby N York 161 G5
Cowesfield Green Wilts 34 B6
Cowfold W Susx 37 K6
Cowgill Cumb 158 C5
Cow Green Suffk 90 C2
Cowhill S Glos 45 J1
Cowie Stirlg 209 M1
Cowlam E R Yk 152 E3
Cowley Devon 13 L3
Cowley Gloucs 64 D4
Cowley Gt Lon 50 D3
Cowley Oxon 66 D6
Cowling Lancs 139 J4
Cowling N York 149 H7
Cowling N York 160 C5
Cowlinge Suffk 88 E4
Cowmes Kirk 141 J4
Cowpe Lancs 140 C4
Cowpen Nthumb 181 H3
Cowpen Bewley S on T 170 B5
Cowplain Hants 19 M2
Cowshill Dur 167 K3
Cowslip Green N Som 44 F6
Cowthorpe N York 150 F5
Coxall Herefs 95 J8
Coxbank Ches E 113 L3
Coxbench Derbys 116 C3
Coxbridge Somset 31 J3
Cox Common Suffk 107 H7

Coxford Cnwll 11 H3
Coxford Norfk 121 J5
Coxgreen Staffs 97 H6
Coxheath Kent 39 J3
Coxhoe Dur 169 J3
Coxley Somset 31 H2
Coxley Wakefd 141 L4
Coxley Wick Somset 31 H2
Coxpark Cnwll 12 A8
Coxtie Green Essex 70 E7
Coxwold N York 161 H7
Coychurch Brdgnd 42 E6
Coychurch Crematorium Brdgnd 42 D5
Coylton S Ayrs 196 E7
Coylumbridge Highld 242 B1
Coytrahen Brdgnd 42 D4
Crabbs Cross Worcs 82 B2
Crab Orchard Dorset 17 L1
Crabtree W Susx 37 K6
Crabtree Green Wrexhm 112 E3
Crackenthorpe Cumb 166 F6
Crackington Haven Cnwll 11 G3
Crackley Staffs 114 C2
Crackley Warwks 99 J8
Crackleybank Shrops 97 G1
Crackpot N York 159 H3
Cracoe N York 149 H4
Craddock Devon 29 K8
Cradle End Herts 70 C3
Cradley Dudley 97 L6
Cradley Herefs 81 G6
Cradley Heath Sandw 97 L6
Cradoc Powys 60 F1
Crafthole Cnwll 6 D4
Crafton Bucks 67 L3
Crag Foot Lancs 157 G7
Craggan Highld 253 K6
Cragganmore Moray 254 D4
Cragg Hill Leeds 150 B8
Cragg Vale Calder 140 F3
Craghead Dur 180 F8
Crai Powys 60 D2
Craibstone Moray 267 K4
Craichie Angus 234 D6
Craig Angus 235 H4
Craig Highld 249 H2
Craigbank E Ayrs 197 H8
Craigburn Border 200 B2
Craigcefnparc Swans 57 J4
Craigcleuch D & G 177 K2
Craigdam Abers 256 F5
Craigdhu Ag & B 216 C6
Craigearn Abers 245 G1
Craigellachie Moray 254 F3
Craigend P & K 221 K3
Craigend Rens 208 D5
Craigendoran Ag & B 208 A3
Craigends Rens 208 C6
Craighlaw D & G 173 H3
Craighouse Ag & B 205 H3
Craigie P & K 233 H6
Craigie S Ayrs 196 E4
Craigiefold Abers 269 G3
Craigley D & G 175 J3
Craig Llangiwg Neath 57 K4
Craiglockhart C Edin 211 H5
Craigmillar C Edin 211 J4
Craignant Shrops 112 C4
Craigneston D & G 185 J3
Craigneuk N Lans 209 K6
Craigneuk N Lans 209 K7
Craignure Ag & B 227 L5
Craigo Angus 235 H3
Craig Penllyn V Glam 42 E6
Craigrothie Fife 222 F5
Craigruie Stirlg 219 H3
Craig's End Essex 88 E7
Craigton Angus 234 D7
Craigton C Aber 245 J3
Craigton E Rens 208 E8
Craigton Crematorium C Glas 208 F6
Craigton of Airlie Angus 233 M5
Craig-y-Duke Neath 57 K4
Craig-y-nos Powys 60 C4
Craik Border 188 B4
Crail Fife 223 L5
Crailing Border 189 J1
Craiselound N Linc 143 J8
Crakehall N York 160 C5
Crakehill N York 160 F7
Crakemarsh Staffs 115 H4
Crambe N York 151 M3
Cramlington Nthumb 181 G3
Cramond C Edin 211 G4
Cramond Bridge C Edin 211 G4
Crampmoor Hants 34 E6
Cranage Ches E 130 E6
Cranberry Staffs 114 C4

Cranborne Dorset 33 H8
Cranbourne Br For 50 A4
Cranbrook Devon 14 A4
Cranbrook Kent 39 J6
Cranbrook Common Kent 39 K5
Crane Moor Barns 141 M7
Crane's Corner Norfk 105 J1
Cranfield C Beds 85 J6
Cranford Devon 26 F6
Cranford Gt Lon 50 E4
Cranford St Andrew Nhants 101 K7
Cranford St John Nhants 101 K8
Cranham Gloucs 64 C4
Cranham Gt Lon 52 C2
Cranhill Warwks 82 D4
Crank St Hel 139 G7
Cranleigh Surrey 37 G3
Cranmer Green Suffk 89 L1
Cranmore IoW 18 F5
Cranmore Somset 31 L2
Cranoe Leics 101 G4
Cransford Suffk 91 H2
Cranshaws Border 212 F6
Cranstal IoM 154 f2
Cranswick E R Yk 152 F5
Crantock Cnwll 4 C3
Cranwell Lincs 118 D2
Cranwich Norfk 104 F4
Cranworth Norfk 105 K3
Craobh Haven Ag & B 216 B5
Crapstone Devon 6 F1
Crarae Ag & B 216 F7
Crask Inn Highld 272 D3
Crask of Aigas Highld 250 E3
Craster Nthumb 191 K2
Craswall Herefs 79 K8
Crateford Staffs 97 K2
Cratfield Suffk 107 G8
Crathes Abers 245 G4
Crathes Crematorium Abers 245 G4
Crathie Abers 243 J4
Crathie Highld 241 G5
Crathorne N York 161 G1
Craven Arms Shrops 95 K6
Crawcrook Gatesd 180 D6
Crawford Lancs 139 G2
Crawford S Lans 186 E2
Crawfordjohn S Lans 186 C2
Crawley Hants 34 F4
Crawley Oxon 65 M4
Crawley W Susx 37 L4
Crawley Down W Susx 38 A6
Crawleyside Dur 168 C3
Crawshawbooth Lancs 140 B3
Crawton Abers 245 J7
Craxe's Green Essex 72 D3
Cray N York 159 G6
Crayford Gt Lon 52 B4
Crayke N York 151 J2
Craymere Beck Norfk 122 B5
Crays Hill Essex 71 H8
Cray's Pond Oxon 48 F3
Craythorne Staffs 115 L6
Crazies Hill Wokham 49 J3
Creacombe Devon 28 E7
Creagan Inn Ag & B 228 F6
Creag Ghoraidh W Isls 283 c9
Creagorry W Isls 283 c9
Creaguaineach Lodge Highld 230 B2
Creamore Bank Shrops 113 H5
Creaton Nhants 84 D1
Creca D & G 177 H5
Credenhill Herefs 80 B6
Crediton Devon 13 J3
Creebank D & G 183 J7
Creebridge D & G 173 K2
Creech Dorset 17 H6
Creech Heathfield Somset 30 D5
Creech St Michael Somset 30 C6
Creed Cnwll 4 F5
Creekmoor Poole 17 K4
Creekmouth Gt Lon 51 M3
Creeksea Essex 72 D7
Creeting St Mary Suffk 90 C4
Creeton Lincs 118 D7
Creetown D & G 174 D3
Cregneash IoM 154 b8
Creg ny Baa IoM 154 e5
Cregrina Powys 79 G5
Creich Fife 222 E3
Creigiau Cardif 43 G5
Cremyll Cnwll 6 E4
Cressage Shrops 96 D3
Cressbrook Derbys 132 C5
Cresselly Pembks 55 H5
Cressex Bucks 67 K8
Cressing Essex 71 J3
Cresswell Nthumb 191 K7

Cresswell Pembks 55 H5
Cresswell Staffs 114 F4
Creswell Derbys 133 K5
Creswell Green Staffs 98 D1
Cretingham Suffk 90 F3
Cretshengan Ag & B 206 A5
Crewe Ches E 130 D8
Crewe-by-Farndon Ches W 112 F1
Crewe Crematorium Ches E 130 D8
Crewe Green Ches E 130 E8
Crew Green Powys 112 D8
Crewkerne Somset 15 K1
Crews Hill Station Gt Lon 69 J7
Crewton C Derb 116 C5
Crianlarich Stirlg 218 F2
Cribyn Cerdgn 76 F5
Criccieth Gwynd 109 J4
Crich Derbys 116 B1
Crich Carr Derbys 116 B1
Crichton Mdloth 211 L6
Crick Mons 44 F1
Crick Nhants 84 B1
Crickadarn Powys 78 F6
Cricket St Thomas Somset 15 J1
Crickheath Shrops 112 D7
Crickhowell Powys 61 K3
Cricklade Wilts 65 G8
Cricklewood Gt Lon 51 G2
Cridling Stubbs N York 142 E3
Crieff P & K 220 F3
Criggan Cnwll 5 G3
Criggion Powys 112 D8
Crigglestone Wakefd 141 M4
Crimble Rochdl 140 C5
Crimond Abers 269 K5
Crimplesham Norfk 104 C3
Crimscote Warwks 82 F5
Crinaglack Highld 250 D4
Crinan Ag & B 216 B8
Crindledyke N Lans 209 L7
Cringleford Norfk 106 D2
Cringles C Brad 149 J6
Crinow Pembks 55 K4
Cripplesease Cnwll 2 D4
Cripplestyle Dorset 33 J8
Cripp's Corner E Susx 24 D3
Croachy Highld 251 H6
Croanford Cnwll 10 E8
Crockenhill Kent 52 B5
Crocker End Oxon 49 H2
Crockerhill W Susx 20 F5
Crockernwell Devon 13 H4
Crocker's Ash Herefs 63 G4
Crockerton Wilts 32 E2
Crocketford D & G 185 K8
Crockey Hill C York 151 K6
Crockham Hill Kent 38 C3
Crockhurst Street Kent 39 G4
Crockleford Heath Essex 72 F2
Crock Street Somset 30 D8
Croeserw Neath 42 C3
Croes-goch Pembks 74 D6
Croes-lan Cerdgn 76 C6
Croesor Gwynd 110 B3
Croesyceiliog Carmth 58 D5
Croesyceiliog Torfn 62 C7
Croes-y-mwyalch Torfn 62 C8
Croes-y-pant Mons 62 C6
Croft Leics 100 B4
Croft Lincs 137 J7
Croft Warrtn 130 C1
Croftamie Stirlg 208 E2
Croft Mitchell Cnwll 3 H4
Crofton Cumb 165 J1
Crofton Wakefd 142 B4
Crofton Wilts 47 K6
Croft-on-Tees N York 160 D1
Croftown Highld 261 K3
Crofts Moray 266 F6
Crofts Bank Traffd 139 M8
Crofts of Dipple Moray 267 G4
Crofts of Savoch Abers 269 J4
Crofty Swans 56 F6
Crogen Gwynd 111 K4
Croggan Ag & B 227 K7
Croglin Cumb 166 D2
Croick Highld 262 D2
Cromarty Highld 264 B6
Crombie Fife 210 E2
Cromdale Highld 253 L6
Cromer Herts 69 J2
Cromer Norfk 122 E3
Cromford Derbys 132 F8
Cromhall S Glos 45 K1
Cromhall Common S Glos 45 K1
Cromor W Isls 282 g4
Crompton Fold Oldham 140 E6
Cromwell Notts 134 F7
Cronberry E Ayrs 197 H6

Crondall Hants 36 B1
Cronkbourne IoM 154 e6
Cronk-y-Voddy IoM 154 d5
Cronton Knows 129 L2
Crook Cumb 157 G4
Crook Dur 168 F4
Crookdake Cumb 165 G2
Crooke Wigan 139 H6
Crooked End Gloucs 63 J3
Crookedholm E Ayrs 196 E3
Crooked Soley Wilts 47 L4
Crookes Sheff 132 F2
Crookhall Dur 180 E1
Crookham Nthumb 202 E5
Crookham W Berk 48 D6
Crookham Village Hants 49 J8
Crook Inn Border 199 J7
Crooklands Cumb 157 H6
Crook of Devon P & K 221 J7
Cropper Derbys 115 L4
Cropredy Oxon 83 L6
Cropston Leics 100 C1
Cropthorne Worcs 82 B6
Cropton N York 162 D5
Cropwell Bishop Notts 117 H4
Cropwell Butler Notts 117 J4
Cros W Isls 282 h1
Crosbost W Isls 282 g4
Crosby Cumb 164 E3
Crosby IoM 154 d6
Crosby N Linc 143 M5
Crosby Sefton 138 C8
Crosby Garret Cumb 158 C1
Crosby Ravensworth Cumb 166 E3
Crosby Villa Cumb 164 E3
Croscombe Somset 31 K2
Crosemere Shrops 113 G5
Crosland Edge Kirk 141 H5
Crosland Hill Kirk 141 H5
Cross Somset 44 E8
Crossaig Ag & B 194 C1
Crossapol Ag & B 224 C6
Cross Ash Mons 62 E3
Cross-at-Hand Kent 39 K4
Crossbost W Isls 282 g4
Crossbush W Susx 21 H5
Crosscanonby Cumb 164 E3
Cross Coombe Cnwll 4 B4
Crossdale Street Norfk 122 E4
Cross End Bed 85 L4
Cross End Essex 89 G8
Crossens Sefton 138 D4
Cross Flatts C Brad 149 K7
Crossford Fife 210 E2
Crossford S Lans 198 D4
Crossgate Cnwll 11 L7
Crossgate Lincs 119 H6
Crossgate Staffs 114 E6
Crossgatehall E Loth 211 L5
Crossgates E Ayrs 196 D2
Crossgates Fife 210 F1
Cross Gates Leeds 142 B1
Crossgates N York 163 J6
Crossgates Powys 78 F2
Crossgill Lancs 147 L3
Cross Green Devon 11 M7
Cross Green Leeds 141 M2
Cross Green Staffs 97 K2
Cross Green Suffk 89 G4
Cross Green Suffk 89 H4
Cross Green Suffk 89 K4
Crosshands Carmth 55 L2
Cross Hands Carmth 59 G6
Crosshands E Ayrs 196 F3
Cross Hands Pembks 55 H4
Cross Hill Derbys 116 C2
Crosshill Fife 222 B7
Crosshill S Ayrs 183 J2
Cross Hills N York 149 H6
Crosshouse E Ayrs 196 D3
Cross Houses Shrops 96 C2
Cross Houses Shrops 96 C2
Cross in Hand E Susx 23 J3
Cross Inn Cerdgn 76 D6
Cross Inn Cerdgn 77 G4
Cross Inn Pembks 55 J5
Cross Inn Rhondd 43 G5
Cross Keys Ag & B 208 B2
Crosskeys Caerph 43 K1
Cross Keys Wilts 46 C5
Crosskirk Highld 279 H2
Crosslands Cumb 156 E1
Cross Lane IoW 19 H5
Cross Lane Head Shrops 97 G4
Cross Lanes Cnwll 3 H6
Cross Lanes Cnwll 4 C6
Cross Lanes N York 151 H3
Crosslanes Shrops 112 E7
Cross Lanes Wrexhm 112 E2

Crosslee Rens 208 C6
Crossley Kirk 141 K3
Crossmichael D & G 175 J2
Cross Oak Powys 61 H2
Cross of Jackston Abers 256 D5
Cross o' th' hands Derbys 115 M2
Crosspost W Susx 37 L6
Crossroads Abers 244 D2
Crossroads Abers 245 G5
Cross Roads C Brad 149 J8
Cross Street Suffk 106 D8
Crosston Angus 234 E4
Cross Town Ches E 130 E4
Crossway Mons 62 F3
Crossway Powys 78 E4
Crossway Green Mons 63 G8
Crossway Green Worcs 81 J2
Crossways Dorset 16 E5
Crosswell Pembks 75 J5
Crosthwaite Cumb 156 F4
Croston Lancs 138 F4
Crostwick Norfk 122 E8
Crostwight Norfk 123 G5
Crouch Kent 38 F2
Crouch Kent 40 D4
Crouch End Gt Lon 51 J1
Croucheston Wilts 33 J6
Crouch Hill Dorset 32 B8
Crough House Green Kent 38 C4
Croughton Nhants 84 A8
Crovie Abers 268 E3
Crow Hants 18 B3
Crowan Cnwll 3 G4
Crowborough E Susx 38 D7
Crowborough Warren E Susx 38 D7
Crowcombe Somset 29 L3
Crowdecote Derbys 132 B6
Crowden Derbys 141 G7
Crowden Devon 12 C3
Crowdhill Hants 35 G6
Crowdleham Kent 52 C7
Crow Edge Barns 141 J6
Crowell Oxon 67 H7
Crow End Cambs 87 G4
Crowfield Nhants 84 B7
Crowfield Suffk 90 D4
Crowfield Green Suffk 90 D4
Crowgate Street Norfk 123 G7
Crow Green Essex 70 E7
Crowhill E Loth 213 G4
Crow Hill Herefs 63 J2
Crowhole Derbys 133 G4
Crowhurst E Susx 24 D5
Crowhurst Surrey 38 B4
Crowhurst Lane End Surrey 38 B4
Crowland Lincs 102 E2
Crowland Suffk 89 K1
Crowlas Cnwll 2 E4
Crowle N Linc 143 K5
Crowle Worcs 81 L4
Crowle Green Worcs 81 L4
Crowmarsh Gifford Oxon 48 F1
Crown Corner Suffk 90 F1
Crownhill C Plym 6 F3
Crownhill Crematorium M Keyn 84 F7
Crownpits Surrey 36 E2
Crownthorpe Norfk 106 B3
Crowntown Cnwll 3 G5
Crows-an-Wra Cnwll 2 B5
Crow's Green Essex 71 G2
Crowshill Norfk 105 J2
Crow's Nest Cnwll 6 B1
Crowsnest Shrops 95 J3
Crowthorne Wokham 49 K6
Crowton Ches W 130 B5
Croxall Staffs 99 G1
Croxby Lincs 144 F8
Croxdale Dur 169 H3
Croxden Staffs 115 H4
Croxley Green Herts 68 D7
Croxteth Lpool 138 E8
Croxton Cambs 86 E3
Croxton N Linc 144 E5
Croxton Norfk 105 H6
Croxton Norfk 121 K5
Croxton Staffs 114 B5
Croxtonbank Staffs 114 B5
Croxton Green Ches E 113 J1
Croxton Kerrial Leics 117 L5
Croy Highld 252 E2
Croy N Lans 209 J4
Croyde Devon 27 H3
Croyde Bay Devon 27 G3
Croydon Cambs 87 G5
Croydon Gt Lon 51 J6
Croydon Crematorium Gt Lon 51 J5
Crubenmore Highld 241 J5
Cruckmeole Shrops 95 K2

Cruckton Shrops 95 K1
Cruden Bay Abers 257 K4
Crudgington Wrekin 113 K7
Crudie Abers 268 E5
Crudwell Wilts 64 D8
Cruft Devon 12 C3
Crûg Powys 79 H1
Crugmeer Cnwll 10 C7
Crugybar Carmth 77 J7
Crug-y-byddar Powys 94 E7
Crumlin Caerph 43 K2
Crumplehorn Cnwll 5 L4
Crumpsall Manch 140 C7
Crundale Kent 40 E5
Crundale Pembks 54 F3
Crunwear Pembks 55 L5
Cruwys Morchard Devon 28 F8
Crux Easton Hants 48 B7
Cruxton Dorset 16 B3
Crwbin Carmth 58 E6
Cryers Hill Bucks 67 L7
Crymych Pembks 75 L5
Crynant Neath 60 B6
Crystal Palace Gt Lon 51 J5
Cuaig Highld 260 A8
Cuan Ag & B 215 L2
Cubbington Warwks 83 H2
Cubert Cnwll 4 C3
Cubley Barns 141 K7
Cublington Bucks 67 K3
Cublington Herefs 79 M7
Cuckfield W Susx 22 D2
Cucklington Somset 32 C5
Cuckney Notts 133 L5
Cuckoo Bridge Lincs 119 G7
Cuckoo's Corner Hants 35 M3
Cuckoo's Nest Ches W 129 J7
Cuddesdon Oxon 66 F6
Cuddington Bucks 67 H5
Cuddington Ches W 130 B5
Cuddington Heath Ches W 113 G2
Cuddy Hill Lancs 147 J4
Cudham Gt Lon 51 L7
Cudliptown Devon 12 C6
Cudnell Bmouth 17 L3
Cudworth Barns 142 B6
Cudworth Somset 30 F8
Cuerdley Cross Warrtn 130 A2
Cufaude Hants 49 G3
Cuffley Herts 69 J6
Cuil Highld 228 F4
Culbokie Highld 263 G7
Culbone Somset 28 E1
Culburnie Highld 250 E3
Culcabock Highld 251 J3
Culcharry Highld 253 G2
Culcheth Warrtn 130 C1
Culdrain Abers 255 K5
Culduie Highld 248 A4
Culford Suffk 89 G1
Culgaith Cumb 166 E5
Culham Oxon 66 D8
Culkein Highld 270 D2
Culkein Drumbeg Highld 270 F1
Culkerton Gloucs 64 D7
Cullen Moray 267 K3
Cullercoats N Tyne 181 J4
Cullerlie Abers 245 G3
Cullicudden Highld 263 H7
Cullingworth C Brad 149 J8
Cullipool Ag & B 215 L2
Cullivoe Shet 281 e2
Culloden Highld 252 D3
Cullompton Devon 14 M1
Culm Davy Devon 29 L7
Culmington Shrops 96 B7
Culmstock Devon 29 K8
Culnacraig Highld 270 E7
Culnaightrie D & G 175 J5
Culnaknock Highld 259 J4
Culpho Suffk 90 F5
Culrain Highld 263 L1
Culross Fife 210 C2
Culroy S Ayrs 196 C8
Culsalmond Abers 256 B5
Culscadden D & G 174 D5
Culshabbin D & G 173 H4
Culswick Shet 281 c6
Cultercullen Abers 257 G7
Cults C Aber 245 K3
Culverstone Green Kent 52 D6
Culverthorpe Lincs 118 D3
Culworth Nhants 84 A6
Cumbernauld N Lans 209 K4
Cumbernauld Village N Lans 209 K4
Cumberworth Lincs 137 J5
Cumdivock Cumb 165 K1
Cuminestown Abers 268 E6
Cumledge Border 202 B2

Cummersdale Cumb 177 L8
Cummertrees D & G 176 F5
Cummingston Moray 266 C2
Cumnock E Ayrs 197 H7
Cumnor Oxon 66 C6
Cumrew Cumb 178 D8
Cumrue D & G 176 E2
Cumwhinton Cumb 178 B8
Cumwhitton Cumb 178 C8
Cundall N York 150 F1
Cunninghamhead N Ayrs 196 D3
Cunningsburgh Shet 281 e7
Cupar Fife 222 F4
Cupar Muir Fife 222 F4
Curbar Derbys 132 E5
Curbridge Hants 19 J1
Curbridge Oxon 65 M5
Curdridge Hants 35 H8
Curdworth Warwks 98 F5
Curland Somset 30 C7
Curridge W Berk 48 C4
Currie C Edin 211 G5
Curry Mallet Somset 30 E6
Curry Rivel Somset 30 F6
Curteis Corner Kent 39 L5
Curtisden Green Kent 39 J5
Curtisknowle Devon 7 L4
Cury Cnwll 3 H6
Cushnie Abers 244 C1
Cushuish Somset 30 B5
Cusop Herefs 79 J7
Cusworth Donc 142 E7
Cutcloy D & G 174 C7
Cutcombe Somset 29 G3
Cutgate Rochdl 140 C5
Cuthill Highld 263 K2
Cutiau Gwynd 110 B8
Cutler's Green Essex 70 E1
Cutmadoc Cnwll 5 J2
Cutmere Cnwll 6 C3
Cutnall Green Worcs 81 K2
Cutsdean Gloucs 65 G1
Cutsyke Wakefd 142 C3
Cutthorpe Derbys 133 G5
Cuttivett Cnwll 6 D2
Cuxham Oxon 67 G8
Cuxton Medway 52 F5
Cuxwold Lincs 144 F7
Cwm Blae G 61 J6
Cwm Denbgs 128 C4
Cwmafan Neath 57 L6
Cwmaman Rhondd 60 F7
Cwmann Carmth 77 G6
Cwmavon Torfn 62 B6
Cwmbach Carmth 56 E4
Cwmbach Carmth 75 M7
Cwmbâch Powys 79 G7
Cwmbach Rhondd 60 F6
Cwmbach Llechrhyd Powys 78 E4
Cwmbelan Powys 93 K7
Cwmbran Torfn 62 C8
Cwmbrwyno Cerdgn 92 F7
Cwm Capel Carmth 56 E4
Cwmcarn Caerph 43 K3
Cwmcarvan Mons 62 F6
Cwm-celyn Blae G 61 K5
Cwm-Cewydd Gwynd 93 J1
Cwm-cou Cerdgn 76 B6
Cwm Crawnon Powys 61 J3
Cwmdare Rhondd 60 F6
Cwmdu Carmth 59 H3
Cwmdu Powys 61 J2
Cwmdu Swans 57 H6
Cwmduad Carmth 58 D2
Cwm Dulais Swans 57 H4
Cwmdwr Carmth 59 K2
Cwmfelin Brdgnd 42 C4
Cwmfelin Myr Td 61 H6
Cwmfelin Boeth Carmth 55 L3
Cwmfelinfach Caerph 43 J3
Cwmfelin Mynach Carmth 75 L7
Cwmffrwd Carmth 58 D5
Cwmgiedd Powys 59 L6
Cwmgorse Carmth 57 K3
Cwm Gwaun Pembks 75 H5
Cwmgwili Carmth 57 G3
Cwmgwrach Neath 60 C6
Cwmhiraeth Carmth 76 C7
Cwm-Ifor Carmth 59 J4
Cwm Irfon Powys 78 A5
Cwmisfael Carmth 58 F5
Cwm Llinau Powys 93 J2
Cwmllynfell Neath 59 K6
Cwmmawr Carmth 58 F6
Cwm Morgan Carmth 58 B2
Cwmparc Rhondd 42 E3
Cwmpengraig Carmth 58 C2
Cwm Penmachno Conwy 110 E2
Cwmpennar Rhondd 61 G7

Cwmrhos Powys 61 J2
Cwmrhydyceirw Swans 57 J5
Cwmsychbant Cerdgn 76 E6
Cwmtillery Blae G 61 K6
Cwm-twrch Isaf Powys 57 L3
Cwm-twrch Uchaf Powys 59 L6
Cwm-y-glo Carmth 59 G6
Cwm-y-glo Gwynd 125 K7
Cwmyoy Mons 62 C3
Cwmystwyth Cerdgn 93 G8
Cwrt Gwynd 92 E3
Cwrt-newydd Cerdgn 76 E5
Cwrt-y-gollen Powys 61 K4
Cyfronydd Powys 94 E2
Cylibebyll Neath 57 K4
Cymau Flints 129 G8
Cymer Neath 42 C3
Cymmer Rhondd 42 F3
Cynghordy Carmth 77 M7
Cynheidre Carmth 56 E3
Cynonville Neath 42 C3
Cynwyd Denbgs 111 K3
Cynwyl Elfed Carmth 58 C3

D

Daccombe Devon 8 D1
Dacre Cumb 166 B5
Dacre N York 150 B4
Dacre Banks N York 150 B3
Daddry Shield Dur 167 K3
Dadford Bucks 84 C7
Dadlington Leics 99 L4
Dafen Carmth 56 F4
Daffy Green Norfk 105 J2
Dagenham Gt Lon 52 B2
Daglingworth Gloucs 64 E6
Dagnall Bucks 68 C4
Dagworth Suffk 89 L3
Dail bho Dheas W Isls 282 g1
Dailly S Ayrs 183 H3
Dainton Devon 8 C2
Dairsie Fife 223 G4
Daisy Hill Bolton 139 K6
Daisy Hill Leeds 141 L2
Dalabrog W Isls 283 b11
Dalavich Ag & B 216 F5
Dalbeattie D & G 175 L3
Dalbury Derbys 115 M5
Dalby IoM 154 b6
Dalby Lincs 137 H5
Dalby N York 151 K2
Dalcapon P & K 232 E4
Dalchalm Highld 274 B6
Dalchreichart Highld 240 A1
Dalchruin P & K 220 C4
Dalcrue P & K 221 J2
Dalderby Lincs 136 E6
Dalditch Devon 14 B6
Daldowie Crematorium C Glas 209 H6
Dale Cumb 166 D2
Dale Derbys 116 D4
Dale Pembks 54 C5
Dale Bottom Cumb 165 J6
Dale End Derbys 132 D7
Dale End N York 149 G6
Dale Hill E Susx 39 H7
Dalehouse N York 171 H7
Dalelia Highld 237 L6
Dalgarven N Ayrs 196 B2
Dalgety Bay Fife 211 G2
Dalgig E Ayrs 197 G8
Dalginross P & K 220 D3
Dalguise P & K 232 E6
Dalhalvaig Highld 278 F5
Dalham Suffk 88 E3
Daliburgh W Isls 283 b11
Dalkeith Mdloth 211 K5
Dallas Moray 266 C5
Dallinghoo Suffk 91 G4
Dallington E Susx 24 B3
Dallington Nhants 84 E3
Dallow N York 150 B2
Dalmally Ag & B 217 K2
Dalmary Stirlg 219 H8
Dalmellington E Ayrs 184 D2
Dalmeny C Edin 210 F3
Dalmore Highld 263 H6
Dalmuir W Duns 208 E5
Dalnabreck Highld 237 K6
Dalnacardoch P & K 231 K1
Dalnahaitnach Highld 252 F7
Dalnaspidal P & K 231 J1
Dalnawillan Lodge Highld 279 H8
Daloist P & K 231 L4
Dalqueich P & K 221 K6
Dalquhairn S Ayrs 183 J4

Dalreavoch Highld	273	H6
Dalry N Ayrs	196	B1
Dalrymple E Ayrs	196	D8
Dalserf S Lans	198	C3
Dalsmeran Ag & B	192	D5
Dalston Cumb	165	L1
Dalston Gt Lon	51	J2
Dalswinton D & G	176	B2
Dalton Cumb	157	H7
Dalton D & G	176	F4
Dalton Lancs	139	G6
Dalton N York	159	K1
Dalton N York	160	F7
Dalton Nthumb	180	D4
Dalton Rothm	133	J1
Dalton-in-Furness Cumb	156	B7
Dalton-le-Dale Dur	169	L1
Dalton Magna Rothm	133	J1
Dalton-on-Tees N York	160	D1
Dalton Parva Rothm	133	J1
Dalton Piercy Hartpl	170	B4
Dalveich Stirlg	219	K2
Dalwhinnie Highld	241	H6
Dalwood Devon	14	F3
Damask Green Herts	69	H1
Damerham Hants	33	J7
Damgate Norfk	107	H2
Dam Green Norfk	105	L6
Damnaglaur D & G	172	E7
Danaway Kent	53	J6
Danbury Essex	71	J6
Danby N York	162	C1
Danby Bottom N York	162	B2
Danby Wiske N York	160	E3
Dandaleith Moray	254	F3
Danderhall Mdloth	211	J5
Danebridge Ches E	131	J6
Dane End Herts	69	J3
Danegate E Susx	38	E6
Danehill E Susx	22	F2
Dane Hills C Leic	100	C3
Danemoor Green Norfk	105	L2
Danesford Shrops	97	G5
Danesmoor Derbys	133	H7
Dane Street Kent	40	D5
Daniel's Water Kent	40	C7
Danshillock Abers	268	D6
Danskine E Loth	212	C5
Danthorpe E R Yk	145	H1
Danzey Green Warwks	82	D2
Dapple Heath Staffs	115	G6
Darby Green Hants	49	K7
Darcy Lever Bolton	139	L6
Dardy Powys	61	K3
Darenth Kent	52	C5
Daresbury Halton	130	B3
Darfield Barns	142	C6
Darfoulds Notts	133	L4
Dargate Kent	40	E3
Dargavel Rens	208	D5
Darite Cnwll	6	B1
Darland Medway	53	G6
Darland Wrexhm	129	J8
Darlaston Wsall	98	B4
Darlaston Green Wsall	98	B4
Darley N York	150	B4
Darley Abbey C Derb	116	B4
Darley Bridge Derbys	132	E7
Darley Dale Derbys	132	E7
Darley Green Solhll	98	F8
Darleyhall Herts	68	F3
Darley Head N York	150	B4
Darlingscott Warwks	82	F6
Darlington Darltn	169	H7
Darlington Crematorium Darltn	169	H7
Darliston Shrops	113	J5
Darlton Notts	134	F5
Darnford Staffs	98	E2
Darnick Border	201	H6
Darowen Powys	93	H3
Darra Abers	268	D6
Darracott Devon	26	D7
Darracott Devon	27	H3
Darras Hall Nthumb	180	E5
Darrington Wakefd	142	D4
Darsham Suffk	91	K1
Darshill Somset	31	K2
Dartford Kent	52	B4
Dartford Crossing Kent	52	C4
Dartington Devon	8	B2
Dartmeet Devon	12	F7
Dartmouth Devon	8	C4
Darton Barns	141	M5
Darvel E Ayrs	197	H3
Darwell Hole E Susx	24	C3
Darwen Bl w D	139	K3
Datchet W & M	50	C3
Datchworth Herts	69	H3
Datchworth Green Herts	69	H3
Daubhill Bolton	139	L6
Daugh of Kinermony Moray	254	E3
Dauntsey Wilts	46	E3
Dava Highld	253	J4
Davenham Ches W	130	C5
Davenport Stockp	131	H2
Davenport Green Ches E	131	G4
Davenport Green Traffd	130	F2
Daventry Nhants	84	B3
Davidson's Mains C Edin	211	H4
Davidstow Cnwll	11	G5
David Street Kent	52	E6
Davington D & G	187	K5
Davington Hill Kent	40	D3
Daviot Abers	256	D6
Daviot Highld	252	D4
Daviot House Highld	252	D4
Davis's Town E Susx	23	J4
Davoch of Grange Moray	267	K6
Davyhulme Traffd	139	M8
Daw End Wsall	98	C3
Dawesgreen Surrey	37	K2
Dawley Wrekin	96	F2
Dawlish Devon	13	M7
Dawlish Warren Devon	14	A7
Dawn Conwy	127	G5
Daws Green Somset	30	B6
Daws Heath Essex	53	H1
Daw's House Cnwll	11	K6
Daybrook Notts	116	F3
Day Green Ches E	130	F8
Dayhills Staffs	114	F5
Dayhouse Bank Worcs	98	B7
Daylesford Gloucs	65	K2
Ddol Flints	128	D5
Ddol-Cownwy Powys	111	K8
Deal Kent	41	L5
Dean Cumb	164	E5
Dean Devon	7	L2
Dean Devon	27	L2
Dean Devon	28	C1
Dean Dorset	33	G7
Dean Hants	34	F4
Dean Hants	35	H7
Dean Lancs	140	C3
Dean Oxon	65	M3
Dean Somset	31	L2
Dean Bottom Kent	52	C5
Deanburnhaugh Border	188	C4
Deancombe Devon	7	L2
Dean Court Oxon	66	C6
Deane Bolton	139	K6
Deane Hants	35	H1
Dean End Dorset	33	G7
Dean Head Barns	141	L7
Deanhead Kirk	141	G4
Deanland Dorset	33	G7
Deanlane End W Susx	20	B4
Dean Prior Devon	7	L2
Deanraw Nthumb	179	J6
Dean Row Ches E	131	G3
Deans W Loth	210	D5
Deanscales Cumb	164	E5
Deanshanger Nhants	84	E7
Deanshaugh Moray	267	G6
Deanston Stirlg	220	C6
Dean Street Kent	39	J3
Dearham Cumb	164	E3
Dearnley Rochdl	140	D4
Debach Suffk	90	F4
Debden Essex	70	C7
Debden Essex	87	L8
Debden Green Essex	70	E1
Debenham Suffk	90	E3
Deblin's Green Worcs	81	J5
Dechmont W Loth	210	D5
Dechmont Road W Loth	210	D5
Deddington Oxon	66	C1
Dedham Essex	90	C8
Dedham Heath Essex	72	F1
Dedworth W & M	50	B4
Deene Nhants	101	L5
Deenethorpe Nhants	101	L5
Deepcar Sheff	141	L8
Deepcut Surrey	49	L7
Deepdale Cumb	158	C5
Deepdale N York	158	F6
Deeping Gate C Pete	102	C2
Deeping St James Lincs	102	D2
Deeping St Nicholas Lincs	119	H8
Deerhurst Gloucs	64	C1
Deerhurst Walton Gloucs	64	C2
Deerton Street Kent	40	C3
Defford Worcs	81	L6
Defynnog Powys	60	D2
Deganwy Conwy	126	F4
Degnish Ag & B	216	B5
Deighton C York	151	K7
Deighton N York	160	E2
Deiniolen Gwynd	125	K7
Delabole Cnwll	10	F6
Delamere Ches W	130	A6
Delfrigs Abers	257	H7
Delley Devon	27	K6
Delliefure Highld	253	L5
Dell Quay W Susx	20	D6
Delly End Oxon	65	M4
Delnabo Moray	254	C8
Delny Highld	263	K5
Delph Oldham	140	E6
Delves Dur	168	E1
Delvin End Essex	88	F4
Dembleby Lincs	118	D4
Demelza Cnwll	5	G2
Denaby Donc	142	D7
Denaby Main Donc	142	D7
Denbies Surrey	37	H1
Denbigh Denbgs	128	C6
Denbighshire Crematorium Denbgs	127	K5
Denbrae Fife	222	F3
Denbury Devon	8	B1
Denby Derbys	116	C2
Denby Bottles Derbys	116	C2
Denby Dale Kirk	141	K6
Denchworth Oxon	48	A1
Dendron Cumb	146	E2
Denel End C Beds	85	K8
Denfield P & K	221	G4
Denford Nhants	101	L8
Dengie Essex	72	E6
Denham Bucks	50	D2
Denham Suffk	88	B3
Denham Suffk	106	D8
Denham End Suffk	88	F3
Denham Green Bucks	50	D1
Denham Green Suffk	106	D8
Denhead Abers	269	J5
Denhead Fife	223	H4
Denhead of Gray C Dund	222	F1
Denholm Border	189	G1
Denholme C Brad	141	G1
Denholme Clough C Brad	141	G1
Denio Gwynd	108	F4
Denmead Hants	19	L1
Denmore C Aber	245	L1
Denne Park W Susx	37	J5
Dennington Suffk	91	G2
Denny Falk	209	L3
Dennyloanhead Falk	209	L3
Den of Lindores Fife	222	D4
Denshaw Oldham	140	E5
Denside Abers	245	H4
Densole Kent	41	G7
Denston Suffk	88	F5
Denstone Staffs	115	H3
Denstroude Kent	40	E3
Dent Cumb	158	B5
Denton Cambs	102	C6
Denton Darltn	169	G7
Denton E Susx	23	G7
Denton Kent	41	G6
Denton Kent	52	E4
Denton Lincs	117	M5
Denton N York	149	L6
Denton Nhants	85	G4
Denton Norfk	106	F5
Denton Oxon	66	C6
Denton Tamesd	131	H1
Denver Norfk	104	C3
Denwick Nthumb	191	J3
Deopham Norfk	105	L3
Deopham Green Norfk	105	L4
Depden Suffk	88	F4
Depden Green Suffk	88	F4
Deptford Gt Lon	51	K3
Deptford Wilts	33	H3
Derby C Derb	116	B4
Derby Devon	27	K4
Derbyhaven IoM	154	C8
Derculich P & K	232	C5
Dereham Norfk	105	K1
Deri Caerph	61	H6
Derril Devon	11	K2
Derringstone Kent	41	G5
Derrington Staffs	114	D7
Derriton Devon	11	L2
Derry Hill Wilts	46	D5
Derrythorpe N Linc	143	L6
Dersingham Norfk	120	F5
Dervaig Ag & B	226	E2
Derwen Denbgs	111	L2
Derwenlas Powys	92	F4
Derwydd Carmth	59	H5
Desborough Nhants	101	H6
Desford Leics	100	B3
Deskford Moray	267	K4
Detchant Nthumb	203	H6
Detling Kent	53	G7
Deuxhill Shrops	96	F6
Devauden Mons	62	F7
Devil's Bridge Cerdgn	92	F8
Devitts Green Warwks	99	H5
Devizes Wilts	46	E5
Devonport C Plym	6	E4
Devonside Clacks	221	G7
Devoran Cnwll	3	K3
Dewarton Mdloth	211	L6
Dewlish Dorset	16	E3
Dewsbury Kirk	141	K3
Dewsbury Moor Kirk	141	K3
Dewsbury Moor Crematorium Kirk	141	K3
Deytheur Powys	112	C8
Dial N Som	45	G5
Dial Green W Susx	36	D5
Dial Post W Susx	21	K3
Dibberford Dorset	15	K2
Dibden Hants	18	F2
Dibden Purlieu Hants	18	F2
Dickens Heath Solhll	98	E8
Dickleburgh Norfk	106	D7
Didbrook Gloucs	64	F1
Didcot Oxon	48	D7
Diddington Cambs	86	D2
Diddlebury Shrops	96	C6
Didley Herefs	62	F1
Didling W Susx	20	D3
Didmarton Gloucs	46	B2
Didsbury Manch	131	G1
Didworthy Devon	7	K2
Digby Lincs	135	M8
Digg Highld	259	H3
Diggle Oldham	140	F6
Digmoor Lancs	139	G6
Digswell Herts	69	H4
Digswell Water Herts	69	H4
Dihewyd Cerdgn	76	E4
Dilham Norfk	123	G6
Dilhorne Staffs	114	F3
Dill Hall Lancs	139	M2
Dillington Cambs	86	C2
Dilston Nthumb	180	A6
Dilton Wilts	32	E1
Dilton Marsh Wilts	32	D1
Dilwyn Herefs	80	A4
Dimple Bolton	139	L4
Dimple Derbys	132	E7
Dinas Carmth	58	A3
Dinas Cnwll	10	C7
Dinas Gwynd	108	D4
Dinas Pembks	75	G4
Dinas Rhondd	42	F3
Dinas Dinlle Gwynd	125	H8
Dinas-Mawddwy Gwynd	111	J8
Dinas Powys V Glam	43	G7
Dinder Somset	31	J2
Dinedor Herefs	80	C7
Dingestow Mons	62	F5
Dingle Lpool	129	J2
Dingleden Kent	39	K7
Dingley Nhants	101	G6
Dingwall Highld	262	F8
Dinmael Conwy	111	J3
Dinnet Abers	244	A4
Dinnington N u Ty	180	F4
Dinnington Rothm	133	K3
Dinnington Somset	30	F8
Dinorwic Gwynd	125	L7
Dinton Bucks	67	J5
Dinton Wilts	33	H4
Dinwoodie D & G	187	H8
Dinworthy Devon	26	E7
Dipford Somset	30	B6
Dipley Hants	49	H7
Dippen Ag & B	194	B3
Dippen N Ayrs	195	G6
Dippenhall Surrey	36	B2
Dippermill Devon	12	B1
Dippertown Devon	12	B5
Dipple Moray	267	G4
Dipple S Ayrs	182	F2
Diptford Devon	7	L3
Dipton Dur	180	E8
Diptonmill Nthumb	179	L6
Dirleton E Loth	212	B2
Dirt Pot Nthumb	167	K2
Discoed Powys	79	K2
Diseworth Leics	116	D6
Dishforth N York	160	E8
Disley Ches E	131	J3
Diss Norfk	106	C7
Disserth Powys	78	E4
Distington Cumb	164	D6
Distington Hall Crematorium Cumb	164	D6

Ditchampton Wilts 33 J4
Ditcheat Somset 31 K4
Ditchingham Norfk 107 G5
Ditchling E Susx 22 E4
Ditherington Shrops 113 H8
Ditteridge Wilts 46 B3
Dittisham Devon 8 C4
Ditton Kent 52 F7
Ditton Green Cambs 88 D4
Ditton Priors Shrops 96 E5
Dixton Gloucs 64 E1
Dixton Mons 63 G4
Dizzard Cnwll 11 H3
Dobcross Oldham 140 F6
Dobwalls Cnwll 5 L2
Doccombe Devon 13 H5
Dochgarroch Highld 251 H3
Dockenfield Surrey 36 B3
Docker Lancs 157 J7
Docking Norfk 121 G4
Docklow Herefs 80 D4
Dockray Cumb 165 J1
Dockray Cumb 165 L6
Dodbrooke Devon 7 L6
Doddinghurst Essex 70 E7
Doddington Cambs 103 H5
Doddington Kent 40 B4
Doddington Lincs 135 H5
Doddington Nthumb 202 F6
Doddington Shrops 96 E8
Doddiscombsleigh Devon 13 K5
Dodd's Green Ches E 113 K3
Doddshill Norfk 120 F5
Doddy Cross Cnwll 6 C2
Dodford Nhants 84 B3
Dodford Worcs 97 L8
Dodington S Glos 45 L3
Dodington Somset 30 A3
Dodleston Ches W 129 J7
Dodscott Devon 27 K7
Dodside E Rens 208 E8
Dod's Leigh Staffs 115 G4
Dodworth Barns 141 M6
Dodworth Bottom Barns 141 M7
Dodworth Green Barns 141 M6
Doe Bank Birm 98 E4
Doe Lea Derbys 133 J6
Dogdyke Lincs 136 D8
Dogley Lane Kirk 141 J5
Dogmersfield Hants 49 J8
Dogridge Wilts 47 G2
Dogsthorpe C Pete 102 D3
Dog Village Devon 14 A3
Dolanog Powys 94 C1
Dolau Powys 79 G2
Dolaucothi Carmth 77 J7
Dolbenmaen Gwynd 109 J3
Doley Staffs 114 A5
Dolfach Powys 93 K3
Dol-fôr Powys 93 H2
Dolfor Powys 94 D6
Dolgarrog Conwy 126 F6
Dolgellau Gwynd 110 D7
Dolgoch Gwynd 92 E3
Dol-gran Carmth 58 D2
Doll Highld 273 L7
Dollar Clacks 221 G7
Dollarfield Clacks 221 G7
Dolley Green Powys 79 K2
Dollwen Cerdgn 92 E7
Dolphin Flints 128 E5
Dolphinholme Lancs 147 K5
Dolphinton S Lans 199 J4
Dolton Devon 27 K8
Dolwen Conwy 127 H5
Dolwyddelan Conwy 110 D1
Dolybont Cerdgn 92 D5
Dolyhir Powys 79 J4
Domgay Powys 112 D7
Donaldson's Lodge Nthumb 202 D5
Doncaster Donc 142 F7
Doncaster Carr Donc 142 F7
Donhead St Andrew Wilts 32 F6
Donhead St Mary Wilts 32 F6
Donibristle Fife 211 G1
Doniford Somset 29 K2
Donington Lincs 119 H4
Donington on Bain Lincs 136 D3
Donington Southing Lincs 119 G5
Donisthorpe Leics 99 J1
Donkey Street Kent 25 L1
Donkey Town Surrey 50 B6
Donnington Gloucs 65 J2
Donnington Herefs 81 G8
Donnington Shrops 96 D2
Donnington W Berk 48 C5
Donnington W Susx 20 D6
Donnington Wrekin 113 M8
Donnington Wood Wrekin 97 G1

Donyatt Somset 30 E8
Doomsday Green W Susx 37 J5
Doonfoot S Ayrs 196 C7
Dora's Green Hants 36 B1
Dorback Lodge Highld 253 L8
Dorchester Dorset 16 D4
Dorchester-on-Thames Oxon 66 E8
Dordon Warwks 99 H3
Dore Sheff 132 F3
Dores Highld 251 G5
Dorking Surrey 37 J1
Dorking Tye Suffk 89 J7
Dormansland Surrey 38 B5
Dormans Park Surrey 38 B5
Dormington Herefs 80 D7
Dormston Worcs 82 A4
Dorn Gloucs 82 F8
Dorney Bucks 50 B3
Dornie Highld 248 D6
Dornoch Highld 264 B2
Dornock D & G 177 H5
Dorrery Highld 279 J5
Dorridge Solhll 98 F8
Dorrington Lincs 118 E1
Dorrington Shrops 96 B3
Dorrington Shrops 114 A3
Dorsington Warwks 82 D5
Dorstone Herefs 79 K7
Dorton Bucks 67 G4
Dosthill Staffs 99 G3
Dothan IoA 124 F5
Dottery Dorset 15 K4
Doublebois Cnwll 5 L2
Doughton Gloucs 46 C1
Douglas IoM 154 e6
Douglas S Lans 198 D7
Douglas and Angus C Dund 234 C8
Douglas Crematorium IoM 154 e6
Douglas Pier Ag & B 217 K7
Douglastown Angus 234 B6
Douglas Water S Lans 198 E6
Douglas West S Lans 198 D7
Doulting Somset 31 L2
Dounby Ork 275 b4
Doune Highld 272 B7
Doune Stirlg 220 C6
Dounepark S Ayrs 182 F3
Dounie Highld 263 G2
Dousland Devon 7 G1
Dovaston Shrops 112 E7
Dove Green Notts 116 D1
Dove Holes Derbys 131 L4
Dovenby Cumb 164 E4
Dover Kent 41 K7
Dover Wigan 139 J7
Dovercourt Essex 73 K1
Doverdale Worcs 81 K2
Doveridge Derbys 115 J5
Doversgreen Surrey 37 L1
Dowally P & K 232 F5
Dowbridge Lancs 138 E2
Dowdeswell Gloucs 64 E3
Dowlais Myr Td 61 G5
Dowland Devon 12 D1
Dowlish Ford Somset 30 E8
Dowlish Wake Somset 30 E8
Down Ampney Gloucs 65 G7
Downderry Cnwll 6 C4
Downe Gt Lon 51 L6
Downend Gloucs 64 B7
Downend IoW 19 J6
Downend S Glos 45 K3
Downend W Berk 48 C4
Downfield C Dund 223 G1
Downgate Cnwll 11 K8
Downgate Cnwll 11 L8
Downham Essex 71 H7
Downham Gt Lon 51 K4
Downham Lancs 148 D7
Downham Market Norfk 104 C3
Down Hatherley Gloucs 64 C3
Downhead Somset 31 J6
Downhead Somset 32 A2
Downhill Cnwll 4 D1
Downhill P & K 221 K1
Downholland Cross Lancs 138 D6
Downholme N York 159 K3
Downicary Devon 11 M4
Downies Abers 245 K4
Downing Flints 128 D4
Downley Bucks 67 K8
Down St Mary Devon 13 H2
Downs Crematorium Br & H 22 E6
Downs Crematorium Br & H 22 E6
Downside Somset 31 K2
Downside Somset 31 L1
Downside Surrey 50 E7
Down Thomas Devon 6 F5
Downton Hants 18 D5

Downton Wilts 33 L6
Dowsby Lincs 118 F5
Dowsdale Lincs 102 F2
Doxey Staffs 114 D6
Doxford Nthumb 191 H2
Doynton S Glos 45 L4
Draethen Caerph 43 K4
Draffan S Lans 198 C4
Dragonby N Linc 143 M5
Dragons Green W Susx 37 H6
Drakeholes Notts 134 E2
Drakelow Worcs 97 J7
Drakemyre N Ayrs 196 B1
Drakes Broughton Worcs 81 L5
Drakewalls Cnwll 12 B8
Draughton N York 149 J5
Draughton Nhants 101 G8
Drax N York 143 H3
Drax Hales N York 143 H3
Draycote Warwks 83 K1
Draycot Foliat Swindn 47 J3
Draycott Derbys 116 D5
Draycott Gloucs 82 E8
Draycott Shrops 97 H5
Draycott Somset 31 G1
Draycott Somset 31 K6
Draycott Worcs 81 K5
Draycott in the Clay Staffs 115 J6
Draycott in the Moors Staffs 114 F3
Drayford Devon 28 D8
Drayton C Port 19 L3
Drayton Leics 101 H5
Drayton Lincs 119 H4
Drayton Norfk 106 D1
Drayton Oxon 66 C8
Drayton Oxon 83 K7
Drayton Somset 30 F6
Drayton Worcs 97 K8
Drayton Bassett Staffs 99 G3
Drayton Beauchamp Bucks 67 L5
Drayton Parslow Bucks 67 K2
Drayton St Leonard Oxon 66 E7
Drebley N York 149 J4
Dreemskerry IoM 154 g4
Dreen Hill Pembks 54 F4
Drefach Carmth 58 F6
Drefach Carmth 76 C7
Drefach Cerdgn 76 F6
Drefelin Carmth 76 C7
Dreghorn N Ayrs 196 C3
Drellingore Kent 41 H7
Drem E Loth 212 B3
Dresden C Stke 114 E3
Drewsteignton Devon 13 H4
Driby Lincs 137 G5
Driffield E R Yk 152 F4
Driffield Gloucs 65 G7
Driffield Cross Roads Gloucs 64 F7
Drift Cnwll 2 C5
Drigg Cumb 155 K3
Drighlington Leeds 141 K2
Drimnin Highld 227 G2
Drimpton Dorset 15 K2
Drimsallie Highld 238 F7
Dringhouses C York 151 J6
Drinkstone Suffk 89 J3
Drinkstone Green Suffk 89 J3
Drive End Dorset 16 B1
Driver's End Herts 69 G3
Drointon Staffs 115 G6
Droitwich Spa Worcs 81 K3
Dron P & K 221 L4
Dronfield Derbys 133 G4
Dronfield Woodhouse Derbys 133 G4
Drongan E Ayrs 196 E7
Dronley Angus 234 A8
Droop Dorset 16 E1
Dropping Well Rothm 133 H1
Droxford Hants 35 J7
Droylsden Tamesd 140 D8
Druid Denbgs 111 K3
Druidston Pembks 54 E3
Druimarbin Highld 229 H1
Druimavuic Ag & B 229 G6
Druimdrishaig Ag & B 206 A5
Druimindarroch Highld 237 K4
Drum Ag & B 206 E4
Drum P & K 221 J7
Drumalbin S Lans 198 F5
Drumbeg Highld 270 F2
Drumblade Abers 255 M4
Drumbreddon D & G 172 D6
Drumbuie Highld 248 B5
Drumburgh Cumb 177 J7
Drumburn D & G 175 L4
Drumburn D & G 176 C6
Drumchapel C Glas 208 E5
Drumchastle P & K 231 J4
Drumclog S Lans 197 J3

Drumeldrie Fife 223 G6
Drumelzier Border 199 K6
Drumfearn Highld 247 L5
Drumfrennie Abers 244 F4
Drumgley Angus 234 C5
Drumguish Highld 241 L3
Drumin Moray 254 D5
Drumjohn D & G 184 E3
Drumlamford S Ayrs 183 H7
Drumlasie Abers 244 E2
Drumleaning Cumb 177 J8
Drumlemble Ag & B 192 D4
Drumlithie Abers 245 H7
Drummoddie D & G 173 K6
Drummore D & G 172 E7
Drummuir Moray 255 H3
Drumnadrochit Highld 250 E5
Drumnagorrach Moray 267 L5
Drumpark D & G 185 L7
Drumrunie Lodge Highld 271 G7
Drumshang S Ayrs 195 L8
Drumuie Highld 259 G7
Drumuillie Highld 253 H7
Drumvaich Stirlg 220 B6
Drunzie P & K 221 L5
Druridge Nthumb 191 K7
Drury Flints 129 G6
Drybeck Cumb 166 F7
Drybridge Moray 267 J4
Drybridge N Ayrs 196 D4
Drybrook Gloucs 63 J4
Dryburgh Border 201 J6
Dry Doddington Lincs 117 M2
Dry Drayton Cambs 87 H3
Drymen Stirlg 208 E1
Drymuir Abers 257 G3
Drynoch Highld 246 F2
Dry Sandford Oxon 66 C7
Dryslwyn Carmth 59 G5
Dry Street Essex 52 E2
Dryton Shrops 96 D2
Dubford Abers 268 E3
Dublin Suffk 90 E1
Duchally Highld 271 L4
Duck End Bed 85 L6
Duck End Cambs 86 E2
Duck End Essex 71 G2
Duck End Essex 88 D8
Duckend Green Essex 71 H3
Duckington Ches W 113 H1
Ducklington Oxon 65 M5
Duck's Cross Bed 86 C4
Duddenhoe End Essex 87 J7
Duddingston C Edin 211 J4
Duddington Nhants 101 L3
Duddlestone Somset 30 C6
Duddleswell E Susx 38 C7
Duddlewick Shrops 96 F6
Duddo Nthumb 202 E4
Duddon Ches W 129 L6
Duddon Bridge Cumb 156 B5
Duddon Common Ches W 129 M6
Dudleston Shrops 112 E4
Dudleston Heath Shrops 112 E4
Dudley Dudley 97 L5
Dudley N Tyne 181 G4
Dudley Hill C Brad 141 J2
Dudley Port Sandw 98 B5
Dudnill Shrops 96 E8
Dudsbury Dorset 17 L3
Dudswell Herts 68 B5
Duffield Derbys 116 B3
Duffryn Neath 42 C3
Dufftown Moray 255 G4
Duffus Moray 266 D3
Dufton Cumb 166 F5
Duggleby N York 152 D2
Duirinish Highld 248 C5
Duisdalemore Highld 247 L5
Duisky Highld 239 G8
Dukestown Blae G 61 J5
Duke Street Suffk 90 C6
Dukinfield Tamesd 140 E8
Dukinfield Crematorium Tamesd 140 E8
Dulas IoA 125 H2
Dulcote Somset 31 J2
Dulford Devon 14 C2
Dull P & K 232 B5
Dullatur N Lans 209 K4
Dullingham Cambs 88 C4
Dullingham Ley Cambs 88 C4
Dulnain Bridge Highld 253 J6
Duloe Bed 86 D3
Duloe Cnwll 5 M3
Dulsie Bridge Highld 253 H3
Dulverton Somset 29 G5
Dulwich Gt Lon 51 J4
Dumbarton W Duns 208 C4

Dumbleton Gloucs ... 82 B8
Dumfries D & G ... 176 C4
Dumgoyne Stirlg ... 208 E2
Dummer Hants ... 35 J2
Dumpton Kent ... 41 L2
Dun Angus ... 235 G3
Dunalastair P & K ... 231 K4
Dunan Ag & B ... 207 J5
Dunan Highld ... 247 J3
Dunan P & K ... 230 E4
Dunaverty Ag & B ... 192 E6
Dunball Somset ... 30 D3
Dunbar E Loth ... 212 E3
Dunbeath Highld ... 275 G2
Dunbeg Ag & B ... 228 D8
Dunblane Stirlg ... 220 D7
Dunbog Fife ... 222 D4
Dunbridge Hants ... 34 D5
Duncanston Highld ... 263 G8
Duncanstone Abers ... 255 L6
Dunchideock Devon ... 13 K5
Dunchurch Warwks ... 83 L1
Duncote Nhants ... 84 C5
Duncow D & G ... 176 C2
Duncrievie P & K ... 221 L5
Duncton W Susx ... 20 F3
Dundee C Dund ... 223 G1
Dundee Crematorium C Dund ... 222 F1
Dundon Somset ... 31 G4
Dundonald S Ayrs ... 196 D4
Dundonnell Highld ... 261 J2
Dundraw Cumb ... 165 H1
Dundreggan Highld ... 240 B1
Dundrennan D & G ... 175 J5
Dundry N Som ... 45 H5
Dunecht Abers ... 245 G2
Dunfermline Fife ... 210 E2
Dunfermline Crematorium
Fife ... 210 F2
Dunfield Gloucs ... 65 H7
Dunford Bridge Barns ... 141 J7
Dungate Kent ... 40 B3
Dungavel S Lans ... 197 J3
Dunge Wilts ... 46 C8
Dungworth Sheff ... 132 E2
Dunham-on-the-Hill Ches W ... 129 L5
Dunham-on-Trent Notts ... 135 G5
Dunhampstead Worcs ... 81 L3
Dunhampton Worcs ... 81 J2
Dunham Town Traffd ... 130 E2
Dunham Woodhouses Traffd ... 130 E2
Dunholme Lincs ... 135 L4
Dunino Fife ... 223 J5
Dunipace Falk ... 209 L2
Dunkeld P & K ... 232 F6
Dunkerton BaNES ... 45 L7
Dunkeswell Devon ... 14 D1
Dunkeswick N York ... 150 D6
Dunkirk Ches W ... 129 J5
Dunkirk Kent ... 40 E3
Dunkirk S Glos ... 46 A2
Dunkirk Wilts ... 46 E6
Dunk's Green Kent ... 38 F3
Dunlappie Angus ... 234 F2
Dunley Hants ... 48 C8
Dunley Worcs ... 81 H2
Dunlop E Ayrs ... 196 E1
Dunmaglass Highld ... 251 G7
Dunmere Cnwll ... 5 H1
Dunmore Falk ... 210 A1
Dunnet Highld ... 280 B2
Dunnichen Angus ... 234 D5
Dunning P & K ... 221 J4
Dunnington C York ... 151 L5
Dunnington E R Yk ... 153 J5
Dunnington Warwks ... 82 C4
Dunnockshaw Lancs ... 140 B2
Dunn Street Kent ... 53 G6
Dunoon Ag & B ... 207 K4
Dunphail Moray ... 253 J2
Dunragit D & G ... 172 E3
Duns Border ... 202 B2
Dunsa Derbys ... 132 E5
Dunsby Lincs ... 118 E6
Dunscar Bolton ... 139 L5
Dunscore D & G ... 185 L6
Dunscroft Donc ... 143 G6
Dunsdale R & Cl ... 170 E6
Dunsden Green Oxon ... 49 H3
Dunsdon Devon ... 11 K1
Dunsfold Surrey ... 36 F4
Dunsford Devon ... 13 J5
Dunshalt Fife ... 222 D5
Dunshillock Abers ... 269 H6
Dunsill Notts ... 133 J7
Dunsley N York ... 171 K8
Dunsley Staffs ... 97 J6
Dunsmore Bucks ... 67 L6
Dunsop Bridge Lancs ... 148 B6

Dunstable C Beds ... 68 C3
Dunstall Staffs ... 115 K7
Dunstall Common Worcs ... 81 K6
Dunstall Green Suffk ... 88 E3
Dunstan Nthumb ... 191 K2
Dunstan Steads Nthumb ... 191 K2
Dunster Somset ... 29 H2
Duns Tew Oxon ... 66 C2
Dunston Gatesd ... 180 F6
Dunston Lincs ... 135 L7
Dunston Norfk ... 106 D3
Dunston Staffs ... 114 E8
Dunstone Devon ... 7 H4
Dunstone Devon ... 13 G7
Dunston Heath Staffs ... 114 E8
Dunsville Donc ... 143 G6
Dunswell E R Yk ... 144 D1
Dunsyre S Lans ... 199 J3
Dunterton Devon ... 11 M6
Dunthrop Oxon ... 65 M2
Duntisbourne Abbots
Gloucs ... 64 E5
Duntisbourne Leer Gloucs ... 64 E5
Duntisbourne Rouse Gloucs ... 64 E6
Duntish Dorset ... 16 D2
Duntocher W Duns ... 208 E4
Dunton Bucks ... 67 K2
Dunton C Beds ... 86 E6
Dunton Norfk ... 121 J5
Dunton Bassett Leics ... 100 C5
Dunton Green Kent ... 38 D2
Dunton Wayletts Essex ... 52 E1
Duntulm Highld ... 259 G2
Dunure S Ayrs ... 195 L7
Dunvant Swans ... 57 G6
Dunvegan Highld ... 258 C7
Dunwich Suffk ... 91 L1
Dunwood Staffs ... 131 J8
Durdar Cumb ... 177 L8
Durgan Cnwll ... 3 K5
Durham Dur ... 169 H2
Durham Crematorium Dur ... 169 H3
Durisdeer D & G ... 186 C5
Durisdeermill D & G ... 186 C5
Durkar Wakefd ... 141 M4
Durleigh Somset ... 30 C4
Durley Hants ... 35 G7
Durley Wilts ... 47 K6
Durley Street Hants ... 35 H7
Durlock Kent ... 41 J2
Durlock Kent ... 41 J4
Durlow Common Herefs ... 80 E7
Durn Rochdl ... 140 E4
Durness Highld ... 276 F3
Durno Abers ... 256 C6
Duror Highld ... 228 F4
Durran Ag & B ... 216 F5
Durrington W Susx ... 21 J6
Durrington Wilts ... 33 K2
Durris Abers ... 245 G4
Dursley Gloucs ... 63 M7
Dursley Cross Gloucs ... 63 K3
Durston Somset ... 30 D5
Durweston Dorset ... 17 G1
Duston Nhants ... 84 D3
Duthil Highld ... 253 H6
Dutlas Powys ... 94 F7
Duton Hill Essex ... 70 F2
Dutson Cnwll ... 11 L5
Dutton Ches W ... 130 B4
Duxford Cambs ... 87 K6
Duxford Oxon ... 66 A7
Dwygyfylchi Conwy ... 126 E4
Dwyran IoA ... 125 H6
Dyce C Aber ... 245 K1
Dyer's End Essex ... 88 E7
Dyfatty Carmth ... 56 E5
Dyffrydan Gwynd ... 110 D8
Dyffryn Brdgnd ... 42 C3
Dyffryn Myr Td ... 61 G6
Dyffryn V Glam ... 43 H7
Dyffryn Ardudwy Gwynd ... 109 K7
Dyffryn Castell Cerdgn ... 93 G7
Dyffryn Cellwen Neath ... 60 C5
Dyke Lincs ... 118 E7
Dyke Moray ... 264 F8
Dykehead Angus ... 233 K4
Dykehead Angus ... 234 B3
Dykehead N Lans ... 210 A7
Dykehead Stirlg ... 219 K7
Dykelands Abers ... 235 H2
Dykends Angus ... 233 K4
Dykeside Abers ... 256 C3
Dylife Powys ... 93 J4
Dymchurch Kent ... 25 L1
Dymock Gloucs ... 63 K1
Dyrham S Glos ... 45 L4
Dysart Fife ... 222 E8
Dyserth Denbgs ... 128 C4

Eachway Worcs ... 98 C8
Eachwick Nthumb ... 180 D4
Eagland Hill Lancs ... 147 H6
Eagle Lincs ... 135 H6
Eagle Barnsdale Lincs ... 135 H6
Eagle Moor Lincs ... 135 H6
Eaglescliffe S on T ... 169 L7
Eaglesfield Cumb ... 164 E5
Eaglesfield D & G ... 177 H4
Eaglesham E Rens ... 208 F8
Eagley Bolton ... 139 L5
Eairy IoM ... 154 d6
Eakring Notts ... 134 D7
Ealand N Linc ... 143 K5
Ealing Gt Lon ... 50 F3
Eals Nthumb ... 178 F7
Eamont Bridge Cumb ... 166 C5
Earby Lancs ... 148 F6
Earcroft Bl w D ... 139 K3
Eardington Shrops ... 97 G5
Eardisland Herefs ... 80 A4
Eardisley Herefs ... 79 K5
Eardiston Shrops ... 112 E6
Eardiston Worcs ... 80 F2
Earith Cambs ... 103 H8
Earle Nthumb ... 202 F7
Earlestown St Hel ... 130 B1
Earley Wokham ... 49 H4
Earlham Norfk ... 106 D2
Earlham Crematorium Norfk ... 106 E2
Earlish Highld ... 258 F4
Earls Barton Nhants ... 85 G3
Earls Colne Essex ... 71 L1
Earls Common Worcs ... 81 M3
Earl's Croome Worcs ... 81 K6
Earlsditton Shrops ... 96 E8
Earlsdon Covtry ... 99 J7
Earl's Down E Susx ... 23 L3
Earlsferry Fife ... 223 H7
Earlsfield Gt Lon ... 51 H4
Earlsford Abers ... 256 E5
Earl's Green Suffk ... 90 B2
Earlsheaton Kirk ... 141 L3
Earl Shilton Leics ... 100 A4
Earl Soham Suffk ... 90 F3
Earl Sterndale Derbys ... 132 B6
Earlston Border ... 201 J5
Earlston E Ayrs ... 196 D4
Earl Stonham Suffk ... 90 D3
Earlswood Surrey ... 37 L1
Earlswood Warwks ... 98 E8
Earlswood Common Mons ... 62 F8
Earnley W Susx ... 20 D7
Earnshaw Bridge Lancs ... 139 G3
Earsdon N Tyne ... 181 H4
Earsdon Nthumb ... 191 J7
Earsham Norfk ... 107 G5
Earswick C York ... 151 K4
Eartham W Susx ... 20 F5
Earthcott S Glos ... 45 K2
Easby N York ... 161 J1
Easdale Ag & B ... 215 L1
Easebourne W Susx ... 36 D6
Easenhall Warwks ... 100 A7
Eashing Surrey ... 36 E2
Easington Bucks ... 67 G5
Easington Dur ... 169 L2
Easington E R Yk ... 145 K4
Easington Nthumb ... 203 J6
Easington Oxon ... 67 G7
Easington R & Cl ... 171 H7
Easington Colliery Dur ... 169 L2
Easington Lane Sundld ... 169 K2
Easingwold N York ... 151 H2
Easole Street Kent ... 41 H5
Eassie and Nevay Angus ... 233 M6
East Aberthaw V Glam ... 42 F8
East Allington Devon ... 7 M5
East Anstey Devon ... 28 F5
East Anton Hants ... 34 E1
East Appleton N York ... 160 C3
East Ashey IoW ... 19 K6
East Ashling W Susx ... 20 D5
East Aston Hants ... 34 F2
East Ayton N York ... 163 H5
East Balsdon Cnwll ... 11 K3
East Bank Blae G ... 61 K6
East Barkwith Lincs ... 136 C3
East Barming Kent ... 39 H3
East Barnby N York ... 171 J8
East Barnet Gt Lon ... 69 H8
East Barns E Loth ... 212 F4
East Barsham Norfk ... 121 K5
East Beckham Norfk ... 122 D4
East Bedfont Gt Lon ... 50 D4
East Bergholt Suffk ... 90 C8

East Bierley Kirk ... 141 J2
East Bilney Norfk ... 121 L7
East Blatchington E Susx ... 23 H7
East Bloxworth Dorset ... 17 H4
East Boldon S Tyne ... 181 J6
East Boldre Hants ... 18 F4
East Bolton Nthumb ... 191 J6
Eastbourne Darltn ... 169 J7
Eastbourne E Susx ... 23 K7
Eastbourne Crematorium
E Susx ... 23 L6
East Bower Somset ... 30 D3
East Bradenham Norfk ... 105 J2
East Brent Somset ... 44 D8
Eastbridge Suffk ... 91 K2
East Bridgford Notts ... 117 J3
East Briscoe Dur ... 168 B6
Eastbrook V Glam ... 43 J7
East Buckland Devon ... 28 A4
East Budleigh Devon ... 14 C5
Eastburn C Brad ... 149 J7
Eastburn E R Yk ... 152 F4
East Burnham Bucks ... 50 B3
East Burton Dorset ... 16 F5
Eastbury Herts ... 68 E8
Eastbury W Berk ... 47 M3
East Butsfield Dur ... 168 C2
East Butterwick N Linc ... 143 L6
Eastby N York ... 149 J5
East Calder W Loth ... 210 E5
East Carleton Norfk ... 106 D3
East Carlton Leeds ... 150 B7
East Carlton Nhants ... 101 H5
East Chaldon Dorset ... 16 F6
East Challow Oxon ... 48 A1
East Charleton Devon ... 7 L6
East Chelborough Dorset ... 16 A2
East Chiltington E Susx ... 22 F4
East Chinnock Somset ... 31 H8
East Chisenbury Wilts ... 47 H8
East Cholderton Hants ... 34 C2
Eastchurch Kent ... 53 L5
East Clandon Surrey ... 50 D8
East Claydon Bucks ... 67 H2
East Clevedon N Som ... 44 E5
East Coker Somset ... 31 J8
Eastcombe Gloucs ... 64 C6
Eastcombe Somset ... 29 L4
East Compton Somset ... 31 K3
East Cornworthy Devon ... 8 C4
East Cote Cumb ... 176 F7
Eastcote Gt Lon ... 50 E1
Eastcote Nhants ... 84 D4
Eastcote Solhll ... 99 G7
Eastcott Cnwll ... 26 D7
Eastcott Wilts ... 46 F7
East Cottingwith E R Yk ... 151 L7
Eastcourt Wilts ... 47 K6
Eastcourt Wilts ... 64 E8
East Cowes IoW ... 19 H4
East Cowick E R Yk ... 143 G4
East Cowton N York ... 160 D2
East Cramlington Nthumb ... 181 G4
East Cranmore Somset ... 31 L2
East Creech Dorset ... 17 H6
East Curthwaite Cumb ... 165 K1
East Dean E Susx ... 23 J7
East Dean Gloucs ... 63 K3
East Dean Hants ... 34 C5
East Dean W Susx ... 20 E4
East Devon Crematorium
Devon ... 14 B3
Eastdown Devon ... 8 B5
East Down Devon ... 27 L3
East Drayton Notts ... 134 F4
East Dulwich Gt Lon ... 51 J4
East Dundry N Som ... 45 H5
East Ella C KuH ... 144 D2
East End Bed ... 86 C4
East End C Beds ... 85 J4
East End E R Yk ... 145 G2
East End E R Yk ... 145 J4
East End Essex ... 70 D8
Eastend Essex ... 72 D4
East End Hants ... 18 E4
East End Hants ... 48 B6
East End Herts ... 70 C2
East End Kent ... 39 L6
East End Kent ... 53 L4
East End M Keyn ... 85 J6
East End Oxon ... 66 B4
East End Somset ... 31 L2
East End Suffk ... 90 C8
Easter Balmoral Abers ... 243 J5
Easter Compton S Glos ... 45 H2
Easter Dalziel Highld ... 252 E2
Eastergate W Susx ... 20 F6
Easterhouse C Glas ... 209 J6
Easter Howgate Mdloth ... 211 H6

Easter Kinkell Highld 251 G1
Easter Moniack Highld 250 F3
Eastern Green Covtry 99 H7
Easter Ord Abers 245 J3
Easter Pitkierie Fife 223 K6
Easter Skeld Shet 281 d6
Easter Softlaw Border 202 B6
Easterton Wilts 46 F8
Eastertown Somset 44 D8
East Everleigh Wilts 47 J8
East Farleigh Kent 39 J3
East Farndon Nhants 100 F6
East Ferry Lincs 143 K7
Eastfield N Lans 210 A6
Eastfield N York 163 J6
East Firsby Lincs 135 K3
East Fortune E Loth 212 C3
East Garforth Leeds 142 C1
East Garston W Berk 47 M4
Eastgate Dur 168 B3
Eastgate Lincs 118 F7
Eastgate Norfk 122 C7
East Ginge Oxon 48 C2
East Goscote Leics 100 E1
East Grafton Wilts 47 K6
East Green Suffk 91 J2
East Grimstead Wilts 34 B5
East Grinstead W Susx 38 B5
East Guldeford E Susx 25 H3
East Haddon Nhants 84 C2
East Hagbourne Oxon 48 D1
East Halton N Linc 144 E4
East Ham Gt Lon 51 L2
Eastham Wirral 129 H4
Eastham Ferry Wirral 129 J3
Easthampstead Park
   Crematorium Br For 49 K5
Easthampton Herefs 80 A3
East Hanney Oxon 66 B8
East Hanningfield Essex 71 J6
East Hardwick Wakefd 142 D4
East Harling Norfk 105 K6
East Harlsey N York 160 F3
East Harnham Wilts 33 K5
East Harptree BaNES 45 H7
East Hartford Nthumb 181 G3
East Harting W Susx 20 C3
East Hatch Wilts 32 F5
East Hatley Cambs 86 F5
East Hauxwell N York 159 L4
East Haven Angus 234 F8
Eastheath Wokham 49 J5
East Heckington Lincs 119 G3
East Hedleyhope Dur 168 F3
East Helmsdale Highld 274 D5
East Hendred Oxon 48 C1
East Heslerton N York 163 G7
East Hewish N Som 44 E6
East Hoathly E Susx 23 H4
East Holme Dorset 17 H5
East Hope Dur 159 J1
Easthope Shrops 96 D4
Easthorpe Essex 72 C3
Easthorpe Notts 117 J1
East Horrington Somset 31 J2
East Horsley Surrey 50 E8
East Horton Nthumb 203 J6
East Howe Bmouth 17 L3
East Huntington C York 151 K5
East Huntspill Somset 30 E2
East Hyde C Beds 68 E4
East Ilkerton Devon 28 C2
East Ilsley W Berk 48 D3
Eastington Devon 13 H1
Eastington Gloucs 63 M6
Eastington Gloucs 65 H4
East Keal Lincs 137 G7
East Kennett Wilts 47 G5
East Keswick Leeds 150 E7
East Kilbride S Lans 209 H8
East Kimber Devon 12 C3
East Kirkby Lincs 136 F7
East Knighton Dorset 16 F5
East Knowstone Devon 28 E6
East Knoyle Wilts 32 E5
East Lambrook Somset 31 G7
East Lancashire Crematorium
   Bury 140 A6
Eastlands D & G 185 K8
East Langdon Kent 41 K6
East Langton Leics 100 F5
East Lavant W Susx 20 D5
East Lavington W Susx 20 F4
East Layton N York 159 L1
Eastleach Martin Gloucs 65 J6
Eastleach Turville Gloucs 65 J6
East Leake Notts 116 F6
East Learmouth Nthumb 202 D5
East Leigh Devon 7 K4

East Leigh Devon 7 L3
East Leigh Devon 13 G2
Eastleigh Devon 27 J5
Eastleigh Hants 34 F7
East Lexham Norfk 121 J8
Eastling Kent 40 C4
East Linton E Loth 212 D3
East Liss Hants 36 A5
East Lockinge Oxon 48 B2
East London Crematorium
   Gt Lon 51 L2
East Lound N Linc 143 K7
East Lulworth Dorset 17 G6
East Lutton N York 152 E2
East Lydeard Somset 30 B5
East Lydford Somset 31 J4
East Malling Kent 39 H2
East Malling Heath Kent 39 H2
East Marden W Susx 20 C4
East Markham Notts 134 E5
East Martin Hants 33 J7
East Marton N York 148 F5
East Meon Hants 35 L6
East Mere Devon 29 H7
East Mersea Essex 72 F4
East Molesey Surrey 50 F5
Eastmoor Norfk 104 E3
East Morden Dorset 17 H4
East Morton C Brad 149 K7
East Morton D & G 186 C6
East Ness N York 162 B7
East Newton E R Yk 153 L8
Eastney C Port 19 L4
Eastnor Herefs 81 G7
East Norton Leics 101 G3
Eastoft N Linc 143 K4
East Ogwell Devon 13 J8
Easton Cambs 86 C1
Easton Cumb 177 J7
Easton Devon 13 G5
Easton Dorset 16 D8
Easton Hants 35 G4
Easton Lincs 118 B6
Easton Norfk 106 C1
Easton Somset 31 H2
Easton Suffk 91 G3
Easton W Berk 48 B4
Easton Wilts 46 C5
Easton Grey Wilts 46 C2
Easton-in-Gordano N Som 45 G4
Easton Maudit Nhants 85 H3
Easton-on-the-Hill Nhants 101 M3
Easton Royal Wilts 47 J7
East Orchard Dorset 32 D7
East Ord Nthumb 202 F3
East Panson Devon 11 L4
East Parley Dorset 17 M3
East Peckham Kent 39 G4
East Pennar Pembks 54 F6
East Pennard Somset 31 K3
East Perry Cambs 86 C2
East Portlemouth Devon 7 L7
East Prawle Devon 8 A7
East Preston W Susx 21 J6
East Pulham Dorset 16 D1
East Putford Devon 26 F7
East Quantoxhead Somset 29 L2
East Rainham Medway 53 H5
East Rainton Sundld 169 J1
East Ravendale NE Lin 145 G7
East Raynham Norfk 121 J6
Eastrea Cambs 102 F4
East Riding Crematorium
   E R Yk 152 F2
Eastriggs D & G 177 H5
East Rigton Leeds 150 E7
Eastrington E R Yk 143 K2
East Rolstone N Som 44 E6
Eastrop Swindn 65 J8
East Rounton N York 160 F7
East Rudham Norfk 121 H6
East Runton Norfk 122 D3
East Ruston Norfk 123 G6
Eastry Kent 41 J4
East Saltoun E Loth 212 B5
Eastshaw W Susx 36 C6
East Sheen Gt Lon 51 G4
East Shefford W Berk 48 A4
East Sleekburn Nthumb 181 G2
East Somerton Norfk 123 K7
East Stockwith Lincs 134 F1
East Stoke Dorset 17 G5
East Stoke Notts 117 K2
East Stour Dorset 32 D6
East Stour Common Dorset 32 D6
East Stourmouth Kent 41 H3
East Stowford Devon 27 L5
East Stratton Hants 35 H3
East Studdal Kent 41 J5

East Sutton Kent 39 L3
East Taphouse Cnwll 5 L2
East-the-Water Devon 27 H5
East Thirston Nthumb 191 J6
East Tilbury Thurr 52 E3
East Tisted Hants 35 L4
East Torrington Lincs 136 B3
East Tuddenham Norfk 106 B1
East Tytherley Hants 34 C5
East Tytherton Wilts 46 D4
East Village Devon 13 K2
Eastville Bristl 45 J4
Eastville Lincs 137 H8
East Wall Shrops 96 C4
East Walton Norfk 121 G8
East Water Somset 31 J1
East Week Devon 12 F4
Eastwell Leics 117 K6
East Wellow Hants 34 C6
East Wemyss Fife 222 F7
East Whitburn W Loth 210 C6
Eastwick Herts 70 B5
East Wickham Gt Lon 51 M3
East Williamston Pembks 55 J6
East Winch Norfk 120 F8
East Winterslow Wilts 34 B4
East Wittering W Susx 20 C7
East Witton N York 159 L5
Eastwood Notts 116 D2
Eastwood Sthend 53 H1
East Woodburn Nthumb 179 L2
Eastwood End Cambs 103 J5
East Woodhay Hants 48 B6
East Woodlands Somset 32 C2
East Worldham Hants 35 M3
East Wretham Norfk 105 J5
East Youlstone Devon 26 D7
Eathorpe Warwks 83 J2
Eaton Ches E 131 G6
Eaton Ches W 130 B7
Eaton Leics 117 L5
Eaton Norfk 106 C2
Eaton Notts 134 E4
Eaton Oxon 66 C6
Eaton Shrops 95 J5
Eaton Shrops 96 B5
Eaton Bishop Herefs 80 B7
Eaton Bray C Beds 68 B3
Eaton Constantine Shrops 96 D2
Eaton Ford Cambs 86 D3
Eaton Green C Beds 68 B3
Eaton Hastings Oxon 65 K7
Eaton Mascott Shrops 96 C2
Eaton Socon Cambs 86 D3
Eaton upon Tern Shrops 113 L7
Eaves Brow Warrtn 130 C1
Eaves Green Solhll 99 H6
Ebberston N York 162 F6
Ebbesborne Wake Wilts 33 G6
Ebbw Vale Blae G 61 J5
Ebchester Dur 180 D7
Ebdon N Som 44 D6
Ebford Devon 14 A5
Ebley Gloucs 64 B6
Ebnal Ches W 113 H2
Ebnal Herefs 80 B3
Ebrington Gloucs 82 E7
Ebsworthy Devon 12 C4
Ecchinswell Hants 48 D7
Ecclaw Border 213 G5
Ecclefechan D & G 177 G2
Eccles Border 202 B5
Eccles Kent 52 F6
Eccles Salfd 140 A8
Ecclesall Sheff 132 F3
Ecclesfield Sheff 133 G1
Eccles Green Herefs 79 L5
Eccleshall Staffs 114 C5
Eccleshill C Brad 149 M8
Ecclesmachan W Loth 210 E4
Eccles on Sea Norfk 123 H5
Eccles Road Norfk 105 L5
Eccleston Ches W 129 J3
Eccleston Lancs 139 G4
Eccleston St Hel 138 F8
Eccleston Green Lancs 139 G4
Echt Abers 245 G2
Eckford Border 201 L7
Eckington Derbys 133 H4
Eckington Worcs 81 L7
Ecton Nhants 84 F3
Ecton Staffs 132 B8
Edale Derbys 132 B3
Eday Ork 275 d3
Edburton W Susx 22 C5
Edderside Cumb 164 E2
Edderton Highld 263 J3
Eddington Kent 41 G2
Eddleston Border 200 B4

Eddlewood S Lans 209 J8
Edenbridge Kent 38 C4
Edenfield Lancs 140 B4
Edenhall Cumb 166 D4
Edenham Lincs 118 E7
Eden Mount Cumb 156 F7
Eden Park Gt Lon 51 K5
Edensor Derbys 132 E5
Edentaggart Ag & B 218 D8
Edenthorpe Donc 143 G6
Edern Gwynd 108 E4
Edgarley Somset 31 H3
Edgbaston Birm 98 D6
Edgcombe Cnwll 3 J4
Edgcott Bucks 67 G3
Edgcott Somset 28 E3
Edge Gloucs 64 B5
Edge Shrops 95 K2
Edgebolton Shrops 113 J7
Edge End Gloucs 63 H4
Edgefield Norfk 122 B5
Edgefield Green Norfk 122 B4
Edgefold Bolton 139 L6
Edge Green Ches W 113 H1
Edgehill Warwks 83 J5
Edgerley Shrops 112 E7
Edgerton Kirk 141 H4
Edgeside Lancs 140 C3
Edgeworth Gloucs 64 D6
Edgeworthy Devon 28 E8
Edginswell Torbay 8 C2
Edgmond Wrekin 114 A7
Edgmond Marsh Wrekin 114 A7
Edgton Shrops 95 J6
Edgware Gt Lon 51 G1
Edgworth Bl w D 139 L4
Edinbane Highld 258 E6
Edinburgh C Edin 211 J4
Edingale Staffs 99 G1
Edingham D & G 175 L2
Edingley Notts 134 D8
Edingthorpe Norfk 123 G5
Edingthorpe Green Norfk 122 F5
Edington Border 202 D2
Edington Nthumb 180 E2
Edington Somset 30 F3
Edington Wilts 46 D8
Edington Burtle Somset 30 F2
Edingworth Somset 44 D8
Edistone Devon 26 D6
Edithmead Somset 30 E1
Edith Weston Rutlnd 101 K2
Edlesborough Bucks 68 B3
Edlingham Nthumb 191 G4
Edlington Lincs 136 D5
Edmond Castle Cumb 178 C7
Edmondsham Dorset 33 J8
Edmondsley Dur 169 G1
Edmondthorpe Leics 117 M8
Edmonton Cnwll 10 D8
Edmonton Gt Lon 69 J8
Edmundbyers Dur 168 C1
Ednam Border 202 A5
Ednaston Derbys 115 L3
Edney Common Essex 71 G6
Edradynate P & K 232 C2
Edrom Border 202 C2
Edstaston Shrops 113 H5
Edstone Warwks 82 E3
Edvin Loach Herefs 80 F3
Edwalton Notts 117 G4
Edwardstone Suffk 89 J6
Edwardsville Myr Td 43 G2
Edwinsford Carmth 59 H2
Edwinstowe Notts 134 C6
Edworth C Beds 86 E7
Edwyn Ralph Herefs 80 F4
Edzell Angus 234 F2
Edzell Woods Abers 234 F2
Efail-fach Neath 57 L6
Efail Isaf Rhondd 43 H5
Efailnewydd Gwynd 108 F4
Efail-Rhyd Powys 112 A6
Efailwen Carmth 75 K7
Efenechtyd Denbgs 128 D8
Effgill D & G 187 L7
Effingham Surrey 50 E7
Effingham Junction Surrey 50 E7
Efflinch Staffs 115 K8
Efford Devon 13 K2
Efford Crematorium C Plym 6 F3
Egbury Hants 48 B8
Egdean W Susx 21 G3
Egerton Bolton 139 L5
Egerton Kent 40 B6
Egerton Forstal Kent 40 A6
Eggborough N York 142 E3
Eggbuckland C Plym 6 F3

Eggesford Devon 28 B8
Eggington C Beds 68 B2
Egginton Derbys 115 M6
Egglescliffe S on T 169 L7
Eggleston Dur 168 C6
Egham Surrey 50 C5
Egham Wick Surrey 50 B5
Egleton Rutlnd 101 J2
Eglingham Nthumb 191 G2
Egloshayle Cnwll 10 D8
Egloskerry Cnwll 11 K5
Eglwysbach Conwy 126 F5
Eglwys-Brewis V Glam 42 F7
Eglwys Cross Wrexhm 113 G3
Eglwys Fach Cerdgn 92 F4
Eglwyswrw Pembks 75 K4
Egmanton Notts 134 E6
Egremont Cumb 164 D8
Egremont Wirral 129 H1
Egton N York 162 E2
Egton Bridge N York 162 D2
Egypt Bucks 50 B2
Egypt Hants 34 F3
Eigg Highld 236 F3
Eight Ash Green Essex 72 D2
Eilanreach Highld 248 C8
Eisteddfa Gurig Cerdgn 93 H6
Elan Village Powys 78 C2
Elberton S Glos 45 J1
Elbridge W Susx 20 F6
Elburton C Plym 7 G4
Elcombe Swindn 47 H3
Elcot W Berk 48 B5
Eldernell Cambs 103 G4
Eldersfield Worcs 64 A1
Elderslie Rens 208 D6
Elder Street Essex 88 B8
Eldon Dur 169 G5
Eldwick C Brad 149 L7
Elerch Cerdgn 92 E6
Elfhill Abers 245 H6
Elford Nthumb 203 K7
Elford Staffs 98 F1
Elgin Moray 266 E4
Elgol Highld 247 H6
Elham Kent 41 G6
Elie Fife 223 J7
Elilaw Nthumb 190 D4
Elim IoA 124 F3
Eling Hants 18 F1
Elkesley Notts 134 D4
Elkstone Gloucs 64 D4
Ella Abers 268 B4
Ellacombe Torbay 8 D2
Elland Calder 141 H4
Elland Lower Edge Calder 141 H3
Ellary Ag & B 206 A4
Ellastone Staffs 115 J3
Ellel Lancs 147 J4
Ellemford Border 212 F7
Ellenabeich Ag & B 215 L1
Ellenborough Cumb 164 D3
Ellenbrook Salfd 139 L7
Ellenhall Staffs 114 C6
Ellen's Green Surrey 37 G4
Ellerbeck N York 160 F3
Ellerby N York 171 J7
Ellerdine Heath Wrekin 113 K7
Ellerhayes Devon 14 A2
Elleric Ag & B 229 G5
Ellerker E R Yk 144 A2
Ellers N York 149 H7
Ellerton E R Yk 151 L7
Ellerton N York 160 C3
Ellerton Shrops 114 A6
Ellesborough Bucks 67 K6
Ellesmere Shrops 112 F4
Ellesmere Port Ches W 129 J4
Ellingham Hants 18 A2
Ellingham Norfk 107 H5
Ellingham Nthumb 203 K8
Ellingstring N York 159 M6
Ellington Cambs 86 D1
Ellington Nthumb 191 K7
Ellington Thorpe Cambs 86 D1
Elliots Green Somset 32 D2
Ellisfield Hants 35 K2
Ellishader Highld 259 H3
Ellistown Leics 99 L1
Ellon Abers 257 H5
Ellonby Cumb 166 A4
Ellough Suffk 107 J6
Elloughton E R Yk 144 B2
Ellwood Gloucs 63 H5
Elm Cambs 103 K2
Elmbridge Worcs 81 K2
Elmdon Essex 87 J7
Elmdon Solhll 98 F6
Elmdon Heath Solhll 98 F7

Elmer W Susx 21 G6
Elmers End Gt Lon 51 K5
Elmer's Green Lancs 139 G6
Elmesthorpe Leics 100 A4
Elm Green Essex 71 J6
Elmhurst Staffs 98 E1
Elmley Castle Worcs 82 A7
Elmley Lovett Worcs 81 K1
Elmore Gloucs 64 A4
Elmore Back Gloucs 63 M4
Elm Park Gt Lon 52 B2
Elmscott Devon 26 D6
Elmsett Suffk 90 C6
Elmstead Heath Essex 72 F3
Elmstead Market Essex 72 F2
Elmstead Row Essex 72 F3
Elmsted Kent 40 F6
Elmstone Kent 41 H3
Elmstone Hardwicke Gloucs 64 D2
Elmswell E R Yk 152 F4
Elmswell Suffk 89 K2
Elmton Derbys 133 K5
Elphin Highld 271 H6
Elphinstone E Loth 211 L5
Elrick Abers 245 H2
Elrig D & G 173 J5
Elrington Nthumb 179 K6
Elsdon Nthumb 190 C7
Elsecar Barns 142 B7
Elsenham Essex 70 D2
Elsfield Oxon 66 D5
Elsham N Linc 144 C5
Elsing Norfk 122 B8
Elslack N York 149 G6
Elson Hants 19 K3
Elson Shrops 112 F4
Elsrickle S Lans 199 J4
Elstead Surrey 36 D2
Elsted W Susx 20 D3
Elsthorpe Lincs 118 E6
Elstob Dur 169 J6
Elston Lancs 139 J1
Elston Notts 117 K2
Elston Wilts 33 J2
Elstone Devon 28 B7
Elstow Bed 85 L6
Elstree Herts 68 F8
Elstronwick E R Yk 145 G1
Elswick Lancs 147 H8
Elswick N u Ty 180 F6
Elsworth Cambs 87 G3
Elterwater Cumb 156 D2
Eltham Gt Lon 51 L4
Eltham Crematorium Gt Lon 51 L4
Eltisley Cambs 86 F3
Elton Bury 140 B5
Elton Cambs 102 B4
Elton Ches W 129 K4
Elton Derbys 132 D7
Elton Gloucs 63 K4
Elton Herefs 80 B1
Elton Notts 117 K4
Elton S on T 169 L7
Elton Green Ches W 129 K5
Eltringham Nthumb 180 C6
Elvanfoot S Lans 186 E3
Elvaston Derbys 116 C5
Elveden Suffk 105 G7
Elvetham Heath Hants 49 K7
Elvingston E Loth 212 A4
Elvington C York 151 L6
Elvington Kent 41 J5
Elwell Devon 28 B4
Elwick Hartpl 170 B4
Elwick Nthumb 203 J5
Elworth Ches E 130 E7
Elworthy Somset 29 K4
Ely Cambs 103 L7
Ely Cardif 43 J6
Emberton M Keyn 85 H5
Embleton Cumb 165 G4
Embleton Dur 169 L5
Embleton Nthumb 191 J2
Embo Highld 264 C1
Emborough Somset 31 K1
Embo Street Highld 264 C2
Embsay N York 149 H5
Emery Down Hants 18 D2
Emley Kirk 141 K5
Emley Moor Kirk 141 K5
Emmbrook Wokham 49 J5
Emmer Green Readg 49 H4
Emmett Carr Derbys 133 J4
Emmington Oxon 67 H6
Emneth Norfk 103 K2
Emneth Hungate Norfk 103 K2
Empingham Rutlnd 101 L2
Empshott Hants 35 M4

Empshott Green Hants 35 M5
Emstrey Crematorium Shrops 96 C1
Emsworth Hants 20 B5
Enborne W Berk 48 B6
Enborne Row W Berk 48 C6
Enchmarsh Shrops 96 B4
Enderby Leics 100 C3
Endmoor Cumb 157 H5
Endon Staffs 114 E1
Endon Bank Staffs 114 E1
Enfield Gt Lon 69 K7
Enfield Crematorium Gt Lon 69 K7
Enfield Lock Gt Lon 69 K7
Enfield Wash Gt Lon 69 K7
Enford Wilts 47 H8
Engine Common S Glos 45 K2
England's Gate Herefs 80 D5
Englefield W Berk 48 F4
Englefield Green Surrey 50 C4
Engleseabrook Ches E 114 B1
English Bicknor Gloucs 63 H4
Englishcombe BaNES 45 L6
English Frankton Shrops 113 G5
Engollan Cnwll 10 B8
Enham-Alamein Hants 34 D1
Enmore Somset 30 C4
Enmore Green Dorset 32 E6
Ennerdale Bridge Cumb 164 E7
Enniscaven Cnwll 4 F3
Enochdhu P & K 233 G3
Ensay Ag & B 226 D3
Ensbury Bmouth 17 L3
Ensdon Shrops 112 F8
Ensis Devon 27 K5
Enson Staffs 114 E6
Enstone Oxon 66 A2
Enterkinfoot D & G 186 C5
Enterpen N York 161 G2
Enville Staffs 97 J6
Eòlaigearraidh W Isls 283 b12
Eoligarry W Isls 283 b12
Epney Gloucs 63 M5
Epperstone Notts 117 H2
Epping Essex 70 C6
Epping Green Essex 70 B6
Epping Green Herts 69 J5
Epping Upland Essex 70 C6
Eppleby N York 168 F8
Eppleworth E R Yk 144 C2
Epsom Surrey 51 G6
Epwell Oxon 83 H7
Epworth N Linc 143 K7
Epworth Turbary N Linc 143 J7
Erbistock Wrexhm 112 E3
Erdington Birm 98 E5
Eridge Green E Susx 38 E6
Eridge Station E Susx 38 E6
Erines Ag & B 206 D4
Eriska Ag & B 228 D6
Eriswell Suffk 104 E7
Erith Gt Lon 52 B3
Erlestoke Wilts 46 E8
Ermington Devon 7 J4
Erpingham Norfk 122 D5
Erriottwood Kent 40 B3
Errogie Highld 250 F7
Errol P & K 222 D3
Erskine Rens 208 D5
Erskine Bridge Rens 208 D4
Ervie D & G 172 B1
Erwarton Suffk 90 F8
Erwood Powys 78 F6
Eryholme N York 160 D1
Eryrys Denbgs 128 E8
Escalls Cnwll 2 B5
Escomb Dur 168 F4
Escott Somset 29 K3
Escrick N York 151 K7
Esgair Carmth 58 C3
Esgair Cerdgn 77 G2
Esgairgeiliog Powys 93 G2
Esgerdawe Carmth 77 H7
Esgyryn Conwy 126 F4
Esh Dur 169 G2
Esher Surrey 50 E6
Esholt C Brad 150 A7
Eshott Nthumb 191 J6
Eshton N York 149 G4
Esh Winning Dur 169 G2
Eskadale Highld 250 D4
Eskbank Mdloth 211 K5
Eskdale Green Cumb 155 L3
Eskdalemuir D & G 187 K6
Eske E R Yk 153 G7
Eskham Lincs 145 K8
Eskholme Donc 143 G4
Esperley Lane Ends Dur 168 E6
Esprick Lancs 147 H8
Essendine Rutlnd 102 A1

Essendon Herts 69 H5
Essich Highld 251 H4
Essington Staffs 98 B3
Esslemont Abers 257 G6
Eston R & Cl 170 D7
Etal Nthumb 202 E5
Etchilhampton Wilts 46 F7
Etchingham E Susx 24 C2
Etchinghill Kent 41 G7
Etchinghill Staffs 115 G7
Etchingwood E Susx 23 H7
Etling Green Norfk 121 M8
Etloe Gloucs 63 K6
Eton W & M 50 B3
Eton Wick W & M 50 B3
Etruria C Stke 114 D2
Etteridge Highld 241 J5
Ettersgill Dur 167 K5
Ettiley Heath Ches E 130 E7
Ettingshall Wolves 97 L4
Ettington Warwks 83 G5
Etton C Pete 102 C2
Etton E R Yk 152 E5
Ettrick Border 187 L3
Ettrickbridge Border 188 C4
Ettrickhill Border 187 L3
Etwall Derbys 115 M5
Eudon George Shrops 96 F5
Euston Suffk 105 H7
Euximoor Drove Cambs 103 K4
Euxton Lancs 139 K4
Evancoyd Powys 79 J3
Evanton Highld 263 G6
Evedon Lincs 118 E2
Evelith Shrops 97 G3
Evelix Highld 263 L2
Evenjobb Powys 79 J1
Evenley Nhants 84 B8
Evenlode Gloucs 65 J3
Evenwood Dur 168 F5
Evenwood Gate Dur 168 F6
Evercreech Somset 31 L1
Everingham E R Yk 152 B5
Everleigh Wilts 47 J8
Everley N York 163 H4
Eversholt C Beds 85 K5
Evershot Dorset 16 A2
Eversley Hants 49 J6
Eversley Cross Hants 49 J6
Everthorpe E R Yk 144 A2
Everton C Beds 86 D5
Everton Hants 18 D5
Everton Lpool 129 H4
Everton Notts 134 D2
Evertown D & G 177 K4
Evesbatch Herefs 80 F5
Evesham Worcs 82 B6
Evington C Leic 100 D3
Ewden Village Sheff 141 G6
Ewell Surrey 51 G6
Ewell Minnis Kent 41 H6
Ewelme Oxon 48 F7
Ewen Gloucs 64 E7
Ewenny V Glam 42 D6
Ewerby Lincs 118 F2
Ewerby Thorpe Lincs 118 F2
Ewhurst Surrey 37 G2
Ewhurst Green E Susx 24 E5
Ewhurst Green Surrey 37 G3
Ewloe Flints 129 G6
Ewloe Green Flints 129 G6
Ewood Bl w D 139 K3
Ewood Bridge Lancs 140 B3
Eworthy Devon 12 B3
Ewshot Hants 36 B2
Ewyas Harold Herefs 62 D2
Exbourne Devon 12 E3
Exbury Hants 19 G4
Exceat E Susx 23 H7
Exebridge Somset 29 G4
Exelby N York 160 D5
Exeter Devon 13 L4
Exeter & Devon Crematorium Devon 13 L4
Exford Somset 28 E4
Exfordsgreen Shrops 95 L2
Exhall Warwks 82 D5
Exhall Warwks 99 K6
Exlade Street Oxon 49 G3
Exley Head C Brad 149 J7
Exminster Devon 13 M5
Exmouth Devon 14 A5
Exning Suffk 88 C3
Exted Kent 41 G7
Exton Devon 14 A4
Exton Hants 35 J5
Exton Rutlnd 101 K8
Exton Somset 29 G4
Exwick Devon 13 L4

Eyam Derbys 132 D4
Eydon Nhants 83 M5
Eye C Pete 102 E3
Eye Herefs 80 C2
Eye Suffk 106 C8
Eye Green C Pete 102 E3
Eye Kettleby Leics 117 K8
Eyemouth Border 213 L6
Eyeworth C Beds 86 E6
Eyhorne Street Kent 39 L2
Eyke Suffk 91 H5
Eynesbury Cambs 86 D3
Eynsford Kent 52 C6
Eynsham Oxon 66 B5
Eype Dorset 15 K4
Eyre Highld 259 G6
Eythorne Kent 41 J5
Eyton Herefs 80 B3
Eyton Shrops 95 J6
Eyton Shrops 112 F8
Eyton Shrops 113 G7
Eyton Wrexhm 112 E3
Eyton on Severn Shrops 96 D2
Eyton upon the Weald Moors Wrekin 113 L8

F

Faccombe Hants 48 A7
Faceby N York 161 H2
Fachwen Powys 111 K8
Facit Lancs 140 D4
Fackley Notts 133 J7
Faddiley Ches E 113 K1
Fadmoor N York 161 L5
Faerdre Swans 57 J4
Fagwyr Swans 57 J4
Faifley W Duns 208 E4
Failand N Som 45 G4
Failford S Ayrs 196 F5
Failsworth Oldham 140 D7
Fairbourne Gwynd 92 D1
Fairburn N York 142 D2
Fairfield Derbys 131 L5
Fairfield Kent 25 H2
Fairfield Worcs 97 L8
Fairfield Park Herts 86 D8
Fairford Gloucs 65 H6
Fairford Park Gloucs 65 H6
Fairgirth D & G 175 L3
Fair Green Norfk 120 E8
Fairhaven Lancs 138 C2
Fair Isle Shet 281 b8
Fairlands Surrey 50 B8
Fairlie N Ayrs 207 L8
Fairlight E Susx 24 F5
Fairlight Cove E Susx 24 F5
Fairmile Devon 14 C3
Fairmile Surrey 50 E6
Fairnilee Border 200 F6
Fair Oak Hants 35 G7
Fairoak Staffs 114 B5
Fair Oak Green Hants 49 G6
Fairseat Kent 52 D6
Fairstead Essex 71 J4
Fairstead Norfk 120 E7
Fairstead Norfk 122 F6
Fairwarp E Susx 23 G2
Fairwater Cardif 43 J6
Fairy Cross Devon 27 G6
Fakenham Norfk 121 K5
Fakenham Magna Suffk 105 H8
Fala Mdloth 211 M6
Fala Dam Mdloth 211 M6
Falcut Nhants 84 B6
Faldingworth Lincs 135 L3
Faldouët Jersey 9 f2
Falfield S Glos 63 K8
Falkenham Suffk 91 G7
Falkirk Falk 210 A3
Falkirk Crematorium Falk 210 A3
Falkland Fife 222 D5
Fallburn S Lans 199 G5
Fallgate Derbys 133 G7
Fallin Stirlg 209 L1
Fallodon Nthumb 191 H2
Fallowfield Manch 131 G1
Fallowfield Nthumb 179 L5
Falls of Blarghour Ag & B 216 F4
Falmer E Susx 22 E5
Falmouth Cnwll 3 K4
Falnash Border 188 C5
Falsgrave N York 163 J5
Falstone Nthumb 179 G2
Fanagmore Highld 276 B6
Fancott C Beds 68 C2
Fanellan Highld 250 E3

Fangdale Beck N York 161 J4
Fangfoss E R Yk 152 A5
Fanmore Ag & B 226 E3
Fannich Lodge Highld 261 L6
Fans Border 201 J5
Far Bletchley M Keyn 85 G8
Farcet Cambs 102 D4
Far Cotton Nhants 84 E3
Farden Shrops 96 D8
Fareham Hants 19 K2
Farewell Staffs 98 D1
Far Forest Worcs 97 G8
Farforth Lincs 136 F4
Far Green Gloucs 63 M7
Faringdon Oxon 65 L8
Farington Lancs 139 G3
Farlam Cumb 178 D7
Farleigh N Som 45 G5
Farleigh Surrey 51 K7
Farleigh Hungerford Somset 46 A7
Farleigh Wallop Hants 35 J2
Farlesthorpe Lincs 137 J5
Farleton Cumb 157 H6
Farleton Lancs 147 L2
Farley Derbys 132 F7
Farley Staffs 115 H3
Farley Wilts 34 B5
Farley Green Suffk 88 E4
Farley Green Surrey 37 G2
Farley Hill Wokham 49 H6
Farleys End Gloucs 63 M4
Farlington C Port 19 M3
Farlington N York 151 K2
Farlow Shrops 96 E7
Farmborough BaNES 45 K7
Farmbridge End Essex 70 F5
Farmcote Gloucs 64 F1
Farmcote Shrops 97 H5
Farmers Carmth 77 J6
Farmington Gloucs 65 H4
Farmoor Oxon 66 C5
Far Moor Wigan 139 G2
Farms Common Cnwll 3 H4
Farm Town Leics 116 C8
Farmtown Moray 267 K6
Farnah Green Derbys 116 B2
Farnborough Gt Lon 51 L6
Farnborough Hants 49 L8
Farnborough W Berk 48 B3
Farnborough Warwks 83 K5
Farnborough Park Hants 49 L7
Farncombe Surrey 36 E2
Farndish Bed 85 H3
Farndon Ches W 112 F1
Farndon Notts 117 K1
Farne Islands Nthumb 203 L5
Farnell Angus 235 G4
Farnham Dorset 33 G7
Farnham Essex 70 C2
Farnham N York 150 E4
Farnham Suffk 91 H3
Farnham Surrey 36 B2
Farnham Common Bucks 50 B2
Farnham Green Essex 70 C2
Farnham Royal Bucks 50 B2
Farningham Kent 52 C5
Farnley Leeds 141 L1
Farnley N York 150 B6
Farnley Tyas Kirk 141 J5
Farnsfield Notts 134 C8
Farnworth Bolton 139 L6
Farnworth Halton 129 L2
Far Oakridge Gloucs 64 D6
Farr Highld 241 L3
Farr Highld 251 J5
Farr Highld 278 B4
Farraline Highld 251 G7
Farringdon Devon 14 B4
Farrington Gurney BaNES 45 J7
Far Sawrey Cumb 156 E4
Farsley Leeds 141 K1
Farther Howegreen Essex 71 K6
Farthing Green Kent 39 K4
Farthinghoe Nhants 83 M7
Farthingloe Kent 41 J7
Farthingstone Nhants 84 B4
Farthing Street Gt Lon 51 L6
Fartown Kirk 141 J4
Farway Devon 14 E3
Fasnacloich Ag & B 229 G6
Fasnakyle Highld 250 B6
Fassfern Highld 239 G7
Fatfield Sundld 181 H8
Faugh Cumb 178 C7
Fauld Staffs 115 K6
Fauldhouse W Loth 210 B6
Faulkbourne Essex 71 J4
Faulkland Somset 45 L8
Fauls Shrops 113 K5

Faversham Kent 40 D3
Fawdington N York 150 F1
Fawdon N u Ty 180 F5
Fawdon Nthumb 190 E3
Fawfieldhead Staffs 131 L7
Fawkham Green Kent 52 C6
Fawler Oxon 66 A4
Fawley Bucks 49 J2
Fawley Hants 19 G3
Fawley W Berk 48 B3
Fawley Chapel Herefs 63 H1
Fawnog Flints 128 F6
Fawsley Nhants 84 A4
Faxfleet E R Yk 143 L3
Faygate W Susx 37 K4
Fazakerley Lpool 138 D8
Fazeley Staffs 99 G3
Fearby N York 160 B6
Fearn Highld 264 C4
Fearnan P & K 231 K6
Fearnbeg Highld 260 B7
Fearnhead Warrtn 130 C2
Fearnmore Highld 260 A7
Fearnoch Ag & B 206 E3
Featherstone Staffs 97 L2
Featherstone Wakefd 142 C4
Feckenham Worcs 82 B3
Feering Essex 72 C3
Feetham N York 159 H3
Feizor N York 148 D2
Felbridge Surrey 38 B5
Felbrigg Norfk 122 E4
Felcourt Surrey 38 B5
Felden Herts 68 D6
Felindre Carmth 59 G4
Felindre Carmth 59 K3
Felindre Carmth 76 C7
Felindre Cerdgn 77 G4
Felindre Powys 61 J2
Felindre Powys 94 E7
Felindre Swans 57 H4
Felindre Farchog Pembks 75 J4
Felin Fach Cerdgn 76 F4
Felinfach Powys 78 F8
Felinfoel Carmth 56 F4
Felingwm Isaf Carmth 58 F4
Felingwm Uchaf Carmth 58 F4
Felin-newydd Powys 78 F8
Felixkirk N York 161 G5
Felixstowe Suffk 91 G8
Felixstowe Ferry Suffk 91 H7
Felkington Nthumb 202 E4
Felkirk Wakefd 142 B5
Felling Gatesd 181 G6
Fell Lane C Brad 149 J7
Fell Side Cumb 165 J3
Felmersham Bed 85 K4
Felmingham Norfk 122 E5
Felpham W Susx 20 F7
Felsham Suffk 89 J4
Felsted Essex 71 G3
Feltham Gt Lon 50 E4
Felthamhill Surrey 50 E5
Felthorpe Norfk 122 D7
Felton Herefs 80 D5
Felton N Som 45 G6
Felton Nthumb 191 H6
Felton Butler Shrops 112 F8
Feltwell Norfk 104 E5
Fenay Bridge Kirk 141 J4
Fence Lancs 148 E8
Fence Rothm 133 J3
Fence Houses Sundld 169 J1
Fencott Oxon 66 E4
Fendike Corner Lincs 137 H7
Fen Ditton Cambs 87 K3
Fen Drayton Cambs 87 G2
Fen End Lincs 119 H7
Fen End Solhll 99 G8
Fenham Nthumb 203 H5
Feniscliffe Bl w D 139 K2
Feniscowles Bl w D 139 K3
Feniton Devon 14 D3
Fenland Crematorium Cambs 103 H4
Fenn Green Shrops 97 H6
Fenn Street Medway 53 G4
Fenny Bentley Derbys 115 K2
Fenny Bridges Devon 14 D3
Fenny Compton Warwks 83 K5
Fenny Drayton Leics 99 K4
Fenny Stratford M Keyn 85 G8
Fenrother Nthumb 191 H7
Fenstanton Cambs 87 G2
Fenstead End Suffk 88 F5
Fen Street Norfk 105 K4
Fen Street Suffk 90 E3
Fenton C Stke 114 D3
Fenton Cambs 103 G7
Fenton Cumb 178 C7

Fenton Lincs 118 A1
Fenton Lincs 135 G4
Fenton Notts 134 F3
Fenton Nthumb 202 F6
Fenton Barns E Loth 212 B3
Fenwick Donc 142 F4
Fenwick E Ayrs 196 F2
Fenwick Nthumb 180 C4
Fenwick Nthumb 203 H5
Feock Cnwll 3 L3
Feolin Ferry Ag & B 205 G3
Fergushill N Ayrs 196 C2
Feriniquarrie Highld 258 B6
Fermain Bay Guern 9 k3
Fern Angus 234 D3
Ferndale Rhondd 42 F2
Ferndown Dorset 17 L3
Ferness Highld 253 J3
Fernham Oxon 65 L8
Fernhill Heath Worcs 81 K3
Fernhurst W Susx 36 D5
Fernie Fife 222 E4
Ferniegair S Lans 209 K8
Fernilea Highld 246 E2
Fernilee Derbys 131 K4
Fernwood Notts 117 L2
Ferrensby N York 150 E4
Ferriby Sluice N Linc 144 B4
Ferrindonald Highld 247 L7
Ferring W Susx 21 J6
Ferrybridge Wakefd 142 D3
Ferryden Angus 235 H4
Ferryhill Dur 169 H4
Ferryhill Station Dur 169 J4
Ferry Point Highld 263 K3
Ferryside Carmth 56 C3
Ferrytown Highld 263 K2
Fersfield Norfk 106 B7
Fersit Highld 240 B7
Feshiebridge Highld 241 M3
Fetcham Surrey 50 F7
Fetlar Shet 281 f3
Fetterangus Abers 269 H6
Fettercairn Abers 235 G1
Fewcott Oxon 66 D2
Fewston N York 150 B5
Ffairfach Carmth 59 H4
Ffair Rhos Cerdgn 77 K2
Ffald-y-Brenin Carmth 77 H6
Ffawyddog Powys 61 K3
Ffestiniog Gwynd 110 D3
Ffordd-las Denbgs 128 D6
Fforest Carmth 57 G4
Fforest Mons 62 B3
Fforest Fach Swans 57 H5
Fforest Göch Neath 57 K4
Ffostrasol Cerdgn 76 C5
Ffrith Flints 129 G8
Ffynnonddewi Cerdgn 76 C4
Ffynnongroyw Flints 128 D3
Ffynnon-oer Cerdgn 76 F4
Fickleshole Surrey 51 K6
Fiddington Gloucs 64 D1
Fiddington Somset 30 B3
Fiddleford Dorset 32 D8
Fiddlers Green Cnwll 4 D4
Fiddlers Hamlet Essex 70 C6
Field Staffs 115 G5
Field Broughton Cumb 156 E6
Field Dalling Norfk 121 M4
Fieldhead Cumb 166 B3
Field Head Leics 100 B2
Fifehead Magdalen Dorset 32 C6
Fifehead Neville Dorset 32 C8
Fifehead St Quintin Dorset 16 E1
Fife Keith Moray 267 H6
Fifield Oxon 65 K3
Fifield W & M 49 L4
Fifield Wilts 33 K2
Figheldean Wilts 33 K2
Filands Wilts 46 D1
Filby Norfk 107 K1
Filey N York 163 L6
Filgrave M Keyn 85 G5
Filkins Oxon 65 K6
Filleigh Devon 28 B5
Filleigh Devon 28 C8
Fillingham Lincs 135 J3
Fillongley Warwks 99 H6
Filmore Hill Hants 35 K5
Filton S Glos 45 J3
Fimber E R Yk 152 D4
Finavon Angus 234 D4
Fincham Norfk 104 D2
Finchampstead Wokham 49 J6
Fincharn Ag & B 216 D6
Finchdean Hants 20 B4
Finchingfield Essex 88 D8
Finchley Gt Lon 51 H1

Place	Page	Grid
Findern Derbys	116	A5
Findhorn Moray	265	G7
Findhorn Bridge Highld	252	E6
Findochty Moray	267	J3
Findo Gask P & K	221	H3
Findon Abers	245	L4
Findon W Susx	21	J5
Findon Mains Highld	263	G7
Findrack House Abers	244	D3
Finedon Nhants	85	H1
Fingal Street Suffk	90	F1
Fingask P & K	222	B3
Fingest Bucks	49	J1
Finghall N York	160	B5
Fingland Cumb	177	H7
Fingland D & G	197	L7
Finglesham Kent	41	K4
Fingringhoe Essex	72	F3
Finkle Green Essex	88	D7
Finkle Street Barns	141	M7
Finlarig Stirlg	231	G8
Finmere Oxon	84	C8
Finnart P & K	230	F4
Finningham Suffk	90	C2
Finningley Donc	143	H7
Finsbay W Isls	282	e6
Finstall Worcs	82	A1
Finsthwaite Cumb	156	E5
Finstock Oxon	66	A4
Finstown Ork	275	C4
Fintry Abers	268	D5
Fintry Stirlg	209	G2
Finzean Abers	244	D5
Fionnphort Ag & B	226	B7
Fionnsbhagh W Isls	282	e6
Firbank Cumb	157	K4
Firbeck Rothm	133	L2
Firby N York	152	A3
Firby N York	160	C5
Firgrove Rochdl	140	D5
Firle E Susx	23	G6
Firsby Lincs	137	H7
Firsdown Wilts	34	B4
Fir Tree Dur	168	F4
Fishbourne IoW	19	J5
Fishbourne W Susx	20	D6
Fishburn Dur	169	K4
Fishcross Clacks	220	F8
Fisher W Susx	20	E6
Fisherford Abers	256	B4
Fisherrow E Loth	211	K4
Fisher's Pond Hants	35	G6
Fisher's Row Lancs	147	H6
Fisherstreet W Susx	36	E4
Fisherton Highld	252	D2
Fisherton S Ayrs	196	B7
Fisherton de la Mere Wilts	33	G3
Fisherwick Staffs	98	F2
Fishery Estate W & M	49	L3
Fishguard Pembks	74	F5
Fishlake Donc	143	G5
Fishleigh Devon	12	D2
Fishmere End Lincs	119	J4
Fishnish Pier Ag & B	227	J4
Fishpond Bottom Dorset	15	J3
Fishponds Bristl	45	J4
Fishtoft Lincs	119	K3
Fishtoft Drove Lincs	119	K2
Fishwick Lancs	139	H2
Fiskavaig Highld	246	D2
Fiskerton Lincs	135	L5
Fiskerton Notts	117	K1
Fitling E R Yk	145	H1
Fittleton Wilts	33	K1
Fittleworth W Susx	21	G3
Fitton End Cambs	103	J1
Fitz Shrops	113	G7
Fitzhead Somset	29	L5
Fitzroy Somset	30	B5
Fitzwilliam Wakefd	142	C5
Five Ash Down E Susx	23	H3
Five Ashes E Susx	23	J2
Five Bells Somset	29	K2
Five Bridges Herefs	80	F6
Fivecrosses Ches W	129	M4
Fivehead Somset	30	E6
Fivelanes Cnwll	11	J6
Five Lanes Mons	44	F1
Five Oak Green Kent	39	G4
Five Oaks Jersey	9	e3
Five Oaks W Susx	37	G5
Five Roads Carmth	56	E4
Five Wents Kent	39	K3
Flack's Green Essex	71	J4
Flackwell Heath Bucks	49	L1
Fladbury Worcs	82	A6
Fladdabister Shet	281	e7
Flagg Derbys	132	C6
Flamborough E R Yk	153	K2
Flamstead Herts	68	D4
Flamstead End Herts	69	J6
Flansham W Susx	20	F6
Flanshaw Wakefd	141	M4
Flappit Spring C Brad	149	J8
Flasby N York	149	G4
Flash Staffs	131	K6
Flashader Highld	258	E6
Flaunden Herts	68	C7
Flawborough Notts	117	K3
Flawith N York	151	L3
Flax Bourton N Som	45	G5
Flaxby N York	150	E4
Flaxley Gloucs	63	K4
Flaxmere Ches W	130	A5
Flaxpool Somset	29	L4
Flaxton N York	151	L3
Fleckney Leics	100	E5
Flecknoe Warwks	83	M3
Fledborough Notts	134	F5
Fleet Dorset	16	C6
Fleet Hants	20	B6
Fleet Hants	49	K8
Fleet Lincs	119	L6
Fleetend Hants	19	H3
Fleet Hargate Lincs	119	L6
Fleetwood Lancs	146	F6
Fleggburgh Norfk	123	J8
Flemingston V Glam	42	F7
Flemington S Lans	209	H7
Flempton Suffk	89	G1
Fletchersbridge Cnwll	5	J2
Fletcher's Green Kent	38	E3
Fletchertown Cumb	165	G2
Fletching E Susx	23	G3
Flexbury Cnwll	11	J1
Flexford Surrey	36	D1
Flimby Cumb	164	D4
Flimwell E Susx	39	H7
Flint Flints	128	F5
Flintham Notts	117	K2
Flint Mountain Flints	128	F5
Flinton E R Yk	153	K8
Flint's Green Solhll	99	H7
Flishinghurst Kent	39	J6
Flitcham Norfk	120	F6
Flitton C Beds	85	L8
Flitwick C Beds	85	K8
Flixborough N Linc	143	L5
Flixborough Stather N Linc	143	L5
Flixton N York	163	J6
Flixton Suffk	107	G6
Flixton Traffd	130	E1
Flockton Kirk	141	K5
Flockton Green Kirk	141	L5
Flodden Nthumb	202	E6
Flodigarry Highld	259	H2
Flookburgh Cumb	156	E7
Flordon Norfk	106	D4
Flore Nhants	84	C3
Flotterton Nthumb	190	E5
Flowers Green E Susx	23	K5
Flowton Suffk	90	C6
Flushdyke Wakefd	141	L3
Flushing Cnwll	3	K4
Fluxton Devon	14	C4
Flyford Flavell Worcs	82	A4
Fobbing Thurr	52	F2
Fochabers Moray	267	G4
Fochriw Caerph	61	H6
Fockerby N Linc	143	L4
Foddington Somset	31	J5
Foel Powys	94	B1
Foelgastell Carmth	59	G6
Foel y Dyffryn Brdgnd	42	C3
Foggathorpe E R Yk	152	A8
Fogo Border	202	B3
Fogwatt Moray	266	E5
Foindle Highld	276	B6
Folda Angus	233	J3
Fole Staffs	115	G4
Foleshill Covtry	99	K7
Folke Dorset	31	L8
Folkestone Kent	41	H8
Folkingham Lincs	118	E5
Folkington E Susx	23	J6
Folksworth Cambs	102	C5
Folkton N York	163	J6
Folla Rule Abers	256	C5
Follifoot N York	150	D5
Folly Gate Devon	12	D3
Folly Hill Surrey	36	B1
Fonmon V Glam	43	G8
Fonthill Bishop Wilts	32	F4
Fonthill Gifford Wilts	32	F4
Fontmell Magna Dorset	32	E7
Fontmell Parva Dorset	20	D7
Fontwell W Susx	20	F5
Font-y-gary V Glam	43	G8
Foolow Derbys	132	D4
Foots Cray Gt Lon	52	A5
Forbestown Abers	243	L1
Forcett N York	168	F8
Ford Ag & B	216	D6
Ford Bucks	67	J5
Ford Derbys	133	H4
Ford Devon	7	J5
Ford Devon	8	B6
Ford Devon	27	G6
Ford Gloucs	65	G1
Ford Nthumb	202	E5
Ford Shrops	95	K1
Ford Somset	29	K5
Ford Somset	45	H8
Ford Staffs	115	H1
Ford W Susx	21	G6
Ford Wilts	33	L4
Ford Wilts	46	B4
Forda Devon	12	D4
Fordcombe Kent	38	E5
Fordell Fife	211	G1
Forden Powys	94	F3
Ford End Essex	71	G4
Forder Green Devon	8	B2
Ford Green Lancs	147	J6
Fordham Cambs	88	C1
Fordham Essex	72	D2
Fordham Norfk	104	C3
Fordham Heath Essex	72	D2
Ford Heath Shrops	95	K1
Fordingbridge Hants	33	K8
Fordon E R Yk	163	J7
Fordoun Abers	245	G8
Ford's Green Suffk	90	C2
Fordstreet Essex	72	D2
Ford Street Somset	29	L7
Fordton Devon	13	J3
Fordwells Oxon	65	L4
Fordwich Kent	41	G3
Fordyce Abers	267	L3
Forebridge Staffs	114	E7
Foremark Derbys	116	B6
Forest Guern	9	j4
Forest N York	160	C3
Forest Becks Lancs	148	D5
Forestburn Gate Nthumb	190	F7
Forest Chapel Ches E	131	J5
Forest Gate Gt Lon	51	L2
Forest Green Surrey	37	H3
Forest Hall N Tyne	181	G5
Forest Head Cumb	178	D7
Forest Hill Gt Lon	51	K4
Forest Hill Oxon	66	E5
Forest-in-Teesdale Dur	167	K4
Forest Lane Head N York	150	D4
Forest Mill Clacks	221	G8
Forest of Dean Crematorium Gloucs	63	J4
Forest Park Crematorium Gt Lon	70	C8
Forest Row E Susx	38	C6
Forest Side IoW	19	H5
Forestside W Susx	20	C4
Forest Town Notts	133	L7
Forfar Angus	234	C5
Forgandenny P & K	221	K3
Forge Powys	93	G3
Forge Hammer Torfn	62	B7
Forge Side Torfn	61	L5
Forgie Moray	267	H5
Forgieside Moray	267	H5
Forgue Abers	256	A3
Forhill Worcs	98	D8
Formby Sefton	138	C6
Forncett End Norfk	106	C4
Forncett St Mary Norfk	106	D4
Forncett St Peter Norfk	106	D5
Fornham All Saints Suffk	89	G2
Fornham St Martin Suffk	89	G2
Fornighty Highld	253	H2
Forres Moray	265	G8
Forsbrook Staffs	114	F3
Forse Highld	275	H1
Forshaw Heath Warwks	98	E8
Forsinard Highld	278	F7
Forss Highld	279	J3
Forston Dorset	16	C3
Fort Augustus Highld	240	C2
Forteviot P & K	221	J4
Forth S Lans	198	F2
Forthampton Gloucs	64	B1
Fort Hommet Guern	9	i2
Forth Road Bridge Fife	210	F3
Fortingall P & K	231	K6
Fort le Marchant Guern	9	k1
Forton Hants	34	F2
Forton Lancs	147	J5
Forton Shrops	113	G8
Forton Somset	15	H1
Forton Staffs	114	B7
Fortrie Abers	256	B3
Fortrose Highld	263	K8
Fortuneswell Dorset	16	D7
Fort William Highld	239	G3
Forty Green Bucks	68	B8
Forty Hill Gt Lon	69	J7
Forward Green Suffk	90	C3
Fosbury Wilts	47	L7
Foscot Oxon	65	J3
Foscote Nhants	84	C6
Fosdyke Lincs	119	K5
Fosdyke Bridge Lincs	119	K5
Foss P & K	231	L4
Fossebridge Gloucs	65	G5
Foss-y-ffin Cerdgn	76	E3
Fosterhouses Donc	143	G5
Foster Street Essex	70	C5
Foston Derbys	115	K5
Foston Leics	100	D4
Foston Lincs	117	M3
Foston N York	151	L3
Foston on the Wolds E R Yk	153	H4
Fotherby Lincs	136	F2
Fothergill Cumb	164	D5
Fotheringhay Nhants	102	B5
Foula Shet	281	a7
Foulbridge Cumb	165	M1
Foulby Wakefd	142	F5
Foulden Border	202	E2
Foulden Norfk	104	F4
Foul End Warwks	99	H4
Foul Mile E Susx	23	K4
Foulness Island Essex	53	L1
Foulon Vale Crematorium Guern	9	j3
Foulridge Lancs	148	F7
Foulsham Norfk	122	A6
Fountainhall Border	200	F3
Four Ashes Solhll	98	F5
Four Ashes Staffs	97	H6
Four Ashes Staffs	97	L2
Four Ashes Suffk	89	K1
Four Cabots Guern	9	j3
Four Crosses Powys	112	C7
Four Crosses Staffs	98	B2
Four Elms Kent	38	C4
Four Foot Somset	31	J4
Four Forks Somset	30	C4
Four Gates Bolton	139	J6
Four Gotes Cambs	120	A8
Four Lane Ends Barns	141	L7
Four Lane Ends Ches W	130	A4
Four Lanes Cnwll	3	H3
Fourlanes End Ches E	130	F7
Four Marks Hants	35	K4
Four Mile Bridge IoA	124	E4
Four Oaks Birm	98	E4
Four Oaks E Susx	24	F2
Four Oaks Gloucs	63	K2
Four Oaks Solhll	99	H7
Fourpenny Highld	264	C1
Four Points W Berk	48	E3
Four Roads Carmth	56	E3
Four Shire Stone Warwks	65	K1
Fourstones Nthumb	179	K5
Four Throws Kent	39	J7
Four Wents Kent	38	F3
Fovant Wilts	33	H5
Foveran Abers	257	H7
Fowey Cnwll	5	K4
Fowley Common Warrtn	139	K8
Fowlhall Kent	39	H4
Fowlis Angus	233	M8
Fowlis Wester P & K	221	G2
Fowlmere Cambs	87	J6
Fownhope Herefs	80	D8
Foxbar Rens	208	D6
Foxcombe Devon	12	C5
Fox Corner Surrey	50	B7
Foxcote Gloucs	64	D5
Foxcote Somset	45	L7
Foxdale IoM	154	C6
Foxearth Essex	89	G6
Foxendown Kent	52	E5
Foxfield Cumb	156	B5
Foxham Wilts	46	E3
Fox Hatch Essex	70	E7
Foxhills Hants	18	E1
Foxhole Cnwll	4	F4
Foxholes N York	163	H8
Foxhunt Green E Susx	23	J4
Foxley Nhants	84	C5
Foxley Norfk	122	A7
Foxley Wilts	46	C1
Foxlydiate Worcs	82	B2
Fox Street Essex	72	F2

Foxt Staffs 115 G2
Foxton Cambs 87 H5
Foxton Dur 169 K5
Foxton Leics 100 F5
Foxton N York 160 F3
Foxup N York 158 F7
Foxwist Green Ches W 130 C6
Foxwood Shrops 96 E8
Foy Herefs 63 H2
Foyers Highld 250 E7
Foynesfield Highld 253 G1
Fraddam Cnwll 2 F4
Fraddon Cnwll 4 E3
Fradley Staffs 98 F1
Fradswell Staffs 114 F5
Fraisthorpe E R Yk 153 J3
Framfield E Susx 23 H3
Framingham Earl Norfk 106 F3
Framingham Pigot Norfk 106 F3
Framlingham Suffk 91 G3
Frampton Dorset 16 B4
Frampton Lincs 119 K4
Frampton Cotterell S Glos 45 K3
Frampton Mansell Gloucs 64 D6
Frampton-on-Severn Gloucs 63 L5
Frampton West End Lincs 119 J3
Framsden Suffk 90 E3
Framwellgate Moor Dur 169 H2
Franche Worcs 97 J7
Frandley Ches W 130 C4
Frankaborough Devon 11 M4
Frankby Wirral 128 F2
Frankfort Norfk 122 F6
Franklands Gate Herefs 80 C6
Frankley Worcs 98 C7
Franksbridge Powys 78 F4
Frankton Warwks 83 K1
Frant E Susx 38 F6
Fraserburgh Abers 269 J3
Frating Essex 73 G3
Frating Green Essex 73 G2
Fratton C Port 19 L4
Freathy Cnwll 6 D4
Freckenham Suffk 88 D1
Freckleton Lancs 138 E2
Freebirch Derbys 132 F5
Freeby Leics 117 L7
Freefolk Hants 35 G1
Freehay Staffs 115 G3
Freeland Oxon 66 B4
Freethorpe Norfk 107 H2
Freethorpe Common Norfk 107 H2
Freiston Lincs 119 L3
Fremington Devon 27 J4
Fremington N York 159 J3
Frenchay S Glos 45 J3
Frenchbeer Devon 12 F5
French Street Kent 51 M8
Frenich P & K 232 B4
Frensham Surrey 36 C3
Freshfield Sefton 138 C6
Freshford Wilts 46 A7
Freshwater IoW 18 E6
Freshwater Bay IoW 18 E6
Freshwater East Pembks 55 G7
Fressingfield Suffk 106 F7
Freston Suffk 90 E7
Freswick Highld 280 E3
Fretherne Gloucs 63 L5
Frettenham Norfk 122 E8
Freuchie Fife 222 D6
Freystrop Pembks 54 F4
Friar Park Sandw 98 C4
Friar's Gate E Susx 38 D6
Friars' Hill N York 162 C5
Friar Waddon Dorset 16 C5
Friday Bridge Cambs 103 K2
Friday Street Suffk 90 F3
Friday Street Suffk 91 H5
Friday Street Suffk 91 J3
Friday Street Surrey 37 H2
Fridaythorpe E R Yk 152 D4
Friden Derbys 132 C7
Friendly Calder 141 G3
Friern Barnet Gt Lon 69 H8
Friesthorpe Lincs 135 M3
Frieston Lincs 118 B2
Frieth Bucks 49 J1
Friezeland Notts 116 D2
Frilford Oxon 66 B7
Frilsham W Berk 48 E4
Frimley Surrey 49 L7
Frimley Green Surrey 49 L7
Frindsbury Medway 52 F5
Fring Norfk 121 G4
Fringford Oxon 66 F1
Frinsted Kent 40 A4
Frinton-on-Sea Essex 73 K3
Friockheim Angus 234 F5

Friog Gwynd 92 D1
Frisby on the Wreake Leics 117 J8
Friskney Lincs 137 J8
Friskney Eaudike Lincs 137 J8
Friston E Susx 23 J7
Friston Suffk 91 J3
Fritchley Derbys 116 B1
Fritham Hants 34 B8
Frith Bank Lincs 119 K2
Frith Common Worcs 80 F1
Frithelstock Devon 27 H7
Frithelstock Stone Devon 27 H7
Frithend Hants 36 B3
Frithsden Herts 68 C5
Frithville Lincs 119 K2
Frittenden Kent 39 K5
Frittiscombe Devon 8 B6
Fritton Norfk 106 E5
Fritton Norfk 107 K3
Fritwell Oxon 66 D1
Frizinghall C Brad 149 L8
Frizington Cumb 164 D7
Frocester Gloucs 63 M6
Frodesley Shrops 96 C3
Frodsham Ches W 129 M4
Frogden Border 202 B7
Frog End Cambs 87 H6
Frog End Cambs 87 L3
Froggatt Derbys 132 E4
Froghall Staffs 115 G2
Frogham Hants 33 L8
Frogham Kent 41 H5
Frogmore Devon 7 M6
Frognall Lincs 102 D2
Frogpool Cnwll 3 J3
Frog Pool Worcs 81 J2
Frogwell Cnwll 6 C1
Frolesworth Leics 100 B5
Frome Somset 32 C1
Frome St Quintin Dorset 16 B2
Fromes Hill Herefs 80 F6
Fron Denbgs 128 C6
Fron Gwynd 108 F4
Fron Gwynd 109 J1
Fron Powys 94 E4
Fron Powys 94 F3
Froncysyllte Denbgs 112 C3
Fron-goch Gwynd 111 H4
Fron Isaf Wrexhm 112 C3
Frostenden Suffk 107 K7
Frosterley Dur 168 C3
Froxfield C Beds 85 J8
Froxfield Wilts 47 L5
Froxfield Green Hants 35 L5
Fryern Hill Hants 34 F6
Fryerning Essex 70 F7
Fryton N York 162 B7
Fuinary Highld 227 J3
Fulbeck Lincs 118 B2
Fulbourn Cambs 87 L4
Fulbrook Oxon 65 K4
Fulflood Hants 35 G5
Fulford C York 151 K6
Fulford Somset 30 B5
Fulford Staffs 114 E4
Fulham Gt Lon 51 H4
Fulking W Susx 22 C5
Fullaford Devon 28 B3
Fullarton N Ayrs 196 C3
Fuller's End Essex 70 D2
Fuller's Moor Ches W 113 H1
Fuller Street Essex 71 H4
Fuller Street Kent 38 E2
Fullerton Hants 34 E3
Fulletby Lincs 136 E5
Fullready Warwks 83 G6
Full Sutton E R Yk 152 A5
Fullwood E Ayrs 196 E1
Fulmer Bucks 50 C2
Fulmodeston Norfk 121 M5
Fulnetby Lincs 136 B4
Fulney Lincs 119 J6
Fulstone Kirk 141 J6
Fulstow Lincs 145 J2
Fulwell Oxon 66 A3
Fulwell Sundld 181 J7
Fulwood Lancs 139 H2
Fulwood Notts 133 J8
Fulwood Sheff 132 F3
Fulwood Somset 30 B6
Fundenhall Norfk 106 C4
Funtington W Susx 20 C5
Funtley Hants 19 J2
Funtullich P & K 220 C2
Furley Devon 15 G2
Furnace Ag & B 217 G7
Furnace Carmth 56 F4
Furnace Cerdgn 92 E4
Furnace End Warwks 99 H5

Furner's Green E Susx 22 F2
Furness Vale Derbys 131 K3
Furneux Pelham Herts 70 B2
Further Quarter Kent 39 M5
Furtho Nhants 84 E6
Furzehill Devon 28 C2
Furzehill Dorset 17 K2
Furzehills Lincs 136 E5
Furzeley Corner Hants 19 L2
Furzley Hants 34 C7
Fyfett Somset 30 C7
Fyfield Essex 70 E5
Fyfield Hants 34 C2
Fyfield Oxon 66 B7
Fyfield Wilts 47 H5
Fyfield Wilts 47 H6
Fyfield Bavant Wilts 33 H6
Fylingthorpe N York 163 G2
Fyning W Susx 36 B6
Fyvie Abers 256 D4

G

Gabroc Hill E Ayrs 196 E1
Gaddesby Leics 100 F1
Gaddesden Row Herts 68 D4
Gadfa IoA 125 H2
Gadgirth S Ayrs 196 E6
Gadlas Shrops 112 E4
Gaer Powys 61 J3
Gaerllwyd Mons 62 F7
Gaerwen IoA 125 H5
Gagingwell Oxon 66 B2
Gailes N Ayrs 196 C4
Gailey Staffs 97 K1
Gainford Dur 168 F7
Gainsborough Lincs 135 G2
Gainsford End Essex 88 E8
Gairloch Highld 260 C4
Gairlochy Highld 239 K6
Gairneybridge P & K 221 L7
Gaisgill Cumb 157 K2
Gaitsgill Cumb 165 L1
Galashiels Border 201 G6
Galgate Lancs 147 J5
Galhampton Somset 31 K5
Gallanachbeg Ag & B 216 C2
Gallanachmore Ag & B 216 C2
Gallantry Bank Ches E 113 H1
Gallatown Fife 222 E8
Galley Common Warwks 99 J5
Galleywood Essex 71 H6
Gallovie Highld 240 F5
Gallowfauld Angus 234 C7
Gallowhill P & K 233 J8
Gallows Green Essex 72 D2
Gallows Green Worcs 81 L3
Gallowstree Common Oxon 49 G3
Galltair Highld 248 C7
Gallt-y-foel Gwynd 125 K7
Gally Hill Hants 49 K8
Gallypot Street E Susx 38 D6
Galmisdale Highld 236 F4
Galmpton Devon 7 K6
Galmpton Torbay 8 D4
Galphay N York 150 C1
Galston E Ayrs 196 F4
Gamballs Green Staffs 131 L6
Gamblesby Cumb 166 E3
Gambles Green Essex 71 J4
Gamelsby Cumb 177 H8
Gamesley Derbys 131 K1
Gamlingay Cambs 86 E5
Gamlingay Cinques Cambs 86 E4
Gamlingay Great Heath Cambs 86 E5
Gammersgill N York 159 J6
Gamrie Abers 268 E4
Gamston Notts 117 G4
Gamston Notts 134 E4
Ganarew Herefs 63 G4
Ganavan Bay Ag & B 216 D1
Gang Cnwll 6 C1
Ganllwyd Gwynd 110 D6
Gannachy Angus 234 F1
Ganstead E R Yk 144 F1
Ganthorpe N York 151 L2
Ganton N York 163 H7
Ganwick Corner Herts 69 H7
Gappah Devon 13 K7
Garbity Moray 266 F5
Garboldisham Norfk 105 K7
Garbole Highld 252 E7
Garchory Abers 243 J2
Garden City Flints 129 H6
Gardeners Green Wokham 49 K5

Garden of England Crematorium Kent 53 J5
Gardenstown Abers 268 E3
Garden Village Sheff 141 L8
Garderhouse Shet 281 d6
Gardham E R Yk 152 E7
Gare Hill Somset 32 C3
Garelochhead Ag & B 207 L1
Garford Oxon 66 B7
Garforth Leeds 142 B1
Gargrave N York 149 G5
Gargunnock Stirlg 220 B8
Garizim Conwy 126 D4
Garlic Street Norfk 106 E6
Garlieston D & G 174 D5
Garlinge Kent 41 K2
Garlinge Green Kent 40 F5
Garlogie Abers 245 H2
Garmond Abers 268 E5
Garmouth Moray 267 G3
Garmston Shrops 96 E2
Garnant Carmth 59 J6
Garn-Dolbenmaen Gwynd 109 J3
Garnett Bridge Cumb 157 H3
Garnfadryn Gwynd 108 E5
Garnswllt Swans 57 H3
Garn-yr-erw Torfn 61 K5
Garrabost W Isls 282 h3
Garrallan E Ayrs 197 G7
Garras Cnwll 3 H6
Garreg Gwynd 109 L3
Garrigill Cumb 167 H2
Garriston N York 159 L4
Garroch D & G 184 F6
Garrochtrie D & G 172 D7
Garrochty Ag & B 207 H8
Garros Highld 259 H4
Garsdale Cumb 158 C5
Garsdale Head Cumb 158 D4
Garsdon Wilts 46 D2
Garshall Green Staffs 114 F5
Garsington Oxon 66 E6
Garstang Lancs 147 J6
Garston Herts 68 E7
Garston Lpool 129 J3
Garswood St Hel 139 H7
Gartachossan Ag & B 204 E4
Gartcosh N Lans 209 J5
Garth Brdgnd 42 C4
Garth Mons 62 D8
Garth Powys 78 C5
Garth Powys 79 J1
Garth Wrexhm 112 C3
Garthamlock C Glas 209 H5
Garthbrengy Powys 78 E8
Gartheli Cerdgn 77 G4
Garthmyl Powys 94 F3
Garthorpe Leics 117 L7
Garthorpe N Linc 143 L4
Garth Row Cumb 157 H3
Garths Cumb 157 H5
Gartly Abers 255 K5
Gartmore Stirlg 219 H7
Gartness N Lans 209 K6
Gartness Stirlg 208 E2
Gartocharn W Duns 208 D2
Garton E R Yk 145 H1
Garton-on-the-Wolds E R Yk 152 F4
Gartymore Highld 274 D5
Garva Bridge Highld 240 F4
Garvald E Loth 212 D5
Garvan Highld 238 F8
Garvard Ag & B 214 D6
Garve Highld 262 C7
Garvellachs Ag & B 215 J2
Garvestone Norfk 105 L2
Garvock Inver 207 L5
Garway Herefs 62 F3
Garway Common Herefs 62 F3
Garway Hill Herefs 62 F2
Garyvard W Isls 282 g4
Gasper Wilts 32 C4
Gastard Wilts 46 C5
Gasthorpe Norfk 105 K7
Gaston Green Essex 70 D4
Gatcombe IoW 19 H6
Gatebeck Cumb 157 J5
Gate Burton Lincs 135 G3
Gateford Notts 134 B3
Gateforth N York 142 E2
Gatehead E Ayrs 196 D4
Gate Helmsley N York 151 L5
Gatehouse Nthumb 179 H1
Gatehouse of Fleet D & G 174 F4
Gateley Norfk 121 L6
Gatenby N York 160 D5
Gatesgarth Cumb 165 G4
Gateshaw Border 189 L2
Gateshead Gatesd 181 G6

Gates Heath Ches W 129 L7
Gateside Angus 234 C6
Gateside E Rens 208 E7
Gateside Fife 222 B5
Gateside N Ayrs 208 B8
Gateslack D & G 186 C5
Gathurst Wigan 139 G6
Gatley Stockp 131 G2
Gatton Surrey 51 H8
Gattonside Border 201 H6
Gaufron Powys 78 D2
Gaulby Leics 100 F3
Gauldry Fife 222 F2
Gauldswell P & K 233 K5
Gaulkthorn Lancs 139 M3
Gaultree Norfk 103 K2
Gaunton's Bank Ches E 113 J2
Gaunt's Common Dorset 17 K2
Gaunt's End Essex 70 E2
Gautby Lincs 136 C5
Gavinton Border 202 B3
Gawber Barns 141 M6
Gawcott Bucks 67 G1
Gawsworth Ches E 131 H5
Gawthorpe Wakefd 141 L3
Gawthrop Cumb 158 B5
Gawthwaite Cumb 156 C5
Gay Bowers Essex 71 J6
Gaydon Warwks 83 J4
Gayhurst M Keyn 85 G6
Gayle N York 158 F5
Gayles N York 159 L1
Gay Street W Susx 21 J3
Gayton Nhants 84 D4
Gayton Norfk 120 F7
Gayton Staffs 114 F6
Gayton Wirral 129 G4
Gayton le Marsh Lincs 137 H3
Gayton Thorpe Norfk 121 G7
Gaywood Norfk 120 E7
Gazeley Suffk 88 E2
Gear Cnwll 3 J6
Gearraidh Bhaird W Isls 282 g4
Geary Highld 258 D4
Gedding Suffk 89 J4
Geddington Nhants 101 K6
Gedling Notts 117 G3
Gedney Lincs 119 L6
Gedney Broadgate Lincs 119 L7
Gedney Drove End Lincs 120 A5
Gedney Dyke Lincs 119 L6
Gedney Hill Lincs 103 G1
Gee Cross Tamesd 131 J1
Geeston Rutlnd 101 L3
Geldeston Norfk 107 H5
Gelli Rhondd 42 E3
Gelli Torfn 62 B8
Gellifor Denbgs 128 D7
Gelligaer Caerph 43 H2
Gelligroes Caerph 43 J3
Gelligron Neath 57 K4
Gellilydan Gwynd 110 C4
Gellinudd Neath 57 K4
Gelly Pembks 55 J3
Gellyburn P & K 233 G7
Gellywen Carmth 58 A4
Gelston D & G 175 J3
Gelston Lincs 118 B3
Gembling E R Yk 153 H4
Gentleshaw Staffs 98 D1
Georgefield D & G 187 L7
George Green Bucks 50 C3
Georgeham Devon 27 H3
Georgemas Junction Station
    Highld 279 L4
George Nympton Devon 28 B6
Georgetown Blae G 61 J5
Georgia Cnwll 2 D4
Georth Ork 275 c3
Gerlan Gwynd 126 C6
Germansweek Devon 12 B4
Germoe Cnwll 2 F5
Gerrans Cnwll 3 M4
Gerrards Cross Bucks 50 C1
Gerrick R & Cl 171 G8
Gestingthorpe Essex 89 G7
Geuffordd Powys 112 B8
Gib Hill Ches W 130 C4
Gibraltar Lincs 137 K7
Gibsmere Notts 117 J2
Giddeahall Wilts 46 B4
Giddy Green Dorset 16 F5
Gidea Park Gt Lon 52 B1
Gidleigh Devon 12 F5
Giffnock E Rens 208 F7
Gifford E Loth 212 C5
Giffordtown Fife 222 E5
Giggleswick N York 148 D3
Gigha Ag & B 205 L6

Gilberdyke E R Yk 143 L2
Gilbert's End Worcs 81 J6
Gilbert Street Hants 35 K4
Gilchriston E Loth 212 B6
Gilcrux Cumb 164 F3
Gildersome Leeds 141 K2
Gildingwells Rothm 133 L3
Gilesgate Moor Dur 169 J2
Gileston V Glam 42 F8
Gilfach Caerph 43 J2
Gilfach Goch Brdgnd 42 E4
Gilfachrheda Cerdgn 76 D3
Gilgarran Cumb 164 D6
Gill Cumb 166 B5
Gillamoor N York 162 B4
Gillan Cnwll 3 K6
Gillen Highld 258 D5
Gillesbie D & G 187 J7
Gilling East N York 161 K4
Gillingham Dorset 32 D5
Gillingham Medway 53 G5
Gillingham Norfk 107 H5
Gilling West N York 160 B2
Gillock Highld 280 B4
Gillow Heath Staffs 131 H7
Gills Highld 280 D2
Gill's Green Kent 39 J7
Gilmanscleuch Border 188 B2
Gilmerton C Edin 211 J5
Gilmerton P & K 220 F2
Gilmonby Dur 168 C8
Gilmorton Leics 100 C6
Gilroes Crematorium C Leic 100 C2
Gilsland Nthumb 178 E5
Gilson Warwks 99 G5
Gilstead C Brad 149 L7
Gilston Border 200 F2
Gilston Herts 70 C4
Gilston Park Herts 70 B4
Giltbrook Notts 116 E2
Gilwern Mons 61 L4
Gimingham Norfk 122 F4
Ginclough Ches E 131 J4
Gingers Green E Susx 23 K5
Gipping Suffk 90 C3
Gipsey Bridge Lincs 119 J2
Girdle Toll N Ayrs 196 C3
Girlington C Brad 141 H1
Girlsta Shet 281 e6
Girsby N York 160 E1
Girtford C Beds 86 D5
Girthon D & G 174 F4
Girton Cambs 87 J3
Girton Notts 135 G6
Girvan S Ayrs 182 F5
Gisburn Lancs 148 E6
Gisleham Suffk 107 K5
Gislingham Suffk 90 C1
Gissing Norfk 106 C6
Gittisham Devon 14 D3
Gladestry Powys 79 J4
Gladsmuir E Loth 212 A4
Glais Swans 57 K5
Glaisdale N York 162 D2
Glamis Angus 234 B6
Glanaber Gwynd 110 B1
Glanaman Carmth 59 J4
Glandford Norfk 122 A3
Glan-Duar Carmth 76 F6
Glandwr Pembks 75 L6
Glan-Dwyfach Gwynd 109 J3
Glandyfi Cerdgn 92 F4
Glangrwyney Powys 61 K4
Glanllynfi Brdgnd 42 C3
Glanmule Powys 94 E5
Glanrhyd Pembks 75 K4
Glan-rhyd Powys 57 L3
Glanton Nthumb 190 F3
Glanton Pike Nthumb 190 F3
Glanvilles Wootton Dorset 16 C1
Glan-y-don Flints 128 E4
Glan-y-llyn Rhondd 43 H5
Glan-y-nant Powys 93 K6
Glan-yr-afon Gwynd 111 H3
Glan-yr-afon Gwynd 111 K3
Glan-yr-afon IoA 126 B4
Glan-yr-afon Swans 57 H4
Glapthorn Nhants 101 M5
Glapwell Derbys 133 J6
Glasbury Powys 79 H7
Glascoed Denbgs 127 K5
Glascoed Mons 62 C6
Glascote Staffs 99 G3
Glascwm Powys 79 G5
Glasfryn Conwy 111 H2
Glasgow C Glas 209 G6
Glasinfryn Gwynd 125 K6
Glasnacardoch Bay Highld 237 K2
Glasnakille Highld 247 H6

Glaspwll Powys 92 F4
Glassenbury Kent 39 J6
Glassford S Lans 197 L3
Glass Houghton Wakefd 142 C3
Glasshouse Gloucs 63 L3
Glasshouse Hill Gloucs 63 L3
Glasshouses N York 149 L3
Glasslaw Abers 268 F4
Glasson Cumb 177 H6
Glasson Lancs 147 J4
Glassonby Cumb 166 D3
Glasterlaw Angus 234 F5
Glaston Rutlnd 101 K3
Glastonbury Somset 31 H3
Glatton Cambs 102 C6
Glazebrook Warrtn 130 D1
Glazebury Warrtn 139 K8
Glazeley Shrops 96 F5
Gleadless Sheff 133 G3
Gleadsmoss Ches E 130 F6
Gleaston Cumb 146 E2
Glebe Highld 250 F8
Gledhow Leeds 150 D8
Gledpark D & G 175 G5
Gledrid Shrops 112 D4
Glemsford Suffk 89 G5
Glenallachie Moray 254 E3
Glenancross Highld 237 K2
Glenaros House Ag & B 227 G4
Glen Auldyn IoM 154 f4
Glenbarr Ag & B 192 D1
Glenbarry Abers 267 L5
Glenbeg Highld 237 H8
Glenbervie Abers 245 G7
Glenboig N Lans 209 J5
Glenborrodale Highld 237 H8
Glenbranter Ag & B 217 J7
Glenbreck Border 187 G2
Glenbrittle Highld 246 F4
Glenbuck E Ayrs 198 B7
Glencally Angus 234 A3
Glencaple D & G 176 C5
Glencarse P & K 222 C3
Glencoe Highld 229 H4
Glencothe Border 199 J7
Glencraig Fife 222 B8
Glencrosh D & G 185 J5
Glendale Highld 258 B6
Glendaruel Ag & B 206 F2
Glendevon P & K 221 H6
Glendoe Lodge Highld 240 C2
Glendoick P & K 222 C3
Glenduckie Fife 222 D3
Glenegedale Ag & B 204 E6
Glenelg Highld 248 C7
Glenerney Moray 253 K2
Glenfarg P & K 221 L5
Glenfield Leics 100 C2
Glenfinnan Highld 238 E7
Glenfintaig Lodge Highld 239 L6
Glenfoot P & K 222 B4
Glenfyne Lodge Ag & B 218 B4
Glengarnock N Ayrs 208 B8
Glengolly Highld 279 K3
Glengorm Castle Ag & B 226 E1
Glengrasco Highld 259 G7
Glenholm Border 199 J6
Glenhoul D & G 184 F2
Glenisla Angus 233 K3
Glenkin Ag & B 207 J3
Glenkindie Abers 243 M1
Glenlivet Moray 254 D6
Glenlochar D & G 175 J2
Glenlomond P & K 222 B6
Glenluce D & G 172 F3
Glenmassen Ag & B 207 H2
Glenmavis N Lans 209 K5
Glen Maye IoM 154 b6
Glen Mona IoM 154 f4
Glenmore Highld 259 G8
Glenmore Lodge Highld 242 C2
Glen Nevis House Highld 229 J1
Glenochil Clacks 220 F8
Glen Parva Leics 100 C4
Glenquiech Angus 234 C3
Glenralloch Ag & B 206 D5
Glenridding Cumb 165 L2
Glenrothes Fife 222 D7
Glenshero Lodge Highld 240 F5
Glenstriven Ag & B 207 H3
Glentham Lincs 135 K2
Glentrool D & G 183 J7
Glen Trool Lodge D & G 183 K7
Glentruim Highld 241 J4
Glentworth Lincs 135 J2
Glenuig Highld 237 K5
Glenvarragill Highld 259 H8
Glen Vine IoM 154 d6
Glenwhilly D & G 182 F8

Glespin S Lans 198 D7
Glewstone Herefs 63 H3
Glinton C Pete 102 G4
Glooston Leics 101 G4
Glossop Derbys 131 L3
Gloster Hill Nthumb 191 K5
Gloucester Gloucs 64 B3
Gloucester Crematorium
    Gloucs 64 B4
Glusburn N York 149 H6
Glutt Lodge Highld 274 D7
Gluvian Cnwll 4 D4
Glympton Oxon 66 B3
Glynarthen Cerdgn 76 B5
Glyn Ceiriog Wrexhm 112 B4
Glyncorrwg Neath 60 C2
Glynde E Susx 23 J7
Glyndebourne E Susx 23 J6
Glyndyfrdwy Denbgs 112 A2
Glynneath Neath 60 D5
Glynn Valley Crematorium
    Cnwll 5 J3
Glyntaff Rhondd 43 H4
Glyntaff Crematorium
    Rhondd 43 H4
Glyntawe Powys 60 C5
Glynteg Carmth 76 C5
Gnosall Staffs 114 C7
Gnosall Heath Staffs 114 C7
Goadby Leics 101 G3
Goadby Marwood Leics 117 K6
Goatacre Wilts 46 F4
Goatham Green E Susx 24 D5
Goathill Dorset 31 L7
Goathland N York 162 E2
Goathurst Somset 30 C4
Goathurst Common Kent 38 D3
Goat Lees Kent 40 D6
Gobowen Shrops 112 D5
Godalming Surrey 36 G2
Goddard's Corner Suffk 91 G2
Goddard's Green Kent 39 K5
Goddards Green W Susx 22 D3
Godden Green Kent 38 D3
Godford Cross Devon 14 C2
Godington Oxon 66 F2
Godley Tamesd 140 C7
Godmanchester Cambs 86 D8
Godmanstone Dorset 16 C3
Godmersham Kent 40 D5
Godney Somset 31 H3
Godolphin Cross Cnwll 2 F5
Godre'r-graig Neath 57 L4
Godshill Hants 33 L2
Godshill IoW 19 J7
Godstone Staffs 115 G5
Godstone Surrey 51 K8
Godsworthy Devon 12 C5
Godwinscroft Hants 18 C4
Goetre Mons 62 C5
Goff's Oak Herts 69 J7
Gogar C Edin 211 G5
Goginan Cerdgn 92 D2
Golan Gwynd 109 J3
Golant Cnwll 5 J4
Golberdon Cnwll 11 L5
Golborne Wigan 139 J3
Golcar Kirk 141 G5
Goldcliff Newpt 44 D1
Golden Cross E Susx 23 K5
Golden Green Kent 39 G4
Golden Grove Carmth 59 G5
Goldenhill C Stke 114 E1
Golden Hill Pembks 55 G5
Golden Pot Hants 35 L2
Golden Valley Derbys 116 C2
Golders Green Gt Lon 51 H3
Golders Green Crematorium
    Gt Lon 51 H3
Goldfinch Bottom W Berk 48 E6
Goldhanger Essex 72 E5
Gold Hill Cambs 103 L4
Gold Hill Dorset 32 C7
Golding Shrops 96 D2
Goldington Bed 86 C4
Goldsborough N York 150 D5
Goldsborough N York 171 H8
Golds Green Sandw 98 C4
Goldsithney Cnwll 2 E5
Goldstone Kent 41 L3
Goldstone Shrops 113 M6
Goldsworth Park Surrey 50 C8
Goldthorpe Barns 142 C6
Goldworthy Devon 27 G5
Golford Kent 39 K6
Golford Green Kent 39 K6
Gollanfield Highld 252 E2
Gollinglith Foot N York 159 L4
Golly Wrexhm 129 G8

Golsoncott Somset	29	J3	
Golspie Highld	273	K8	
Gomeldon Wilts	33	L4	
Gomersal Kirk	141	K3	
Gomshall Surrey	37	G1	
Gonalston Notts	117	H2	
Gonerby Hill Foot Lincs	118	B4	
Gonfirth Shet	281	d5	
Goodameavy Devon	7	G2	
Good Easter Essex	70	F5	
Gooderstone Norfk	104	F3	
Goodleigh Devon	27	L4	
Goodmanham E R Yk	152	D7	
Goodmayes Gt Lon	51	M2	
Goodnestone Kent	40	D3	
Goodnestone Kent	41	H4	
Goodrich Herefs	63	H3	
Goodrington Torbay	8	D3	
Goodshaw Lancs	140	B3	
Goodshaw Fold Lancs	140	B2	
Goodstone Devon	13	H8	
Goodwick Pembks	74	F4	
Goodworth Clatford Hants	34	D2	
Goodyers End Warwks	99	J6	
Goole E R Yk	143	J3	
Goole Fields E R Yk	143	J3	
Goom's Hill Worcs	82	B4	
Goonbell Cnwll	4	B5	
Goonhavern Cnwll	4	C4	
Goonvrea Cnwll	4	B5	
Goosecruives Abers	245	G7	
Gooseford Devon	12	F4	
Goose Green Essex	73	H2	
Goose Green Kent	39	G3	
Goose Green Kent	39	L6	
Goose Green S Glos	45	K4	
Goose Green W Susx	21	J3	
Goose Green Wigan	139	H7	
Gooseham Cnwll	26	D7	
Gooseham Mill Cnwll	26	D7	
Goosehill Green Worcs	81	L3	
Goose Pool Herefs	80	B7	
Goosey Oxon	47	M1	
Goosnargh Lancs	147	L8	
Goostrey Ches E	130	F5	
Gorddinog Conwy	126	D5	
Gordon Border	201	K4	
Gordon Arms Hotel Border	200	C8	
Gordonstown Abers	256	C4	
Gordonstown Abers	267	L5	
Gore Powys	79	J3	
Gorebridge Mdloth	211	K6	
Gorefield Cambs	103	J1	
Gore Pit Essex	72	C3	
Gores Wilts	47	G7	
Gore Street Kent	41	J2	
Gorey Jersey	9	f3	
Goring Oxon	48	F3	
Goring-by-Sea W Susx	21	J6	
Goring Heath Oxon	49	G3	
Gorleston on Sea Norfk	107	L3	
Gornal Wood Crematorium Dudley	97	K5	
Gorrachie Abers	268	D4	
Gorran Churchtown Cnwll	5	G6	
Gorran Haven Cnwll	5	G6	
Gorran High Lanes Cnwll	5	G6	
Gorrig Cerdgn	76	D6	
Gors Cerdgn	92	D7	
Gorsedd Flints	128	E4	
Gorse Hill Swindn	47	H3	
Gorseinon Swans	57	G5	
Gorseybank Derbys	115	M1	
Gorsgoch Cerdgn	76	E5	
Gorslas Carmth	59	G6	
Gorsley Gloucs	63	K2	
Gorsley Common Herefs	63	K2	
Gorstage Ches W	130	B5	
Gorstan Highld	262	G6	
Gorstella Ches W	129	H7	
Gorsten Ag & B	227	L6	
Gorst Hill Worcs	81	G1	
Gorsty Hill Staffs	115	H6	
Gorthleck Highld	250	F7	
Gorton Manch	140	C8	
Gosbeck Suffk	90	D4	
Gosberton Lincs	119	H5	
Gosberton Clough Lincs	119	G5	
Gosfield Essex	71	J1	
Gosford Devon	14	C3	
Gosford Oxon	66	D4	
Gosforth Cumb	155	J2	
Gosforth N u Ty	180	F5	
Gosling Street Somset	31	J4	
Gosmore Herts	68	F2	
Gospel End Staffs	97	K4	
Gospel Green W Susx	36	D4	
Gosport Hants	19	K4	
Gossard's Green C Beds	85	J6	
Gossington Gloucs	63	L6	
Goswick Nthumb	203	G4	
Gotham Notts	116	F5	
Gotherington Gloucs	64	D1	
Gotton Somset	30	C5	
Goudhurst Kent	39	H6	
Goulceby Lincs	136	E4	
Gourdas Abers	256	D3	
Gourdie C Dund	222	F1	
Gourdon Abers	235	K1	
Gourock Inver	207	L3	
Govan C Glas	208	F6	
Goveton Devon	7	L5	
Govilon Mons	61	L4	
Gowdall E R Yk	143	G3	
Gower Highld	262	E8	
Gowerton Swans	57	G5	
Gowkhall Fife	210	E1	
Gowthorpe E R Yk	152	A5	
Goxhill E R Yk	153	K6	
Goxhill N Linc	144	E3	
Goytre Neath	57	L7	
Grabhair W Isls	282	g4	
Graby Lincs	118	E5	
Grade Cnwll	3	H8	
Gradeley Green Ches E	113	K1	
Graffham W Susx	20	F3	
Grafham Cambs	86	D2	
Grafham Surrey	36	F3	
Grafton Herefs	80	C7	
Grafton N York	150	F3	
Grafton Oxon	65	K7	
Grafton Shrops	113	G7	
Grafton Worcs	80	D3	
Grafton Worcs	82	A7	
Grafton Flyford Worcs	81	M4	
Grafton Regis Nhants	84	E6	
Grafton Underwood Nhants	101	K7	
Grafty Green Kent	39	L4	
Graianrhyd Denbgs	128	F8	
Graig Conwy	126	F5	
Graig Denbgs	128	C5	
Graigfechan Denbgs	112	A1	
Grain Medway	53	J4	
Grains Bar Oldham	140	E6	
Grainsby Lincs	145	H7	
Grainthorpe Lincs	145	K8	
Grampound Cnwll	4	F5	
Grampound Road Cnwll	4	E5	
Gramsdal W Isls	283	c9	
Gramsdale W Isls	283	c9	
Granborough Bucks	67	J2	
Granby Notts	117	K4	
Grandborough Warwks	83	L2	
Grand Chemins Jersey	9	e3	
Grandes Rocques Guern	9	j2	
Grandtully P & K	232	D5	
Grange Cumb	165	H7	
Grange Medway	53	G5	
Grange P & K	222	D2	
Grange Wirral	128	F2	
Grange Crossroads Moray	267	K5	
Grange Hall Moray	265	H7	
Grangehall S Lans	199	G4	
Grange Hill Essex	70	C8	
Grangemill Derbys	132	E8	
Grange Moor Kirk	141	K4	
Grangemouth Falk	210	B3	
Grange of Lindores Fife	222	D4	
Grange-over-Sands Cumb	156	F7	
Grangepans Falk	210	D3	
Grange Park Nhants	84	E4	
Grangetown R & Cl	170	D6	
Grangetown Sundld	181	K8	
Grange Villa Dur	180	F8	
Gransmoor E R Yk	153	H4	
Gransmore Green Essex	71	G3	
Granston Pembks	74	E5	
Grantchester Cambs	87	J4	
Grantham Lincs	118	B4	
Grantham Crematorium Lincs	118	B4	
Granton C Edin	211	H4	
Grantown-on-Spey Highld	253	K6	
Grantsfield Herefs	80	C3	
Grantshouse Border	213	H6	
Grappenhall Warrtn	130	C2	
Grasby Lincs	144	D6	
Grasmere Cumb	156	D1	
Grasscroft Oldham	140	E6	
Grassendale Lpool	129	J3	
Grassgarth Cumb	165	K2	
Grass Green Essex	88	E7	
Grassington N York	149	H3	
Grassmoor Derbys	133	H6	
Grassthorpe Notts	134	F6	
Grateley Hants	34	C3	
Gratwich Staffs	115	G5	
Graveley Cambs	86	E3	
Graveley Herts	69	G2	
Gravelly Hill Birm	98	E5	
Gravelsbank Shrops	95	H3	
Graveney Kent	40	D3	
Gravesend Kent	52	E4	
Gravir W Isls	282	g4	
Grayingham Lincs	144	A8	
Grayrigg Cumb	157	J3	
Grays Thurr	52	D3	
Grayshott Hants	36	C4	
Grayson Green Cumb	164	C5	
Grayswood Surrey	36	D4	
Graythorpe Hartpl	170	C5	
Grazeley Wokham	49	G5	
Greasbrough Rothm	142	C8	
Greasby Wirral	128	F2	
Greasley Notts	116	E2	
Great Abington Cambs	87	L5	
Great Addington Nhants	101	L8	
Great Alne Warwks	82	D3	
Great Altcar Lancs	138	C6	
Great Amwell Herts	69	K4	
Great Asby Cumb	166	F8	
Great Ashfield Suffk	89	K2	
Great Ayton N York	170	D8	
Great Baddow Essex	71	H6	
Great Badminton S Glos	46	A2	
Great Bardfield Essex	71	G1	
Great Barford Bed	86	C5	
Great Barr Sandw	98	D4	
Great Barrington Gloucs	65	J4	
Great Barrow Ches W	129	L6	
Great Barton Suffk	89	H2	
Great Barugh N York	162	C6	
Great Bavington Nthumb	180	B3	
Great Bealings Suffk	90	F5	
Great Bedwyn Wilts	47	K6	
Great Bentley Essex	73	G3	
Great Billing Nhants	84	F3	
Great Bircham Norfk	121	G5	
Great Blakenham Suffk	90	D5	
Great Blencow Cumb	166	B4	
Great Bolas Wrekin	113	L7	
Great Bookham Surrey	50	E8	
Great Bosullow Cnwll	2	C4	
Great Bourton Oxon	83	K6	
Great Bowden Leics	101	G5	
Great Bradley Suffk	88	D4	
Great Braxted Essex	72	B4	
Great Bricett Suffk	90	B5	
Great Brickhill Bucks	67	L1	
Great Bridgeford Staffs	114	D6	
Great Brington Nhants	84	C2	
Great Bromley Essex	73	G2	
Great Broughton Cumb	164	E4	
Great Broughton N York	161	J2	
Great Budworth Ches W	130	C4	
Great Burdon Darltn	169	J7	
Great Burstead Essex	71	G8	
Great Busby N York	161	H2	
Great Canfield Essex	70	E3	
Great Carlton Lincs	137	H3	
Great Casterton Rutlnd	101	M2	
Great Chalfield Wilts	46	B6	
Great Chart Kent	40	C7	
Great Chatwell Staffs	114	B8	
Great Chell C Stke	114	D1	
Great Chesterford Essex	87	K6	
Great Cheverell Wilts	46	E8	
Great Chishill Cambs	87	J7	
Great Clacton Essex	73	J4	
Great Cliffe Wakefd	141	M4	
Great Clifton Cumb	164	D5	
Great Coates NE Lin	145	G6	
Great Comberton Worcs	81	L6	
Great Comp Kent	39	G2	
Great Corby Cumb	178	B7	
Great Cornard Suffk	89	H7	
Great Cowden E R Yk	153	L7	
Great Coxwell Oxon	65	K8	
Great Cransley Nhants	101	H8	
Great Cressingham Norfk	105	G3	
Great Crosthwaite Cumb	165	J6	
Great Cubley Derbys	115	K6	
Great Cumbrae Island N Ayrs	207	K7	
Great Dalby Leics	117	K8	
Great Denham Bed	85	K5	
Great Doddington Nhants	85	H2	
Great Doward Herefs	63	G4	
Great Dunham Norfk	121	J8	
Great Dunmow Essex	70	F3	
Great Durnford Wilts	33	K3	
Great Easton Essex	70	F2	
Great Easton Leics	101	J5	
Great Eccleston Lancs	147	H7	
Great Edstone N York	162	C6	
Great Ellingham Norfk	105	L4	
Great Elm Somset	32	C1	
Great Everdon Nhants	84	B4	
Great Eversden Cambs	87	H4	
Great Fencote N York	160	D4	
Greatfield Wilts	47	G2	
Great Finborough Suffk	89	K4	
Greatford Lincs	102	B1	
Great Fransham Norfk	105	H1	
Great Gaddesden Herts	68	C5	
Greatgate Staffs	115	G3	
Great Gidding Cambs	102	C6	
Great Givendale E R Yk	152	B5	
Great Glemham Suffk	91	H3	
Great Glen Leics	100	E4	
Great Gonerby Lincs	118	B4	
Great Gransden Cambs	86	F4	
Great Green Cambs	86	F6	
Great Green Norfk	106	C5	
Great Green Suffk	89	J2	
Great Green Suffk	89	J4	
Great Habton N York	162	D7	
Great Hale Lincs	118	F4	
Great Hallingbury Essex	70	D3	
Greatham Hants	36	A5	
Greatham Hartpl	170	C5	
Greatham W Susx	21	H4	
Great Hampden Bucks	67	K6	
Great Harrowden Nhants	85	G1	
Great Harwood Lancs	139	L1	
Great Haseley Oxon	66	F6	
Great Hatfield E R Yk	153	K7	
Great Haywood Staffs	114	F7	
Great Heck N York	142	F3	
Great Henny Essex	89	H7	
Great Hinton Wilts	46	C7	
Great Hockham Norfk	105	J5	
Great Holland Essex	73	J3	
Great Hollands Br For	49	L5	
Great Horkesley Essex	72	E1	
Great Hormead Herts	69	L1	
Great Horton C Brad	141	J2	
Great Horwood Bucks	67	J1	
Great Houghton Barns	142	C6	
Great Houghton Nhants	84	F3	
Great Hucklow Derbys	132	D4	
Great Kelk E R Yk	153	H4	
Great Kimble Bucks	67	K6	
Great Kingshill Bucks	67	L7	
Great Langdale Cumb	156	D2	
Great Langton N York	160	D3	
Great Leighs Essex	71	H4	
Great Limber Lincs	144	E6	
Great Linford M Keyn	85	G6	
Great Livermere Suffk	89	H1	
Great Longstone Derbys	132	D5	
Great Lumley Dur	169	J1	
Great Lyth Shrops	95	L2	
Great Malvern Worcs	81	H6	
Great Maplestead Essex	89	G7	
Great Marton Bpool	138	C1	
Great Massingham Norfk	121	H7	
Great Melton Norfk	106	C2	
Great Meols Wirral	128	F2	
Great Milton Oxon	66	F6	
Great Missenden Bucks	67	L6	
Great Mitton Lancs	148	C3	
Great Mongeham Kent	41	K5	
Great Moulton Norfk	106	D5	
Great Munden Herts	69	K2	
Great Musgrave Cumb	167	H7	
Great Ness Shrops	112	F7	
Great Notley Essex	71	H3	
Great Oak Mons	62	D5	
Great Oakley Essex	73	J2	
Great Oakley Nhants	101	J6	
Great Offley Herts	68	F2	
Great Ormside Cumb	167	G7	
Great Orton Cumb	177	K7	
Great Ouseburn N York	150	F3	
Great Oxendon Nhants	100	F6	
Great Oxney Green Essex	71	G6	
Great Palgrave Norfk	105	G1	
Great Park N u Ty	180	E5	
Great Parndon Essex	70	B5	
Great Pattenden Kent	39	J4	
Great Paxton Cambs	86	E2	
Great Plumpton Lancs	138	C1	
Great Plumstead Norfk	106	F2	
Great Ponton Lincs	118	B5	
Great Potheridge Devon	27	J7	
Great Preston Leeds	142	B2	
Great Purston Nhants	83	M7	
Great Raveley Cambs	102	E7	
Great Rissington Gloucs	65	J4	
Great Rollright Oxon	65	L1	
Great Ryburgh Norfk	121	L6	
Great Ryle Nthumb	190	E4	
Great Ryton Shrops	96	B3	
Great Saling Essex	71	G2	
Great Salkeld Cumb	166	D3	
Great Sampford Essex	88	C8	
Great Saredon Staffs	98	B2	

Great Saughall Ches W 129 H5
Great Saxham Suffk 88 F3
Great Shefford W Berk 48 A4
Great Shelford Cambs 87 J5
Great Smeaton N York 160 E2
Great Snoring Norfk 121 L4
Great Somerford Wilts 46 D2
Great Soudley Shrops 114 A5
Great Stainton Darltn 169 J6
Great Stambridge Essex 53 J1
Great Staughton Cambs 86 C2
Great Steeping Lincs 137 H6
Great Stoke S Glos 45 J3
Great Stonar Kent 41 K3
Greatstone-on-Sea Kent......... 25 K3
Great Strickland Cumb 166 D6
Great Stukeley Cambs 102 E8
Great Sturton Lincs 136 D4
Great Sutton Ches W 129 J4
Great Sutton Shrops 96 C6
Great Swinburne Nthumb 179 L4
Great Tew Oxon 66 B1
Great Tey Essex 72 C2
Great Thurlow Suffk 88 D5
Great Torrington Devon 27 J7
Great Tosson Nthumb 190 E6
Great Totham Essex 72 B5
Great Totham Essex 72 C4
Great Tows Lincs 136 D2
Great Urswick Cumb 156 C7
Great Wakering Essex 53 K2
Great Waldingfield Suffk 89 H6
Great Walsingham Norfk 121 L4
Great Waltham Essex 71 G4
Great Warford Ches E 130 F4
Great Warley Essex 52 C1
Great Washbourne Gloucs 82 A8
Great Weeke Devon 13 G5
Great Welnetham Suffk 89 H3
Great Wenham Suffk 90 C7
Great Whittington Nthumb 180 B5
Great Wigborough Essex 72 D4
Great Wilbraham Cambs 87 L4
Great Wilne Derbys 116 D5
Great Wishford Wilts 33 J4
Great Witchingham Norfk 122 C7
Great Witcombe Gloucs 64 D4
Great Witley Worcs 81 H2
Great Wolford Warwks 82 F8
Greatworth Nhants 84 A6
Great Wratting Suffk 88 D5
Great Wymondley Herts 69 G2
Great Wyrley Staffs 98 C2
Great Wytheford Shrops 113 J7
Great Yarmouth Norfk 107 L2
Great Yarmouth
    Crematorium Norfk 107 K3
Great Yeldham Essex 88 F7
Grebby Lincs 137 H6
Greeba IoM 154 d6
Green Denbgs 128 C6
Green Bank Cumb 156 E6
Greenbottom Cnwll 4 C6
Greenburn W Loth 210 B7
Greencroft Hall Dur 168 F1
Green Cross Surrey 36 C3
Green Down Somset 45 H8
Green End Bed 85 K5
Green End Bed 86 B2
Green End Bed 86 B3
Green End Bed 86 C5
Green End Cambs 87 H4
Green End Cambs 87 K2
Green End Cambs 87 K3
Green End Cambs 102 D6
Green End Cambs 102 E8
Green End Herts 69 H1
Green End Herts 69 J3
Green End Herts 87 G8
Greenend Oxon 65 L3
Green End Warwks 99 H6
Greenfield Ag & B 207 L1
Greenfield C Beds 85 L8
Greenfield Flints 128 E4
Greenfield Highld 239 L3
Greenfield Oldham 140 F7
Greenfield Oxon 49 H1
Greenford Gt Lon 50 F3
Greengairs N Lans 209 L5
Greengates C Brad 150 B8
Greengill Cumb 164 F3
Greenhalgh Lancs 147 H8
Greenham Somset 29 K6
Greenham W Berk 48 C6
Green Hammerton N York 151 G4
Greenhaugh Nthumb 179 J2
Green Head Cumb 165 L1
Greenhead Nthumb 178 F6
Green Heath Staffs 98 C1

Greenheys Salfd 139 L7
Greenhill D & G 176 F3
Greenhill Falk 209 L3
Greenhill Herefs 81 G5
Greenhill Kent 40 F2
Greenhill S Lans 198 F6
Green Hill Wilts 46 F2
Greenhillocks Derbys 116 C2
Greenhills S Lans 209 G8
Greenhithe Kent 52 C4
Greenholm E Ayrs 197 G3
Greenholme Cumb 157 J2
Greenhouse Border 188 F2
Greenhow Hill N York 149 K3
Greenland Highld 280 B3
Greenland Sheff 133 H2
Greenlands Bucks 49 J2
Green Lane Devon 13 H7
Green Lane Worcs 82 C2
Greenlaw Border 201 L4
Greenlea D & G 176 D4
Greenloaning P & K 220 E5
Green Moor Barns 141 L7
Greenmount Bury 140 A5
Green Oak E R Yk 143 K2
Greenock Inver 207 M4
Greenodd Cumb 156 D6
Green Ore Somset 31 J1
Green Quarter Cumb 157 G2
Greensgate Norfk 122 B8
Greenshields S Lans 199 H4
Greenside Gatesd 180 E6
Greenside Kirk 141 J4
Greens Norton Nhants 84 C5
Greenstead Green Essex 71 K2
Greensted Essex 70 D6
Green Street E Susx 24 D5
Green Street Gloucs 64 C4
Green Street Herts 69 G7
Green Street Herts 70 C3
Green Street Worcs 81 K5
Green Street Green Gt Lon 51 M6
Green Street Green Kent 52 C5
Greenstreet Green Suffk 90 B5
Green Tye Herts 70 C3
Greenway Gloucs 81 G8
Greenway Somset 30 D6
Greenway V Glam 43 G5
Greenway Worcs 81 G1
Greenwich Gt Lon 51 K3
Greet Gloucs 64 F1
Greete Shrops 80 D1
Greetham Lincs 136 F5
Greetham Rutlnd 118 B8
Greetland Calder 141 G3
Gregson Lane Lancs 139 J2
Greinton Somset 30 F4
Grenaby IoM 154 c7
Grendon Nhants 85 G3
Grendon Warwks 99 H3
Grendon Green Herefs 80 E4
Grendon Underwood Bucks 67 G3
Grenofen Devon 12 C8
Grenoside Sheff 133 G1
Grenoside Crematorium Sheff .. 132 F1
Greosabhagh W Isls 282 e6
Gresford Wrexhm 112 E1
Gresham Norfk 122 D4
Greshornish Highld 258 E6
Gressenhall Norfk 121 L8
Gressenhall Green Norfk 121 L8
Gressingham Lancs 147 L2
Gresty Green Ches E 113 M1
Greta Bridge Dur 168 D8
Gretna D & G 177 K5
Gretna Green D & G 177 K5
Gretton Gloucs 64 E1
Gretton Nhants 101 K4
Gretton Shrops 96 C4
Grewelthorpe N York 160 C7
Grey Friars Suffk 91 L1
Greygarth N York 150 A1
Grey Green N Linc 143 K6
Greylake Somset 30 F4
Greylees Lincs 118 D3
Greyrigg D & G 176 E1
Greys Green Oxon 49 H2
Greysouthen Cumb 164 E5
Greystoke Cumb 166 B4
Greystone Angus 234 E6
Greywell Hants 35 L1
Gribb Dorset 15 J2
Gribthorpe E R Yk 143 J1
Griff Warwks 99 K5
Griffithstown Torfn 62 C7
Griffydam Leics 116 C7
Griggs Green Hants 36 B4
Grimeford Village Lancs 139 J5
Grimesthorpe Sheff 133 G2

Grimethorpe Barns 142 C6
Grimley Worcs 81 J3
Grimmet S Ayrs 183 J1
Grimoldby Lincs 137 G2
Grimpo Shrops 112 E6
Grimsargh Lancs 139 H1
Grimsby NE Lin 145 H5
Grimsby Crematorium NE Lin .. 145 H6
Grimscote Nhants 84 C4
Grimscott Cnwll 11 J1
Grimshader W Isls 282 g4
Grimshaw Bl w D 139 L3
Grimshaw Green Lancs 139 G5
Grimsthorpe Lincs 118 D7
Grimston E R Yk 145 H1
Grimston Leics 117 J7
Grimston Norfk 120 F7
Grimstone Dorset 16 C4
Grimstone End Suffk 89 J2
Grinacombe Moor Devon 12 A4
Grindale E R Yk 153 J2
Grindle Shrops 97 G3
Grindleford Derbys 132 E4
Grindleton Lancs 148 D6
Grindley Brook Shrops 113 H3
Grindlow Derbys 132 D4
Grindon Nthumb 202 E4
Grindon S on T 169 K5
Grindon Staffs 115 H1
Grindon Hill Nthumb 179 J5
Grindonrigg Nthumb 202 E4
Gringley on the Hill Notts 134 E2
Grinsdale Cumb 177 L7
Grinshill Shrops 113 H6
Grinton N York 159 J3
Griomaisiadar W Isls 282 g4
Grishipoll Ag & B 224 F3
Grisling Common E Susx 23 G3
Gristhorpe N York 163 K6
Griston Norfk 105 J4
Gritley Ork 275 d5
Grittenham Wilts 46 F2
Grittleton Wilts 46 B3
Grizebeck Cumb 156 C5
Grizedale Cumb 156 D4
Groby Leics 100 B2
Groes Conwy 127 K6
Groes-faen Rhondd 43 G5
Groesffordd Gwynd 108 D4
Groesffordd Powys 61 G2
Groesffordd Marli Denbgs 127 K5
Groeslwyd Powys 94 F1
Groeslon Gwynd 125 H8
Groeslon Gwynd 125 J7
Groes-Wen Caerph 43 H4
Grogarry W Isls 283 c10
Grogport Ag & B 194 C2
Groigearraidh W Isls 283 c10
Gromford Suffk 91 J3
Gronant Flints 128 C3
Groombridge E Susx 38 E6
Grosebay W Isls 282 e6
Grosmont Mons 62 E2
Grosmont N York 162 E2
Groton Suffk 89 J7
Grotton Oldham 140 E6
Grouville Jersey 9 e3
Grove Bucks 67 M3
Grove Dorset 16 D8
Grove Kent 41 H3
Grove Notts 134 E4
Grove Oxon 48 B1
Grove Pembks 55 G6
Grove Green Kent 39 K2
Grovenhurst Kent 39 H5
Grove Park Gt Lon 51 L4
Grovesend S Glos 45 K1
Grovesend Swans 57 G5
Grubb Street Kent 52 C5
Gruinard Highld 260 F2
Gruinart Ag & B 204 D3
Grula Highld 246 E3
Gruline Ag & B 227 G4
Grumbla Cnwll 2 C5
Grundisburgh Suffk 90 F5
Gruting Shet 281 c6
Grutness Shet 281 d9
Gualachulain Highld 229 J6
Guanockgate Lincs 103 H2
Guardbridge Fife 223 H3
Guarlford Worcs 81 J6
Guay P & K 232 F5
Guernsey Guern 9 j3
Guestling Green E Susx 24 F4
Guestling Thorn E Susx 24 F4
Guestwick Norfk 122 B6
Guide Bridge Tamesd 140 D8
Guide Post Nthumb 181 G2
Guilden Morden Cambs 86 F6

Guilden Sutton Ches W .... 129 K
Guildford Surrey .... 36 F
Guildford Crematorium Surrey .... 36 F
Guildstead Kent .... 53 H
Guildtown P & K .... 221 L
Guilsborough Nhants .... 84 D
Guilsfield Powys .... 94 F
Guilton Kent .... 41 J
Guiltreehill S Ayrs .... 183 J
Guineaford Devon .... 27 K
Guisborough R & Cl .... 170 E
Guiseley Leeds .... 150 E
Guist Norfk .... 121 M
Guiting Power Gloucs .... 65 G
Gullane E Loth .... 212 B
Gulling Green Suffk .... 89 D
Gulval Cnwll .... 2 D
Gulworthy Devon .... 12 B
Gumfreston Pembks .... 55 J
Gumley Leics .... 100 F
Gummow's Shop Cnwll .... 4 E
Gunby E R Yk .... 143 H
Gunby Lincs .... 118 B
Gunby Lincs .... 137 J
Gundleton Hants .... 35 J
Gun Green Kent .... 39 J
Gun Hill E Susx .... 23 J
Gun Hill Warwks .... 99 H
Gunn Devon .... 27 J
Gunnerside N York .... 159 G
Gunnerton Nthumb .... 179 L
Gunness N Linc .... 143 L
Gunnislake Cnwll .... 12 B
Gunnista Shet .... 281 L
Gunthorpe C Pete .... 102 D
Gunthorpe N Linc .... 143 K
Gunthorpe Norfk .... 121 M
Gunthorpe Notts .... 117 L
Gunton Suffk .... 107 L
Gunwalloe Cnwll .... 3 C
Gupworthy Somset .... 29 H
Gurnard IoW .... 19 H
Gurnett Ches E .... 131 H
Gurney Slade Somset .... 31 L
Gurnos Powys .... 57 L
Gushmere Kent .... 40 D
Gussage All Saints Dorset ...... 33 C
Gussage St Andrew Dorset ..... 33 C
Gussage St Michael Dorset ..... 33 C
Guston Kent .... 41 L
Gutcher Shet .... 281 E
Guthrie Angus .... 234 E
Guyhirn Cambs .... 103 H
Guyhirn Gull Cambs .... 103 H
Guy's Marsh Dorset .... 32 D
Guyzance Nthumb .... 191 J
Gwaenysgor Flints .... 128 C
Gwalchmai IoA .... 125 C
Gwastadnant Gwynd .... 126 C
Gwaun-Cae-Gurwen Carmth ... 59 H
Gwbert on Sea Cerdgn .... 75 M
Gwealavellan Cnwll .... 2 F
Gweek Cnwll .... 3 H
Gwehelog Mons .... 62 D
Gwenddwr Powys .... 78 C
Gwennap Cnwll .... 3 J
Gwent Crematorium Mons ..... 62 C
Gwenter Cnwll .... 3 J
Gwernaffield Flints .... 128 F
Gwernesney Mons .... 62 D
Gwernogle Carmth .... 58 F
Gwernymynydd Flints .... 128 F
Gwersyllt Wrexhm .... 112 E
Gwespyr Flints .... 128 D
Gwindra Cnwll .... 4 F
Gwinear Cnwll .... 2 F
Gwithian Cnwll .... 2 F
Gwredog IoA .... 125 G
Gwrhay Caerph .... 61 J
Gwyddelwern Denbgs .... 111 H
Gwyddgrug Carmth .... 58 E
Gwynfryn Wrexhm .... 112 E
Gwystre Powys .... 78 B
Gwytherin Conwy .... 127 H
Gyfelia Wrexhm .... 112 D
Gyrn-gôch Gwynd .... 109 G

H

Habberley Shrops .... 95 H
Habberley Worcs .... 97 H
Habergham Lancs .... 140 F
Habertoft Lincs 137
Habin W Susx .... 36 C
Habrough NE Lin 144
Hacconby Lincs 118
Haceby Lincs 118

Place	County	Page	Grid
Hacheston	Suffk	91	G3
Hackbridge	Gt Lon	51	H5
Hackenthorpe	Sheff	133	H3
Hackford	Norfk	106	B3
Hackforth	N York	160	C4
Hack Green	Ches E	113	L2
Hackland	Ork	275	c4
Hackleton	Nhants	84	F4
Hacklinge	Kent	41	K4
Hackman's Gate	Worcs	97	K7
Hackness	N York	163	H4
Hackness	Somset	30	E2
Hackney	Gt Lon	51	K2
Hackthorn	Lincs	135	K3
Hackthorpe	Cumb	166	D6
Hacton	Gt Lon	52	C2
Hadden	Border	202	B6
Haddenham	Bucks	67	H5
Haddenham	Cambs	103	J8
Haddington	E Loth	212	B4
Haddington	Lincs	135	H7
Haddiscoe	Norfk	107	J4
Haddo	Abers	256	E4
Haddon	Cambs	102	C5
Hade Edge	Kirk	141	J6
Hadfield	Derbys	140	F8
Hadham Cross	Herts	70	B3
Hadham Ford	Herts	70	B3
Hadleigh	Essex	53	H2
Hadleigh	Suffk	89	H4
Hadleigh Heath	Suffk	89	K7
Hadley	Worcs	81	K2
Hadley	Wrekin	96	F1
Hadley End	Staffs	115	J7
Hadley Wood	Gt Lon	69	H7
Hadlow	Kent	39	G3
Hadlow Down	E Susx	23	J2
Hadnall	Shrops	113	H7
Hadstock	Essex	88	B6
Hadzor	Worcs	81	L3
Haffenden Quarter	Kent	39	M5
Hafodunos	Conwy	127	H6
Hafod-y-bwch	Wrexhm	112	D2
Hafod-y-coed	Blae G	61	K7
Hafodyrynys	Caerph	61	K7
Haggate	Lancs	140	C1
Haggbeck	Cumb	178	B4
Haggersta	Shet	281	d6
Haggerston	Nthumb	203	G4
Haggington Hill	Devon	27	K2
Haggs	Falk	209	L3
Hagley	Herefs	80	D7
Hagley	Worcs	97	K7
Hagmore Green	Suffk	89	J7
Hagnaby	Lincs	136	F7
Hagnaby	Lincs	137	J4
Hagworthingham	Lincs	136	F6
Haigh	Wigan	139	J6
Haighton Green	Lancs	139	H1
Haile	Cumb	155	J1
Hailes	Gloucs	64	F1
Hailey	Herts	69	K5
Hailey	Oxon	48	F2
Hailey	Oxon	65	M4
Hailsham	E Susx	23	K5
Hail Weston	Cambs	86	D3
Hainault	Gt Lon	70	C8
Haine	Kent	41	K2
Hainford	Norfk	122	E7
Hainton	Lincs	136	C3
Hainworth	C Brad	149	J8
Haisthorpe	E R Yk	153	H3
Hakin	Pembks	54	E5
Halam	Notts	117	H1
Halbeath	Fife	210	F1
Halberton	Devon	29	H8
Halcro	Highld	280	B4
Hale	Cumb	157	H7
Hale	Halton	129	L3
Hale	Hants	33	L7
Hale	Somset	32	C5
Hale	Surrey	36	C1
Hale	Traffd	130	F2
Hale Bank	Halton	129	L3
Halebarns	Traffd	130	F3
Hale Green	E Susx	23	J4
Hale Nook	Lancs	147	G7
Hales	Norfk	107	H4
Hales	Staffs	113	M5
Halesgate	Lincs	119	K6
Hales Green	Derbys	115	K3
Halesowen	Dudley	98	B6
Hales Place	Kent	40	F3
Hale Street	Kent	39	G3
Halesville	Essex	72	C8
Halesworth	Suffk	107	H7
Halewood	Knows	129	K3
Halford	Devon	13	J7
Halford	Shrops	95	K6
Halford	Warwks	83	G6
Halfpenny	Cumb	157	H5
Halfpenny Green	Staffs	97	J5
Halfpenny Houses	N York	160	B5
Halfway	Carmth	59	J3
Halfway	Carmth	59	M2
Halfway	Sheff	133	J3
Halfway	W Berk	48	B5
Halfway Bridge	W Susx	36	D6
Halfway House	Shrops	95	H1
Halfway Houses	Kent	53	K4
Halifax	Calder	141	H3
Halket	E Ayrs	208	D8
Halkirk	Highld	279	K4
Halkyn	Flints	128	F5
Hall	E Rens	208	C8
Hallam Fields	Derbys	116	D4
Halland	E Susx	23	H4
Hallaton	Leics	101	H4
Hallatrow	BaNES	45	J7
Hallbankgate	Cumb	178	D7
Hallbeck	Cumb	157	K5
Hall Cliffe	Wakefd	141	L4
Hall Cross	Lancs	138	E2
Hall Dunnerdale	Cumb	156	B3
Hallen	S Glos	45	H3
Hall End	Bed	85	K6
Hall End	C Beds	86	B7
Hallfield Gate	Derbys	133	H8
Hallgarth	Dur	169	J2
Hallglen	Falk	210	A3
Hall Green	Birm	98	E7
Hallin	Highld	258	C5
Halling	Medway	52	F6
Hallington	Lincs	136	F3
Hallington	Nthumb	180	B4
Halliwell	Bolton	139	L5
Halloughton	Notts	117	J1
Hallow	Worcs	81	J3
Hallow Heath	Worcs	81	J3
Hallsands	Devon	8	B7
Hall's Green	Essex	69	L5
Hall's Green	Herts	69	H2
Hallthwaites	Cumb	156	A5
Hallworthy	Cnwll	11	H5
Hallyne	Border	199	L5
Halmer End	Staffs	114	B2
Halmond's Frome	Herefs	80	F5
Halmore	Gloucs	63	K6
Halnaker	W Susx	20	E5
Halsall	Lancs	138	D5
Halse	Nhants	84	A7
Halse	Somset	29	L5
Halsetown	Cnwll	2	D3
Halsham	E R Yk	145	H2
Halsinger	Devon	27	J3
Halstead	Essex	71	K1
Halstead	Kent	52	A6
Halstead	Leics	101	G2
Halstock	Dorset	15	M1
Halsway	Somset	29	L3
Haltcliff Bridge	Cumb	165	L3
Haltemprice Crematorium	E R Yk	144	C2
Haltham	Lincs	136	D7
Haltoft End	Lincs	119	L3
Halton	Bucks	67	L5
Halton	Halton	129	M3
Halton	Lancs	147	K3
Halton	Leeds	142	A1
Halton	Nthumb	180	B5
Halton	Wrexhm	112	D3
Halton East	N York	149	J5
Halton Fenside	Lincs	137	H7
Halton Gill	N York	158	F7
Halton Green	Lancs	147	K3
Halton Holegate	Lincs	137	H6
Halton Lea Gate	Nthumb	178	F7
Halton Quay	Cnwll	6	E2
Halton Shields	Nthumb	180	B5
Halton West	N York	148	E5
Haltwhistle	Nthumb	179	G6
Halvana	Cnwll	11	J6
Halvergate	Norfk	107	J2
Halwell	Devon	8	A4
Halwill	Devon	12	B3
Halwill Junction	Devon	12	B3
Ham	Devon	14	F2
Ham	Gloucs	63	K7
Ham	Gloucs	64	E3
Ham	Gt Lon	50	F4
Ham	Kent	41	K4
Ham	Somset	30	D6
Ham	Somset	31	L1
Ham	Wilts	47	L6
Hambleden	Bucks	49	J2
Hambledon	Hants	35	K7
Hambledon	Surrey	36	E3
Hamble-le-Rice	Hants	19	H2
Hambleton	Lancs	147	G7
Hambleton	N York	142	H5
Hambleton Moss Side	Lancs	147	G7
Hambridge	Somset	30	F6
Hambrook	S Glos	45	J3
Hambrook	W Susx	20	C5
Ham Common	Dorset	32	D5
Hameringham	Lincs	136	F6
Hamerton	Cambs	102	C7
Ham Green	Herefs	81	H6
Ham Green	Kent	25	G2
Ham Green	Kent	53	H5
Ham Green	N Som	45	G4
Ham Green	Worcs	82	B3
Ham Hill	Kent	52	F6
Hamilton	S Lans	209	J7
Hamlet	Dorset	16	B1
Hamlins	E Susx	23	K5
Hammerpot	W Susx	21	H5
Hammersmith	Gt Lon	51	G3
Hammerwich	Staffs	98	D2
Hammerwood	E Susx	38	C5
Hammond Street	Herts	69	J2
Hammoon	Dorset	32	D7
Hamnavoe	Shet	281	d7
Hampden Park	E Susx	23	K6
Hamperden End	Essex	70	E1
Hampnett	Gloucs	65	G4
Hampole	Donc	142	D5
Hampreston	Dorset	17	L3
Hampsfield	Cumb	156	F6
Hampson Green	Lancs	147	J5
Hampstead	Gt Lon	51	H2
Hampstead Norreys	W Berk	48	D4
Hampsthwaite	N York	150	C4
Hampton	C Pete	102	D4
Hampton	Devon	15	G3
Hampton	Gt Lon	50	F5
Hampton	Kent	40	F2
Hampton	Shrops	97	G6
Hampton	Swindn	65	J8
Hampton	Worcs	82	B6
Hampton Bishop	Herefs	80	D7
Hampton Fields	Gloucs	64	C7
Hampton Green	Ches W	113	H2
Hampton Heath	Ches W	113	H2
Hampton-in-Arden	Solhll	99	G7
Hampton Loade	Shrops	97	G6
Hampton Lovett	Worcs	81	K2
Hampton Lucy	Warwks	83	G4
Hampton Magna	Warwks	83	G2
Hampton on the Hill	Warwks	82	F2
Hampton Poyle	Oxon	66	D4
Hampton Wick	Gt Lon	50	F5
Hamptworth	Wilts	34	B7
Hamrow	Norfk	121	K6
Hamsey	E Susx	22	F5
Hamsey Green	Surrey	51	K7
Hamstall Ridware	Staffs	115	H7
Hamstead	Birm	98	D5
Hamstead	IoW	18	F5
Hamstead Marshall	W Berk	48	B6
Hamsterley	Dur	168	E4
Hamsterley	Dur	180	D7
Hamstreet	Kent	40	C8
Ham Street	Somset	31	J4
Hamwood	N Som	44	D7
Hamworthy	Poole	17	K4
Hanbury	Staffs	115	K6
Hanbury	Worcs	81	M2
Hanby	Lincs	118	D5
Hanchet End	Suffk	88	C6
Hanchurch	Staffs	114	C3
Handa Island	Highld	276	A6
Handale	N & Cl	171	G2
Hand and Pen	Devon	14	B3
Handbridge	Ches W	129	J6
Handcross	W Susx	37	L5
Handforth	Ches E	131	G3
Hand Green	Ches W	130	A7
Handley	Ches W	129	L8
Handley	Derbys	133	G7
Handley Green	Essex	71	G6
Handsacre	Staffs	115	H8
Handsworth	Birm	98	D5
Handsworth	Sheff	133	H2
Handy Cross	Bucks	49	K1
Hanford	C Stke	114	D3
Hanford	Dorset	32	D8
Hanging Heaton	Kirk	141	L3
Hanging Houghton	Nhants	84	E1
Hanging Langford	Wilts	33	H3
Hangleton	Br & H	22	D6
Hangleton	W Susx	21	J6
Hanham	S Glos	45	J4
Hankelow	Ches E	113	L2
Hankerton	Wilts	46	E1
Hankham	E Susx	23	K6
Hanley	C Stke	114	D2
Hanley Castle	Worcs	81	J6
Hanley Child	Worcs	80	F2
Hanley Swan	Worcs	81	J6
Hanley William	Worcs	80	F2
Hanlith	N York	148	F3
Hanmer	Wrexhm	113	G3
Hannaford	Devon	27	L5
Hannah	Lincs	137	J4
Hannington	Hants	48	D7
Hannington	Nhants	84	F1
Hannington	Swindn	65	H8
Hannington Wick	Swindn	65	H8
Hanscombe End	C Beds	86	C8
Hanslope	M Keyn	84	F6
Hanthorpe	Lincs	118	E6
Hanwell	Gt Lon	50	F3
Hanwell	Oxon	83	K6
Hanwood	Shrops	95	K2
Hanworth	Gt Lon	50	E5
Hanworth	Norfk	122	D4
Happendon	S Lans	198	E6
Happisburgh	Norfk	123	H5
Happisburgh Common	Norfk	123	H5
Hapsford	Ches W	129	L5
Hapton	Lancs	140	B2
Hapton	Norfk	106	D4
Harberton	Devon	8	A3
Harbertonford	Devon	8	A4
Harbledown	Kent	40	F4
Harborne	Birm	98	C6
Harborough Magna	Warwks	100	B7
Harbottle	Nthumb	190	C5
Harbourneford	Devon	7	K2
Harbours Hill	Worcs	81	M2
Harbridge	Hants	18	A2
Harbridge Green	Hants	33	K8
Harbury	Warwks	83	J3
Harby	Leics	117	K5
Harby	Notts	135	H5
Harcombe	Devon	13	K6
Harcombe	Devon	14	D4
Harcombe Bottom	Devon	15	H3
Harden	C Brad	149	K8
Harden	Wsall	98	C3
Hardendale	Cumb	166	D7
Hardenhuish	Wilts	46	C4
Hardgate	Abers	245	H3
Hardgate	D & G	175	K2
Hardgate	N York	150	C3
Hardgate	W Duns	208	E4
Hardham	W Susx	21	H3
Hardhorn	Lancs	147	G8
Hardingham	Norfk	105	L3
Hardingstone	Nhants	84	E4
Hardington	Somset	45	L8
Hardington Mandeville	Somset	31	H8
Hardington Marsh	Somset	15	L1
Hardington Moor	Somset	31	H8
Hardisworthy	Devon	26	D6
Hardley	Hants	19	G3
Hardley Street	Norfk	107	H3
Hardmead	M Keyn	85	H5
Hardraw	N York	158	F4
Hardsough	Lancs	140	B4
Hardstoft	Derbys	133	J7
Hardway	Hants	19	K3
Hardway	Somset	32	B4
Hardwick	Bucks	67	K3
Hardwick	Cambs	87	H3
Hardwick	Nhants	85	G1
Hardwick	Norfk	106	E5
Hardwick	Oxon	66	A6
Hardwick	Oxon	66	E1
Hardwick	Rothm	133	K3
Hardwick	Wsall	98	D4
Hardwicke	Gloucs	64	A4
Hardwicke	Gloucs	64	C2
Hardwick Village	Notts	134	C4
Hardy's Green	Essex	72	D3
Harebeating	E Susx	23	K5
Hareby	Lincs	136	F6
Hare Croft	C Brad	149	K8
Harefield	Gt Lon	50	D1
Hare Green	Essex	73	G2
Hare Hatch	Wokham	49	J3
Harehill	Derbys	115	K4
Harehills	Leeds	141	M1
Harehope	Nthumb	191	G2
Harelaw	Border	188	F2
Harelaw	D & G	178	B3
Harelaw	Dur	180	E8
Hareplain	Kent	39	L5
Haresceugh	Cumb	166	E2
Harescombe	Gloucs	64	B5
Haresfield	Gloucs	64	A5
Harestock	Hants	34	F4
Hare Street	Essex	70	B5
Hare Street	Essex	70	D7

Place	County	Page	Grid
Hare Street	Herts	69	K1
Harewood	Leeds	150	D6
Harewood End	Herefs	63	G2
Harford	Devon	7	J3
Hargate	Norfk	106	C5
Hargatewall	Derbys	132	B4
Hargrave	Ches W	129	L7
Hargrave	Nhants	85	K1
Hargrave	Suffk	88	F3
Harker	Cumb	177	L6
Harkstead	Suffk	90	E8
Harlaston	Staffs	99	G1
Harlaxton	Lincs	118	A5
Harlech	Gwynd	109	K5
Harlescott	Shrops	113	H8
Harlesden	Gt Lon	51	G2
Harlesthorpe	Derbys	133	K4
Harleston	Devon	8	B6
Harleston	Norfk	106	E6
Harleston	Suffk	89	L3
Harlestone	Nhants	84	D2
Harle Syke	Lancs	140	C1
Harley	Rothm	142	B8
Harley	Shrops	96	D3
Harlington	C Beds	68	D1
Harlington	Donc	142	D7
Harlington	Gt Lon	50	E3
Harlosh	Highld	258	D8
Harlow	Essex	70	C5
Harlow Hill	Nthumb	180	C5
Harlthorpe	E R Yk	151	M8
Harlton	Cambs	87	H5
Harlyn	Cnwll	10	B7
Harman's Cross	Dorset	17	J6
Harmby	N York	159	L5
Harmer Green	Herts	69	H4
Harmer Hill	Shrops	113	H7
Harmondsworth	Gt Lon	50	D3
Harmston	Lincs	135	K7
Harnage	Shrops	96	D3
Harnham	Nthumb	180	C3
Harnhill	Gloucs	64	F7
Harold Hill	Gt Lon	70	D8
Haroldston West	Pembks	54	D4
Haroldswick	Shet	281	f1
Harold Wood	Gt Lon	52	C1
Harome	N York	161	L6
Harpenden	Herts	68	E4
Harpford	Devon	14	C4
Harpham	E R Yk	153	H3
Harpley	Norfk	121	H6
Harpley	Worcs	80	F3
Harpole	Nhants	84	D3
Harpsdale	Highld	279	K5
Harpsden	Oxon	49	J3
Harpswell	Lincs	135	J2
Harpurhey	Manch	140	C7
Harpur Hill	Derbys	131	L5
Harraby	Cumb	177	M7
Harracott	Devon	27	K5
Harrapool	Highld	247	K4
Harrietfield	P & K	221	H1
Harrietsham	Kent	39	L3
Harringay	Gt Lon	51	J1
Harrington	Cumb	164	C5
Harrington	Lincs	137	G5
Harrington	Nhants	101	G7
Harringworth	Nhants	101	K4
Harris	W Isls	282	e6
Harriseahead	Staffs	131	G8
Harriston	Cumb	165	G2
Harrogate	N York	150	D5
Harrogate Crematorium N York		150	D5
Harrold	Bed	85	J4
Harrop Dale	Oldham	140	F6
Harrow	Gt Lon	50	F1
Harrowbarrow	Cnwll	11	M8
Harrowden	Bed	86	B5
Harrowgate Village	Darltn	169	H7
Harrow Green	Suffk	89	H4
Harrow Hill	Gloucs	63	K4
Harrow on the Hill	Gt Lon	50	F2
Harrow Weald	Gt Lon	50	F1
Harston	Cambs	87	J5
Harston	Leics	117	L5
Harswell	E R Yk	152	C7
Hart	Hartpl	170	B4
Hartburn	Nthumb	180	D2
Hartburn	S on T	169	L7
Hartest	Suffk	89	G5
Hartfield	E Susx	38	D6
Hartford	Cambs	86	E1
Hartford	Ches W	130	C6
Hartford	Somset	29	G5
Hartfordbridge	Hants	49	J7
Hartford End	Essex	71	G3
Hartforth	N York	159	L2
Hartgrove	Dorset	32	D7
Harthill	Ches W	129	L8
Harthill	N Lans	210	B6
Harthill	Rothm	133	K3
Hartington	Derbys	132	C7
Hartington	Nthumb	180	B1
Hartland	Devon	26	D6
Hartland Quay	Devon	26	C6
Hartlebury	Worcs	81	J1
Hartlepool	Hartpl	170	C4
Hartlepool Crematorium Hartpl		170	C4
Hartley	Cumb	158	D1
Hartley	Kent	39	J6
Hartley	Kent	52	D5
Hartley	Nthumb	181	H4
Hartley Green	Kent	52	D5
Hartley Green	Staffs	114	F5
Hartley Wespall	Hants	49	G7
Hartley Wintney	Hants	49	J7
Hartlip	Kent	53	H6
Hartoft End	N York	162	C4
Harton	N York	151	L1
Harton	S Tyne	181	J6
Harton	Shrops	96	B5
Hartpury	Gloucs	64	A2
Hartshead	Kirk	141	J3
Hartshill	C Stke	114	D2
Hartshill	Warwks	99	J4
Hartshorne	Derbys	116	B7
Hartside	Nthumb	190	D3
Hartsop	Cumb	165	L8
Hart Station	Hartpl	170	B3
Hartswell	Somset	29	K5
Hartwell	Nhants	84	F5
Hartwith	N York	150	B3
Hartwood	N Lans	209	M7
Hartwoodmyres	Border	188	D1
Harvel	Kent	52	E6
Harvington	Worcs	82	C5
Harvington	Worcs	97	K8
Harwell	Notts	134	D2
Harwell	Oxon	48	C1
Harwich	Essex	73	K1
Harwood	Bolton	139	L5
Harwood	Dur	167	J4
Harwood Dale	N York	163	H3
Harwood Lee	Bolton	139	L5
Harwood Park Crematorium Herts		69	H3
Harworth	Notts	134	C2
Hasbury	Dudley	98	B6
Hascombe	Surrey	36	F3
Haselbech	Nhants	100	F7
Haselbury Plucknett	Somset	31	L2
Haseley	Warwks	82	F2
Haseley Green	Warwks	82	F1
Haseley Knob	Warwks	82	F1
Haselor	Warwks	82	D4
Hasfield	Gloucs	64	B2
Hasguard	Pembks	54	D5
Hasholme	E R Yk	143	L1
Haskayne	Lancs	138	D6
Hasketon	Suffk	90	F5
Hasland	Derbys	133	H5
Haslemere	Surrey	36	D4
Haslingden	Lancs	140	B3
Haslingfield	Cambs	87	H5
Haslington	Ches E	130	E8
Hassall	Ches E	130	E8
Hassall Green	Ches E	130	F7
Hassell Street	Kent	40	E6
Hassingham	Norfk	107	H2
Hassness	Cumb	165	G7
Hassocks	W Susx	22	D4
Hassop	Derbys	132	D5
Haste Hill	Surrey	36	D4
Haster	Highld	280	D6
Hasthorpe	Lincs	137	J5
Hastingleigh	Kent	40	E6
Hastings	E Susx	24	E5
Hastings	Somset	30	D7
Hastings Crematorium E Susx		24	E5
Hastingwood	Essex	70	C5
Hastoe	Herts	68	A5
Haswell	Dur	169	K2
Haswell Plough	Dur	169	K2
Hatch	C Beds	86	D5
Hatch Beauchamp	Somset	30	D6
Hatch End	Bed	86	B3
Hatch End	Gt Lon	50	E1
Hatchet Gate	Hants	18	F3
Hatching Green	Herts	68	E4
Hatchmere	Ches W	130	A5
Hatcliffe	NE Lin	145	G7
Hatfield	Donc	143	G6
Hatfield	Herefs	80	E3
Hatfield	Herts	69	G5
Hatfield	Worcs	81	K5
Hatfield Broad Oak	Essex	70	E4
Hatfield Heath	Essex	70	D4
Hatfield Peverel	Essex	71	J5
Hatfield Woodhouse	Donc	143	H6
Hatford	Oxon	65	M8
Hatherden	Hants	34	D1
Hatherleigh	Devon	12	D2
Hathern	Leics	116	E7
Hatherop	Gloucs	65	H6
Hathersage	Derbys	132	E3
Hathersage Booths	Derbys	132	E3
Hatherton	Ches E	113	L2
Hatherton	Staffs	98	B1
Hatley St George	Cambs	86	F5
Hatt	Cnwll	6	D2
Hattersley	Tamesd	131	K1
Hattingley	Hants	35	K3
Hatton	Abers	257	K4
Hatton	Angus	234	C6
Hatton	Derbys	115	L5
Hatton	Gt Lon	50	E4
Hatton	Lincs	136	C4
Hatton	Shrops	95	L5
Hatton	Warrtn	130	B3
Hatton	Warwks	82	F2
Hatton Heath	Ches W	129	K7
Hatton of Fintray	Abers	256	F8
Haugh	E Ayrs	196	F6
Haugh	Lincs	137	H4
Haugh	Rochdl	140	D5
Haugham	Lincs	136	F3
Haughhead	E Duns	209	G3
Haugh Head	Nthumb	202	F7
Haughley	Suffk	89	L3
Haughley Green	Suffk	89	L2
Haugh of Glass	Moray	255	H4
Haugh of Urr	D & G	175	K2
Haughs of Kinnaird	Angus	235	G4
Haughton	Ches E	130	B8
Haughton	Notts	134	D5
Haughton	Powys	112	D7
Haughton	Shrops	96	F4
Haughton	Shrops	97	G2
Haughton	Shrops	112	F6
Haughton	Shrops	113	J8
Haughton	Staffs	114	D7
Haughton Green	Tamesd	131	J1
Haughton le Skerne	Darltn	169	J7
Haultwick	Herts	69	J3
Haunton	Staffs	99	G1
Hautes Croix	Jersey	9	d1
Hauxton	Cambs	87	J5
Havannah	Ches E	131	G6
Havant	Hants	20	B5
Havant Crematorium	Hants	20	B5
Haven	Herefs	79	M4
Haven Bank	Lincs	119	H1
Haven Side	E R Yk	144	F2
Havenstreet	IoW	19	J5
Havercroft	Wakefd	142	B5
Haverfordwest	Pembks	54	F4
Haverhill	Suffk	88	D6
Haverigg	Cumb	155	L7
Havering-atte-Bower	Gt Lon	70	D8
Haversham	M Keyn	84	F6
Haverthwaite	Cumb	156	E6
Haverton Hill	S on T	170	C6
Havyatt	N Som	44	F6
Havyatt	Somset	31	H3
Hawarden	Flints	129	H6
Hawbridge	Worcs	81	L5
Hawbush Green	Essex	71	J3
Hawcoat	Cumb	146	D2
Hawen	Cerdgn	76	C6
Hawes	N York	158	F5
Hawe's Green	Norfk	106	E4
Hawford	Worcs	81	J3
Hawick	Border	188	E3
Hawkchurch	Devon	15	H3
Hawkedon	Suffk	88	F4
Hawkenbury	Kent	39	K4
Hawkeridge	Wilts	46	B8
Hawkerland	Devon	14	C5
Hawker's Cove	Cnwll	10	C7
Hawkesbury	S Glos	45	M2
Hawkesbury	Warwks	99	K6
Hawkesbury Upton	S Glos	45	M2
Hawkes End	Covtry	99	J6
Hawk Green	Stockp	131	J2
Hawkhill	Nthumb	191	J4
Hawkhurst	Kent	39	J7
Hawkhurst Common	E Susx	23	J4
Hawkinge	Kent	41	H7
Hawkinge Crematorium	Kent	41	G7
Hawkley	Hants	35	M5
Hawkley	Wigan	139	H6
Hawkridge	Somset	28	F5
Hawksdale	Cumb	165	L1
Hawkshaw	Bury	139	M5
Hawkshead	Cumb	156	E3
Hawkshead Hill	Cumb	156	D3
Hawksland	S Lans	198	D5
Hawkspur Green	Essex	71	G1
Hawkstone	Shrops	113	J5
Hawkswick	N York	149	G2
Hawksworth	Leeds	149	L7
Hawksworth	Notts	117	K3
Hawkwell	Essex	53	J1
Hawkwell	Nthumb	180	C4
Hawley	Hants	49	L7
Hawley	Kent	52	C4
Hawling	Gloucs	64	F3
Hawnby	N York	161	J5
Haworth	C Brad	149	J8
Hawridge	Bucks	68	B6
Hawstead	Suffk	89	G3
Hawstead Green	Suffk	89	H3
Hawthorn	Dur	169	L2
Hawthorn	Hants	35	K4
Hawthorn	Rhondd	43	H4
Hawthorn Hill	Br For	49	L4
Hawthorn Hill	Lincs	136	D6
Hawthorpe	Lincs	118	D6
Hawton	Notts	117	L1
Haxby	C York	151	K4
Haxey	N Linc	143	J7
Haxey Carr	N Linc	143	J7
Haxted	Surrey	38	C4
Haxton	Wilts	33	K1
Hay	Cnwll	4	D8
Hay	Cnwll	10	D8
Haycombe Crematorium BaNES		45	L6
Haydock	St Hel	139	H8
Haydon	BaNES	45	K8
Haydon	Dorset	31	L7
Haydon	Somset	30	C6
Haydon Bridge	Nthumb	179	J7
Haydon Wick	Swindn	47	H2
Haye	Cnwll	11	L8
Hayes	Gt Lon	50	E3
Hayes	Gt Lon	51	L7
Hayes End	Gt Lon	50	D3
Hayfield	Ag & B	217	H2
Hayfield	Derbys	131	L2
Hayfield Green	Donc	143	G7
Haygate	Wrekin	96	E1
Hay Green	Norfk	120	C7
Hayhillock	Angus	234	E7
Hayle	Cnwll	2	E4
Hayley Green	Dudley	98	B6
Hayling Island	Hants	20	B6
Haymoor Green	Ches E	113	L2
Hayne	Devon	13	H5
Hayne	Devon	29	G7
Haynes (Church End)	C Beds	86	B7
Haynes (Northwood End) C Beds		86	B6
Haynes (Silver End)	C Beds	86	B6
Haynes (West End)	C Beds	85	L7
Hay-on-Wye	Powys	79	J6
Hayscastle	Pembks	74	E7
Hayscastle Cross	Pembks	74	E7
Haysden	Kent	38	F4
Hay Street	Herts	69	K2
Hayton	Cumb	164	F2
Hayton	Cumb	178	C7
Hayton	E R Yk	152	C6
Hayton	Notts	134	E3
Hayton's Bent	Shrops	96	C5
Haytor Vale	Devon	13	H7
Haytown	Devon	26	F7
Haywards Heath	W Susx	22	E2
Haywood	Donc	142	F5
Haywood	Herefs	80	B8
Haywood Oaks	Notts	134	C8
Hazards Green	E Susx	24	C5
Hazelbank	S Lans	198	D4
Hazelbury Bryan	Dorset	16	E1
Hazeleigh	Essex	71	K6
Hazeley	Hants	49	H7
Hazelford	Notts	117	K2
Hazel Grove	Stockp	131	H2
Hazelhurst	Tamesd	140	E7
Hazelslade	Staffs	98	C1
Hazel Street	Kent	39	H5
Hazel Stub	Suffk	88	D6
Hazelton Walls	Fife	222	E3
Hazelwood	Derbys	116	B2
Hazlemere	Bucks	67	L3
Hazlerigg	N u Ty	180	F4
Hazles	Staffs	114	F2
Hazleton	Gloucs	65	G3
Heacham	Norfk	120	C4
Headbourne Worthy	Hants	35	G4
Headbrook	Herefs	79	K4
Headcorn	Kent	39	L4
Headingley	Leeds	150	C8

Headington Oxon	66	D5	
Headlam Dur	168	F7	
Headlesscross N Lans	210	B7	
Headless Cross Worcs	82	B2	
Headley Hants	36	B4	
Headley Hants	48	D6	
Headley Surrey	51	G8	
Headley Down Hants	36	B4	
Headley Heath Worcs	98	D8	
Headon Devon	11	M2	
Headon Notts	134	E4	
Heads Nook Cumb	178	C7	
Heage Derbys	116	B2	
Healaugh N York	151	G6	
Healaugh N York	159	H3	
Heald Green Stockp	131	G3	
Heale Devon	28	A2	
Heale Somset	30	C6	
Heale Somset	30	F5	
Healey N York	160	B6	
Healey Nthumb	180	B7	
Healey Rochdl	140	D4	
Healey Wakefd	141	L4	
Healeyfield Dur	168	D1	
Healing NE Lin	145	G5	
Heamoor Cnwll	2	D5	
Heanor Derbys	116	D2	
Heanton Punchardon Devon	27	J4	
Heapham Lincs	135	H2	
Hearn Hants	36	B3	
Heart of England Crematorium Warwks	99	K5	
Hearts Delight Kent	53	J6	
Heasley Mill Devon	28	C4	
Heaste Highld	247	K5	
Heath Derbys	133	J6	
Heath Wakefd	142	A4	
Heath and Reach C Beds	68	L4	
Heath Common W Susx	21	J4	
Heathcote Derbys	132	C7	
Heathcote Shrops	113	L6	
Heath End Bucks	67	L4	
Heath End Hants	48	B6	
Heath End Leics	116	B7	
Heath End Warwks	82	F3	
Heather Leics	99	K1	
Heathfield Cambs	87	J6	
Heathfield Devon	13	J7	
Heathfield E Susx	23	K3	
Heathfield N York	149	L2	
Heathfield Somset	29	L5	
Heathfield Village Oxon	66	D4	
Heath Green Worcs	82	C1	
Heath Hall D & G	176	C3	
Heath Hayes & Wimblebury Staffs	98	C2	
Heath Hill Shrops	97	H1	
Heath House Somset	30	D5	
Heathstock Devon	14	F2	
Heathton Shrops	97	H5	
Heath Town Wolves	97	L3	
Heathwaite N York	161	G2	
Heatley Staffs	115	H6	
Heatley Warrtn	130	D2	
Heaton Bolton	139	L6	
Heaton C Brad	149	L8	
Heaton Lancs	147	J4	
Heaton N u Ty	181	G5	
Heaton Staffs	131	J7	
Heaton Chapel Stockp	131	H1	
Heaton Mersey Stockp	131	G2	
Heaton Norris Stockp	131	H2	
Heaton's Bridge Lancs	138	E5	
Heaverham Kent	52	C7	
Heaviley Stockp	131	H2	
Heavitree Devon	13	L4	
Hebburn S Tyne	181	H6	
Hebden N York	149	J3	
Hebden Bridge Calder	140	F2	
Hebden Green Ches W	130	C6	
Hebing End Herts	69	J3	
Hebron Carmth	75	L6	
Hebron IoA	125	H3	
Hebron Nthumb	191	J8	
Heckfield Hants	49	H6	
Heckfield Green Suffk	106	D8	
Heckfordbridge Essex	72	D3	
Heckington Lincs	118	F3	
Heckmondwike Kirk	141	K3	
Heddington Wilts	46	E5	
Heddon-on-the-Wall Nthumb	180	D5	
Hedenham Norfk	107	G5	
Hedge End Hants	19	H1	
Hedgerley Bucks	50	B2	
Hedgerley Green Bucks	50	B2	
Hedging Somset	30	D5	
Hedley on the Hill Nthumb	180	C7	
Hednesford Staffs	98	C1	
Hedon E R Yk	145	F2	
Hedsor Bucks	49	L2	
Heeley Sheff	133	G3	
Hegdon Hill Herefs	80	D4	
Heglibister Shet	281	d6	
Heighington Darltn	169	H6	
Heighington Lincs	135	L6	
Heightington Worcs	81	H1	
Heiton Border	201	L7	
Hele Devon	13	H8	
Hele Devon	14	A2	
Hele Devon	27	J2	
Hele Somset	30	B6	
Helebridge Cnwll	11	J2	
Hele Lane Devon	28	D8	
Helensburgh Ag & B	208	A3	
Helenton S Ayrs	196	D5	
Helford Cnwll	3	J6	
Helford Passage Cnwll	3	J5	
Helhoughton Norfk	121	J6	
Helions Bumpstead Essex	88	C7	
Hellaby Rothm	133	K1	
Helland Cnwll	10	F8	
Hellandbridge Cnwll	10	F8	
Hell Corner W Berk	48	A6	
Hellescott Cnwll	11	K5	
Hellesdon Norfk	106	L1	
Hellesveor Cnwll	2	D3	
Hellidon Nhants	83	M4	
Hellifield N York	148	E4	
Hellingly E Susx	23	K5	
Hellington Norfk	107	G3	
Helm Nthumb	191	H7	
Helmdon Nhants	84	B6	
Helme Kirk	141	H5	
Helmingham Suffk	90	E4	
Helmington Row Dur	168	F4	
Helmsdale Highld	274	D5	
Helmshore Lancs	140	B3	
Helmsley N York	161	K6	
Helperby N York	150	F2	
Helperthorpe N York	152	E2	
Helpringham Lincs	118	F3	
Helpston C Pete	102	C2	
Helsby Ches W	129	L4	
Helsey Lincs	137	K5	
Helston Cnwll	3	G5	
Helstone Cnwll	10	F6	
Helton Cumb	166	C6	
Helwith N York	159	K2	
Helwith Bridge N York	148	D2	
Hemblington Norfk	107	G1	
Hembridge Somset	31	K3	
Hemel Hempstead Herts	68	D5	
Hemerdon Devon	7	H3	
Hemingbrough N York	143	H2	
Hemingby Lincs	136	D5	
Hemingfield Barns	142	B7	
Hemingford Abbots Cambs	86	F1	
Hemingford Grey Cambs	86	F1	
Hemingstone Suffk	90	D4	
Hemington Leics	116	D6	
Hemington Nhants	102	B6	
Hemington Somset	45	L8	
Hemley Suffk	91	G6	
Hemlington Middsb	170	C7	
Hempholme E R Yk	153	H5	
Hempnall Norfk	106	E4	
Hempnall Green Norfk	106	E5	
Hempriggs Moray	266	B3	
Hempstead Essex	88	C7	
Hempstead Medway	53	G6	
Hempstead Norfk	122	C4	
Hempstead Norfk	123	H6	
Hempsted Gloucs	64	B4	
Hempton Norfk	121	K5	
Hempton Oxon	66	C1	
Hemsby Norfk	123	K8	
Hemswell Lincs	135	J2	
Hemswell Cliff Lincs	135	J2	
Hemsworth Wakefd	142	C5	
Hemyock Devon	29	L8	
Henbury Bristl	45	H3	
Henbury Ches E	131	H5	
Hendham Devon	7	L5	
Hendomen Powys	94	F4	
Hendon Gt Lon	51	G1	
Hendon Sundld	181	J8	
Hendon Crematorium Gt Lon	51	G1	
Hendra Cnwll	3	J4	
Hendra Cnwll	10	E7	
Hendre Brdgnd	42	E5	
Hendre Flints	128	E6	
Hendre Mons	62	F4	
Hendy Carmth	57	G4	
Heneglwys IoA	125	G4	
Henfield W Susx	22	C4	
Henford Devon	11	M4	
Henfynyw Cerdgn	76	E3	
Henghurst Kent	40	B8	
Hengoed Caerph	43	J3	
Hengoed Powys	79	J4	
Hengoed Shrops	112	D5	
Hengrave Suffk	89	G2	
Henham Essex	70	E2	
Heniarth Powys	94	D2	
Henlade Somset	30	C6	
Henley Dorset	16	D2	
Henley Gloucs	64	C4	
Henley Shrops	95	L5	
Henley Shrops	96	C8	
Henley Somset	30	F4	
Henley Suffk	90	E5	
Henley W Susx	36	D5	
Henley Green Covtry	99	K7	
Henley-in-Arden Warwks	82	E2	
Henley-on-Thames Oxon	49	J2	
Henley Park Surrey	50	B8	
Henley's Down E Susx	24	D5	
Henley Street Kent	52	E5	
Henllan Cerdgn	76	C7	
Henllan Denbgs	127	L6	
Henllan Amgoed Carmth	55	L3	
Henllys Torfn	44	B1	
Henlow C Beds	86	D7	
Hennock Devon	13	J6	
Henny Street Essex	89	H7	
Henryd Conwy	126	F5	
Henry's Moat (Castell Hendre) Pembks	75	H6	
Hensall N York	142	F3	
Henshaw Nthumb	179	H6	
Hensingham Cumb	164	C7	
Henstead Suffk	107	K6	
Hensting Hants	35	G6	
Henstridge Somset	32	B7	
Henstridge Ash Somset	32	B6	
Henstridge Marsh Somset	32	B6	
Henton Oxon	67	J6	
Henton Somset	31	H2	
Henwick Worcs	81	J4	
Henwood Cnwll	11	K7	
Henwood Oxon	66	C6	
Heol-las Swans	57	J5	
Heol Senni Powys	60	D2	
Heol-y-Cyw Brdgnd	42	E5	
Hepburn Nthumb	190	F1	
Hepple Nthumb	190	E6	
Hepscott Nthumb	180	F2	
Heptonstall Calder	140	E2	
Hepworth Kirk	141	J6	
Hepworth Suffk	105	K8	
Herbrandston Pembks	54	E5	
Hereford Herefs	80	C7	
Hereford Crematorium Herefs	80	C7	
Hereson Kent	41	L2	
Heribusta Highld	258	F3	
Heriot Border	200	E2	
Hermiston C Edin	211	G5	
Hermitage Border	188	E7	
Hermitage Dorset	16	C1	
Hermitage W Berk	48	D4	
Hermitage W Susx	20	B5	
Hermit Hill Barns	141	M7	
Hermon Carmth	58	C3	
Hermon IoA	125	G6	
Hermon Pembks	75	L6	
Herne Kent	41	G2	
Herne Bay Kent	41	G2	
Herne Common Kent	41	G2	
Herne Hill Gt Lon	51	J4	
Herne Pound Kent	39	G3	
Herner Devon	27	K5	
Hernhill Kent	40	E3	
Herodsfoot Cnwll	5	L1	
Heronden Kent	41	J4	
Herongate Essex	52	D1	
Heronsford S Ayrs	182	E6	
Heronsgate Herts	68	C3	
Herriard Hants	35	K2	
Herringfleet Suffk	107	K4	
Herring's Green Bed	86	B6	
Herringswell Suffk	88	E1	
Herringthorpe Rothm	133	J1	
Herrington Sundld	181	J8	
Hersden Kent	41	G3	
Hersham Cnwll	11	J1	
Hersham Surrey	50	E6	
Herstmonceux E Susx	23	L5	
Herston Dorset	17	K6	
Herston Ork	275	c6	
Hertford Herts	69	J4	
Hertford Heath Herts	69	K5	
Hertingfordbury Herts	69	J5	
Hesketh Bank Lancs	138	F3	
Hesketh Lane Lancs	147	M7	
Hesket Newmarket Cumb	165	K3	
Heskin Green Lancs	139	G4	
Hesleden Dur	170	B3	
Hesleden N York	158	F7	
Hesley Donc	134	C1	
Hesleyside Nthumb	179	J2	
Heslington C York	151	K5	
Hessay C York	151	H5	
Hessenford Cnwll	6	C3	
Hessett Suffk	89	J3	
Hessle E R Yk	144	C3	
Hessle Wakefd	142	C4	
Hest Bank Lancs	147	J3	
Hestley Green Suffk	90	D2	
Heston Gt Lon	50	E3	
Hestwall Ork	275	b4	
Heswall Wirral	129	G3	
Hethe Oxon	66	E1	
Hethersett Norfk	106	C2	
Hethersgill Cumb	178	B5	
Hetherside Cumb	178	B5	
Hetherson Green Ches W	113	H2	
Hethpool Nthumb	202	D7	
Hett Dur	169	H3	
Hetton N York	149	G4	
Hetton-le-Hole Sundld	169	K1	
Hetton Steads Nthumb	203	G6	
Heugh Nthumb	180	D4	
Heughhead Abers	243	L1	
Heugh Head Border	213	J6	
Heveningham Suffk	91	H1	
Hever Kent	38	D4	
Heversham Cumb	157	H6	
Hevingham Norfk	122	D7	
Hewas Water Cnwll	4	F5	
Hewelsfield Gloucs	63	H6	
Hewenden C Brad	149	K3	
Hewish N Som	44	E6	
Hewish Somset	15	K1	
Hewood Dorset	15	H2	
Hexham Nthumb	179	L6	
Hextable Kent	52	B5	
Hexthorpe Donc	142	F7	
Hexton Herts	68	E1	
Hexworthy Cnwll	11	L6	
Hexworthy Devon	12	F8	
Hey Lancs	148	F7	
Heybridge Essex	70	F7	
Heybridge Essex	71	L5	
Heybridge Basin Essex	72	C5	
Heybrook Bay Devon	6	F5	
Heydon Cambs	87	J7	
Heydon Norfk	122	C6	
Heydour Lincs	118	D4	
Heyhead Manch	131	G3	
Hey Houses Lancs	138	D2	
Heylipoll Ag & B	224	B6	
Heylor Shet	281	d4	
Heyrod Tamesd	140	E7	
Heysham Lancs	147	H4	
Heyshaw N York	149	L3	
Heyshott W Susx	20	E3	
Heyside Oldham	140	D6	
Heytesbury Wilts	32	F2	
Heythrop Oxon	65	M2	
Heywood Rochdl	140	C5	
Heywood Wilts	46	C8	
Hibaldstow N Linc	144	B7	
Hickleton Donc	142	D6	
Hickling Norfk	123	J6	
Hickling Notts	117	J6	
Hickling Green Norfk	123	H6	
Hickling Heath Norfk	123	H7	
Hickling Pastures Notts	117	H6	
Hickmans Green Kent	40	E4	
Hicks Forstal Kent	41	G3	
Hickstead W Susx	22	D3	
Hidcote Bartrim Gloucs	82	E6	
Hidcote Boyce Gloucs	82	E6	
High Ackworth Wakefd	142	C4	
Higham Barns	141	M6	
Higham Derbys	133	H7	
Higham Kent	38	F4	
Higham Kent	52	F5	
Higham Lancs	148	E8	
Higham Suffk	88	E2	
Higham Suffk	89	L8	
Higham Dykes Nthumb	180	D4	
Higham Ferrers Nhants	85	J2	
Higham Gobion C Beds	86	C8	
Higham Hill Gt Lon	51	K1	
Higham on the Hill Leics	99	K4	
Highampton Devon	12	C2	
Highams Park Gt Lon	69	K8	
High Angerton Nthumb	180	D2	
High Ardwell D & G	172	D5	
High Auldgirth D & G	176	B1	
High Bankhill Cumb	166	D2	
High Beach Essex	69	L7	
High Bentham N York	148	B2	
High Bewaldeth Cumb	165	H4	
High Bickington Devon	27	L6	

Hoe Hants ... 35 H7
Hoe Norfk ... 121 M8
Hoe Benham W Berk ... 48 B5
Hoe Gate Hants ... 35 K8
Hoff Cumb ... 166 F7
Hogben's Hill Kent ... 40 D4
Hoggards Green Suffk ... 89 H4
Hoggeston Bucks ... 67 K2
Hoggrill's End Warwks ... 99 G5
Hog Hill E Susx ... 25 G4
Hoghton Lancs ... 139 J2
Hoghton Bottoms Lancs ... 139 J2
Hognaston Derbys ... 115 L2
Hogsthorpe Lincs ... 137 K5
Holbeach Lincs ... 119 K6
Holbeach Bank Lincs ... 119 K6
Holbeach Clough Lincs ... 119 K6
Holbeach Drove Lincs ... 103 G1
Holbeach Hurn Lincs ... 119 L6
Holbeach St Johns Lincs ... 119 K7
Holbeach St Mark's Lincs ... 119 L5
Holbeach St Matthew Lincs ... 119 L5
Holbeck Notts ... 133 L5
Holbeck Woodhouse Notts ... 133 L5
Holberrow Green Worcs ... 82 B3
Holbeton Devon ... 7 J5
Holborn Gt Lon ... 51 J3
Holborough Kent ... 52 F6
Holbrook Derbys ... 116 B3
Holbrook Sheff ... 133 J3
Holbrook Suffk ... 90 E7
Holbrook Moor Derbys ... 116 B3
Holbrooks Covtry ... 99 J6
Holburn Nthumb ... 203 G6
Holbury Hants ... 19 G3
Holcombe Devon ... 13 M7
Holcombe Somset ... 31 L1
Holcombe Rogus Devon ... 29 J7
Holcot Nhants ... 84 F1
Holden Lancs ... 148 D6
Holdenby Nhants ... 84 D2
Holden Gate Calder ... 140 D3
Holder's Green Essex ... 70 F1
Holdgate Shrops ... 96 D5
Holdingham Lincs ... 118 E2
Holditch Dorset ... 15 H2
Holdsworth Calder ... 141 G2
Holehouse Derbys ... 131 K1
Hole-in-the-Wall Herefs ... 63 J2
Holemoor Devon ... 12 A2
Hole Street W Susx ... 21 K4
Holford Somset ... 29 L3
Holgate C York ... 151 J5
Holker Cumb ... 156 E7
Holkham Norfk ... 121 K3
Hollacombe Devon ... 11 M2
Holland Fen Lincs ... 119 H2
Holland Lees Lancs ... 139 G6
Holland-on-Sea Essex ... 73 J4
Hollandstoun Ork ... 275 f1
Hollee D & G ... 177 J5
Hollesley Suffk ... 91 H6
Hollicombe Torbay ... 8 D2
Hollingbourne Kent ... 39 L2
Hollingdon Br & H ... 22 D5
Hollingdon Bucks ... 67 L2
Hollingthorpe Leeds ... 142 B2
Hollington Derbys ... 115 L4
Hollington Staffs ... 115 G4
Hollingworth Tamesd ... 140 F8
Hollinlane Ches E ... 131 G3
Hollins Bury ... 140 B6
Hollins Derbys ... 132 F5
Hollins Staffs ... 114 F2
Hollinsclough Staffs ... 131 L6
Hollins End Sheff ... 133 H3
Hollins Green Warrtn ... 130 D2
Hollins Lane Lancs ... 147 K5
Hollinswood Wrekin ... 96 F2
Hollinwood Shrops ... 113 H4
Hollingrove E Susx ... 24 C3
Hollocombe Devon ... 27 L8
Holloway Derbys ... 132 F8
Holloway Gt Lon ... 51 J2
Holloway Wilts ... 32 E5
Hollowell Nhants ... 84 D1
Hollowmoor Heath Ches W ... 129 L6
Hollows D & G ... 177 L3
Hollybush Caerph ... 61 J6
Hollybush E Ayrs ... 196 D7
Hollybush Herefs ... 81 H7
Holly End Norfk ... 103 K2
Holly Green Worcs ... 81 K7
Hollyhurst Ches E ... 113 J3
Hollywood Worcs ... 98 D7
Holmbridge Kirk ... 141 H6
Holmbury St Mary Surrey ... 37 H2
Holmbush Cnwll ... 5 H4

Holmcroft Staffs ... 114 E6
Holme Cambs ... 102 D6
Holme Cumb ... 157 H7
Holme Kirk ... 141 H6
Holme N Linc ... 144 A6
Holme N York ... 160 E6
Holme Notts ... 134 F7
Holme Chapel Lancs ... 140 C2
Holme Green N York ... 151 J7
Holme Hale Norfk ... 105 H2
Holme Lacy Herefs ... 80 D8
Holme Marsh Herefs ... 79 L4
Holme next the Sea Norfk ... 120 F3
Holme on the Wolds E R Yk ... 152 E6
Holme Pierrepont Notts ... 117 G4
Holmer Herefs ... 80 C6
Holmer Green Bucks ... 67 L7
Holme St Cuthbert Cumb ... 164 F1
Holmes Chapel Ches E ... 130 E6
Holmesfield Derbys ... 132 F4
Holmes Hill E Susx ... 23 J4
Holmeswood Lancs ... 138 E4
Holmethorpe Surrey ... 51 H8
Holme upon Spalding Moor
E R Yk ... 152 B8
Holmewood Derbys ... 133 H6
Holmfield Calder ... 141 G2
Holmfirth Kirk ... 141 H6
Holmhead E Ayrs ... 197 H7
Holmpton E R Yk ... 145 K3
Holmrook Cumb ... 155 K3
Holmsford Bridge
Crematorium N Ayrs ... 196 D3
Holmshurst E Susx ... 23 L2
Holmside Dur ... 169 G1
Holmwrangle Cumb ... 166 C1
Holne Devon ... 7 K1
Holnest Dorset ... 16 C1
Holnicote Somset ... 29 G2
Holsworthy Devon ... 11 L2
Holsworthy Beacon Devon ... 11 L1
Holt Dorset ... 17 K2
Holt Norfk ... 122 B4
Holt Wilts ... 46 B6
Holt Worcs ... 81 J3
Holt Wrexhm ... 112 F1
Holtby C York ... 151 L5
Holt End Worcs ... 82 C1
Holt Fleet Worcs ... 81 J3
Holt Green Lancs ... 138 E6
Holt Heath Dorset ... 17 L2
Holt Heath Worcs ... 81 J3
Holton Oxon ... 66 F5
Holton Somset ... 31 L5
Holton Suffk ... 107 H7
Holton cum Beckering Lincs ... 136 B3
Holton Heath Dorset ... 17 J4
Holton Hill E Susx ... 24 B2
Holton le Clay Lincs ... 145 H7
Holton le Moor Lincs ... 144 D8
Holton St Mary Suffk ... 90 C7
Holt Street Kent ... 41 H5
Holtye E Susx ... 38 C5
Holway Flints ... 128 E4
Holwell Dorset ... 32 B8
Holwell Herts ... 86 D8
Holwell Leics ... 117 J6
Holwell Oxon ... 65 K5
Holwick Dur ... 167 L5
Holworth Dorset ... 16 E6
Holybourne Hants ... 35 M3
Holy Cross Worcs ... 97 L7
Holyfield Essex ... 69 K6
Holyhead IoA ... 124 D3
Holy Island IoA ... 124 D3
Holy Island Nthumb ... 203 J4
Holy Island Nthumb ... 203 J5
Holymoorside Derbys ... 133 G6
Holyport W & M ... 49 L3
Holystone Nthumb ... 190 D5
Holytown N Lans ... 209 K6
Holytown Crematorium
N Lans ... 209 K6
Holywell C Beds ... 68 C4
Holywell Cambs ... 87 G1
Holywell Cnwll ... 4 C3
Holywell Dorset ... 16 B2
Holywell Flints ... 128 E4
Holywell Nthumb ... 181 H4
Holywell Warwks ... 82 E2
Holywell Green Calder ... 141 G4
Holywell Lake Somset ... 29 K6
Holywell Row Suffk ... 104 E7
Holywood D & G ... 176 B3
Holywood Village D & G ... 176 C3
Homer Shrops ... 96 E3
Homer Green Sefton ... 138 D7
Homersfield Suffk ... 106 F6
Homescales Cumb ... 157 J5

Hom Green Herefs ... 63 H3
Homington Wilts ... 33 K5
Honeyborough Pembks ... 54 F5
Honeybourne Worcs ... 82 D6
Honeychurch Devon ... 12 E2
Honey Hill Kent ... 40 F3
Honeystreet Wilts ... 47 G6
Honey Tye Suffk ... 89 J8
Honiley Warwks ... 82 F1
Honing Norfk ... 123 G6
Honingham Norfk ... 106 C1
Honington Lincs ... 118 B3
Honington Suffk ... 105 H8
Honington Warwks ... 83 G6
Honiton Devon ... 14 E3
Honley Kirk ... 141 H5
Honnington Wrekin ... 114 A8
Honor Oak Crematorium
Gt Lon ... 51 K4
Hoo Kent ... 41 J2
Hoobrook Worcs ... 97 J3
Hood Green Barns ... 141 M7
Hood Hill Rothm ... 142 B8
Hooe C Plym ... 6 F4
Hooe E Susx ... 24 C5
Hoo End Herts ... 68 F3
Hoo Green Ches E ... 130 D3
Hoohill Bpool ... 146 F8
Hook Cambs ... 103 J5
Hook Devon ... 15 G2
Hook E R Yk ... 143 J3
Hook Gt Lon ... 50 F6
Hook Hants ... 19 H3
Hook Hants ... 49 H8
Hook Pembks ... 55 G4
Hook Wilts ... 47 G2
Hook-a-Gate Shrops ... 95 L2
Hook Bank Worcs ... 81 J7
Hooke Dorset ... 15 M3
Hook End Essex ... 70 E7
Hookgate Staffs ... 114 A4
Hook Green Kent ... 39 G6
Hook Green Kent ... 52 D5
Hook Norton Oxon ... 83 H8
Hook Street Gloucs ... 63 K7
Hook Street Wilts ... 47 G2
Hookway Devon ... 13 K3
Hookwood Surrey ... 37 L2
Hooley Surrey ... 51 H7
Hooley Bridge Rochdl ... 140 C5
Hoo Meavy Devon ... 7 G2
Hoo St Werburgh Medway ... 53 G4
Hooton Ches W ... 129 J4
Hooton Levitt Rothm ... 133 K2
Hooton Pagnell Donc ... 142 D6
Hooton Roberts Rothm ... 142 D8
Hopcrofts Holt Oxon ... 66 C2
Hope Derbys ... 132 C3
Hope Devon ... 7 K6
Hope Flints ... 129 G7
Hope Powys ... 95 G2
Hope Shrops ... 95 H3
Hope Staffs ... 132 B8
Hope Bagot Shrops ... 96 D8
Hope Bowdler Shrops ... 95 L5
Hope End Green Essex ... 70 E3
Hopehouse Border ... 187 L3
Hopeman Moray ... 266 C2
Hope Mansell Herefs ... 63 J3
Hopesay Shrops ... 95 J6
Hopetown Wakefd ... 142 B3
Hope under Dinmore Herefs ... 80 C5
Hopgrove C York ... 151 K5
Hopperton N York ... 150 F4
Hop Pole Lincs ... 102 D1
Hopsford Warwks ... 99 L6
Hopstone Shrops ... 97 H4
Hopton Derbys ... 115 L1
Hopton Shrops ... 112 F7
Hopton Staffs ... 114 E6
Hopton Suffk ... 105 K7
Hopton Cangeford Shrops ... 96 C7
Hopton Castle Shrops ... 95 J7
Hoptonheath Shrops ... 95 J7
Hopton on Sea Norfk ... 107 L3
Hopton Wafers Shrops ... 96 E8
Hopwas Staffs ... 98 F3
Hopwood Rochdl ... 140 C6
Hopwood Worcs ... 98 C8
Horam E Susx ... 23 K4
Horbling Lincs ... 118 F4
Horbury Wakefd ... 141 L4
Horcott Gloucs ... 65 H7
Horden Dur ... 170 B3
Horderley Shrops ... 95 K6
Hordle Hants ... 18 D4
Hordley Shrops ... 112 F5
Horeb Carmth ... 56 H7
Horeb Cerdgn ... 76 D2

Horfield Bristl ... 45 H4
Horham Suffk ... 90 F1
Horkesley Heath Essex ... 72 E1
Horkstow N Linc ... 144 B4
Horley Oxon ... 83 K6
Horley Surrey ... 37 L2
Hornblotton Green Somset ... 31 K4
Hornby Lancs ... 147 L2
Hornby N York ... 160 B4
Hornby N York ... 160 E2
Horncastle Lincs ... 136 E6
Hornchurch Gt Lon ... 52 B2
Horncliffe Nthumb ... 202 E3
Horndean Border ... 202 D3
Horndean Hants ... 35 L8
Horndon Devon ... 12 C6
Horndon on the Hill Thurr ... 52 E2
Horne Surrey ... 38 A4
Horner Somset ... 28 F2
Horne Row Essex ... 71 J6
Horners Green Suffk ... 89 K7
Horney Common E Susx ... 23 G2
Horn Hill Bucks ... 68 C8
Horning Norfk ... 123 G8
Horninghold Leics ... 101 H4
Horninglow Staffs ... 115 L6
Horningsea Cambs ... 87 K3
Horningsham Wilts ... 32 D3
Horningtoft Norfk ... 121 K6
Horningtops Cnwll ... 6 B3
Hornsbury Somset ... 30 E8
Hornsby Cumb ... 166 C1
Hornsbygate Cumb ... 166 C1
Horns Cross Devon ... 27 G6
Horns Cross E Susx ... 24 E3
Hornsea E R Yk ... 153 K6
Hornsey Gt Lon ... 51 J1
Horn's Green Gt Lon ... 51 M7
Horn Street Kent ... 41 G8
Hornton Oxon ... 83 J6
Horpit Swindn ... 47 J2
Horra Shet ... 281 e3
Horrabridge Devon ... 7 G1
Horringer Suffk ... 89 G3
Horringford IoW ... 19 J6
Horrocks Fold Bolton ... 139 L5
Horrocksford Lancs ... 148 C7
Horsacott Devon ... 27 J4
Horsebridge Devon ... 12 A7
Horsebridge E Susx ... 23 K5
Horsebridge Hants ... 34 D5
Horsebridge Shrops ... 95 J2
Horsebridge Staffs ... 114 F1
Horsebrook Staffs ... 97 K1
Horsecastle N Som ... 44 E5
Horsedown Cnwll ... 3 G4
Horsehay Wrekin ... 96 F2
Horseheath Cambs ... 88 C5
Horsehouse N York ... 159 J6
Horsell Surrey ... 50 C7
Horseman's Green Wrexhm ... 113 G3
Horsenden Bucks ... 67 J6
Horsey Norfk ... 123 J7
Horsey Somset ... 30 D3
Horsey Corner Norfk ... 123 J6
Horsford Norfk ... 122 D8
Horsforth Leeds ... 150 B8
Horsham W Susx ... 37 J5
Horsham Worcs ... 81 G4
Horsham St Faith Norfk ... 122 E8
Horsington Lincs ... 136 C6
Horsington Somset ... 32 B6
Horsley Derbys ... 116 C3
Horsley Gloucs ... 64 B7
Horsley Nthumb ... 180 D5
Horsley Nthumb ... 190 B6
Horsley Cross Essex ... 73 H2
Horsleycross Street Essex ... 73 G1
Horsley-Gate Derbys ... 132 F4
Horsleyhill Border ... 188 F2
Horsley's Green Bucks ... 67 J8
Horsley Woodhouse Derbys ... 116 C3
Horsmonden Kent ... 39 H5
Horspath Oxon ... 66 E6
Horstead Norfk ... 122 F7
Horsted Keynes W Susx ... 22 F2
Horton Bucks ... 68 A3
Horton Dorset ... 17 K1
Horton Lancs ... 148 E6
Horton Nhants ... 84 F4
Horton S Glos ... 45 M2
Horton Shrops ... 113 H5
Horton Somset ... 30 D7
Horton Staffs ... 131 J8
Horton Surrey ... 51 G6
Horton Swans ... 56 E7
Horton W & M ... 50 C4
Horton Wilts ... 46 F6
Horton Wrekin ... 113 L8

Horton Cross Somset	30 E7	Hoylake Wirral	128 F2
Horton-cum-Studley Oxon	66 F4	Hoyland Barns	142 B7
Horton Green Ches W	113 G2	Hoyland Common Barns	142 B7
Horton Heath Hants	35 G7	Hoylandswaine Barns	141 L6
Horton-in-Ribblesdale N York	148 D2	Hoyle W Susx	20 E3
Horton Kirby Kent	52 C5	Hoyle Mill Barns	142 A6
Horwich Bolton	139 J5	Hubberholme N York	159 G7
Horwich End Derbys	131 K3	Hubberston Pembks	54 E5
Horwood Devon	27 J5	Hubbert's Bridge Lincs	119 J3
Hoscar Lancs	138 F5	Huby N York	150 C6
Hoscote Border	188 C4	Huby N York	151 J3
Hose Leics	117 J5	Huccaby Devon	12 F8
Hosey Hill Kent	51 M8	Hucclecote Gloucs	64 C4
Hosh P & K	220 E3	Hucking Kent	53 H7
Hoswick Shet	281 e8	Hucknall Notts	116 F2
Hotham E R Yk	143 M1	Huddersfield Kirk	141 H4
Hothfield Kent	40 C6	Huddersfield Crematorium	
Hoton Leics	116 F7	Kirk	141 J4
Hott Nthumb	179 H2	Huddington Worcs	81 L4
Hough Ches E	113 M1	Hudnall Herts	68 C4
Hough Ches E	131 G4	Hudswell N York	159 L3
Hougham Lincs	118 A3	Huggate E R Yk	152 D5
Hough End Leeds	141 K1	Hugglescote Leics	99 L1
Hough Green Halton	129 L2	Hughenden Valley Bucks	67 L7
Hough-on-the-Hill Lincs	118 B2	Hughley Shrops	96 D4
Houghton Cambs	86 F1	Hugh Town IoS	10 c3
Houghton Cumb	177 L7	Huish Devon	27 J8
Houghton Hants	34 D4	Huish Wilts	47 H6
Houghton Nthumb	180 D5	Huish Champflower Somset	29 J5
Houghton Pembks	55 G5	Huish Episcopi Somset	31 G5
Houghton W Susx	21 H4	Hùisinis W Isls	282 d5
Houghton Conquest C Beds	85 L7	Huisinish W Isls	282 d5
Houghton Gate Dur	181 .H8	Hulcote C Beds	85 J7
Houghton Green E Susx	25 G3	Hulcote Nhants	84 D5
Houghton Green Warrtn	130 C1	Hulcott Bucks	67 K4
Houghton le Side Darltn	169 G6	Hulham Devon	14 B6
Houghton-le-Spring Sundld	169 J1	Hulland Derbys	115 L2
Houghton on the Hill Leics	100 E3	Hulland Ward Derbys	115 L2
Houghton Regis C Beds	68 C2	Hullavington Wilts	46 C3
Houghton St Giles Norfk	121 K4	Hull Bridge E R Yk	153 G7
Hound Green Hants	49 H7	Hullbridge Essex	71 K8
Houndslow Border	201 K4	Hull, Kingston upon C KuH	144 D2
Houndsmoor Somset	29 L5	Hulme Manch	140 C8
Houndwood Border	213 J6	Hulme Staffs	114 E2
Hounslow Gt Lon	50 F4	Hulme Warrtn	130 B2
Househill Highld	253 G1	Hulme End Staffs	132 B7
Houses Hill Kirk	141 K4	Hulme Walfield Ches E	131 G6
Housieside Abers	257 G6	Hulse Heath Ches E	130 E3
Houston Rens	208 C5	Hulton Lane Ends Bolton	139 K6
Houstry Highld	275 G1	Hulverstone IoW	18 F6
Houton Ork	275 b5	Hulver Street Norfk	105 J1
Hove Br & H	22 D6	Hulver Street Suffk	107 K6
Hove Edge Calder	141 H3	Humber Devon	13 L7
Hoveringham Notts	117 J2	Humber Herefs	80 C4
Hoveton Norfk	122 F7	Humber Bridge N Linc	144 C3
Hovingham N York	161 L7	Humberston NE Lin	145 J6
Howbrook Barns	141 M8	Humberstone C Leic	100 E2
How Caple Herefs	63 J1	Humberton N York	150 F2
Howden E R Yk	143 J2	Humbie E Loth	212 A6
Howden-le-Wear Dur	168 F4	Humbleton E R Yk	145 G1
Howe Highld	280 D4	Humbleton Nthumb	202 F7
Howe IoM	154 b8	Humby Lincs	118 D5
Howe N York	160 E6	Hume Border	201 L5
Howe Norfk	106 F3	Humshaugh Nthumb	179 L4
Howe Bridge Wigan	139 K7	Huna Highld	280 E2
Howe Bridge Crematorium		Huncoat Lancs	140 A2
Wigan	139 K7	Huncote Leics	100 B4
Howe Green Essex	71 H6	Hundalee Border	189 H3
Howegreen Essex	71 K6	Hundall Derbys	133 H4
Howell Lincs	118 F2	Hunderthwaite Dur	168 C6
How End C Beds	85 K7	Hundleby Lincs	137 G6
Howe of Teuchar Abers	268 E6	Hundle Houses Lincs	119 H1
Howes D & G	177 G5	Hundleton Pembks	54 F6
Howe Street Essex	71 G4	Hundon Suffk	88 E5
Howe Street Essex	88 D8	Hundred End Lancs	138 E3
Howey Powys	78 E3	Hundred House Powys	78 F4
Howgate Cumb	164 C6	Hungarton Leics	100 F2
Howgate Mdloth	211 H7	Hungerford Hants	33 L8
Howgill Lancs	148 E6	Hungerford Somset	29 J3
Howick Nthumb	191 K3	Hungerford W Berk	47 M5
Howle Wrekin	113 M6	Hungerford Newtown W Berk	47 M4
Howle Hill Herefs	63 J3	Hunger Hill Bolton	139 K6
Howlett End Essex	88 B8	Hunger Hill Lancs	139 G5
Howley Somset	15 G1	Hungerstone Herefs	80 B8
How Mill Cumb	178 C7	Hungerton Lincs	118 A5
Howmore W Isls	283 b10	Hungryhatton Shrops	113 L6
Hownam Border	189 L2	Hunmanby N York	163 K7
Howrigg Cumb	165 K1	Hunningham Warwks	83 J2
Howsham N Linc	144 D6	Hunnington Worcs	98 B7
Howsham N York	151 M3	Hunsbury Hill Nhants	84 E4
Howtel Nthumb	202 D6	Hunsdon Herts	69 L1
Howt Green Kent	53 J6	Hunsingore N York	150 F5
Howton Herefs	62 E1	Hunslet Leeds	141 M2
Howtown Cumb	166 B6	Hunsonby Cumb	166 D4
How Wood Herts	68 F6	Hunstanton Norfk	120 E3
Howwood Rens	208 C7	Hunstanworth Dur	168 B1
Hoxa Ork	275 c6	Hunsterson Ches E	113 M2
Hoxne Suffk	106 D7	Hunston Suffk	89 K2
Hoy Ork	275 b5	Hunston W Susx	20 D6
Hunston Green Suffk	89 K2	Hutton Sessay N York	161 G7
Hunstrete BaNES	45 J6	Hutton Wandesley N York	151 H5
Hunsworth Kirk	141 J2	Huxham Devon	13 M3
Hunt End Worcs	82 B2	Huxham Green Somset	31 K4
Hunter's Inn Devon	28 B1	Huxley Ches W	129 L7
Hunter's Quay Ag & B	207 K3	Huyton Knows	129 K5
Huntham Somset	30 E5	Hycemoor Cumb	155 K5
Hunthill Lodge Angus	234 D1	Hyde Gloucs	64 C6
Huntingdon Cambs	86 E1	Hyde Hants	33 L8
Huntingfield Suffk	107 G8	Hyde Tamesd	131 J1
Huntingford Dorset	32 D5	Hyde Heath Bucks	68 B7
Huntington C York	151 K4	Hyde Lea Staffs	114 E7
Huntington Ches W	129 K6	Hydestile Surrey	36 E3
Huntington E Loth	212 B4	Hykeham Moor Lincs	135 K4
Huntington Herefs	79 J4	Hyndford Bridge S Lans	198 F5
Huntington Herefs	80 B6	Hynish Ag & B	224 C7
Huntington Staffs	98 B1	Hyssington Powys	95 H4
Huntingtowerfield P & K	221 K2	Hystfield Gloucs	63 K7
Huntley Gloucs	63 L3	Hythe Essex	72 E2
Huntly Abers	255 L4	Hythe Hants	19 G2
Hunton Hants	35 G3	Hythe Kent	41 G8
Hunton Kent	39 H3	Hythe Somset	44 F8
Hunton N York	160 B4	Hythe End W & M	50 C4
Hunton Bridge Herts	68 D7	Hyton Cumb	155 K5
Hunt's Corner Norfk	105 L5		
Huntscott Somset	29 G2		
Hunt's Cross Lpool	129 K3		
Hunts Green Bucks	67 L6		
Hunts Green Warwks	98 F4	I	
Huntsham Devon	29 H6		
Huntshaw Devon	27 J6	Ibberton Dorset	16 F1
Huntshaw Cross Devon	27 J6	Ible Derbys	132 E8
Huntspill Somset	30 D2	Ibsley Hants	18 A2
Huntstile Somset	30 C4	Ibstock Leics	99 L2
Huntworth Somset	30 D4	Ibstone Bucks	67 J8
Hunwick Dur	168 F4	Ibthorpe Hants	48 A8
Hunworth Norfk	122 B4	Iburndale N York	162 F1
Hurcott Somset	30 F7	Ibworth Hants	48 E1
Hurdcott Wilts	33 L4	Icelton N Som	44 D6
Hurdsfield Ches E	131 H5	Ichrachan Ag & B	217 G1
Hurley W & M	49 K2	Ickburgh Norfk	105 G4
Hurley Warwks	99 H4	Ickenham Gt Lon	50 D2
Hurley Bottom W & M	49 K2	Ickford Bucks	66 F5
Hurley Common Warwks	99 H4	Ickham Kent	41 H4
Hurlford E Ayrs	196 F4	Ickleford Herts	68 F1
Hurlston Green Lancs	138 E5	Icklesham E Susx	24 F4
Hurn Dorset	18 A4	Ickleton Cambs	87 K6
Hurn's End Lincs	119 M2	Icklingham Suffk	88 F1
Hursley Hants	34 F6	Ickornshaw N York	149 G7
Hurst Dorset	16 F4	Ickwell Green C Beds	86 C6
Hurst N York	159 J2	Icomb Gloucs	65 J3
Hurst Somset	31 G7	Idbury Oxon	65 K3
Hurst Wokham	49 J4	Iddesleigh Devon	12 D1
Hurstbourne Priors Hants	34 F2	Ide Devon	13 L4
Hurstbourne Tarrant Hants	48 A8	Ideford Devon	13 K7
Hurst Green E Susx	24 D2	Ide Hill Kent	38 D3
Hurst Green Essex	73 G4	Iden E Susx	25 G3
Hurst Green Lancs	148 B8	Iden Green Kent	39 J6
Hurst Green Surrey	38 B3	Iden Green Kent	39 K7
Hurst Hill Dudley	97 L4	Idle C Brad	149 M8
Hurstley Herefs	79 L5	Idless Cnwll	4 D5
Hurstpierpoint W Susx	22 D4	Idlicote Warwks	83 G6
Hurst Wickham W Susx	22 D4	Idmiston Wilts	33 L3
Hurstwood Lancs	140 C2	Idole Carmth	58 D5
Hurtiso Ork	275 d5	Idridgehay Derbys	115 M2
Hurtmore Surrey	36 E2	Idrigill Highld	258 F4
Hurworth Burn Dur	169 L4	Idstone Oxon	47 K2
Hurworth-on-Tees Darltn	169 J8	Iffley Oxon	66 D6
Hurworth Place Darltn	160 D1	Ifield W Susx	37 K3
Hury Dur	168 B6	Ifold W Susx	36 F4
Husbands Bosworth Leics	100 E6	Iford Bmouth	18 A5
Husborne Crawley C Beds	85 J8	Iford E Susx	22 F5
Husthwaite N York	161 H7	Ifton Mons	44 F1
Hutcherleigh Devon	8 A5	Ifton Heath Shrops	112 E4
Hutcliffe Wood Crematorium		Ightfield Shrops	113 K4
Sheff	133 G3	Ightham Kent	38 F2
Hut Green N York	142 F3	Iken Suffk	91 J4
Huthwaite Notts	133 J7	Ilam Staffs	115 J2
Huttoft Lincs	137 K4	Ilchester Somset	31 H6
Hutton Border	202 E2	Ilderton Nthumb	190 E2
Hutton Cumb	166 B5	Ilford Gt Lon	51 L2
Hutton E R Yk	152 F5	Ilford Somset	30 E7
Hutton Essex	70 F4	Ilfracombe Devon	27 J2
Hutton Lancs	139 G2	Ilkeston Derbys	116 D3
Hutton N Som	44 D7	Ilketshall St Andrew Suffk	107 H6
Hutton Bonville N York	160 E3	Ilketshall St John Suffk	107 H6
Hutton Buscel N York	163 H6	Ilketshall St Lawrence Suffk	107 H6
Hutton Conyers N York	160 D7	Ilketshall St Margaret Suffk	107 G6
Hutton Cranswick E R Yk	153 G5	Ilkley C Brad	149 K6
Hutton End Cumb	166 B3	Illand Cnwll	11 K7
Hutton Hang N York	159 L5	Illey Dudley	98 B7
Hutton Henry Dur	169 L3	Illidge Green Ches E	130 F7
Hutton-le-Hole N York	162 B4	Illingworth Calder	141 G2
Hutton Lowcross R & Cl	170 D4	Illogan Cnwll	3 H2
Hutton Magna Dur	168 E8	Ilmington Warwks	82 F6
Hutton Mulgrave N York	162 E1	Ilminster Somset	30 E7
Hutton Roof Cumb	157 J7	Ilsington Devon	13 H7
Hutton Roof Cumb	165 L4	Ilsington Dorset	16 E4
Hutton Rudby N York	161 G2		

Ilston Swans 57 G6
Ilton N York 160 B7
Ilton Somset 30 E7
Imachar N Ayrs 194 D3
Immingham NE Lin 144 F5
Immingham Dock NE Lin 145 G4
Impington Cambs 87 J3
Ince Ches W 129 K4
Ince Blundell Sefton 138 C7
Ince-in-Makerfield Wigan 139 J6
Inchbae Lodge Hotel Highld 262 C6
Inchbare Angus 234 F2
Inchberry Moray 266 F5
Incheril Highld 261 G7
Inchinnan Rens 208 E5
Inchlaggan Highld 239 K3
Inchmichael P & K 222 D2
Inchmore Highld 251 G3
Inchnacardoch Hotel Highld 240 C2
Inchnadamph Highld 271 H4
Inchture P & K 222 D2
Inchvuilt Highld 249 L4
Inchyra P & K 222 C3
Indian Queens Cnwll 4 E3
Ingatestone Essex 70 F7
Ingbirchworth Barns 141 K6
Ingerthorpe N York 150 C3
Ingestre Staffs 114 F6
Ingham Lincs 135 J3
Ingham Norfk 123 H6
Ingham Suffk 89 G1
Ingham Corner Norfk 123 H6
Ingleborough Norfk 120 B8
Ingleby Derbys 116 B6
Ingleby Arncliffe N York 161 G3
Ingleby Barwick S on T 170 B7
Ingleby Cross N York 161 G3
Ingleby Greenhow N York 161 J2
Ingleigh Green Devon 12 E1
Inglesbatch BaNES 45 L6
Inglesham Swindn 65 J7
Ingleston D & G 176 C6
Ingleton Dur 168 F6
Ingleton N York 158 B8
Inglewhite Lancs 147 L7
Ingmanthorpe N York 150 F5
Ingoe Nthumb 180 C4
Ingol Lancs 139 G1
Ingoldisthorpe Norfk 120 F5
Ingoldmells Lincs 137 K6
Ingoldsby Lincs 118 D5
Ingram Nthumb 190 E3
Ingrave Essex 52 D1
Ingrow C Brad 149 J7
Ings Cumb 157 G3
Ingst S Glos 45 H2
Ingthorpe Rutlnd 101 M2
Ingworth Norfk 122 D5
Inkberrow Worcs 82 B4
Inkerman Dur 168 E3
Inkhorn Abers 257 G4
Inkpen W Berk 48 A6
Inkstack Highld 280 C2
Inmarsh Wilts 46 D6
Innellan Ag & B 207 J5
Innerleithen Border 200 D6
Innerleven Fife 222 F7
Innermessan D & G 172 D2
Innerwick E Loth 212 F4
Innesmill Moray 266 F3
Innsworth Gloucs 64 B3
Insch Abers 256 A6
Insh Highld 241 L3
Inskip Lancs 147 J8
Inskip Moss Side Lancs 147 J8
Instow Devon 27 H5
Insworke Cnwll 6 E4
Intake Sheff 133 H3
Inver Abers 243 H5
Inver Highld 264 D3
Inver P & K 232 F7
Inverailort Highld 238 B7
Inveralligin Highld 260 D8
Inverallochy Abers 269 J3
Inveran Highld 272 E8
Inveraray Ag & B 217 H5
Inverarish Highld 247 H2
Inverarity Angus 234 C6
Inverarnan Stirlg 218 D3
Inverasdale Highld 260 C3
Inverbeg Ag & B 218 E7
Inverbervie Abers 235 K1
Inverboyndie Abers 268 B3
Invercreran House Hotel
  Ag & B 229 G6
Inverdruie Highld 242 B1
Inveresk E Loth 211 K5
Inveresragan Ag & B 228 F8
Inverey Abers 242 E4

Inverfarigaig Highld 250 F7
Inverfolla Ag & B 228 E6
Invergarry Highld 240 A3
Invergeldie P & K 220 C2
Invergloy Highld 239 L6
Invergordon Highld 263 J6
Invergowrie P & K 222 F1
Inverguseran Highld 238 B2
Inverhadden P & K 231 J4
Inverherive Hotel Stirlg 218 E2
Inverie Highld 238 B3
Inverinan Ag & B 216 F4
Inverinate Highld 248 E7
Inverkeilor Angus 235 G5
Inverkeithing Fife 210 F2
Inverkeithny Abers 268 A6
Inverkip Inver 207 K4
Inverkirkaig Highld 270 E4
Inverlael Highld 261 K3
Inverlair Highld 240 B7
Inverliever Lodge Ag & B 216 D6
Inverlochy Ag & B 217 K2
Invermark Angus 244 A7
Invermoriston Highld 250 D8
Invernaver Highld 278 B4
Inverneill Ag & B 206 D3
Inverness Highld 251 H3
Inverness Crematorium
  Highld 251 H3
Invernettie Abers 257 L3
Invernoaden Ag & B 217 J7
Inveroran Hotel Ag & B 229 M7
Inverquharity Angus 234 B4
Inverquhomery Abers 257 J2
Inverroy Highld 239 M7
Inversanda Highld 228 E3
Invershiel Highld 248 F7
Invershin Highld 272 E6
Invershore Highld 275 H1
Inversnaid Hotel Stirlg 218 E5
Inverugie Abers 269 L6
Inveruglas Ag & B 218 D5
Inveruglass Highld 241 L3
Inverurie Abers 256 D7
Inwardleigh Devon 12 D3
Inworth Essex 72 C3
Iochdar W Isls 283 b9
Iona Ag & B 226 B7
Iping W Susx 36 C6
iPort Logistics Park Donc 142 F8
Ipplepen Devon 8 B2
Ipsden Oxon 48 F2
Ipstones Staffs 115 G2
Ipswich Suffk 90 E6
Ipswich Crematorium Suffk 90 E6
Irby Wirral 128 F3
Irby in the Marsh Lincs 137 J7
Irby upon Humber NE Lin 145 G6
Irchester Nhants 85 H2
Ireby Cumb 165 H3
Ireby Lancs 157 L7
Ireland C Beds 86 C7
Ireleth Cumb 156 B7
Ireshopeburn Dur 167 K3
Irlam Salfd 130 E1
Irnham Lincs 118 D6
Iron Acton S Glos 45 K2
Iron Bridge Cambs 103 K4
Ironbridge Wrekin 96 F3
Iron Cross Warwks 82 C5
Ironmacannie D & G 185 G7
Irons Bottom Surrey 37 K2
Ironville Derbys 116 D1
Irstead Norfk 123 H7
Irthington Cumb 178 C6
Irthlingborough Nhants 85 J1
Irton N York 163 H6
Irvine N Ayrs 196 C3
Isauld Highld 279 G3
Isbister Shet 281 d3
Isbister Shet 281 f5
Isfield E Susx 23 G4
Isham Nhants 101 J8
Isington Hants 36 A2
Islandpool Worcs 97 K7
Islay Ag & B 204 E1
Isle Abbotts Somset 30 E6
Isle Brewers Somset 30 E6
Isleham Cambs 104 C8
Isle of Dogs Gt Lon 51 K3
Isle of Lewis W Isls 282 f3
Isle of Man IoM 154 e5
Isle of Mull Ag & B 227 H6
Isle of Sheppey Kent 40 C2
Isle of Skye Highld 246 F1
Isle of Walney Cumb 146 D3
Isle of Whithorn D & G 174 D7
Isle of Wight IoW 19 J6

Isle of Wight Crematorium
  IoW 19 J5
Isleornsay Highld 247 L6
Isles of Scilly IoS 10 c2
Islesteps D & G 176 C4
Islet Village Guern 9 k2
Isleworth Gt Lon 50 F4
Isley Walton Leics 116 C6
Islibhig W Isls 282 d3
Islington Gt Lon 51 J2
Islington Crematorium Gt Lon 51 H1
Islip Nhants 101 L7
Islip Oxon 66 D4
Islivig W Isls 282 d3
Isombridge Wrekin 96 E1
Istead Rise Kent 52 D5
Itchen Abbas Hants 35 H4
Itchen Stoke Hants 35 H4
Itchingfield W Susx 37 H5
Itchington S Glos 45 K2
Itteringham Norfk 122 C5
Itton Devon 12 F3
Itton Mons 62 F8
Itton Common Mons 62 F7
Ivegill Cumb 165 M2
Ivelet N York 159 G3
Iver Bucks 50 D3
Iver Heath Bucks 50 C2
Iveston Dur 168 E1
Ivinghoe Bucks 68 B3
Ivinghoe Aston Bucks 68 B3
Ivington Herefs 80 B4
Ivington Green Herefs 80 B4
Ivybridge Devon 7 J4
Ivychurch Kent 25 J2
Ivy Cross Dorset 32 E6
Ivy Hatch Kent 38 F3
Ivy Todd Norfk 105 H2
Iwade Kent 40 A2
Iwerne Courtney Dorset 32 E8
Iwerne Minster Dorset 32 E8
Ixworth Suffk 89 J1
Ixworth Thorpe Suffk 89 J1

J

Jack Green Lancs 139 J3
Jack Hill N York 150 B5
Jack-in-the-Green Devon 14 B3
Jack's Bush Hants 34 C3
Jacksdale Notts 116 D1
Jackson Bridge Kirk 141 J6
Jackton S Lans 209 G8
Jacobstow Cnwll 11 H3
Jacobstowe Devon 12 E2
Jacobs Well Surrey 50 C8
Jameston Pembks 55 H7
Jamestown Highld 262 E8
Jamestown W Duns 208 C3
Janetstown Highld 275 G2
Janetstown Highld 280 D6
Jardine Hall D & G 176 E1
Jarrow S Tyne 181 H6
Jarvis Brook E Susx 38 E7
Jasper's Green Essex 71 H2
Jawcraig Falk 209 M4
Jaywick Essex 73 H4
Jealott's Hill Br For 49 L4
Jeater Houses N York 160 F4
Jedburgh Border 189 H2
Jeffreyston Pembks 55 J5
Jemimaville Highld 263 K7
Jerbourg Guern 9 k4
Jersey Jersey 9 d2
Jersey Crematorium Jersey 9 d3
Jersey Marine Neath 57 K6
Jerusalem Lincs 135 J5
Jesmond N u Ty 181 G5
Jevington E Susx 23 J7
Jingle Street Mons 62 F5
Jockey End Herts 68 D4
Jodrell Bank Ches E 130 F5
Johnby Cumb 166 B4
John o' Groats Highld 280 E2
Johns Cross E Susx 24 D3
Johnshaven Abers 235 K2
Johnson Street Norfk 123 H8
Johnston Pembks 54 F5
Johnstone D & G 187 K6
Johnstone Rens 208 D6
Johnstonebridge D & G 187 G7
Johnstown Carmth 58 D6
Johnstown Wrexhm 112 D2
Joppa C Edin 211 K4
Joppa Cerdgn 77 G2
Joppa S Ayrs 196 E7
Jordans Bucks 50 B1

Jordanston Pembks 74 F5
Jordanthorpe Sheff 133 G3
Joyden's Wood Kent 52 B4
Jubilee Corner Kent 39 L4
Jump Barns 142 B7
Jumper's Town E Susx 38 C6
Juniper Nthumb 179 L7
Juniper Green C Edin 211 G5
Jura Ag & B 215 G7
Jurby IoM 154 e3
Jurston Devon 13 G5

K

Kaber Cumb 167 J8
Kaimend S Lans 199 G4
Kames Ag & B 206 F5
Kames E Ayrs 197 K5
Kea Cnwll 4 C6
Keadby N Linc 143 L5
Keal Cotes Lincs 137 G7
Kearby Town End N York 150 E6
Kearsley Bolton 139 M6
Kearsley Nthumb 180 B4
Kearsney Kent 41 J6
Kearstwick Cumb 157 K6
Kearton N York 159 H3
Keasden N York 148 C3
Keaton Devon 7 J4
Keckwick Halton 130 B3
Keddington Lincs 136 F2
Keddington Corner Lincs 137 G2
Kedington Suffk 88 E6
Kedleston Derbys 116 A3
Keelby Lincs 144 F5
Keele Staffs 114 C3
Keele University Staffs 114 C3
Keeley Green Bed 85 K6
Keelham C Brad 141 G1
Keeres Green Essex 70 F4
Keeston Pembks 54 E3
Keevil Wilts 46 D7
Kegworth Leics 116 E6
Kehelland Cnwll 3 G3
Keig Abers 256 A7
Keighley C Brad 149 J7
Keighley Crematorium C Brad 149 J8
Keilarsbrae Clacks 220 F8
Keillour P & K 221 H2
Keiloch Abers 243 G5
Keils Ag & B 205 H3
Keinton Mandeville Somset 31 J5
Keir Mill D & G 186 C7
Keirsleywell Row Nthumb 179 H8
Keisby Lincs 118 D6
Keisley Cumb 167 G6
Keiss Highld 280 D4
Keith Moray 267 J6
Keithick P & K 233 J7
Keithock Angus 234 F3
Keithtown Highld 262 F8
Kelbrook Lancs 148 F7
Kelby Lincs 118 D3
Keld Cumb 166 D7
Keld N York 158 F3
Keld Head N York 162 D5
Keldholme N York 162 C5
Kelfield N Linc 143 L7
Kelfield N York 151 J8
Kelham Notts 134 F8
Kelhead D & G 176 F5
Kellacott Devon 12 A5
Kellamergh Lancs 138 E2
Kellas Angus 234 C8
Kellas Moray 266 D5
Kellaton Devon 8 B7
Kelleth Cumb 157 L2
Kelling Norfk 122 B3
Kellington N York 142 E3
Kelloe Dur 169 K3
Kelloholm D & G 185 J1
Kells Cumb 164 C7
Kelly Devon 11 M6
Kelly Bray Cnwll 11 L8
Kelmarsh Nhants 101 J2
Kelmscott Oxon 65 K7
Kelsale Suffk 91 J2
Kelsall Ches W 129 M6
Kelshall Herts 87 G7
Kelsick Cumb 165 G1
Kelso Border 201 M6
Kelstedge Derbys 133 G7
Kelstern Lincs 136 D2
Kelsterton Flints 129 G5
Kelston BaNES 45 K5
Keltneyburn P & K 231 L5
Kelton D & G 176 C5

Place	County	Page	Grid
Kelty Fife		221	L8
Kelvedon Essex		72	C3
Kelvedon Hatch Essex		70	E7
Kelynack Cnwll		2	B5
Kemacott Devon		28	B2
Kemback Fife		223	G4
Kemberton Shrops		97	G3
Kemble Gloucs		64	E7
Kemble Wick Gloucs		64	E7
Kemerton Worcs		81	L7
Kemeys Commander Mons		62	D6
Kemnay Abers		256	D8
Kempe's Corner Kent		40	D6
Kempley Gloucs		63	K1
Kempley Green Gloucs		63	K1
Kempsey Worcs		81	J5
Kempsford Gloucs		65	H7
Kemps Green Warwks		82	D1
Kempshott Hants		35	J1
Kempston Bed		85	K5
Kempston Hardwick Bed		85	K6
Kempton Shrops		95	J6
Kemp Town Br & H		22	E6
Kemsing Kent		52	C7
Kemsley Kent		40	B2
Kemsley Street Kent		53	H6
Kenardington Kent		25	H1
Kenchester Herefs		80	B6
Kencot Oxon		65	K6
Kendal Cumb		157	H4
Kenderchurch Herefs		62	E2
Kendleshire S Glos		45	K3
Kenfig Brdgnd		42	B5
Kenfig Hill Brdgnd		42	C5
Kenilworth Warwks		83	G1
Kenley Gt Lon		51	J7
Kenley Shrops		96	D3
Kenmore Highld		260	B8
Kenmore P & K		231	L6
Kenn Devon		13	L5
Kenn N Som		44	E5
Kennacraig Ag & B		206	C6
Kennards House Cnwll		11	K6
Kenneggy Cnwll		2	F5
Kennerleigh Devon		13	J1
Kennessee Green Sefton		138	D7
Kennet Clacks		210	B1
Kennethmont Abers		255	L6
Kennett Cambs		88	D2
Kennford Devon		13	L5
Kenninghall Norfk		105	L6
Kennington Kent		40	D6
Kennington Oxon		66	D6
Kennoway Fife		222	F6
Kenny Somset		30	D7
Kenny Hill Suffk		104	D7
Kennythorpe N York		152	B3
Kenovay Ag & B		224	C6
Kensaleyre Highld		259	G6
Kensington Gt Lon		51	H3
Kensworth Common C Beds		68	C3
Kentallen Highld		228	F4
Kent and Sussex Crematorium Kent		38	F6
Kentchurch Herefs		62	E2
Kentford Suffk		88	E2
Kent Green Ches E		131	G8
Kentisbeare Devon		14	C1
Kentisbury Devon		27	L2
Kentisbury Ford Devon		27	L2
Kentish Town Gt Lon		51	H2
Kentmere Cumb		157	G2
Kenton Devon		13	M6
Kenton Gt Lon		50	F1
Kenton N u Ty		180	F5
Kenton Suffk		90	E2
Kenton Bankfoot N u Ty		180	F5
Kentra Highld		237	G2
Kents Bank Cumb		156	F7
Kent's Green Gloucs		63	L2
Kent's Oak Hants		34	D6
Kent Street E Susx		24	E4
Kent Street Kent		39	G2
Kenwick Shrops		112	F5
Kenwyn Cnwll		4	D5
Kenyon Warrtn		139	J8
Keoldale Highld		276	F3
Keppoch Highld		248	E6
Kepwick N York		161	G4
Keresley Covtry		99	J6
Kermincham Ches E		130	F6
Kernborough Devon		8	B6
Kerne Bridge Herefs		63	H3
Kerrera Ag & B		216	C2
Kerridge Ches E		131	J4
Kerridge-end Ches E		131	J4
Kerris Cnwll		2	C5
Kerry Powys		94	E5
Kerrycroy Ag & B		207	J6
Kersall Notts		134	E7
Kersbrook Devon		14	C6
Kerscott Devon		27	L5
Kersey Suffk		89	K6
Kersey Tye Suffk		89	K6
Kersey Upland Suffk		89	K6
Kershader W Isls		282	f4
Kershopefoot Cumb		178	B2
Kersoe Worcs		82	A7
Kerswell Devon		14	C2
Kerswell Green Worcs		81	K6
Kerthen Wood Cnwll		2	F4
Kesgrave Suffk		90	F6
Kessingland Suffk		107	L6
Kessingland Beach Suffk		107	L6
Kestle Cnwll		5	G5
Kestle Mill Cnwll		4	D3
Keston Gt Lon		51	L6
Keswick Cumb		165	J6
Keswick Norfk		106	E2
Ketsby Lincs		137	G4
Kettering Nhants		101	J7
Kettering Crematorium Nhants		101	J7
Ketteringham Norfk		106	D3
Kettins P & K		233	K7
Kettlebaston Suffk		89	K5
Kettlebridge Fife		222	E5
Kettlebrook Staffs		99	G3
Kettleburgh Suffk		91	G3
Kettle Green Herts		69	L3
Kettleholm D & G		176	F3
Kettleness N York		171	J7
Kettleshulme Ches E		131	K4
Kettlesing N York		150	B4
Kettlesing Bottom N York		150	B4
Kettlestone Norfk		121	L5
Kettlethorpe Lincs		135	G4
Kettletoft Ork		275	e2
Kettlewell N York		149	H2
Ketton Rutlnd		101	L3
Kew Gt Lon		50	F4
Kewstoke N Som		44	C6
Kexbrough Barns		141	M6
Kexby C York		151	L5
Kexby Lincs		135	H3
Key Green Ches E		131	H7
Key Green N York		162	D2
Keyham Leics		100	E2
Keyhaven Hants		18	D5
Keyingham E R Yk		145	H3
Keymer W Susx		22	D4
Keynsham BaNES		45	K5
Keysoe Bed		86	B3
Keysoe Row Bed		86	B3
Keyston Cambs		102	A8
Key Street Kent		53	J6
Keyworth Notts		117	G5
Kibbear Somset		30	B6
Kibblesworth Gatesd		181	G7
Kibworth Beauchamp Leics		100	F4
Kibworth Harcourt Leics		100	F4
Kidbrooke Gt Lon		51	L4
Kidburngill Cumb		164	E6
Kiddemore Green Staffs		97	J2
Kidderminster Worcs		97	J8
Kiddington Oxon		66	B3
Kidd's Moor Norfk		106	C3
Kidlington Oxon		66	D4
Kidmore End Oxon		49	G3
Kidsdale D & G		174	C7
Kidsgrove Staffs		131	G8
Kidstones N York		159	G6
Kidwelly Carmth		56	D3
Kiel Crofts Ag & B		228	D7
Kielder Nthumb		189	H7
Kiells Ag & B		204	F3
Kilbarchan Rens		208	C6
Kilbeg Highld		247	K7
Kilberry Ag & B		206	A6
Kilbirnie N Ayrs		208	A8
Kilbride Ag & B		207	G5
Kilbride Ag & B		215	L8
Kilbuiack Moray		266	B4
Kilburn Derbys		116	C2
Kilburn Gt Lon		51	H1
Kilburn N York		161	H6
Kilby Leics		100	D4
Kilchamaig Ag & B		206	C6
Kilchattan Ag & B		207	H8
Kilchattan Ag & B		214	D5
Kilcheran Ag & B		228	C7
Kilchoan Highld		236	F7
Kilchoman Ag & B		204	B4
Kilchrenan Ag & B		217	G3
Kilconquhar Fife		223	H6
Kilcot Gloucs		63	K2
Kilcoy Highld		251	G2
Kilcreggan Ag & B		207	L3
Kildale N York		161	K1
Kildalloig Ag & B		192	F4
Kildary Highld		263	K5
Kildavaig Ag & B		206	F6
Kildavanan Ag & B		207	G5
Kildonan Highld		274	B4
Kildonan N Ayrs		195	G6
Kildonan Lodge Highld		274	B4
Kildonnan Highld		236	F3
Kildrochet House D & G		172	D4
Kildrummy Abers		255	J8
Kildwick N York		149	H6
Kilfinan Ag & B		206	E3
Kilfinnan Highld		239	M4
Kilford Denbgs		128	C6
Kilgetty Pembks		55	K5
Kilgrammie S Ayrs		183	G3
Kilgwrrwg Common Mons		62	F7
Kilham E R Yk		153	G3
Kilham Nthumb		202	D6
Kilkenneth Ag & B		224	B6
Kilkenzie Ag & B		192	D3
Kilkerran Ag & B		192	E4
Kilkhampton Cnwll		26	D8
Killamarsh Derbys		133	J3
Killay Swans		57	H6
Killearn Stirlg		208	E2
Killen Highld		263	J8
Killerby Darltn		169	G6
Killerton Devon		14	A3
Killichonan P & K		231	G4
Killiechonate Highld		239	L7
Killiechronan Ag & B		227	G4
Killiecrankie P & K		232	D3
Killilan Highld		248	F5
Killimster Highld		280	D5
Killin Stirlg		231	G8
Killinghall N York		150	C4
Killington Cumb		157	K5
Killington Devon		28	B2
Killingworth N Tyne		181	G5
Killiow Cnwll		4	C6
Killochyett Border		200	F4
Kilmacolm Inver		208	B5
Kilmahog Stirlg		219	K5
Kilmahumaig Ag & B		216	B8
Kilmaluag Highld		259	G2
Kilmany Fife		222	F3
Kilmarnock E Ayrs		196	E3
Kilmartin Ag & B		216	C7
Kilmaurs E Ayrs		196	E3
Kilmelford Ag & B		216	C4
Kilmersdon Somset		45	K8
Kilmeston Hants		35	J5
Kilmichael Ag & B		192	E4
Kilmichael Glassary Ag & B		216	D8
Kilmichael of Inverlussa Ag & B		206	B2
Kilmington Devon		15	G3
Kilmington Wilts		32	C3
Kilmington Common Wilts		32	C4
Kilmington Street Wilts		32	C4
Kilmorack Highld		250	E3
Kilmore Ag & B		216	D2
Kilmore Highld		247	K7
Kilmory Ag & B		205	M2
Kilmory Highld		237	G6
Kilmory N Ayrs		193	K4
Kilmuir Highld		251	J2
Kilmuir Highld		258	D7
Kilmuir Highld		258	F3
Kilmuir Highld		263	K5
Kilmun Ag & B		207	K3
Kilnave Ag & B		204	D2
Kilncadzow S Lans		198	E3
Kilndown Kent		39	H6
Kiln Green Wokham		49	K3
Kilnhill Cumb		165	H4
Kilnhouses Ches W		130	C6
Kilnhurst Rothm		142	C8
Kilninver Ag & B		216	C3
Kiln Pit Hill Nthumb		180	C7
Kilnsea E R Yk		145	L4
Kilnsey N York		149	H2
Kilnwick E R Yk		152	F6
Kilnwick Percy E R Yk		152	C6
Kiloran Ag & B		214	D5
Kilpatrick N Ayrs		194	D5
Kilpeck Herefs		62	F1
Kilpin E R Yk		143	K2
Kilpin Pike E R Yk		143	J2
Kilrenny Fife		223	K6
Kilsby Nhants		84	A1
Kilspindie P & K		222	C2
Kilstay D & G		172	E7
Kilsyth N Lans		209	J3
Kiltarlity Highld		250	E3
Kilton R & Cl		171	G7
Kilton Thorpe R & Cl		171	G7
Kilvaxter Highld		258	F3
Kilve Somset		29	L2
Kilvington Notts		117	L3
Kilwinning N Ayrs		196	B2
Kimberley Norfk		106	B3
Kimberley Notts		116	E3
Kimberworth Rothm		133	H1
Kimblesworth Dur		169	H1
Kimble Wick Bucks		67	J5
Kimbolton Cambs		86	B2
Kimbolton Herefs		80	C3
Kimcote Leics		100	D6
Kimmeridge Dorset		17	J1
Kimmerston Nthumb		202	E6
Kimpton Hants		34	C2
Kimpton Herts		68	F3
Kimworthy Devon		26	E8
Kinbrace Highld		273	L2
Kinbuck Stirlg		220	D6
Kincaple Fife		223	H3
Kincardine Fife		210	B2
Kincardine Highld		263	G2
Kincardine Bridge Fife		210	B2
Kincardine O'Neil Abers		244	D4
Kinclaven P & K		233	H7
Kincorth C Aber		245	L3
Kincorth House Moray		265	G7
Kincraig Highld		241	M2
Kincraigie P & K		232	E5
Kindallachan P & K		232	E5
Kinerarach Ag & B		205	L5
Kineton Gloucs		65	G2
Kineton Warwks		83	H5
Kinfauns P & K		222	B3
Kingarth Ag & B		207	H7
Kingcausie Abers		245	J3
Kingcoed Mons		62	E6
Kingerby Lincs		135	L1
Kingford Devon		11	K2
Kingham Oxon		65	K2
Kingholm Quay D & G		176	C4
Kinghorn Fife		211	J2
Kinglassie Fife		222	C7
Kingoodie P & K		222	F1
King's Acre Herefs		80	B7
Kingsand Cnwll		6	L6
Kingsash Bucks		67	L6
Kingsbarns Fife		223	K5
Kingsbridge Devon		7	L6
Kingsbridge Somset		29	H4
Kings Bridge Swans		57	G5
King's Bromley Staffs		115	J8
Kingsburgh Highld		258	F5
Kingsbury Gt Lon		51	G1
Kingsbury Warwks		99	G4
Kingsbury Episcopi Somset		31	G6
King's Caple Herefs		63	H2
Kingsclere Hants		48	D7
King's Cliffe Nhants		101	M4
Kings Clipstone Notts		134	C6
Kingscote Gloucs		64	B7
Kingscott Devon		27	K7
King's Coughton Warwks		82	C3
Kingscross N Ayrs		195	G5
Kingsdon Somset		31	H5
Kingsdown Kent		41	L5
Kingsdown Swindn		47	H1
Kingsdown Wilts		46	A5
Kingsdown Crematorium Swindn		47	H1
Kingseat Abers		257	G7
Kingseat Fife		210	F1
Kingsey Bucks		67	H6
Kingsfold W Susx		37	J4
Kingsford C Aber		245	J2
Kingsford E Ayrs		196	E2
Kingsford Worcs		97	J7
Kingsgate Kent		41	L1
Kings Green Gloucs		81	H8
Kingshall Street Suffk		89	J3
Kingsheanton Devon		27	K3
King's Heath Birm		98	D7
Kings Hill Kent		39	H2
King's Hill Wsall		98	C4
Kings House Hotel Highld		229	L4
Kingshouse Hotel Stirlg		219	J3
Kingshurst Solhll		98	F5
Kingside Hill Cumb		177	G8
Kingskerswell Devon		8	C1
Kingskettle Fife		222	E6
Kingsland Dorset		15	K3
Kingsland Herefs		80	B3
Kingsland IoA		124	D3
Kings Langley Herts		68	D6
Kingsley Ches W		130	A5
Kingsley Hants		36	B3
Kingsley Staffs		115	G2
Kingsley Green W Susx		36	D5
Kingsley Park Nhants		84	E3

Kingslow Shrops	97	H4
King's Lynn Norfk	120	D7
Kings Meaburn Cumb	166	E6
Kingsmead Hants	35	J8
King's Mills Guern	9	i3
King's Moss St Hel	139	G7
Kingsmuir Angus	234	D5
Kings Muir Border	200	B5
Kingsmuir Fife	223	J5
Kings Newnham Warwks	99	M7
King's Newton Derbys	116	C6
Kingsnorth Kent	40	C7
King's Norton Birm	98	D7
King's Norton Leics	100	F3
Kings Nympton Devon	28	B7
King's Pyon Herefs	80	B5
Kings Ripton Cambs	102	F8
King's Somborne Hants	34	D4
King's Stag Dorset	32	B8
King's Stanley Gloucs	64	A6
King's Sutton Nhants	83	L8
Kingstanding Birm	98	D4
Kingsteignton Devon	13	K8
King Sterndale Derbys	132	B5
Kingsthorne Herefs	63	G1
Kingsthorpe Nhants	84	E3
Kingston Cambs	87	G4
Kingston Cnwll	11	L7
Kingston Devon	7	J5
Kingston Devon	14	C5
Kingston Dorset	16	E1
Kingston Dorset	17	J6
Kingston E Loth	212	C3
Kingston Hants	18	A3
Kingston IoW	19	H7
Kingston Kent	41	G5
Kingston W Susx	21	J6
Kingston Bagpuize Oxon	66	B7
Kingston Blount Oxon	67	H7
Kingston Deverill Wilts	32	D3
Kingstone Herefs	80	A8
Kingstone Somset	30	E8
Kingstone Staffs	115	H5
Kingstone Winslow Oxon	47	K2
Kingston Lisle Oxon	47	L2
Kingston near Lewes E Susx	22	F5
Kingston on Soar Notts	116	E6
Kingston on Spey Moray	267	G3
Kingston Russell Dorset	16	A4
Kingston St Mary Somset	30	B5
Kingston Seymour N Som	44	E5
Kingston Stert Oxon	67	H7
Kingston upon Hull C KuH	144	D2
Kingston upon Thames Gt Lon	50	F5
Kingston upon Thames Crematorium Gt Lon	51	G5
Kingstown Cumb	177	L7
King's Walden Herts	68	F2
Kingswear Devon	8	C4
Kingswells C Aber	245	J2
Kings Weston Bristl	45	G3
Kingswinford Dudley	97	K5
Kingswood Bucks	67	G3
Kingswood Gloucs	63	L8
Kingswood Kent	39	L3
Kingswood Powys	94	F3
Kingswood S Glos	45	J4
Kingswood Somset	29	K3
Kingswood Surrey	51	H7
Kingswood Warwks	82	E1
Kingswood Brook Warwks	82	E1
Kingswood Common Herefs	79	K4
Kingswood Common Staffs	97	J3
Kings Worthy Hants	35	G4
Kingthorpe Lincs	136	B4
Kington Herefs	79	K4
Kington S Glos	45	J1
Kington Worcs	82	A4
Kington Langley Wilts	46	D3
Kington Magna Dorset	32	C6
Kington St Michael Wilts	46	C3
Kingussie Highld	241	K3
Kingweston Somset	31	H5
Kinharrachie Abers	257	G5
Kinharvie D & G	176	B5
Kinkell Bridge P & K	221	G4
Kinknockie Abers	257	J3
Kinleith C Edin	211	G5
Kinlet Shrops	97	G7
Kinloch Highld	246	E8
Kinloch Highld	271	K1
Kinloch Highld	277	J5
Kinloch P & K	233	H6
Kinlochard Stirlg	219	G6
Kinlochbervie Highld	276	C5
Kinlocheil Highld	238	F7
Kinlochewe Highld	261	G7
Kinloch Hourn Highld	238	F2
Kinlochlaggan Highld	240	F5
Kinlochleven Highld	229	K3
Kinlochmoidart Highld	237	K6
Kinlochnanuagh Highld	237	L4
Kinloch Rannoch P & K	231	J4
Kinloss Moray	265	H7
Kinmel Bay Conwy	127	K4
Kinmuck Abers	256	E7
Kinmundy Abers	256	F8
Kinnabus Ag & B	204	D7
Kinnadie Abers	257	H3
Kinnaird P & K	232	E4
Kinneff Abers	245	J8
Kinnelhead D & G	186	F6
Kinnell Angus	234	F5
Kinnerley Shrops	112	E7
Kinnersley Herefs	79	L5
Kinnersley Worcs	81	K6
Kinnerton Powys	79	J3
Kinnerton Shrops	95	J4
Kinnerton Green Flints	129	H7
Kinnesswood P & K	222	B6
Kinninvie Dur	168	D6
Kinnordy Angus	234	B4
Kinoulton Notts	117	H5
Kinross P & K	221	K6
Kinrossie P & K	222	C1
Kinsbourne Green Herts	68	E4
Kinsey Heath Ches E	113	L3
Kinsham Herefs	79	L2
Kinsham Worcs	81	L8
Kinsley Wakefd	142	C5
Kinson Bmouth	17	L3
Kintbury W Berk	48	A5
Kintessack Moray	264	F7
Kintillo P & K	221	L4
Kinton Herefs	95	K8
Kinton Shrops	112	E7
Kintore Abers	256	E8
Kintour Ag & B	205	G6
Kintra Ag & B	204	D6
Kintra Ag & B	226	C7
Kintraw Ag & B	216	C6
Kinveachy Highld	253	G7
Kinver Staffs	97	J6
Kiplin N York	160	C3
Kippax Leeds	142	C2
Kippen Stirlg	219	L8
Kippford D & G	175	L4
Kipping's Cross Kent	39	G5
Kirbister Ork	275	c5
Kirby Bedon Norfk	106	F2
Kirby Bellars Leics	117	J7
Kirby Cane Norfk	107	H5
Kirby Corner Covtry	99	J8
Kirby Cross Essex	73	J3
Kirby Fields Leics	100	B3
Kirby Grindalythe N York	152	D2
Kirby Hill N York	150	E2
Kirby Hill N York	159	L2
Kirby Knowle N York	161	G5
Kirby-le-Soken Essex	73	J3
Kirby Misperton N York	162	D6
Kirby Muxloe Leics	100	B3
Kirby Sigston N York	160	F4
Kirby Underdale E R Yk	152	B4
Kirby Wiske N York	160	E5
Kirdford W Susx	36	F5
Kirk Highld	280	C4
Kirkabister Shet	281	e7
Kirkandrews D & G	174	F5
Kirkandrews upon Eden Cumb	177	K7
Kirkbampton Cumb	177	J7
Kirkbean D & G	176	C7
Kirk Bramwith Donc	143	G5
Kirkbride Cumb	177	H7
Kirkbridge N York	160	C4
Kirkbuddo Angus	234	D6
Kirkburn Border	200	C5
Kirkburn E R Yk	152	F5
Kirkburton Kirk	141	K5
Kirkby Knows	138	E7
Kirkby Lincs	135	L1
Kirkby N York	161	H2
Kirkby Fleetham N York	160	D4
Kirkby Green Lincs	136	A8
Kirkby-in-Ashfield Notts	133	K8
Kirkby-in-Furness Cumb	156	B6
Kirkby la Thorpe Lincs	118	E2
Kirkby Lonsdale Cumb	157	K7
Kirkby Malham N York	148	F4
Kirkby Mallory Leics	99	M3
Kirkby Malzeard N York	160	C7
Kirkby Mills N York	162	C5
Kirkbymoorside N York	162	B5
Kirkby on Bain Lincs	136	D7
Kirkby Overblow N York	150	D6
Kirkby Stephen Cumb	158	D1
Kirkby Thore Cumb	166	E5
Kirkby Underwood Lincs	118	E6
Kirkby Wharf N York	151	H7
Kirkby Woodhouse Notts	116	E1
Kirkcaldy Fife	211	J1
Kirkcaldy Crematorium Fife	222	D8
Kirkcambeck Cumb	178	C5
Kirkchrist D & G	175	G4
Kirkcolm D & G	172	C1
Kirkconnel D & G	197	L8
Kirkconnell D & G	176	C5
Kirkcowan D & G	173	J3
Kirkcudbright D & G	175	H5
Kirkdale Lpool	129	H1
Kirk Deighton N York	150	F5
Kirk Ella E R Yk	144	C2
Kirkfieldbank S Lans	198	E4
Kirkgunzeon D & G	175	L2
Kirk Hallam Derbys	116	D3
Kirkham Lancs	138	E1
Kirkham N York	151	M3
Kirkhamgate Wakefd	141	L3
Kirk Hammerton N York	151	G5
Kirkharle Nthumb	180	B2
Kirkhaugh Nthumb	167	G1
Kirkheaton Kirk	141	J4
Kirkheaton Nthumb	180	B3
Kirkhill Highld	250	F3
Kirkhope S Lans	186	E5
Kirkhouse Cumb	178	D7
Kirkhouse Green Donc	143	G5
Kirkibost Highld	247	H5
Kirkinch P & K	233	L6
Kirkinner D & G	174	C4
Kirkintilloch E Duns	209	H4
Kirk Ireton Derbys	115	M2
Kirkland Cumb	164	E7
Kirkland Cumb	166	F4
Kirkland D & G	185	K5
Kirkland D & G	186	F8
Kirkland D & G	197	L8
Kirkland Guards Cumb	165	G3
Kirk Langley Derbys	115	M4
Kirkleatham R & Cl	170	E6
Kirkleatham Crematorium R & Cl	170	E6
Kirklevington S on T	160	F1
Kirkley Suffk	107	L5
Kirklington N York	160	D6
Kirklington Notts	134	D8
Kirklinton Cumb	178	B5
Kirkliston C Edin	210	F4
Kirkmabreck D & G	174	D4
Kirkmaiden D & G	172	E7
Kirk Merrington Dur	169	H4
Kirk Michael IoM	154	d4
Kirkmichael P & K	233	G3
Kirkmichael S Ayrs	183	J1
Kirkmuirhill S Lans	198	C4
Kirknewton Nthumb	202	E7
Kirknewton W Loth	210	F5
Kirkney Abers	255	K5
Kirk of Shotts N Lans	209	M6
Kirkoswald Cumb	166	D3
Kirkoswald S Ayrs	183	G2
Kirkpatrick D & G	186	D8
Kirkpatrick Durham D & G	175	K1
Kirkpatrick-Fleming D & G	177	J5
Kirk Sandall Donc	142	F6
Kirksanton Cumb	155	L6
Kirk Smeaton N York	142	E4
Kirkstall Leeds	150	C8
Kirkstead Lincs	136	C7
Kirkstile Abers	255	L5
Kirkstone Pass Inn Cumb	156	F1
Kirkstyle Highld	280	D2
Kirkthorpe Wakefd	142	B3
Kirkton Abers	256	B6
Kirkton D & G	176	C3
Kirkton Fife	222	F2
Kirkton Highld	248	C6
Kirkton Highld	248	E3
Kirkton P & K	221	G3
Kirkton Manor Border	200	B5
Kirkton of Airlie Angus	233	M5
Kirkton of Auchterhouse Angus	234	A7
Kirkton of Barevan Highld	252	F2
Kirkton of Collace P & K	222	C1
Kirkton of Glenbuchat Abers	255	H8
Kirkton of Kingoldrum Angus	234	A4
Kirkton of Logie Buchan Abers	257	H6
Kirkton of Maryculter Abers	245	J4
Kirkton of Menmuir Angus	234	E3
Kirkton of Monikie Angus	234	D7
Kirkton of Rayne Abers	256	C5
Kirkton of Skene Abers	245	H2
Kirkton of Tealing Angus	234	B7
Kirkton of Tough Abers	244	D1
Kirktown Abers	269	J3
Kirktown Abers	269	K6
Kirktown of Alvah Abers	268	B4
Kirktown of Bourtie Abers	256	E6
Kirktown of Fetteresso Abers	245	J6
Kirktown of Mortlach Moray	255	G4
Kirktown of Slains Abers	257	J6
Kirkurd Border	199	K4
Kirkwall Ork	275	c4
Kirkwhelpington Nthumb	180	B2
Kirk Yetholm Border	202	C7
Kirmington N Linc	144	E5
Kirmond le Mire Lincs	136	C1
Kirn Ag & B	207	K3
Kirriemuir Angus	234	B4
Kirstead Green Norfk	106	F4
Kirtlebridge D & G	177	H4
Kirtling Cambs	88	D4
Kirtling Green Cambs	88	D4
Kirtlington Oxon	66	D3
Kirtomy Highld	278	C3
Kirton Lincs	119	J4
Kirton Notts	134	D6
Kirton Suffk	91	G7
Kirton End Lincs	119	J3
Kirtonhill W Duns	208	C4
Kirton Holme Lincs	119	J3
Kirton in Lindsey N Linc	144	A8
Kirwaugh D & G	173	K4
Kishorn Highld	248	D4
Kislingbury Nhants	84	D3
Kitebrook Warwks	65	K1
Kite Green Warwks	82	E2
Kites Hardwick Warwks	83	L2
Kitleigh Cnwll	11	J3
Kitt Green Wigan	139	H6
Kittisford Somset	29	K6
Kittle Swans	57	G7
Kitt's Green Birm	98	F6
Kittybrewster C Aber	245	K2
Kitwood Hants	35	K4
Kivernoll Herefs	62	F1
Kiveton Park Rothm	133	K3
Knaith Lincs	135	G3
Knaith Park Lincs	135	G3
Knap Corner Dorset	32	D6
Knaphill Surrey	50	B7
Knapp Somset	30	D5
Knapp Hill Hants	34	E6
Knapthorpe Notts	134	E7
Knapton C York	151	J5
Knapton N York	162	F7
Knapton Norfk	122	F5
Knapton Green Herefs	80	B5
Knapwell Cambs	87	G3
Knaresborough N York	150	E4
Knarsdale Nthumb	178	F8
Knaven Abers	257	G3
Knayton N York	160	F5
Knebworth Herts	69	H3
Knedlington E R Yk	143	J2
Kneesall Notts	134	D6
Kneeton Notts	117	J2
Knelston Swans	56	E7
Knenhall Staffs	114	E4
Knettishall Suffk	105	K7
Knightacott Devon	28	B3
Knightcote Warwks	83	J4
Knightley Staffs	114	C6
Knightley Dale Staffs	114	C6
Knighton C Leic	100	D3
Knighton Devon	7	G5
Knighton Dorset	31	K8
Knighton Poole	17	L3
Knighton Powys	79	K1
Knighton Somset	30	B2
Knighton Staffs	114	A3
Knighton Staffs	114	B6
Knighton Wilts	47	L4
Knighton on Teme Worcs	80	E1
Knightsbridge Gloucs	64	C2
Knightsmill Cnwll	10	F6
Knightwick Worcs	81	G4
Knill Herefs	79	K3
Knipoch Ag & B	216	C3
Knipton Leics	117	L5
Knitsley Dur	168	E1
Kniveton Derbys	115	K2
Knock Cumb	166	F5
Knock Highld	247	L6
Knock Moray	267	L5
Knock W Isls	282	g3
Knockally Highld	274	F2
Knockan Highld	271	H6
Knockando Moray	254	D3
Knockbain Highld	250	F3
Knockbain Highld	263	H8
Knock Castle N Ayrs	207	K6

Knockdee Highld......279 L4
Knockdow Ag & B......207 J5
Knockdown Wilts......46 B1
Knockeen S Ayrs......183 H4
Knockenkelly N Ayrs......195 G5
Knockentiber E Ayrs......196 D3
Knockhall Kent......52 C4
Knockholt Kent......51 M7
Knockholt Pound Kent......52 A7
Knockin Shrops......112 E7
Knockinlaw E Ayrs......196 E3
Knockmill Kent......52 C6
Knockrome Ag & B......205 J2
Knocksharry IoM......154 c5
Knocksheen D & G......184 F6
Knockvennie Smithy D & G...185 J8
Knodishall Suffk......91 K3
Knodishall Common Suffk....91 K3
Knole Somset......31 G6
Knole Park S Glos......45 H2
Knolls Green Ches E......130 F4
Knolton Wrexhm......112 F4
Knook Wilts......32 F3
Knossington Leics......101 H2
Knott End-on-Sea Lancs......147 G6
Knotting Bed......85 K3
Knotting Green Bed......85 K3
Knottingley Wakefd......142 D3
Knotty Ash Lpool......129 J1
Knotty Green Bucks......68 B8
Knowbury Shrops......96 D8
Knowe D & G......183 H8
Knowehead D & G......184 F5
Knoweside S Ayrs......195 L8
Knowle Bristl......45 J5
Knowle Devon......13 H2
Knowle Devon......14 B1
Knowle Devon......14 B6
Knowle Devon......27 J3
Knowle Shrops......96 D8
Knowle Solhll......98 F8
Knowle Somset......29 H2
Knowle Cross Devon......14 B3
Knowlefield Cumb......177 L7
Knowle Green Lancs......148 A8
Knowle Hill Surrey......50 C5
Knowle St Giles Somset......30 E8
Knowle Village Hants......19 J2
Knowle Wood Calder......140 D3
Knowl Green Essex......88 F7
Knowl Hill W & M......49 K3
Knowlton Dorset......17 K1
Knowlton Kent......41 J4
Knowsley Knows......138 E8
Knowstone Devon......28 E6
Knox N York......150 C4
Knox Bridge Kent......39 K5
Knucklas Powys......95 G8
Knuston Nhants......85 H2
Knutsford Ches E......130 E4
Knutton Staffs......114 C2
Krumlin Calder......141 G4
Kuggar Cnwll......3 J7
Kyleakin Highld......248 B6
Kyle of Lochalsh Highld......248 B6
Kylerhea Highld......248 C7
Kylesku Highld......271 H1
Kylesmorar Highld......238 C5
Kyles Scalpay W Isls......282 f6
Kylestrome Highld......271 H1
Kynaston Herefs......80 E8
Kynaston Shrops......112 E7
Kynnersley Wrekin......113 L8
Kyre Green Worcs......80 E3
Kyre Park Worcs......80 E3
Kyrewood Worcs......80 E2
Kyrle Somset......29 J6

L

La Bellieuse Guern......9 j3
Lacasaigh W Isls......282 f4
Lacasdal W Isls......282 g3
Laceby NE Lin......145 G6
Lacey Green Bucks......67 K7
Lach Dennis Ches W......130 D5
Lackenby R & Cl......170 D6
Lackford Suffk......88 F1
Lackford Green Suffk......88 F1
Lacock Wilts......46 C5
Ladbroke Warwks......83 K3
Ladderedge Staffs......114 F1
Laddingford Kent......39 H4
Lade Bank Lincs......119 L1
Ladock Cnwll......4 E5
Lady Ork......275 e2

Ladybank Fife......222 E5
Ladycross Cnwll......11 L5
Ladygill S Lans......198 F7
Lady Hall Cumb......156 B5
Ladykirk Border......202 D3
Ladyridge Herefs......63 H1
Lady's Green Suffk......88 E3
Ladywood Birm......98 D6
Ladywood Worcs......81 K3
La Fontenelle Guern......9 k1
La Fosse Guern......9 j4
Lag D & G......185 L5
Laga Highld......237 J8
Lagavulin Ag & B......204 F7
Lagg N Ayrs......193 K4
Laggan Highld......240 A4
Laggan Highld......241 G5
Lagganlia Highld......241 M3
La Greve Guern......9 k2
La Grève de Lecq Jersey......9 b1
La Hougue Bie Jersey......9 e3
La Houguette Guern......9 h3
Laid Highld......277 G4
Laide Highld......260 E2
Laig Highld......236 F3
Laigh Clunch E Ayrs......196 F2
Laigh Fenwick E Ayrs......196 F3
Laigh Glenmuir E Ayrs......197 J7
Laighstonehall S Lans......209 J8
Laindon Essex......52 E1
Lairg Highld......272 E6
Laisterdyke C Brad......141 J1
Laithes Cumb......166 B4
Lake Devon......12 C5
Lake Devon......27 K4
Lake IoW......19 K7
Lake Wilts......33 K3
Lakenheath Suffk......104 E6
Laker's Green Surrey......36 F4
Lakesend Norfk......103 L4
Lakeside Cumb......156 E5
Laleham Surrey......50 D5
Laleston Brdgnd......42 C5
Lamanva Cnwll......3 J5
Lamarsh Essex......89 H8
Lamas Norfk......122 E7
Lambden Border......202 A4
Lamberhurst Kent......39 H6
Lamberhurst Down Kent......39 G6
Lamberton Border......213 L7
Lambeth Gt Lon......51 J3
Lambeth Crematorium Gt Lon...51 H4
Lambfair Green Suffk......88 E4
Lambley Notts......117 H2
Lambley Nthumb......178 F7
Lambourn W Berk......47 L3
Lambourne End Essex......70 C8
Lambourn Woodlands W Berk...47 L4
Lamb Roe Lancs......148 C8
Lambs Green W Susx......37 K3
Lambston Pembks......54 E3
Lamellion Cnwll......6 A2
Lamerton Devon......12 B7
Lamesley Gatesd......181 G7
Lamington S Lans......199 G7
Lamlash N Ayrs......195 G5
Lamonby Cumb......165 L3
Lamorick Cnwll......5 H2
Lamorna Cnwll......2 C6
Lamorran Cnwll......4 E6
Lampen Cnwll......5 L2
Lampeter Cerdgn......77 G5
Lampeter Velfrey Pembks......55 K4
Lamphey Pembks......55 G6
Lamplugh Cumb......164 E6
Lamport Nhants......101 G8
Lamyatt Somset......31 L4
Lana Devon......11 K1
Lana Devon......11 L3
Lanark S Lans......198 E4
Lancaster Lancs......147 J3
Lancaster & Morecambe
  Crematorium Lancs......147 J3
Lancaut Gloucs......63 G7
Lanchester Dur......168 F1
Lancing W Susx......21 L6
L'Ancresse Guern......9 k1
Landbeach Cambs......87 K2
Landcross Devon......27 H6
Landerberry Abers......245 G3
Landford Wilts......34 B7
Land-hallow Highld......275 H4
Landican Crematorium Wirral...129 G3
Landimore Swans......56 E6
Landkey Devon......27 L4
Landore Swans......57 J5
Landrake Cnwll......6 D3
Landscove Devon......7 M2
Land's End Cnwll......2 A6

Landshipping Pembks......55 G4
Landue Cnwll......11 L6
Landulph Cnwll......6 E3
Landwade Suffk......88 C2
Lane Cnwll......4 D3
Laneast Cnwll......11 J6
Lane Bottom Lancs......140 C1
Lane End Bucks......49 K1
Lane End Cnwll......5 H1
Lane End Hants......35 H5
Lane End Kent......52 C4
Lane End Lancs......148 F6
Lane End Warrtn......130 D2
Lane End Wilts......32 D2
Lane Ends Derbys......115 L4
Lane Ends Lancs......140 B2
Lane Ends N York......149 H7
Lane Green Staffs......97 K3
Laneham Notts......134 F4
Lanehead Dur......167 J2
Lane Head Dur......168 E8
Lanehead Nthumb......179 H2
Lane Head Wigan......139 J8
Lane Head Wsall......98 B3
Lane Heads Lancs......147 H7
Lanercost Cumb......178 D6
Laneshaw Bridge Lancs......149 G7
Lane Side Lancs......140 B3
Langaford Devon......12 A3
Langal Highld......237 K6
Langaller Somset......30 C5
Langar Notts......117 J4
Langbank Rens......208 C4
Langbar N York......149 K5
Langbaurgh N York......170 D8
Langcliffe N York......148 E3
Langdale End N York......163 G4
Langdon Cnwll......11 K5
Langdon Beck Dur......167 K4
Langdown Hants......19 G2
Langdyke Fife......222 E6
Langenhoe Essex......72 E3
Langford C Beds......86 D7
Langford Devon......14 B2
Langford Essex......71 K5
Langford N Som......44 F6
Langford Notts......135 G7
Langford Oxon......65 K6
Langford Budville Somset......29 K6
Langham Dorset......32 C5
Langham Essex......72 F1
Langham Norfk......121 M3
Langham Rutlnd......101 J1
Langham Suffk......89 K1
Langho Lancs......139 L1
Langholm D & G......177 L2
Langland Swans......57 H7
Langlee Border......201 G6
Langley Ches E......131 J5
Langley Derbys......116 D2
Langley Gloucs......64 E2
Langley Hants......19 G3
Langley Herts......69 G3
Langley Kent......39 K3
Langley Nthumb......179 J6
Langley Oxon......65 L4
Langley Rochdl......140 C6
Langley Slough......50 C3
Langley Somset......29 K5
Langley W Susx......36 B5
Langley Warwks......82 E3
Langley Burrell Wilts......46 D4
Langley Castle Nthumb......179 J6
Langley Common Derbys......115 M4
Langley Green Derbys......115 M4
Langley Green Essex......72 C3
Langley Green Warwks......82 E3
Langley Heath Kent......39 K3
Langley Lower Green Essex...87 J8
Langley Marsh Somset......29 K5
Langley Mill Derbys......116 D2
Langley Moor Dur......169 H3
Langley Park Dur......169 G2
Langley Street Norfk......107 H3
Langley Upper Green Essex...87 J8
Langney E Susx......23 L6
Langold Notts......134 B2
Langore Cnwll......11 K5
Langport Somset......30 F5
Langrick Lincs......119 J2
Langridge BaNES......45 L5
Langridgeford Devon......27 K6
Langrigg Cumb......165 G2
Langrish Hants......35 L6
Langsett Barns......141 K7
Langside P & K......220 D4
Langstone Hants......20 B6
Langstone Newpt......44 D1
Langthorne N York......160 C4

Langthorpe N York......150 E2
Langthwaite N York......159 H2
Langtoft E R Yk......152 F3
Langtoft Lincs......102 C1
Langton Dur......168 F6
Langton Lincs......136 D6
Langton Lincs......137 G5
Langton N York......152 B2
Langton by Wragby Lincs......136 C4
Langton Green Kent......38 C5
Langton Green Suffk......106 C8
Langton Herring Dorset......16 B6
Langton Long Blandford
  Dorset......17 H2
Langton Matravers Dorset......17 K6
Langtree Devon......27 H7
Langtree Week Devon......27 H7
Langwathby Cumb......166 D4
Langwell House Highld......274 F1
Langwith Derbys......133 K5
Langwith Junction Derbys......133 K6
Langworth Lincs......135 L4
Lanivet Cnwll......5 H3
Lanjeth Cnwll......5 G4
Lank Cnwll......10 F7
Lanlivery Cnwll......5 J3
Lanner Cnwll......3 H3
Lanoy Cnwll......11 K7
Lanreath Cnwll......5 L3
Lansallos Cnwll......5 K4
Lanteglos Cnwll......10 C8
Lanteglos Highway Cnwll......5 K4
Lanton Border......189 G2
Lanton Nthumb......202 E6
La Passee Guern......9 j2
Lapford Devon......13 G1
Laphroaig Ag & B......204 F7
Lapley Staffs......97 K1
Lapworth Warwks......82 E1
Larachbeg Highld......227 K3
Larbert Falk......209 M3
Larbreck Lancs......147 H7
Largie Abers......256 A5
Largiemore Ag & B......206 E2
Largoward Fife......223 H5
Largs N Ayrs......207 K7
Largybeg N Ayrs......195 G6
Largymore N Ayrs......195 G6
Larkbeare Devon......14 C3
Larkfield Inver......207 L4
Larkfield Kent......52 F7
Larkhall S Lans......198 C3
Larkhill Wilts......33 K2
Larling Norfk......105 K5
La Rocque Jersey......9 f4
La Rousaillerie Guern......9 j2
Lartington Dur......168 C7
Lasborough Gloucs......64 B8
Lasham Hants......35 K2
Lashbrook Devon......12 A1
Lashbrook Devon......12 B2
Lashenden Kent......39 L5
Lask Edge Staffs......131 H8
Lasswade Mdloth......211 J6
Lastingham N York......162 C4
Latcham Somset......31 G2
Latchford Herts......69 K3
Latchford Oxon......67 G6
Latchford Warrtn......130 C2
Latchingdon Essex......72 C7
Latchley Cnwll......12 A7
Lately Common Warrtn......139 K8
Lathbury M Keyn......85 G6
Latheron Highld......275 G2
Latheronwheel Highld......275 G2
Lathones Fife......223 H5
Latimer Bucks......68 C7
Latteridge S Glos......45 K2
Lattiford Somset......32 B5
Latton Wilts......65 G7
Lauder Border......201 H4
Laugharne Carmth......56 B3
Laughterton Lincs......135 G4
Laughton E Susx......23 H4
Laughton Leics......100 E5
Laughton Lincs......118 E5
Laughton Lincs......143 L8
Laughton-en-le-Morthen
  Rothm......133 K2
Launcells Cnwll......11 J2
Launcells Cross Cnwll......11 K2
Launceston Cnwll......11 L5
Launton Oxon......66 F3
Laurencekirk Abers......235 H1
Laurieston D & G......175 G2
Laurieston Falk......210 B3
Lavendon M Keyn......85 H4
Lavenham Suffk......89 J5

Lavernock V Glam 43 J8
Laversdale Cumb 178 B6
Laverstock Wilts 33 L5
Laverstoke Hants 35 G1
Laverton Gloucs 82 C8
Laverton N York 160 B7
Laverton Somset 45 M8
La Villette Guern 9 j3
Lavister Wrexhm 129 J8
Law S Lans 209 L8
Lawers P & K 231 J7
Lawford Essex 73 G1
Lawford Somset 29 L4
Law Hill S Lans 209 L8
Lawhitton Cnwll 11 L6
Lawkland N York 148 D3
Lawkland Green N York 148 D3
Lawley Wrekin 96 F2
Lawnhead Staffs 114 C6
Lawns Wood Crematorium
   Leeds 150 C8
Lawrenny Pembks 55 G5
Lawshall Suffk 89 H4
Lawshall Green Suffk 89 H4
Lawton Herefs 80 B3
Laxay W Isls 282 f4
Laxdale W Isls 282 g3
Laxey IoM 154 f5
Laxfield Suffk 91 G1
Laxford Bridge Highld 276 C7
Laxo Shet 281 e5
Laxton E R Yk 143 K3
Laxton Nhants 101 L4
Laxton Notts 134 C6
Laycock C Brad 149 J7
Layer Breton Essex 72 D3
Layer-de-la-Haye Essex 72 D3
Layer Marney Essex 72 D4
Layham Suffk 89 L7
Layland's Green W Berk 48 A5
Laymore Dorset 15 J2
Layter's Green Bucks 50 C1
Laytham E R Yk 152 A7
Laythes Cumb 177 H7
Lazenby R & Cl 170 D6
Lazonby Cumb 166 D3
Lea Derbys 132 F8
Lea Herefs 63 K3
Lea Lincs 135 G2
Lea Shrops 95 J5
Lea Shrops 95 K2
Lea Wilts 46 D2
Leachkin Highld 251 H3
Leadburn Border 200 B2
Leadenham Lincs 118 B1
Leaden Roding Essex 70 E4
Leadgate Dur 180 D8
Leadgate Nthumb 180 D8
Leadhills S Lans 186 C3
Leadingcross Green Kent 39 M3
Leadmill Derbys 132 E4
Leafield Oxon 65 L4
Leagrave Luton 68 D2
Leahead Ches W 130 D6
Lea Heath Staffs 115 G6
Leake N York 160 F4
Leake Common Side Lincs 119 L1
Lealholm N York 162 D1
Lealholm Side N York 162 D1
Lealt Highld 259 H4
Leam Derbys 132 E4
Lea Marston Warwks 99 G5
Leamington Hastings Warwks 83 K2
Leamington Spa Warwks 83 H2
Leamside Dur 169 J1
Leap Cross E Susx 23 K5
Leasgill Cumb 157 H6
Leasingham Lincs 118 E2
Leasingthorne Dur 169 H4
Leatherhead Surrey 50 F7
Leathley N York 150 B6
Leaton Shrops 113 G7
Leaton Wrekin 96 E1
Lea Town Lancs 138 F2
Leaveland Kent 40 C4
Leavenheath Suffk 89 J7
Leavening N York 152 B3
Leaves Green Gt Lon 51 L6
Lea Yeat Cumb 158 D5
Lebberston N York 163 K6
Le Bigard Guern 9 i4
Le Bourg Guern 9 j4
Le Bourg Jersey 9 f4
Lechlade on Thames Gloucs 65 J7
Lecht Gruinart Ag & B 204 D3
Leck Lancs 157 K7
Leckbuie P & K 231 K7
Leckford Hants 34 E3
Leckhampstead Bucks 84 D7

Leckhampstead W Berk 48 B4
Leckhampstead Thicket
   W Berk 48 B4
Leckhampton Gloucs 64 D3
Leckmelm Highld 261 K2
Leckwith V Glam 43 J6
Leconfield E R Yk 152 F7
Ledaig Ag & B 228 E7
Ledburn Bucks 67 L3
Ledbury Herefs 81 G7
Leddington Gloucs 80 F8
Ledgemoor Herefs 79 M5
Ledicot Herefs 80 A3
Ledmore Junction Highld 271 H5
Ledsham Ches W 129 H5
Ledsham Leeds 142 C2
Ledston Leeds 142 C2
Ledstone Devon 7 L5
Ledston Luck Leeds 142 C2
Ledwell Oxon 66 B2
Lee Devon 27 H2
Lee Gt Lon 51 K4
Lee Hants 34 D7
Lee Shrops 112 F5
Leebotwood Shrops 96 B4
Lee Brockhurst Shrops 113 J6
Leece Cumb 146 E2
Lee Chapel Essex 52 E2
Lee Clump Bucks 67 M6
Lee Common Bucks 67 M6
Leeds Kent 39 K3
Leeds Leeds 141 L1
Leedstown Cnwll 2 F4
Lee Green Ches E 130 C7
Leek Staffs 131 K8
Leek Wootton Warwks 83 G2
Lee Mill Devon 7 H4
Leeming C Brad 141 G1
Leeming N York 160 D5
Leeming Bar N York 160 D4
Lee Moor Devon 7 H3
Lee-on-the-Solent Hants 19 J3
Lees C Brad 149 J8
Lees Derbys 115 L4
Lees Oldham 140 E6
Lees Green Derbys 115 L4
Leesthorpe Leics 101 H1
Leeswood Flints 129 G7
Leetown P & K 222 C3
Leftwich Ches W 130 C5
Legar Powys 61 K4
Legbourne Lincs 137 G3
Legburthwaite Cumb 165 K6
Legerwood Border 201 J4
Le Gron Guern 9 i3
Legsby Lincs 136 B3
Le Haguais Jersey 9 e4
Le Hocq Jersey 9 e4
Leicester C Leic 100 D3
Leicester Forest East Leics 100 B3
Leigh Devon 28 C8
Leigh Dorset 16 B1
Leigh Gloucs 64 C2
Leigh Kent 38 E4
Leigh Shrops 95 H3
Leigh Surrey 37 K2
Leigh Wigan 139 K7
Leigh Wilts 64 F8
Leigh Worcs 81 H4
Leigh Beck Essex 53 H2
Leigh Delamere Wilts 46 C3
Leigh Green Kent 40 A8
Leigh Knoweglass S Lans 197 J1
Leighland Chapel Somset 29 J4
Leigh-on-Sea Sthend 53 H2
Leigh Park Dorset 17 K3
Leigh Park Hants 20 B5
Leigh Sinton Worcs 81 H5
Leighswood Wsall 98 D3
Leighterton Gloucs 46 B1
Leighton N York 159 L6
Leighton Powys 94 F2
Leighton Shrops 96 E2
Leighton Somset 32 B2
Leighton Bromswold Cambs 102 C8
Leighton Buzzard C Beds 68 A2
Leigh upon Mendip Somset 31 M2
Leigh Woods N Som 45 H4
Leinthall Earls Herefs 80 B2
Leinthall Starkes Herefs 80 A1
Leintwardine Herefs 95 K8
Leire Leics 100 B5
Leiston Suffk 91 K3
Leith C Edin 211 J4
Leitholm Border 202 B4
Lelant Cnwll 2 E4
Lelley E R Yk 145 G1
Lem Hill Worcs 97 G8
Lempitlaw Border 202 B6

Lemreway W Isls 282 g5
Lemsford Herts 69 G4
Lenchwick Worcs 82 B6
Lendalfoot S Ayrs 182 E5
Lendrick Stirlg 219 J6
Lendrum Terrace Abers 257 L3
Lenham Kent 40 A5
Lenham Heath Kent 40 B5
Lenie Highld 250 F6
Lennel Border 202 C5
Lennox Plunton D & G 174 F4
Lennoxtown E Duns 209 G3
Lent Bucks 50 A3
Lenton C Nott 116 F4
Lenton Lincs 118 D5
Lenwade Norfk 122 B7
Lenzie E Duns 209 H4
Leochel-Cushnie Abers 244 C2
Leomansley Staffs 98 E2
Leominster Herefs 80 C3
Leonard Stanley Gloucs 64 A6
Leoville Jersey 9 b1
Lepe Hants 19 G4
Lephin Highld 258 B6
Leppington N York 152 A4
Lepton Kirk 141 K5
Lerags Ag & B 216 C2
L'Erée Guern 9 h3
Lerryn Cnwll 5 K3
Lerwick Shet 281 e6
Les Arquêts Guern 9 h3
Lesbury Nthumb 191 J4
Les Hubits Guern 9 k3
Leslie Abers 255 M6
Leslie Fife 222 D6
Les Lohiers Guern 9 i3
Lesmahagow S Lans 198 D5
Les Murchez Guern 9 i4
Lesnewth Cnwll 11 G4
Les Nicolles Guern 9 j4
Les Quartiers Guern 9 j2
Les Quennevais Jersey 9 b3
Les Sages Guern 9 i3
Lessingham Norfk 123 H6
Lessonhall Cumb 165 H1
Lestowder Cnwll 3 K6
Les Villets Guern 9 i4
Leswalt D & G 172 C2
L'Etacq Jersey 9 a2
Letchmore Heath Herts 68 F7
Letchworth Garden City Herts 86 E8
Letcombe Bassett Oxon 48 A2
Letcombe Regis Oxon 48 A2
Letham Angus 234 E5
Letham Border 189 J4
Letham Falk 210 B2
Letham Fife 222 E4
Letham Grange Angus 235 G6
Lethendy P & K 233 H7
Lethenty Abers 255 M7
Lethenty Abers 256 E4
Letheringham Suffk 91 G4
Letheringsett Norfk 122 B4
Lettaford Devon 13 G6
Letterewe Highld 260 F5
Letterfearn Highld 248 D7
Letterfinlay Lodge Hotel
   Highld 239 L5
Lettermorar Highld 237 L3
Letters Highld 261 K2
Lettershaw S Lans 186 D2
Letterston Pembks 74 F6
Lettoch Highld 253 K7
Lettoch Highld 254 B5
Letton Herefs 79 L1
Letton Herefs 79 L6
Lett's Green Kent 51 M7
Letty Green Herts 69 H5
Letwell Rothm 133 L2
Leuchars Fife 223 H3
Leumrabhagh W Isls 282 g5
Leurbost W Isls 282 g4
Levalsa Meor Cnwll 5 G5
Levedale Staffs 114 D8
Level's Green Essex 70 C2
Leven E R Yk 153 H6
Leven Fife 222 F7
Levens Cumb 157 G5
Levens Green Herts 69 K3
Levenshulme Manch 131 G1
Levenwick Shet 281 d8
Leverburgh W Isls 282 d6
Leverington Cambs 103 J1
Leverstock Green Herts 68 D5
Leverton Lincs 119 L2
Le Villocq Guern 9 j2
Levington Suffk 90 F7
Levisham N York 162 E4
Lew Oxon 65 L6

Lewannick Cnwll 11 K6
Lewdown Devon 12 B5
Lewes E Susx 22 F5
Leweston Pembks 54 F2
Lewisham Gt Lon 51 K4
Lewisham Crematorium
   Gt Lon 51 L4
Lewiston Highld 250 F6
Lewistown Brdgnd 42 E4
Lewis Wych Herefs 79 L4
Lewknor Oxon 67 H7
Leworthy Devon 11 L2
Leworthy Devon 28 B3
Lewson Street Kent 40 C3
Lewth Lancs 147 J8
Lewtrenchard Devon 12 B5
Lexden Essex 72 D2
Lexworthy Somset 30 C4
Ley Cnwll 5 K2
Leybourne Kent 52 E7
Leyburn N York 159 K4
Leycett Staffs 114 B2
Leygreen Herts 68 F2
Ley Hill Bucks 68 C6
Leyland Lancs 139 H3
Leyland Green St Hel 139 H7
Leylodge Abers 245 G1
Leys Abers 269 J5
Leys P & K 233 K7
Leysdown-on-Sea Kent 53 M5
Leysmill Angus 234 F6
Leys of Cossans Angus 234 B5
Leysters Herefs 80 D2
Leyton Gt Lon 51 K2
Leytonstone Gt Lon 51 K2
Lezant Cnwll 11 L6
Lezerea Cnwll 3 H4
Lhanbryde Moray 266 F4
Libanus Powys 60 F2
Libberton S Lans 199 G4
Libbery Worcs 81 L4
Liberton C Edin 211 J5
Lichfield Staffs 98 E2
Lichfield & District
   Crematorium Staffs 98 F1
Lickey Worcs 98 C8
Lickey End Worcs 81 M1
Lickey Rock Worcs 98 B8
Lickfold W Susx 36 D5
Liddaton Green Devon 12 B6
Liddesdale Highld 228 B3
Liddington Swindn 47 J3
Lidgate Derbys 132 F4
Lidgate Suffk 88 E4
Lidget Donc 143 G7
Lidgett Notts 134 C6
Lidham Hill E Susx 24 F4
Lidlington C Beds 85 K7
Lidsey W Susx 20 F6
Lidsing Kent 53 G6
Liff Angus 222 E1
Lifford Birm 98 D7
Lifton Devon 11 M5
Liftondown Devon 11 M5
Lighthorne Warwks 83 H4
Lighthorne Heath Warwks 83 H4
Lightwater Surrey 50 B6
Lightwood C Stke 114 E3
Lightwood Green Ches E 113 L3
Lightwood Green Wrexhm 112 F3
Lilbourne Nhants 100 C8
Lilburn Tower Nthumb 190 E1
Lilleshall Wrekin 114 A8
Lilley Herts 68 E2
Lilley W Berk 48 C3
Lilliesleaf Border 201 H8
Lillingstone Dayrell Bucks 84 D7
Lillingstone Lovell Bucks 84 D7
Lillington Dorset 31 K8
Lilliput Poole 17 K5
Lilstock Somset 29 L2
Lilyhurst Shrops 97 G1
Limbrick Lancs 139 L4
Limbury Luton 68 D2
Limebrook Herefs 79 L2
Limefield Bury 140 B5
Limekilnburn S Lans 197 K1
Limekilns Fife 210 E2
Limerigg Falk 209 M5
Limerstone IoW 19 G7
Limestone Brae Nthumb 167 J3
Lime Street Worcs 64 A1
Limington Somset 31 J6
Limmerhaugh E Ayrs 197 J5
Limpenhoe Norfk 107 H3
Limpley Stoke Wilts 45 M6
Limpsfield Surrey 51 L8
Limpsfield Chart Surrey 51 L8
Linby Notts 116 F1

Linchmere W Susx 36 C5
Lincluden D & G 176 C3
Lincoln Lincs 135 K5
Lincoln Crematorium Lincs ... 135 K5
Lincomb Worcs 81 J2
Lincombe Devon 7 L6
Lincombe Devon 27 J2
Lindale Cumb 156 F6
Lindal in Furness Cumb ... 156 C7
Lindfield W Susx 22 E2
Lindford Hants 36 B4
Lindley Kirk 141 H4
Lindley N York 150 B6
Lindores D & G 222 D4
Lindow End Ches E 130 F4
Lindridge Worcs 80 F2
Lindsell Essex 70 F2
Lindsey Suffk 89 K6
Lindsey Tye Suffk 89 K6
Liney Somset 30 E4
Linford Hants 18 B2
Linford Thurr 52 E3
Lingbob C Brad 149 K8
Lingdale R & Cl 170 F7
Lingen Herefs 79 L2
Lingfield Surrey 38 B4
Lingwood Norfk 107 G2
Liniclate W Isls 283 c9
Linicro Highld 258 F3
Linkend Worcs 64 B1
Linkenholt Hants 48 A7
Linkhill Kent 24 E2
Linkinhorne Cnwll 11 L7
Linktown Fife 211 J1
Linkwood Moray 266 E4
Linley Shrops 95 J5
Linley Green Herefs 80 F4
Linleygreen Shrops 96 F4
Linlithgow W Loth 210 C4
Linn Crematorium E Rens ... 209 G7
Linshiels Nthumb 190 C5
Linsidemore Highld 272 D8
Linslade C Beds 67 M2
Linstead Parva Suffk 107 G7
Linstock Cumb 178 A7
Linthurst Worcs 82 B1
Linthwaite Kirk 141 H5
Lintlaw Border 213 H7
Lintmill Moray 267 K3
Linton Border 202 B7
Linton Cambs 88 B6
Linton Derbys 115 M8
Linton Herefs 63 K2
Linton Kent 39 J3
Linton Leeds 150 E6
Linton N York 149 H3
Linton Nthumb 191 K7
Linton Heath Derbys 115 M8
Linton Hill Herefs 63 K2
Linton-on-Ouse N York 151 G4
Linwood Hants 18 B2
Linwood Lincs 136 B2
Linwood Rens 208 D6
Lionacleit W Isls 283 c9
Lional W Isls 282 h1
Lions Green E Susx 23 J4
Liphook Hants 36 C4
Lipley Shrops 114 A5
Liscard Wirral 129 G1
Liscombe Somset 28 F4
Liskeard Cnwll 6 B2
Lismore Ag & B 228 C7
Liss Hants 36 A5
Lissett E R Yk 153 J4
Liss Forest Hants 36 A5
Lissington Lincs 136 B3
Liston Essex 89 G6
Lisvane Cardif 43 J5
Liswerry Newpt 44 D2
Litcham Norfk 121 J8
Litchard Brdgnd 42 D5
Litchborough Nhants 84 C4
Litchfield Hants 48 C8
Litherland Sefton 138 D8
Litlington Cambs 87 G6
Litlington E Susx 23 J7
Little Abington Cambs 87 L5
Little Addington Nhants 101 L8
Little Airies D & G 173 K5
Little Almshoe Herts 69 G2
Little Alne Warwks 82 D3
Little Altcar Sefton 138 C6
Little Amwell Herts 69 K5
Little Asby Cumb 158 B1
Little Aston Staffs 98 E3
Little Atherfield IoW 19 G7
Little Ayton N York 170 D8
Little Baddow Essex 71 J5
Little Badminton S Glos 46 A2

Little Bampton Cumb 177 J7
Little Bardfield Essex 71 G1
Little Barford Bed 86 D4
Little Barningham Norfk 122 C5
Little Barrington Gloucs 65 J4
Little Barrow Ches W 129 L5
Little Barugh N York 162 D6
Little Bavington Nthumb 180 B3
Little Bealings Suffk 90 F5
Littlebeck N York 162 F2
Little Bedwyn Wilts 47 L5
Little Bentley Essex 73 G2
Little Berkhamsted Herts 69 H5
Little Billing Nhants 84 F3
Little Billington C Beds 68 B3
Little Birch Herefs 63 G1
Little Bispham Bpool 146 F7
Little Blakenham Suffk 90 C5
Little Blencow Cumb 166 B4
Little Bloxwich Wsall 98 C3
Little Bognor W Susx 21 G3
Little Bolehill Derbys 116 A1
Little Bollington Ches E 130 E2
Little Bookham Surrey 50 E8
Littleborough Devon 28 E8
Littleborough Notts 135 G3
Littleborough Rochdl 140 E4
Littlebourne Kent 41 G4
Little Bourton Oxon 83 K6
Little Bowden Leics 101 L6
Little Bradley Suffk 88 D5
Little Brampton Herefs 79 K3
Little Brampton Shrops 95 J7
Little Braxted Essex 71 K4
Little Brechin Angus 234 F3
Littlebredy Dorset 16 B5
Little Brickhill M Keyn 67 L1
Little Bridgeford Staffs 114 D6
Little Brington Nhants 84 C3
Little Bromley Essex 73 G2
Little Broughton Cumb 164 E4
Little Budworth Ches W 130 B6
Littleburn Highld 251 H1
Little Burstead Essex 71 G8
Littlebury Essex 87 L7
Littlebury Green Essex 87 K7
Little Bytham Lincs 118 D7
Little Canfield Essex 70 E3
Little Carlton Lincs 137 G3
Little Carlton Notts 134 F8
Little Casterton Rutlnd 101 M2
Little Catwick E R Yk 153 H6
Little Catworth Cambs 86 B1
Little Cawthorpe Lincs 137 G3
Little Chalfont Bucks 68 C7
Little Chart Kent 40 B6
Little Chesterford Essex 87 L7
Little Cheveney Kent 39 H4
Little Cheverell Wilts 46 E8
Little Chishill Cambs 87 J7
Little Clacton Essex 73 H3
Little Clanfield Oxon 65 K6
Little Clifton Cumb 164 E5
Little Coates NE Lin 145 H6
Little Comberton Worcs 81 M6
Little Common E Susx 24 C5
Little Comp Kent 39 G2
Little Compton Warwks 65 K1
Little Corby Cumb 178 B7
Little Cornard Suffk 89 H7
Littlecott Wilts 47 H8
Little Cowarne Herefs 80 E5
Little Coxwell Oxon 65 L8
Little Crakehall N York 160 C4
Little Cransley Nhants 101 H8
Little Cressingham Norfk 105 H3
Little Crosby Sefton 138 C7
Little Crosthwaite Cumb 165 H5
Little Cubley Derbys 115 J4
Little Dalby Leics 117 K8
Littledean Gloucs 63 K4
Little Dewchurch Herefs 63 G1
Little Ditton Cambs 88 D3
Little Doward Herefs 63 G4
Littledown Hants 47 M7
Little Downham Cambs 103 L6
Little Driffield E R Yk 152 F4
Little Dunham Norfk 105 H1
Little Dunkeld P & K 232 F7
Little Dunmow Essex 71 G3
Little Durnford Wilts 33 K4
Little Easton Essex 70 F2
Little Eaton Derbys 116 B3
Little Ellingham Norfk 105 K3
Little Elm Somset 32 B2
Little Everdon Nhants 84 B4
Little Eversden Cambs 87 H4
Little Faringdon Oxon 65 J6
Little Fencote N York 160 D4

Little Fenton N York 142 E1
Little Fransham Norfk 105 H1
Little Gaddesden Herts 68 C4
Little Garway Herefs 62 F2
Little Gidding Cambs 102 C7
Little Glemham Suffk 91 H4
Little Gorsley Herefs 63 K2
Little Gransden Cambs 86 F4
Little Green Notts 117 J3
Little Green Somset 32 B1
Little Grimsby Lincs 136 F2
Little Gringley Notts 134 E3
Little Habton N York 162 C7
Little Hadham Herts 70 B3
Little Hale Lincs 118 F3
Little Hallam Derbys 116 D3
Little Hallingbury Essex 70 D4
Littleham Devon 14 B6
Littleham Devon 27 H6
Little Hampden Bucks 67 L6
Littlehampton W Susx 21 H6
Little Hanford Dorset 32 D8
Little Harrowden Nhants 85 G1
Little Haseley Oxon 66 F7
Little Hatfield E R Yk 153 J7
Little Hautbois Norfk 122 E7
Little Haven Pembks 54 D4
Littlehaven W Susx 37 J4
Little Hay Staffs 98 E3
Little Hayfield Derbys 131 K2
Little Haywood Staffs 115 G7
Little Heath Staffs 114 D8
Little Heath W Berk 49 G4
Littlehempston Devon 8 B2
Little Hereford Herefs 80 D2
Little Horkesley Essex 72 D1
Little Hormead Herts 69 L2
Little Horsted E Susx 23 G4
Little Horton C Brad 141 J2
Little Horton Wilts 46 F6
Little Horwood Bucks 67 J1
Little Houghton Barns 142 C6
Little Houghton Nhants 84 F3
Littlehoughton Nthumb 191 J3
Little Hucklow Derbys 132 C4
Little Hulton Salfd 139 L7
Little Hungerford W Berk 48 D4
Little Hutton N York 161 G7
Little Irchester Nhants 85 H2
Little Kelk E R Yk 153 H4
Little Keyford Somset 32 C2
Little Kimble Bucks 67 K5
Little Kineton Warwks 83 H5
Little Kingshill Bucks 67 L7
Little Knox D & G 175 K3
Little Langdale Cumb 156 D2
Little Langford Wilts 33 H4
Little Laver Essex 70 E5
Little Leigh Ches W 130 B4
Little Leighs Essex 71 H4
Little Lever Bolton 139 M6
Little Linford M Keyn 85 G6
Little Load Somset 31 G6
Little London Bucks 66 F4
Little London Cambs 103 J4
Little London E Susx 23 J3
Little London Essex 70 C1
Little London Essex 88 D8
Little London Gloucs 63 L3
Little London Hants 34 E1
Little London Hants 48 F7
Little London Leeds 150 B7
Little London Lincs 119 H7
Little London Lincs 119 M6
Little London Lincs 136 F5
Little London Norfk 120 C7
Little London Powys 94 C5
Little Longstone Derbys 132 D5
Little Madeley Staffs 114 B3
Little Malvern Worcs 81 H7
Little Mancot Flints 129 H6
Little Maplestead Essex 89 G8
Little Marcle Herefs 80 F7
Little Marland Devon 27 J8
Little Marlow Bucks 49 L2
Little Massingham Norfk 121 H6
Little Melton Norfk 106 D2
Littlemill Abers 243 K4
Littlemill Highld 253 H2
Little Mill Mons 62 C6
Little Milton Oxon 66 F7
Little Missenden Bucks 68 A7
Little Mongeham Kent 41 K5
Littlemoor Derbys 133 G7
Little Moor Somset 30 D4
Littlemore Oxon 66 D6
Little Musgrave Cumb 167 H8
Little Ness Shrops 112 F7
Little Neston Ches W 129 G4

Little Newcastle Pembks 75 G6
Little Newsham Dur 168 E7
Little Norton Somset 31 G8
Little Oakley Essex 73 J1
Little Oakley Nhants 101 K6
Little Odell Bed 85 J4
Little Offley Herts 68 F3
Little Ormside Cumb 167 G7
Little Orton Cumb 177 K7
Little Ouse Cambs 104 C5
Little Ouseburn N York 150 F4
Littleover C Derb 116 B5
Little Oxendon Nhants 100 F6
Little Packington Warwks 99 G6
Little Pattenden Kent 39 J4
Little Paxton Cambs 86 D3
Little Petherick Cnwll 10 C8
Little Plumpton Lancs 138 D1
Little Plumstead Norfk 107 G5
Little Ponton Lincs 118 B5
Littleport Cambs 104 B6
Littleport Bridge Cambs 104 B6
Little Posbrook Hants 19 J3
Little Potheridge Devon 27 J8
Little Preston Leeds 142 B2
Little Preston Nhants 84 B4
Littler Ches W 130 C6
Little Raveley Cambs 102 E7
Little Reedness E R Yk 143 K3
Little Ribston N York 150 E5
Little Rissington Gloucs 65 J3
Little Rollright Oxon 65 L1
Little Rowsley Derbys 132 E6
Little Ryburgh Norfk 121 L6
Little Ryle Nthumb 190 E4
Little Ryton Shrops 96 B3
Little Salkeld Cumb 166 D3
Little Sampford Essex 88 C8
Little Sandhurst Br For 49 K6
Little Saredon Staffs 97 L2
Little Saughall Ches W 129 J6
Little Saxham Suffk 88 F3
Little Scatwell Highld 262 C9
Little Shelford Cambs 87 J5
Little Shrewley Warwks 82 F2
Little Silver Devon 13 L1
Little Singleton Lancs 147 E2
Little Skipwith N York 151 K8
Little Smeaton N York 142 E4
Little Snoring Norfk 121 L5
Little Sodbury S Glos 45 M2
Little Sodbury End S Glos 45 L2
Little Somborne Hants 34 E4
Little Somerford Wilts 46 D2
Little Soudley Shrops 114 A6
Little Stainforth N York 148 E4
Little Stainton Darltn 169 K6
Little Stanion Nhants 101 K6
Little Stanney Ches W 129 J5
Little Staughton Bed 86 B3
Little Steeping Lincs 137 H7
Little Stoke Staffs 114 E5
Littlestone-on-Sea Kent 25 K2
Little Stonham Suffk 90 D3
Little Stretton Leics 100 E3
Little Stretton Shrops 95 K5
Little Strickland Cumb 166 C6
Little Stukeley Cambs 102 E8
Little Sugnall Staffs 114 C5
Little Sutton Ches W 129 J4
Little Sutton Shrops 96 C6
Little Swinburne Nthumb 179 M3
Little Sypland D & G 175 H4
Little Tew Oxon 66 A2
Little Tey Essex 72 C2
Little Thetford Cambs 103 L8
Little Thirkleby N York 161 G7
Little Thornage Norfk 122 B4
Little Thornton Lancs 147 G2
Little Thorpe Dur 169 L2
Littlethorpe Leics 100 C4
Littlethorpe N York 150 D3
Little Thurlow Suffk 88 D5
Little Thurlow Green Suffk 88 D5
Little Thurrock Thurr 52 D3
Littleton Angus 234 A5
Littleton BaNES 45 H6
Littleton Ches W 129 K6
Littleton D & G 175 G4
Littleton Dorset 17 H2
Littleton Hants 34 F4
Littleton Somset 31 H5
Littleton Surrey 36 E2
Littleton Surrey 50 D5
Littleton Drew Wilts 46 B3
Littleton-on-Severn S Glos 45 H1
Littleton Pannell Wilts 46 E8
Little Torrington Devon 27 J8
Little Totham Essex 72 C5

Little Town Cumb 165 H6
Littletown Dur. 169 J2
Little Town Lancs 148 B8
Little Town Warrtn 130 C1
Little Twycross Leics 99 J2
Little Urswick Cumb. 156 C7
Little Wakering Essex 53 K1
Little Walden Essex 87 L7
Little Waldingfield Suffk 89 J6
Little Walsingham Norfk 121 K4
Little Waltham Essex 71 H4
Little Warley Essex 52 D1
Little Washbourne Gloucs 82 A8
Little Weighton E R Yk. 144 B1
Little Welnetham Suffk 89 H3
Little Welton Lincs 136 F2
Little Wenham Suffk 90 C7
Little Wenlock Wrekin 96 E2
Little Weston Somset 31 K5
Little Whitefield IoW 19 K5
Little Whittingham Green
  Suffk 106 F8
Little Whittington Nthumb 180 B5
Littlewick Green W & M 49 K3
Little Wilbraham Cambs 87 L3
Littlewindsor Dorset 15 K2
Little Witcombe Gloucs 64 C4
Little Witley Worcs 81 H3
Little Wittenham Oxon 66 E8
Little Wolford Warwks 83 G8
Littlewood Staffs 98 C2
Little Woodcote Gt Lon 51 H6
Littleworth Bucks 67 L3
Littleworth Oxon 65 L7
Littleworth Staffs 98 C1
Littleworth Staffs 114 E7
Littleworth W Susx 21 L3
Littleworth Worcs 81 K5
Littleworth Worcs 82 B3
Littleworth Common Bucks 50 B2
Little Wratting Suffk 88 D5
Little Wymington Bed 85 L2
Little Wymondley Herts. 69 G2
Little Wyrley Staffs 98 C2
Little Wytheford Shrops 113 J7
Little Yeldham Essex 88 F7
Littley Green Essex 71 G4
Litton Derbys 132 C4
Litton N York 158 F7
Litton Somset 45 H8
Litton Cheney Dorset 15 M4
Liurbost W Isls 282 g4
Liverpool Lpool 129 H2
Liversedge Kirk 141 J3
Liverton Devon 13 J7
Liverton R & Cl 171 G7
Liverton Mines R & Cl 171 G7
Liverton Street Kent 39 L3
Livingston W Loth 210 E5
Livingston Village W Loth 210 D5
Lixwm Flints 128 E5
Lizard Cnwll 3 H8
Llaingoch IoA 124 D3
Llaithddu Powys 94 C7
Llan Powys 93 J3
Llanaber Gwynd 109 L7
Llanaelhaearn Gwynd 109 G3
Llanafan Cerdgn 77 J1
Llanafan-Fawr Powys 78 D4
Llanafan-fechan Powys 78 D5
Llanallgo IoA 125 J3
Llanarmon Gwynd 109 G4
Llanarmon Dyffryn Ceiriog
  Wrexhm 112 A5
Llanarmon-yn-Ial Denbgs 128 E8
Llanarth Cerdgn 76 D4
Llanarth Mons 62 D5
Llanarthne Carmth 58 F5
Llanasa Flints 128 D3
Llanbabo IoA 124 F2
Llanbadarn Fawr Cerdgn 92 D7
Llanbadarn Fynydd Powys 94 D7
Llanbadarn-y-garreg Powys 78 F5
Llanbadoc Mons 62 D7
Llanbadrig IoA 124 F1
Llanbeder Newpt 44 D1
Llanbedr Gwynd 109 K6
Llanbedr Powys 61 K3
Llanbedr Powys 79 G6
Llanbedr-Dyffryn-Clwyd
  Denbgs 128 D7
Llanbedrgoch IoA 125 J4
Llanbedrog Gwynd 108 F5
Llanbedr-y-Cennin Conwy 126 E6
Llanberis Gwynd 125 K7
Llanbethêry V Glam 43 G7
Llanbister Powys 94 D8
Llanblethian V Glam 42 F7
Llanboidy Carmth 55 L2

Llanbradach Caerph 43 J4
Llanbrynmair Powys 93 K3
Llancadle V Glam 42 F8
Llancarfan V Glam 43 G7
Llancayo Mons 62 D6
Llancloudy Herefs 63 G3
Llancynfelyn Cerdgn 92 E5
Llandaff Cardif 43 J6
Llandanwg Gwynd 109 K6
Llandarcy Neath 57 K6
Llandawke Carmth 58 A6
Llanddaniel Fab IoA 125 J5
Llanddarog Carmth 58 F5
Llanddeiniol Cerdgn 77 J1
Llanddeiniolen Gwynd 125 K6
Llanddderfel Gwynd 111 J4
Llanddeusant Carmth 59 L4
Llanddeusant IoA 124 F3
Llanddew Powys 61 G1
Llanddewi Swans 56 E7
Llanddewi Brefi Cerdgn 77 J4
Llanddewi'r Cwm Powys 78 E5
Llanddewi Rhydderch Mons 62 D4
Llanddewi Velfrey Pembks 55 K3
Llanddewi Ystradenni Powys 78 F2
Llanddoget Conwy 126 F7
Llanddona IoA 125 K4
Llanddowror Carmth 58 A6
Llanddulas Conwy 127 H4
Llanddwywe Gwynd 109 K6
Llanddyfnan IoA 125 J4
Llandecwyn Gwynd 110 B4
Llandefaelog Powys 60 F1
Llandefaelog-Tre'r-Graig
  Powys 61 H1
Llandefalle Powys 78 F8
Llandegfan IoA 125 K5
Llandegla Denbgs 112 B1
Llandegley Powys 79 G3
Llandegveth Mons 62 C8
Llandegwning Gwynd 108 D5
Llandeilo Carmth 59 H4
Llandeilo Graban Powys 78 F6
Llandeilo'r Fan Powys 78 B8
Llandeloy Pembks 74 D6
Llandenny Mons 62 E6
Llandevaud Newpt 44 E1
Llandevenny Mons 44 E2
Llandinabo Herefs 63 G2
Llandinam Powys 94 B3
Llandissilio Pembks 55 J3
Llandogo Mons 63 G6
Llandough V Glam 42 F7
Llandough V Glam 43 J7
Llandovery Carmth 59 L2
Llandow V Glam 42 E7
Llandre Carmth 77 J6
Llandre Cerdgn 92 D6
Llandre Isaf Pembks 75 K6
Llandrillo Denbgs 111 K4
Llandrillo-yn-Rhos Conwy 127 G4
Llandrindod Wells Powys 78 E3
Llandrinio Powys 112 D8
Llandudno Conwy 126 F3
Llandudno Junction Conwy 126 F4
Llandulas Powys 78 B7
Llandwrog Gwynd 125 H6
Llandybie Carmth 59 H6
Llandyfaelog Carmth 58 D6
Llandyfan Carmth 59 H5
Llandyfriog Cerdgn 76 B7
Llandyfrydog IoA 125 H3
Llandygai Gwynd 126 B5
Llandygwydd Cerdgn 75 M3
Llandynan Denbgs 112 B3
Llandyrnog Denbgs 128 D6
Llandyssil Powys 94 F4
Llandysul Cerdgn 76 D7
Llanedeyrn Cardif 43 K5
Llanedi Carmth 57 G3
Llaneglwys Powys 78 E7
Llanegryn Gwynd 92 D2
Llanegwad Carmth 58 F4
Llaneilian IoA 125 H1
Llanelian-yn-Rhôs Conwy 127 G4
Llanelidan Denbgs 111 L2
Llanelieu Powys 79 H8
Llanellen Mons 62 C5
Llanelli Carmth 56 F5
Llanelli Crematorium Carmth 56 F4
Llanelltyd Gwynd 110 D7
Llanelly Mons 61 K4
Llanelly Hill Mons 61 K4
Llanelwedd Powys 78 E5
Llanenddwyn Gwynd 109 L6
Llanengan Gwynd 108 E6
Llanerch Gwynd 111 G8
Llanerch Powys 95 H4
Llanerchymedd IoA 125 G3

Llanerfyl Powys 94 B2
Llanfachraeth IoA 124 E3
Llanfachreth Gwynd 110 E7
Llanfaelog IoA 124 F5
Llanfaelrhys Gwynd 108 C6
Llanfaenor Mons 62 E4
Llanfaes IoA 126 B4
Llanfaes Powys 61 G2
Llanfaethlu IoA 124 E2
Llanfair Gwynd 109 K6
Llanfair Caereinion Powys 94 D2
Llanfair Clydogau Cerdgn 77 H5
Llanfair Dyffryn Clwyd
  Denbgs 128 D8
Llanfairfechan Conwy 126 D5
Llanfair Kilgeddin Mons 62 D5
Llanfair-Nant-Gwyn Pembks 75 K5
Llanfairpwllgwyngyll IoA 125 J5
Llanfair Talhaiarn Conwy 127 J5
Llanfair Waterdine Shrops 94 F8
Llanfairynghornwy IoA 124 E2
Llanfair-yn-Neubwll IoA 124 E4
Llanfallteg Carmth 55 K3
Llanfallteg West Carmth 55 K3
Llanfarian Cerdgn 92 D7
Llanfechain Powys 112 B7
Llanfechell IoA 124 F2
Llanferres Denbgs 128 E7
Llanfflewyn IoA 124 F2
Llanfigael IoA 124 F3
Llanfihangel-ar-arth Carmth 76 E7
Llanfihangel Glyn Myfyr
  Conwy 111 J2
Llanfihangel Nant Bran Powys 78 C8
Llanfihangel-nant-Melan
  Powys 79 H4
Llanfihangel Rhydithon
  Powys 79 G2
Llanfihangel Rogiet Mons 44 F2
Llanfihangel Tal-y-llyn Powys 61 H2
Llanfihangel-uwch-Gwili
  Carmth 58 E4
Llanfihangel-y-Creuddyn
  Cerdgn 92 E8
Llanfihangel-yng-Ngwynfa
  Powys 111 L8
Llanfihangel yn Nhowyn IoA 124 E4
Llanfihangel-y-pennant
  Gwynd 92 E2
Llanfihangel-y-pennant
  Gwynd 109 J3
Llanfihangel-y-traethau
  Gwynd 109 L4
Llanfilo Powys 78 F8
Llanfoist Mons 62 B4
Llanfor Gwynd 111 H4
Llanfrechfa Torfn 62 C8
Llanfrothen Gwynd 110 B3
Llanfrynach Powys 61 G2
Llanfwrog Denbgs 128 D8
Llanfwrog IoA 124 E3
Llanfyllin Powys 112 A7
Llanfynydd Carmth 59 G3
Llanfynydd Flints 129 G8
Llanfyrnach Pembks 75 L6
Llangadfan Powys 94 B1
Llangadog Carmth 56 D3
Llangadog Carmth 59 K3
Llangadwaladr IoA 125 G6
Llangadwaladr Powys 112 B5
Llangaffo IoA 125 H6
Llangain Carmth 58 C5
Llangammarch Wells Powys 78 C6
Llangan V Glam 42 E6
Llangarron Herefs 63 G3
Llangasty-Talyllyn Powys 61 H2
Llangathen Carmth 59 G4
Llangattock Powys 61 K3
Llangattock Lingoed Mons 62 D3
Llangattock-Vibon-Avel Mons 62 F4
Llangedwyn Powys 112 B6
Llangefni IoA 125 H4
Llangeinor Brdgnd 42 E5
Llangeitho Cerdgn 77 H3
Llangeler Carmth 76 C7
Llangelynin Gwynd 92 C2
Llangendeirne Carmth 58 E6
Llangennech Carmth 57 G4
Llangenny Powys 61 K3
Llangennith Swans 56 D6
Llangenny Powys 61 K3
Llangernyw Conwy 127 H6
Llangian Gwynd 108 E5
Llangiwg Neath 57 K4
Llangloffan Pembks 74 E5
Llanglydwen Carmth 75 L6
Llangoed IoA 126 C4
Llangoedmor Cerdgn 75 L3
Llangollen Denbgs 112 B3
Llangolman Pembks 75 J6

Llangors Powys 61 H2
Llangovan Mons 62 F6
Llangower Gwynd 111 G5
Llangrannog Cerdgn 76 B4
Llangristiolus IoA 125 H5
Llangrove Herefs 63 G5
Llangua Mons 62 E2
Llangunllo Powys 79 H1
Llangunnor Carmth 58 D5
Llangurig Powys 93 K7
Llangwm Conwy 111 J3
Llangwm Mons 62 E7
Llangwm Pembks 55 G5
Llangwnnadl Gwynd 108 D7
Llangwyfan Denbgs 128 D6
Llangwyllog IoA 125 H4
Llangwyryfon Cerdgn 77 H1
Llangybi Cerdgn 77 H4
Llangybi Gwynd 109 G3
Llangybi Mons 62 D7
Llangyfelach Swans 57 H5
Llangynhafal Denbgs 128 D7
Llangynidr Powys 61 J3
Llangynin Carmth 55 M3
Llangynllo Cerdgn 76 C6
Llangynog Carmth 58 C6
Llangynog Powys 111 K6
Llangynwyd Brdgnd 42 C4
Llanhamlach Powys 61 H2
Llanharan Rhondd 42 F5
Llanharry Rhondd 42 F5
Llanhennock Mons 62 D8
Llanhilleth Blae G 61 K7
Llanidan IoA 125 J6
Llanidloes Powys 93 L6
Llaniestyn Gwynd 108 D5
Llanigon Powys 79 H7
Llanilar Cerdgn 92 D7
Llanilid Rhondd 42 E5
Llanina Cerdgn 76 D3
Llanio Cerdgn 77 H4
Llanishen Cardif 43 J5
Llanishen Mons 62 F6
Llanllechid Gwynd 126 C6
Llanlleonfel Powys 78 C5
Llanllowell Mons 62 D7
Llanllugan Powys 94 C3
Llanllwch Carmth 58 C5
Llanllwchaiarn Powys 94 D5
Llanllwni Carmth 76 E7
Llanllyfni Gwynd 109 H1
Llanmadoc Swans 56 D6
Llanmaes V Glam 42 E7
Llanmartin Newpt 44 E1
Llanmerewig Powys 94 E5
Llanmihangel V Glam 42 E7
Llanmiloe Carmth 55 M5
Llanmorlais Swans 56 F6
Llannefydd Conwy 127 K5
Llannon Carmth 56 F3
Llannor Gwynd 108 F4
Llanon Cerdgn 76 F2
Llanover Mons 62 C5
Llanpumsaint Carmth 58 D3
Llanrhaeadr-ym-Mochnant
  Powys 111 M6
Llanrhian Pembks 74 D6
Llanrhidian Swans 56 F6
Llanrhos Conwy 126 F4
Llanrhychwyn Conwy 126 F7
Llanrhyddlad IoA 124 F2
Llanrhystud Cerdgn 76 F1
Llanrothal Herefs 62 F3
Llanrug Gwynd 125 J7
Llanrumney Cardif 43 K5
Llanrwst Conwy 126 F7
Llansadurnen Carmth 56 A3
Llansadwrn Carmth 59 J3
Llansadwrn IoA 125 K4
Llansaint Carmth 56 C3
Llansamlet Swans 57 J5
Llansanffraid Glan Conwy
  Conwy 126 F4
Llansannan Conwy 127 J6
Llansannor V Glam 42 F6
Llansantffraed Powys 61 H2
Llansantffraed-Cwmdeuddwr
  Powys 78 D2
Llansantffraed-in-Elvel Powys 78 F4
Llansantffraid Cerdgn 76 F2
Llansantffraid-ym-Mechain
  Powys 112 C7
Llansawel Carmth 59 H2
Llansilin Powys 112 B6
Llansoy Mons 62 E6
Llanspyddid Powys 60 F2
Llanstadwell Pembks 54 F6
Llansteffan Carmth 56 C3
Llanstephan Powys 78 F6

Place	County	Page	Grid
Llantarnam	Torfn	62	C8
Llanteg	Pembks	55	L5
Llanthewy Skirrid	Mons	62	D4
Llanthony	Mons	62	B2
Llantilio-Crossenny	Mons	62	E4
Llantilio Pertholey	Mons	62	C4
Llantood	Pembks	75	K4
Llantrisant	IoA	124	F3
Llantrisant	Mons	62	D7
Llantrisant	Rhondd	43	G5
Llantrithyd	V Glam	43	G5
Llantwit Fardre	Rhondd	43	G4
Llantwit Major	V Glam	42	E7
Llantysilio	Denbgs	112	B3
Llanuwchllyn	Gwynd	111	G5
Llanvaches	Newpt	44	E1
Llanvair Discoed	Mons	62	F8
Llanvapley	Mons	62	D4
Llanvetherine	Mons	62	D4
Llanveynoe	Herefs	62	C1
Llanvihangel Crucorney	Mons	62	C3
Llanvihangel Gobion	Mons	62	D5
Llanvihangel-Ystern-Llewern Mons		62	E4
Llanwarne	Herefs	63	G2
Llanwddyn	Powys	111	K7
Llanwenarth	Mons	62	B4
Llanwenog	Cerdgn	76	F6
Llanwern	Newpt	44	D2
Llanwinio	Carmth	58	A4
Llanwnda	Gwynd	125	H8
Llanwnda	Pembks	74	F4
Llanwnnen	Cerdgn	76	F6
Llanwnog	Powys	94	B4
Llanwonno	Rhondd	42	F3
Llanwrda	Carmth	59	K3
Llanwrin	Powys	93	G3
Llanwrthwl	Powys	78	D3
Llanwrtyd	Powys	78	B5
Llanwrtyd Wells	Powys	78	B6
Llanwyddelan	Powys	94	C3
Llanyblodwel	Shrops	112	C4
Llanybri	Carmth	58	B6
Llanybydder	Carmth	76	F6
Llanycefn	Pembks	55	J2
Llanychaer	Pembks	75	G5
Llanycil	Gwynd	111	H4
Llanycrwys	Carmth	77	H6
Llanymawddwy	Gwynd	111	G7
Llanymynech	Powys	112	C7
Llanynghenedl	IoA	124	E3
Llanynys	Denbgs	128	C7
Llan-y-pwll	Wrexhm	112	F1
Llanyre	Powys	78	E4
Llanystumdwy	Gwynd	109	H4
Llanywern	Powys	61	H2
Llawhaden	Pembks	55	H3
Llawnt	Shrops	112	C5
Llawryglyn	Powys	93	K5
Llay	Wrexhm	129	H8
Llechcynfarwy	IoA	125	G3
Llechfaen	Powys	61	G4
Llechrhyd	Caerph	61	H5
Llechryd	Cerdgn	75	L3
Llechylched	IoA	124	F4
Lledrod	Cerdgn	77	H1
Llidiardau	Gwynd	111	G4
Llidiartnenog	Carmth	77	G7
Llidiart-y-parc	Denbgs	111	M3
Llithfaen	Gwynd	108	F3
Lloc	Flints	128	C5
Llowes	Powys	79	H7
Llwydcoed	Rhondd	60	F6
Llwydcoed Crematorium Rhondd		60	F6
Llwydiarth	Powys	111	K8
Llwyn	Denbgs	128	C6
Llwyncelyn	Cerdgn	76	E3
Llwyndafydd	Cerdgn	76	C4
Llwynderw	Powys	94	F3
Llwyn-drain	Pembks	58	A2
Llwyn-du	Mons	62	C4
Llwyndyrys	Gwynd	108	F2
Llwyngwril	Gwynd	92	D2
Llwynhendy	Carmth	56	F5
Llwynmawr	Wrexhm	112	C4
Llwyn-on	Myr Td	60	F5
Llwyn-y-brain	Carmth	55	L4
Llwyn-y-groes	Cerdgn	77	G4
Llwynypia	Rhondd	42	F3
Llynclys	Shrops	112	D6
Llynfaes	IoA	125	G4
Llyn-y-pandy	Flints	128	E6
Llysfaen	Conwy	127	H4
Llyswen	Cerdgn	76	E3
Llyswen	Powys	79	G7
Llysworney	V Glam	42	E6
Llys-y-frân	Pembks	55	H2
Llywel	Powys	60	C1
Load Brook	Sheff	132	E2
Loan	Falk	210	L4
Loanend	Nthumb	202	E3
Loanhead	Mdloth	211	J6
Loaningfoot	D & G	176	C7
Loans	S Ayrs	196	C4
Lobb	Devon	27	H3
Lobhillcross	Devon	12	B5
Lochailort	Highld	238	B7
Lochaline	Highld	227	K1
Lochans	D & G	172	D3
Locharbriggs	D & G	176	C3
Lochavich	Ag & B	216	E4
Lochawe	Ag & B	217	J2
Loch Baghasdail	W Isls	283	c11
Lochboisdale	W Isls	283	c11
Lochbuie	Ag & B	227	H7
Lochcarron	Highld	248	E4
Lochdon	Ag & B	227	L6
Lochdonhead	Ag & B.	227	L5
Lochead	Ag & B	206	B3
Lochearnhead	Stirlg	219	K2
Lochee	C Dund	222	F1
Locheilside Station	Highld	239	G7
Lochend	Highld	251	G4
Lochfoot	D & G	176	B4
Lochgair	Ag & B	206	E1
Lochgelly	Fife	222	C8
Lochgilphead	Ag & B	206	D2
Lochgoilhead	Ag & B	217	K7
Lochieheads	Fife	222	D4
Lochill	Moray	266	C3
Lochindorb Lodge	Highld	253	J4
Lochinver	Highld	270	E4
Loch Loyal Lodge	Highld	277	L7
Lochluichart	Highld	262	B7
Lochmaben	D & G	176	E2
Lochmaddy	W Isls	283	d8
Loch nam Madadh	W Isls	283	d8
Lochore	Fife	222	B7
Lochranza	N Ayrs	194	E1
Loch Sgioport	W Isls	283	c10
Lochside	Abers	235	J3
Lochside	D & G	176	C3
Lochside	Highld	252	F1
Lochskipport	W Isls	283	c10
Lochslin	Highld	264	C4
Lochton	S Ayrs	183	G7
Lochty	Angus	234	E3
Lochty	Fife	223	J5
Lochuisge	Highld	228	B4
Lochwinnoch	Rens	208	B7
Lochwood	D & G	187	G6
Lockengate	Cnwll	5	H3
Lockerbie	D & G	176	F3
Lockeridge	Wilts	47	H5
Lockerley	Hants	34	C5
Locking	N Som	44	D7
Locking Stumps	Warrtn	130	C1
Lockington	E R Yk	152	F6
Lockington	Leics	116	D6
Lockleywood	Shrops	113	M6
Locksbottom	Gt Lon	51	L6
Locksgreen	IoW	19	G5
Locks Heath	Hants	19	H2
Lockton	N York	162	E5
Loddington	Leics	101	H3
Loddington	Nhants	101	H7
Loddiswell	Devon	7	L5
Loddon	Norfk	107	G4
Lode	Cambs	87	L3
Lode Heath	Solhll	98	F7
Loders	Dorset	15	L4
Lodge Hill Crematorium	Birm	98	C7
Lodsworth	W Susx	36	D6
Lofthouse	Leeds	142	A3
Lofthouse	N York	159	K8
Lofthouse Gate	Wakefd	142	A3
Loftus	R & Cl	171	G7
Logan	E Ayrs	197	H6
Loganbeck	Cumb	156	A4
Loganlea	W Loth	210	C6
Loggerheads	Staffs	114	A4
Logie	Angus	235	H3
Logie	Fife	223	K2
Logie	Moray	253	K2
Logie Coldstone	Abers	243	M3
Logie Newton	Abers	256	B4
Logie Pert	Angus	235	G3
Logierait	P & K	232	E5
Logierieve	Abers	257	G6
Login	Carmth	55	K2
Lolworth	Cambs	87	H2
Lonbain	Highld	259	M6
Londesborough	E R Yk	152	C6
London	Gt Lon	51	J3
London Apprentice	Cnwll	5	G5
London Beach	Kent	39	M6
London Colney	Herts	68	F6
Londonderry	N York	160	D5
London End	Nhants	85	H2
Londonthorpe	Lincs	118	C4
Londubh	Highld	260	D4
Lonemore	Highld	260	C4
Long Ashton	N Som	45	H5
Long Bank	Worcs	97	H8
Long Bennington	Lincs	117	L3
Longbenton	N Tyne	181	G5
Longborough	Gloucs	65	J1
Long Bredy	Dorset	16	A4
Longbridge	Birm	98	C6
Longbridge	Warwks	83	G3
Longbridge Deverill	Wilts	32	E3
Long Buckby	Nhants	84	C2
Longburgh	Cumb	177	J2
Longburton	Dorset	31	L8
Long Cause	Devon	8	B3
Long Clawson	Leics	117	J6
Longcliffe	Derbys	132	D8
Longcombe	Devon	8	C3
Long Common	Hants	35	G7
Long Compton	Staffs	114	D7
Long Compton	Warwks	83	G8
Longcot	Oxon	47	K1
Long Crendon	Bucks	67	G5
Long Crichel	Dorset	17	J1
Longcroft	Cumb	177	H7
Longcross	Surrey	50	C6
Longden	Shrops	95	K2
Longden Common	Shrops	95	K2
Long Ditton	Surrey	50	F5
Longdon	Staffs	115	H8
Longdon	Worcs	81	J7
Longdon Green	Staffs	98	D1
Longdon Heath	Worcs	81	J7
Longdon upon Tern	Wrekin	113	K8
Longdown	Devon	13	K4
Longdowns	Cnwll	3	J4
Long Drax	N York	143	H2
Long Duckmanton	Derbys	133	J5
Long Eaton	Derbys	116	E5
Longfield	Kent	52	D5
Longford	Covtry	99	K6
Longford	Derbys	115	L4
Longford	Gloucs	64	B3
Longford	Gt Lon	50	D4
Longford	Kent	38	D2
Longford	Shrops	113	L5
Longford	Wrekin	114	A7
Longforgan	P & K	222	E1
Longformacus	Border	212	F7
Longframlington	Nthumb	191	G6
Long Green	Ches W	129	L5
Long Green	Worcs	81	J8
Longham	Dorset	17	L3
Longham	Norfk	121	L8
Long Hanborough	Oxon	66	B4
Longhaven	Abers	257	L4
Long Hedges	Lincs	119	K2
Longhirst	Nthumb	191	J8
Longhope	Gloucs	63	K3
Longhope	Ork	275	b6
Longhorsley	Nthumb	191	H7
Longhoughton	Nthumb	191	J3
Long Itchington	Warwks	83	K2
Longlands	Cumb	165	J3
Longlane	Derbys	115	L4
Long Lawford	Warwks	100	A8
Longlevens	Gloucs	64	B3
Longley	Calder	141	G3
Longley	Kirk	141	J6
Longley Green	Worcs	81	G5
Longleys	P & K	233	L6
Long Load	Somset	31	G6
Longmanhill	Abers	268	D4
Long Marston	Herts	67	L4
Long Marston	N York	151	H5
Long Marston	Warwks	82	E5
Long Marton	Cumb	166	F5
Long Meadowend	Shrops	95	K7
Long Melford	Suffk	89	H6
Longmoor Camp	Hants	36	B4
Longmorn	Moray	266	F5
Longmoss	Ches E	131	H5
Long Newnton	Gloucs	64	C8
Longnewton	Border	201	J7
Long Newton	E Loth	212	B6
Longnewton	S on T	169	K7
Longney	Gloucs	63	M4
Longniddry	E Loth	212	A4
Longnor	Shrops	96	B3
Longnor	Staffs	132	B6
Longparish	Hants	34	F2
Longpark	Cumb	178	A6
Long Preston	N York	148	E4
Longridge	Lancs	147	M8
Longridge	Staffs	114	E8
Longridge	W Loth	210	C6
Longriggend	N Lans	209	L5
Long Riston	E R Yk	153	H7
Longrock	Cnwll	2	D5
Longsdon	Staffs	114	F1
Longshaw	Wigan	139	G2
Longside	Abers	269	J6
Long Sight	Oldham	140	D6
Longslow	Shrops	113	L4
Longstanton	Cambs	87	H2
Longstock	Hants	34	D3
Longstone	Pembks	55	K5
Longstowe	Cambs	86	F4
Long Stratton	Norfk	106	D5
Long Street	M Keyn	84	F5
Longstreet	Wilts	47	H8
Long Sutton	Hants	35	M2
Long Sutton	Lincs	119	M7
Long Sutton	Somset	31	G6
Longthorpe	C Pete	102	D4
Long Thurlow	Suffk	89	K2
Longthwaite	Cumb	166	B6
Longton	C Stke	114	E3
Longton	Lancs	138	F3
Longtown	Cumb	177	L5
Longtown	Herefs	62	C1
Longueville	Jersey	9	e3
Longville in the Dale	Shrops	96	C4
Long Waste	Wrekin	113	K8
Long Whatton	Leics	116	D6
Longwick	Bucks	67	J6
Long Wittenham	Oxon	66	E8
Longwitton	Nthumb	180	C1
Longwood	D & G	175	H3
Longwood	Shrops	96	D2
Longworth	Oxon	66	A7
Longyester	E Loth	212	C6
Lôn-las	Swans	57	K5
Lonmay	Abers	269	J4
Lonmore	Highld	258	D7
Looe	Cnwll	6	B4
Loose	Kent	39	L3
Loosebeare	Devon	13	G2
Loosegate	Lincs	119	K6
Loosley Row	Bucks	67	K7
Lootcherbrae	Abers	268	A5
Lopcombe Corner	Wilts	34	B4
Lopen	Somset	30	F8
Loppington	Shrops	113	G6
Lorbottle	Nthumb	190	E5
Lordington	W Susx	20	C5
Lordsbridge	Norfk	104	B1
Lordshill	C Sotn	34	E7
Lords Wood	Medway	53	C6
Lornty	P & K	233	J6
Loscoe	Derbys	116	C2
Loscombe	Dorset	15	L3
Losgaintir	W Isls	282	e6
Lossiemouth	Moray	266	E2
Lostford	Shrops	113	K5
Lostock Gralam	Ches W	130	D5
Lostock Green	Ches W	130	D5
Lostock Hall	Lancs	139	H3
Lostock Hall Fold	Bolton	139	K6
Lostock Junction	Bolton	139	K6
Lostwithiel	Cnwll	5	J4
Lothbeg	Highld	274	C6
Lothersdale	N York	149	G6
Lothmore	Highld	274	C6
Loudwater	Bucks	49	L1
Loughborough	Leics	116	F7
Loughborough Crematorium Leics		116	F7
Loughor	Swans	57	H5
Loughton	Essex	70	B7
Loughton	M Keyn	85	G7
Loughton	Shrops	96	E6
Lound	Lincs	102	E1
Lound	Notts	134	D2
Lound	Suffk	107	K4
Lounston	Devon	13	J7
Lount	Leics	116	C7
Louth	Lincs	136	F2
Loveclough	Lancs	140	B2
Lovedean	Hants	19	M1
Lover	Wilts	34	B6
Loversall	Donc	142	C4
Loves Green	Essex	70	F6
Lovesome Hill	N York	160	E3
Loveston	Pembks	55	J5
Lovington	Somset	31	K5
Low Ackworth	Wakefd	142	C4
Low Angerton	Nthumb	180	D2
Lowbands	Gloucs	63	M1
Low Barbeth	D & G	172	C2
Low Barlings	Lincs	136	A5
Low Bell End	N York	162	C3
Low Bentham	N York	148	A2

Place	Page	Grid
Low Biggins Cumb.	157	K7
Low Borrowbridge Cumb	157	K2
Low Bradfield Sheff	132	E2
Low Bradley N York	149	H6
Low Braithwaite Cumb	166	A2
Low Burnham N Linc	143	K7
Low Buston Nthumb	191	J5
Lowca Cumb	164	C6
Low Catton E R Yk	151	L5
Low Coniscliffe Darltn	169	H7
Low Crosby Cumb	178	B7
Lowdham Notts	117	H2
Low Dinsdale Darltn	169	K8
Lowe Shrops	113	H5
Lowe Hill Staffs	131	K8
Low Ellington N York	160	B6
Lower Aisholt Somset	30	B4
Lower Ansty Dorset	16	E2
Lower Apperley Gloucs	64	B2
Lower Arncott Oxon	66	F3
Lower Ashton Devon	13	K6
Lower Assendon Oxon	49	H2
Lower Ballam Lancs	138	D2
Lower Bartle Lancs	139	G1
Lower Basildon W Berk	48	F3
Lower Bearwood Herefs	79	M4
Lower Beeding W Susx	37	K5
Lower Benefield Nhants	101	L5
Lower Bentley Worcs	82	A2
Lower Beobridge Shrops	97	H5
Lower Birchwood Derbys	116	D1
Lower Boddington Nhants	83	L5
Lower Boscaswell Cnwll	2	B4
Lower Bourne Surrey	36	C2
Lower Brailes Warwks	83	H7
Lower Breakish Highld	247	L4
Lower Bredbury Stockp	131	H2
Lower Broadheath Worcs	81	J4
Lower Broxwood Herefs	79	L4
Lower Buckenhill Herefs	80	E8
Lower Bullingham Herefs	80	C7
Lower Burgate Hants	33	K7
Lower Burrowton Devon	14	B3
Lower Burton Herefs	80	A4
Lower Caldecote C Beds	86	D6
Lower Cam Gloucs	63	L7
Lower Canada N Som	44	D7
Lower Catesby Nhants	83	M3
Lower Chapel Powys	78	E8
Lower Chicksgrove Wilts	33	G5
Lower Chute Wilts	47	L8
Lower Clapton Gt Lon	51	K2
Lower Clent Worcs	97	L7
Lower Common Hants	49	J6
Lower Creedy Devon	13	K2
Lower Crossings Derbys	131	L4
Lower Cumberworth Kirk	141	K6
Lower Darwen Bl w D	139	K3
Lower Dean Bed	85	L2
Lower Denby Kirk	141	K6
Lower Diabaig Highld	260	C7
Lower Dicker E Susx	23	J5
Lower Dinchope Shrops	95	L6
Lower Down Shrops	95	H6
Lower Dunsforth N York	150	F3
Lower Egleton Herefs	80	E6
Lower Elkstone Staffs	131	L8
Lower Ellastone Staffs	115	J3
Lower End Bucks	67	G5
Lower End M Keyn	85	H7
Lower End Nhants	84	F3
Lower End Nhants	85	H3
Lower Everleigh Wilts	47	J8
Lower Exbury Hants	19	G4
Lower Eythorne Kent	41	J5
Lower Failand N Som	45	G4
Lower Farringdon Hants	35	L4
Lower Feltham Gt Lon	50	E4
Lower Fittleworth W Susx	21	G3
Lower Foxdale IoM	154	c6
Lower Frankton Shrops	112	E5
Lower Freystrop Pembks	54	F4
Lower Froyle Hants	35	M2
Lower Gabwell Devon	8	D1
Lower Gledfield Highld	263	G2
Lower Godney Somset	31	G4
Lower Gornal Dudley	97	L5
Lower Gravenhurst C Beds	86	C8
Lower Green Herts	86	D8
Lower Green Herts	87	J8
Lower Green Kent	38	E5
Lower Green Kent	39	G5
Lower Green Norfk	121	L4
Lower Green Staffs	97	K2
Lower Green Suffk	88	E2
Lower Hacheston Suffk	91	H4
Lower Halliford Surrey	50	E5
Lower Halstock Leigh Dorset	15	M1
Lower Halstow Kent	53	J5
Lower Hamworthy Poole	17	K4
Lower Hardres Kent	40	F5
Lower Harpton Herefs	79	K3
Lower Hartlip Kent	53	H6
Lower Hartshay Derbys	116	C1
Lower Hartwell Bucks	67	J4
Lower Hatton Staffs	114	C4
Lower Hawthwaite Cumb	156	B5
Lower Hergest Herefs	79	K4
Lower Heyford Oxon	66	C2
Lower Heysham Lancs	147	H4
Lower Higham Kent	52	F4
Lower Holbrook Suffk	90	E8
Lower Hordley Shrops	112	F5
Lower Horncroft W Susx	21	G3
Lowerhouse Lancs	140	B1
Lower Houses Kirk	141	J5
Lower Howsell Worcs	81	H5
Lower Irlam Salfd	130	D1
Lower Kilburn Derbys	116	C3
Lower Kilcott Gloucs	46	A1
Lower Killeyan Ag & B	204	D7
Lower Kingcombe Dorset	16	A3
Lower Kingswood Surrey	51	H8
Lower Kinnerton Ches W	129	H7
Lower Langford N Som	44	F6
Lower Largo Fife	223	G6
Lower Leigh Staffs	115	G4
Lower Lemington Gloucs	82	F8
Lower Llanfadog Powys	78	C2
Lower Lovacott Devon	27	J5
Lower Loxhore Devon	27	L3
Lower Lydbrook Gloucs	63	H4
Lower Lye Herefs	79	M2
Lower Machen Newpt	43	K4
Lower Maes-coed Herefs	62	D1
Lower Mannington Dorset	17	L2
Lower Marston Somset	32	C2
Lower Meend Gloucs	63	H6
Lower Merridge Somset	30	B4
Lower Middleton Cheney Nhants	83	L7
Lower Milton Somset	31	J2
Lower Moor Worcs	82	A6
Lower Morton S Glos	63	J8
Lower Nazeing Essex	69	K6
Lower Norton Warwks	82	F3
Lower Nyland Dorset	32	C6
Lower Penarth V Glam	43	J7
Lower Penn Staffs	97	K4
Lower Pennington Hants	18	E5
Lower Penwortham Lancs	139	G2
Lower Peover Ches E	130	E5
Lower Place Rochdl	140	D5
Lower Pollicott Bucks	67	H4
Lower Quinton Warwks	82	E6
Lower Rainham Medway	53	H5
Lower Raydon Suffk	90	B7
Lower Roadwater Somset	29	J3
Lower Salter Lancs	147	M3
Lower Seagry Wilts	46	D3
Lower Sheering Essex	70	C4
Lower Shelton C Beds	85	K6
Lower Shiplake Oxon	49	J3
Lower Shuckburgh Warwks	83	L3
Lower Slaughter Gloucs	65	H3
Lower Soothill Kirk	141	L3
Lower Soudley Gloucs	63	K5
Lower Standen Kent	41	H7
Lower Stanton St Quintin Wilts	46	D3
Lower Stoke Medway	53	H4
Lower Stone Gloucs	63	K8
Lower Stonnall Staffs	98	D3
Lower Stow Bedon Norfk	105	K4
Lower Street Dorset	17	G3
Lower Street E Susx	24	C5
Lower Street Norfk	122	F4
Lower Street Suffk	88	F5
Lower Street Suffk	90	D5
Lower Stretton Warrtn	130	C3
Lower Stroud Dorset	15	K3
Lower Sundon C Beds	68	D2
Lower Swanwick Hants	19	H2
Lower Swell Gloucs	65	H2
Lower Tadmarton Oxon	83	J7
Lower Tale Devon	14	C2
Lower Tean Staffs	115	G4
Lower Thurlton Norfk	107	J3
Lower Town Cnwll	3	G5
Lower Town Devon	13	G8
Lower Town Herefs	80	E6
Lower Town Pembks	74	F5
Lower Trebullett Cnwll	11	L7
Lower Treluswell Cnwll	3	K4
Lower Tysoe Warwks	83	H6
Lower Ufford Suffk	91	G5
Lower Upcott Devon	13	K6
Lower Upham Hants	35	H7
Lower Upnor Medway	53	G5
Lower Vexford Somset	29	L4
Lower Walton Warrtn	130	B3
Lower Waterston Dorset	16	E4
Lower Weare Somset	44	E8
Lower Weedon Nhants	84	C3
Lower Welson Herefs	79	K5
Lower Westmancote Worcs	81	L7
Lower Whatcombe Dorset	17	G2
Lower Whatley Somset	32	B2
Lower Whitley Ches W	130	B4
Lower Wick Gloucs	63	L7
Lower Wick Worcs	81	J5
Lower Wield Hants	35	K3
Lower Willingdon E Susx	23	K6
Lower Withington Ches E	130	F5
Lower Woodend Bucks	49	K2
Lower Woodford Wilts	33	K4
Lower Wraxhall Dorset	16	A2
Lower Wyche Worcs	81	H6
Lower Wyke C Brad	141	J3
Lowesby Leics	100	F2
Lowestoft Suffk	107	L5
Loweswater Cumb	164	F6
Low Fell Gatesd	181	G7
Lowfield Heath W Susx	37	L3
Low Gartachorrans Stirlg	208	D2
Low Gate Nthumb	179	L6
Low Gettbridge Cumb	178	C7
Lowgill Cumb	157	K3
Lowgill Lancs	148	A3
Low Grantley N York	150	B2
Low Green N York	150	B4
Low Habberley Worcs	97	H7
Low Ham Somset	30	F5
Low Harrogate N York	150	C5
Low Hawsker N York	163	G1
Low Hesket Cumb	166	B2
Low Hutton N York	152	A2
Lowick Cumb	156	D5
Lowick Nhants	101	L7
Lowick Nthumb	203	G5
Lowick Bridge Cumb	156	D5
Lowick Green Cumb	156	D5
Low Knipe Cumb	166	C6
Low Laithe N York	150	B3
Lowlands Dur	168	E5
Lowlands Torfn	62	C7
Low Langton Lincs	136	C4
Low Leighton Derbys	131	K3
Low Lorton Cumb	164	F5
Low Marishes N York	162	E7
Low Marnham Notts	134	F6
Low Middleton Nthumb	203	H6
Low Mill N York	161	L4
Low Moor C Brad	141	J2
Low Moorsley Sundld	169	J2
Low Moresby Cumb	164	C6
Low Newton Cumb	156	F6
Low Row Cumb	165	G2
Low Row Cumb	165	K3
Low Row Cumb	178	D6
Low Row N York	159	H3
Low Salchrie D & G	172	C2
Low Santon N Linc	144	B5
Lowsonford Warwks	82	E2
Low Street Norfk	123	G6
Low Street Thurr	52	E3
Low Tharston Norfk	106	D4
Lowther Cumb	166	D6
Lowther Castle Cumb	166	C6
Lowthorpe E R Yk	153	H4
Lowton Devon	12	F2
Lowton Somset	30	B7
Lowton Wigan	139	J8
Lowton Common Wigan	139	J8
Lowton St Mary's Wigan	139	J8
Low Torry Fife	210	D2
Low Toynton Lincs	136	E5
Low Valley Barns	142	B7
Low Wood Cumb	156	E6
Low Worsall N York	160	F1
Low Wray Cumb	156	E2
Loxbeare Devon	29	G7
Loxhill Surrey	36	F3
Loxhore Devon	27	L3
Loxhore Cott Devon	27	L3
Loxley Warwks	83	G4
Loxley Green Staffs	115	H5
Loxter Herefs	81	G7
Loxton N Som	44	D7
Loxwood W Susx	36	F4
Lubenham Leics	100	F6
Lucasgate Lincs	119	M2
Lucas Green Surrey	50	B7
Luccombe Somset	29	G4
Luccombe Village IoW	19	K7
Lucker Nthumb	203	J7
Luckett Cnwll	11	M7
Lucking Street Essex	89	G8
Luckington Wilts	46	B2
Lucklawhill Fife	223	G3
Lucknam Wilts	46	B4
Luckwell Bridge Somset	28	F3
Lucton Herefs	80	B2
Lucy Cross N York	169	G8
Ludag W Isls	283	c12
Ludborough Lincs	145	H8
Ludbrook Devon	7	J4
Ludchurch Pembks	55	K4
Luddenden Calder	141	G3
Luddenden Foot Calder	140	F3
Luddenham Court Kent	40	C3
Luddesdown Kent	52	E5
Luddington N Linc	143	L4
Luddington Warwks	82	E5
Luddington in the Brook Nhants	102	C6
Ludford Lincs	136	D2
Ludford Shrops	96	C8
Ludgershall Bucks	67	G4
Ludgershall Wilts	34	B1
Ludgvan Cnwll	2	D4
Ludham Norfk	123	H7
Ludlow Shrops	96	C8
Ludney Somset	30	F8
Ludwell Wilts	32	F6
Ludworth Dur	169	K2
Luffenhall Herts	69	J1
Luffincott Devon	11	L4
Luffness E Loth	212	B3
Lugar E Ayrs	197	H6
Luggate Burn E Loth	212	D4
Lugg Green Herefs	80	B3
Luggiebank N Lans	209	K4
Lugton E Ayrs	208	C8
Lugwardine Herefs	80	D7
Luib Highld	247	J3
Luing Ag & B	215	L2
Lulham Herefs	80	A7
Lullington Derbys	99	H1
Lullington E Susx	23	J6
Lullington Somset	45	M8
Lulsgate Bottom N Som	45	G6
Lulsley Worcs	81	G4
Lulworth Camp Dorset	16	F6
Lumb Calder	140	F3
Lumb Lancs	140	C3
Lumbutts Calder	140	E3
Lumby N York	142	D2
Lumphanan Abers	244	D3
Lumphinnans Fife	222	B8
Lumsden Abers	255	K7
Lunan Angus	235	H5
Lunanhead Angus	234	D5
Luncarty P & K	221	K1
Lund E R Yk	152	E6
Lund N York	143	G1
Lundie Angus	233	L8
Lundin Links Fife	223	G6
Lundin Mill Fife	223	G6
Lundy Devon	26	B2
Lundy Green Norfk	106	E5
Lunga Ag & B	215	K3
Lunna Shet	281	e4
Lunsford Kent	52	F7
Lunsford's Cross E Susx	24	C5
Lunt Sefton	138	D7
Luntley Herefs	79	M4
Luppitt Devon	14	E1
Lupridge Devon	7	L4
Lupset Wakefd	141	M4
Lupton Cumb	157	J6
Lurgashall W Susx	36	D5
Lurley Devon	29	G7
Lusby Lincs	136	F6
Luscombe Devon	8	B3
Luson Devon	7	H5
Luss Ag & B	218	E8
Lussagiven Ag & B	215	J7
Lusta Highld	258	D5
Lustleigh Devon	13	H6
Luston Herefs	80	B3
Luthermuir Abers	235	G2
Luthrie Fife	222	E3
Lutley Dudley	97	L6
Luton Devon	13	L7
Luton Devon	14	C2
Luton Luton	68	E3
Luton Medway	53	G5
Lutterworth Leics	100	C6
Lutton Devon	7	H3
Lutton Devon	7	K3
Lutton Lincs	119	M6
Lutton Nhants	102	C6
Luxborough Somset	29	H3
Luxulyan Cnwll	5	H3
Luzley Tamesd	140	E7

Lybster Highld 275 H1
Lydbury North Shrops 95 J6
Lydcott Devon 28 B4
Lydd Kent 25 K3
Lydden Kent 41 H6
Lydden Kent 41 K2
Lyddington Rutlnd 101 J4
Lydd-on-Sea Kent 25 K3
Lydeard St Lawrence Somset 29 L4
Lyde Green Hants 49 H7
Lydford Devon 12 C5
Lydford on Fosse Somset 31 J5
Lydgate Calder 140 D3
Lydgate Rochdl 140 E4
Lydham Shrops 95 H5
Lydiard Green Wilts 47 G2
Lydiard Millicent Wilts 47 G2
Lydiard Tregoze Swindn 47 G2
Lydiate Sefton 138 D7
Lydiate Ash Worcs 98 B8
Lydlinch Dorset 32 B8
Lydney Gloucs 63 J6
Lydstep Pembks 55 J7
Lye Dudley 97 L6
Lye Cross N Som 44 F6
Lye Green Bucks 68 B6
Lye Green E Susx 38 D6
Lye Green Warwks 82 E2
Lye Head Worcs 97 G8
Lye's Green Wilts 32 D2
Lyford Oxon 66 B8
Lymbridge Green Kent 40 F6
Lyme Regis Dorset 15 H4
Lyminge Kent 40 F7
Lymington Hants 18 E4
Lyminster W Susx 21 H6
Lymm Warrtn 130 D2
Lympne Kent 40 F8
Lympsham Somset 44 C8
Lympstone Devon 14 A6
Lynbridge Devon 28 C1
Lynchat Highld 241 L3
Lynch Green Norfk 106 C2
Lyndhurst Hants 18 D2
Lyndon Rutlnd 101 K3
Lyndon Green Birm 98 F6
Lyne Border 199 L5
Lyne Surrey 50 C5
Lyneal Shrops 113 G5
Lyne Down Herefs 63 J1
Lyneham Devon 13 K6
Lyneham Oxon 65 K3
Lyneham Wilts 46 F3
Lyneholmford Cumb 178 C4
Lynemouth Nthumb 191 K7
Lyne of Skene Abers 245 G2
Lynesack Dur 168 E5
Lyness Ork 275 b6
Lyng Norfk 122 B7
Lyng Somset 30 E5
Lynmouth Devon 28 C1
Lynn Staffs 98 D3
Lynn Wrekin 114 B8
Lynsted Kent 40 B3
Lynstone Cnwll 11 H2
Lynton Devon 28 C1
Lynton Cross Devon 27 K2
Lyon's Gate Dorset 16 C2
Lyonshall Herefs 79 L4
Lytchett Matravers Dorset 17 J3
Lytchett Minster Dorset 17 J4
Lyth Highld 280 C4
Lytham Lancs 138 D2
Lytham St Anne's Lancs 138 D2
Lythbank Shrops 95 L2
Lythe N York 171 K8
Lythmore Highld 279 J3

M

Mabe Burnthouse Cnwll 3 J4
Mablethorpe Lincs 137 J3
Macclesfield Ches E 131 H5
Macclesfield Crematorium
Ches E 131 H5
Macduff Abers 268 C3
Macharioch Ag & B 192 E6
Machen Caerph 43 K4
Machrie N Ayrs 194 D4
Machrihanish Ag & B 192 D4
Machrins Ag & B 214 D5
Machynlleth Powys 93 G3
Machynys Carmth 56 F5
Mackworth Derbys 116 A4
Macmerry E Loth 211 M4
Maddaford Devon 12 D4
Madderty P & K 221 G3

Maddington Wilts 33 J2
Maddiston Falk 210 B4
Madehurst W Susx 21 G5
Madeley Staffs 114 B3
Madeley Wrekin 96 F3
Madeley Heath Staffs 114 B2
Madford Devon 29 L8
Madingley Cambs 87 H3
Madley Herefs 80 A7
Madresfield Worcs 81 J5
Madron Cnwll 2 C5
Maenaddwyn IoA 125 H3
Maenan Conwy 126 F6
Maenclochog Pembks 75 J6
Maendy V Glam 42 F6
Maenporth Cnwll 3 K5
Maentwrog Gwynd 110 C3
Maen-y-groes Cerdgn 76 C3
Maer Cnwll 11 H1
Maer Staffs 114 B4
Maerdy Carmth 59 J3
Maerdy Rhondd 42 E2
Maesbrook Shrops 112 D6
Maesbury Shrops 112 D6
Maesbury Marsh Shrops 112 D6
Maes-glas Newpt 44 C2
Maesgwynne Carmth 55 L2
Maeshafn Denbgs 128 E7
Maesllyn Cerdgn 76 C6
Maesmynis Powys 78 D6
Maesmynis Powys 78 E5
Maesteg Brdgnd 42 C3
Maesybont Carmth 59 G5
Maesycwmmer Caerph 43 J3
Maggieknockater Moray 254 C4
Maggots End Essex 70 C2
Magham Down E Susx 23 K5
Maghull Sefton 138 D7
Magna Park Leics 100 B6
Magor Mons 44 E2
Maidenbower W Susx 37 L4
Maiden Bradley Wilts 32 D3
Maidencombe Torbay 8 D1
Maidenhayne Devon 15 G3
Maiden Head N Som 45 H5
Maidenhead W & M 49 L3
Maiden Law Dur 168 F1
Maiden Newton Dorset 16 B3
Maidens S Ayrs 182 F1
Maiden's Green Br For 49 L4
Maidenwell Lincs 136 F4
Maiden Wells Pembks 55 G7
Maidford Nhants 84 B5
Maids Moreton Bucks 84 D8
Maidstone Kent 39 J2
Maidwell Nhants 101 G8
Mail Shet 281 e6
Maindee Newpt 44 C1
Mainland Ork 275 c4
Mainland Shet 281 d6
Mainsforth Dur 169 J4
Mains of Balhall Angus 234 D3
Mains of Balnakettle Abers 244 E8
Mains of Dalvey Highld 254 B5
Mains of Haulkerton Abers 235 H1
Mains of Lesmoir Abers 255 J6
Mains of Melgunds Angus 234 E4
Mainsriddle D & G 176 B7
Mainstone Shrops 95 G6
Maisemore Gloucs 64 A3
Major's Green Worcs 98 E7
Makeney Derbys 116 B3
Malborough Devon 7 K7
Malcoff Derbys 131 L3
Malden Rushett Gt Lon 50 F6
Maldon Essex 71 K5
Malham N York 148 F3
Maligar Highld 259 H4
Mallaig Highld 237 K1
Mallaigvaig Highld 237 K1
Malleny Mills C Edin 211 G6
Mallows Green Essex 70 C2
Malltraeth IoA 125 G6
Mallwyd Gwynd 93 J1
Malmesbury Wilts 46 D2
Malmsmead Devon 28 D1
Malpas Ches W 113 H2
Malpas Cnwll 4 D6
Malpas Newpt 44 C1
Malshanger Hants 48 E8
Malswick Gloucs 63 L2
Maltby Lincs 136 F3
Maltby Rothm 133 K1
Maltby S on T 170 B8
Maltby le Marsh Lincs 137 J3
Malting Green Essex 72 E3
Maltman's Hill Kent 40 A6
Malton N York 152 B2

Malvern Worcs 81 H6
Malvern Link Worcs 81 H5
Malvern Wells Worcs 81 H6
Mamble Worcs 80 F1
Mamhilad Mons 62 C6
Manaccan Cnwll 3 J6
Manafon Powys 94 D3
Manais W Isls 282 e6
Manaton Devon 13 H6
Manby Lincs 137 G2
Mancetter Warwks 99 J4
Manchester Manch 140 C8
Manchester Crematorium
Manch 131 G1
Mancot Flints 129 H6
Mandally Highld 240 A3
Manea Cambs 103 K5
Maney Birm 98 E4
Manfield N York 169 G8
Mangerton Dorset 15 L3
Mangotsfield S Glos 45 K4
Mangrove Green Herts 68 E2
Manhay Cnwll 3 H5
Manish W Isls 282 e6
Mankinholes Calder 140 E3
Manley Ches W 129 L5
Manmoel Caerph 61 J6
Mannal Ag & B 224 C7
Manningford Bohune Wilts 47 H7
Manningford Bruce Wilts 47 H7
Manningham C Brad 141 J1
Mannings Heath W Susx 37 K5
Mannington Dorset 17 L2
Manningtree Essex 73 G1
Mannofield C Aber 245 K3
Manorbier Pembks 55 H7
Manorbier Newton Pembks 55 H6
Manordeilo Carmth 59 J4
Manorhill Border 201 K6
Manorowen Pembks 74 F5
Manor Park Gt Lon 51 L2
Manor Park Crematorium
Gt Lon 51 L2
Mansell Gamage Herefs 79 M6
Mansell Lacy Herefs 80 A6
Mansergh Cumb 157 K6
Mansfield E Ayrs 197 J8
Mansfield Notts 133 K7
Mansfield & District
Crematorium Notts 133 K7
Mansfield Woodhouse Notts 133 K7
Mansriggs Cumb 156 D6
Manston Dorset 32 D7
Manston Kent 41 K2
Manston Leeds 142 B1
Manswood Dorset 17 J1
Manthorpe Lincs 118 B4
Manthorpe Lincs 118 E8
Manton N Linc 144 A7
Manton Notts 134 C4
Manton Rutlnd 101 J3
Manton Wilts 47 H5
Manuden Essex 70 C2
Manwood Green Essex 70 E4
Maperton Somset 31 L5
Maplebeck Notts 134 E7
Maple Cross Herts 68 C8
Mapledurham Oxon 49 G4
Mapledurwell Hants 49 G8
Maplehurst W Susx 37 J6
Maplescombe Kent 52 C6
Mapleton Derbys 115 K2
Mapleton Kent 38 C3
Mapperley Derbys 116 D3
Mapperley Park C Nott 117 G3
Mapperton Dorset 15 L3
Mappleborough Green
Warwks 82 C2
Mappleton E R Yk 153 K7
Mapplewell Barns 141 M5
Mappowder Dorset 16 E2
Marazanvose Cnwll 4 C5
Marazion Cnwll 2 E5
Marbury Ches E 113 J2
March Cambs 103 J4
March S Lans 186 E3
Marcham Oxon 66 C2
Marchamley Shrops 113 K5
Marchamley Wood Shrops 113 K5
Marchington Staffs 115 J5
Marchington Woodlands
Staffs 115 J6
Marchros Gwynd 108 E6
Marchwiel Wrexhm 112 E2
Marchwood Hants 18 F2
Marcross V Glam 42 D7
Marden Herefs 80 C6
Marden Kent 39 J4
Marden Wilts 47 G7

Marden Ash Essex 70 E6
Marden Beech Kent 39 J5
Marden's Hill E Susx 38 D7
Marden Thorn Kent 39 J5
Mardlebury Herts 69 H3
Mardy Mons 62 C4
Marefield Leics 101 G2
Mareham le Fen Lincs 136 E7
Mareham on the Hill Lincs 136 E6
Marehay Derbys 116 C2
Marehill W Susx 21 H3
Maresfield E Susx 23 G2
Marfleet C KuH 144 F2
Marford Wrexhm 129 H8
Margam Neath 57 L7
Margam Crematorium Neath 42 B7
Margaret Marsh Dorset 32 D7
Margaret Roding Essex 70 F5
Margaretting Essex 71 G6
Margaretting Tye Essex 71 G6
Margate Kent 41 K1
Margnaheglish N Ayrs 195 G4
Margrie D & G 174 F5
Margrove Park R & Cl 170 F7
Marham Norfk 104 E2
Marhamchurch Cnwll 11 J2
Marholm C Pete 102 C3
Marian-glas IoA 125 J3
Mariansleigh Devon 28 C6
Marine Town Kent 53 K4
Marionburgh Abers 244 F2
Marishader Highld 259 H4
Maristow Devon 6 F2
Marjoriebanks D & G 176 E2
Mark Somset 30 F1
Markbeech Kent 38 D5
Markby Lincs 137 J4
Mark Causeway Somset 30 E2
Mark Cross E Susx 38 F7
Markeaton C Derb 116 B4
Markeaton Crematorium
C Derb 116 B4
Market Bosworth Leics 99 L3
Market Deeping Lincs 102 C2
Market Drayton Shrops 113 L5
Market Harborough Leics 100 F6
Market Lavington Wilts 46 F8
Market Overton Rutlnd 118 A8
Market Rasen Lincs 136 B2
Market Stainton Lincs 136 D4
Market Warsop Notts 133 L6
Market Weighton E R Yk 152 D5
Market Weston Suffk 105 K7
Markfield Leics 100 B2
Markham Caerph 61 J6
Markham Moor Notts 134 E5
Markinch Fife 222 E6
Markington N York 150 C3
Markle E Loth 212 C3
Marksbury BaNES 45 K6
Mark's Corner IoW 19 H5
Marks Tey Essex 72 C2
Markwell Cnwll 6 D4
Markyate Herts 68 C4
Marlborough Wilts 47 J5
Marlbrook Herefs 80 C4
Marlbrook Worcs 98 B8
Marlcliff Warwks 82 C5
Marldon Devon 8 C2
Marle Green E Susx 23 K4
Marlesford Suffk 91 H3
Marley Kent 41 G5
Marley Kent 41 G4
Marley Green Ches E 113 J2
Marley Hill Gatesd 180 F7
Marlingford Norfk 106 C2
Marloes Pembks 54 C5
Marlow Bucks 49 K2
Marlow Herefs 95 K8
Marlow Bottom Bucks 49 K1
Marlpit Hill Kent 38 C4
Marlpits E Susx 24 C4
Marlpits E Susx 38 C7
Marlpool Derbys 116 D3
Marnhull Dorset 32 C7
Marple Stockp 131 J2
Marple Bridge Stockp 131 J2
Marr Donc 142 E6
Marrick N York 159 K3
Marros Carmth 55 L5
Marsden Kirk 141 G5
Marsden S Tyne 181 K6
Marsden Height Lancs 148 F5
Marsett N York 158 F5
Marsh Bucks 67 K5
Marsh C Brad 149 J8
Marsh Devon 30 C8
Marshall's Heath Herts 68 F4
Marshalswick Herts 68 F5

Marsham Norfk 122 D6
Marsh Baldon Oxon 66 E7
Marsh Benham W Berk 48 B5
Marshborough Kent 41 J4
Marshbrook Shrops 95 K5
Marshchapel Lincs 145 K7
Marsh Farm Luton 68 D2
Marshfield Newpt 43 L5
Marshfield S Glos 45 M4
Marshgate Cnwll 11 G4
Marsh Gibbon Bucks 66 F3
Marsh Green Devon 14 B4
Marsh Green Kent 38 C4
Marsh Green Wrekin 113 K8
Marshland St James Norfk 103 L2
Marsh Lane Derbys 133 H4
Marsh Lane Gloucs 63 H5
Marshside Sefton 138 D4
Marsh Street Somset 29 H2
Marshwood Dorset 15 J3
Marske N York 159 K3
Marske-by-the-Sea R & Cl 170 E6
Marsland Green Wigan 139 H4
Marston Ches W 130 D5
Marston Herefs 79 L4
Marston Lincs 118 A3
Marston Oxon 66 D5
Marston Staffs 97 J1
Marston Staffs 114 E6
Marston Warwks 99 G4
Marston Wilts 46 D7
Marston Green Solhll 98 F6
Marston Jabbet Warwks 99 K5
Marston Magna Somset 31 K6
Marston Meysey Wilts 65 H7
Marston Montgomery Derbys 115 J4
Marston Moretaine C Beds 85 K7
Marston on Dove Derbys 115 L5
Marston St Lawrence Nhants 84 A7
Marston Stannett Herefs 80 D4
Marston Trussell Nhants 100 F6
Marstow Herefs 63 H3
Marsworth Bucks 68 A4
Marten Wilts 47 L7
Marthall Ches E 130 F4
Martham Norfk 123 J7
Martin Hants 33 J7
Martin Kent 41 K6
Martin Lincs 136 B7
Martin Lincs 136 D6
Martindale Cumb 166 B6
Martin Dales Lincs 136 C7
Martin Drove End Hants 33 H6
Martinhoe Devon 28 B1
Martin Hussingtree Worcs 81 K3
Martinscroft Warrtn 130 C2
Martinstown Dorset 16 C5
Martlesham Suffk 90 F6
Martlesham Heath Suffk 90 F6
Martletwy Pembks 55 H5
Martley Worcs 81 H3
Martock Somset 31 G7
Marton Ches E 131 G4
Marton Ches W 130 C6
Marton Cumb 156 C7
Marton E R Yk 153 J7
Marton E R Yk 153 K2
Marton Lincs 135 G3
Marton Middsb 170 C7
Marton N York 150 F3
Marton N York 162 C6
Marton Shrops 95 G3
Marton Warwks 83 J2
Marton-le-Moor N York 150 E2
Martyr's Green Surrey 50 E7
Martyr Worthy Hants 35 G4
Marwick Ork 275 b3
Marwood Devon 27 K3
Marybank Highld 250 E1
Maryburgh Highld 262 F8
Marygold Border 213 H7
Maryhill C Glas 208 F5
Maryhill Crematorium C Glas 208 F5
Marykirk Abers 235 H2
Maryland Mons 63 G6
Marylebone Gt Lon 51 H4
Marylebone Wigan 139 H6
Marypark Moray 254 D4
Maryport Cumb 164 D3
Maryport D & G 172 E7
Marystow Devon 12 B6
Mary Tavy Devon 12 C6
Maryton Angus 235 H4
Marywell Abers 244 D4
Marywell Abers 245 L4
Marywell Angus 235 G6
Masham N York 160 B6
Mashbury Essex 71 G5
Mason N u Ty 180 F4

Masongill N York 157 L7
Masonhill Crematorium S Ayrs 196 D7
Mastin Moor Derbys 133 J4
Matching Essex 70 D5
Matching Green Essex 70 D5
Matching Tye Essex 70 D5
Matfen Nthumb 180 C4
Matfield Kent 39 G5
Mathern Mons 45 G1
Mathon Herefs 81 G6
Mathry Pembks 74 E6
Matlask Norfk 122 C4
Matlock Derbys 132 F7
Matlock Bank Derbys 132 F7
Matlock Bath Derbys 132 F8
Matlock Dale Derbys 132 F7
Matson Gloucs 64 B4
Matterdale End Cumb 165 L6
Mattersey Notts 134 D2
Mattersey Thorpe Notts 134 D2
Mattingley Hants 49 H7
Mattishall Norfk 105 L1
Mattishall Burgh Norfk 105 L1
Mauchline E Ayrs 196 F5
Maud Abers 269 G6
Maufant Jersey 9 e2
Maugersbury Gloucs 65 J2
Maughold IoM 154 g4
Mauld Highld 250 C4
Maulden C Beds 85 L7
Maulds Meaburn Cumb 166 E7
Maunby N York 160 E5
Maund Bryan Herefs 80 D5
Maundown Somset 29 J5
Mautby Norfk 107 K1
Mavesyn Ridware Staffs 115 H8
Mavis Enderby Lincs 137 G6
Mawbray Cumb 164 E1
Mawdesley Lancs 139 G5
Mawdlam Brdgnd 42 B5
Mawgan Cnwll 3 H6
Mawgan Porth Cnwll 4 D2
Maw Green Ches E 130 D8
Mawla Cnwll 4 A5
Mawnan Cnwll 3 K5
Mawnan Smith Cnwll 3 K5
Mawsley Nhants 101 H8
Mawthorpe Lincs 137 J5
Maxey C Pete 102 C2
Maxstoke Warwks 99 G6
Maxted Street Kent 40 F6
Maxton Border 201 J7
Maxton Kent 41 J7
Maxwelltown D & G 176 C4
Maxworthy Cnwll 11 J4
Mayals Swans 57 H6
May Bank Staffs 114 D2
Maybole S Ayrs 183 H1
Maybury Surrey 50 C7
Mayes Green Surrey 37 H3
Mayfield E Susx 23 K2
Mayfield Mdloth 211 K6
Mayfield Staffs 115 J2
Mayford Surrey 50 C7
May Hill Gloucs 63 L3
Mayland Essex 72 D6
Maylandsea Essex 72 C6
Maynard's Green E Susx 23 K3
Maypole Birm 98 D7
Maypole Kent 41 G2
Maypole Mons 62 F4
Maypole Green Norfk 107 J4
Maypole Green Suffk 89 J3
Maypole Green Suffk 91 G2
May's Green Oxon 49 H3
May's Green Surrey 50 E7
Mead Devon 26 C7
Meadgate BaNES 45 K7
Meadle Bucks 67 K6
Meadowfield Dur 169 H3
Meadowtown Shrops 95 H3
Meadwell Devon 12 A6
Meaford Staffs 114 D4
Meal Bank Cumb 157 H4
Mealrigg Cumb 164 F2
Mealsgate Cumb 165 H2
Meanwood Leeds 150 C8
Mearbeck N York 148 E4
Meare Somset 31 G3
Meare Green Somset 30 D6
Meare Green Somset 30 E5
Mearns E Rens 208 F7
Mears Ashby Nhants 85 G2
Measham Leics 99 J1
Meath Green Surrey 37 L2
Meathop Cumb 156 F6
Meaux E R Yk 153 H7
Meavaig W Isls 282 e3
Meavy Devon 7 G2

Medbourne Leics 101 H5
Medburn Nthumb 180 D5
Meddon Devon 26 D7
Meden Vale Notts 134 B5
Medlam Lincs 136 F8
Medlar Lancs 147 H8
Medmenham Bucks 49 K2
Medomsley Dur 180 D7
Medstead Hants 35 K3
Medway Crematorium Kent 53 G6
Meerbrook Staffs 131 K7
Meer Common Herefs 79 L5
Meesden Herts 70 B1
Meeson Wrekin 113 L6
Meeth Devon 12 D1
Meeting Green Suffk 88 E4
Meeting House Hill Norfk 122 F6
Meifod Powys 94 E1
Meigle P & K 233 L6
Meikle Carco D & G 186 A3
Meikle Earnock S Lans 209 J8
Meikle Kilmory Ag & B 207 G6
Meikle Obney P & K 232 F7
Meikleour P & K 233 J7
Meikle Wartle Abers 256 C5
Meinciau Carmth 56 E3
Meir C Stke 114 E3
Meir Heath Staffs 114 E3
Melbourn Cambs 87 H6
Melbourne Derbys 116 C6
Melbourne E R Yk 152 A7
Melbur Cnwll 4 F4
Melbury Devon 26 F7
Melbury Abbas Dorset 32 E6
Melbury Bubb Dorset 16 B2
Melbury Osmond Dorset 16 A1
Melbury Sampford Dorset 16 A2
Melchbourne Bed 85 K2
Melcombe Bingham Dorset 16 E2
Meldon Devon 12 D4
Meldon Nthumb 180 D2
Meldon Park Nthumb 180 D2
Meldreth Cambs 87 H6
Meldrum Stirlg 220 C7
Melfort Ag & B 216 C4
Meliden Denbgs 128 C3
Melinau Pembks 55 K4
Melin-byrhedyn Powys 93 H4
Melincourt Neath 60 D7
Melin-y-coed Conwy 127 G7
Melin-y-ddol Powys 94 D2
Melin-y-wig Denbgs 111 K2
Melkinthorpe Cumb 166 D5
Melkridge Nthumb 179 G7
Melksham Wilts 46 C6
Mellangoose Cnwll 3 H5
Mell Green W Berk 48 C3
Mellguards Cumb 166 B2
Melling Lancs 147 M2
Melling Sefton 138 E7
Melling Mount Sefton 138 E7
Mellis Suffk 106 B8
Mellon Charles Highld 260 D2
Mellon Udrigle Highld 260 E1
Mellor Lancs 139 K2
Mellor Stockp 131 K2
Mellor Brook Lancs 139 J2
Mells Somset 32 B1
Mells Suffk 107 H8
Melmerby Cumb 166 E3
Melmerby N York 159 K5
Melmerby N York 160 E7
Melness Highld 277 K4
Melon Green Suffk 89 G4
Melplash Dorset 15 L3
Melrose Border 201 H6
Melsetter Ork 275 b6
Melsonby N York 160 B1
Meltham Kirk 141 H5
Meltham Mills Kirk 141 H5
Melton E R Yk 144 B2
Melton Suffk 91 G1
Meltonby E R Yk 152 B5
Melton Constable Norfk 122 A5
Melton Mowbray Leics 117 K7
Melton Ross N Linc 144 D1
Melvaig Highld 260 B3
Melverley Shrops 112 E8
Melverley Green Shrops 112 E7
Melvich Highld 278 D3
Membury Devon 15 G2
Memsie Abers 269 H4
Memus Angus 234 C4
Menabilly Cnwll 5 J4
Menagissey Cnwll 4 B5
Menai Bridge IoA 125 K5
Mendham Suffk 106 F6
Mendip Crematorium Somset 31 K2

Mendlesham Suffk 90 D2
Mendlesham Green Suffk 90 C3
Menheniot Cnwll 6 C4
Menithwood Worcs 81 G2
Menna Cnwll 4 E4
Mennock D & G 185 K2
Menston C Brad 149 L7
Menstrie Clacks 220 E7
Menthorpe N York 143 H1
Mentmore Bucks 67 M3
Meoble Highld 238 C6
Meole Brace Shrops 96 B1
Meonstoke Hants 35 J7
Meopham Kent 52 D5
Meopham Green Kent 52 D6
Meopham Station Kent 52 D5
Mepal Cambs 103 J7
Meppershall C Beds 86 C8
Merbach Herefs 79 K6
Mere Ches E 130 E3
Mere Wilts 32 D4
Mere Brow Lancs 138 E4
Mereclough Lancs 140 C2
Mere Green Birm 98 E4
Mere Green Worcs 81 L3
Mere Heath Ches W 130 C5
Meresborough Medway 53 H6
Mereworth Kent 39 G3
Meriden Solhll 99 G7
Merkadale Highld 246 E2
Merley Poole 17 K3
Merlin's Bridge Pembks 54 F4
Merrington Shrops 113 G7
Merrion Pembks 54 F7
Merriott Somset 31 G8
Merrivale Devon 12 D7
Merrow Surrey 36 F1
Merry Field Hill Dorset 17 K2
Merry Hill Herts 68 E8
Merryhill Wolves 97 K4
Merry Lees Leics 100 A2
Merrymeet Cnwll 6 B2
Mersea Island Essex 72 F4
Mersey Crossing Halton 129 L3
Mersham Kent 40 D7
Merstham Surrey 51 H8
Merston W Susx 20 E6
Merstone IoW 19 J6
Merther Cnwll 4 D6
Merthyr Carmth 58 C5
Merthyr Cynog Powys 78 D7
Merthyr Dyfan V Glam 43 H7
Merthyr Mawr Brdgnd 42 D6
Merthyr Tydfil Myr Td 61 G6
Merthyr Vale Myr Td 61 G7
Merton Devon 27 J8
Merton Gt Lon 51 H5
Merton Norfk 105 H4
Merton Oxon 66 E3
Meshaw Devon 28 D7
Messing Essex 72 C3
Messingham N Linc 143 M6
Metfield Suffk 106 F7
Metherell Cnwll 6 E1
Metheringham Lincs 135 L7
Methil Fife 222 F7
Methilhill Fife 222 F7
Methley Leeds 142 B2
Methley Junction Leeds 142 B3
Methlick Abers 256 F4
Methven P & K 221 J2
Methwold Norfk 104 E4
Methwold Hythe Norfk 104 E4
Mettingham Suffk 107 H5
Metton Norfk 122 D4
Mevagissey Cnwll 5 G6
Mexborough Donc 142 D7
Mey Highld 280 C2
Meysey Hampton Gloucs 65 G7
Miabhaig W Isls 282 e3
Michaelchurch Herefs 63 G2
Michaelchurch Escley Herefs 79 K8
Michaelchurch-on-Arrow
    Powys 79 J5
Michaelstone-y-Fedw Newpt 43 K5
Michaelston-le-Pit V Glam 43 J7
Michaelstow Cnwll 10 F6
Michelcombe Devon 7 K1
Micheldever Hants 35 G3
Micheldever Station Hants 35 G2
Michelmersh Hants 34 D5
Mickfield Suffk 90 D3
Micklebring Donc 133 K7
Mickleby N York 171 J8
Micklefield Leeds 142 C1
Micklefield Green Herts 68 D7
Mickleham Surrey 50 F8
Mickleover C Derb 116 A5
Micklethwaite C Brad 149 K7

Micklethwaite Cumb...... 165 J1
Mickleton Dur...... 168 B6
Mickleton Gloucs...... 82 E6
Mickletown Leeds...... 142 B2
Mickle Trafford Ches W...... 129 K5
Mickley Derbys...... 132 F4
Mickley N York...... 160 C7
Mickley Green Suffk...... 89 G4
Mickley Square Nthumb...... 180 C6
Mid Ardlaw Abers...... 269 H3
Midbea Ork...... 275 c2
Mid Beltie Abers...... 244 E3
Mid Bockhampton Dorset...... 18 B4
Mid Calder W Loth...... 210 E5
Mid Clyth Highld...... 280 C8
Mid Culbeuchly Abers...... 268 B4
Middle Assendon Oxon...... 49 H2
Middle Aston Oxon...... 66 C2
Middle Barton Oxon...... 66 B2
Middlebie D & G...... 177 H4
Middlebridge P & K...... 232 C2
Middle Chinnock Somset...... 31 G8
Middle Claydon Bucks...... 67 H2
Middlecliffe Barns...... 142 C6
Middlecott Devon...... 13 G5
Middle Duntisbourne Gloucs...... 64 E6
Middleham N York...... 159 L5
Middle Handley Derbys...... 133 H4
Middle Harling Norfk...... 105 K6
Middlehill Cnwll...... 6 B1
Middlehill Wilts...... 46 B5
Middlehope Shrops...... 96 B5
Middle Kames Ag & B...... 206 E1
Middle Littleton Worcs...... 82 C6
Middle Madeley Staffs...... 114 B3
Middle Maes-coed Herefs...... 79 L8
Middlemarsh Dorset...... 16 C1
Middle Mayfield Staffs...... 115 J3
Middle Mill Pembks...... 74 C7
Middlemore Devon...... 12 C8
Middle Quarter Kent...... 40 A7
Middle Rasen Lincs...... 136 A2
Middle Rocombe Devon...... 8 D1
Middle Salter Lancs...... 147 M3
Middlesbrough Middsb...... 170 C6
Middlesceugh Cumb...... 165 L2
Middleshaw Cumb...... 157 J5
Middlesmoor N York...... 159 K7
Middle Stoford Somset...... 30 B6
Middle Stoke Medway...... 53 H4
Middlestone Dur...... 169 H4
Middlestone Moor Dur...... 169 H4
Middle Stoughton Somset...... 30 F1
Middlestown Wakefd...... 141 L4
Middle Street Gloucs...... 63 M6
Middle Taphouse Cnwll...... 5 K2
Middlethird Border...... 201 L4
Middleton Ag & B...... 224 B6
Middleton Cumb...... 157 K5
Middleton Derbys...... 132 D7
Middleton Derbys...... 132 E8
Middleton Essex...... 89 H7
Middleton Hants...... 34 F2
Middleton Herefs...... 80 D1
Middleton Lancs...... 147 H4
Middleton Leeds...... 141 M2
Middleton N York...... 149 L6
Middleton N York...... 162 D5
Middleton Nhants...... 101 J5
Middleton Norfk...... 120 E8
Middleton Nthumb...... 180 C2
Middleton Nthumb...... 203 H6
Middleton P & K...... 221 L6
Middleton Rochdl...... 140 C6
Middleton Shrops...... 96 C7
Middleton Shrops...... 112 D5
Middleton Suffk...... 91 K2
Middleton Swans...... 56 D7
Middleton Warwks...... 98 F4
Middleton Cheney Nhants...... 83 L7
Middleton Crematorium
     Rochdl...... 140 C6
Middleton Green Staffs...... 114 E4
Middleton Hall Nthumb...... 202 F8
Middleton-in-Teesdale Dur...... 168 B5
Middleton Moor Suffk...... 91 J2
Middleton One Row Darltn...... 169 K8
Middleton-on-Leven N York...... 161 G1
Middleton-on-Sea W Susx...... 20 F6
Middleton on the Hill Herefs...... 80 C2
Middleton on the Wolds
     E R Yk...... 152 E6
Middleton Park C Aber...... 245 K1
Middleton Priors Shrops...... 96 E5
Middleton Quernhow N York...... 160 E7
Middleton Scriven Shrops...... 96 F6
Middleton Stoney Oxon...... 66 D2
Middleton Tyas N York...... 160 B2

Middletown Cumb...... 155 H1
Middle Town IoS...... 10 b3
Middletown N Som...... 44 F4
Middletown Powys...... 95 H1
Middle Tysoe Warwks...... 83 H6
Middle Wallop Hants...... 34 C3
Middlewich Ches E...... 130 D6
Middle Winterslow Wilts...... 34 B4
Middlewood Cnwll...... 11 K7
Middlewood Herefs...... 79 K6
Middle Woodford Wilts...... 33 K4
Middlewood Green Suffk...... 90 C3
Middleyard E Ayrs...... 197 G4
Middle Yard Gloucs...... 64 B6
Middlezoy Somset...... 30 E4
Middridge Dur...... 169 H5
Midford BaNES...... 45 M6
Midge Hall Lancs...... 139 G3
Midgeholme Cumb...... 178 E7
Midgham W Berk...... 48 E5
Midgley Calder...... 140 F3
Midgley Wakefd...... 141 L5
Mid Holmwood Surrey...... 37 J2
Midhopestones Sheff...... 141 K7
Midhurst W Susx...... 36 C6
Mid Lavant W Susx...... 20 D5
Midlem Border...... 201 H7
Mid Mains Highld...... 250 D4
Midney Somset...... 31 H5
Midpark Ag & B...... 207 G7
Midsomer Norton BaNES...... 45 K8
Midtown Highld...... 277 K4
Midville Lincs...... 137 G8
Mid Warwickshire
     Crematorium Warwks...... 83 G3
Midway Ches E...... 131 H3
Mid Yell Shet...... 281 e3
Migvie Abers...... 244 A2
Milborne Port Somset...... 31 L7
Milborne St Andrew Dorset...... 16 F3
Milborne Wick Somset...... 31 L6
Milbourne Nthumb...... 180 D4
Milbourne Wilts...... 46 D2
Milburn Cumb...... 166 F5
Milbury Heath S Glos...... 45 K1
Milby N York...... 150 F2
Milcombe Oxon...... 83 K8
Milden Suffk...... 89 J6
Mildenhall Suffk...... 104 E8
Mildenhall Wilts...... 47 J5
Milebrook Powys...... 79 K1
Milebush Kent...... 39 J4
Mile Elm Wilts...... 46 E5
Mile End Essex...... 72 E2
Mile End Gloucs...... 63 H5
Mile End Suffk...... 107 G5
Mileham Norfk...... 121 K7
Mile Oak Br & H...... 22 C5
Mile Oak Kent...... 39 H4
Mile Oak Staffs...... 98 F3
Miles Hope Herefs...... 80 D2
Milesmark Fife...... 210 E1
Miles Platting Manch...... 140 C7
Mile Town Kent...... 53 K4
Milfield Nthumb...... 202 E6
Milford Derbys...... 116 B3
Milford Devon...... 26 D6
Milford Powys...... 94 D5
Milford Staffs...... 114 F7
Milford Surrey...... 36 E2
Milford Haven Pembks...... 54 E5
Milford on Sea Hants...... 18 D5
Milkwall Gloucs...... 63 H5
Millais Jersey...... 9 a1
Milland W Susx...... 36 B5
Milland Marsh W Susx...... 36 C5
Mill Bank Calder...... 140 F3
Millbeck Cumb...... 165 H5
Millbreck Abers...... 257 J3
Millbridge Surrey...... 36 C2
Millbrook C Beds...... 85 K7
Millbrook C Sotn...... 34 E8
Millbrook Cnwll...... 6 E4
Millbrook Jersey...... 9 c3
Millbrook Tamesd...... 140 E7
Mill Brow Stockp...... 131 J2
Millbuie Abers...... 245 H2
Millbuie Highld...... 250 F1
Millcombe Devon...... 8 B5
Mill Common Norfk...... 107 G3
Mill Common Suffk...... 107 H7
Millcorner E Susx...... 24 E3
Millcraig Highld...... 263 H5
Mill Cross Devon...... 7 L3
Milldale Staffs...... 115 J1
Mill End Bucks...... 49 J2
Mill End Cambs...... 103 G7
Millend Gloucs...... 63 L7
Mill End Herts...... 87 G8

Millerhill Mdloth...... 211 K5
Miller's Dale Derbys...... 132 C5
Millers Green Derbys...... 115 M1
Miller's Green Essex...... 70 E5
Millerston C Glas...... 209 H5
Millgate Lancs...... 140 D4
Mill Green Cambs...... 88 C6
Mill Green Essex...... 70 F6
Mill Green Herts...... 69 G5
Mill Green Lincs...... 119 H6
Mill Green Norfk...... 106 C6
Millgreen Shrops...... 113 L6
Mill Green Staffs...... 98 D3
Mill Green Staffs...... 115 H7
Mill Green Suffk...... 89 J6
Mill Green Suffk...... 89 K4
Mill Green Suffk...... 90 D3
Mill Green Suffk...... 91 H3
Millhalf Herefs...... 79 K5
Millhayes Devon...... 14 F2
Millhead Lancs...... 147 K2
Millheugh S Lans...... 198 B3
Mill Hill E Susx...... 23 L6
Mill Hill Gt Lon...... 69 G8
Millhouse Ag & B...... 206 F5
Millhouse Cumb...... 165 K3
Millhousebridge D & G...... 176 F2
Millhouse Green Barns...... 141 K7
Millhouses Barns...... 142 C6
Millhouses Sheff...... 133 G3
Milliken Park Rens...... 208 C6
Millin Cross Pembks...... 55 G4
Millington E R Yk...... 152 C5
Mill Lane Hants...... 36 A1
Millmeece Staffs...... 114 C5
Millness Cumb...... 157 H6
Mill of Drummond P & K...... 220 E4
Mill of Haldane W Duns...... 208 C3
Millom Cumb...... 155 M6
Millook Cnwll...... 11 H3
Millpool Cnwll...... 2 F5
Millpool Cnwll...... 11 G8
Millport N Ayrs...... 207 K8
Mill Side Cumb...... 157 G6
Mill Street Kent...... 39 H2
Mill Street Norfk...... 122 B7
Mill Street Suffk...... 90 C1
Millthorpe Derbys...... 132 F4
Millthrop Cumb...... 157 L4
Milltimber C Aber...... 245 J3
Milltown Abers...... 243 J2
Milltown Abers...... 255 J8
Milltown Cnwll...... 5 J3
Milltown D & G...... 177 K4
Milltown Derbys...... 133 G7
Milltown Devon...... 27 K3
Milltown of Auchindoun
     Moray...... 255 G4
Milltown of Campfield Abers...... 244 E3
Milltown of Edinvillie Moray...... 254 F4
Milltown of Learney Abers...... 244 E3
Milltown of Rothiemay Moray...... 267 L6
Milnathort P & K...... 221 L6
Milngavie E Duns...... 208 F4
Milnrow Rochdl...... 140 D5
Milnthorpe Cumb...... 157 H6
Milnthorpe Wakefd...... 142 A4
Milovaig Highld...... 258 B6
Milson Shrops...... 80 E1
Milstead Kent...... 40 A3
Milston Wilts...... 33 L2
Milthorpe Lincs...... 118 F5
Milthorpe Nhants...... 84 B6
Milton C Stke...... 114 E2
Milton Cambs...... 87 K3
Milton Cumb...... 178 D6
Milton D & G...... 172 F4
Milton D & G...... 175 L1
Milton Derbys...... 116 A6
Milton Highld...... 248 A3
Milton Highld...... 250 E5
Milton Highld...... 251 G2
Milton Highld...... 263 K5
Milton Highld...... 280 D6
Milton Inver...... 208 B5
Milton Kent...... 52 E4
Milton Moray...... 254 D7
Milton Moray...... 267 K4
Milton N Som...... 44 D6
Milton Newpt...... 44 D1
Milton Notts...... 134 E5
Milton Oxon...... 66 C8
Milton Oxon...... 83 K8
Milton P & K...... 233 G3
Milton Pembks...... 55 H6
Milton Somset...... 31 G6
Milton Stirlg...... 219 H7
Milton W Duns...... 208 D4
Milton Abbas Dorset...... 16 F2

Milton Abbot Devon...... 12 A6
Milton Bridge Mdloth...... 211 H6
Milton Bryan C Beds...... 68 B3
Milton Clevedon Somset...... 31 L3
Milton Combe Devon...... 6 F2
Milton Common Oxon...... 67 G6
Milton Damerel Devon...... 27 G4
Milton End Gloucs...... 63 L5
Milton End Gloucs...... 65 H7
Milton Ernest Bed...... 85 K4
Milton Green Ches W...... 129 K7
Milton Hill Oxon...... 48 C1
Milton Keynes M Keyn...... 85 G7
Milton Lilbourne Wilts...... 47 J7
Milton Malsor Nhants...... 84 E4
Milton Morenish P & K...... 231 H8
Milton of Auchinhove Abers...... 244 C3
Milton of Balgonie Fife...... 222 E7
Milton of Buchanan Stirlg...... 208 D2
Milton of Campsie E Duns...... 209 H4
Milton of Finavon Angus...... 234 D4
Milton of Leys Highld...... 251 J3
Milton of Murtle C Aber...... 245 J4
Milton on Stour Dorset...... 32 D5
Milton Regis Kent...... 40 A2
Milton Street E Susx...... 23 J6
Milton-under-Wychwood
     Oxon...... 65 K3
Milverton Somset...... 29 L5
Milverton Warwks...... 83 H2
Milwich Staffs...... 114 E5
Milwr Flints...... 128 E5
Minard Ag & B...... 216 F7
Minchington Dorset...... 33 G7
Minchinhampton Gloucs...... 64 C7
Mindrum Nthumb...... 202 C6
Minehead Somset...... 29 H2
Minera Wrexhm...... 112 C1
Minety Wilts...... 46 F1
Minffordd Gwynd...... 109 L4
Mingarrypark Highld...... 237 K6
Miningsby Lincs...... 136 F6
Minions Cnwll...... 11 C8
Minishant S Ayrs...... 196 C6
Minllyn Gwynd...... 111 G8
Minnigaff D & G...... 173 K2
Minnonie Abers...... 268 C4
Minshull Vernon Ches E...... 130 D7
Minskip N York...... 150 E3
Minstead Hants...... 18 D2
Minsted W Susx...... 20 D5
Minster Kent...... 41 J2
Minsterley Shrops...... 95 J2
Minster Lovell Oxon...... 65 L5
Minster-on-Sea Kent...... 53 L4
Minsterworth Gloucs...... 64 A4
Minterne Magna Dorset...... 16 C2
Minterne Parva Dorset...... 16 C2
Minting Lincs...... 136 C5
Mintlaw Abers...... 269 J6
Mintlyn Crematorium Norfk...... 120 E7
Minto Border...... 188 F2
Minton Shrops...... 95 K5
Minwear Pembks...... 55 H4
Minworth Birm...... 98 F5
Mirehouse Cumb...... 164 C7
Mireland Highld...... 280 D4
Mirfield Kirk...... 141 K4
Miserden Gloucs...... 64 D5
Miskin Rhondd...... 43 G3
Miskin Rhondd...... 43 G5
Misson Notts...... 134 D7
Misterton Leics...... 100 C8
Misterton Notts...... 134 F7
Misterton Somset...... 15 K1
Mistley Essex...... 73 G4
Mistley Heath Essex...... 73 H4
Mitcham Gt Lon...... 51 H5
Mitcheldean Gloucs...... 63 K3
Mitchell Cnwll...... 4 D4
Mitchellslacks D & G...... 186 E1
Mitchel Troy Mons...... 62 F7
Mitford Nthumb...... 180 E2
Mithian Cnwll...... 4 D3
Mitton Staffs...... 114 D8
Mixbury Oxon...... 84 B8
Mixenden Calder...... 141 G3
Moats Tye Suffk...... 90 B4
Mobberley Ches E...... 130 F4
Mobberley Staffs...... 115 G2
Moccas Herefs...... 79 L6
Mochdre Conwy...... 127 G4
Mochdre Powys...... 94 C7
Mochrum D & G...... 173 J7
Mockbeggar Hants...... 18 B3
Mockbeggar Kent...... 39 H4
Mockerkin Cumb...... 164 E6
Modbury Devon...... 7 H5
Moddershall Staffs...... 114 D4

Moelfre IoA	125	J2	
Moelfre Powys	112	B6	
Moel Tryfan Gwynd	125	J8	
Moffat D & G	187	G5	
Mogador Surrey	51	H8	
Moggerhanger C Beds	86	C5	
Moira Leics	116	A8	
Molash Kent	40	D5	
Mol-chlach Highld	246	F6	
Mold Flints	128	F7	
Moldgreen Kirk	141	J4	
Molehill Green Essex	70	E2	
Molehill Green Essex	71	H3	
Molescroft E R Yk	152	F7	
Molesden Nthumb	180	E2	
Molesworth Cambs	102	B8	
Moll Highld	247	J3	
Molland Devon	28	E5	
Mollington Ches W	129	J5	
Mollington Oxon	83	K5	
Mollinsburn N Lans	209	J5	
Monachty Cerdgn	76	F3	
Mondynes Abers	245	H7	
Monewden Suffk	90	F3	
Moneydie P & K	221	J1	
Moneyrow Green W & M	49	L3	
Moniaive D & G	185	J5	
Monifieth Angus	223	J1	
Monikie Angus	234	D7	
Monimail Fife	222	E4	
Monington Pembks	75	K3	
Monk Bretton Barns	142	B6	
Monken Hadley Gt Lon	69	H7	
Monk Fryston N York	142	D2	
Monkhide Herefs	80	E6	
Monkhill Cumb	177	K7	
Monkhopton Shrops	96	E5	
Monkland Herefs	80	B4	
Monkleigh Devon	27	H6	
Monknash V Glam	42	D7	
Monkokehampton Devon	12	E2	
Monkseaton N Tyne	181	J4	
Monks Eleigh Suffk	89	K5	
Monk's Gate W Susx	37	K5	
Monks Heath Ches E	131	G5	
Monk Sherborne Hants	48	F7	
Monks Horton Kent	40	E7	
Monksilver Somset	29	K3	
Monks Kirby Warwks	100	A6	
Monk Soham Suffk	90	F2	
Monkspath Solhll	98	E8	
Monks Risborough Bucks	67	K6	
Monksthorpe Lincs	137	H6	
Monk Street Essex	70	E2	
Monkswood Mons	62	D6	
Monkton Devon	14	E2	
Monkton Kent	41	J2	
Monkton S Ayrs	196	D5	
Monkton S Tyne	181	H6	
Monkton V Glam	42	D7	
Monkton Combe BaNES	45	M6	
Monkton Deverill Wilts	32	E3	
Monkton Farleigh Wilts	46	A6	
Monkton Heathfield Somset	30	C5	
Monkton Up Wimborne Dorset	33	H8	
Monkton Wyld Dorset	15	H3	
Monkwearmouth Sundld	181	K7	
Monkwood Hants	35	K5	
Monmore Green Wolves	97	L4	
Monmouth Mons	63	G4	
Monnington on Wye Herefs	79	L6	
Monreith D & G	173	J6	
Montacute Somset	31	H7	
Montcliffe Bolton	139	K5	
Montford Shrops	112	F8	
Montford Bridge Shrops	113	G8	
Montgarrie Abers	255	L8	
Montgomery Powys	94	F4	
Monton Salfd	140	A7	
Montrose Angus	235	H4	
Mont Saint Guern	9	i3	
Monxton Hants	34	C2	
Monyash Derbys	132	C6	
Monymusk Abers	256	C8	
Monzie P & K	220	F2	
Moodiesburn N Lans	209	J5	
Moonzie Fife	222	F4	
Moor Allerton Leeds	150	D8	
Moorbath Dorset	15	K4	
Moorby Lincs	136	E6	
Moorcot Herefs	79	L4	
Moor Crichel Dorset	17	K1	
Moordown Bmouth	17	L4	
Moore Halton	130	B3	
Moor End C Beds	68	B3	
Moor End Calder	141	G2	
Moor End Devon	12	F1	
Moorend Gloucs	63	L6	
Moor End Lancs	147	G6	
Moor End N York	151	J8	
Moorends Donc	143	H4	
Moorgreen Hants	35	G7	
Moor Green Herts	69	J2	
Moorgreen Notts	116	E2	
Moorhall Derbys	132	F5	
Moorhampton Herefs	79	M6	
Moorhead C Brad	149	L8	
Moor Head Leeds	141	K2	
Moorhouse Cumb	177	H8	
Moorhouse Cumb	177	K7	
Moorhouse Donc	142	D5	
Moorhouse Notts	134	E6	
Moorhouse Bank Surrey	51	L8	
Moorland Somset	30	E4	
Moorlinch Somset	30	F3	
Moor Monkton N York	151	H4	
Moor Row Cumb	164	D7	
Moor Row Cumb	165	H1	
Moorsholm R & Cl	170	F7	
Moorside Dorset	32	D7	
Moorside Dur	168	D1	
Moor Side Lancs	138	E1	
Moor Side Lancs	147	K8	
Moorside Leeds	150	C8	
Moor Side Lincs	136	E8	
Moorside Oldham	140	E6	
Moorstock Kent	40	E7	
Moor Street Birm	98	C6	
Moor Street Medway	53	H6	
Moorswater Cnwll	5	M2	
Moorthorpe Wakefd	142	C5	
Moortown Devon	12	C7	
Moortown Hants	18	A3	
Moortown IoW	19	G7	
Moortown Leeds	150	D7	
Moortown Lincs	144	D7	
Moortown Wrekin	113	K7	
Morangie Highld	263	K3	
Morar Highld	237	K2	
Moray Crematorium Moray	267	H4	
Morborne Cambs	102	C5	
Morchard Bishop Devon	13	H1	
Morchard Road Devon	13	H2	
Morcombelake Dorset	15	J4	
Morcott Rutlnd	101	K3	
Morda Shrops	112	D6	
Morden Dorset	17	H3	
Morden Gt Lon	51	H5	
Mordiford Herefs	80	D7	
Mordon Dur	169	J5	
More Shrops	95	H5	
Morebath Devon	29	G6	
Morebattle Border	189	K1	
Morecambe Lancs	147	H3	
Moredon Swindn	47	H2	
Morefield Highld	261	J1	
Morehall Kent	41	G7	
Moreleigh Devon	7	L4	
Morenish P & K	231	H8	
Moresby Parks Cumb	164	C6	
Morestead Hants	35	G6	
Moreton Dorset	16	F5	
Moreton Essex	70	D5	
Moreton Herefs	80	C2	
Moreton Oxon	67	G6	
Moreton Staffs	114	B8	
Moreton Staffs	115	J5	
Moreton Wirral	129	G2	
Moreton Corbet Shrops	113	J6	
Moretonhampstead Devon	13	H5	
Moreton-in-Marsh Gloucs	65	J1	
Moreton Jeffries Herefs	80	E5	
Moretonmill Shrops	113	J7	
Moreton Morrell Warwks	83	H4	
Moreton on Lugg Herefs	80	C6	
Moreton Paddox Warwks	83	H4	
Moreton Pinkney Nhants	84	B5	
Moreton Say Shrops	113	K4	
Moreton Valence Gloucs	63	M5	
Morfa Cerdgn	76	B4	
Morfa Bychan Gwynd	109	K4	
Morfa Dinlle Gwynd	125	H8	
Morfa Glas Neath	60	C6	
Morfa Nefyn Gwynd	108	E3	
Morganstown Cardif	43	H5	
Morgan's Vale Wilts	33	L6	
Morham E Loth	212	C5	
Moriah Cerdgn	92	D7	
Morland Cumb	166	E6	
Morley Ches E	130	F3	
Morley Derbys	116	C3	
Morley Dur	168	E5	
Morley Leeds	141	L2	
Morley Green Ches E	130	F3	
Morley St Botolph Norfk	106	B3	
Mornick Cnwll	11	L8	
Morningside C Edin	211	H5	
Morningside N Lans	209	L7	
Morningthorpe Norfk	106	E5	
Morpeth Nthumb	180	F2	
Morphie Abers	235	H3	
Morrey Staffs	115	J7	
Morridge Side Staffs	115	G1	
Morriston Swans	57	J5	
Morston Norfk	121	M3	
Mortehoe Devon	27	H2	
Morthen Rothm	133	J2	
Mortimer W Berk	49	G6	
Mortimer Common W Berk	49	G6	
Mortimer's Cross Herefs	80	A3	
Mortimer West End Hants	48	F6	
Mortlake Gt Lon	51	G4	
Mortlake Crematorium Gt Lon	51	G4	
Morton Cumb	166	B3	
Morton Cumb	177	L7	
Morton Derbys	133	H7	
Morton IoW	19	K6	
Morton Lincs	118	E6	
Morton Lincs	134	F1	
Morton Notts	117	J1	
Morton Shrops	112	D6	
Morton Hall Lincs	135	H7	
Mortonhall Crematorium C Edin	211	J5	
Morton-on-Swale N York	160	D4	
Morton on the Hill Norfk	122	C8	
Morton Tinmouth Dur	168	F6	
Morvah Cnwll	2	B4	
Morval Cnwll	6	B3	
Morvich Highld	248	F7	
Morville Shrops	96	F4	
Morville Heath Shrops	96	F4	
Morwenstow Cnwll	26	C7	
Mosborough Sheff	133	H3	
Moscow E Ayrs	196	F3	
Mose Shrops	97	G5	
Mosedale Cumb	165	K4	
Moseley Birm	98	D6	
Moseley Wolves	97	L4	
Moseley Worcs	81	J3	
Moses Gate Bolton	139	L6	
Moss Ag & B	224	B6	
Moss Donc	142	F5	
Moss Wrexhm	112	D1	
Mossbank Shet	281	e4	
Moss Bank St Hel	139	G8	
Mossbay Cumb	164	C5	
Mossblown S Ayrs	196	D6	
Mossbrow Traffd	130	D2	
Mossburnford Border	189	H3	
Mossdale D & G	175	G1	
Mossdale E Ayrs	184	D2	
Moss Edge Lancs	147	H7	
Moss End Ches E	130	D4	
Mossend N Lans	209	K7	
Mosser Mains Cumb	164	F5	
Mossley Ches E	131	H7	
Mossley Tamesd	140	E7	
Mosspaul Hotel Border	188	C6	
Moss Side Cumb	177	G8	
Moss-side Highld	253	G1	
Moss Side Lancs	138	D2	
Moss Side Sefton	138	D7	
Mosstodloch Moray	267	G4	
Mossyard D & G	174	E4	
Mossy Lea Lancs	139	G5	
Mosterton Dorset	15	K2	
Moston Manch	140	C7	
Moston Shrops	113	J6	
Moston Green Ches E	130	E7	
Mostyn Flints	128	E4	
Motcombe Dorset	32	E6	
Mothecombe Devon	7	H5	
Motherby Cumb	166	A5	
Motherwell N Lans	209	K7	
Motspur Park Gt Lon	51	G5	
Mottingham Gt Lon	51	L4	
Mottisfont Hants	34	D5	
Mottistone IoW	18	F7	
Mottram in Longdendale Tamesd	140	F8	
Mottram St Andrew Ches E	131	G4	
Mouilpied Guern	9	J2	
Mouldsworth Ches W	129	L5	
Moulin P & K	232	D3	
Moulsecoomb Br & H	22	E6	
Moulsford Oxon	48	E2	
Moulsoe M Keyn	85	H7	
Moultavie Highld	263	H5	
Moulton Ches W	130	C5	
Moulton Lincs	119	J6	
Moulton N York	160	C4	
Moulton Nhants	84	F2	
Moulton Suffk	88	D2	
Moulton V Glam	43	G7	
Moulton Chapel Lincs	119	J7	
Moulton St Mary Norfk	107	H2	
Moulton Seas End Lincs	119	K6	
Mount Cnwll	4	C4	
Mount Cnwll	5	K1	
Mount Kirk	141	H4	
Mountain C Brad	141	G2	
Mountain Ash Rhondd	61	G7	
Mountain Cross Border	199	K4	
Mountain Street Kent	40	E5	
Mount Ambrose Cnwll	4	B6	
Mount Bures Essex	89	H8	
Mountfield E Susx	24	D3	
Mountgerald Highld	263	G7	
Mount Hawke Cnwll	4	B5	
Mount Hermon Cnwll	3	H7	
Mountjoy Cnwll	4	E3	
Mount Lothian Mdloth	200	C2	
Mountnessing Essex	70	F7	
Mounton Mons	63	G8	
Mount Pleasant Ches E	131	G8	
Mount Pleasant Derbys	115	M8	
Mount Pleasant Derbys	116	B2	
Mount Pleasant Dur	169	H4	
Mount Pleasant E R Yk	153	L7	
Mount Pleasant E Susx	23	G4	
Mount Pleasant Norfk	105	K4	
Mount Pleasant Suffk	88	E5	
Mount Pleasant Worcs	82	B2	
Mountsett Crematorium Dur	180	E7	
Mountsorrel Leics	116	F8	
Mount Sorrel Wilts	33	H6	
Mount Tabor Calder	141	G2	
Mousehole Cnwll	2	D5	
Mouswald D & G	176	E4	
Mow Cop Ches E	131	G8	
Mowhaugh Border	189	L2	
Mowmacre Hill C Leic	100	D2	
Mowsley Leics	100	E5	
Moy Highld	240	D7	
Moy Highld	252	E5	
Moyle Highld	248	D7	
Moylegrove Pembks	75	J3	
Muasdale Ag & B	205	L8	
Muchalls Abers	245	K5	
Much Birch Herefs	63	G1	
Much Cowarne Herefs	80	E6	
Much Dewchurch Herefs	62	F1	
Muchelney Somset	30	F6	
Muchelney Ham Somset	31	G6	
Much Hadham Herts	70	B3	
Much Hoole Lancs	138	F3	
Much Hoole Town Lancs	138	F3	
Muchlarnick Cnwll	5	L3	
Much Marcle Herefs	63	K1	
Much Wenlock Shrops	96	E3	
Muck Highld	236	E4	
Mucking Thurr	52	E3	
Muckingford Thurr	52	E3	
Muckleford Dorset	16	C4	
Mucklestone Staffs	114	A4	
Muckley Shrops	96	E4	
Muckton Lincs	137	G3	
Muddiford Devon	27	K3	
Muddles Green E Susx	23	J4	
Mudeford Dorset	18	B5	
Mudford Somset	31	J7	
Mudford Sock Somset	31	J7	
Mudgley Somset	31	G2	
Mud Row Kent	53	M4	
Mugdock Stirlg	208	F4	
Mugeary Highld	246	F1	
Mugginton Derbys	115	M3	
Muggintonlane End Derbys	115	M3	
Muggleswick Dur	168	D1	
Muirden Abers	268	C5	
Muirdrum Angus	234	E7	
Muiresk Abers	268	C6	
Muirhead Angus	233	M8	
Muirhead Fife	222	D6	
Muirhead N Lans	209	J5	
Muirkirk E Ayrs	197	K5	
Muirmill Stirlg	209	J2	
Muir of Fowlis Abers	244	C1	
Muir of Miltonduff Moray	266	D4	
Muir of Ord Highld	250	F2	
Muirshearlich Highld	239	J7	
Muirtack Abers	257	J4	
Muirton P & K	221	G5	
Muirton Mains Highld	250	E1	
Muirton of Ardblair P & K	233	J6	
Muker N York	158	F3	
Mulbarton Norfk	106	D3	
Mulben Moray	267	G6	
Mulfra Cnwll	2	C4	
Mull Ag & B	227	H5	
Mullacott Cross Devon	27	J2	
Mullion Cnwll	3	H7	
Mullion Cove Cnwll	3	H7	

Mumby Lincs ... 137 K5
Munderfield Row Herefs ... 80 F5
Munderfield Stocks Herefs ... 80 F5
Mundesley Norfk ... 123 G4
Mundford Norfk ... 104 F4
Mundham Norfk ... 107 G4
Mundon Hill Essex ... 72 C6
Mundy Bois Kent ... 40 B6
Mungrisdale Cumb ... 165 L4
Munlochy Highld ... 251 H1
Munnoch N Ayrs ... 195 L1
Munsley Herefs ... 80 F7
Munslow Shrops ... 96 C6
Murchington Devon ... 13 G5
Murcot Worcs ... 82 C7
Murcott Oxon ... 66 E4
Murcott Wilts ... 46 D1
Murkle Highld ... 279 L3
Murlaggan Highld ... 239 G5
Murrell Green Hants ... 49 H7
Murroes Angus ... 234 C8
Murrow Cambs ... 103 H2
Mursley Bucks ... 67 K2
Murston Kent ... 40 B2
Murthill Angus ... 234 C4
Murthly P & K ... 233 G7
Murton C York ... 151 K5
Murton Cumb ... 167 G6
Murton Dur ... 169 K1
Murton N Tyne ... 181 H5
Murton Nthumb ... 202 F3
Murton Swans ... 57 G7
Musbury Devon ... 15 G4
Muscoates N York ... 162 B6
Musselburgh E Loth ... 211 K4
Muston Leics ... 117 L4
Muston N York ... 163 K6
Mustow Green Worcs ... 97 K8
Muswell Hill Gt Lon ... 51 H1
Mutehill D & G ... 175 H5
Mutford Suffk ... 107 K5
Muthill P & K ... 220 F4
Mutterton Devon ... 14 B2
Muxton Wrekin ... 114 A8
Mybster Highld ... 279 L5
Myddfai Carmth ... 59 L3
Myddle Shrops ... 113 G6
Mydroilyn Cerdgn ... 76 E4
Myerscough Lancs ... 147 K7
Mylor Cnwll ... 3 L4
Mylor Bridge Cnwll ... 3 K4
Mynachlog ddu Pembks ... 75 K6
Myndd-llan Flints ... 128 D5
Myndtown Shrops ... 95 J5
Mynydd-bach Mons ... 62 F8
Mynydd-Bach Swans ... 57 J5
Mynydd Buch Cerdgn ... 92 F8
Mynyddgarreg Carmth ... 56 D3
Mynydd Isa Flints ... 128 F7
Mynydd Llandygai Gwynd ... 126 B6
Mynytho Gwynd ... 108 E5
Myrebird Abers ... 245 G4
Myredykes Border ... 189 G6
Mytchett Surrey ... 49 L7
Mytholm Calder ... 140 E2
Mytholmroyd Calder ... 140 F3
Mythop Lancs ... 138 D1
Myton-on-Swale N York ... 150 F3

N

Naast Highld ... 260 C3
Nab's Head Lancs ... 139 J2
Na Buirgh W Isls ... 282 d6
Naburn C York ... 151 J6
Nab Wood Crematorium C Brad ... 149 L8
Naccolt Kent ... 40 D6
Nackington Kent ... 40 F4
Nacton Suffk ... 90 F7
Nafferton E R Yk ... 153 L4
Nag's Head Gloucs ... 64 C7
Nailbridge Gloucs ... 63 J4
Nailsbourne Somset ... 30 B5
Nailsea N Som ... 44 F5
Nailstone Leics ... 99 L2
Nailsworth Gloucs ... 64 B7
Nairn Highld ... 264 D8
Nalderswood Surrey ... 37 K2
Nancegollan Cnwll ... 3 G4
Nancledra Cnwll ... 2 D4
Nanhoron Gwynd ... 108 E5
Nannerch Flints ... 128 E5
Nanpantan Leics ... 116 E8
Nanpean Cnwll ... 4 F4
Nanquidno Cnwll ... 2 B5
Nanstallon Cnwll ... 5 H2

Nant-ddu Powys ... 60 F4
Nanternis Cerdgn ... 76 C4
Nantgaredig Carmth ... 58 F4
Nantgarw Rhondd ... 43 H4
Nant-glas Powys ... 78 D2
Nantglyn Denbgs ... 127 K7
Nantgwyn Powys ... 93 L8
Nant Gwynant Gwynd ... 110 B2
Nantlle Gwynd ... 109 J1
Nantmawr Shrops ... 112 C6
Nantmel Powys ... 78 E2
Nantmor Gwynd ... 109 L2
Nant Peris Gwynd ... 126 B7
Nantwich Ches E ... 113 L1
Nant-y-Bwch Blae G ... 61 H5
Nantycaws Carmth ... 58 E5
Nant-y-derry Mons ... 62 C6
Nantyffyllon Brdgnd ... 42 C3
Nantyglo Blae G ... 61 K5
Nant-y-gollen Shrops ... 112 C5
Nant-y-moel Brdgnd ... 42 D3
Nant-y-pandy Conwy ... 126 D5
Naphill Bucks ... 67 K7
Napleton Worcs ... 81 K5
Nappa N York ... 148 E5
Napton on the Hill Warwks ... 83 L3
Narberth Pembks ... 55 J4
Narborough Leics ... 100 C4
Narborough Norfk ... 104 E1
Narkurs Cnwll ... 6 C4
Nasareth Gwynd ... 109 H2
Naseby Nhants ... 100 F7
Nash Bucks ... 84 F8
Nash Gt Lon ... 51 L6
Nash Herefs ... 79 K3
Nash Newpt ... 44 D2
Nash Shrops ... 80 E1
Nash End Worcs ... 97 H7
Nashes Green Hants ... 35 K2
Nash Lee Bucks ... 67 K5
Nash Street Kent ... 52 D5
Nassington Nhants ... 102 B4
Nastend Gloucs ... 64 A6
Nasty Herts ... 69 K2
Nateby Cumb ... 158 D1
Nateby Lancs ... 147 J7
Natland Cumb ... 157 H5
Naughton Suffk ... 89 L5
Naunton Gloucs ... 65 G2
Naunton Worcs ... 81 K7
Naunton Beauchamp Worcs ... 81 M5
Navenby Lincs ... 135 K8
Navestock Essex ... 70 D7
Navestock Side Essex ... 70 E7
Navidale Highld ... 274 D5
Navity Highld ... 264 B7
Nawton N York ... 161 L5
Nayland Suffk ... 89 K8
Nazeing Essex ... 69 L6
Nazeing Gate Essex ... 69 L6
Neacroft Hants ... 18 B4
Neal's Green Warwks ... 99 J6
Neap Shet ... 281 e5
Near Cotton Staffs ... 115 H2
Near Sawrey Cumb ... 156 E3
Neasden Gt Lon ... 51 G2
Neasham Darltn ... 169 J8
Neath Neath ... 57 L5
Neatham Hants ... 35 M3
Neatishead Norfk ... 123 G7
Nebo Cerdgn ... 77 G2
Nebo Conwy ... 127 G8
Nebo Gwynd ... 109 H2
Nebo IoA ... 125 H2
Necton Norfk ... 105 H2
Nedd Highld ... 270 F2
Nedderton Nthumb ... 180 F2
Nedging Suffk ... 89 K5
Nedging Tye Suffk ... 89 L5
Needham Norfk ... 106 E7
Needham Market Suffk ... 90 C4
Needham Street Suffk ... 88 E2
Needingworth Cambs ... 87 G1
Neen Savage Shrops ... 96 F7
Neen Sollars Shrops ... 80 F1
Neenton Shrops ... 96 E6
Nefyn Gwynd ... 108 E3
Neilston E Rens ... 208 E7
Nelson Caerph ... 43 H3
Nelson Lancs ... 148 F8
Nemphlar S Lans ... 198 E4
Nempnett Thrubwell BaNES ... 45 G7
Nenthall Cumb ... 167 H2
Nenthead Cumb ... 167 H2
Nenthorn Border ... 201 L5
Neopardy Devon ... 13 J3
Nep Town W Susx ... 22 B4
Nercwys Flints ... 128 F7
Nereabolls Ag & B ... 204 C5

Nerston S Lans ... 209 H7
Nesbit Nthumb ... 202 F6
Nesfield N York ... 149 K6
Ness Ches W ... 129 G4
Nesscliffe Shrops ... 112 F7
Neston Ches W ... 129 G4
Neston Wilts ... 46 B5
Netchwood Shrops ... 96 E5
Nether Alderley Ches E ... 131 G4
Netheravon Wilts ... 33 K1
Nether Blainslie Border ... 201 H4
Netherbrae Abers ... 268 E4
Nether Broughton Leics ... 117 J6
Netherburn S Lans ... 198 C4
Netherbury Dorset ... 15 L3
Netherby Cumb ... 177 L4
Netherby N York ... 150 D6
Nether Cerne Dorset ... 16 C3
Nethercleuch D & G ... 176 F2
Nether Compton Dorset ... 31 K7
Nethercote Warwks ... 83 M2
Nethercott Devon ... 11 L3
Nethercott Devon ... 27 H3
Nether Crimond Abers ... 256 E7
Nether Dallachy Moray ... 267 G3
Netherend Gloucs ... 63 H7
Nether Exe Devon ... 13 L3
Netherfield E Susx ... 24 C3
Netherfield Leics ... 117 G8
Netherfield Notts ... 117 G5
Nether Fingland S Lans ... 186 D4
Nethergate N Linc ... 143 J7
Nethergate Norfk ... 122 B5
Netherhampton Wilts ... 33 K5
Nether Handley Derbys ... 133 H4
Nether Handwick Angus ... 234 B7
Nether Haugh Rothm ... 142 C8
Netherhay Dorset ... 15 J2
Nether Headon Notts ... 134 E4
Nether Heage Derbys ... 116 B2
Nether Heyford Nhants ... 84 C3
Nether Howcleugh S Lans ... 186 F4
Nether Kellet Lancs ... 147 K2
Nether Kinmundy Abers ... 257 K3
Netherland Green Staffs ... 115 H5
Nether Langwith Notts ... 133 K5
Netherlaw D & G ... 175 J6
Netherley Abers ... 245 J5
Nethermill D & G ... 176 D1
Nethermuir Abers ... 257 G3
Netherne-on-the-Hill Surrey ... 51 J7
Netheroyd Hill Kirk ... 141 H4
Nether Padley Derbys ... 132 E4
Nether Poppleton C York ... 151 J5
Nether Row Cumb ... 165 K3
Netherseal Derbys ... 99 H1
Nether Silton N York ... 161 G4
Nether Skyborry Shrops ... 95 G8
Nether Stowey Somset ... 30 B3
Nether Street Essex ... 70 E5
Netherstreet Wilts ... 46 E6
Netherthong Kirk ... 141 H6
Netherthorpe Derbys ... 133 J5
Netherton Angus ... 234 E4
Netherton Devon ... 13 L8
Netherton Dudley ... 97 L5
Netherton Hants ... 48 A7
Netherton Herefs ... 63 G2
Netherton Kirk ... 141 H5
Netherton N Lans ... 209 K8
Netherton Nthumb ... 190 E4
Netherton Oxon ... 66 B7
Netherton P & K ... 233 H5
Netherton Sefton ... 138 D7
Netherton Shrops ... 97 G6
Netherton Stirlg ... 208 F3
Netherton Wakefd ... 141 L4
Netherton Worcs ... 82 A7
Nethertown Cumb ... 155 H1
Nethertown Highld ... 280 E1
Nethertown Lancs ... 148 C8
Nethertown Staffs ... 115 J8
Netherurd Border ... 199 J4
Nether Wallop Hants ... 34 C4
Nether Wasdale Cumb ... 155 L2
Nether Welton Cumb ... 165 K2
Nether Westcote Gloucs ... 65 J3
Nether Whitacre Warwks ... 99 G5
Nether Whitecleuch S Lans ... 186 B2
Nether Winchendon Bucks ... 67 H4
Netherwitton Nthumb ... 191 G8
Nethy Bridge Highld ... 253 J7
Netley Hants ... 19 G2
Netley Marsh Hants ... 34 D8
Nettlebed Oxon ... 49 G2
Nettlebridge Somset ... 31 L1
Nettlecombe Dorset ... 15 L3
Nettlecombe IoW ... 19 J8
Nettleden Herts ... 68 C5

Nettleham Lincs ... 135 K4
Nettlestead Kent ... 39 H3
Nettlestead Green Kent ... 39 H3
Nettlestone IoW ... 19 L5
Nettlesworth Dur ... 169 H1
Nettleton Lincs ... 144 E7
Nettleton Wilts ... 46 B3
Nettleton Shrub Wilts ... 46 B3
Netton Devon ... 7 G5
Netton Wilts ... 33 K4
Neuadd Carmth ... 59 K4
Neuadd-ddu Powys ... 93 K8
Nevendon Essex ... 53 G1
Nevern Pembks ... 75 J4
Nevill Holt Leics ... 101 K4
New Abbey D & G ... 176 C5
New Aberdour Abers ... 268 F3
New Addington Gt Lon ... 51 K6
Newall Leeds ... 150 D6
New Alresford Hants ... 35 J4
New Alyth P & K ... 233 K6
Newark C Pete ... 102 C3
Newark Ork ... 275 f2
Newark-on-Trent Notts ... 117 L1
New Arram E R Yk ... 153 G7
Newarthill N Lans ... 209 L7
New Ash Green Kent ... 52 B6
New Balderton Notts ... 117 L1
Newbarn Kent ... 40 F7
New Barn Kent ... 52 D5
New Barnet Gt Lon ... 69 H7
New Barton Nhants ... 85 G2
Newbattle Mdloth ... 211 K6
New Bewick Nthumb ... 190 F2
Newbie D & G ... 177 H6
Newbiggin Cumb ... 146 E2
Newbiggin Cumb ... 155 K4
Newbiggin Cumb ... 166 B5
Newbiggin Cumb ... 166 D1
Newbiggin Cumb ... 166 E5
Newbiggin Dur ... 167 L5
Newbiggin Dur ... 168 F1
Newbiggin N York ... 159 G4
Newbiggin N York ... 159 H5
Newbiggin-by-the-Sea Nthumb ... 181 H1
Newbigging Angus ... 233 H7
Newbigging Angus ... 234 C7
Newbigging Angus ... 234 D8
Newbigging S Lans ... 199 H4
Newbiggin-on-Lune Cumb ... 158 C2
New Bilton Warwks ... 100 B8
Newbold Derbys ... 133 G5
Newbold Leics ... 116 C7
Newbold on Avon Warwks ... 100 B8
Newbold on Stour Warwks ... 82 F6
Newbold Pacey Warwks ... 83 G4
Newbold Revel Warwks ... 99 M7
Newbold Verdon Leics ... 99 L3
New Bolingbroke Lincs ... 136 F8
Newborough C Pete ... 102 D2
Newborough IoA ... 125 G6
Newborough Staffs ... 115 J6
Newbottle Nhants ... 83 M7
Newbottle Sundld ... 181 H8
New Boultham Lincs ... 135 K5
Newbourne Suffk ... 91 G6
New Bradwell M Keyn ... 84 F2
New Brampton Derbys ... 133 G6
New Brancepeth Dur ... 169 G2
Newbridge C Edin ... 210 F4
Newbridge Caerph ... 43 K3
Newbridge Cerdgn ... 76 B6
Newbridge Cnwll ... 2 C5
Newbridge Cnwll ... 4 D4
Newbridge D & G ... 176 C3
Newbridge Hants ... 34 C7
Newbridge IoW ... 18 F6
New Bridge N York ... 162 D6
Newbridge Oxon ... 66 B6
Newbridge Wrexhm ... 112 D3
Newbridge Green Worcs ... 81 J2
Newbridge-on-Usk Mons ... 62 D3
Newbridge-on-Wye Powys ... 78 C4
New Brighton Flints ... 128 F6
New Brighton Wirral ... 129 G6
New Brinsley Notts ... 116 D1
New Brotton R & Cl ... 171 G6
Newbrough Nthumb ... 179 K5
New Broughton Wrexhm ... 112 D1
New Buckenham Norfk ... 106 B5
Newbuildings Devon ... 13 J3
Newburgh Abers ... 257 J4
Newburgh Abers ... 269 H5
Newburgh Fife ... 222 E4
Newburgh Lancs ... 138 F5
Newburgh Priory N York ... 161 J5
Newburn N u Ty ... 180 F6
New Bury Bolton ... 139 L6

Newbury Somset 32 B1
Newbury W Berk 48 C5
Newbury Wilts 32 D3
Newbury Park Gt Lon 51 L1
Newby Cumb 166 E6
Newby Lancs 148 E6
Newby N York 148 C2
Newby N York 163 J4
Newby N York 170 C8
Newby Bridge Cumb 156 E5
Newby Cross Cumb 177 L8
Newby East Cumb 178 B7
Newby Head Cumb 166 E6
New Byth Abers 268 E5
Newby West Cumb 177 L8
Newby Wiske N York 160 E5
Newcastle Mons 62 F4
Newcastle Shrops 95 G7
Newcastle Emlyn Carmth 76 B7
Newcastleton Border 178 C2
Newcastle-under-Lyme Staffs 114 D2
Newcastle upon Tyne N u Ty 181 G6
Newchapel Pembks 75 L4
Newchapel Staffs 131 G8
Newchapel Surrey 38 A5
Newchurch Blae G 61 J5
Newchurch Herefs 79 L5
Newchurch IoW 19 J6
Newchurch Kent 25 K1
Newchurch Mons 62 F7
Newchurch Powys 79 H5
Newchurch Staffs 115 J7
Newchurch in Pendle Lancs 148 E7
New Costessey Norfk 106 D2
New Cowper Cumb 164 F2
Newcraighall C Edin 211 K4
New Crofton Wakefd 142 B4
New Cross Cerdgn 92 D8
New Cross Gt Lon 51 K4
New Cross Somset 30 F7
New Cumnock E Ayrs 197 J8
New Cut E Susx 24 E4
New Deer Abers 268 F6
New Delaval Nthumb 181 H3
New Delph Oldham 140 F6
New Denham Bucks 50 D2
Newdigate Surrey 37 J3
New Duston Nhants 84 D3
New Earswick C York 151 K5
New Eastwood Notts 116 D2
New Edlington Donc 142 E7
New Elgin Moray 266 E4
New Ellerby E R Yk 153 J7
Newell Green Br For 49 L5
New Eltham Gt Lon 51 L4
New End Worcs 82 C3
Newenden Kent 24 F2
New England C Pete 102 D3
New England Essex 88 E6
Newent Gloucs 63 L2
New Farnley Leeds 141 L2
New Ferry Wirral 129 H3
Newfield Dur 169 G4
Newfield Dur 181 G8
Newfield Highld 264 B4
New Fletton C Pete 102 D4
Newfound Hants 48 E8
New Fryston Wakefd 142 C2
Newgale Pembks 54 D2
New Galloway D & G 185 G7
Newgate Norfk 122 A3
Newgate Street Herts 69 J6
New Gilston Fife 223 G5
New Grimsby IoS 10 b2
Newhall Ches E 113 K2
Newhall Derbys 115 M7
Newham Nthumb 203 K7
New Hartley Nthumb 181 H3
Newhaven C Edin 211 H4
Newhaven Derbys 132 C7
Newhaven E Susx 23 G7
New Haw Surrey 50 D6
New Hedges Pembks 55 K6
New Herrington Sundld 181 H8
Newhey Rochdl 140 E5
New Holkham Norfk 121 J4
New Holland N Linc 144 H4
Newholm N York 171 K8
New Houghton Derbys 133 K6
New Houghton Norfk 121 H6
Newhouse N Lans 209 L6
New Houses N York 158 D7
New Houses Wigan 139 H7
New Hutton Cumb 157 J4
New Hythe Kent 52 F7
Newick E Susx 22 F3
Newingreen Kent 40 F8
Newington Kent 41 G7
Newington Kent 53 J6

Newington Oxon 66 F7
Newington Shrops 95 K6
Newington Bagpath Gloucs 64 B8
New Inn Carmth 58 E2
New Inn Torfn 62 C7
New Invention Shrops 95 H8
New Lakenham Norfk 106 E2
New Lanark S Lans 198 E4
Newland C KuH 144 D2
Newland Cumb 156 D6
Newland E R Yk 143 K2
Newland Gloucs 63 H5
Newland N York 143 H3
Newland Oxon 66 A5
Newland Somset 28 E3
Newland Worcs 81 H5
Newlandrig Mdloth 211 L6
Newlands Border 188 E7
Newlands Cumb 165 K3
Newlands Nthumb 180 D7
Newlands of Dundurcas
    Moray 266 F6
New Lane Lancs 138 E5
New Lane End Warrtn 130 C1
New Langholm D & G 177 K2
New Leake Lincs 137 G8
New Leeds Abers 269 H5
New Lodge Barns 142 A6
New Longton Lancs 139 G3
New Luce D & G 172 F2
Newlyn Cnwll 2 D5
Newmachar Abers 256 F7
Newmains N Lans 209 L7
New Malden Gt Lon 51 G5
Newman's End Essex 70 D4
Newman's Green Suffk 89 H6
Newmarket Suffk 88 C3
Newmarket W Isls 282 g3
New Marske R & Cl 170 E6
New Marston Oxon 66 D5
New Marton Shrops 112 E4
New Mill Abers 245 H7
Newmill Border 188 D4
New Mill Cnwll 2 D4
New Mill Herts 68 A4
New Mill Kirk 141 J6
Newmill Moray 267 J5
Newmillerdam Wakefd 141 M4
Newmill of Inshewan Angus 234 C3
Newmills C Edin 211 G5
New Mills Cnwll 4 E4
New Mills Derbys 131 K3
Newmills Fife 210 D2
Newmills Mons 63 G5
New Mills Powys 94 D3
Newmiln P & K 221 L1
Newmilns E Ayrs 197 G3
New Milton Hants 18 C4
New Mistley Essex 73 H1
New Moat Pembks 75 H7
Newnes Shrops 112 F5
Newney Green Essex 71 G5
Newnham Hants 49 H8
Newnham Herts 86 E7
Newnham Kent 40 B4
Newnham Nhants 84 B3
Newnham Bridge Worcs 80 E2
Newnham on Severn Gloucs 63 K5
New Ollerton Notts 134 D6
New Oscott Birm 98 E4
New Pitsligo Abers 268 F5
New Polzeath Cnwll 10 C6
Newport Cnwll 11 L5
Newport Dorset 17 G4
Newport E R Yk 143 L2
Newport Essex 87 L8
Newport Gloucs 63 K7
Newport Highld 274 F3
Newport IoW 19 H6
Newport Newpt 44 C1
Newport Norfk 123 K8
Newport Pembks 75 H4
Newport Wrekin 114 A7
Newport-on-Tay Fife 223 G2
Newport Pagnell M Keyn 85 G6
Newpound Common W Susx 37 G5
New Prestwick S Ayrs 196 C6
New Quay Cerdgn 76 D3
Newquay Cnwll 4 D3
New Quay Essex 72 F2
New Rackheath Norfk 106 F1
New Radnor Powys 79 H3
New Rent Cumb 166 B3
New Ridley Nthumb 180 C7
New Road Side N York 149 H7
New Romney Kent 25 K2
New Rossington Donc 143 G8
New Row Cerdgn 92 F8
New Row Lancs 148 A8

New Sauchie Clacks 220 F8
Newsbank Ches E 131 G6
Newseat Abers 256 C5
Newsham Lancs 147 K8
Newsham N York 160 E5
Newsham N York 168 E8
Newsham Nthumb 181 H3
New Sharlston Wakefd 142 B4
Newsholme E R Yk 143 H2
Newsholme Lancs 148 E5
New Shoreston Nthumb 203 K6
New Silksworth Sundld 181 J8
New Skelton R & Cl 170 F7
Newsome Kirk 141 J5
New Somerby Lincs 118 B4
New Southgate Crematorium
    Gt Lon 69 H8
New Springs Wigan 139 J6
Newstead Border 201 H6
Newstead Notts 116 E1
Newstead Nthumb 203 J7
New Stevenston N Lans 209 K7
New Street Herefs 79 L4
New Swannington Leics 116 D8
Newthorpe N York 142 D1
Newthorpe Notts 116 E2
New Thundersley Essex 53 G1
Newtimber W Susx 22 D4
Newtoft Lincs 135 L2
Newton Ag & B 217 G7
Newton Border 189 G2
Newton Brdgnd 42 C6
Newton C Beds 86 E6
Newton Cambs 87 J5
Newton Cambs 119 M8
Newton Cardif 43 K6
Newton Ches W 129 J6
Newton Ches W 129 L7
Newton Ches W 129 M4
Newton Cumb 146 D2
Newton Derbys 133 J7
Newton Herefs 79 L1
Newton Herefs 79 L8
Newton Herefs 80 C4
Newton Highld 251 G2
Newton Highld 252 D2
Newton Highld 263 L6
Newton Highld 280 D6
Newton Lancs 147 G8
Newton Lancs 157 J7
Newton Lincs 118 D4
Newton Mdloth 211 K5
Newton Moray 266 C3
Newton Moray 267 G4
Newton N York 152 D1
Newton Nhants 101 J6
Newton Norfk 121 H8
Newton Notts 117 J3
Newton Nthumb 180 C6
Newton Nthumb 190 D5
Newton S Lans 198 F6
Newton S Lans 209 H6
Newton Sandw 98 C4
Newton Shrops 112 F4
Newton Somset 29 K3
Newton Staffs 115 G6
Newton Suffk 89 J7
Newton W Loth 210 E3
Newton Warwks 100 C7
Newton Wilts 34 B6
Newton Abbot Devon 13 K8
Newton Arlosh Cumb 177 G7
Newton Aycliffe Dur 169 H5
Newton Bewley Hartpl 170 B5
Newton Blossomville M Keyn 85 H5
Newton Bromswold Nhants 85 K2
Newton Burgoland Leics 99 K2
Newton-by-the-Sea Nthumb 203 L8
Newton by Toft Lincs 135 L2
Newton Ferrers Devon 7 G5
Newton Ferry W Isls 282 c7
Newton Flotman Norfk 106 E4
Newtongrange Mdloth 211 K6
Newton Green Mons 45 G1
Newton Harcourt Leics 100 E4
Newton Heath Manch 140 C7
Newtonhill Abers 245 K5
Newton Hill Wakefd 141 M3
Newton-in-Bowland Lancs 148 B5
Newton Kyme N York 151 G6
Newton-le-Willows Lancs 160 E5
Newton-le-Willows St Hel 139 H8
Newtonloan Mdloth 211 K6
Newton Longville Bucks 67 K1
Newton Mearns E Rens 208 F7
Newtonmill Angus 234 F3
Newtonmore Highld 241 J4
Newton Morrell N York 160 C1
Newton Mountain Pembks 55 G5

Newton Mulgrave N York 171 H7
Newton of Balcanquhal P & K 222 B5
Newton of Balcormo Fife 223 J6
Newton-on-Ouse N York 151 H4
Newton-on-Rawcliffe N York 162 E4
Newton on the Hill Shrops 113 H7
Newton-on-the-Moor
    Nthumb 191 H5
Newton on Trent Lincs 135 G5
Newton Poppleford Devon 14 C5
Newton Purcell Oxon 66 F1
Newton Regis Warwks 99 H2
Newton Reigny Cumb 166 B4
Newton St Cyres Devon 13 K3
Newton St Faith Norfk 122 E8
Newton St Loe BaNES 45 L6
Newton St Petrock Devon 27 G8
Newton Solney Derbys 115 M6
Newton Stacey Hants 34 E3
Newton Stewart D & G 173 K2
Newton Tony Wilts 34 B3
Newton Tracey Devon 27 J5
Newton under Roseberry
    R & Cl 170 D8
Newton Underwood Nthumb 180 E2
Newton upon Derwent E R Yk 151 M6
Newton Valence Hants 35 L4
Newton Wamphray D & G 187 H7
Newton with Scales Lancs 138 F2
Newtown Blae G 61 J5
Newtown Ches W 129 M4
Newtown Cnwll 2 F5
Newtown Cnwll 11 K7
Newtown Cumb 164 E1
Newtown Cumb 166 C6
Newtown Cumb 177 L6
Newtown Cumb 178 C6
Newtown D & G 185 J1
Newtown Derbys 131 K3
Newtown Devon 14 C3
Newtown Devon 28 D6
Newtown Dorset 15 L2
New Town Dorset 17 K1
New Town Dorset 32 F7
New Town Dorset 33 G7
New Town E Susx 23 H3
Newtown Gloucs 63 K6
Newtown Hants 18 D2
Newtown Hants 35 J8
Newtown Hants 48 C6
Newtown Herefs 80 B4
Newtown Herefs 80 C8
Newtown Herefs 80 E6
Newtown Highld 240 B3
Newtown IoW 19 G5
Newtown Lancs 139 G4
New Town Nhants 101 L7
Newtown Nthumb 190 E6
Newtown Nthumb 202 E6
Newtown Nthumb 203 G8
Newtown Poole 17 K4
Newtown Powys 94 D5
Newtown Rhondd 61 G7
Newtown Shrops 112 F7
Newtown Shrops 113 H5
Newtown Somset 30 C8
Newtown Staffs 98 C3
Newtown Staffs 131 H7
Newtown Wigan 139 H6
Newtown Wilts 32 F5
New Town Wilts 47 L4
Newtown Wilts 47 L6
Newtown Worcs 81 K4
Newtown Worcs 98 B7
Newtown-in-St Martin Cnwll 3 J6
Newtown Linford Leics 100 B2
Newtown of Beltrees Rens 208 C7
Newtown St Boswells Border 201 J6
Newtown Unthank Leics 100 B3
New Tredegar Caerph 61 J6
New Trows S Lans 198 D5
New Tupton Derbys 133 H6
Newtyle Angus 233 L7
New Walsoken Cambs 103 K2
New Waltham NE Lin 145 H6
New Whittington Derbys 133 H4
New Winton E Loth 211 M5
New Yatt Oxon 66 A4
Newyears Green Gt Lon 50 D1
Newyork Ag & B 216 F5
New York Lincs 136 D8
New York N Tyne 181 H5
New York N York 150 B3
Nextend Herefs 79 L4
Neyland Pembks 54 F6
Niarbyl IoM 154 b6
Nibley Gloucs 63 K5
Nibley S Glos 45 K3
Nibley Green Gloucs 63 L7

Nicholashayne Devon	29	K7	
Nicholaston Swans	56	F7	
Nickies Hill Cumb	178	D5	
Nidd N York	150	D4	
Nigg C Aber	245	L3	
Nigg Highld	264	C5	
Nigg Ferry Highld	264	B6	
Nimlet BaNES	45	L5	
Ninebanks Nthumb	179	H8	
Nine Elms Swindn	47	G2	
Nine Wells Pembks	74	C7	
Ninfield E Susx	24	C5	
Ningwood IoW	18	F6	
Nisbet Border	201	L8	
Nisbet Hill Border	202	B3	
Niton IoW	19	H8	
Nitshill C Glas	208	E7	
Noah's Ark Kent	52	C7	
Noak Bridge Essex	52	E1	
Noak Hill Gt Lon	70	D8	
Noblethorpe Barns	141	L6	
Nobold Shrops	95	L2	
Nobottle Nhants	84	C3	
Nocton Lincs	135	L6	
Nogdam End Norfk	107	H3	
Noke Oxon	66	E4	
Nolton Pembks	54	E3	
Nolton Haven Pembks	54	D3	
No Man's Heath Ches W	113	H2	
No Man's Heath Warwks	99	H4	
No Man's Land Cnwll	6	B3	
Nomansland Devon	28	E8	
Nomansland Wilts	34	B7	
Noneley Shrops	113	H6	
Nonington Kent	41	H5	
Nook Cumb	157	H6	
Nook Cumb	178	B3	
Norbiton Gt Lon	51	G5	
Norbreck Bpool	146	F7	
Norbridge Herefs	81	G6	
Norbury Ches E	113	J2	
Norbury Derbys	115	J3	
Norbury Gt Lon	51	J5	
Norbury Shrops	95	J5	
Norbury Staffs	114	B6	
Norbury Common Ches E	113	J2	
Norbury Junction Staffs	114	B7	
Norchard Worcs	81	J2	
Norcott Brook Ches W	130	B4	
Norcross Lancs	146	F7	
Nordelph Norfk	103	L3	
Norden Rochdl	140	C5	
Nordley Shrops	96	F4	
Norham Nthumb	202	D4	
Norland Town Calder	141	G3	
Norley Ches W	130	B5	
Norleywood Hants	18	E4	
Norlington E Susx	23	G4	
Normanby Lincs	135	K2	
Normanby N Linc	143	M4	
Normanby N York	162	C6	
Normanby R & Cl	170	D7	
Normanby le Wold Lincs	136	B1	
Norman Cross Cambs	102	D5	
Normandy Surrey	50	B8	
Normans Bay E Susx	24	C6	
Norman's Green Devon	14	C2	
Normanton C Derb	116	B5	
Normanton Leics	117	L3	
Normanton Notts	134	E8	
Normanton Rutlnd	101	K2	
Normanton Wakefd	142	B3	
Normanton Wilts	33	K3	
Normanton le Heath Leics	99	K1	
Normanton on Cliffe Lincs	118	B2	
Normanton on Soar Notts	116	E7	
Normanton on the Wolds Notts	117	G5	
Normanton on Trent Notts	134	F6	
Normoss Lancs	147	G8	
Norney Surrey	36	D2	
Norrington Common Wilts	46	C6	
Norris Green Cnwll	6	E1	
Norris Green Lpool	129	J1	
Norris Hill Leics	116	B8	
Norristhorpe Kirk	141	K3	
Northacre Norfk	105	J4	
Northall Bucks	68	B3	
Northallerton N York	160	E4	
Northall Green Norfk	121	M8	
Northam C Sotn	19	G1	
Northam Devon	27	H5	
Northampton Nhants	84	E3	
Northampton Worcs	81	J2	
North Anston Rothm	133	K3	
North Ascot Br For	49	M5	
North Aston Oxon	66	C1	
Northaw Herts	69	H6	
Northay Somset	30	D8	

North Baddesley Hants	34	E6	
North Ballachulish Highld	229	G3	
North Barrow Somset	31	K5	
North Barsham Norfk	121	K4	
Northbay W Isls	283	b13	
North Benfleet Essex	53	G1	
North Berwick E Loth	212	C2	
North Bitchburn Dur	168	F4	
North Blyth Nthumb	181	H2	
North Boarhunt Hants	19	K2	
North Bockhampton Dorset	18	B4	
Northborough C Pete	102	C2	
Northbourne Kent	41	K5	
North Bovey Devon	13	H6	
North Bradley Wilts	46	B7	
North Brentor Devon	12	C6	
North Brewham Somset	32	B3	
North Bridge Surrey	36	E3	
Northbridge Street E Susx	24	D2	
Northbrook Hants	35	G3	
Northbrook Oxon	66	D3	
North Brook End Cambs	86	F6	
North Buckland Devon	27	H3	
North Burlingham Norfk	107	H2	
North Cadbury Somset	31	K5	
North Carlton Lincs	135	J4	
North Carlton Notts	134	B3	
North Cave E R Yk	143	M1	
North Cerney Gloucs	64	E5	
North Chailey E Susx	22	F3	
Northchapel W Susx	36	E5	
North Charford Hants	33	L7	
North Charlton Nthumb	191	H2	
North Cheam Gt Lon	51	G6	
North Cheriton Somset	31	M5	
North Chideock Dorset	15	K4	
Northchurch Herts	68	B5	
North Cliffe E R Yk	152	D8	
North Clifton Notts	135	G5	
North Close Dur	169	H4	
North Cockerington Lincs	137	G2	
North Connel Ag & B	228	E8	
North Cornelly Brdgnd	42	B5	
North Corner Cnwll	3	K7	
North Cotes Lincs	145	J7	
Northcott Devon	11	L4	
Northcott Devon	14	D1	
Northcott Devon	29	K8	
North Country Cnwll	4	A6	
Northcourt Oxon	66	D7	
North Cove Suffk	107	K5	
North Cowton N York	160	D2	
North Crawley M Keyn	85	H6	
North Cray Gt Lon	52	A4	
North Creake Norfk	121	J4	
North Curry Somset	30	D6	
North Dalton E R Yk	152	E5	
North Deighton N York	150	E5	
North Devon Crematorium Devon	27	K4	
Northdown Kent	41	L1	
North Duffield N York	151	L8	
North East Surrey Crematorium Gt Lon	51	G5	
Northedge Derbys	133	G6	
North Elham Kent	41	G6	
North Elkington Lincs	136	E2	
North Elmham Norfk	121	L7	
North Elmsall Wakefd	142	D5	
Northend Bucks	67	H8	
North End C Port	19	L3	
North End Cumb	177	K7	
North End Dorset	32	D5	
North End E R Yk	145	H2	
North End E R Yk	153	K7	
North End Essex	71	G3	
North End Hants	33	J7	
North End Hants	35	J5	
North End Leics	116	F8	
North End Lincs	119	H3	
North End Lincs	137	H2	
North End Lincs	144	D7	
North End Lincs	145	J7	
North End N Linc	144	E3	
North End N Som	44	E5	
North End Nhants	85	J2	
North End Norfk	105	K5	
North End Nthumb	191	G6	
North End Sefton	138	C6	
North End W Susx	21	G6	
North End W Susx	21	J5	
Northend Warwks	83	J5	
Northenden Manch	131	G2	
Northend Woods Bucks	49	L1	
North Erradale Highld	260	B4	
North Evington C Leic	100	D3	
North Fambridge Essex	71	K7	
North Featherstone Wakefd	142	C3	
North Ferriby E R Yk	144	B3	

Northfield Birm	98	C7	
Northfield C Aber	245	K2	
Northfield E R Yk	144	C2	
Northfields Lincs	102	A2	
Northfleet Kent	52	D4	
North Frodingham E R Yk	153	H5	
North Gorley Hants	33	L8	
North Green Norfk	106	E5	
North Green Suffk	91	G3	
North Green Suffk	91	J2	
North Greetwell Lincs	135	K5	
North Grimston N York	152	C2	
North Halling Medway	52	F6	
North Haven Shet	281	b8	
North Hayling Hants	20	B6	
North Hazelrigg Nthumb	203	G6	
North Heasley Devon	28	C4	
North Heath W Susx	37	G6	
North Hele Devon	29	J6	
North Hertfordshire Memorial Park & Crematorium Herts	86	D8	
North Hill Cnwll	11	K7	
North Hillingdon Gt Lon	50	D2	
North Hinksey Village Oxon	66	D6	
North Holmwood Surrey	37	J2	
North Huish Devon	7	K3	
North Hykeham Lincs	135	J6	
Northiam E Susx	24	E2	
Northill C Beds	86	C6	
Northington Gloucs	63	L5	
Northington Hants	35	H3	
North Kelsey Lincs	144	D7	
North Kessock Highld	251	H2	
North Killingholme N Linc	144	F4	
North Kilvington N York	160	F5	
North Kilworth Leics	100	D6	
North Kingston Hants	18	B3	
North Kyme Lincs	118	F1	
North Lancing W Susx	21	L5	
North Landing E R Yk	153	L2	
Northlands Lincs	119	K1	
Northleach Gloucs	65	G4	
North Lee Bucks	67	K5	
North Lees N York	160	D7	
Northleigh Devon	14	E3	
Northleigh Devon	27	L4	
North Leigh Kent	40	F6	
North Leigh Oxon	66	A4	
North Leverton with Habblesthorpe Notts	134	F3	
Northlew Devon	12	C3	
North Littleton Worcs	82	C5	
Northload Bridge Somset	31	H3	
North Lopham Norfk	105	L6	
North Luffenham Rutlnd	101	K3	
North Marden W Susx	20	C4	
North Marston Bucks	67	J3	
North Middleton Mdloth	211	K7	
North Middleton Nthumb	190	E1	
North Millbrex Abers	256	E3	
North Milmain D & G	172	D4	
North Molton Devon	28	C5	
Northmoor Oxon	66	B6	
North Moreton Oxon	48	E1	
Northmuir Angus	234	B4	
North Mundham W Susx	20	E6	
North Muskham Notts	134	F7	
North Newbald E R Yk	152	D8	
North Newington Oxon	83	K7	
North Newnton Wilts	47	H7	
North Newton Somset	30	D4	
Northney Hants	20	B6	
North Nibley Gloucs	63	L7	
North Oakley Hants	48	D8	
North Ockendon Gt Lon	52	C2	
Northolt Gt Lon	50	E2	
Northop Flints	128	F6	
Northop Hall Flints	129	G6	
North Ormesby Middsb	170	C6	
North Ormsby Lincs	136	E1	
Northorpe Kirk	141	K3	
Northorpe Lincs	118	E8	
Northorpe Lincs	119	G4	
Northorpe Lincs	143	M8	
North Otterington N York	160	E5	
Northover Somset	31	H3	
Northover Somset	31	H6	
North Owersby Lincs	135	L1	
Northowram Calder	141	H2	
North Perrott Somset	15	L1	
North Petherton Somset	30	D4	
North Petherwin Cnwll	11	K5	
North Pickenham Norfk	105	H2	
North Piddle Worcs	81	M4	
North Poorton Dorset	15	M3	
Northport Dorset	17	H5	
North Poulner Hants	18	B2	
North Queensferry Fife	210	F3	

North Radworthy Devon	28	C4	
North Rauceby Lincs	118	D3	
Northrepps Norfk	122	E4	
North Reston Lincs	137	G3	
North Rigton N York	150	C6	
North Ripley Hants	18	B4	
North Rode Ches E	131	H6	
North Ronaldsay Ork	275	f1	
North Row Cumb	165	H4	
North Runcton Norfk	120	E8	
North Scale Cumb	146	C2	
North Scarle Lincs	135	G6	
North Seaton Nthumb	181	H4	
North Seaton Colliery Nthumb	181	H4	
North Shian Ag & B	228	E6	
North Shields N Tyne	181	J5	
North Shoebury Sthend	53	K2	
North Shore Bpool	146	F8	
North Side C Pete	102	C4	
North Side Cumb	164	C5	
North Skelton R & Cl	170	F7	
North Somercotes Lincs	145	L8	
North Stainley N York	160	D3	
North Stainmore Cumb	167	J7	
North Stifford Thurr	52	D3	
North Stoke BaNES	45	L5	
North Stoke Oxon	48	F3	
North Stoke W Susx	21	H5	
Northstowe Cambs	87	H2	
North Street Cambs	88	B2	
North Street Hants	33	K7	
North Street Hants	35	K4	
North Street Kent	40	D4	
North Street Medway	53	H4	
North Street W Berk	48	F4	
North Sunderland Nthumb	203	K6	
North Tamerton Cnwll	11	K3	
North Tawton Devon	12	F2	
North Third Stirlg	209	L1	
North Thoresby Lincs	145	H8	
North Togston Nthumb	191	K5	
North Tolsta W Isls	282	h2	
Northton W Isls	282	d6	
North Town Devon	12	C1	
North Town Somset	31	J2	
North Town W & M	49	L3	
North Tuddenham Norfk	122	A8	
North Uist W Isls	283	b8	
North Walbottle N u Ty	180	E5	
North Walsham Norfk	122	F5	
North Waltham Hants	35	H4	
North Warnborough Hants	35	M1	
North Way Somset	29	L5	
North Weald Bassett Essex	70	D6	
North Wheatley Notts	134	F3	
North Whilborough Devon	8	C2	
Northwich Ches W	130	C5	
North Wick BaNES	45	H6	
Northwick S Glos	45	E1	
Northwick Somset	30	E1	
Northwick Worcs	81	J4	
North Widcombe BaNES	45	H7	
North Willingham Lincs	136	C2	
North Wingfield Derbys	133	H6	
North Witham Lincs	118	B7	
Northwold Norfk	104	E2	
Northwood C Stke	114	D7	
Northwood Derbys	132	E6	
Northwood Gt Lon	50	E1	
Northwood IoW	19	H5	
Northwood Shrops	113	H6	
Northwood Green Gloucs	63	L4	
North Wootton Dorset	31	L7	
North Wootton Norfk	120	E6	
North Wootton Somset	31	H4	
North Wraxall Wilts	46	B4	
North Wroughton Swindn	47	H3	
Norton Donc	142	D5	
Norton E Susx	23	G7	
Norton Gloucs	64	B2	
Norton Halton	130	A3	
Norton Hants	34	F3	
Norton Herts	86	D7	
Norton IoW	18	E5	
Norton Mons	62	F3	
Norton N Som	44	D6	
Norton Nhants	84	B3	
Norton Notts	133	L5	
Norton Powys	79	K2	
Norton S on T	170	B6	
Norton Sheff	133	G3	
Norton Shrops	95	L7	
Norton Shrops	96	D2	
Norton Shrops	96	E6	
Norton Shrops	97	G3	
Norton Suffk	89	J2	
Norton Swans	57	H7	
Norton W Susx	20	F5	
Norton Wilts	46	C2	

Norton Worcs 81 K5
Norton Worcs 82 B5
Norton Bavant Wilts 32 F2
Norton Bridge Staffs 114 D5
Norton Canes Staffs 98 C2
Norton Canon Herefs 79 M6
Norton Corner Norfk 122 B6
Norton Disney Lincs 135 H7
Norton Ferris Wilts 32 C4
Norton Fitzwarren Somset 30 B5
Norton Green IoW 18 E6
Norton Hawkfield BaNES 45 H6
Norton Heath Essex 70 F6
Norton in Hales Shrops 113 M4
Norton-Juxta-Twycross Leics 99 J2
Norton-le-Clay N York 150 F2
Norton-le-Moors C Stke 114 D1
Norton Lindsey Warwks 82 F3
Norton Little Green Suffk 89 K2
Norton Malreward BaNES 45 J6
Norton Mandeville Essex 70 E6
Norton-on-Derwent N York 152 B2
Norton St Philip Somset 45 M7
Norton Subcourse Norfk 107 H4
Norton sub Hamdon Somset 31 G7
Norton Wood Herefs 79 L5
Norwell Notts 134 F7
Norwell Woodhouse Notts 134 E7
Norwich Norfk 106 E2
Norwich (St Faith)
    Crematorium Norfk 122 E8
Norwick Shet 281 f1
Norwood Clacks 220 F8
Norwood Derbys 133 J3
Norwood Kent 25 K1
Norwood End Essex 70 E5
Norwood Green Calder 141 H2
Norwood Green Gt Lon 50 E3
Norwood Hill Surrey 37 K2
Norwoodside Cambs 103 H4
Noseley Leics 101 G4
Noss Mayo Devon 7 G5
Nosterfield N York 160 C6
Nosterfield End Cambs 88 C6
Nostie Highld 248 D6
Notgrove Gloucs 65 G3
Nottage Brdgnd 42 B6
Notter Cnwll 6 D3
Nottingham C Nott 116 F4
Nottington Dorset 16 C6
Notton Wakefd 142 A5
Notton Wilts 46 C5
Nounsley Essex 71 J5
Noutard's Green Worcs 81 J2
Nowton Suffk 89 H3
Nox Shrops 95 K1
Nuffield Oxon 49 G2
Nunburnholme E R Yk 152 C6
Nuncargate Notts 116 E1
Nunclose Cumb 166 C2
Nuneaton Warwks 99 K5
Nuneham Courtenay Oxon 66 E7
Nunhead Gt Lon 51 K4
Nunkeeling E R Yk 153 J6
Nun Monkton N York 151 J4
Nunney Somset 32 B2
Nunney Catch Somset 32 B2
Nunnington Herefs 80 D6
Nunnington N York 161 L6
Nunsthorpe NE Lin 145 H6
Nunthorpe C York 151 J6
Nunthorpe Middsb 170 C7
Nunthorpe Village Middsb 170 D8
Nunton Wilts 33 K5
Nunwick N York 160 D7
Nunwick Nthumb 179 K4
Nupdown S Glos 63 J7
Nup End Bucks 67 L3
Nupend Gloucs 64 A5
Nuptown Br For 49 L4
Nursling Hants 34 E7
Nursted Hants 36 A6
Nursteed Wilts 46 F6
Nurton Staffs 97 J3
Nutbourne W Susx 20 C6
Nutbourne W Susx 21 J3
Nutfield Surrey 37 M1
Nuthall Notts 116 E3
Nuthampstead Herts 87 H8
Nuthurst W Susx 37 J5
Nutley E Susx 23 G2
Nutley Hants 35 J2
Nuttall Bury 140 B4
Nutwell Donc 143 G7
Nybster Highld 280 E3
Nyetimber W Susx 20 E7
Nyewood W Susx 36 B6
Nymet Rowland Devon 13 G1
Nymet Tracey Devon 13 G3

Nympsfield Gloucs 64 A7
Nynehead Somset 29 L6
Nythe Somset 30 F4
Nyton W Susx 20 F5

O

Oadby Leics 100 D3
Oad Street Kent 53 J6
Oakall Green Worcs 81 J3
Oakamoor Staffs 115 G3
Oakbank W Loth 210 E5
Oak Cross Devon 12 D3
Oakdale Caerph 43 J2
Oake Somset 29 L6
Oaken Staffs 97 J3
Oakenclough Lancs 147 K6
Oakengates Wrekin 96 F1
Oakenholt Flints 129 G5
Oakenshaw Dur 169 G3
Oakenshaw Kirk 141 J2
Oakerthorpe Derbys 133 H8
Oakford Cerdgn 76 E4
Oakford Devon 29 G6
Oakfordbridge Devon 29 G6
Oakgrove Ches E 131 H6
Oakham Rutlnd 101 J2
Oakhanger Ches E 114 B1
Oakhanger Hants 36 A4
Oakhill Somset 31 K2
Oakhurst Kent 38 E3
Oakington Cambs 87 H2
Oaklands Powys 78 E5
Oakle Street Gloucs 63 M4
Oakley Bed 85 K4
Oakley Bucks 66 F4
Oakley Fife 210 D1
Oakley Hants 35 H1
Oakley Oxon 67 H7
Oakley Poole 17 K3
Oakley Suffk 106 D7
Oakley Green W & M 50 A4
Oakley Park Powys 93 L6
Oakridge Lynch Gloucs 64 C6
Oaks Lancs 139 K1
Oaks Shrops 95 K2
Oaksey Wilts 64 E8
Oaks Green Derbys 115 J5
Oakshaw Ford Cumb 178 C4
Oakshott Hants 35 M5
Oakthorpe Leics 99 J1
Oak Tree Darltn 169 K8
Oakwood C Derb 116 C4
Oakwood Nthumb 179 L5
Oakworth C Brad 149 J8
Oare Kent 40 C3
Oare Somset 28 D2
Oare Wilts 47 H6
Oasby Lincs 118 D4
Oath Somset 30 F5
Oathlaw Angus 234 D4
Oatlands Park Surrey 50 E6
Oban Ag & B 216 D1
Obley Shrops 95 H7
Obney P & K 232 F8
Oborne Dorset 31 L7
Obthorpe Lincs 118 E8
Occold Suffk 90 D1
Occumster Highld 275 J1
Ochiltree E Ayrs 196 F6
Ockbrook Derbys 116 C4
Ocker Hill Sandw 98 B4
Ockeridge Worcs 81 H3
Ockham Surrey 50 D7
Ockle Highld 237 G6
Ockley Surrey 37 H3
Ocle Pychard Herefs 80 E6
Octon E R Yk 153 G2
Odcombe Somset 31 H7
Odd Down BaNES 45 L6
Oddendale Cumb 166 E8
Oddingley Worcs 81 L3
Oddington Gloucs 65 J2
Oddington Oxon 66 E4
Odell Bed 85 J4
Odham Devon 12 C2
Odiham Hants 49 H8
Odsal C Brad 141 J2
Odsey Cambs 86 F7
Odstock Wilts 33 K5
Odstone Leics 99 K2
Offchurch Warwks 83 J2
Offenham Worcs 82 C6
Offerton Stockp 131 H2
Offerton Sundld 181 J7
Offham E Susx 22 F5
Offham Kent 39 G2

Offham W Susx 21 H5
Offleymarsh Staffs 114 B5
Offord Cluny Cambs 86 E2
Offord D'Arcy Cambs 86 E2
Offton Suffk 90 C5
Offwell Devon 14 E3
Ogbourne Maizey Wilts 47 J4
Ogbourne St Andrew Wilts 47 J4
Ogbourne St George Wilts 47 J4
Ogden Calder 141 G2
Ogle Nthumb 180 E3
Ogmore V Glam 42 D6
Ogmore-by-Sea V Glam 42 C6
Ogmore Vale Brdgnd 42 E4
Ogwen Bank Gwynd 126 C6
Okeford Fitzpaine Dorset 32 D8
Okehampton Devon 12 E4
Oker Side Derbys 132 E7
Okewood Hill Surrey 37 H3
Olchard Devon 13 K7
Old Nhants 84 F1
Old Aberdeen C Aber 245 L2
Old Alresford Hants 35 J4
Oldany Highld 270 E2
Old Auchenbrack D & G 185 J3
Old Basford C Nott 116 F3
Old Basing Hants 49 G8
Old Beetley Norfk 121 L7
Oldberrow Warwks 82 D2
Old Bewick Nthumb 190 F4
Old Bolingbroke Lincs 136 F6
Old Bramhope Leeds 150 B7
Old Brampton Derbys 133 G5
Old Bridge of Urr D & G 175 J1
Old Buckenham Norfk 106 B5
Old Burghclere Hants 48 C7
Oldbury Kent 38 F2
Oldbury Sandw 98 C5
Oldbury Shrops 97 G5
Oldbury Warwks 99 J4
Oldbury Naite S Glos 63 J8
Oldbury-on-Severn S Glos 63 J8
Oldbury on the Hill Gloucs 46 B1
Old Byland N York 161 J5
Old Cantley Donc 143 G7
Old Cassop Dur 169 J3
Oldcastle Mons 62 C2
Oldcastle Heath Ches W 113 G2
Old Catton Norfk 106 E1
Old Churchstoke Powys 95 G4
Old Clee NE Lin 145 H6
Old Cleeve Somset 29 J3
Old Colwyn Conwy 127 H4
Oldcotes Notts 134 B2
Old Coulsdon Gt Lon 51 J7
Old Dailly S Ayrs 183 G3
Old Dalby Leics 117 H6
Old Dam Derbys 132 B4
Old Deer Abers 269 H6
Old Ditch Somset 31 H1
Old Edlington Donc 142 E8
Old Eldon Dur 169 H5
Old Ellerby E R Yk 153 J8
Old Felixstowe Suffk 91 H8
Oldfield C Brad 149 H8
Oldfield Worcs 81 J2
Old Fletton C Pete 102 D4
Oldford Somset 32 C1
Old Forge Herefs 63 H3
Old Furnace Herefs 62 F2
Old Glossop Derbys 131 L1
Old Goole E R Yk 143 J3
Old Grimsby IoS 10 b2
Old Hall Green Herts 69 K3
Oldhall Green Suffk 89 H4
Old Hall Street Norfk 122 F5
Oldham Oldham 140 D6
Oldham Crematorium Oldham 140 D7
Oldhamstocks E Loth 213 G5
Old Harlow Essex 70 C5
Old Heath Essex 72 E3
Old Hunstanton Norfk 120 F3
Old Hurst Cambs 102 F7
Old Hutton Cumb 157 J5
Old Kea Cnwll 4 D6
Old Kilpatrick W Duns 208 D4
Old Knebworth Herts 69 G3
Old Lakenham Norfk 106 E2
Oldland S Glos 45 K4
Old Langho Lancs 148 B8
Old Laxey IoM 154 f5
Old Leake Lincs 119 L2
Old Malton N York 152 B1
Oldmeldrum Abers 256 E6
Oldmill Cnwll 11 M7
Old Milverton Warwks 83 G2
Oldmixon N Som 44 C7
Old Newton Suffk 90 B3

Old Oxted Surrey 51 K8
Old Portlethen Abers 245 L4
Old Quarrington Dur 169 J3
Old Radford C Nott 116 F3
Old Radnor Powys 79 J3
Old Rayne Abers 256 B6
Old Romney Kent 25 J2
Old Shoreham W Susx 22 B6
Oldshoremore Highld 276 C4
Old Soar Kent 38 F3
Old Sodbury S Glos 45 L3
Old Somerby Lincs 118 C5
Oldstead N York 161 H6
Old Stratford Nhants 84 E7
Old Struan P & K 232 B2
Old Swarland Nthumb 191 H6
Old Swinford Dudley 97 K6
Old Tebay Cumb 157 K2
Old Thirsk N York 160 F6
Old Town Calder 140 F2
Old Town Cumb 157 J6
Old Town Cumb 166 B2
Old Town E Susx 23 K7
Old Town IoS 10 c3
Old Trafford Traffd 140 B8
Old Tupton Derbys 133 H6
Oldwall Cumb 178 B6
Oldwalls Swans 56 E6
Old Warden C Beds 86 C6
Oldways End Somset 28 F6
Old Weston Cambs 102 B7
Old Wick Highld 280 E6
Old Windsor W & M 50 C4
Old Wives Lees Kent 40 E4
Old Woking Surrey 50 C7
Old Wolverton M Keyn 84 F7
Old Woodhall Lincs 136 D6
Old Woods Shrops 113 G7
Olgrinmore Highld 279 K5
Olive Green Staffs 115 J7
Oliver's Battery Hants 34 F5
Ollaberry Shet 281 d4
Ollach Highld 247 H1
Ollerton Ches E 130 F4
Ollerton Notts 134 D6
Ollerton Shrops 113 L6
Olmarch Cerdgn 77 H4
Olmstead Green Cambs 88 C7
Olney M Keyn 85 H5
Olrig House Highld 279 L3
Olton Solhll 98 E7
Olveston S Glos 45 J2
Ombersley Worcs 81 J3
Ompton Notts 134 D6
Once Brewed Nthumb 179 H5
Onchan IoM 154 e6
Onecote Staffs 131 L8
Onehouse Suffk 89 K3
Onen Mons 62 E4
Ongar Street Herefs 79 M2
Onibury Shrops 95 L7
Onich Highld 229 G3
Onllwyn Neath 60 C5
Onneley Staffs 114 B3
Onslow Green Essex 71 G3
Onslow Village Surrey 36 E1
Onston Ches W 130 B5
Openwoodgate Derbys 116 B2
Opinan Highld 260 B5
Orbliston Moray 266 F5
Orbost Highld 258 D7
Orby Lincs 137 J6
Orchard Portman Somset 30 C6
Orcheston Wilts 33 J2
Orcop Herefs 62 F2
Orcop Hill Herefs 62 F2
Ord Abers 268 A4
Ordhead Abers 244 E2
Ordie Abers 244 A3
Ordiequish Moray 267 G5
Ordley Nthumb 179 L7
Ordsall Notts 134 D4
Ore E Susx 24 F5
Oreleton Common Herefs 80 B2
Oreton Shrops 96 E7
Orford Suffk 91 K5
Orford Warrtn 130 B2
Organford Dorset 17 H4
Orgreave Staffs 115 J8
Orkney Islands Ork 275 C4
Orlestone Kent 40 C8
Orleton Herefs 80 C2
Orleton Worcs 81 G2
Orlingbury Nhants 85 G1
Ormathwaite Cumb 165 J5
Ormesby R & Cl 170 C2
Ormesby St Margaret Norfk 123 K8
Ormesby St Michael Norfk 123 K8
Ormiscaig Highld 260 D2

Place	County	Page	Grid
Ormiston	E Loth	211	M5
Ormsaigmore	Highld	236	F7
Ormsary	Ag & B	206	A4
Ormskirk	Lancs	138	E6
Ornsby Hill	Dur	168	F1
Oronsay	Ag & B	214	C6
Orphir	Ork	275	b5
Orpington	Gt Lon	51	M5
Orrell	Sefton	138	D8
Orrell	Wigan	139	G7
Orrell Post	Wigan	139	G6
Orrisdale	IoM	154	d4
Orroland	D & G	175	J5
Orsett	Thurr	52	D3
Orsett Heath	Thurr	52	D3
Orslow	Staffs	114	C8
Orston	Notts	117	K3
Orthwaite	Cumb	165	H4
Ortner	Lancs	147	K5
Orton	Cumb	157	K1
Orton	Nhants	101	H7
Orton	Staffs	97	K4
Orton Longueville	C Pete	102	D4
Orton-on-the-Hill	Leics	99	J3
Orton Rigg	Cumb	177	K8
Orton Waterville	C Pete	102	C4
Orwell	Cambs	87	H5
Osbaldeston	Lancs	139	K2
Osbaldeston Green	Lancs	139	K1
Osbaldwick	C York	151	K5
Osbaston	Leics	99	L3
Osbaston	Shrops	112	D7
Osborne	IoW	19	H5
Osbournby	Lincs	118	E4
Oscroft	Ches W	129	L6
Ose	Highld	258	E8
Osgathorpe	Leics	116	D7
Osgodby	Lincs	135	M1
Osgodby	N York	143	G1
Osgodby	N York	163	J5
Oskaig	Highld	247	H1
Oskamull	Ag & B	226	E4
Osmaston	Derbys	115	K3
Osmington	Dorset	16	D6
Osmington Mills	Dorset	16	D6
Osmondthorpe	Leeds	142	A1
Osmotherley	N York	161	G3
Osney	Oxon	66	D6
Ospringe	Kent	40	C3
Ossett	Wakefd	141	L4
Ossington	Notts	134	E6
Ostend	Essex	72	D7
Osterley	Gt Lon	50	F3
Oswaldkirk	N York	161	K6
Oswaldtwistle	Lancs	139	L2
Oswestry	Shrops	112	D5
Otford	Kent	52	B7
Otham	Kent	39	K3
Otham Hole	Kent	39	K3
Othery	Somset	30	F4
Otley	Leeds	150	B6
Otley	Suffk	90	E4
Otley Green	Suffk	90	F4
Otterbourne	Hants	34	F6
Otterburn	N York	148	F4
Otterburn	Nthumb	190	C7
Otter Ferry	Ag & B	206	E2
Otterham	Cnwll	11	H4
Otterhampton	Somset	30	C2
Otterham Quay	Kent	53	H5
Otterham Station	Cnwll	11	G5
Otternish	W Isls	282	c7
Ottershaw	Surrey	50	C6
Otterswick	Shet	281	e3
Otterton	Devon	14	C5
Otterwood	Hants	18	F3
Ottery St Mary	Devon	14	C3
Ottinge	Kent	41	G6
Ottringham	E R Yk	145	H3
Oughterby	Cumb	177	J7
Oughtershaw	N York	158	F6
Oughterside	Cumb	164	F3
Oughtibridge	Sheff	132	F1
Oughtrington	Warrtn	130	D2
Oulston	N York	161	J7
Oulton	Cumb	177	H8
Oulton	Leeds	142	B2
Oulton	Norfk	122	C6
Oulton	Staffs	114	B7
Oulton	Staffs	114	E4
Oulton	Suffk	107	L4
Oulton Broad	Suffk	107	L5
Oulton Street	Norfk	122	C6
Oundle	Nhants	102	A5
Ounsdale	Staffs	97	K5
Ousby	Cumb	166	E4
Ousden	Suffk	88	E3
Ousefleet	E R Yk	143	L3
Ouston	Dur	181	G8
Outchester	Nthumb	203	J6
Out Elmstead	Kent	41	G5
Outgate	Cumb	156	E3
Outhgill	Cumb	158	D2
Outhill	Warwks	82	D2
Outlands	Staffs	114	B5
Outlane	Kirk	141	G4
Out Newton	E R Yk	145	K3
Out Rawcliffe	Lancs	147	H7
Outwell	Norfk	103	K3
Outwick	Hants	33	K7
Outwood	Surrey	37	M2
Outwood	Wakefd	142	A3
Outwood Gate	Bury	140	B6
Outwoods	Leics	116	C7
Outwoods	Staffs	114	B7
Ouzlewell Green	Leeds	142	A3
Ovenden	Calder	141	G2
Over	Cambs	87	H1
Over	Ches W	130	C6
Over	Gloucs	64	A3
Over	S Glos	45	H2
Over Burrows	Derbys	115	L4
Overbury	Worcs	81	M7
Overcombe	Dorset	16	D6
Over Compton	Dorset	31	K7
Overdale Crematorium	Bolton	139	K6
Over End	Cambs	102	B5
Overgreen	Derbys	132	F5
Over Green	Warwks	98	F4
Over Haddon	Derbys	132	D6
Over Kellet	Lancs	147	K2
Over Kiddington	Oxon	66	B3
Overleigh	Somset	31	G4
Overley	Staffs	115	J8
Over Monnow	Mons	63	G4
Over Norton	Oxon	65	L2
Over Peover	Ches E	130	F5
Overpool	Ches W	129	J4
Overscaig	Highld	272	B3
Overseal	Derbys	115	M8
Over Silton	N York	161	G4
Oversland	Kent	40	D4
Oversley Green	Warwks	82	C4
Overstone	Nhants	84	F2
Over Stowey	Somset	30	B3
Overstrand	Norfk	122	E3
Over Stratton	Somset	31	G7
Overstreet	Wilts	33	J3
Over Tabley	Ches E	130	E4
Overthorpe	Nhants	83	L7
Overton	C Aber	245	J1
Overton	Ches W	129	M4
Overton	Hants	35	G1
Overton	Lancs	147	H4
Overton	N York	151	J5
Overton	Shrops	80	C1
Overton	Swans	56	E7
Overton	Wakefd	141	L4
Overton	Wrexhm	112	E3
Overton Bridge	Wrexhm	112	E3
Overton Green	Ches E	130	F7
Overtown	Lancs	140	C2
Overtown	Lancs	157	K7
Overtown	N Lans	209	L8
Overtown	Swindn	47	H3
Overtown	Wakefd	142	A4
Over Wallop	Hants	34	C3
Over Whitacre	Warwks	99	H5
Over Woodhouse	Derbys	133	J5
Over Worton	Oxon	66	B1
Overy	Oxon	66	E8
Oving	Bucks	67	J3
Oving	W Susx	20	E6
Ovingdean	Br & H	22	E6
Ovingham	Nthumb	180	D6
Ovington	Dur	168	E7
Ovington	Essex	88	F6
Ovington	Hants	35	H4
Ovington	Norfk	105	J3
Ovington	Nthumb	180	C6
Ower	Hants	19	H3
Ower	Hants	34	D7
Owermoigne	Dorset	16	E5
Owlbury	Shrops	95	H5
Owlerton	Sheff	133	G2
Owlpen	Gloucs	64	A7
Owl's Green	Suffk	91	G1
Owlsmoor	Br For	49	K6
Owlswick	Bucks	67	J6
Owmby	Lincs	135	K2
Owmby	Lincs	144	D6
Owslebury	Hants	35	G6
Owston	Donc	142	E5
Owston	Leics	101	K2
Owston Ferry	N Linc	143	K7
Owstwick	E R Yk	145	H1
Owthorne	E R Yk	145	J2
Owthorpe	Notts	117	H5
Owton Manor	Hartpl	170	C5
Oxborough	Norfk	104	E3
Oxbridge	Dorset	15	L3
Oxcombe	Lincs	136	F4
Oxcroft	Derbys	133	J5
Oxen End	Essex	71	G1
Oxenholme	Cumb	157	H5
Oxenhope	C Brad	140	F1
Oxen Park	Cumb	156	D5
Oxenpill	Somset	31	G3
Oxenton	Gloucs	64	D1
Oxenwood	Wilts	47	L7
Oxford	Oxon	66	D6
Oxford Crematorium	Oxon	66	E5
Oxhey	Herts	68	E8
Oxhill	Dur	180	F8
Oxhill	Warwks	83	H6
Oxley	Wolves	97	K3
Oxley Green	Essex	72	C4
Oxley's Green	E Susx	24	C3
Oxlode	Cambs	103	K6
Oxnam	Border	189	J3
Oxnead	Norfk	122	E6
Oxshott	Surrey	50	F6
Oxshott Heath	Surrey	50	E6
Oxspring	Barns	141	L7
Oxted	Surrey	51	K8
Oxton	Border	201	G2
Oxton	N York	151	H7
Oxton	Notts	117	G1
Oxton	Wirral	129	G2
Oxwich	Swans	56	F7
Oxwich Green	Swans	56	F7
Oxwick	Norfk	121	K6
Oykel Bridge	Highld	271	L7
Oyne	Abers	256	B6
Oystermouth	Swans	57	H7
Ozleworth	Gloucs	64	A8

P

Place	County	Page	Grid
Pabail	W Isls	282	h3
Packers Hill	Dorset	16	D1
Packington	Leics	116	B8
Packmoor	C Stke	114	D1
Packmores	Warwks	83	G2
Padanaram	Angus	234	C5
Padbury	Bucks	67	H1
Paddington	Gt Lon	51	H3
Paddington	Warrtn	130	C2
Paddlesworth	Kent	41	G7
Paddlesworth	Kent	52	E6
Paddock Wood	Kent	39	G4
Paddolgreen	Shrops	113	H5
Padfield	Derbys	140	F8
Padgate	Warrtn	130	C2
Padhams Green	Essex	70	F7
Padiham	Lancs	140	B1
Padside	N York	149	L4
Padstow	Cnwll	10	C7
Padworth	W Berk	48	F5
Page Bank	Dur	169	G4
Pagham	W Susx	20	E7
Paglesham	Essex	72	D8
Paignton	Torbay	8	C3
Pailton	Warwks	100	A7
Paine's Cross	E Susx	23	K3
Painleyhill	Staffs	115	G5
Painscastle	Powys	79	G6
Painshawfield	Nthumb	180	C6
Painsthorpe	E R Yk	152	B4
Painswick	Gloucs	64	C5
Painter's Forstal	Kent	40	C3
Paisley	Rens	208	E6
Paisley Woodside Crematorium	Rens	208	D6
Pakefield	Suffk	107	L5
Pakenham	Suffk	89	J2
Pale	Gwynd	111	J4
Pale Green	Essex	88	D6
Palestine	Hants	34	B3
Paley Street	W & M	49	L4
Palfrey	Wsall	98	C4
Palgrave	Suffk	106	C7
Pallington	Dorset	16	E4
Palmersbridge	Cnwll	11	H7
Palmers Green	Gt Lon	69	J8
Palmerston	E Ayrs	196	F7
Palmerstown	V Glam	43	H7
Palnackie	D & G	175	K3
Palnure	D & G	174	C2
Palterton	Derbys	133	J6
Pamber End	Hants	48	F7
Pamber Green	Hants	48	F7
Pamber Heath	Hants	48	F6
Pamington	Gloucs	81	L8
Pamphill	Dorset	17	K3
Pampisford	Cambs	87	K5
Panborough	Somset	31	G2
Panbride	Angus	234	E8
Pancrasweek	Devon	11	K2
Pancross	V Glam	43	G7
Pandy	Caerph	43	J4
Pandy	Gwynd	92	D3
Pandy	Gwynd	111	K6
Pandy	Mons	62	C3
Pandy	Powys	93	K3
Pandy	Wrexhm	112	B4
Pandy'r Capel	Denbgs	111	L2
Pandy Tudur	Conwy	127	G6
Panfield	Essex	71	H2
Pangbourne	W Berk	48	F4
Pangdean	W Susx	22	D5
Panks Bridge	Herefs	80	E5
Pannal	N York	150	D5
Pannal Ash	N York	150	C5
Pant	Shrops	112	D7
Pantasaph	Flints	128	E4
Panteg	Pembks	74	F5
Pantersbridge	Cnwll	5	K1
Pant-ffrwyth	Brdgnd	42	E5
Pant Glas	Gwynd	109	H2
Pantglas	Powys	93	G4
Pant-Gwyn	Carmth	59	G4
Pant-lasau	Swans	57	J3
Pant Mawr	Powys	93	J7
Panton	Lincs	136	C4
Pant-pastynog	Denbgs	128	B7
Pantperthog	Gwynd	93	G3
Pant-y-dwr	Powys	93	L8
Pant-y-ffridd	Powys	94	E3
Pantyffynnon	Carmth	57	H3
Pantygaseg	Torfn	61	J4
Pant-y-gog	Brdgnd	42	D3
Pantymenyn	Carmth	75	K7
Pant-y-mwyn	Flints	128	E6
Panxworth	Norfk	107	G3
Papcastle	Cumb	164	F4
Papigoe	Highld	280	E6
Papple	E Loth	212	D4
Papplewick	Notts	116	F1
Papworth Everard	Cambs	86	F3
Papworth St Agnes	Cambs	86	F2
Par	Cnwll	5	H4
Paramour Street	Kent	41	J4
Parbold	Lancs	139	G5
Parbrook	Somset	31	J4
Parbrook	W Susx	37	G6
Parc	Gwynd	111	J4
Parc Gwyn Crematorium	Pembks	55	K4
Parcllyn	Cerdgn	75	M2
Parc Seymour	Newpt	44	D4
Pardshaw	Cumb	164	E5
Parham	Suffk	91	G3
Park	D & G	186	D7
Park	Nthumb	178	E6
Park Bottom	Cnwll	3	H3
Park Bridge	Tamesd	140	E7
Park Corner	E Susx	38	E6
Park Corner	Oxon	49	G4
Park Corner	W & M	49	K2
Park Crematorium	Hants	36	C1
Park Crematorium	Lancs	138	D2
Park End	Bed	85	K4
Parkend	Gloucs	63	J5
Park End	Nthumb	179	K4
Parker's Green	Kent	38	F2
Parkeston	Essex	73	K1
Parkeston Quay	Essex	90	F8
Park Farm	Kent	40	D7
Parkgate	Ches W	129	G4
Parkgate	Cumb	165	H1
Parkgate	D & G	176	D1
Parkgate	E Susx	24	C4
Parkgate	Essex	71	C2
Park Gate	Hants	19	J2
Parkgate	Kent	39	L5
Parkgate	Kent	52	B6
Park Gate	Leeds	150	A4
Parkgate	Surrey	37	L2
Park Gate	Worcs	81	L1
Park Green	Essex	70	C2
Park Green	Suffk	90	D4
Parkgrove Crematorium	Angus	234	F5
Parkhall	W Duns	208	E4
Parkham	Devon	27	G6
Parkham Ash	Devon	26	F6
Park Head	Derbys	116	B1
Park Hill	Gloucs	63	H2
Parkhouse	Mons	63	G6
Parkmill	Swans	57	G6
Park Royal	Gt Lon	51	K4
Parkside	Dur	169	K5
Parkside	N Lans	209	K5

Place	Page	Grid
Parkside Wrexhm	129	J8
Parkstone Poole	17	K4
Park Street Herts	68	F6
Park Street W Susx	37	H4
Parkway Herefs	81	G8
Park Wood Crematorium Calder	141	H3
Parley Green Dorset	17	M3
Parmoor Bucks	49	J1
Parndon Wood Crematorium Essex	70	C5
Parracombe Devon	28	B2
Parrog Pembks	75	H4
Parsonby Cumb	164	F3
Parson Cross Sheff	133	G1
Parson Drove Cambs	103	H2
Parson's Heath Essex	72	F2
Parson's Hill Derbys	116	A6
Partick C Glas	208	F5
Partington Traffd	130	D2
Partney Lincs	137	H6
Parton Cumb	164	C6
Partridge Green W Susx	22	B3
Partrishow Powys	62	B3
Parwich Derbys	115	K1
Paslow Wood Common Essex	70	C6
Passenham Nhants	84	F7
Passfield Hants	36	B4
Passingford Bridge Essex	70	D7
Paston C Pete	102	D3
Paston Norfk	123	G4
Pasturefields Staffs	114	F6
Patchacott Devon	12	B3
Patcham Br & H	22	D5
Patchetts Green Herts	68	F7
Patching W Susx	21	J5
Patchole Devon	27	L2
Patchway S Glos	45	J3
Pateley Bridge N York	149	L3
Paternoster Heath Essex	72	D4
Pathe Somset	30	F5
Pathhead Fife	222	E8
Pathhead Mdloth	211	L6
Pathlow Warwks	82	E3
Path of Condie P & K	221	K5
Patmore Heath Herts	70	B2
Patna E Ayrs	183	K1
Patney Wilts	47	G7
Patrick IoM	154	c5
Patrick Brompton N York	160	B4
Patricroft Salfd	139	M8
Patrington E R Yk	145	J3
Patrington Haven E R Yk	145	J3
Patrixbourne Kent	41	G4
Patterdale Cumb	165	L7
Pattingham Staffs	97	J4
Pattishall Nhants	84	C4
Pattiswick Green Essex	71	K2
Patton Shrops	96	D4
Patton Bridge Cumb	157	J3
Paul Cnwll	2	D5
Paulerspury Nhants	84	D6
Paull E R Yk	144	F3
Paulton BaNES	45	K7
Paunton Herefs	80	F5
Pauperhaugh Nthumb	191	G6
Pave Lane Wrekin	114	B8
Pavenham Bed	85	K4
Pawlett Somset	30	D2
Pawston Nthumb	202	C6
Paxford Gloucs	82	E7
Paxton Border	202	E3
Payden Street Kent	40	B4
Payhembury Devon	14	C2
Paynter's Lane End Cnwll	3	H2
Paythorne Lancs	148	E5
Paytoe Herefs	80	A1
Peacehaven E Susx	22	F7
Peak Dale Derbys	132	B4
Peak Forest Derbys	132	B4
Peak Hill Lincs	119	J8
Peakirk C Pete	102	D2
Pearson's Green Kent	39	H4
Peartree Green Herefs	80	E8
Peasedown St John BaNES	45	K7
Peasehill Derbys	116	C2
Peaseland Green Norfk	122	B8
Peasemore W Berk	48	C3
Peasenhall Suffk	91	H2
Pease Pottage W Susx	37	L4
Peaslake Surrey	37	G2
Peasley Cross St Hel	129	M1
Peasmarsh E Susx	25	G3
Peasmarsh Somset	30	E8
Peasmarsh Surrey	36	E2
Peathill Abers	269	G3
Peat Inn Fife	223	H5
Peatling Magna Leics	100	D5
Peatling Parva Leics	100	D5
Peaton Shrops	96	C6
Pebmarsh Essex	89	G8
Pebsham E Susx	24	D5
Pebworth Worcs	82	D6
Pecket Well Calder	140	F2
Peckforton Ches E	129	M8
Peckham Gt Lon	51	J4
Peckleton Leics	100	A3
Pedairffordd Powys	111	M6
Pedlinge Kent	40	F8
Pedmore Dudley	97	K7
Pedwell Somset	30	F4
Peebles Border	200	B5
Peel IoM	154	c5
Peel Lancs	138	D2
Peel Common Hants	19	K3
Peel Green Crematorium Salfd	139	M8
Peene Kent	41	G7
Peening Quarter Kent	39	M7
Peggs Green Leics	116	C7
Pegsdon C Beds	68	E1
Pegswood Nthumb	180	F2
Pegwell Kent	41	K3
Peinchorran Highld	247	H2
Peinlich Highld	259	G5
Pelcomb Pembks	54	F3
Pelcomb Bridge Pembks	54	F3
Pelcomb Cross Pembks	54	F3
Peldon Essex	72	E4
Pell Green E Susx	39	G6
Pelsall Wsall	98	C3
Pelsall Wood Wsall	98	C3
Pelton Dur	181	G8
Pelton Fell Dur	181	G8
Pelutho Cumb	164	F1
Pelynt Cnwll	5	L4
Pemberton Carmth	56	F5
Pemberton Wigan	139	H7
Pembles Cross Kent	39	M4
Pembrey Carmth	56	D4
Pembridge Herefs	79	M4
Pembroke Pembks	55	G6
Pembroke Dock Pembks	54	F6
Pembury Kent	39	G5
Pen-allt Herefs	63	H1
Penallt Mons	63	G5
Penally Pembks	55	J7
Penare Cnwll	5	G6
Penarth V Glam	43	J7
Penblewin Pembks	55	J4
Pen-bont Rhydybeddau Cerdgn	92	E6
Penbryn Cerdgn	76	B5
Pencader Carmth	58	E2
Pencaenewydd Gwynd	109	G3
Pencaitland E Loth	212	A5
Pencarnisiog IoA	124	F5
Pencarreg Carmth	76	F6
Pencarrow Cnwll	10	F6
Pencelli Powys	61	H2
Penclawdd Swans	57	G5
Pencoed Brdgnd	42	E5
Pencombe Herefs	80	E5
Pencoyd Herefs	63	G2
Pencraig Herefs	63	H3
Pencraig Powys	111	K6
Pendeen Cnwll	2	B4
Penderyn Rhondd	60	E5
Pendine Carmth	55	L5
Pendlebury Salfd	140	B7
Pendleton Lancs	148	D7
Pendock Worcs	81	H8
Pendoggett Cnwll	10	E6
Pendomer Somset	31	H8
Pendoylan V Glam	43	G6
Penegoes Powys	93	G3
Penelewey Cnwll	3	K3
Pen-ffordd Pembks	55	J2
Pengam Caerph	43	J2
Pengam Cardif	43	K6
Penge Gt Lon	51	K5
Pengelly Cnwll	10	F6
Pengorffwysfa IoA	125	H1
Pengover Green Cnwll	6	B2
Pen-groes-oped Mons	62	C5
Pengwern Denbgs	127	K4
Penhale Cnwll	3	H7
Penhale Cnwll	4	E3
Penhale Cnwll	5	J3
Penhale Cnwll	6	E4
Penhallow Cnwll	4	C4
Penhalurick Cnwll	3	H3
Penhalvean Cnwll	3	H3
Penhill Swindn	47	H1
Penhow Newpt	44	E1
Penhurst E Susx	24	C4
Peniarth Gwynd	92	D2
Penicuik Mdloth	211	H7
Peniel Carmth	58	D4
Peniel Denbgs	127	L7
Penifiler Highld	259	H8
Peninver Ag & B	192	F3
Penisarwaun Gwynd	125	K7
Penistone Barns	141	K7
Penjerrick Cnwll	3	K5
Penketh Warrtn	130	A2
Penkill S Ayrs	183	G3
Penkridge Staffs	97	L1
Penlean Cnwll	11	H3
Penleigh Wilts	32	E1
Penley Wrexhm	112	F3
Penllergaer Swans	57	H5
Pen-llyn IoA	124	F3
Penllyn V Glam	42	E6
Pen-lôn IoA	125	G6
Penmachno Conwy	110	E2
Penmaen Caerph	43	J2
Penmaen Swans	56	F7
Penmaenan Conwy	126	E4
Penmaenmawr Conwy	126	E4
Penmaenpool Gwynd	110	C7
Penmark V Glam	43	G7
Penmon IoA	126	C3
Penmorfa Gwynd	109	K3
Penmount Crematorium Cnwll	4	D5
Penmynydd IoA	125	J5
Penn Bucks	67	M8
Penn Wolves	97	K4
Pennal Gwynd	92	F3
Pennan Abers	268	F3
Pennant Cerdgn	76	F3
Pennant Denbgs	111	K5
Pennant Powys	93	J4
Pennant-Melangell Powys	111	K6
Pennard Swans	57	G7
Pennerley Shrops	95	J3
Pennicott Devon	13	K2
Pennington Cumb	156	C7
Pennington Hants	18	D4
Pennington Green Wigan	139	J6
Pennorth Powys	61	H2
Penn Street Bucks	68	A7
Pennsylvania S Glos	45	L4
Penny Bridge Cumb	156	D6
Pennycross Ag & B	226	F7
Pennygate Norfk	123	G7
Pennyghael Ag & B	227	G7
Pennyglen S Ayrs	183	H1
Penny Green Derbys	133	L4
Penny Hill Lincs	119	K6
Pennymoor Devon	28	F8
Pennywell Sundld	181	J7
Penparc Cerdgn	75	L3
Penparcau Cerdgn	92	D7
Penpedairheol Caerph	43	J2
Penpedairheol Mons	62	C6
Penpergwm Mons	62	C5
Penperlleni Mons	62	C6
Penpethy Cnwll	10	F5
Penpillick Cnwll	5	J4
Penpol Cnwll	3	K3
Penpoll Cnwll	5	K4
Penponds Cnwll	3	G3
Penpont Cnwll	10	F7
Penpont D & G	186	C7
Penpont Powys	60	E2
Penquit Devon	7	J4
Penrest Cnwll	11	L7
Penrherber Carmth	76	B7
Pen-rhiw Pembks	75	M4
Penrhiwceiber Rhondd	43	G2
Pen Rhiwfawr Neath	57	K3
Penrhiwllan Cerdgn	76	C6
Penrhiw-pal Cerdgn	76	C6
Penrhos Gwynd	108	F5
Penrhos IoA	124	D3
Penrhos Mons	62	E5
Penrhos Powys	59	L6
Penrhos garnedd Gwynd	125	K5
Penrhyn Bay Conwy	127	G3
Penrhyncoch Cerdgn	92	D6
Penrhyn-coch Cerdgn	92	E6
Penrhyndeudraeth Gwynd	109	L4
Penrhyn-side Conwy	126	F3
Penrice Swans	56	F7
Penrioch N Ayrs	194	D2
Penrith Cumb	166	C4
Penrose Cnwll	10	B8
Penruddock Cumb	166	A5
Penryn Cnwll	3	K4
Pensarn Conwy	127	J4
Pensax Worcs	81	G2
Pensby Wirral	129	G3
Penselwood Somset	32	C4
Pensford BaNES	45	J6
Pensham Worcs	81	L6
Penshaw Sundld	181	H8
Penshurst Kent	38	E4
Penshurst Station Kent	38	E4
Pensilva Cnwll	11	K8
Pensnett Dudley	97	K5
Penstone Devon	13	H3
Penstrowed Powys	94	C5
Pentewan Cnwll	5	G5
Pentir Gwynd	125	K6
Pentire Cnwll	4	C3
Pentlepoir Pembks	55	J5
Pentlow Essex	89	G6
Pentlow Street Essex	89	G6
Pentney Norfk	120	F8
Pentonbridge Cumb	178	B3
Penton Grafton Hants	34	D2
Penton Mewsey Hants	34	D2
Pentraeth IoA	125	J4
Pentre Denbgs	128	C7
Pentre Flints	129	H6
Pentre Mons	62	C6
Pentre Mons	62	E7
Pentre Powys	94	C6
Pentre Powys	94	E5
Pentre Powys	95	G5
Pentre Rhondd	42	E2
Pentre Shrops	112	E7
Pentre Wrexhm	112	D3
Pentre-bâch Cerdgn	77	G6
Pentre Bach Flints	128	F4
Pentrebach Myr Td	61	G6
Pentre-bach Powys	78	B8
Pentrebeirdd Powys	94	E1
Pentre Berw IoA	125	H5
Pentre-bont Conwy	110	D1
Pentrebychan Crematorium Wrexhm	112	D2
Pentre-cagel Carmth	76	C7
Pentrecelyn Denbgs	112	A1
Pentre-celyn Powys	93	J2
Pentre-chwyth Swans	57	J6
Pentre-clawdd Shrops	112	D5
Pentre-cwrt Carmth	76	D7
Pentredwr Denbgs	112	B2
Pentrefelin Gwynd	109	J4
Pentrefelin IoA	125	H1
Pentre Ffwrndan Flints	128	F5
Pentrefoelas Conwy	111	G1
Pentregalar Pembks	75	L6
Pentregat Cerdgn	76	C5
Pentre-Gwenlais Carmth	59	H5
Pentre Gwynfryn Gwynd	109	L6
Pentre Halkyn Flints	128	E5
Pentre Hodrey Shrops	95	H7
Pentre Isaf Conwy	127	K5
Pentre Llanrhaeadr Denbgs	128	C7
Pentre Llifior Powys	94	E4
Pentre-llwyn-llwyd Powys	78	C4
Pentre-llyn Cerdgn	92	D8
Pentre-llyn-cymmer Conwy	111	J1
Pentre-Maw Powys	93	J3
Pentre Meyrick V Glam	42	E6
Pentre-piod Torfn	62	B6
Pentre-poeth Newpt	44	B2
Pentre'rbryn Cerdgn	76	D4
Pentre'r-felin Cerdgn	77	H5
Pentre'r Felin Conwy	126	F6
Pentre'r-felin Powys	60	D1
Pentre Saron Denbgs	127	L7
Pentre-tafarn-y-fedw Conwy	126	F7
Pentre ty gwyn Carmth	59	M2
Pentrich Derbys	116	C1
Pentridge Dorset	33	H7
Pen-twyn Caerph	61	K7
Pen-twyn Mons	63	G5
Pen-twyn Torfn	61	L6
Pentwynmaur Caerph	43	K2
Pentyrch Cardif	43	H5
Penwithick Cnwll	5	H4
Penwood Hants	48	C6
Penwyllt Powys	60	C4
Penybanc Carmth	59	H4
Penybont Powys	78	F2
Pen-y-bont Powys	112	B6
Pen-y-bont-fawr Powys	111	L6
Pen-y-bryn Pembks	75	L4
Pen-y-cae Powys	60	C4
Penycae Wrexhm	112	D3
Pen-y-cae-mawr Mons	62	E8
Penycaerau Gwynd	108	C6
Pen-y-cefn Flints	128	D4
Pen-y-clawdd Mons	62	F5
Pen-y-coedcae Rhondd	43	G4
Penycwn Pembks	54	D4
Pen-y-fai Brdgnd	42	D5
Pen-y-felin Flints	128	D5
Penyffordd Flints	129	G7
Penyffridd Gwynd	125	J8
Pen-y-garn Cerdgn	92	D6
Pen-y-Garnedd Powys	111	L6

Pen-y-genffordd Powys 61 J1
Pen-y-graig Gwynd 108 C5
Penygraig Rhondd 42 F3
Penygroes Carmth 59 G6
Penygroes Gwynd 109 H1
Pen-y-Gwryd Gwynd 126 D8
Pen-y-lan V Glam 42 F6
Pen-y-Mynydd Carmth 56 E4
Penymynydd Flints 129 G7
Pen-y-pass Gwynd 126 C8
Pen-yr-Heol Mons 62 E5
Pen-yr-Heolgerrig Myr Td 60 F6
Penysarn IoA 125 H2
Pen-y-stryt Denbgs 112 E1
Penywaun Rhondd 60 E6
Penzance Cnwll 2 D5
Peopleton Worcs 81 L5
Peover Heath Ches E 130 F4
Peper Harow Surrey 36 D2
Peplow Shrops 113 K6
Pepper's Green Essex 70 F5
Pepperstock C Beds 68 D3
Perceton N Ayrs 196 C3
Percyhorner Abers 269 H3
Perelle Guern 9 i3
Perham Down Wilts 34 B1
Periton Somset 29 G2
Perivale Gt Lon 50 F2
Perkins Village Devon 14 B4
Perkinsville Dur 181 G8
Perlethorpe Notts 134 C5
Perranarworthal Cnwll 3 K3
Perranporth Cnwll 4 B4
Perranuthnoe Cnwll 2 E5
Perranwell Cnwll 3 K3
Perranwell Cnwll 4 C4
Perran Wharf Cnwll 3 K3
Perranzabuloe Cnwll 4 C4
Perrott's Brook Gloucs 64 E6
Perry Birm 98 D5
Perry Barr Birm 98 D5
Perry Barr Crematorium Birm 98 D5
Perry Green Essex 71 K3
Perry Green Herts 70 B4
Perry Green Wilts 46 E1
Perrystone Hill Herefs 63 J1
Perry Street Somset 15 H2
Pershall Staffs 114 C5
Pershore Worcs 81 L6
Pertenhall Bed 86 B2
Perth P & K 221 K3
Perth Crematorium P & K 221 K2
Perthy Shrops 112 E5
Perton Herefs 80 E7
Perton Staffs 97 J3
Pertwood Wilts 32 E4
Peterborough C Pete 102 D4
Peterborough Crematorium
 C Pete 102 D3
Peterchurch Herefs 79 L7
Peterculter C Aber 245 J3
Peterhead Abers 257 L2
Peterlee Dur 169 L2
Petersfield Hants 35 M6
Peter's Green Herts 68 F3
Petersham Gt Lon 50 F4
Peters Marland Devon 27 H8
Peterstone Wentlooge Newpt 43 L5
Peterston-super-Ely V Glam 43 G6
Peterstow Herefs 63 H2
Peters Village Kent 52 F6
Peter Tavy Devon 12 C7
Petham Kent 40 F5
Petherwin Gate Cnwll 11 K5
Petrockstow Devon 12 C1
Petsoe End M Keyn 85 H5
Pet Street Kent 40 E6
Pett E Susx 24 F4
Pettaugh Suffk 90 E3
Pett Bottom Kent 40 F5
Petterden Angus 234 C7
Pettinain S Lans 198 F4
Pettistree Suffk 91 G4
Petton Devon 29 H6
Petton Shrops 113 G6
Petts Wood Gt Lon 51 M5
Pettycur Fife 211 J2
Petty France S Glos 46 A2
Pettymuk Abers 257 G7
Petworth W Susx 36 E6
Pevensey E Susx 23 L6
Pevensey Bay E Susx 24 B6
Pewsey Wilts 47 H7
Pheasant's Hill Bucks 49 J2
Phepson Worcs 81 L3
Philadelphia Sundld 181 H8
Philham Devon 26 D6
Philiphaugh Border 200 F7
Phillack Cnwll 2 F3

Philleigh Cnwll 3 L3
Philpot End Essex 70 F3
Philpstoun W Loth 210 E4
Phocle Green Herefs 63 J2
Phoenix Green Hants 49 J7
Pibsbury Somset 31 G5
Pica Cumb 164 D6
Piccadilly Warwks 99 G4
Piccotts End Herts 68 D5
Pickburn Donc 142 E6
Pickering N York 162 H6
Picket Piece Hants 34 E2
Picket Post Hants 18 B2
Picket Twenty Hants 34 E2
Pickford Covtry 99 H7
Pickford Green Covtry 99 H7
Pickhill N York 160 E6
Picklescott Shrops 95 K3
Pickmere Ches E 130 D4
Pickney Somset 30 B5
Pickstock Wrekin 114 A6
Pickup Bank Bl w D 139 L3
Pickwell Devon 27 H3
Pickwell Leics 101 G1
Pickwick Wilts 46 B5
Pickworth Lincs 118 D5
Pickworth Rutlnd 101 L1
Picton Ches W 129 K5
Picton Flints 128 D3
Picton N York 160 F1
Piddinghoe E Susx 23 G6
Piddington Bucks 67 K8
Piddington Nhants 84 F4
Piddington Oxon 66 H4
Piddlehinton Dorset 16 D3
Piddletrenthide Dorset 16 D3
Pidley Cambs 103 G7
Piercebridge Darltn 169 G2
Pierowall Ork 275 C1
Piff's Elm Gloucs 64 C2
Pigdon Nthumb 180 E1
Pigeon Green Warwks 82 F3
Pig Oak Dorset 17 K2
Pig Street Herefs 79 L5
Pikehall Derbys 132 D7
Pilford Dorset 17 K2
Pilgrims Hatch Essex 70 E4
Pilham Lincs 135 H1
Pill N Som 45 G4
Pillaton Cnwll 6 D2
Pillatonmill Cnwll 6 D2
Pillerton Hersey Warwks 83 G5
Pillerton Priors Warwks 83 G5
Pilleth Powys 79 J2
Pilley Barns 142 A7
Pilley Hants 18 E4
Pilley Bailey Hants 18 E4
Pillgwenlly Newpt 44 C2
Pillhead Devon 27 H5
Pilling Lancs 147 H6
Pilling Lane Lancs 147 G6
Pilning S Glos 45 H2
Pilot Inn Kent 25 K4
Pilsbury Derbys 132 B7
Pilsdon Dorset 15 J3
Pilsgate C Pete 102 B2
Pilsley Derbys 132 E5
Pilsley Derbys 133 H7
Pilson Green Norfk 107 H1
Piltdown E Susx 23 G3
Pilton Devon 27 K4
Pilton Nhants 101 M6
Pilton Rutlnd 101 K3
Pilton Somset 31 K3
Pilton Green Swans 56 E7
Pimbo Lancs 139 G7
Pimlico Herts 68 E6
Pimlico Lancs 148 C7
Pimlico Nhants 84 B7
Pimperne Dorset 17 H1
Pinchbeck Lincs 119 H6
Pinchbeck Bars Lincs 119 G6
Pincheon Green Donc 143 G4
Pinchinthorpe R & Cl 170 D7
Pincock Lancs 139 H4
Pinfold Lancs 138 E5
Pinford End Suffk 89 G3
Pinged Carmth 56 D4
Pingewood W Berk 49 G5
Pin Green Herts 69 H2
Pinhoe Devon 13 M4
Pinkett's Booth Covtry 99 H6
Pinkney Wilts 46 B2
Pinkneys Green W & M 49 L3
Pinley Covtry 99 K7
Pinley Green Warwks 82 F3
Pin Mill Suffk 90 E7
Pinminnoch S Ayrs 182 F4
Pinmore S Ayrs 182 F4

Pinn Devon 14 C5
Pinner Gt Lon 50 E1
Pinner Green Gt Lon 50 E1
Pinsley Green Ches E 113 K2
Pinvin Worcs 81 M5
Pinwherry S Ayrs 182 F5
Pinxton Derbys 133 J8
Pipe and Lyde Herefs 80 C6
Pipe Aston Herefs 80 B1
Pipe Gate Shrops 114 A3
Pipehill Staffs 98 D2
Piperhill Highld 253 G2
Pipers Pool Cnwll 11 J6
Pipewell Nhants 101 J6
Pippacott Devon 27 J3
Pippin Street Lancs 139 H3
Pipton Powys 79 G7
Pirbright Surrey 50 B7
Pirbright Camp Surrey 50 B7
Pirnie Border 201 K7
Pirnmill N Ayrs 194 D2
Pirton Herts 68 F1
Pirton Worcs 81 K5
Pisgah Cerdgn 92 E7
Pishill Oxon 49 H1
Pistyll Gwynd 108 E3
Pitblae Abers 269 H3
Pitcairngreen P & K 221 J2
Pitcalnie Highld 264 C5
Pitcaple Abers 256 C6
Pitcarity Angus 233 M2
Pitchcombe Gloucs 64 B5
Pitchcott Bucks 67 J3
Pitcher Row Lincs 119 J5
Pitchford Shrops 96 C3
Pitch Green Bucks 67 J6
Pitch Place Surrey 36 C3
Pitch Place Surrey 50 B8
Pitchroy Moray 254 D4
Pitcombe Somset 31 L4
Pitcot V Glam 42 D6
Pitcox E Loth 212 E4
Pitfichie Abers 256 B8
Pitglassie Abers 256 C3
Pitgrudy Highld 264 B2
Pitlessie Fife 222 E5
Pitlochry P & K 232 D4
Pitmachie Abers 256 B6
Pitmain Highld 241 K3
Pitmedden Abers 256 F6
Pitminster Somset 30 B7
Pitmuies Angus 234 E5
Pitmunie Abers 256 B8
Pitney Somset 31 G5
Pitroddie P & K 222 C2
Pitscottie Fife 223 G4
Pitsea Essex 52 F1
Pitses Oldham 140 E7
Pitsford Nhants 84 E2
Pitstone Bucks 68 B4
Pitt Devon 29 J7
Pitt Hants 34 F5
Pittarrow Abers 245 G8
Pitt Court Gloucs 63 L7
Pittenweem Fife 223 K6
Pitteuchar Fife 222 D7
Pittington Dur 169 J2
Pittodrie House Hotel Abers 256 C6
Pitton Wilts 34 B4
Pitt's Wood Kent 38 F3
Pittulie Abers 269 H3
Pityme Cnwll 10 E7
Pity Me Dur 169 H2
Pivington Kent 40 B6
Pixey Green Suffk 106 E8
Pixham Surrey 37 J1
Plains N Lans 209 L5
Plain Street Cnwll 10 D6
Plaish Shrops 96 C4
Plaistow Gt Lon 51 L2
Plaistow W Susx 36 F5
Plaitford Hants 34 C7
Plank Lane Wigan 139 J7
Plas Cymyran IoA 124 E4
Plastow Green Hants 48 D6
Platt Bridge Wigan 139 J7
Platt Lane Shrops 113 L4
Platts Heath Kent 39 L3
Plawsworth Dur 169 H1
Plaxtol Kent 38 F3
Playden E Susx 25 G3
Playford Suffk 90 F5
Play Hatch Oxon 49 H4
Playing Place Cnwll 4 C6
Playley Green Gloucs 63 M1
Plealey Shrops 95 K2
Plean Stirlg 209 M2
Pleasance Fife 222 C4
Pleasington Bl w D 139 J2

Pleasington Crematorium
 Bl w D 139 K2
Pleasley Derbys 133 K6
Pleasleyhill Notts 133 K6
Pleck Dorset 32 B8
Pledgdon Green Essex 70 E2
Pledwick Wakefd 142 A4
Pleinheaume Guern 9 J2
Plemont Jersey 9 a1
Plemstall Ches W 129 K5
Plenmeller Nthumb 179 G6
Pleshey Essex 71 G4
Plockton Highld 248 C5
Plowden Shrops 95 J6
Plox Green Shrops 95 J6
Pluckley Kent 40 B6
Pluckley Station Kent 40 B6
Pluckley Thorne Kent 40 B6
Plucks Gutter Kent 41 J3
Plumbland Cumb 164 F3
Plumgarths Cumb 157 G4
Plumley Ches E 130 E5
Plump Hill Gloucs 63 K4
Plumpton Cumb 156 D7
Plumpton Cumb 166 C3
Plumpton E Susx 22 E4
Plumpton Nhants 84 B5
Plumpton End Nhants 84 D6
Plumpton Green E Susx 22 E4
Plumpton Head Cumb 166 C4
Plumstead Gt Lon 51 L3
Plumstead Norfk 122 C4
Plumstead Green Norfk 122 C4
Plumtree Notts 117 G5
Plumtree Green Kent 39 K4
Plungar Leics 117 K5
Plurenden Kent 40 B7
Plush Dorset 16 D2
Plusha Cnwll 11 J6
Plushabridge Cnwll 11 K8
Plwmp Cerdgn 76 C5
Plymouth C Plym 6 F4
Plympton C Plym 7 G4
Plymstock C Plym 7 G4
Plymtree Devon 14 B2
Pockley N York 161 K5
Pocklington E R Yk 152 B6
Pode Hole Lincs 119 H7
Podimore Somset 31 J6
Podington Bed 85 J3
Podmore Staffs 114 B4
Point Clear Essex 73 G4
Pointon Lincs 118 F5
Pokesdown Bmouth 18 A5
Polbain Highld 270 C6
Polbathic Cnwll 6 C3
Polbeth W Loth 210 D6
Polbrock Cnwll 5 G1
Polebrook Nhants 102 B4
Pole Elm Worcs 81 J5
Polegate E Susx 23 K6
Pole Moor Kirk 141 G4
Polesworth Warwks 99 H3
Polgigga Cnwll 2 B6
Polglass Highld 270 D6
Polgooth Cnwll 5 G5
Polgown D & G 185 H2
Poling W Susx 21 H6
Poling Corner W Susx 21 H5
Polkerris Cnwll 5 J4
Pollard Street Norfk 123 G5
Pollington E R Yk 142 F4
Polloch Highld 228 B2
Pollokshaws C Glas 208 F6
Pollokshields C Glas 208 F6
Polmassick Cnwll 5 G5
Polmear Cnwll 5 J4
Polmont Falk 210 B3
Polnish Highld 237 L2
Polperro Cnwll 5 L4
Polruan Cnwll 5 K5
Polsham Somset 31 H2
Polstead Suffk 89 K7
Polstead Heath Suffk 89 K7
Poltalloch Ag & B 216 C7
Poltescoe Cnwll 3 J7
Poltimore Devon 13 M3
Polton Mdloth 211 J6
Polwarth Border 202 A3
Polyphant Cnwll 11 J6
Polzeath Cnwll 10 C6
Pomathorn Mdloth 211 H6
Pomeroy Derbys 132 B6
Ponde Powys 78 F7
Pondersbridge Cambs 102 F5
Ponders End Gt Lon 69 K7
Ponsanooth Cnwll 3 J3
Ponsonby Cumb 155 J2
Ponsongath Cnwll 3 J7

Ponsworthy Devon 13 G7
Pontac Jersey 9 e4
Pontamman Carmth 59 H6
Pontantwn Carmth 58 E6
Pontardawe Neath 57 K4
Pontarddulais Swans 57 G4
Pont-ar-gothi Carmth 58 F4
Pont-ar-Hydfer Powys 60 C2
Pont-ar-llechau Carmth 59 K4
Pontarsais Carmth 58 E3
Pontblyddyn Flints 129 G7
Pont Cyfyng Conwy 126 E8
Pont Dolgarrog Conwy 126 F6
Pontdolgoch Powys 94 B5
Pont-Ebbw Newpt 44 C2
Pontefract Wakefd 142 C3
Pontefract Crematorium
Wakefd 142 C4
Ponteland Nthumb 180 E4
Ponterwyd Cerdgn 93 G7
Pontesbury Shrops 95 K2
Pontesbury Hill Shrops 95 K2
Pontesford Shrops 95 K2
Pontfadog Wrexhm 112 C4
Pontfaen Pembks 75 G5
Pont-faen Powys 78 D8
Pontgarreg Cerdgn 76 B4
Pontgarreg Pembks 75 K4
Ponthenri Carmth 56 E3
Ponthir Torfn 62 C8
Ponthirwaun Cerdgn 76 A6
Pontllanfraith Caerph 43 J3
Pontlliw Swans 57 H5
Pontlottyn Caerph 61 K6
Pontlyfni Gwynd 109 H1
Pont Morlais Carmth 56 F3
Pontnêddféchan Neath 60 D5
Pontnewydd Torfn 62 B7
Pontnewynydd Torfn 62 B6
Pont Pen-y-benglog Gwynd 126 C7
Pontrhydfendigaid Cerdgn 77 K2
Pont Rhyd-sarn Gwynd 111 G6
Pont Rhyd-y-cyff Brdgnd 42 C4
Pont-rhyd-y-fen Neath 42 B3
Pontrhydygroes Cerdgn 77 K1
Pontrhydyrun Torfn 62 C7
Pontrilas Herefs 62 E2
Pont Robert Powys 94 D1
Pont-rug Gwynd 125 J7
Ponts Green E Susx 24 B4
Pontshaen Cerdgn 76 D6
Pontshill Herefs 63 J3
Pontsticill Myr Td 61 G5
Pont Walby Neath 60 D6
Pontwelly Carmth 76 D7
Pontyates Carmth 56 E3
Pontyberem Carmth 58 F6
Pont-y-blew Wrexhm 112 D4
Pontybodkin Flints 129 G7
Pontyclun Rhondd 42 F5
Pontycymer Brdgnd 42 D3
Pontyglasier Pembks 75 K5
Pontygwaith Rhondd 42 F3
Pontygynon Pembks 75 K5
Pont-y-pant Conwy 110 E1
Pontypool Torfn 62 B7
Pontypridd Rhondd 43 G4
Pont-yr-hafod Pembks 74 E7
Pont-yr-Rhyl Brdgnd 42 D4
Pontywaun Caerph 43 K3
Pool Cnwll 3 H3
Pool IoS 10 b2
Poole Poole 17 K4
Poole Crematorium Poole 17 K3
Poole Keynes Gloucs 64 E8
Poolewe Highld 260 D4
Pooley Bridge Cumb 166 B6
Pooley Street Norfk 105 J7
Poolfold Staffs 131 H7
Pool Head Herefs 80 D5
Poolhill Gloucs 63 L1
Pool in Wharfedale Leeds 150 C6
Pool of Muckhart Clacks 221 H7
Pool Quay Powys 95 G1
Pool Street Essex 88 F7
Pooting's Kent 38 C3
Popham Hants 35 H2
Poplar Gt Lon 51 K3
Poplar Street Suffk 91 K2
Porchfield IoW 19 G5
Poringland Norfk 106 F3
Porkellis Cnwll 3 H4
Porlock Somset 28 F2
Porlock Weir Somset 28 F1
Portachoillan Ag & B 206 B7
Port-an-Eorna Highld 248 B5
Port Appin Ag & B 228 D6
Port Askaig Ag & B 205 G3
Portavadie Ag & B 206 E5

Port Bannatyne Ag & B 207 H5
Portbury N Som 45 G4
Port Carlisle Cumb 177 H6
Port Charlotte Ag & B 204 C4
Portchester Hants 19 K3
Portchester Crematorium
Hants 19 K2
Port Clarence S on T 170 C6
Port Driseach Ag & B 206 F4
Port Ellen Ag & B 204 E7
Port Elphinstone Abers 256 D7
Portencalzie D & G 182 C8
Portencross N Ayrs 195 K1
Port Erin IoM 154 b8
Portesham Dorset 16 B5
Portessie Moray 267 J3
Port e Vullen IoM 154 g4
Port Eynon Swans 56 E7
Portfield Gate Pembks 54 F4
Portgate Devon 12 A5
Port Gaverne Cnwll 10 D6
Port Glasgow Inver 208 B4
Portgordon Moray 267 H3
Portgower Highld 274 D5
Porth Cnwll 4 D2
Porth Rhondd 42 F3
Porthallow Cnwll 3 K6
Porthallow Cnwll 5 L4
Porthcawl Brdgnd 42 B6
Porthcothan Cnwll 10 B8
Porthcurno Cnwll 2 B6
Porthdinllaen Gwynd 108 D3
Port Henderson Highld 260 B5
Porthgain Pembks 74 D7
Porthgwarra Cnwll 2 B6
Porthill Staffs 114 D2
Porthkea Cnwll 4 D6
Porthkerry V Glam 43 G8
Porthleven Cnwll 3 G6
Porthmadog Gwynd 109 K4
Porthmeor Cnwll 2 C4
Porth Navas Cnwll 3 J5
Portholland Cnwll 4 F6
Porthoustock Cnwll 3 K6
Porthpean Cnwll 5 H5
Porthtowan Cnwll 3 H2
Porthwgan Wrexhm 112 F2
Porthyrhyd Carmth 58 F5
Porth-y-Waen Shrops 112 C6
Portincaple Ag & B 218 C8
Portinfer Jersey 9 a1
Portington E R Yk 143 K2
Portinnisherrich Ag & B 216 F5
Portinscale Cumb 165 H6
Port Isaac Cnwll 10 D6
Portishead N Som 44 F4
Portknockie Moray 267 K3
Portlethen Abers 245 K4
Portling D & G 175 L4
Portloe Cnwll 4 F7
Port Logan D & G 172 D6
Portlooe Cnwll 6 A4
Portmahomack Highld 264 E3
Portmellon Cnwll 5 G6
Port Mòr Highld 236 E4
Portmore Hants 18 E4
Port Mulgrave N York 171 J7
Portnacroish Ag & B 228 E6
Portnaguran W Isls 282 h3
Portnahaven Ag & B 204 B6
Portnalong Highld 246 D2
Port nan Giuran W Isls 282 h3
Port nan Long W Isls 282 c7
Port Nis W Isls 282 h1
Portobello C Edin 211 J4
Portobello Gatesd 181 G7
Portobello Wolves 98 B4
Port of Menteith Stirlg 219 J7
Port of Ness W Isls 282 h1
Porton Wilts 33 L4
Portontown Devon 12 A7
Portpatrick D & G 172 B4
Port Quin Cnwll 10 D6
Port Ramsay Ag & B 228 D6
Portreath Cnwll 3 G2
Portree Highld 259 H7
Port Righ Ag & B 194 C3
Port St Mary IoM 154 b8
Portscatho Cnwll 3 M4
Portsea C Port 19 L4
Portskerra Highld 278 E3
Portskewett Mons 45 G1
Portslade Br & H 22 C6
Portslade-by-Sea Br & H 22 C6
Portslogan D & G 172 B3
Portsmouth C Port 19 L4
Portsmouth Calder 140 D3
Portsmouth Arms Devon 27 L7
Port Soderick IoM 154 d7

Port Solent C Port 19 L3
Portsonachan Hotel Ag & B 217 G3
Portsoy Abers 267 M3
Port Sunlight Wirral 129 H3
Portswood C Sotn 34 F8
Port Talbot Neath 57 L7
Port Tennant Swans 57 J6
Portuairk Highld 236 E7
Portway Herefs 80 B6
Portway Herefs 80 B6
Portway Sandw 98 B6
Portway Worcs 82 C1
Port Wemyss Ag & B 204 B6
Port William D & G 173 J6
Portwrinkle Cnwll 6 D4
Portyerrock D & G 174 D7
Posbury Devon 13 J3
Posenhall Shrops 96 E3
Poslingford Suffk 88 F5
Posso Border 199 L6
Postbridge Devon 12 F6
Postcombe Oxon 67 H7
Post Green Dorset 17 J4
Postling Kent 40 F7
Postwick Norfk 106 F2
Potarch Abers 244 D4
Potsgrove C Beds 68 B1
Potten End Herts 68 C5
Potten Street Kent 41 H2
Potter Brompton N York 163 H7
Pottergate Street Norfk 106 D5
Potterhanworth Lincs 135 L6
Potterhanworth Booths Lincs 135 M6
Potter Heigham Norfk 123 J7
Potterne Wilts 46 E7
Potterne Wick Wilts 46 E7
Potter Row Bucks 67 L6
Potters Bar Herts 69 H6
Potters Brook Lancs 147 J5
Potter's Cross Staffs 97 J6
Potters Crouch Herts 68 E6
Potter's Forstal Kent 39 M4
Potters Green Covtry 99 K7
Potter's Green E Susx 23 H3
Potter's Green Herts 69 K3
Pottersheath Herts 69 G3
Potters Marston Leics 100 B4
Potter Somersal Derbys 115 J4
Potterspury Nhants 84 E6
Potter Street Essex 70 C5
Potterton Abers 257 H8
Potterton Leeds 150 F8
Potthorpe Norfk 121 L7
Pottle Street Wilts 32 D3
Potto N York 161 G2
Potton C Beds 86 E5
Pott Row Norfk 120 F7
Pott's Green Essex 72 C3
Pott Shrigley Ches E 131 J4
Poughill Cnwll 11 J1
Poughill Devon 13 K1
Poulner Hants 18 B2
Poulshot Wilts 46 E7
Poulton Gloucs 65 G7
Poulton Wirral 129 G2
Poulton-le-Fylde Lancs 147 G7
Poulton Priory Gloucs 65 G7
Pound Bank Worcs 97 G8
Poundbury Dorset 16 C4
Poundffald Swans 57 G6
Poundgate E Susx 38 D7
Pound Green E Susx 23 H3
Pound Green Suffk 88 E4
Pound Green Worcs 97 G7
Pound Hill W Susx 37 L3
Poundon Bucks 66 F2
Poundsbridge Kent 38 E5
Poundsgate Devon 13 G8
Poundstock Cnwll 11 H3
Pound Street Hants 48 C6
Pounsley E Susx 23 J3
Pouton D & G 174 C5
Pouy Street Suffk 91 H1
Povey Cross Surrey 37 L3
Powburn Nthumb 190 F3
Powderham Devon 13 M5
Powerstock Dorset 15 L3
Powfoot D & G 176 F5
Pow Green Herefs 81 G6
Powhill Cumb 177 H7
Powick Worcs 81 J5
Powmill P & K 221 J7
Poxwell Dorset 16 E6
Poyle Slough 50 C4
Poynings W Susx 22 C5
Poyntington Dorset 31 L6
Poynton Ches E 131 H3
Poynton Wrekin 113 J8
Poynton Green Wrekin 113 J7

Poyston Cross Pembks 55 G3
Poystreet Green Suffk 89 K4
Praa Sands Cnwll 2 F5
Pratt's Bottom Gt Lon 52 A6
Praze-an-Beeble Cnwll 3 G4
Predannack Wollas Cnwll 3 H7
Prees Shrops 113 J5
Preesall Lancs 147 G6
Prees Green Shrops 113 J5
Preesgweene Shrops 112 D4
Prees Heath Shrops 113 J4
Prees Higher Heath Shrops 113 J4
Prees Lower Heath Shrops 113 J5
Prendwick Nthumb 190 E4
Pren-gwyn Cerdgn 76 D6
Prenteg Gwynd 109 K3
Prenton Wirral 129 G2
Prescot Knows 129 L1
Prescott Devon 29 K8
Prescott Shrops 96 F7
Prescott Shrops 112 F7
Presnerb Angus 233 J2
Pressen Nthumb 202 C6
Prestatyn Denbgs 128 C3
Prestbury Ches E 131 H4
Prestbury Gloucs 64 C2
Presteigne Powys 79 K2
Prestleigh Somset 31 K3
Prestolee Bolton 139 M6
Preston Border 213 H6
Preston Br & H 22 D6
Preston Devon 13 K7
Preston Dorset 16 D6
Preston E R Yk 144 F2
Preston Gloucs 64 F7
Preston Herts 68 F2
Preston Kent 40 D3
Preston Kent 41 H3
Preston Lancs 139 G2
Preston Nthumb 203 K8
Preston Rutlnd 101 J3
Preston Shrops 96 C1
Preston Somset 29 K4
Preston Torbay 8 D3
Preston Wilts 46 F3
Preston Wilts 47 K4
Preston Bagot Warwks 82 E2
Preston Bissett Bucks 67 G1
Preston Bowyer Somset 29 L5
Preston Brockhurst Shrops 113 J6
Preston Brook Halton 130 B4
Preston Candover Hants 35 J3
Preston Capes Nhants 84 B4
Preston Crematorium Lancs 139 H1
Preston Crowmarsh Oxon 48 F1
Preston Deanery Nhants 84 F4
Preston Green Warwks 82 E2
Preston Gubbals Shrops 113 H7
Preston Montford Shrops 113 G8
Preston on Stour Warwks 82 F5
Preston on Tees S on T 169 L7
Preston on the Hill Halton 130 B3
Preston on Wye Herefs 79 M7
Prestonpans E Loth 211 L4
Preston Patrick Cumb 157 H6
Preston Plucknett Somset 31 H7
Preston St Mary Suffk 89 J5
Preston Street Kent 41 H3
Preston-under-Scar N York 159 K4
Preston upon the Weald
Moors Wrekin 113 L8
Preston Wynne Herefs 80 D6
Prestwich Bury 140 B6
Prestwick Nthumb 180 E4
Prestwick S Ayrs 196 C6
Prestwood Bucks 67 L7
Prestwood Staffs 97 K6
Price Town Brdgnd 42 E3
Prickwillow Cambs 104 B7
Priddy Somset 31 H1
Priestacott Devon 12 B1
Priestcliffe Derbys 132 C5
Priestcliffe Ditch Derbys 132 C5
Priest Hutton Lancs 157 H7
Priestland E Ayrs 197 H3
Priestley Green Calder 141 H3
Priest Weston Shrops 95 H4
Priestwood Green Kent 52 E6
Primethorpe Leics 100 B5
Primrose Green Norfk 122 B8
Primrosehill Border 213 H5
Primrose Hill Cambs 103 H5
Primrose Hill Derbys 133 J8
Primrose Hill Dudley 97 L6
Primrose Hill Lancs 138 E6
Primrose Hill Lancs 202 C7
Primsidemill Border 202 C7
Princes Gate Pembks 55 K4
Princes Risborough Bucks 67 K6
Princethorpe Warwks 83 J1

Princetown Devon 12 E7
Prinsted W Susx 20 C5
Prion Denbgs 128 C7
Prior Rigg Cumb 178 B5
Priors Halton Shrops 96 B8
Priors Hardwick Warwks 83 L4
Priorslee Wrekin 97 G1
Priors Marston Warwks 83 L4
Priors Norton Gloucs 64 C2
Priory Wood Herefs 79 J6
Prisk V Glam 42 F6
Priston BaNES 45 K7
Pristow Green Norfk 106 C5
Prittlewell Sthend 53 J2
Privett Hants 35 L5
Prixford Devon 27 K3
Probus Cnwll 4 E5
Prora E Loth 212 B3
Prospect Cumb 164 F3
Prospidnick Cnwll 3 G5
Protstonhill Abers 268 E3
Prudhoe Nthumb 180 D6
Prussia Cove Cnwll 2 E7
Publow BaNES 45 J6
Puckeridge Herts 69 K2
Puckington Somset 30 E7
Pucklechurch S Glos 45 K4
Puckrup Gloucs 81 K7
Puddinglake Ches W 130 E5
Puddington Ches W 129 H5
Puddington Devon 28 E8
Puddledock Norfk 105 L5
Puddletown Dorset 16 E4
Pudleston Herefs 80 D3
Pudsey Leeds 141 K1
Pulborough W Susx 21 H3
Puleston Wrekin 114 A7
Pulford Ches W 129 J7
Pulham Dorset 16 D1
Pulham Market Norfk 106 D6
Pulham St Mary Norfk 106 E6
Pullens Green S Glos 63 J8
Pulloxhill C Beds 85 L8
Pulverbatch Shrops 95 K3
Pumpherston W Loth 210 E5
Pumsaint Carmth 77 J7
Puncheston Pembks 75 G6
Puncknowle Dorset 15 M5
Punnett's Town E Susx 23 K3
Purbrook Hants 19 M2
Purfleet Thurr 52 C3
Puriton Somset 30 D3
Purleigh Essex 71 K6
Purley Gt Lon 51 J6
Purley W Berk 49 G4
Purlogue Shrops 95 G7
Purlpit Wilts 46 C5
Purls Bridge Cambs 103 K6
Purse Caundle Dorset 32 B7
Purshull Green Worcs 81 K1
Purslow Shrops 95 J7
Purston Jaglin Wakefd 142 C4
Purtington Somset 15 J1
Purton Gloucs 63 K6
Purton Gloucs 63 K6
Purton Wilts 47 G2
Purton Stoke Wilts 47 G1
Pury End Nhants 84 D6
Pusey Oxon 65 M7
Putley Herefs 80 E7
Putley Green Herefs 80 F7
Putloe Gloucs 64 A5
Putney Gt Lon 51 G4
Putney Vale Crematorium Gt Lon 51 G4
Putsborough Devon 27 H3
Puttenham Herts 67 L4
Puttenham Surrey 36 D2
Puttock End Essex 89 G7
Putton Dorset 16 C6
Putts Corner Devon 14 D3
Puxley Nhants 84 E6
Puxton N Som 44 E6
Pwll Carmth 56 E4
Pwllcrochan Pembks 54 F6
Pwll-du Mons 61 L5
Pwll-glâs Denbgs 111 M1
Pwllgloyw Powys 78 E8
Pwllheli Gwynd 108 F4
Pwllmeyric Mons 63 G8
Pwll-trap Carmth 58 A5
Pwll-y-glaw Neath 42 B3
Pydew Conwy 126 F4
Pye Bridge Derbys 116 D1
Pyecombe W Susx 22 D4
Pye Corner Newpt 44 D2
Pye Green Staffs 114 F8
Pyle Brdgnd 42 B5
Pyleigh Somset 29 L5

Pylle Somset 31 K3
Pymoor Cambs 103 K6
Pymore Dorset 15 L4
Pyrford Surrey 50 D7
Pyrton Oxon 67 G7
Pytchley Nhants 101 J8
Pyworthy Devon 11 K2

Q

Quabbs Shrops 94 F7
Quadring Lincs 119 H5
Quadring Eaudike Lincs 119 H5
Quainton Bucks 67 H3
Quaker's Yard Myr Td 43 H3
Quaking Houses Dur 180 F8
Quarff Shet 281 e7
Quarley Hants 34 C2
Quarndon Derbys 116 B3
Quarr Hill IoW 19 K5
Quarrier's Village Inver 208 B5
Quarrington Lincs 118 E3
Quarrington Hill Dur 169 J3
Quarrybank Ches W 130 A6
Quarry Bank Dudley 97 L6
Quarrywood Moray 266 D3
Quarter N Ayrs 207 K6
Quarter S Lans 197 L1
Quatford Shrops 97 G5
Quatt Shrops 97 G5
Quebec Dur 168 F2
Quedgeley Gloucs 64 A4
Queen Adelaide Cambs 104 B7
Queenborough Kent 53 K4
Queen Camel Somset 31 K6
Queen Charlton BaNES 45 J5
Queen Dart Devon 28 E7
Queenhill Worcs 81 K7
Queen Oak Dorset 32 C4
Queen's Bower IoW 19 J6
Queensbury C Brad 141 H2
Queensferry Flints 129 H6
Queensferry Crossing Fife 210 F3
Queen's Head Shrops 112 E6
Queen's Hills Norfk 106 D1
Queenslie C Glas 209 H6
Queen's Park Bed 85 L5
Queen's Park Nhants 84 E3
Queen Street Kent 39 H4
Queen Street Wilts 46 F2
Queenzieburn N Lans 209 J3
Quendon Essex 70 D1
Queniborough Leics 100 E1
Quenington Gloucs 65 H6
Quernmore Lancs 147 K4
Queslett Birm 98 D4
Quethiock Cnwll 6 C2
Quick's Green W Berk 48 E4
Quidenham Norfk 105 L6
Quidhampton Hants 35 G1
Quidhampton Wilts 33 K5
Quina Brook Shrops 113 H5
Quinbury End Nhants 84 B5
Quinton Dudley 98 C6
Quinton Nhants 84 E4
Quinton Green Nhants 84 F4
Quintrell Downs Cnwll 4 D3
Quixhall Staffs 115 H3
Quixwood Border 213 H6
Quoditch Devon 12 A3
Quoig P & K 220 E3
Quorn Leics 116 F8
Quothquan S Lans 199 G5
Quoyburray Ork 275 d5
Quoyloo Ork 275 b4

R

Raasay Highld 259 K8
Rabbit's Cross Kent 39 K4
Rableyheath Herts 69 G3
Raby Cumb 177 G8
Raby Wirral 129 H4
Rachan Mill Border 199 K6
Rachub Gwynd 126 C6
Rackenford Devon 28 E7
Rackham W Susx 21 H4
Rackheath Norfk 122 F8
Racks D & G 176 D4
Rackwick Ork 275 a5
Radbourne Derbys 115 M4
Radcliffe Bury 140 B6
Radcliffe Nthumb 191 K5
Radcliffe on Trent Notts 117 H4
Radclive Bucks 84 D8

Radcot Oxon 65 L7
Raddery Highld 263 J7
Raddington Somset 29 J5
Radernie Fife 223 H5
Radford Covtry 99 J7
Radford Semele Warwks 83 H2
Radlet Somset 30 B3
Radlett Herts 68 F7
Radley Devon 28 C6
Radley Oxon 66 D7
Radley W Berk 48 A5
Radley Green Essex 70 F6
Radmore Green Ches E 130 B8
Radnage Bucks 67 J7
Radstock BaNES 45 K8
Radstone Nhants 84 B7
Radway Warwks 83 J5
Radwell Bed 85 K4
Radwell Herts 86 E8
Radwinter Essex 88 C7
Radwinter End Essex 88 C7
Radyr Cardif 43 H5
RAF College (Cranwell) Lincs 118 D2
Rafford Moray 265 H8
Ragdale Leics 117 H7
Ragdon Shrops 95 L5
Raginnis Cnwll 2 D6
Raglan Mons 62 E5
Ragnall Notts 134 F5
Raigbeg Highld 252 F6
Rainbow Hill Worcs 81 K4
Rainford St Hel 138 F7
Rainham Gt Lon 52 B3
Rainham Medway 53 H6
Rainhill St Hel 129 L2
Rainhill Stoops St Hel 129 L2
Rainow Ches E 131 J4
Rainsbrook Crematorium Warwks 83 M1
Rainsough Bury 140 B7
Rainton N York 160 E7
Rainworth Notts 134 B8
Raisbeck Cumb 157 K1
Raise Cumb 167 G2
Raisthorpe N York 152 C3
Rait P & K 222 C2
Raithby Lincs 136 F3
Raithby Lincs 137 G6
Raithwaite N York 171 K8
Rake Hants 36 B5
Rakewood Rochdl 140 E5
Ralia Highld 241 J4
Ram Carmth 77 G6
Ramasaig Highld 258 B7
Rame Cnwll 3 J4
Rame Cnwll 6 E5
Ram Hill S Glos 45 K3
Ram Lane Kent 40 C6
Rampisham Dorset 16 A2
Rampside Cumb 146 E3
Rampton Cambs 87 J2
Rampton Notts 134 F4
Ramsbottom Bury 140 B4
Ramsbury Wilts 47 K4
Ramscraigs Highld 274 F3
Ramsdean Hants 35 L4
Ramsdell Hants 48 E7
Ramsden Oxon 65 M4
Ramsden Worcs 81 L6
Ramsden Bellhouse Essex 71 H8
Ramsden Heath Essex 71 H7
Ramsey Cambs 102 F6
Ramsey Essex 73 J1
Ramsey IoM 154 f3
Ramsey Forty Foot Cambs 102 F6
Ramsey Heights Cambs 102 E6
Ramsey Island Essex 72 D6
Ramsey Island Pembks 74 A7
Ramsey Mereside Cambs 102 F5
Ramsey St Mary's Cambs 102 E6
Ramsgate Kent 41 L2
Ramsgill N York 149 K2
Ramshaw Dur 168 B1
Ramshaw Dur 168 F5
Ramsholt Suffk 91 H7
Ramshope Nthumb 189 K5
Ramshorn Staffs 115 H3
Ramsley Devon 12 F4
Ramsnest Common Surrey 36 E4
Ranby Lincs 136 D3
Ranby Notts 134 C3
Rand Lincs 136 B4
Randalls Park Crematorium Surrey 50 F7
Randwick Gloucs 64 B5
Ranfurly Rens 208 C6
Rangemore Staffs 115 K7
Rangeworthy S Glos 45 K2
Rankinston E Ayrs 196 E8

Ranksborough Rutlnd 101 H1
Rank's Green Essex 71 H3
Rannoch Station P & K 230 D4
Ranscombe Somset 29 G2
Ranskill Notts 134 C2
Ranton Staffs 114 D6
Ranton Green Staffs 114 D7
Ranworth Norfk 123 G8
Raploch Stirlg 220 D8
Rapness Ork 275 d2
Rapps Somset 30 E7
Rascarrel D & G 175 K5
Rashfield Ag & B 207 J2
Rashwood Worcs 81 L2
Raskelf N York 151 G2
Rassau Blae G 61 J5
Rastrick Calder 141 H3
Ratagan Highld 248 E7
Ratby Leics 100 B2
Ratcliffe Culey Leics 99 J3
Ratcliffe on Soar Notts 116 E6
Ratcliffe on the Wreake Leics 117 G8
Rathen Abers 269 J4
Rathillet Fife 222 F3
Rathmell N York 148 D4
Ratho C Edin 210 F5
Ratho Station C Edin 210 F5
Rathven Moray 267 J3
Ratlake Hants 34 E6
Ratley Warwks 83 J5
Ratling Kent 41 H4
Ratlinghope Shrops 95 K4
Rattar Highld 280 C2
Ratten Row Cumb 165 K3
Ratten Row Cumb 165 L1
Ratten Row Lancs 147 H7
Rattery Devon 7 L3
Rattlesden Suffk 89 K3
Ratton Village E Susx 23 K7
Rattray P & K 233 J6
Raughton Cumb 165 L1
Raughton Head Cumb 165 L2
Raunds Nhants 85 K1
Ravenfield Rothm 133 J1
Ravenglass Cumb 155 K3
Ravenhills Green Worcs 81 G4
Raveningham Norfk 107 H4
Ravenscar N York 163 H2
Ravenscraig N Lans 209 K7
Ravensdale IoM 154 e4
Ravensden Bed 86 B4
Ravenseat N York 158 E2
Ravenshead Notts 133 L8
Ravensmoor Ches E 113 K2
Ravensthorpe Kirk 141 K4
Ravensthorpe Nhants 84 C1
Ravenstone Leics 99 L1
Ravenstone M Keyn 85 G5
Ravenstonedale Cumb 158 C2
Ravenstruther S Lans 198 F4
Ravensworth N York 159 L1
Raw N York 163 G2
Rawcliffe C York 151 J5
Rawcliffe E R Yk 143 H3
Rawcliffe Bridge E R Yk 143 H3
Rawdon Leeds 150 B7
Rawdon Crematorium Leeds 150 B8
Rawling Street Kent 40 B3
Rawmarsh Rothm 142 C8
Rawnsley Staffs 98 C1
Rawreth Essex 71 J3
Rawridge Devon 14 E2
Rawtenstall Lancs 140 B3
Raydon Suffk 90 B7
Raylees Nthumb 190 C7
Rayleigh Essex 53 H1
Raymond's Hill Devon 15 H3
Rayne Essex 71 H3
Raynes Park Gt Lon 51 G5
Reach Cambs 88 B2
Read Lancs 140 A1
Reading Readg 49 H4
Reading Crematorium Readg 49 H4
Reading Street Kent 25 G1
Reading Street Kent 41 L2
Reagill Cumb 166 E2
Realwa Cnwll 2 F4
Rearquhar Highld 263 K1
Rearsby Leics 117 H8
Rease Heath Ches E 113 L1
Reay Highld 279 G3
Reculver Kent 41 H2
Red Ball Devon 29 K7
Redberth Pembks 55 J6
Redbourn Herts 68 E4
Redbourne N Linc 144 B7
Redbrook Gloucs 63 G5
Redbrook Wrexhm 113 H3
Redbrook Street Kent 40 B8

Redburn Highld 253 H2
Redburn Nthumb 179 H6
Redcar R & Cl 170 E6
Redcastle D & G 175 K2
Redcastle Highld 251 G2
Red Dial Cumb 165 H2
Redding Falk 210 B3
Reddingmuirhead Falk 210 B3
Reddish Stockp 131 H1
Redditch Worcs 82 B2
Redditch Crematorium Worcs .. 82 B2
Rede Suffk 88 F4
Redenhall Norfk 106 F6
Redenham Hants 34 C1
Redesmouth Nthumb 179 K3
Redford Abers 235 J2
Redford Angus 234 E6
Redford W Susx 36 C5
Redfordgreen Border 188 C3
Redgate Rhondd 42 F4
Redgorton P & K 221 K2
Redgrave Suffk 105 L7
Redhill Abers 245 H3
Red Hill Bmouth 17 L3
Redhill Herts 86 F8
Redhill N Som 45 G6
Redhill Surrey 37 L1
Red Hill Warwks 82 D4
Redisham Suffk 107 H6
Redland Bristl 45 H4
Redland Ork 275 c3
Redlingfield Suffk 90 E1
Redlingfield Green Suffk .. 90 E1
Red Lodge Suffk 88 D1
Red Lumb Rochdl 140 C4
Redlynch Somset 32 B4
Redlynch Wilts 33 L6
Redmain Cumb 164 F4
Redmarley Worcs 81 H6
Redmarley D'Abitot Gloucs .. 63 L1
Redmarshall S on T 169 K6
Redmile Leics 117 L4
Redmire N York 159 J4
Redmyre Abers 245 G8
Rednal Birm 98 C8
Rednal Shrops 112 E6
Redpath Border 201 J6
Redpoint Highld 260 B6
Red Post Cnwll 11 K2
Red Rock Wigan 139 H6
Red Roses Carmth 55 L4
Red Row Nthumb 191 K6
Redruth Cnwll 4 A6
Redstocks Wilts 46 D6
Redstone P & K 233 J8
Redstone Cross Pembks .. 55 J4
Red Street Staffs 114 C1
Redvales Bury 140 B6
Red Wharf Bay IoA 125 J3
Redwick Newpt 44 E2
Redwick S Glos 45 H2
Redworth Darltn 169 G6
Reed Herts 87 H8
Reedham Norfk 107 J3
Reedness E R Yk 143 K3
Reeds Beck Lincs 136 D6
Reeds Holme Lancs 140 B3
Reepham Lincs 135 L5
Reepham Norfk 122 B7
Reeth N York 159 J3
Reeves Green Solhll 99 H7
Regaby IoM 154 f3
Regil N Som 45 G6
Reiff Highld 270 C5
Reigate Surrey 37 L1
Reighton N York 163 L7
Reisque Abers 256 F7
Reiss Highld 280 D5
Rejerrah Cnwll 4 C4
Releath Cnwll 3 G4
Relubbus Cnwll 2 F4
Relugas Moray 253 J2
Remenham Wokham 49 J2
Remenham Hill Wokham .. 49 J2
Rempstone Notts 116 F6
Rendcomb Gloucs 64 E5
Rendham Suffk 91 H2
Rendlesham Suffk 91 H4
Renfrew Rens 208 E5
Renhold Bed 86 B5
Renishaw Derbys 133 J4
Rennington Nthumb 191 J3
Renton W Duns 208 C3
Renwick Cumb 166 E2
Repps Norfk 123 J8
Repton Derbys 116 A6
Reraig Highld 248 C6
Resaurie Highld 251 J3
Rescassa Cnwll 5 G6

Rescorla Cnwll 5 G5
Resipole Burn Highld 237 L7
Reskadinnick Cnwll 3 G3
Resolis Highld 263 J6
Resolven Neath 60 C6
Rest and be thankful Ag & B .. 218 C5
Reston Border 213 J6
Restronguet Cnwll 3 K4
Reswallie Angus 234 D5
Reterth Cnwll 4 F2
Retford Notts 134 D3
Retire Cnwll 5 G2
Rettendon Essex 71 J7
Retyn Cnwll 4 E3
Revesby Lincs 136 E7
Rew Devon 7 K7
Rew Devon 13 H8
Rewe Devon 13 M3
Rew Street IoW 19 H5
Rexon Devon 12 A5
Reydon Suffk 107 K7
Reymerston Norfk 105 L2
Reynalton Pembks 55 J5
Reynoldston Swans 56 E6
Rezare Cnwll 11 L7
Rhadyr Mons 62 D6
Rhandirmwyn Carmth 77 L6
Rhayader Powys 78 D2
Rheindown Highld 250 F2
Rhes-y-cae Flints 128 E5
Rhewl Denbgs 112 B3
Rhewl Denbgs 128 D7
Rhewl-fawr Flints 128 D3
Rhewl Mostyn Flints 128 D4
Rhicarn Highld 270 E3
Rhiconich Highld 276 D5
Rhicullen Highld 263 J5
Rhigos Rhondd 60 D6
Rhireavach Highld 261 G1
Rhives Highld 273 K7
Rhiwbina Cardif 43 J5
Rhiwbryfdir Gwynd 110 D2
Rhiwderyn Newpt 43 L4
Rhiwen Gwynd 125 K7
Rhiwinder Rhondd 42 F4
Rhiwlas Gwynd 111 H4
Rhiwlas Gwynd 125 K6
Rhiwlas Powys 112 B5
Rhiwsaeson Rhondd 43 G5
Rhode Somset 30 C4
Rhoden Green Kent 39 H4
Rhodesia Notts 133 L4
Rhodes Minnis Kent 40 F6
Rhodiad-y-brenin Pembks .. 74 C6
Rhonehouse D & G 175 J3
Rhoose V Glam 43 G8
Rhos Carmth 58 C2
Rhos Denbgs 128 D7
Rhos Neath 57 K4
Rhosaman Carmth 59 K6
Rhosbeirio IoA 125 G2
Rhoscefnhir IoA 125 J4
Rhoscolyn IoA 124 D4
Rhoscrowther Pembks ... 54 E6
Rhosesmor Flints 128 F6
Rhos-fawr Gwynd 109 G4
Rhosgadfan Gwynd 125 J8
Rhosgoch IoA 125 G2
Rhosgoch Powys 79 H5
Rhos Haminiog Cerdgn .. 76 F2
Rhoshill Pembks 75 L4
Rhoshirwaun Gwynd 108 C5
Rhoslan Gwynd 109 H3
Rhoslefain Gwynd 92 C2
Rhosllanerchrugog Wrexhm .. 112 D2
Rhôs Lligwy IoA 125 J2
Rhosmaen Carmth 59 H4
Rhosmeirch IoA 125 H4
Rhosneigr IoA 124 E5
Rhosnesni Wrexhm 112 E2
Rhôs-on-Sea Conwy 127 G4
Rhosrobin Wrexhm 112 E1
Rhossili Swans 56 D7
Rhostryfan Gwynd 125 J8
Rhostyllen Wrexhm 112 D2
Rhosybol IoA 125 G2
Rhos y-brithdir Powys 111 M7
Rhosygadfa Shrops 112 D4
Rhos-y-garth Cerdgn 77 H1
Rhos-y-gwaliau Gwynd .. 111 H4
Rhos-y-llan Gwynd 108 D4
Rhosymedre Wrexhm 112 D3
Rhos-y-meirch Powys 79 K1
Rhu Ag & B 207 M2
Rhuallt Denbgs 128 C5
Rhubodach Ag & B 207 G4
Rhuddall Heath Ches W .. 130 A7
Rhuddlan Cerdgn 76 F6
Rhuddlan Denbgs 127 L4

Rhulen Powys 79 G5
Rhunahaorine Ag & B 205 M6
Rhyd Gwynd 110 B3
Rhydargaeau Carmth 58 D4
Rhydcymerau Carmth 77 G7
Rhydd Worcs 81 J6
Rhyd-Ddu Gwynd 109 K1
Rhydding Neath 57 K5
Rhydgaled Conwy 127 K6
Rhydlanfair Conwy 110 F1
Rhydlewis Cerdgn 76 C5
Rhydlios Gwynd 108 C5
Rhyd-lydan Conwy 111 G2
Rhydowen Cerdgn 76 E6
Rhydrosser Cerdgn 77 G2
Rhydspence Herefs 79 J5
Rhydtalog Flints 128 F8
Rhyd-uchaf Gwynd 111 G4
Rhyd-y-clafdy Gwynd 108 E4
Rhydycroesau Shrops 112 C5
Rhydyfelin Cerdgn 92 D7
Rhydyfelin Rhondd 43 H4
Rhyd-y-foel Conwy 127 H4
Rhydyfro Neath 57 K4
Rhyd-y-groes Gwynd 125 K6
Rhydymain Gwynd 110 F7
Rhyd-y-meirch Mons 62 C5
Rhydymwyn Flints 128 E6
Rhyd-y-pennau Cerdgn .. 92 D6
Rhyd-yr-onnen Gwynd ... 92 D3
Rhyd-y-sarn Gwynd 110 C3
Rhyl Denbgs 127 K3
Rhymney Caerph 61 H5
Rhynd P & K 222 B3
Rhynie Abers 255 K6
Rhynie Highld 264 C4
Ribbesford Worcs 97 H8
Ribbleton Lancs 139 H2
Ribby Lancs 138 E2
Ribchester Lancs 139 K1
Riber Derbys 132 F7
Riby Lincs 144 F6
Riccall N York 151 K8
Riccarton Border 188 F7
Riccarton E Ayrs 196 E4
Richards Castle Herefs .. 80 C1
Richings Park Bucks 50 C3
Richmond Gt Lon 50 F4
Richmond N York 159 M2
Richmond Sheff 133 H3
Richmond Fort Guern 9 i2
Rich's Holford Somset ... 29 L4
Rickerscote Staffs 114 E7
Rickford N Som 44 F7
Rickham Devon 7 L1
Rickinghall Suffk 105 L8
Rickling Essex 70 D1
Rickling Green Essex 70 D1
Rickmansworth Herts ... 68 D8
Riddell Border 188 E1
Riddings Derbys 116 C1
Riddlecombe Devon 27 L8
Riddlesden C Brad 149 K7
Ridge BaNES 45 H7
Ridge Dorset 17 H5
Ridge Herts 69 G7
Ridge Wilts 33 G4
Ridge Green Surrey 37 L1
Ridge Lane Warwks 99 J4
Ridge Row Kent 41 G6
Ridgeway Derbys 133 H3
Ridgeway Worcs 82 B3
Ridgeway Cross Herefs .. 81 G5
Ridgewell Essex 88 E7
Ridgewood E Susx 23 H3
Ridgmont C Beds 85 J8
Riding Mill Nthumb 180 B6
Ridley Kent 52 D6
Ridley Nthumb 179 H6
Ridley Green Ches E 113 J1
Ridlington Norfk 123 G5
Ridlington Rutlnd 101 J3
Ridlington Street Norfk .. 123 G5
Ridsdale Nthumb 179 L2
Rievaulx N York 161 J5
Rigg D & G 177 J5
Riggend N Lans 209 K5
Righoul Highld 253 G2
Rigmadon Park Cumb ... 157 K5
Rigsby Lincs 137 H5
Rigside S Lans 198 E6
Riley Green Lancs 139 J3
Rileyhill Staffs 115 J8
Rilla Mill Cnwll 11 K7
Rillaton Cnwll 11 K7
Rillington N York 162 E7
Rimington Lancs 148 D6
Rimpton Somset 31 K6

Rimswell E R Yk 145 J2
Rinaston Pembks 75 G7
Rindleford Shrops 97 G4
Ringford D & G 175 H3
Ringinglow Sheff 132 F5
Ringland Norfk 106 C1
Ringles Cross E Susx 23 H3
Ringlestone Kent 39 L2
Ringley Bolton 139 M6
Ringmer E Susx 23 G5
Ringmore Devon 7 J5
Ringmore Devon 13 L8
Ring o'Bells Lancs 138 F5
Ringorm Moray 254 E3
Ring's End Cambs 103 H3
Ringsfield Suffk 107 H5
Ringsfield Corner Suffk .. 107 H6
Ringshall Herts 68 C4
Ringshall Suffk 90 B4
Ringshall Stocks Suffk .. 90 B5
Ringstead Nhants 101 L8
Ringstead Norfk 120 F3
Ringwood Hants 18 A3
Ringwould Kent 41 K5
Rinmore Abers 255 H8
Rinsey Cnwll 2 F5
Rinsey Croft Cnwll 2 F5
Ripe E Susx 23 H5
Ripley Derbys 116 C2
Ripley Hants 18 B4
Ripley N York 150 G4
Ripley Surrey 50 D7
Riplingham E R Yk 144 B2
Riplington Hants 35 K6
Ripon N York 150 D2
Rippingale Lincs 118 E6
Ripple Kent 41 K5
Ripple Worcs 81 K7
Ripponden Calder 140 F4
Risabus Ag & B 204 D7
Risbury Herefs 80 D4
Risby N Linc 144 A5
Risby Suffk 88 F2
Risca Caerph 43 K3
Rise E R Yk 153 J7
Riseden E Susx 38 F7
Riseden Kent 39 H6
Risegate Lincs 119 H5
Riseholme Lincs 135 K5
Risehow Cumb 164 D4
Riseley Bed 85 L3
Riseley Wokham 49 H6
Rishangles Suffk 90 E2
Rishton Lancs 139 L2
Rishworth Calder 140 F4
Rising Bridge Lancs 140 A3
Risley Derbys 116 D4
Risley Warrtn 130 C1
Risplith N York 150 B2
Rivar Wilts 47 L6
Rivenhall End Essex ... 71 K4
River Kent 41 J6
River W Susx 36 D6
River Bank Cambs 87 L2
Riverford Highld 250 F1
Riverhead Kent 38 D2
Rivers Corner Dorset .. 32 C8
Rivington Lancs 139 J5
Roachill Devon 28 E6
Roade Nhants 84 E5
Road Green Norfk 106 F4
Roadhead Cumb 178 C4
Roadmeetings S Lans .. 198 E3
Roadside E Ayrs 197 H7
Roadside Highld 279 L4
Roadwater Somset 29 J3
Roag Highld 258 D7
Roa Island Cumb 146 D3
Roan of Craigoch S Ayrs .. 183 H2
Roast Green Essex 87 J8
Roath Cardif 43 K6
Roberton Border 188 D3
Roberton S Lans 198 F7
Robertsbridge E Susx .. 24 D3
Roberttown Kirk 141 J3
Robeston Wathen Pembks .. 55 J4
Robgill Tower D & G ... 177 H4
Robin Hill Staffs 131 H7
Robin Hood Lancs ... 139 G5
Robin Hood Leeds ... 141 M2
Robin Hood Crematorium
Solhll 98 E7
Robinhood End Essex .. 88 E7
Robin Hood's Bay N York .. 163 G2
Roborough Devon 6 F2
Roborough Devon 27 K7
Robroyston C Glas ... 209 H5
Roby Knows 129 K2
Roby Mill Lancs 139 G6

Rocester Staffs ... 115 J4
Roch Pembks ... 54 E3
Rochdale Rochdl ... 140 D5
Rochdale Crematorium
  Rochdl ... 140 C5
Roche Cnwll ... 5 G3
Rochester Medway ... 52 F5
Rochester Nthumb ... 189 M6
Rochford Essex ... 53 J1
Rochford Worcs ... 80 E2
Roch Gate Pembks ... 54 E3
Rock Cnwll ... 10 C7
Rock Neath ... 57 L6
Rock Nthumb ... 191 J2
Rock W Susx ... 21 K4
Rock Worcs ... 81 G1
Rockbeare Devon ... 14 B4
Rockbourne Hants ... 33 K7
Rockcliffe Cumb ... 177 K6
Rockcliffe D & G ... 175 L4
Rockcliffe Cross Cumb ... 177 K6
Rock End Staffs ... 131 H8
Rockend Torbay ... 8 D2
Rock Ferry Wirral ... 129 H2
Rockfield Highld ... 264 E3
Rockfield Mons ... 62 F4
Rockford Devon ... 28 D1
Rockford Hants ... 18 B2
Rockgreen Shrops ... 96 C8
Rockhampton S Glos ... 63 K8
Rockhead Cnwll ... 10 D7
Rockhill Shrops ... 95 G7
Rock Hill Worcs ... 81 L1
Rockingham Nhants ... 101 J5
Rockland All Saints Norfk ... 105 K4
Rockland St Mary Norfk ... 107 G3
Rockland St Peter Norfk ... 105 K4
Rockley Notts ... 134 E5
Rockley Wilts ... 47 H4
Rockliffe Lancs ... 140 C3
Rockville Ag & B ... 207 L1
Rockwell End Bucks ... 49 J1
Rockwell Green Somset ... 29 L6
Rodborough Gloucs ... 64 B6
Rodbourne Swindn ... 47 H2
Rodbourne Wilts ... 46 D2
Rodd Herefs ... 79 K3
Roddam Nthumb ... 190 E2
Rodden Dorset ... 16 B5
Roddymoor Dur ... 168 F3
Rode Somset ... 46 A8
Rode Heath Ches E ... 130 F8
Rode Heath Ches E ... 131 G6
Rodel W Isls ... 282 d7
Roden Wrekin ... 113 J8
Rodhuish Somset ... 29 J3
Rodington Wrekin ... 113 K8
Rodington Heath Wrekin ... 113 K8
Rodley Gloucs ... 63 L5
Rodley Leeds ... 150 B8
Rodmarton Gloucs ... 64 D7
Rodmell E Susx ... 22 F6
Rodmersham Kent ... 40 B3
Rodmersham Green Kent ... 40 B3
Rodney Stoke Somset ... 31 H1
Rodsley Derbys ... 115 K3
Rodway Somset ... 30 C3
Roecliffe N York ... 150 E3
Roe Cross Tamesd ... 140 E8
Roe Green Herts ... 69 G5
Roe Green Herts ... 87 G8
Roe Green Salfd ... 139 L7
Roehampton Gt Lon ... 51 G4
Roffey W Susx ... 37 J4
Rogart Highld ... 273 H7
Rogate W Susx ... 36 B6
Roger Ground Cumb ... 156 E3
Rogerstone Newpt ... 44 B2
Roghadal W Isls ... 282 d7
Rogiet Mons ... 44 F2
Roke Oxon ... 66 F8
Roker Sundld ... 181 K7
Rollesby Norfk ... 123 J8
Rolleston Leics ... 100 F3
Rolleston Notts ... 117 K1
Rollestone Wilts ... 33 J2
Rolleston on Dove Staffs ... 115 L6
Rolston E R Yk ... 153 K6
Rolstone N Som ... 44 D6
Rolvenden Kent ... 39 L7
Rolvenden Layne Kent ... 39 L7
Romaldkirk Dur ... 168 C6
Romanby N York ... 160 E4
Romanno Bridge Border ... 199 K3
Romansleigh Devon ... 28 C6
Romden Castle Kent ... 40 A7
Romesdal Highld ... 258 F6
Romford Dorset ... 17 L1
Romford Gt Lon ... 52 B1

Romiley Stockp ... 131 J2
Romney Street Kent ... 52 C6
Romsey Cambs ... 87 K4
Romsey Hants ... 34 D6
Romsley Shrops ... 97 H6
Romsley Worcs ... 98 B7
Rona Highld ... 259 L5
Ronachan Ag & B ... 206 B8
Rood Ashton Wilts ... 46 C7
Rookhope Dur ... 167 L2
Rookley IoW ... 19 H6
Rookley Green IoW ... 19 H7
Rooks Bridge Somset ... 44 D8
Rooks Nest Somset ... 29 K4
Rookwith N York ... 160 B5
Roos E R Yk ... 145 H2
Roose Cumb ... 146 D2
Roosebeck Cumb ... 146 E2
Roothams Green Bed ... 86 B4
Ropley Hants ... 35 K4
Ropley Dean Hants ... 35 K4
Ropley Soke Hants ... 35 K4
Ropsley Lincs ... 118 C5
Rora Abers ... 269 K6
Rorrington Shrops ... 95 H3
Rosarie Moray ... 267 H6
Rose Cnwll ... 4 C4
Roseacre Lancs ... 147 H8
Rose Ash Devon ... 28 D6
Rosebank S Lans ... 198 D3
Rosebush Pembks ... 75 J4
Rosecare Cnwll ... 11 H3
Rosecliston Cnwll ... 4 D3
Rosedale Abbey N York ... 162 C3
Rose Green Essex ... 72 C2
Rose Green Suffk ... 89 J7
Rose Green Suffk ... 89 K6
Rose Green W Susx ... 20 E7
Rosehall Highld ... 272 C7
Rosehearty Abers ... 269 K3
Rose Hill E Susx ... 23 G4
Rose Hill Lancs ... 140 B2
Rosehill Shrops ... 113 G8
Rose Hill Crematorium Donc ... 142 F7
Roseisle Moray ... 266 C3
Roselands E Susx ... 23 K7
Rosemarket Pembks ... 54 F5
Rosemarkie Highld ... 263 K8
Rosemary Lane Devon ... 29 L7
Rosemount P & K ... 233 J6
Rosenannon Cnwll ... 4 F2
Rosenithon Cnwll ... 3 K6
Roser's Cross E Susx ... 23 J3
Rosevean Cnwll ... 5 H3
Rosevine Cnwll ... 3 M4
Rosewarne Cnwll ... 2 F4
Rosewell Mdloth ... 211 J6
Roseworth S on T ... 169 L6
Roseworthy Cnwll ... 3 G3
Rosgill Cumb ... 166 D7
Roskestal Cnwll ... 2 B6
Roskhill Highld ... 258 D7
Roskorwell Cnwll ... 3 K6
Rosley Cumb ... 165 K2
Roslin Mdloth ... 211 J6
Rosliston Derbys ... 115 L8
Rosneath Ag & B ... 207 L2
Ross D & G ... 175 G6
Ross Nthumb ... 203 J5
Rossett Wrexhm ... 129 J8
Rossett Green N York ... 150 D5
Rossington Donc ... 143 G8
Ross-on-Wye Herefs ... 63 J2
Roster Highld ... 280 C8
Rostherne Ches E ... 130 E3
Rosthwaite Cumb ... 165 H7
Roston Derbys ... 115 J3
Rosudgeon Cnwll ... 2 E5
Rosyth Fife ... 210 F2
Rothbury Nthumb ... 190 F6
Rotherby Leics ... 117 H8
Rotherfield E Susx ... 38 E7
Rotherfield Greys Oxon ... 49 H3
Rotherfield Peppard Oxon ... 49 H3
Rotherham Rothm ... 133 H1
Rotherham Crematorium
  Rothm ... 133 J1
Rothersthorpe Nhants ... 84 D4
Rotherwick Hants ... 49 H7
Rothes Moray ... 266 F6
Rothesay Ag & B ... 207 H6
Rothiebrisbane Abers ... 256 D4
Rothiemurchus Lodge Highld ... 242 C2
Rothienorman Abers ... 256 C4
Rothley Leics ... 100 D1
Rothley Nthumb ... 180 C1
Rothmaise Abers ... 256 B5
Rothwell Leeds ... 142 A2
Rothwell Lincs ... 144 F7

Rothwell Nhants ... 101 H7
Rotsea E R Yk ... 153 G5
Rottal Lodge Angus ... 234 B2
Rottingdean Br & H ... 22 F6
Rottington Cumb ... 164 C8
Roucan D & G ... 176 D3
Roucan Loch Crematorium
  D & G ... 176 D3
Roud IoW ... 19 H7
Rougham Norfk ... 121 H7
Rougham Suffk ... 89 H3
Rough Close Staffs ... 114 E4
Rough Common Kent ... 40 F3
Roughlee Lancs ... 148 E7
Roughpark Abers ... 243 K1
Roughton Lincs ... 136 D6
Roughton Norfk ... 122 E4
Roughton Shrops ... 97 G4
Roughway Kent ... 38 F3
Roundbush Essex ... 72 B6
Round Bush Herts ... 68 F7
Roundbush Green Essex ... * ... 70 E4
Round Green Luton ... 68 E3
Roundham Somset ... 15 K1
Roundhay Leeds ... 150 D8
Rounds Green Sandw ... 98 C5
Round Street Kent ... 52 E5
Roundstreet Common W Susx ... 37 G5
Roundswell Devon ... 27 K4
Roundway Wilts ... 46 E6
Roundyhill Angus ... 234 B5
Rousay Ork ... 275 c3
Rousdon Devon ... 15 G4
Rousham Oxon ... 66 C2
Rous Lench Worcs ... 82 B4
Routenburn N Ayrs ... 207 K6
Routh E R Yk ... 153 H7
Rout's Green Bucks ... 67 J7
Row Cnwll ... 10 F7
Row Cumb ... 157 G5
Row Cumb ... 166 E4
Rowanburn D & G ... 177 L3
Rowardennan Stirlg ... 218 E2
Rowarth Derbys ... 131 K2
Row Ash Hants ... 35 H8
Rowberrow Somset ... 44 F7
Rowborough IoW ... 19 G6
Rowde Wilts ... 46 E6
Rowden Devon ... 12 F3
Rowen Conwy ... 126 E5
Rowfield Derbys ... 115 K2
Rowfoot Nthumb ... 178 F6
Rowford Somset ... 30 C5
Row Green Essex ... 71 H3
Rowhedge Essex ... 72 F3
Rowhook W Susx ... 37 H4
Rowington Warwks ... 82 F2
Rowland Derbys ... 132 D5
Rowland's Castle Hants ... 20 B5
Rowlands Gill Gatesd ... 180 E7
Rowledge Surrey ... 36 B2
Rowley Dur ... 168 E1
Rowley E R Yk ... 144 B1
Rowley Shrops ... 95 H2
Rowley Hill Kirk ... 141 J5
Rowley Regis Sandw ... 98 B6
Rowley Regis Crematorium
  Sandw ... 98 B6
Rowlstone Herefs ... 62 D2
Rowly Surrey ... 37 G3
Rowner Hants ... 19 K3
Rowney Green Worcs ... 82 B1
Rownhams Hants ... 34 E7
Rowrah Cumb ... 164 E7
Rowsham Bucks ... 67 K3
Rowsley Derbys ... 132 E6
Rowstock Oxon ... 48 C1
Rowston Lincs ... 136 A8
Rowthorne Derbys ... 133 J6
Rowton Ches W ... 129 K6
Rowton Shrops ... 95 J1
Rowton Shrops ... 95 K7
Rowton Wrekin ... 113 K7
Row Town Surrey ... 50 D6
Roxburgh Border ... 201 L7
Roxby N Linc ... 144 A4
Roxby N York ... 171 H7
Roxton Bed ... 86 C4
Roxwell Essex ... 70 F5
Royal Leamington Spa
  Warwks ... 83 H2
Royal Oak Darltn ... 169 G6
Royal Oak Lancs ... 138 F7
Royal's Green Ches E ... 113 K3
Royal Sutton Coldfield Birm ... 98 E4
Royal Tunbridge Wells Kent ... 38 F5
Royal Wootton Bassett Wilts ... 46 E2
Roy Bridge Highld ... 239 M7
Roydhouse Kirk ... 141 K5

Roydon Essex ... 69 L5
Roydon Norfk ... 106 C7
Roydon Norfk ... 120 F7
Roydon Hamlet Essex ... 69 L5
Royston Barns ... 142 B5
Royston Herts ... 87 G7
Royton Oldham ... 140 D6
Rozel Jersey ... 9 e2
Ruabon Wrexhm ... 112 D3
Ruaig Ag & B ... 224 D5
Ruan High Lanes Cnwll ... 4 E6
Ruan Lanihorne Cnwll ... 4 E6
Ruan Major Cnwll ... 3 H7
Ruan Minor Cnwll ... 3 J8
Ruardean Gloucs ... 63 J3
Ruardean Hill Gloucs ... 63 J4
Ruardean Woodside Gloucs ... 63 J4
Rubery Birm ... 98 C7
Rubha Ban W Isls ... 283 c12
Ruckcroft Cumb ... 166 C2
Ruckhall Herefs ... 80 B7
Ruckinge Kent ... 40 D8
Ruckland Lincs ... 136 F4
Ruckley Shrops ... 96 C3
Rudbaxton Pembks ... 54 F3
Rudby N York ... 161 G1
Rudchester Nthumb ... 180 D5
Ruddington Notts ... 116 F5
Ruddle Gloucs ... 63 K5
Ruddlemoor Cnwll ... 5 G4
Rudford Gloucs ... 63 M3
Rudge Somset ... 46 B8
Rudgeway S Glos ... 45 J2
Rudgwick W Susx ... 37 G4
Rudhall Herefs ... 63 J2
Rudheath Ches W ... 130 D5
Rudheath Woods Ches E ... 130 E5
Rudley Green Essex ... 71 K6
Rudloe Wilts ... 46 B5
Rudry Caerph ... 43 J5
Rudston E R Yk ... 153 H2
Rudyard Staffs ... 131 J8
Ruecastle Border ... 189 G2
Rufford Lancs ... 138 F4
Rufforth C York ... 151 H5
Rug Denbgs ... 111 K3
Rugby Warwks ... 100 B8
Rugeley Staffs ... 115 G7
Ruishton Somset ... 30 C6
Ruislip Gt Lon ... 50 E2
Rùm Highld ... 236 D1
Rumbach Moray ... 267 H5
Rumbling Bridge P & K ... 221 J7
Rumburgh Suffk ... 107 G7
Rumby Hill Dur ... 168 F4
Rumford Cnwll ... 10 C7
Rumford Falk ... 210 B4
Rumney Cardif ... 43 K6
Rumwell Somset ... 30 B6
Runcorn Halton ... 129 L3
Runcton W Susx ... 20 E6
Runcton Holme Norfk ... 104 C2
Runfold Surrey ... 36 C2
Runhall Norfk ... 105 L2
Runham Norfk ... 107 J1
Runham Norfk ... 107 L2
Runnington Somset ... 29 L6
Runsell Green Essex ... 71 J6
Runshaw Moor Lancs ... 139 G4
Runswick N York ... 171 J7
Runtaleave Angus ... 233 L2
Runwell Essex ... 71 J2
Ruscombe Wokham ... 49 J4
Rushall Herefs ... 80 E8
Rushall Norfk ... 106 D6
Rushall Wilts ... 47 H7
Rushall Wsall ... 98 C3
Rushbrooke Suffk ... 89 H3
Rushbury Shrops ... 96 C5
Rushden Herts ... 69 J1
Rushden Nhants ... 85 J2
Rushenden Kent ... 53 K5
Rusher's Cross E Susx ... 38 F7
Rushford Devon ... 12 B7
Rushford Norfk ... 105 J7
Rush Green Essex ... 73 H4
Rush Green Gt Lon ... 52 B2
Rush Green Herts ... 69 G2
Rush Green Warrtn ... 130 D2
Rushlake Green E Susx ... 23 L3
Rushmere Suffk ... 107 K6
Rushmere St Andrew Suffk ... 90 E6
Rushmoor Surrey ... 36 C3
Rushock Herefs ... 79 K3
Rushock Worcs ... 81 K1
Rusholme Manch ... 131 G1
Rushton Ches W ... 130 B7
Rushton Nhants ... 101 J6
Rushton Shrops ... 96 D2

Rushton Spencer Staffs 131 J7
Rushwick Worcs 81 J4
Rushyford Dur 169 H5
Ruskie Stirlg 219 K7
Ruskington Lincs 118 E1
Rusland Cross Cumb 156 E5
Rusper W Susx 37 K3
Ruspidge Gloucs 63 K5
Russel Green Essex 71 H4
Russell's Water Oxon 49 H1
Russel's Green Suffk 90 F1
Russ Hill Surrey 37 K3
Rusthall Kent 38 E5
Rustington W Susx 21 H6
Ruston N York 163 G6
Ruston Parva E R Yk 153 G3
Ruswarp N York 162 F1
Ruthall Shrops 96 D5
Rutherford Border 201 K7
Rutherglen S Lans 209 G6
Ruthernbridge Cnwll 5 G2
Ruthin Denbgs 128 D8
Ruthrieston C Aber 245 K3
Ruthven Abers 267 K6
Ruthven Angus 233 L5
Ruthven Highld 241 K4
Ruthven Highld 252 F5
Ruthvoes Cnwll 4 F3
Ruthwaite Cumb 165 H3
Ruthwell D & G 176 E5
Ruxley Corner Gt Lon 52 A5
Ruxton Green Herefs 63 G3
Ruyton-XI-Towns Shrops 112 F7
Ryal Nthumb 180 B4
Ryall Dorset 15 J4
Ryall Worcs 81 K7
Ryarsh Kent 52 E7
Rycote Oxon 67 G6
Rydal Cumb 156 E2
Ryde IoW 19 K5
Rye E Susx 25 G3
Ryebank Shrops 113 H5
Ryeford Herefs 63 J3
Rye Foreign E Susx 25 G3
Rye Harbour E Susx 25 H3
Ryehill E R Yk 145 G3
Ryeish Green Wokham 49 H5
Rye Street Worcs 81 H8
Ryhall Rutlnd 102 A1
Ryhill Wakefd 142 B5
Ryhope Sundld 181 K8
Rylah Derbys 133 J6
Ryland Lincs 135 K4
Rylands Notts 116 F4
Rylstone N York 149 H4
Ryme Intrinseca Dorset 31 J8
Ryther N York 151 J7
Ryton Gatesd 180 E6
Ryton N York 162 D7
Ryton Shrops 97 G3
Ryton Warwks 99 L6
Ryton-on-Dunsmore Warwks 99 K8
Ryton Woodside Gatesd 180 E6

S

Sabden Lancs 148 D8
Sabine's Green Essex 70 E7
Sacombe Herts 69 J3
Sacombe Green Herts 69 J3
Sacriston Dur 169 G1
Sadberge Darltn 169 J7
Saddell Ag & B 194 B4
Saddington Leics 100 E5
Saddlebow Norfk 120 D8
Saddlescombe W Susx 22 D5
Sadgill Cumb 157 G2
Saffron Walden Essex 87 H7
Sageston Pembks 55 H6
Saham Hills Norfk 105 H3
Saham Toney Norfk 105 H3
Saighton Ches W 129 K7
St Abbs Border 213 K5
St Agnes Border 212 F6
St Agnes Cnwll 4 B5
St Agnes IoS 10 b3
St Albans Herts 68 F5
St Allen Cnwll 4 D5
St Andrew Guern 9 j3
St Andrews Fife 223 J4
St Andrews Major V Glam 43 H7
St Andrews Well Dorset 15 L4
St Anne's Lancs 138 C2
St Ann's D & G 187 J3
St Ann's Chapel Cnwll 12 A8
St Ann's Chapel Devon 7 J5
St Anthony-in-Meneage Cnwll 3 K6

St Anthony's Hill E Susx 23 L7
St Arvans Mons 63 G7
St Asaph Denbgs 128 B5
St Athan V Glam 42 F8
St Aubin Jersey 9 c3
St Austell Cnwll 5 G4
St Bees Cumb 164 C8
St Blazey Cnwll 5 H4
St Blazey Gate Cnwll 5 H4
St Boswells Border 201 J7
St Brelade Jersey 9 b3
St Brelade's Bay Jersey 9 b3
St Breock Cnwll 10 D8
St Breward Cnwll 10 F7
St Briavels Gloucs 63 H6
St Brides Pembks 54 C5
St Bride's Major V Glam 42 D6
St Brides Netherwent Mons 44 E1
St Brides-super-Ely V Glam 43 H6
St Brides Wentlooge Newpt 44 C3
St Budeaux C Plym 6 E3
Saintbury Gloucs 82 D7
St Buryan Cnwll 2 C6
St Catherine BaNES 45 M5
St Catherines Ag & B 217 J5
St Chloe Gloucs 64 B6
St Clears Carmth 58 A5
St Cleer Cnwll 6 A1
St Clement Cnwll 4 D6
St Clement Jersey 9 e4
St Clether Cnwll 11 H5
St Colmac Ag & B 207 G5
St Columb Major Cnwll 4 E2
St Columb Minor Cnwll 4 D2
St Columb Road Cnwll 4 E3
St Combs Abers 269 K4
St Cross South Elmham Suffk 106 F6
St Cyrus Abers 235 J2
St David's P & K 221 G3
St Davids Pembks 74 B7
St Day Cnwll 4 B6
St Decumans Somset 29 K2
St Dennis Cnwll 4 F3
St Devereux Herefs 62 E1
St Dogmaels Pembks 75 K3
St Dogwells Pembks 75 G6
St Dominick Cnwll 6 D1
St Donats V Glam 42 E8
St Edith's Marsh Wilts 46 E6
St Endellion Cnwll 10 D6
St Enoder Cnwll 4 D5
St Erme Cnwll 4 D5
St Erney Cnwll 6 D3
St Erth Cnwll 2 E4
St Erth Praze Cnwll 2 F4
St Ervan Cnwll 10 B8
St Eval Cnwll 4 E1
St Ewe Cnwll 5 G5
St Fagans Cardif 43 H6
St Fergus Abers 269 K6
St Fillans P & K 220 B2
St Florence Pembks 55 J6
St Gennys Cnwll 11 G3
St George Conwy 127 K4
St Georges N Som 44 D6
St George's V Glam 43 H6
St George's Hill Surrey 50 D6
St Germans Cnwll 6 D3
St Giles in the Wood Devon 27 J7
St Giles-on-the-Heath Devon 11 L4
St Gluvia's Cnwll 3 K4
St Harmon Powys 78 D1
St Helen Auckland Dur 168 F5
St Helens Cumb 164 D4
St Helen's E Susx 24 E5
St Helens IoW 19 L6
St Helens St Hel 139 G8
St Helens Crematorium St Hel 139 G8
St Helier Gt Lon 51 H5
St Helier Jersey 9 d3
St Hilary Cnwll 2 E5
St Hilary V Glam 42 F7
Saint Hill Devon 14 C1
Saint Hill W Susx 38 B6
St Illtyd Blae G 61 K6
St Ippollitts Herts 69 G2
St Ishmael's Pembks 54 D5
St Issey Cnwll 10 C8
St Ive Cnwll 6 C2
St Ive Cross Cnwll 6 C2
St Ives Cambs 87 G1
St Ives Cnwll 2 E3
St Ives Dorset 17 M2
St James Norfk 122 F7
St James's End Nhants 84 E3
St James South Elmham Suffk 107 H7
St Jidgey Cnwll 4 F1
St John Cnwll 6 E4
St John Jersey 9 c1

St Johns Dur 168 D4
St John's E Susx 38 D7
St John's IoM 154 c5
St John's Kent 38 E2
St Johns Surrey 50 C7
St Johns Worcs 81 J4
St John's Chapel Devon 27 J5
St John's Chapel Dur 167 K3
St John's Fen End Norfk 103 L1
St John's Highway Norfk 120 C8
St John's Kirk S Lans 199 G6
St John's Town of Dalry D & G 184 F6
St John's Wood Gt Lon 51 H2
St Judes IoM 154 e3
St Just Cnwll 2 B5
St Just-in-Roseland Cnwll 3 L4
St Katherines Abers 256 D5
St Keverne Cnwll 3 K6
St Kew Cnwll 10 E7
St Kew Highway Cnwll 10 E7
St Keyne Cnwll 6 A3
St Lawrence Cnwll 5 H2
St Lawrence Essex 72 D6
St Lawrence IoW 19 J8
St Lawrence Jersey 9 c2
St Lawrence Kent 41 K2
St Leonards Bucks 67 M5
St Leonards Dorset 17 M2
St Leonards E Susx 24 E5
St Leonard's Street Kent 39 H2
St Levan Cnwll 2 B6
St Lythans V Glam 43 H7
St Mabyn Cnwll 10 E7
St Madoes P & K 222 C3
St Margarets Herefs 79 L8
St Margarets Herts 69 K5
St Margaret's at Cliffe Kent 41 K6
St Margaret's Hope Ork 275 c6
St Margaret South Elmham Suffk 107 G6
St Marks IoM 154 d7
St Martin Cnwll 3 J6
St Martin Cnwll 6 B4
St Martin Guern 9 j3
St Martin Jersey 9 e2
St Martin's IoS 10 C1
St Martin's P & K 221 L1
St Martin's Shrops 112 D4
St Martin's Moor Shrops 112 D4
St Mary Jersey 9 c2
St Mary Bourne Hants 34 F1
St Marychurch Torbay 8 D2
St Mary Church V Glam 42 F7
St Mary Cray Gt Lon 52 A5
St Mary Hill V Glam 42 E6
St Mary in the Marsh Kent 25 K2
St Marylebone Crematorium Gt Lon 51 H1
St Mary's IoS 10 c3
St Mary's Ork 275 d5
St Mary's Bay Kent 25 K2
St Mary's Hoo Medway 53 H4
St Mary's Platt Kent 39 G2
St Maughans Mons 62 F4
St Maughans Green Mons 62 F4
St Mawes Cnwll 3 L4
St Mawgan Cnwll 4 E2
St Mellion Cnwll 6 D2
St Mellons Cardif 43 K5
St Merryn Cnwll 10 B7
St Mewan Cnwll 5 G4
St Michael Caerhays Cnwll 4 F6
St Michael Church Somset 30 D5
St Michael Penkevil Cnwll 4 D6
St Michaels Kent 39 M6
St Michaels Worcs 80 D2
St Michael's on Wyre Lancs 147 J7
St Michael South Elmham Suffk 107 G6
St Minver Cnwll 10 D7
St Monans Fife 223 J6
St Neot Cnwll 5 L1
St Neots Cambs 86 D3
St Newlyn East Cnwll 4 D3
St Nicholas Pembks 74 E5
St Nicholas V Glam 43 H6
St Nicholas-at-Wade Kent 41 J2
St Ninians Stirlg 209 L1
St Olaves Norfk 107 J3
St Osyth Essex 73 H4
St Ouen Jersey 9 b2
St Owen's Cross Herefs 63 G2
St Paul's Cray Gt Lon 52 A5
St Paul's Walden Herts 69 G3
St Peter Jersey 9 b2
St Peter Port Guern 9 k3
St Peter's Guern 9 i3
St Peter's Kent 41 L2
St Peter's Hill Cambs 86 E1

St Petrox Pembks 55 G7
St Pinnock Cnwll 5 L2
St Quivox S Ayrs 196 D6
St Ruan Cnwll 3 J8
St Sampson Guern 9 k2
St Saviour Guern 9 i3
St Saviour Jersey 9 d3
St Stephen Cnwll 4 F4
St Stephens Cnwll 6 E3
St Stephens Cnwll 11 L5
St Teath Cnwll 10 F6
St Thomas Devon 13 L4
St Margaret's Bay Kent 41 K6
St Tudy Cnwll 10 F7
St Twynnells Pembks 54 F7
St Veep Cnwll 5 K4
St Vigeans Angus 235 G6
St Wenn Cnwll 5 G2
St Weonards Herefs 63 G2
St y-Nyll V Glam 43 H6
Salcombe Devon 7 L7
Salcombe Regis Devon 14 D5
Salcott-cum-Virley Essex 72 D4
Sale Traffd 130 F2
Saleby Lincs 137 J4
Sale Green Worcs 81 L4
Salehurst E Susx 24 D2
Salem Carmth 59 H4
Salem Cerdgn 92 E6
Salen Ag & B 227 H4
Salen Highld 237 K7
Salesbury Lancs 139 K1
Salford C Beds 85 H7
Salford Oxon 65 L2
Salford Salfd 140 B8
Salford Priors Warwks 82 C5
Salfords Surrey 37 L2
Salhouse Norfk 123 G8
Saline Fife 221 J8
Salisbury Wilts 33 K5
Salisbury Crematorium Wilts 33 K4
Salkeld Dykes Cumb 166 D3
Salle Norfk 122 C6
Salmonby Lincs 136 F5
Salperton Gloucs 65 G3
Salph End Bed 86 B5
Salsburgh N Lans 209 L6
Salt Staffs 114 F6
Salta Cumb 164 E2
Saltaire C Brad 149 L8
Saltash Cnwll 6 E3
Saltburn Highld 263 K6
Saltburn-by-the-Sea R & Cl 170 F6
Saltby Leics 117 M6
Salt Coates Cumb 177 G8
Saltcoats Cumb 155 K3
Saltcoats N Ayrs 195 L3
Saltcotes Lancs 138 D2
Saltdean Br & H 22 F6
Salterbeck Cumb 164 C5
Salterforth Lancs 148 F6
Salterswall Ches W 130 C6
Salterton Wilts 33 K4
Saltfleet Lincs 137 H1
Saltfleetby All Saints Lincs 137 H2
Saltfleetby St Clement Lincs 137 J1
Saltfleetby St Peter Lincs 137 H2
Saltford BaNES 45 K5
Salthouse Norfk 122 B3
Saltley Birm 98 E5
Saltmarsh Newpt 44 D2
Saltmarshe E R Yk 143 K3
Saltney Flints 129 J6
Salton N York 162 C6
Saltrens Devon 27 H6
Saltwell Crematorium Gatesd 181 G6
Saltwick Nthumb 180 E3
Saltwood Kent 40 F8
Salvington W Susx 21 K6
Salwarpe Worcs 81 K3
Salway Ash Dorset 15 K3
Sambourne Warwks 82 C3
Sambrook Wrekin 113 M6
Samlesbury Lancs 139 H2
Samlesbury Bottoms Lancs 139 J2
Sampford Arundel Somset 29 K7
Sampford Brett Somset 29 K3
Sampford Courtenay Devon 12 F2
Sampford Moor Somset 29 K7
Sampford Peverell Devon 29 J8
Sampford Spiney Devon 12 D8
Samsonlane Ork 275 e3
Samson's Corner Essex 73 G3
Samuelston E Loth 212 B5
Sanaigmore Ag & B 204 C2
Sancreed Cnwll 2 C5
Sancton E R Yk 152 D7
Sand Somset 31 G2
Sandaig Highld 247 M8

Sandale Cumb	165	H3
Sandal Magna Wakefd	142	A4
Sanday Ork	275	e2
Sandbach Ches E	130	E7
Sandbank Ag & B	207	K3
Sandbanks Poole	17	K5
Sandend Abers	267	L3
Sanderstead Gt Lon	51	J6
Sandford Cumb	167	G7
Sandford Devon	13	J2
Sandford Dorset	17	H5
Sandford Hants	18	B3
Sandford IoW	19	J7
Sandford N Som	44	E7
Sandford S Lans	197	L2
Sandford Shrops	112	E6
Sandford Shrops	113	J5
Sandford-on-Thames Oxon	66	D6
Sandford Orcas Dorset	31	K6
Sandford St Martin Oxon	66	B2
Sandgate Kent	41	G8
Sandhaven Abers	269	H3
Sandhead D & G	172	D5
Sandhill Rothm	142	C8
Sandhills Dorset	16	B3
Sandhills Dorset	31	L8
Sand Hills Leeds	150	E7
Sandhills Oxon	66	E5
Sandhills Surrey	36	D3
Sandhoe Nthumb	180	A5
Sandhole Ag & B	216	F7
Sand Hole E R Yk	152	B8
Sandholme E R Yk	143	L2
Sandholme Lincs	119	K4
Sandhurst Br For	49	K6
Sandhurst Gloucs	64	B2
Sandhurst Kent	39	K7
Sandhurst Cross Kent	24	E2
Sand Hutton N York	151	L4
Sandhutton N York	160	E4
Sandiacre Derbys	116	E4
Sandilands Lincs	137	K3
Sandiway Ches W	130	B5
Sandleheath Hants	33	K7
Sandleigh Oxon	66	C6
Sandley Dorset	32	C6
Sandling Kent	53	G7
Sandlow Green Ches E	130	F6
Sandness Shet	281	c5
Sandon Essex	71	H6
Sandon Herts	87	G2
Sandon Staffs	114	E5
Sandon Bank Staffs	114	E6
Sandown IoW	19	K6
Sandplace Cnwll	6	A3
Sandridge Herts	68	F5
Sandridge Wilts	46	D6
Sandringham Norfk	120	F5
Sands Bucks	67	K8
Sandsend N York	171	K8
Sand Side Cumb	156	B6
Sandside Cumb	157	G6
Sandtoft N Linc	143	J6
Sandway Kent	39	M3
Sandwell Valley Crematorium Sandw	98	C5
Sandwich Kent	41	K4
Sandwich Bay Kent	41	K4
Sandwick Cumb	166	A6
Sandwick Shet	281	e8
Sandwick W Isls	282	g3
Sandwith Cumb	164	C7
Sandwith Newtown Cumb	164	C7
Sandy C Beds	86	D5
Sandy Bank Lincs	136	E8
Sandycroft Flints	129	H6
Sandy Cross E Susx	23	K3
Sandy Cross Herefs	80	F4
Sandyford D & G	187	J7
Sandygate Devon	13	K7
Sandygate IoM	154	e3
Sandy Haven Pembks	54	D5
Sandyhills D & G	175	M4
Sandylands Lancs	147	H3
Sandy Lane C Brad	149	K8
Sandylane Staffs	113	M4
Sandylane Swans	57	G2
Sandy Lane Wilts	46	D5
Sandy Lane Wrexhm	112	F3
Sandy Park Devon	13	G5
Sandysike Cumb	177	L5
Sandyway Herefs	63	G2
Sangobeg Highld	277	G3
Sangomore Highld	276	F3
Sankey Bridges Warrtn	130	B2
Sankyn's Green Worcs	81	H2
Sanna Highld	236	E6
Sanndabhaig W Isls	282	g3
Sannox N Ayrs	195	G2
Sanquhar D & G	185	K1
Santon Cumb	155	K2
Santon IoM	154	d7
Santon Bridge Cumb	155	K2
Santon Downham Suffk	105	G6
Sapcote Leics	100	E5
Sapey Common Herefs	81	G2
Sapiston Suffk	105	J8
Sapley Cambs	102	E8
Sapperton Derbys	115	K4
Sapperton Gloucs	64	D6
Sapperton Lincs	118	D5
Saracen's Head Lincs	119	K6
Sarclet Highld	280	D7
Sarisbury Hants	19	H2
Sarn Brdgnd	42	D5
Sarn Powys	93	L4
Sarn Powys	94	F5
Sarnau Carmth	58	B5
Sarnau Cerdgn	76	B5
Sarnau Gwynd	111	J4
Sarnau Powys	78	E8
Sarnau Powys	112	C5
Sarn Bach Gwynd	108	E6
Sarnesfield Herefs	79	L5
Sarn Meyllteyrn Gwynd	108	D5
Sarn-wen Powys	112	D7
Saron Carmth	59	H6
Saron Carmth	76	C7
Saron Gwynd	125	H7
Saron Gwynd	125	J6
Sarratt Herts	68	D7
Sarre Kent	41	H2
Sarsden Oxon	65	L3
Sarson Hants	34	C2
Satley Dur	168	E2
Satmar Kent	41	H7
Satron N York	159	G3
Satterleigh Devon	28	B6
Satterthwaite Cumb	156	D4
Satwell Oxon	49	H2
Sauchen Abers	244	F1
Saucher P & K	233	J8
Sauchieburn Abers	235	G2
Saul Gloucs	63	L5
Saundby Notts	134	F2
Saundersfoot Pembks	55	K6
Saunderton Bucks	67	J6
Saunderton Station Bucks	67	K7
Saunton Devon	27	H3
Sausthorpe Lincs	137	G6
Saverley Green Staffs	114	F4
Savile Town Kirk	141	K4
Sawbridge Warwks	83	L2
Sawbridgeworth Herts	70	C4
Sawdon N York	163	G5
Sawley Derbys	116	D5
Sawley Lancs	148	D6
Sawley N York	150	C2
Sawston Cambs	87	K5
Sawtry Cambs	102	D6
Saxby Leics	117	L7
Saxby Lincs	135	K3
Saxby All Saints N Linc	144	C4
Saxelbye Leics	117	J7
Saxham Street Suffk	90	C3
Saxilby Lincs	135	H4
Saxlingham Norfk	122	A4
Saxlingham Green Norfk	106	E4
Saxlingham Nethergate Norfk	106	E4
Saxlingham Thorpe Norfk	106	E4
Saxmundham Suffk	91	J3
Saxondale Notts	117	H3
Saxon Street Cambs	88	D3
Saxtead Suffk	91	G2
Saxtead Green Suffk	90	F2
Saxtead Little Green Suffk	90	F2
Saxthorpe Norfk	122	C5
Saxton N York	151	G8
Sayers Common W Susx	22	D4
Scackleton N York	161	L8
Scaftworth Notts	134	D2
Scagglethorpe N York	152	C1
Scalasaig Ag & B	214	D5
Scalby E R Yk	143	L2
Scalby N York	163	H4
Scald End Bed	85	L4
Scaldwell Nhants	84	E1
Scaleby Cumb	178	B6
Scalebyhill Cumb	178	B6
Scale Houses Cumb	166	E2
Scales Cumb	146	E2
Scales Cumb	165	K5
Scalesceugh Cumb	166	B1
Scalford Leics	117	K6
Scaling N York	171	H7
Scaling Dam R & Cl	171	H8
Scalloway Shet	281	d7
Scalpay Highld	247	J2
Scamblesby Lincs	136	E4
Scammonden Kirk	141	H4
Scamodale Highld	228	C1
Scampston N York	162	F7
Scampton Lincs	135	J4
Scaniport Highld	251	H4
Scapegoat Hill Kirk	141	G4
Scarba Ag & B	215	K3
Scarborough N York	163	J5
Scarcewater Cnwll	4	F4
Scarcliffe Derbys	133	K6
Scarcroft Leeds	150	E7
Scarfskerry Highld	280	C2
Scargill Dur	168	D8
Scarinish Ag & B	224	D6
Scarisbrick Lancs	138	D5
Scarness Cumb	165	H4
Scarning Norfk	105	J1
Scarrington Notts	117	J3
Scarth Hill Lancs	138	E6
Scarthingwell N York	151	G8
Scartho NE Lin	145	H6
Scaur D & G	175	L4
Scawby N Linc	144	B6
Scawsby Donc	142	E6
Scawthorpe Donc	142	E6
Scawton N York	161	J6
Scayne's Hill W Susx	22	F3
Scethrog Powys	61	H2
Scholar Green Ches E	131	G8
Scholemoor Crematorium C Brad	141	H1
Scholes Kirk	141	J3
Scholes Kirk	141	J6
Scholes Leeds	150	E8
Scholes Rothm	142	B8
Scholes Wigan	139	J6
School Aycliffe Dur	169	H6
School Green C Brad	141	H1
School Green Ches W	130	C6
Schoolgreen Wokham	49	H5
School House Dorset	15	J2
Scissett Kirk	141	L5
Scleddau Pembks	74	F5
Scofton Notts	134	C4
Scole Norfk	106	C7
Scone P & K	221	L2
Sconser Highld	247	H2
Scoonie Fife	222	F6
Scopwick Lincs	135	M8
Scoraig Highld	261	G1
Scorborough E R Yk	152	F6
Scorrier Cnwll	4	B6
Scorriton Devon	7	K1
Scorton Lancs	147	K6
Scorton N York	160	C3
Sco Ruston Norfk	122	F7
Scotby Cumb	178	B7
Scotch Corner N York	160	B2
Scotforth Lancs	147	J4
Scot Hay Staffs	114	B2
Scothern Lincs	135	L4
Scotland Lincs	118	C5
Scotland Gate Nthumb	181	G2
Scotlandwell P & K	222	C7
Scot Lane End Bolton	139	J6
Scotscalder Station Highld	279	K5
Scotsdike Cumb	177	L4
Scot's Gap Nthumb	180	C2
Scotsmill Abers	255	L7
Scotstoun C Glas	208	F5
Scotswood N u Ty	180	F6
Scotter Lincs	143	M7
Scotterthorpe Lincs	143	L7
Scottlethorpe Lincs	118	D7
Scotton Lincs	143	M7
Scotton N York	150	D4
Scotton N York	160	B3
Scottow Norfk	122	F6
Scott Willoughby Lincs	118	D4
Scoulton Norfk	105	K3
Scounslow Green Staffs	115	H5
Scourie Highld	276	B7
Scourie More Highld	276	A7
Scousburgh Shet	281	d8
Scouthead Oldham	140	E6
Scrabster Highld	279	K2
Scraesburgh Border	189	J3
Scrafield Lincs	136	F6
Scrainwood Nthumb	190	D4
Scrane End Lincs	119	L3
Scraptoft Leics	100	E2
Scratby Norfk	123	K8
Scrayingham N York	152	A4
Scrays E Susx	24	F3
Scredington Lincs	118	E3
Scremby Lincs	137	H6
Scremerston Nthumb	202	F3
Screveton Notts	117	J3
Scrivelsby Lincs	136	E6
Scriven N York	150	E4
Scrooby Notts	134	C2
Scropton Derbys	115	K5
Scrub Hill Lincs	136	D8
Scruton N York	160	D4
Scuggate Cumb	178	B4
Scullomie Highld	277	L4
Sculthorpe Norfk	121	K5
Scunthorpe N Linc	143	M5
Scurlage Swans	56	E7
Sea Somset	30	E8
Seaborough Dorset	15	K2
Seabridge Staffs	114	C3
Seabrook Kent	41	G8
Seaburn Sundld	181	K6
Seacombe Wirral	129	H2
Seacroft Leeds	150	E8
Seacroft Lincs	137	K5
Seadyke Lincs	119	K4
Seafield W Loth	210	D6
Seafield Crematorium C Edin	211	J4
Seaford E Susx	23	H7
Seaforth Sefton	138	C8
Seagrave Leics	117	G8
Seagry Heath Wilts	46	D3
Seaham Dur	169	L2
Seahouses Nthumb	203	L6
Seal Kent	38	E2
Sealand Flints	129	H6
Seale Surrey	36	D4
Seamer N York	163	J6
Seamer N York	170	C8
Seamill N Ayrs	195	K2
Sea Palling Norfk	123	K6
Searby Lincs	144	D6
Seasalter Kent	40	E2
Seascale Cumb	155	J2
Seathwaite Cumb	156	B3
Seathwaite Cumb	165	H8
Seatle Cumb	156	E6
Seatoller Cumb	165	H7
Seaton Cnwll	6	C4
Seaton Cumb	164	D4
Seaton Devon	14	F4
Seaton Dur	169	L1
Seaton E R Yk	153	J2
Seaton Kent	41	H4
Seaton Nthumb	181	H3
Seaton Rutlnd	101	K4
Seaton Burn N Tyne	181	G4
Seaton Carew Hartpl	170	C5
Seaton Delaval Nthumb	181	H4
Seaton Ross E R Yk	152	B7
Seaton Sluice Nthumb	181	H3
Seatown Dorset	15	K4
Seave Green N York	161	J3
Seaview IoW	19	L5
Seaville Cumb	177	G8
Seavington St Mary Somset	30	F7
Seavington St Michael Somset	30	F7
Sebastopol Torfn	62	C2
Sebergham Cumb	165	K2
Seckington Warwks	99	H2
Second Severn Crossing Mons	45	G2
Sedbergh Cumb	157	L4
Sedbury Gloucs	63	H8
Sedbusk N York	158	F4
Sedgeberrow Worcs	82	B7
Sedgebrook Lincs	117	M4
Sedge Fen Suffk	104	D6
Sedgefield Dur	169	K5
Sedgeford Norfk	120	F4
Sedgehill Wilts	32	E5
Sedgemoor Crematorium Somset	30	D2
Sedgley Dudley	97	L4
Sedgley Park Bury	140	B7
Sedgwick Cumb	157	H5
Sedlescombe E Susx	24	E4
Sedrup Bucks	67	J5
Seed Kent	40	B4
Seend Wilts	46	D6
Seend Cleeve Wilts	46	D6
Seer Green Bucks	68	B8
Seething Norfk	107	G4
Sefton Sefton	138	D7
Seghill Nthumb	181	H4
Seighford Staffs	114	D6
Seion Gwynd	125	K6
Seisdon Staffs	97	J4
Selattyn Shrops	112	C5
Selborne Hants	35	M4
Selby N York	142	F1
Selham W Susx	20	F3
Selhurst Gt Lon	51	J5
Selkirk Border	201	G7
Sellack Herefs	63	H2
Sellafield Station Cumb	155	J2

Sellafirth Shet	281	e2
Sellan Cnwll	2	C5
Sellick's Green Somset	30	B7
Sellindge Kent	40	E7
Selling Kent	40	D4
Sells Green Wilts	46	D6
Selly Oak Birm	98	D7
Selmeston E Susx	23	H6
Selsdon Gt Lon	51	K6
Selsey W Susx	20	D8
Selsfield Common W Susx	38	A6
Selside Cumb	157	H3
Selside N York	158	D7
Selsley Gloucs	64	B6
Selsted Kent	41	H6
Selston Notts	116	D1
Selworthy Somset	29	G2
Semer Suffk	89	K6
Semington Wilts	46	C6
Semley Wilts	32	E5
Sempringham Lincs	118	F5
Send Surrey	50	C7
Send Marsh Surrey	50	C7
Senghenydd Caerph	43	H3
Sennen Cnwll	2	B6
Sennen Cove Cnwll	2	B6
Sennybridge Powys	60	D2
Serlby Notts	134	C2
Sessay N York	161	G7
Setchey Norfk	104	C1
Setley Hants	18	D3
Seton Mains E Loth	211	M4
Settle N York	148	E3
Settrington N York	152	C2
Seven Ash Somset	29	L4
Sevenhampton Gloucs	64	F3
Sevenhampton Swindn	47	J1
Seven Hills Crematorium Suffk	90	F7
Seven Kings Gt Lon	51	M2
Sevenoaks Kent	38	E2
Sevenoaks Weald Kent	38	E3
Seven Sisters Neath	60	B5
Seven Springs Gloucs	64	D4
Seven Star Green Essex	72	D2
Severn Beach S Glos	45	G2
Severn Bridge S Glos	45	H1
Severn Stoke Worcs	81	K6
Sevick End Bed	86	B4
Sevington Kent	40	D7
Sewards End Essex	88	B7
Sewardstonebury Essex	69	K7
Sewell C Beds	68	C3
Sewerby E R Yk	153	K2
Seworgan Cnwll	3	H5
Sewstern Leics	118	A7
Sexhow N York	161	G2
Sezincote Gloucs	65	H1
Sgiogarstaigh W Isls	282	h1
Shabbington Bucks	67	G5
Shackerley Shrops	97	J2
Shackerstone Leics	99	K2
Shacklecross Derbys	116	C5
Shackleford Surrey	36	D2
Shade Calder	140	D3
Shader W Isls	282	g1
Shadforth Dur	169	J3
Shadingfield Suffk	107	H2
Shadoxhurst Kent	40	C7
Shadwell Leeds	150	D7
Shadwell Norfk	105	J6
Shaftenhoe End Herts	87	H1
Shaftesbury Dorset	32	E6
Shaftholme Donc	142	F6
Shafton Barns	142	B5
Shafton Two Gates Barns	142	B5
Shakerley Wigan	139	K7
Shalbourne Wilts	47	L6
Shalcombe IoW	18	F6
Shalden Hants	35	L4
Shalden Green Hants	35	L2
Shaldon Devon	13	L8
Shalfleet IoW	18	F6
Shalford Essex	71	H3
Shalford Surrey	36	F2
Shalford Green Essex	71	H2
Shallowford Staffs	114	D5
Shalmsford Street Kent	40	E4
Shalstone Bucks	84	C7
Shamley Green Surrey	36	F2
Shandford Angus	234	D3
Shandon Ag & B	207	L2
Shandwick Highld	264	D5
Shangton Leics	100	F4
Shankhouse Nthumb	181	G3
Shanklin IoW	19	K7
Shantron Ag & B	208	B2
Shap Cumb	166	D7
Shapinsay Ork	275	d4
Shapwick Dorset	17	H2
Shapwick Somset	30	F3
Shard End Birm	98	F5
Shardlow Derbys	116	C5
Shareshill Staffs	97	L2
Sharlston Wakefd	142	B4
Sharlston Common Wakefd	142	B4
Sharman's Cross Solhll	98	E7
Sharnal Street Medway	53	G4
Sharnbrook Bed	85	K3
Sharneyford Lancs	140	C3
Sharnford Leics	100	B5
Sharnhill Green Dorset	16	D2
Sharoe Green Lancs	139	G1
Sharow N York	150	D2
Sharpenhoe C Beds	68	D3
Sharperton Nthumb	190	D5
Sharp Green Norfk	123	H7
Sharpness Gloucs	63	K6
Sharpthorne W Susx	38	B6
Sharptor Cnwll	11	J8
Sharpway Gate Worcs	81	L2
Sharrington Norfk	122	A4
Shatterford Worcs	97	H7
Shatterling Kent	41	J4
Shatton Derbys	132	D3
Shaugh Prior Devon	7	G2
Shave Cross Dorset	15	J3
Shavington Ches E	113	M1
Shaw C Brad	140	F1
Shaw Oldham	140	D6
Shaw Swindn	47	G2
Shaw W Berk	48	C5
Shaw Wilts	46	C6
Shawbirch Wrekin	113	L8
Shawbost W Isls	282	f2
Shawbury Shrops	113	J7
Shawclough Rochdl	140	D5
Shaw Common Gloucs	63	K2
Shawdon Hill Nthumb	190	F3
Shawell Leics	100	C7
Shawford Hants	34	F6
Shawforth Lancs	140	D4
Shaw Green Herts	69	J1
Shaw Green Lancs	139	G4
Shaw Green N York	150	C5
Shawhead D & G	185	L7
Shaw Mills N York	150	C3
Shawsburn S Lans	198	C3
Shear Cross Wilts	32	E3
Shearington D & G	176	D5
Shearsby Leics	100	D5
Shearston Somset	30	D5
Shebbear Devon	12	B1
Shebdon Staffs	114	B6
Shebster Highld	279	H3
Sheddens E Rens	208	F7
Shedfield Hants	35	H8
Sheen Staffs	132	B7
Sheepbridge Derbys	133	G5
Sheep Hill Dur	180	E7
Sheepridge Kirk	141	J4
Sheepscar Leeds	141	M1
Sheepscombe Gloucs	64	C5
Sheepstor Devon	7	G1
Sheepwash Devon	12	C2
Sheepwash Nthumb	181	G2
Sheepway N Som	45	G4
Sheepy Magna Leics	99	J3
Sheepy Parva Leics	99	J3
Sheering Essex	70	D4
Sheerness Kent	53	K4
Sheerwater Surrey	50	D6
Sheet Hants	36	A6
Sheffield Cnwll	2	D5
Sheffield Sheff	133	G2
Sheffield Bottom W Berk	49	G5
Sheffield City Road Crematorium Sheff	133	G3
Sheffield Green E Susx	22	F2
Shefford C Beds	86	C7
Shefford Woodlands W Berk	48	A4
Sheigra Highld	276	B4
Sheinton Shrops	96	E3
Shelderton Shrops	95	K7
Sheldon Birm	98	F6
Sheldon Derbys	132	C6
Sheldon Devon	14	D1
Sheldwich Kent	40	D4
Sheldwich Lees Kent	40	D4
Shelf Calder	141	H2
Shelfanger Norfk	106	C6
Shelfield Warwks	82	D3
Shelfield Wsall	98	C3
Shelfield Green Warwks	82	D3
Shelford Notts	117	H3
Shelford Warwks	99	L5
Shellacres Nthumb	202	D4
Shelley Essex	70	E6
Shelley Kirk	141	K5
Shelley Suffk	89	L7
Shelley Far Bank Kirk	141	K5
Shellingford Oxon	65	L8
Shellow Bowells Essex	70	F5
Shelsley Beauchamp Worcs	81	G3
Shelsley Walsh Worcs	81	G3
Shelton Bed	85	K2
Shelton Norfk	106	E5
Shelton Notts	117	K3
Shelton Shrops	95	L1
Shelton Green Norfk	106	E5
Shelton Lock C Derb	116	C5
Shelton Under Harley Staffs	114	C4
Shelve Shrops	95	H4
Shelwick Herefs	80	C6
Shenfield Essex	70	F8
Shenington Oxon	83	J6
Shenley Herts	68	F7
Shenley Brook End M Keyn	85	G8
Shenleybury Herts	68	F6
Shenley Church End M Keyn	85	G7
Shenmore Herefs	79	M7
Shennanton D & G	173	J2
Shenstone Staffs	98	E3
Shenstone Worcs	97	J8
Shenstone Woodend Staffs	98	E3
Shenton Leics	99	K3
Shenval Moray	254	E6
Shepeau Stow Lincs	102	F1
Shephall Herts	69	H2
Shepherd's Bush Gt Lon	51	J3
Shepherd's Green Oxon	49	H2
Shepherds Patch Gloucs	63	L6
Shepherdswell Kent	41	H5
Shepley Kirk	141	J6
Shepperdine S Glos	63	J8
Shepperton Surrey	50	D5
Shepperton Green Surrey	50	D5
Shepreth Cambs	87	H5
Shepshed Leics	116	E7
Shepton Beauchamp Somset	30	F7
Shepton Mallet Somset	31	K2
Shepton Montague Somset	31	L4
Shepway Kent	39	J3
Sheraton Dur	170	B4
Sherborne Dorset	31	L7
Sherborne Gloucs	65	H4
Sherborne Somset	45	H7
Sherborne St John Hants	48	F7
Sherbourne Warwks	83	G3
Sherburn Dur	169	J2
Sherburn N York	163	G7
Sherburn Hill Dur	169	J2
Sherburn in Elmet N York	142	D1
Shere Surrey	37	G1
Shereford Norfk	121	K5
Sherfield English Hants	34	C6
Sherfield on Loddon Hants	49	G7
Sherfin Lancs	140	B3
Sherford Devon	8	A6
Sherford Dorset	17	H4
Sheriffhales Shrops	97	G1
Sheriff Hutton N York	151	K3
Sheringham Norfk	122	D3
Sherington M Keyn	85	H6
Shermanbury W Susx	22	B3
Shernborne Norfk	120	F5
Sherrington Wilts	33	G3
Sherston Wilts	46	B2
Sherwood C Nott	116	F3
Sherwood Forest Crematorium Notts	134	D6
Shetland Islands Shet	281	d6
Shettleston C Glas	209	H6
Shevington Wigan	139	H6
Shevington Moor Wigan	139	H5
Shevington Vale Wigan	139	G6
Sheviock Cnwll	6	D4
Shibden Head C Brad	141	H2
Shide IoW	19	H6
Shidlaw Nthumb	202	C5
Shiel Bridge Highld	248	F7
Shieldaig Highld	248	D4
Shieldhill D & G	176	D2
Shieldhill Falk	210	B4
Shieldhill House Hotel S Lans	199	G5
Shields N Lans	209	K7
Shielfoot Highld	237	J6
Shielhill Angus	234	C4
Shielhill Inver	207	L4
Shifford Oxon	66	A4
Shifnal Shrops	97	G2
Shilbottle Nthumb	191	J4
Shildon Dur	169	G5
Shillford E Rens	208	D7
Shillingford Devon	29	H6
Shillingford Oxon	66	E8
Shillingford Abbot Devon	13	L5
Shillingford St George Devon	13	L5
Shillingstone Dorset	32	D8
Shillington C Beds	86	C8
Shillmoor Nthumb	190	B4
Shilton Oxon	65	K5
Shilton Warwks	99	L6
Shimpling Norfk	106	D6
Shimpling Suffk	89	H5
Shimpling Street Suffk	89	H4
Shincliffe Dur	169	H3
Shiney Row Sundld	181	H8
Shinfield Wokham	49	H6
Shingay Cambs	86	F6
Shingle Street Suffk	91	J6
Shinnersbridge Devon	8	B2
Shinness Highld	272	D5
Shipbourne Kent	38	F3
Shipdham Norfk	105	J2
Shipham Somset	44	E7
Shiphay Torbay	8	D2
Shiplake Oxon	49	J3
Shiplake Row Oxon	49	H3
Shiplate N Som	44	D7
Shipley C Brad	149	L8
Shipley Derbys	116	D3
Shipley Shrops	97	H4
Shipley W Susx	37	H6
Shipley Bridge Surrey	37	M3
Shipley Hatch Kent	40	C7
Shipmeadow Suffk	107	H5
Shippea Hill Station Cambs	104	C6
Shippon Oxon	66	C7
Shipston-on-Stour Warwks	83	G7
Shipton Bucks	67	J2
Shipton Gloucs	64	F3
Shipton N York	151	H4
Shipton Shrops	96	D5
Shipton Bellinger Hants	34	B2
Shipton Gorge Dorset	15	L4
Shipton Green W Susx	20	C7
Shipton Moyne Gloucs	46	C1
Shipton-on-Cherwell Oxon	66	C4
Shiptonthorpe E R Yk	152	C7
Shipton-under-Wychwood Oxon	65	L3
Shirburn Oxon	67	G7
Shirdley Hill Lancs	138	D5
Shire Cumb	166	E4
Shirebrook Derbys	133	K6
Shiregreen Sheff	133	G1
Shirehampton Bristl	45	G4
Shiremoor N Tyne	181	H4
Shirenewton Mons	62	F8
Shire Oak Wsall	98	D3
Shireoaks Notts	133	L3
Shirkoak Kent	40	B8
Shirland Derbys	133	H8
Shirlett Shrops	96	E4
Shirley C Sotn	34	E8
Shirley Derbys	115	L3
Shirley Gt Lon	51	K6
Shirley Solhll	98	E7
Shirl Heath Herefs	80	A3
Shirrell Heath Hants	35	H8
Shirvan Ag & B	206	D2
Shirwell Devon	27	L3
Shiskine N Ayrs	194	E5
Shittlehope Dur	168	C3
Shobdon Herefs	79	M3
Shobley Hants	18	B2
Shobrooke Devon	13	K2
Shoby Leics	117	H7
Shocklach Ches W	113	G2
Shocklach Green Ches W	113	G2
Shoeburyness Sthend	53	K2
Sholden Kent	41	K5
Sholing C Sotn	19	G2
Shoot Hill Shrops	95	K1
Shop Cnwll	10	B7
Shop Cnwll	26	D7
Shopwyke W Susx	20	E6
Shore Rochdl	140	D4
Shoreditch Gt Lon	51	J2
Shoreditch Somset	30	C6
Shoreham Kent	52	B6
Shoreham-by-Sea W Susx	22	C6
Shoreswood Nthumb	202	E4
Shorley Hants	35	J4
Shorncote Gloucs	64	F5
Shorne Kent	52	E5
Shortacross Cnwll	6	B3
Shortbridge E Susx	23	G3
Shortfield Common Surrey	36	C2
Shortgate E Susx	23	H4
Short Heath Birm	98	E5
Shortheath Hants	36	A4
Short Heath Wsall	98	B3
Shortlanesend Cnwll	4	C5
Shortlees E Ayrs	196	E4
Shortstown Bed	86	B6

Shorwell IoW 19 G7
Shoscombe BaNES 45 L7
Shotesham Norfk 106 E4
Shotgate Essex 71 J8
Shotley Suffk 90 F8
Shotley Bridge Dur 180 D8
Shotleyfield Nthumb 180 C8
Shotley Gate Suffk 90 F8
Shotley Street Suffk 90 F8
Shottenden Kent 40 D4
Shottermill Surrey 36 C4
Shottery Warwks 82 K6
Shotteswell Warwks 83 K6
Shottisham Suffk 91 H6
Shottle Derbys 116 A2
Shottlegate Derbys 116 A2
Shotton Dur 169 K5
Shotton Dur 169 L3
Shotton Flints 129 H6
Shotton Nthumb 180 F3
Shotton Nthumb 202 C7
Shotton Colliery Dur 169 K3
Shotts N Lans 210 A7
Shotwick Ches W 129 H5
Shougle Moray 266 D5
Shouldham Norfk 104 D2
Shouldham Thorpe Norfk 104 D2
Shoulton Worcs 81 J3
Shover's Green E Susx 39 G7
Shraleybrook Staffs 114 B2
Shrawardine Shrops 112 H4
Shrawley Worcs 81 J2
Shreding Green Bucks 50 C3
Shrewley Warwks 82 F2
Shrewsbury Shrops 96 B1
Shrewton Wilts 33 J2
Shripney W Susx 20 F6
Shrivenham Oxon 47 K1
Shropham Norfk 105 K5
Shroton Dorset 32 E8
Shrub End Essex 72 E2
Shucknall Herefs 80 D6
Shudy Camps Cambs 88 C6
Shuna Ag & B 216 B5
Shurdington Gloucs 64 D3
Shurlock Row W & M 49 K4
Shurnock Worcs 82 B3
Shurrery Highld 279 J4
Shurrery Lodge Highld 279 J5
Shurton Somset 30 B2
Shustoke Warwks 99 G5
Shute Devon 13 L3
Shute Devon 14 F3
Shutford Oxon 83 J7
Shut Heath Staffs 114 D7
Shuthonger Gloucs 81 K8
Shutlanger Nhants 84 E5
Shutterton Devon 13 M6
Shutt Green Staffs 97 K2
Shuttington Warwks 99 H2
Shuttlewood Derbys 133 J5
Shuttleworth Bury 140 B4
Siabost W Isls 282 f2
Siadar W Isls 282 g1
Sibbertoft Nhants 100 E6
Sibdon Carwood Shrops 95 K6
Sibford Ferris Oxon 83 H7
Sibford Gower Oxon 83 H7
Sible Hedingham Essex 88 F8
Sibley's Green Essex 70 F2
Siblyback Cnwll 11 J8
Sibsey Lincs 119 K2
Sibsey Fenside Lincs 119 K1
Sibson Cambs 102 B4
Sibson Leics 99 K3
Sibster Highld 280 D5
Sibthorpe Notts 117 K2
Sibthorpe Notts 134 E5
Sibton Suffk 91 J2
Sicklesmere Suffk 89 H3
Sicklinghall N York 150 E6
Sidbrook Somset 30 C5
Sidbury Devon 14 D4
Sidbury Shrops 96 F6
Sid Cop Barns 142 B6
Sidcot N Som 44 E7
Sidcup Gt Lon 51 M4
Siddick Cumb 164 D4
Siddington Ches E 131 G5
Siddington Gloucs 64 F7
Sidemoor Worcs 81 L1
Sidestrand Norfk 122 F3
Sidford Devon 14 D4
Sidlesham W Susx 20 D7
Sidlesham Common W Susx 20 D6
Sidley E Susx 24 C4
Sidmouth Devon 14 D5
Siefton Shrops 96 B6
Sigford Devon 13 H7

Sigglesthorne E R Yk 153 J6
Sigingstone V Glam 42 E7
Signet Oxon 65 K5
Silchester Hants 48 F6
Sileby Leics 117 G8
Silecroft Cumb 155 L6
Silfield Norfk 106 C3
Silian Cerdgn 77 G5
Silkstead Hants 34 F6
Silkstone Barns 141 L6
Silkstone Common Barns 141 L6
Silk Willoughby Lincs 118 E3
Silloth Cumb 176 F8
Silpho N York 163 H4
Silsden C Brad 149 J6
Silsoe C Beds 86 B8
Silton Dorset 32 C5
Silverburn Mdloth 211 G7
Silverdale Lancs 157 G7
Silverdale Staffs 114 C2
Silver End Essex 71 K3
Silverford Abers 268 D3
Silvergate Norfk 122 D6
Silverlace Green Suffk 91 H3
Silverley's Green Suffk 106 F8
Silverstone Nhants 84 C6
Silver Street Kent 53 J7
Silver Street Somset 31 J4
Silverton Devon 13 M2
Silverwell Cnwll 4 B5
Silvington Shrops 96 E7
Simister Bury 140 C6
Simmondley Derbys 131 K1
Simonburn Nthumb 179 K4
Simonsbath Somset 28 D3
Simonsburrow Devon 29 L7
Simonstone Lancs 140 A1
Simonstone N York 158 F4
Simprim Border 202 C4
Simpson M Keyn 85 H8
Simpson Cross Pembks 54 E3
Sinclair's Hill Border 202 C3
Sinclairston E Ayrs 196 F7
Sinderby N York 160 E6
Sinderhope Nthumb 179 K8
Sinderland Green Traffd 130 E2
Sindlesham Wokham 49 J5
Sinfin C Derb 116 B5
Singleborough Bucks 67 J1
Single Street Gt Lon 51 L7
Singleton Kent 40 C7
Singleton Lancs 147 G8
Singleton W Susx 20 E4
Singlewell Kent 52 E5
Sinkhurst Green Kent 39 K5
Sinnarhard Abers 244 B1
Sinnington N York 162 C5
Sinope Leics 116 C8
Sinton Worcs 81 J3
Sinton Worcs 81 J3
Sinton Green Worcs 81 J3
Sipson Gt Lon 50 D3
Sirhowy Blae G 61 J5
Sissinghurst Kent 39 K6
Siston S Glos 45 K4
Sitcott Devon 11 L4
Sithney Cnwll 3 G5
Sithney Common Cnwll 3 G5
Sithney Green Cnwll 3 G5
Sittingbourne Kent 40 B3
Six Ashes Shrops 97 H5
Six Bells Blae G 61 K6
Six Hills Leics 117 H7
Sixhills Lincs 136 C2
Six Mile Bottom Cambs 88 B4
Sixmile Cottages Kent 40 F6
Sixpenny Handley Dorset 33 G7
Six Rues Jersey 9 C2
Sizewell Suffk 91 L3
Skaill Ork 275 d5
Skares E Ayrs 197 G7
Skateraw Abers 245 K5
Skateraw E Loth 213 G4
Skeabost Highld 259 D7
Skeeby N York 160 B2
Skeffington Leics 101 G3
Skeffling E R Yk 145 K4
Skegby Notts 133 K7
Skegby Notts 134 F5
Skegness Lincs 137 L7
Skelbo Highld 264 B1
Skelbo Street Highld 264 B1
Skelbrooke Donc 142 D5
Skeldyke Lincs 119 K4
Skellingthorpe Lincs 135 J5
Skellorn Green Ches E 131 H3
Skellow Donc 142 E5
Skelmanthorpe Kirk 141 K5
Skelmersdale Lancs 138 F6

Skelmorlie N Ayrs 207 K5
Skelpick Highld 278 B5
Skelston D & G 185 K6
Skelton C York 151 J4
Skelton Cumb 166 B4
Skelton E R Yk 143 J3
Skelton N York 159 K3
Skelton R & Cl 170 F7
Skelton on Ure N York 150 E2
Skelwith Bridge Cumb 156 E2
Skendleby Lincs 137 H5
Skene House Abers 245 G2
Skenfrith Mons 62 F3
Skerne E R Yk 153 J3
Skerray Highld 277 L4
Skerricha Highld 276 C6
Skerton Lancs 147 J3
Sketchley Leics 99 L5
Sketty Swans 57 H6
Skewen Neath 57 K5
Skewsby N York 151 K2
Skeyton Norfk 122 E6
Skeyton Corner Norfk 122 E6
Skiall Highld 279 H3
Skidbrooke Lincs 137 H1
Skidbrooke North End Lincs 137 H1
Skidby E R Yk 144 C1
Skigersta W Isls 282 h1
Skilgate Somset 29 H5
Skillington Lincs 118 A6
Skinburness Cumb 176 F7
Skinflats Falk 210 B2
Skinidin Highld 258 C7
Skinners Green W Berk 48 C6
Skinningrove R & Cl 171 G6
Skipness Ag & B 206 E7
Skipper's Bridge D & G 177 L2
Skiprigg Cumb 165 L2
Skipsea E R Yk 153 J5
Skipsea Brough E R Yk 153 J5
Skipton N York 149 H5
Skipton-on-Swale N York 160 E6
Skipwith N York 151 L8
Skirlaugh E R Yk 153 J7
Skirling Border 199 J5
Skirmett Bucks 49 J1
Skirpenbeck E R Yk 152 A4
Skirwith Cumb 166 E4
Skirwith N York 158 C7
Skirza Highld 280 D2
Skitby Cumb 178 B5
Skittle Green Bucks 67 J6
Skokholm Island Pembks 54 B6
Skomer Island Pembks 54 B5
Skulamus Highld 247 L4
Skyborry Green Shrops 95 G8
Skye Green Essex 72 C3
Skye of Curr Highld 253 J6
Skyreholme N York 149 J4
Slack Calder 140 E2
Slackcote Oldham 140 E6
Slack Head Cumb 157 G6
Slackholme End Lincs 137 K5
Slacks of Cairnbanno Abers 256 F3
Slad Gloucs 64 C5
Slade Devon 14 D1
Slade Devon 27 J2
Slade Devon 28 E5
Slade End Oxon 48 E1
Slade Green Gt Lon 52 B4
Slade Heath Staffs 97 L2
Slade Hooton Rothm 133 K2
Sladesbridge Cnwll 10 E8
Slades Green Worcs 81 J8
Slaggyford Nthumb 178 F8
Slaidburn Lancs 148 C5
Slaithwaite Kirk 141 G5
Slaley Derbys 132 E8
Slaley Nthumb 180 A7
Slamannan Falk 209 M4
Slapton Bucks 68 B3
Slapton Devon 8 B6
Slapton Nhants 84 C6
Slattocks Rochdl 140 D6
Slaugham W Susx 37 L5
Slaughterford Wilts 46 B4
Slawston Leics 101 G4
Sleaford Hants 36 B3
Sleaford Lincs 118 E2
Sleagill Cumb 166 E6
Sleap Shrops 113 H6
Sleapford Wrekin 113 L8
Sleapshyde Herts 69 G5
Sleasdairidh Highld 272 F8
Slebech Pembks 55 H4
Sledge Green Worcs 81 J8
Sledmere E R Yk 152 E3
Sleetbeck Cumb 178 C3
Sleight Dorset 17 J3

Sleightholme Dur 168 B8
Sleights N York 162 F1
Slepe Dorset 17 H4
Slickly Highld 280 C3
Sliddery N Ayrs 193 J4
Sligachan Ag & B 247 G3
Sligrachan Ag & B 207 K1
Slimbridge Gloucs 63 L6
Slindon Staffs 114 C5
Slindon W Susx 20 F5
Slinfold W Susx 37 H4
Sling Gwynd 126 B6
Slingsby N York 162 B7
Slip End C Beds 68 D3
Slip End Herts 86 F7
Slipton Nhants 101 L7
Slitting Mill Staffs 115 G8
Slockavullin Ag & B 216 C7
Sloley Norfk 122 H6
Sloncombe Devon 13 H5
Sloothby Lincs 137 J5
Slough Slough 50 C3
Slough Crematorium Bucks 50 B3
Slough Green Somset 30 C7
Slough Green W Susx 37 L5
Slumbay Highld 248 E4
Slyfield Green Surrey 50 C8
Slyne Lancs 147 J3
Smailholm Border 201 K6
Smallbridge Rochdl 140 D5
Smallbrook Devon 13 K3
Smallbrook Gloucs 63 H7
Smallburgh Norfk 123 G6
Smalldale Derbys 132 B4
Smalldale Derbys 132 C3
Small Dole W Susx 22 C5
Smalley Derbys 116 C3
Smalley Common Derbys 116 C3
Smalley Green Derbys 116 C3
Smallfield Surrey 37 M2
Small Heath Birm 98 E6
Small Hythe Kent 25 G1
Smallridge Devon 15 G2
Smallthorne C Stke 114 D2
Smallways N York 168 E8
Smallwood Ches E 130 F7
Small Wood Hey Lancs 147 H6
Smallworth Norfk 105 K7
Smannell Hants 34 E1
Smardale Cumb 158 C1
Smarden Kent 39 L5
Smarden Bell Kent 39 L5
Smart's Hill Kent 38 E5
Smeafield Nthumb 203 H5
Smearisary Highld 237 J5
Smeatharpe Devon 14 E1
Smeeth Kent 40 E7
Smeeton Westerby Leics 100 E5
Smelthouses N York 150 B3
Smerral Highld 275 G2
Smestow Staffs 97 J5
Smethwick Sandw 98 C6
Smethwick Green Ches E 130 F7
Smisby Derbys 116 B7
Smith End Green Worcs 81 H5
Smithfield Cumb 178 B6
Smith Green Lancs 147 J5
Smithies Barns 142 A6
Smithincott Devon 29 J8
Smith's End Herts 87 H7
Smith's Green Essex 70 E3
Smith's Green Essex 88 D7
Smithstown Highld 260 C4
Smithton Highld 252 D3
Smithy Bridge Rochdl 140 D5
Smithy Green Ches E 130 E5
Smithy Green Stockp 131 G3
Smithy Houses Derbys 116 C2
Smockington Leics 99 M5
Smoo Highld 277 G3
Smythe's Green Essex 72 D3
Snade D & G 185 L2
Snailbeach Shrops 95 J3
Snailwell Cambs 88 C2
Snainton N York 163 G6
Snaith E R Yk 143 G3
Snake Pass Inn Derbys 132 B2
Snape N York 160 C6
Snape Suffk 91 J3
Snape Green Lancs 138 D5
Snape Street Suffk 91 J4
Snaresbrook Gt Lon 51 L1
Snarestone Leics 99 K2
Snarford Lincs 135 L3
Snargate Kent 25 J2
Snave Kent 25 J1
Sneachill Worcs 81 L4
Snead Powys 95 H5

Sneath Common Norfk......106 D5
Sneaton N York......162 F1
Sneatonthorpe N York......162 F2
Snelland Lincs......135 M4
Snelson Ches E......130 F5
Snelston Derbys......115 J3
Snetterton Norfk......105 K5
Snettisham Norfk......120 F4
Snibston Leics......116 C8
Snig's End Gloucs......64 A1
Snitter Nthumb......190 E5
Snitterby Lincs......135 K1
Snitterfield Warwks......82 F3
Snitterton Derbys......132 G4
Snitton Shrops......96 D8
Snoadhill Kent......40 B6
Snodhill Herefs......79 K7
Snodland Kent......52 F6
Snoll Hatch Kent......39 G4
Snowden Hill Barns......141 L7
Snowdon Kent......41 H5
Snow End Herts......69 L1
Snowshill Gloucs......82 C8
Snow Street Norfk......106 B7
Soake Hants......19 L2
Soar Cardif......43 H5
Soar Devon......7 K7
Soar Powys......60 E1
Soay Highld......246 F6
Soberton Hants......35 J7
Soberton Heath Hants......35 J7
Sockbridge Cumb......166 C5
Sockburn Darltn......160 E1
Sodom Denbgs......128 C5
Sodylt Bank Shrops......112 E3
Soham Cambs......104 B8
Soham Cotes Cambs......104 B8
Solas W Isls......282 c7
Solbury Pembks......54 E4
Soldon Devon......26 E8
Soldon Cross Devon......26 E8
Soldridge Hants......35 K4
Sole Street Kent......40 E5
Sole Street Kent......52 E5
Solihull Solhll......98 F7
Sollers Dilwyn Herefs......80 A4
Sollers Hope Herefs......80 E8
Sollom Lancs......138 F4
Solva Pembks......74 C7
Solwaybank D & G......177 J3
Somerby Leics......101 G1
Somerby Lincs......144 D6
Somercotes Derbys......116 C1
Somerford Dorset......18 B5
Somerford Keynes Gloucs......64 F6
Somerley W Susx......20 D7
Somerleyton Suffk......107 K4
Somersal Herbert Derbys......115 J4
Somersby Lincs......136 F5
Somersham Cambs......103 G7
Somersham Suffk......90 C5
Somerton Oxon......66 D2
Somerton Somset......31 H5
Somerton Suffk......89 G4
Somerwood Shrops......113 J8
Sompting W Susx......21 K6
Sompting Abbotts W Susx......21 K6
Sonning Wokham......49 J4
Sonning Common Oxon......49 H3
Sonning Eye Oxon......49 H4
Sontley Wrexhm......112 E2
Sopley Hants......18 B4
Sopwell Herts......68 F6
Sopworth Wilts......46 B2
Sorbie D & G......174 C5
Sordale Highld......279 L4
Sorisdale Ag & B......225 H3
Sorn E Ayrs......197 G5
Sortat Highld......280 C4
Sotby Lincs......136 D4
Sots Hole Lincs......136 B6
Sotterley Suffk......107 J6
Soughton Flints......128 F6
Soulbury Bucks......67 L2
Soulby Cumb......166 B5
Soulby Cumb......167 H8
Souldern Oxon......66 D1
Souldrop Bed......85 J3
Sound Ches E......113 K2
Sound Muir Moray......267 G5
Soundwell S Glos......45 J4
Sourton Devon......12 D4
Soutergate Cumb......156 B6
South Acre Norfk......121 H8
South Alkham Kent......41 H7
Southall Gt Lon......50 E3
South Allington Devon......8 B7
South Alloa Falk......210 A1
Southam Gloucs......64 E2

Southam Warwks......83 K3
South Ambersham W Susx......20 F3
Southampton C Sotn......19 G1
Southampton Crematorium
   Hants......34 F7
South Anston Rothm......133 K3
South Ascot W & M......50 A5
South Ashford Kent......40 C7
South Baddesley Hants......18 E4
South Ballachulish Highld......229 G4
South Bank C York......151 J5
South Bank R & Cl......170 C6
South Barrow Somset......31 K5
South Beddington Gt Lon......51 H6
South Beer Cnwll......11 K4
South Benfleet Essex......53 G2
Southborough Gt Lon......51 L5
Southborough Kent......38 F5
Southbourne Bmouth......18 A5
Southbourne W Susx......20 C5
South Bowood Dorset......15 K3
South Bramwith Donc......143 G5
South Brent Devon......7 K3
South Brewham Somset......32 B4
South Bristol Crematorium
   Bristl......45 H5
South Broomhill Nthumb......191 K6
Southburgh Norfk......105 K2
South Burlingham Norfk......107 K2
Southburn E R Yk......152 F5
South Cadbury Somset......31 K5
South Carlton Lincs......135 J4
South Carlton Notts......134 B3
South Cave E R Yk......144 A2
South Cerney Gloucs......64 F7
South Chailey E Susx......22 F4
South Chard Somset......15 H2
South Charlton Nthumb......191 H2
South Cheriton Somset......32 B6
South Church Dur......169 G5
Southchurch Sthend......53 J2
South Cleatlam Dur......168 E7
South Cliffe E R Yk......152 D8
South Clifton Notts......135 G5
South Cockerington Lincs......137 G2
South Cornelly Brdgnd......42 B5
Southcott Cnwll......11 H3
Southcott Devon......12 D4
Southcott Devon......13 H6
Southcott Devon......27 H7
Southcott Wilts......47 H7
Southcourt Bucks......67 K5
South Cove Suffk......107 K7
South Creake Norfk......121 J4
South Crosland Kirk......141 H5
South Croxton Leics......100 F2
South Dalton E R Yk......152 E6
South Darenth Kent......52 C5
South Dell W Isls......282 g1
South Duffield N York......143 H1
South Earlswood Surrey......37 L1
Southease E Susx......23 G6
South Elkington Lincs......136 E2
South Elmsall Wakefd......142 D5
Southend Ag & B......192 E6
Southend E R Yk......145 K4
South End Hants......33 J7
South End Herefs......81 G6
South End N Linc......144 E4
South End Norfk......105 K5
Southend Wilts......47 J4
Southend Crematorium
   Sthend......53 J2
Southend-on-Sea Sthend......53 J2
Southernby Cumb......165 L3
Southernden Kent......39 L4
Southerndown V Glam......42 D7
Southerness D & G......176 C7
South Erradale Highld......260 B5
Southerton Devon......14 C4
Southery Norfk......104 C4
South Essex Crematorium
   Gt Lon......52 C2
South Fambridge Essex......72 B8
South Fawley W Berk......48 A3
South Ferriby N Linc......144 B4
South Field E R Yk......144 C3
Southfield Falk......209 M4
Southfleet Kent......52 D5
Southford IoW......19 J7
Southgate Gt Lon......69 J8
Southgate Norfk......120 E5
Southgate Norfk......121 J4
Southgate Norfk......122 C6
Southgate Swans......57 G7
South Godstone Surrey......38 A4
South Gorley Hants......18 B2
South Gosforth N u Ty......181 G5

South Green Essex......71 G8
South Green Essex......72 F3
South Green Kent......53 J7
South Green Norfk......105 L1
South Green Suffk......106 D8
South Gyle C Edin......211 G4
South Hanningfield Essex......71 H7
South Harting W Susx......20 C3
South Hayling Hants......20 B6
South Hazelrigg Nthumb......203 G6
South Heath Bucks......67 M6
South Heighton E Susx......23 G6
South Hetton Dur......169 K2
South Hiendley Wakefd......142 B5
South Hill Cnwll......11 L8
South Hill Somset......31 G5
South Hinksey Oxon......66 D6
South Hole Devon......26 C6
South Holmwood Surrey......37 J2
South Hornchurch Gt Lon......52 B2
South Horrington Somset......31 J2
South Huish Devon......7 K6
South Hykeham Lincs......135 J6
South Hylton Sundld......181 J7
Southill C Beds......86 C6
Southington Hants......35 G1
South Kelsey Lincs......144 D8
South Kessock Highld......251 H2
South Killingholme N Linc......144 F4
South Kilvington N York......160 F6
South Kilworth Leics......100 D7
South Kirkby Wakefd......142 C5
South Knighton Devon......13 J8
South Kyme Lincs......119 G2
South Lanarkshire
   Crematorium S Lans......209 H7
South Leicestershire
   Crematorium Leics......100 D4
Southleigh Devon......14 E4
South Leigh Oxon......66 B5
South Leverton Notts......134 F3
South Lincolnshire
   Crematorium Lincs......119 H6
South Littleton Worcs......82 C6
South London Crematorium
   Gt Lon......51 H5
South Lopham Norfk......105 L7
South Luffenham Rutlnd......101 K3
South Lynn Norfk......120 D7
South Malling E Susx......23 G5
South Marston Swindn......47 J2
South Merstham Surrey......51 H8
South Middleton Nthumb......190 E2
South Milford N York......142 D2
South Milton Devon......7 K6
South Mimms Herts......69 G6
Southminster Essex......72 D7
South Molton Devon......28 C5
South Moor Dur......180 F8
Southmoor Oxon......66 B7
South Moreton Oxon......48 E1
Southmuir Angus......234 B5
South Mundham W Susx......20 E6
South Muskham Notts......134 F8
South Newbald E R Yk......152 D8
South Newington Oxon......83 J8
South Newton Wilts......33 J4
South Normanton Derbys......133 J8
South Norwood Gt Lon......51 J5
South Nutfield Surrey......37 M1
South Ockendon Thurr......52 D2
Southoe Cambs......86 D2
Southolt Suffk......90 E2
South Ormsby Lincs......137 G4
Southorpe C Pete......102 B3
South Ossett Wakefd......141 L4
South Otterington N York......160 E5
Southover Dorset......16 B4
Southover E Susx......24 B2
South Owersby Lincs......135 L1
Southowram Calder......141 H3
South Oxfordshire
   Crematorium Oxon......66 B8
South Park Surrey......37 K1
South Perrott Dorset......15 L1
South Petherton Somset......31 G7
South Petherwin Cnwll......11 K6
South Pickenham Norfk......105 G3
South Pill Cnwll......6 E3
South Pool Devon......7 M6
South Poorton Dorset......15 M3
Southport Sefton......138 D4
Southport Crematorium Lancs......138 D5
South Queensferry C Edin......210 F3
South Radworthy Devon......28 C4
South Rauceby Lincs......118 D2
South Raynham Norfk......121 J6
South Reddish Stockp......131 H1
Southrepps Norfk......122 E4

South Reston Lincs......137 G3
Southrey Lincs......136 B6
South Ronaldsay Ork......275 c6
Southrop Gloucs......65 J6
Southrope Hants......35 K2
South Runcton Norfk......104 C2
South Scarle Notts......135 G7
Southsea C Port......19 L4
Southsea Wrexhm......112 D1
South Shian Ag & B......228 E7
South Shields S Tyne......181 J5
South Shields Crematorium
   S Tyne......181 J6
South Shore Bpool......138 C1
Southside Dur......168 E5
South Somercotes Lincs......137 H1
South Stainley N York......150 D3
South Stifford Thurr......52 D3
South Stoke BaNES......45 L6
South Stoke Oxon......48 F2
South Stoke W Susx......21 H5
South Stour Kent......40 D7
South Street Kent......40 D4
South Street Kent......40 F2
South Street Kent......52 D6
South Tarbrax S Lans......199 H3
South Tawton Devon......12 F4
South Tehidy Cnwll......3 G3
South Thoresby Lincs......137 G4
South Thorpe Dur......168 E7
South Town Hants......35 K4
Southtown Norfk......107 L2
Southtown Somset......30 D7
South Uist W Isls......283 c10
Southwaite Cumb......166 B2
South Walsham Norfk......107 H1
Southwark Gt Lon......51 J3
South Warnborough Hants......35 L2
Southwater W Susx......37 J5
Southwater Street W Susx......37 H5
Southway Somset......31 H2
South Weald Essex......70 E8
Southwell Dorset......16 D8
Southwell Notts......117 J1
South West Middlesex
   Crematorium Gt Lon......50 E4
South Weston Oxon......67 H7
South Wheatley Cnwll......11 J4
South Wheatley Notts......134 F3
Southwick Hants......19 L2
Southwick Nhants......101 M5
Southwick Somset......30 E2
Southwick Sundld......181 J7
Southwick W Susx......22 C6
Southwick Wilts......46 B7
South Widcombe BaNES......45 H7
South Wigston Leics......100 D4
South Willesborough Kent......40 D7
South Willingham Lincs......136 C3
South Wingate Dur......169 L4
South Wingfield Derbys......133 G8
South Witham Lincs......118 B7
Southwold Suffk......107 K8
South Wonston Hants......34 F4
Southwood Norfk......107 H2
Southwood Somset......31 J4
South Woodham Ferrers
   Essex......71 K7
South Wootton Norfk......120 E7
South Wraxall Wilts......46 B6
South Zeal Devon......12 F4
Sovereign Harbour E Susx......23 L6
Sowerby Calder......141 G3
Sowerby N York......160 F6
Sowerby Bridge Calder......141 G3
Sowerby Row Cumb......165 L3
Sower Carr Lancs......147 G7
Sowerhill Somset......28 F6
Sowhill Torfn......62 B7
Sowley Green Suffk......88 D5
Sowood Calder......141 G4
Sowton Devon......6 F2
Sowton Devon......14 A4
Soyland Town Calder......140 F4
Spa Common Norfk......122 F5
Spain's End Essex......88 D7
Spalding Lincs......119 H7
Spaldington E R Yk......143 J1
Spaldwick Cambs......86 C1
Spalford Notts......135 G6
Spanby Lincs......118 E4
Spanish Green Hants......49 G7
Sparham Norfk......122 B7
Sparhamill Norfk......122 B7
Spark Bridge Cumb......156 C6
Sparket Cumb......166 B5
Sparkford Somset......31 K5
Sparkhill Birm......98 E6
Sparkwell Devon......7 H3

Sparrow Green Norfk	121	L8
Sparrowpit Derbys	132	B4
Sparrows Green E Susx	39	G6
Sparsholt Hants	34	F4
Sparsholt Oxon	47	M2
Spartylea Nthumb	167	K1
Spath Staffs	115	H4
Spaunton N York	162	C5
Spaxton Somset	30	C3
Spean Bridge Highld	239	L7
Spear Hill W Susx	21	K3
Spearywell Hants	34	D5
Speen Bucks	67	K7
Speen W Berk	48	C3
Speeton N York	163	L7
Speke Lpool	129	K3
Speldhurst Kent	38	E5
Spellbrook Herts	70	C4
Spelmonden Kent	39	H6
Spelsbury Oxon	65	M3
Spen Kirk	141	K3
Spencers Wood Wokham	49	H5
Spen Green Ches E	130	F7
Spennithorne N York	159	L5
Spennymoor Dur	169	H4
Spernall Warwks	82	C3
Spetchley Worcs	81	K4
Spetisbury Dorset	17	H2
Spexhall Suffk	107	H7
Spey Bay Moray	267	J2
Speybridge Highld	253	K6
Speyview Moray	254	E3
Spilsby Lincs	137	G6
Spindlestone Nthumb	203	J6
Spinkhill Derbys	133	J4
Spinningdale Highld	263	J2
Spion Kop Notts	133	L6
Spirthill Wilts	46	E4
Spital Wirral	129	H3
Spital Hill Donc	134	C1
Spital in the Street Lincs	135	K2
Spithurst E Susx	23	G4
Spittal E Loth	212	A4
Spittal E R Yk	152	B5
Spittal Highld	279	L5
Spittal Nthumb	202	F3
Spittal Pembks	55	G2
Spittalfield P & K	233	H7
Spittal of Glenmuick Abers	243	K6
Spittal of Glenshee P & K	233	H7
Spittal-on-Rule Border	189	G2
Spixworth Norfk	122	E8
Splatt Cnwll	10	C7
Splatt Cnwll	11	J5
Splatt Devon	12	E2
Splayne's Green E Susx	23	G2
Splottlands Cardif	43	K6
Spofforth N York	150	E5
Spondon C Derb	116	C4
Spon Green Flints	129	G7
Spooner Row Norfk	106	B4
Sporle Norfk	105	G1
Spott E Loth	212	E4
Spottiswoode Border	201	J3
Spratton Nhants	84	D1
Spreakley Surrey	36	B3
Spreyton Devon	13	G5
Spriddlestone Devon	7	G4
Spridlington Lincs	135	K3
Springburn C Glas	209	G5
Springfield D & G	177	K5
Springfield Essex	71	H5
Springfield Fife	222	F5
Springhill Staffs	98	B3
Springhill Staffs	98	D2
Springholm D & G	175	K1
Springside N Ayrs	196	D3
Springthorpe Lincs	135	H2
Spring Vale Barns	141	L7
Springwell Sundld	181	G7
Springwood Crematorium Lpool	129	K3
Sproatley E R Yk	145	F1
Sproston Green Ches W	130	E6
Sprotbrough Donc	142	E7
Sproughton Suffk	90	D6
Sprouston Border	202	B6
Sprowston Norfk	106	E1
Sproxton Leics	117	M6
Sproxton N York	161	K6
Spunhill Shrops	112	F5
Spurstow Ches E	130	A8
Spyway Dorset	15	M4
Square & Compass Pembks	74	D6
Stableford Shrops	97	G4
Stableford Staffs	114	C4
Stacey Bank Sheff	132	F2
Stackhouse N York	148	E3
Stackpole Pembks	55	G7
Stackpole Elidor Pembks	55	G7
Stacksford Norfk	105	L5
Stacksteads Lancs	140	C3
Staddiscombe C Plym	7	G4
Staddlethorpe E R Yk	143	L2
Staden Derbys	131	L5
Stadhampton Oxon	66	F7
Stadhlaigearraidh W Isls	283	b10
Staffield Cumb	166	D2
Staffin Highld	259	H3
Stafford Staffs	114	E7
Stafford Crematorium Staffs	114	E6
Stagsden Bed	85	J5
Stainborough Barns	141	M4
Stainburn Cumb	164	D5
Stainburn N York	150	C6
Stainby Lincs	118	B7
Staincross Barns	141	M5
Staindrop Dur	168	E6
Staines-upon-Thames Surrey	50	D5
Stainfield Lincs	118	E6
Stainfield Lincs	136	B5
Stainforth Donc	143	G5
Stainforth N York	148	E2
Staining Lancs	147	G8
Stainland Calder	141	G4
Stainsacre N York	163	G1
Stainsby Derbys	133	J6
Stainton Cumb	157	H5
Stainton Cumb	166	C5
Stainton Cumb	177	L7
Stainton Donc	133	L1
Stainton Dur	168	D7
Stainton Middsb	170	B4
Stainton N York	159	K3
Stainton by Langworth Lincs	135	L4
Staintondale N York	163	H3
Stainton le Vale Lincs	136	C1
Stainton with Adgarley Cumb	146	E1
Stair Cumb	165	H6
Stair E Ayrs	196	E6
Stairfoot Barns	142	B6
Stairhaven D & G	172	F4
Staithes N York	171	H7
Stakeford Nthumb	181	G2
Stake Pool Lancs	147	H6
Stakes Hants	19	M2
Stalbridge Dorset	32	B7
Stalbridge Weston Dorset	32	B7
Stalham Norfk	123	H6
Stalham Green Norfk	123	H6
Stalisfield Green Kent	40	B5
Stalland Common Norfk	105	L4
Stallen Dorset	31	K7
Stallingborough NE Lin	145	G5
Stalling Busk N York	159	G5
Stallington Staffs	114	E4
Stalmine Lancs	147	G6
Stalmine Moss Side Lancs	147	G6
Stalybridge Tamesd	140	E8
Stambourne Essex	88	E7
Stambourne Green Essex	88	D7
Stamford Lincs	102	A2
Stamford Nthumb	191	J2
Stamford Bridge Ches W	129	L6
Stamford Bridge E R Yk	151	M5
Stamfordham Nthumb	180	C4
Stamford Hill Gt Lon	51	J2
Stanah Lancs	147	G7
Stanborough Herts	69	G5
Stanbridge C Beds	68	B2
Stanbridge Dorset	17	K2
Stanbury C Brad	149	H8
Stand Bury	140	B6
Stand N Lans	209	K5
Standburn Falk	210	B4
Standeford Staffs	97	K2
Standen Kent	39	L5
Standen Street Kent	39	K7
Standerwick Somset	32	D1
Standford Hants	36	B4
Standingstone Cumb	164	D4
Standish Gloucs	64	A5
Standish Wigan	139	H5
Standish Lower Ground Wigan	139	H6
Standlake Oxon	66	B6
Standon Hants	34	F5
Standon Herts	69	K3
Standon Staffs	114	C4
Standon Green End Herts	69	K3
Standwell Green Suffk	90	D1
Stane N Lans	210	A7
Stanfield Norfk	121	K7
Stanford C Beds	86	D7
Stanford Kent	40	F7
Stanford Shrops	95	H1
Stanford Bishop Herefs	80	F5
Stanford Bridge Worcs	81	G2
Stanford Bridge Wrekin	113	M6
Stanford Dingley W Berk	48	E4
Stanford in the Vale Oxon	65	M8
Stanford le Hope Thurr	52	E3
Stanford on Avon Nhants	100	D7
Stanford on Soar Notts	116	F7
Stanford on Teme Worcs	81	G2
Stanford Rivers Essex	70	D7
Stanfree Derbys	133	J5
Stanghow R & Cl	170	F7
Stanground C Pete	102	D4
Stanhill Lancs	139	L2
Stanhoe Norfk	121	H4
Stanhope Border	199	K7
Stanhope Dur	168	C3
Stanhope Kent	40	C7
Stanhope Bretby Derbys	116	A7
Stanion Nhants	101	K6
Stanklin Worcs	97	J8
Stanley Derbys	116	C3
Stanley Dur	180	F8
Stanley Notts	133	J7
Stanley P & K	221	K1
Stanley Shrops	97	G6
Stanley Staffs	114	E1
Stanley Wakefd	142	A3
Stanley Common Derbys	116	C3
Stanley Crook Dur	168	F3
Stanley Ferry Wakefd	142	A3
Stanley Gate Lancs	138	F6
Stanley Moor Staffs	114	E1
Stanley Pontlarge Gloucs	64	E1
Stanmer Br & H	22	E5
Stanmore Gt Lon	68	F8
Stanmore Hants	34	F5
Stanmore W Berk	48	C3
Stannersburn Nthumb	179	G2
Stanningfield Suffk	89	H4
Stanningley Leeds	141	K1
Stannington Nthumb	180	F3
Stannington Sheff	132	F2
Stannington Station Nthumb	180	F3
Stansbatch Herefs	79	L3
Stansfield Suffk	88	F5
Stanshope Staffs	115	J1
Stanstead Suffk	89	G5
Stanstead Abbotts Herts	69	K5
Stansted Kent	52	D6
Stansted Mountfitchet Essex	70	D2
Stanton Derbys	115	M7
Stanton Gloucs	82	C8
Stanton Mons	62	C3
Stanton Nthumb	191	G8
Stanton Staffs	115	J2
Stanton Suffk	105	K8
Stanton by Bridge Derbys	116	B6
Stanton by Dale Derbys	116	D4
Stanton Drew BaNES	45	H6
Stanton Fitzwarren Swindn	47	J1
Stanton Harcourt Oxon	66	B6
Stanton Hill Notts	133	J7
Stanton in Peak Derbys	132	E6
Stanton Lacy Shrops	96	B7
Stanton Lees Derbys	132	E7
Stanton Long Shrops	96	D5
Stanton-on-the-Wolds Notts	117	G5
Stanton Prior BaNES	45	K6
Stanton St Bernard Wilts	47	G6
Stanton St John Oxon	66	E5
Stanton St Quintin Wilts	46	C3
Stanton Street Suffk	89	J2
Stanton under Bardon Leics	100	A1
Stanton upon Hine Heath Shrops	113	J6
Stanton Wick BaNES	45	J6
Stantway Gloucs	63	L4
Stanwardine in the Field Shrops	112	F6
Stanwardine in the Wood Shrops	113	G6
Stanway Essex	72	D2
Stanway Gloucs	64	F1
Stanway Green Essex	72	D2
Stanway Green Suffk	90	F1
Stanwell Surrey	50	D4
Stanwell Moor Surrey	50	D4
Stanwick Nhants	85	J2
Stanwick St John N York	168	F8
Stanwix Cumb	177	L7
Staoinebrig W Isls	283	b10
Stape N York	162	D4
Stapehill Dorset	17	L3
Stapeley Ches E	113	L2
Stapenhill Staffs	115	L7
Staple Kent	41	J4
Staple Cross Devon	29	J6
Staplecross E Susx	24	E3
Staplefield W Susx	37	L5
Staple Fitzpaine Somset	30	C7
Stapleford Cambs	87	K5
Stapleford Herts	69	J4
Stapleford Leics	117	L7
Stapleford Lincs	135	H8
Stapleford Notts	116	E4
Stapleford Wilts	33	J3
Stapleford Abbotts Essex	70	D8
Stapleford Tawney Essex	70	D7
Staplegrove Somset	30	B5
Staplehay Somset	30	B6
Staple Hill Worcs	98	B8
Staplehurst Kent	39	K5
Staplers IoW	19	H6
Staplestreet Kent	40	D3
Stapleton Cumb	178	C4
Stapleton Herefs	79	L3
Stapleton Leics	99	L4
Stapleton N York	169	H8
Stapleton Shrops	95	L3
Stapleton Somset	31	G6
Stapley Somset	30	B8
Staploe Bed	86	C3
Staplow Herefs	80	F7
Star Fife	222	E6
Star IoA	125	J5
Star Pembks	75	M5
Star Somset	44	E7
Starbeck N York	150	E4
Starbotton N York	159	G7
Starcross Devon	14	A6
Stareton Warwks	83	H1
Starkholmes Derbys	132	F7
Starlings Green Essex	70	C1
Starr's Green E Susx	24	D4
Starston Norfk	106	E6
Start Devon	8	B7
Startforth Dur	168	D7
Startley Wilts	46	D3
Statenborough Kent	41	J4
Statham Warrtn	130	D2
Stathe Somset	30	E5
Stathern Leics	117	K5
Station Town Dur	169	L3
Staughton Green Cambs	86	C2
Staughton Highway Cambs	86	C2
Staunton Gloucs	63	H4
Staunton Gloucs	64	A1
Staunton in the Vale Notts	117	L3
Staunton on Arrow Herefs	79	L3
Staunton on Wye Herefs	79	L6
Staveley Cumb	157	G3
Staveley Derbys	133	H5
Staveley N York	150	E3
Staveley-in-Cartmel Cumb	156	E5
Staverton Devon	8	B2
Staverton Gloucs	64	C2
Staverton Nhants	83	M3
Staverton Wilts	46	B6
Staverton Bridge Gloucs	64	C3
Stawell Somset	30	E4
Stawley Somset	29	J6
Staxigoe Highld	280	E5
Staxton N York	163	J6
Staylittle Cerdgn	92	E5
Staylittle Powys	93	J5
Staynall Lancs	147	G7
Staythorpe Notts	117	K1
Stead C Brad	149	L6
Stean N York	159	K8
Stearsby N York	151	K2
Steart Somset	30	C2
Stebbing Essex	71	G2
Stebbing Green Essex	71	G2
Stechford Birm	98	E6
Stede Quarter Kent	39	L5
Stedham W Susx	36	C6
Steel Nthumb	179	L7
Steel Cross E Susx	38	E7
Steelend Fife	210	D1
Steele Road Border	188	F7
Steel Green Cumb	155	L6
Steel Heath Shrops	113	J4
Steen's Bridge Herefs	80	C4
Steep Hants	35	M6
Steephill IoW	19	J8
Steep Lane Calder	140	F3
Steeple Dorset	17	H6
Steeple Essex	72	D6
Steeple Ashton Wilts	46	C7
Steeple Aston Oxon	66	C2
Steeple Barton Oxon	66	C2
Steeple Bumpstead Essex	88	D7
Steeple Claydon Bucks	67	H2
Steeple Gidding Cambs	102	C7
Steeple Langford Wilts	33	H3
Steeple Morden Cambs	86	F6
Steep Marsh Hants	35	M5
Steeton C Brad	149	J7
Stein Highld	258	D5
Stella Gatesd	180	E6

Stelling Minnis Kent........40 F6
Stembridge Somset........30 F6
Stenalees Cnwll........5 G3
Stenhouse D & G........185 K4
Stenhousemuir Falk........210 A2
Stenigot Lincs........136 D3
Stenscholl Highld........259 H3
Stenson Fields Derbys........116 B5
Stenton E Loth........212 D4
Steornabhagh W Isls........282 g3
Stepaside Pembks........55 K5
Stepford D & G........185 L6
Stepney Gt Lon........51 K3
Stepping Hill Stockp........131 H2
Steppingley C Beds........85 K8
Stepps N Lans........209 H5
Sternfield Suffk........91 J3
Stert Wilts........46 F7
Stetchworth Cambs........88 C3
Stevenage Herts........69 G2
Steven's Crouch E Susx........24 C4
Stevenston N Ayrs........196 B3
Steventon Hants........35 H1
Steventon Oxon........48 C1
Steventon End Essex........88 B6
Stevington Bed........85 K4
Stewartby Bed........85 K6
Stewartfield S Lans........209 G7
Stewarton Ag & B........192 E4
Stewarton E Ayrs........196 E2
Stewkley Bucks........67 K2
Stewley Somset........30 D7
Stewton Lincs........137 G2
Steyne Cross IoW........19 L6
Steyning W Susx........21 L4
Steynton Pembks........54 E5
Stibb Cnwll........26 C8
Stibbard Norfk........121 L6
Stibb Cross Devon........27 G7
Stibb Green Wilts........47 J6
Stibbington Cambs........102 B4
Stichill Border........201 L5
Sticker Cnwll........5 G5
Stickford Lincs........136 F7
Sticklepath Devon........12 F4
Sticklepath Somset........29 J4
Stickling Green Essex........87 K8
Stickney Lincs........136 F8
Stiffkey Norfk........121 L3
Stifford Clays Thurr........52 D3
Stifford's Bridge Herefs........81 G5
Stiff Street Kent........53 J6
Stile Bridge Kent........39 J4
Stileway Somset........31 G3
Stilligarry W Isls........283 b10
Stillingfleet N York........151 J7
Stillington N York........151 J2
Stillington S on T........169 K6
Stilton Cambs........102 D5
Stinchcombe Gloucs........63 L7
Stinsford Dorset........16 D4
Stiperstones Shrops........95 J3
Stirchley Birm........98 D7
Stirchley Wrekin........96 F2
Stirling Abers........257 L3
Stirling Stirlg........220 D8
Stirtloe Cambs........86 D2
Stirton N York........149 H5
Stisted Essex........71 J2
Stitchcombe Wilts........47 K5
Stithians Cnwll........3 J4
Stivichall Covtry........99 J8
Stixwould Lincs........136 C6
St Michaels Fife........223 H3
Stoak Ches W........129 K5
Stobo Border........199 L5
Stoborough Dorset........17 H5
Stoborough Green Dorset........17 H5
Stobs Castle Border........188 E4
Stobswood Nthumb........191 J7
Stock Essex........71 G7
Stock N Som........44 F6
Stockbridge Hants........34 D4
Stockbriggs S Lans........198 C6
Stockbury Kent........53 H6
Stockcross W Berk........48 B5
Stockdalewath Cumb........165 L2
Stocker's Hill Kent........40 C5
Stockerston Leics........101 H4
Stock Green Worcs........82 A3
Stocking Herefs........63 J1
Stockingford Warwks........99 J5
Stocking Pelham Herts........70 C1
Stockland Devon........14 F2
Stockland Bristol Somset........30 C2
Stockland Green Kent........38 E5
Stockleigh English Devon........13 K2
Stockleigh Pomeroy Devon........13 K2
Stockley Wilts........46 E5

Stockley Hill Herefs........79 L7
Stocklinch Somset........30 F7
Stockmoor Herefs........79 M4
Stockport Stockp........131 H2
Stockport Crematorium
    Stockp........131 H2
Stocksbridge Sheff........141 L8
Stocksfield Nthumb........180 C6
Stockton Herefs........80 C3
Stockton Norfk........107 H4
Stockton Shrops........95 G3
Stockton Shrops........97 G3
Stockton Warwks........83 K3
Stockton Wilts........33 G3
Stockton Wrekin........114 B8
Stockton Brook Staffs........114 E1
Stockton Heath Warrtn........130 B3
Stockton-on-Tees S on T........170 B6
Stockton on Teme Worcs........81 G2
Stockton on the Forest C York........151 L4
Stockwell Gloucs........64 D4
Stockwell End Wolves........97 K3
Stockwell Heath Staffs........115 G7
Stockwood Bristl........45 J5
Stockwood Dorset........16 B1
Stock Wood Worcs........82 B3
Stodday Lancs........147 J4
Stodmarsh Kent........41 H3
Stody Norfk........122 B4
Stoer Highld........270 D2
Stoford Somset........31 J4
Stoford Wilts........33 J4
Stogumber Somset........29 K3
Stogursey Somset........30 B2
Stoke Covtry........99 K7
Stoke Devon........26 D6
Stoke Hants........20 B6
Stoke Hants........48 B8
Stoke Medway........53 H4
Stoke Abbott Dorset........15 K3
Stoke Albany Nhants........101 H5
Stoke Ash Suffk........90 D1
Stoke Bardolph Notts........117 H4
Stoke Bliss Worcs........80 F3
Stoke Bruerne Nhants........84 E5
Stoke-by-Clare Suffk........88 E6
Stoke-by-Nayland Suffk........89 K7
Stoke Canon Devon........13 L3
Stoke Charity Hants........35 G3
Stoke Climsland Cnwll........11 L7
Stoke Cross Herefs........80 E5
Stoke D'Abernon Surrey........50 E7
Stoke Doyle Nhants........102 A6
Stoke Dry Rutlnd........101 J4
Stoke Edith Herefs........80 E7
Stoke End Warwks........98 F4
Stoke Farthing Wilts........33 H5
Stoke Ferry Norfk........104 D3
Stoke Fleming Devon........8 C5
Stokeford Dorset........17 G5
Stoke Gabriel Devon........8 C3
Stoke Gifford S Glos........45 J3
Stoke Golding Leics........99 L4
Stoke Goldington M Keyn........85 G5
Stoke Green Bucks........50 B3
Stokeham Notts........134 F4
Stoke Hammond Bucks........67 L1
Stoke Heath Shrops........113 L5
Stoke Heath Worcs........81 L2
Stoke Holy Cross Norfk........106 E3
Stokeinteignhead Devon........13 L8
Stoke Lacy Herefs........80 E5
Stoke Lyne Oxon........66 E2
Stoke Mandeville Bucks........67 K5
Stokenchurch Bucks........67 J7
Stoke Newington Gt Lon........51 J2
Stokenham Devon........8 B6
Stoke-on-Trent C Stke........114 D2
Stoke Orchard Gloucs........64 D2
Stoke Poges Bucks........50 B2
Stoke Pound Worcs........81 M2
Stoke Prior Herefs........80 C4
Stoke Prior Worcs........81 L2
Stoke Rivers Devon........27 L4
Stoke Rochford Lincs........118 B6
Stoke Row Oxon........49 G2
Stoke St Gregory Somset........30 E5
Stoke St Mary Somset........30 C6
Stoke St Michael Somset........31 L2
Stoke St Milborough Shrops........96 D7
Stokesay Shrops........95 M4
Stokesby Norfk........107 J1
Stokesley N York........161 H1
Stoke sub Hamdon Somset........31 G7
Stoke Talmage Oxon........67 G2
Stoke Trister Somset........32 B5
Stoke upon Tern Shrops........113 L6
Stoke-upon-Trent C Stke........114 D3
Stoke Wake Dorset........16 E1

Stoke Wharf Worcs........81 L2
Stolford Somset........30 C2
Stondon Massey Essex........70 E7
Stone Bucks........67 J4
Stone Gloucs........63 K8
Stone Kent........52 C4
Stone Rothm........133 L2
Stone Somset........31 J4
Stone Staffs........114 E5
Stone Worcs........97 J8
Stonea Cambs........103 J5
Stone Allerton Somset........30 F1
Ston Easton Somset........45 J8
Stonebridge N Som........44 D7
Stonebridge Norfk........105 J3
Stonebridge Warwks........99 G6
Stone Bridge Corner C Pete........102 F3
Stonebroom Derbys........133 H7
Stone Chair Calder........141 H2
Stone Cross E Susx........23 K6
Stone Cross E Susx........38 D7
Stone Cross E Susx........39 G7
Stone Cross Kent........38 E5
Stone Cross Kent........40 D7
Stone Cross Kent........41 K4
Stonecross Green Suffk........89 G4
Stonecrouch Kent........39 H6
Stone-edge-Batch N Som........44 F4
Stoneferry C KuH........144 E2
Stonefield Castle Hotel Ag & B........206 D5
Stonegate E Susx........39 G7
Stonegate N York........162 D1
Stonegrave N York........161 L7
Stonehall Worcs........81 K5
Stonehaugh Nthumb........179 J4
Stonehaven Abers........245 J6
Stone Hill Donc........143 H6
Stonehouse C Plym........6 F4
Stone House Cumb........158 D5
Stonehouse Gloucs........64 A6
Stonehouse Nthumb........179 G7
Stonehouse S Lans........198 C4
Stone in Oxney Kent........25 M2
Stoneleigh Warwks........83 H1
Stoneley Green Ches E........113 K1
Stonely Cambs........86 C2
Stoner Hill Hants........35 M5
Stonesby Leics........117 L6
Stonesfield Oxon........66 B4
Stones Green Essex........73 H2
Stone Street Kent........38 F2
Stone Street Suffk........89 K6
Stone Street Suffk........89 K7
Stone Street Suffk........107 H7
Stonestreet Green Kent........40 E7
Stonethwaite Cumb........165 J7
Stonewells Moray........266 F3
Stonewood Kent........52 D4
Stoneybridge W Isls........283 b10
Stoneybridge Worcs........97 L8
Stoneyburn W Loth........210 C6
Stoney Cross Hants........18 D1
Stoneygate C Leic........100 D3
Stoneyhills Essex........72 D7
Stoneykirk D & G........172 D4
Stoney Middleton Derbys........132 E4
Stoney Stanton Leics........100 B4
Stoney Stoke Somset........32 B4
Stoney Stratton Somset........31 L3
Stoney Stretton Shrops........95 J2
Stoneywood C Aber........245 K1
Stoneywood Falk........209 L2
Stonham Aspal Suffk........90 D3
Stonnall Staffs........98 D3
Stonor Oxon........49 H1
Stonton Wyville Leics........101 G4
Stony Cross Herefs........80 D2
Stony Cross Herefs........81 G5
Stonyford Hants........34 D7
Stony Houghton Derbys........133 K6
Stony Stratford M Keyn........84 F7
Stonywell Staffs........98 D1
Stoodleigh Devon........28 B4
Stoodleigh Devon........29 G7
Stopham W Susx........21 H3
Stopsley Luton........68 E2
Stoptide Cnwll........10 C7
Storeton Wirral........129 G3
Storeyard Green Herefs........81 G6
Storey Arms Powys........60 E3
Stornoway W Isls........282 g3
Storridge Herefs........81 H5
Storrington W Susx........21 J4
Storth Cumb........157 G2
Storwood E R Yk........151 M7
Stotfield Moray........266 E2
Stotfold C Beds........86 E7
Stottesdon Shrops........96 F6
Stoughton Leics........100 E3

Stoughton Surrey........50 C8
Stoughton W Susx........20 C4
Stoulton Worcs........81 L5
Stourbridge Dudley........97 K6
Stourbridge Crematorium
    Dudley........97 K6
Stourpaine Dorset........17 G1
Stourport-on-Severn Worcs........81 J1
Stour Provost Dorset........32 C6
Stour Row Dorset........32 D6
Stourton Leeds........141 M2
Stourton Staffs........97 K6
Stourton Warwks........83 G7
Stourton Wilts........32 C4
Stourton Caundle Dorset........32 B7
Stout Somset........31 G4
Stove Shet........281 e8
Stoven Suffk........107 J7
Stow Border........200 F4
Stow Lincs........135 H3
Stow Bardolph Norfk........104 C2
Stow Bedon Norfk........105 J4
Stowbridge Norfk........104 B2
Stow-cum-Quy Cambs........87 L3
Stowe Gloucs........63 H5
Stowe Shrops........95 H8
Stowe by Chartley Staffs........114 F6
Stowehill Nhants........84 C3
Stowell Somset........31 L6
Stowey BaNES........45 H7
Stowford Devon........12 B3
Stowford Devon........12 B5
Stowford Devon........14 D5
Stowford Devon........28 B3
Stowlangtoft Suffk........89 J2
Stow Longa Cambs........86 C1
Stow Maries Essex........71 K7
Stowmarket Suffk........90 B3
Stow-on-the-Wold Gloucs........65 J2
Stowting Kent........41 F7
Stowting Common Kent........40 F6
Stowupland Suffk........90 C3
Straanruie Highld........253 J8
Strachan Abers........244 F5
Strachur Ag & B........217 H7
Stradbroke Suffk........106 E8
Stradbrook Wilts........46 D3
Stradishall Suffk........88 E5
Stradsett Norfk........104 D2
Stragglethorpe Lincs........118 B1
Stragglethorpe Notts........117 H4
Straight Soley Wilts........47 L4
Straiton Mdloth........211 J5
Straiton S Ayrs........183 K2
Straloch Abers........256 F7
Straloch P & K........232 F3
Stramshall Staffs........115 H4
Strang IoM........154 e6
Strangeways Salfd........140 B7
Strangford Herefs........63 H2
Stranraer D & G........172 C3
Strata Florida Cerdgn........77 K2
Stratfield Mortimer W Berk........49 G6
Stratfield Saye Hants........49 G6
Stratfield Turgis Hants........49 M7
Stratford C Beds........86 D5
Stratford Gt Lon........51 K2
Stratford St Andrew Suffk........91 H3
Stratford St Mary Suffk........90 B8
Stratford sub Castle Wilts........33 K4
Stratford Tony Wilts........33 J5
Stratford-upon-Avon Warwks........82 F4
Strath Highld........260 C4
Strathan Highld........270 E4
Strathan Highld........277 K3
Strathaven S Lans........197 K2
Strathblane Stirlg........208 F3
Strathcanaird Highld........270 F7
Strathcarron Highld........248 F3
Strathcoil Ag & B........227 K6
Strathdon Abers........243 K1
Strathkinness Fife........223 H4
Strathloanhead W Loth........210 B4
Strathmashie House Highld........241 G5
Strathmiglo Fife........222 C5
Strathpeffer Highld........262 E8
Strathtay P & K........232 D4
Strathwhillan N Ayrs........195 G4
Strathy Highld........278 E3
Strathy Inn Highld........278 E3
Strathyre Stirlg........219 J4
Stratton Cnwll........11 J1
Stratton Dorset........16 C4
Stratton Gloucs........64 E6
Stratton Audley Oxon........66 F2
Stratton-on-the-Fosse
    Somset........31 L1
Stratton St Margaret Swindn........47 H2
Stratton St Michael Norfk........106 D4

Stratton Strawless Norfk 122 E7
Stream Somset 29 K3
Streat E Susx 22 E4
Streatham Gt Lon 51 J4
Streatley C Beds 68 D2
Streatley W Berk 48 E3
Street Devon 14 E5
Street Lancs 147 K5
Street N York 162 C2
Street Somset 31 H3
Street Ashton Warwks 99 M7
Street Dinas Shrops 112 E4
Street End E Susx 23 K3
Street End Kent 40 F4
Street End W Susx 20 D7
Street Gate Gatesd 180 F7
Streethay Staffs 98 F1
Street Houses N York 151 H6
Streetlam N York 160 D3
Street Lane Derbys 116 C2
Streetly Wsall 98 D4
Streetly Crematorium Wsall 98 D4
Streetly End Cambs 88 C5
Street on the Fosse Somset 31 K3
Strefford Shrops 95 K6
Strelitz P & K 233 J8
Strelley Notts 116 E3
Strensall C York 151 K4
Strensham Worcs 81 L7
Stretcholt Somset 30 D2
Strete Devon 8 C5
Stretford Herefs 80 B4
Stretford Herefs 80 C4
Stretford Traffd 130 F1
Strethall Essex 87 K7
Stretham Cambs 103 K8
Strettington W Susx 20 E5
Stretton Ches W 113 G1
Stretton Derbys 133 H7
Stretton Rutlnd 118 B8
Stretton Staffs 97 K1
Stretton Staffs 115 L6
Stretton Warrtn 130 C3
Stretton en le Field Leics 99 J1
Stretton Grandison Herefs 80 E6
Stretton-on-Dunsmore
    Warwks 83 J1
Stretton on Fosse Warwks 82 F7
Stretton Sugwas Herefs 80 B6
Stretton under Fosse Warwks 99 M7
Stretton Westwood Shrops 96 D4
Strichen Abers 269 H5
Strines Stockp 131 J2
Stringston Somset 30 B2
Strixton Nhants 85 H3
Stroat Gloucs 63 H7
Strollamus Highld 247 J3
Stroma Highld 280 E1
Stromeferry Highld 248 D5
Stromness Ork 275 b4
Stronaba Highld 239 L6
Stronachlachar Stirlg 218 F5
Stronafian Ag & B 207 G3
Stronchrubie Highld 271 H4
Strone Ag & B 207 K3
Strone Highld 239 J7
Strone Highld 250 F6
Stronmilchan Ag & B 217 J2
Stronsay Ork 275 e3
Strontian Highld 228 C3
Strood Kent 39 L7
Strood Medway 52 F5
Strood Green Surrey 37 J1
Strood Green W Susx 36 F6
Stroud Gloucs 64 B6
Stroud Hants 35 L6
Stroude Surrey 50 C5
Stroud Green Essex 53 J1
Stroud Green Gloucs 64 A5
Stroxton Lincs 118 B5
Struan Highld 246 D1
Struan P & K 232 B2
Strubby Lincs 137 H3
Strumpshaw Norfk 107 G2
Strutherhill S Lans 198 C3
Struthers Fife 222 F5
Struy Highld 250 C4
Stryd-y-Facsen IoA 124 F3
Stryt-issa Wrexhm 112 D2
Stuartfield Abers 257 H3
Stubbers Green Wsall 98 D3
Stubbington Hants 19 J3
Stubbins Lancs 140 B4
Stubbs Green Norfk 106 E4
Stubhampton Dorset 32 F8
Stubley Derbys 133 G4
Stubshaw Cross Wigan 139 H7
Stubton Lincs 118 A2
Stuckton Hants 33 L8

Studfold N York 148 E2
Stud Green W & M 49 L3
Studham C Beds 68 C4
Studholme Cumb 177 H7
Studland Dorset 17 K6
Studley Warwks 82 C2
Studley Wilts 46 D4
Studley Common Warwks 82 C2
Studley Roger N York 150 C2
Studley Royal N York 150 C2
Stuntney Cambs 103 L7
Stunts Green E Susx 23 K4
Sturbridge Staffs 114 C5
Sturgate Lincs 135 H2
Sturmer Essex 88 D6
Sturminster Common Dorset 32 C8
Sturminster Marshall Dorset 17 J3
Sturminster Newton Dorset 32 C8
Sturry Kent 41 G3
Sturton N Linc 144 B7
Sturton by Stow Lincs 135 H4
Sturton le Steeple Notts 134 F3
Stuston Suffk 106 C7
Stutton N York 151 G7
Stutton Suffk 90 D8
Styal Ches E 131 G3
Stydd Lancs 148 A8
Stynie Moray 267 G4
Styrrup Notts 134 C2
Succoth Ag & B 218 D6
Suckley Worcs 81 G5
Suckley Green Worcs 81 G4
Sudborough Nhants 101 L7
Sudbourne Suffk 91 J4
Sudbrook Lincs 118 C3
Sudbrook Mons 45 G2
Sudbrooke Lincs 135 L4
Sudbury Derbys 115 K5
Sudbury Gt Lon 50 F2
Sudbury Suffk 89 H7
Sudden Rochdl 140 C5
Sudgrove Gloucs 64 D5
Suffield N York 163 H4
Suffield Norfk 122 E5
Sugdon Wrekin 113 K8
Sugnall Staffs 114 B5
Sugwas Pool Herefs 80 B6
Suisnish Highld 247 J5
Sulby IoM 154 e3
Sulgrave Nhants 84 A6
Sulham W Berk 48 F4
Sulhamstead W Berk 48 F5
Sulhamstead Abbots W Berk 48 F5
Sulhamstead Bannister
    W Berk 48 F5
Sullington W Susx 21 J4
Sullom Shet 281 d4
Sullom Voe Shet 281 d4
Sully V Glam 43 J8
Summerbridge N York 150 B3
Summercourt Cnwll 4 E4
Summerfield Norfk 121 G4
Summerfield Worcs 97 J8
Summer Heath Bucks 49 H1
Summerhill Pembks 55 K5
Summerhill Staffs 98 D3
Summer Hill Wrexhm 112 D1
Summerhouse Darltn 169 G6
Summerlands Cumb 157 H5
Summerley Derbys 133 G4
Summersdale W Susx 20 D5
Summerseat Bury 140 B5
Summertown Oxon 66 D5
Summit Oldham 140 D6
Summit Rochdl 140 E4
Sunbiggin Cumb 157 L1
Sunbury-on-Thames Surrey 50 E5
Sundaywell D & G 185 K6
Sunderland Ag & B 204 C3
Sunderland Cumb 165 G4
Sunderland Lancs 147 H4
Sunderland Sundld 181 K7
Sunderland Bridge Dur 169 H3
Sunderland Crematorium
    Sundld 181 J7
Sundhope Border 200 D8
Sundon Park Luton 68 D2
Sundridge Kent 38 D2
Sunk Island E R Yk 145 H4
Sunningdale W & M 50 B5
Sunninghill W & M 50 B5
Sunningwell Oxon 66 D7
Sunniside Dur 168 F3
Sunniside Gatesd 180 F7
Sunny Brow Dur 169 G4
Sunnyhill C Derb 116 B5
Sunnyhurst Bl w D 139 K3
Sunnylaw Stirlg 220 D7
Sunnymead Oxon 66 D5

Sunton Wilts 47 K8
Surbiton Gt Lon 50 F5
Surfleet Lincs 119 H6
Surfleet Seas End Lincs 119 J6
Surlingham Norfk 107 G2
Surrex Essex 72 C3
Surrey & Sussex Crematorium
    W Susx 37 L3
Sustead Norfk 122 D4
Susworth Lincs 143 L7
Sutcombe Devon 26 F8
Sutcombemill Devon 26 F8
Suton Norfk 106 B4
Sutterby Lincs 137 G5
Sutterton Lincs 119 J4
Sutton C Beds 86 E5
Sutton C Pete 102 B4
Sutton Cambs 103 J7
Sutton Devon 7 K6
Sutton Devon 13 G2
Sutton Donc 142 E5
Sutton E Susx 23 H7
Sutton Gt Lon 51 H6
Sutton Kent 41 K5
Sutton N York 142 D3
Sutton Norfk 123 H6
Sutton Notts 117 K4
Sutton Oxon 66 B6
Sutton Pembks 54 E4
Sutton Shrops 96 C1
Sutton Shrops 97 G6
Sutton Shrops 112 E6
Sutton Shrops 113 L5
Sutton St Hel 129 M1
Sutton Staffs 114 B7
Sutton Suffk 91 G6
Sutton W Susx 21 G4
Sutton Abinger Surrey 37 H2
Sutton-at-Hone Kent 52 C5
Sutton Bassett Nhants 101 G5
Sutton Benger Wilts 46 D3
Sutton Bingham Somset 31 J8
Sutton Bonington Notts 116 E6
Sutton Bridge Lincs 120 B7
Sutton Cheney Leics 99 L3
Sutton Coldfield Birm 98 E4
Sutton Coldfield
    Crematorium Birm 98 F4
Sutton Courtenay Oxon 66 D8
Sutton Crosses Lincs 119 M7
Sutton cum Lound Notts 134 D3
Sutton Fields Notts 116 E6
Sutton Green Surrey 50 C8
Sutton Green Wrexhm 112 F2
Sutton Howgrave N York 160 D6
Sutton-in-Ashfield Notts 133 K7
Sutton-in-Craven N York 149 H7
Sutton in the Elms Leics 100 B4
Sutton Lane Ends Ches E 131 H5
Sutton Maddock Shrops 97 G3
Sutton Mallet Somset 30 E3
Sutton Mandeville Wilts 33 G5
Sutton Manor St Hel 129 L2
Sutton Marsh Herefs 80 D6
Sutton Montis Somset 31 K6
Sutton-on-Hull C KuH 144 E1
Sutton on Sea Lincs 137 K3
Sutton-on-the-Forest N York 151 J3
Sutton on the Hill Derbys 115 L5
Sutton on Trent Notts 134 F6
Sutton Poyntz Dorset 16 D6
Sutton St Edmund Lincs 103 H1
Sutton St James Lincs 119 L7
Sutton St Nicholas Herefs 80 C6
Sutton Scotney Hants 34 F3
Sutton Street Kent 39 K2
Sutton-under-Brailes Warwks 83 G7
Sutton-under-
    Whitestonecliffe N York 161 G6
Sutton upon Derwent E R Yk 151 L6
Sutton Valence Kent 39 K3
Sutton Veny Wilts 32 E3
Sutton Waldron Dorset 32 E7
Sutton Weaver Ches W 130 A4
Sutton Wick BaNES 45 H7
Sutton Wick Oxon 66 C8
Swaby Lincs 137 G4
Swadlincote Derbys 116 A7
Swaffham Norfk 105 G2
Swaffham Bulbeck Cambs 87 L3
Swaffham Prior Cambs 88 B2
Swafield Norfk 122 F5
Swainby N York 161 G2
Swainshill Herefs 80 B7
Swainsthorpe Norfk 106 E3
Swainswick BaNES 45 M5
Swalcliffe Oxon 83 J7
Swalecliffe Kent 40 F2
Swallow Lincs 144 F7

Swallow Beck Lincs 135 J6
Swallowcliffe Wilts 33 G5
Swallowfield Wokham 49 J6
Swallownest Rothm 133 J3
Swallows Cross Essex 70 F7
Swampton Hants 34 E1
Swanage Dorset 17 K6
Swanbourne Bucks 67 K2
Swanbridge V Glam 43 J8
Swancote Shrops 97 G4
Swan Green Ches W 130 E6
Swanland E R Yk 144 C2
Swanley Kent 52 B5
Swanley Village Kent 52 B5
Swanmore Hants 35 J4
Swannington Leics 116 C8
Swannington Norfk 122 C7
Swanpool Lincs 135 J6
Swanscombe Kent 52 D4
Swansea Swans 57 J6
Swansea Crematorium Swans 57 J5
Swan Street Essex 72 C2
Swanton Abbot Norfk 122 F6
Swanton Morley Norfk 121 M8
Swanton Novers Norfk 121 M5
Swanton Street Kent 53 J7
Swan Valley Nhants 84 D4
Swan Village Sandw 98 C5
Swanwick Derbys 116 C1
Swanwick Hants 19 H2
Swarby Lincs 118 D3
Swardeston Norfk 106 D3
Swarkestone Derbys 116 B6
Swarland Nthumb 191 H5
Swarraton Hants 35 H3
Swartha C Brad 149 J6
Swarthmoor Cumb 156 C7
Swaton Lincs 118 F4
Swavesey Cambs 87 G2
Sway Hants 18 D4
Swayfield Lincs 118 C7
Swaythling C Sotn 34 F7
Sweet Green Worcs 80 F3
Sweetham Devon 13 K3
Sweethaws E Susx 38 D7
Sweetlands Corner Kent 39 K4
Sweets Cnwll 11 G3
Sweetshouse Cnwll 5 J3
Swefling Suffk 91 H3
Swepstone Leics 99 K1
Swerford Oxon 66 A1
Swettenham Ches E 130 F6
Swffryd Blae G 61 K7
Swift's Green Kent 39 L4
Swilland Suffk 90 E4
Swillbrook Lancs 138 F1
Swillington Leeds 142 B2
Swimbridge Devon 27 L5
Swimbridge Newland Devon 27 L5
Swinbrook Oxon 65 L4
Swincliffe Kirk 141 K2
Swincliffe N York 150 C4
Swincombe Devon 28 B3
Swinden N York 148 E5
Swinderby Lincs 135 H7
Swindon Gloucs 64 D2
Swindon Nthumb 190 D6
Swindon Staffs 97 J5
Swindon Swindn 47 H2
Swine E R Yk 153 J8
Swinefleet E R Yk 143 J3
Swineford S Glos 45 K5
Swineshead Bed 85 L2
Swineshead Lincs 119 H3
Swineshead Bridge Lincs 119 H3
Swiney Highld 275 H1
Swinford Leics 100 C7
Swinford Oxon 66 C5
Swingfield Minnis Kent 41 G6
Swingfield Street Kent 41 H6
Swingleton Green Suffk 89 K6
Swinhoe Nthumb 203 K7
Swinhope Lincs 145 G6
Swinithwaite N York 159 J5
Swinmore Common Herefs 80 F7
Swinscoe Staffs 115 J2
Swinside Cumb 165 H6
Swinstead Lincs 118 D7
Swinthorpe Lincs 135 L4
Swinton Border 202 C4
Swinton N York 160 B6
Swinton N York 162 D8
Swinton Rothm 142 C7
Swinton Salfd 140 A7
Swithland Leics 100 C1
Swordale Highld 263 G6
Swordland Highld 238 B5
Swordly Highld 278 C4
Sworton Heath Ches E 130 D3

Swyddffynnon Cerdgn 77 J2
Swyncombe Oxon 49 G1
Swynnerton Staffs 114 D4
Swyre Dorset 15 M5
Sycharth Powys 112 B6
Sychnant Powys 93 L7
Sychtyn Powys 94 B2
Sydallt Wrexhm 129 H8
Syde Gloucs 64 D5
Sydenham Gt Lon 51 K4
Sydenham Oxon 67 H6
Sydenham Damerel Devon ... 12 A7
Sydenhurst Surrey 36 E4
Syderstone Norfk 121 H5
Sydling St Nicholas Dorset ... 16 C3
Sydmonton Hants 48 C7
Sydnal Lane Shrops 97 H2
Syerston Notts 117 K2
Syke Rochdl 140 D4
Sykehouse Donc 143 G4
Syleham Suffk 106 E7
Sylen Carmth 56 F3
Symbister Shet 281 e5
Symington S Ayrs 196 D5
Symington S Lans 199 G6
Symondsbury Dorset 15 K4
Symonds Yat (East) Herefs 63 H4
Symonds Yat (West) Herefs ... 63 H4
Sympson Green C Brad 150 A8
Synderford Dorset 15 J2
Synod Inn Cerdgn 76 D4
Syre Highld 278 B7
Syreford Gloucs 64 F3
Syresham Nhants 84 C7
Syston Leics 100 D1
Syston Lincs 118 B3
Sytchampton Worcs 81 J2
Sywell Nhants 84 F2

T

Tabley Hill Ches E 130 E4
Tackley Oxon 66 C3
Tacolneston Norfk 106 C4
Tadcaster N York 151 G7
Taddington Derbys 132 C5
Taddington Gloucs 65 G1
Taddiport Devon 27 H7
Tadley Hants 48 F6
Tadlow Cambs 86 F5
Tadmarton Oxon 83 J7
Tadwick BaNES 45 L5
Tadworth Surrey 51 L2
Tafarnaubach Blae G 61 H5
Tafarn-y-bwlch Pembks 75 J5
Tafarn-y-Gelyn Denbgs 128 E7
Taff's Well Rhondd 43 H5
Tafolwern Powys 93 J3
Taibach Neath 57 L7
Tain Highld 263 L3
Tain Highld 280 D3
Tai'n Lôn Gwynd 109 H2
Tairbeart W Isls 282 e5
Tai'r Bull Powys 60 F2
Tairgwaith Neath 59 K6
Takeley Essex 70 E3
Takeley Street Essex 70 E3
Talachddu Powys 78 F8
Talacre Flints 128 D3
Talaton Devon 14 C3
Talbenny Pembks 54 D4
Talbot Green Rhondd 43 G5
Talbot Village Bmouth 17 L4
Taleford Devon 14 C3
Talerddig Powys 93 K3
Talgarreg Cerdgn 76 D5
Talgarth Powys 79 G8
Talisker Highld 246 D3
Talke Staffs 114 C1
Talke Pits Staffs 114 C1
Talkin Cumb 178 D7
Talladale Highld 260 E6
Talla Linnfoots Border 187 H2
Tallaminnock S Ayrs 183 K3
Tallarn Green Wrexhm 113 C5
Tallentire Cumb 164 F4
Talley Carmth 59 H2
Tallington Lincs 102 B2
Tallwrn Wrexhm 112 D2
Talmine Highld 277 K4
Talog Carmth 58 B4
Talsarn Cerdgn 77 G4
Talsarnau Gwynd 109 L4
Talskiddy Cnwll 4 E2
Talwrn IoA 125 J4
Talwrn Wrexhm 112 F2
Tal-y-bont Cerdgn 92 E5

Tal-y-Bont Conwy 126 F6
Tal-y-bont Gwynd 109 L7
Tal-y-bont Gwynd 126 C5
Talybont-on-Usk Powys 61 H3
Tal-y-Cafn Conwy 126 F5
Tal-y-coed Mons 62 E4
Tal-y-garn Rhondd 42 F5
Tal-y-llyn Gwynd 92 F2
Talysarn Gwynd 109 J1
Tal-y-Waun Torfn 61 L6
Talywern Powys 93 H3
Tamer Lane End Wigan 139 J7
Tamerton Foliot C Plym 6 F3
Tamworth Staffs 99 G3
Tamworth Green Lincs 119 L3
Tancred N York 151 G4
Tancredston Pembks 74 E7
Tandridge Surrey 38 B3
Tanfield Dur 180 F7
Tanfield Lea Dur 180 F8
Tangasdale W Isls 283 b13
Tangiers Pembks 54 F3
Tangley Hants 47 L8
Tangmere W Susx 20 E5
Tan Hill N York 158 F1
Tankerness Ork 275 d4
Tankersley Barns 142 A7
Tankerton Kent 40 F2
Tannach Highld 280 D6
Tannachie Abers 245 H6
Tannadice Angus 234 D4
Tanner's Green Worcs 98 D8
Tannington Suffk 90 F2
Tannochside N Lans 209 J6
Tansley Derbys 132 F7
Tansor Nhants 102 B5
Tantobie Dur 180 E7
Tanton N York 170 C8
Tanwood Worcs 97 K8
Tanworth in Arden Warwks 82 D1
Tan-y-Bwlch Gwynd 110 C3
Tan-y-fron Conwy 127 J6
Tan-y-fron Wrexhm 112 D1
Tan-y-grisiau Gwynd 110 C3
Tan-y-groes Cerdgn 76 B5
Taobh Tuath W Isls 282 d6
Taplow Bucks 49 M3
Tarbert Ag & B 205 L6
Tarbert Ag & B 206 D5
Tarbert W Isls 282 e5
Tarbet Ag & B 218 D6
Tarbet Highld 238 C5
Tarbet Highld 276 B6
Tarbock Green Knows 129 K2
Tarbolton S Ayrs 196 E5
Tarbrax S Lans 199 H2
Tardebigge Worcs 82 B2
Tarfside Angus 244 B7
Tarland Abers 244 B3
Tarleton Lancs 138 F4
Tarlscough Lancs 138 E5
Tarlton Gloucs 64 D7
Tarnock Somset 44 D8
Tarns Cumb 164 F1
Tarnside Cumb 156 F4
Tarporley Ches W 130 A7
Tarr Somset 28 F4
Tarrant Crawford Dorset 17 H2
Tarrant Gunville Dorset 32 F8
Tarrant Hinton Dorset 32 F8
Tarrant Keyneston Dorset 17 H2
Tarrant Launceston Dorset 17 J1
Tarrant Monkton Dorset 17 J1
Tarrant Rawston Dorset 17 H1
Tarrant Rushton Dorset 17 H2
Tarring Neville E Susx 23 G6
Tarrington Herefs 80 E7
Tarskavaig Highld 247 J6
Tarves Abers 256 F5
Tarvin Ches W 129 L6
Tarvin Sands Ches W 129 L6
Tasburgh Norfk 106 D4
Tasley Shrops 96 F4
Taston Oxon 65 M3
Tatenhill Staffs 115 K7
Tathall End M Keyn 84 F6
Tatham Lancs 147 M2
Tathwell Lincs 136 F3
Tatsfield Surrey 51 L7
Tattenhall Ches W 129 L7
Tatterford Norfk 121 J6
Tattersett Norfk 121 J5
Tattershall Lincs 136 D8
Tattershall Bridge Lincs 136 C8
Tattershall Thorpe Lincs 136 D7
Tattingstone Suffk 90 D7
Tattingstone White Horse
    Suffk 90 D7
Tatworth Somset 15 H2

Tauchers Moray 267 H6
Taunton Somset 30 C6
Taunton Deane Crematorium
    Somset 30 B6
Taverham Norfk 106 D1
Taverners Green Essex 70 E3
Tavernspite Pembks 55 L4
Tavistock Devon 12 C7
Taw Green Devon 12 F3
Tawstock Devon 27 K5
Taxal Derbys 131 K4
Tay Bridge C Dund 223 G1
Taychreggan Hotel Ag & B 217 G3
Tayinloan Ag & B 205 M7
Taynton Gloucs 63 L3
Taynton Oxon 65 K4
Taynuilt Ag & B 216 F1
Tayport Fife 223 H2
Tayvallich Ag & B 215 L7
Tealby Lincs 136 C2
Tealing Angus 234 B7
Team Valley Gatesd 181 G7
Teangue Highld 247 K6
Teanord Highld 263 G7
Tebay Cumb 157 K2
Tebworth C Beds 68 C2
Tedburn St Mary Devon 13 J4
Teddington Gloucs 81 M8
Teddington Gt Lon 50 F5
Tedstone Delamere Herefs 80 F3
Tedstone Wafer Herefs 80 F3
Teesport R & Cl 170 D6
Teesside Crematorium Middsb .. 170 C7
Teesside Park S on T 170 B7
Teeton Nhants 84 D1
Teffont Evias Wilts 33 G4
Teffont Magna Wilts 33 G4
Tegryn Pembks 75 L5
Teigh Rutlnd 117 M8
Teigncombe Devon 12 F5
Teigngrace Devon 13 K7
Teignmouth Devon 13 L8
Teindside Border 188 D4
Telford Wrekin 96 F2
Telford Crematorium Wrekin 97 G1
Tellisford Somset 46 A7
Telscombe E Susx 22 F6
Telscombe Cliffs E Susx 22 F7
Tempar P & K 231 J4
Templand D & G 176 E2
Temple Cnwll 11 G7
Temple Mdloth 211 K7
Temple Balsall Solhll 99 G8
Temple Bar Cerdgn 76 F4
Temple Cloud BaNES 45 J7
Templecombe Somset 32 B6
Temple End Suffk 88 D5
Temple Ewell Kent 41 J6
Temple Grafton Warwks 82 D4
Temple Guiting Gloucs 65 G2
Temple Herdewyke Warwks 83 J5
Temple Hirst N York 142 F3
Temple Normanton Derbys 133 H6
Temple of Fiddes Abers 245 H7
Temple Sowerby Cumb 166 E5
Templeton Devon 28 F8
Templeton Pembks 55 J4
Templetown Dur 168 E1
Tempsford C Beds 86 D4
Tenbury Wells Worcs 80 E2
Tenby Pembks 55 K6
Tendring Essex 73 H2
Tendring Green Essex 73 H2
Tendring Heath Essex 73 H2
Ten Mile Bank Norfk 104 B4
Tenpenny Heath Essex 73 G3
Tenterden Kent 39 M6
Terling Essex 71 J4
Tern Wrekin 113 K8
Ternhill Shrops 113 L5
Terregles D & G 176 B3
Terrington N York 151 L2
Terrington St Clement Norfk .. 120 C7
Terrington St John Norfk 104 A1
Terry's Green Warwks 98 E8
Teston Kent 39 H3
Testwood Hants 34 D7
Tetbury Gloucs 64 C8
Tetbury Upton Gloucs 64 C8
Tetchill Shrops 112 F5
Tetcott Devon 11 L3
Tetford Lincs 136 F5
Tetney Lincs 145 J7
Tetney Lock Lincs 145 J7
Tetsworth Oxon 67 G6
Tettenhall Wolves 97 K3
Tettenhall Wood Wolves 97 K3
Teversal Notts 133 J7
Teversham Cambs 87 K3

Teviothead Border 188 C5
Tewin Herts 69 H4
Tewin Wood Herts 69 H4
Tewkesbury Gloucs 81 K8
Teynham Kent 40 B3
Thackley C Brad 149 M8
Thackthwaite Cumb 164 F6
Thackthwaite Cumb 166 A5
Thainstone Abers 256 D8
Thakeham W Susx 21 J3
Thame Oxon 67 H6
Thames Ditton Surrey 50 F5
Thamesmead Gt Lon 52 A3
Thamesport Medway 53 J4
Thanet Crematorium Kent 41 K2
Thanington Kent 40 F4
Thankerton S Lans 199 G5
Tharston Norfk 106 D4
Thatcham W Berk 48 D5
Thatto Heath St Hel 129 L1
Thaxted Essex 70 F1
Theakston N York 160 D5
Thealby N Linc 143 M4
Theale Somset 31 G2
Theale W Berk 48 F5
Thearne E R Yk 153 G8
The Bank Ches E 131 G8
The Beeches Gloucs 64 F6
Theberton Suffk 91 K2
The Blythe Staffs 115 G6
The Bog Shrops 95 J4
The Bourne Worcs 82 A4
The Braes Highld 247 H2
The Bratch Staffs 97 K4
The Broad Herefs 80 C3
The Brunt E Loth 212 F4
The Bryn Mons 62 C5
The Bungalow IoM 154 e5
The Burf Worcs 81 J2
The Camp Gloucs 64 C5
The Chequer Wrexhm 113 H3
The City Bed. 86 C3
The City Bucks 67 J7
The Common Oxon 65 L2
The Common Wilts 34 B4
The Common Wilts 46 F2
The Corner Kent 39 H5
The Cronk IoM 154 d3
Theddingworth Leics 100 E6
Theddlethorpe All Saints Lincs .. 137 J2
Theddlethorpe St Helen Lincs .. 137 J2
The Den N Ayrs 196 C1
The Forge Herefs 79 L3
The Forstal Kent 40 D7
The Fouralls Shrops 113 L5
The Green Cumb 156 A5
The Green Essex 71 J3
The Green N York 162 D2
The Green Wilts 32 E4
The Grove Worcs 81 K7
The Haven W Susx 37 G5
The Haw Gloucs 64 B2
The Headland Hartpl 170 C4
The Hill Cumb 156 A6
The Holt Wokham 49 K3
The Hundred Herefs 80 C2
Thelbridge Cross Devon 28 D8
The Leacon Kent 40 C8
The Lee Bucks 67 L6
The Lhen IoM 154 e2
Thelnetham Suffk 105 L7
The Lochs Moray 266 F4
Thelveton Norfk 106 D7
Thelwall Warrtn 130 C2
The Marsh Powys 95 H4
Themelthorpe Norfk 122 B6
The Middles Dur 180 F8
The Moor Kent 39 J7
The Mumbles Swans 57 H7
The Murray S Lans 209 H8
The Mythe Gloucs 81 K8
The Narth Mons 63 G6
The Neuk Abers 245 G4
Thenford Nhants 83 M7
Theobald's Green Wilts 46 F5
The Quarry Gloucs 63 L7
The Quarter Kent 39 M4
The Reddings Gloucs 64 C3
Therfield Herts 87 G7
The Rhôs Powys 61 J1
The Ross P & K 220 D3
The Sands Surrey 36 C2
The Shoe Wilts 46 A4
The Smithies Shrops 96 F4
The Spring Warwks 83 G1
The Square Torfn 62 B7
The Stair Kent 38 F4
The Stocks Kent 25 G2
The Straits Hants 36 A3

The Strand Wilts............... 46 D7
Thetford Norfk............. 105 H6
Thethwaite Cumb.......... 165 L2
The Towans Cnwll............. 2 E3
The Vauld Herefs........... 80 C5
The Wyke Shrops........... 97 G2
Theydon Bois Essex........ 70 C7
Theydon Mount Essex...... 70 C7
Thicket Priory N York...... 151 L7
Thickwood Wilts............ 46 B4
Thimbleby Lincs........... 136 D5
Thimbleby N York.......... 161 G3
Thingwall Wirral........... 129 G3
Thirkleby N York........... 161 G6
Thirlby N York............. 161 G6
Thirlestane Border......... 201 H4
Thirn N York.............. 160 B5
Thirsk N York............. 160 H6
Thirtleby E R Yk.......... 144 F1
Thistleton Lancs.......... 147 H8
Thistleton Rutlnd......... 118 B7
Thistley Green Suffk...... 104 D8
Thixendale N York......... 152 C4
Thockrington Nthumb...... 179 M3
Tholomas Drove Cambs..... 103 H2
Tholthorpe N York......... 151 G2
Thomas Chapel Pembks..... 55 J5
Thomas Close Cumb........ 166 B3
Thomastown Abers......... 255 L4
Thomas Town Warwks....... 82 C3
Thompson Norfk........... 105 J4
Thong Kent............... 52 E5
Thongsbridge Kirk........ 141 J6
Thoralby N York........... 159 H5
Thoresby Notts........... 134 C5
Thoresthorpe Lincs........ 137 J4
Thoresway Lincs.......... 144 F8
Thorganby Lincs.......... 145 G8
Thorganby N York......... 151 L7
Thorgill N York........... 162 C3
Thorington Suffk......... 107 J8
Thorington Street Suffk.... 89 K8
Thorlby N York........... 149 H5
Thorley Herts............. 70 C3
Thorley IoW.............. 18 F6
Thorley Houses Herts...... 70 C3
Thorley Street IoW........ 18 F6
Thormanby N York......... 161 H7
Thornaby-on-Tees S on T... 170 B7
Thornage Norfk........... 122 B4
Thornborough Bucks........ 84 E8
Thornborough N York...... 160 D6
Thornbury C Brad......... 141 J1
Thornbury Devon........... 12 A1
Thornbury Herefs.......... 80 E3
Thornbury S Glos.......... 45 J1
Thornby Cumb............ 177 J8
Thornby Nhants........... 100 E8
Thorncliff Staffs......... 131 K7
Thorncliffe Crematorium
    Cumb............... 146 D2
Thorncombe Dorset......... 15 J2
Thorncombe Street Surrey... 36 F3
Thorncott Green C Beds..... 86 C5
Thorncross IoW........... 19 G7
Thorndon Suffk........... 90 D1
Thorndon Cross Devon...... 12 D4
Thorne Donc............. 143 H5
Thorne Coffin Somset...... 31 H7
Thornecroft Devon.......... 7 M2
Thornehillhead Devon...... 27 G7
Thorner Leeds........... 150 E7
Thornes Staffs............ 98 D3
Thornes Wakefd.......... 141 M4
Thorne St Margaret Somset.. 29 K6
Thorney Bucks............ 50 D3
Thorney C Pete.......... 102 F3
Thorney Notts........... 135 G5
Thorney Somset........... 30 F6
Thorney Hill Hants......... 18 B4
Thorney Island W Susx..... 20 C6
Thorney Toll Cambs....... 103 G3
Thornfalcon Somset........ 30 D6
Thornford Dorset.......... 31 K8
Thorngrafton Nthumb...... 179 H6
Thorngrove Somset......... 30 E4
Thorngumbald E R Yk...... 145 G3
Thornham Norfk.......... 121 G3
Thornham Magna Suffk..... 90 C1
Thornham Parva Suffk...... 90 D1
Thornhaugh C Pete........ 102 B3
Thornhill C Sotn.......... 19 G1
Thornhill Caerph.......... 43 J5
Thornhill Cumb.......... 155 H1
Thornhill D & G.......... 186 C2
Thornhill Derbys......... 132 D3
Thornhill Kirk............ 141 L4
Thornhill Stirlg.......... 219 L7
Thornhill Lees Kirk....... 141 K4

Thornhills Calder......... 141 J3
Thornholme E R Yk....... 153 H3
Thornicombe Dorset........ 17 G2
Thornington Nthumb...... 202 D6
Thornley Dur............. 168 E3
Thornley Dur............. 169 K3
Thornley Gate Nthumb.... 179 J7
Thornliebank E Rens...... 208 F7
Thorns Suffk............. 88 E4
Thornsett Derbys......... 131 K2
Thorns Green Ches E...... 130 F3
Thornthwaite Cumb........ 165 H5
Thornthwaite N York...... 149 L4
Thornton Angus.......... 234 B6
Thornton Bucks........... 84 E8
Thornton C Brad.......... 141 H1
Thornton E R Yk......... 152 A6
Thornton Fife........... 222 E7
Thornton Lancs.......... 146 F2
Thornton Leics.......... 100 A2
Thornton Lincs.......... 136 D6
Thornton Middsb........ 170 B7
Thornton Nthumb........ 202 E4
Thornton Pembks......... 54 E5
Thornton Sefton......... 138 D7
Thornton Curtis N Linc.... 144 D4
Thornton Garden of Rest
    Crematorium Sefton.... 138 D7
Thorntonhall S Lans...... 209 G8
Thornton Heath Gt Lon..... 51 J5
Thornton Hough Wirral.... 129 G3
Thornton-in-Craven N York. 148 F6
Thornton in Lonsdale N York. 158 B8
Thornton-le-Beans N York.. 160 F4
Thornton-le-Clay N York... 151 L3
Thornton-le-Dale N York... 162 E6
Thornton le Moor Lincs.... 144 D8
Thornton-le-Moor N York... 160 F5
Thornton-le-Moors Ches W.. 129 K5
Thornton-le-Street N York.. 160 F5
Thorntonloch E Loth...... 213 G4
Thornton Rust N York..... 159 G5
Thornton Steward N York... 160 A5
Thornton Watlass N York... 160 C5
Thornwood Common Essex... 70 C6
Thornydykes Border....... 201 J3
Thornythwaite Cumb....... 165 L6
Thoroton Notts.......... 117 K3
Thorp Arch Leeds........ 150 F6
Thorpe Derbys........... 115 J2
Thorpe E R Yk.......... 152 F6
Thorpe Lincs............ 137 J3
Thorpe N York.......... 149 H3
Thorpe Norfk............ 107 J4
Thorpe Notts............ 117 K2
Thorpe Surrey........... 50 C5
Thorpe Abbotts Norfk..... 106 D7
Thorpe Acre Leics....... 116 E2
Thorpe Arnold Leics...... 117 K7
Thorpe Audlin Wakefd..... 142 D4
Thorpe Bassett N York.... 162 F8
Thorpe Bay Sthend........ 53 K2
Thorpe by Water Rutlnd... 101 K4
Thorpe Common Rothm.... 133 G1
Thorpe Constantine Staffs.. 99 H2
Thorpe End Norfk......... 106 F1
Thorpe Green Essex....... 73 H3
Thorpe Green Lancs...... 139 H3
Thorpe Green Suffk....... 89 J4
Thorpe Hesley Rothm..... 142 B8
Thorpe in Balne Donc..... 142 F5
Thorpe Langton Leics..... 101 G5
Thorpe Larches Dur...... 169 K5
Thorpe Lea Surrey........ 50 C5
Thorpe le Fallows Lincs.... 135 H4
Thorpe-le-Soken Essex..... 73 J3
Thorpe le Street E R Yk... 152 C7
Thorpe Malsor Nhants..... 101 H7
Thorpe Mandeville Nhants.. 83 M6
Thorpe Market Norfk...... 122 E4
Thorpe Marriot Norfk..... 122 D8
Thorpe Morieux Suffk..... 89 J4
Thorpeness Suffk......... 91 L3
Thorpe on the Hill Leeds... 141 M2
Thorpe on the Hill Lincs... 135 H6
Thorpe St Andrew Norfk... 106 F2
Thorpe St Peter Lincs..... 137 J7
Thorpe Salvin Rothm...... 133 K3
Thorpe Satchville Leics.... 100 F1
Thorpe Thewles S on T.... 169 L6
Thorpe Tilney Lincs....... 136 B8
Thorpe Underwood N York.. 151 G4
Thorpe Underwood Nhants.. 101 H7
Thorpe Waterville Nhants... 102 A7
Thorpe Willoughby N York.. 142 F2
Thorpland Norfk......... 104 C2
Thorrington Essex......... 73 G3
Thorverton Devon......... 13 L2
Thrales End C Beds........ 68 E4

Thrandeston Suffk....... 106 C8
Thrapston Nhants........ 101 M7
Threapland Cumb......... 165 G3
Threapland N York....... 149 H4
Threapwood Ches W...... 113 G3
Threapwood Staffs....... 115 G3
Threapwood Head Staffs... 115 G3
Threave S Ayrs.......... 183 J2
Three Ashes Herefs........ 63 G3
Three Bridges W Susx...... 37 L3
Three Burrows Cnwll........ 4 B5
Three Chimneys Kent....... 39 K5
Three Cocks Powys........ 79 G7
Three Counties Crematorium
    Essex............... 71 J2
Three Crosses Swans....... 57 G6
Three Cups Corner E Susx... 23 L3
Three Gates Worcs........ 80 F3
Threehammer Common Norfk. 123 G7
Three Hammers Cnwll....... 11 J5
Three Holes Norfk........ 103 K3
Threekingham Lincs....... 118 A4
Three Leg Cross E Susx..... 39 H7
Three Legged Cross Dorset.. 17 L2
Three Mile Cross Wokham.. 49 H5
Threemilestone Cnwll........ 4 C6
Threemiletown W Loth..... 210 E4
Three Oaks E Susx......... 24 F4
Threlkeld Cumb.......... 165 K5
Threshers Bush Essex...... 70 D5
Threshfield N York....... 149 H3
Thrigby Norfk........... 107 J1
Thringarth Dur.......... 167 L6
Thringstone Leics........ 116 D4
Thrintoft N York......... 160 D4
Thriplow Cambs.......... 87 J6
Throapham Rothm........ 133 K2
Throckenhalt Lincs....... 103 G2
Throcking Herts.......... 69 J1
Throckley N u Ty........ 180 E5
Throckmorton Worcs....... 82 A5
Throop Bmouth........... 17 M3
Throop Dorset............ 16 F4
Throphill Nthumb........ 180 D2
Thropton Nthumb........ 190 E5
Throsk Stirlg........... 209 M1
Througham Gloucs......... 64 D5
Throughgate D & G....... 185 L6
Throwleigh Devon......... 12 F4
Throwley Kent........... 40 C4
Throwley Forstal Kent..... 40 C4
Thrumpton Notts......... 116 E5
Thrumpton Notts......... 134 D4
Thrumster Highld........ 280 D7
Thrunscoe NE Lin........ 145 J6
Thrunton Nthumb........ 190 F4
Thrup Oxon.............. 65 L7
Thrupp Gloucs........... 64 B6
Thrupp Oxon............. 66 C4
Thrushelton Devon........ 12 B5
Thrussington Leics....... 117 H8
Thruxton Hants.......... 34 C2
Thruxton Herefs.......... 80 B8
Thrybergh Rothm........ 142 D8
Thulston Derbys......... 116 C5
Thundersley Essex......... 53 G1
Thurcaston Leics........ 100 C1
Thurcroft Rothm......... 133 K2
Thurdon Cnwll........... 26 E8
Thurgarton Norfk........ 122 D4
Thurgarton Notts........ 117 J2
Thurgoland Barns........ 141 L7
Thurlaston Leics........ 100 B4
Thurlaston Warwks........ 83 L1
Thurlbear Somset......... 30 C6
Thurlby Lincs........... 118 E8
Thurlby Lincs........... 135 H7
Thurlby Lincs........... 137 J4
Thurleigh Bed........... 85 L3
Thurlestone Devon.......... 7 K6
Thurloxton Somset........ 30 C5
Thurlstone Barns........ 141 K7
Thurlton Norfk.......... 107 J4
Thurlwood Ches E........ 130 F8
Thurmaston Leics........ 100 D2
Thurnby Leics........... 100 E3
Thurne Norfk........... 123 H8
Thurnham Kent........... 53 H7
Thurning Nhants......... 102 B6
Thurning Norfk.......... 122 B5
Thurnscoe Barns......... 142 C6
Thursby Cumb........... 165 K1
Thursden Lancs.......... 140 D1
Thursford Norfk......... 121 L5
Thursley Surrey.......... 36 D3
Thurso Highld........... 279 K3
Thurstaston Wirral....... 128 F3
Thurston Suffk........... 89 J2
Thurston Clough Oldham... 140 E6

Thurstonfield Cumb....... 177 K7
Thurstonland Kirk....... 141 J5
Thurston Planch Suffk..... 89 J2
Thurton Norfk........... 107 G3
Thurvaston Derbys....... 115 L4
Thuxton Norfk........... 105 L2
Thwaite N York.......... 158 F3
Thwaite Suffk............ 90 D2
Thwaite Head Cumb....... 156 E4
Thwaites C Brad......... 149 K7
Thwaite St Mary Norfk.... 107 G4
Thwaites Brow C Brad..... 149 K7
Thwing E R Yk.......... 153 G2
Tibbermore P & K........ 221 J3
Tibbers D & G.......... 186 C6
Tibberton Gloucs......... 63 M3
Tibberton Worcs.......... 81 L4
Tibberton Wrekin........ 113 L7
Tibbie Shiels Inn Border... 187 K2
Tibenham Norfk.......... 106 C5
Tibshelf Derbys......... 133 J7
Tibthorpe E R Yk........ 152 E5
Ticehurst E Susx......... 39 H7
Tichborne Hants.......... 35 H5
Tickencote Rutlnd....... 101 L2
Tickenham N Som......... 44 F4
Tickford End M Keyn...... 85 H6
Tickhill Donc........... 134 B1
Ticklerton Shrops........ 96 B5
Ticknall Derbys......... 116 B6
Tickton E R Yk.......... 153 H6
Tidbury Green Solhll...... 98 E8
Tidcombe Wilts.......... 47 L7
Tiddington Oxon......... 67 G6
Tiddington Warwks........ 82 F4
Tiddleywink Wilts........ 46 C4
Tidebrook E Susx......... 38 F7
Tideford Cnwll............ 6 C3
Tideford Cross Cnwll....... 6 C3
Tidenham Gloucs......... 63 H7
Tideswell Derbys........ 132 C4
Tidmarsh W Berk......... 48 F4
Tidmington Warwks........ 83 G7
Tidpit Hants............ 33 J7
Tidworth Wilts.......... 34 B1
Tiers Cross Pembks....... 54 E5
Tiffield Nhants.......... 84 D5
Tigerton Angus......... 234 E3
Tigh a' Ghearraidh W Isls.. 282 b7
Tigharry W Isls......... 282 b7
Tighnabruaich Ag & B..... 206 F4
Tigley Devon.............. 7 L3
Tilbrook Cambs.......... 86 B2
Tilbury Thurr........... 52 D4
Tilbury Dock Thurr....... 52 D4
Tilbury Green Essex....... 88 E7
Tilbury Juxta Clare Essex... 88 F7
Tile Cross Birm.......... 98 F6
Tile Hill Covtry......... 99 H7
Tilehouse Green Solhll.... 98 E8
Tilehurst Readg.......... 49 G4
Tilford Surrey........... 36 C2
Tilgate W Susx.......... 37 L4
Tilgate Forest Row W Susx.. 37 L4
Tilham Street Somset...... 31 J4
Tillers Green Gloucs...... 80 F8
Tillicoultry Clacks....... 221 G7
Tillietudlem S Lans...... 198 D4
Tillingham Essex......... 72 E6
Tillington Herefs........ 80 B6
Tillington W Susx........ 36 E6
Tillington Common Herefs.. 80 B6
Tillybirloch Abers....... 244 F2
Tillyfourie Abers........ 244 E1
Tillygreig Abers......... 256 F7
Tillyrie P & K.......... 221 K6
Tilmanstone Kent........ 41 J5
Tilney All Saints Norfk... 120 C7
Tilney High End Norfk.... 120 C8
Tilney St Lawrence Norfk.. 120 C8
Tilshead Wilts.......... 33 H1
Tilstock Shrops......... 113 J4
Tilston Ches W.......... 113 G1
Tilstone Bank Ches W..... 130 A7
Tilstone Fearnall Ches W... 130 A7
Tilsworth C Beds........ 68 B2
Tilton on the Hill Leics... 101 G2
Tiltups End Gloucs....... 64 B7
Tilty Essex............. 70 E2
Timberland Lincs........ 136 B7
Timbersbrook Ches E...... 131 H7
Timberscombe Somset...... 29 G2
Timble N York.......... 149 M5
Timewell Devon.......... 29 H5
Timpanheck D & G....... 177 K4
Timperley Traffd........ 130 F2
Timsbury BaNES......... 45 K7
Timsbury Hants.......... 34 D6
Timsgarry W Isls........ 282 d3

Timsgearraidh W Isls 282 d3
Timworth Suffk 89 H2
Timworth Green Suffk 89 H2
Tincleton Dorset 16 E4
Tindale Cumb 178 E7
Tingewick Bucks 84 C8
Tingley Leeds 141 L3
Tingrith C Beds 68 C1
Tingwell Ork 275 c3
Tinhay Devon 12 A5
Tinker's Hill Hants 34 E2
Tinkersley Derbys 132 E6
Tinsley Sheff 133 H2
Tinsley Green W Susx 37 L3
Tintagel Cnwll 10 F5
Tintern Mons 63 G7
Tintinhull Somset 31 H7
Tintwistle Derbys 140 F8
Tinwald D & G 176 D3
Tinwell Rutlnd 101 M2
Tippacott Devon 28 D2
Tipp's End Norfk 103 K4
Tiptoe Hants 18 C4
Tipton Sandw 98 B5
Tipton Green Sandw 98 B5
Tipton St John Devon 14 C4
Tiptree Essex 72 C4
Tiptree Heath Essex 72 C4
Tirabad Powys 78 B7
Tiree Ag & B 224 C6
Tiretigan Ag & B 206 A6
Tirley Gloucs 64 B2
Tiroran Ag & B 226 F6
Tirphil Caerph 61 H6
Tirril Cumb 166 C5
Tir-y-fron Flints 129 G7
Tisbury Wilts 32 F5
Tisman's Common W Susx 37 G4
Tissington Derbys 115 K1
Titchberry Devon 26 D5
Titchfield Hants 19 J3
Titchfield Common Hants 19 J2
Titchmarsh Nhants 102 A7
Titchwell Norfk 121 G3
Tithby Notts 117 J4
Titley Herefs 79 L3
Titmore Green Herts 69 G2
Titsey Surrey 51 L7
Titson Cnwll 11 J2
Tittensor Staffs 114 D4
Tittleshall Norfk 121 K7
Titton Worcs 81 J1
Tiverton Ches W 130 A7
Tiverton Devon 29 G8
Tivetshall St Margaret Norfk 106 D6
Tivetshall St Mary Norfk 106 D6
Tivington Somset 29 G2
Tivy Dale Barns 141 L6
Tixall Staffs 114 F7
Tixover Rutlnd 101 L3
Toab Shet 281 d9
Toadhole Derbys 133 H8
Toadmoor Derbys 116 B1
Tobermory Ag & B 226 F1
Toberonochy Ag & B 215 L3
Tobha Mòr W Isls 283 b10
Tocher Abers 256 C5
Tochieneal Moray 267 K3
Tockenham Wilts 46 F3
Tockenham Wick Wilts 46 F3
Tocketts R & Cl 170 E7
Tockholes Bl w D 139 K3
Tockington S Glos 45 J2
Tockwith N York 151 G5
Todber Dorset 32 D7
Todburn Nthumb 191 G7
Toddington C Beds 68 C2
Toddington Gloucs 82 B8
Todds Green Herts 69 G2
Todenham Gloucs 82 F8
Todhills Angus 234 C7
Todhills Cumb 177 L6
Todhills Dur 169 G4
Todmorden Calder 140 E3
Todwick Rothm 133 K3
Toft Cambs 87 G4
Toft Ches E 130 E4
Toft Lincs 118 E8
Toft Shet 281 e4
Toft Warwks 83 L1
Toft Hill Dur 168 F5
Toft Hill Lincs 136 D7
Toft Monks Norfk 107 J4
Toft next Newton Lincs 135 L2
Toftrees Norfk 121 K6
Toftwood Norfk 105 K1
Togston Nthumb 191 J6
Tokavaig Highld 247 J6
Tokers Green Oxon 49 H3

Tolastadh bho Thuath W Isls 282 h2
Toldish Cnwll 4 F3
Tolland Somset 29 K4
Tollard Farnham Dorset 32 F7
Tollard Royal Wilts 32 F7
Toll Bar Donc 142 E6
Tollbar End Covtry 99 K8
Toller Fratrum Dorset 16 B3
Toller Porcorum Dorset 16 A3
Tollerton N York 151 H3
Tollerton Notts 117 G4
Toller Whelme Dorset 15 L2
Tollesbury Essex 72 D5
Tolleshunt D'Arcy Essex 72 D5
Tolleshunt Knights Essex 72 D4
Tolleshunt Major Essex 72 C5
Tollingham E R Yk 152 C8
Toll of Birness Abers 257 J5
Tolpuddle Dorset 16 F4
Tolworth Gt Lon 51 G5
Tomatin Highld 252 E6
Tomchrasky Highld 239 M1
Tomdoun Highld 239 K3
Tomich Highld 250 B6
Tomich Highld 250 F2
Tomich Highld 263 J5
Tomich Highld 272 F7
Tomintoul Moray 254 D7
Tomlow Warwks 83 K3
Tomnacross Highld 250 F3
Tomnavoulin Moray 254 D6
Tompkin Staffs 114 E1
Ton Mons 62 C6
Ton Mons 62 D7
Tonbridge Kent 38 F4
Tondu Brdgnd 42 D5
Tonedale Somset 29 L6
Ton fanau Gwynd 92 C3
Tong C Brad 141 K2
Tong Kent 40 C4
Tong Shrops 97 H2
Tong W Isls 282 g3
Tonge Leics 116 C7
Tong Green Kent 40 C4
Tongham Surrey 36 C1
Tongland D & G 175 H4
Tong Norton Shrops 97 H2
Tongue Highld 277 K5
Tongue End Lincs 118 F7
Tongwynlais Cardif 43 H5
Tonmawr Neath 42 B2
Tonna Neath 57 L5
Tonwell Herts 69 J4
Tonypandy Rhondd 42 F3
Tonyrefail Rhondd 42 F4
Toot Baldon Oxon 66 E7
Toot Hill Essex 70 D6
Toothill Hants 34 E7
Toothill Swindn 47 G2
Tooting Gt Lon 51 H5
Tooting Bec Gt Lon 51 H4
Topcliffe N York 160 F7
Topcroft Norfk 106 F5
Topcroft Street Norfk 106 F5
Top End Bed 85 L3
Topham Donc 143 G4
Top of Hebers Rochdl 140 C6
Toppesfield Essex 88 E7
Toprow Norfk 106 D4
Topsham Devon 13 M5
Top-y-rhos Flints 128 F7
Torbeg N Ayrs 194 D5
Torboll Highld 273 H8
Torbreck Highld 251 H3
Torbryan Devon 8 B2
Torcastle Highld 239 J7
Torcross Devon 8 B6
Tore Highld 251 G1
Torfrey Cnwll 5 J4
Torinturk Ag & B 206 C6
Torksey Lincs 135 G4
Torlundy Highld 239 K8
Tormarton S Glos 45 M3
Tormore N Ayrs 194 D4
Tornagrain Highld 252 E2
Tornaveen Abers 244 D2
Torness Highld 251 G6
Toronto Dur 169 G4
Torpenhow Cumb 165 G3
Torphichen W Loth 210 C4
Torphins Abers 244 E3
Torpoint Cnwll 6 E4
Torquay Torbay 8 D2
Torquay Crematorium Torbay 8 D2
Torquhan Border 200 F3
Torr Devon 7 H4
Torran Highld 259 K6
Torrance E Duns 209 G4

Torranyard N Ayrs 196 D2
Torre Somset 29 J3
Torridon Highld 260 E8
Torridon House Highld 260 D8
Torrin Highld 247 J4
Torrisdale Ag & B 194 B4
Torrisdale Highld 278 B4
Torrish Highld 274 C4
Torrisholme Lancs 147 J3
Torrobull Highld 272 E7
Torry C Aber 245 L3
Torryburn Fife 210 D2
Torteval Guern 9 h4
Torthorwald D & G 176 D3
Tortington W Susx 21 G6
Torton Worcs 81 J1
Tortworth S Glos 63 L8
Torvaig Highld 259 H7
Torver Cumb 156 C4
Torwood Falk 209 M2
Torwoodlee Border 201 G5
Torworth Notts 134 D2
Tosberry Devon 26 D6
Toscaig Highld 247 L1
Toseland Cambs 86 E3
Tosside Lancs 148 D4
Tostock Suffk 89 J3
Totaig Highld 258 B6
Tote Highld 259 G6
Tote Highld 259 J4
Tote Hill W Susx 36 C6
Totford Hants 35 H3
Tothill Lincs 137 H3
Totland IoW 18 E6
Totley Sheff 132 F4
Totley Brook Sheff 132 F4
Totnes Devon 8 B3
Toton Notts 116 E4
Totronald Ag & B 224 F4
Totscore Highld 258 F3
Tottenham Gt Lon 51 J1
Tottenhill Norfk 104 C1
Totteridge Gt Lon 69 H8
Totternhoe C Beds 68 C3
Tottington Bury 140 A5
Tottleworth Lancs 139 L2
Totton Hants 34 D8
Touchen End W & M 49 L4
Toulston N York 151 G7
Toulton Somset 30 B4
Toulvaddie Highld 264 D4
Tovil Kent 39 J3
Towan Cnwll 5 G5
Towan Cnwll 10 B7
Toward Ag & B 207 J5
Toward Quay Ag & B 207 J5
Towcester Nhants 84 D5
Towednack Cnwll 2 D3
Towersey Oxon 67 H6
Towie Abers 244 A1
Tow Law Dur 168 E3
Town End Cambs 103 J4
Town End Cumb 156 E1
Town End Cumb 156 F6
Town End Cumb 166 E5
Townend W Duns 208 C4
Towngate Cumb 166 C1
Towngate Lincs 102 C1
Town Green Lancs 138 E6
Town Green Norfk 107 G1
Townhead Barns 141 J7
Town Head Cumb 156 F2
Townhead Cumb 164 E3
Townhead Cumb 166 E4
Townhead D & G 176 D1
Town Head N York 148 E4
Townhead of Greenlaw D & G 175 J2
Townhill Fife 210 F1
Town Kelloe Dur 169 K3
Townlake Devon 12 A7
Town Lane Wigan 139 K7
Town Littleworth E Susx 22 F4
Town of Lowton Wigan 139 J8
Town Row E Susx 38 E7
Towns End Hants 48 E7
Townsend Somset 30 E7
Townshend Cnwll 2 F4
Town Street Suffk 104 F6
Townwell S Glos 45 K1
Town Yetholm Border 202 C7
Towthorpe C York 151 K4
Towthorpe E R Yk 152 D3
Towton N York 151 G7
Towyn Conwy 127 K4
Toxteth Lpool 129 H2
Toynton All Saints Lincs 137 G7
Toynton Fen Side Lincs 137 G7
Toynton St Peter Lincs 137 G7
Toy's Hill Kent 38 D3

Trabboch E Ayrs 196 E6
Trabbochburn E Ayrs 196 F6
Traboe Cnwll 3 J6
Tracebridge Somset 29 K6
Tradespark Highld 264 D8
Trafford Park Traffd 140 B8
Trallong Powys 60 E1
Tranent E Loth 211 L4
Tranmere Wirral 129 H2
Trantelbeg Highld 278 F5
Trantlemore Highld 278 F5
Tranwell Nthumb 180 F2
Trap Carmth 59 J5
Traprain E Loth 212 D4
Trap's Green Warwks 82 D1
Trapshill W Berk 48 A6
Traquair Border 200 D6
Trash Green W Berk 49 G5
Trawden Lancs 148 F8
Trawscoed Cerdgn 77 J1
Trawsfynydd Gwynd 110 D4
Trealaw Rhondd 42 F3
Treales Lancs 138 F1
Trearddur Bay IoA 124 D4
Treaslane Highld 258 F6
Treator Cnwll 10 C7
Tre Aubrey V Glam 43 G7
Trebanog Rhondd 42 F4
Trebanos Neath 57 K4
Trebartha Cnwll 11 K7
Trebarwith Cnwll 10 E5
Trebeath Cnwll 11 J5
Trebetherick Cnwll 10 C7
Treborough Somset 29 H4
Trebudannon Cnwll 4 E3
Trebullett Cnwll 11 L7
Treburgett Cnwll 10 E6
Treburley Cnwll 11 L7
Treburrick Cnwll 10 B8
Trebyan Cnwll 5 J2
Trecastle Powys 60 C1
Trecogo Cnwll 11 K6
Trecott Devon 12 F3
Trecwn Pembks 74 F5
Trecynon Rhondd 60 F6
Tredaule Cnwll 11 J6
Tredavoe Cnwll 2 C5
Tredegar Blae G 61 J5
Tredethy Cnwll 10 F8
Tredington Gloucs 64 C1
Tredington Warwks 83 G6
Tredinnick Cnwll 5 H3
Tredinnick Cnwll 5 K2
Tredinnick Cnwll 5 M3
Tredinnick Cnwll 6 B3
Tredinnick Cnwll 10 C8
Tredomen Powys 61 H1
Tredrissi Pembks 75 J4
Tredrizzick Cnwll 10 D7
Tredunnock Mons 62 D8
Tredustan Powys 61 H1
Treen Cnwll 2 B6
Treen Cnwll 2 C3
Treesmill Cnwll 5 J4
Treeton Rothm 133 J2
Trefasser Pembks 74 E4
Trefdraeth IoA 125 G5
Trefecca Powys 61 J1
Trefeglwys Powys 93 L5
Trefenter Cerdgn 77 H2
Treffgarne Pembks 54 F2
Treffgarne Owen Pembks 74 E7
Trefforest Rhondd 43 G4
Treffynnon Pembks 74 D6
Trefil Blae G 61 H4
Trefilan Cerdgn 77 G4
Trefin Pembks 74 D5
Treflach Wood Shrops 112 C6
Trefnannau Powys 112 C8
Trefnant Denbgs 128 C5
Trefonen Shrops 112 C6
Trefor Gwynd 108 F2
Trefor IoA 124 F4
Trefrew Cnwll 10 F5
Trefriw Conwy 126 F7
Tregadillett Cnwll 11 K6
Tre-gagle Mons 63 G5
Tregaian IoA 125 H4
Tregare Mons 62 E5
Tregarne Cnwll 3 K6
Tregaron Cerdgn 77 J3
Tregarth Gwynd 126 B6
Tregaswith Cnwll 4 E2
Tregatta Cnwll 10 F5
Tregawne Cnwll 5 G2
Tregeare Cnwll 11 J5
Tregeiriog Wrexhm 112 B5
Tregele IoA 124 F1
Tregellist Cnwll 10 E7

Tregenna Cnwll....4 E6
Tregeseal Cnwll....2 B5
Tregew Cnwll....3 K4
Tre-Gibbon Rhondd....60 F6
Tregidden Cnwll....3 J6
Tregiskey Cnwll....5 G5
Treglemais Pembks....74 D6
Tregole Cnwll....11 H3
Tregolls Cnwll....3 J4
Tregonce Cnwll....10 C7
Tregonetha Cnwll....4 F2
Tregony Cnwll....4 F6
Tregoodwell Cnwll....11 G6
Tregorrick Cnwll....5 G4
Tregoss Cnwll....4 F3
Tregoyd Powys....79 H7
Tregrehan Mills Cnwll....5 H4
Tre-groes Cerdgn....76 D6
Tregullon Cnwll....5 H4
Tregunna Cnwll....10 D7
Tregunnon Cnwll....11 J6
Tregurrian Cnwll....4 D2
Tregynon Powys....94 D4
Tre-gynwr Carmth....58 D5
Trehafod Rhondd....43 G3
Trehan Cnwll....6 D3
Treharris Myr Td....43 H2
Treharrock Cnwll....10 E6
Trehemborne Cnwll....10 B7
Treherbert Carmth....77 G6
Treherbert Rhondd....42 E2
Trehunist Cnwll....6 C2
Trekenner Cnwll....11 L7
Treknow Cnwll....10 E5
Trelan Cnwll....3 J7
Trelash Cnwll....11 H4
Trelassick Cnwll....4 E4
Trelawne Cnwll....5 L4
Trelawnyd Flints....128 C4
Treleague Cnwll....3 K6
Treleaver Cnwll....3 K7
Trelech Carmth....58 A3
Trelech a'r Betws Carmth....58 B3
Treleddyd-fawr Pembks....74 B6
Trelew Cnwll....3 K4
Trelewis Myr Td....43 H2
Treligga Cnwll....10 E5
Trelights Cnwll....10 D6
Trelill Cnwll....10 E7
Trelinnoe Cnwll....11 K6
Trelion Cnwll....4 F4
Trelissick Cnwll....3 L3
Trellech Mons....63 G6
Trelleck Grange Mons....62 F6
Trelogan Flints....128 D4
Trelow Cnwll....4 F1
Trelowarren Cnwll....3 J6
Trelowia Cnwll....6 B3
Treluggan Cnwll....3 M3
Trelystan Powys....95 G3
Tremadog Gwynd....109 K3
Tremail Cnwll....11 H5
Tremain Cerdgn....75 M3
Tremaine Cnwll....11 J5
Tremar Cnwll....6 B1
Trematon Cnwll....6 D3
Trembraze Cnwll....6 B2
Tremeirchion Denbgs....128 C5
Tremethick Cross Cnwll....2 C5
Tremore Cnwll....5 G2
Tre-Mostyn Flints....128 D4
Trenance Cnwll....3 K6
Trenance Cnwll....4 D1
Trenance Cnwll....10 C8
Trenarren Cnwll....5 H5
Trench Wrekin....96 F1
Trench Green Oxon....49 G3
Trendeal Cnwll....4 E4
Trendrine Cnwll....2 D3
Treneague Cnwll....10 D8
Trenear Cnwll....3 H5
Treneglos Cnwll....11 H5
Trenerth Cnwll....2 F4
Trenewan Cnwll....5 K4
Trenewth Cnwll....10 F7
Trengune Cnwll....11 H4
Treninnick Cnwll....4 D3
Trenowah Cnwll....4 C3
Trenoweth Cnwll....3 J4
Trent Dorset....31 K7
Trentham C Stke....114 D3
Trentishoe Devon....28 A1
Trentlock Derbys....116 E5
Trent Port Lincs....135 G2
Trent Vale C Stke....114 D3
Trenwheal Cnwll....3 G4
Treoes V Glam....42 E6
Treorchy Rhondd....42 E2
Trequite Cnwll....10 E7

Tre'r-ddol Cerdgn....92 E5
Trerhyngyll V Glam....42 F6
Trerulefoot Cnwll....6 C3
Tresaith Cerdgn....76 A5
Tresawle Cnwll....4 E5
Tresco IoS....10 b2
Trescott Staffs....97 J4
Trescowe Cnwll....2 F5
Tresean Cnwll....4 C3
Tresham Gloucs....46 A1
Treshnish Isles Ag & B....225 H7
Tresillian Cnwll....4 E5
Tresinney Cnwll....10 F6
Treskinnick Cross Cnwll....11 H3
Tresmeer Cnwll....11 J5
Tresparrett Cnwll....11 G4
Tressait P & K....232 B3
Tresta Shet....281 d6
Tresta Shet....281 f3
Treswell Notts....134 F4
Treswithian Cnwll....3 G3
Treswithian Downs Crematorium Cnwll....3 G3
Tre Taliesin Cerdgn....92 E5
Trethevey Cnwll....10 F5
Trethewey Cnwll....2 B6
Trethomas Caerph....43 J4
Trethosa Cnwll....4 F4
Trethurgy Cnwll....5 H4
Tretio Pembks....74 C6
Tretire Herefs....63 G2
Tretower Powys....61 J3
Treuddyn Flints....128 F8
Trevadlock Cnwll....11 K6
Trevalga Cnwll....10 F4
Trevalyn Wrexhm....129 J8
Trevanger Cnwll....10 D7
Trevanson Cnwll....10 D8
Trevarrack Cnwll....2 D5
Trevarren Cnwll....4 E3
Trevarrian Cnwll....4 D2
Trevarrick Cnwll....5 G6
Trevarth Cnwll....3 J3
Trevaughan Carmth....55 L4
Tre-vaughan Carmth....58 D4
Treveal Cnwll....2 D3
Treveal Cnwll....4 C3
Treveighan Cnwll....10 F6
Trevellas Downs Cnwll....4 B4
Trevelmond Cnwll....5 L2
Trevemper Cnwll....4 D3
Treveor Cnwll....5 G6
Treverbyn Cnwll....4 E5
Treverbyn Cnwll....5 G3
Treverva Cnwll....3 J5
Trevescan Cnwll....2 B6
Trevethin Torfn....62 B6
Trevia Cnwll....10 F6
Trevigro Cnwll....6 C1
Trevilla Cnwll....3 L3
Trevilson Cnwll....4 D4
Treviscoe Cnwll....4 F4
Treviskey Cnwll....4 F6
Trevithick Cnwll....4 E2
Trevithick Cnwll....4 F6
Trevoll Cnwll....4 D4
Trevone Cnwll....10 B7
Trevor Wrexhm....112 C3
Trevorgans Cnwll....2 B6
Trevorrick Cnwll....10 C7
Trevose Cnwll....10 B7
Trew Cnwll....3 G5
Trewalder Cnwll....10 F6
Trewalkin Powys....61 J1
Trewarmett Cnwll....10 F5
Trewassa Cnwll....11 G5
Trewavas Cnwll....2 F5
Treween Cnwll....11 J6
Trewellard Cnwll....2 B4
Trewen Cnwll....11 J6
Trewennack Cnwll....3 H5
Trewent Pembks....55 G7
Trewern Powys....95 G3
Trewetha Cnwll....10 E6
Trewethern Cnwll....10 E7
Trewidland Cnwll....6 B3
Trewillis Cnwll....3 K7
Trewint Cnwll....6 B2
Trewint Cnwll....11 J6
Trewithian Cnwll....3 M4
Trewoodloe Cnwll....11 L8
Trewoon Cnwll....3 H7
Trewoon Cnwll....5 G4
Treworga Cnwll....4 E6
Treworgan Cnwll....4 D5
Treworlas Cnwll....4 E5
Treworld Cnwll....11 G4
Treworthal Cnwll....3 M3
Tre-wyn Mons....62 C3

Treyarnon Cnwll....10 B7
Treyford W Susx....20 D3
Trickett's Cross Dorset....17 L2
Triermain Cumb....178 E5
Triffleton Pembks....75 G7
Trillacott Cnwll....11 K4
Trimdon Dur....169 K4
Trimdon Colliery Dur....169 K4
Trimdon Grange Dur....169 K3
Trimingham Norfk....122 F4
Trimley Lower Street Suffk....91 G7
Trimley St Martin Suffk....91 G7
Trimley St Mary Suffk....91 G7
Trimpley Worcs....97 H7
Trimsaran Carmth....56 F2
Trims Green Herts....70 C4
Trimstone Devon....27 J2
Trinafour P & K....231 K3
Trinant Caerph....61 K7
Tring Herts....68 A5
Tringford Herts....67 M4
Tring Wharf Herts....68 A4
Trinity Angus....234 F3
Trinity Jersey....9 d2
Trinity Gask P & K....221 G3
Triscombe Somset....29 L4
Trislaig Highld....239 H8
Trispen Cnwll....4 D5
Tritlington Nthumb....191 J7
Troan Cnwll....4 E3
Trochry P & K....232 E7
Troedrhiwfuwch Caerph....61 H6
Troedyraur Cerdgn....76 B6
Troedyrhiw Myr Td....61 G6
Trofarth Conwy....127 G5
Trois Bois Jersey....9 c2
Troon Cnwll....3 G3
Troon S Ayrs....196 G5
Trossachs Pier Stirlg....219 H5
Troston Suffk....89 H1
Troswell Cnwll....11 J4
Trotshill Worcs....81 K4
Trottiscliffe Kent....52 D7
Trotton W Susx....36 B6
Troughend Nthumb....190 B7
Trough Gate Lancs....140 D3
Troutbeck Cumb....156 F2
Troutbeck Cumb....165 L5
Troutbeck Bridge Cumb....156 F3
Troway Derbys....133 H4
Trowbridge Wilts....46 B7
Trowell Notts....116 E3
Trowle Common Wilts....46 B7
Trowley Bottom Herts....68 D4
Trowse Newton Norfk....106 C2
Troy Leeds....150 C8
Trudoxhill Somset....32 C2
Trull Somset....30 B6
Trumfleet Donc....142 F7
Trumpan Highld....258 C4
Trumpet Herefs....80 F7
Trumpington Cambs....87 J4
Trumpsgreen Surrey....50 C5
Trunch Norfk....122 F4
Trunnah Lancs....147 G7
Truro Cnwll....4 D6
Truscott Cnwll....11 K5
Trusham Devon....13 K6
Trusley Derbys....115 L4
Trusthorpe Lincs....137 K3
Trysull Staffs....97 J4
Tubney Oxon....66 B7
Tuckenhay Devon....8 B4
Tuckhill Shrops....97 H5
Tuckingmill Cnwll....3 G3
Tuckingmill Wilts....32 F5
Tuckton Bmouth....18 A5
Tucoyse Cnwll....4 F5
Tuddenham Suffk....88 E1
Tuddenham Suffk....90 E5
Tudeley Kent....38 F4
Tudhoe Dur....169 H3
Tudorville Herefs....63 H3
Tudweiliog Gwynd....108 D4
Tuesley Surrey....36 E3
Tuffley Gloucs....64 B4
Tufton Hants....34 F2
Tufton Pembks....75 H6
Tugby Leics....101 G3
Tugford Shrops....96 D6
Tughall Nthumb....203 K7
Tullibody Clacks....220 E8
Tullich Abers....243 L4
Tullich Highld....251 H6
Tullich Highld....264 D7
Tulliemet P & K....232 F5
Tulloch Abers....256 E5
Tullochgorm Ag & B....216 F8
Tulloch Station Highld....240 B7

Tullymurdoch P & K....233 J5
Tullynessle Abers....255 L7
Tulse Hill Gt Lon....51 J4
Tumble Carmth....58 F6
Tumbler's Green Essex....71 K2
Tumby Lincs....136 D7
Tumby Woodside Lincs....136 C6
Tummel Bridge P & K....231 L4
Tunbridge Wells Kent....38 F5
Tundergarth D & G....177 G3
Tunga W Isls....282 g3
Tungate Norfk....122 F5
Tunley BaNES....45 K7
Tunstall C Stke....114 D1
Tunstall E R Yk....145 L2
Tunstall Kent....40 A3
Tunstall Lancs....157 K8
Tunstall N York....160 B3
Tunstall Norfk....107 J2
Tunstall Staffs....114 B6
Tunstall Suffk....91 H4
Tunstall Sundld....181 J8
Tunstead Derbys....132 B5
Tunstead Norfk....122 F7
Tunstead Milton Derbys....131 K4
Tunworth Hants....35 K1
Tupsley Herefs....80 C7
Turgis Green Hants....49 G7
Turkdean Gloucs....65 G4
Tur Langton Leics....100 F4
Turleigh Wilts....46 A6
Turleygreen Shrops....97 H6
Turn Lancs....140 B4
Turnastone Herefs....79 L7
Turnberry S Ayrs....182 F6
Turnchapel C Plym....6 F4
Turnditch Derbys....116 A2
Turner Green Lancs....139 J2
Turner's Green E Susx....23 L3
Turner's Green Warwks....82 E2
Turner's Hill W Susx....38 A6
Turners Puddle Dorset....16 F4
Turnford Herts....69 K6
Turnhouse C Edin....211 G4
Turnworth Dorset....16 F1
Turriff Abers....268 C6
Turton Bottoms Bl w D....139 L4
Turves Cambs....103 G4
Turvey Bed....85 J5
Turville Bucks....49 J1
Turville Heath Bucks....49 H1
Turweston Bucks....84 B7
Tushielaw Inn Border....187 L3
Tutbury Staffs....115 L6
Tutnall Worcs....82 A1
Tutshill Gloucs....63 G8
Tuttington Norfk....122 E6
Tutwell Cnwll....11 M7
Tuxford Notts....134 E5
Twatt Ork....275 b3
Twatt Shet....281 d6
Twechar E Duns....209 J4
Tweedbank Border....201 H6
Tweedmouth Nthumb....202 F3
Tweedsmuir Border....187 G1
Twelveheads Cnwll....4 B6
Twelve Oaks E Susx....24 C3
Twemlow Green Ches E....130 F6
Twenty Lincs....118 F7
Twerton BaNES....45 L6
Twickenham Gt Lon....50 F4
Twigworth Gloucs....64 B3
Twineham W Susx....22 C3
Twineham Green W Susx....22 C3
Twinhoe BaNES....45 L7
Twinstead Essex....89 H7
Twitchen Devon....28 D5
Twitchen Shrops....95 J7
Twitham Kent....41 H4
Two Bridges Devon....12 E7
Two Dales Derbys....132 E7
Two Gates Staffs....99 G3
Two Mile Oak Cross Devon....8 C1
Two Pots Devon....27 J2
Two Waters Herts....68 D6
Twycross Leics....99 G2
Twyford Bucks....67 G2
Twyford Hants....35 G6
Twyford Leics....100 F2
Twyford Lincs....118 B6
Twyford Norfk....121 M6
Twyford Wokham....49 J4
Twyford Common Herefs....80 C8
Twyn-carno Caerph....61 H5
Twynholm D & G....175 G4
Twyning Green Gloucs....81 L7
Twynllanan Carmth....59 L4
Twyn-yr-Odyn V Glam....43 H7
Twyn-y-Sheriff Mons....62 E6

Twywell Nhants 101 L7
Tyberton Herefs 79 M7
Tyburn Birm 98 E5
Tycroes Carmth 57 H3
Ty Croes IoA 124 F5
Tycrwyn Powys 111 L7
Tydd Gote Lincs 120 A7
Tydd St Giles Cambs 119 M8
Tydd St Mary Lincs 119 M7
Tye Hants 20 B6
Tye Green Essex 70 D2
Tye Green Essex 71 J3
Tye Green Essex 88 B8
Tyersal C Brad 141 J1
Tyldesley Wigan 139 K7
Tyler Hill Kent 40 F3
Tylers Green Bucks 67 L8
Tyler's Green Essex 70 D6
Tylers Green Surrey 51 K8
Tylorstown Rhondd 42 F3
Tylwch Powys 93 L7
Ty-nant Conwy 111 J3
Ty-nant Gwynd 111 H6
Tyndrum Stirlg 218 E1
Ty'n-dwr Denbgs 112 C3
Tyneham Dorset 17 G6
Tynemouth N Tyne 181 J5
Tynemouth Crematorium
N Tyne 181 J5
Tyne Tunnel S Tyne 181 H5
Tynewydd Rhondd 60 E7
Tyninghame E Loth 212 D3
Tynron D & G 185 K4
Ty'n-y-bryn Rhondd 42 F4
Ty'n-y-coedcae Caerph 43 K4
Tynygongl IoA 125 J3
Tynygraig Cerdgn 77 J1
Ty'n-y-Groes Conwy 126 F5
Tyn-y-nant Rhondd 43 G4
Tyrie Abers 269 G4
Tyringham M Keyn 85 G6
Tyseley Birm 98 E6
Tythegston Brdgnd 42 C6
Tytherington Ches E 131 H4
Tytherington S Glos 45 K1
Tytherington Somset 32 C2
Tytherington Wilts 32 F3
Tytherleigh Devon 15 H2
Tytherton Lucas Wilts 46 D4
Tyttenhanger Herts 68 F6
Tywardreath Cnwll 5 J4
Tywardreath Highway Cnwll 5 J4
Tywyn Conwy 126 F4
Tywyn Gwynd 92 C3

U

Ubbeston Green Suffk 91 H1
Ubley BaNES 45 G7
Uckerby N York 160 C2
Uckfield E Susx 23 H3
Uckinghall Worcs 81 K7
Uckington Gloucs 64 C2
Uckington Shrops 96 D2
Uddingston S Lans 209 J6
Uddington S Lans 198 E6
Udimore E Susx 24 F3
Udny Green Abers 256 F6
Udny Station Abers 257 G6
Uffcott Wilts 47 H3
Uffculme Devon 29 K8
Uffington Lincs 102 B2
Uffington Oxon 47 L1
Uffington Shrops 96 C1
Ufford C Pete 102 B3
Ufford Suffk 91 G5
Ufton Warwks 83 J3
Ufton Nervet W Berk 48 F5
Ugadale Ag & B 194 B5
Ugborough Devon 7 K4
Uggeshall Suffk 107 J7
Ugglebarnby N York 162 F1
Ughill Sheff 132 E2
Ugley Essex 70 D2
Ugley Green Essex 70 D2
Ugthorpe N York 171 J8
Uibhist A Deas W Isls 283 c10
Uibhist A Tuath W Isls 283 b8
Uig Ag & B 224 F4
Uig Highld 258 B6
Uig Highld 258 F4
Uig W Isls 282 d3
Uigshader Highld 259 G7
Uisken Ag & B 226 D8
Uisken Highld 280 D7
Ulcat Row Cumb 165 L6
Ulceby Lincs 137 H5

Ulceby N Linc 144 E5
Ulceby Skitter N Linc 144 E5
Ulcombe Kent 39 L4
Uldale Cumb 165 H3
Uley Gloucs 63 M7
Ulgham Nthumb 191 J7
Ullapool Highld 261 J1
Ullenhall Warwks 82 D2
Ullenwood Gloucs 64 D4
Ulleskelf N York 151 H7
Ullesthorpe Leics 100 B6
Ulley Rothm 133 J2
Ullingswick Herefs 80 E5
Ullinish Lodge Hotel Highld 246 D1
Ullock Cumb 164 E6
Ulpha Cumb 156 B4
Ulpha Cumb 157 G6
Ulrome E R Yk 153 J4
Ulsta Shet 281 e4
Ulting Wick Essex 71 K5
Ulva Ag & B 226 D4
Ulverley Green Solhll 98 E7
Ulverston Cumb 156 C7
Ulwell Dorset 17 K6
Ulzieside D & G 185 J1
Umberleigh Devon 27 L6
Unapool Highld 271 H2
Underbarrow Cumb 157 G4
Under Burnmouth Border 178 B2
Undercliffe C Brad 141 J1
Underdale Shrops 96 B1
Underling Green Kent 39 J4
Underriver Kent 38 E3
Underwood Newpt 44 D1
Underwood Notts 116 D2
Undley Suffk 104 D7
Undy Mons 44 E2
Union Mills IoM 154 e6
Union Street E Susx 39 H7
Unst Shet 281 f2
Unstone Derbys 133 G4
Unstone Green Derbys 133 G4
Unthank Cumb 165 L1
Unthank Cumb 166 B3
Unthank Cumb 166 E3
Unthank Derbys 132 F4
Unthank Nthumb 202 F3
Upavon Wilts 47 H7
Up Cerne Dorset 16 C2
Upchurch Kent 53 H5
Upcott Devon 28 D5
Upcott Herefs 79 K5
Upend Cambs 88 D3
Up Exe Devon 13 L2
Upgate Norfk 122 C7
Upgate Street Norfk 106 B5
Upgate Street Norfk 106 F5
Uphall Dorset 16 A2
Uphall W Loth 210 E5
Upham Devon 13 K1
Upham Hants 35 H6
Uphampton Herefs 79 M3
Uphampton Worcs 81 J2
Uphill N Som 44 C7
Up Holland Lancs 139 G6
Uplawmoor E Rens 208 D8
Upleadon Gloucs 63 L2
Upleatham R & Cl 170 E6
Uplees Kent 40 C2
Uploders Dorset 15 L4
Uplowman Devon 29 J7
Uplyme Devon 15 H4
Up Marden W Susx 20 C4
Upminster Gt Lon 52 C2
Up Mudford Somset 31 J7
Up Nately Hants 49 G8
Upottery Devon 14 E1
Upper Affcot Shrops 95 K6
Upper Ardchronie Highld 263 G3
Upper Arley Worcs 97 H7
Upper Arncott Oxon 66 F4
Upper Astrop Nhants 83 L7
Upper Basildon W Berk 48 F4
Upper Batley Kirk 141 K3
Upper Beeding W Susx 22 B5
Upper Benefield Nhants 101 L5
Upper Bentley Worcs 82 B2
Upper Bighouse Highld 278 F5
Upper Birchwood Derbys 133 J8
Upper Boat Rhondd 43 H4
Upper Boddington Nhants 83 L5
Upper Borth Cerdgn 92 D5
Upper Brailes Warwks 83 G7
Upper Breinton Herefs 80 B7
Upper Broadheath Worcs 81 J4
Upper Broughton Notts 117 J6
Upper Bucklebury W Berk 48 D5
Upper Burgate Hants 33 K7
Upper Bush Medway 52 E5

Upperby Cumb 177 L8
Upper Caldecote C Beds 86 D6
Upper Canada N Som 44 D7
Upper Canterton Hants 18 D1
Upper Catesby Nhants 83 M3
Upper Catshill Worcs 98 B8
Upper Chapel Powys 78 D7
Upper Cheddon Somset 30 C5
Upper Chicksgrove Wilts 33 C5
Upper Chute Wilts 47 L8
Upper Clapton Gt Lon 51 K2
Upper Clatford Hants 34 D2
Upper Coberley Gloucs 64 E4
Upper Cotton Staffs 115 G2
Upper Cound Shrops 96 C2
Upper Cudworth Barns 142 B6
Upper Cumberworth Kirk 141 K6
Upper Dallachy Moray 267 G4
Upper Deal Kent 41 K5
Upper Dean Bed 85 L2
Upper Denby Kirk 141 K6
Upper Denton Cumb 178 E5
Upper Dicker E Susx 23 J5
Upper Dinchope Shrops 95 L6
Upper Dounreay Highld 279 H3
Upper Dovercourt Essex 73 K1
Upper Drumbane Stirlg 219 L6
Upper Dunsforth N York 150 F3
Upper Eashing Surrey 36 E2
Upper Eathie Highld 263 K7
Upper Egleton Herefs 80 E6
Upper Elkstone Staffs 131 L7
Upper Ellastone Staffs 115 J3
Upper End Derbys 132 B4
Upper Enham Hants 34 E1
Upper Farmcote Shrops 97 H5
Upper Farringdon Hants 35 L4
Upper Framilode Gloucs 63 L5
Upper Froyle Hants 35 M2
Upperglen Highld 258 E6
Upper Godney Somset 31 H2
Upper Gravenhurst C Beds 86 C8
Upper Green Mons 62 D3
Upper Green Suffk 88 E2
Upper Green W Berk 48 A6
Upper Grove Common Herefs 63 H2
Upper Hackney Derbys 132 F7
Upper Hale Surrey 36 B1
Upper Halliford Surrey 50 E5
Upper Halling Medway 52 E6
Upper Hambleton Rutlnd 101 K2
Upper Harbledown Kent 40 F4
Upper Hardres Court Kent 40 F5
Upper Hardwick Herefs 79 M4
Upper Hartfield E Susx 38 C6
Upper Hartshay Derbys 116 C2
Upper Hatherley Gloucs 64 D3
Upper Hatton Staffs 114 C4
Upper Haugh Rothm 142 C8
Upper Hayton Shrops 96 C7
Upper Heaton Kirk 141 J4
Upper Helmsley N York 151 L4
Upper Hergest Herefs 79 J4
Upper Heyford Nhants 84 C3
Upper Heyford Oxon 66 D2
Upper Hill Herefs 80 B4
Upper Hockenden Kent 52 B5
Upper Hopton Kirk 141 K4
Upper Howsell Worcs 81 H5
Upper Hulme Staffs 131 K7
Upper Ifold Surrey 36 F4
Upper Inglesham Swindn 65 J7
Upper Kilcott Gloucs 46 A1
Upper Killay Swans 57 G6
Upper Kinchrackine Ag & B 217 J2
Upper Knockando Moray 254 D3
Upper Lambourn W Berk 47 L3
Upper Landywood Staffs 98 C2
Upper Langford N Som 44 F7
Upper Langwith Derbys 133 K5
Upper Largo Fife 223 G6
Upper Leigh Staffs 115 G4
Upper Leigh N Som 45 H6
Upper Lochton Abers 244 F4
Upper Longdon Staffs 115 H8
Upper & Lower Stondon
C Beds 86 D8
Upper Ludstone Shrops 97 H4
Upper Lybster Highld 275 H1
Upper Lydbrook Gloucs 63 J4
Upper Lyde Herefs 80 C6
Upper Lye Herefs 79 M2
Upper Maes-coed Herefs 79 L8
Upper Midhope Sheff 141 J6
Uppermill Oldham 140 F6
Upper Milton Worcs 81 J1
Upper Minety Wilts 46 E1
Upper Moor Worcs 82 A5
Upper Moor Side Leeds 141 K2

Upper Mulben Moray 267 G6
Upper Netchwood Shrops 96 E5
Upper Nobut Staffs 115 G4
Upper Norwood W Susx 20 F3
Upper Padley Derbys 132 E4
Upper Pennington Hants 18 D4
Upper Pollicott Bucks 67 H4
Upper Poppleton C York 151 J5
Upper Quinton Warwks 82 E6
Upper Ratley Hants 34 D6
Upper Rissington Gloucs 65 J3
Upper Rochford Worcs 80 E2
Upper Ruscoe D & G 174 E3
Upper Sapey Herefs 80 F3
Upper Saxondale Notts 117 K6
Upper Seagry Wilts 46 D3
Upper Shelton C Beds 85 K6
Upper Sheringham Norfk 122 C3
Upper Skelmorlie N Ayrs 207 K5
Upper Slaughter Gloucs 65 H3
Upper Soudley Gloucs 63 K5
Upper Spond Herefs 79 K4
Upper Standen Kent 41 H7
Upper Staploe Bed 86 C3
Upper Stoke Norfk 106 E3
Upper Stowe Nhants 84 C4
Upper Street Hants 33 K7
Upper Street Norfk 106 D7
Upper Street Norfk 123 G7
Upper Street Norfk 123 G8
Upper Street Suffk 88 F5
Upper Street Suffk 90 C5
Upper Street Suffk 90 D8
Upper Strensham Worcs 81 K7
Upper Sundon C Beds 68 D2
Upper Swell Gloucs 65 H2
Upper Tankersley Barns 142 A7
Upper Tasburgh Norfk 106 E4
Upper Tean Staffs 115 G2
Upperthong Kirk 141 H6
Upperthorpe Derbys 133 J4
Upperthorpe N Linc 143 J7
Upper Threapwood Ches W 113 G3
Upperton W Susx 36 E6
Upper Town Derbys 115 L1
Uppertown Derbys 132 F6
Upper Town Dur 168 D3
Upper Town Herefs 80 D5
Uppertown Highld 280 D1
Upper Town N Som 45 G6
Upper Town Suffk 89 J2
Upper Tumble Carmth 59 G6
Upper Tysoe Warwks 83 H6
Upper Ufford Suffk 91 G4
Upperup Gloucs 64 F7
Upper Upham Wilts 47 J3
Upper Upnor Medway 53 G5
Upper Victoria Angus 234 E8
Upper Vobster Somset 32 B1
Upper Wardington Oxon 83 L6
Upper Weald M Keyn 84 F7
Upper Weedon Nhants 84 B3
Upper Welland Worcs 81 H7
Upper Wellingham E Susx 23 G4
Upper Weston BaNES 45 L5
Upper Weybread Suffk 106 E7
Upper Wick Worcs 81 J5
Upper Wield Hants 35 K3
Upper Winchendon Bucks 67 H4
Upperwood Derbys 132 F8
Upper Woodford Wilts 33 K3
Upper Wootton Hants 48 E7
Upper Wraxall Wilts 46 A4
Upper Wyche Worcs 81 H6
Uppincott Devon 13 L2
Uppingham Rutlnd 101 J3
Uppington Dorset 17 K2
Uppington Shrops 96 D2
Upsall N York 161 G5
Upsettlington Border 202 D4
Upshire Essex 69 L7
Up Somborne Hants 34 E4
Upstreet Kent 41 H3
Up Sydling Dorset 16 B2
Upthorpe Suffk 89 K1
Upton Bucks 67 J5
Upton C Pete 102 C3
Upton Cambs 102 D7
Upton Ches W 129 J6
Upton Cnwll 11 H2
Upton Cnwll 11 K8
Upton Cumb 165 K3
Upton Devon 7 K6
Upton Devon 14 C2
Upton Dorset 16 E6
Upton Dorset 17 J4
Upton E R Yk 153 J5
Upton Halton 129 L2
Upton Hants 34 E7

Upton Hants 47 M7
Upton Leics 99 K3
Upton Lincs 135 H2
Upton Nhants 84 D3
Upton Norfk 107 H1
Upton Notts 117 J1
Upton Notts 134 E4
Upton Oxon 48 D2
Upton Oxon 65 K4
Upton Pembks 55 G6
Upton R & Cl 171 G6
Upton Slough 50 B3
Upton Somset 29 H5
Upton Somset 31 G5
Upton Wakefd 142 D5
Upton Warwks 82 D4
Upton Wilts 32 E4
Upton Wirral 129 G2
Upton Bishop Herefs 63 K2
Upton Cheyney S Glos 45 K5
Upton Cressett Shrops 96 E5
Upton Crews Herefs 63 J2
Upton Cross Cnwll 11 K8
Upton End C Beds 86 C8
Upton Grey Hants 35 L1
Upton Heath Ches W 129 J5
Upton Hellions Devon 13 K2
Upton Lovell Wilts 32 F3
Upton Magna Shrops 96 C1
Upton Noble Somset 32 B3
Upton Pyne Devon 13 L3
Upton St Leonards Gloucs 64 B4
Upton Scudamore Wilts 32 E1
Upton Snodsbury Worcs 81 L4
Upton Towans Cnwll 2 F3
Upton-upon-Severn Worcs 81 K7
Upton Warren Worcs 81 L2
Upwaltham W Susx 20 F4
Upware Cambs 87 L1
Upwell Norfk 103 K3
Upwey Dorset 16 C5
Upwick Green Herts 70 C2
Upwood Cambs 102 E6
Urchfont Wilts 46 F7
Urdimarsh Herefs 80 C5
Ure Bank N York 150 D1
Urlay Nook S on T 169 L7
Urmston Traffd 130 E1
Urpeth Dur 181 G7
Urquhart Moray 266 F4
Urra N York 161 J2
Urray Highld 250 E1
Usan Angus 235 H4
Ushaw Moor Dur 169 G2
Usk Mons 62 D7
Usselby Lincs 136 A1
Usworth Sundld 181 H7
Utkinton Ches W 130 A6
Utley C Brad 149 J7
Uton Devon 13 J3
Utterby Lincs 136 F1
Uttoxeter Staffs 115 H5
Uwchmynydd Gwynd 108 B6
Uxbridge Gt Lon 50 D2
Uyeasound Shet 281 f2
Uzmaston Pembks 54 F4

V

Vale Guern 9 k2
Vale Crematorium Luton 68 E2
Vale of Glamorgan
   Crematorium V Glam 43 H7
Valley IoA 124 E4
Valley End Surrey 50 B6
Valley Truckle Cnwll 10 F6
Valtos Highld 259 J4
Valtos W Isls 282 e3
Vange Essex 52 F2
Varteg Torfn 61 L6
Vatsetter Shet 281 e3
Vatten Highld 258 D7
Vaynor Myr Td 61 G5
Vazon Bay Guern 9 i2
Veensgarth Shet 281 e6
Velindre Powys 79 H7
Vellow Somset 29 K3
Velly Devon 26 E6
Venngreen Devon 26 F8
Vennington Shrops 95 H2
Venn Ottery Devon 14 C4
Venny Tedburn Devon 13 J3
Venterdon Cnwll 11 L7
Ventnor IoW 19 J8
Venton Devon 7 H3
Vernham Dean Hants 47 M7
Vernham Street Hants 47 M7

Vernolds Common Shrops 95 L7
Verwood Dorset 17 L1
Veryan Cnwll 4 E7
Veryan Green Cnwll 4 F6
Vicarage Devon 14 E5
Vickerstown Cumb 146 C2
Victoria Barns 141 J6
Victoria Blae G 61 J5
Victoria Cnwll 5 G3
Vidlin Shet 281 e5
Viewfield Moray 266 F3
Viewpark N Lans 209 J6
Vigo Kent 52 D6
Village de Putron Guern 9 k3
Ville la Bas Jersey 9 a1
Villiaze Guern 9 i3
Vinehall Street E Susx 24 D3
Vines Cross E Susx 23 K4
Vinters Park Crematorium
   Kent 39 K2
Virginia Water Surrey 50 C5
Virginstow Devon 11 M4
Vobster Somset 32 B1
Voe Shet 281 d5
Vowchurch Herefs 79 L7
Vulcan Village St Hel 130 B1

W

Waberthwaite Cumb 155 K4
Wackerfield Dur 168 F6
Wacton Norfk 106 D5
Wadborough Worcs 81 K5
Waddesdon Bucks 67 H4
Waddeton Devon 8 C3
Waddicar Sefton 138 E7
Waddingham Lincs 144 B8
Waddington Lancs 148 C7
Waddington Lincs 135 K6
Waddon Devon 13 K6
Waddon Dorset 16 B5
Waddon Gt Lon 51 J6
Wadebridge Cnwll 10 D8
Wadeford Somset 30 D8
Wadenhoe Nhants 101 M6
Wadesmill Herts 69 K4
Wadhurst E Susx 39 G7
Wadshelf Derbys 132 F5
Wadswick Wilts 46 B5
Wadworth Donc 142 F8
Waen Denbgs 127 K7
Waen Denbgs 128 D6
Waen Powys 112 C7
Waen Fach Powys 112 B8
Waen-pentir Gwynd 125 K6
Waen-wen Gwynd 125 K6
Wagbeach Shrops 95 J3
Wainfelin Torfn 62 B6
Wainfleet All Saints Lincs 137 J7
Wainfleet Bank Lincs 137 J7
Wainfleet St Mary Lincs 137 J8
Wainford Norfk 107 G5
Wainhouse Corner Cnwll 11 H3
Wainscott Medway 52 F5
Wain's Hill N Som 44 E5
Wainstalls Calder 141 G2
Waitby Cumb 158 C1
Waithe Lincs 145 H7
Wakefield Wakefd 142 A4
Wakefield Crematorium
   Wakefd 141 M4
Wake Green Birm 98 E6
Wakerley Nhants 101 L3
Wakes Colne Essex 72 C2
Walberswick Suffk 107 K8
Walberton W Susx 21 G5
Walbottle N u Ty 180 E5
Walbutt D & G 175 J1
Walby Cumb 178 B6
Walcombe Somset 31 J2
Walcot Lincs 118 E4
Walcot N Linc 143 M3
Walcot Shrops 95 J6
Walcot Shrops 96 D1
Walcot Swindn 47 H2
Walcot Warwks 82 D4
Walcote Leics 100 C6
Walcot Green Norfk 106 C7
Walcott Lincs 136 B8
Walcott Norfk 123 G5
Walden N York 159 H6
Walden Head N York 159 H6
Walden Stubbs N York 142 E4
Walderslade Medway 53 G6
Walderton W Susx 20 C5
Walditch Dorset 15 L4
Waldley Derbys 115 J4

Waldridge Dur 169 H1
Waldringfield Suffk 91 G6
Waldron E Susx 23 J3
Wales Rothm 133 J3
Wales Somset 31 K6
Walesby Lincs 136 B1
Walesby Notts 134 D5
Walford Herefs 63 H3
Walford Herefs 79 M1
Walford Shrops 113 G7
Walford Staffs 114 C5
Walford Heath Shrops 113 G7
Walgherton Ches E 113 M2
Walgrave Nhants 84 F1
Walhampton Hants 18 E4
Walkden Salfd 139 L7
Walker N u Ty 181 H6
Walkerburn Border 200 D5
Walker Fold Lancs 148 B7
Walkeringham Notts 134 F1
Walkerith Lincs 134 F1
Walkern Herts 69 H2
Walker's Green Herefs 80 C5
Walker's Heath Birm 98 D7
Walkerton Fife 222 C7
Walkford Dorset 18 C5
Walkhampton Devon 7 G1
Walkington E R Yk 152 F8
Walkley Sheff 133 G2
Walk Mill Lancs 140 C2
Walkwood Worcs 82 B2
Wall Nthumb 179 L5
Wall Staffs 98 E2
Wallacetown S Ayrs 183 H2
Wallacetown S Ayrs 196 C6
Wallands Park E Susx 22 F5
Wallasey Wirral 129 G1
Wallasey (Kingsway) Tunnel
   Wirral 129 H2
Wall End Cumb 156 B6
Wall End Herefs 80 B4
Wallend Medway 53 J4
Waller's Green Herefs 80 F7
Wallhead Cumb 178 B6
Wall Heath Dudley 97 K5
Wall Houses Nthumb 180 C5
Wallingford Oxon 48 F1
Wallington Gt Lon 51 H6
Wallington Hants 19 K2
Wallington Herts 86 F8
Wallington Heath Wsall 98 C3
Wallis Pembks 75 G7
Wallisdown Poole 17 L4
Walliswood Surrey 37 H3
Walls Shet 281 c6
Wallsend N Tyne 181 H5
Wallthwaite Cumb 165 K5
Wall under Haywood Shrops 96 C5
Wallyford E Loth 211 L4
Walmer Kent 41 L5
Walmer Bridge Lancs 138 F3
Walmersley Bury 140 B5
Walmestone Kent 41 H3
Walmley Birm 98 F5
Walmley Ash Birm 98 F5
Walmsgate Lincs 137 G4
Walney Cumb 146 C2
Walpole Somset 30 D3
Walpole Suffk 107 H8
Walpole Cross Keys Norfk 120 B7
Walpole Highway Norfk 120 B8
Walpole St Andrew Norfk 120 B8
Walpole St Peter Norfk 120 B8
Walrow Somset 30 E2
Walsall Wsall 98 C4
Walsall Wood Wsall 98 D3
Walsden Calder 140 D3
Walsgrave on Sowe Covtry 99 K7
Walsham le Willows Suffk 89 K1
Walshaw Bury 140 A5
Walshford N York 150 F5
Walsoken Norfk 103 K1
Walston S Lans 199 H4
Walsworth Herts 69 G1
Walter's Ash Bucks 67 K7
Walters Green Kent 38 D5
Walterston V Glam 43 G7
Walterstone Herefs 62 D2
Waltham Kent 40 E5
Waltham NE Lin 145 H7
Waltham Abbey Essex 69 K7
Waltham Chase Hants 35 H7
Waltham Cross Herts 69 K7
Waltham on the Wolds Leics 117 L6
Waltham St Lawrence W & M 49 K4
Waltham's Cross Essex 71 G1
Walthamstow Gt Lon 51 K1
Walton C Pete 102 D3
Walton Cumb 178 C6

Walton Derbys 133 G6
Walton Leeds 150 F6
Walton Leics 100 C4
Walton M Keyn 85 H7
Walton Powys 79 J3
Walton Shrops 95 L7
Walton Somset 31 G4
Walton Staffs 114 D5
Walton Staffs 114 D6
Walton Suffk 91 G8
Walton W Susx 20 D6
Walton Wakefd 142 A4
Walton Warwks 83 G4
Walton Wrekin 113 K7
Walton Cardiff Gloucs 64 C1
Walton East Pembks 55 H2
Walton Elm Dorset 32 C7
Walton Grounds Nhants 83 L8
Walton Highway Norfk 103 K1
Walton-in-Gordano N Som 44 E4
Walton Lea Crematorium
   Warrtn 130 B3
Walton-le-Dale Lancs 139 H2
Walton-on-Thames Surrey 50 E5
Walton-on-the-Hill Staffs 114 F7
Walton on the Hill Surrey 51 G7
Walton-on-the-Naze Essex 73 K7
Walton on the Wolds Leics 117 G7
Walton-on-Trent Derbys 115 L7
Walton Park N Som 44 E4
Walton West Pembks 54 E4
Waltonwrays Crematorium
   N York 149 H5
Walwen Flints 128 D4
Walwen Flints 128 E4
Walwen Flints 128 E5
Walwick Nthumb 179 L5
Walworth Darltn 169 G7
Walworth Gt Lon 51 J3
Walworth Gate Darltn 169 G6
Walwyn's Castle Pembks 54 E4
Wambrook Somset 15 G1
Wampool Cumb 177 H1
Wanborough Surrey 36 D1
Wanborough Swindn 47 J2
Wandon End Herts 68 E3
Wandsworth Gt Lon 51 H4
Wangford Suffk 107 J7
Wanlip Leics 100 D1
Wanlockhead D & G 186 C4
Wannock E Susx 23 K6
Wansford C Pete 102 B3
Wansford E R Yk 153 G4
Wanshurst Green Kent 39 J4
Wanstead Gt Lon 51 L1
Wanstrow Somset 32 B3
Wanswell Gloucs 63 K6
Wantage Oxon 48 B1
Wants Green Worcs 81 H4
Wapley S Glos 45 L3
Wappenbury Warwks 83 J2
Wappenham Nhants 84 C6
Warbleton E Susx 23 K4
Warborough Oxon 66 F8
Warboys Cambs 102 F7
Warbreck Bpool 146 F8
Warbstow Cnwll 11 H4
Warburton Traffd 130 D2
Warcop Cumb 167 H7
Warden Kent 53 M5
Warden Nthumb 179 L5
Ward End Birm 98 E5
Warden Street C Beds 86 C6
Ward Green Suffk 90 B2
Ward Green Cross Lancs 148 B7
Wardhedges C Beds 85 L8
Wardington Oxon 83 L6
Wardle Ches E 130 B8
Wardle Rochdl 140 D4
Wardley Gatesd 181 H6
Wardley Rutlnd 101 H3
Wardley Salfd 140 A7
Wardlow Derbys 132 D5
Wardsend Ches E 131 J3
Wardy Hill Cambs 103 K7
Ware Herts 69 K4
Wareham Dorset 17 H5
Warehorne Kent 25 J1
Warenford Nthumb 203 J7
Waren Mill Nthumb 203 J6
Warenton Nthumb 203 J7
Wareside Herts 69 K4
Waresley Cambs 86 E4
Waresley Worcs 81 J1
Ware Street Kent 39 K2
Warfield Br For 49 L4
Warfleet Devon 8 C5
Wargate Lincs 119 H5
Wargrave Wokham 49 J3

Warham Herefs 80 B7
Warham Norfk 121 L3
Wark Nthumb 179 K3
Wark Nthumb 202 C5
Warkleigh Devon 27 M6
Warkton Nhants 101 K7
Warkworth Nhants 83 L7
Warkworth Nthumb 191 K5
Warlaby N York 160 E4
Warland Calder 140 E4
Warleggan Cnwll 5 K1
Warleigh BaNES 46 A6
Warley Town Calder 141 G3
Warlingham Surrey 51 K7
Warmbrook Derbys 115 M1
Warmfield Wakefd 142 B4
Warmingham Ches E 130 D7
Warmington Nhants 102 B5
Warmington Warwks 83 K5
Warminster Wilts 32 E2
Warmley S Glos 45 K4
Warmsworth Donc 142 E7
Warmwell Dorset 16 E5
Warndon Worcs 81 K4
Warnford Hants 35 J6
Warnham W Susx 37 J4
Warnham Court W Susx 37 J4
Warningcamp W Susx 21 H5
Warninglid W Susx 37 K5
Warren Ches E 131 H5
Warren Pembks 54 F7
Warrenby R & Cl 170 D5
Warrenhill S Lans 198 F5
Warren Row W & M 49 K3
Warren's Green Herts 69 H4
Warren Street Kent 40 B5
Warrington M Keyn 85 H4
Warrington Warrtn 130 B2
Warriston C Edin 211 H4
Warriston Crematorium
  C Edin 211 H4
Warsash Hants 19 H2
Warslow Staffs 132 B7
Warsop Vale Notts 133 L6
Warter E R Yk 152 D5
Warthermaske N York 160 B6
Warthill N York 151 L5
Wartling E Susx 24 B5
Wartnaby Leics 117 J7
Warton Lancs 138 E2
Warton Lancs 147 K2
Warton Nthumb 190 E5
Warton Warwks 99 H3
Warwick Warwks 83 G2
Warwick Bridge Cumb 178 B7
Warwick-on-Eden Cumb 178 B7
Warwicksland Cumb 178 B3
Wasbister Ork 275 C3
Wasdale Head Cumb 156 E4
Wash Derbys 131 L3
Washall Green Herts 70 C1
Washaway Cnwll 5 H1
Washbourne Devon 8 B4
Washbrook Somset 30 F1
Washbrook Suffk 90 D6
Washfield Devon 29 G7
Washfold N York 159 J2
Washford Somset 29 J3
Washford Pyne Devon 28 E8
Washingborough Lincs 135 L5
Washington Sundld 181 H7
Washington W Susx 21 J4
Washwood Heath Birm 98 E5
Wasing W Berk 48 E6
Waskerley Dur 168 D2
Wasperton Warwks 83 G3
Wasps Nest Lincs 135 M6
Wass N York 161 J6
Watchet Somset 29 K2
Watchfield Oxon 47 K1
Watchfield Somset 30 E2
Watchgate Cumb 157 H3
Watchill Cumb 165 G2
Watcombe Torbay 8 D2
Watendlath Cumb 165 J7
Water Devon 13 H6
Water Lancs 140 C3
Waterbeach Cambs 87 K2
Waterbeach W Susx 20 E5
Waterbeck D & G 177 H3
Waterden Norfk 121 J4
Water Eaton Oxon 66 D5
Water Eaton Staffs 97 K1
Water End Bed 86 C5
Water End Bed 86 C5
Water End C Beds 85 L7
Waterend Cumb 164 F6
Water End E R Yk 152 B8
Water End Essex 88 B7

Water End Herts 68 D5
Water End Herts 69 G6
Waterfall Staffs 115 H1
Waterfoot Ag & B 194 C3
Waterfoot E Rens 208 F7
Waterford Herts 69 J4
Water Fryston Wakefd 142 D2
Watergate Cnwll 11 G6
Waterhead Cumb 156 E2
Waterheads Border 200 B3
Waterhouses Dur 168 F3
Waterhouses Staffs 115 H2
Wateringbury Kent 39 H3
Waterlane Gloucs 64 D3
Waterloo Cnwll 10 F8
Waterloo Derbys 133 H7
Waterloo Herefs 79 L5
Waterloo Highld 247 K4
Waterloo N Lans 209 L8
Waterloo Norfk 122 E7
Waterloo P & K 233 G7
Waterloo Pembks 55 G6
Waterloo Sefton 138 C8
Waterloo Cross Devon 29 J8
Waterloo Port Gwynd 125 J6
Waterlooville Hants 19 M2
Watermillock Cumb 166 B6
Water Newton Cambs 102 C4
Water Orton Warwks 98 F5
Waterperry Oxon 66 F6
Waterrow Somset 29 J6
Watersfield W Susx 21 G4
Waterside Bl w D 139 L3
Waterside Bucks 68 B7
Waterside Cumb 165 H2
Waterside Donc 143 H5
Waterside E Ayrs 184 C1
Waterside E Ayrs 196 F2
Waterside E Duns 209 H4
Water's Nook Bolton 139 K6
Waterstein Highld 258 A7
Waterstock Oxon 66 F6
Waterston Pembks 54 F5
Water Stratford Bucks 84 C8
Water Street Neath 42 B4
Waters Upton Wrekin 113 K7
Water Yeat Cumb 156 D5
Watford Herts 68 E7
Watford Nhants 84 B2
Wath N York 149 L2
Wath N York 160 D7
Wath upon Dearne Rothm 142 C7
Watlington Norfk 104 C1
Watlington Oxon 67 G8
Watnall Notts 116 E2
Watten Highld 280 B5
Wattisfield Suffk 105 K8
Wattisham Suffk 89 K5
Watton Dorset 15 K4
Watton E R Yk 152 F6
Watton Norfk 105 J3
Watton-at-Stone Herts 69 J3
Watton Green Norfk 105 J3
Wattons Green Essex 70 D8
Wattston N Lans 209 K5
Wattstown Rhondd 42 F3
Wattsville Caerph 43 K3
Wauldby E R Yk 144 B2
Waulkmill Abers 244 F3
Waunarlwydd Swans 57 H6
Waunfawr Cerdgn 92 D7
Waunfawr Gwynd 125 J7
Waungron Swans 57 G4
Waunlwyd Blae G 61 J5
Wavendon M Keyn 85 H7
Waveney Crematorium Suffk 107 J6
Waverbridge Cumb 165 H1
Waverton Ches W 129 K7
Waverton Cumb 165 H1
Wawne E R Yk 153 H8
Waxham Norfk 123 J6
Waxholme E R Yk 145 K2
Way Kent 41 K2
Waye Devon 13 H8
Wayford Somset 15 J1
Waytown Dorset 15 L3
Way Village Devon 13 K1
Way Wick N Som 44 D6
Weacombe Somset 29 K3
Weald Oxon 65 L6
Wealdstone Gt Lon 50 F1
Weardley Leeds 150 D7
Weare Somset 44 E8
Weare Giffard Devon 27 H6
Wearhead Dur 167 K3
Wearne Somset 30 F5
Wear Valley Crematorium Dur 169 H4
Weasdale Cumb 158 B2

Weasenham All Saints Norfk 121 J7
Weasenham St Peter Norfk 121 J7
Weaste Salfd 140 B8
Weatheroak Hill Worcs 98 D8
Weaverham Ches W 130 B5
Weaverslake Staffs 115 J7
Weaverthorpe N York 152 E2
Webbington Somset 44 D7
Webb's Heath S Glos 45 K4
Webheath Worcs 82 B2
Webton Herefs 80 A7
Wedderlairs Abers 256 F5
Wedding Hall Fold N York 149 G6
Weddington Kent 41 J3
Weddington Warwks 99 K5
Wedhampton Wilts 46 F7
Wedmore Somset 31 G1
Wednesbury Sandw 98 C4
Wednesfield Wolves 97 L3
Weecar Notts 135 G6
Weedon Bucks 67 K3
Weedon Bec Nhants 84 C3
Weedon Lois Nhants 84 B6
Weeford Staffs 98 F3
Week Devon 8 A2
Week Devon 27 K5
Week Devon 28 C7
Weeke Devon 13 H2
Weeke Hants 34 F5
Weekley Nhants 101 J7
Week St Mary Cnwll 11 J3
Weel E R Yk 153 G7
Weeley Essex 73 H3
Weeley Crematorium Essex 73 H3
Weeley Heath Essex 73 H3
Weem P & K 232 C5
Weeping Cross Staffs 114 E7
Weethley Warwks 82 C4
Weeting Norfk 104 F5
Weeton E R Yk 145 K4
Weeton Lancs 138 D1
Weeton N York 150 C6
Weetwood Leeds 150 C8
Weir Lancs 140 C3
Weirbrook Shrops 112 E6
Weir Quay Devon 6 E2
Weisdale Shet 281 d5
Welborne Norfk 106 B2
Welbourn Lincs 118 C1
Welburn N York 151 M2
Welbury N York 160 F2
Welby Lincs 118 C4
Welches Dam Cambs 103 K6
Welcombe Devon 26 D7
Weldon Nhants 101 K5
Weldon Bridge Nthumb 191 G6
Welford Nhants 100 E7
Welford W Berk 48 B4
Welford-on-Avon Warwks 82 D5
Welham Leics 101 G5
Welham Notts 134 E3
Welham Bridge E R Yk 143 K1
Welham Green Herts 69 G6
Well Hants 36 A2
Well Lincs 137 H5
Well N York 160 C6
Welland Worcs 81 H7
Wellbank Angus 234 D7
Well End Bucks 49 L1
Well End Herts 69 G7
Wellesbourne Warwks 83 G4
Wellesbourne Mountford
  Warwks 83 G4
Well Head Herts 68 F2
Well Hill Kent 52 B6
Wellhouse W Berk 48 D4
Welling Gt Lon 51 M4
Wellingborough Nhants 85 H2
Wellingham Norfk 121 J7
Wellingore Lincs 135 K8
Wellington Cumb 155 K2
Wellington Herefs 80 C5
Wellington Somset 29 L6
Wellington Wrekin 96 E1
Wellington Heath Herefs 81 G7
Wellington Marsh Herefs 80 C6
Wellow BaNES 45 L7
Wellow IoW 18 F6
Wellow Notts 134 D6
Wellpond Green Herts 69 L3
Wells Somset 31 J2
Wellsborough Leics 99 K3
Wells Green Ches E 113 M1
Wells Head C Brad 141 G4
Wells-next-the-Sea Norfk 121 K3
Wellstye Green Essex 70 F3
Well Town Devon 13 L1
Welltree P & K 221 G3
Wellwood Fife 210 E1

Welney Norfk 103 L4
Welshampton Shrops 113 G6
Welsh Bicknor Herefs 63 H4
Welsh End Shrops 113 H4
Welsh Frankton Shrops 112 E5
Welsh Hook Pembks 74 F5
Welsh Newton Herefs 63 G3
Welshpool Powys 94 F2
Welsh St Donats V Glam 42 F6
Welton Cumb 165 K2
Welton E R Yk 144 B2
Welton Lincs 135 K4
Welton Nhants 84 B2
Welton le Marsh Lincs 137 J6
Welton le Wold Lincs 136 E2
Welwick E R Yk 145 J3
Welwyn Herts 69 G4
Welwyn Garden City Herts 69 G4
Wem Shrops 113 H5
Wembdon Somset 30 D3
Wembley Gt Lon 50 F2
Wembury Devon 7 G5
Wembworthy Devon 12 F1
Wemyss Bay Inver 207 K5
Wenallt Cerdgn 77 J1
Wendens Ambo Essex 87 K8
Wendlebury Oxon 66 E3
Wendling Norfk 105 J1
Wendover Bucks 67 L5
Wendron Cnwll 3 H5
Wendy Cambs 87 G5
Wenfordbridge Cnwll 10 F7
Wenhaston Suffk 107 J8
Wennington Cambs 102 E7
Wennington Gt Lon 52 B3
Wennington Lancs 147 M2
Wensley Derbys 132 E7
Wensley N York 159 K5
Wentbridge Wakefd 142 D4
Wentnor Shrops 95 J5
Wentworth Cambs 103 K7
Wentworth Rothm 142 B8
Wentworth Castle Barns 141 M7
Wenvoe V Glam 43 H7
Weobley Herefs 79 M5
Weobley Marsh Herefs 80 A5
Wepham W Susx 21 H5
Wereham Norfk 104 D3
Wergs Wolves 97 K3
Wern Gwynd 109 K4
Wern Powys 61 H3
Wern Powys 95 G1
Wern Shrops 112 D4
Werneth Low Tamesd 131 J1
Wernffrwd Swans 56 F6
Wern-y-gaer Flints 128 F6
Werrington C Pete 102 D3
Werrington Cnwll 11 L5
Werrington Staffs 114 E2
Wervin Ches W 129 K5
Wesham Lancs 138 E1
Wessex Vale Crematorium
  Hants 35 G7
Wessington Derbys 133 G8
West Aberthaw V Glam 42 F8
West Acre Norfk 121 G6
West Allerdean Nthumb 202 F4
West Alvington Devon 7 L6
West Amesbury Wilts 33 K3
West Anstey Devon 28 E5
West Appleton N York 160 B4
West Ashby Lincs 136 E5
West Ashling W Susx 20 D5
West Ashton Wilts 46 C7
West Auckland Dur 168 F5
West Ayton N York 163 H5
West Bagborough Somset 30 A4
West Bank Blae G 61 K6
West Bank Halton 129 L3
West Barkwith Lincs 136 C4
West Barnby N York 171 J8
West Barns E Loth 212 B3
West Barsham Norfk 121 K5
West Bay Dorset 15 K4
West Beckham Norfk 122 C4
West Bedfont Surrey 50 D4
Westbere Kent 41 J2
West Bergholt Essex 72 D2
West Berkshire Crematorium
  W Berk 48 D5
West Bexington Dorset 15 M5
West Bilney Norfk 120 F8
West Blatchington Br & H 22 D6
West Boldon S Tyne 181 J6
Westborough Lincs 117 M3
Westbourne Bmouth 17 L4
Westbourne W Susx 20 B5
West Bourton Dorset 32 C5
West Bowling C Brad 141 J2

West Brabourne Kent ... 40 E6
West Bradenham Norfk ... 105 J2
West Bradford Lancs ... 148 C7
West Bradley Somset ... 31 J3
West Bretton Wakefd ... 141 L5
West Bridgford Notts ... 117 G4
West Briscoe Dur ... 168 B6
West Bromwich Sandw ... 98 C5
Westbrook Kent ... 41 K1
Westbrook W Berk ... 48 B4
Westbrook Wilts ... 46 D5
West Buckland Devon ... 28 B4
West Buckland Somset ... 30 B6
West Burrafirth Shet ... 281 c5
West Burton N York ... 159 H5
West Burton W Susx ... 21 G4
Westbury Bucks ... 84 B8
Westbury Shrops ... 95 J2
Westbury Wilts ... 46 C8
Westbury Leigh Wilts ... 32 E1
Westbury-on-Severn Gloucs ... 63 L4
Westbury-on-Trym Bristl ... 45 H3
Westbury-sub-Mendip Somset ... 31 H1
West Butsfield Dur ... 168 E2
West Butterwick N Linc ... 143 L6
Westby Lancs ... 138 D2
West Byfleet Surrey ... 50 D6
West Cairngaan D & G ... 172 E8
West Caister Norfk ... 107 K1
West Calder W Loth ... 210 D6
West Camel Somset ... 31 J6
West Chaldon Dorset ... 16 E6
West Challow Oxon ... 48 A1
West Charleton Devon ... 7 L6
West Chelborough Dorset ... 15 M2
West Chevington Nthumb ... 191 J6
West Chiltington W Susx ... 21 J3
West Chinnock Somset ... 31 G8
West Chisenbury Wilts ... 47 H8
West Clandon Surrey ... 50 D8
West Cliffe Kent ... 41 K6
Westcliff-on-Sea Sthend ... 53 J2
West Coker Somset ... 31 H8
West Combe Devon ... 7 L2
Westcombe Somset ... 31 L3
West Compton Somset ... 31 K2
West Compton Abbas Dorset ... 16 A4
Westcote Gloucs ... 65 J3
Westcote Barton Oxon ... 66 B2
Westcott Bucks ... 67 H4
Westcott Devon ... 14 B2
Westcott Surrey ... 37 H1
West Cottingwith N York ... 151 L7
Westcourt Wilts ... 47 J6
West Cowick E R Yk ... 143 G3
West Cross Swans ... 57 H7
West Curry Cnwll ... 11 K4
West Curthwaite Cumb ... 165 K1
Westdean E Susx ... 23 J7
West Dean W Susx ... 20 E4
West Dean Wilts ... 34 B5
West Deeping Lincs ... 102 C2
West Derby Lpool ... 129 J1
West Dereham Norfk ... 104 D3
West Ditchburn Nthumb ... 191 G2
West Down Devon ... 27 J3
Westdown Camp Wilts ... 33 H2
Westdowns Cnwll ... 10 F6
West Drayton Gt Lon ... 50 D3
West Drayton Notts ... 134 E5
West Dunnet Highld ... 280 B2
Wested Kent ... 52 B5
West Ella E R Yk ... 144 C2
West End Bed ... 85 J4
West End Br For ... 49 L5
West End Caerph ... 43 K3
West End Cambs ... 87 G2
West End Cumb ... 177 K7
West End E R Yk ... 144 A2
West End E R Yk ... 144 F2
West End E R Yk ... 145 H2
Westend Gloucs ... 64 A5
West End Hants ... 34 F7
West End Hants ... 35 K4
West End Herts ... 69 H5
West End Herts ... 69 J6
West End Lancs ... 139 L2
West End Leeds ... 150 B8
West End Lincs ... 145 K8
West End N Som ... 44 F5
West End N York ... 151 H7
West End Norfk ... 105 H2
West End Norfk ... 107 K1
West End Oxon ... 48 E2
West End S Glos ... 45 L1
West End Somset ... 31 L4
West End Surrey ... 50 B6
West End Surrey ... 50 E6
West End W & M ... 49 K4

West End W Susx ... 22 B4
West End Wilts ... 32 F6
West End Wilts ... 33 G6
West End Wilts ... 46 E3
West End Green Hants ... 49 G6
Westend Town Nthumb ... 179 H6
Westenhanger Kent ... 40 F7
Wester Aberchalder Highld ... 250 F7
Westerdale Highld ... 279 K6
Westerdale N York ... 161 L2
Westerfield Suffk ... 90 E5
Westergate W Susx ... 20 F6
Westerham Kent ... 51 L8
Westerhope N u Ty ... 180 F5
Westerland Devon ... 8 C2
Westerleigh S Glos ... 45 K3
Westerleigh Crematorium
    S Glos ... 45 L3
Western Isles W Isls ... 282 e6
Wester Ochiltree W Loth ... 210 D4
Wester Pitkierie Fife ... 223 K6
Westerton W Susx ... 20 E5
Westerton of Rossie Angus ... 235 G4
Westerwick Shet ... 281 c6
West Ewell Surrey ... 51 G6
West Farleigh Kent ... 39 H3
West Farndon Nhants ... 83 M5
West Felton Shrops ... 112 E6
Westfield BaNES ... 45 K8
Westfield Cumb ... 164 C5
Westfield E Susx ... 24 E4
Westfield Highld ... 279 J3
Westfield N Lans ... 209 J4
Westfield Norfk ... 105 K2
Westfield W Loth ... 210 B4
Westfields Dorset ... 16 D2
Westfields Herefs ... 80 C7
Westfields of Rattray P & K ... 233 J6
Westfield Sole Kent ... 53 G6
West Flotmanby N York ... 163 K6
Westford Somset ... 29 L6
Westgate Dur ... 167 L3
Westgate N Linc ... 143 K6
Westgate Norfk ... 121 L3
Westgate Hill C Brad ... 141 K2
Westgate-on-Sea Kent ... 41 K1
Westgate Street Norfk ... 122 D7
West Ginge Oxon ... 48 C2
West Grafton Wilts ... 47 K7
West Green Hants ... 49 H7
West Grimstead Wilts ... 33 L5
West Grinstead W Susx ... 37 J6
West Haddlesey N York ... 142 E2
West Haddon Nhants ... 84 C1
West Hagbourne Oxon ... 48 D2
West Hagley Worcs ... 97 K7
Westhall Suffk ... 107 J7
West Hallam Derbys ... 116 D3
West Hallam Common Derbys ... 116 C3
West Halton N Linc ... 144 A4
Westham Dorset ... 16 C6
Westham E Susx ... 23 L6
West Ham Gt Lon ... 51 K2
Westham Somset ... 30 F2
Westhampnett W Susx ... 20 E5
West Handley Derbys ... 133 H4
West Hanney Oxon ... 66 B8
West Hanningfield Essex ... 71 H7
West Harnham Wilts ... 33 K5
West Harptree BaNES ... 45 H7
West Harting W Susx ... 20 C3
West Hatch Somset ... 30 D6
West Hatch Wilts ... 32 F5
West Haven Angus ... 234 E8
Westhay Somset ... 31 G2
Westhead Lancs ... 138 F6
West Head Norfk ... 104 B2
West Heath Birm ... 98 C7
West Heath Hants ... 48 E7
West Helmsdale Highld ... 274 D5
West Hendred Oxon ... 48 C1
West Hertfordshire
    Crematorium Herts ... 68 E6
West Heslerton N York ... 163 G7
West Hewish N Som ... 44 D6
Westhide Herefs ... 80 D6
Westhill Abers ... 245 J4
West Hill Devon ... 14 C4
West Hoathly W Susx ... 38 A6
West Holme Dorset ... 17 G5
Westholme Somset ... 31 J4
Westhope Herefs ... 80 B5
Westhope Shrops ... 95 L6
West Horndon Essex ... 52 D1
Westhorp Nhants ... 83 L5
Westhorpe Lincs ... 119 H5
Westhorpe Suffk ... 90 B2
West Horrington Somset ... 31 J2
West Horsley Surrey ... 50 D8

West Horton Nthumb ... 203 G7
West Hougham Kent ... 41 H7
Westhoughton Bolton ... 139 K6
Westhouse N York ... 157 L7
Westhouses Derbys ... 133 H8
West Howe Bmouth ... 17 L3
West Howetown Somset ... 29 G4
Westhumble Surrey ... 50 F8
West Huntingtower P & K ... 221 K2
West Huntspill Somset ... 30 D2
West Hyde C Beds ... 68 E4
West Hyde Herts ... 50 C1
West Hythe Kent ... 40 F8
West Ilkerton Devon ... 28 C2
West Ilsley W Berk ... 48 C3
West Itchenor W Susx ... 20 C6
West Keal Lincs ... 137 G7
West Kennett Wilts ... 47 G5
West Kilbride N Ayrs ... 195 K1
West Kingsdown Kent ... 52 C6
West Kington Wilts ... 46 A3
West Kirby Wirral ... 128 F2
West Knapton N York ... 162 F7
West Knighton Dorset ... 16 D5
West Knoyle Wilts ... 32 E4
West Kyloe Nthumb ... 203 G5
Westlake Devon ... 7 J4
West Lambrook Somset ... 30 F7
West Lancashire
    Crematorium Lancs ... 138 E5
Westland Green Herts ... 70 B3
West Langdon Kent ... 41 K6
West Lavington W Susx ... 20 E3
West Lavington Wilts ... 46 E8
West Layton N York ... 168 F8
West Leake Notts ... 116 E6
West Learmouth Nthumb ... 202 C5
West Lees N York ... 161 G2
West Leigh Devon ... 13 G2
Westleigh Devon ... 27 H5
Westleigh Devon ... 29 J7
West Leigh Somset ... 29 L5
Westleton Suffk ... 91 K6
West Lexham Norfk ... 121 J8
Westley Shrops ... 95 J2
Westley Suffk ... 89 G2
Westley Waterless Cambs ... 88 C4
West Lilling N York ... 151 K3
Westlington Bucks ... 67 J5
West Linton Border ... 199 K3
Westlinton Cumb ... 177 L6
West Littleton S Glos ... 45 M4
West Lockinge Oxon ... 48 B2
West London Crematorium
    Gt Lon ... 51 G3
West Lothian Crematorium
    W Loth ... 210 D5
West Lulworth Dorset ... 16 F6
West Lutton N York ... 152 E2
West Lydford Somset ... 31 J4
West Lyn Devon ... 28 C1
West Lyng Somset ... 30 D5
West Lynn Norfk ... 120 D7
West Malling Kent ... 52 E7
West Malvern Worcs ... 81 H6
West Marden W Susx ... 20 C4
West Markham Notts ... 134 E5
Westmarsh Kent ... 41 J3
West Marsh NE Lin ... 145 H5
West Marton N York ... 148 F5
West Melbury Dorset ... 32 E6
West Melton Rothm ... 142 C7
West Meon Hants ... 35 K6
West Meon Hut Hants ... 35 K5
West Meon Woodlands Hants ... 35 K5
West Mersea Essex ... 72 E4
Westmeston E Susx ... 22 E4
Westmill Herts ... 69 J4
Westmill Herts ... 69 K2
West Milton Dorset ... 15 L3
Westminster Gt Lon ... 51 J3
West Molesey Surrey ... 50 E6
West Monkton Somset ... 30 C5
West Moors Dorset ... 17 L2
West Morden Dorset ... 17 H3
West Morriston Border ... 201 J3
West Morton C Brad ... 149 K7
West Mudford Somset ... 31 J6
Westmuir Angus ... 234 A5
West Ness N York ... 162 B6
West Newbiggin Darltn ... 169 K7
Westnewton Cumb ... 164 F2
West Newton E R Yk ... 153 K8
West Newton Norfk ... 120 F6
West Newton Somset ... 30 D5
West Norwood Gt Lon ... 51 J4
West Norwood Crematorium
    Gt Lon ... 51 J4

Westoe S Tyne ... 181 J5
West Ogwell Devon ... 13 J8
Weston BaNES ... 45 L5
Weston Ches E ... 114 A1
Weston Devon ... 14 D3
Weston Devon ... 14 E5
Weston Dorset ... 16 D8
Weston Halton ... 129 L3
Weston Hants ... 35 M6
Weston Herefs ... 79 L4
Weston Herts ... 69 H1
Weston Lincs ... 119 J4
Weston N York ... 149 M6
Weston Nhants ... 84 B6
Weston Notts ... 134 F6
Weston Shrops ... 95 H8
Weston Shrops ... 96 D5
Weston Shrops ... 112 D6
Weston Staffs ... 114 F6
Weston W Berk ... 48 B4
Weston Beggard Herefs ... 80 D7
Westonbirt Gloucs ... 46 B1
Weston by Welland Nhants ... 101 G5
Weston Colley Hants ... 35 K3
Weston Colville Cambs ... 88 C4
Weston Corbett Hants ... 35 L2
Weston Coyney C Stke ... 114 E3
Weston Favell Nhants ... 84 F4
Weston Green Cambs ... 88 C5
Weston Heath Shrops ... 97 H1
Weston Hills Lincs ... 119 J3
Weston in Arden Warwks ... 99 K6
Westoning C Beds ... 85 K8
Weston-in-Gordano N Som ... 44 F4
Westoning Woodend C Beds ... 68 C1
Weston Jones Staffs ... 114 B6
Weston Longville Norfk ... 122 C8
Weston Lullingfields Shrops ... 112 F6
Weston Mill Crematorium
    C Plym ... 6 F3
Weston-on-Avon Warwks ... 82 E5
Weston-on-the-Green Oxon ... 66 D3
Weston Patrick Hants ... 35 L2
Weston Rhyn Shrops ... 112 D4
Weston-sub-Edge Gloucs ... 82 D7
Weston-super-Mare N Som ... 44 C6
Weston-super-Mare
    Crematorium N Som ... 44 D6
Weston Turville Bucks ... 67 K5
Weston-under-Lizard Staffs ... 97 H1
Weston under Penyard Herefs ... 63 J3
Weston-under-Redcastle
    Shrops ... 113 J5
Weston under Wetherley
    Warwks ... 83 J1
Weston Underwood Derbys ... 116 A3
Weston Underwood M Keyn ... 85 G5
Weston-upon-Trent Derbys ... 116 C6
Westonzoyland Somset ... 30 E4
West Orchard Dorset ... 32 D2
West Overton Wilts ... 47 H5
Westow N York ... 152 A3
West Panson Devon ... 11 L4
West Park Abers ... 245 H6
West Parley Dorset ... 17 L3
West Peckham Kent ... 39 G3
West Peeke Devon ... 11 L4
West Pelton Dur ... 180 F7
West Pennard Somset ... 31 J3
West Pentire Cnwll ... 4 C3
West Perry Cambs ... 86 C2
West Pinchbeck Lincs ... 119 J6
West Porlock Somset ... 28 F2
Westport Somset ... 30 F6
West Pulham Dorset ... 16 D1
West Putford Devon ... 26 F7
West Quantoxhead Somset ... 29 K3
Westquarter Falk ... 210 B3
Westra V Glam ... 43 J7
West Raddon Devon ... 13 L2
West Rainton Dur ... 169 J1
West Rasen Lincs ... 135 L2
West Ravendale NE Lin ... 145 G7
Westray Ork ... 275 c2
West Raynham Norfk ... 121 J6
West Retford Notts ... 134 D3
Westridge Green W Berk ... 48 E3
Westrigg W Loth ... 210 B5
West Road Crematorium
    N u Ty ... 180 F6
Westrop Swindn ... 65 J8
West Rounton N York ... 160 F2
West Row Suffk ... 104 D8
West Rudham Norfk ... 121 H6
West Runton Norfk ... 122 D3
Westruther Border ... 201 K3
Westry Cambs ... 103 H4
West Saltoun E Loth ... 212 A5
West Sandford Devon ... 13 J2

West Sandwick Shet....281 e3
West Scrafton N York....159 K6
West Sleekburn Nthumb....181 G2
West Somerton Norfk....123 K7
West Stafford Dorset....16 D5
West Stockwith Notts....134 F1
West Stoke W Susx....20 D5
West Stonesdale N York....158 F2
West Stoughton Somset....30 F1
West Stour Dorset....32 C6
West Stourmouth Kent....41 H3
West Stow Suffk....89 G1
West Stowell Wilts....47 H6
West Stratton Hants....35 H3
West Street Kent....40 A4
West Street Kent....41 K4
West Street Medway....52 F4
West Street Suffk....89 K1
West Suffolk Crematorium
    Suffk....89 G2
West Tanfield N York....160 C7
West Taphouse Cnwll....5 K2
West Tarbert Ag & B....206 D5
West Tarring W Susx....21 J6
West Thirston Nthumb....191 H6
West Thorney W Susx....20 C6
Westthorpe Derbys....133 J4
West Thorpe Notts....117 G6
West Thurrock Thurr....52 C3
West Tilbury Thurr....52 E3
West Tisted Hants....35 K5
West Torrington Lincs....136 B3
West Town BaNES....45 G6
West Town Hants....20 B7
West Town Herefs....80 B3
West Town N Som....44 F5
West Town Somset....31 J4
West Town Somset....32 B3
West Tytherley Hants....34 C5
West Walton Norfk....103 K1
Westward Cumb....165 J2
Westward Ho! Devon....27 G5
Westwell Kent....40 C6
Westwell Oxon....65 J5
Westwell Leacon Kent....40 C5
West Wellow Hants....34 C7
West Wembury Devon....7 G5
West Wemyss Fife....222 E8
Westwick Cambs....87 J2
Westwick Dur....168 D7
West Wick N Som....44 D6
Westwick Norfk....122 F6
West Wickham Cambs....88 C5
West Wickham Gt Lon....51 K5
West Williamston Pembks....55 H5
West Wiltshire Crematorium
    Wilts....46 C7
West Winch Norfk....120 E8
West Winterslow Wilts....34 B4
West Wittering W Susx....20 C7
West Witton N York....159 J5
Westwood Devon....14 B3
Westwood Kent....41 K2
Westwood Kent....52 D5
Westwood Notts....116 D1
Westwood Nthumb....179 H6
Westwood Wilts....46 A7
West Woodburn Nthumb....179 K2
West Woodhay W Berk....48 B6
Westwood Heath Covtry....99 H6
West Woodlands Somset....32 C2
Westwoodside N Linc....143 J7
West Worldham Hants....35 M3
West Worthing W Susx....21 K6
West Wratting Cambs....88 C5
West Wycombe Bucks....67 K8
West Wylam Nthumb....180 D6
West Yatton Wilts....46 B4
West Yoke Kent....52 D5
West Youlstone Cnwll....26 D7
Wetham Green Kent....53 H5
Wetheral Cumb....178 B2
Wetherby Leeds....150 F6
Wetherden Suffk....89 K3
Wetheringsett Suffk....90 D2
Wethersfield Essex....71 H1
Wetherup Street Suffk....90 D2
Wetley Rocks Staffs....114 F2
Wettenhall Ches E....130 C7
Wetton Staffs....132 B8
Wetwang E R Yk....152 E4
Wetwood Staffs....114 B5
Wexcombe Wilts....47 K7
Wexham Slough....50 C3
Wexham Street Bucks....50 C2
Weybourne Norfk....122 C3
Weybourne Surrey....36 C1
Weybread Suffk....106 E7
Weybread Street Suffk....106 E7

Weybridge Surrey....50 D6
Weycroft Devon....15 G3
Weydale Highld....279 L3
Weyhill Hants....34 D2
Weymouth Dorset....16 C6
Weymouth Crematorium
    Dorset....16 C6
Whaddon Bucks....84 F8
Whaddon Cambs....87 G6
Whaddon Gloucs....64 B4
Whaddon Wilts....33 L5
Whaddon Wilts....46 C6
Whale Cumb....166 C6
Whaley Derbys....133 K5
Whaley Bridge Derbys....131 K3
Whaley Thorns Derbys....133 K5
Whaligoe Highld....280 D8
Whalley Lancs....148 C8
Whalley Banks Lancs....139 L1
Whalsay Shet....281 f5
Whalton Nthumb....180 D3
Whaplode Lincs....119 K6
Whaplode Drove Lincs....103 G1
Wharf Warwks....83 K5
Wharfe N York....148 D2
Wharles Lancs....147 J8
Wharley End C Beds....85 J6
Wharncliffe Side Sheff....132 F1
Wharram-le-Street N York....152 C3
Wharton Ches W....130 C6
Wharton Herefs....80 C4
Whashton N York....159 L2
Whasset Cumb....157 H6
Whatcote Warwks....83 G6
Whateley Warwks....99 G3
Whatfield Suffk....89 L6
Whatley Somset....15 H1
Whatley Somset....32 B2
Whatley's End S Glos....45 K3
Whatlington E Susx....24 D4
Whatsole Street Kent....40 F6
Whatstandwell Derbys....116 B1
Whatton Notts....117 K4
Whauphill D & G....173 K5
Whaw N York....159 H2
Wheal Rose Cnwll....4 B6
Wheatacre Norfk....107 J4
Wheatfield Oxon....67 G7
Wheathampstead Herts....68 F4
Wheathill Shrops....96 E7
Wheathill Somset....31 J5
Wheatley Calder....141 G3
Wheatley Hants....36 A3
Wheatley Oxon....66 E6
Wheatley Hill Dur....169 K3
Wheatley Hills Donc....142 F6
Wheatley Lane Lancs....148 E8
Wheaton Aston Staffs....97 J1
Wheatsheaf Wrexhm....112 D1
Wheddon Cross Somset....29 G3
Wheelbarrow Town Kent....40 F6
Wheeler End Bucks....67 K8
Wheeler's Green Wokham....49 J4
Wheelerstreet Surrey....36 E3
Wheelock Ches E....130 E7
Wheelock Heath Ches E....130 E8
Wheelton Lancs....139 J3
Wheldale Wakefd....142 C3
Wheldrake C York....151 L6
Whelford Gloucs....65 H7
Whelpley Hill Bucks....68 C6
Whelpo Cumb....165 J3
Whelston Flints....128 F4
Whempstead Herts....69 J3
Whenby N York....151 K2
Whepstead Suffk....89 G4
Wherstead Suffk....90 E7
Wherwell Hants....34 E3
Wheston Derbys....132 C4
Whetsted Kent....39 G4
Whetstone Gt Lon....69 H8
Whetstone Leics....100 C4
Wheyrigg Cumb....165 G1
Whicham Cumb....155 L6
Whichford Warwks....83 H8
Whickham Gatesd....181 G8
Whiddon Devon....12 B3
Whiddon Down Devon....13 G4
Whigstreet Angus....234 D6
Whilton Nhants....84 C2
Whimble Devon....11 L2
Whimple Devon....14 B3
Whimpwell Green Norfk....123 H5
Whinburgh Norfk....105 K2
Whin Lane End Lancs....147 H7
Whinnieliggate D & G....175 H4
Whinnow Cumb....177 J8
Whinnyfold Abers....257 K5
Whinny Hill S on T....169 K7

Whippingham IoW....19 H5
Whipsnade C Beds....68 C3
Whipton Devon....13 M4
Whirlow Sheff....132 F3
Whisby Lincs....135 H6
Whissendine Rutlnd....117 L8
Whissonsett Norfk....121 K7
Whistlefield Ag & B....218 C8
Whistlefield Inn Ag & B....217 J8
Whistley Green Wokham....49 J4
Whiston Knows....129 L2
Whiston Nhants....85 G3
Whiston Rothm....133 J2
Whiston Staffs....114 D8
Whiston Staffs....115 G2
Whiston Cross Shrops....97 H3
Whiston Eaves Staffs....115 G2
Whitacre Fields Warwks....99 H5
Whitbeck Cumb....155 K5
Whitbourne Herefs....81 G4
Whitburn S Tyne....181 K6
Whitburn W Loth....210 C6
Whitby Ches W....129 J4
Whitby N York....171 K8
Whitbyheath Ches W....129 J5
Whitchester Border....212 F7
Whitchurch BaNES....45 J5
Whitchurch Bucks....67 J3
Whitchurch Cardif....43 J5
Whitchurch Devon....12 C8
Whitchurch Hants....34 F1
Whitchurch Herefs....63 H4
Whitchurch Oxon....48 F3
Whitchurch Pembks....74 C7
Whitchurch Shrops....113 J3
Whitchurch Canonicorum
    Dorset....15 J3
Whitchurch Hill Oxon....48 F3
Whitcombe Dorset....16 D5
Whitcot Shrops....95 J5
Whitcott Keysett Shrops....95 G6
Whiteacre Kent....40 E5
Whiteacre Heath Warwks....99 G5
Whiteash Green Essex....71 J1
White Ball Somset....29 K7
Whitebridge Highld....250 E8
Whitebrook Mons....63 G6
Whitebushes Surrey....37 L1
Whitecairns Abers....257 G8
Whitechapel Gt Lon....51 J3
White Chapel Lancs....147 L7
Whitechurch Pembks....75 K5
Whitecliffe Gloucs....63 H5
White Colne Essex....72 C1
White Coppice Lancs....139 J4
Whitecraig E Loth....211 K5
Whitecroft Gloucs....63 J6
Whitecrook D & G....172 F3
Whitecross Cnwll....2 E4
White Cross Cnwll....3 H6
Whitecross Cnwll....10 D8
Whitecross Falk....210 C4
White End Worcs....81 H8
Whiteface Highld....263 J2
Whitefarland N Ayrs....194 D3
Whitefaulds S Ayrs....183 H1
Whitefield Bury....140 B6
Whitefield Devon....28 C4
Whitefield Somset....29 K5
Whitefield Lane End Knows....129 K2
Whiteford Abers....256 C6
Whitegate Ches W....130 C6
Whitehall Hants....49 H8
Whitehall Ork....275 e3
Whitehall W Susx....37 H6
Whitehaven Cumb....164 C7
Whitehill Kent....40 C3
Whitehill Leics....99 L1
Whitehill and Bordon Hants....36 A4
Whitehills Abers....268 B3
Whitehouse Abers....256 A8
Whitehouse Ag & B....206 C6
Whitehouse Common Birm....98 E4
Whitekirk E Loth....212 D3
White Kirkley Dur....168 C3
White Lackington Dorset....16 D3
Whitelackington Somset....30 F7
White Ladies Aston Worcs....81 L4
Whiteleaf Bucks....67 K6
White-le-Head Dur....180 E7
Whiteley Hants....19 J2
Whiteley Bank IoW....19 J7
Whiteley Green Ches E....131 H4
Whiteley Village Surrey....50 D7
Whitemans Green W Susx....22 D2
White Mill Carmth....58 E4
Whitemire Moray....253 J1
Whitemoor C Nott....116 F3
Whitemoor Cnwll....5 G3

Whitemoor Derbys....116 B2
Whitemoor Staffs....131 H7
Whiteness Shet....281 d6
White Notley Essex....71 J3
Whiteoak Green Oxon....65 M4
White Ox Mead BaNES....45 L7
Whiteparish Wilts....34 B6
White Pit Lincs....137 G4
Whiterashes Abers....256 F7
White Roding Essex....70 E4
Whiterow Highld....280 E6
Whiterow Moray....265 G8
Whiteshill Gloucs....64 B5
Whitesmith E Susx....23 J4
White Stake Lancs....139 G3
Whitestaunton Somset....30 D8
Whitestone Devon....13 K4
White Stone Herefs....80 D6
Whitestone Cross Devon....13 L4
Whitestreet Green Suffk....89 K7
Whitewall Corner N York....152 B2
White Waltham W & M....49 K3
Whiteway BaNES....45 L6
Whiteway Gloucs....64 C5
Whitewell Lancs....148 B6
Whiteworks Devon....12 E8
Whitfield C Dund....234 C8
Whitfield Kent....41 J6
Whitfield Nhants....84 B7
Whitfield Nthumb....179 H7
Whitfield S Glos....63 K8
Whitfield Hall Nthumb....179 H7
Whitford Devon....14 F3
Whitford Flints....128 D4
Whitgift E R Yk....143 K3
Whitgreave Staffs....114 D6
Whithorn D & G....174 C6
Whiting Bay N Ayrs....195 G6
Whitkirk Leeds....142 B1
Whitland Carmth....55 L3
Whitlaw Border....188 E4
Whitletts S Ayrs....196 D6
Whitley N York....142 E4
Whitley Readg....49 H5
Whitley Sheff....133 G1
Whitley Wilts....46 C5
Whitley Bay N Tyne....181 J4
Whitley Bay Crematorium
    N Tyne....181 J4
Whitley Chapel Nthumb....179 L7
Whitley Heath Staffs....114 C6
Whitley Lower Kirk....141 K4
Whitley Row Kent....38 D3
Whitlock's End Solhll....98 E6
Whitminster Gloucs....63 M5
Whitmore Dorset....17 L1
Whitmore Staffs....114 C3
Whitnage Devon....29 J7
Whitnash Warwks....83 H3
Whitney-on-Wye Herefs....79 J5
Whitrigg Cumb....165 G3
Whitrigg Cumb....177 H7
Whitrigglees Cumb....177 H7
Whitsbury Hants....33 K7
Whitsome Border....202 D3
Whitson Newpt....44 D2
Whitstable Kent....40 E2
Whitstone Cnwll....11 K3
Whittingham Nthumb....190 F4
Whittingslow Shrops....95 K5
Whittington Derbys....133 H4
Whittington Gloucs....64 E3
Whittington Lancs....157 K7
Whittington Norfk....104 E3
Whittington Shrops....112 E5
Whittington Staffs....97 J6
Whittington Staffs....98 F2
Whittington Warwks....99 J4
Whittington Worcs....81 K4
Whittington Moor Derbys....133 G5
Whittlebury Nhants....84 D6
Whittle-le-Woods Lancs....139 H3
Whittlesey Cambs....102 F4
Whittlesford Cambs....87 K5
Whittlestone Head Bl w D....139 L4
Whitton N Linc....143 M3
Whitton Nthumb....190 F6
Whitton Powys....79 J2
Whitton S on T....169 K6
Whitton Shrops....80 D1
Whitton Suffk....90 D5
Whittonditch Wilts....47 L4
Whittonstall Nthumb....180 C7
Whitway Hants....48 C7
Whitwell Derbys....133 K4
Whitwell Herts....68 F3
Whitwell IoW....19 J8
Whitwell N York....160 D3
Whitwell Rutlnd....101 K2

Whitwell-on-the-Hill N York 151 M3
Whitwell Street Norfk 122 B7
Whitwick Leics 116 D8
Whitwood Wakefd 142 B3
Whitworth Lancs 140 D4
Whixall Shrops 113 H4
Whixley N York 150 F4
Whorlton Dur 168 E7
Whorlton N York 161 G2
Whyle Herefs 80 D3
Whyteleafe Surrey 51 J7
Wibdon Gloucs 63 H7
Wibsey C Brad 141 J2
Wibtoft Warwks 100 B6
Wichenford Worcs 81 H3
Wichling Kent 40 B4
Wick Bmouth 18 B5
Wick Devon 14 E2
Wick Highld 280 E6
Wick S Glos 45 K4
Wick Somset 30 B2
Wick Somset 30 F5
Wick V Glam 42 D7
Wick W Susx 21 H6
Wick Wilts 33 L6
Wick Worcs 81 M6
Wicken Cambs 88 B1
Wicken Nhants 84 E7
Wicken Bonhunt Essex 87 K8
Wickenby Lincs 136 A3
Wick End Bed 85 K5
Wicken Green Village Norfk 121 J5
Wickersley Rothm 133 J2
Wicker Street Green Suffk 89 K6
Wickford Essex 71 H8
Wickham Hants 19 K2
Wickham W Berk 48 B5
Wickham Bishops Essex 71 K5
Wickhambreaux Kent 41 H3
Wickhambrook Suffk 88 E4
Wickhamford Worcs 82 C7
Wickham Green Suffk 90 C2
Wickham Green W Berk 48 B4
Wickham Heath W Berk 48 B5
Wickham Market Suffk 91 G4
Wickhampton Norfk 107 J2
Wickham St Paul Essex 89 G7
Wickham Skeith Suffk 90 C2
Wickham Street Suffk 88 F4
Wickham Street Suffk 90 C1
Wickhurst Green W Susx 37 H5
Wicklewood Norfk 106 B3
Wickmere Norfk 122 D5
Wick St Lawrence N Som 44 D6
Wickstreet E Susx 23 J5
Wickwar S Glos 45 L1
Widdington Essex 70 D1
Widdop Calder 140 D1
Widdrington Nthumb 191 K7
Widdrington Station Nthumb 191 J7
Widecombe in the Moor
   Devon 13 G7
Widegates Cnwll 6 B3
Widemouth Bay Cnwll 11 H2
Wide Open N Tyne 181 G4
Widford Essex 71 G6
Widford Herts 70 B4
Widham Wilts 47 G1
Widley Hants 19 M2
Widmer End Bucks 67 L7
Widmerpool Notts 117 G6
Widmore Gt Lon 51 L5
Widnes Halton 129 L3
Widnes Crematorium Halton 129 L2
Widworthy Devon 14 F3
Wigan Wigan 139 H6
Wigan Crematorium Wigan 139 H7
Wigborough Somset 31 G7
Wiggaton Devon 14 C4
Wiggenhall St Germans Norfk 120 D8
Wiggenhall St Mary Magdalen
   Norfk 104 B1
Wiggenhall St Mary the
   Virgin Norfk 104 B1
Wiggenhall St Peter Norfk 104 C1
Wiggens Green Essex 88 D6
Wiggenstall Staffs 132 B7
Wiggington Shrops 112 E4
Wigginton C York 151 J4
Wigginton Herts 68 B5
Wigginton Oxon 83 J8
Wigginton Staffs 99 G2
Wigginton Bottom Herts 68 B5
Wigglesworth N York 148 N4
Wiggonby Cumb 177 J8
Wiggonholt W Susx 21 H3
Wighill N York 151 G6
Wighton Norfk 121 L3
Wightwick Wolves 97 K4

Wigley Derbys 132 F5
Wigley Hants 34 D7
Wigmore Herefs 80 A2
Wigmore Medway 53 G6
Wigsley Notts 135 G5
Wigsthorpe Nhants 102 A6
Wigston Leics 100 D4
Wigston Fields Leics 100 D3
Wigston Parva Leics 100 A5
Wigthorpe Notts 134 B3
Wigtoft Lincs 119 J4
Wigton Cumb 165 H1
Wigtown D & G 174 C4
Wigtwizzle Sheff 141 L8
Wike Leeds 150 D7
Wilbarston Nhants 101 H5
Wilberfoss E R Yk 151 M5
Wilburton Cambs 103 K8
Wilby Nhants 85 G2
Wilby Norfk 105 L5
Wilby Suffk 90 F1
Wilcot Wilts 47 H6
Wilcott Shrops 112 F7
Wilcrick Newpt 44 E2
Wilday Green Derbys 132 F5
Wildboarclough Ches E 131 K6
Wilden Bed 86 B4
Wilden Worcs 81 J1
Wilde Street Suffk 104 D7
Wildhern Hants 34 D1
Wildhill Herts 69 H5
Wildmanbridge S Lans 209 L8
Wildmill Brdgnd 42 D5
Wildmoor Hants 49 G7
Wildmoor Worcs 98 B8
Wildsworth Lincs 143 K8
Wilford C Nott 116 F4
Wilford Hill Crematorium
   Notts 116 F4
Wilkesley Ches E 113 K3
Wilkhaven Highld 264 E3
Wilkieston W Loth 210 F5
Wilkin's Green Herts 69 G5
Wilksby Lincs 136 E7
Willand Devon 29 J8
Willards Hill E Susx 24 C2
Willaston Ches E 113 L1
Willaston Ches W 129 H4
Willen M Keyn 85 G7
Willenhall Covtry 99 K8
Willenhall Wsall 98 B4
Willerby E R Yk 144 C2
Willerby N York 163 H6
Willersey Gloucs 82 D7
Willersley Herefs 79 K6
Willesborough Kent 40 D7
Willesborough Lees Kent 40 D7
Willesden Gt Lon 51 G2
Willesleigh Devon 27 L4
Willesley Wilts 46 B1
Willett Somset 29 K4
Willey Shrops 96 F3
Willey Warwks 100 B6
Willey Green Surrey 50 B8
Williamscot Oxon 83 L6
Williamstown Rhondd 42 F4
Willian Herts 69 G1
Willicote Warwks 82 E5
Willingale Essex 70 E5
Willingdon E Susx 23 K6
Willingham Cambs 87 H1
Willingham by Stow Lincs 135 H3
Willingham Green Cambs 88 C4
Willington Bed 86 C5
Willington Derbys 116 A6
Willington Dur 169 G4
Willington Kent 39 K3
Willington N Tyne 181 H5
Willington Warwks 83 G7
Willington Corner Ches W 129 M6
Willitoft E R Yk 143 J1
Williton Somset 29 K3
Willoughby Lincs 137 J5
Willoughby Warwks 83 M2
Willoughby Hills Lincs 119 K2
Willoughby-on-the-Wolds
   Notts 117 H6
Willoughby Waterleys Leics 100 C5
Willoughton Lincs 135 J1
Willow Green Ches W 130 B4
Willows Green Essex 71 H3
Willsbridge S Glos 45 K5
Willsworthy Devon 12 D6
Willtown Somset 30 F6
Wilmcote Warwks 82 K4
Wilmington BaNES 45 K6
Wilmington Devon 14 F3
Wilmington E Susx 23 J6
Wilmington Kent 52 B4

Wilmslow Ches E 131 G3
Wilnecote Staffs 99 G3
Wilpshire Lancs 139 K1
Wilsden C Brad 149 K8
Wilsford Lincs 118 D3
Wilsford Wilts 33 K3
Wilsford Wilts 47 G7
Wilsham Devon 28 D1
Wilshaw Kirk 141 H6
Wilsill N York 150 A3
Wilsley Green Kent 39 K6
Wilsley Pound Kent 39 K6
Wilson Herefs 63 H2
Wilson Leics 116 C6
Wilsontown S Lans 198 F2
Wilstead Bed 85 L6
Wilsthorpe Lincs 102 B1
Wilstone Herts 67 L4
Wilstone Green Herts 67 M4
Wilton Cumb 164 D8
Wilton Herefs 63 H2
Wilton N York 162 F6
Wilton R & Cl 170 D6
Wilton Wilts 33 J4
Wilton Wilts 47 K6
Wilton Dean Border 188 C3
Wimbish Essex 88 B7
Wimbish Green Essex 88 C8
Wimbledon Gt Lon 51 G5
Wimblington Cambs 103 J5
Wimboldsley Ches W 130 D7
Wimborne Minster Dorset 17 K3
Wimborne St Giles Dorset 33 H8
Wimbotsham Norfk 104 C2
Wimpole Cambs 87 G5
Wimpstone Warwks 82 F5
Wincanton Somset 32 B5
Winceby Lincs 136 F6
Wincham Ches W 130 C4
Winchburgh W Loth 210 E4
Winchcombe Gloucs 64 F2
Winchelsea E Susx 25 G4
Winchelsea Beach E Susx 25 G4
Winchester Hants 35 G5
Winchet Hill Kent 39 J5
Winchfield Hants 49 J8
Winchmore Hill Bucks 68 B8
Winchmore Hill Gt Lon 69 J8
Wincle Ches E 131 J6
Wincobank Sheff 133 G1
Winder Cumb 164 D7
Windermere Cumb 156 F3
Winderton Warwks 83 H7
Windhill Highld 250 F2
Windlehurst Stockp 131 J3
Windlesham Surrey 50 A6
Windmill Cnwll 10 B7
Windmill Derbys 132 C4
Windmill Hill E Susx 23 L5
Windmill Hill Somset 30 D7
Windrush Gloucs 65 J4
Windsole Abers 267 L4
Windsor W & M 50 B4
Windsoredge Gloucs 64 B7
Windsor Green Suffk 89 H4
Windygates Fife 222 F7
Windyharbour Ches E 131 G5
Windy Hill Wrexhm 129 G8
Wineham W Susx 22 C3
Winestead E R Yk 145 J3
Winewall Lancs 148 F7
Winfarthing Norfk 106 C6
Winford IoW 19 J6
Winford N Som 45 G6
Winforton Herefs 79 K6
Winfrith Newburgh Dorset 16 F5
Wing Bucks 67 L3
Wing Rutlnd 101 K3
Wingate Dur 169 L3
Wingates Bolton 139 K6
Wingates Nthumb 191 G7
Wingerworth Derbys 133 G6
Wingfield C Beds 68 C3
Wingfield Suffk 106 E7
Wingfield Wilts 46 B7
Wingfield Green Suffk 106 E7
Wingham Kent 41 H4
Wingland Lincs 120 B6
Wingmore Kent 41 G6
Wingrave Bucks 67 L3
Winkburn Notts 134 E7
Winkfield Br For 49 L4
Winkfield Row Br For 49 L5
Winkhill Staffs 115 H7
Winkhurst Green Kent 38 D3
Winkleigh Devon 12 F1
Winksley N York 150 C2
Winkton Dorset 18 B4
Winlaton Gatesd 180 E6

Winlaton Mill Gatesd 180 E6
Winless Highld 280 D5
Winllan Powys 112 C7
Winmarleigh Lancs 147 J6
Winnall Hants 35 G5
Winnersh Wokham 49 J5
Winnington Ches W 130 C5
Winscales Cumb 164 D5
Winscombe N Som 44 E7
Winsford Ches W 130 C6
Winsford Somset 28 F4
Winsham Devon 27 J3
Winsham Somset 15 J2
Winshill Staffs 115 M7
Winshwen Swans 57 J5
Winskill Cumb 166 D4
Winslade Hants 35 K1
Winsley Wilts 46 A6
Winslow Bucks 67 J2
Winson Gloucs 65 G5
Winsor Hants 34 D8
Winster Cumb 156 F4
Winster Derbys 132 E7
Winston Dur 168 F7
Winston Suffk 90 E3
Winstone Gloucs 64 D5
Winswell Devon 27 J4
Winterborne Came Dorset 16 D5
Winterborne Clenston Dorset 17 G2
Winterborne Herringston
   Dorset 16 D5
Winterborne Houghton
   Dorset 16 F2
Winterborne Kingston Dorset 17 G3
Winterborne Monkton Dorset 16 D5
Winterborne Stickland Dorset 16 F2
Winterborne Tomson Dorset 17 G3
Winterborne Whitechurch
   Dorset 17 G3
Winterborne Zelston Dorset 17 H3
Winterbourne S Glos 45 J3
Winterbourne W Berk 48 C4
Winterbourne Abbas Dorset 16 B4
Winterbourne Bassett Wilts 47 G4
Winterbourne Dauntsey Wilts 33 L4
Winterbourne Earls Wilts 33 L4
Winterbourne Gunner Wilts 33 L4
Winterbourne Monkton Wilts 47 G4
Winterbourne Steepleton
   Dorset 16 B4
Winterbourne Stoke Wilts 33 J3
Winterbrook Oxon 48 F1
Winterburn N York 149 G4
Winteringham N Linc 144 A3
Winterley Ches E 130 B4
Wintersett Wakefd 142 B4
Winterslow Wilts 34 B4
Winterton N Linc 144 A4
Winterton-on-Sea Norfk 123 K7
Winthorpe Lincs 137 K6
Winthorpe Notts 135 G8
Winton Bmouth 17 L4
Winton Cumb 167 H8
Winton E Susx 23 H6
Winton N York 160 F3
Wintringham N York 162 F8
Winwick Cambs 102 B7
Winwick Nhants 100 D8
Winwick Warrtn 130 B1
Wirksworth Derbys 115 M1
Wirswall Ches E 113 J3
Wisbech Cambs 103 J2
Wisbech St Mary Cambs 103 J2
Wisborough Green W Susx 37 G5
Wiseman's Bridge Pembks 55 K5
Wiseton Notts 134 E2
Wishanger Gloucs 64 D5
Wishaw N Lans 209 L7
Wisley Surrey 50 D7
Wispington Lincs 136 D5
Wissenden Kent 40 B7
Wissett Suffk 107 H7
Wissington Norfk 104 D4
Wissington Suffk 89 J8
Wistanstow Shrops 95 K6
Wistanswick Shrops 113 L5
Wistaston Ches E 113 L1
Wistaston Green Ches E 130 D8
Wisterfield Ches E 131 G5
Wiston Pembks 55 H3
Wiston S Lans 198 F6
Wiston W Susx 21 K4
Wistow Cambs 102 F7
Wistow Leics 100 E4
Wistow N York 142 F1
Wiswell Lancs 148 C8
Witcham Cambs 103 J7
Witchampton Dorset 17 J2
Witchford Cambs 103 K7

Witcombe Somset 31 G6
Witham Essex 71 K4
Witham Friary Somset 32 B3
Witham on the Hill Lincs 118 D8
Witham St Hughs Lincs 135 H7
Withcall Lincs 136 E3
Withdean Br & H 22 D5
Witherenden Hill E Susx 23 L2
Witheridge Devon 28 D8
Witherley Leics 99 J4
Withern Lincs 137 H3
Withernsea E R Yk 145 J2
Withernwick E R Yk 153 K7
Withersdale Street Suffk 106 F7
Withersfield Suffk 88 D5
Witherslack Cumb 156 F5
Withiel Cnwll 5 G2
Withiel Florey Somset 29 H4
Withielgoose Cnwll 5 G2
Withington Gloucs 64 F4
Withington Herefs 80 D6
Withington Manch 131 G1
Withington Shrops 96 D1
Withington Staffs 115 G4
Withington Green Ches E 130 F5
Withington Marsh Herefs 80 D6
Withleigh Devon 28 F8
Withnell Lancs 139 J3
Withnell Fold Lancs 139 J3
Withybed Green Worcs 82 B1
Withybrook Warwks 99 L6
Withycombe Somset 29 J3
Withyham E Susx 38 D6
Withy Mills BaNES 45 K7
Withypool Somset 28 E4
Withywood Bristl 45 H5
Witley Surrey 36 E3
Witnesham Suffk 90 E5
Witney Oxon 65 M5
Wittering C Pete 102 B3
Wittersham Kent 25 G2
Witton Birm 98 D5
Witton Norfk 107 G2
Witton Norfk 123 G5
Witton Gilbert Dur 169 G2
Witton Green Norfk 107 J3
Witton le Wear Dur 168 F4
Witton Park Dur 168 F4
Wiveliscombe Somset 29 K5
Wivelrod Hants 35 K3
Wivelsfield E Susx 22 E3
Wivelsfield Green E Susx 22 E3
Wivelsfield Station W Susx 22 E3
Wivenhoe Essex 72 F3
Wivenhoe Cross Essex 72 F2
Wiveton Norfk 122 A3
Wix Essex 73 H2
Wixams Bed 85 L6
Wixford Warwks 82 C4
Wix Green Essex 73 H2
Wixhill Shrops 113 J6
Wixoe Suffk 88 E6
Woburn C Beds 85 J8
Woburn Sands M Keyn 85 H8
Wokefield Park W Berk 49 G6
Woking Surrey 50 C7
Woking Crematorium Surrey 50 B7
Wokingham Wokham 49 K5
Wolborough Devon 13 K8
Woldingham Surrey 51 K7
Wold Newton E R Yk 163 J8
Wold Newton NE Lin 145 G8
Wolfclyde S Lans 199 H6
Wolferlow Herefs 80 F3
Wolferton Norfk 120 E6
Wolfhampcote Warwks 83 M2
Wolfhill P & K 233 H8
Wolf Hills Nthumb 179 G2
Wolf's Castle Pembks 74 F6
Wolfsdale Pembks 54 F3
Wollaston Dudley 97 K6
Wollaston Nhants 85 H3
Wollaston Shrops 95 H1
Wollaton C Nott 116 E4
Wolleigh Devon 13 J6
Wollerton Shrops 113 K5
Wollescote Dudley 97 L6
Wolseley Bridge Staffs 115 G7
Wolsingham Dur 168 D3
Wolstanton Staffs 114 D2
Wolstenholme Rochdl 140 C5
Wolston Warwks 99 L8
Wolsty Cumb 176 E8
Wolvercote Oxon 66 D5
Wolverhampton Wolves 97 K4
Wolverley Shrops 113 G5
Wolverley Worcs 97 J7
Wolverton Hants 48 E7
Wolverton Kent 41 H6

Wolverton M Keyn 84 F7
Wolverton Warwks 82 F3
Wolverton Wilts 32 C4
Wolverton Common Hants 48 E7
Wolvesnewton Mons 62 F7
Wolvey Warwks 99 L6
Wolvey Heath Warwks 99 L5
Wolviston S on T 170 B5
Wombleton N York 161 L6
Wombourne Staffs 97 K5
Wombwell Barns 142 B7
Womenswold Kent 41 H5
Womersley N York 142 E4
Wonastow Mons 62 F5
Wonersh Surrey 36 F2
Wonford Devon 13 L4
Wonson Devon 12 F5
Wonston Dorset 16 E1
Wonston Hants 35 G3
Wooburn Green Bucks 49 M1
Wooburn Moor Bucks 49 M1
Woodacott Devon 11 M1
Woodale N York 159 J6
Woodall Rothm 133 J3
Woodbank Ches W 129 H5
Woodbastwick Norfk 123 G8
Woodbeck Notts 134 F4
Wood Bevington Warwks 82 C4
Woodborough Notts 117 G2
Woodborough Wilts 47 G7
Woodbridge Devon 14 E4
Woodbridge Dorset 32 E7
Woodbridge Suffk 91 G5
Wood Burcote Nhants 84 D6
Woodbury Devon 14 B5
Woodbury Salterton Devon 14 B5
Woodchester Gloucs 64 B6
Woodchurch Kent 40 B8
Woodchurch Wirral 129 G2
Woodcombe Somset 29 G2
Woodcote Gt Lon 51 J6
Woodcote Oxon 48 F3
Woodcote Wrekin 114 B8
Woodcote Green Worcs 81 L1
Woodcott Hants 48 B7
Woodcroft Gloucs 63 G7
Woodcutts Dorset 33 G7
Wood Dalling Norfk 122 B6
Woodditton Cambs 88 D3
Woodeaton Oxon 66 D5
Wood Eaton Staffs 114 C7
Wooden Pembks 55 J6
Wood End Bed 85 K6
Wood End Bed 86 B2
Wood End C Beds 85 J7
Wood End Cambs 103 H8
Wood End Gt Lon 50 E3
Wood End Herts 69 J2
Woodend Highld 228 B3
Woodend Nhants 84 B5
Woodend Staffs 115 K6
Woodend W Loth 210 B5
Woodend W Susx 20 D5
Wood End Warwks 82 D1
Wood End Warwks 99 H4
Wood End Warwks 99 J6
Wood End Wolves 97 L3
Wood Enderby Lincs 136 E6
Woodend Green Essex 70 E2
Woodfalls Wilts 33 L6
Woodford Cnwll 26 C8
Woodford Devon 8 B5
Woodford Gloucs 63 K7
Woodford Gt Lon 69 L8
Woodford Nhants 101 L8
Woodford Stockp 131 H3
Woodford Bridge Gt Lon 51 L1
Woodford Green Gt Lon 69 L8
Woodford Halse Nhants 84 A5
Woodford Wells Gt Lon 69 L8
Woodgate Birm 98 C6
Woodgate Devon 29 K7
Woodgate Norfk 121 K8
Woodgate Norfk 121 M8
Woodgate W Susx 20 F6
Woodgate Worcs 81 M2
Wood Green Gt Lon 51 J1
Woodgreen Hants 33 L7
Woodgreen Oxon 66 A5
Woodhall Inver 159 H4
Woodhall Hill Leeds 141 K1
Woodhall Spa Lincs 136 C7
Woodham Bucks 67 H3
Woodham Dur 169 H5
Woodham Surrey 50 D6
Woodham Ferrers Essex 71 J7
Woodham Mortimer Essex 71 K6
Woodham Walter Essex 71 K5
Wood Hayes Wolves 97 L3

Woodhead Abers 256 E4
Woodhill Shrops 97 G6
Woodhill Somset 30 E5
Woodhorn Nthumb 181 H1
Woodhorn Demesne Nthumb 181 H1
Woodhouse Leeds 141 L1
Woodhouse Leics 116 F8
Woodhouse Sheff 133 H3
Woodhouse Wakefd 142 B3
Woodhouse Eaves Leics 116 F8
Woodhouse Green Staffs 131 H7
Woodhouselee Mdloth 211 H6
Woodhouselees D & G 177 L4
Woodhouse Mill Sheff 133 H3
Woodhouses Cumb 177 K8
Woodhouses Oldham 140 D7
Woodhouses Staffs 98 D2
Woodhouses Staffs 115 J7
Woodhuish Devon 8 D4
Woodhurst Cambs 103 G8
Woodingdean Br & H 22 E6
Woodkirk Leeds 141 L3
Woodland Abers 256 F7
Woodland Devon 7 J4
Woodland Devon 8 B1
Woodland Dur 168 D5
Woodland Kent 40 F7
Woodland S Ayrs 182 F4
Woodland Head Devon 13 H3
Woodlands Abers 245 H4
Woodlands Donc 142 E6
Woodlands Dorset 17 L1
Woodlands Hants 18 E1
Woodlands Kent 52 C6
Woodlands N York 150 D5
Woodlands Somset 29 L3
Woodlands (Coleshill)
    Crematorium Warwks 98 F5
Woodlands Park W & M 49 L3
Woodlands St Mary W Berk 47 M4
Woodlands (Scarborough)
    Crematorium N York 163 J5
Woodlands (Scunthorpe)
    Crematorium N Linc 143 M5
Woodland Street Somset 31 J3
Woodland View Sheff 132 F2
Wood Lane Shrops 112 F5
Wood Lane Staffs 114 C2
Woodleigh Devon 7 L5
Woodlesford Leeds 142 B2
Woodley Stockp 131 J1
Woodley Wokham 49 J4
Woodmancote Gloucs 63 M7
Woodmancote Gloucs 64 E2
Woodmancote Gloucs 64 E5
Woodmancote W Susx 20 C5
Woodmancote W Susx 22 C4
Woodmancote Worcs 81 L6
Woodmancott Hants 35 H2
Woodmansey E R Yk 153 G8
Woodmansgreen W Susx 36 C5
Woodmansterne Surrey 51 H7
Woodmanton Devon 14 B5
Woodmarsh Wilts 46 B7
Woodmill Staffs 115 J7
Woodminton Wilts 33 H6
Woodnesborough Kent 41 J4
Woodnewton Nhants 102 A4
Woodnook Notts 116 D1
Wood Norton Norfk 121 M6
Woodplumpton Lancs 139 G1
Woodrising Norfk 105 K3
Wood Row Leeds 142 B2
Woodrow Worcs 97 K8
Wood's Corner E Susx 24 B3
Woods Eaves Herefs 79 K5
Woodseaves Shrops 113 M5
Woodseaves Staffs 114 B6
Woodsend Wilts 47 J4
Woodsetts Rothm 133 L3
Woodsford Dorset 16 E4
Wood's Green E Susx 39 G6
Woodside Br For 50 B5
Woodside Cumb 164 D4
Woodside Essex 70 C6
Woodside Fife 223 G5
Woodside Gt Lon 51 J5
Woodside Hants 18 E5
Woodside Herts 69 H5
Woodside P & K 233 J7
Woodside Crematorium Inver 207 M4
Woodside Green Kent 40 B4
Woodstock Oxon 66 C4
Woodstock Pembks 75 H7
Woodston C Pete 102 D4
Wood Street Norfk 123 H7
Wood Street Village Surrey 36 E1
Woodthorpe Derbys 133 J5
Woodthorpe Leics 116 F8

Woodthorpe Lincs 137 H4
Woodton Norfk 106 F4
Woodtown Devon 27 G6
Woodvale Sefton 138 C5
Woodvale Crematorium
    Br & H 22 E6
Woodville Derbys 116 A7
Woodwall Green Staffs 114 B5
Wood Walton Cambs 102 E7
Woodyates Dorset 33 H7
Woody Bay Devon 28 B1
Woofferton Shrops 80 C2
Wookey Somset 31 H2
Wookey Hole Somset 31 H2
Wool Dorset 17 G5
Woolacombe Devon 27 H2
Woolage Green Kent 41 H5
Woolage Village Kent 41 H5
Woolaston Gloucs 63 H7
Woolaston Common Gloucs 63 H6
Woolavington Somset 30 E3
Woolbeding W Susx 36 C6
Woolbrook Devon 14 D5
Woolcotts Somset 29 H4
Wooldale Kirk 141 J6
Wooler Nthumb 202 F7
Woolfardisworthy Devon 13 J1
Woolfardisworthy Devon 26 F6
Woolfold Bury 140 B5
Woolfords S Lans 199 G2
Woolhampton W Berk 48 E5
Woolhope Herefs 80 E8
Woolland Dorset 16 E1
Woollard BaNES 45 J6
Woollensbrook Herts 69 K5
Woolley BaNES 45 L5
Woolley Cambs 102 C8
Woolley Cnwll 26 D7
Woolley Derbys 133 G7
Woolley Wakefd 141 M5
Woolley Bridge Derbys 131 K1
Woolley Green W & M 49 K3
Woolmere Green Worcs 81 M3
Woolmerston Somset 30 D4
Woolminstone Somset 15 J1
Woolpack Kent 39 L6
Woolpit Suffk 89 K3
Woolpit Green Suffk 89 K3
Woolscott Warwks 83 L2
Woolsgrove Devon 13 J2
Woolsington N u Ty 180 F5
Woolstaston Shrops 95 L4
Woolsthorpe Lincs 117 L5
Woolsthorpe-by-
    Colsterworth Lincs 118 B6
Woolston C Sotn 19 G2
Woolston Devon 7 L5
Woolston Devon 7 L6
Woolston Shrops 95 K6
Woolston Shrops 112 D6
Woolston Somset 29 K3
Woolston Somset 31 L5
Woolston Warrtn 130 C2
Woolstone Gloucs 64 D1
Woolstone M Keyn 85 G7
Woolstone Oxon 47 L2
Woolston Green Devon 8 A2
Woolton Lpool 129 K2
Woolton Hill Hants 48 B6
Woolverstone Suffk 90 E7
Woolverton Somset 46 A8
Woolwich Gt Lon 51 L3
Woonton Herefs 79 L5
Woonton Herefs 80 D3
Wooperton Nthumb 190 F2
Woore Shrops 114 A3
Wootten Green Suffk 90 F1
Wootton Bed 85 K6
Wootton Hants 18 C4
Wootton Herefs 79 L5
Wootton IoW 19 J5
Wootton Kent 41 H6
Wootton N Linc 144 D4
Wootton Nhants 84 E4
Wootton Oxon 66 B3
Wootton Oxon 66 C6
Wootton Shrops 112 E6
Wootton Staffs 114 C6
Wootton Staffs 115 H3
Wootton Bassett Wilts 46 F3
Wootton Bridge IoW 19 J5
Wootton Broadmead Bed 85 K6
Wootton Common IoW 19 J5
Wootton Courtenay Somset 29 G2
Wootton Fitzpaine Dorset 15 J3
Wootton Rivers Wilts 47 I6
Wootton St Lawrence Hants 48 E8
Wootton Wawen Warwks 82 E3

Worcester Worcs ... 81 K4
Worcester Crematorium
    Worcs ... 81 K4
Worcester Park Gt Lon ... 51 G6
Wordsley Dudley ... 97 K6
Worfield Shrops ... 97 G4
Worgret Dorset ... 17 H5
Workhouse End Bed ... 86 B5
Workhouse Green Suffk ... 89 H7
Workington Cumb ... 164 D5
Worksop Notts ... 134 B4
Worlaby Lincs ... 136 F4
Worlaby N Linc ... 144 C5
Worlds End Bucks ... 67 L5
Worlds End Hants ... 19 L1
World's End W Berk ... 48 C3
Worlds End W Susx ... 22 E3
Worle N Som ... 44 D6
Worleston Ches E ... 130 C8
Worlingham Suffk ... 107 J5
Worlington Devon ... 28 D8
Worlington Suffk ... 104 D8
Worlingworth Suffk ... 90 F2
Wormald Green N York ... 150 D3
Wormbridge Herefs ... 62 E1
Wormegay Norfk ... 104 D1
Wormelow Tump Herefs ... 62 F1
Wormhill Derbys ... 132 C5
Wormhill Herefs ... 80 A7
Wormingford Essex ... 72 D1
Worminghall Bucks ... 66 F5
Wormington Gloucs ... 82 B7
Worminster Somset ... 31 J2
Wormit Fife ... 223 G2
Wormleighton Warwks ... 83 K4
Wormley Herts ... 69 K6
Wormley Surrey ... 36 E3
Wormleybury Herts ... 69 K6
Wormley Hill Donc ... 143 G4
Wormshill Kent ... 39 M2
Wormsley Herefs ... 80 A5
Worplesdon Surrey ... 50 B8
Worrall Sheff ... 132 F1
Worrall Hill Gloucs ... 63 J4
Worsbrough Barns ... 142 A7
Worsbrough Bridge Barns ... 142 A7
Worsbrough Dale Barns ... 142 B7
Worsley Salfd ... 139 M7
Worstead Norfk ... 122 F6
Worsthorne Lancs ... 140 C1
Worston Devon ... 7 H4
Worston Lancs ... 148 D7
Worth Kent ... 41 K4
Worth Somset ... 31 H4
Worth W Susx ... 37 L4
Wortham Suffk ... 106 B7
Worthen Shrops ... 95 H2
Worthenbury Wrexhm ... 112 F2
Worthing Norfk ... 121 M7
Worthing W Susx ... 21 K6
Worthing Crematorium
    W Susx ... 21 J5
Worthington Leics ... 116 C7
Worth Matravers Dorset ... 17 J7
Worthybrook Mons ... 62 F5
Worting Hants ... 48 F8
Wortley Barns ... 141 M7
Wortley Leeds ... 141 L1
Worton N York ... 159 G5
Worton Wilts ... 46 E7
Wortwell Norfk ... 106 F6
Wotherton Shrops ... 95 G3
Wothorpe C Pete ... 101 M2
Wotter Devon ... 7 H3
Wotton Surrey ... 37 H2
Wotton-under-Edge Gloucs ... 63 M8
Wotton Underwood Bucks ... 67 G4
Woughton on the Green
    M Keyn ... 85 G7
Wouldham Kent ... 52 F6
Woundale Shrops ... 97 H5
Wrabness Essex ... 73 J1
Wrafton Devon ... 27 J4
Wragby Lincs ... 136 B4
Wragby Wakefd ... 142 C4
Wramplingham Norfk ... 106 C2
Wrangaton Devon ... 7 K3
Wrangbrook Wakefd ... 142 D5
Wrangle Lincs ... 119 M2
Wrangle Common Lincs ... 119 M1
Wrangle Lowgate Lincs ... 119 M1
Wrangway Somset ... 29 L7
Wrantage Somset ... 30 D6
Wrawby N Linc ... 144 C6
Wraxall N Som ... 44 F4
Wraxall Somset ... 31 K4
Wray Lancs ... 147 M2
Wray Castle Cumb ... 156 E3
Wraysbury W & M ... 50 C4

Wrayton Lancs ... 147 M2
Wrea Green Lancs ... 138 E2
Wreaks End Cumb ... 156 B5
Wreay Cumb ... 166 B1
Wreay Cumb ... 166 B6
Wrecclesham Surrey ... 36 B2
Wrekenton Gatesd ... 181 G7
Wrelton N York ... 162 D5
Wrenbury Ches E ... 113 K2
Wrench Green N York ... 163 H5
Wreningham Norfk ... 106 D4
Wrentham Suffk ... 107 K6
Wrenthorpe Wakefd ... 141 M3
Wrentnall Shrops ... 95 K3
Wressle E R Yk ... 143 H2
Wressle N Linc ... 144 B6
Wrestlingworth C Beds ... 86 E5
Wretton Norfk ... 104 D3
Wrexham Wrexhm ... 112 E2
Wrexham Industrial Estate
    Wrexhm ... 112 F2
Wribbenhall Worcs ... 97 H8
Wrickton Shrops ... 96 E6
Wrightington Bar Lancs ... 139 G5
Wright's Green Essex ... 70 D4
Wrinehill Staffs ... 114 B2
Wrington N Som ... 44 F6
Writhlington BaNES ... 45 K8
Writtle Essex ... 71 G6
Wrockwardine Wrekin ... 96 E1
Wroot N Linc ... 143 H7
Wrose C Brad ... 149 L8
Wrotham Kent ... 52 D7
Wrotham Heath Kent ... 52 D7
Wrottesley Staffs ... 97 J3
Wroughton Swindn ... 47 H3
Wroxall IoW ... 19 J7
Wroxall Warwks ... 82 F1
Wroxeter Shrops ... 96 D2
Wroxham Norfk ... 122 F8
Wroxton Oxon ... 83 K7
Wyaston Derbys ... 115 K3
Wyatt's Green Essex ... 70 F7
Wyberton East Lincs ... 119 K3
Wyberton West Lincs ... 119 J3
Wyboston Bed ... 86 D4
Wybunbury Ches E ... 113 M2
Wychbold Worcs ... 81 L2
Wych Cross E Susx ... 38 C7
Wychnor Staffs ... 115 K8
Wyck Hants ... 35 M3
Wyck Rissington Gloucs ... 65 J3
Wycliffe Dur ... 168 E7
Wycoller Lancs ... 149 G8
Wycomb Leics ... 117 K6
Wycombe Marsh Bucks ... 67 L8
Wyddial Herts ... 69 K1
Wye Kent ... 40 D6
Wyesham Mons ... 63 G4
Wyfordby Leics ... 117 L7
Wyke C Brad ... 141 J2
Wyke Devon ... 13 K3
Wyke Devon ... 15 J4
Wyke Dorset ... 32 D5
Wyke Shrops ... 96 E3
Wyke Surrey ... 50 A8
Wyke Champflower Somset ... 31 L4
Wykeham N York ... 163 H6
Wyken Covtry ... 99 K7
Wyken Shrops ... 97 H4
Wyke Regis Dorset ... 16 C7
Wykey Shrops ... 112 F6
Wykin Leics ... 99 L4
Wylam Nthumb ... 180 D6
Wylde Green Birm ... 98 E4
Wylye Wilts ... 33 H3
Wymeswold Leics ... 117 G6
Wymington Bed ... 85 J2
Wymondham Leics ... 117 M7
Wymondham Norfk ... 106 C3
Wyndham Brdgnd ... 42 E3
Wynford Eagle Dorset ... 16 B3
Wynyard Park S on T ... 169 L5
Wynyard Village S on T ... 169 L5
Wyre Forest Crematorium
    Worcs ... 97 J8
Wyre Piddle Worcs ... 81 M5
Wysall Notts ... 117 G6
Wyson Herefs ... 80 C2
Wythall Worcs ... 98 D8
Wytham Oxon ... 66 C5
Wythburn Cumb ... 165 K7
Wythenshawe Manch ... 131 G2
Wythop Mill Cumb ... 165 G5
Wyton Cambs ... 86 F1
Wyton E R Yk ... 144 F1
Wyverstone Suffk ... 90 B2
Wyverstone Street Suffk ... 89 L2
Wyville Lincs ... 118 A5

Y

Yaddlethorpe N Linc ... 143 M6
Yafford IoW ... 19 G7
Yafforth N York ... 160 E4
Yalberton Torbay ... 8 C3
Yalding Kent ... 39 H3
Yanwath Cumb ... 166 C5
Yanworth Gloucs ... 65 G4
Yapham E R Yk ... 152 B5
Yapton W Susx ... 21 G6
Yarborough N Som ... 44 D7
Yarbridge IoW ... 19 K6
Yarburgh Lincs ... 136 F1
Yarcombe Devon ... 14 F1
Yard Devon ... 28 D6
Yardley Birm ... 98 E6
Yardley Crematorium Birm ... 98 E6
Yardley Gobion Nhants ... 84 E6
Yardley Hastings Nhants ... 85 G4
Yardley Wood Birm ... 98 E7
Yardro Powys ... 79 J3
Yarford Somset ... 30 B5
Yarkhill Herefs ... 80 E6
Yarley Somset ... 31 H2
Yarlington Somset ... 31 L5
Yarm S on T ... 169 L8
Yarmouth IoW ... 18 E5
Yarnacott Devon ... 27 L5
Yarnbrook Wilts ... 46 C7
Yarner Devon ... 13 H7
Yarnfield Staffs ... 114 D5
Yarnscombe Devon ... 27 K6
Yarnton Oxon ... 66 C5
Yarpole Herefs ... 80 B2
Yarrow Border ... 200 D7
Yarrow Somset ... 30 E2
Yarrow Feus Border ... 200 D7
Yarrowford Border ... 200 E7
Yarsop Herefs ... 80 A6
Yarwell Nhants ... 102 B4
Yate S Glos ... 45 L3
Yateley Hants ... 49 K6
Yatesbury Wilts ... 46 F4
Yattendon W Berk ... 48 E4
Yatton Herefs ... 80 A2
Yatton N Som ... 44 E6
Yatton Keynell Wilts ... 46 C4
Yaverland IoW ... 19 K6
Yawl Devon ... 15 H4
Yawthorpe Lincs ... 135 H1
Yaxham Norfk ... 105 K1
Yaxley Cambs ... 102 D5
Yaxley Suffk ... 106 C8
Yazor Herefs ... 79 M6
Yeading Gt Lon ... 50 E3
Yeadon Leeds ... 150 B7
Yealand Conyers Lancs ... 157 H7
Yealand Redmayne Lancs ... 157 H7
Yealand Storrs Lancs ... 157 H7
Yealmbridge Devon ... 7 H4
Yealmpton Devon ... 7 H4
Yearby R & Cl ... 170 E6
Yearngill Cumb ... 164 F2
Yearsley N York ... 161 J7
Yeaton Shrops ... 113 G7
Yeaveley Derbys ... 115 K3
Yeavering Nthumb ... 202 E7
Yedingham N York ... 162 F6
Yelford Oxon ... 66 A6
Yell Shet ... 281 e3
Yelland Devon ... 27 J4
Yelling Cambs ... 86 F3
Yelvertoft Nhants ... 100 D8
Yelverton Devon ... 7 G1
Yelverton Norfk ... 106 F3
Yenston Somset ... 32 B6
Yeoford Devon ... 13 H3
Yeolmbridge Cnwll ... 11 L5
Yeo Mill Devon ... 28 E5
Yeo Vale Devon ... 27 G6
Yeovil Somset ... 31 J7
Yeovil Crematorium Somset ... 31 H7
Yeovil Marsh Somset ... 31 J7
Yeovilton Somset ... 31 J6
Yerbeston Pembks ... 55 H5
Yesnaby Ork ... 275 b4
Yetlington Nthumb ... 190 E4
Yetminster Dorset ... 16 B1
Yetson Devon ... 8 B4
Yettington Devon ... 14 B5
Yetts o'Muckhart Clacks ... 221 H6
Yews Green C Brad ... 141 H2
Yew Tree Sandw ... 98 C4
Y Felinheli Gwynd ... 125 J6
Y Ferwig Cerdgn ... 75 L2
Y Ffôr Gwynd ... 109 G4
Y Gyffylliog Denbgs ... 128 C8

Yielden Bed ... 85 K2
Yieldingtree Worcs ... 97 K7
Yieldshields S Lans ... 198 E3
Yiewsley Gt Lon ... 50 D3
Y Maerdy Conwy ... 111 K3
Y Nant Wrexhm ... 112 D2
Ynysboeth Rhondd ... 43 G3
Ynysddu Caerph ... 43 J3
Ynysforgan Swans ... 57 J5
Ynyshir Rhondd ... 42 F3
Ynyslas Cerdgn ... 92 D5
Ynysmaerdy Rhondd ... 42 F4
Ynysmeudwy Neath ... 57 K4
Ynystawe Swans ... 57 J5
Ynyswen Powys ... 60 C4
Ynyswen Rhondd ... 42 E2
Ynysybwl Rhondd ... 43 G3
Ynysymaengwyn Gwynd ... 92 D3
Yockenthwaite N York ... 158 F6
Yockleton Shrops ... 95 K2
Yokefleet E R Yk ... 143 K3
Yoker C Glas ... 208 E5
York C York ... 151 J1
York Lancs ... 139 L1
York City Crematorium C York ... 151 J6
Yorkletts Kent ... 40 E3
Yorkley Gloucs ... 63 J5
York Town Surrey ... 49 L7
Yorton Heath Shrops ... 113 H7
Youlgreave Derbys ... 132 D6
Youlthorpe E R Yk ... 152 B5
Youlton N York ... 151 G3
Youngsbury Herts ... 69 K3
Young's End Essex ... 71 H3
Yoxall Staffs ... 115 J7
Yoxford Suffk ... 91 J2
Y Rhiw Gwynd ... 108 D6
Ysbyty Cynfyn Cerdgn ... 93 G7
Ysbyty Ifan Conwy ... 110 K3
Ysbyty Ystwyth Cerdgn ... 77 K1
Ysceifiog Flints ... 128 D5
Ysgubor-y-Coed Cerdgn ... 92 E4
Ystalyfera Neath ... 57 L3
Ystrad Rhondd ... 42 F3
Ystrad Aeron Cerdgn ... 76 F4
Ystradfellte Powys ... 60 D4
Ystrad Ffin Carmth ... 77 L6
Ystradgynlais Powys ... 60 B5
Ystrad Meurig Cerdgn ... 77 K2
Ystrad Mynach Caerph ... 43 J3
Ystradowen V Glam ... 42 F5
Ystumtuen Cerdgn ... 92 F7
Ythanbank Abers ... 257 G5
Ythanwells Abers ... 256 B4
Ythsie Abers ... 256 D3

Z

Zeal Monachorum Devon ... 13 G2
Zeals Wilts ... 32 C4
Zelah Cnwll ... 4 C4
Zennor Cnwll ... 2 C3
Zoar Cnwll ... 3 J7
Zouch Notts ... 116 E6

Map pages north

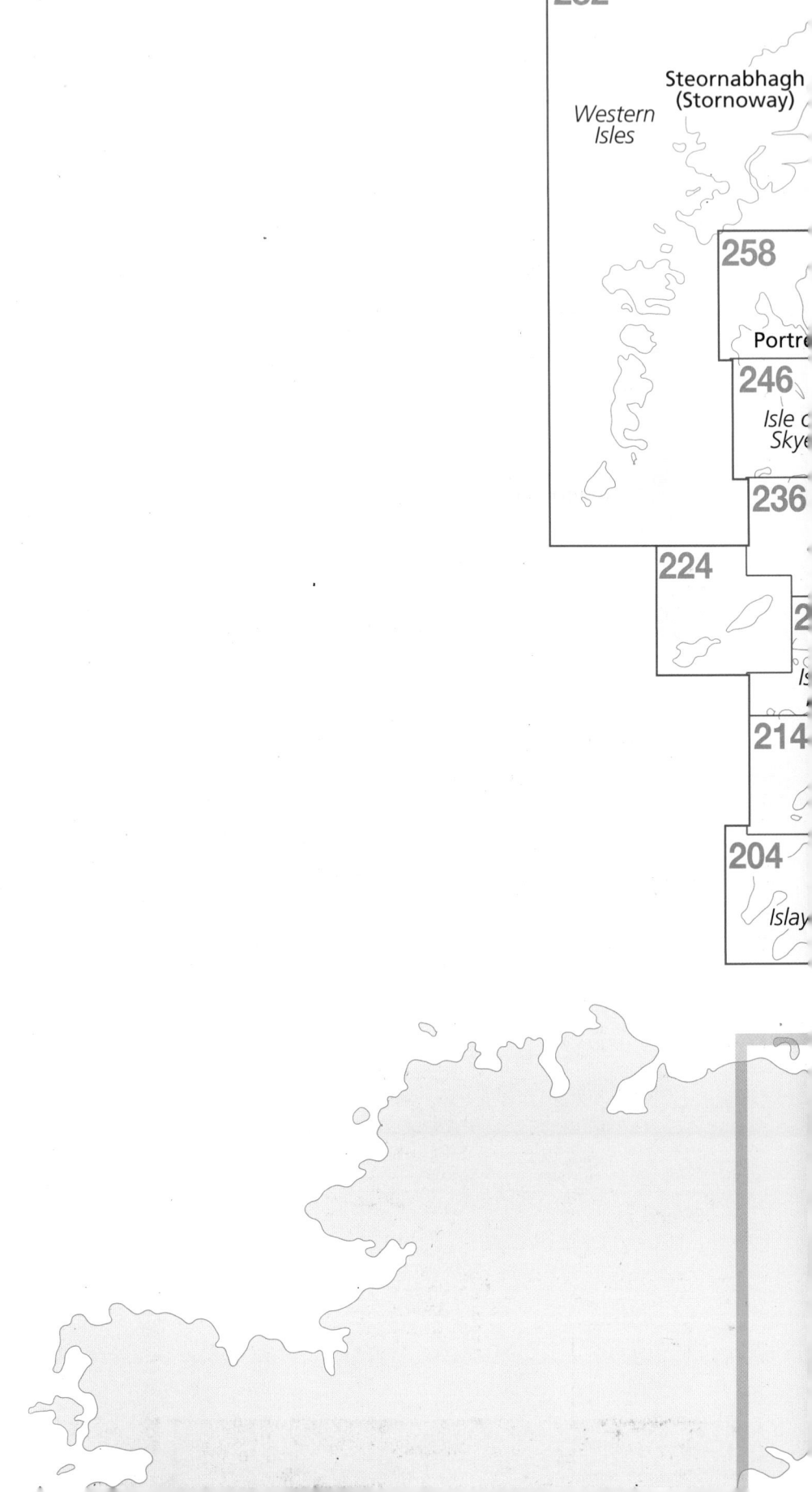

282

Steornabhagh
(Stornoway)

Western
Isles

258

Portre

246

Isle o
Skye

236

224

214

204

Islay